ECONOMICS

CANADA IN THE GLOBAL ENVIRONMENT

ECONOMICS

CANADA IN THE GLOBAL ENVIRONMENT

SIXTH EDITION

MICHAEL PARKIN ◆ ROBIN BADE

University of Western Ontario

PEARSON

Addison
Wesley

Toronto

Library and Archives Canada Cataloguing in Publication

Parkin, Michael, 1939–
    Economics : Canada in the global environment / Michael Parkin, Robin Bade.—6th ed.

Includes index.
ISBN 0-321-31268-6

1. Economics—Textbooks. 2. Canada—Economic conditions—1991–
—Textbooks. I. Bade, Robin II. Title.

HB171.5.P26 2006   330   C2005-905353-4

0-321-31268-6

Vice President, Editorial Director: Michael J. Young
Editor in Chief, Business and Economics: Gary Bennett
Director of Marketing, Business and Economics: Bill Todd
Associate Editor: Stephen Broadbent
Production Editor: Jennifer Handel
Copy Editor: Lu Cormier
Proofreader: Edie Franks
Production Coordinator: Deborah Starks
Page Layout: Carolyn E. Sebestyen
Technical Illustrator: Richard Parkin
Indexer: Belle Wong
Permissions and Photo Research: Lisa Brant
Art Director: Julia Hall
Interior and Cover Design: Anthony Leung
Cover Image: Background, Ron Stroud/Masterfile; Centre, Greg Stott/Masterfile

Statistics Canada information is used with the permission of the Minister of Industry, as Minister responsible for Statistics Canada. Information on the availability of the wide range of data from Statistics Canada can be obtained from Statistics Canada's Regional Offices, its World Wide Web site at http://www.statcan.ca, and its toll-free access number 1-800-263-1136. The Statistics Canada CANSIM II database can be accessed at http://cansim2.statcan.ca/cgi-win/CNSMCGI.EXE.

    3 4 5   10 09 08 07 06

Printed and bound in the United States of America.

The cover depicts a Canadian urban scene viewed through the lens of the Parkin–Bade icon. You can look at this cover in many different ways. Here is what we see.

First, we see a metaphor for what our text, Web site, and other supplements seek to be—a window that gives students a sharply focused view of the world based on a clear and compelling account of timeless principles.

Second, we see a symbol of what economics (and all scientific endeavour) is about. The Parkin–Bade icon is like an economic model. We use models to understand reality. The model is abstract, like the diamond shape and its hole or aperture. The model distorts our view of the world by omitting some details. But it permits us to see the focus of our interest in the brightest and clearest possible light.

 To our students

ABOUT THE AUTHORS

Michael Parkin received his training as an economist at the Universities of Leicester and Essex in England. Currently in the Department of Economics at the University of Western Ontario, Professor Parkin has held faculty appointments at Brown University, the University of Manchester, the University of Essex, and Bond University. He is a past president of the Canadian Economics Association and has served on the editorial boards of the *American Economic Review* and the *Journal of Monetary Economics* and as managing editor of the *Canadian Journal of Economics*. Professor Parkin's research on macroeconomics, monetary economics, and international economics has resulted in over 160 publications in journals and edited volumes, including the *American Economic Review*, the *Journal of Political Economy*, the *Review of Economic Studies*, the *Journal of Monetary Economics*, and the *Journal of Money, Credit and Banking*. He became most visible to the public with his work on inflation that discredited the use of wage and price controls. Michael Parkin also spearheaded the movement towards European monetary union.

Robin Bade earned degrees in mathematics and economics at the University of Queensland and her Ph.D. at the Australian National University. She has held faculty appointments in the business schools at the University of Edinburgh and Bond University and in the economics departments at the University of Manitoba, the University of Toronto, and the University of Western Ontario. Her research on international capital flows appears in the *International Economic Review* and the *Economic Record*.

Professor Parkin and Dr. Bade are the joint authors of *Modern Macroeconomics* (Pearson Education Canada), an intermediate text, and *Foundations of Economics* (Pearson Education Canada), and have collaborated on many research and textbook writing projects. They are both experienced and dedicated teachers of introductory economics.

PREFACE

This book presents economics as a serious, lively, and evolving science. Its goal is to open students' eyes to the "economic way of thinking" and to help them gain insights into how the economy works and how it might be made to work better.

We provide a thorough and complete coverage of the subject, using a straightforward, precise, and clear writing style.

We are conscious that many students find economics hard, so we place the student at centre stage and write for the student. We use language that doesn't intimidate and that allows the student to concentrate on the substance.

We open each chapter with a clear statement of learning objectives, a real-world student-friendly vignette to grab attention, and a brief preview. We illustrate principles with examples that are selected to hold the student's interest and to make the subject lively. And we put principles to work by using them to illuminate current real-world problems and issues.

We present some advanced topics, such as game theory, the modern theory of the firm, public choice theory, rational expectations, and new growth theory. But we explain these topics with familiar core ideas and tools.

Today's course springs from today's issues—the information revolution, the Asian economic boom, the Kyoto debate, and the expansion of international trade and investment. But the principles that we use to understand these issues remain the core principles of our science.

Governments and international agencies place renewed emphasis on long-term fundamentals as they seek to sustain economic growth. This book reflects this emphasis.

To help promote a rich, active learning experience, we have developed MyEconLab, a comprehensive online learning environment that features tests, personalized study plans, a dynamic eText, interactive tutorials, frequent news updates, and more.

The Sixth Edition Revision

ECONOMICS, SIXTH EDITION, RETAINS ALL OF the improvements achieved in its predecessor with its thorough and detailed presentation of modern economics, emphasis on real-world examples and critical thinking skills, diagrams renowned for pedagogy and precision, and path-breaking technology.

We organize our description of what is new in the sixth edition in four sections:

■ Refocused and revised introductory chapters

■ Revised and updated microeconomics content

■ Revised and updated macroeconomics content

■ MyEconLab

Refocused and Revised Introductory Chapters

1. We have refocused Chapter 1 to place greater emphasis on the role of incentives in influencing people's choices and on the question: Can choices made in the pursuit of self-interest also serve the social interest? This central question of economics is introduced through eight pressing issues in today's world that are explored further at various later points in the text. They are central planning versus the market, globalization, the new economy, the post 9/11 economy, corporate scandals, HIV/AIDS, disappearing tropical rainforests, and water shortages.

   These issues grab the student's attention and provide an early signal that economics is not a narrow business oriented subject but one that addresses issues of major social concern.

2. We have heavily revised our explanation of the gains from trade (Chapter 2), which we now begin with a numerical example and follow with a graphical analysis. The example has absolute advantage built into it so that the role of comparative advantage is demonstrated more vividly.

Revised and Updated Microeconomics Content

In addition to thorough and extensive updating, the microeconomics chapters feature the following eight revisions, some of them major:

1. Efficiency and Equity (Chapter 5) has been extensively revised. We have deleted the short refresher on efficiency and now refer the reader back to Chapter 2, where this topic is introduced and explained.

   We have added a new section that describes the eight alternative methods that might be used to allocate scarce resources: market price, command, majority rule, contest, first-come-first-served, lottery, personal characteristics, and force. By laying out these alternatives, we are better able to evaluate the ability of the market to achieve an efficient outcome. We return to these alternatives later in the chapter and ask whether there are situations in which one of them might improve on the market allocation.

   The sections that show the equivalence of demand and marginal social benefit and supply and marginal social cost have been rewritten to place the emphasis on moving from the individual to society. Consequently, we now derive the market demand and supply curves in this chapter. We also explain the connections between individual and economy-wide consumer surplus and producer surplus.

   We have rewritten the case study on a water shortage in a natural disaster to review the fairness and efficiency of the market compared with its alternatives.

2. Markets in Action (Chapter 6) has an expanded discussion of the inequity of rent ceilings, which also examines the equity implications of the alternative allocation methods. We have added an explicit graphical analysis of the inefficiency of the minimum wage and added brief discussion of living wage laws. A new section explicitly (and graphically) analyzes taxes levied on the seller and the buyer to demonstrate their equivalence.

3. Utility and Demand (Chapter 7) now opens with an explanation of how a change in income or prices changes the budget line (similar to what is done in the parallel indifference curve chapter, Chapter 8, but less technically and without equations. The section on individual demand and market demand has been removed from this chapter because it is now covered in Chapter 5—see above).

4. A new appendix to Chapter 8 explains the connection between marginal utility theory and indifference

curve theory for those wishing to teach both approaches to consumer theory.

5. Perfect Competition (Chapter 11) has a new explanation of the efficiency of perfect competition illustrated graphically with a figure of both the market and the individual firm in long-run equilibrium.

6. Monopolistic Competition and Oligopoly (Chapter 13) has an expanded discussion of short-run loss (as well as profit) and exit (as well as entry). It also has an expanded comparison of monopolistic competition and perfect competition covering both the markup over marginal cost and the excess capacity result. We have expanded the discussions of the efficiency of monopolistic competition and advertising. We also explain advertising as a signal and the role of brand names.

A new introduction to oligopoly explains the cost and demand conditions in which it arises and gives some examples. The game theory section now includes an R&D game of chicken, which we contrast with the prisoners' dilemma.

7. Competition Policy (Chapter 14) includes new material on price cap regulation, which shows that a price cap with monopoly can lower the price and increase output.

8. Public Goods and Common Resources (Chapter 16) has a new introduction on classifying goods and resources and identifies common resources—rival and nonexcludable resources. It also notes that nonrival and excludable goods and services are produced by natural monopoly. The chapter now explores the tragedy of the commons (along with the free-rider problem). We have removed the section on taxes from this chapter and now cover them only in Chapter 6.

Revised and Updated Macroeconomics Content

In addition to thorough and extensive updating, the macroeconomics chapters feature the following eight major revisions:

1. A First Look at Macroeconomics (Chapter 19) has new material on the Lucas wedge and Okun gap—the wedge created by growth slowdown and the gap created by recession. This description serves to emphasize the vital importance of economic growth and the ability of small changes to make a big difference.

2. Fiscal Policy (Chapter 24) has been revised to explain the government expenditures multiplier and autonomous tax/transfer payments multiplier more generally in terms of the slope of the aggregate expenditure curve rather than the marginal propensity to consume. We have also improved our explanation of the role of induced taxes and transfer payments in affecting the multipliers and of the distinction between cyclical and structural budget balance.

3. Money, Banking, and Interest Rates (Chapter 25) is now the first of three chapters that pave the way towards an explanation of how the Bank of Canada conducts its monetary policy. The section on the banking system is broader than in the previous editions. As before, it describes the functions of the depository institutions. But it now also provides a brief description of the role played in the banking system by the Bank of Canada. It describes and explains of the functions of the Large Value Transfer System (LVTS) and the Automated Clearing Settlement System (ACCS), which lay an institutional foundation for a later (new) description and analysis of the Bank of Canada's monetary policy.

Substantially rewritten material on how banks create money now unifies two sections of the fifth edition to explain the money multiplier. (The separate deposits multiplier is gone.)

4. The Exchange Rate (Chapter 26) is now placed before the discussion of monetary policy. This placement serves to emphasize the role of a flexible exchange rate as a foundation for the conduct of monetary policy. The chapter has a new section on exchange rate policy that reviews the four options: flexible, fixed, crawling peg, and currency union, and explains that only a flexible exchange rate leaves monetary policy free to pursue domestic goals.

5. Monetary Policy (Chapter 28) is the most heavily revised chapter in the new edition. It begins with a new discussion of the Bank of Canada's monetary policy objective, its achievement, and its rationale. A new description and analysis of the conduct of monetary policy explains how the overnight rate target is set and how it is achieved using the operating band between

bank rate and the settlements balances rate and open market operations. This section includes an explanation of the crucial distinction between an instrument rule and a targeting rule for the conduct of monetary policy. We have written a new explanation of the monetary policy transmission mechanism (building on that of the fifth edition but in the context of the Bank's current operating procedures) that includes the explanation of the interest-sensitive expenditure curve from the fifth edition Chapter 25. We also provide a new discussion of alternative approaches to monetary policy including Taylor and McCallum rules, exchange rate targeting, and money stock targeting and we explain why a rule for monetary policy is necessary.

6. Fiscal and Monetary Interactions (Chapter 29) has a new section on "Policy Coordination, Conflict, and Risk" that explains the risks of using an interest rate instrument if the response of the interest rate is too little or too slow and the difficulty of determining the appropriate level for the interest rate when fiscal policy changes.

7. The fifth edition chapters on the Business Cycle, Policy Challenges, and the Stock Market have been removed. (Web-based versions of these chapters are available for those who want to cover them).

8. Trading with the World (Chapter 32) now has a section on the balance of payments (from Chapter 34 in the previous edition).

MyEconLab

MyEconLab is a turnkey, online solution for your economics course. Featuring a new and powerful graphing engine and testing bank, students are able to self-test and generate a study plan, and instructors are able to assign homework and capture grades. With a tight, everything-in-one-place organization around the new testing tool, questions include true and false, fill-in-the-blank, multiple-choice, numerical, and complete-the-graph. Because questions are generated algorithmically, there are about 40,000 questions per chapter!

Users of our previous Web site will find MyEconLab an exciting and powerful resource. Practice Tests for each section of the textbook enable students to test their ability and identify the areas in which they need further work. Based on a student's performance on a practice test, a personalized study plan shows where further study needs to focus. Once students have received their study plan, additional practice exercises, keyed to the textbook, provide extensive practice and link directly to the eText, with animated graphs and other resources.

Users of MyEconLab will revel in the powerful graphing tool integrated into both the practice tests and practice exercises. This tool enables students to manipulate graphs and see how the concepts, numbers, and graphs are connected. A new, powerful feature is that questions using the graphing tool (like all other questions) can be submitted and graded.

For review and self-assessment, MyEconLab provides tutorials launched directly from the practice exercises. Using the tutorial instruction, students can see a demonstration of step-by-step solutions to practice problems, or they can participate in guided, step-by-step tutorials that promote self-discovery.

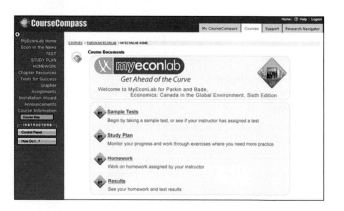

Features to Enhance Teaching and Learning

HERE, WE DESCRIBE THE CHAPTER FEATURES THAT are designed to enhance the learning process. Each chapter contains the following learning aids.

Chapter Opener

Each chapter opens with a one-page student-friendly, attention-grabbing vignette. The vignette raises questions that both motivate the student and focus the chapter. The sixth edition carries this story into the main body of the chapter, and relates it to the chapter-ending *Reading Between the Lines* feature.

Chapter Objectives

A list of learning objectives enables students to see exactly where the chapter is going and to set their goals before they begin the chapter. We link the objectives directly to the chapter's major headings.

After studying this chapter,
you will be able to
- Describe a competitive market and think about a price as an opportunity cost
- Explain the influences on demand
- Explain the influences on supply
- Explain how demand and supply determine prices and quantities bought and sold
- Use demand and supply to make predictions about changes in prices and quantities

In-Text Review Quizzes

A review quiz at the end of most major sections enables students to determine whether a topic needs further study before moving on. The review quiz includes the corresponding Study Plan in MyEconLab.

REVIEW QUIZ

1 What is the distinction between a money price and a relative price?
2 Why is a relative price an opportunity cost?
3 Can you think of an example of a good whose money price and relative price have risen?
4 Can you think of an example of a good whose money price and relative price have fallen?

myeconlab Study Plan 3.1

Key Terms

Highlighted terms within the text simplify the student's task of learning the vocabulary of economics. Each highlighted term appears in an end-of-chapter list and an end-of-book glossary with page numbers, boldfaced in the index, and on Flashcards on MyEconLab.

ffee by the price of a pack of gum and find f one price to the other. The ratio of one other is called a **relative price**, and a *relative opportunity co*

KEY TERMS

Change in demand, 62
Change in supply, 67
demanded, 65

Above full-employment equilibrium A macroeconomic equilibrium in which real GDP exceeds potential GDP. (p. 519)

Absolute advantage A person has an absolute advantage if that person is more productive than another person. (p. 42)

Diagrams That Show the Action

This book has set new standards of clarity in its diagrams. Our goal has always been to show "where the economic action is." The diagrams in this book continue to generate an enormously positive response, which confirms our view that graphical analysis is the most powerful tool available for teaching and learning economics. But many students find graphs hard to work with. For this reason, we have developed the entire art program with the study and review needs of the student in mind. The diagrams feature

- Shifted curves, equilibrium points, and other important features highlighted in red
- Colour-blended arrows to suggest movement
- Graphs paired with data tables
- Diagrams labelled with boxed notes
- Extended captions that make each diagram and its caption a self-contained object for study and review

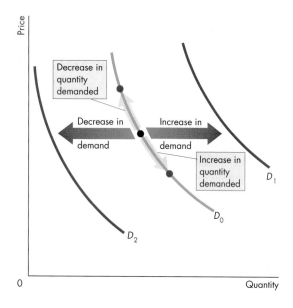

Reading Between the Lines

Each chapter ends with an economic analysis of a significant news article from the popular press together with a thorough economic analysis of the issues raised in the article. The sixth edition features 22 new *Reading Between the Lines* articles and analysis along with 8 classics from the fifth edition that remain relevant today. We chose each article because it sheds additional light on the questions first raised in the chapter opener.

Special "You're the Voter" sections in selected chapters invite students to analyze typical campaign topics and to probe their own stances on key public policy issues. Critical thinking questions about the article appear with the end-of-chapter questions and problems.

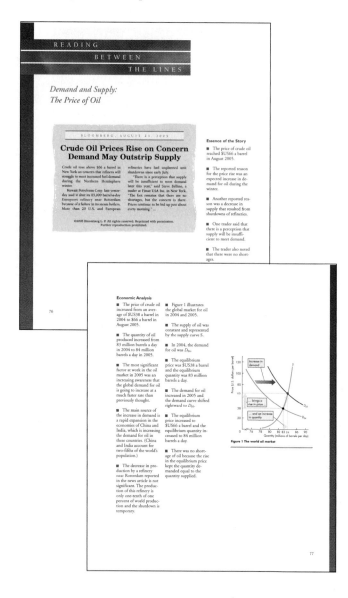

End-of-Chapter Study Material

Each chapter closes with a concise summary organized by major topics, lists of key figures, tables, and terms (all with page references), problems, critical thinking questions, and Web exercises. The problems are arranged in parallel pairs with solutions to the odd-numbered problems provided in MyEconLab.

Each problem also appears on MyEconLab, where it can be worked online in the chapter Test and Study Plan. We also provide the links needed for the Web exercises in MyEconLab.

SUMMARY

KEY POINTS

Production Possibilities and Opportunity Cost (pp. 34–36)

- The production possibilities frontier, *PPF*, is the boundary between production levels that are attainable and those that are not attainable when all the available resources are used to their limit.
- Production efficiency occurs at points on the *PPF*.
- Along the *PPF*, the opportunity cost of producing more of one good is the amount of the other good that must be given up.
- The opportunity cost of a good increases as production of the good increases.

Using Resources Efficiently (pp. 37–39)

- The marginal cost of a good is the opportunity cost of producing one more unit.
- The marginal benefit from a good is the maximum amount of another good that a person is willing to forgo to obtain more of the first good.
- The marginal benefit of a good decreases as the amount of the good available increases.
- Resources are used efficiently when the marginal cost of each good is equal to its marginal benefit.

Economic Growth (pp. 40–41)

- Economic growth, which is the expansion of production possibilities, results from capital accumulation and technological change.
- The opportunity cost of economic growth is forgone current consumption.

Gains from Trade (pp. 42–45)

- A person has a comparative advantage in producing a good if that person can produce the good at a lower opportunity cost than everyone else.
- People gain by specializing in the activity in which they have a comparative advantage and trading with others.
- Dynamic comparative advantage arises from learning-by-doing.

Economic Coordination (pp. 45–47)

- Firms coordinate a large amount of economic activity, but there is a limit to the efficient size of a firm.
- Markets coordinate the economic choices of people and firms.
- Markets can work efficiently only when property rights exist.
- Money makes trading in markets more efficient.

KEY FIGURES

Figure 2.1   Production Possibilities Frontier, 34
Figure 2.4   Efficient Use of Resources, 39
Figure 2.7   The Gains from Trade, 44
Figure 2.8   Circular Flows in the Market Economy, 47

KEY TERMS

Absolute advantage, 42
Allocative efficiency, 39
Capital accumulation, 40
Comparative advantage, 42
Dynamic comparative advantage, 45
Economic growth, 40
Firm, 45
Learning-by-doing, 45
Marginal benefit, 38
Marginal benefit curve, 38
Marginal cost, 57
Market, 46
Money, 46
Preferences, 38
Production efficiency, 35
Production possibilities frontier, 34
Property rights, 46
Technological change, 40

PROBLEMS

Go to **MyEconLab** for solutions to odd-numbered problems and additional exercises.

1. Calculate Wendell's opportunity cost of one hour of tennis when he increases the time he plays tennis from
   a. 6 hours a week.
   b. 8 hours a week.

2. Calculate Tina's opportunity cost of a day of skiing when she increases her time spent skiing from
   a. 2 to 4 days a month.
   b. 4 to 6 days a month.

3. Wendell, in problem 1, has the following marginal benefit curve:

   a. If Wendell is efficient, what is his grade?
   b. Why would Wendell be worse off getting a higher grade?

4. Tina in problem 2, has the following marginal benefit curve:

   a. If Tina is efficient, how much does she ski?
   b. Why would Tina be worse off spending more days a month skiing?

5. Sunland's production possibilities are

Food (kilograms per month)		Sunscreen (litres per month)
300	and	0
200	and	50
100	and	100
0	and	150

   a. Draw a graph of Sunland's *PPF*.

---

   b. What are Sunland's opportunity costs of producing food and sunscreen at each output?

6. Jane's Island's production possibilities are

Corn (kilograms per month)		Cloth (metres per month)
6	and	0
4	and	2
2	and	4
0	and	6

   a. Draw a graph of the *PPF* on Jane's Island.
   b. What are Jane's opportunity costs of producing corn and cloth at each output in the table?

7. In problem 5, to get a litre of sunscreen the people of Sunland are willing to give up 5 kilograms of food if they have 25 litres of sunscreen, 2 kilograms of food if they have 75 litres of sunscreen, and 1 kilogram of food if they have 125 litres of sunscreen.
   a. Draw a graph of Sunland's marginal benefit from sunscreen.
   b. What is the efficient quantity of sunscreen?

8. In problem 6, to get a metre of cloth Jane is willing to give up 1.5 kilograms of corn if she has 2 metres of cloth; 1.0 kilogram of corn if she has 4 metres of cloth; and 0.5 kilogram of corn if she has 6 metres of cloth.
   a. Draw a graph of Jane's marginal benefit from cloth.
   b. What is Jane's efficient quantity of cloth?

9. Busyland's production possibilities are

Food (kilograms per month)		Sunscreen (litres per month)
150	and	0
100	and	100
50	and	200
0	and	300

   Calculate Busyland's opportunity costs of food and sunscreen at each output in the table.

10. Joe Island's production possibilities are

Corn (kilograms per month)		Cloth (metres per month)
12	and	0
8	and	1
4	and	2
0	and	3

   What are Joe's opportunity costs of producing corn and cloth at each output in the table?

11. In problems 5 and 9, Sunland and Busyland each produce and consume 100 kilograms of food and 100 litres of sunscreen per month, and they do not trade. Now the countries begin to trade with each other.
   a. What good does Sunland sell to Busyland and what good does it buy from Busyland?
   b. If Sunland and Busyland divide the total output of food and sunscreen equally, what are the gains from trade?

12. In problems 6 and 10, Jane's Island and Joe's Island each produce and consume 4 kilograms of corn and 2 metres of cloth and they do not trade. Now the islands begin to trade.
   a. What good does Jane sell to Joe and what good does Jane buy from Joe?
   b. If Jane and Joe divide the total output of corn and cloth equally, what are the gains from trade?

CRITICAL THINKING

1. After you have studied *Reading Between the Lines* on pp. 48–49, answer the following questions:
   a. At what point on the blue *PPF* in Fig. 1 on p. 49 is the combination of education goods and services and consumption goods and services efficient? Explain your answer.
   b. Students are facing rising tuition. How does higher tuition change the opportunity cost of education and how does it change the *PPF*s in Fig. 1 and Fig. 2?
   c. Who receives the benefits from education? Is the marginal cost of education equal to the marginal benefit of education? Is resource use in the market for education efficient?

WEB EXERCISES

Use the links on **MyEconLab** to work the following exercise.

1. Obtain data on the tuition and other costs of enrolling in the MBA program at a school that interests you.
   a. Draw a *PPF* that shows the tradeoff that you would face if you decided to enroll in the MBA program.
   b. Do you think the marginal benefit of an MBA exceeds the marginal cost?

For the Instructor

THIS BOOK ENABLES YOU TO ACHIEVE THREE objectives in your principles course:

- Focus on the economic way of thinking
- Explain the issues and problems of our time
- Choose your own course structure

Focus on the Economic Way of Thinking

You know how hard it is to encourage a student to think like an economist. But that is your goal. Consistent with this goal, the text focuses on and repeatedly uses the central ideas: choice; tradeoff; opportunity cost; the margin; incentives; the gains from voluntary exchange; the forces of demand, supply, and equilibrium; the pursuit of economic rent; and the effects of government actions on the economy.

Explain the Issues and Problems of Our Time

Students must use the central ideas and tools if they are to begin to *understand* them. There is no better way to motivate students than by using the tools of economics to explain the issues that confront today's world. Issues such as central planning versus the market; globalization and the emergence of China as a major economic force; the new economy with new near monopolies such as eBay and the widening income gap between rich and poor; the post-9/11 economy and the reallocation of resources towards counterterrorism and the defence that it entails; corporate scandals and the principal-agent problems and incentives faced by corporate managers; HIV/AIDS and the enormous cost of drugs for treating it; the disappearing tropical rainforests and the challenge that this tragedy of the commons creates; the challenge of managing the world's water resources.

Choose Your Own Course Structure

You want to teach your own course. We have organized this book to enable you to do so. We demonstrate the book's flexibility in the flexibility chart and alternative sequences table that appear on pp. xxii–xxv. You can use this book to teach a traditional course that blends theory and policy or a current policy issues course. Your micro course can emphasize theory or policy. You can structure your macro course to emphasize long-term growth and supply-side fundamentals. Or you can follow a traditional macro sequence and emphasize short-term fluctuations. The choices are yours.

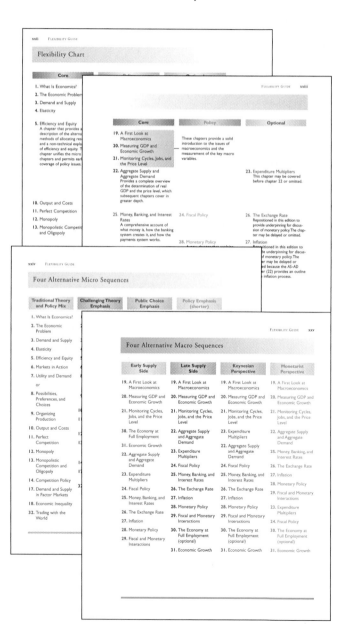

Instructor's Manual

The Instructor's Manual, written by Torben Drewes of Trent University, integrates the teaching and learning package and is a guide to all the supplements. Each chapter contains a chapter outline, what's new in the sixth edition, teaching suggestions, a look at where we have been and where we are going, descriptions of the electronic supplements, and additional discussion questions. The chapter outline and teaching suggestions sections are keyed to the PowerPoint lecture notes. Solutions to end-of-chapter problems are provided in a separate section.

New Lecture Notes This edition of the Instructor's Manual offers two new exciting features. Extensive lecture notes that incorporate alternative teaching examples— "Points of Interest"—enable a new user of Parkin and Bade to walk into the classroom well armed with engaging stories and explanations and a seasoned user to access a whole new set of fresh examples.

New Worksheets Another new and innovative feature is a set of worksheets. These Worksheets ask the student to contemplate real-world problems that illustrate economic principles. Examples include showing the effect of the catastropic events of 9/11 using a marginal cost/marginal benefit diagram and calculating the effects of funding social security for the huge number of baby-boomer retirees. Instructors can assign these as in-class group projects or as homework. There is a Worksheet for every chapter.

Two Test Banks

To provide lots of choice when preparing tests and exams, we offer two Test Banks in TestGen with a total of more than 8,700 questions. Test Bank 1, prepared by Morteza Haghiri of Mount Allison University and Wilson Wong of Champlain College, contains over 4,500 multiple-choice questions. Test Bank 2, prepared by Sigrid Ewender of Kwantlen University College and Ariel Lade of the University of Victoria, contains about 4,200 multiple-choice, true-false, and short-answer questions. Both testbanks are thoroughly revised, upgraded, and improved.

Personal Response System Questions

Gauge your students' course progress with clicker questions that enable instructors to pose questions, record results, and display those results instantly in the classroom. Questions are provided in PowerPoint® format.

Image Library

Nearly all of the tables and figures from the text are available for viewing in the Image Library included on the Instructor's Resource CD-ROM.

PowerPoint® Resources

We have developed a full-colour Microsoft PowerPoint Lecture Presentation for each chapter that includes all the figures from the text, animated graphs, and speaking notes. The slide outlines are based on the chapter outlines in the Instructor's Manual, and the speaking notes are based on the Instructor's Manual teaching suggestions. The presentations can be used electronically in the classroom or can be printed to create hard-copy transparency masters, and they can be accessed using Windows or Macintosh. We have also prepared a set of PowerPoint lecture notes for students. Students can download these from MyEconLab, print them, and bring them to class. The instructor's set contains the option to present full-screen-size graphs.

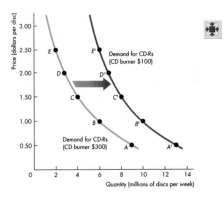

Instructor's Resource CD-ROM with Computerized Test Banks

This CD contains Computerized Test Bank files, Personal Response System questions, Instructor's Manual files in Microsoft Word, PowerPoint files, and an Image Library. Our two test banks are available in Test Generator Software (TestGen-EQ with QuizMaster-EQ). Fully networkable, they are available for Windows and Macintosh. TestGen-EQ's new graphical interface enables instructors to view, edit, and add questions; transfer questions to tests; and print different forms of tests. Tests can be formatted with varying fonts and styles, margins, and headers and footers, as in any word-processing document. Search and sort features let the instructor quickly locate questions and arrange them in a preferred order. QuizMaster-EQ, working with your school's computer network, automatically grades the exams, stores the results on disk, and allows the instructor to view or print a variety of reports.

Course Management Systems

We offer three alternative course management systems—CourseCompass, Blackboard, and WebCT. Each system provides a dynamic, interactive, content-rich, and flexible online course management tool that enables instructors to easily and effectively customize online course materials to suit their needs. Instructors can track and analyze student performance on an array of Internet activities. Please contact your Pearson Education Canada representative for more details.

MyEconLab

The Web site that accompanies *Economics*, Sixth Edition, breaks new ground by providing a structured environment in which students can practice what they learn and test their understanding and then pursue a study plan that is generated from their performance on practice tests. Every new copy of Parkin/Bade, *Economics: Canada in the Global Environment*, Sixth Edition, comes with a student code to access the power of MyEconLab.

MyEconLab provides rich content resources keyed to the eText as well as flexible tools that enable instructors to easily and effectively customize online course materials to suit their needs.

Instructors can create and assign tests, quizzes, or graded homework assignments that incorporate graphing questions and online versions of the end-of-chapter problems in the textbook. MyEconLab saves instructors time by automatically grading all questions and tracking results in an online grade book. Now available from within MyEconLab is the added testing capability of over 4,000 multiple-choice questions derived from the sixth edition of the Parkin/Bade Test Bank 1.

Once registered for MyEconLab, instructors have access to downloadable supplements such as Instructor's Manuals, PowerPoint lecture notes, and Test Banks. Instructors also have access to a "Consult the Author" feature that allows them to ask questions of and make suggestions to the author via e-mail and receive a response within 24 hours.

For more information about MyEconLab, or to request an Instructor Access Code, visit **http://www.myeconlab.com.**

For the Student

Study Guide

The sixth edition Study Guide by Avi Cohen of York University and Harvey King of the University of Regina is carefully coordinated with the main text. Each chapter of the Study Guide contains

- Key concepts
- Helpful hints
- True-false questions that ask students to explain their answers
- Multiple-choice questions
- Short-answer questions

Each part allows students to test their cumulative understanding with questions that go across chapters and work a sample midterm examination.

MyEconLab

MyEconLab—the online homework and tutorial system that is packaged with every new copy of *Economics*—puts students in control of their own learning through a suite of study and practice tools correlated with the online, interactive version of the textbook and other media tools. Every new copy of Parkin/Bade, *Economics: Canada in the Global Environment*, Sixth Edition, comes with a student code to access the power of MyEconLab.

Within MyEconLab's structured environment, students practice what they learn, test their understanding, and then pursue a Study Plan that MyEconLab generates for them based on their performance on practice tests.

At the core of MyEconLab are the following features:

- **Practice Tests**—Practice tests for every chapter section enable students to test their understanding and identify the areas in which they need to do further work. Practice Test questions based directly on the review quizzes and end-of-chapter problems ask students to work with graphs: interpreting them, manipulating them, and even drawing them. Instructors can let students use the supplied pre-built tests or create their own tests.

- **Personalized Study Plan**—Based on a student's performance on a practice test, MyEconLab generates a Personalized Study Plan that shows where further study is needed. The correlation between the text and MyEconLab is perfect and seamless.

- **Additional Practice Exercises**—The Personalized Study Plans direct students to additional exercises for each topic. Additional practice exercises are keyed to each section of the textbook and link students to the eText with animated graphs.

- **Tutorial Instruction**—Launched from the additional practice exercises, tutorial instruction is provided in the form of solutions to problems, step-by-step explanations, and other media-based explanations.

- **Powerful Graphing Tool**—Integrated into the practice tests and additional practice exercises, the graphing tool lets students manipulate and even draw graphs so that they grasp how the concepts, numbers, and graphs are connected.

- Three types of graphing problems:

  1. **Draw Graphs**—MyEconLab's Draw Graph problems automatically grade the graphs students draw.

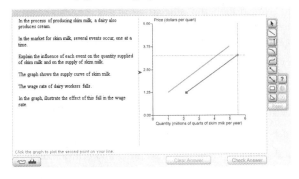

  2. **Model-based Graphs**—Students can change data inputs and watch curves shift. Multiple-choice, true-false, and short-answer questions quiz students on their interpretations of the graph.

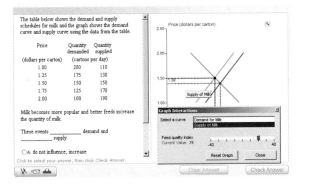

3. **Data Graphs**—Students can plot up to five variables against each other to give a clear picture of how economic indicators relate to each other.

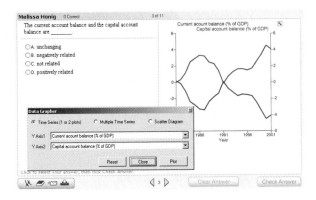

MyEconLab Study Plan links to the following resources:

- **eText**—Quick reference to specific pages of the textbook that correspond to each Study Plan exercise.

- **Animated Figures**—Step-by-step animations of every figure from the textbook with audio explanations of the action.

- **Glossary**—A searchable version of the textbook glossary with additional examples and links to related terms.

Additional MyEconLab Resources

- **Ask the Authors**—Virtual office hours with Robin Bade and Michael Parkin.

- **Glossary Flashcards**—Every key term available as a flash-card, allowing students to quiz themselves on vocabulary from one or more chapters at a time.

- **Economics in the News**—Updated every week during the school year, news items with links to sources for further reading and discussion questions.

- **Links for Web Exercises**—All the links needed for answering the Web Exercises in the textbook—checked and updated regularly so that they don't disappear.

PowerPoints Lecture Notes

We have prepared a full set of PowerPoint lecture notes for students. These notes contain an outline of each chapter with the textbook figures animated. Students can downloaded these lecture notes from MyEconLab, print them, and bring them to class or use them in creating their own set of notes for use when preparing for tests and exams.

Acknowledgments

WE THANK OUR CURRENT AND FORMER COLLEAGUES AND friends at the University of Western Ontario who have taught us so much. They are Jim Davies, Jeremy Greenwood, Ig Horstmann, Peter Howitt, Greg Huffman, David Laidler, Phil Reny, Chris Robinson, John Whalley, and Ron Wonnacott. We also thank Doug McTaggart and Christopher Findlay, co-authors of the Australian edition, and Melanie Powell and Kent Matthews, co-authors of the European edition. Suggestions arising from their adaptations of earlier editions have been helpful to us in preparing this edition.

We thank the several thousand students whom we have been privileged to teach. The instant response that comes from the look of puzzlement or enlightenment has taught us how to teach economics.

It is an especial joy to thank the many outstanding managers, editors, and others at Pearson Education Canada who have contributed to the concerted publishing effort that brought this edition to completion. Allan Reynolds, President and CEO, and Steve O'Hern, President of Higher Education, have once again provided outstanding corporate direction. They have worked hard to build a corporate culture that brings the best out of its editors and authors. Michael Young, Vice President and Editorial Director for Higher Education, has been a devoted contributor through his appointment and management of the outstanding editors with whom we've worked. Gary Bennett, now Editor in Chief of Business and Economics, has played a major role in bringing this revision to completion and in finding and managing a team of outstanding supplements authors. Stephen Broadbent brought his experience and dedicated professionalism to the development effort. Matthew Christian and Laura Canning built MyEconLab. Bill Todd, Marketing Manager, provided inspired marketing direction. His brochures and, more important, his thoughtful questions and prodding for material had a significant impact on the shape of the text. Anthony Leung, Designer, designed the cover, text,

and package and surpassed the challenge of ensuring that we meet the highest design standards. Jennifer Handel, our Production Editor, worked miracles on a tight production schedule and coped calmly with late-changing content. Lu Cormier copyedited the text manuscript and Edie Franks proofread the final pages. We thank all of these wonderful people. It has been inspiring to work with them and to share in creating what we believe is a truly outstanding educational tool.

We thank our supplements authors, Avi Cohen, Harvey King, Torben Drewes, Sigrid Ewender, Morteza Haghiri, Ariel Lade, and Wilson Wong. And we thank Kit Pasula for the extraordinarily careful accuracy review of near-final pages. Kit caught many slips and even some errors of substance that we are relieved to have had the opportunity of correcting.

We thank the people who work directly with us. Jeannie Gillmore provided outstanding research assistance on many topics, including the *Reading Between the Lines* news articles and worked long and diligently to create the MyEconLab test questions and guided solutions. Jane McAndrew provided excellent library help. Richard Parkin created the electronic art files and offered many ideas that improved the figures in this book. And Laurel Davies managed an ever-growing and more complex coding of draw-graph objects, feedback, and many other features of the MyEconLab question database.

As with the previous editions, this one owes an enormous debt to our students. We dedicate this book to them and again thank them for their careful reading and critical comments on the previous edition.

Classroom experience will continue to test the value of this book. We would appreciate hearing from instructors and students about how we can continue to improve it in future editions.

Michael Parkin
Robin Bade
London, Ontario, Canada
michael.parkin@uwo.ca
robin@econ100.com

Reviewers

Ather H. Akbari, Saint Mary's University
Iris Au, University of Toronto
Bogdan Buduru, Concordia University
Beverly J. Cameron, University of Manitoba
Jason Childs, University of New Brunswick, Saint John
Marilyn Cottrell, Brock University
Livio Di Matteo, Lakehead University
Torben Drewes, Trent University
Oliver Franke, Athabasca University
Bruno Fullone, George Brown College
Philippe Ghayad, Dawson College and Concordia University
David Gray, University of Ottawa
Eric Kam, Ryerson University
Cevat Burc Kayahan, University of Guelph
Eva Lau, University of Waterloo
Anastasia M. Lintner, University of Guelph
Christian Marfels, Dalhousie University
Roberto Martínez-Espiñeira, St. Francis Xavier University
Rob Moir, University of New Brunswick Saint John
Saeed Moshiri, University of Manitoba
Derek Pyne, Memorial University of Newfoundland
Jim Sentance, University of Prince Edward Island
Lance Shandler, Kwantlen University College
Peter W. Sinclair, Wilfrid Laurier University
Glen Stirling, University of Western Ontario
Irene Trela, University of Western Ontario
Jane Waples, Memorial University of Newfoundland
Andrew Wong, Grant MacEwan College
Peter Wylie, University of British Colombia, Okanagan
Ayoub Yousefi, University of Western Ontario

Flexibility Chart

Core	Policy	Optional

Core

1. What Is Economics?
2. The Economic Problem
3. Demand and Supply
4. Elasticity

5. Efficiency and Equity
A chapter that provides a description of the alternative methods of allocating resources and a non-technical explanation of efficiency and equity. The chapter unifies the micro chapters and permits early coverage of policy issues.

Policy

6. Markets in Action
A unique chapter that gives extensive applications of demand and supply.

Optional

1. Appendix: Graphs in Economics
A good appendix to assign to the student with a fear of graphs.

7. Utility and Demand
Although this chapter is optional, it may be covered if desired *before* demand in Chapter 3.

8. Possibilities, Preferences, and Choices
A full chapter on this strictly optional topic to ensure that it is covered clearly with intuitive explanations and illustrations.

9. Organizing Production
This chapter may be skipped or assigned as a reading.

---

10. Output and Costs
11. Perfect Competition
12. Monopoly
13. Monopolistic Competition and Oligopoly

14. Competition Policy

15. Externalities
Describes the full range of externalities, explains the Coase theorem, and the use of taxes, subsidies, and market solutions.

16. Public Goods and Common Resources
Describes the four types of goods and explains the free-rider problem and the tragedy of the commons.

18. Economic Inequality

17. Demand and Supply in Factor Markets
Enables you to cover all the factor market issues in a single chapter. Includes an explanation of present value.

17. Appendix: Labour Unions

Core	Policy	Optional
19. A First Look at Macroeconomics	These chapters provide a solid introduction to the issues of macroeconomics and the measurement of the key macro variables.	
20. Measuring GDP and Economic Growth		
21. Monitoring Cycles, Jobs, and the Price Level		
22. Aggregate Supply and Aggregate Demand Provides a complete overview of the determination of real GDP and the price level, which subsequent chapters cover in greater depth.		**23.** Expenditure Multipliers This chapter may be covered before chapter 22 or omitted.
25. Money, Banking, and Interest Rates A comprehensive account of what money is, how the banking system creates it, and how the payments system works.	**24.** Fiscal Policy	**26.** The Exchange Rate Repositioned in this edition to provide underpinning for discussion of monetary policy. The chapter may be delayed or omitted.
	28. Monetary Policy A new chapter that explains what the Bank of Canada does and how its actions influence the economy.	**27.** Inflation Repositioned in this edition to provide underpinning for discussion of monetary policy. The chapter may be delayed or omitted because the *AS–AD* chapter (22) provides an outline of the inflation process.
	29. Fiscal and Monetary Interactions	
30. The Economy at Full Employment A unique chapter that explains the forces that determine potential GDP.	These chapters may be covered before Chapter 22.	
31. Economic Growth Although optional, this chapter is crucial for understanding Canada's productivity growth slowdown.		
		32. Trading with the World

Four Alternative Micro Sequences

Traditional Theory and Policy Mix	Challenging Theory Emphasis	Public Choice Emphasis	Policy Emphasis (shorter)
1. What Is Economics?	1. What Is Economics?	1. What Is Economics?	1. What Is Economics?
2. The Economic Problem	2. The Economic Problem	2. The Economic Problem	2. The Economic Problem
3. Demand and Supply	3. Demand and Supply	3. Demand and Supply	3. Demand and Supply
4. Elasticity	4. Elasticity	4. Elasticity	4. Elasticity
5. Efficiency and Equity	5. Efficiency and Equity	5. Efficiency and Equity	5. Efficiency and Equity
6. Markets in Action	6. Markets in Action	6. Markets in Action	6. Markets in Action
7. Utility and Demand	8. Possibilities, Preferences, and Choices	7. Utility and Demand	15. Externalities
or	9. Organizing Production	9. Organizing Production	16. Public Goods and Common Resources
8. Possibilities, Preferences, and Choices	10. Output and Costs	10. Output and Costs	17. Demand and Supply in Factor Markets
9. Organizing Production	11. Perfect Competition	11. Perfect Competition	18. Economic Inequality
10. Output and Costs	12. Monopoly	12. Monopoly	32. Trading with the World
11. Perfect Competition	13. Monopolistic Competition and Oligopoly	13. Monopolistic Competition and Oligopoly	
12. Monopoly	14. Competition Policy	14. Competition Policy	
13. Monopolistic Competition and Oligopoly	17. Demand and Supply in Factor Markets	15. Externalities	
14. Competition Policy	32. Trading with the World	16. Public Goods and Common Resources	
17. Demand and Supply in Factor Markets			
18. Economic Inequality			
32. Trading with the World			

Four Alternative Macro Sequences

Early Supply Side	Late Supply Side	Keynesian Perspective	Monetarist Perspective
19. A First Look at Macroeconomics	19. A First Look at Macroeconomics	19. A First Look at Macroeconomics	19. A First Look at Macroeconomics
20. Measuring GDP and Economic Growth	20. Measuring GDP and Economic Growth	20. Measuring GDP and Economic Growth	20. Measuring GDP and Economic Growth
21. Monitoring Cycles, Jobs, and the Price Level	21. Monitoring Cycles, Jobs, and the Price Level	21. Monitoring Cycles, Jobs, and the Price Level	21. Monitoring Cycles, Jobs, and the Price Level
30. The Economy at Full Employment	22. Aggregate Supply and Aggregate Demand	23. Expenditure Multipliers	22. Aggregate Supply and Aggregate Demand
31. Economic Growth	23. Expenditure Multipliers	22. Aggregate Supply and Aggregate Demand	25. Money, Banking, and Interest Rates
22. Aggregate Supply and Aggregate Demand	24. Fiscal Policy	24. Fiscal Policy	26. The Exchange Rate
23. Expenditure Multipliers	25. Money, Banking, and Interest Rates	25. Money, Banking, and Interest Rates	27. Inflation
24. Fiscal Policy	26. The Exchange Rate	26. The Exchange Rate	28. Monetary Policy
25. Money, Banking, and Interest Rates	27. Inflation	27. Inflation	29. Fiscal and Monetary Interactions
26. The Exchange Rate	28. Monetary Policy	28. Monetary Policy	23. Expenditure Multipliers
27. Inflation	29. Fiscal and Monetary Interactions	29. Fiscal and Monetary Interactions	24. Fiscal Policy
28. Monetary Policy	30. The Economy at Full Employment (optional)	30. The Economy at Full Employment (optional)	30. The Economy at Full Employment (optional)
29. Fiscal and Monetary Interactions	31. Economic Growth	31. Economic Growth	31. Economic Growth

BRIEF CONTENTS

Part 1   **Introduction**   1

Chapter 1   What Is Economics?   1
Chapter 2   The Economic Problem   33

Part 2   **How Markets Work**   59

Chapter 3   Demand and Supply   59
Chapter 4   Elasticity   83
Chapter 5   Efficiency and Equity   103
Chapter 6   Markets in Action   123

Part 3   **Households' Choices**   153

Chapter 7   Utility and Demand   153
Chapter 8   Possibilities, Preferences, and Choices   171

Part 4   **Firms and Markets**   197

Chapter 9   Organizing Production   197
Chapter 10   Output and Costs   219
Chapter 11   Perfect Competition   239
Chapter 12   Monopoly   263
Chapter 13   Monopolistic Competition and Oligopoly   285

Part 5   **Market Failure and Government**   323

Chapter 14   Competition Policy   323
Chapter 15   Externalities   345
Chapter 16   Public Goods and Common Resources   363

Part 6   **Factor Markets and Inequality**   387

Chapter 17   Demand and Supply in Factor Markets   387
Chapter 18   Economic Inequality   419

Part 7   **Macroeconomic Overview**   445

Chapter 19   A First Look at Macroeconomics   445
Chapter 20   Measuring GDP and Economic Growth   465
Chapter 21   Monitoring Cycles, Jobs, and the Price Level   485
Chapter 22   Aggregate Supply and Aggregate Demand   507

Part 8   **Aggregate Demand and Inflation**   535

Chapter 23   Expenditure Multipliers   535
Chapter 24   Fiscal Policy   563
Chapter 25   Money, Banking, and Interest Rates   589
Chapter 26   The Exchange Rate   611
Chapter 27   Inflation   631
Chapter 28   Monetary Policy   655
Chapter 29   Fiscal and Monetary Interactions   677

Part 9   **Aggregate Supply, Economic Growth, and International Trade**   705

Chapter 30   The Economy at Full Employment   705
Chapter 31   Economic Growth   733
Chapter 32   Trading with the World   755

CONTENTS

Part 1 Introduction 1

Chapter 1 What Is Economics? 1

Understanding Our Changing World 1

Definition of Economics 2
  Microeconomics 2
  Macroeconomics 2

Two Big Economic Questions 3
  What, How, and For Whom? 3
  When Is the Pursuit of Self-Interest in the Social
    Interest? 5

The Economic Way of Thinking 9
  Choices and Tradeoffs 9
  What, How, and For Whom Tradeoffs 9
  Choices Bring Change 10
  Opportunity Cost 10
  Choosing at the Margin 11
  Responding to Incentives 11
  Human Nature, Incentives, and Institutions 11

Economics: A Social Science 12
  Observation and Measurement 12
  Model Building 12
  Testing Models 12
  Obstacles and Pitfalls in Economics 13
  Agreement and Disagreement 14

Chapter 1 Appendix Graphs in Economics 17

Graphing Data 17
  Time-Series Graphs 18
  Cross-Section Graphs 18
  Scatter Diagrams 19

Graphs Used in Economic Models 20
  Variables That Move in the Same Direction 20
  Variables That Move in Opposite Directions 21
  Variables That Have a Maximum or a Minimum 22
  Variables That Are Unrelated 23

The Slope of a Relationship 24
  The Slope of a Straight Line 24
  The Slope of a Curved Line 25

Graphing Relationships Among More Than
Two Variables 26

MATHEMATICAL NOTE
  Equations to Straight Lines 28

Summary (Key Points, Key Figures and Tables, and Key Terms), Problems, Critical Thinking, and Web Exercises appear at the end of each chapter.

Chapter 2 **The Economic Problem** 33

Good, Better, Best! **33**

Production Possibilities and Opportunity Cost **34**
Production Possibilities Frontier **34**
Production Efficiency **35**
Tradeoff Along the *PPF* **35**
Opportunity Cost **35**

Using Resources Efficiently **37**
The *PPF* and Marginal Cost **37**
Preferences and Marginal Benefit **38**
Efficient Use of Resources **39**

Economic Growth **40**
The Cost of Economic Growth **40**
Economic Growth in Canada and
Hong Kong **41**

Gains from Trade **42**
Comparative Advantage and Absolute Advantage **42**
Achieving the Gains from Trade **43**
Dynamic Comparative Advantage **45**

Economic Coordination **45**
Firms **45**
Property Rights **46**
Markets **46**
Money **46**
Circular Flows Through Markets **46**
Coordinating Decisions **46**

READING BETWEEN THE LINES
POLICY WATCH
The Cost and Benefit of Education **48**

Part 1 Wrap Up
Understanding the Scope of Economics 53
Probing the Ideas:
The Sources of Economic Wealth **54**
Talking with Lawrence H. Summers **56**

Part 2 **How Markets Work** 59

Chapter 3 **Demand and Supply** 59

Slide, Rocket, and Roller Coaster **59**

Markets and Prices **60**

Demand **61**
The Law of Demand **61**
Demand Curve and Demand Schedule **61**
A Change in Demand **62**
A Change in the Quantity Demanded Versus a Change
in Demand **64**

Supply **66**
The Law of Supply **66**
Supply Curve and Supply Schedule **66**
A Change in Supply **67**
A Change in the Quantity Supplied Versus a Change in
Supply **68**

Market Equilibrium **70**
Price as a Regulator **70**
Price Adjustments **71**

Predicting Changes in Price and Quantity **72**
A Change in Demand **72**
A Change in Supply **73**
A Change in Both Demand and Supply **74**

READING BETWEEN THE LINES
Demand and Supply: The Price of Oil **76**

MATHEMATICAL NOTE
Demand, Supply, and Equilibrium **78**

Chapter 4 **Elasticity** 83

Tough Times in the Recording Industry   83

Price Elasticity of Demand   **84**
  Calculating Price Elasticity of Demand   **85**
  Inelastic and Elastic Demand   **86**
  Elasticity Along a Straight-Line
    Demand Curve   **87**
  Total Revenue and Elasticity   **88**
  Your Expenditure and Your Elasticity   **89**
  The Factors That Influence the
    Elasticity of Demand   **89**

More Elasticities of Demand   **91**
  Cross Elasticity of Demand   **91**
  Income Elasticity of Demand   **92**
  Real-World Income Elasticities of Demand   **93**

Elasticity of Supply   **94**
  Calculating the Elasticity of Supply   **94**
  The Factors That Influence the
    Elasticity of Supply   **95**

READING BETWEEN THE LINES
  Elasticities of Demand for CDs   **98**

Chapter 5 **Efficiency and Equity** 103

Self-Interest and the Social Interest   **103**

Resource Allocation Methods   **104**
  Market Price   **104**
  Command   **104**
  Majority Rule   **104**
  Contest   **104**
  First-Come, First-Served   **104**
  Lottery   **105**
  Personal Characteristics   **105**
  Force   **105**

Demand and Marginal Benefit   **106**
  Demand, Willingness to Pay, and Value   **106**
  Individual Demand and Market Demand   **106**
  Consumer Surplus   **107**

Supply and Marginal Cost   **108**
  Supply, Cost, and Minimum Supply-Price   **108**
  Individual Supply and Market Supply   **108**
  Producer Surplus   **109**

Is the Competitive Market Efficient?   **110**
  Efficiency of Competitive Equilibrium   **110**
  The Invisible Hand   **111**
  The Invisible Hand at Work Today   **111**
  Underproduction and Overproduction   **111**
  Obstacles to Efficiency   **112**
  Alternatives to the Market   **113**

Are Markets Fair?   **114**
  It's Not Fair If the *Result* Isn't Fair   **114**
  It's Not Fair If the *Rules* Aren't Fair   **116**
  Case Study: A Water Shortage in a
    Natural Disaster   **116**

READING BETWEEN THE LINES
POLICY WATCH
  Inefficiency in Global Water Use   **118**

Chapter 6 Markets in Action 123

Turbulent Times 123

Housing Markets and Rent Ceilings 124
The Market Before and After the Earthquake 124
Long-Run Adjustments 125
A Regulated Housing Market 125
Search Activity 126
Black Markets 126
Inefficiency of Rent Ceilings 127
Are Rent Ceilings Fair? 127
Rent Ceilings in Practice 128

The Labour Market and the Minimum Wage 128
A Minimum Wage 130
Inefficiency of a Minimum Wage 130
Provincial Minimum Wage Laws and Their Effects 131
A Living Wage 131

Taxes 132
Tax Incidence 132
A Tax on Sellers 132
A Tax on Buyers 133
Equivalence of Tax on Buyers and Sellers 133
Tax Division and Elasticity of Demand 134
Tax Division and Elasticity of Supply 135
Taxes in Practice 136
Taxes and Efficiency 136

Subsidies and Quotas 137
Harvest Fluctuations 137
Subsidies 138
Production Quotas 139

Markets for Illegal Goods 140
A Free Market for Drugs 140
A Market for Illegal Drugs 140
Legalizing and Taxing Drugs 141

READING BETWEEN THE LINES
POLICY WATCH
The Minimum Wage in Action 142

Part 2 Wrap Up
Understanding How Markets Work 147
Probing the Ideas:
Discovering the Laws of Demand
and Supply 148
Talking with Paul Beaudry 150

Part 3 Households' Choices 153

Chapter 7 Utility and Demand 153

Water, Water, Everywhere 153

The Household's Budget 154
Consumption Possibilities 154
Relative Price 154
Real Income 155

Preferences and Utility 156
Total Utility 156
Marginal Utility 156
Diminishing Marginal Utility 156

Maximizing Utility 158
The Utility-Maximizing Choice 158
Equalizing Marginal Utility per Dollar 158

Predictions of Marginal Utility Theory 160
A Fall in the Price of a Movie 160
A Rise in the Price of Pop 161
A Rise in Income 163
Temperature: An Analogy 164

Efficiency, Price, and Value 164
Consumer Efficiency and Consumer Surplus 164
The Paradox of Value 164

READING BETWEEN THE LINES
What's the Marginal Utility of a Boat Ride? 166

Chapter 8 **Possibilities, Preferences, and Choices 171**

Subterranean Movements **171**

Consumption Possibilities **172**
   The Budget Equation **173**

Preferences and Indifference Curves **175**
   Marginal Rate of Substitution **176**
   Degree of Substitutability **177**

Predicting Consumer Behaviour **178**
   A Change in Price **179**
   A Change in Income **180**
   Substitution Effect and Income Effect **181**
   Back to the Facts **182**

Work–Leisure Choices **182**
   Labour Supply **182**
   The Labour Supply Curve **183**

READING BETWEEN THE LINES
The Marginal Rate of Substitution Between Printed Books and E-Books **184**

Chapter 8 Appendix **Marginal Utility and Indifference Curves 189**

Two Ways of Describing Preferences **189**

Maximizing Utility Is Choosing the Best Affordable Point **190**

Utility Exists! **190**

 Part 3 Wrap Up
Understanding Households' Choices 191
   Probing the Ideas:
      People as Rational Decision Makers **192**
   Talking with Steven D. Levitt **194**

Part 4   Firms and Markets   197

Chapter 9   Organizing Production   197

Spinning a Web   197

The Firm and Its Economic Problem   198
 The Firm's Goal   198
 Measuring the Firm's Profit   198
 Opportunity Cost   198
 Economic Profit   199
 Economic Accounting: A Summary   199
 The Firm's Constraints   200

Technological and Economic Efficiency   201
 Technological Efficiency   201
 Economic Efficiency   201

Information and Organization   203
 Command Systems   203
 Incentive Systems   203
 Mixing the Systems   203
 The Principal–Agent Problem   204
 Coping with the Principal–Agent Problem   204
 Types of Business Organization   204
 Pros and Cons of Different
  Types of Firms   205
 The Relative Importance of Different
  Types of Firms   206

Markets and the Competitive Environment   207
 Measures of Concentration   208
 Concentration Measures for the
  Canadian Economy   209
 Limitations of Concentration Measures   209
 Market Structures in the North American
  Economy   211

Markets and Firms   212
 Market Coordination   212
 Why Firms?   212

READING BETWEEN THE LINES
 Nortel's Challenges and Opportunities   214

Chapter 10   Output and Costs   219

Technologies Converging   219

Decision Time Frames   220
 The Short Run   220
 The Long Run   220

Short-Run Technology Constraint   221
 Product Schedules   221
 Product Curves   221
 Total Product Curve   222
 Marginal Product Curve   222
 Average Product Curve   224
 Marginal Grade and Grade
  Point Average   224

Short-Run Cost   225
 Total Cost   225
 Marginal Cost   226
 Average Cost   226
 Why the Average Total Cost Curve
  Is U-Shaped   226
 Cost Curves and Product Curves   228
 Shifts in the Cost Curves   228

Long-Run Cost   230
 The Production Function   230
 Short-Run Cost and Long-Run Cost   230
 The Long-Run Average Cost Curve   232
 Economies and Diseconomies of Scale   232

READING BETWEEN THE LINES
 Traditional Phone Versus VoIP   234

Chapter 11 **Perfect Competition**   239

Sweet Competition   239

Competition   240
How Perfect Competition Arises   240
Price Takers   240
Economic Profit and Revenue   240

The Firm's Decisions in Perfect Competition   242
Profit-Maximizing Output   242
Marginal Analysis   244
Profits and Losses in the Short Run   245
The Firm's Short-Run Supply Curve   246
Short-Run Industry Supply Curve   247

Output, Price, and Profit in Perfect Competition   248
Short-Run Equilibrium   248
A Change in Demand   248
Long-Run Adjustments   249
Entry and Exit   249
Changes in Plant Size   250
Long-Run Equilibrium   251

Changing Tastes and Advancing Technology   252
A Permanent Change in Demand   252
External Economies and Diseconomies   253
Technological Change   255

Competition and Efficiency   256
Efficient Use of Resources   256
Choices, Equilibrium, and Efficiency   256

READING BETWEEN THE LINES
Perfect Competition in Maple Syrup   258

Chapter 12 **Monopoly**   263

Dominating the Internet   263

Market Power   264
How Monopoly Arises   264
Monopoly Price-Setting Strategies   265

A Single-Price Monopoly's Output and Price Decision   266
Price and Marginal Revenue   266
Marginal Revenue and Elasticity   267
Output and Price Decision   268

Single-Price Monopoly and Competition Compared   270
Comparing Output and Price   270
Efficiency Comparison   271
Redistribution of Surpluses   272
Rent Seeking   272
Rent-Seeking Equilibrium   272

Price Discrimination   273
Price Discrimination and Consumer Surplus   273
Profiting by Price Discriminating   274
Perfect Price Discrimination   275
Efficiency and Rent Seeking with Price Discrimination   276

Monopoly Policy Issues   277
Gains from Monopoly   277
Regulating Natural Monopoly   278

READING BETWEEN THE LINES POLICY WATCH
eBay Is a Monopoly But Google Isn't!   280

Chapter 13 Monopolistic Competition and Oligopoly   285

Searching the Globe for a Niche   285

What Is Monopolistic Competition?   286
    Large Number of Firms   286
    Product Differentiation   286
    Competing on Quality, Price, and Marketing   286
    Entry and Exit   287
    Examples of Monopolistic Competition   287

Price and Output in Monopolistic Competition   288
    The Firm's Short-Run Output and
        Price Decision   288
    Profit Maximizing Might Be Loss Minimizing   288
    Long Run: Zero Economic Profit   289
    Monopolistic Competition and Perfect
        Competition   290
    Is Monopolistic Competition Efficient?   291

Product Development and Marketing   292
    Innovation and Product Development   292
    Advertising   292
    Using Advertising to Signal Quality   294
    Brand Names   295
    Efficiency of Advertising and
        Brand Names   295

What Is Oligopoly?   296
    Barriers to Entry   296
    Small Number of Firms   297
    Examples of Oligopoly   297

Two Traditional Oligopoly Models   298
    The Kinked Demand Curve Model   298
    Dominant Firm Oligopoly   298

Oligopoly Games   300
    What Is a Game?   300
    The Prisoners' Dilemma   300
    An Oligopoly Price-Fixing Game   302
    Other Oligopoly Games   306
    An R&D Game   306
    The Disappearing Invisible Hand   307
    A Game of Chicken   308

Repeated Games and Sequential Games   309
    A Repeated Duopoly Game   309
    A Sequential Entry Game in a
        Contestable Market   310

READING BETWEEN THE LINES
Monopolistic Competition in China's
    Juice Market   312

Part 4 Wrap Up
Understanding Firms and Markets   317
    Probing the Ideas:
        Market Power   318
    Talking with Bengt Holmstrom   320

Part 5   Market Failure and Government   323

Chapter 14   Competition Policy   323

Social Interest or Special Interests?   323

The Economic Theory of Government   324
Monopoly and Oligopoly Regulation   324
Externalities   324
The Provision of Public Goods   324
The Use of Common Resources   324
Income Redistribution   325
Public Choice and the Political Marketplace   325
Political Equilibrium   326

Monopoly and Oligopoly Regulation   326
The Economic Theory of Regulation   326

Regulation and Deregulation   327
The Scope of Regulation   327
The Regulatory Process   327
Natural Monopoly   328
Social Interest or Capture in Natural Monopoly
  Regulation?   332
Cartel Regulation   332
Social Interest or Capture in Cartel
  Regulation?   333
Making Predictions   334

Public Ownership   335
Efficient Crown Corporation   335
A Bureaucracy Model of Public Enterprise   336
A Profit-Maximizing Public Enterprise   337
Compromise Outcome   337
Crown Corporations in Reality   337
Privatization   337

Anti-Combine Law   338
Canada's Anti-Combine Law   338
Some Major Anti-Combine Cases   338
Social or Special Interest?   339

READING BETWEEN THE LINES
POLICY WATCH
Market Power of Broadband Providers   340

Chapter 15   Externalities   345

Greener and Smarter   345

Externalities in Our Lives   346
Negative Production Externalities   346
Positive Production Externalities   346
Negative Consumption Externalities   346
Positive Consumption Externalities   346

Negative Externalities: Pollution   347
The Demand for a Pollution-Free Environment   347
The Sources of Pollution   347
Private Costs and Social Costs   349
Production and Pollution: How Much?   350
Property Rights   350
The Coase Theorem   351
Government Actions in the Face of External
  Costs   352

Positive Externalities: Knowledge   353
Private Benefits and Social Benefits   353
Government Actions in the Face of
  External Benefits   355

READING BETWEEN THE LINES
The Air Pollution Debate   358

Chapter 16 **Public Goods and Common Resources   363**

Free Riding and Overusing the Commons   363

Classifying Goods and Resources   364
  A Four-Fold Classification   364
  Two Problems   364

Public Goods and the Free-Rider Problem   365
  The Benefit of a Public Good   365
  The Efficient Quantity of a Public Good   366
  Private Provision by Market   366
  Public Provision by Majority Vote   366
  The Role of Bureaucrats   368
  Rational Ignorance   368
  Two Types of Political Equilibrium   369
  Why Government Is Large and Grows   369
  Voters Strike Back   369

Common Resources   370
  The Tragedy of the Commons   370
  Sustainable Production   370
  An Overfishing Equilibrium   371
  The Efficient Use of the Commons   372
  Achieving an Efficient Outcome   373
  Public Choice and the Political Equilibrium   375

READING BETWEEN THE LINES
POLICY WATCH
  Rainforests: A Tragedy of the Commons   376

Part 5 Wrap Up
Understanding Market Failure and Government   381
  Probing the Ideas:
    Externalities and Property Rights   382
  Talking with Caroline M. Hoxby   384

Part 6 **Factor Markets and Inequality   387**

Chapter 17 **Demand and Supply in Factor Markets   387**

Many Happy Returns   387

Factor Prices and Incomes   388

Labour Markets   389
  The Demand for Labour   389
  Marginal Revenue Product   390
  The Labour Demand Curve   391
  Equivalence of Two Conditions for Profit
    Maximization   392
  Changes in the Demand for Labour   393
  Market Demand   394
  Elasticity of Demand for Labour   394
  The Supply of Labour   394
  Labour Market Equilibrium   396

Capital Markets   397
  The Demand for Capital   397
  Discounting and Present Value   398
  Demand Curve for Capital   401
  The Supply of Capital   402
  Supply Curve of Capital   402
  The Interest Rate   402
  Changes in Demand and Supply   403

Natural Resource Markets   403
  The Supply of a Renewable Natural Resource   403
  The Supply of a Nonrenewable Natural
    Resource   404
  Price and the Hotelling Principle   404

Income, Economic Rent, and Opportunity Cost   406
  Large and Small Incomes   406

READING BETWEEN THE LINES
  A Resource Market in Action   408

Chapter 17 Appendix Labour Unions 413

Market Power in the Labour Market 413
  Union Objectives and Constraints 413
  A Union in a Competitive
    Labour Market 414
  How Unions Try to Change the Demand for
    Labour 415
  The Scale of Union–Nonunion
    Wage Differentials 415

Monopsony 416
  Monopsony Tendencies 417
  Monopsony and a Union 417
  Monopsony and the Minimum Wage 417

Chapter 18 Economic Inequality 419

Rags and Riches 419

Measuring Economic Inequality 420
  The Distribution of After-Tax Income 420
  The Income Lorenz Curve 421
  The Distribution of Wealth 422
  Wealth Versus Income 422
  Annual or Lifetime Income and Wealth? 423
  Trends in Inequality 423
  Poverty 424
  Who Are the Poor? 424
  How Long Does Poverty Last? 425

The Sources of Economic Inequality 426
  Human Capital 426
  Discrimination 429
  Unequal Ownership of Capital 430

Income Redistribution 431
  Income Taxes 431
  Income Maintenance Programs 431
  Subsidized Services 431
  The Scale of Income Redistribution 432
  The Big Tradeoff 433

READING BETWEEN THE LINES
Changing Inequality and Redistribution 434

Part 6 Wrap Up
Understanding Factor Markets 439
  Probing the Ideas:
    Running Out of Resources 440
  Talking with Janet Currie 442

Part 7 Macroeconomic Overview 445

Chapter 19 A First Look at Macroeconomics 445

What Will Your World Be Like? 445

Origins and Issues of Macroeconomics 446
 Short-Term Versus Long-Term Goals 446
 The Road Ahead 446

Growth and Fluctuations 447
 Growth and Fluctuations in Canada 447
 Economic Growth Around the World 449
 The Lucas Wedge and the Okun Gap 451
 Benefits and Costs of Economic Growth 452

Jobs and Unemployment 452
 Jobs 452
 Unemployment 452
 Unemployment in Canada 453
 Unemployment Around the World 454
 Why Unemployment Is a Problem 454

Inflation 455
 Inflation in Canada 455
 Inflation Around the World 456
 Is Inflation a Problem? 456

Surpluses and Deficits 457
 Government Budget Surplus and Deficit 457
 International Surplus and Deficit 457
 Do Surpluses and Deficits Matter? 458

Macroeconomic Policy Challenges and Tools 459
 Policy Challenges and Tools 459

READING BETWEEN THE LINES
Unemployment, Inflation, and Growth 460

Chapter 20 Measuring GDP and Economic Growth 465

An Economic Barometer 465

Gross Domestic Product 466
 GDP Defined 466
 GDP and the Circular Flow of Expenditure and Income 467
 Financial Flows 468
 How Investment Is Financed 468
 Gross and Net Domestic Product 469

Measuring Canada's GDP 471
 The Expenditure Approach 471
 The Income Approach 471

Real GDP and the Price Level 473
 Calculating Real GDP 473
 Calculating the Price Level 474
 Deflating the GDP Balloon 475

Measuring Economic Growth 476
 Economic Welfare Comparisons 476
 International Comparisons 478
 Business Cycle Forecasts 479

READING BETWEEN THE LINES
The Quarterly GDP Report 480

Chapter 21 **Monitoring Cycles, Jobs, and the Price Level 485**

Vital Signs **485**

The Business Cycle **486**
Business Cycle Dates **486**
Growth Rate Cycles **486**

Jobs and Wages **488**
Population Survey **488**
Four Labour Market Indicators **488**
Aggregate Hours **491**
Real Wage Rate **492**

Unemployment and Full Employment **493**
The Anatomy of Unemployment **493**
Types of Unemployment **495**
Full Employment **496**
Real GDP and Unemployment
Over the Cycle **497**

The Consumer Price Index **498**
Reading the CPI Numbers **498**
Constructing the CPI **498**
Measuring Inflation **500**
The Biased CPI **501**
The Magnitude of the Bias **501**
Some Consequences of the Bias **501**

READING BETWEEN THE LINES
The Monthly CPI Report **502**

Chapter 22 **Aggregate Supply and Aggregate Demand 507**

Production and Prices **507**

Aggregate Supply **508**
Aggregate Supply Fundamentals **508**
Long-Run Aggregate Supply **508**
Short-Run Aggregate Supply **509**
Movements Along the *LAS* and
SAS Curves **510**
Changes in Aggregate Supply **511**

Aggregate Demand **513**
The Aggregate Demand Curve **513**
Changes in Aggregate Demand **514**

Macroeconomic Equilibrium **516**
Short-Run Macroeconomic Equilibrium **516**
Long-Run Macroeconomic Equilibrium **517**
Economic Growth and Inflation **518**
The Business Cycle **518**
Fluctuations in Aggregate Demand **520**
Fluctuations in Aggregate Supply **521**

Canadian Economic Growth, Inflation, and Cycles **522**
Economic Growth **522**
Inflation **523**
Business Cycles **523**
The Evolving Economy: 1961–2004 **523**

READING BETWEEN THE LINES
POLICY WATCH
Kyoto in the *AS–AD* Model **524**

Part 7 Wrap Up
Understanding the Themes of Macroeconomics 529
Probing the Ideas:
Macroeconomic Revolutions **530**
Talking with Peter Howitt **532**

Part 8   Aggregate Demand and Inflation   535

Chapter 23   Expenditure Multipliers   535

Economic Amplifier or Shock Absorber?   535

Expenditure Plans and GDP   536
   Consumption and Saving Plans   536
   Marginal Propensity to Consume   538
   Marginal Propensity to Save   538
   Other Influences on Consumption Expenditure and
     Saving   539
   The Canadian Consumption Function   540
   Consumption as a Function of Real GDP   540
   Import Function   541

Equilibrium Expenditure at a Fixed Price Level   541
   The Aggregate Implications of Fixed Prices   541
   The Aggregate Expenditure Model   542
   Aggregate Planned Expenditure and Real GDP   543
   Actual Expenditure, Planned Expenditure, and Real
     GDP   543
   Equilibrium Expenditure   544
   Convergence to Equilibrium   545

The Multiplier   546
   The Basic Idea of the Multiplier   546
   The Multiplier Effect   546
   Why Is the Multiplier Greater Than 1?   547
   The Size of the Multiplier   547
   The Multiplier and the Slope of the *AE* Curve   548
   Imports and Income Taxes   548
   Business Cycle Turning Points   549

The Multiplier and the Price Level   551
   Aggregate Expenditure and Aggregate
     Demand   551
   Aggregate Expenditure and the
     Price Level   551
   Equilibrium GDP and the Price Level   553

READING BETWEEN THE LINES
   The Aggregate Expenditure Multiplier in Action   556

MATHEMATICAL NOTE
   The Algebra of the Multiplier   558

Chapter 24   Fiscal Policy   563

Balancing Acts on Parliament Hill   563

Government Budgets   564
   Budget Making   564
   Highlights of the 2005 Budget   564
   The Budget in Historical Perspective   565
   Provincial and Local Government Budgets   568
   The Canadian Government Budget in Global
     Perspective   569

Fiscal Policy Multipliers   570
   Government Expenditures Multiplier   570
   Autonomous Tax Multiplier   572
   Induced Taxes and Transfer Payments   573
   International Trade and Fiscal Policy Multipliers   574
   Automatic Stabilizers   574

Fiscal Policy Multipliers and the Price Level   576
   Fiscal Policy and Aggregate Demand   576
   Fiscal Expansion at Potential GDP   578
   Limitations of Fiscal Policy   579

Supply-Side Effects of Fiscal Policy   579
   Fiscal Policy and Potential GDP   579
   Supply Effects and Demand Effects   580

READING BETWEEN THE LINES
POLICY WATCH
   A Winter Heating Multiplier   582

MATHEMATICAL NOTE
   The Algebra of the Fiscal Policy Multipliers   584

Chapter 25 **Money, Banking, and Interest Rates** 589

Money Makes the World Go Around   589

What Is Money?   590
Medium of Exchange   590
Unit of Account   590
Store of Value   591
Money in Canada Today   591

The Banking System   593
Depository Institutions   593
The Bank of Canada   595
The Payments System   595

How Banks Create Money   596
Creating Deposits by Making Loans   596
The Money Creation Process   597
The Money Multiplier   599

The Demand for Money   601
The Influences on Money Holding   601
The Demand for Money Curve   602
Shifts in the Demand for Money Curve   602
The Demand for Money in Canada   603

Interest Rate Determination   604
Money Market Equilibrium   605

READING BETWEEN THE LINES
Canada's Changing Demand for Money   606

Chapter 26 **The Exchange Rate**   611

Many Monies!   611

Currencies and Exchange Rates   612
The Foreign Exchange Market   612
Foreign Exchange Rates   612
Cross Exchange Rates   613

The Foreign Exchange Market   615
The Demand for One Money Is the Supply of Another Money   615
Demand in the Foreign Exchange Market   615
The Law of Demand for Foreign Exchange   615
Demand Curve for Canadian Dollars   616
Supply in the Foreign Exchange Market   617
The Law of Supply of Foreign Exchange   617
Supply Curve for Canadian Dollars   617
Market Equilibrium   618
Equilibrium Cross Exchange Rates   618

Changes in Demand and Supply: Exchange Rate Fluctuations   619
Changes in the Demand for Dollars   619
Changes in the Supply of Dollars   620
Changes in the Exchange Rate   620
Exchange Rate Expectations   622

Exchange Rate Policy   623
Flexible Exchange Rate   623
Fixed Exchange Rate   623
Crawling Peg   624
Currency Union   624

READING BETWEEN THE LINES
The Strengthening Canadian Dolar   626

Chapter 27 Inflation 631

From Rome to Rio de Janeiro 631

Inflation: Demand-Pull and Cost-Push 632
   Inflation and a Change in the Price Level 632
   Demand-Pull Inflation 633
   Cost-Push Inflation 635

The Quantity Theory of Money 638
   Evidence on the Quantity Theory 638

Effects of Inflation 640
   Unanticipated Inflation in the Labour
      Market 640
   Unanticipated Inflation in the Market for Financial
      Capital 640
   Forecasting Inflation 641
   Anticipated Inflation 641
   Unanticipated Inflation 642
   The Costs of Anticipated Inflation 642

Inflation and Unemployment: The Phillips Curve 644
   The Short-Run Phillips Curve 644
   The Long-Run Phillips Curve 646
   Changes in the Natural Rate of Unemployment 646
   The Canadian Phillips Curve 647

Interest Rates and Inflation 648
   How Interest Rates Are Determined 649
   Why Inflation Influences the Nominal
      Interest Rate 649

READING BETWEEN THE LINES
Inflation–Unemployment Tradeoff 650

Chapter 28 Monetary Policy 655

Fiddling with the Knobs 655

Monetary Policy Objective and Framework 656
   Monetary Policy Objective 656
   Responsibility for Monetary Policy 657

The Conduct of Monetary Policy 658
   Choosing a Policy Instrument 658
   The Overnight Rate 658
   The Bank's Decision-Making Process 659
   Hitting the Overnight Rate Target 660
   How an Open Market Operation Works 660
   Equilibrium in the Market for Reserves 662

Monetary Policy Transmission 663
   Quick Overview 663
   Interest Rate Fluctuations 663
   Exchange Rate Fluctuations 665
   Money and Loans 665
   The Interest Rate and Expenditure Plans 665
   The Change in Aggregate Demand, Real GDP, and the
      Price Level 668

Alternative Monetary Policy Strategies 670
   Overnight Rate Instrument Rule 670
   Monetary Base Instrument Rule 670
   Exchange Rate Targeting Rule 671
   Money Targeting Rule 671
   Why Rules? 671

READING BETWEEN THE LINES
POLICY WATCH
Monetary Policy in Action 672

Chapter 29 **Fiscal and Monetary
              Interactions 677**

Sparks Fly in Ottawa **677**

Macroeconomic Equilibrium **678**
    Two Markets in Short-Run Equilibrium **678**
    Simultaneous Equilibrium **678**

Fiscal Policy in the Short Run **680**
    First Round Effects of Fiscal Policy **680**
    Second Round Effects of Fiscal Policy **680**
    Other Fiscal Policies **683**
    Crowding Out and Crowding In **683**
    The Exchange Rate and International
        Crowding Out **683**

Monetary Policy in the Short Run **684**
    Second Round Effects **685**
    Money and the Exchange Rate **687**

Relative Effectiveness of Policies **687**
    Effectiveness of Fiscal Policy **687**
    Effectiveness of Monetary Policy **688**
    Keynesian–Monetarist Controversy **688**
    Sorting Out the Competing Claims **689**
    Interest Rate and Exchange Rate Effectiveness **689**

Policy Actions at Full Employment **690**
    Expansionary Fiscal Policy at Full Employment **690**
    Crowding Out at Full Employment **690**
    Expansionary Monetary Policy at
        Full Employment **691**
    Long-Run Neutrality **691**

Policy Coordination, Conflict, and Risk **692**
    Policy Coordination **692**
    Policy Conflict **692**
    A Policy Interaction Risk **693**

READING BETWEEN THE LINES
POLICY WATCH
    Monetary and Fiscal Tensions **694**

Part 8 Wrap Up
    **Understanding Aggregate Demand and
    Inflation 699**
        Probing the Ideas:
            Understanding Inflation **700**
        Talking with Michael Woodford **702**

**Part 9   Aggregate Supply,
           Economic Growth, and
           International Trade 705**

Chapter 30 **The Economy at
              Full Employment 705**

Production and Jobs **705**

Real GDP and Employment **706**
    Production Possibilities **706**
    The Production Function **706**
    Changes in Productivity **707**
    Shifts in the Production Function **708**

The Labour Market and Aggregate Supply **709**
    The Demand for Labour **709**
    The Supply of Labour **711**
    Labour Market Equilibrium **712**
    Potential GDP **712**
    Aggregate Supply **713**

Changes in Potential GDP **714**
    An Increase in Population **714**
    An Increase in Labour Productivity **715**
    Population and Productivity in Canada **717**

Unemployment at Full Employment **719**
    Job Search **719**
    Job Rationing **720**

READING BETWEEN THE LINES
POLICY WATCH
    Canada–U.S. Productivity Gap **722**

Chapter 30 Appendix Deriving the Long-Run and Short-Run Aggregate Supply Curves 724

The Aggregate Supply Curves 724

Deriving the Long-Run Aggregate Supply Curve 724
Changes in Long-Run Aggregate Supply 726

Short-Run Aggregate Supply 726
Short-Run Equilibrium in the
Labour Market 726
Deriving the Short-Run Aggregate Supply Curve 727
Changes in Short-Run Aggregate Supply 729
Short-Run Changes in the Quantity of Real GDP
Supplied 729
The Shape of the Short-Run Aggregate
Supply Curve 729

Chapter 31 Economic Growth 733

Transforming People's Lives 733

Long-Term Growth Trends 734
Growth in the Canadian Economy 734
Real GDP Growth in the World Economy 735

The Causes of Economic Growth: A First Look 737
Preconditions for Economic Growth 737
Saving and Investment in New Capital 737
Investment in Human Capital 738
Discovery of New Technologies 738

Growth Accounting 739
Labour Productivity 739
The Productivity Curve 739
Accounting for the Productivity Growth Slowdown and
Speedup 741
Technological Change During the Productivity Growth
Slowdown 742
Achieving Faster Growth 742

Growth Theories 743
Classical Growth Theory 743
Neoclassical Growth Theory 745
New Growth Theory 747
Sorting Out the Theories 749

READING BETWEEN THE LINES
Forecasting Economic Growth 750

Chapter 32 **Trading with the World** **755**

Silk Routes and Sucking Sounds **755**

Patterns and Trends in International Trade **756**
Trade in Goods **756**
Trade in Services **756**
Geographical Patterns of International Trade **756**
Trends in the Volume of Trade **756**
Net Exports and International Borrowing **756**

The Gains from International Trade **757**
Opportunity Cost in Farmland **757**
Opportunity Cost in Mobilia **758**
Comparative Advantage **758**
The Gains from Trade: Cheaper to Buy Than to Produce **758**
The Terms of Trade **758**
Balanced Trade **759**
Changes in Production and Consumption **759**
Calculating the Gains from Trade **761**
Gains for Both Countries **761**
Gains from Trade in Reality **761**

International Trade Restrictions **763**
The History of Tariffs **763**
How Tariffs Work **764**
Nontariff Barriers **766**
How Quotas and VERs Work **766**

The Case Against Protection **767**
The Employment Argument **767**
The Infant-Industry Argument **767**
The Dumping Argument **768**
Maintains National Security **768**
Allows Us to Compete with Cheap Foreign Labour **768**
Brings Diversity and Stability **769**
Penalizes Lax Environmental Standards **769**
Protects National Culture **769**
Prevents Rich Countries from Exploiting Developing Countries **769**
Why Is International Trade Restricted? **769**
Compensating Losers **770**
Protection to Avoid a Trade Deficit **771**

The Balance of International Payments **772**
Balance of Payments Accounts **772**
Borrowers and Lenders, Debtors and Creditors **774**
Current Account Balance **774**
The Twin Deficits **775**

The North American Free Trade Agreement **776**
The Terms of the Canada–United States Agreement **776**
The Extension of the Agreement: NAFTA **777**
Effects of the Free Trade Agreement **777**

READING BETWEEN THE LINES
POLICY WATCH
Tariffs in Action: Lumber **778**

Part 9 Wrap Up
Aggregate Supply, Economic Growth, and International Trade **783**
Probing the Ideas:
Gains from International Trade **784**
Talking with Dan Trefler **786**

Canadian Economy Database **789**

Glossary **G–I**

Index **I–I**

Credits **C–I**

What Is Economics?

Understanding Our Changing World

You are studying economics at a time of enormous change and uncertainty. Much of the change is for the better. The information age of laptop computers with wireless connection to the Internet, MP3 music, DVD movies, cell phones, Palm Pilots, iPods, and a host of other gadgets and toys have transformed the way we work and play.

But some change is for the worse. After the hype of the new millennium, the global economy slipped into recession. The September 11 terrorist attacks slashed business and vacation travel, shrank our airlines, and tightened security at the Canada-U.S. border and at airports and seaports. SARS, mad cow disease, and disputes with the United States about softwood lumber, all sent shockwaves through the Canadian economy.

◆ The information age, global recession, and the effects of terrorism are just some of the forces that are changing today's world. Your course in economics will help you to understand how these powerful forces shape our world. This chapter takes the first step. It describes the questions that economists try to answer, the way they think about those questions, and the methods they use in the search for answers. Economics makes extensive use of graphs, and an appendix provides a guide to these graphical methods.

After studying this chapter, you will be able to

- **Define economics and distinguish between microeconomics and macroeconomics**
- **Explain the big questions of economics**
- **Explain the key ideas that define the economic way of thinking**
- **Explain how economists go about their work as social scientists**

Definition of Economics

ALL ECONOMIC QUESTIONS ARISE BECAUSE WE want more than we can get. We want a peaceful and secure world. We want clean air, lakes, and rivers. We want long and healthy lives. We want good schools, colleges, and universities. We want spacious and comfortable homes. We want an enormous range of sports and recreational gear from running shoes to jet skis. We want the time to enjoy sports, games, novels, movies, music, travel, and hanging out with our friends.

What each one of us can get is limited by time, by the income we earn, and by the prices we must pay. Everyone ends up with some unsatisfied wants. What as a society we can get is limited by our productive resources. These resources include the gifts of nature, human labour and ingenuity, and tools and equipment that we have produced.

Our inability to satisfy all our wants is called **scarcity**. The poor and the rich alike face scarcity. A child wants a $1.00 can of pop and two 50¢ packs of gum but has only $1.00 in his pocket. He faces scarcity. A millionaire wants to spend the weekend playing golf *and* spend the same weekend at the office attending a business strategy meeting. She faces scarcity. A society wants to provide improved health care, install a computer in every classroom, explore space, clean polluted lakes and rivers, and so on. Society faces scarcity. Even parrots face scarcity!

Faced with scarcity, we must *choose* among the available alternatives. The child must *choose* the pop *or* the gum. The millionaire must *choose* the golf game *or* the meeting. As a society, we must *choose* among health care, national defence, and the environment.

The choices that we make depend on the incentives that we face. An **incentive** is a reward that encourages or a penalty that discourages an action. If the price of pop falls, the child has an *incentive* to choose more pop. If a profit of $10 million is at stake, the millionaire has an *incentive* to skip the golf game. As computer prices tumble, school boards have an *incentive* to connect more classrooms to the Internet.

Economics is the social science that studies the *choices* that individuals, businesses, governments, and entire societies make as they cope with *scarcity* and the *incentives* that influence and reconcile those choices. The subject divides into two main parts:

- Microeconomics
- Macroeconomics

Microeconomics

Microeconomics is the study of the choices that individuals and businesses make, the way these choices interact in markets, and the influence of governments. Some examples of microeconomic issues are: Why are people buying more SUVs and fewer minivans? How would a tax on e-commerce affect Amazon.com?

Macroeconomics

Macroeconomics is the study of the performance of the national economy and the global economy. Some examples of macroeconomic issues are: Why did production and jobs shrink in 2001? Why has Japan's economy stagnated? Can the government bring prosperity by cutting tax rates?

Not only do I want a cracker—we all want a cracker!

© The New Yorker Collection 1985, Frank Modell from cartoonbank.com. All Rights Reserved.

REVIEW QUIZ

1 List some examples of choices being made in Canada today.
2 Use the headlines in today's news to provide some examples of scarcity around the world.
3 Use today's news to illustrate the distinction between microeconomics and macroeconomics.

myeconlab **Study Plan 1.1**

Two Big Economic Questions

TWO BIG QUESTIONS SUMMARIZE THE SCOPE OF economics:

- How do choices end up determining *what, how,* and *for whom* goods and services get produced?
- When do choices made in the pursuit of *self-interest* also promote the *social interest?*

What, How, and For Whom?

Goods and services are the objects that people value and produce to satisfy human wants. Goods are physical objects such as basketballs. Services are tasks performed for people such as haircuts. By far the largest part of what Canada produces today is services such as retail and wholesale trade, health care, and education. Goods are a small part of total production.

What? What we produce changes over time. Sixty years ago, almost 20 percent of Canadians worked on farms. That number has shrunk to less than 3 percent today. Over the same period, the number of people who produce goods—in mining, construction, and manufacturing—has shrunk from 60 percent to less than 25 percent. The decrease in farming and manufacturing is reflected in an increase in services. Sixty years ago, 20 percent of the population produced services. Today, more than 75 percent of working Canadians have service jobs. Figure 1.1 shows these trends.

What determines the quantities of corn, DVDs, and haircuts and all the other millions of items that we produce?

How? Goods and services are produced by using productive resources that economists call **factors of production**. Factors of production are grouped into four categories:

- Land
- Labour
- Capital
- Entrepreneurship

Land The "gifts of nature" that we use to produce goods and services are called **land**. In economics, land

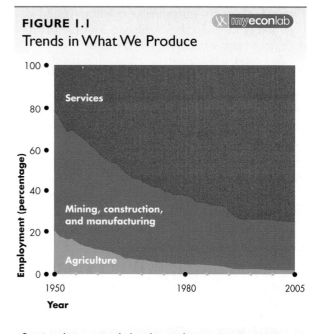

FIGURE 1.1
Trends in What We Produce

Services have expanded and agriculture, mining, construction, and manufacturing have shrunk.

Source of data: Statistics Canada.

is what in everyday language we call *natural resources*. It includes land in the everyday sense together with metal ores, oil, gas and coal, water, and air.

Our land surface and water resources are renewable and some of our mineral resources can be recycled. But the resources that we use to create energy are nonrenewable—they can be used only once.

Labour The work time and work effort that people devote to producing goods and services is called **labour**. Labour includes the physical and the mental efforts of all the people who work on farms and construction sites and in factories, shops, and offices.

The *quality* of labour depends on **human capital**, which is the knowledge and skill that people obtain from education, on-the-job training, and work experience. You are building your own human capital right now as you work on your economics course, and your human capital will continue to grow as you become better at your job.

Human capital expands over time. Today, more than 85 percent of the population of Canada has completed high school and more than 43 percent have a college or university degree. Figure 1.2 shows a measure of the growth of human capital in Canada over the past few decades.

Capital The tools, instruments, machines, buildings, and other items that businesses now use to produce goods and services are called **capital**.

In everyday language, we talk about money, stocks, and bonds as being capital. These items are financial capital. They play an important role in enabling people to lend to businesses and provide businesses with financial resources, but they are not used to produce goods and services. Because they are not productive resources, they are not capital.

Entrepreneurship The human resource that organizes labour, land, and capital is called **entrepreneurship**. Entrepreneurs come up with new ideas about what and how to produce, make business decisions, and bear the risks that arise from these decisions.

How do the quantities of factors of production that get used to produce the many different goods and services get determined?

For Whom? Who gets the goods and services that are produced depends on the incomes that people earn. A large income enables a person to buy large quantities of goods and services. A small income leaves a person with few options and small quantities of goods and services.

People earn their incomes by selling the services of the factors of production they own:

- Land earns **rent**.
- Labour earns **wages**.
- Capital earns **interest**.
- Entrepreneurship earns **profit**.

Which factor of production earns the most income? The answer is labour. Wages and fringe benefits are around 70 percent of total income. Land, capital, and entrepreneurship share the rest. These percentages have been remarkably constant over time.

Knowing how income is shared among the factors of production doesn't tell us how it is shared among individuals. You know of lots of people who earn very large incomes. The average baseball salary in 2005 was about $3 million, and some stars such as Roy Halladay of the Toronto Blue Jays get a bit more than $13 million.

You know of even more people who earn very small incomes. Servers at McDonald's average around $7 an hour; checkout clerks, gas station attendants, and textile and leather workers all earn less than $10 an hour.

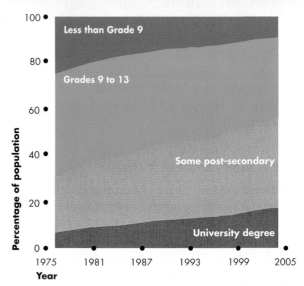

FIGURE 1.2
A Measure of Human Capital

Today, more than 43 percent of the Canadian population has post-secondary certificates, diplomas, or university degrees. A further 42 percent have completed high school.

Source of data: Statistics Canada.

You probably know about other persistent differences in incomes. Men, on the average, earn more than women; university and college graduates, on the average, earn more than high school graduates.

We can get a good sense of who consumes the goods and services produced by looking at the percentages of total income earned by different groups of people. The 20 percent of people with the lowest incomes receive 5 percent of total income, while the richest 20 percent receive 45 percent of total income. So on the average, people in the top 20 percent earn almost 9 times the incomes of those in the 20 percent who earn the least.

Why is the distribution of income so unequal? Why do women earn less than men?

Economics provides some answers to these questions about what, how, and for whom goods and services get produced.

The second big question of economics that we'll now examine is a harder question both to appreciate and to answer.

When Is the Pursuit of Self-Interest in the Social Interest?

Every day, you and 32 million other Canadians, along with 6.5 billion people in the rest of the world, make economic choices that result in "What," "How," and "For Whom" goods and services get produced.

Are the goods and services produced, and the quantities in which they are produced, the right ones? Do the factors of production employed get used in the best possible way? And do the goods and services that we produce go to the people who benefit most from them?

You know that your own choices are the best ones for you—or at least you think they're the best at the time that you make them. You use your time and other resources in the way that makes most sense to you. But you don't think much about how your choices affect other people. You order a home delivery pizza because you're hungry and want to eat. You don't order it thinking that the delivery person or the cook needs an income. You make choices that are in your self-interest. Choices made in **self-interest** are choices that are best for the person making them.

When you act on your economic decisions, you come into contact with thousands of other people who produce and deliver the goods and services that you decide to buy or who buy the things that you sell. These people have made their own decisions— what to produce and how to produce it, whom to hire or whom to work for, and so on. Like you, everyone else makes choices that they think are best for them. When the pizza delivery person shows up at your home, he's not doing you a favour. He's earning his income and hoping for a nice tip.

Could it be possible that when each one of us makes choices that are in our own best interest, it turns out that these choices are also the best for society as a whole? Choices that are the best for society as a whole are said to be in the **social interest**.

Economists have been trying to find the answer to this question since 1776, the year in which Adam Smith's monumental book, *An Inquiry into the Nature and the Causes of the Wealth of Nations*, was published. The question is a hard one to answer, but a lot of progress has been made. Much of the rest of this book helps you to learn what we know about this question and its answer. To help you start thinking about the question, we're going to illustrate it with eight topics that generate heated discussion in today's world. You're already at least a little bit familiar with each one of them. They are

- Central planning versus the market
- Globalization
- The new economy
- The post 9/11 economy
- Corporate scandals
- HIV/AIDS
- Disappearing tropical rainforests
- Water shortages

Central Planning Versus the Market The Soviet Union was founded in 1924 and the People's Republic of China in 1948. These two nations operated the world's largest centrally planned economies.

The antithesis of central planning is the market economy in which resources are privately owned and people are free to trade in markets at prices that are determined by market forces.

From the 1920s until the 1980s, many people believed that self-interest and the social interest could be reconciled only by central economic planning and that the Soviet Union and China had adopted a superior economic system.

As it turned out these economies performed only modestly and China's decade-long so-called "Cultural Revolution" (1966–1976) was an economic disaster.

China began to transform its economy in 1978 when Deng Xiaoping succeeded Mao Zedong. Deng's dictum was to "seek truth from facts" and do what works. He could see Canada, the United States, Europe, Japan, Australia, and Taiwan and Hong Kong, the latter two of which he regarded as part of China, growing richer and richer while China stagnated. He had no time for poverty and said (he has many memorable sayings): "Poverty is not socialism. To be rich is glorious." And in line with his basic outlook: "It doesn't matter if a cat is black or white so long as it catches mice."

In the almost 30 years since China began developing markets and private enterprise, the Chinese economy has performed like no other. Output has grown at an average rate of around 8 percent a year, with living standards doubling every decade or so. All the expansion has occurred in the private market sector of the economy. The market economy continues to be a resounding success for China.

The experiment with central economic planning in the Soviet Union and Eastern Europe lasted a bit longer. But not much longer. On November 9, 1989, a date that will long be written about in economic history books, the Berlin Wall tumbled and with its destruction, two Germanys embarked on a path towards unity.

West Germany had a market economy and East Germany a centrally planned economy. The integration of the economies of the two Germanys took the form of converting the East German economy to capitalism. State-owned enterprises were sold and markets were freed. People previously completely banned from moving between East and West Germany became free to move to any part of Germany (and indeed to any part of the European Union).

Part of Germany's economic problem today stems from a heavy dose of socialism in the form of extraordinarily high wages and benefits as well as rigid employment regulations that make it hard for firms to fire workers (and so firms are cautious to hire them).

Soon after the collapse of the Berlin Wall, the Soviet Union collapsed. It splintered into a number of independent states, each of which embarked on a process of building free markets and the development of the ethics needed to operate an efficient capitalist economy.

Most Chinese and Eastern Europeans are in no doubt that despite a long and difficult adjustment process from central planning to a market economy, the move is worthwhile.

But are they correct? And if they are correct, how do markets manage to do a better job than central economic planning?

Globalization Whenever world leaders hold summit meetings, anti-globalization protests accompany them. Globalization—the expansion of international trade and investment—has been going on for centuries, but during the 1990s, advances in microchip, satellite, and fibre-optic technologies brought a dramatic fall in the cost of communication and accelerated the process. A phone call or even a video conference between people on different continents has become an everyday and easily affordable event. Every day, 20,000 people travel by air between North America and East Asia, and close to that number travel between North America and Europe.

The result of this explosion of communication is a globalization of production decisions. When Nike decides to increase the production of sports shoes, people who live in China, Indonesia, or Malaysia get

more work. As more and more people use credit cards, people in Barbados get hired to key in the data from sales slips. When Sony wants to create a new game for PlayStation 2, or when Steven Spielberg wants a movie animation sequence, programmers in India or New Zealand write the code. And when China Airlines wants some new regional jets, it is most likely that Canadians who work for Bombardier will build them.

As part of the process of globalization, Canada produces more services and fewer manufactured goods. And China and the small economies in East Asia produce an expanding volume of manufactures.

The economies of Asia are also growing more rapidly than are those of North America and Europe. China is already the world's second largest economy in terms of production and, on current trends, by 2013 it will be the world's largest economy. This rapid economic expansion in Asia will bring further changes to the global economy as the wealthier Chinese and other Asians begin to travel and buy more of the goods and services that Canada and other parts of the world produce. Globalization will proceed at an accelerated pace.

But globalization is leaving some behind. The nations of Africa and parts of South America are not sharing in the prosperity that globalization is bringing to other parts of the world.

Is globalization a good thing? Whom does it benefit? Globalization is pretty clearly in the interest of the owners of multinational firms that profit by producing in low-cost regions and selling in high-price regions. But is globalization in your interest and the interest of the young worker in Malaysia who sews your new running shoes? Is it in the social interest?

The New Economy The 1980s and 1990s were years of extraordinary economic change that have been called the *Information Revolution*. Economic revolutions don't happen very often. The previous one, the *Industrial Revolution*, occurred between 1760 and 1830 and saw the transformation from rural farm life to urban industrial life for most people. The revolution before that, the *Agricultural Revolution*, occurred around 10,000 years ago and saw the transformation from a life of hunting and gathering to a life of settled farming.

Placing the events of the last 20 years of the twentieth century on the status of those two previous revolutions might be a stretch. But the changes that occurred during those years were incredible. And they were based on one major technology: the microprocessor or computer chip. Moore's law predicted that the number of transistors that could be placed on one integrated chip would double every 18 months. This prediction turned out to be remarkably accurate. In 1980, a PC chip had 60,000 transistors. By 2000, chips with more than 40 million transistors were in machines like the one that sits on your lap.

The spinoffs from faster and cheaper computing were widespread. Telecommunications became much faster and cheaper, music and movie recording became more realistic and cheaper, millions of routine tasks that previously required human decision and action were automated. You encounter these automated tasks every day when you check out at the supermarket, call directory assistance, or call a government department or large business.

All the new products and processes and the low-cost computing power that made them possible were produced by people who made choices in the pursuit of self-interest. They did not result from any grand design or government economic plan.

When Gordon Moore set up Intel and started making chips, no one had told him to do so, and he wasn't thinking how much easier it would be for you to turn in your essay on time if you had a faster PC. When Bill Gates quit Harvard to set up Microsoft, he wasn't trying to create the best operating system and improve people's computing experience. Moore and Gates and thousands of other entrepreneurs were in hot pursuit of the big payoffs that many of them achieved. Yet their actions did make everyone else better off. They did advance the social interest.

But could more have been done? Were resources used in the best possible way during the information revolution? Did Intel make the best possible chips and sell them in the right quantities for the right prices? Or was the quality of the chips too low and the price too high? And what about Microsoft? Did Bill Gates have to be paid $US46 billion to produce the successive generations of Windows and Word? Were these programs developed in the social interest?

The Economic Response to 9/11 The awful events of September 11, 2001 created economic shockwaves that will last for some years and changed "What," "How," and "For Whom."

The biggest changes in production occurred in the travel, accommodation, and security industries. Much business travel was replaced by teleconferencing. Much vacation travel left the air and went onto the highway. Foreign trips were cut back. Airlines lost business and cut back on their orders for new airplanes. Banks that had lent money to airlines wrote off millions of dollars in losses.

But sales of SUVs and RVs increased. And airports, although operating at lower capacity, beefed up their security services. Thousands of new security agents were hired and state-of-the-art scanners were installed.

Thousands of people made choices in pursuit of their self-interest that led to these changes in production. But were these changes also in the social interest?

Corporate Scandals In 2000, the names Enron and WorldCom meant corporate integrity and spectacular success. But today, they are tainted with scandal.

Founded in 1985, Enron expanded to become the seventh largest U.S. business by 2001. But its expansion was built on an elaborate web of lies, deceit, and fraud. In October 2001, after revelations by one of its former executives, Enron's directors acknowledged that by inflating reported income and hiding debts, they had made the firm appear to be worth considerably more than it actually was. One Enron executive, Michael Kopper, pleaded guilty to charges of money laundering and wire fraud and helped federal investigators uncover the fraud that made millions of dollars for the firm's executives and wiped out its stockholders' wealth.

Scott Sullivan, a highly respected financial officer, joined WorldCom in 1992 and helped turn it into one of the world's telecommunications giants. In his last year with the company, Sullivan's salary was $US700,000 and his bonus (in stock options) was $US10 million. But just ten years after joining the company, Sullivan was fired and arrested for allegedly falsifying the company's accounts, inflating its book profits by almost $US4 billion, and inflating his own bonus in the process. Shortly after these events, WorldCom filed for bankruptcy protection in the largest bankruptcy filing in U.S. history, laid off 17,000 workers, and, like Enron, wiped out its stockholders' wealth.

These cases illustrate the fact that sometimes, in the pursuit of self-interest, people break the law. Such behaviour is not in the social interest. Indeed, the law was established precisely to limit such behaviour.

But some corporate behaviour is legal yet regarded by some as inappropriate. For example, many people think that top executive salaries are out of control. In some cases, executives who have received huge incomes have brought ruin to the companies that they manage.

The people who hired the executives acted in their own self-interest and appointed the best people they could find. The executives acted in their own self-interest. But what became of the self-interest of the stockholders and the customers of these firms? Didn't they suffer? Aren't these glaring examples of conflict between self-interest and the social interest?

HIV/AIDS   The World Health Organization and United Nations estimate that 42 million people were suffering from HIV/AIDS in 2002. During that year, 3 million died from the disease and there were 5 million new cases. Most of the HIV/AIDS cases—30 million of them in 2002—were in Africa, where incomes average around $7 a day. The most effective treatment for this disease is an antiretroviral drug made by the large multinational drug companies. The cost of this treatment is around $2,700 a year—more than $7 a day. For sales to poor countries, the cost has been lowered to around $1,200 a year—$3.30 a day.

Developing new drugs is a high-cost and high-risk activity. And if the activity were not in the self-interest of the drug companies, they would stop the effort. But once developed, the cost of producing a drug is just a few cents a dose. Would it be in the social interest for drugs to be made available at the low cost of producing them?

Disappearing Tropical Rainforests   Tropical rainforests in South America, Africa, and Asia support the lives of 30 million species of plants, animals, and insects—approaching 50 percent of all species on the planet. These rainforests provide us with the ingredients for many goods including soaps, mouthwashes, shampoos, food preservatives, rubber, nuts, and fruits. The Amazon rainforest alone converts about 450 million tonnes of carbon dioxide into oxygen each year.

Yet tropical rainforests cover less than two percent of the Earth's surface and are heading for extinction. Logging, cattle ranching, mining, oil extraction, hydroelectric dams, and subsistence farming are destroying the equivalent of two football fields every second or an area larger than New York City every day. At the current rate of destruction, almost all the tropical rainforest ecosystems will be gone by 2030.

Each one of us makes economic choices that are in our self-interest to consume products, some of which are destroying this natural resource. Are our choices damaging the social interest? And if they are, what can be done to change the incentives we face and change our behaviour?

Water Shortages   The world is awash with water—it is our most abundant resource. But 97 percent of it is seawater. Another 2 percent is frozen in glaciers and ice. The 1 percent of the earth's water that is available for human consumption would be sufficient if only it were in the right places. Canada, Finland, and a few other places have more water than they can use, but Australia, Africa, and California (and many other places) could use much more water than they can get. Some people pay less for water than others. California farmers, for example, pay less than California households. Some of the highest prices for water are faced by people in the poorest countries who must either buy from a water dealer's truck or carry water in buckets over long distances.

In the United Kingdom, water is provided by private water companies. In Canada, public enterprises deliver the water.

In India and Bangladesh, plenty of rain falls, but it falls during a short wet season and the rest of the year is dry. Dams could help to reduce the shortage in the dry season, but not enough have been built in those countries.

Are the nations' and the world's water resources being managed properly? Are the decisions that we each make in our self-interest to use, conserve, and transport water also in the social interest?

We've just looked at eight topics that illustrate the big question: Do choices made in the pursuit of self-interest also serve the social interest?

You'll discover, as you work through this book, that much of what we do in the pursuit of our self-interest does indeed further the social interest. But there are areas in which the social interest and self-interest come into conflict. You'll discover the principles that help economists to figure out when the social interest is being served, when it is not, and what might be done when it is not.

REVIEW QUIZ

1   Describe the broad facts about "What," "How," and "For Whom" goods and services get produced.
2   Use headlines from the recent news to illustrate the potential for conflict between self-interest and the social interest.

⊗ myeconlab   Study Plan 1.2

The Economic Way of Thinking

THE DEFINITION OF ECONOMICS AND THE questions that you've just reviewed tell you about the *scope of economics*. But they don't tell you how economists *think* about these questions and go about seeking answers to them.

You're now going to begin to see how economists approach economic questions. First, in this section, we'll look at the ideas that define the *economic way of thinking*. This way of thinking needs practice, but it is powerful and as you become more familiar with it, you'll begin to see the world around you with a new and sharp focus.

Choices and Tradeoffs

Because we face scarcity, we must make choices. And when we make a choice, we select from the available alternatives. For example, you can spend the weekend studying for your next economics test and having fun with your friends, but you can't do both of these activities at the same time. You must choose how much time to devote to each. Whatever choice you make, you could have chosen something else instead.

You can think about your choice as a tradeoff. A **tradeoff** is an exchange—giving up one thing to get something else. When you choose how to spend your weekend, you face a tradeoff between studying and hanging out with your friends.

Guns Versus Butter

The classic tradeoff is between guns and butter. "Guns" and "butter" stand for any pair of goods. They might actually be guns and butter. Or they might be broader categories such as national defence and food. Or they might be any pair of specific goods or services such as cola and bottled water, baseball bats and tennis rackets, universities and hospitals, realtor services and career counselling.

Regardless of the specific objects that guns and butter represent, the guns-versus-butter tradeoff captures a hard fact of life: If we want more of one thing, we must trade something else in exchange for it.

The idea of a tradeoff is central to the whole of economics. We'll look at some examples, beginning with the big questions: What, How, and For Whom? We can view each of these questions about the goods and services that get produced in terms of tradeoffs.

What, How, and For Whom Tradeoffs

The questions what, how, and for whom goods and services are produced all involve tradeoffs that are similar to that between guns and butter.

"What" Tradeoffs What goods and services get produced depends on choices made by each one of us, by our government, and by the businesses that produce the things we buy.

Each of these choices involves a tradeoff. Each one of us faces a tradeoff when we choose how to spend our income. You go to the movies this week, but you forgo a few cups of coffee to buy the ticket. You trade off coffee for a movie.

The federal government faces a tradeoff when it chooses how to spend our tax dollars. Parliament votes for more hospitals but cuts back on educational programs. The federal government trades off education for hospitals.

Businesses face a tradeoff when they decide what to produce. Nike hires Tiger Woods and allocates resources to designing and marketing a new golf ball but cuts back on its development of a new running shoe. Nike trades off running shoes for golf balls.

"How" Tradeoffs How goods and services get produced depends on choices made by the businesses that produce the things we buy. These choices involve a tradeoff. For example, Tim Hortons opens a new doughnut store with an automated production line and closes an older store with a traditional kitchen— Tim Hortons trades off labour for capital.

"For Whom" Tradeoffs For whom goods and services are produced depends on the distribution of buying power. Buying power can be redistributed —transferred from one person to another—in three ways: by voluntary payments, by theft, or through taxes and benefits organized by governments. Redistribution brings tradeoffs.

Each of us faces a "for whom" tradeoff when we choose how much to contribute to the United Nations' famine relief fund. You cut your spending and donate $50. You trade off your own spending for a small increase in economic equality.

We make choices that influence redistribution by theft when we vote to make theft illegal and devote resources to law enforcement. We trade off some goods and services for an increase in the security of our property.

We also vote for taxes and social programs that redistribute buying power from the rich to the poor. Government redistribution confronts society with what has been called the **big tradeoff**—the tradeoff between equality and efficiency. Taxing the rich and making transfers to the poor bring greater economic equality. But taxing productive activities such as running a business, working hard, and saving and investing in capital discourages these activities. So taxing productive activities means producing less. A more equal distribution means there is less to share.

You can think of the big tradeoff as being the problem of how to share a pie that everyone contributes to baking. If each person receives a share of the pie that reflects the size of her or his effort, everyone will work hard and the pie will be as large as possible. But if the pie is shared equally, regardless of contribution, some talented bakers will slacken off and the pie will shrink. The big tradeoff is one between the size of the pie and how equally it is shared. We trade off some production for increased equality.

Choices Bring Change

What, how, and for whom goods and services are produced changes over time. And choices bring change. The quantity and range of goods and services available today in Canada is much greater than that in Africa. And the economic condition of Canada today is much better than it was a generation ago. But the quality of economic life (and its rate of improvement) doesn't depend purely on nature and on luck. It depends on many of the choices made by each one of us, by governments, and by businesses. And these choices involve tradeoffs.

One choice is that of how much of our income to consume and how much to save. Our saving can be channelled through the financial system to finance businesses and to pay for new capital that increases production. The more we save and invest, the more goods and services we'll be able to produce in the future. When you decide to save an extra $1,000 and forgo a vacation, you trade off the vacation for a higher future income. If everyone saves an extra $1,000 and businesses invest in more equipment that increases production, the average consumption per person rises. As a society, we trade off current consumption for economic growth and higher future consumption.

A second choice is how much effort to devote to education and training. By becoming better educated and more highly skilled, we become more productive

and are able to produce more goods and services. When you decide to remain in school for another two years to complete a professional degree and forgo a huge chunk of leisure time, you trade off leisure today for a higher future income. If everyone becomes better educated, production increases and income per person rises. As a society, we trade off current consumption and leisure time for economic growth and higher future consumption.

A third choice, usually made by businesses, is how much effort to devote to research and the development of new products and production methods. Ford Motor Company can hire engineers to do research on a new robotic assembly line or to operate the existing plant and produce cars. More research brings greater productivity in the future but means smaller current production—a tradeoff of current production for greater future production.

Seeing choices as tradeoffs emphasizes the idea that to get something, we must give up something. What we give up is the cost of what we get. Economists call this cost the opportunity cost.

Opportunity Cost

The highest-valued alternative that we give up to get something is the **opportunity cost** of the activity chosen. "There's no such thing as a free lunch" is not just a clever throwaway line. It expresses the central idea of economics: that every choice involves a cost.

You can quit school, or you can remain in school. If you quit school and take a job at McDonald's, you earn enough to buy some CDs, go to the movies, and spend lots of free time with your friends. If you remain in school, you can't afford these things. You will be able to buy these things and more when you graduate, and that is one of the payoffs from being in school. But for now, when you've bought your books, you have nothing left for CDs and movies. And doing assignments leaves no time for hanging around with your friends. The opportunity cost of being in school is the highest-valued alternative that you would have done if you had quit school.

All the "what," "how," and "for whom" tradeoffs that we've just considered involve opportunity cost. The opportunity cost of some guns is the butter forgone; the opportunity cost of a movie ticket is the number of cups of coffee forgone.

And the choices that bring change also involve opportunity cost. The opportunity cost of more goods and services in the future is less consumption today.

Choosing at the Margin

You can allocate the next hour between studying and e-mailing your friends. But the choice is not all or nothing. You must decide how many minutes to allocate to each activity. To make this decision, you compare the benefit of a little bit more study time with its cost—you make your choice at the **margin**.

The benefit that arises from an increase in an activity is called **marginal benefit**. For example, suppose that you're spending four nights a week studying and your grade point average is 3.0. You decide that you want a higher grade and decide to study an extra night each week. Your grade now rises to 3.5. The marginal benefit from studying for one additional night a week is the 0.5 increase in your grade. It is *not* the 3.5 grade. The reason is that you already have the benefit from studying for four nights a week, so we don't count this benefit as resulting from the decision you are now making.

The cost of an increase in an activity is called **marginal cost**. For you, the marginal cost of increasing your study time by one night a week is the cost of the additional night not spent with your friends (if that is your best alternative use of the time). It does not include the cost of the four nights you are already studying.

To make your decision, you compare the marginal benefit from an extra night of study with its marginal cost. If the marginal benefit exceeds the marginal cost, you study the extra night. If the marginal cost exceeds the marginal benefit, you do not study the extra night.

By evaluating marginal benefits and marginal costs and choosing only those actions that bring greater benefit than cost, we use our scarce resources in the way that makes us as well off as possible.

Responding to Incentives

Our choices respond to incentives. A change in marginal cost or a change in marginal benefit changes the incentives that we face and leads us to change our choice.

For example, suppose your economics instructor gives you a problem set and tells you that all the problems will be on the next test. The marginal benefit from working these problems is large, so you diligently work them all. In contrast, if your math instructor gives you a problem set and tells you that none of the problems will be on the next test, the marginal benefit from working these problems is lower, so you skip most of them.

The central idea of economics is that we can predict how choices will change by looking at changes in incentives. More of an activity is undertaken when its marginal cost falls or marginal benefit rises; less of an activity is undertaken when its marginal cost rises or marginal benefit falls.

Incentives are also the key to reconciling self-interest and the social interest. When our choices are *not* in the social interest, it is because we face the wrong incentives. One of the central challenges for economists is to figure out the incentive systems that result in self-interested choices leading to the social interest.

Human Nature, Incentives, and Institutions

Economists take human nature as given and view people as acting in their self-interest. All people—consumers, producers, politicians, and public servants—pursue their self-interest.

Self-interested actions are not necessarily *selfish* actions. You might decide to use your resources in ways that bring pleasure to others as well as to yourself. But a self-interested act gets the most value for *you* based on *your* view about value.

If human nature is given and if people act in their self-interest, how can we take care of the social interest? Economists answer this question by emphasizing the crucial role that institutions play in influencing the incentives that people face as they pursue their self-interest.

The key institution is a legal system that protects personal security and private property and enables people to specialize and trade in markets. You will learn as you progress with your study of economics that where these institutions exist, self-interest can indeed promote the social interest.

Economics: A Social Science

ECONOMICS IS A SOCIAL SCIENCE (ALONG WITH political science, psychology, and sociology). Economists try to discover how the economic world works, and in pursuit of this goal (like all scientists), they distinguish between two types of statements:

- What *is*
- What *ought to be*

Statements about what *is* are called *positive* statements and they might be right or wrong. We can test a positive statement by checking it against the facts. When a chemist does an experiment in her laboratory, she is attempting to check a positive statement against the facts.

Statements about what *ought to be* are called *normative* statements. These statements depend on values and cannot be tested. When Parliament debates a motion, it is ultimately trying to decide what ought to be. It is making a normative statement.

To see the distinction between positive and normative statements, consider the controversy over global warming. Some scientists believe that centuries of the burning of coal and oil are increasing the carbon dioxide content of the earth's atmosphere and leading to higher temperatures that eventually will have devastating consequences for life on this planet. "Our planet is warming because of an increased carbon dioxide buildup in the atmosphere" is a positive statement. It can (in principle and with sufficient data) be tested. "We ought to cut back on our use of carbon-based fuels such as coal and oil" is a normative statement. You can agree with or disagree with this statement, but you can't test it. It is based on values. Health-care reform provides an economic example of the distinction. "Universal health care cuts the amount of work time lost to illness" is a positive statement. "All Canadians should have equal access to health care" is a normative statement.

The task of economic science is to discover positive statements that are consistent with what we observe and that help us to understand the economic world. This task can be broken into three steps:

- Observation and measurement
- Model building
- Testing models

Observation and Measurement

Economists observe and measure data on such things as the quantities of natural and human resources, wages and work hours, the prices and quantities of the different goods and services produced, taxes and government spending, and the quantities of goods and services bought from and sold to other countries.

Model Building

The second step towards understanding how the economic world works is to build a model. An **economic model** is a description of some aspect of the economic world that includes only those features of the world that are needed for the purpose at hand. A model is simpler than the reality it describes. What a model includes and what it leaves out result from assumptions about what is essential and what are inessential details.

You can see how ignoring details is useful—even essential—to our understanding by thinking about a model that you see every day: the TV weather map. The weather map is a model that helps to predict the temperature, wind speed and direction, and precipitation over a future period. The weather map shows lines called isobars—lines of equal barometric pressure. It doesn't show the highways. The reason is that our theory of the weather tells us that the pattern of air pressure, not the location of the highways, determines the weather.

An economic model is similar to a weather map. For example, an economic model of a cell phone network might tell us the effects of the development of a new low-cost technology on the number of cell phone subscribers and the volume of cell phone use. But the model would ignore such details as the colours of the covers on people's cell phones and the tunes they use for ring tones.

Testing Models

The third step is testing the model. A model's predictions might correspond to the facts or be in conflict with them. By comparing the model's predictions with the facts, we can test a model and develop an economic theory. An **economic theory** is a generalization that summarizes what we think we understand about the economic choices that people make and the performance of industries and entire economies. Economic theory is a bridge between an economic model and the real economy.

The process of building and testing models creates theories. For example, meteorologists have a theory that if the isobars form a particular pattern at a particular time of the year (a model), then it will snow (reality). They have developed this theory by repeated observation and by carefully recording the weather that follows specific pressure patterns.

Economics is a young science. It was born in 1776 with the publication of Adam Smith's *Wealth of Nations* (see p. 54). Over the years since then, economists have discovered many useful theories. But in many areas, economists are still looking for answers. The gradual accumulation of economic knowledge gives most economists some faith that their methods will, eventually, provide usable answers to the big economic questions.

But progress in economics comes slowly. Let's look at some of the obstacles to progress in economics.

Obstacles and Pitfalls in Economics

We cannot easily do economic experiments. And most economic behaviour has many simultaneous causes. For these two reasons, it is difficult in economics to unscramble cause and effect.

Unscrambling Cause and Effect By changing one factor at a time and holding all the other relevant factors constant, we isolate the factor of interest and are able to investigate its effects in the clearest possible way. This logical device, which all scientists use to identify cause and effect, is called *ceteris paribus*. **Ceteris paribus** is a Latin term that means "other things being equal" or "if all other relevant things remain the same." Ensuring that other things are equal is crucial in many activities, and all successful attempts to make scientific progress use this device.

Economic models (like the models in all other sciences) enable the influence of one factor at a time to be isolated in the imaginary world of the model. When we use a model, we are able to imagine what would happen if only one factor changed. But *ceteris paribus* can be a problem in economics when we try to test a model.

Laboratory scientists, such as chemists and physicists, perform experiments by actually holding all the relevant factors constant except for the one under investigation. In non-experimental sciences such as economics (and astronomy), we usually observe the outcomes of the simultaneous operation of many factors. Consequently, it is hard to sort out the effects of each individual factor and to compare them with what a model predicts. To cope with this problem, economists take three complementary approaches.

First, they look for pairs of events in which other things were equal (or similar). An example might be to study the effects of unemployment insurance on the unemployment rate by comparing the United States with Canada on the presumption that the people in the two economies are sufficiently similar. Second, economists use statistical tools—called econometrics. Third, when economists can, they perform experiments. This relatively new approach puts real subjects (usually students) in a decision-making situation and varies their incentives in some way to discover how they respond to a change in one factor at a time.

Economists try to avoid fallacies—errors of reasoning that lead to a wrong conclusion. But two fallacies are common, and you need to be on your guard to avoid them. They are the

- Fallacy of composition
- *Post hoc* fallacy

Fallacy of Composition The fallacy of composition is the (false) statement that what is true of the parts is true of the whole or that what is true of the whole is true of the parts. There are many everyday examples of this fallacy. Standing at a ball game to get a better view works for one person but not for all—what is true for a part of a crowd is not true for the whole crowd.

The fallacy of composition arises in many economic situations that stem from the fact that the parts interact with each other to produce an outcome for the whole that might differ from the intent of the parts.

For example, a firm fires some workers to cut costs and improve its profits. If all firms take similar actions, income falls and so does spending. The firm sells less, and its profits don't improve.

Or suppose that a firm thinks it can gain market share by cutting its price and mounting a large advertising campaign. Again, if the one firm takes these actions they work. But if all the firms in an industry take the same actions, they all end up with the same market share as before and lower profits.

Post Hoc Fallacy Another Latin phrase—*post hoc ergo propter hoc*—means "after this, therefore because of this." The *post hoc* fallacy is the error of reasoning that a first event *causes* a second event because the first occurred before the second. Suppose you are a visitor from a far-off world. You observe lots of people shopping in early December, and then you see them opening gifts and partying in the holiday season. "Does the shopping cause the holiday season?" you wonder. After a deeper study, you discover that the holiday season causes the shopping. A later event causes an earlier event.

Unravelling cause and effect is difficult in economics. And just looking at the timing of events often doesn't help. For example, the stock market booms, and some months later the economy expands—jobs and incomes grow. Did the stock market boom cause the economy to expand? Possibly, but perhaps businesses started to plan the expansion of production because a new technology that lowered costs had become available. As knowledge of the plans spread, the stock market reacted to *anticipate* the economic expansion. To disentangle cause and effect, economists use economic models and data and, to the extent that they can, perform experiments.

Economics is a challenging science. Does the difficulty of getting answers in economics mean that anything goes and that economists disagree on most questions? Perhaps you've heard the joke "If you laid all the economists in the world end to end, they still wouldn't reach a conclusion." Surprisingly, perhaps, the joke does not describe reality.

Agreement and Disagreement

Economists have reached conclusions and agree on a wide range of questions. And often the agreed-upon view of economists disagrees with the popular and sometimes politically correct view. When Bank of Canada Governor David Dodge testifies before Parliament, his words are rarely controversial among economists, even when they generate endless debate in the media and Parliament.

Here are 12 propositions with which at least 7 out of every 10 economists broadly agree:

■ Tariffs and import restrictions make most people worse off.

■ A large budget deficit has an adverse effect on the economy.

■ A minimum wage increases unemployment among young workers and low-skilled workers.

■ Cash payments to welfare recipients make them better off than do transfers-in-kind of equal cash value.

■ A tax cut can help to lower unemployment when the unemployment rate is high.

■ The distribution of income should be more equal.

■ Inflation is primarily caused by a rapid rate of money creation.

■ The government should restructure welfare along the lines of a "negative income tax."

■ Rent ceilings cut the availability of housing.

■ Pollution taxes are more effective than pollution limits.

■ The redistribution of income is a legitimate role for the government.

■ The federal budget should be balanced on the average over the business cycle but not every year.

Which of these propositions are positive and which are normative? Notice that economists are willing to offer their opinions on normative issues as well as their professional views on positive questions. Be on the lookout for normative propositions dressed up as positive propositions.

REVIEW QUIZ

1 What is the distinction between a positive statement and a normative statement? Provide an example (different from those in the chapter) of each type of statement.
2 What is a model? Can you think of a model that you might use (probably without thinking of it as a model) in your everyday life?
3 What is a theory? Why is the statement "It might work in theory, but it doesn't work in practice" a silly statement?
4 What is the *ceteris paribus* assumption and how is it used?
5 Try to think of some everyday examples of the fallacy of composition and the *post hoc* fallacy.

myeconlab   **Study Plan 1.4**

SUMMARY

KEY POINTS

A Definition of Economics (p. 2)

- All economic questions arise from scarcity—from the fact that wants exceed the resources available to satisfy them.
- Economics is the social science that studies the choices that people make as they cope with scarcity.
- The subject divides into microeconomics and macroeconomics.

Two Big Economic Questions (pp. 3–8)

- Two big questions summarize the scope of economics:
  1. How do choices end up determining *what, how*, and *for whom* goods and services get produced?
  2. When do choices made in the pursuit of *self-interest* also promote the *social interest*?

The Economic Way of Thinking (pp. 9–11)

- Every choice is a tradeoff—exchanging more of something for less of something else.
- The classic guns-versus-butter tradeoff represents all tradeoffs.
- All economic questions involve tradeoffs.
- The big social tradeoff is that between equality and efficiency.
- The highest-valued alternative forgone is the opportunity cost of what is chosen.
- Choices are made at the margin and respond to incentives.

Economics: A Social Science (pp. 12–14)

- Economists distinguish between positive statements—what is—and normative statements—what ought to be.

- To explain the economic world, economists develop theories by building and testing economic models.
- Economists use the *ceteris paribus* assumption to try to disentangle cause and effect and are careful to avoid the fallacy of composition and the *post hoc* fallacy.
- Economists agree on a wide range of questions about how the economy works.

KEY TERMS

Big tradeoff, 10
Capital, 4
Ceteris paribus, 13
Economic model, 12
Economics, 2
Economic theory, 12
Entrepreneurship, 4
Factors of production, 3
Goods and services, 3
Human capital, 3
Incentive, 2
Interest, 4
Labour, 3
Land, 3
Macroeconomics, 2
Margin, 11
Marginal benefit, 11
Marginal cost, 11
Microeconomics, 2
Opportunity cost, 10
Profit, 4
Rent, 4
Scarcity, 2
Self-interest, 5
Social interest, 5
Tradeoff, 9
Wages, 4

PROBLEMS

Go to myeconlab **for solutions to odd-numbered problems and additional exercises.**

1. Your friends go the movies one evening and you decide to stay home and do your economics assignment and practice test. You get 80 percent on your next economics exam compared with the 70 percent that you normally score. What is the opportunity cost of your extra points?

2. You go to the movies one evening instead of studying for your economics test. You get 50 percent on your next economics test rather than the 70 percent that you usually get. What is the opportunity cost of going to the movies?

3. You plan to go to school this summer. If you do, you won't be able to take your usual job that pays $6,000 for the summer, and you won't be able to live at home for free. The cost of tuition is $2,000 and textbooks is $200, and living expenses are $1,400. What is the opportunity cost of going to summer school?

4. You plan to go skiing next weekend. If you do, you'll have to miss doing your usual weekend job that pays $100. You won't be able to study for 8 hours and you won't be able to use your prepaid college meal plan. The cost of travel and accommodations will be $350, the ski rental will cost $60, and your food will cost $40. What is the opportunity cost of the ski trip?

5. The local mall has free parking, but the mall is always very busy, and it usually takes 30 minutes to find a parking space. Today when you found a vacant spot, Harry also wanted it. Is parking really free at this mall? If not, what did it cost you to park today? When you parked your car today, did you impose any costs on Harry? Explain your answers.

6. The university has built a new movie house. Admission for students is free and there are always plenty of empty seats. But when the movie house screened *Lord of the Rings*, the lines were long. So the movie house decided to charge $4 per student. Cadbury Schweppes offered students a free soft drink. Compare the student's opportunity cost of seeing the movie *Lord of the Rings* with that of any other movie screened in the year. Which is less costly and by how much?

CRITICAL THINKING

1. Use the two big questions of economics and the economic way of thinking to organize a short essay about the economic life of a homeless man. Does he face scarcity? Does he make choices? Can you interpret his choices as being in his own best interest? Can either his own choices or the choices of others make him better off? If so, how?

WEB EXERCISES

Use the links on myeconlab **to work the following exercises.**

1. Visit the CBC.
   a. What is the top economic news story today?
   b. With which of the big questions does it deal? (It must deal with at least one of them and might deal with more than one.)
   c. What tradeoffs does the news item discuss?
   d. Write a brief summary of the news item in a few bulleted points using as much as possible of the economic vocabulary that you have learned in this chapter and that is in the key terms list on p. 15.

2. Visit *Resources for Economists on the Internet.* This site is a good place from which to search for economic information on the Internet.
   a. Scroll down the page and click on General Interest.
   b. Visit the "general interest" sites and become familiar with the types of information they contain.

3. Visit Statistics Canada.
   a. What is the number of people employed (nonfarm employment) in your area?
   b. Has employment increased or decreased?
   c. What is income per person (per capita income) in your area?

Graphs in Economics

After studying this appendix, you will be able to

- Make and interpret a time-series graph, a cross-section graph, and a scatter diagram

- Distinguish between linear and nonlinear relationships and between relationships that have a maximum and a minimum

- Define and calculate the slope of a line

- Graph relationships among more than two variables

Graphing Data

A GRAPH REPRESENTS A QUANTITY AS A DISTANCE on a line. Figure A1.1 shows two examples. Here, a distance on the horizontal line represents temperature, measured in degrees Celsius. A movement from left to right shows an increase in temperature. The point marked 0 represents zero degrees Celsius. To the right of 0, the temperature is positive. To the left of 0 (as indicated by the minus sign), the temperature is negative. A distance on the vertical line represents altitude or height, measured in thousands of metres above sea level. The point marked 0 represents sea level. Points above 0 represent metres above sea level. Points below 0 (indicated by a minus sign) represent metres below sea level.

By setting two scales perpendicular to each other, as in Fig. A1.1, we can visualize the relationship between two variables. The scale lines are called *axes*. The vertical line is the *y-axis*, and the horizontal line is the *x-axis*. Each axis has a zero point, which is shared by the two axes. This zero point, common to both axes, is called the *origin*.

To show something in a two-variable graph, we need two pieces of information: the value of the *x*-variable and the value of the *y*-variable. For example, off the coast of British Columbia on a winter's day, the temperature is 10 degrees—the value of *x*. A fishing boat is located at 0 metres above sea level—the value of *y*. These two bits of information appear as point *A* in Fig. A1.1. A climber at the top of Mt. McKinley on a cold day is 6,194 metres above sea level in a zero-degree gale. These two pieces of information appear as point *B*. The position of the

FIGURE A1.1
Making a Graph

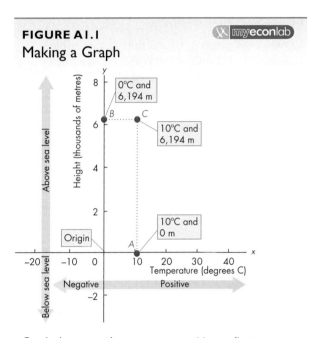

Graphs have axes that measure quantities as distances. Here, the horizontal axis (*x*-axis) measures temperature, and the vertical axis (*y*-axis) measures height. Point *A* represents a fishing boat at sea level (0 on the *y*-axis) on a day when the temperature is 10°C. Point *B* represents a climber on Mt. McKinley, 6,194 metres above sea level, at a temperature of 0°C. Point *C* represents a climber on Mt. McKinley, 6,194 metres above sea level, at a temperature of 10°C.

climber on a warmer day might be at the point marked *C*. This point represents the peak of Mt. McKinley at a temperature of 10 degrees.

We can draw two lines, called *coordinates*, from point *C*. One, called the *y*-coordinate, runs from *C* to the horizontal axis. Its length is the same as the value marked off on the *y*-axis. The other, called the *x*-coordinate, runs from *C* to the vertical axis. Its length is the same as the value marked off on the *x*-axis. We describe a point in a graph by the values of its *x*-coordinate and its *y*-coordinate.

Graphs like that in Fig. A1.1 can show any type of quantitative data on two variables. Economists use three types of graphs based on the principles in Fig. A1.1 to reveal and describe the relationships among variables. They are

- Time-series graphs
- Cross-section graphs
- Scatter diagrams

17

Time-Series Graphs

A **time-series graph** measures time (for example, months or years) on the *x*-axis and the variable or variables in which we are interested on the *y*-axis. Figure A1.2 is an example of a time-series graph. It provides some information on the average price of unleaded gasoline across Canada.

In Fig. A1.2, we measure time in years running from 1990 to 2005. We measure the price of gasoline (the variable that we are interested in) on the *y*-axis.

The point of a time-series graph is to enable us to visualize how a variable has changed over time and how its value in one period relates to its value in another period.

A time-series graph conveys an enormous amount of information quickly and easily, as this example illustrates. It shows

- The *level* of the price of gasoline—when it is *high* and *low*. When the line is a long way from the *x*-axis, the price is high. When the line is close to the *x*-axis, the price is low.
- How the price *changes*—whether it *rises* or *falls*. When the line slopes upward, as in 2000, the price is rising. When the line slopes downward, as in 1993, the price is falling.
- The *speed* with which the price changes—whether it rises or falls *quickly* or *slowly*. If the line is steep, then the price rises or falls quickly. If the line is not steep, the price rises or falls slowly. For example, the price rose quickly from 2003 to 2004 and slowly from 1995 to 1996. The price fell quickly from 2001 to 2002 and slowly from 1991 to 1994.

A time-series graph also reveals whether there is a trend. A trend is a general tendency for a variable to move in one direction. A **trend** might be upward or downward. In Fig. A1.2, you can see that the price of gasoline had a general tendency to rise from the mid-1990s to 2005. That is, although the price rose and fell, the general tendency was for it to rise—the price had an upward trend.

A time-series graph also helps us detect cycles in variables. You can see some peaks and troughs in the price of gasoline in Fig. A1.2. You can see a trough in 1998 and a peak in 2001.

Finally, a time-series graph also lets us compare the variable in different periods quickly. Figure A1.2 shows that the 1990s were different from the 2000s. The

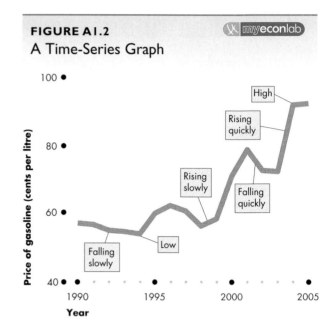

FIGURE A1.2
A Time-Series Graph

A time-series graph plots the level of a variable on the *y*-axis against time (day, week, month, or year) on the *x*-axis. This graph shows the average price of gasoline each year from 1990 to 2005. It shows us when the price of gasoline was *high* and when it was *low*, when the price *increased* and when it *decreased*, and when it changed *quickly* and when it changed *slowly*.

price of gasoline fluctuated more in the 2000s than it did in the 1990s.

You can see that a time-series graph conveys a wealth of information. And it does so in much less space than we have used to describe only some of its features. But you do have to "read" the graph to obtain all this information.

Cross-Section Graphs

A **cross-section graph** shows the values of an economic variable for different groups in a population at a point in time. Figure A1.3, called a *bar chart*, is an example of a cross-section graph.

The bar chart in Fig. A1.3 shows the number of visitors to each province in 2004. The length of each bar indicates the number of visitors. This figure enables you to compare the number of visitors across the provinces. And you can do so much more quickly and clearly than you could by looking at a list of numbers.

FIGURE A1.3
A Cross-Section Graph

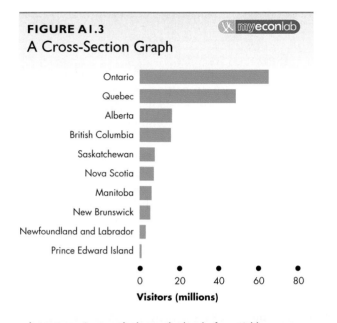

A cross-section graph shows the level of a variable across the members of a population. This bar chart shows the number of visitors to each province in 2004.

Scatter Diagrams

A **scatter diagram** plots the value of one variable against the value of another variable. Such a graph reveals whether a relationship exists between two variables and describes their relationship. Figure A1.4(a) shows the relationship between expenditure and income. Each point shows expenditure per person and income per person in a given year from 1990 to 2004. The points are "scattered" within the graph. The point labelled *A* tells us that in 1999, income per person was $19,610 and expenditure per person was $18,448. The dots in this graph form a pattern, which reveals that as income increases, expenditure increases.

Figure A1.4(b) shows the relationship between the number of international phone calls and the price of a call. This graph shows that as the price per minute falls, the number of calls increases.

Figure A1.4(c) shows a scatter diagram of inflation and unemployment in Canada. Here, the dots show no clear relationship between these two variables. The dots in this graph reveal that there is no simple relationship between these variables.

FIGURE A1.4
Scatter Diagrams

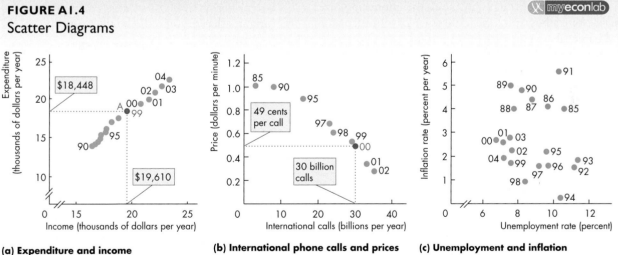

(a) Expenditure and income

(b) International phone calls and prices

(c) Unemployment and inflation

A scatter diagram reveals the relationship between two variables. Part (a) shows the relationship between expenditure and income. Each point shows the values of the two variables in a specific year. For example, point A shows that in 1999, average income was $19,610 and average expenditure was $18,448. The pattern formed by the points shows that as income increases, expenditure increases.

Part (b) shows the relationship between the price of an international phone call and the number of calls made. This graph shows that as the price of a phone call falls, the number of calls made increases. Part (c) shows the inflation rate and unemployment rate in Canada. This graph shows that the inflation rate and the unemployment rate are not closely related.

Breaks in the Axes Two of the graphs you've just looked at, Fig. A1.4(a) and Fig. A1.4(c), have breaks in their axes, as shown by the small gaps. The breaks indicate that there are jumps from the origin, 0, to the first values recorded.

In Fig. A1.4(a), the breaks are used because the lowest value of expenditure exceeds $13,000 and the lowest value of income exceeds $17,000. With no breaks in the axes of this graph, there would be a lot of empty space, all the points would be crowded into the top right corner, and we would not be able to see whether a relationship exists between these two variables. By breaking the axes, we are able to bring the relationship into view.

Putting a break in the axes is like using a zoom lens to bring the relationship into the centre of the graph and magnify it so that it fills the graph.

Misleading Graphs Breaks can be used to highlight a relationship. But they can also be used to mislead—to make a graph that lies. The most common way of making a graph lie is to use axis breaks either to stretch or to compress a scale. For example, suppose that in Fig. A1.4(a), the *y*-axis ran from zero to $45,000 while the *x*-axis was the same as the one shown. The graph would now create the impression that despite a huge increase in income, expenditure had barely changed.

To avoid being misled, it is a good idea to get into the habit of always looking closely at the values and the labels on the axes of a graph before you start to interpret it.

Correlation and Causation A scatter diagram that shows a clear relationship between two variables, such as Fig. A1.4(a) or Fig. A1.4(b), tells us that the two variables have a high correlation. When a high correlation is present, we can predict the value of one variable from the value of the other variable. But correlation does not imply causation.

Sometimes a high correlation is a coincidence, but sometimes it does arise from a causal relationship. It is likely, for example, that rising income causes rising expenditure (Fig. A1.4a) and that the falling price of a phone call causes more calls to be made (Fig. A1.4b).

You've now seen how we can use graphs in economics to show economic data and to reveal relationships between variables. Next, we'll learn how economists use graphs to construct and display economic models.

Graphs Used in Economic Models

THE GRAPHS USED IN ECONOMICS ARE NOT ALWAYS designed to show real-world data. Often they are used to show general relationships among the variables in an economic model.

An *economic model* is a stripped down, simplified description of an economy or of a component of an economy, such as a business or a household. It consists of statements about economic behaviour that can be expressed as equations or as curves in a graph. Economists use models to explore the effects of different policies or other influences on the economy in ways that are similar to the use of model airplanes in wind tunnels and models of the climate.

You will encounter many different kinds of graphs in economic models, but there are some repeating patterns. Once you've learned to recognize these patterns, you will instantly understand the meaning of a graph. Here, we'll look at the different types of curves that are used in economic models, and we'll see some everyday examples of each type of curve. The patterns to look for in graphs are the four cases:

- Variables that move in the same direction
- Variables that move in opposite directions
- Variables that have a maximum or a minimum
- Variables that are unrelated

Let's look at these four cases.

Variables That Move in the Same Direction

Figure A1.5 shows graphs of the relationships between two variables that move up and down together. A relationship between two variables that move in the same direction is called a **positive relationship** or a **direct relationship**. A line that slopes upward shows such a relationship.

Figure A1.5 shows three types of relationships: one that has a straight line and two that have curved lines. But all the lines in these three graphs are called curves. Any line on a graph—no matter whether it is straight or curved—is called a *curve*.

A relationship shown by a straight line is called a **linear relationship**. Figure A1.5(a) shows a linear rela-

FIGURE A1.5

Positive (Direct) Relationships

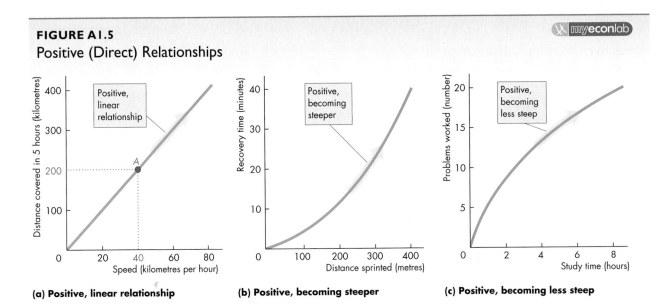

(a) Positive, linear relationship   **(b) Positive, becoming steeper**   **(c) Positive, becoming less steep**

Each part of this figure shows a positive (direct) relationship between two variables. That is, as the value of the variable measured on the x-axis increases, so does the value of the variable measured on the y-axis. Part (a) shows a linear relationship—as the two variables increase together, we move along a straight line. Part (b) shows a positive relationship such that as the two variables increase together, we move along a curve that becomes steeper. Part (c) shows a positive relationship such that as the two variables increase together, we move along a curve that becomes less steep.

tionship between the number of kilometres travelled in 5 hours and speed. For example, point *A* shows that we will travel 200 kilometres in 5 hours if our speed is 40 kilometres an hour. If we double our speed to 80 kilometres an hour, we will travel 400 kilometres in 5 hours.

Figure A1.5(b) shows the relationship between distance sprinted and recovery time (the time it takes the heart rate to return to its normal resting value). This relationship is an upward-sloping one that starts out quite flat but then becomes steeper as we move along the curve away from the origin. The reason this curve slopes upward and becomes steeper is because the additional recovery time needed from sprinting an additional 100 metres increases. It takes less than 5 minutes to recover from the first 100 metres, but it takes more than 10 minutes to recover from the second 100 metres.

Figure A1.5(c) shows the relationship between the number of problems worked by a student and the amount of study time. This relationship is an upward-sloping one that starts out quite steep and becomes flatter as we move away from the origin. Study time becomes less productive as the student spends more hours studying and becomes more tired.

Variables That Move in Opposite Directions

Figure A1.6 shows relationships between things that move in opposite directions. A relationship between variables that move in opposite directions is called a **negative relationship** or an **inverse relationship**.

Figure A1.6(a) shows the relationship between the number of hours available for playing squash and the number of hours for playing tennis when the total is 5 hours. One extra hour spent playing tennis means one hour less playing squash and vice versa. This relationship is negative and linear.

Figure A1.6(b) shows the relationship between the cost per kilometre travelled and the length of a journey. The longer the journey, the lower is the cost per kilometre. But as the journey length increases, the cost per kilometre decreases, and the fall in the cost is smaller, the longer the journey. This feature of the relationship is shown by the fact that the curve slopes downward, starting out steep at a short journey length and then becoming flatter as the journey length increases. This relationship arises because some of the costs are fixed (such as auto insurance), and the fixed cost is spread over a longer journey.

FIGURE A1.6
Negative (Inverse) Relationships

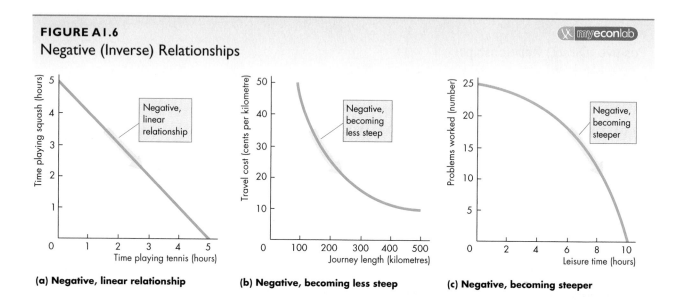

(a) **Negative, linear relationship**   (b) **Negative, becoming less steep**   (c) **Negative, becoming steeper**

Each part of this figure shows a negative (inverse) relationship between two variables. That is, as the value of the variable measured on the x-axis increases, the value of the variable measured on the y-axis decreases. Part (a) shows a linear relationship. The total time spent playing tennis and squash is 5 hours. As the time spent playing tennis increases, the time spent playing squash decreases, and we move along a straight line. Part (b) shows a negative relationship such that as the journey length increases, the curve becomes less steep. Part (c) shows a negative relationship such that as leisure time increases, the curve becomes steeper.

Figure A1.6(c) shows the relationship between the amount of leisure time and the number of problems worked by a student. Increasing leisure time produces an increasingly large reduction in the number of problems worked. This relationship is a negative one that starts out with a gentle slope at a small number of leisure hours and becomes steeper as the number of leisure hours increases. This relationship is a different view of the idea shown in Fig. A1.5(c).

Variables That Have a Maximum or a Minimum

Many relationships in economic models have a maximum or a minimum. For example, firms try to make the maximum possible profit and to produce at the lowest possible cost. Figure A1.7 shows relationships that have a maximum or a minimum.

Figure A1.7(a) shows the relationship between rainfall and wheat yield. When there is no rainfall, wheat will not grow, so the yield is zero. As the rainfall increases up to 10 days a month, the wheat yield increases. With 10 rainy days each month, the wheat yield reaches its maximum at 2 tonnes per hectare (point A). Rain in excess of 10 days a month starts to lower the yield of wheat. If every day is rainy, the wheat suffers from a lack of sunshine and the yield decreases to zero. This relationship is one that starts out sloping upward, reaches a maximum, and then slopes downward.

Figure A1.7(b) shows the reverse case—a relationship that begins sloping downward, falls to a minimum, and then slopes upward. Most economic costs are like this relationship. An example is the relationship between the cost per kilometre and speed for a car trip. At low speeds, the car is creeping in a traffic jam. The number of kilometres per litre is low, so the cost per kilometre is high. At high speeds, the car is travelling faster than its efficient speed, using a large quantity of gasoline, and again the number of kilometres per litre is low and the cost per kilometre is high. At a speed of 100 kilometres an hour, the cost per kilometre is at its minimum (point B). This relationship is one that starts out sloping downward, reaches a minimum, and then slopes upward.

FIGURE A1.7
Maximum and Minimum Points

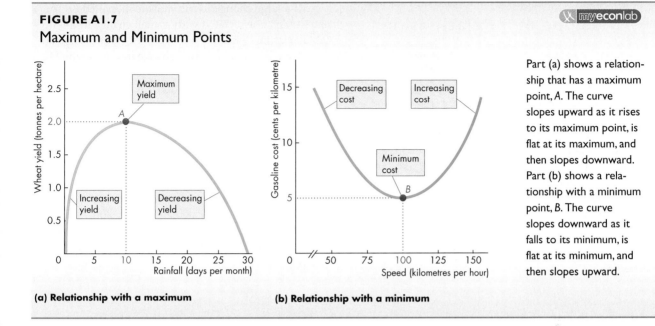

Part (a) shows a relationship that has a maximum point, A. The curve slopes upward as it rises to its maximum point, is flat at its maximum, and then slopes downward. Part (b) shows a relationship with a minimum point, B. The curve slopes downward as it falls to its minimum, is flat at its minimum, and then slopes upward.

(a) Relationship with a maximum   **(b) Relationship with a minimum**

Variables That Are Unrelated

There are many situations in which no matter what happens to the value of one variable, the other variable remains constant. Sometimes we want to show the independence between two variables in a graph, and Fig. A1.8 shows two ways of achieving this.

In describing the graphs in Figs. A1.5 through A1.7, we have talked about curves that slope upward and downward, and curves that become less steep or steeper. Let's spend a little time discussing exactly what we mean by slope and how we measure the slope of a curve.

FIGURE A1.8
Variables That Are Unrelated

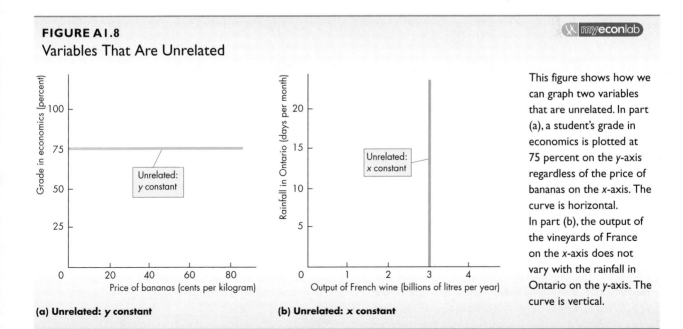

This figure shows how we can graph two variables that are unrelated. In part (a), a student's grade in economics is plotted at 75 percent on the y-axis regardless of the price of bananas on the x-axis. The curve is horizontal.
In part (b), the output of the vineyards of France on the x-axis does not vary with the rainfall in Ontario on the y-axis. The curve is vertical.

(a) Unrelated: y constant   **(b) Unrelated: x constant**

The Slope of a Relationship

WE CAN MEASURE THE INFLUENCE OF ONE variable on another by the slope of the relationship. The **slope** of a relationship is the change in the value of the variable measured on the y-axis divided by the change in the value of the variable measured on the x-axis. We use the Greek letter Δ (*delta*) to represent "change in." Thus Δy means the change in the value of the variable measured on the y-axis, and Δx means the change in the value of the variable measured on the x-axis. Therefore the slope of the relationship is

$$\Delta y/\Delta x$$

If a large change in the variable measured on the y-axis (Δy) is associated with a small change in the variable measured on the x-axis (Δx), the slope is large and the curve is steep. If a small change in the variable measured on the y-axis (Δy) is associated with a large change in the variable measured on the x-axis (Δx), the slope is small and the curve is flat.

We can make the idea of slope sharper by doing some calculations.

The Slope of a Straight Line

The slope of a straight line is the same regardless of where on the line you calculate it. The slope of a straight line is constant. Let's calculate the slopes of the lines in Fig. A1.9. In part (a), when x increases from 2 to 6, y increases from 3 to 6. The change in x

---

FIGURE A1.9
The Slope of a Straight Line

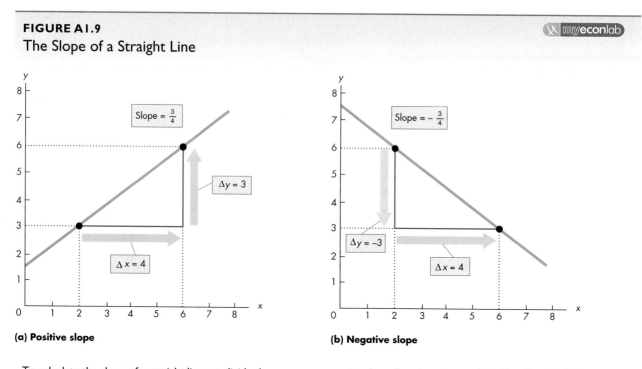

(a) Positive slope

(b) Negative slope

To calculate the slope of a straight line, we divide the change in the value of the variable measured on the y-axis (Δy) by the change in the value of the variable measured on the x-axis (Δx), as we move along the curve. Part (a) shows the calculation of a positive slope. When x increases from 2 to 6, Δx equals 4. That change in x brings about an increase in y from 3 to 6, so Δy equals 3. The slope ($\Delta y/\Delta x$) equals 3/4. Part (b) shows the calculation of a negative slope. When x increases from 2 to 6, Δx equals 4. That increase in x brings about a decrease in y from 6 to 3, so Δy equals −3. The slope ($\Delta y/\Delta x$) equals −3/4.

is +4—that is, Δx is 4. The change in y is +3—that is, Δy is 3. The slope of that line is

$$\frac{\Delta y}{\Delta x} = \frac{3}{4}.$$

In part (b), when x increases from 2 to 6, y decreases from 6 to 3. The change in y is *minus* 3—that is, Δy is –3. The change in x is *plus* 4—that is, Δx is 4. The slope of the curve is

$$\frac{\Delta y}{\Delta x} = \frac{-3}{4}.$$

Notice that the two slopes have the same magnitude (3/4) but the slope of the line in part (a) is positive (+3/+4 = 3/4), while that in part (b) is negative (–3/+4 = –3/4). The slope of a positive relationship is positive; the slope of a negative relationship is negative.

The Slope of a Curved Line

The slope of a curved line is trickier. The slope of a curved line is not constant. Its slope depends on where on the line we calculate it. There are two ways to calculate the slope of a curved line: You can calculate the slope at a point, or you can calculate the slope across an arc of the curve. Let's look at the two alternatives.

Slope at a Point To calculate the slope at a point on a curve, you need to construct a straight line that has the same slope as the curve at the point in question. Figure A1.10 shows how this is done. Suppose you want to calculate the slope of the curve at point A. Place a ruler on the graph so that it touches point A and no other point on the curve, then draw a straight line along the edge of the ruler. The straight red line is this line, and it is the tangent to the curve at point A. If the ruler touches the curve only at point A, then the slope of the curve at point A must be the same as the slope of the edge of the ruler. If the curve and the ruler do not have the same slope, the line along the edge of the ruler will cut the curve instead of just touching it.

Now that you have found a straight line with the same slope as the curve at point A, you can calculate the slope of the curve at point A by calculating the slope of the straight line. Along the straight line, as x

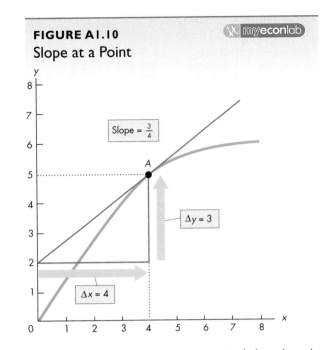

FIGURE A1.10
Slope at a Point

To calculate the slope of the curve at point A, draw the red line that just touches the curve at A—the tangent. The slope of this straight line is calculated by dividing the change in y by the change in x along the red line. When x increases from 0 to 4, Δx equals 4. That change in x is associated with an increase in y from 2 to 5, so Δy equals 3. The slope of the red line is 3/4. So the slope of the curve at point A is 3/4.

increases from 0 to 4 ($\Delta x = 4$) y increases from 2 to 5 ($\Delta y = 3$). Therefore the slope of the line is

$$\frac{\Delta y}{\Delta x} = \frac{3}{4}.$$

Thus the slope of the curve at point A is 3/4.

Slope Across an Arc An arc of a curve is a piece of a curve. In Fig. A1.11, you are looking at the same curve as in Fig. A1.10. But instead of calculating the slope at point A, we are going to calculate the slope across the arc from B to C. You can see that the slope at B is greater than the slope at C. When we calculate the slope across an arc, we are calculating the average slope between two points. As we move along the arc from B to C, x increases from 3 to 5 and y increases from 4 to 5.5. The change in x is 2 ($\Delta x = 2$), and the

FIGURE A1.11
Slope Across an Arc

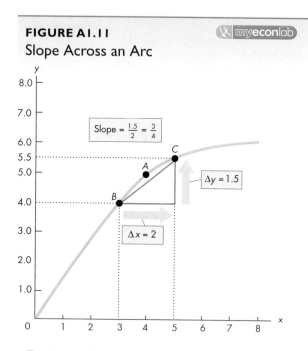

To calculate the average slope of the curve along the arc *BC*, draw a straight line from *B* to *C*. The slope of the line *BC* is calculated by dividing the change in *y* by the change in *x*. In moving from *B* to *C*, Δ*x* equals 2 and Δ*y* equals 1.5. The slope of the line *BC* is 1.5 divided by 2, or 3/4. So the slope of the curve across the arc *BC* is 3/4.

change in *y* is 1.5 (Δ*y* = 1.5). Therefore the slope of the line is

$$\frac{\Delta y}{\Delta x} = \frac{1.5}{2} = \frac{3}{4}.$$

Thus the slope of the curve across the arc *BC* is 3/4.

This calculation gives us the slope of the curve between points *B* and *C*. The actual slope calculated is the slope of the straight line from *B* to *C*. This slope approximates the average slope of the curve along the arc *BC*. In this particular example, the slope across the arc *BC* is identical to the slope of the curve at point *A*. But the calculation of the slope of a curve does not always work out so neatly. You might have some fun constructing some more examples and some counter-examples.

You now know how to make and interpret a graph. But so far, we've limited our attention to graphs of two variables. We're now going to learn how to graph more than two variables.

Graphing Relationships Among More Than Two Variables

WE HAVE SEEN THAT WE CAN GRAPH THE relationship between two variables as a point formed by the *x*- and *y*-coordinates in a two-dimensional graph. You may be thinking that although a two-dimensional graph is informative, most of the things in which you are likely to be interested involve relationships among many variables, not just two. For example, the amount of ice cream consumed depends on the price of ice cream and the temperature. If ice cream is expensive and the temperature is low, people eat much less ice cream than when ice cream is inexpensive and the temperature is high. For any given price of ice cream, the quantity consumed varies with the temperature; and for any given temperature, the quantity of ice cream consumed varies with its price.

Figure A1.12 shows a relationship among three variables. The table shows the number of litres of ice cream consumed each day at various temperatures and ice cream prices. How can we graph these numbers?

To graph a relationship that involves more than two variables, we use the *ceteris paribus* assumption.

Ceteris Paribus We noted in the chapter (see p. 13) that every laboratory experiment is an attempt to create *ceteris paribus* and isolate the relationship of interest. We use the same method to make a graph when more than two variables are involved.

Figure A1.12(a) shows an example. There, you can see what happens to the quantity of ice cream consumed when the price of ice cream varies and the temperature is held constant. The line labelled 21°C shows the relationship between ice cream consumption and the price of ice cream if the temperature remains at 21°C. The numbers used to plot that line are those in the third column of the table in Fig. A1.12. For example, if the temperature is 21°C, 10 litres are consumed when the price is 60¢ a scoop and 18 litres are consumed when the price is 30¢ a scoop. The curve labelled 32°C shows consumption as the price varies if the temperature remains at 32°C.

We can also show the relationship between ice cream consumption and temperature when the price of ice cream remains constant, as shown

FIGURE A1.12

Graphing a Relationship Among Three Variables

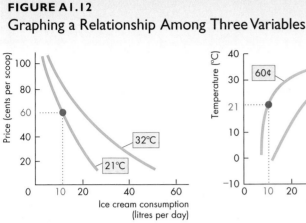

(a) Price and consumption at a given temperature

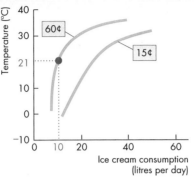

(b) Temperature and consumption at a given price

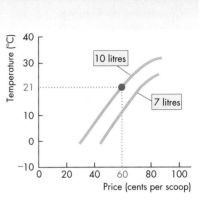

(c) Temperature and price at a given consumption

Price	Ice cream consumption (litres per day)			
(cents per scoop)	–10°C	10°C	21°C	32°C
15	12	18	25	50
30	10	12	18	37
45	7	10	13	27
60	5	7	10	20
75	3	5	7	14
90	2	3	5	10
105	1	2	3	6

The quantity of ice cream consumed depends on its price and the temperature. The table gives some hypothetical numbers that tell us how many litres of ice cream are consumed each day at different prices and different temperatures. For example, if the price is 60¢ a scoop and the temperature is 21°C, 10 litres of ice cream are consumed. This set of values is highlighted in the table and each part of the figure.

To graph a relationship among three variables, the value of one variable is held constant. Part (a) shows the relationship between price and consumption when temperature is held constant. One curve holds temperature at 32°C and the other at 21°C. Part (b) shows the relationship between temperature and consumption when price is held constant. One curve holds the price at 60¢ a scoop and the other at 15¢ a scoop. Part (c) shows the relationship between temperature and price when consumption is held constant. One curve holds consumption at 10 litres a day and the other at 7 litres a day.

in Fig. A1.12(b). The curve labelled 60¢ shows how the consumption of ice cream varies with the temperature when ice cream costs 60¢ a scoop, and a second curve shows the relationship when ice cream costs 15¢ a scoop. For example, at 60¢ a scoop, 10 litres are consumed when the temperature is 21°C and 20 litres when the temperature is 32°C.

Figure A1.12(c) shows the combinations of temperature and price that result in a constant consumption of ice cream. One curve shows the combination that results in 10 litres a day being consumed, and

the other shows the combination that results in 7 litres a day being consumed. A high price and a high temperature lead to the same consumption as a lower price and a lower temperature. For example, 10 litres of ice cream are consumed at 21°C and 60¢ a scoop, 32°C and 90¢ a scoop, and at 10°C and 45¢ a scoop.

With what you have learned about graphs, you can move forward with your study of economics. There are no graphs in this book that are more complicated than those that have been explained in this appendix.

Mathematical Note
Equations to Straight Lines

IF A STRAIGHT LINE IN A GRAPH DESCRIBES THE relationship between two variables, we call it a *linear relationship*. Figure 1 shows the linear relationship between a person's expenditure and income. This person spends $100 a week (by borrowing or spending previous savings) when income is zero. And out of each dollar earned, this person spends 50 cents (and saves 50 cents).

All linear relationships are described by the same general equation. We call the quantity that is measured on the horizontal (or *x*-axis) *x* and we call the quantity that is measured on the vertical (or *y*-axis) *y*. In the case of Fig. 1, *x* is income and *y* is expenditure.

A Linear Equation

The equation that describes a straight-line relationship between *x* and *y* is

$$y = a + bx.$$

In this equation, *a* and *b* are fixed numbers and they are called constants. The values of *x* and *y* vary so these numbers are called variables. Because the equation describes a straight line, it is called a *linear equation*.

The equation tells us that when the value of *x* is zero, the value of *y* is *a*. We call the constant *a* the *y*-axis intercept. The reason is that on the graph the straight line hits the *y*-axis at a value equal to *a*. Figure 1 illustrates the *y*-axis intercept.

For positive values of *x*, the value of *y* exceeds *a*. The constant *b* tells us by how much *y* increases above *a* as *x* increases. The constant *b* is the slope of the line.

Slope of Line

As we explain in the chapter, the *slope* of a relationship is the change in the value of *y* divided by the change in the value of *x* as we move along the line. We use the Greek letter Δ (*delta*) to represent "change in." Thus Δy means the change in the value of the variable measured on the *y*-axis, and Δx means the change in the value of the variable measured on the *x*-axis. Therefore the slope of the relationship is

$$\Delta y/\Delta x.$$

To see why the slope is *b*, suppose that initially the value of *x* is x_1, or $200 in Fig. 2. The corresponding value of *y* is y_1, also $200 in Fig. 2. The equation to the line tells us that

$$y_1 = a + bx_1. \tag{1}$$

Now the value of *x* increases by Δx to $x_1 + \Delta x$ (or $400 in Fig. 2). And the value of *y* increases by Δy to $y_1 + \Delta y$ (or $300 in Fig. 2).

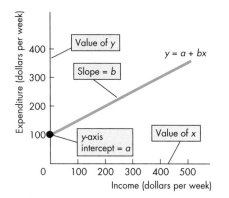

Figure 1 Linear relationship

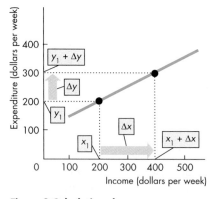

Figure 2 Calculating slope

The equation to the line now tells us that

$$y_1 + \Delta y = a + b(x_1 + \Delta x). \qquad (2)$$

To calculate the slope of the line, subtract equation (1) from equation (2) to obtain

$$\Delta y = b\Delta x \qquad (3)$$

and now divide equation (3) by Δx to obtain

$$\frac{\Delta y}{\Delta x} = b.$$

So, the slope of the line is b.

Position of Line

The y-axis intercept determines the position of the line on the graph. Figure 3 illustrates the relationship between the y-axis intercept and the position of the line on the graph. The y-axis measures saving and the x-axis measures income. When the y-axis intercept, a, is positive, the line hits the y-axis at a positive value of y—as the blue line does. When the y-axis intercept, a, is zero, the line hits the y-axis at the origin—as the purple line does. When the y-axis intercept, a, is negative, the line hits the y-axis at a negative value of y—as the red line does. As the equations to the three lines show, the value of the y-axis intercept does not influence the slope of the line.

Positive Relationships

Figure 1 shows a positive relationship—the two variables x and y move in the same direction. All positive relationships have a slope that is positive. In the equation to the line, the constant b is positive. In this example, the y-axis intercept, a, is 100. The slope b equals $\Delta y/\Delta x$, which is 100/200 or 0.5. The equation to the line is

$$y = 100 + 0.5x.$$

Negative Relationships

Figure 4 shows a negative relationship—the two variables x and y move in the opposite direction. All negative relationships have a slope that is negative. In the equation to the line, the constant b is negative. In the example in Fig. 4, the y-axis intercept, a, is 30. The slope, b, equals $\Delta y/\Delta x$, which is −20/2 or −10. The equation to the line is

$$y = 30 + (-10)x$$

or,

$$y = 30 - 10x.$$

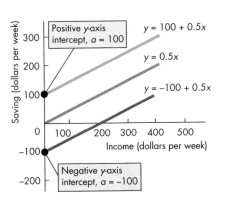

Figure 3 The *y*-axis intercept

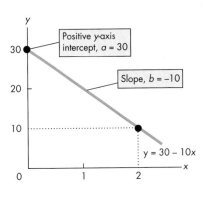

Figure 4 Negative relationship

SUMMARY

KEY POINTS

Graphing Data (pp. 17–20)

- A time-series graph shows the trend and fluctuations in a variable over time.
- A cross-section graph shows how variables change across the members of a population.
- A scatter diagram shows the relationship between two variables. It shows whether two variables are positively related, negatively related, or unrelated.

Graphs Used in Economic Models (pp. 20–23)

- Graphs are used to show relationships among variables in economic models.
- Relationships can be positive (an upward-sloping curve), negative (a downward-sloping curve), positive and then negative (have a maximum point), negative and then positive (have a minimum point), or unrelated (a horizontal or vertical curve).

The Slope of a Relationship (pp. 24–26)

- The slope of a relationship is calculated as the change in the value of the variable measured on the y-axis divided by the change in the value of the variable measured on the x-axis—that is, $\Delta y/\Delta x$.
- A straight line has a constant slope.
- A curved line has a varying slope. To calculate the slope of a curved line, we calculate the slope at a point or across an arc.

Graphing Relationships Among More Than Two Variables (pp. 26–27)

- To graph a relationship among more than two variables, we hold constant the values of all the variables except two.
- We then plot the value of one of the variables against the value of another.

KEY FIGURES

Figure A1.1   Making a Graph, 17
Figure A1.5   Positive (Direct) Relationships, 21
Figure A1.6   Negative (Inverse) Relationships, 22
Figure A1.7   Maximum and Minimum Points, 23
Figure A1.9   The Slope of a Straight Line, 24
Figure A1.10 Slope at a Point, 25
Figure A1.11 Slope Across an Arc, 26

KEY TERMS

Cross-section graph, 18
Direct relationship, 20
Inverse relationship, 21
Linear relationship, 20
Negative relationship, 21
Positive relationship, 20
Scatter diagram, 19
Slope, 24
Time-series graph, 18
Trend, 18

REVIEW QUIZ

1. What are the three types of graphs used to show economic data?
2. Give an example of a time-series graph.
3. List three things that a time-series graph shows quickly and easily.
4. Give examples, not those in the chapter, of scatter diagrams that show a positive relationship, a negative relationship, and no relationship.
5. Draw some graphs to show the relationships between two variables that
   a. Move in the same direction.
   b. Move in opposite directions.
   c. Have a maximum.
   d. Have a minimum.
6. Which relationship in question 5 is a positive relationship and which is a negative relationship?
7. What are the two ways of calculating the slope of a curved line?
8. How do we graph a relationship among more than two variables?

myeconlab **Study Plan 1.5**

PROBLEMS

Go to (X myeconlab) for solutions to odd-numbered problems and additional exercises.

The spreadsheet provides data on the Canadian economy: Column A is the year, column B is the inflation rate, column C is the interest rate, column D is the growth rate, and column E is the unemployment rate. Use this spreadsheet to answer problems 1, 2, 3, and 4.

	A	B	C	D	E
1	1995	2.2	7.2	2.9	9.6
2	1996	1.6	4.3	1.6	9.7
3	1997	1.6	3.6	4.2	9.2
4	1998	0.9	5.0	4.1	8.4
5	1999	1.7	4.9	5.6	7.6
6	2000	3.1	5.7	5.2	6.8
7	2001	2.1	3.9	1.8	7.2
8	2002	2.1	2.7	3.1	7.7
9	2003	3.0	2.9	2.1	7.6
10	2004	1.7	2.3	2.8	7.2

1. Draw a time-series graph of the inflation rate.
   a. In which year(s) (i) was inflation highest, (ii) was inflation lowest, (iii) did it increase, (iv) did it decrease most?
   b. What was the main trend in inflation?

2. Draw a time-series graph of the interest rate.
   a. In which year(s) (i) was the interest rate lowest, (ii) was it highest, (iii) did it increase, (iv) did it increase most?
   b. What was the main trend in the interest rate?

3. Draw a scatter diagram to show the relationship between the inflation rate and the interest rate. Describe the relationship.

4. Draw a scatter diagram to show the relationship between the growth rate and the unemployment rate. Describe the relationship.

5. Draw a graph to show the relationship between the two variables x and y:

x	0	1	2	3	4	5	6	7	8
y	0	1	4	9	16	25	36	49	64

   a. Is the relationship positive or negative?
   b. Does the slope of the relationship increase or decrease as the value of x increases?
   c. Think of some economic relationships that might be similar to this one.

6. Draw a graph that shows the relationship between the two variables x and y:

x	0	1	2	3	4	5
y	25	24	22	16	8	0

   a. Is the relationship positive or negative?
   b. Does the slope of the relationship increase or decrease as the value of x increases?
   c. Think of some economic relationships that might be similar to this one.

7. In problem 5, calculate the slope of the relationship between x and y when x equals 4.

8. In problem 6, calculate the slope of the relationship between x and y when x equals 3.

9. In problem 5, calculate the slope of the relationship across the arc when x increases from 3 to 4.

10. In problem 6, calculate the slope of the relationship across the arc when x increases from 4 to 5.

11. Calculate the slope of the relationship shown at point A in the following figure.

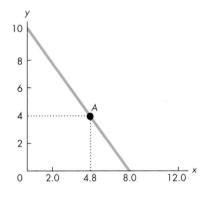

12. Calculate the slope of the relationship shown at point A in the following figure.

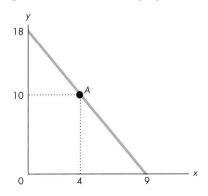

13. Calculate the slope of the relationship:

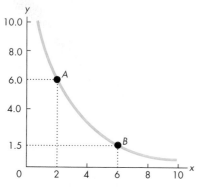

a. At points *A* and *B*.
b. Across the arc *AB*.

14. Calculate the slope of the relationship:

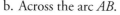
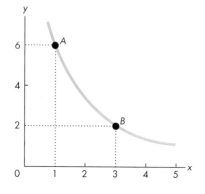

a. At points *A* and *B*.
b. Across the arc *AB*.

15. The table gives the price of a balloon ride, the temperature, and the number of rides a day.

Price	Balloon rides (number per day)		
(dollars per ride)	10°C	20°C	30°C
5.00	32	40	50
10.00	27	32	40
15.00	18	27	32
20.00	10	18	27

Draw graphs to show the relationship between

a. The price and the number of rides, holding the temperature constant.
b. The number of rides and temperature, holding the price constant.
c. The temperature and price, holding the number of rides constant.

16. The table gives the price of an umbrella, the amount of rainfall, and the number of umbrellas purchased.

Price	Umbrellas (number per day)		
(dollars per umbrella)	0	2	10
	(mm of rainfall)		
10	7	8	12
20	4	7	8
30	2	4	7
40	1	2	4

Draw graphs to show the relationship between

a. The price and the number of umbrellas purchased, holding the amount of rainfall constant.
b. The number of umbrellas purchased and the amount of rainfall, holding the price constant.
c. The amount of rainfall and the price, holding the number of umbrellas purchased constant.

WEB EXERCISES

Use the links on **myeconlab** to work the following exercises.

1. Find the Consumer Price Index (CPI) for the latest 12 months. Make a graph of the CPI. During the most recent month, was the CPI rising or falling? Was the rate of rise or fall increasing or decreasing?

2. Find the unemployment rate for the latest 12 months. Graph the unemployment rate. During the most recent month, was it rising or falling? Was the rate of rise or fall increasing or decreasing?

3. Use the data that you obtained in exercises 1 and 2. Make a graph to show whether the CPI and the unemployment rate are related.

4. Use the data that you obtained in exercises 1 and 2. Calculate the percentage change in the CPI each month. Make a graph to show whether the percentage change in the CPI and the unemployment rate are related to each other.

The Economic Problem

CHAPTER 2

Good, Better, Best!

We live in a style that surprises our grandparents and would have astonished our great-grandparents. MP3s, video games, cell phones, gene splicing, personal computers, and iPods, which did not exist even 25 years ago, have transformed our daily lives. For most of us, life is good and getting better. But we still make choices and face costs.

Perhaps the biggest choice that you will make is when to quit school and begin full-time work. When you've completed your current program, will you remain in school and work towards a postgraduate degree or a professional degree? What are the costs and consequences of this choice? We'll return to this question in *Reading Between the Lines* at the end of this chapter.

We see an incredible amount of specialization and trade in the world. Each one of us specializes in a particular job—as a lawyer, a journalist, a homemaker. Why? How do we benefit from specialization and trade?

Over many centuries, social institutions have evolved that we take for granted. They include firms, markets, and a political and legal system that protects private property. Why have these institutions evolved?

◆ These are the questions that we study in this chapter. We begin with the core economic problem—scarcity and choice—and the concept of the production possibilities frontier. We then learn about the central idea of economics: using resources efficiently. We also discover how we can expand production by accumulating capital, expanding our knowledge, and specializing and trading with each other. What you will learn in this chapter is the foundation on which all economics is built.

After studying this chapter, you will be able to

■ Define the production possibilities frontier and calculate opportunity cost

■ Distinguish between production possibilities and preferences and describe an efficient allocation of resources

■ Explain how current production choices expand future production possibilities

■ Explain how specialization and trade expand our production possibilities

■ Explain why property rights and markets have evolved

Production Possibilities and Opportunity Cost

EVERY WORKING DAY, IN MINES, FACTORIES, SHOPS, and offices and on farms and construction sites across Canada, 16.5 million people produce a vast variety of goods and services valued at $4 billion. But the quantities of goods and services that we can produce are limited by both our available resources and by technology. And if we want to increase our production of one good, we must decrease our production of something else—we face tradeoffs. You are going to learn about the production possibilities frontier, which describes the limit to what we can produce and provides a neat way of thinking about and illustrating the idea of a tradeoff.

The **production possibilities frontier** *(PPF)* is the boundary between those combinations of goods and services that can be produced and those that cannot. To illustrate the *PPF*, we focus on two goods at a time and hold the quantities produced of all the other goods and services constant. That is, we look at a *model* economy in which everything remains the same (*ceteris paribus*) except for the production of the two goods we are considering.

Let's look at the production possibilities frontier for CDs and pizza, which stand for *any* pair of goods or services.

Production Possibilities Frontier

The *production possibilities frontier* for CDs and pizza shows the limits to the production of these two goods, given the total resources available to produce them. Figure 2.1 shows this production possibilities frontier. The table lists some combinations of the quantities of pizzas and CDs that can be produced in a month given the resources available. The figure graphs these combinations. The *x*-axis shows the quantity of pizzas produced, and the *y*-axis shows the quantity of CDs produced.

The *PPF* illustrates *scarcity* because we cannot attain the points outside the frontier. They are points that describe wants that can't be satisfied. We can produce at all the points *inside* the *PPF* and *on* the *PPF*. They are attainable points. Suppose that in a typical month, we produce 4 million pizzas and 5 million CDs. Figure 2.1 shows this combination as point *E* and as possibility *E* in the table. The figure also shows

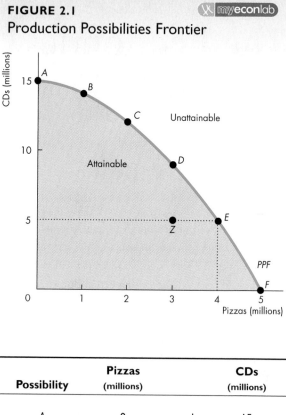

FIGURE 2.1   myeconlab

Production Possibilities Frontier

Possibility	Pizzas (millions)		CDs (millions)
A	0	and	15
B	1	and	14
C	2	and	12
D	3	and	9
E	4	and	5
F	5	and	0

The table lists six points on the production possibilities frontier for CDs and pizza. Row *A* tells us that if we produce no pizza, the maximum quantity of CDs we can produce is 15 million. Points *A, B, C, D, E,* and *F* in the figure represent the rows of the table. The line passing through these points is the production possibilities frontier (*PPF*). The *PPF* separates the attainable from the unattainable. Production is possible at any point *inside* the orange area or *on* the frontier. Points outside the frontier are unattainable. Points inside the frontier such as point *Z* are inefficient because resources are wasted or misallocated. At such points, it is possible to use the available resources to produce more of either or both goods.

other production possibilities. For example, we might stop producing pizza and move all the people who produce it into producing CDs. Point A in the figure and possibility A in the table show this case. The quantity of CDs produced increases to 15 million, and pizza production dries up. Alternatively, we might close the CD factories and switch all the resources into producing pizza. In this situation, we produce 5 million pizzas. Point F in the figure and possibility F in the table show this case.

Production Efficiency

We achieve **production efficiency** if we cannot produce more of one good without producing less of some other good. When production is efficient, we are at a point *on* the PPF. If we are at a point *inside* the PPF, such as point Z, production is *inefficient* because we have some *unused* resources or we have some *misallocated* resources or both.

Resources are unused when they are idle but could be working. For example, we might leave some of the factories idle or some workers unemployed.

Resources are *misallocated* when they are assigned to tasks for which they are not the best match. For example, we might assign skilled pizza makers to work in a CD factory and skilled CD makers to work in a pizza shop. We could get more pizza *and* more CDs from these same workers if we reassigned them to the tasks that more closely match their skills.

If we produce at a point inside the PPF such as Z, we can use our resources more efficiently to produce more pizzas, more CDs, or more of *both* pizzas and CDs. But if we produce at a point *on* the PPF, we are using our resources efficiently and we can produce more of one good only if we produce less of the other. That is, along the PPF, we face a *tradeoff.*

Tradeoff Along the *PPF*

Every choice *along* the PPF involves a *tradeoff*—we must give up something to get something else. On the PPF in Fig. 2.1, we must give up some CDs to get more pizza or give up some pizza to get more CDs.

Tradeoffs arise in every imaginable real-world situation, and you reviewed several of them in Chapter 1. At any given point in time, we have a fixed amount of labour, land, capital, and entrepreneurship. By using our available technologies, we can employ these resources to produce goods and services. But we are

limited in what we can produce. This limit defines a boundary between what we can attain and what we cannot attain. This boundary is the real-world's production possibilities frontier, and it defines the tradeoffs that we must make. On our real-world PPF, we can produce more of any one good or service only if we produce less of some other goods or services.

When doctors say that we must spend more on AIDS and cancer research, they are suggesting a tradeoff: more medical research for less of some other things. When the prime minister says that he wants to spend more on education and health care, he is suggesting a tradeoff: more education and health care for less national defence or less private spending (because of higher taxes). When an environmental group argues for less logging, it is suggesting a tradeoff: greater conservation of endangered wildlife for less paper. When your parents say that you should study more, they are suggesting a tradeoff: more study time for less leisure or sleep.

All tradeoffs involve a cost—an opportunity cost.

Opportunity Cost

The *opportunity cost* of an action is the highest-valued alternative forgone. The *PPF* helps us to make the concept of opportunity cost precise and enables us to calculate it. Along the *PPF*, there are only two goods, so there is only one alternative forgone: some quantity of the other good. Given our current resources and technology, we can produce more pizzas only if we produce fewer CDs. The opportunity cost of producing an additional pizza is the number of CDs we *must* forgo. Similarly, the opportunity cost of producing an additional CD is the quantity of pizzas we *must* forgo.

For example, at point C in Fig. 2.1, we produce fewer pizzas and more CDs than at point D. If we choose point D over point C, the additional 1 million pizzas *cost* 3 million CDs. One pizza costs 3 CDs.

We can also work out the opportunity cost of choosing point C over point D in Fig. 2.1. If we move from point D to point C, the quantity of CDs produced increases by 3 million and the quantity of pizzas produced decreases by 1 million. So if we choose point C over point D, the additional 3 million CDs *cost* 1 million pizzas. One CD costs 1/3 of a pizza.

Opportunity Cost Is a Ratio Opportunity cost is a ratio. It is the decrease in the quantity produced of one good divided by the increase in the quantity produced of another good as we move along the production possibilities frontier.

Because opportunity cost is a ratio, the opportunity cost of producing an additional CD is equal to the *inverse* of the opportunity cost of producing an additional pizza. Check this proposition by returning to the calculations we've just worked through. When we move along the *PPF* from *C* to *D*, the opportunity cost of a pizza is 3 CDs. The inverse of 3 is 1/3, so if we decrease the production of pizza and increase the production of CDs by moving from *D* to *C*, the opportunity cost of a CD must be 1/3 of a pizza. You can check that this number is correct. If we move from *D* to *C*, we produce 3 million more CDs and 1 million fewer pizzas. Because 3 million CDs cost 1 million pizzas, the opportunity cost of 1 CD is 1/3 of a pizza.

Increasing Opportunity Cost The opportunity cost of a pizza increases as the quantity of pizzas produced increases. Also, the opportunity cost of a CD increases as the quantity of CDs produced increases. This phenomenon of increasing opportunity cost is reflected in the shape of the *PPF*—it is bowed outward.

When a large quantity of CDs and a small quantity of pizzas are produced—between points *A* and *B* in Fig. 2.1—the frontier has a gentle slope. A given increase in the quantity of pizzas *costs* a small decrease in the quantity of CDs, so the opportunity cost of a pizza is a small quantity of CDs.

When a large quantity of pizzas and a small quantity of CDs are produced—between points *E* and *F* in Fig. 2.1—the frontier is steep. A given increase in the quantity of pizzas *costs* a large decrease in the quantity of CDs, so the opportunity cost of a pizza is a large quantity of CDs.

The *PPF* is bowed outward because resources are not all equally productive in all activities. People with several years of experience working for Sony are good at producing CDs but not very good at making pizzas. So if we move some of these people from Sony to Domino's, we get a small increase in the quantity of pizzas but a large decrease in the quantity of CDs.

Similarly, people who have spent years working at Domino's are good at producing pizzas, but they have no idea how to produce CDs. So if we move some of these people from Domino's to Sony, we get a small increase in the quantity of CDs but a large decrease in the quantity of pizzas. The more of either good we try to produce, the less productive are the additional

resources we use to produce that good and the larger is the opportunity cost of a unit of that good.

Increasing Opportunity Costs Are Everywhere Just about every activity that you can think of is one with an increasing opportunity cost. We allocate the most skillful farmers and the most fertile land to the production of food. And we allocate the best doctors and the least fertile land to the production of health-care services. If we shift fertile land and tractors away from farming to hospitals and ambulances and ask farmers to become hospital porters, the production of food drops drastically and the increase in the production of health-care services is small. The opportunity cost of a unit of health-care services rises. Similarly, if we shift our resources away from health care towards farming, we must use more doctors and nurses as farmers and more hospitals as hydroponic tomato factories. The decrease in the production of health-care services is large, but the increase in food production is small. The opportunity cost of a unit of food rises.

This example is extreme and unlikely, but these same considerations apply to any pair of goods that you can imagine.

REVIEW QUIZ

1 How does the production possibilities frontier illustrate scarcity?
2 How does the production possibilities frontier illustrate production efficiency?
3 How does the production possibilities frontier show that every choice involves a tradeoff?
4 How does the production possibilities frontier illustrate opportunity cost?
5 Why is opportunity cost a ratio?
6 Why does the *PPF* for most goods bow outward so that opportunity cost increases as the quantity produced of a good increases?

ⓧ myeconlab   **Study Plan 2.1**

We've seen that what we can produce is limited by the production possibilities frontier. We've also seen that production on the *PPF* is efficient. But we can produce many different quantities on the *PPF*. How do we choose among them? How do we know which point on the *PPF* is the best one?

Using Resources Efficiently

YOU'VE SEEN THAT WE ACHIEVE PRODUCTION efficiency at every point on the *PPF*. But which point is best? What quantities of CDs and pizzas best serve the social interest?

This question is an example of real-world questions of enormous consequence such as: How much should we spend on treating AIDS and how much on cancer research? Should we expand education and health-care programs or cut taxes? Should we spend more on the preservation of rainforests and the conservation of endangered wildlife?

To answer these questions, we must find a way of measuring and comparing costs and benefits.

The *PPF* and Marginal Cost

The **marginal cost** of a good is the opportunity cost of producing *one more unit* of it. We calculate marginal cost from the *slope* of the *PPF*. As the quantity of pizza produced increases, the *PPF* gets steeper and marginal cost increases. Figure 2.2 illustrates the calculation of the marginal cost of a pizza.

Begin by finding the opportunity cost of pizza in blocks of 1 *million* pizzas. The first million pizzas cost 1 million CDs, the second million pizzas cost 2 million CDs, the third million pizzas cost 3 million CDs, and so on. The bars in part (a) illustrate these calculations.

The bars in part (b) show the cost of an average pizza in each of the 1 million pizza blocks. Focus on the 3rd million pizzas—the move from *C* to *D* in part (a). Over this range, because the 1 million pizzas cost 3 million CDs, one of these pizzas, on the average, costs 3 CDs—the height of the bar in part (b).

Next, find the opportunity cost of *each* additional pizza—the marginal cost of a pizza. The marginal cost of a pizza is increasing as the quantity of pizza produced increases. The marginal cost at point *C* is less than it is at point *D*. On the average over the range from *C* to *D*, the marginal cost of a pizza is 3 CDs. But it exactly equals 3 CDs only in the middle of the range between *C* and *D*. The red dot in part (b) indicates that the marginal cost of a pizza is 3 CDs when 2.5 million pizzas are produced. Each black dot in part (b) is interpreted in the same way. The orange curve that passes through these dots, labelled *MC*, is the marginal cost curve. It shows the marginal cost of a pizza at each quantity of pizza as we move along the *PPF*.

FIGURE 2.2
The *PPF* and Marginal Cost

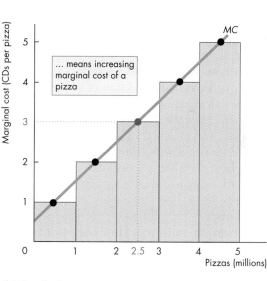

(a) *PPF* and opportunity cost

(b) Marginal cost

Marginal cost is calculated from the slope of the *PPF*. As the quantity of pizza produced increases, the *PPF* gets steeper and the marginal cost of a pizza increases. The bars in part (a) show the opportunity cost of pizza in blocks of 1 million pizzas. The bars in part (b) show the cost of an average pizza in each of these 1 million blocks. The orange curve, *MC*, shows the marginal cost of a pizza at each point along the *PPF*. This curve passes through the centre of each of the bars in part (b).

Preferences and Marginal Benefit

Look around your classroom and notice the wide variety of shirts, caps, pants, and shoes that you and your fellow students are wearing today. Why is there such a huge variety? Why don't you all wear the same styles and colours? The answer lies in what economists call preferences. **Preferences** are a description of a person's likes and dislikes.

You've seen that we have a concrete way of describing the limits to production: the *PPF*. We need a similarly concrete way of describing preferences. To describe preferences, economists use the concept of marginal benefit. The **marginal benefit** of a good or service is the benefit received from consuming one more unit of it.

We measure the marginal benefit of a good or service by the most that people are *willing to pay* for an additional unit of it. The idea is that you are not willing to pay more for a good than it is worth to you. But you are willing to pay an amount up to what it is worth. So the willingness to pay for something measures its marginal benefit.

Economists use the marginal benefit curve to illustrate preferences. The **marginal benefit curve** shows the relationship between the marginal benefit of a good and the quantity of that good consumed. It is a general principle that the more we have of any good or service, the smaller is its marginal benefit and the less we are willing to pay for an additional unit of it. This tendency is so widespread and strong that we call it a principle—the *principle of decreasing marginal benefit*.

The basic reason why marginal benefit of a good or service decreases as we consume more of it is that we like variety. The more we consume of any one good or service, the more of other things we see that we would like better.

Think about your willingness to pay for pizza (or any other item). If pizza is hard to come by and you can buy only a few slices a year, you might be willing to pay a high price to get an additional slice. But if pizza is all you've eaten for the past few days, you are willing to pay almost nothing for another slice.

In everyday life, we think of what we pay for goods and services as the money that we give up—dollars. But you've learned to think about cost as other goods or services forgone, not a dollar cost. You can think about willingness to pay in the same terms. The price you are willing to pay for something is the quantity of other goods and services that you are willing to forgo. Let's continue with the example of CDs and pizzas and illustrate preferences this way.

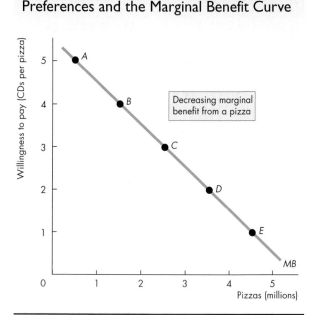

FIGURE 2.3 myeconlab
Preferences and the Marginal Benefit Curve

Possibility	Pizzas (millions)	Willingness to pay (CDs per pizza)
A	0.5	5
B	1.5	4
C	2.5	3
D	3.5	2
E	4.5	1

The smaller the quantity of pizzas produced, the more CDs people are willing to give up for an additional pizza. If pizza production is 0.5 million, people are willing to pay 5 CDs per pizza. But if pizza production is 4.5 million, people are willing to pay only 1 CD per pizza. Willingness to pay measures marginal benefit. And decreasing marginal benefit is a universal feature of people's preferences.

Figure 2.3 illustrates preferences as the willingness to pay for pizza in terms of CDs. In row *A*, pizza production is 0.5 million, and at that quantity, people are willing to pay 5 CDs per pizza. As the quantity of pizza produced increases, the amount that people are willing to pay for it falls. When pizza production is 4.5 million, people are willing to pay only 1 CD per pizza.

Let's now use the concepts of marginal cost and marginal benefit to describe the efficient quantity of pizzas to produce.

Efficient Use of Resources

When we cannot produce more of any one good without giving up some other good, we have achieved *production efficiency*, and we're producing at a point on the *PPF*. When we cannot produce more of any good without giving up some other good that we *value more highly*, we have achieved **allocative efficiency** and we are producing at the point on the *PPF* that we prefer above all other points.

Suppose in Fig. 2.4, we produce 1.5 million pizzas at point *A* on the *PPF*. The marginal cost of a pizza is 2 CDs and the marginal benefit from a pizza is 4 CDs. Because someone values an additional pizza more highly than it costs to produce, we can get more value from our resources by moving some of them out of producing CDs and into producing pizzas.

Now suppose we produce 3.5 million pizzas at point *C* on the *PPF*. The marginal cost of a pizza is now 4 CDs but the marginal benefit is only 2 CDs. Because the additional pizza costs more to produce than anyone thinks it is worth, we can get more value from our resources by moving some of them away from producing pizzas and into producing CDs.

But suppose we produce 2.5 million pizzas at point *B* on the *PPF*. Marginal cost and marginal benefit are now equal at 3 CDs. This allocation of resources is efficient. If more pizzas are produced, the forgone CDs are worth more than the additional pizzas. If fewer pizzas are produced, the forgone pizzas are worth more than the additional CDs.

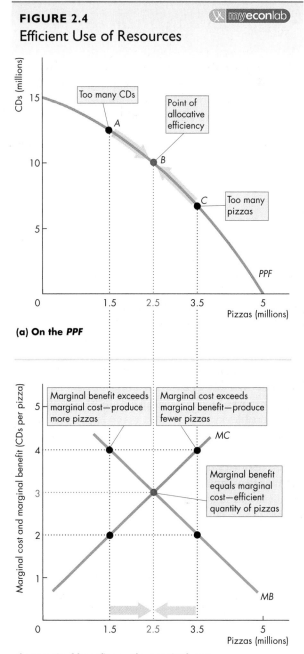

FIGURE 2.4
Efficient Use of Resources

(a) On the PPF

(b) Marginal benefit equals marginal cost

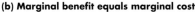

The greater the quantity of pizzas produced, the smaller is the marginal benefit (*MB*) from pizza—the fewer CDs people are willing to give up to get an additional pizza. But the greater the quantity of pizzas produced, the greater is the marginal cost (*MC*) of pizza—the more CDs people must give up to get an additional pizza. When marginal benefit equals marginal cost, resources are being used efficiently.

REVIEW QUIZ

1 What is marginal cost? How is it measured?
2 What is marginal benefit? How is it measured?
3 How does the marginal benefit from a good change as the quantity of that good increases?
4 What is production efficiency and how does it relate to the production possibilities frontier?
5 What conditions must be satisfied if resources are used efficiently?

myeconlab **Study Plan 2.2**

You now understand the limits to production and the conditions under which resources are used efficiently. Your next task is to study the expansion of production possibilities.

Economic Growth

DURING THE PAST 30 YEARS, PRODUCTION PER person in the Canada has doubled. Such an expansion of production is called **economic growth**. Economic growth increases our *standard of living*, but it doesn't overcome scarcity and avoid opportunity cost. To make our economy grow, we face a trade-off—the faster we make production grow, the greater is the opportunity cost of economic growth.

The Cost of Economic Growth

Two key factors influence economic growth: technological change and capital accumulation. **Technological change** is the development of new goods and of better ways of producing goods and services. **Capital accumulation** is the growth of capital resources, which includes *human capital*.

As a consequence of technological change and capital accumulation, we have an enormous quantity of cars that enable us to produce more transportation than was available when we had only horses and carriages; we have satellites that make global communications possible on a scale that is much larger than that produced by the earlier cable technology. But new technologies and new capital have an opportunity cost. To use resources in research and development and to produce new capital, we must decrease our production of consumption goods and services. Let's look at this opportunity cost.

Instead of studying the *PPF* of pizzas and CDs, we'll hold the quantity of CDs produced constant and examine the *PPF* for pizzas and pizza ovens. Figure 2.5 shows this *PPF* as the blue curve *ABC*. If we devote no resources to producing pizza ovens, we produce at point *A*. If we produce 3 million pizzas, we can produce 6 pizza ovens at point *B*. If we produce no pizza, we can produce 10 ovens at point *C*.

The amount by which our production possibilities expand depends on the resources we devote to technological change and capital accumulation. If we devote no resources to this activity (point *A*), our *PPF* remains at *ABC*—the blue curve in Fig. 2.5. If we cut the current production of pizza and produce 6 ovens (point *B*), then in the future, we'll have more capital and our *PPF* will rotate outward to the position shown by the red curve. The fewer resources we devote to producing pizza and the more resources we

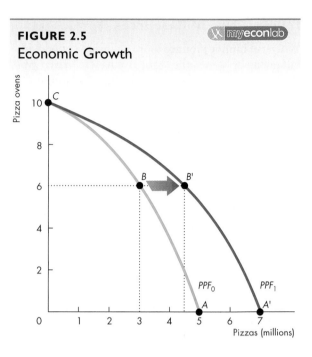

FIGURE 2.5
Economic Growth

PPF_0 shows the limits to the production of pizza and pizza ovens, with the production of all other goods and services remaining the same. If we devote no resources to producing pizza ovens and produce 5 million pizzas, we remain at point *A*. But if we decrease pizza production to 3 million and produce 6 ovens, at point *B*, our production possibilities expand. After one period, the *PPF* rotates outward to PPF_1 and we can produce at point *B'*, a point outside the original *PPF*. We can rotate the *PPF* outward, but we cannot avoid opportunity cost. The opportunity cost of producing more pizzas in the future is fewer pizzas today.

devote to producing ovens, the greater is the expansion of our production possibilities.

Economic growth is not free. To make it happen, we devote resources to producing new ovens and less to producing pizza. In Fig. 2.5, we move from *A* to *B*. There is no free lunch. The opportunity cost of more pizzas in the future is fewer pizzas today. Also, economic growth is no magic formula for abolishing scarcity. On the new production possibilities frontier, we continue to face a tradeoff and opportunity cost.

The ideas about economic growth that we have explored in the setting of the pizza industry also apply to nations. Let's look at two examples.

Economic Growth in Canada and Hong Kong

If as a nation we devote all our resources to producing consumption goods and none to research and capital accumulation, our production possibilities in the future will be the same as they are today. To expand our production possibilities in the future, we must devote fewer resources to producing consumption goods and some resources to accumulating capital and developing technologies so that we can produce more consumption goods in the future. The decrease in today's consumption is the opportunity cost of an increase in future consumption.

The experiences of Canada and Hong Kong make a striking example of the effects of our choices on the rate of economic growth. In 1965, the production possibilities per person in Canada were three times those in Hong Kong (see Fig. 2.6). Canada devoted one-fifth of its resources to accumulating capital and the other four-fifths to consumption. In 1965, Canada was at point *A* on its *PPF*. Hong Kong devoted one-third of its resources to accumulating capital and two-thirds to consumption. In 1965, Hong Kong was at point *A* on its *PPF*.

Since 1965, both countries have experienced economic growth, but growth in Hong Kong has been more rapid than that in Canada. Because Hong Kong devoted a bigger fraction of its resources to accumulating capital, its production possibilities have expanded more quickly.

By 2005, the production possibilities per person in Hong Kong and Canada were similar. If Hong Kong continues to devote more resources to accumulating capital than we do (at point *B* on its 2005 *PPF*), Hong Kong will continue to grow more rapidly than Canada. But if Hong Kong increases consumption and decreases capital accumulation (moving to point *D* on its 2005 *PPF*), then its rate of economic growth will slow.

Canada is typical of the rich industrial countries, which include the United States, Western Europe, and Japan. Hong Kong is typical of the fast-growing Asian economies, which include Taiwan, Thailand, South Korea, and China. Growth in these countries slowed during the Asia crisis of 1998 but quickly rebounded. Production possibilities expand in these countries by between 5 and almost 10 percent a year. If these high growth rates are maintained, these other Asian countries will eventually close the gap on Canada as Hong Kong has done.

FIGURE 2.6
Economic Growth in Canada and Hong Kong

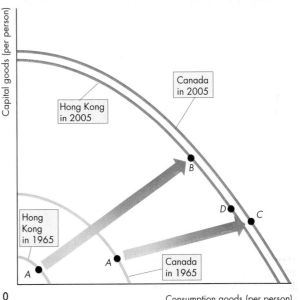

In 1965, the production possibilities per person in Canada were much larger than those in Hong Kong. But Hong Kong devoted more of its resources to accumulating capital than did Canada, so Hong Kong's production possibilities frontier has shifted outward more quickly than has that of Canada. In 2005, Hong Kong's production possibilities per person were similar to those in Canada.

REVIEW QUIZ

1 What are the two key factors that generate economic growth?
2 How does economic growth influence the production possibilities frontier?
3 What is the opportunity cost of economic growth?
4 Why has Hong Kong experienced faster economic growth than Canada has?

myeconlab   Study Plan 2.3

Next, we're going to study another way in which we expand our production possibilities—the amazing fact that *both* buyers and sellers gain from specialization and trade.

Gains from Trade

PEOPLE CAN PRODUCE FOR THEMSELVES ALL THE goods that they consume, or they can concentrate on producing one good (or perhaps a few goods) and then trade with others—exchange some of their own goods for those of others. Concentrating on the production of only one good or a few goods is called *specialization*. We are going to discover how people gain by specializing in the production of the good in which they have a *comparative advantage* and trading with each other.

Comparative Advantage and Absolute Advantage

A person has a **comparative advantage** in an activity if that person can perform the activity at a lower opportunity cost than anyone else. Differences in opportunity costs arise from differences in individual abilities and from differences in the characteristics of capital and land.

No one excels at everything. One person is an outstanding pitcher but a poor catcher; another person is a brilliant lawyer but a poor teacher. In almost all human endeavours, what one person does easily, someone else finds difficult. The same applies to land and capital. One plot of land is fertile but has no mineral deposits; another plot of land has outstanding views but is infertile. One machine has great precision but is difficult to operate; another is fast but often breaks down.

Although no one excels at everything, some people excel and can outperform others in a large number of activities—and perhaps even in all activities. A person who is more productive than others has an **absolute advantage**.

Absolute advantage involves comparing productivities—production per hour—while comparative advantage involves comparing opportunity costs.

Notice that a person who has an absolute advantage does not have a *comparative* advantage in every activity. John Grisham is a better lawyer and a better writer of fast-paced thrillers than most people. He has an absolute advantage in these two activities. But compared to others, he is a better writer than lawyer, so his *comparative* advantage is in writing.

Because people's abilities and the quality of their resources differ, they have different opportunity costs of producing various goods. These differences in opportunity cost are the source of comparative advantage.

Let's explore the idea of comparative advantage by looking at two smoothie bars: one operated by Liz and the other operated by Joe.

Liz's Smoothie Bar Liz produces smoothies and salads. In Liz's high-tech bar, she can turn out either a smoothie or a salad every 90 seconds. If she spends all her time making smoothies, she produces 40 an hour. And if she spends all her time making salads, she also produces 40 an hour. If she splits her time equally between the two, she can produce 20 smoothies and 20 salads an hour. For each additional smoothie Liz produces, she must decrease her production of salads by one and for each additional salad she produces, she must decrease her production of smoothies by one. So

Liz's opportunity cost of producing 1 smoothie is 1 salad,

and

Liz's opportunity cost of producing 1 salad is 1 smoothie.

Liz's customers buy smoothies and salads in equal quantities, so she splits her time equally between the two items and produces 20 smoothies and 20 salads an hour.

Joe's Smoothie Bar Joe also produces both smoothies and salads. But Joe's bar is smaller than Liz's. Also, Joe has only one blender and it's a slow old machine. Even if Joe uses all his resources to produce smoothies, he can produce only 6 an hour. But Joe is pretty good in the salad department so if he uses all his resources to make salads, he can produce 30 an hour.

TABLE 2.1	Liz's Production Possibilities	
Item	Minutes to produce 1	Quantity per hour
Smoothies	1.5	40
Salads	1.5	40

TABLE 2.2	Joe's Production Possibilities	
Item	Minutes to produce 1	Quantity per hour
Smoothies	10	6
Salads	2	30

Joe's ability to make smoothies and salads is the same regardless of how he splits an hour between the two tasks. He can make a salad in 2 minutes or a smoothie in 10 minutes. For each additional smoothie Joe produces, he must decrease his production of salads by 5. And for each additional salad he produces, he must decrease his production of smoothies by 1/5 of a smoothie. So

Joe's opportunity cost of producing 1 smoothie is 5 salads,

and

Joe's opportunity cost of producing 1 salad is 1/5 of a smoothie.

Joe's customers, like Liz's, buy smoothies and salads in equal quantities. So Joe spends 50 minutes of each hour making smoothies and 10 minutes of each hour making salads. With this division of his time, Joe produces 5 smoothies and 5 salads an hour.

Liz's Absolute Advantage You can see from the numbers that describe the two smoothie bars that Liz is four times as productive as Joe—her 20 smoothies and salads an hour are four times Joe's 5. Liz has an absolute advantage—she is more productive than Joe in producing both smoothies and salads. But Liz has a comparative advantage in only one of the activities.

Liz's Comparative Advantage In which of the two activities does Liz have a comparative advantage? Recall that comparative advantage is a situation in which one person's opportunity cost of producing a good is lower than another person's opportunity cost of producing that same good. Liz has a comparative advantage in producing smoothies. Her opportunity cost of a smoothie is 1 salad, whereas Joe's opportunity cost of a smoothie is 5 salads.

Joe's Comparative Advantage If Liz has a comparative advantage in producing smoothies, Joe must have a comparative advantage in producing salads. His opportunity cost of a salad is 1/5 of a smoothie, while Liz's opportunity cost of a salad is 1 smoothie.

Achieving the Gains from Trade

Liz and Joe run into each other one evening in a singles bar. After a few minutes of getting acquainted, Liz tells Joe about her amazingly profitable smoothie business that is selling 20 smoothies and 20 salads an hour. Her only problem, she tells Joe, is that she wishes she could produce more because potential customers leave when her lines get too long.

Joe isn't sure whether to risk spoiling his chances by telling Liz about his own struggling business. But he takes the risk. When he explains to Liz that he spends 50 minutes of every hour making 5 smoothies and 10 minutes making 5 salads, Liz's eyes pop. "Have I got a deal for you!" she exclaims.

Here's the deal that Liz sketches on a table napkin. Joe stops making smoothies and allocates all his time to producing salads. And Liz increases her production of smoothies to 35 an hour and cuts her production of salads to 5 an hour—see Table 2.3(a).

TABLE 2.3	Liz and Joe Gain from Trade	
(a) Production	**Liz**	**Joe**
Smoothies	35	0
Salads	5	30
(b) Trade	**Liz**	**Joe**
Smoothies	sell 10	buy 10
Salads	buy 20	sell 20
(c) After trade	**Liz**	**Joe**
Smoothies	25	10
Salads	25	10
(d) Gains from trade	**Liz**	**Joe**
Smoothies	+5	+5
Salads	+5	+5

They then trade. Liz sells Joe 10 smoothies and Joe sells Liz 20 salads—the price of a smoothie is 2 salads—see Table 2.3(b).

After the trade, Joe has 10 salads—the 30 he produces minus the 20 he sells to Liz. And he has the 10 smoothies that he buys from Liz. So Joe doubles the quantities of smoothies and salads he can sell—see Table 2.3(c).

Liz has 25 smoothies— the 35 she produces minus the 10 she sells to Joe. And she has 25 salads—the 5 she produces plus the 20 she buys from Joe—see Table 2.3(c). Both Liz and Joe gain 5 smoothies and 5 salads—see Table 2.3(d).

Liz draws a graph (Fig. 2.7) to illustrate her suggestion. The blue *PPF* in part (a) shows Joe's production possibilities. He is producing at 5 smoothies and 5 salads an hour at point *A*. The blue *PPF* in part (b)

shows Liz's production possibilities. She is producing at 20 smoothies and 20 salads an hour at point *A*.

Liz's proposal is that they each produce more of the good in which they have a comparative advantage. Joe produces 30 salads and no smoothies at point *B* on his *PPF*. Liz produces 35 smoothies and 5 salads at the point *B* on her *PPF*.

Liz and Joe then trade— exchange—smoothies and salads at a price of 2 salads per smoothie, or 1/2 of a smoothie per salad. Joe gets smoothies for 2 salads each, which is less than the 5 salads it costs him to produce a smoothie. And Liz gets salads for 1/2 a smoothie each, which is less than the 1 smoothie that it costs her to produce a salad.

With trade, Joe has 10 smoothies and 10 salads at point *C*—a gain of 5 smoothies and 5 salads. Joe moves to a point *outside* his *PPF*.

FIGURE 2.7
The Gains from Trade

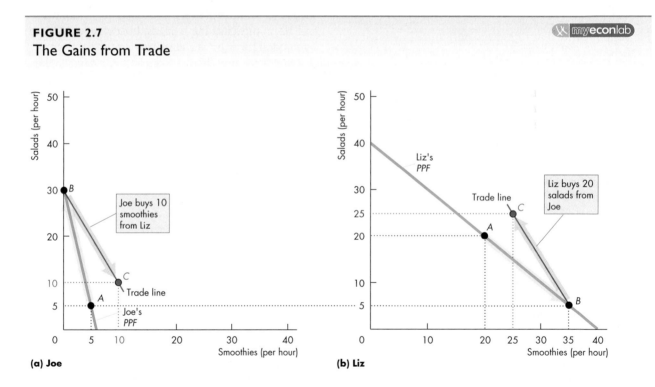

(a) Joe

(b) Liz

Joe initially produces at point *A* on his *PPF* in part (a), and Liz initially produces at point *A* on her *PPF* in part (b). Joe's opportunity cost of producing a salad is less than Liz's, so Joe has a comparative advantage in producing salad. Liz's opportunity cost of producing a smoothie is less than Joe's, so Liz has a comparative advantage in producing smoothies. If Joe specializes in salad, he produces 30 salads and no smoothies at point *B* on his *PPF*. If Liz produces 35 smoothies

and 5 salads, she produces at point *B* on her *PPF*. They exchange salads for smoothies along the red "Trade line." Liz buys salads from Joe for less than her opportunity cost of producing them, and Joe buys smoothies from Liz for less than his opportunity cost of producing them. Each goes to point *C*—a point outside his or her *PPF*. Both Joe and Liz increase production by 5 smoothies and 5 salads with no change in resources.

With trade, Liz has 25 smoothies and 25 salads at point *C*—a gain of 5 smoothies and 5 salads. Liz moves to a point *outside* her *PPF.*

Despite Liz's absolute advantage in producing smoothies and salads, both Liz and Joe gain from producing more of the good in which they have a comparative advantage and trading.

The gains that we achieve from international trade are similar to those achieved by Joe and Liz in this example. When Canadians buy T-shirts from China and when China buys regional jets from Canada, both countries gain. We get our shirts at a lower cost than that at which we can produce them, and China gets its regional jets at a lower cost than that at which it can produce them.

Dynamic Comparative Advantage

At any given point in time, the resources and technologies available determine the comparative advantages that individuals and nations have. But just by repeatedly producing a particular good or service, people become more productive in that activity, a phenomenon called **learning-by-doing**. Learning-by-doing is the basis of *dynamic* comparative advantage. **Dynamic comparative advantage** is a comparative advantage that a person (or country) possesses as a result of having specialized in a particular activity and, as a result of learning-by-doing, having become the producer with the lowest opportunity cost.

Singapore, for example, pursued dynamic comparative advantage vigorously when it decided to begin a bio-technology industry in which it initially didn't have a comparative advantage.

REVIEW QUIZ

1 What gives a person a comparative advantage?
2 Distinguish between comparative advantage and absolute advantage.
3 Is production still efficient when people specialize?
4 Why do people specialize and trade?
5 What are the gains from specialization and trade?
6 What is the source of the gains from trade?
7 How does dynamic comparative advantage arise?

myeconlab **Study Plan 2.4**

Economic Coordination

PEOPLE GAIN BY SPECIALIZING IN THE PRODUCTION of those goods and services in which they have a comparative advantage and then trading with each other. Liz and Joe, whose production of salads and smoothies we studied earlier in this chapter, can get together and make a deal that enables them to enjoy the gains from specialization and trade. But for billions of individuals to specialize and produce millions of different goods and services, their choices must somehow be coordinated.

Two competing economic coordination systems have been used—central economic planning and decentralized markets.

Central economic planning might appear to be the best system because it can express national priorities. But when this system was tried, as it was for 60 years in Russia, and for 30 years in China, it was a miserable failure. Today, these and most other previously planned economies are adopting a decentralized market system.

To make decentralized coordination work, four complementary social institutions that have evolved over many centuries are required. They are

- Firms
- Property rights
- Markets
- Money

Firms

A **firm** is an economic unit that hires factors of production and organizes those factors to produce and sell goods and services. Examples of firms are your local gas station, Wal-Mart, and Roots.

Firms coordinate a huge amount of economic activity. The coffee shop Second Cup, for example, might buy the machines and labour services of Liz and Joe and start to produce salads *and* smoothies at all its outlets.

But if a firm gets too big, it can't keep track of all the information that is needed to coordinate its activities. For this reason, firms themselves specialize and trade with each other. For example, Wal-Mart could produce all the things that it sells in its stores. And it could produce all the raw materials that are used to produce the things that it sells. But Sam Walton would not have become one of the wealthiest people in the world if he had followed that path. Instead, Wal-Mart buys from other firms that specialize in the production of a narrow range of items. And this trade takes place in markets.

Property Rights

The social arrangements that govern the ownership, use, and disposal of resources, goods, and services are called **property rights**. *Real property* includes land and buildings—the things we call property in ordinary speech—and durable goods such as plant and equipment. *Financial property* includes stocks and bonds and money in the bank. *Intellectual property* is the intangible product of creative effort. This type of property includes books, music, computer programs, and inventions of all kinds and is protected by copyrights and patents.

Where property rights are enforced, people have the incentive to specialize and produce the goods in which each person has a comparative advantage. Where people can easily steal the production of others, then time, energy, and resources are devoted not to production but to protecting possessions. If we had not developed property rights, we would still be hunting and gathering like our Stone Age ancestors.

Markets

In ordinary speech, the word *market* means a place where people buy and sell goods such as fish, meat, fruits, and vegetables. In economics, a *market* has a more general meaning. A **market** is any arrangement that enables buyers and sellers to get information and to do business with each other. An example is the market in which oil is bought and sold—the world oil market. The world oil market is not a place. It is the network of oil producers, oil users, wholesalers, and brokers who buy and sell oil. In the world oil market, decision makers do not meet physically. They make deals throughout the world by telephone, fax, and direct computer link.

Markets have evolved because they facilitate trade. Without organized markets, we would miss out on a substantial part of the potential gains from trade. Enterprising individuals and firms, each pursuing their own self-interest, have profited from making markets—standing ready to buy or sell the items in which they specialize. But markets can work only when property rights exist.

Money

Money is any commodity or token that is generally acceptable as a means of payment. Liz and Joe didn't use money in the example above. They exchanged salads and smoothies. In principle, trade in markets can exchange any item for any other item. But you can perhaps imagine how complicated life would be if we exchanged goods for other goods. The "invention" of money makes trading in markets much more efficient.

Circular Flows Through Markets

Figure 2.8 shows the flows that result from the choices that households and firms make. Households specialize and choose the quantities of labour, land, capital, and entrepreneurship to sell or rent to firms. Firms choose the quantities of factors of production to hire. These (red) flows go through the *factor markets*. Households choose the quantities of goods and services to buy, and firms choose the quantities to produce. These (red) flows go through the *goods markets*. Households receive incomes and make expenditures on goods and services (green flows). These green flows are payments for the corresponding real (red) flows.

How do markets coordinate all these decisions?

Coordinating Decisions

Markets coordinate individual decisions through price adjustments. To see how, think about your local market for hamburgers. Suppose that some people who want to buy hamburgers are not able to do so. To make the choices of buyers and sellers compatible, buyers must scale down their appetites or more hamburgers must be offered for sale (or both must happen). A rise in the price of a hamburger produces this outcome. A higher price encourages producers to offer more hamburgers for sale. It also encourages some people to change their lunch plans. Fewer people buy hamburgers, and more buy hot dogs. More hamburgers (and more hot dogs) are offered for sale.

Alternatively, suppose that more hamburgers are available than people want to buy. In this case, to make the choices of buyers and sellers compatible, more hamburgers must be bought or fewer hamburgers must be offered for sale (or both). A fall in the price of a hamburger achieves this outcome. A lower price encourages firms to produce fewer hamburgers. It also encourages people to buy more hamburgers.

FIGURE 2.8

Circular Flows in the Market Economy

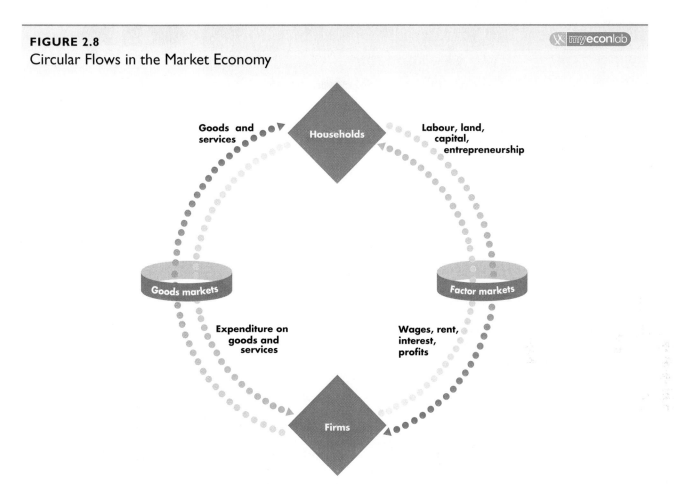

Households and firms make economic choices and markets coordinate these choices.

Households choose the quantities of labour, land, capital, and entrepreneurship to sell or rent to firms in exchange for wages, rent, interest, and profit. Households also choose how to spend their incomes on the various types of goods and services available.

Firms choose the quantities of factors of production to hire and the quantities of the goods and services to produce.

Goods markets and factor markets coordinate these choices of households and firms. The clockwise red flows are real flows—the flows of factors of production from households to firms and the flows of goods and services from firms to households. The counterclockwise green flows are the payments for the red flows—the flow of income for the factors of production and the flow of expenditure on goods and services.

◆ You have now begun to see how economists approach economic questions. Scarcity, choice, and divergent opportunity costs explain why we specialize and trade and why firms, property rights, markets, and money have developed. You can see all around you the lessons you've learned in this chapter. *Reading Between the Lines* on pp. 48–49 gives an example. It explores the *PPF* of a student like you and the choices that students must make that influence their own economic growth—the growth of their incomes.

The Cost and Benefit of Education

GLOBE AND MAIL, AUGUST 28, 2002

Academics leap to defence of the MBA

They don't come with a guarantee, but business degrees offer students well-paying jobs with reputable companies, say many of Canada's top business schools, throwing coldwater on a new study questioning the value of an MBA. ...

After surveying decades of research, Jeffrey Pfeffer and Christina Fong of Stanford's graduate school of business have concluded that, with the possible exception of the most elite programs, master's degrees in business administration teach little that would be of real use in the business world. ...

The salaries for these graduates are a telling story. At Queen's University's School of Business, for example, the average starting salary is $95,000. Before joining the program, the average salary of students is $59,750. And at the Rotman School of Management at the University of Toronto, students entering the two-year program have salaries in the $50,000 [range] on average. But the average starting salary for this year's graduate was $89,000. ...

Brian Bemmels, associate dean for academic programs at the University of British Columbia's faculty of commerce, said the research article forces schools to evaluate their programs. He added that the article is based on a lot of opinion.

UBC's business school made a major change in 1995, restructuring its MBA program and reducing it to 15 months from two years to minimize losses of income to students. The average age of students in the program is 31.

Mr. Bemmels said the demand for an MBA degree speaks for itself. UBC had well over 700 applicants for 100 seats this year. Only 17 per cent of the incoming class has a business degree, he said. The rest are graduates of medicine, engineering and general arts.

"All these people wouldn't be doing it if they didn't think it was valuable," Mr. Bemmels said.

"I don't believe the notion that they have been fooled and tricked into something that's no good for them," he added.

Reprinted with permission from *The Globe and Mail.*

Essence of the Story

■ Jeffrey Pfeffer and Christina Fong of the Stanford Graduate School of Business say that MBA programs teach little of use in the business world.

■ The salaries earned by MBA graduates tell a different story.

■ The average starting salary for an MBA is $95,000, up from $59,750 before the MBA.

■ At the Rotman School of Management at the University of Toronto, students entering the two-year program have an average salary of $50,000 and an average starting salary of $89,000 after graduation.

■ Brian Bemmels said the UBC business school had over 700 applicants for 100 places and most were graduates of medicine, engineering, and general arts.

Economic Analysis

■ Education increases human capital and expands production possibilities.

■ The opportunity cost of a degree is forgone consumption. The payoff is an increase in lifetime production possibilities.

■ Figure 1 shows the choices facing a high school graduate who can consume education goods and services and consumption goods and services on the blue *PPF*.

■ Working full time, this person can consume at point *A* on the blue *PPF* in Fig. 1.

■ By attending university, the student moves from point *A* to point *B* along her *PPF*, forgoes current consumption (the opportunity cost of education), and increases the use of educational goods and services.

■ On graduating from university, earnings jump, so production possibilities expand to the red *PPF* in Fig. 1.

■ Figure 2 shows a university graduate's choices. The blue curve is the same *PPF* as the red *PPF* in Fig. 1.

■ Working full time, this person earns enough to consume at point *C* on the blue *PPF* in Fig. 2.

■ By pursuing an MBA, the student moves from point *C* to point *D* along her *PPF*, forgoes current consumption (the opportunity cost of an MBA), and increases the use of educational goods and services.

■ With an MBA, a person's earnings jump again, so production possibilities expand to the red *PPF* in Fig. 2.

■ For people who have the required ability, the benefits of post-secondary and post-graduate education exceed the costs.

You're the Voter

■ The Canada Millennium Scholarship Foundation, funded by the federal government, provides $4,000 a year to 900 young Canadians.

■ Do you think the Canada Millennium Scholarship Foundation should be expanded so that more students can benefit from it?

■ With the huge return from post-secondary and post-graduate education, why don't more people remain in school for longer?

■ Would you vote for or against a tax increase to provide greater funding for the Canada Millennium Scholarship Foundation? Why?

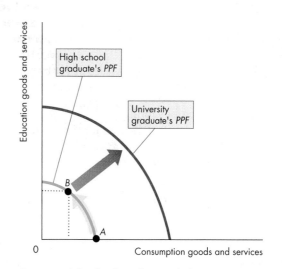

Figure 1 High school graduate's choices

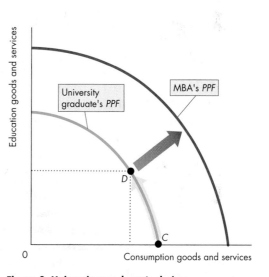

Figure 2 University graduate's choices

KEY POINTS

Production Possibilities and Opportunity Cost (pp. 34–36)

- The production possibilities frontier, *PPF*, is the boundary between production levels that are attainable and those that are not attainable when all the available resources are used to their limit.
- Production efficiency occurs at points on the *PPF*.
- Along the *PPF*, the opportunity cost of producing more of one good is the amount of the other good that must be given up.
- The opportunity cost of a good increases as production of the good increases.

Using Resources Efficiently (pp. 37–39)

- The marginal cost of a good is the opportunity cost of producing one more unit.
- The marginal benefit from a good is the maximum amount of another good that a person is willing to forgo to obtain more of the first good.
- The marginal benefit of a good decreases as the amount of the good available increases.
- Resources are used efficiently when the marginal cost of each good is equal to its marginal benefit.

Economic Growth (pp. 40–41)

- Economic growth, which is the expansion of production possibilities, results from capital accumulation and technological change.
- The opportunity cost of economic growth is forgone current consumption.

Gains from Trade (pp. 42–45)

- A person has a comparative advantage in producing a good if that person can produce the good at a lower opportunity cost than everyone else.
- People gain by specializing in the activity in which they have a comparative advantage and trading with others.
- Dynamic comparative advantage arises from learning-by-doing.

Economic Coordination (pp. 45–47)

- Firms coordinate a large amount of economic activity, but there is a limit to the efficient size of a firm.
- Markets coordinate the economic choices of people and firms.
- Markets can work efficiently only when property rights exist.
- Money makes trading in markets more efficient.

KEY FIGURES

Figure 2.1   Production Possibilities Frontier, 34
Figure 2.4   Efficient Use of Resources, 39
Figure 2.7   The Gains from Trade, 44
Figure 2.8   Circular Flows in the Market Economy, 47

KEY TERMS

Absolute advantage, 42
Allocative efficiency, 39
Capital accumulation, 40
Comparative advantage, 42
Dynamic comparative advantage, 45
Economic growth, 40
Firm, 45
Learning-by-doing, 45
Marginal benefit, 38
Marginal benefit curve, 38
Marginal cost, 37
Market, 46
Money, 46
Preferences, 38
Production efficiency, 35
Production possibilities frontier, 34
Property rights, 46
Technological change, 40

PROBLEMS

Go to ⓧ myeconlab **for solutions to odd-numbered problems and additional exercises.**

1. Calculate Wendell's opportunity cost of one hour of tennis when he increases the time he plays tennis from
   a. 4 to 6 hours a week.
   b. 6 to 8 hours a week.

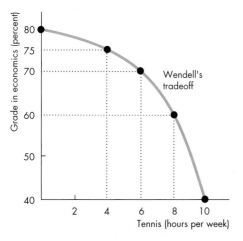

2. Calculate Tina's opportunity cost of a day of skiing when she increases her time spent skiing from
   a. 2 to 4 days a month.
   b. 4 to 6 days a month.

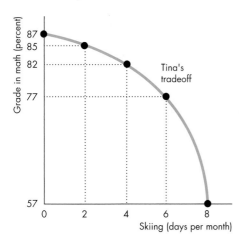

3. Wendell, in problem 1, has the following marginal benefit curve:

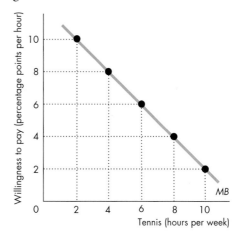

   a. If Wendell is efficient, what is his grade?
   b. Why would Wendell be worse off getting a higher grade?

4. Tina in problem 2, has the following marginal benefit curve:

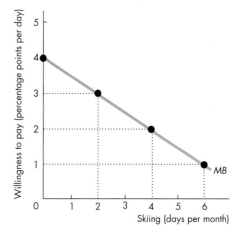

   a. If Tina is efficient, how much does she ski?
   b. Why would Tina be worse off spending more days a month skiing?

5. Sunland's production possibilities are

Food (kilograms per month)		Sunscreen (litres per month)
300	and	0
200	and	50
100	and	100
0	and	150

   a. Draw a graph of Sunland's *PPF.*

b. What are Sunland's opportunity costs of producing food and sunscreen at each output?

6. Jane's Island's production possibilities are

Corn (kilograms per month)		Cloth (metres per month)
6	and	0
4	and	2
2	and	4
0	and	6

a. Draw a graph of the *PPF* on Jane's Island.
b. What are Jane's opportunity costs of producing corn and cloth at each output in the table?

7. In problem 5, to get a litre of sunscreen the people of Sunland are willing to give up 5 kilograms of food if they have 25 litres of sunscreen, 2 kilograms of food if they have 75 litres of sunscreen, and 1 kilogram of food if they have 125 litres of sunscreen.

a. Draw a graph of Sunland's marginal benefit from sunscreen.
b. What is the efficient quantity of sunscreen?

8. In problem 6, to get a metre of cloth Jane is willing to give up 1.5 kilograms of corn if she has 2 metres of cloth; 1.0 kilogram of corn if she has 4 metres of cloth; and 0.5 kilograms of corn if she has 6 metres of cloth.

a. Draw a graph of Jane's marginal benefit from cloth.
b. What is Jane's efficient quantity of cloth?

9. Busyland's production possibilities are

Food (kilograms per month)		Sunscreen (litres per month)
150	and	0
100	and	100
50	and	200
0	and	300

Calculate Busyland's opportunity costs of food and sunscreen at each output in the table.

10. Joe Island's production possibilities are

Corn (kilograms per month)		Cloth (metres per month)
12	and	0
8	and	1
4	and	2
0	and	3

What are Joe's opportunity costs of producing corn and cloth at each output in the table?

11. In problems 5 and 9, Sunland and Busyland each produce and consume 100 kilograms of food and 100 litres of sunscreen per month, and they do not trade. Now the countries begin to trade with each other.

a. What good does Sunland sell to Busyland and what good does it buy from Busyland?
b. If Sunland and Busyland divide the total output of food and sunscreen equally, what are the gains from trade?

12. In problems 6 and 10, Jane's Island and Joe's Island each produce and consume 4 kilograms of corn and 2 metres of cloth and they do not trade. Now the islands begin to trade.

a. What good does Jane sell to Joe and what good does Jane buy from Joe?
b. If Jane and Joe divide the total output of corn and cloth equally, what are the gains from trade?

CRITICAL THINKING

1. After you have studied *Reading Between the Lines* on pp. 48–49, answer the following questions:

a. At what point on the blue *PPF* in Fig. 1 on p. 49 is the combination of education goods and services and consumption goods and services efficient? Explain your answer.
b. Students are facing rising tuition. How does higher tuition change the opportunity cost of education and how does it change the *PPF*s in Fig. 1 and Fig. 2?
c. Who receives the benefits from education? Is the marginal cost of education equal to the marginal benefit of education? Is resource use in the market for education efficient?

WEB EXERCISES

Use the links on (X myeconlab) **to work the following exercise.**

1. Obtain data on the tuition and other costs of enrolling in the MBA program at a school that interests you.

a. Draw a *PPF* that shows the tradeoff that you would face if you decided to enroll in the MBA program.
b. Do you think the marginal benefit of an MBA exceeds the marginal cost?

Your Economic Revolution

You are making progress in your study of economics. You've already encountered the big questions and big ideas of economics. And you've learned about the key insight that specialization and exchange create economic wealth.

You are studying economics at a time that future historians might call the *Information Revolution*. We reserve the word *Revolution* for big events that influence all future generations.

During the *Agricultural Revolution*, which occurred 10,000 years ago, people learned to domesticate animals and plant crops. They stopped roaming in search of food and settled in villages and eventually towns and cities, where they developed markets in which to exchange their products.

During the *Industrial Revolution*, which began 240 years ago, people used science to create new technologies. This revolution brought extraordinary wealth for some but created conditions in which others were left behind. It brought social and political tensions that we still face today.

During today's *Information Revolution*, people who embraced the new technologies prospered on an unimagined scale. But the incomes and living standards of the less educated are falling behind, and social and political tensions are increasing. Today's revolution has a global dimension. Some of the winners live in previously poor countries in Asia, and some of the losers live here in North America.

So you are studying economics at an interesting time. Whatever *your* motivation is for studying economics, *our* objective is to help you do well in your course, to enjoy it, and to develop a deeper understanding of the economic world around you.

Three reasons why we hope that we both succeed: First, a decent understanding of economics will help you to become a full participant in the Information Revolution. Second, an understanding of economics will help you play a more effective role as a citizen and voter and enable you to add your voice to those who are looking for solutions to our social and political problems. Third, you will enjoy the sheer fun of *understanding* the forces at play and how they are shaping our world.

If you are finding economics interesting, think seriously about majoring in the subject. A degree in economics gives the best training available in problem solving, offers lots of opportunities to develop conceptual skills, and opens doors to a wide range of graduate courses, including the MBA, and to a wide range of jobs. You can read more about the benefits of an economics degree in the essay by Robert Whaples and Harvey King in your *Study Guide*.

Economics was born during the Industrial Revolution. We'll look at its birth and meet its founder, Adam Smith. Then we'll talk about the progress that economists have made and some of the outstanding policy problems of today with one of today's most distinguished economists, Lawrence H. Summers, President of Harvard University.

The Sources of Economic Wealth

THE FATHER OF ECONOMICS

Adam Smith *was a giant of a scholar who contributed to ethics and jurisprudence as well as economics. Born in 1723 in Kirkcaldy, a small fishing town near Edinburgh, Scotland, Smith was the only child of the town's customs officer (who died before Adam was born).*

His first academic appointment, at age 28, was as Professor of Logic at the University of Glasgow. He subsequently became tutor to a wealthy Scottish duke, whom he accompanied on a two-year grand European tour, following which he received a pension of £300 a year—ten times the average income at that time.

With the financial security of his pension, Smith devoted ten years to writing An Inquiry into the Nature and Causes of the Wealth of Nations, *which was published in 1776. Many people had written on economic issues before Adam Smith, but he made economics a science. Smith's account was so broad and authoritative that no subsequent writer on economics could advance ideas without tracing their connections to those of Adam Smith.*

THE ISSUES

Why are some nations wealthy while others are poor? This question lies at the heart of economics. And it leads directly to a second question: What can poor nations do to become wealthy?

Adam Smith, who is regarded by many scholars as the founder of economics, attempted to answer these questions in his book *The Wealth of Nations*, published in 1776. Smith was pondering these questions at the height of the Industrial Revolution. During these years, new technologies were invented and applied to the manufacture of cotton and wool cloth, iron, transportation, and agriculture.

Smith wanted to understand the sources of economic wealth, and he brought his acute powers of observation and abstraction to bear on the question. His answer:

- The division of labour
- Free markets

The division of labour—breaking tasks down into simple tasks and becoming skilled in those tasks—is the source of "the greatest improvement in the productive powers of labour," said Smith. The division of labour became even more productive when it was applied to creating new technologies. Scientists and engineers, trained in extremely narrow fields, became specialists at inventing. Their powerful skills accelerated the advance of technology, so by the 1820s, machines could make consumer goods faster and more accurately than any craftsman could. And by the 1850s, machines could make other machines that labour alone could never have made.

But, said Smith, the fruits of the division of labour are limited by the extent of the market. To make the market as large as possible, there must be no impediments to free trade both within a country and among countries. Smith argued that when each person makes the best possible economic choice, that choice leads as if by "an invisible hand" to the best outcome for society as a whole. The butcher, the brewer, and the baker each pursue their own interests but, in doing so, also serve the interests of everyone else.

THEN

Adam Smith speculated that one person, working hard, using the hand tools available in the 1770s, might possibly make 20 pins a day. Yet, he observed, by using those same hand tools but breaking the process into a number of individually small operations in which people specialize —by the *division of labour*—ten people could make a staggering 48,000 pins a day. One draws out the wire, another straightens it, a third cuts it, a fourth points it, a fifth grinds it. Three specialists make the head, and a fourth attaches it. Finally, the pin is polished and packaged. But a large market is needed to support the division of labour: one factory employing ten workers would need to sell more than 15 million pins a year to stay in business.

NOW

If Adam Smith were here today, the computer chip would fascinate him. He would see it as an extraordinary example of the productivity of the division of labour and of the use of machines to make machines that make other machines. From a design of a chip's intricate circuits, cameras transfer an image to glass plates that work like stencils. Workers prepare silicon wafers on which the circuits are printed. Some slice the wafers, others polish them, others bake them, and yet others coat them with a light-sensitive chemical. Machines transfer a copy of the circuit onto the wafer. Chemicals then etch the design onto the wafer. Further processes deposit atom-sized transistors and aluminum connectors. Finally, a laser separates the hundreds of chips on the wafer. Every stage in the process of creating a computer chip uses other computer chips. And like the pin of the 1770s, the computer chip of today benefits from a large market—a global market—to buy chips in the huge quantities in which they are produced efficiently.

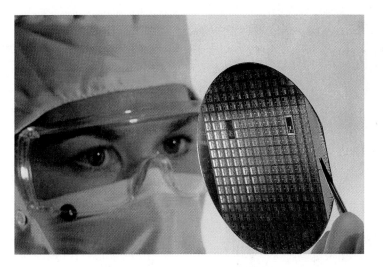

Many economists have worked on the big themes that Adam Smith began. One of these is Lawrence H. Summers, President of Harvard University and a distinguished economist.

TALKING WITH

Lawrence H. Summers is President of Harvard University. Born in 1954 in New Haven, Connecticut, into a family of distinguished economists, he was an undergraduate at the Massachusetts Institute of Technology and a graduate student at Harvard University. While still in his 20s, he became one of the youngest tenured economics professors at Harvard University. In Washington, he has held a succession of public service jobs at the World Bank and in the U.S. government, culminating in 1999 with his appointment as Secretary of the Treasury—the chief financial officer of the United States and the president's highest-ranking advisor.

Dr. Summers's research has covered an enormous range of macroeconomic and public policy issues that include capital taxation, unemployment, global financial crises, the transition to a market economy in Eastern Europe, and the problem of speeding progress in the developing countries.

Michael Parkin and Robin Bade talked with Lawrence Summers about his career and the progress that economists have made since the pioneering days of Adam Smith.

Lawrence H. Summers

How does Adam Smith's assessment of the "nature and causes of the wealth of nations" look today in light of the lessons that economists have learned over the past two centuries?

Adam Smith is looking very good today. I think one of the most important insights of the social sciences of the last several centuries is Smith's idea that good things can come from the invisible hand—from decentralization rather than from central planning and direction. But Smith is also prescient in recognizing the various qualifications to the argument for the invisible hand, whether involving fairness, externalities, or monopoly.

What do we know today that Adam Smith didn't know?

We know today much more than Smith did about economic fluctuations and about the role of money—about what we today call macroeconomics. We know more today about economic situations that involve bargaining, whether between two individuals or between small numbers of firms in an industry, or between a buyer and a seller. We know much more today about markets without perfect information. I know how good my used car is when I sell it—you don't when you buy it. I know whether I'm sick when I buy medical insurance, but the insurance company has to try to figure it out. The role of information in markets, which turns out to be quite profound, is something we understand much better today. And we also understand much better today the role of politics and governments in shaping the economy, which is far larger than it was in Smith's day.

Coincidentally, a few days before we're holding this conversation, a new nation was born—East Timor. What advice can economists offer a new and extremely poor nation as it takes its first steps?

Much of economic success involves strong rights to property. Has anyone ever washed a rented car or taken as good care of their hotel room as their home? When people own their farmlands, they're much more likely to farm them sustainably. When businesses own their machinery, they're much more likely to take care of it. When individuals own what they produce, they're much more likely to work hard.

Strong property rights and the framework of laws that support them are profoundly important to the market-based exchanges that are essential to economic success. So also is stable money that can be a basis for exchange. So also is an educated and capable population. But if there is a single lesson that is important for a starting economy, it is that strong property rights can motivate individuals.

One lesson that we've learned from your work at the World Bank is that the return to educating girls in developing countries is very high. What did you discover in that work?

Primary education, and especially for girls, may be the highest return investment available in the developing world. Those who read produce more and therefore earn more. Girls who are educated grow up to be better mothers who have smaller, happier, healthier families. Women who are educated are empowered with greater career options. They are less likely to fall into prostitution, and that reduces the spread of AIDS.

Women who are educated are much more likely to take care of the environment. So it is in many respects that primary education, and especially that of girls, generates very large returns.

Are there any other activities that yield comparable returns for developing countries?

Maybe some investments in health care that generate very large returns—it's a difficult evaluation to make. The really crucial lesson is that a country's most precious assets are its people, and investments in people are likely to be the most important investments of all.

Some of your earliest research was on taxing the income from capital. Why isn't the income from capital just like the income from labour?

Think about it this way: Two individuals both earn a hundred dollars. One spends it all this year; the other saves half of it and earns 10 percent interest next year. Who should pay more total taxes? Plausibly, for fairness, both should pay the same tax. A tax on income will lead to the same taxes in the first year for the two individuals; and higher taxes in the second year for the individual who saved.

In effect, taxes on capital income are taxes on future consumption, and it is far from clear why a society should want to tax future consumption more highly than present consumption.

On the other hand, very large fortunes often show up as capital income, and so designing a workable and fair tax system that doesn't tax investment income is something that is very difficult to do.

> **"** *The really crucial lesson is that a country's most precious assets are its people, and investments in people are likely to be the most important investments of all.* **"**

Would you say that we have not yet managed to figure this one out?

We'll all be working on finding the best tax systems for a long time to come. And it may mean that the income tax is, as Churchill said of democracy, terrible but the best alternative.

The United States has a large and persistent current account deficit, a low personal saving rate, and a projected deficit in the Social Security and Medicare trust funds. Are you concerned about these problems?

Herb Stein, who was a leading American policy economist, once said that the unsustainable cannot be sustained and must surely end!

This is a concern, given that U.S. national debt to foreigners is rising faster than U.S. income. And it's a concern in terms of the financing of Social Security and Medicare as our population ages. In a way, the solution to both these problems is more American saving, because that will put us in a stronger position as our population ages, and will allow us to have investment in the United States without incurring debts to foreigners.

Probably the most potent way of increasing a country's national savings is to improve the position of its budget. Whether to increase taxes or cut expenditures is a judgment for the congress to debate. My guess is that some combination would be appropriate. There are aspects of expenditures that are going to be hard to control. On the other hand, there are other aspects in terms of transfer payments and terms of various subsidies where economies probably are possible. And one virtue of a strong fiscal position is that it reduces interest expense down the road.

Did you always want to be an economist? How did you choose economics?

I thought I would be a mathematician or a physicist, but found myself very interested in questions of public policy. I was very involved in debate when I was in college. So I found myself wanting very much to combine an interest in public policy issues with an analytical approach, and economics gave me a way to do that. I also found that I had some aptitude, relative to my aptitude for pure mathematics or physics, so I gravitated to economics.

What led a brilliant academic economist to Washington? What did you want to achieve?

I hoped to put to use some of what I had learned in my studies in a direct way and to enhance my understanding of the way actual economies work by seeing how the policy process operated. I had a great time in Washington and feel that my economics training made a huge difference in everything I did. Whether it was thinking about how to respond to the Mexican and Asian financial crises or working on financial deregulation. Whether it was choosing optimal investments for the Customs Department in protecting our borders or designing tax incentives to promote saving. Whether it was supporting the protection of the Social Security trust fund or thinking about enforcement policies against corporate tax shelters. Principles of economics—in terms of maximizing benefits relative to costs, in terms of always thinking of the margin, in terms of always recognizing the opportunity cost of choices taken, in terms of always needing to see things add up—was quite valuable.

And what insights does economics bring to the task of running a major university?

I came to Harvard because I thought after my time in government the two most important resources that were going to shape the economies of the future were leaders and new ideas, and those are the two things that a university produces.

Successful leadership in a university is all about what economists think about all the time—incentives—whether it's for professors to do a good job teaching, attracting the best scholars in a particular area, or motivating concern and research about the most important problems.

Leadership and management for the university are very much about economics because they're very much about incentives. Some of them are pecuniary and involve money, but other incentives come from people's feelings of being appreciated; they come from the teams in which people have an opportunity to work; they come from the way in which the university is organized. If working at the treasury was heavily about applied macroeconomics, leadership in the university is heavily about applied microeconomics.

What is your advice to a student who is just setting out to become an economist? What other subjects work well with economics?

The best advice to students is, don't be a commodity that's available in a perfectly competitive market. Stand out by developing your own distinctive expertise in something you care deeply about. It matters much less what it is and much more that it be yours and it not be a hundred other people's.

I think there is enormous potential in almost every area of economics, but I think that the people who will contribute the most to economics over the next quarter century will be those who have some keen understanding of the context in which economics is playing out—the international context, the technological context, and the political context. So my hope would be that those interested in economics would understand that economics is very different from physics in that it is tracking a changing reality and that in order to do the best economics in a given period, you have to be able to track that changing reality, and that means understanding international, technological, and political contexts.

Demand and Supply

Slide, Rocket, and Roller Coaster

Slide, rocket, and roller coaster—Canada's Wonderland rides? No, they are commonly used descriptions of price changes.

The price of a personal computer took a dramatic slide from around $3,000 in 2000 to around $500 in 2005. The price of gasoline rocketed in the summer of 2005. The prices of coffee, bananas, and other agricultural products rise and fall like a roller coaster.

You've learned that economics is about the choices people make to cope with scarcity, and how those choices respond to incentives. Prices are one of the incentives to which people respond. You're now going to see how prices are determined by demand and supply.

The demand and supply model is the main tool of economics. It helps us to answer the big economic question: What, how, and for whom are goods and services produced. It also helps us to say when the pursuit of self-interest promotes the social interest.

◆ Your careful study of this topic will bring big rewards both in your further study of economics and in your everyday life. When you have completed your study of demand and supply, you will be able to explain how prices are determined and make predictions about price slides, rockets, and roller coasters. Once you understand demand and supply, you will view the world through new eyes.

After studying this chapter, you will be able to

- ■ **Describe a competitive market and think about a price as an opportunity cost**
- ■ **Explain the influences on demand**
- ■ **Explain the influences on supply**
- ■ **Explain how demand and supply determine prices and quantities bought and sold**
- ■ **Use demand and supply to make predictions about changes in prices and quantities**

Markets and Prices

WHEN YOU NEED A NEW PAIR OF RUNNING SHOES, want a bagel and a latte, plan to upgrade your stereo system, or need to fly home for Thanksgiving, you must find a place where people sell those items or offer those services. The place in which you find them is a *market*. You learned in Chapter 2 (p. 46) that a market is any arrangement that enables buyers and sellers to get information and to do business with each other.

A market has two sides: buyers and sellers. There are markets for *goods* such as apples and hiking boots, for *services* such as haircuts and tennis lessons, for *resources* such as computer programmers and earthmovers, and for other manufactured *inputs* such as memory chips and auto parts. There are also markets for money such as Japanese yen and for financial securities such as Yahoo! stock. Only our imagination limits what can be traded in markets.

Some markets are physical places where buyers and sellers meet and where an auctioneer or a broker helps to determine the prices. Examples of this type of market are the wholesale fish, meat, and produce markets and car auction markets.

Some markets are groups of people spread around the world who never meet and know little about each other but are connected through the Internet or by telephone and fax. Examples are the e-commerce markets and currency markets.

But most markets are unorganized collections of buyers and sellers. You do most of your trading in this type of market. An example is the market for basketball shoes. The buyers in this $3 billion-a-year market are the 45 million North Americans who play basketball (or who want to make a fashion statement). The sellers are the tens of thousands of retail sports equipment and footwear stores. Each buyer can visit several different stores, and each seller knows that the buyer has a choice of stores.

Markets vary in the intensity of competition that buyers and sellers face. In this chapter, we're going to study a **competitive market**—a market that has many buyers and many sellers, so no single buyer or seller can influence the price.

Producers offer items for sale only if the price is high enough to cover their opportunity cost. And consumers respond to changing opportunity cost by seeking cheaper alternatives to expensive items.

We are going to study the way people respond to *prices* and the forces that determine prices. But to pur-sue these tasks, we need to understand the relationship between a price and an opportunity cost.

In everyday life, the *price* of an object is the number of dollars that must be given up in exchange for it. Economists refer to this price as the **money price**.

The *opportunity cost* of an action is the highest-valued alternative forgone. If, when you buy a coffee, the highest-valued thing you forgo is some gum, then the opportunity cost of the coffee is the *quantity* of gum forgone. We can calculate the quantity of gum forgone from the money prices of coffee and gum.

If the money price of coffee is $1 a cup and the money price of gum is 50¢ a pack, then the opportunity cost of one cup of coffee is two packs of gum. To calculate this opportunity cost, we divide the price of a cup of coffee by the price of a pack of gum and find the *ratio* of one price to the other. The ratio of one price to another is called a **relative price**, and a *relative price is an opportunity cost.*

We can express the relative price of coffee in terms of gum or any other good. The normal way of expressing a relative price is in terms of a "basket" of all goods and services. To calculate this relative price, we divide the money price of a good by the money price of a "basket" of all goods (called a *price index*). The resulting relative price tells us the opportunity cost of the good in terms of how much of the "basket" we must give up to buy it.

The theory of demand and supply that we are about to study determines *relative prices,* and the word "price" means *relative* price. When we predict that a price will fall, we do not mean that its *money* price will fall—although it might. We mean that its *relative* price will fall. That is, its price will fall *relative* to the average price of other goods and services.

REVIEW QUIZ

1 What is the distinction between a money price and a relative price?
2 Why is a relative price an opportunity cost?
3 Can you think of an example of a good whose money price and relative price have risen?
4 Can you think of an example of a good whose money price and relative price have fallen?

myeconlab **Study Plan 3.1**

Let's begin our study of demand and supply, starting with demand.

Demand

IF YOU DEMAND SOMETHING, THEN YOU

1. Want it,
2. Can afford it, and
3. Plan to buy it.

Wants are the unlimited desires or wishes that people have for goods and services. How many times have you thought that you would like something "if only you could afford it" or "if it weren't so expensive"? Scarcity guarantees that many—perhaps most—of our wants will never be satisfied. Demand reflects a decision about which wants to satisfy.

The **quantity demanded** of a good or service is the amount that consumers plan to buy during a given time period at a particular price. The quantity demanded is not necessarily the same as the quantity actually bought. Sometimes the quantity demanded exceeds the amount of goods available, so the quantity bought is less than the quantity demanded.

The quantity demanded is measured as an amount per unit of time. For example, suppose that you buy one cup of coffee a day. The quantity of coffee that you demand can be expressed as 1 cup per day, 7 cups per week, or 365 cups per year. Many factors influence buying plans and one of them is price. We look first at the relationship between the quantity demanded of a good and its price. To study this relationship, we keep all other influences on buying plans the same and we ask: How, other things remaining the same, does the quantity demanded of a good change as its price changes?

The law of demand provides the answer.

The Law of Demand

The **law of demand** states

Other things remaining the same, the higher the price of a good, the smaller is the quantity demanded; and the lower the price of a good, the greater is the quantity demanded.

Why does a higher price reduce the quantity demanded? For two reasons:

- Substitution effect
- Income effect

Substitution Effect When the price of a good rises, other things remaining the same, its *relative* price—its opportunity cost—rises. Although each good is unique, it has *substitutes*—other goods that can be used in its place. As the opportunity cost of a good rises, people buy less of that good and more of its substitutes.

Income Effect When a price rises and all other influences on buying plans remain unchanged, the price rises *relative* to people's incomes. So faced with a higher price and an unchanged income, people cannot afford to buy all the things they previously bought. They must decrease the quantities demanded of at least some goods and services, and normally, the good whose price has increased will be one of the goods that people buy less of.

To see the substitution effect and the income effect at work, think about the effects of a change in the price of a recordable compact disc—a CD-R. Several different goods are substitutes for a CD-R. For example, an audiotape and prerecorded CD provide services similar to those of a CD-R.

Suppose that a CD-R initially sells for $3.00 and then its price falls to $1.50. People now substitute CD-Rs for audiotapes and prerecorded CDs—the substitution effect. And with a budget that now has some slack from the lower price of a CD-R, people buy more CD-Rs—the income effect. The quantity of CD-Rs demanded increases for these two reasons.

Now suppose that a CD-R initially sells for $3.00 and then the price doubles to $6.00. People now substitute prerecorded CDs and audiotapes for CD-Rs—the substitution effect. And faced with a tighter budget, people buy fewer CD-Rs—the income effect. The quantity of CD-Rs demanded decreases for these two reasons.

Demand Curve and Demand Schedule

You are now about to study one of the two most used curves in economics: the demand curve. And you are going to encounter one of the most critical distinctions: the distinction between *demand* and *quantity demanded*.

The term **demand** refers to the entire relationship between the price of the good and the quantity demanded of the good. Demand is illustrated by the demand curve and the demand schedule. The term *quantity demanded* refers to a point on a demand curve—the quantity demanded at a particular price.

Figure 3.1 shows the demand curve for CD-Rs. A **demand curve** shows the relationship between the quantity demanded of a good and its price when all other influences on consumers' planned purchases remain the same.

The table in Fig. 3.1 is the demand schedule for CD-Rs. A *demand schedule* lists the quantities demanded at each price when all the other influences on consumers' planned purchases remain the same. For example, if the price of a CD-R is 50¢, the quantity demanded is 9 million a week. If the price is $2.50, the quantity demanded is 2 million a week. The other rows of the table show the quantities demanded at prices of $1.00, $1.50, and $2.00.

We graph the demand schedule as a demand curve with the quantity demanded of CD-Rs on the *x*-axis and the price of a CD-R on the *y*-axis. The points on the demand curve labelled *A* through *E* correspond to the rows of the demand schedule. For example, point *A* on the graph shows a quantity demanded of 9 million CD-Rs a week at a price of 50¢ a disc.

Willingness and Ability to Pay Another way of looking at the demand curve is as a willingness-and-ability-to-pay curve. And the willingness and ability to pay is a measure of *marginal benefit.*

If a small quantity is available, the highest price that someone is willing and able to pay for one more unit is high. But as the quantity available increases, the marginal benefit of each additional unit falls and the highest price that someone is willing and able to pay also falls along the demand curve.

In Fig. 3.1, if only 2 million CD-Rs are available each week, the highest price that someone is willing to pay for the 2 millionth CD-R is $2.50. But if 9 million CD-Rs are available each week, someone is willing to pay 50¢ for the last CD-R bought.

A Change in Demand

When any factor that influences buying plans other than the price of the good changes, there is a **change in demand**. Figure 3.2 illustrates an increase in demand. When demand increases, the demand curve shifts rightward and the quantity demanded is greater at each and every price. For example, at a price of $2.50, on the original (blue) demand curve, the quantity demanded is 2 million discs a week. On the new (red) demand curve, the quantity demanded is 6 million discs a week. Look closely at the numbers in the table in Fig. 3.2 and check that the quantity demanded is greater at each price.

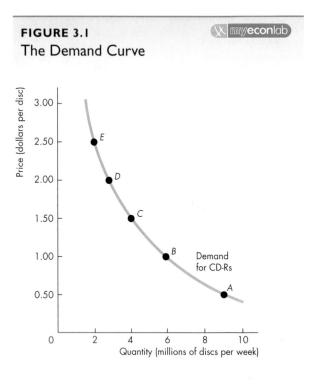

FIGURE 3.1
The Demand Curve

	Price (dollars per disc)	Quantity demanded (millions of discs per week)
A	0.50	9
B	1.00	6
C	1.50	4
D	2.00	3
E	2.50	2

The table shows a demand schedule for CD-Rs. At a price of 50¢ a disc, 9 million a week are demanded; at a price of $1.50 a disc, 4 million a week are demanded. The demand curve shows the relationship between quantity demanded and price, everything else remaining the same. The demand curve slopes downward: As price decreases, the quantity demanded increases.

The demand curve can be read in two ways. For a given price, the demand curve tells us the quantity that people plan to buy. For example, at a price of $1.50 a disc, the quantity demanded is 4 million discs a week. For a given quantity, the demand curve tells us the maximum price that consumers are willing and able to pay for the last disc available. For example, the maximum price that consumers will pay for the 6 millionth disc is $1.00.

Six main factors bring changes in demand. They are changes in

1. The prices of related goods
2. Expected future prices
3. Income
4. Expected future income
5. Population
6. Preferences

1. Prices of Related Goods The quantity of CD-Rs that consumers plan to buy depends in part on the prices of substitutes for CD-Rs. A **substitute** is a good that can be used in place of another good. For example, a bus ride is a substitute for a train ride; a prerecorded CD is a substitute for a CD-R, and a hamburger is a substitute for a hot dog. If the price of a substitute for a CD-R rises, people buy less of the substitute and more CD-Rs. For example, if the price of a prerecorded CD rises, people buy fewer CDs and more CD-Rs. The demand for CD-Rs increases.

The quantity of CD-Rs that people plan to buy also depends on the prices of complements with CD-Rs. A **complement** is a good that is used in conjunction with another good. Hamburgers and fries are complements. So are spaghetti and meat sauce, and so are CD-Rs and CD burners. If the price of a CD burner falls, people buy more CD burners *and more* CD-Rs. A fall in the price of a CD burner increases the demand for CD-Rs in Fig. 3.2.

2. Expected Future Prices If the price of a good is expected to rise in the future and if the good can be stored, the opportunity cost of obtaining the good for future use is lower today than it will be when the price has increased. So people retime their purchases—they substitute over time. They buy more of the good now before its price is expected to rise (and less after), so the current demand for the good increases. For example, suppose that Florida is hit by a frost that damages the season's orange crop. You expect the price of orange juice to rise in the future. So you fill your freezer with enough frozen juice to get you through the next six months. Your current demand for frozen orange juice has increased, and your future demand has decreased.

Similarly, if the price of a good is expected to fall in the future, the opportunity cost of buying the good today is high relative to what it is expected to be in the future. So again, people retime their purchases. They buy less of the good now before its price

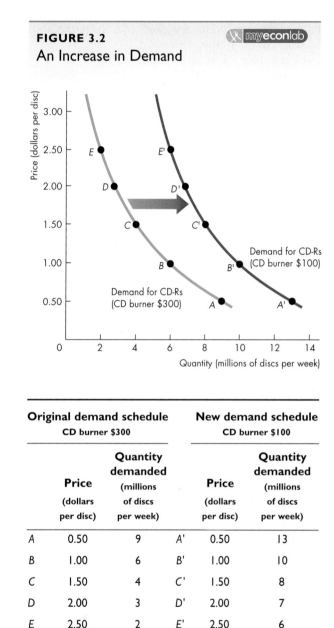

FIGURE 3.2   myeconlab

An Increase in Demand

Original demand schedule			New demand schedule		
CD burner $300			**CD burner $100**		
	Price (dollars per disc)	**Quantity demanded** (millions of discs per week)		**Price** (dollars per disc)	**Quantity demanded** (millions of discs per week)
A	0.50	9	A'	0.50	13
B	1.00	6	B'	1.00	10
C	1.50	4	C'	1.50	8
D	2.00	3	D'	2.00	7
E	2.50	2	E'	2.50	6

A change in any influence on buyers' plans other than the price of the good itself results in a new demand schedule and a shift of the demand curve. A change in the price of a CD burner changes the demand for CD-Rs. At a price of $1.50 a disc, 4 million discs a week are demanded when a CD burner costs $300 (row C of the table) and 8 million CD-Rs a week are demanded when a CD burner costs $100. A *fall* in the price of a CD burner *increases* the demand for CD-Rs. The demand curve shifts *rightward*, as shown by the shift arrow and the resulting red curve.

falls, so the demand for the good decreases today and increases in the future.

Computer prices are constantly falling, and this fact poses a dilemma. Will you buy a new computer now, in time for the start of the school year, or will you wait until the price has fallen some more? Because people expect computer prices to keep falling, the current demand for computers is less (the future demand is greater) than it otherwise would be.

3. Income Consumers' income influences demand. When income increases, consumers buy more of most goods, and when income decreases, consumers buy less of most goods. Although an increase in income leads to an increase in the demand for *most* goods, it does not lead to an increase in the demand for *all* goods. A **normal good** is one for which demand increases as income increases. An **inferior good** is one for which demand decreases as income increases. Long-distance transportation has examples of both normal goods and inferior goods. As incomes increase, the demand for air travel (a normal good) increases and the demand for long-distance bus trips (an inferior good) decreases.

4. Expected future income When expected future income increases, demand might increase. For example, a sales person gets the news that she will receive a big bonus at the end of the year, so she decides to buy a new car right now.

5. Population Demand also depends on the size and the age structure of the population. The larger the population, the greater is the demand for all goods and services; the smaller the population, the smaller is the demand for all goods and services.

For example, the demand for parking spaces or movies or CD-Rs or just about anything that you can imagine is much greater in the Greater Toronto Area (population 4.6 million) than it is in North Bay (population 110,000).

Also, the larger the proportion of the population in a given age group, the greater is the demand for the goods and services used by that age group.

For example, in 2001, there were 2.1 million 20–24-year-olds in Canada compared with 2.5 million in 1981. As a result, the demand for university places decreased during those years. During those same years, the number of Canadians aged 85 years and over increased by 235,000. As a result, the demand for nursing home services increased.

TABLE 3.1   The Demand for CD-Rs

The Law of Demand

The quantity of CD-Rs demanded

Decreases if:	Increases if:
■ The price of a CD-R rises	■ The price of a CD-R falls

Changes in Demand

The demand for CD-Rs

Decreases if:	Increases if:
■ The price of a substitute falls	■ The price of a substitute rises
■ The price of a complement rises	■ The price of a complement falls
■ The price of a CD-R is expected to fall in the future	■ The price of a CD-R is expected to rise in the future
■ Income falls*	■ Income rises*
■ Expected future income falls	■ Expected future income rises
■ The population decreases	■ The population increases

*A CD-R is a normal good.

6. Preferences Demand depends on preferences. *Preferences* are an individual's attitudes towards goods and services. For example, a rock music fanatic has a much greater preference for CD-Rs than does a tone-deaf technophobe. As a consequence, even if they have the same incomes, their demands for CD-Rs will be very different.

Table 3.1 summarizes the influences on demand and the direction of those influences.

A Change in the Quantity Demanded Versus a Change in Demand

Changes in the factors that influence buyers' plans cause either a change in the quantity demanded or a change in demand. Equivalently, they cause either a movement along the demand curve or a shift of the demand curve. The distinction between a change in the quantity demanded and a change in demand is the same as that between a movement along the demand curve and a shift of the demand curve.

A point on the demand curve shows the quantity demanded at a given price. So a movement along the demand curve shows a **change in the quantity demanded**. The entire demand curve shows demand. So a shift of the demand curve shows a *change in demand*. Figure 3.3 summarizes these distinctions.

Movement Along the Demand Curve If the price of a good changes but everything else remains the same, there is a movement along the demand curve. Because the demand curve slopes downward, a fall in the price of a good increases the quantity demanded of it and a rise in the price of the good decreases the quantity demanded of it—the law of demand.

In Fig. 3.3, if the price of a good falls when everything else remains the same, the quantity demanded of that good increases and there is a movement down the demand curve D_0. If the price rises when everything else remains the same, the quantity demanded of that good decreases and there is a movement up the demand curve D_0.

A Shift of the Demand Curve If the price of a good remains constant but some other influence on buyers' plans changes, there is a change in demand for that good. We illustrate a change in demand as a shift of the demand curve. For example, if the price of a CD burner falls, consumers buy more CD-Rs regardless of the price of a CD-R. That is what a rightward shift of the demand curve shows—more CD-Rs are bought at each and every price.

In Fig. 3.3, when any factor that influences buying plans, other than the price of the good, changes, there is a *change in demand* and the demand curve shifts. Demand *increases* and the demand curve *shifts rightward* (to the red demand curve D_1) if the price of a substitute rises, the price of a complement falls, the expected future price of the good rises, income increases (for a normal good), expected future income increases, or the population increases. Demand *decreases* and the demand curve *shifts leftward* (to the red demand curve D_2) if the price of a substitute falls, the price of a complement rises, the expected future price of the good falls, income decreases (for a normal good), expected future income decreases, or the population decreases. (For an inferior good, the effects of changes in income are in the direction opposite to those described above.)

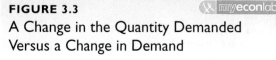

FIGURE 3.3

A Change in the Quantity Demanded Versus a Change in Demand

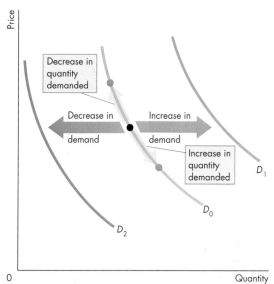

When the price of the good changes, there is a movement along the demand curve and *a change in the quantity demanded,* shown by the blue arrows on demand curve D_0. When any other influence on buyers' plans changes, there is a shift of the demand curve and a *change in demand.* An increase in demand shifts the demand curve rightward (from D_0 to D_1). A decrease in demand shifts the demand curve leftward (from D_0 to D_2).

REVIEW QUIZ

1 What is the law of demand and how do we illustrate it?

2 If a fixed amount of a good is available, what does the demand curve tell us about the price that consumers are willing to pay for that fixed quantity?

3 List all the influences on buying plans that change demand, and for each influence say whether it increases or decreases demand.

4 What happens to the quantity of Palm Pilots demanded and the demand for Palm Pilots if the price of a Palm Pilot falls and all other influences on buying plans remain the same?

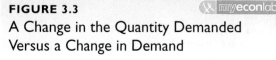 **Study Plan 3.2**

Supply

⌐ IF A FIRM SUPPLIES A GOOD OR SERVICE, THE FIRM

1. Has the resources and technology to produce it,
2. Can profit from producing it, and
3. Plans to produce it and sell it.

A supply is more than just having the *resources* and the *technology* to produce something. *Resources and technology* are the constraints that limit what is possible.

Many useful things can be produced, but they are not produced unless it is profitable to do so. Supply reflects a decision about which technologically feasible items to produce.

The **quantity supplied** of a good or service is the amount that producers plan to sell during a given time period at a particular price. The quantity supplied is not necessarily the same amount as the quantity actually sold. Sometimes the quantity supplied is greater than the quantity demanded, so the quantity bought is less than the quantity supplied.

Like the quantity demanded, the quantity supplied is measured as an amount per unit of time. For example, suppose that GM produces 1,000 cars a day. The quantity of cars supplied by GM can be expressed as 1,000 a day, 7,000 a week, or 365,000 a year. Without the time dimension, we cannot tell whether a particular number is large or small.

Many factors influence selling plans and again, one of them is price. We look first at the relationship between the quantity supplied of a good and its price. And again, as we did when we studied demand, to isolate this relationship, we keep all other influences on selling plans the same and we ask: How, other things remaining the same, does the quantity supplied of a good change as its price changes?

The law of supply provides the answer.

The Law of Supply

The **law of supply** states:

Other things remaining the same, the higher the price of a good, the greater is the quantity supplied; and the lower the price of a good, the smaller is the quantity supplied.

Why does a higher price increase the quantity supplied? It is because *marginal cost increases.* As the quantity produced of any good increases, the marginal cost of producing the good increases. (You can refresh your memory of increasing marginal cost in Chapter 2, p. 37.)

It is never worth producing a good if the price received for it does not at least cover the marginal cost of producing it. So when the price of a good rises, other things remaining the same, producers are willing to incur a higher marginal cost and increase production. The higher price brings forth an increase in the quantity supplied.

Let's now illustrate the law of supply with a supply curve and a supply schedule.

Supply Curve and Supply Schedule

You are now going to study the second of the two most used curves in economics: the supply curve. And you're going to learn about the critical distinction between *supply* and *quantity supplied*.

The term **supply** refers to the entire relationship between the quantity supplied and the price of a good. Supply is illustrated by the supply curve and the supply schedule. The term *quantity supplied* refers to a point on a supply curve—the quantity supplied at a particular price.

Figure 3.4 shows the supply curve of CD-Rs. A **supply curve** shows the relationship between the quantity supplied of a good and its price when all other influences on producers' planned sales remain the same. The supply curve is a graph of a supply schedule.

The table in Fig. 3.4 sets out the supply schedule for CD-Rs. A *supply schedule* lists the quantities supplied at each price when all the other influences on producers' planned sales remain the same. For example, if the price of a CD-R is 50¢, the quantity supplied is zero—in row *A* of the table. If the price of a CD-R is $1.00, the quantity supplied is 3 million CD-Rs a week—in row *B*. The other rows of the table show the quantities supplied at prices of $1.50, $2.00, and $2.50.

To make a supply curve, we graph the quantity supplied on the *x*-axis and the price on the *y*-axis, just as in the case of the demand curve. The points on the supply curve labelled *A* through *E* correspond to the rows of the supply schedule. For example, point *A* on the graph shows a quantity supplied of zero at a price of 50¢ a CD-R.

FIGURE 3.4

The Supply Curve

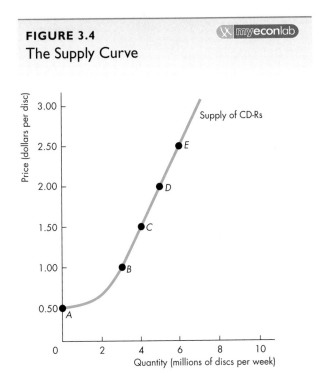

	Price (dollars per disc)	Quantity supplied (millions of discs per week)
A	0.50	0
B	1.00	3
C	1.50	4
D	2.00	5
E	2.50	6

The table shows the supply schedule of CD-Rs. For example, at a price of $1.00, 3 million discs a week are supplied; at a price of $2.50, 6 million discs a week are supplied. The supply curve shows the relationship between the quantity supplied and price, everything else remaining the same. The supply curve usually slopes upward: As the price of a good increases, so does the quantity supplied.

A supply curve can be read in two ways. For a given price, it tells us the quantity that producers plan to sell at that price. And for a given quantity, it tells us the minimum price that producers are willing to accept for that quantity.

Minimum Supply Price Just as the demand curve has two interpretations, so too does the supply curve. The demand curve can be interpreted as a willingness-and-ability-to-pay curve. The supply curve can be interpreted as a minimum-supply-price curve. It tells us the lowest price at which someone is willing to sell another unit.

If a small quantity is produced, the lowest price at which someone is willing to sell one more unit is low. But if a large quantity is produced, the lowest price at which someone is willing to sell one more unit is high.

In Fig. 3.4, if 6 million CD-Rs a week are produced, the lowest price that a producer is willing to accept for the 6 millionth disc is $2.50. But if only 4 million CD-Rs are produced each week, the lowest price that a producer is willing to accept for the 4 millionth disc is $1.50.

A Change in Supply

When any factor that influences selling plans other than the price of the good changes, there is a **change in supply**. Five main factors bring changes in supply. They are changes in

1. The prices of resources used to produce the good
2. The prices of related goods produced
3. Expected future prices
4. The number of suppliers
5. Technology

1. Prices of Productive Resources The prices of productive resources influence supply. The easiest way to see this influence is to think about the supply curve as a minimum-supply-price curve. If the price of a productive resource rises, the lowest price a producer of a good that uses that resource is willing to accept rises, so supply of the good decreases. For example, during 2005, the price of jet fuel increased and the supply of air transportation decreased. Similarly, a rise in the minimum wage decreases the supply of hamburgers. If the wages of disc producers rise, the supply of CD-Rs decreases.

2. Prices of Related Goods Produced The prices of related goods and services that firms produce influence supply. For example, if the price of a prerecorded CD rises, the supply of CD-Rs decreases. CD-Rs and prerecorded CDs are *substitutes in production*—goods that can be produced by using the same resources. If the price of beef rises, the supply of cowhide increases. Beef and cowhide are *complements in production*—goods that must be produced together.

3. Expected Future Prices If the price of a good is expected to rise, the return from selling the good in the future is higher than it is today. So supply of the good decreases today and increases in the future.

4. The Number of Suppliers The larger the number of firms that produce a good, the greater is the supply of the good. And as firms enter an industry, the supply in that industry increases. As firms leave an industry, the supply in that industry decreases.

5. Technology The term "technology" is used broadly to mean the way that factors of production are used to produce a good. Technology changes both positively and negatively. A positive technology change occurs when a new method is discovered that lowers the cost of producing a good. An example is new methods used in the factories that make CDs. A negative technology change occurs when an event such as extreme weather or natural disaster increases the cost of producing a good. A positive technology change increases supply, and a negative technology change decreases supply.

   Figure 3.5 illustrates an increase in supply. When supply increases, the supply curve shifts rightward and the quantity supplied is larger at each and every price. For example, at a price of $1, on the original (blue) supply curve, the quantity supplied is 3 million discs a week. On the new (red) supply curve, the quantity supplied is 6 million discs a week. Look closely at the numbers in the table in Fig. 3.5 and check that the quantity supplied is larger at each price.

   Table 3.2 summarizes the influences on supply and the directions of those influences.

A Change in the Quantity Supplied Versus a Change in Supply

Changes in the factors that influence sellers' plans cause either a change in the quantity supplied or a change in supply. Equivalently, they cause either a movement along the supply curve or a shift of the supply curve.

   A point on the supply curve shows the quantity supplied at a given price. A movement along the supply curve shows a **change in the quantity supplied**. The entire supply curve shows supply. A shift of the supply curve shows a *change in supply*.

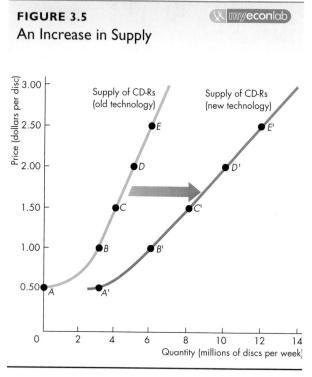

FIGURE 3.5

An Increase in Supply

A change in any influence on sellers' plans other than the price of the good itself results in a new supply schedule and a shift of the supply curve. For example, if Imation Enterprises invents a new, cost-saving technology for producing CD-Rs, the supply of CD-Rs changes. At a price of $1.50 a disc, 4 million discs a week are supplied when producers use the old technology (row C of the table) and 8 million CD-Rs a week are supplied when producers use the new technology. An advance in technology *increases* the supply of CD-Rs. The supply curve shifts *rightward*, as shown by the shift arrow and the resulting red curve.

| Original supply schedule | | New supply schedule | |
| Old technology | | New technology | |
Price (dollars per disc)	Quantity supplied (millions of discs per week)	Price (dollars per disc)	Quantity supplied (millions of discs per week)
A 0.50	0	A' 0.50	3
B 1.00	3	B' 1.00	6
C 1.50	4	C' 1.50	8
D 2.00	5	D' 2.00	10
E 2.50	6	E' 2.50	12

Figure 3.6 illustrates and summarizes these distinctions. If the price of a good falls and everything else remains the same, the quantity supplied of that good decreases and there is a movement down the supply curve S_0. If the price of a good rises and everything else remains the same, the quantity supplied increases and there is a movement up the supply curve S_0. When any other influence on selling plans changes, the supply curve shifts and there is a *change in supply*. If the supply curve is S_0 and if production costs fall, supply increases and the supply curve shifts to the red supply curve S_1. If production costs rise, supply decreases and the supply curve shifts to the red supply curve S_2.

TABLE 3.2   The Supply of CD-Rs

The Law of Supply

The quantity of CD-Rs supplied

Decreases if:	*Increases if:*
▪ The price of a CD-R falls	▪ The price of a CD-R rises

Changes in Supply

The supply of CD-Rs

Decreases if:	*Increases if:*
▪ The price of a resource used to produce CD-Rs rises	▪ The price of a resource used to produce CD-Rs falls
▪ The price of a substitute in production rises	▪ The price of a substitute in production falls
▪ The price of a complement in production falls	▪ The price of a complement in production rises
▪ The price of a CD-R is expected to rise in the future	▪ The price of a CD-R is expected to fall in the future
▪ The number of CD-R producers decreases	▪ The number of CD-R producers increases
▪ A less efficient technology for producing CD-Rs is used	▪ A more efficient technology for producing CD-Rs is used

FIGURE 3.6
A Change in the Quantity Supplied Versus a Change in Supply

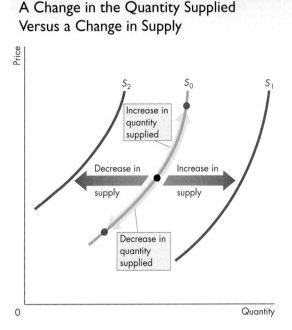

When the price of the good changes, there is a movement along the supply curve and *a change in the quantity supplied,* shown by the blue arrows on supply curve S_0. When any other influence on selling plans changes, there is a shift of the supply curve and a *change in supply.* An increase in supply shifts the supply curve rightward (from S_0 to S_1), and a decrease in supply shifts the supply curve leftward (from S_0 to S_2).

REVIEW QUIZ

1 What is the law of supply and how do we illustrate it?
2 What does the supply curve tell us about the price at which firms will supply a given quantity of a good?
3 List all the influences on selling plans, and for each influence say whether it changes supply.
4 What happens to the quantity of Palm Pilots supplied and the supply of Palm Pilots if the price of a Palm Pilot falls?

myeconlab **Study Plan 3.3**

Your next task is to use what you've learned about demand and supply and understand how prices and quantities are determined.

Market Equilibrium

WE HAVE SEEN THAT WHEN THE PRICE OF A GOOD rises, the quantity demanded *decreases* and the quantity supplied *increases*. We are now going to see how prices coordinate the plans of buyers and sellers and achieve an equilibrium.

An *equilibrium* is a situation in which opposing forces balance each other. Equilibrium in a market occurs when the price balances the plans of buyers and sellers. The **equilibrium price** is the price at which the quantity demanded equals the quantity supplied. The **equilibrium quantity** is the quantity bought and sold at the equilibrium price. A market moves towards its equilibrium because

- Price regulates buying and selling plans.
- Price adjusts when plans don't match.

Price as a Regulator

The price of a good regulates the quantities demanded and supplied. If the price is too high, the quantity supplied exceeds the quantity demanded. If the price is too low, the quantity demanded exceeds the quantity supplied. There is one price at which the quantity demanded equals the quantity supplied. Let's work out what that price is.

Figure 3.7 shows the market for CD-Rs. The table shows the demand schedule (from Fig. 3.1) and the supply schedule (from Fig. 3.4). If the price of a disc is 50¢, the quantity demanded is 9 million discs a week, but no discs are supplied. There is a shortage of 9 million discs a week. This shortage is shown in the final column of the table. At a price of $1.00 a disc, there is still a shortage, but only of 3 million discs a week. If the price of a disc is $2.50, the quantity supplied is 6 million discs a week, but the quantity demanded is only 2 million. There is a surplus of 4 million discs a week. The one price at which there is neither a shortage nor a surplus is $1.50 a disc. At that price, the quantity demanded is equal to the quantity supplied: 4 million discs a week. The equilibrium price is $1.50 a disc, and the equilibrium quantity is 4 million discs a week.

Figure 3.7 shows that the demand curve and the supply curve intersect at the equilibrium price of $1.50 a disc. At each price *above* $1.50 a disc, there is a surplus of discs. For example, at $2.00 a disc, the surplus

FIGURE 3.7
Equilibrium

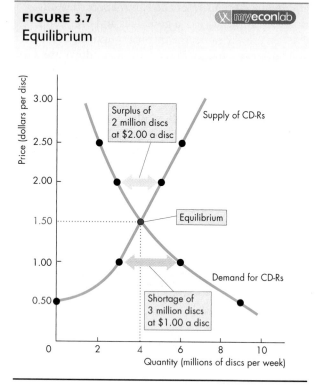

Price (dollars per disc)	Quantity demanded	Quantity supplied	Shortage (–) or surplus (+)
	(millions of discs per week)		
0.50	9	0	–9
1.00	6	3	–3
1.50	4	4	0
2.00	3	5	+2
2.50	2	6	+4

The table lists the quantities demanded and quantities supplied as well as the shortage or surplus of discs at each price. If the price is $1.00 a disc, 6 million discs a week are demanded and 3 million are supplied. There is a shortage of 3 million discs a week, and the price rises.

If the price is $2.00 a disc, 3 million discs a week are demanded and 5 million are supplied. There is a surplus of 2 million discs a week, and the price falls.

If the price is $1.50 a disc, 4 million discs a week are demanded and 4 million are supplied. There is neither a shortage nor a surplus. Neither buyers nor sellers have any incentive to change the price. The price at which the quantity demanded equals the quantity supplied is the equilibrium price.

is 2 million discs a week, as shown by the blue arrow. At each price *below* $1.50 a disc, there is a shortage of discs. For example, at $1.00 a disc, the shortage is 3 million discs a week, as shown by the red arrow.

Price Adjustments

You've seen that if the price is below equilibrium, there is a shortage and that if the price is above equilibrium, there is a surplus. But can we count on the price to change and eliminate a shortage or surplus? We can, because such price changes are beneficial to both buyers and sellers. Let's see why the price changes when there is a shortage or a surplus.

A Shortage Forces the Price Up Suppose the price of a CD-R is $1. Consumers plan to buy 6 million discs a week, and producers plan to sell 3 million discs a week. Consumers can't force producers to sell more than they plan, so the quantity that is actually offered for sale is 3 million discs a week. In this situation, powerful forces operate to increase the price and move it towards the equilibrium price. Some producers, noticing lines of unsatisfied consumers, raise the price. Some producers increase their output. As producers push the price up, the price rises towards its equilibrium. The rising price reduces the shortage because it decreases the quantity demanded and increases the quantity supplied. When the price has increased to the point at which there is no longer a shortage, the forces moving the price stop operating and the price comes to rest at its equilibrium.

A Surplus Forces the Price Down Suppose the price of a CD-R is $2. Producers plan to sell 5 million discs a week, and consumers plan to buy 3 million discs a week. Producers cannot force consumers to buy more than they plan, so the quantity that is actually bought is 3 million discs a week. In this situation, powerful forces operate to lower the price and move it towards the equilibrium price. Some producers, unable to sell the quantities of CD-Rs they planned to sell, cut their prices. In addition, some producers scale back production. As producers cut the price, the price falls towards its equilibrium. The falling price decreases the surplus because it increases the quantity demanded and decreases the quantity supplied. When the price has fallen to the point at which there is no longer a surplus, the forces moving the price stop operating and the price comes to rest at its equilibrium.

The Best Deal Available for Buyers and Sellers When the price is below equilibrium, it is forced up towards the equilibrium. Why don't buyers resist the increase and refuse to buy at the higher price? Because they value the good more highly than the current price and they cannot satisfy all their demands at the current price. In some markets—for example, the auction markets that operate on eBay—the buyers might even be the ones who force the price up by offering to pay higher prices.

When the price is above equilibrium, it is bid down towards the equilibrium. Why don't sellers resist this decrease and refuse to sell at the lower price? Because their minimum supply price is below the current price and they cannot sell all they would like to at the current price. Normally, it is the sellers who force the price down by offering lower prices to gain market share from their competitors.

At the price at which the quantity demanded and the quantity supplied are equal, neither buyers nor sellers can do business at a better price. Buyers pay the highest price they are willing to pay for the last unit bought, and sellers receive the lowest price at which they are willing to supply the last unit sold.

When people freely make offers to buy and sell and when demanders try to buy at the lowest possible price and suppliers try to sell at the highest possible price, the price at which trade takes place is the equilibrium price—the price at which the quantity demanded equals the quantity supplied. The price coordinates the plans of buyers and sellers, and no one has an incentive to change it.

REVIEW QUIZ

1 What is the equilibrium price of a good or service?
2 Over what range of prices does a shortage arise?
3 Over what range of prices does a surplus arise?
4 What happens to the price when there is a shortage?
5 What happens to the price when there is a surplus?
6 Why is the price at which the quantity demanded equals the quantity supplied the equilibrium price?

myeconlab **Study Plan 3.4**

Predicting Changes in Price and Quantity

THE DEMAND AND SUPPLY THEORY THAT WE HAVE just studied provides us with a powerful way of analyzing influences on prices and the quantities bought and sold. According to the theory, a change in price stems from a change in demand, a change in supply, or a change in both demand and supply. Let's look first at the effects of a change in demand.

A Change in Demand

What happens to the price and quantity of CD-Rs if the demand for CD-Rs increases? We can answer this question with a specific example. Between 1998 and 2001, the price of a CD burner fell from $300 to $100. Because the CD burner and CD-R discs are complements, the demand for discs increased, as is shown in the table in Fig. 3.8. The original demand schedule and the new one are set out in the first three columns of the table. The table also shows the supply schedule for CD-Rs.

When demand increases, there is a shortage at the original equilibrium price of $1.50 a disc. To eliminate the shortage, the price must rise. The price that makes the quantity demanded and quantity supplied equal again is $2.50 a disc. At this price, 6 million discs are bought and sold each week. When demand increases, both the price and the quantity increase.

Figure 3.8 shows these changes. The figure shows the original demand for and supply of CD-Rs. The original equilibrium price is $1.50 a disc, and the quantity is 4 million discs a week. When demand increases, the demand curve shifts rightward. The equilibrium price rises to $2.50 a disc, and the quantity supplied increases to 6 million discs a week, as highlighted in the figure. There is an *increase in the quantity supplied* but *no change in supply*—a movement along, but no shift of, the supply curve.

We can reverse this change in demand. Start at a price of $2.50 a disc with 6 million discs a week being bought and sold, and then work out what happens if demand decreases to its original level. Such a decrease in demand might arise from a fall in the price of an MP3 player (a substitute for CD-R technology). The decrease in demand shifts the demand curve leftward. The equilibrium price falls to $1.50 a disc, and the equilibrium quantity decreases to 4 million discs a week.

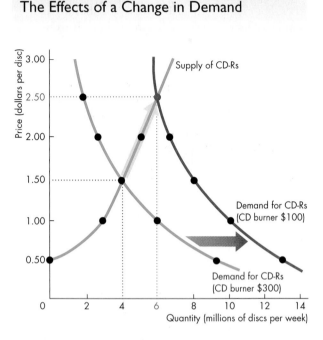

FIGURE 3.8 🅧 myeconlab

The Effects of a Change in Demand

Price	Quantity demanded (millions of discs per week)		Quantity supplied
(dollars per disc)	CD burner $300	CD burner $100	(millions of discs per week)
0.50	9	13	0
1.00	6	10	3
1.50	**4**	**8**	**4**
2.00	3	7	5
2.50	**2**	**6**	**6**

With the price of a CD burner at $300, the demand for CD-Rs is the blue demand curve. The equilibrium price is $1.50 a disc, and the equilibrium quantity is 4 million discs a week. When the price of a CD burner falls from $300 to $100, the demand for CD-Rs increases and the demand curve shifts rightward to become the red curve.

At $1.50 a disc, there is now a shortage of 4 million discs a week. The price of a disc rises to a new equilibrium of $2.50. As the price rises to $2.50, the quantity supplied increases—shown by the blue arrow on the supply curve—to the new equilibrium quantity of 6 million discs a week. Following an increase in demand, the quantity supplied increases but supply does not change—the supply curve does not shift.

We can now make our first two predictions:

1. When demand increases, both the price and the quantity increase.
2. When demand decreases, both the price and the quantity decrease.

A Change in Supply

When Imation and other producers introduce new cost-saving technologies in their CD-R production plants, the supply of CD-Rs increases. The new supply schedule (the same one that was shown in Fig. 3.5) is presented in the table in Fig. 3.9. What are the new equilibrium price and quantity? The answer is highlighted in the table: The price falls to $1.00 a disc, and the quantity increases to 6 million a week. You can see why by looking at the quantities demanded and supplied at the old price of $1.50 a disc. The quantity supplied at that price is 8 million discs a week, and there is a surplus of discs. The price falls. Only when the price is $1.00 a disc does the quantity supplied equal the quantity demanded.

Figure 3.9 illustrates the effect of an increase in supply. It shows the demand curve for CD-Rs and the original and new supply curves. The initial equilibrium price is $1.50 a disc, and the quantity is 4 million discs a week. When the supply increases, the supply curve shifts rightward. The equilibrium price falls to $1.00 a disc, and the quantity demanded increases to 6 million discs a week, highlighted in the figure. There is an *increase in the quantity demanded* but *no change in demand*—a movement along, but no shift of, the demand curve.

We can reverse this change in supply. If we start out at a price of $1.00 a disc with 6 million discs a week being bought and sold, we can work out what happens if supply decreases to its original level. Such a decrease in supply might arise from an increase in the cost of labour or raw materials. The decrease in supply shifts the supply curve leftward. The equilibrium price rises to $1.50 a disc, and the equilibrium quantity decreases to 4 million discs a week.

We can now make two more predictions:

1. When supply increases, the quantity increases and the price falls.
2. When supply decreases, the quantity decreases and the price rises.

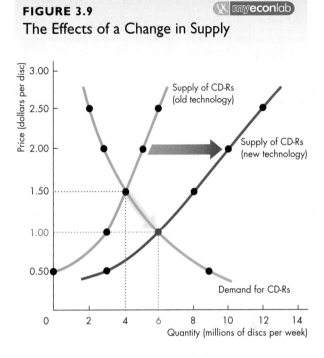

FIGURE 3.9   myeconlab

The Effects of a Change in Supply

Price (dollars per disc)	Quantity demanded (millions of discs per week)	Quantity supplied (millions of discs per week)	
		Old technology	New technology
0.50	9	0	3
1.00	6	3	6
1.50	**4**	**4**	**8**
2.00	3	5	10
2.50	2	6	12

With the old technology, the supply of CD-Rs is shown by the blue supply curve. The equilibrium price is $1.50 a disc, and the equilibrium quantity is 4 million discs a week. When the new technology is adopted, the supply of CD-Rs increases and the supply curve shifts rightward to become the red curve.

At $1.50 a disc, there is now a surplus of 4 million discs a week. The price of a CD-R falls to a new equilibrium of $1.00 a disc. As the price falls to $1.00, the quantity demanded increases—shown by the blue arrow on the demand curve—to the new equilibrium quantity of 6 million discs a week. Following an increase in supply, the quantity demanded increases but demand does not change—the demand curve does not shift.

A Change in Both Demand and Supply

You can now predict the effects of a change in either demand or supply on the price and the quantity. But what happens if *both* demand and supply change together? To answer this question, we look first at the case in which demand and supply move in the same direction—either both increase or both decrease. Then we look at the case in which they move in opposite directions—demand decreases and supply increases or demand increases and supply decreases.

Demand and Supply Change in the Same Direction We've seen that an increase in the demand for CD-Rs raises its price and increases the quantity bought and sold. And we've seen that an increase in the supply of CD-Rs lowers its price and increases the quantity bought and sold. Let's now examine what happens when both of these changes occur together.

The table in Fig. 3.10 brings together the numbers that describe the original quantities demanded and supplied and the new quantities demanded and supplied after the fall in the price of the CD burner and the improved CD-R production technology. These same numbers are illustrated in the graph. The original (blue) demand and supply curves intersect at a price of $1.50 a disc and a quantity of 4 million discs a week. The new (red) supply and demand curves also intersect at a price of $1.50 a disc but at a quantity of 8 million discs a week.

An increase in either demand or supply increases the quantity. So when both demand and supply increase, so does the equilibrium quantity.

An increase in demand raises the price, and an increase in supply lowers the price, so we can't say whether the price will rise or fall when demand and supply increase together. In this example, the price does not change. But notice that if demand increases by slightly more than the amount shown in the figure, the equilibrium price will rise. And if supply increases by slightly more than the amount shown in the figure, the equilibrium price will fall.

We can now make two more predictions:

1. When *both* demand and supply increase, the quantity increases and the price might increase, decrease, or remain the same.
2. When *both* demand and supply decrease, the quantity decreases and the price might increase, decrease, or remain the same.

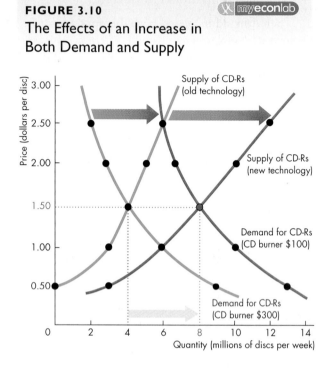

FIGURE 3.10

The Effects of an Increase in Both Demand and Supply

Price	Original quantities (millions of discs per week)		New quantities (millions of discs per week)	
	Quantity demanded	Quantity supplied	Quantity demanded	Quantity supplied
(dollars per disc)	CD burner $300	old technology	CD burner $100	new technology
0.50	9	0	13	3
1.00	6	3	10	6
1.50	4	4	8	8
2.00	3	5	7	10
2.50	2	6	6	12

When a CD burner costs $300 and firms use the old technology to produce discs, the price of a disc is $1.50 and the quantity is 4 million discs a week. A fall in the price of the CD burner increases the demand for CD-Rs, and improved technology increases the supply of CD-Rs. The new supply curve intersects the new demand curve at $1.50 a disc, the same price as before, but the equilibrium quantity increases to 8 million discs a week. These increases in demand and supply increase the quantity but leave the price unchanged.

Demand and Supply Change in Opposite Directions Let's now see what happens when demand and supply change together in *opposite* directions. A new production technology increases the supply of CD-Rs as before. But now the price of an MP3 download rises. An MP3 download is a *complement* of a CD-R. With more costly MP3 downloads, some people switch from buying CD-Rs to buying prerecorded CDs. The demand for CD-Rs decreases.

The table in Fig. 3.11 describes the original and new demand and supply schedules and the original (blue) and new (red) demand and supply curves. The original equilibrium price is $2.50 a disc, and the quantity is 6 million discs a week. The new supply and demand curves intersect at a price of $1.00 a disc and at the original quantity of 6 million discs a week.

A decrease in demand or an increase in supply lowers the price. So when a decrease in demand and an increase in supply occur together, the price falls.

A decrease in demand decreases the quantity, and an increase in supply increases the quantity, so we can't say for sure which way the quantity will change when demand decreases and supply increases at the same time. In this example, the quantity doesn't change. But notice that if demand had decreased by slightly more than is shown in the figure, the quantity would have decreased. And if supply had increased by slightly more than is shown in the figure, the quantity would have increased. So

1. When demand decreases and supply increases, the price falls and the quantity might increase, decrease, or remain the same.

2. When demand increases and supply decreases, the price rises and the quantity might increase, decrease, or remain the same.

REVIEW QUIZ

1 What is the effect on the price of a CD-R and the quantity of CD-Rs if (a) the price of a PC falls or (b) the price of an MP3 download rises or (c) more firms produce CD-Rs or (d) CD-R producers' wages rise or (e) any two of these events occur together? (Draw the diagrams!)

myeconlab **Study Plan 3.5**

◆ To complete your study of demand and supply, take a look at *Reading Between the Lines* on pp. 76–77, which looks at the rocketing price of gasoline in the summer of 2005.

FIGURE 3.11   myeconlab

The Effects of a Decrease in Demand and an Increase in Supply

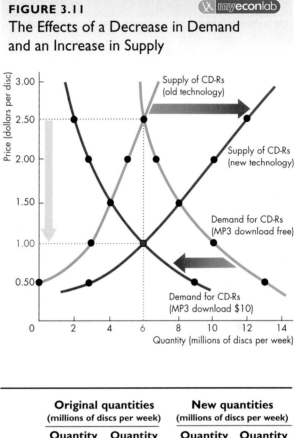

	Original quantities (millions of discs per week)		New quantities (millions of discs per week)	
Price	**Quantity demanded**	**Quantity supplied**	**Quantity demanded**	**Quantity supplied**
(dollars per disc)	MP3 download free	old technology	MP3 download $10	new technology
0.50	13	0	9	3
1.00	10	3	6	6
1.50	8	4	4	8
2.00	7	5	3	10
2.50	6	6	2	12

When MP3 downloads are free and firms use the old technology to produce discs, the price is $2.50 a disc and the quantity is 6 million discs a week. A rise in the price of an MP3 download decreases the demand for CD-Rs, and improved technology increases the supply of CD-Rs. The new equilibrium price is $1.00 a disc, a lower price, but in this case the quantity remains constant at 6 million discs a week. This decrease in demand and increase in supply lower the price but leave the quantity unchanged.

Demand and Supply:
The Price of Oil

BLOOMBERG, AUGUST 23, 2005

Crude Oil Prices Rise on Concern Demand May Outstrip Supply

Crude oil rose above $66 a barrel in New York on concern that refiners will struggle to meet increased fuel demand during the Northern Hemisphere winter.

Kuwait Petroleum Corp. late yesterday said it shut its 85,000 barrel-a-day Europoort refinery near Rotterdam because of a failure in its steam boilers. More than 20 U.S. and European refineries have had unplanned unit shutdowns since early July.

"There is a perception that supply will be insufficient to meet demand later this year," said Steve Bellino, a trader at Fimat USA Inc. in New York. "The fact remains that there are no shortages, but the concern is there. Prices continue to be bid up just about every morning." ...

Essence of the Story

■ The price of crude oil reached $US66 a barrel in August 2005.

■ The reported reason for the price rise was an expected increase in demand for oil during the winter.

■ Another reported reason was a decrease in supply that resulted from shutdowns of refineries.

■ One trader said that there is a perception that supply will be insufficient to meet demand.

■ The trader also noted that there were no shortages.

Economic Analysis

■ The price of crude oil increased from an average of $US38 a barrel in 2004 to $66 a barrel in August 2005.

■ The quantity of oil produced increased from 83 million barrels a day in 2004 to 84 million barrels a day in 2005.

■ The most significant factor at work in the oil market in 2005 was an increasing awareness that the global demand for oil is going to increase at a much faster rate than previously thought.

■ The main source of the increase in demand is a rapid expansion in the economies of China and India, which is increasing the demand for oil in these countries. (China and India account for two-fifths of the world's population.)

■ The decrease in production by a refinery near Rotterdam reported in the news article is not significant. The production of this refinery is only one-tenth of one percent of world production and the shutdown is temporary.

■ Figure 1 illustrates the global market for oil in 2004 and 2005.

■ The supply of oil was constant and represented by the supply curve S.

■ In 2004, the demand for oil was D_{04}.

■ The equilibrium price was $US38 a barrel and the equilibrium quantity was 83 million barrels a day.

■ The demand for oil increased in 2005 and the demand curve shifted rightward to D_{05}.

■ The equilibrium price increased to $US66 a barrel and the equilibrium quantity increased to 84 million barrels a day.

■ There was no shortage of oil because the rise in the equilibrium price kept the quantity demanded equal to the quantity supplied.

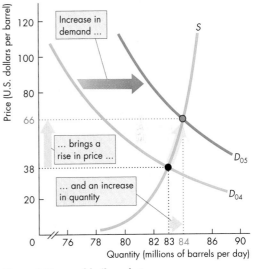

Figure 1 The world oil market

Mathematical Note
Demand, Supply, and Equilibrium

Demand Curve

The law of demand says that as the price of a good or service falls, the quantity demanded of that good or service increases. We illustrate the law of demand by setting out a demand schedule, drawing a graph of the demand curve, or writing down an equation. When the demand curve is a straight line, the following linear equation describes it:

$$P = a - bQ_D$$

where P is the price and Q_D is the quantity demanded. The a and b are positive constants.

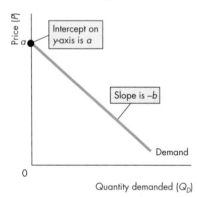

The demand equation tells us three things:

1. The price at which no one is willing to buy the good (Q_D is zero). That is, if the price is a, then the quantity demanded is zero. You can see the price a on the graph. It is the price at which the demand curve hits the y-axis—what we call the demand curve's "intercept on the y-axis."

2. As the price falls, the quantity demanded increases. If Q_D is a positive number, then the price P must be less than a. And as Q_D gets larger, the price P becomes smaller. That is, as the quantity increases, the maximum price that buyers are willing to pay for the good falls.

3. The constant b tells us how fast the maximum price that someone is willing to pay for the good falls as the quantity increases. That is, the constant b tells us about the steepness of the demand curve. The equation tells us that the slope of the demand curve is $-b$.

Supply Curve

The law of supply says that as the price of a good or service rises, the quantity supplied of that good or service increases. We illustrate the law of supply by setting out a supply schedule, drawing a graph of the supply curve, or writing down an equation. When the supply curve is a straight line, the following linear equation describes it:

$$P = c + dQ_S$$

where P is the price and Q_S is the quantity supplied. The c and d are positive constants.

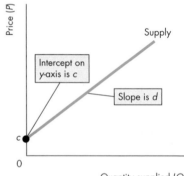

The supply equation tells us three things:

1. The price at which sellers are not willing to supply the good (Q_S is zero). That is, if the price is c, then no one is willing to sell the good. You can see the price c on the graph. It is the price at which the supply curve hits the y-axis—what we call the supply curve's "intercept on the y-axis."

2. As the price rises, the quantity supplied increases. If Q_S is a positive number, then the price P must be greater than c. And as Q_S increases, the price P gets larger. That is, as the quantity increases, the minimum price that sellers are willing to accept rises.

3. The constant d tells us how fast the minimum price at which someone is willing to sell the good rises as the quantity increases. That is, the constant d tells us about the steepness of the supply curve. The equation tells us that the slope of the supply curve is d.

Market Equilibrium

Demand and supply determine market equilibrium. The figure shows the equilibrium price (P^*) and equilibrium quantity (Q^*) at the intersection of the demand curve and the supply curve.

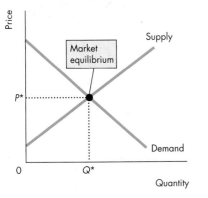

We can use the equations to find the equilibrium price and equilibrium quantity. The price of a good adjusts until the quantity demanded equals the quantity supplied. That is,

$$Q_D = Q_S.$$

So at the equilibrium price (P^*) and equilibrium quantity (Q^*),

$$Q_D = Q_S = Q^*.$$

To find the equilibrium price and equilibrium quantity, substitute Q^* for Q_D in the demand equation and Q^* for Q_S in the supply equation. Then the price is the equilibrium price (P^*), which gives

$$P^* = a - bQ^*$$

$$P^* = c + dQ^*.$$

Notice that

$$a - bQ^* = c + dQ^*.$$

Now solve for Q^*:

$$a - c = bQ^* + dQ^*$$

$$a - c = (b + d)Q^*$$

$$Q^* = \frac{a - c}{b + d}.$$

To find the equilibrium price, (P^*), substitute for Q^* in either the demand equation or the supply equation.

Using the demand equation, we have

$$P^* = a - b\left(\frac{a - c}{b + d}\right)$$

$$P^* = \frac{a(b + d) - b(a - c)}{b + d}$$

$$P^* = \frac{ad + bc}{b + d}.$$

Alternatively, using the supply equation, we have

$$P^* = c + d\left(\frac{a - c}{b + d}\right)$$

$$P^* = \frac{c(b + d) + d(a - c)}{b + d}$$

$$P^* = \frac{ad + bc}{b + d}.$$

An Example

The demand for ice cream cones is

$$P = 800 - 2Q_D.$$

The supply of ice cream cones is

$$P = 200 + 1Q_S.$$

The price of a cone is expressed in cents, and the quantities are expressed in cones per day.

To find the equilibrium price (P^*) and equilibrium quantity (Q^*), substitute Q^* for Q_D and Q_S and P^* for P. That is,

$$P^* = 800 - 2Q^*$$

$$P^* = 200 + 1Q^*.$$

Now solve for Q^*:

$$800 - 2Q^* = 200 + 1Q^*$$

$$600 = 3Q^*$$

$$Q^* = 200.$$

And

$$P^* = 800 - 2(200) = 400.$$

The equilibrium price is $4 a cone, and the equilibrium quantity is 200 cones per day.

SUMMARY

KEY POINTS

Markets and Prices (p. 60)

- A competitive market is one that has so many buyers and sellers that no one can influence the price.
- Opportunity cost is a relative price.
- Demand and supply determine relative prices.

Demand (pp. 61–65)

- Demand is the relationship between the quantity demanded of a good and its price when all other influences on buying plans remain the same.
- The higher the price of a good, other things remaining the same, the smaller is the quantity demanded—the law of demand.
- Demand depends on the prices of substitutes and complements, expected future prices, income, expected future income, population, and preferences.

Supply (pp. 66–69)

- Supply is the relationship between the quantity supplied of a good and its price when all other influences on selling plans remain the same.
- The higher the price of a good, other things remaining the same, the greater is the quantity supplied—the law of supply.
- Supply depends on the prices of resources used to produce a good, the prices of related goods produced, expected future prices, the number of suppliers, and technology.

Market Equilibrium (pp. 70–71)

- At the equilibrium price, the quantity demanded equals the quantity supplied.
- At prices above equilibrium, there is a surplus and the price falls.
- At prices below equilibrium, there is a shortage and the price rises.

Predicting Changes in Price and Quantity (pp. 72–75)

- An increase in demand brings a rise in the price and an increase in the quantity supplied. (A decrease in demand brings a fall in the price and a decrease in the quantity supplied.)
- An increase in supply brings a fall in the price and an increase in the quantity demanded. (A decrease in supply brings a rise in the price and a decrease in the quantity demanded.)
- An increase in demand and an increase in supply bring an increased quantity, but the price might rise, fall, or remain the same. An increase in demand and a decrease in supply bring a higher price, but the quantity might increase, decrease, or remain the same.

KEY FIGURES

Figure 3.1   The Demand Curve, 62
Figure 3.3   A Change in the Quantity Demanded Versus a Change in Demand, 65
Figure 3.4   The Supply Curve, 67
Figure 3.6   A Change in the Quantity Supplied Versus a Change in Supply, 69
Figure 3.7   Equilibrium, 70
Figure 3.8   The Effects of a Change in Demand, 72
Figure 3.9   The Effects of a Change in Supply, 73

KEY TERMS

Change in demand, 62
Change in supply, 67
Change in the quantity demanded, 65
Change in the quantity supplied, 68
Competitive market, 60
Complement, 63
Demand, 61
Demand curve, 62
Equilibrium price, 70
Equilibrium quantity, 70
Inferior good, 64
Law of demand, 61
Law of supply, 66
Money price, 60
Normal good, 64
Quantity demanded, 61
Quantity supplied, 66
Relative price, 60
Substitute, 63
Supply, 66
Supply curve, 66

PROBLEMS

Go to myeconlab for solutions to odd-numbered problems and additional exercises.

1. What is the effect on the price of an audiotape and the quantity of audiotapes sold if
   a. The price of a CD rises?
   b. The price of a Walkman rises?
   c. The supply of CD players increases?
   d. Consumers' incomes increase?
   e. Workers who make audiotapes get a pay raise?
   f. The price of a Walkman rises at the same time as the workers who make audiotapes get a pay raise?

2. What is the effect on the price of a DVD player and the quantity of DVD players sold if
   a. The price of a DVD rises?
   b. The price of a DVD falls?
   c. The supply of DVD players increases?
   d. Consumers' incomes decrease??
   e. The wage rate of workers who produce DVD players increases?
   f. The wage rate of workers who produce DVD players rises and at the same time the price of a DVD falls?

3. The following events occur one at a time:
   i. The price of crude oil rises.
   ii. The price of a car rises.
   iii. All speed limits on highways are abolished.
   iv. Robot technology cuts the cost of producing a car.

   Which of these events will increase or decrease (state which)
   a. The demand for gasoline?
   b. The supply of gasoline?
   c. The quantity of gasoline demanded?
   d. The quantity of gasoline supplied?

4. The following events occur one at a time:
   i. The price of airfares halve.
   ii. The price of beef falls.
   iii. A cheap new strong cloth, a close substitute for leather, is invented.
   iv. A new high-speed technology for cutting leather is invented.

   Which of these events will increase or decrease (state which)
   a. The demand for leather bags?
   b. The supply of leather bags?
   c. The quantity of leather bags demanded?
   d. The quantity of leather bags supplied?

5. The figure illustrates the market for pizza.
   a. Label the curves in the figure.
   b. What are the equilibrium price of a pizza and the equilibrium quantity of pizza?

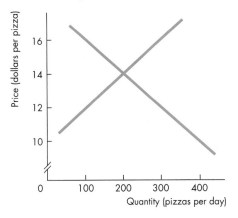

6. The figure illustrates the market for fish.
   a. Label the curves in the figure.
   b. What are the equilibrium price of a fish and the equilibrium quantity of fish?

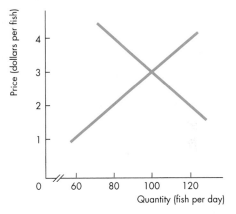

7. The demand and supply schedules for gum are

Price (cents per pack)	Quantity demanded	Quantity supplied
	(millions of packs per week)	
20	180	60
30	160	80
40	140	100
50	120	120
60	100	140
70	80	160
80	60	180

   a. Draw a graph of the gum market and mark in the equilibrium price and quantity.

b. Suppose that gum is 70¢ a pack. Describe the situation in the gum market and explain how the price of gum adjusts.

8. The demand and supply schedules for potato chips are

Price (cents per bag)	Quantity demanded	Quantity supplied
	(millions of bags per week)	
50	160	130
60	150	140
70	140	150
80	130	160
90	120	170
100	110	180

a. Draw a graph of the potato chip market and mark in the equilibrium price and quantity.

b. Suppose that chips are 60¢ a bag. Describe the situation in the market for chips and explain how the price adjusts.

9. In problem 7, suppose that a fire destroys some gum-producing factories and the supply of gum decreases by 40 million packs a week.

a. Has there been a shift of or a movement along the supply curve of gum?

b. Has there been a shift of or a movement along the demand curve for gum?

c. What are the new equilibrium price and equilibrium quantity of gum?

10. In problem 8, suppose a new dip comes onto the market, which is very popular and the demand for potato chips increases by 30 million bags per week.

a. Has there been a shift of or a movement along the supply curve of potato chips?

b. Has there been a shift of or a movement along the demand curve for gum?

c. What are the new equilibrium price and equilibrium quantity of potato chips?

11. In problem 9, suppose an increase in the teenage population increases the demand for gum by 40 million packs per week at the same time as the fire occurs. What are the new equilibrium price and quantity of gum?

12. In problem 10, suppose that a virus destroys several potato farms with the result that the supply of potato chips decreases by 40 million bags a week at the same time as the dip comes onto the market. What are the new equilibrium price and quantity of potato chips?

CRITICAL THINKING

1. After you have studied *Reading Between the Lines* on pp. 76–77, answer the following questions:

a. What happened to the price of oil between 2004 and 2005?

b. Why did the supply-side event reported in the news article have almost no effect on the supply of oil?

c. Why did the demand for oil increase in 2005?

d. Why did the equilibrium quantity of oil increase in 2005?

e. What might eventually decrease the demand for oil and lower its equilibrium price?

WEB EXERCISES

Use the links on myeconlab to work the following exercises.

1. Obtain data on the prices and quantities of wheat.

a. Make a figure similar to Fig. 3.7 on p. 70 to illustrate the market for wheat since 2001.

b. Show the changes in demand and supply and the changes in the quantity demanded and the quantity supplied that are consistent with the price and quantity data.

2. Obtain data on the price of oil.

a. Describe how the price of oil has changed over the past five years.

b. Draw a demand-supply graph to explain what happens to the price when there is an increase or a decrease in supply and no change in demand.

c. What do you predict would happen to the price of oil if a new drilling technology permitted deeper ocean sources to be used?

d. What do you predict would happen to the price of oil if a clean and safe nuclear technology were developed?

e. What do you predict would happen to the price of oil if automobiles were powered by batteries instead of by internal combustion engines?

Elasticity

CHAPTER 4

Tough Times in the Recording Industry

The recording industry is operating in tough times. Faced with the alternatives of paying $12 for a CD or nothing for a download, more and more people are choosing to download. This activity is an example of a conflict between self-interest and the social interest. If artists and recording companies don't get rewarded for their work, the amount of recorded music available will dry up.

Some CD producers are trying to combat the problem by slashing the price of a CD. Will this strategy work? Can lower-priced CDs beat downloads, bring greater revenue to the CD producers and the artists whose work they sell, and help to promote the social interest?

◆ In this chapter, you will learn about a tool that helps us to answer this question. You will learn about the elasticities of demand and supply. At the end of the chapter, we'll return to the question confronting CD producers and see whether lower-priced CDs are the solution to the dilemma of the recorded music industry.

After studying this chapter, you will be able to

■ **Define, calculate, and explain the factors that influence the price elasticity of demand**

■ **Define, calculate, and explain the factors that influence the cross elasticity of demand and the income elasticity of demand**

■ **Define, calculate, and explain the factors that influence the elasticity of supply**

Price Elasticity of Demand

YOU KNOW THAT WHEN SUPPLY INCREASES, THE equilibrium price falls and the equilibrium quantity increases. But does the price fall by a large amount and the quantity increase by a little? Or does the price barely fall and the quantity increase by a large amount?

The answer depends on the responsiveness of the quantity demanded to a change in price. You can see why by studying Fig. 4.1, which shows two possible scenarios in a local pizza market. Figure 4.1(a) shows one scenario, and Fig. 4.1(b) shows the other.

In both cases, supply is initially S_0. In part (a), the demand for pizza is shown by the demand curve D_A. In part (b), the demand for pizza is shown by the demand curve D_B. Initially, in both cases, the price is $20 a pizza and the quantity of pizza produced and consumed is 10 pizzas an hour.

Now a large pizza franchise opens up, and the supply of pizza increases. The supply curve shifts rightward to S_1. In case (a), the price falls by an enormous $15 to $5 a pizza, and the quantity increases by only 3 to 13 pizzas an hour. In contrast, in case (b), the price falls by only $5 to $15 a pizza and the quantity increases by 7 to 17 pizzas an hour.

The different outcomes arise from differing degrees of responsiveness of the quantity demanded to a change in price. But what do we mean by responsiveness? One possible answer is slope. The slope of demand curve D_A is steeper than the slope of demand curve D_B.

In this example, we can compare the slopes of the two demand curves. But we can't always do so. The reason is that the slope of a demand curve depends on the units in which we measure the price and quantity. And we often must compare the demand curves for different goods and services that are measured in unrelated units. For example, a pizza producer might want to compare the demand for pizza with the demand for soft drinks. Which quantity demanded is more responsive to a price change? This question can't be answered by comparing the slopes of two demand curves. The units of measurement of pizza and soft drinks are unrelated. The question can be answered with a measure of responsiveness that is independent of units of measurement. Elasticity is such a measure.

The **price elasticity of demand** is a units-free measure of the responsiveness of the quantity demanded of a good to a change in its price when all other influences on buyers' plans remain the same.

FIGURE 4.1   myeconlab

How a Change in Supply Changes Price and Quantity

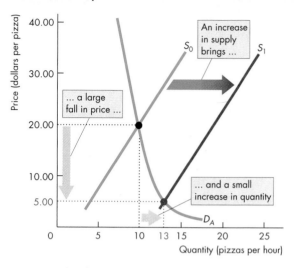

(a) Large price change and small quantity change

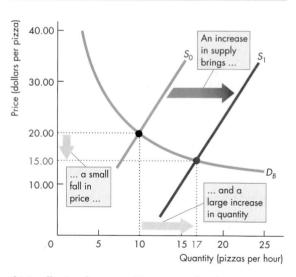

(b) Small price change and large quantity change

Initially the price is $20 a pizza and the quantity sold is 10 pizzas an hour. Then supply increases from S_0 to S_1. In part (a), the price falls by $15 to $5 a pizza, and the quantity increases by 3 to 13 pizzas an hour. In part (b), the price falls by only $5 to $15 a pizza, and the quantity increases by 7 to 17 pizzas an hour. The price change is smaller and the quantity change is larger in case (b) than in case (a). The quantity demanded is more responsive to a change in price in case (b) than in case (a).

Calculating Price Elasticity of Demand

We calculate the *price elasticity of demand* by using the formula:

$$\text{Price elasticity of demand} = \frac{\text{Percentage change in quantity demanded}}{\text{Percentage change in price}}.$$

To use this formula, we need to know the quantities demanded at different prices when all other influences on buyers' plans remain the same. Suppose we have the data on prices and quantities demanded of pizza and we calculate the price elasticity of demand for pizza.

Figure 4.2 zooms in on the demand curve for pizza and shows how the quantity demanded responds to a small change in price. Initially, the price is $20.50 a pizza and 9 pizzas an hour are sold—the original point in the figure. The price then falls to $19.50 a pizza, and the quantity demanded increases to 11 pizzas an hour—the new point in the figure. When the price falls by $1 a pizza, the quantity demanded increases by 2 pizzas an hour.

To calculate the price elasticity of demand, we express the changes in price and quantity demanded as percentages of the *average price* and the *average quantity*. By using the average price and average quantity, we calculate the elasticity at a point on the demand curve midway between the original point and the new point. The original price is $20.50 and the new price is $19.50, so the average price is $20. The $1 price decrease is 5 percent of the average price. That is,

$$\Delta P/P_{ave} = (\$1/\$20) \times 100 = 5\%.$$

The original quantity demanded is 9 pizzas and the new quantity demanded is 11 pizzas, so the average quantity demanded is 10 pizzas. The 2 pizza increase in the quantity demanded is 20 percent of the average quantity. That is,

$$\Delta Q/Q_{ave} = (2/10) \times 100 = 20\%.$$

So the price elasticity of demand, which is the percentage change in the quantity demanded (20 percent) divided by the percentage change in price (5 percent) is 4. That is,

$$\text{Price elasticity of demand} = \frac{\%\Delta Q}{\%\Delta P}$$

$$= \frac{20\%}{5\%} = 4.$$

FIGURE 4.2

Calculating the Elasticity of Demand

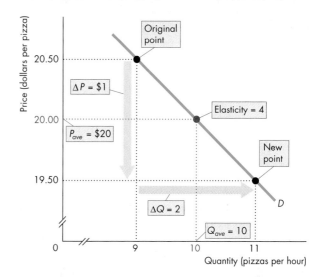

The elasticity of demand is calculated by using the formula:*

$$\text{Price elasticity of demand} = \frac{\text{Percentage change in quantity demanded}}{\text{Percentage change in price}}$$

$$= \frac{\%\Delta Q}{\%\Delta P}$$

$$= \frac{\Delta Q/Q_{ave}}{\Delta P/P_{ave}}$$

$$= \frac{2/10}{1/20}$$

$$= 4.$$

This calculation measures the elasticity at an average price of $20 a pizza and an average quantity of 10 pizzas an hour.

*In the formula, the Greek letter delta (Δ) stands for "change in" and %Δ stands for "percentage change in."

Average Price and Quantity Notice that we use the *average* price and *average* quantity. We do this because it gives the most precise measurement of elasticity—at the midpoint between the original price and the new price. If the price falls from $20.50 to $19.50, the $1 price change is 4.9 percent of $20.50. The 2 pizza change in quantity is 22.2 percent of 9 pizzas, the original quantity. So if we use these numbers, the price elasticity of demand is 22.2 divided by 4.9, which equals 4.5. If the price rises from $19.50 to $20.50, the $1 price change is 5.1 percent of $19.50. The 2 pizza change in quantity is 18.2 percent of 11 pizzas, the original quantity. So if we use these numbers, the price elasticity of demand is 18.2 divided by 5.1, which equals 3.6. By using percentages of the *average* price and *average* quantity, we get the same value for the elasticity regardless of whether the price falls from $20.50 to $19.50 or rises from $19.50 to $20.50.

Percentages and Proportions Elasticity is the ratio of two percentage changes. So when we divide one percentage change by another, the 100s cancel. A percentage change is a *proportionate* change multiplied by 100. The proportionate change in price is $\Delta P/P_{ave}$, and the proportionate change in quantity demanded is $\Delta Q/Q_{ave}$. So if we divide $\Delta Q/Q_{ave}$ by $\Delta P/P_{ave}$ we get the same answer as we get by using percentage changes.

A Units-Free Measure Now that you've calculated a price elasticity of demand, you can see why it is a *units-free measure*. Elasticity is a units-free measure because the percentage change in each variable is independent of the units in which the variable is measured. And the ratio of the two percentages is a number without units.

Minus Sign and Elasticity When the price of a good *rises*, the quantity demanded *decreases* along the demand curve. Because a *positive* change in price brings a *negative* change in the quantity demanded, the price elasticity of demand is a negative number. But it is the magnitude, or *absolute value*, of the price elasticity of demand that tells us how responsive—how elastic—demand is. To compare price elasticities of demand, we use the magnitude of the elasticity and ignore the minus sign.

Inelastic and Elastic Demand

Figure 4.3 shows three demand curves that cover the entire range of possible elasticities of demand. In Fig. 4.3(a), the quantity demanded is constant regardless of the price. If the quantity demanded remains constant when the price changes, then the price elasticity of demand is zero and the good is said to have a **perfectly inelastic demand**. One good that has a very low price elasticity of demand (perhaps zero over some price range) is insulin. Insulin is of such importance to some diabetics that if the price rises or falls, they do not change the quantity they buy.

If the percentage change in the quantity demanded equals the percentage change in price, then the price elasticity equals 1 and the good is said to have a **unit elastic demand**. The demand in Fig. 4.3(b) is an example of unit elastic demand.

Between the cases shown in Fig. 4.3(a) and Fig. 4.3(b) is the general case in which the percentage change in the quantity demanded is less than the percentage change in price. In this case, the price

FIGURE 4.3
Inelastic and Elastic Demand

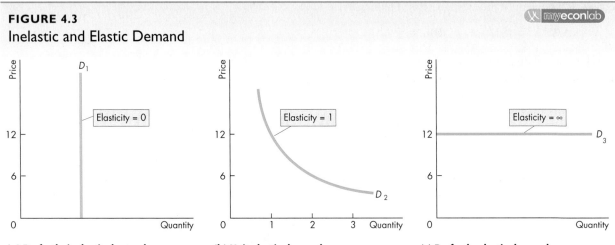

(a) Perfectly inelastic demand   **(b) Unit elastic demand**   **(c) Perfectly elastic demand**

Each demand illustrated here has a constant elasticity. The demand curve in part (a) illustrates the demand for a good that has a zero elasticity of demand. The demand curve in part (b) illustrates the demand for a good with a unit elasticity of demand. And the demand curve in part (c) illustrates the demand for a good with an infinite elasticity of demand.

elasticity of demand is between zero and 1 and the good is said to have an **inelastic demand**. Food and housing are examples of goods with inelastic demand.

If the quantity demanded changes by an infinitely large percentage in response to a tiny price change, then the price elasticity of demand is infinity and the good is said to have a **perfectly elastic demand**. Figure 4.3(c) shows a perfectly elastic demand. An example of a good that has a very high elasticity of demand (almost infinite) is a soft drink from two campus machines located side by side. If the two machines offer the same soft drinks for the same price, some people buy from one machine and some from the other. But if one machine's price is higher than the other's, by even a small amount, no one will buy from the machine with the higher price. Soft drinks from the two machines are perfect substitutes.

Between the cases in Fig. 4.3(b) and Fig. 4.3(c) is the general case in which the percentage change in the quantity demanded exceeds the percentage change in price. In this case, the price elasticity of demand is greater than 1 and the good is said to have an **elastic demand**. Automobiles and furniture are examples of goods that have elastic demand.

Elasticity Along a Straight-Line Demand Curve

Elasticity and slope are not the same, but they are related. To understand how they are related, let's look at elasticity along a straight-line demand curve—a demand curve that has a constant slope.

Figure 4.4 illustrates the calculation of elasticity along a straight-line demand curve. First, suppose the price falls from $25 to $15 a pizza. The quantity demanded increases from zero to 20 pizzas an hour. The average price is $20 a pizza, and the average quantity is 10 pizzas. So

$$\text{Price elasticity of demand} = \frac{\Delta Q/Q_{ave}}{\Delta P/P_{ave}}$$

$$= \frac{20/10}{10/20}$$

$$= 4.$$

That is, the price elasticity of demand at an average price of $20 is 4.

Next, suppose that the price falls from $15 to $10 a pizza. The quantity demanded increases from 20 to 30 pizzas an hour. The average price is now $12.50 a

pizza, and the average quantity is 25 pizzas an hour. So

$$\text{Price elasticity of demand} = \frac{10/25}{5/12.50}$$

$$= 1.$$

That is, the price elasticity of demand at an average price of $12.50 a pizza is 1.

Finally, suppose that the price falls from $10 to zero. The quantity demanded increases from 30 to 50 pizzas an hour. The average price is now $5 and the average quantity is 40 pizzas an hour. So

$$\text{Price elasticity of demand} = \frac{20/40}{10/5}$$

$$= 1/4.$$

That is, the price elasticity of demand at an average price of $5 a pizza is 1/4.

You've now seen how elasticity changes along a straight-line demand curve. At the midpoint of the curve, demand is unit elastic. Above the midpoint, demand is elastic. Below the midpoint, demand is inelastic.

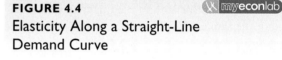

FIGURE 4.4
Elasticity Along a Straight-Line Demand Curve

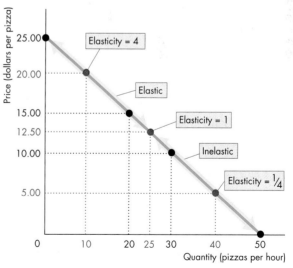

On a straight-line demand curve, elasticity decreases as the price falls and the quantity demanded increases. Demand is unit elastic at the midpoint of the demand curve (elasticity is 1). Above the midpoint, demand is elastic; below the midpoint, demand is inelastic.

Total Revenue and Elasticity

The **total revenue** from the sale of a good equals the price of the good multiplied by the quantity sold. When a price changes, total revenue also changes. But a rise in price does not always increase total revenue. The change in total revenue depends on the elasticity of demand in the following way:

- If demand is elastic, a 1 percent price cut increases the quantity sold by more than 1 percent and total revenue increases.
- If demand is inelastic, a 1 percent price cut increases the quantity sold by less than 1 percent and total revenue decreases.
- If demand is unit elastic, a 1 percent price cut increases the quantity sold by 1 percent and so total revenue does not change.

Figure 4.5 shows how we can use this relationship between elasticity and total revenue to estimate elasticity using the total revenue test. The **total revenue test** is a method of estimating the price elasticity of demand by observing the change in total revenue that results from a change in the price, when all other influences on the quantity sold remain the same.

- If a price cut increases total revenue, demand is elastic.
- If a price cut decreases total revenue, demand is inelastic.
- If a price cut leaves total revenue unchanged, demand is unit elastic.

In Fig. 4.5(a), over the price range from $25 to $12.50, demand is elastic. Over the price range from $12.50 to zero, demand is inelastic. At a price of $12.50, demand is unit elastic.

Figure 4.5(b) shows total revenue. At a price of $25, the quantity sold is zero, so total revenue is zero. At a price of zero, the quantity demanded is 50 pizzas an hour and total revenue is again zero. A price cut in the elastic range brings an increase in total revenue—the percentage increase in the quantity demanded is greater than the percentage decrease in price. A price cut in the inelastic range brings a decrease in total revenue—the percentage increase in the quantity demanded is less than the percentage decrease in price. At unit elasticity, total revenue is at a maximum.

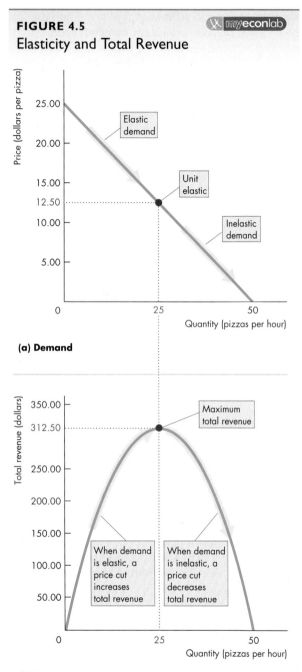

FIGURE 4.5
Elasticity and Total Revenue

(a) Demand

(b) Total revenue

When demand is elastic, in the price range from $25 to $12.50, a decrease in price (part a) brings an increase in total revenue (part b). When demand is inelastic, in the price range from $12.50 to zero, a decrease in price (part a) brings a decrease in total revenue (part b). When demand is unit elastic, at a price of $12.50 (part a), total revenue is at a maximum (part b).

Your Expenditure and Your Elasticity

When a price changes, the change in your expenditure on the good depends on *your* elasticity of demand.

- If your demand is elastic, a 1 percent price cut increases the quantity you buy by more than 1 percent and your expenditure on the item increases.
- If your demand is inelastic, a 1 percent price cut increases the quantity you buy by less than 1 percent and your expenditure on the item decreases.
- If your demand is unit elastic, a 1 percent price cut increases the quantity you buy by 1 percent and your expenditure on the item does not change.

So if you spend more on an item when its price falls, your demand for that item is elastic; if you spend the same amount, your demand is unit elastic; and if you spend less, your demand is inelastic.

The Factors That Influence the Elasticity of Demand

Table 4.1 lists some estimates of actual elasticities in the real world. You can see that these real-world elasticities of demand range from 1.52 for metals, the item with the most elastic demand in the table, to 0.05 for oil, the item with the most inelastic demand in the table. What makes the demand for some goods elastic and the demand for others inelastic?

The magnitude of the elasticity of demand depends on:

- The closeness of substitutes
- The proportion of income spent on the good
- The time elapsed since a price change

Closeness of Substitutes The closer the substitutes for a good or service, the more elastic is the demand for it. For example, oil from which we make gasoline has substitutes but none that are currently very close (imagine a steam-driven, coal-fuelled car). So the demand for oil is inelastic. Plastics are close substitutes for metals, so the demand for metals is elastic.

The degree of substitutability between two goods also depends on how narrowly (or broadly) we define them. For example, the elasticity of demand for meat is low, but the elasticity of demand for beef or pork is high. The elasticity of demand for personal computers is low, but the elasticity of demand for a Dell, IBM, or Hewlett-Packard computer is high.

In everyday language we call some goods, such as food and housing, *necessities* and other goods, such as exotic vacations, *luxuries*. A necessity is a good that

TABLE 4.1   Some Real-World Price Elasticities of Demand

Good or Service	Elasticity
Elastic Demand	
Metals	1.52
Electrical engineering products	1.39
Mechanical engineering products	1.30
Furniture	1.26
Motor vehicles	1.14
Instrument engineering products	1.10
Professional services	1.09
Transportation services	1.03
Inelastic Demand	
Gas, electricity, and water	0.92
Chemicals	0.89
Drinks (all types)	0.78
Clothing	0.64
Tobacco	0.61
Banking and insurance services	0.56
Housing services	0.55
Agricultural and fish products	0.42
Books, magazines, and newspapers	0.34
Food	0.12
Oil	0.05

Sources: Ahsan Mansur and John Whalley, "Numerical Specification of Applied General Equilibrium Models: Estimation, Calibration, and Data," in *Applied General Equilibrium Analysis*, eds. Herbert E. Scarf and John B. Shoven (New York: Cambridge University Press, 1984), 109; and Henri Theil, Ching-Fan Chung, and James L. Seale, Jr., *Advances in Econometrics, Supplement I, 1989, International Evidence on Consumption Patterns* (Greenwich, Conn.: JAI Press Inc., 1989), and Geoffrey Heal, Columbia University, Web site.

has poor substitutes and that is crucial for our well-being. So generally, a necessity has an inelastic demand. In Table 4.1, food and oil might be classified as necessities.

A luxury is a good that usually has many substitutes, one of which is not buying it. So a luxury generally has an elastic demand. In Table 4.1, furniture and motor vehicles might be classified as luxuries.

Proportion of Income Spent on the Good Other things remaining the same, the greater the proportion of income spent on a good, the more elastic is the demand for it.

Think about your own elasticity of demand for chewing gum and housing. If the price of chewing gum doubles, you consume almost as much gum as before. Your demand for gum is inelastic. If apartment rents double, you shriek and look for more students to share accommodation with you. Your demand for housing is more elastic than your demand for gum. Why the difference? Housing takes a large proportion of your budget, and gum takes only a tiny proportion. You don't like either price increase, but you hardly notice the higher price of gum, while the higher rent puts your budget under severe strain.

Figure 4.6 shows the proportion of income spent on food and the price elasticity of demand for food in 10 countries. This figure confirms the general tendency we have just described. The larger the proportion of income spent on food, the larger is the price elasticity of demand for food. For example, in Tanzania, a nation where 62 percent of income is spent on food, the price elasticity of demand for food is 0.77. In contrast, in Canada, where 14 percent of income is spent on food, the price elasticity of demand for food is 0.13.

Time Elapsed Since Price Change The longer the time that has elapsed since a price change, the more elastic is demand. When the price of oil increased by 400 percent during the 1970s, people barely changed the quantity of oil and gasoline they consumed. But gradually, as more efficient auto and airplane engines were developed, the quantity consumed decreased. The demand for oil has become more elastic as more time has elapsed since the huge price hike. Similarly, when the price of a PC fell, the quantity of PCs demanded increased only slightly at first. But as more people have become better informed about the variety of ways of using a PC, the quantity of PCs bought has increased sharply. The demand for PCs has become more elastic.

FIGURE 4.6   myeconlab

Price Elasticities in 10 Countries

As income increases and the proportion of income spent on food decreases, the demand for food becomes less elastic.

Source of data: Henri Theil, Ching-Fan Chung, and James L. Seale, Jr., *Advances in Econometrics, Supplement 1, 1989, International Evidence on Consumption Patterns* (Greenwich, Conn.: JAI Press, Inc., 1989).

REVIEW QUIZ

1 Why do we need a units-free measure of the responsiveness of the quantity demanded of a good or service to a change in its price?
2 Can you define and calculate the price elasticity of demand?
3 Why, when we calculate the price elasticity of demand, do we express the change in price as a percentage of the *average* price and the change in quantity as a percentage of the *average* quantity?
4 What is the total revenue test and why does it work?
5 What are the main influences on the elasticity of demand that make the demand for some goods elastic and the demand for other goods inelastic?
6 Why is the demand for a luxury generally more elastic than the demand for a necessity?

myeconlab   **Study Plan 4.1**

You've now completed your study of the *price* elasticity of demand. Two other elasticity concepts tell us about the effects of other influences on demand. Let's look at these other elasticities of demand.

More Elasticities of Demand

BACK AT THE PIZZERIA, YOU ARE TRYING TO WORK out how a price cut by the burger shop next door will affect the demand for your pizza. You know that pizzas and burgers are substitutes. And you know that when the price of a substitute for pizza falls, the demand for pizza decreases. But by how much?

You also know that pizza and soft drinks are complements. And you know that if the price of a complement of pizza falls, the demand for pizza increases. So you wonder whether you might keep your customers by cutting the price you charge for soft drinks. But again by how much?

To answer these questions, you need to calculate the cross elasticity of demand. Let's examine this elasticity measure.

Cross Elasticity of Demand

We measure the influence of a change in the price of a substitute or complement by using the concept of the cross elasticity of demand. The **cross elasticity of demand** is a measure of the responsiveness of the demand for a good to a change in the price of a substitute or complement, other things remaining the same. We calculate the *cross elasticity of demand* by using the formula:

$$\text{Cross elasticity of demand} = \frac{\text{Percentage change in quantity demanded}}{\text{Percentage change in price of a substitute or complement}}.$$

The cross elasticity of demand can be positive or negative. It is *positive* for a *substitute* and *negative* for a *complement*.

Substitutes Suppose that the price of pizza is constant and 9 pizzas an hour are sold. Then the price of a burger rises from $1.50 to $2.50. No other influence on buying plans changes and the quantity of pizzas sold increases to 11 an hour.

The change in the quantity demanded is +2 pizzas—the new quantity, 11 pizzas, minus the original quantity, 9 pizzas. The average quantity is 10 pizzas. So the quantity of pizzas demanded increases by 20 percent (+20). That is,

$$\Delta Q/Q_{ave} = (+2/10) \times 100 = +20\%.$$

The change in the price of a burger, a substitute for pizza, is +$1—the new price, $2.50, minus the original price, $1.50. The average price is $2 a burger. So the price of a burger rises by 50 percent (+50). That is,

$$\Delta P/P_{ave} = (+\$1/\$2) \times 100 = +50\%.$$

So the cross elasticity of demand for pizza with respect to the price of a burger is

$$\frac{+20\%}{+50\%} = 0.4.$$

Figure 4.7 illustrates the cross elasticity of demand. Pizza and burgers are substitutes. Because they are substitutes, when the price of a burger rises, the demand for pizza increases. The demand curve for pizza shifts rightward from D_0 to D_1. Because a *rise* in the price of a burger brings an *increase* in the demand for pizza, the cross elasticity of demand for pizza with respect to the price of a burger is *positive*. Both the price and the quantity change in the same direction.

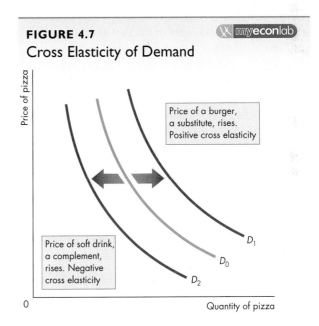

FIGURE 4.7
Cross Elasticity of Demand

A burger is a *substitute* for pizza. When the price of a burger rises, the demand for pizza increases and the demand curve for pizza shifts rightward from D_0 to D_1. The cross elasticity of the demand is *positive*.

Soft drinks are a *complement* of pizza. When the price of soft drinks rises, the demand for pizza decreases and the demand curve for pizza shifts leftward from D_0 to D_2. The cross elasticity of the demand is *negative*.

Complements Now suppose that the price of pizza is constant and 11 pizzas an hour are sold. Then the price of a soft drink rises from $1.50 to $2.50. No other influence on buying plans changes and the quantity of pizzas sold falls to 9 an hour.

The change in the quantity demanded is the opposite of what we've just calculated: The quantity of pizzas demanded decreases by 20 percent (–20).

The change in the price of a soft drink, a complement of pizza, is the same as the percentage change in the price of a burger that we've just calculated: The price rises by 50 percent (+50). So the cross elasticity of demand for pizza with respect to the price of a soft drink is

$$\frac{-20\%}{+50\%} = -0.4.$$

Because pizza and soft drinks are complements, when the price of a soft drink rises, the demand for pizza decreases. The demand curve for pizza shifts leftward from D_0 to D_2. Because a *rise* in the price of a soft drink brings a *decrease* in the demand for pizza, the cross elasticity of demand for pizza with respect to the price of a soft drink is *negative*. The price and quantity change in *opposite* directions.

The magnitude of the cross elasticity of demand determines how far the demand curve shifts. The larger the cross elasticity (absolute value), the greater is the change in demand and the larger is the shift in the demand curve.

If two items are very close substitutes, such as two brands of spring water, the cross elasticity is large. If two items are close complements, such as movies and popcorn, the cross elasticity is large.

If two items are somewhat unrelated to each other, such as newspapers and orange juice, the cross elasticity is small—perhaps even zero.

Income Elasticity of Demand

Suppose the economy is expanding and people are enjoying rising incomes. This prosperity is bringing an increase in the demand for most types of goods and services. But by how much will the demand for pizza increase? The answer depends on the **income elasticity of demand**, which is a measure of the responsiveness of the demand for a good or service to a change in income, other things remaining the same.

The income elasticity of demand is calculated by using the formula:

$$\text{Income elasticity of demand} = \frac{\text{Percentage change in quantity demanded}}{\text{Percentage change in income}}.$$

Income elasticities of demand can be positive or negative and fall into three interesting ranges:

- Greater than 1 (*normal* good, income elastic)
- Positive and less than 1 (*normal* good, income inelastic)
- Negative (*inferior* good)

Income Elastic Demand Suppose that the price of pizza is constant and 9 pizzas an hour are sold. Then incomes rise from $975 to $1,025 a week. No other influence on buying plans changes and the quantity of pizzas sold increases to 11 an hour.

The change in the quantity demanded is +2 pizzas. The average quantity is 10 pizzas, so the quantity demanded increases by 20 percent. The change in income is +$50 and the average income is $1,000, so incomes increase by 5 percent. The income elasticity of demand for pizza is

$$\frac{20\%}{5\%} = 4.$$

As income increases, the quantity of pizza demanded increases faster than income. The demand for pizza is income elastic. Other goods in this category include ocean cruises, international travel, jewellery, and works of art.

Income Inelastic Demand If the percentage increase in the quantity demanded is less than the percentage increase in income, the income elasticity of demand is positive and less than 1. In this case, the quantity demanded increases as income increases, but the quantity demanded does not increase as quickly as income increases. The demand for the good is income inelastic. Goods in this category include food, clothing, newspapers, and magazines.

Inferior Goods If the quantity demanded of a good decreases when income increases, the income elasticity of demand is negative. Goods in this category include small motorcycles, potatoes, and rice. Low-income consumers buy most of these goods.

Real-World Income Elasticities of Demand

Table 4.2 shows estimates of some real-world income elasticities of demand. The demand for a necessity such as food or clothing is income inelastic, while the demand for a luxury such as transportation, which includes airline and foreign travel, is income elastic.

But what is a necessity and what is a luxury depends on the level of income. For people with a low income, food and clothing can be luxuries. So the *level* of income has a big effect on income elasticities of demand. Figure 4.8 shows this effect on the income elasticity of demand for food in 10 countries. In countries with low incomes, such as Tanzania and India, the income elasticity of demand for food is high. In countries with high incomes, such as Canada, the income elasticity of demand for food is low.

TABLE 4.2 Some Real-World Income Elasticities of Demand

Good or Service	Elasticity
Elastic Demand	
Airline travel	5.82
Movies	3.41
Foreign travel	3.08
Electricity	1.94
Restaurant meals	1.61
Local buses and trains	1.38
Haircuts	1.36
Automobiles	1.07
Inelastic Demand	
Tobacco	0.86
Alcoholic drinks	0.62
Furniture	0.53
Clothing	0.51
Newspapers and magazines	0.38
Telephone	0.32
Food	0.14

Sources: H.S. Houthakker and Lester D. Taylor, *Consumer Demand in the United States* (Cambridge, Mass.: Harvard University Press, 1970); and Henri Theil, Ching-Fan Chung, and James L. Seale, Jr., *Advances in Econometrics, Supplement 1, 1989, International Evidence on Consumption Patterns* (Greenwich, Conn.: JAI Press, Inc., 1989).

FIGURE 4.8 myeconlab
Income Elasticities in 10 Countries

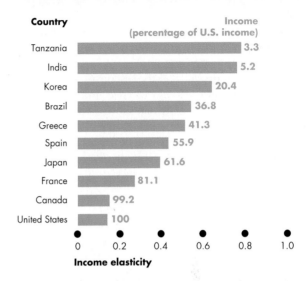

As income increases, the income elasticity of demand for food decreases. Low-income consumers spend a larger percentage of any increase in income on food than do high-income consumers.

Source of data: Henri Theil, Ching-Fan Chung, and James L. Seale, Jr., *Advances in Econometrics, Supplement 1, 1989, International Evidence on Consumption Patterns* (Greenwich, Conn.: JAI Press, Inc., 1989).

REVIEW QUIZ

1 What does the cross elasticity of demand measure?
2 What does the sign (positive versus negative) of the cross elasticity of demand tell us about the relationship between two goods?
3 What does the income elasticity of demand measure?
4 What does the sign (positive versus negative) of the income elasticity of demand tell us about a good?
5 Why does the level of income influence the magnitude of the income elasticity of demand?

myeconlab **Study Plan 4.2**

You've now completed your study of the *cross elasticity* of demand and the *income elasticity* of demand. Let's look at the other side of a market and examine the elasticity of supply.

Elasticity of Supply

YOU KNOW THAT WHEN DEMAND INCREASES, THE price rises and the quantity increases. But does the price rise by a large amount and the quantity increase by a little? Or does the price barely rise and the quantity increase by a large amount?

The answer depends on the responsiveness of the quantity supplied to a change in price. You can see why by studying Fig. 4.9, which shows two possible scenarios in a local pizza market. Figure 4.9(a) shows one scenario, and Fig. 4.9(b) shows the other.

In both cases, demand is initially D_0. In part (a), the supply of pizza is shown by the supply curve S_A. In part (b), the supply of pizza is shown by the supply curve S_B. Initially, in both cases, the price is $20 a pizza and the quantity produced and consumed is 10 pizzas an hour.

Now increases in incomes and population increase the demand for pizza. The demand curve shifts rightward to D_1. In case (a), the price rises by $10 to $30 a pizza, and the quantity increases by only 3 to 13 an hour. In contrast, in case (b), the price rises by only $1 to $21 a pizza, and the quantity increases by 10 to 20 pizzas an hour.

The different outcomes arise from differing degrees of responsiveness of the quantity supplied to a change in price. We measure the degree of responsiveness by using the concept of the elasticity of supply.

Calculating the Elasticity of Supply

The **elasticity of supply** measures the responsiveness of the quantity supplied to a change in the price of a good when all other influences on selling plans remain the same. It is calculated by using the formula:

$$\text{Elasticity of supply} = \frac{\text{Percentage change in quantity supplied}}{\text{Percentage change in price}}.$$

We use the same method that you learned when you studied the elasticity of demand. (Refer back to p. 85 to check this method.) Let's calculate the elasticity of supply along the supply curves in Fig. 4.9.

In Fig. 4.9(a), when the price rises from $20 to $30, the price rise is $10 and the average price is $25, so the price rises by 40 percent of the average price. The quantity increases from 10 to 13 pizzas an

FIGURE 4.9

How a Change in Demand Changes Price and Quantity

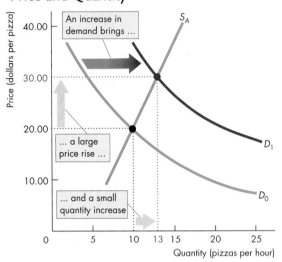

(a) Large price change and small quantity change

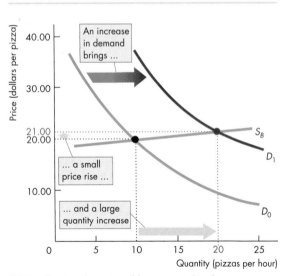

(b) Small price change and large quantity change

Initially, the price is $20 a pizza, and the quantity sold is 10 pizzas an hour. Then increases in incomes and population increase the demand for pizza. The demand curve shifts rightward to D_1. In part (a) the price rises by $10 to $30 a pizza, and the quantity increases by 3 to 13 pizzas an hour. In part (b), the price rises by only $1 to $21 a pizza, and the quantity increases by 10 to 20 pizzas an hour. The price change is smaller and the quantity change is larger in case (b) than in case (a). The quantity supplied is more responsive to a change in price in case (b) than in case (a).

hour, so the increase is 3 pizzas, the average quantity is 11.5 pizzas an hour, and the quantity increases by 26 percent. The elasticity of supply is equal to 26 percent divided by 40 percent, which equals 0.65.

In Fig. 4.9(b), when the price rises from $20 to $21, the price rise is $1 and the average price is $20.50, so the price rises by 4.9 percent of the average price. The quantity increases from 10 to 20 pizzas an hour, so the increase is 10 pizzas, the average quantity is 15 pizzas, and the quantity increases by 67 percent. The elasticity of supply is equal to 67 percent divided by 4.9 percent, which equals 13.67.

Figure 4.10 shows the range of elasticities of supply. If the quantity supplied is fixed regardless of the price, the supply curve is vertical and the elasticity of supply is zero. Supply is perfectly inelastic. This case is shown in Fig. 4.10(a). A special intermediate case is when the percentage change in price equals the percentage change in quantity. Supply is unit elastic. This case is shown in Fig. 4.10(b). No matter how steep the supply curve is, if it is linear and passes through the origin, supply is unit elastic. If there is a price at which sellers are willing to offer any quantity for sale, the supply curve is horizontal and the elasticity of supply is infinite. Supply is perfectly elastic. This case is shown in Fig. 4.10(c).

The Factors That Influence the Elasticity of Supply

The magnitude of the elasticity of supply depends on

- Resource substitution possibilities
- Time frame for the supply decision

Resource Substitution Possibilities Some goods and services can be produced only by using unique or rare productive resources. These items have a low, even perhaps a zero, elasticity of supply. Other goods and services can be produced by using commonly available resources that could be allocated to a wide variety of alternative tasks. Such items have a high elasticity of supply.

A Van Gogh painting is an example of a good with a vertical supply curve and a zero elasticity of supply. At the other extreme, wheat can be grown on land that is almost equally good for growing corn. So it is just as easy to grow wheat as corn, and the opportunity cost of wheat in terms of forgone corn is almost constant. As a result, the supply curve of wheat is almost horizontal and its elasticity of supply is very large. Similarly, when a good is produced in many different countries (for example, sugar and beef), the supply of the good is highly elastic.

FIGURE 4.10
Inelastic and Elastic Supply

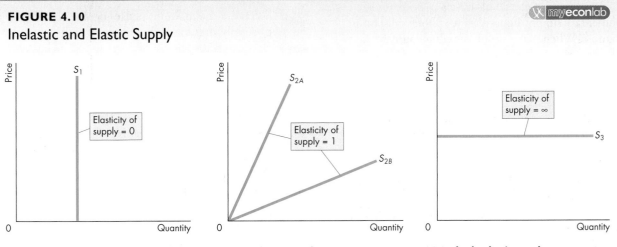

(a) Perfectly inelastic supply   **(b) Unit elastic supply**   **(c) Perfectly elastic supply**

Each supply illustrated here has a constant elasticity. The supply curve in part (a) illustrates the supply of a good that has a zero elasticity of supply. The supply curve in part (b) illustrates the supply for a good with a unit elasticity of supply. All linear supply curves that pass through the origin illustrate supplies that are unit elastic. The supply curve in part (c) illustrates the supply for a good with an infinite elasticity of supply.

The supply of most goods and services lies between these two extremes. The quantity produced can be increased but only by incurring a higher cost. If a higher price is offered, the quantity supplied increases. Such goods and services have an elasticity of supply between zero and infinity.

Time Frame for Supply Decisions To study the influence of the length of time elapsed since a price change, we distinguish three time frames of supply:

1. Momentary supply
2. Long-run supply
3. Short-run supply

When the price of a good rises or falls, the *momentary supply curve* shows the response of the quantity supplied immediately following a price change.

Some goods, such as fruits and vegetables, have a perfectly inelastic momentary supply—a vertical supply curve. The quantities supplied depend on crop-planting decisions made earlier. In the case of oranges, for example, planting decisions have to be made many years in advance of the crop being available. The momentary supply curve is vertical because, on a given day, no matter what the price of oranges, producers cannot change their output. They have picked, packed, and shipped their crop to market, and the quantity available for that day is fixed.

In contrast, some goods have a perfectly elastic momentary supply. Long-distance phone calls are an example. When many people simultaneously make a call, there is a big surge in the demand for telephone cables, computer switching, and satellite time, and the quantity bought increases. But the price remains constant. Long-distance carriers monitor fluctuations in demand and reroute calls to ensure that the quantity supplied equals the quantity demanded without changing the price.

The *long-run supply curve* shows the response of the quantity supplied to a change in price after all the technologically possible ways of adjusting supply have been exploited. In the case of oranges, the long run is the time it takes new plantings to grow to full maturity—about 15 years. In some cases, the long-run adjustment occurs only after a completely new production plant has been built and workers have been trained to operate it—typically a process that might take several years.

The *short-run supply curve* shows how the quantity supplied responds to a price change when only *some* of the technologically possible adjustments to production have been made. The short-run response to a price change is a sequence of adjustments. The first adjustment that is usually made is in the amount of labour employed. To increase output in the short run, firms work their labour force overtime and perhaps hire additional workers. To decrease their output in the short run, firms either lay off workers or reduce their hours of work. With the passage of time, firms can make additional adjustments, perhaps training additional workers or buying additional tools and other equipment.

The short-run supply curve slopes upward because producers can take actions quite quickly to change the quantity supplied in response to a price change. For example, if the price of oranges falls, growers can stop picking and leave oranges to rot on the trees. Or if the price rises, they can use more fertilizer and improved irrigation to increase the yields of their existing trees. In the long run, they can plant more trees and increase the quantity supplied even more in response to a given price rise.

REVIEW QUIZ

1 Why do we need to measure the responsiveness of the quantity supplied of a good or service to a change in its price?

2 Can you define and calculate the elasticity of supply?

3 What are the main influences on the elasticity of supply that make the supply of some goods elastic and the supply of other goods inelastic?

4 Can you provide examples of goods or services whose elasticities of supply are (a) zero, (b) greater than zero but less than infinity, and (c) infinity?

5 How does the time frame over which a supply decision is made influence the elasticity of supply?

myeconlab **Study Plan 4.3**

◆ You have now learned about the elasticities of demand and supply. Table 4.3 summarizes all the elasticities that you've met in this chapter. In the next chapter, we study the efficiency of competitive markets. But before doing that, *Reading Between the Lines* on pp. 98–99 puts the elasticity of demand to work and looks at the dilemma facing the recorded music industry that we described at the beginning of this chapter.

TABLE 4.3   A Compact Glossary of Elasticities

Price Elasticities of Demand

A relationship is described as	When its magnitude is	Which means that
Perfectly elastic or infinitely elastic	Infinity	The smallest possible increase in price causes an infinitely large decrease in the quantity demanded*
Elastic	Less than infinity but greater than 1	The percentage decrease in the quantity demanded exceeds the percentage increase in price
Unit elastic	1	The percentage decrease in the quantity demanded equals the percentage increase in price
Inelastic	Greater than zero but less than 1	The percentage decrease in the quantity demanded is less than the percentage increase in price
Perfectly inelastic or completely inelastic	Zero	The quantity demanded is the same at all prices

Cross Elasticities of Demand

A relationship is described as	When its value is	Which means that
Perfect substitutes	Infinity	The smallest possible increase in the price of one good causes an infinitely large increase in the quantity demanded of the other good
Substitutes	Positive, less than infinity	If the price of one good increases, the quantity demanded of the other good also increases
Independent	Zero	If the price of one good increases, the quantity demanded of the other good remains the same
Complements	Less than zero	If the price of one good increases, the quantity demanded of the other good decreases

Income Elasticities of Demand

A relationship is described as	When its value is	Which means that
Income elastic (normal good)	Greater than 1	The percentage increase in the quantity demanded is greater than the percentage increase in income
Income inelastic (normal good)	Less than 1 but greater than zero	The percentage increase in the quantity demanded is less than the percentage increase in income
Negative income elastic (inferior good)	Less than zero	When income increases, quantity demanded decreases

Elasticities of Supply

A relationship is described as	When its magnitude is	Which means that
Perfectly elastic	Infinity	The smallest possible increase in price causes an infinitely large increase in the quantity supplied
Elastic	Less than infinity but greater than 1	The percentage increase in the quantity supplied exceeds the percentage increase in the price
Inelastic	Greater than zero but less than 1	The percentage increase in the quantity supplied is less than the percentage increase in the price
Perfectly inelastic	Zero	The quantity supplied is the same at all prices

*In each description, the directions of change may be reversed. For example, in this case, the smallest possible *decrease* in price causes an infinitely large *increase* in the quantity demanded.

Elasticity of Demand for CDs

GLOBE AND MAIL, SEPTEMBER 4, 2003

Music giant chops prices to combat downloads

North American record giant Universal Music is slashing prices on its compact discs in a desperate bid to get music fans back into stores and away from downloading music for free on their home computers.

Universal said yesterday it will chop prices starting in October, so that CDs that currently carry a suggested retail price in Canada of $19.98, $20.98 and $21.98 will sell for no more than $14.98.

Will consumers take the bait?

"Don't be too sure," said Josh Bernoff, an analyst at Forrester Research Inc. in Boston. "I think you'll see unit sales go up as prices go down, but this will not change the slide away from CDs towards downloading."

Jason Goorwah, a 17-year-old student in Toronto, agrees. "I've stopped buying a lot of CDs," he said, adding that he prefers to download music onto his MP3 player.

Mr. Goorwah said cheaper prices might persuade him to buy a few extra CDs, but a $5 saving isn't enough to lure him into record stores more often. ...

The new pricing policy will affect Universal's new releases, its top hits and the company's back catalogue. ...

Music sales have dropped 20 per cent in Canada in the past three years, a loss of about $250-million to the industry. ...

Universal Music Canada president Randy Lennox acknowledged that record companies must change their approach. "The industry needs to rethink its business model, and we at Universal are trying to lead that particular charge," he said.

He predicted that the price cut could boost CD sales by as much as 30 per cent.

Mr. Lennox wouldn't say how much the change will cost his company, but the hope is that increased volume will outweigh the decreased margins. ...

Reprinted with permission from *The Globe and Mail.*

Essence of the Story

■ The sale of music CDs has fallen 20 percent in Canada in the past three years and decreased industry total revenue by $250 million.

■ In a bid to combat lower revenue, Universal is slashing CD prices from around $21 to under $15.

■ An analyst says that more CDs will be sold at the lower price, but the move towards music downloading will not stop.

■ Universal Music Canada president Randy Lennox says that the price cut could increase the quantity of CDs sold by as much as 30 percent.

Economic Analysis

■ This news article is about the market for recorded music in Canada, but the problem that it describes applies everywhere.

■ The news article provides enough information for us to find the point on the demand curve for CDs before the price cut.

■ At an average price of $21 per CD, about 48 million CDs a year were demanded.

■ The price is in the news article. To find the quantity, first use the reported fact that $250 million of total revenue represents 20 percent of total revenue three years ago.

■ Total revenue three years ago must have been $250 million ÷ 0.2 = $1.25 billion, so total revenue in 2003 was $1 billion.

■ With total revenue of $1 billion and a price of $21 a CD, the number of CDs sold is a little less than 48 million. This is the quantity demanded at $21 a CD.

■ The news article also provides enough information for us to find what Universal Music thinks is a second point on the demand curve.

■ Randy Lennox says that the quantity of CDs sold will increase by 30 percent if the price is cut to $15 a CD.

■ If the quantity of CDs demanded increases by 30 percent, it becomes 62 million.

■ Figure 1 shows the demand curve for CDs based on the information that we've pulled from the news article.

■ We can calculate the elasticity of demand at the midpoint of the two points identified.

■ The quantity demanded increases by 14 million CDs and the average quantity is 55 million CDs, so the quantity demanded increases by 25.4 percent.

■ The price falls by $6 and the average price is $18 a CD, so the percentage fall in price is 33.3 percent.

■ The price elasticity of demand—percentage change in quantity demanded divided by percentage change in the price—is 25.4 ÷ 33.3 = 0.76.

■ So, according to the information provided in the news article, Universal Music believes that the demand for CDs is inelastic.

■ When a good has an inelastic demand, a price cut *decreases* total revenue.

■ With the price cut, Universal will sell more CDs but will suffer a loss of total revenue.

■ The total revenue test confirms this conclusion. At $21 a CD, total revenue is $21 × 48 million = $1 billion. At $15 a CD, total revenue is $15 × 62 million = $930 million.

■ Because downloads and CDs are substitutes, a rise in the price of a download increases the demand for CDs.

■ So if CD producers can find a way of increasing the price of a download, they can increase the demand for CDs.

■ The amount by which the demand for CDs would increase is determined by the cross elasticity of demand between CDs and downloads.

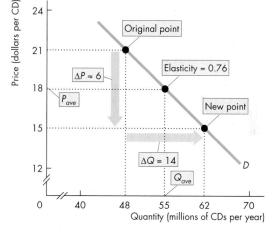

Figure 1 The market for music CDs in Canada

SUMMARY

KEY POINTS

Price Elasticity of Demand (pp. 84–90)

- Elasticity is a measure of the responsiveness of the quantity demanded of a good to a change in its price.
- Price elasticity of demand equals the percentage change in the quantity demanded divided by the percentage change in price.
- The larger the magnitude of the price elasticity of demand, the greater is the responsiveness of the quantity demanded to a given change in price.
- Price elasticity of demand depends on how easily one good serves as a substitute for another, the proportion of income spent on the good, and the length of time elapsed since the price change.
- If demand is elastic, a decrease in price leads to an increase in total revenue. If demand is unit elastic, a decrease in price leaves total revenue unchanged. And if demand is inelastic, a decrease in price leads to a decrease in total revenue.

More Elasticities of Demand (pp. 91–93)

- Cross elasticity of demand measures the responsiveness of demand for one good to a change in the price of a substitute or a complement.
- The cross elasticity of demand with respect to the price of a substitute is positive. The cross elasticity of demand with respect to the price of a complement is negative.
- Income elasticity of demand measures the responsiveness of demand to a change in income. For a normal good, the income elasticity of demand is positive. For an inferior good, the income elasticity of demand is negative.
- When the income elasticity of demand is greater than 1, the percentage of income spent on the good increases as income increases.
- When the income elasticity of demand is less than 1 but greater than zero, the percentage of income spent on the good decreases as income increases.

Elasticity of Supply (pp. 94–96)

- Elasticity of supply measures the responsiveness of the quantity supplied of a good to a change in its price.
- The elasticity of supply is usually positive and ranges between zero (vertical supply curve) and infinity (horizontal supply curve).
- Supply decisions have three time frames: momentary, long run, and short run.
- Momentary supply refers to the response of sellers to a price change at the instant that the price changes.
- Long-run supply refers to the response of sellers to a price change when all the technologically feasible adjustments in production have been made.
- Short-run supply refers to the response of sellers to a price change after some of the technologically feasible adjustments in production have been made.

KEY FIGURES AND TABLE

Figure 4.2   Calculating the Elasticity of Demand, 85
Figure 4.3   Inelastic and Elastic Demand, 86
Figure 4.4   Elasticity Along a Straight-Line Demand Curve, 87
Figure 4.5   Elasticity and Total Revenue, 88
Figure 4.7   Cross Elasticity of Demand, 91
Table 4.3   Compact Glossary of Elasticities, 97

KEY TERMS

Cross elasticity of demand, 91
Elastic demand, 87
Elasticity of supply, 94
Income elasticity of demand, 92
Inelastic demand, 87
Perfectly elastic demand, 87
Perfectly inelastic demand, 86
Price elasticity of demand, 84
Total revenue, 88
Total revenue test, 88
Unit elastic demand, 86

PROBLEMS

Go to ⓧ myeconlab for solutions to odd-numbered problems and additional exercises.

1. Rain spoils the strawberry crop. As a result, the price rises from $4 to $6 a box and the quantity demanded decreases from 1,000 to 600 boxes a week. Over this price range,
   a. What is the price elasticity of demand?
   b. Describe the demand for strawberries.

2. Good weather brings a bumper tomato crop. The price falls from $7 to $5 a basket, and the quantity demanded increases from 300 to 500 baskets a day. Over this price range,
   a. What is the price elasticity of demand?
   b. Describe the demand for tomatoes.

3. The figure shows the demand for videotape rentals.

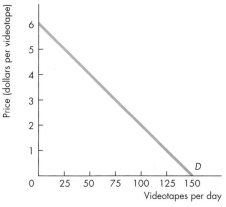

   a. Calculate the elasticity of demand for a rise in rental price from $3 to $5.
   b. At what price is the elasticity of demand equal to 1?

4. The figure shows the demand for pens.

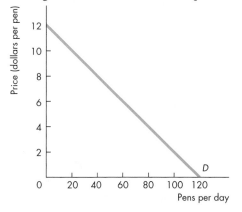

   a. Calculate the elasticity of demand for a rise in price from $6 to $10.
   b. At what prices is the elasticity of demand equal to 1, greater than 1, and less than 1?

5. If the quantity of dental services demanded increases by 10 percent when the price of dental services falls by 10 percent, is the demand for dental service inelastic, elastic, or unit elastic?

6. If the quantity of haircuts demanded decreases by 10 percent when the price of a haircut rises by 5 percent, is the demand for haircuts elastic, inelastic, or unit elastic? Explain your answer.

7. The demand schedule for computer chips is.

Price (dollars per chip)	Quantity demanded (millions of chips per year)
200	50
250	45
300	40
350	35
400	30

   a. What happens to total revenue if the price falls from $400 to $350 a chip?
   b. What happens to total revenue if the price falls from $350 to $300 a chip?
   c. At what price is total revenue at a maximum?
   d. At an average price of $350, is the demand for chips elastic or inelastic? Use the total revenue test to answer this question.

8. The demand schedule for sugar is

Price (dollars per kilogram)	Quantity demanded (millions of kilograms per year)
5	25
10	20
15	15
20	10
25	5

   a. What happens to total revenue if the price of sugar rises from $5 to $15 a kilogram?
   b. What happens to total revenue if the price rises from $15 to $25 a kilogram?
   c. At what price is total revenue at a maximum?
   d. At an average price of $20 a kilogram, is the demand for sugar elastic or inelastic? Use the total revenue test to answer this question.

9. In problem 7, at $250 a chip, is the demand for chips elastic or inelastic? Use the total revenue test to answer this question.

10. In problem 8, at $10 a kilogram, is the demand for sugar elastic or inelastic? Use the total revenue test to answer this question.

11. If a 2 percent rise in the price of orange juice decreases the quantity of orange juice demanded by 22 percent and increases the quantity of apple juice demanded by 14 percent, calculate the cross elasticity of demand between orange juice and apple juice.

12. If a 5 percent fall in the price of chicken decreases the quantity of beef demanded by 20 percent and increases the quantity of chicken demanded by 15 percent, calculate the cross elasticity of demand between chicken and beef.

13. Alex's income has increased from $3,000 to $5,000. Alex increased his consumption of bagels from 4 to 8 a month and decreased his consumption of doughnuts from 12 to 6 a month. Calculate Alex's income elasticity of demand for (a) bagels and (b) doughnuts.

14. Judy's income has increased from $13,000 to $17,000. Judy increased her demand for concert tickets by 15 percent and decreased her demand for bus rides by 10 percent. Calculate Judy's income elasticity of demand for (a) concert tickets and (b) bus rides.

15. The table gives the supply schedule for long-distance phone calls.

Price (cents per minute)	Quantity supplied (millions of minutes per day)
10	200
20	400
30	600
40	800

Calculate the elasticity of supply when
a. The price falls from 40¢ to 30¢.
b. The average price is 20¢ a minute.

16. The table gives the supply schedule for jeans.

Price (dollars per pair)	Quantity supplied (millions of pairs per year)
120	2,400
125	2,800
130	3,200
135	3,600

Calculate the elasticity of supply when
a. The price rises from $125 to $135 a pair.
b. The average price is $125 a pair.

CRITICAL THINKING

1. After you have studied *Reading Between the Lines* (pp. 98–99) on the elasticity of demand for CDs and then answer the following questions:
   a. Do you think that the demand for CDs is inelastic as implied by the numbers in the news article? Explain why or why not.
   b. If the demand for CDs is inelastic, how might the recording industry increase its total revenue?
   c. What elasticity information would you need to predict the change in the demand for CDs and music downloads over the next five years?

2. The demand for illegal drugs is estimated to be inelastic. Much of the expenditure on illegal drugs comes from crime. Assuming these statements to be correct:
   a. How will a successful campaign that decreases the supply of drugs influence the price of drugs and the amount spent on them?
   b. What will happen to the amount of crime?

WEB EXERCISES

Use the links on X myeconlab to work the following exercise.

1. a. Find the price of gasoline in the summer of 2005.
   b. Use the concepts of demand, supply, and elasticity to explain recent changes in the price of gasoline.
   c. Find the price of crude oil.
   d. Use the concepts of demand, supply, and elasticity to explain recent changes in the price of crude oil.

2. a. Find the number of litres in a barrel and the cost of crude oil in a litre of gasoline.
   b. What are the other costs that make up the total cost of a litre of gasoline?
   c. If the price of crude oil falls by 10 percent, by what percentage would you expect the price of gasoline to change, other things remaining the same?
   d. Which demand do you think is more elastic: that for crude oil or gasoline? Why?

Efficiency and Equity

CHAPTER

5

Self-Interest and the Social Interest

Every time you buy a pair of sports shoes or a textbook, fill your gas tank, download some MP3 files and burn a CD, order a pizza, check in at the airport, or even just take a shower, you express *your* view about how scarce resources should be used. You try to spend your income and your time in ways that get the most out of *your* scarce resources—you make choices that further your *self-interest*. And markets coordinate your decisions along with those of everyone else. But do markets do a good job? Do they enable us to allocate resources *efficiently* when we buy shoes, books, gasoline, music, CD-Rs, pizza, airline services, water, and other things? Could we as a *society* be better off if we spent more on some things and less on others?

The market economy generates huge incomes for some people and miserable pickings for others. For example, software sales by Microsoft have generated enough profit over the past ten years to rocket Bill Gates, one of its founders, into the position of being one of the richest people in the world. Is it *fair* that Bill Gates is so incredibly rich while others live in miserable poverty?

The social interest has the two dimensions we've just discussed—efficiency and fairness (or equity). So our central question in this chapter is: Does the market achieve an efficient and fair use of resources?

◆ At the end of the chapter, in *Reading Between the Lines,* we return to the issue that we first raised in Chapter 1 about the use of the world's water resources. Do we use markets and other arrangements that allocate the world's scarce water in the social interest?

After studying this chapter, you will be able to

■ Describe the alternative methods of allocating scarce resources

■ Distinguish between value and price and define consumer surplus

■ Distinguish between cost and price and define producer surplus

■ Explain the conditions under which markets are efficient and describe the sources of inefficiency in our economy

■ Explain the main ideas about fairness and evaluate claims that markets result in unfair outcomes

103

Resource Allocation Methods

THE GOAL OF THIS CHAPTER IS TO EVALUATE THE ability of markets to allocate resources *efficiently* and *fairly*. But to see whether the market does a good job, we must compare it with its alternatives. Resources are scarce, so they must be allocated *somehow*. And trading in markets is just one of several alternative methods.

Resources might be allocated by

- Market price
- Command
- Majority rule
- Contest
- First-come, first-served
- Lottery
- Personal characteristics
- Force

Let's briefly examine each method.

Market Price

When a market price allocates a scarce resource, the people who are willing and able to pay that price get the resource. Two kinds of people decide not to pay the market price: those who can afford to pay but choose not to buy and those who are too poor and simply can't afford to buy.

For many goods and services, distinguishing between those who choose not to buy and those who can't afford to buy doesn't matter. But for a few items, it does matter. For example, poor people can't afford to pay school fees and doctor's fees. Because poor people can't afford items that most people consider to be essential, these items are usually allocated by one of the other methods.

Command

A **command system** allocates resources by the order (command) of someone in authority. In the Canadian economy, the command system is used extensively inside firms and government departments. For example, if you have a job, most likely someone tells you what to do. Your labour is allocated to specific tasks by a command.

A command system works well in organizations in which the lines of authority and responsibility are clear and it is easy to monitor the activities being performed. But a command system works badly when the range of activities to be monitored is large and when it is easy for people to fool those in authority. The system works so badly in North Korea, where it is used extensively in place of markets, that it fails even to deliver an adequate supply of food.

Majority Rule

Majority rule allocates resources in the way that a majority of voters choose. Societies use majority rule to elect representative governments that make some of the biggest decisions. For example, majority rule decides the tax rates that end up allocating scarce resources between private use and public use. And majority rule decides how tax dollars are allocated among competing uses such as education and health care.

Majority rule works well when the decisions being made affect large numbers of people and self-interest must be suppressed to use resources most effectively.

Contest

A contest allocates resources to a winner (or a group of winners). Sporting events use this method. Mike Wier, Tiger Woods, and other golfers compete and the winner gets the biggest payoff.

But contests are more general than those in a sports arena, though we don't normally call them contests. For example, Bill Gates won a contest to provide the world's personal computer operating system.

Contests do a good job when the efforts of the "players" are hard to monitor and reward directly. By dangling the opportunity to win a big prize, people are motivated to work hard and try to become the "winner." Only a few people end up with a big prize, but many people work harder in the process of trying to win. So total production is much greater than it would be without the contest.

First-Come, First-Served

A first-come, first-served method allocates resources to those who are first in line. Many casual restaurants won't accept reservations. They use first-come, first-served to allocate their scarce tables. Highway space is allocated in this way too—the first to arrive at the on-ramp gets the road space. If too many vehicles enter the highway, the speed slows and people wait in line for some space to become available.

First-come, first-served works best when, as in the above examples, a scarce resource can serve just one user at a time in a sequence. By serving the user who arrives first, this method minimizes the time spent waiting for the resource to become free.

Lottery

Lotteries allocate resources to those who pick the winning number, draw the lucky cards, or come up lucky on some other gaming system. Provincial lotteries and casinos reallocate millions of dollars worth of goods and services every year.

But lotteries are more widespread than jackpots and roulette wheels in casinos. They are used to allocate landing slots to airlines at some airports and have been used to allocate fishing rights and the electromagnetic spectrum used by cell phones.

Lotteries work best when there is no effective way to distinguish among potential users of a scarce resource.

Personal Characteristics

When resources are allocated on the basis of personal characteristics, people with the "right" characteristics get the resources. Some of the resources that matter most to you are allocated in this way. For example, you will choose a marriage partner on the basis of personal characteristics. But this method also gets used in unacceptable ways. Allocating the best jobs to white, Anglo-Saxon males and discriminating against visible minorities and women is an example.

Force

Force plays a crucial role, for both good and ill, in allocating scarce resources. Let's start with the ill.

War, the use of military force by one nation against another, has played an enormous role historically in allocating resources. The economic supremacy of European settlers in the Americas and Australia owes much to the use of this method.

Theft, the taking of the property of others without their consent, also plays a large role. Both large-scale

organized crime and small-scale petty crime collectively allocate billions of dollars worth of resources annually.

But force plays a crucial positive role in allocating resources. It provides the state with an effective method of transferring wealth from the rich to the poor, and it provides the legal framework in which voluntary exchange in markets takes place.

A legal system is the foundation on which our market economy functions. Without courts to enforce contracts, it would not be possible to do business. But the courts could not enforce contracts without the ability to apply force if neccesary. The state provides the ultimate force that enables the courts to do their work.

More broadly, the force of the state is essential to uphold the principle of the rule of law. This principle is the bedrock of civilized economic (and social and political) life. With the rule of law upheld, people can go about their daily economic lives with the assurance that their property will be protected—that they can sue for violations of their property (and be sued if they violate the property of others).

Free from the burden of protecting their property and confident in the knowledge that those with whom they trade will honor their agreements, people can get on with focusing on the activity at which they have a comparative advantage and trading for mutual gain.

REVIEW QUIZ

1 Describe the alternative methods of allocating scarce resources.
2 Provide an example of each allocation method that illustrates when it works well.
3 Provide an example of each allocation method that illustrates when it works badly.

 myeconlab **Study Plan 5.1**

In the next sections, we're going to see how a market can achieve an efficient use of resources, examine the obstacles to efficiency, and see how sometimes, an alternative method might improve on the market.

After looking at efficiency, we'll turn our attention to the more difficult issue of fairness.

Demand and Marginal Benefit

RESOURCES ARE ALLOCATED EFFICIENTLY WHEN they are used in the ways that people value most highly. This outcome occurs when marginal benefit equals marginal cost (pp. 37–39). So to determine whether a competitive market is efficient, we need to see whether, at the market equilibrium quantity, marginal benefit equals marginal cost. We begin by seeing how market demand reflects marginal benefit.

Demand, Willingness to Pay, and Value

In everyday life, we talk about "getting value for money." When we use this expression, we are distinguishing between *value* and *price*. Value is what we get, and the price is what we pay.

The value of one more unit of a good or service is its marginal benefit. And we measure marginal benefit by the maximum price that is willingly paid for another unit of the good or service. But willingness to pay determines demand. A *demand curve is a marginal benefit curve.*

In Fig. 5.1(a), Lisa is willing to pay $1 for the 30th slice and $1 is her marginal benefit from that slice. In Fig. 5.1(b), Nick is willing to pay $1 for the 10th slice and $1 is his marginal benefit from that slice. But for which slice is the economy willing to pay $1? The answer is provided by the *market demand curve.*

Individual Demand and Market Demand

The relationship between the price of a good and the quantity demanded by one person is called *individual demand.* And the relationship between the price of a good and the quantity demanded by all buyers is called *market demand.*

The market demand curve is the horizontal sum of the individual demand curves and is formed by adding the quantities demanded by all the individuals at each price.

Figure 5.1(c) illustrates the market demand if Lisa and Nick are the only people. Lisa's demand curve (part a) and Nick's demand curve (part b) sum horizontally to the market demand curve in part (c).

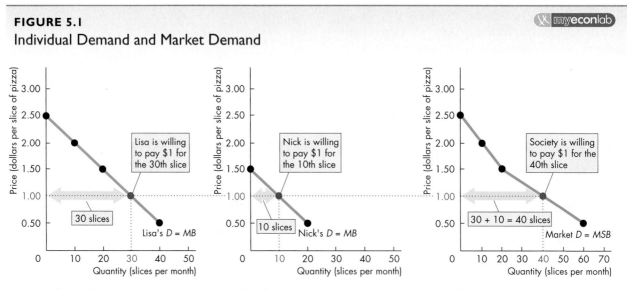

FIGURE 5.1

Individual Demand and Market Demand

(a) Lisa's demand

(b) Nick's demand

(c) Market demand

At a price of $1 a slice, the quantity demanded by Lisa is 30 slices and the quantity demanded by Nick is 10 slices, so the quantity demanded by the market is 40 slices. Lisa's demand curve in part (a) and Nick's demand curve in part (b) sum horizontally to the market demand curve in part (c). The market demand curve is the *marginal social benefit (MSB)* curve.

At a price of $1, Lisa demands 30 slices, Nick demands 10 slices, and the quantity demanded by the market is 40 slices.

So from the market demand curve, we see that the economy (or society) is willing to pay $1 for the 40th slice a month. The market demand curve is the economy's *marginal social benefit* (*MSB*) curve.

Although we're measuring price in dollars, think of it as telling us the number of *dollars' worth of other goods and services willingly forgone* to obtain one more slice of pizza (see Chapter 3, p. 60).

Consumer Surplus

We don't always have to pay what we are willing to pay—we get a bargain. When people buy something for less than it is worth to them, they receive a consumer surplus. A **consumer surplus** is the value (or marginal benefit) of a good minus the price paid for it, summed over the quantity bought.

Figure 5.2(a) shows Lisa's consumer surplus from pizza when the price is $1 a slice. At this price, she buys 30 slices a week because the 30th slice is worth $1 to her. But Lisa is willing to pay $2 for the 10th slice, so her marginal benefit from this slice is $1 more

than she pays for it—she receives a *consumer surplus* of $1 on the 10th slice.

Lisa's consumer surplus is the sum of the surpluses on *all of the slices* she buys. This sum is the area of the green triangle—the area below the demand curve and above the market price line. In Fig. 5.2(a), this area is equal to its base (30 slices) multiplied by its height ($1.50) divided by 2, which is $22.50. The area of the blue rectangle shows what Lisa pays for 30 slices of pizza.

Figure 5.2(b) shows Nick's consumer surplus and part (c) shows the consumer surplus for the economy. You can see that the consumer surplus for the economy is the sum of the consumer surpluses of Lisa and Nick.

All goods and services, like pizza, have decreasing marginal benefit. So people receive more benefit from their consumption than the amount they pay.

REVIEW QUIZ

1 How do we measure the value or marginal benefit of a good or service?
2 What is consumer surplus? How do we measure it?

   myeconlab   **Study Plan 5.2**

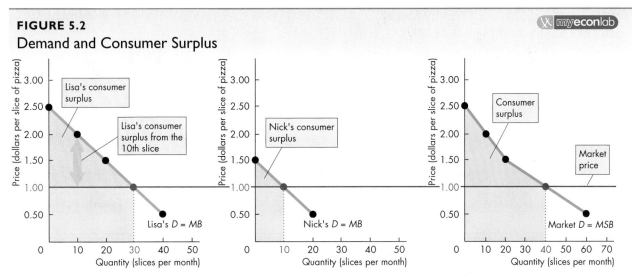

FIGURE 5.2
Demand and Consumer Surplus   **myeconlab**

(a) Lisa's consumer surplus   **(b) Nick's consumer surplus**   **(c) Market consumer surplus**

Lisa is willing to pay $2.00 for her 10th slice of pizza (part a). At a market price of $1 a slice, Lisa gets a consumer surplus of $1 on the 10th slice. The green triangle shows her consumer surplus on the 30 slices she buys at $1 a slice. The

green triangle in part (b) shows Nick's consumer surplus on the 10 slices that he buys at $1 a slice. The green area in part (c) shows the consumer surplus for the economy. The blue rectangles show the amounts spent on pizza.

Supply and Marginal Cost

WE ARE NOW GOING TO SEE HOW MARKET SUPPLY reflects marginal cost. This section closely parallels the related ideas about market demand and marginal benefit that you've just studied. Firms are in business to make a profit. To do so, they must sell their output for a price that exceeds the cost of production. Let's investigate the relationship between cost and price.

Supply, Cost, and Minimum Supply-Price

Earning a profit means receiving more for the sale of a good or service than the cost of producing it. Just as consumers distinguish between *value* and *price*, so producers distinguish between *cost* and *price*. Cost is what a producer gives up, and the price is what a producer receives.

The cost of one more unit of a good or service is its marginal cost. And marginal cost is the minimum price that producers must receive to induce them to offer to sell another unit of the good or service. But the minimum supply-price determines supply. *A supply curve is a marginal cost curve.*

In Fig. 5.3(a), Max is willing to produce the 100th pizza for $15, his marginal cost of that pizza. In Fig. 5.3(b), Mario is willing to produce the 50th pizza for $15, his marginal cost of that pizza. But which pizza is the economy willing to produce for $15? The answer is provided by the *market supply curve.*

Individual Supply and Market Supply

The relationship between the price of a good and the quantity supplied by one producer is called *individual supply.* And the relationship between the price of a good and the quantity supplied by all producers is called *market supply.*

The market supply curve is the horizontal sum of the individual supply curves and is formed by adding the quantities supplied by all the producers at each price.

Figure 5.1(c) illustrates the market supply if Max and Mario are the only producers. Max's supply curve (part a) and Mario's supply curve (part b) sum horizontally to the market supply curve in part (c).

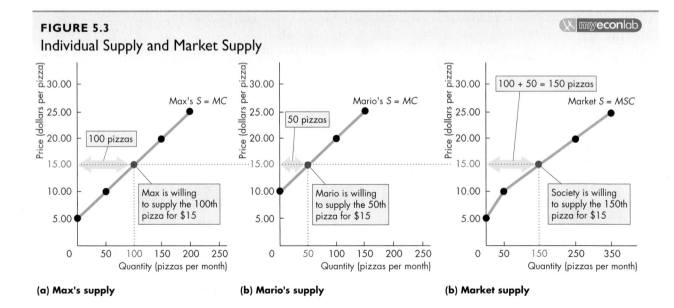

FIGURE 5.3
Individual Supply and Market Supply

(a) Max's supply   **(b) Mario's supply**   **(b) Market supply**

At a price of $15 a pizza, the quantity supplied by Max is 100 pizzas and the quantity supplied by Mario is 50 pizzas, so the quantity supplied by the market is 150 pizzas. Max's supply curve in part (a) and Mario's supply curve in part (b) sum horizontally to the market supply curve in part (c). The market supply curve is the marginal social cost (MSC) curve.

At a price of $15 a pizza, Max supplies 100 pizzas, Mario supplies 50 pizzas and the quantity supplied by the market is 150 pizzas.

So from the market supply curve, we see that the economy (or society) is willing to produce the 150th pizza a month for $15. The market supply curve is the economy's *marginal social cost* (*MSC*) curve.

Again, although we're measuring price in dollars, think of it as telling us the number of *dollars' worth of other goods and services that must be forgone* to obtain one more pizza.

Producer Surplus

When price exceeds marginal cost, the firm receives a producer surplus. A **producer surplus** is the price received for it minus minimum-supply price (or marginal cost) of a good, summed over the quantity sold.

Figure 5.4(a) shows Max's producer surplus from pizza when the price is $15 a pizza. At this price, he sells 100 pizzas a week because the 100th pizza costs him $15 to produce. But Max is willing to produce the 50th pizza for his marginal cost, which is $10. So he receives a *producer surplus* of $5 on this pizza.

Max's producer surplus is the sum of the surpluses on all the pizza he sells. This sum is the area of the blue triangle—the area below the market price and above the supply curve. In Fig. 5.4(a), this area is equal to its base (100) multiplied by its height ($10) divided by 2, which is $500. The red area below the supply curve shows what it costs Max to produce 100 pizzas.

Figure 5.4(b) shows Mario's producer surplus and part (c) shows the producer surplus for the economy. You can see that the producer surplus for the economy is the sum of the producer surpluses of Max and Mario.

Consumer surplus and producer surplus can be used to measure the efficiency of a market. Let's see how we can use these concepts to study the efficiency of a competitive market.

REVIEW QUIZ

1 What is the relationship between marginal cost, minimum supply-price, and supply?
2 What is producer surplus? How do we measure it?

myeconlab **Study Plan 5.3**

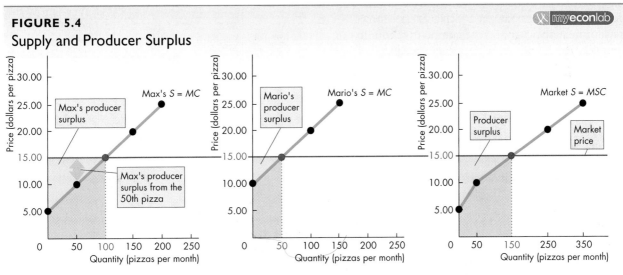

FIGURE 5.4
Supply and Producer Surplus

(a) Max's producer surplus

(b) Mario's producer surplus

(c) Economy producer surplus

Max is willing to produce the 50th pizza for $10 (part a). At a market price of $15 a pizza, Max gets a producer surplus of $5 on the 50th pizza. The blue triangle shows his producer surplus on the 100 pizzas he sells at $15 each. The blue triangle in part (b) shows Mario's producer surplus on the 50 pizzas that he sells at $15 each. The blue area in part (c) shows producer surplus for the economy. The red areas show the cost of producing the pizzas sold.

Is the Competitive Market Efficient?

FIGURE 5.5(a) SHOWS THE MARKET FOR PIZZA. The market forces that you studied in Chapter 3 (pp. 70–71) pull the pizza market to its equilibrium price of $15 a pizza and equilibrium quantity of 10,000 pizzas a day. Buyers enjoy a consumer surplus (green area) and sellers enjoy a producer surplus (blue area). Is this competitive equilibrium efficient?

Efficiency of Competitive Equilibrium

You've seen that the market demand curve for pizza tells us the marginal social benefit from pizza. So in Fig. 5.5(b), we label the demand curve as the marginal social benefit curve, *MSB*.

You've also seen that the market supply curve of pizza tells us the marginal social cost of pizza. So in Fig 5.5(b), we label the supply curve as the marginal social cost curve, *MSC*. You can see that where the demand curve and the supply curve intersect in part (a), the marginal social benefit curve and the marginal social cost curve intersect in part (b). So at the equilibrium price and quantity, marginal social benefit equals marginal social cost. But when marginal social benefit equals marginal social cost, resources are allocated efficiently. So the competitive equilibrium is efficient and resources are allocated to their highest-value uses.

If production is less than 10,000 pizzas a day, the marginal social benefit from pizza exceeds its marginal social cost. If production exceeds 10,000 pizzas a day, the marginal social cost of pizza exceeds its marginal social benefit. Only when 10,000 pizzas a day are produced is the marginal social benefit of pizza equal to its marginal social cost.

The competitive market pushes the quantity of pizza produced to its efficient level of 10,000 a day. If production is less than 10,000 pizzas a day, a shortage raises the price, which increases production. If production exceeds 10,000 pizzas a day, a surplus lowers the price, which decreases production. So, a competitive pizza market is efficient.

Notice that when the efficient quantity is produced, *total surplus* (the sum of consumer surplus and producer surplus) is maximized. Buyers and sellers acting in their self-interest end up promoting the social interest.

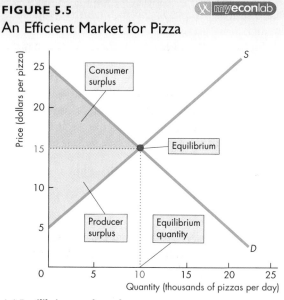

FIGURE 5.5

An Efficient Market for Pizza

(a) Equilibrium and surpluses

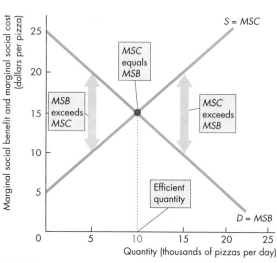

(b) Efficiency

Competitive equilibrium in part (a) occurs when the quantity demanded equals the quantity supplied. Consumer surplus is the area under the demand curve and above the price—the green triangle. Producer surplus is the area above the supply curve and below the price—the blue triangle.

Resources are used efficiently in part (b) when marginal social benefit, *MSB*, equals marginal social cost, *MSC*.

The efficient quantity in part (b) is the same as the equilibrium quantity in part (a). The competitive pizza market produces the efficient quantity of pizza.

The Invisible Hand

Writing in his *Wealth of Nations* in 1776, Adam Smith was the first to suggest that competitive markets send resources to the uses in which they have the highest value (see pp. 54–55). Smith believed that each participant in a competitive market is "led by an invisible hand to promote an end [the efficient use of resources] which was no part of his intention."

You can see the invisible hand at work in the cartoon. The cold drinks vendor has both cold drinks and shade. He has an opportunity cost of each and a minimum supply-price of each. The reader on the park bench has a marginal benefit from each and a willingness to pay for each. You can see from the transaction that occurs that the marginal benefit from shade exceeds the price of shade and the price of a cold drink exceeds its marginal benefit. The transaction creates a producer surplus and a consumer surplus. The vendor obtains a producer surplus from selling the shade for more than its opportunity cost, and the reader obtains a consumer surplus from buying the shade for less than its marginal benefit. In the third frame of the cartoon, both the consumer and the producer are better off than they were in the first frame. The umbrella has moved to its highest-valued use.

The Invisible Hand at Work Today

The market economy relentlessly performs the activity illustrated in the cartoon and in Fig. 5.5 to achieve an efficient allocation of resources. And rarely has the market been working as hard as it is today: Think about some changes taking place that the market is guiding towards an efficient use of resources.

New technologies have cut the cost of producing a computer. As these advances have occurred, the supply of computers has increased and the price has fallen. Lower prices have encouraged an increase in the quantity demanded of this now less costly tool. The marginal social benefit from computers is brought to equality with their marginal social cost.

A Florida frost cuts the supply of oranges. With fewer oranges available, the marginal social benefit from oranges increases. A shortage of oranges raises their price, so the market allocates the smaller quantity to the people who value them most highly.

Market forces persistently bring marginal social cost and marginal social benefit to equality and maximize total surplus (the sum of consumer surplus and producer surplus).

Underproduction and Overproduction

Inefficiency can occur because either too little of an item is produced—underproduction—or too much is produced—overproduction.

Underproduction In Fig. 5.6(a), the quantity of pizza produced is 5,000 a day. At this quantity, consumers are willing to pay $20 for a pizza that costs only $10 to produce. The quantity produced is inefficient—there is underproduction.

The scale of the inefficiency is measured by **deadweight loss**, which is the decrease in total surplus that results from inefficiency. The grey triangle in Fig. 5.6(a) shows the deadweight loss.

FIGURE 5.6
Underproduction and Overproduction

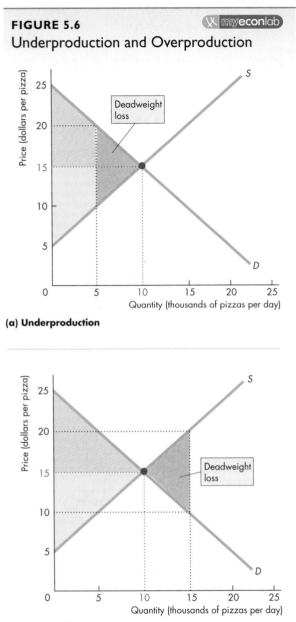

(a) Underproduction

(b) Overproduction

In part (a), if pizza production is cut to 5,000 a day, the benefit of one more pizza exceeds its cost. Total surplus, the sum of the green and blue areas, is reduced and a deadweight loss (the grey triangle) arises.

In part (b), if pizza production increases to 15,000 a day, the cost of the 15,000th pizza exceeds its benefit. A deadweight loss (grey triangle) arises. Total surplus equals the sum of the green and blue areas minus the grey triangle.

Overproduction In Fig. 5.6(b), the quantity of pizza produced is 15,000 a day. At this quantity, consumers are willing to pay only $10 for a pizza that costs $20 to produce. By producing the 15,000th pizza, $10 of resources are wasted. Again, the grey triangle shows the deadweight loss. The total surplus (the sum of consumer surplus and producer surplus) is smaller than its maximum by the amount of the deadweight loss. The deadweight loss is borne by the entire society. It is not a loss for the consumers and a gain for the producer. It is a *social* loss.

Obstacles to Efficiency

The obstacles to efficiency that bring underproduction or overproduction are

- Price and quantity regulations
- Taxes and subsidies
- Externalities
- Public goods and common resources
- Monopoly
- High transactions costs

Price and Quantity Regulations *Price regulations* that put a cap on the rent that a landlord is permitted to charge and laws that require employers to pay a minimum wage sometimes block the price adjustments that balance the quantity demanded and the quantity supplied and lead to underproduction. *Quantity regulations* that limit the amount that a farm is permitted to produce also lead to underproduction.

Taxes and Subsidies *Taxes* increase the prices paid by buyers and lower the prices received by sellers. So taxes decrease the quantity produced and lead to underproduction. *Subsidies*, which are payments by the government to producers, decrease the prices paid by buyers and increase the prices received by sellers. So subsidies increase the quantity produced and lead to overproduction.

Externalities An *externality* is a cost or a benefit that affects someone other than the seller or the buyer of a good. An electric utility creates an *external cost* by burning coal that brings acid rain and crop damage. The utility doesn't consider the cost of pollution when it decides how much power to produce. The result is overproduction. An apartment owner would provide an *external benefit* if she installed a smoke detector. But she doesn't consider her neighbor's marginal benefit and decides not to install a smoke detector. There is underproduction.

Public Goods and Common Resources A *public good is* a good or service that is consumed simultaneously by everyone even if they don't pay for it. Examples are national defence and law enforcement. Competitive markets would underproduce a public good because of a *free-rider problem*—it is in each person's interest to free ride on everyone else and avoid paying for her or his share of a public good.

A common resource is owned by no one but used by everyone. Atlantic salmon is an example. It is in everyone's self-interest to ignore the costs of their own use of a common resource that fall on others (called *the tragedy of the commons*), which leads to overproduction.

Monopoly A *monopoly* is a firm that is the sole provider of a good or service. Local water supply and cable television are supplied by firms that are monopolies. The self-interest of a monopoly is to maximize its profit. And because the monopoly has no competitors, it can set the price to achieve its self-interested goal. To achieve its goal, a monopoly produces too little and charges too high a price. It leads to underproduction.

High Transactions Costs Stroll around a shopping mall and observe the retail markets in which you participate. You'll see that these markets employ enormous quantities of scarce labor and capital resources. It is costly to operate any market. Economists call the opportunity costs of making trades in a market **transactions costs**.

To use market price as the allocator of scarce resources, it must be worth bearing the opportunity cost of establishing a market. Some markets are just too costly to operate. For example, when you want to play tennis on your local "free" court, you don't pay a market price for your slot on the court. You hang around until the court becomes vacant, and you "pay" with your waiting time. When transactions costs are high, the market might underproduce.

You now know the conditions under which resource allocation is efficient. You've seen how a competitive market can be efficient, and you've seen some impediments to efficiency. But can alternative allocation methods improve on the market?

Alternatives to the Market

When a market is inefficient, can one of the alternative non-market methods that we described at the beginning of this chapter do a better job? Sometimes it can.

Often, majority rule might be used in a number of ways in an attempt to improve the allocation of resources. But majority rule has its own shortcomings. A group that pursues the self-interest of its members can become the majority. For example, a price or quantity regulation that creates a deadweight loss is almost always the result of a self-interested group becoming the majority and imposing costs on the minority. Also, with majority rule, votes must be translated into actions by bureaucrats who have their own agendas based on their self-interest.

Managers in firms issue commands and avoid the transactions costs that they would incur if they went to a market every time they needed a job done. First-come, first-served saves a lot of hassle in waiting lines. These lines could have markets in which people trade their place in the line—but someone would have to enforce the agreements. Can you imagine the hassle at a busy ATM if you had to buy your spot at the head of the line?

There is no one efficient mechanism for allocating resources efficiently. But supplemented by majority rule, bypassed inside firms by command systems, and by occasionally using first-come, first-served, markets do an amazingly good job.

REVIEW QUIZ

1 Do competitive markets use resources efficiently? Explain why or why not.
2 What is deadweight loss and under what conditions does it occur?
3 What are the obstacles to achieving an efficient allocation of resources in the market economy?

myeconlab **Study Plan 5.4**

Is an efficient allocation of resources also a fair allocation? Does the competitive market provide people with fair incomes for their work? Do people always pay a fair price for the things they buy? Don't we need the government to step into some competitive markets to prevent the price from rising too high or falling too low? Let's now study these questions.

Are Markets Fair?

WHEN A NATURAL DISASTER STRIKES, SUCH AS A severe winter storm, the prices of many essential items jump. The reason the prices jump is that some people have a greater demand and greater willingness to pay when the items are in limited supply. So the higher prices achieve an efficient allocation of scarce resources. News reports of these price hikes almost never talk about efficiency. Instead, they talk about equity or fairness. The claim often made is that it is unfair for profit-seeking dealers to cheat the victims of natural disaster.

Similarly, when low-skilled people work for a wage that is below what most would regard as a "living wage," the media and politicians talk of employers taking unfair advantage of their workers.

How do we decide whether something is fair or unfair? You know when *you* think something is unfair. But how do you know? What are the *principles* of fairness?

Philosophers have tried for centuries to answer this question. Economists have offered their answers too. But before we look at these answers, you should know that there is no universally agreed upon answer.

Economists agree about efficiency. That is, they agree that it makes sense to make the economic pie as large as possible and to bake it at the lowest possible cost. But they do not agree about equity. That is, they do not agree about what are fair shares of the economic pie for all the people who make it. The reason is that ideas about fairness are not exclusively economic ideas. They touch on politics, ethics, and religion. Nevertheless, economists have thought about these issues and have a contribution to make. So let's examine the views of economists on this topic.

To think about fairness, think of economic life as a game—a serious game. All ideas about fairness can be divided into two broad groups:. They are

■ It's not fair if the *result* isn't fair.
■ It's not fair if the *rules* aren't fair.

It's Not Fair If the *Result* Isn't Fair

The earliest efforts to establish a principle of fairness were based on the view that the result is what matters. And the general idea was that it is unfair if people's incomes are too unequal. It is unfair that a bank president earns millions of dollars a year while a bank teller earns only thousands of dollars a year. It is unfair that a store owner enjoys a larger profit and her customers pay higher prices in the aftermath of a winter storm.

There was a lot of excitement during the nineteenth century when economists thought they had made the incredible discovery that equality, which they regarded as a fair result, was also efficient. They argued that to make the economic pie as large as possible, it must be cut into equal pieces, one for each person. This idea turns out to be wrong, but there is a lesson in the reason why it is wrong. So this nineteenth century idea is worth a closer look.

Utilitarianism   The nineteenth century idea that only equality brings efficiency is called *utilitarianism*. **Utilitarianism** is a principle that states that we should strive to achieve "the greatest happiness for the greatest number." The people who developed this idea were known as utilitarians. They included the most eminent thinkers, such as Jeremy Bentham and John Stuart Mill.

Utilitarians argued that to achieve "the greatest happiness for the greatest number," income must be transferred from the rich to the poor up to the point of complete equality—to the point at which there are no rich and no poor.

They reasoned in the following way: First, everyone has the same basic wants and a similar capacity to enjoy life. Second, the greater a person's income, the smaller is the marginal benefit of a dollar. The millionth dollar spent by a rich person brings a smaller marginal benefit to that person than the marginal benefit of the thousandth dollar spent by a poorer person. So by transferring a dollar from the millionaire to the poorer person, more is gained than is lost and the two people added together are better off.

Figure 5.7 illustrates this utilitarian idea. Tom and Jerry have the same marginal benefit curve, *MB*. (Marginal benefit is measured on the same scale of 1 to 3 for both Tom and Jerry.) Tom earns $5,000 a year and his marginal benefit of a dollar of income is 3 at point *A*. Jerry earns $45,000 a year and his marginal benefit of a dollar of income is 1at point *B*. If a dollar is transferred from Jerry to Tom, Jerry loses 1 unit of marginal benefit and Tom gains 3 units. So together, Tom and Jerry are better off. They are sharing the economic pie more efficiently. If a second dollar is transferred, the same thing happens: Tom gains more than Jerry loses. And the same is true for every dollar transferred until they both reach point *C*. At point *C*,

FIGURE 5.7
Utilitarian Fairness

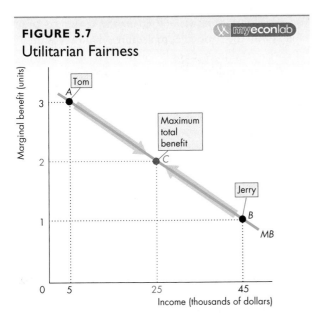

Tom earns $5,000 and has 3 units of marginal benefit at point A. Jerry earns $45,000 and has 1 unit of marginal benefit at point B. If income is transferred from Jerry to Tom, Jerry's loss is less than Tom's gain. Only when each of them has $25,000 and 2 units of marginal benefit (at point C) can the sum of their total benefit increase no further.

Tom and Jerry have $25,000 each and a marginal benefit of 2 units. Now they are sharing the economic pie in the most efficient way. It is bringing the greatest attainable happiness to Tom and Jerry.

The Big Tradeoff One big problem with the utilitarian ideal of complete equality is that it ignores the costs of making income transfers. Recognizing the cost of making income transfers leads to what is called the **big tradeoff**, which is a tradeoff between efficiency and fairness.

The big tradeoff is based on the following facts. Income can be transferred from people with high incomes to people with low incomes only by taxing the high incomes. Taxing people's income from employment makes them work less. It results in the quantity of labour being less than the efficient quantity. Taxing people's income from capital makes them save less. It results in the quantity of capital being less than the efficient quantity. With smaller quantities of both labour and capital, the quantity of goods and services produced is less than the efficient quantity. The economic pie shrinks.

The tradeoff is between the size of the economic pie and the degree of equality with which it is shared. The greater the amount of income redistribution through income taxes, the greater is the inefficiency—the smaller is the economic pie.

There is a second source of inefficiency. A dollar taken from a rich person does not end up as a dollar in the hands of a poorer person. Some of it is spent on administration of the tax and transfer system. The cost of tax-collecting agencies, such as Canada Revenue Agency, and welfare-administering agencies, such as Social Development Canada, must be paid with some of the taxes collected. Also, taxpayers hire accountants, auditors, and lawyers to help them ensure that they pay the correct amount of taxes. These activities use skilled labour and capital resources that could otherwise be used to produce goods and services that people value.

You can see that when all these costs are taken into account, taking a dollar from a rich person does not give a dollar to a poor person. It is even possible that with high taxes, the poor might end up being worse off. Suppose, for example, that highly taxed entrepreneurs decide to work less and close some of their businesses. Low-income workers get fired and must seek other, perhaps even lower-paid, work.

Because of the big tradeoff, those who say that fairness is equality of income propose a modified version of utilitarianism.

Make the Poorest as Well Off as Possible A Harvard philosopher, John Rawls, proposed a modified version of utilitarianism in a classic book entitled *A Theory of Justice*, published in 1971. Rawls says that, taking all the costs of income transfers into account, the fair distribution of the economic pie is the one that makes the poorest person as well off as possible. The incomes of rich people should be taxed, and after paying the costs of administering the tax and transfer system, what is left should be transferred to the poor. But the taxes must not be so high that they make the economic pie shrink to the point at which the poorest person ends up with a smaller piece. A bigger share of a smaller pie can be less than a smaller share of a bigger pie. The goal is to make the piece enjoyed by the poorest person as big as possible. Most likely, this piece will not be an equal share.

The "fair results" idea requires a change in the results after the game is over. Some economists say that these changes are themselves unfair and propose a different way of thinking about fairness.

It's Not Fair If the *Rules* Aren't Fair

The idea that it's not fair if the rules aren't fair is based on a fundamental principle that seems to be hard-wired into the human brain: the symmetry principle. The **symmetry principle** is the requirement that people in similar situations be treated similarly. It is the moral principle that lies at the centre of all the big religions and that says, in some form or other, "behave towards other people in the way you expect them to behave towards you."

In economic life, this principle translates into *equality of opportunity*. But equality of opportunity to do what? This question is answered by the late Harvard philosopher Robert Nozick, in a book entitled *Anarchy, State, and Utopia*, published in 1974.

Nozick argues that the idea of fairness as an outcome or result cannot work and that fairness must be based on the fairness of the rules. He suggests that fairness obeys two rules:

1. The state must enforce laws that establish and protect private property.
2. Private property may be transferred from one person to another only by voluntary exchange.

The first rule says that everything that is valuable must be owned by individuals and that the state must ensure that theft is prevented. The second rule says that the only legitimate way a person can acquire property is to buy it in exchange for something else that the person owns. If these rules, which are the only fair rules, are followed, then the result is fair. It doesn't matter how unequally the economic pie is shared, provided that the pie is baked by people, each one of whom voluntarily provides services in exchange for the share of the pie offered in compensation.

These rules satisfy the symmetry principle. And if these rules are not followed, the symmetry principle is broken. You can see these facts by imagining a world in which the laws are not followed.

First, suppose that some resources or goods are not owned. They are common property. Then everyone is free to participate in a grab to use them. The strongest will prevail. But when the strongest prevails, the strongest effectively *owns* the resources or goods in question and prevents others from enjoying them.

Second, suppose that we do not insist on voluntary exchange for transferring ownership of resources from one person to another. The alternative is *involuntary* transfer. In simple language, the alternative is theft.

Both of these situations violate the symmetry principle. Only the strong get to acquire what they want. The weak end up with only the resources and goods that the strong don't want.

In a majority rule political system, the strong are those in the majority or those with enough resources to influence opinion and achieve a majority.

In contrast, if the two rules of fairness are followed, everyone, strong and weak, is treated in a similar way. Everyone is free to use their resources and human skills to create things that are valued by themselves and others and to exchange the fruits of their efforts with each other. This is the only set of arrangements that obeys the symmetry principle.

Fairness and Efficiency   If private property rights are enforced and if voluntary exchange takes place in a competitive market, resources will be allocated efficiently if there are no

1. Price and quantity regulations
2. Taxes and subsidies
3. Externalities
4. Public goods and common resources
5. Monopolies
6. High transactions costs

And according to the Nozick rules, the resulting distribution of income and wealth will be fair. Let's study a concrete example to examine the claim that if resources are allocated efficiently, they are also allocated fairly.

Case Study: A Water Shortage in a Natural Disaster

An earthquake has broken the pipes that deliver drinking water to a city. Bottled water is available but there is no tap water. What is the fair way to allocate the bottled water?

Market Price   Suppose that if the water is allocated by market price, the price jumps to $8 a bottle—five times its normal price. At this price, the people who own water can make a large profit by selling it. People who are willing and able to pay $8 a bottle get the water. And because most people can't afford the $8 price, they end up either without water or consuming just a few drops a day.

You can see that the water is being used efficiently. There is a fixed amount available, some people are willing to pay $8 to get a bottle, and the water goes to those people. The people who own and sell water receive a large producer surplus and total surplus (the sum of consumer surplus and producer surplus) is maximized.

On the rules view, the outcome is also fair. No one is denied the water they are willing to pay for. But on the results view, the outcome would most likely be regarded as unfair. The lucky owners of water make a killing and the poorest end up being the thirstiest.

Non-Market Methods Suppose that by a majority vote, the citizens decide that the government will buy all the water, pay for it with a tax, and allocate it to the citizens using one of the non-market methods. The possibilities now are:

1. Command Someone decides who is the most deserving and needy. Perhaps everyone is given an equal share. Or perhaps government officials and their families end up with most of the water.

2. Contest Bottles of water are prizes that go to those who are best at the particular contest.

3. First-come-first-served Water goes to the first off the mark or to those who place the lowest value on their time and can afford to wait in line.

4. Lottery Water goes to those in luck.

5. Personal characteristics Water goes to those with the "right" characteristics. Perhaps the old, the young, or pregnant mothers get the water.

Except by chance, none of these methods delivers an allocation of water that is either fair or efficient. It is unfair on the rules view because the tax involves involuntary transfers of resources among citizens. And it is unfair on the results view because the poorest don't end up being made as well off as possible.

The allocation is inefficient for two reasons. First, resources have been used to operate the allocation scheme. Second, some people are willing to pay for more water than they have been allocated and others have been allocated more water than they are willing to pay for.

The second source of inefficiency can be overcome if, after the non-market allocation, the city allows water to be traded at its market price. People who value the water they received at less than the market price sell and people who are willing to pay the market price to obtain more water than they were allocated buy. Those who value the water most highly are the ones who consume it.

Market Price with Taxes Another approach is to allocate the scarce water using the market price but after redistributing buying power by taxing the sellers of water and providing benefits to the poor.

Suppose water owners are taxed on each bottle sold and the revenue from these taxes is given to the poorest people. People are then free, starting from this new distribution of buying power, to trade water at the market price.

Because the owners of water are taxed on what they sell, they have a weaker incentive to offer water for sale and the supply decreases. The equilibrium price rises to more than $8 a bottle. There is now a deadweight loss in the market for water—similar to the loss that arises from underproduction on p. 112. (We study the effects of a tax and show its inefficiency in Chapter 6 on pp. 132–136.)

So the tax is inefficient. On the rules view, the tax is also unfair because it forces the owners of water to make a transfer to others. On the results view, the outcome might be regarded as being fair.

This brief case study illustrates the complexity of ideas about fairness. Economists have a clear criterion of efficiency but no comparably clear criterion of fairness. Most economists regard Nozick as being too extreme and want a fair tax in the rules. But there is no consensus about what would be a fair tax.

REVIEW QUIZ
1 What are the two big approaches to thinking about fairness?
2 What is the utilitarian idea of fairness and what is wrong with it?
3 Explain the big tradeoff. What idea of fairness has been developed to deal with it?
4 What is the main idea of fairness based on fair rules?
myeconlab Study Plan 5.5

◆ You've now studied the two biggest issues that run right through the whole of economics: efficiency and fairness. In the next chapter, we study some sources of inefficiency and unfairness. And at many points throughout this book—and in your life—you will return to and use the ideas about efficiency and fairness that you've learned in this chapter. *Reading Between the Lines* on pp. 118–119 looks at an example of an inefficiency in our economy today.

Inefficiency in Global Water Use

THE WALL STREET JOURNAL, NOVEMBER 26, 2003

Ravaged by Famine, Ethiopia Finally Gets Help From the Nile

MERAWI, Ethiopia—A barefoot farmer named Takele Tarekegn emerged from his cornfields one day this summer and encountered engineers and bankers stumbling through the dense bush in front of his mud-brick shack.

The interlopers, wielding compasses and blueprints, were blazing a trail to the nearby Koga River. They were also charting what could be a historic turn in the turbulent water politics of the Nile River, which have kept millions of Ethiopians on the ragged edge of starvation.

A small dam is to be built on the Koga, Mr. Tarekegn's visitors told him, and a network of canals, too—the first irrigation project for peasant farmers ever constructed in the area. "If we can finally use our water, we'll be able to feed our families all year long," says the 46-year-old farmer. "I have been waiting for this all my life."

For now, he watches water that could be his salvation rush away to another man's fields in another country. ...

In all, rivers originating in Ethiopia's highlands contribute 85% of the Nile water flowing through Egypt—where a vast web of dams and canals first commissioned by the Pharaohs turn millions of desert acres into fertile fields. ...

Essence of the Story

■ The Koga River in Ethiopia's highlands flows into the Nile River, which in turn flows into Egypt.

■ A vast web of dams and canals first built by Egypt's ancient rulers, the Pharaohs, make fertile millions of acres of desert.

■ A small dam with a supporting network of canals is to be built on the Koga.

■ Ethiopian farmers will be able to increase production and feed their families.

Economic Analysis

■ Water is one of the world's most vital resources, and it is used inefficiently.

■ Markets in water are not competitive. They are controlled by governments or private producers, and they do not work like the competitive markets that deliver an efficient use of resources.

■ The major problem in achieving an efficient use of water is to get it from the places where it is most abundant to the places in which it has the most valuable uses.

■ Some places have too little water, and some have too much.

■ The news article highlights two such places—Ethiopia with too little water and Egypt with too much.

■ The figures illustrate what is happening to water use in these two countries.

■ In Fig. 1, the curve D shows the demand for water in Ethiopia and the curve MC shows the marginal cost of providing water through dams and irrigation canals.

■ The absence of dams and irrigation canals means that the quantity of water available in Ethiopia Q_A is less than the efficient quantity. Farmers are willing to pay W, which exceeds the marginal cost C and a deadweight loss arises from underproduction.

■ In Fig. 2, the curve D shows the demand for water in Egypt and the curve MC shows the marginal cost of providing water through dams and irrigation canals.

■ The flow of free water from Ethiopia and the presence of extensive dams and irrigation canals mean that the quantity of water available in Egypt Q_B is greater than the efficient quantity. Farmers are willing to pay W, which is less than the marginal cost C and a deadweight loss arises from overproduction.

■ The situation in Ethiopia and Egypt is replicated in thousands of places around the world.

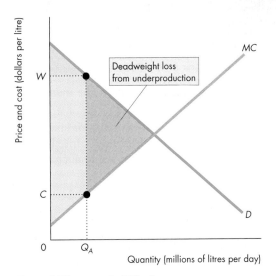

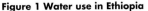

Figure 1 Water use in Ethiopia

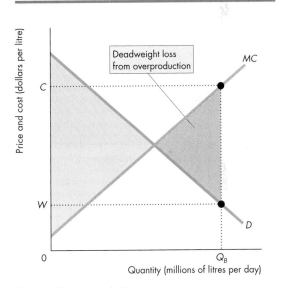

Figure 2 Water use in Egypt

You're the Voter

■ Do you think that water is too important to be left to the market to allocate?

■ Do you think that water should be shipped from Canada to Saudi Arabia?

119

SUMMARY

KEY POINTS

Resource Allocation Methods (pp. 104–105)

- Because resources are scarce, some mechanism must allocate them.
- The alternative allocation methods are: market price; command; majority rule; contest; first-come, first-served; lottery; personal characteristics; and force.

Demand and Marginal Benefit (pp. 106–107)

- Marginal benefit determines demand, and a demand curve is the marginal benefit curve.
- Market demand curve is the horizontal sum of the individual demand curves.
- Value is what people are *willing to* pay; price is what people *must* pay.
- Consumer surplus equals value minus price, summed over the quantity bought.

Supply and Marginal Cost (pp. 108–109)

- The minimum-supply price determines supply and the supply curve is the marginal cost curve.
- Market supply curve is the horizontal sum of the individual supply curves.
- Opportunity cost is what producers pay; price is what producers receive.
- Producer surplus equals price minus minimum supply-price, summed over the quantity sold.

Is the Competitive Market Efficient? (pp. 110–113)

- In a competitive equilibrium, marginal social benefit equals marginal social cost and resource allocation is efficient.
- Buyers and sellers acting in their self-interest end up promoting the social interest.
- Total surplus, the sum of consumer surplus and producer surplus, is maximized.

- Producing less than or more than the efficient quantity creates deadweight loss.
- Price and quantity regulations, taxes and subsidies, externalities, public goods and common resources, monopoly, and high transactions costs create inefficiency and deadweight loss.

Are Markets Fair? (pp. 114–117)

- Ideas about fairness can be divided into two groups: fair *results* and fair *rules*.
- Fair-results ideas require income transfers from the rich to the poor.
- Fair-rules ideas require property rights and voluntary exchange.

KEY FIGURES

Figure 5.1   Individual Demand and Market Demand, 106
Figure 5.2   Demand and Consumer Surplus, 107
Figure 5.3   Individual Supply and Market Supply, 108
Figure 5.4   Supply and Producer Surplus, 109
Figure 5.5   An Efficient Market for Pizza, 110
Figure 5.6   Underproduction and Overproduction, 112

KEY TERMS

Big tradeoff, 115
Command system, 104
Consumer surplus, 107
Deadweight loss, 111
Producer surplus, 109
Symmetry principle, 116
Transactions costs, 113
Utilitarianism, 114

PROBLEMS

Go to 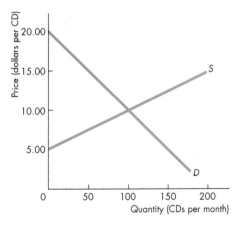 ⓧ myeconlab for solutions to odd-numbered problems and additional exercises.

1. The table gives the demand schedules for train travel for Ben, Beth, and Bo.

Price (cents per kilometre)	Quantity demanded (kilometres)		
	Ben	Beth	Bo
0	50	40	60
10	45	35	50
20	40	30	40
30	35	25	30
40	30	20	20
50	25	15	10
60	20	10	0

a. If the market price is 40 cents a kilometre
   i   What is each traveller's marginal benefit?
   ii   Which traveller has the largest consumer surplus? Explain why.
   iii What is marginal social benefit? Why?
b. Construct the market demand schedule.

2. The table gives the supply schedules of jetski rides by three owners: Ann, Arthur, and Abby.

Price (dollars per ride)	Quantity supplied (rides per day)		
	Ann	Arthur	Abby
10.00	0	0	0
12.50	5	0	0
15.00	10	5	0
17.50	15	10	5
20.00	20	15	10
22.50	25	20	15

a. What is each owner's minimum supply-price of 10 rides a day?
b. Which owner has the largest producer surplus when the price of a ride is $17.50? Explain why.
c. What is marginal social cost of producing 45 rides a day?
d. Construct the market supply schedule.

3. The figure shows the market for floppy discs.

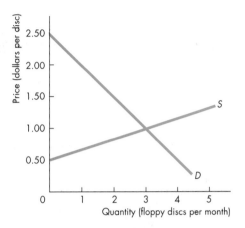

a. What are the equilibrium price and equilibrium quantity of floppy discs?
b. Calculate the consumer surplus.
c. Calculate the producer surplus.
d. Calculate the cost of producing the floppy discs sold.
e. What is the efficient quantity of floppy discs?

4. The figure illustrates the market for CDs.

a. What are the equilibrium price and equilibrium quantity of CDs?
b. Calculate the amount consumers paid for CDs.
c. Calculate the consumer surplus.
d. Calculate the producer surplus.
e. Calculate the cost of producing the CDs sold.
f. What is the efficient quantity of CDs?

5. The table gives the demand and supply schedules for sandwiches.

Price (dollars per sandwich)	Quantity demanded	Quantity supplied
	(sandwiches per day)	
0	300	0
1	250	50
3	200	100
4	150	150
5	100	200
6	50	250
7	0	300

a. What is the maximum price that consumers are willing to pay for the 200th sandwich?
b. What is the minimum price that producers are willing to accept for the 200th sandwich?
c. Are 200 sandwiches a day less than or greater than the efficient quantity?
d. Draw a graph of the sandwich market and mark in the efficient quantity, shade in the consumer surplus and the producer surplus.
e. On the graph of the sandwich market, shade in the deadweight loss created when 200 sandwiches a day are produced.

6. The table gives the demand and supply schedules for sunscreen.

Price (dollars per bottle)	Quantity demanded	Quantity supplied
	(bottles per day)	
0	600	0
1	500	100
2	400	200
3	300	300
4	200	400
5	100	500
6	0	600

a. What is the maximum price that consumers are willing to pay for the 200th bottle?
b. What is the minimum price that producers are willing to accept for the 200th bottle?
c. Are 200 bottles a day less than or greater than the efficient quantity? (Draw the graph.)
d. Draw a graph of the sunscreen market and mark in the efficient quantity, shade in the consumer surplus and the producer surplus.
e. On the graph of the sunscreen market, shade in the deadweight loss created when sunscreen bottlers produce 200 bottles a day.

CRITICAL THINKING

1. After you have studied *Reading Between the Lines* on pp. 118–119, answer the following questions:
   a. What is the major problem in achieving an efficient use of the world's water?
   b. If there were a global market in water, like there is in oil, how do you think the market would work?
   c. Would a free world market in water achieve an efficient use of the world's water resources? Explain why or why not.
   d. Would a free world market in water achieve a fair use of the world's water resources? Explain why or why not and be clear about the concept of fairness that you are using.

WEB EXERCISES

Use the links on ⓧ myeconlab to work the following exercise.

1. Visit the Web site of Health Action International and read the article by Catrin Schulte-Hillen entitled "Study concerning the availability and price of AZT." Then answer the following questions and explain your answers using the concepts of marginal benefit, marginal cost, price, consumer surplus, and producer surplus.
   a. What is the range of retail prices of AZT across the countries covered by the study?
   b. How do you think the range of prices influences the efficiency of the market for AZT?
   c. What, if anything, do you think could be done to increase the quantity of AZT and decrease its price?
   d. Canadian online pharmacies sell AZT to Americans for a price below the U.S. price. Does this practice increase or decrease consumer surplus in (i) Canada and (ii) the United States? Does it increase or decrease producer surplus in (i) Canada and (ii) the United States?
   e. What do you think must be done to make the market for AZT efficient?

Markets in Action

Turbulent Times

Apartment rents are skyrocketing in Toronto, and people are screaming for help. Do rent controls help renters live in affordable housing?

Almost every day, a new machine is invented that increases productivity and replaces some workers. Take a look at the machines in McDonald's that have replaced some low-skilled workers. Do minimum wage laws enable low-skilled people to earn a living wage?

Almost everything we buy is taxed. Beer is one heavily taxed item. How much of the beer tax gets paid by the buyer and how much by the seller? Do taxes help or hinder the market in its attempt to move resources to where they are valued most highly?

In 2003, ideal conditions brought record yields and global grain production increased. But in 2000 and 2001, yields were low and global grain production decreased. How do farm prices and revenues react to such output fluctuations and how do subsidies and production quotas affect farmers?

Trading in drugs is illegal. How do laws that make trading in a good or service illegal affect its price and the quantity bought and sold?

◆ In this chapter, we use the theory of demand and supply (Chapter 3) and the concepts of elasticity (Chapter 4) and efficiency (Chapter 5) to answer questions like those that we've just posed. In *Reading Between the Lines* at the end of the chapter, we explore the effects of an increase in Alberta's minimum wage in 2005.

After studying this chapter, you will be able to

- ■ Explain how housing markets work and how price ceilings create housing shortages and inefficiency

- ■ Explain how labour markets work and how minimum wage laws create unemployment and inefficiency

- ■ Explain the effects of a tax

- ■ Explain why farm prices and revenues fluctuate and how production subsidies and quotas influence farm production, costs, and prices

- ■ Explain how markets for illegal goods work

Housing Markets and Rent Ceilings

TO SEE HOW A HOUSING MARKET WORKS, LET'S transport ourselves to San Francisco in April 1906, as the city is suffering from a massive earthquake and fire. You can sense the enormity of San Francisco's problems by reading a headline from the April 19, 1906, *New York Times* about the first days of the crisis:

Over 500 Dead, $200,000,000 Lost in San Francisco Earthquake
Nearly Half the City Is in Ruins and 50,000 Are Homeless

The commander of federal troops in charge of the emergency described the magnitude of the problem:

> Not a hotel of note or importance was left standing. The great apartment houses had vanished ... two hundred-and-twenty-five thousand people were ... homeless.[1]

Almost overnight, more than half the people in a city of 400,000 had lost their homes. Temporary shelters and camps alleviated some of the problem, but it was also necessary to utilize the apartment buildings and houses left standing. As a consequence, they had to accommodate 40 percent more people than they had before the earthquake.

The *San Francisco Chronicle* was not published for more than a month after the earthquake. When the newspaper reappeared on May 24, 1906, the city's housing shortage—what would seem to be a major news item that would still be of grave importance—was not mentioned. Milton Friedman and George Stigler describe the situation:

> *There is not a single mention of a housing shortage!* The classified advertisements listed sixty-four offers of flats and houses for rent, and nineteen of houses for sale, against five advertisements of flats or houses wanted. Then and thereafter a considerable number of all types of accommodation except hotel rooms were offered for rent.[2]

How did San Francisco cope with such a devastating reduction in the supply of housing?

---

[1] Reported in Milton Friedman and George J. Stigler, "Roofs or Ceilings? The Current Housing Problem," in *Popular Essays on Current Problems*, vol. 1, no. 2 (New York: Foundation for Economic Education, 1946), pp. 3–159.
[2] *Ibid.*, p. 3.

The Market Before and After the Earthquake

Figure 6.1 shows the market for housing in San Francisco. The demand curve for housing is *D*. There is a short-run supply curve, labelled *SS*, and a long-run supply curve, labelled *LS*.

Short-Run Supply The short-run supply curve shows the change in the quantity of housing supplied as the rent changes while the number of houses and apartment buildings remains constant. The short-run supply response arises from changes in the intensity with which existing buildings are used. The higher the rent, the greater is the incentive for families to rent out some of the rooms that they previously used themselves.

Long-Run Supply The long-run supply curve shows how the quantity of housing supplied responds to a change in price after enough time has elapsed for new apartment buildings and houses to be erected or for existing ones to be destroyed. In Fig. 6.1, the long-run supply curve is *perfectly elastic*. The marginal cost of building is the same regardless of the number of houses and apartments in existence. And so long as the rent exceeds the marginal cost of building, developers have an incentive to keep on building. So long-run supply is perfectly elastic at a rent equal to marginal cost.

Equilibrium The equilibrium rent and quantity are determined by demand and *short-run* supply. Before the earthquake, the equilibrium rent is $16 a month and the quantity is 100,000 units of housing.

Figure 6.1(a) shows the situation immediately after the earthquake. Few people died in the earthquake, so demand remains at *D*. But the devastation decreases supply and shifts the short-run supply curve *SS* leftward to *SS_A*. If the rent remains at $16 a month, only 44,000 units of housing are available. But with only 44,000 units of housing available, the maximum rent that someone is willing to pay for the last available apartment is $24 a month. So rents rise. In Fig. 6.1(a), the rent rises to $20 a month.

As the rent rises, the quantity of housing demanded decreases and the quantity supplied increases to 72,000 units. These changes occur because people economize on their use of space and make spare rooms, attics, and basements available to others. The higher rent allocates the scarce housing to the people who value it most highly and are willing to pay the most for it.

But the higher rent has other, long-run effects. Let's look at these long-run effects.

FIGURE 6.1

The San Francisco Housing Market in 1906

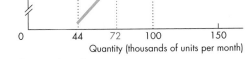

(a) After earthquake

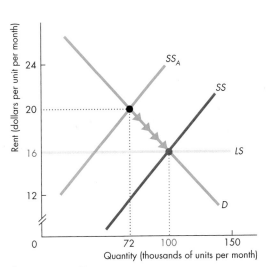

(b) Long-run adjustment

Part (a) shows that before the earthquake, 100,000 housing units were rented at $16 a month. After the earthquake, the short-run supply curve shifts from SS to SS_A. The rent rises to $20 a month, and the quantity of housing decreases to 72,000 units.

With rent at $20 a month, there is profit in building new apartments and houses. As the building proceeds, the short-run supply curve shifts rightward (part b). The rent gradually falls to $16 a month, and the quantity of housing increases to 100,000 units—as the arrowed line shows.

Long-Run Adjustments

With sufficient time for new apartments and houses to be constructed, supply increases. The long-run supply curve tells us that in the long run, housing is supplied at a rent of $16 a month. Because the rent of $20 a month exceeds the long-run supply price of $16 a month, there is a building boom. More apartments and houses are built, and the short-run supply curve shifts gradually rightward.

Figure 6.1(b) shows the long-run adjustment. As more housing is built, the short-run supply curve shifts gradually rightward and intersects the demand curve at lower rents and larger quantities. The market equilibrium follows the arrows down the demand curve. The building boom ends when there is no further profit in building new apartments and houses. The process ends when the rent is back at $16 a month, and 100,000 units of housing are available.

We've just seen how a housing market responds to a decrease in supply. And we've seen that a key part of the adjustment process is a rise in the rent. Suppose the government passes a law to stop the rent from rising. What happens then?

A Regulated Housing Market

We're now going to study the effects of a price ceiling in the housing market. A **price ceiling** is a regulation that makes it illegal to charge a price higher than a specified level. When a price ceiling is applied to housing markets, it is called a **rent ceiling**. How does a rent ceiling affect the housing market?

The effect of a price (rent) ceiling depends on whether it is imposed at a level that is above or below the equilibrium price (rent). A price ceiling set *above* the equilibrium price has no effect. The reason is that the price ceiling does not constrain the market forces. The force of the law and the market forces are not in conflict. But a price ceiling *below* the equilibrium price has powerful effects on a market. The reason is that the price ceiling attempts to prevent the price from regulating the quantities demanded and supplied. The force of the law and the market forces are in conflict, and one (or both) of these forces must yield to some degree.

Let's study the effects of a price ceiling that is set below the equilibrium price by returning to San Francisco. What would have happened in San Francisco if a rent ceiling of $16 a month—the rent before the earthquake—had been imposed?

FIGURE 6.2
A Rent Ceiling

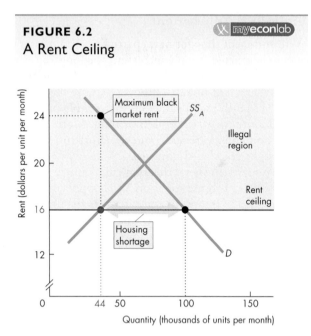

A rent above $16 a month is illegal (in the grey-shaded illegal region). At a rent of $16 a month, the quantity of housing supplied after the earthquake is 44,000 units. Someone is willing to pay $24 a month for the 44,000th unit. Frustrated renters spend time searching for housing and they make deals with landlords in a black market.

Figure 6.2 enables us to answer this question. A rent that exceeds $16 a month is in the grey-shaded illegal region in the figure. At a rent of $16 a month, the quantity of housing supplied is 44,000 units and the quantity demanded is 100,000 units. So there is a shortage of 56,000 units of housing.

But the story does not end here. Somehow, the 44,000 units of available housing must be allocated among people who demand 100,000 units. How is this allocation achieved? When a rent ceiling creates a housing shortage, two developments occur. They are

- Search activity
- Black markets

Search Activity

The time spent looking for someone with whom to do business is called **search activity**. We spend some time in search activity almost every time we buy something. You want the latest hot CD, and you know four stores that stock it. But which store has the best deal? You

need to spend a few minutes on the Internet or calling your friends to find out. In some markets, we spend a lot of time searching. An example is the housing market in which we spend a lot of time checking the alternatives available before making a choice.

But when a price is regulated and there is a shortage, search activity increases. In the case of a rent-controlled housing market, frustrated would-be renters scan the newspapers, not only for housing ads but also for death notices! Any information about newly available housing is useful. And they race to be first on the scene when news of a possible supplier breaks.

The *opportunity cost* of a good is equal not only to its price but also to the value of the search time spent finding the good. So the opportunity cost of housing is equal to the rent (a regulated price) plus the time and other resources spent searching for the restricted quantity available. Search activity is costly. It uses time and other resources, such as telephones, cars, and gasoline that could have been used in other productive ways. A rent ceiling controls the rent portion of the cost of housing, but it does not control the opportunity cost, which might even be *higher* than the rent would be if the market were unregulated.

Black Markets

A **black market** is an illegal market in which the price exceeds the legally imposed price ceiling. Black markets occur in rent-controlled housing, the same way that scalpers run black markets in tickets for big sporting events and rock concerts.

When rent ceilings are in force, frustrated renters and landlords constantly seek ways of increasing rents. One common way is for a new tenant to pay a high price for worthless fittings, such as charging $2,000 for threadbare drapes. Another is for the tenant to pay an exorbitant price for new locks and keys—called "key money."

The level of a black market rent depends on how tightly the rent ceiling is enforced. With loose enforcement, the black market rent is close to the unregulated rent. But with strict enforcement, the black market rent is equal to the maximum price that renters are willing to pay.

With strict enforcement of the rent ceiling in the San Francisco example shown in Fig. 6.2, the quantity of housing available remains at 44,000 units. A small number of people offer housing for rent at $24 a month—the highest rent that someone is willing to pay—and the government detects and punishes some of these black market traders.

Inefficiency of Rent Ceilings

In an unregulated market, the market determines the rent at which the quantity demanded equals the quantity supplied. In this situation, scarce housing resources are allocated efficiently. *Marginal social benefit* equals *marginal social cost* (see Chapter 5, p. 105).

Figure 6.3 shows the inefficiency of a rent ceiling. If the rent is fixed at $16 per month, 44,000 units are supplied. Marginal benefit is $24 a month. The blue triangle above the supply curve and below the rent ceiling line shows producer surplus. Because the quantity of housing is less than the competitive quantity, there is a deadweight loss, shown by the grey triangle. This loss is borne by the consumers who can't find housing and by producers who can't supply housing at the new lower price. Consumers who do find housing at the controlled rent gain. If no one incurs search costs, consumer surplus is shown by the sum of the green triangle and the red rectangle. But search costs might eat up part of the consumer surplus, possibly as much as the amount shown by the red rectangle.

Are Rent Ceilings Fair?

Do rent ceilings achieve a fairer allocation of scarce housing? Chapter 5 (pp. 112–115) explores the complex ideas about fairness. According to the *fair rules* view, anything that blocks voluntary exchange is unfair, so rent ceilings are unfair. But according to the *fair result* view, a fair outcome is one that benefits the less well off. So according to this view, the fairest outcome is the one that allocates scarce housing to the poorest. To see whether rent ceilings help to achieve a fairer outcome in this sense, we need to consider how the market allocates scarce housing resources in the face of a rent ceiling.

Blocking rent adjustments doesn't eliminate scarcity. Rather, because it decreases the quantity of housing available, it creates an even bigger challenge for the housing market. So somehow, the market must ration a smaller quantity of housing and allocate that housing among the people who demand it.

When the rent is not permitted to allocate scarce housing, what other mechanisms are available? Some possibilities are

- A lottery
- A queue
- Discrimination

Are these mechanisms fair?

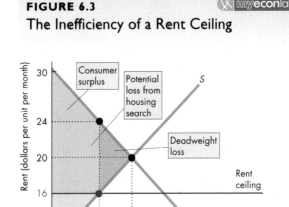

FIGURE 6.3
The Inefficiency of a Rent Ceiling

A rent ceiling of $16 a month decreases the quantity of housing supplied to 44,000 units. Producer surplus shrinks, and a deadweight loss (grey triangle) arises. If people use no resources in search activity, consumer surplus is the green triangle plus the red rectangle. But if people use resources in search activity equal to the amount shown by the red rectangle, the consumer surplus shrinks to the green triangle.

A lottery allocates housing to those who are lucky, not to those who are poor. A queue (a method used to allocate housing in England after World War II) allocates housing to those who have the greatest foresight and who get their names on a list first, not to the poorest. Discrimination allocates scarce housing based on the views and self-interest of the owner of the housing. In the case of public housing, it is the self-interest of the bureaucracy that administers the allocation that counts.

In principle, self-interested owners and bureaucrats could allocate housing to satisfy some criterion of fairness. But they are not likely to do so. Discrimination based on friendship, family ties, and criteria such as race, ethnicity, or sex is more likely to enter the equation. We might make such discrimination illegal, but we would not be able to prevent it from occurring.

It is hard, then, to make a case for rent ceilings on the basis of fairness. When rent adjustments are blocked, other methods of allocating scarce housing resources operate that do not produce a fair outcome.

Rent Ceilings in Practice

London, New York, Paris, and San Francisco, four of the world's great cities, have rent ceilings in some part of their housing markets. Winnipeg has rent ceilings and Toronto had them from 1975 until the late 1990s. Many Canadian cities including Calgary, Edmonton, and Vancouver do not have rent ceilings.

We can test for the effects of rent ceilings by comparing the housing markets in cities with and without ceilings. We learn two main lessons from such a comparison.

First, rent ceilings definitely create a housing shortage. Second, they do lower the rents for some but raise them for others. A survey[3] conducted in the United States in 1997 showed that the rents of housing units *actually available for rent* were 2.5 times the average of all rents in New York but equal to the average rent in Philadelphia where there is no rent ceiling. The winners from rent ceilings in New York City are the families that have lived there for a long time. These families include some rich and famous ones. The losers are mobile newcomers. It is the voting power of the winners that keeps New York's rent ceilings in place.

The bottom line is that in principle and in practice, rent ceilings are inefficient and unfair. They prevent the housing market from operating in the social interest.

REVIEW QUIZ

1 How does a decrease in the supply of housing change the equilibrium rent in the short run?
2 What are the effects of a rise in rent? And who gets the scarce housing resources?
3 What are the long-run effects of higher rents following a decrease in the supply of housing?
4 What is a rent ceiling and what are its effects if it is set above the equilibrium rent?
5 What are the effects of a rent ceiling that is set below the equilibrium rent?
6 How do scarce housing resources get allocated when a rent ceiling is in place?

myeconlab   Study Plan 6.1

You now know how a price ceiling works. Next, we'll learn about the effects of a price floor by studying minimum wages in the labour market.

---

[3] William Tucker, "How Rent Control Drives Out Affordable Housing."

The Labour Market and the Minimum Wage

FOR EACH ONE OF US, THE LABOUR MARKET IS the market that influences the jobs we get and the wages we earn. Firms decide how much labour to demand, and the lower the wage rate, the greater is the quantity of labour demanded. Households decide how much labour to supply, and the higher the wage rate, the greater is the quantity of labour supplied. The wage rate adjusts to make the quantity of labour demanded equal to the quantity supplied.

Equilibrium wage rates give some people high incomes but leave many more people with low incomes. And the labour market is constantly hit by shocks that often hit the lowest paid the hardest. The most pervasive of these shocks is the arrival of new labour-saving technologies that decrease the demand for low-skilled workers and lower their wage rates. During the 1980s and 1990s, for example, the demand for telephone operators and television repair technicians decreased. Throughout the past 200 years, the demand for low-skilled farm labourers has steadily decreased.

How does the labour market cope with this continuous decrease in the demand for low-skilled labour? Doesn't it mean that the wage rate of low-skilled workers is constantly falling?

To answer these questions, we must study the market for low-skilled labour in both the short run and the long run.

In the short run, there are a given number of people who have a given skill, training, and experience. Short-run supply of labour describes how the number of hours of labour supplied by this given number of people changes as the wage rate changes. To get them to work more hours, they must be offered a higher wage rate.

In the long run, people can acquire new skills and find new types of jobs. The number of people in the low-skilled labour market depends on the wage rate in this market compared with other opportunities. If the wage rate of low-skilled labour is high enough, people will enter this market. If the wage rate is too low, people will leave it. Some will seek training to enter higher-skilled labour markets, and others will stop working.

The long-run supply of labour is the relationship between the quantity of labour supplied and the wage rate after enough time has passed for people to enter or leave the low-skilled labour market. If people can freely enter and leave the low-skilled labour market, the long-run supply of labour is *perfectly elastic*.

Figure 6.4 shows the market for low-skilled labour. Other things remaining the same, the lower the wage rate, the greater is the quantity of labour demanded by firms. The demand curve for labour, *D* in part (a), shows this relationship between the wage rate and the quantity of labour demanded. Other things remaining the same, the higher the wage rate, the greater is the quantity of labour supplied by households. But the longer the period of adjustment, the greater is the *elasticity of supply* of labour. The short-run supply curve is *SS*, and the long-run supply curve is *LS*. In the figure, long-run supply is assumed to be perfectly elastic (the *LS* curve is horizontal). This market is in equilibrium at a wage rate of $7 an hour and 22 million hours of labour employed.

What happens if a labour-saving invention decreases the demand for low-skilled labour? Figure 6.4(a) shows the short-run effects of such a change. Before the new technology is introduced, the demand curve is the curve labelled *D*. After the introduction of the new technology, the demand curve shifts leftward to D_A. The wage rate falls to $6 an hour, and the quantity of labour employed decreases to 21 million hours. But this short-run effect on the wage rate and employment is not the end of the story.

People who are now earning only $6 an hour look around for other opportunities. They see many other jobs (in markets for other types of skills) that pay more than $6 an hour. One by one, workers decide to go back to school or take jobs that pay less but offer on-the-job training. As a result, the short-run supply curve begins to shift leftward.

Figure 6.4(b) shows the long-run adjustment. As the short-run supply curve shifts leftward, it intersects the demand curve D_A at higher wage rates and fewer hours employed. The process ends when workers have no incentive to leave the low-skilled labour market and the short-run supply curve has shifted to SS_A. At this point, the wage rate has returned to $7 an hour and employment has decreased to 20 million hours a year.

Concerned about the incomes of low-paid workers, provincial governments have set minimum wage rates and many campaign for a living wage. Let's look at the effects of a minimum wage and a living wage.

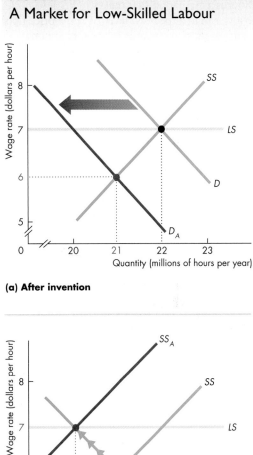

FIGURE 6.4

A Market for Low-Skilled Labour

(a) After invention

(b) Long-run adjustment

Part (a) shows the immediate effect of a labour-saving invention on the market for low-skilled labour. Initially, the wage rate is $7 an hour and 22 million hours are employed. A labour-saving invention shifts the demand curve from *D* to D_A. The wage rate falls to $6 an hour, and employment decreases to 21 million hours. With the lower wage rate, some workers leave this market and the short-run supply curve starts to shift gradually leftward to SS_A in part (b). The wage rate gradually increases, and employment decreases. In the long run, the wage rate returns to $7 an hour and employment decreases to 20 million hours a year.

A Minimum Wage

A **price floor** is a regulation that makes it illegal to trade at a price lower than a specified level. When a price floor is applied to labour markets, it is called a **minimum wage**. If a minimum wage is set *below* the equilibrium wage, the minimum wage has no effect. The minimum wage and market forces are not in conflict. But a minimum wage set *above* the equilibrium wage is in conflict with market forces, and it does have some effects on the labour market. Let's study these effects by returning to the market for low-skilled labour.

Suppose that with an equilibrium wage of $7 an hour (Fig. 6.4a), the government sets a minimum wage at $8 an hour. Figure 6.5 shows the minimum wage as the horizontal red line labelled "Minimum wage." A wage below this level is illegal, in the grey-shaded illegal region. At the minimum wage rate, 20 million hours of labour are demanded (point A) and 22 million hours of labour are supplied (point B), so 2 million hours of available labour are unemployed.

With only 20 million hours demanded, some workers are willing to supply that 20 millionth hour for $6. Frustrated unemployed workers spend time and other resources searching for hard-to-find jobs.

Inefficiency of a Minimum Wage

In an unregulated labour market, everyone who is willing to work for the going wage rate gets a job. And the market allocates the economy's scarce labour resources to the jobs in which they are valued most highly. The minimum wage frustrates the market mechanism and results in unemployment—wasted labour resources—and an inefficient amount of job search.

Figure 6.6 illustrates the inefficiency of the minimum wage. The deadweight loss arises because at the quantity of labour employed—20 million hours—the value to the firm of the marginal worker exceeds that wage rate for which that person is willing to work.

At this level of employment, unemployed people have a big incentive to spend time and effort looking for work. The red rectangle shows the potential loss from this extra job search. This loss arises because someone who finds a job earns $8 an hour (read off from the demand curve) but would have been willing to work for $6 an hour (read off from the supply curve). So everyone who is unemployed has an incentive to search hard and use resources that are worth the $2-an-hour surplus to find a job.

FIGURE 6.5
Minimum Wage and Unemployment

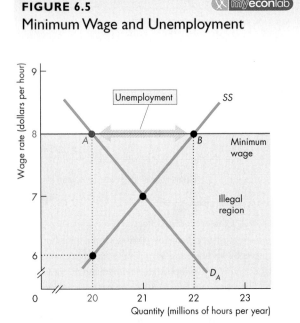

A wage below $8 an hour is illegal (in the grey-shaded illegal region). At the minimum wage of $8 an hour, 20 million hours are hired but 22 million hours are available. Unemployment—*AB*—of 2 million hours a year is created.

FIGURE 6.6
The Inefficiency of a Minimum Wage

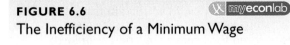

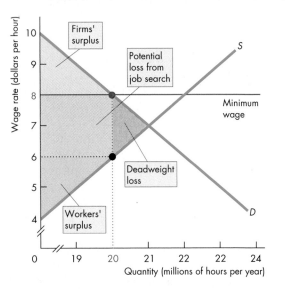

A minimum wage shrinks the firms' surplus (blue) and workers' surplus (green) and creates a deadweight loss (grey). If people use resources in job search equal to the amount they are able to gain by finding a job, the red rectangle is also lost.

Provincial Minimum Wage Laws and Their Effects

Provincial governments in Canada set minimum wage rates. In 2005, minimum wage rates ranged from a low of $6.25 an hour in Newfoundland to highs of $8.00 an hour in British Columbia, $7.45 an hour in Ontario, $7.25 in Manitoba, $7.20 an hour in the Yukon, and $7.00 an hour in Alberta.

You saw in Fig. 6.5 that the minimum wage brings unemployment. But how much unemployment does it bring? Economists do not agree on the answer to this question. Until recently, most economists believed that the minimum wage was a big contributor to high unemployment among low-skilled young workers. But this view has recently been challenged and the challenge rebutted.

David Card of the University of California at Berkeley and Alan Krueger of Princeton University say that increases in the minimum wage have not decreased employment and created unemployment. From their study of minimum wages in California, New Jersey, and Texas, Card and Krueger say that the employment rate of low-income workers increased following an increase in the minimum wage. They suggest three reasons why higher minimum wages might increase employment. First, workers become more conscientious and productive. Second, workers are less likely to quit, so labour turnover, which is costly, is reduced. Third, managers make a firm's operations more efficient.

Most economists are skeptical about Card and Krueger's suggestions. They ask two questions. First, if higher wages make workers more productive and reduce labour turnover, why don't firms freely pay wage rates above the equilibrium wage to encourage more productive work habits? Second, are there other explanations for the employment responses that Card and Krueger have found?

Card and Krueger got the timing wrong according to Daniel Hamermesh of the University of Texas at Austin. He says that firms cut employment *before* the minimum wage is increased in anticipation of the increase. If he is correct, looking for the effects of an increase *after* it has occurred misses its main effects. Finis Welch of Texas A&M University and Kevin Murphy of the University of Chicago say the employment effects that Card and Krueger found are caused by regional differences in economic growth, not by changes in the minimum wage.

One effect of the minimum wage, according to Fig. 6.5, is an increase in the quantity of labour supplied. If this effect occurs, it might show up as an increase in the number of people who quit school before completing high school to look for work. Some economists say that this response does occur.

A Living Wage

You've seen that the provincial minimum wage rates probably cause unemployment and create a deadweight loss. Despite these effects of a price floor in the labour market, a popular movement is seeking to create a more pervasive and much higher floor at a living wage. A **living wage** has been defined as an hourly wage rate that enables a person who works a 40-hour work week to rent adequate housing for not more than 30 percent of the amount earned. For example, if the going market rent for a one-bedroom apartment is $180 a week, the living wage is $15 an hour. (Check: 40 hours at $15 an hour is $600, and $180 is 30 percent of $600.)

Living wage laws are being tried in Peterborough and Waterloo in Ontario and Kamloops in British Columbia. Campaigns to expand the use of living wages are being mounted in many cities and municipalities across the country. The effects of the living wage can be expected to be similar to those of the minimum wage.

REVIEW QUIZ

1 How does a decrease in the demand for low-skilled labour change the wage rate in the short run?

2 What are the long-run effects of a lower wage rate for low-skilled labour?

3 What is a minimum wage? What are the effects of a minimum wage set below the equilibrium wage?

4 What are the effects of a minimum wage or a living wage that is set above the equilibrium wage?

myeconlab   Study Plan 6.2

Next we're going to study a more widespread government action in markets: taxes. We'll see how taxes change prices and quantities. You will discover the surprising fact that while the government can impose a tax, it can't decide who will pay the tax! And you will see that a tax creates a deadweight loss.

Taxes

EVERYTHING YOU EARN AND ALMOST EVERYTHING
you buy is taxed. Income taxes and social security
taxes are deducted from your earnings and sales taxes
and GST are added to the bill when you buy something. Employers also pay a social security tax for
their workers, and producers of tobacco products,
alcoholic drinks, and gasoline pay a tax every time
they sell something.

Who *really* pays these taxes? Because the income
tax and social security tax are deducted from your pay,
and the sales tax is added to the prices that you pay,
isn't it obvious that *you* pay these taxes? And isn't it
equally obvious that your employer pays the
employer's contribution to the social security tax and
that tobacco producers pay the tax on cigarettes?

You're going to discover that it isn't obvious who
really pays a tax and that lawmakers don't make that
decision. We begin with a definition of tax incidence.

Tax Incidence

Tax incidence is the division of the burden of a tax
between the buyer and the seller. When the government imposes a tax on the sale of a good,[4] the price
paid by the buyer might rise by the full amount of the
tax, by a lesser amount, or not at all. If the price paid
by the buyer rises by the full amount of the tax, then
the burden of the tax falls entirely on the buyer—the
buyer pays the tax. If the price paid by the buyer rises
by a lesser amount than the tax, then the burden of
the tax falls partly on the buyer and partly on the
seller. And if the price paid by the buyer doesn't
change at all, then the burden of the tax falls entirely
on the seller.

Tax incidence does not depend on the tax law.
The law might impose a tax on sellers or on buyers,
but the outcome is the same in either case. To see why,
let's look at the tax on cigarettes.

A Tax on Sellers

In January 2005, the government of Ontario upped
the tax on the sale of cigarettes for the third time since
taking office in the fall 2003. To work out the effects

of a tax on the sellers of cigarettes, we begin by examining the effects on demand and supply in the cigarette market.

In Fig. 6.7, the demand curve is *D*, and the supply
curve is *S*. With no tax, the equilibrium price is $6 per
pack and 35 million packs a year are bought and sold.

A tax on sellers is like an increase in cost, so it
decreases supply. To determine the position of the new
supply curve, we add the tax to the minimum price
that sellers are willing to accept for each quantity sold.
You can see that without the tax, sellers are willing to
offer 35 million packs a year for $6 a pack. So with a
$2 tax, sellers will offer 35 million packs a year only if
the price is $8 a pack. The supply curve shifts to the
red curve labelled *S + tax on sellers*.

Equilibrium occurs where the new supply curve
intersects the demand curve at 32 million packs a year.
The price paid by buyers rises by $1.50 to $7.50 a
pack. And the price received by sellers falls by 50¢ to
$5.50 a pack. So buyers pay $1.50 of the tax and sellers pay the other 50¢.

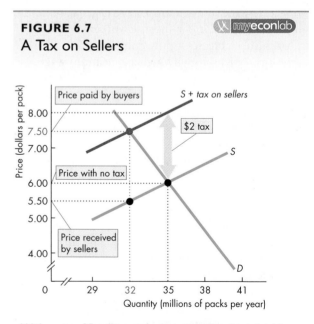

FIGURE 6.7
A Tax on Sellers

With no tax, 35 million packs a year are bought and sold at
$6 a pack. A tax on sellers of $2 a pack shifts the supply
curve leftward to *S + tax on sellers*. The equilibrium quantity
decreases to 32 million packs a year, the price paid by buyers
rises to $7.50 a pack, and the price received by sellers falls
to $5.50 a pack. The tax raises the price paid by buyers by
less than the tax and lowers the price received by sellers, so
buyers and sellers share the burden of the tax.

---

[4] These propositions also apply to services and factors of production (land, labour, capital).

A Tax on Buyers

Suppose that instead of taxing sellers, Ontario taxes cigarette buyers $2 a pack.

A tax on buyers lowers the amount they are willing to pay the seller, so it decreases demand and shifts the demand curve leftward. To determine the position of this new demand curve, we subtract the tax from the maximum price that buyers are willing to pay for each quantity bought. You can see that without the tax, buyers are willing to buy 35 million packs a year for $6 a pack. So with a $2 tax, they will buy 35 packs a year only if the price including the tax is $6 a pack, which means that they're willing to pay the seller only $4 a pack. The demand curve shifts to become the red curve labelled *D – tax on buyers.*

Equilibrium occurs where the new demand curve intersects the supply curve at a quantity of 32 million packs a year. The price received by sellers falls to $5.50 a pack, and the price paid by buyers rises to $7.50 a pack.

FIGURE 6.8
A Tax on Buyers

myeconlab

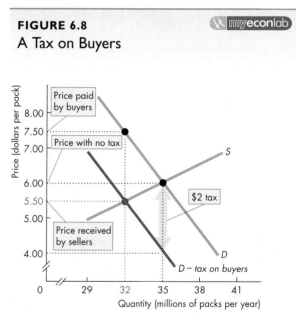

With no tax, 35 million packs a year are bought and sold at $6 a pack. A tax on buyers of $2 a pack shifts the demand curve leftward to *D – tax on buyers.* The equilibrium quantity decreases to 32 million packs a year, the price paid by buyers rises to $7.50 a pack, and the price received by sellers falls to $5.50 a pack. The tax raises the price paid by buyers by less than the tax and lowers the price received by sellers, so buyers and sellers share the burden of the tax.

Equivalence of Tax on Buyers and Sellers

You can see that the tax on buyers in Fig. 6.8 has the same effects as the tax on sellers in Fig. 6.7. In both cases, the equilibrium quantity decreases to 32 million packs a year, the price paid by buyers rises by $1.50 to $7.50 a pack, and the price received by sellers falls by 50¢ to $5.50 a pack. Buyers pay $1.50 of the $2.00 tax, and sellers pay the other 50¢ of the tax.

Can We Share the Burden Equally? Suppose that the government of Ontario wants the burden of the cigarette tax to fall equally on buyers and sellers and declares that a $1 tax be imposed on each. Is the burden of the tax then shared equally?

You can see that it is not. The tax is still $2 a pack. And you've seen that the tax has the same effect regardless of whether it is imposed on sellers or buyers. So imposing half the tax on one and half on the other is like an average of the two cases you've examined. (Draw the demand-supply graph and work out what happens in this case. The demand curve shifts downward by $1 and the supply curve shifts upward by $1. The new equilibrium quantity is still 32 million packs a year. Buyers pay $7.50 a pack, of which $1.50 is tax. Sellers receive from buyers $6.50, but must pay a $1 tax, so they net $5.50 a pack.)

The key point is that when a transaction is taxed, there are two prices: the price paid by buyers, which includes the tax; and the price received by sellers, which excludes the tax. Buyers respond only to the price that includes the tax, because that is the price they pay. Sellers respond only to the price that excludes the tax, because that is the price they receive.

A tax is like a wedge between the buying price and the selling price. It is the size of the wedge, not the side of the market on which the tax is imposed that determines the effects of the tax.

The Employment Insurance tax is an example of a tax that Parliament imposes on *both* buyers of labour (employers) and sellers of labour (employees). The principles you've just learned apply to this tax too. And the market for labour, not Parliament, decides how the burden of the Employment Insurance tax is divided between employers and employees.

In the Ontario cigarette tax example, the buyers bear three times the burden of the tax borne by sellers. But the division of the burden of a tax between buyers and sellers depends on the elasticities of demand and supply, as you will now see.

Tax Division and Elasticity of Demand

The division of the tax between buyers and sellers depends in part on the elasticity of demand. There are two extreme cases:

- Perfectly inelastic demand—buyers pay.
- Perfectly elastic demand—sellers pay.

Perfectly Inelastic Demand Figure 6.9(a) shows the market for insulin, a vital daily medication of diabetics. Demand is perfectly inelastic at 100,000 doses a day, regardless of the price, as shown by the vertical curve D. That is, a diabetic would sacrifice all other goods and services rather than not consume the insulin dose that provides good health. The supply curve of insulin is S. With no tax, the price is $2 a dose and the quantity is 100,000 doses a day.

If insulin is taxed at 20¢ a dose, we must add the tax to the minimum price at which drug companies are willing to sell insulin. The result is the new supply curve $S + tax$. The price rises to $2.20 a dose, but the quantity does not change. Buyers pay the entire sales tax of 20¢ a dose.

Perfectly Elastic Demand Figure 6.9(b) shows the market for pink marker pens. Demand is perfectly elastic at $1 a pen, as shown by the horizontal curve D. If pink pens are less expensive than the others, everyone uses pink. If pink pens are more expensive than the others, no one uses pink. The supply curve is S. With no tax, the price of a pink marker is $1, and the quantity is 4,000 pens a week.

If a tax of 10¢ a pen is imposed on pink marker pens but not on other colours, we add the tax to the minimum price at which sellers are willing to offer pink pens for sale, and the new supply curve is $S + tax$. The price remains at $1 a pen, and the quantity decreases to 1,000 a week. The 10¢ tax leaves the price paid by buyers unchanged but lowers the amount received by sellers by the full amount of the tax. Sellers pay the entire tax of 10¢ a pink pen.

We've seen that when demand is perfectly inelastic, buyers pay the entire tax and when demand is perfectly elastic, sellers pay the entire tax. In the usual case, demand is neither perfectly inelastic nor perfectly elastic and the tax is split between buyers and sellers. But the division depends on the elasticity of demand. The more inelastic the demand, the larger is the amount of the tax paid by buyers.

FIGURE 6.9

Tax and the Elasticity of Demand

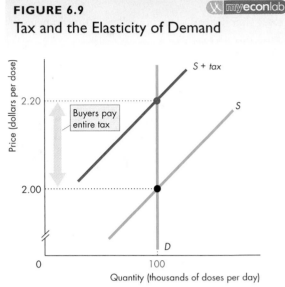

(a) Perfectly inelastic demand

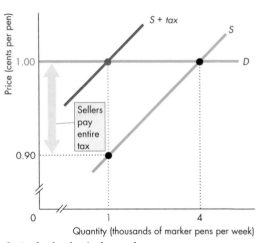

(b) Perfectly elastic demand

Part (a) shows the market for insulin, where demand is perfectly inelastic. With no tax, the price is $2 a dose and the quantity is 100,000 doses a day. A tax of 20¢ a dose shifts the supply curve to $S + tax$. The price rises to $2.20 a dose, but the quantity bought does not change. Buyers pay the entire tax.

Part (b) shows the market for pink pens, in which demand is perfectly elastic. With no tax, the price of a pen is $1 and the quantity is 4,000 pens a week. A tax of 10¢ a pink pen shifts the supply curve to $S + tax$. The price remains at $1 a pen, and the quantity of pink pens sold decreases to 1,000 a week. Sellers pay the entire tax.

Tax Division and Elasticity of Supply

The division of the tax between buyers and sellers also depends, in part, on the elasticity of supply. Again, there are two extreme cases:

- Perfectly inelastic supply—sellers pay.
- Perfectly elastic supply—buyers pay.

Perfectly Inelastic Supply Figure 6.10(a) shows the market for water from a mineral spring that flows at a constant rate that can't be controlled. Supply is perfectly inelastic at 100,000 bottles a week, as shown by the supply curve *S*. The demand curve for the water from this spring is *D*. With no tax, the price is 50¢ a bottle and the 100,000 bottles that flow from the spring are bought.

Suppose this spring water is taxed at 5¢ a bottle. The supply curve does not change because the spring owners still produce 100,000 bottles a week even though the price they receive falls. But buyers are willing to buy the 100,000 bottles only if the price is 50¢ a bottle. So the price remains at 50¢ a bottle. The tax reduces the price received by sellers to 45¢ a bottle, and sellers pay the entire tax.

Perfectly Elastic Supply Figure 6.10(b) shows the market for sand from which computer-chip makers extract silicon. Supply of this sand is perfectly elastic at a price of 10¢ a kilogram, as shown by the supply curve *S*. The demand curve for sand is *D*. With no tax, the price is 10¢ a kilogram and 5,000 kilograms a week are bought.

If this sand is taxed at 1¢ a kilogram, we must add the tax to the minimum supply-price. Sellers are now willing to offer any quantity at 11¢ a kilogram along the curve *S* + *tax*. A new equilibrium is determined where the new supply curve intersects the demand curve: at a price of 11¢ a kilogram and a quantity of 3,000 kilograms a week. The tax has increased the price buyers pay by the full amount of the tax—1¢ a kilogram—and has decreased the quantity sold. Buyers pay the entire tax.

We've seen that when supply is perfectly inelastic, sellers pay the entire tax and when supply is perfectly elastic, buyers pay the entire tax. In the usual case, supply is neither perfectly inelastic nor perfectly elastic and the tax is split between buyers and sellers. But how the tax is split depends on the elasticity of supply. The more elastic the supply, the larger is the amount of the tax paid by buyers.

FIGURE 6.10   myeconlab

Tax and the Elasticity of Supply

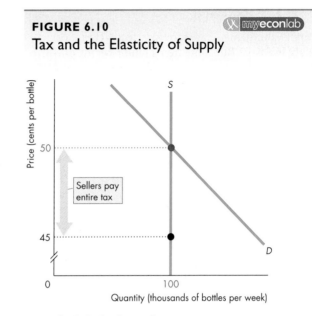

(a) Perfectly inelastic supply

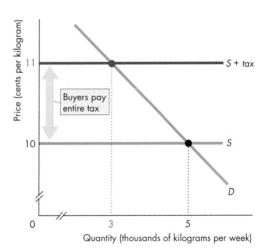

(b) Perfectly elastic supply

Part (a) shows the market for water from a mineral spring. Supply is perfectly inelastic. With no tax, the price is 50¢ a bottle. With a tax of 5¢ a bottle, the price remains at 50¢ a bottle. The number of bottles bought remains the same, but the price received by sellers decreases to 45¢ a bottle. Sellers pay the entire tax.

Part (b) shows the market for sand. Supply is perfectly elastic. With no tax, the price is 10¢ a kilogram. A tax of 1¢ a kilogram increases the minimum supply-price to 11¢ a kilogram. The supply curve shifts to *S* + *tax*. The price increases to 11¢ a kilogram. Buyers pay the entire tax.

Taxes in Practice

Supply and demand are rarely perfectly elastic or perfectly inelastic. But some items tend towards one of the extremes. For example, alcohol, tobacco, and gasoline have low elasticities of demand and high elasticities of supply. So the burden of these taxes falls more heavily on buyers than on sellers. Labour has a low elasticity of supply and a high elasticity of demand. So despite Parliament's desire for employers to pay more of the Employment Insurance tax than do workers, the burden of this tax falls mainly on workers.

The most heavily taxed items are those that have either a low elasticity of demand or a low elasticity of supply. For these items, when a tax is imposed the equilibrium quantity doesn't decrease much. So the government collects a large tax revenue and the deadweight loss from the tax is small.

It is unusual to tax an item heavily if neither its demand nor its supply is inelastic. With an elastic supply *and* demand, a tax brings a large decrease in the equilibrium quantity and a small tax revenue.

Taxes and Efficiency

You've seen that a tax places a wedge between the price that buyers pay and the price that sellers receive. The price that buyers pay is also the buyers' willingness to pay, which measures marginal benefit. The price that sellers receive is also the sellers' minimum supply-price, which equals marginal cost.

So because a tax places a wedge between the buyers' price and the sellers' price, it also puts a wedge between marginal benefit and marginal cost and creates inefficiency. With a higher buyers' price and a lower sellers' price, the tax decreases the quantities produced and consumed and a deadweight loss arises. Figure 6.11 shows the inefficiency of a tax on CD players. With a tax, both consumer surplus and producer surplus shrink. Part of each surplus goes to the government in tax revenue (purple area) and part becomes a deadweight loss—the grey area.

In the extreme cases of perfectly inelastic demand and perfectly inelastic supply, a tax does not change the quantity bought and sold and there is no deadweight loss. The more inelastic is either demand or supply, the smaller is the decrease in quantity and the smaller is the deadweight loss. When demand or supply is perfectly inelastic, the quantity remains constant and no deadweight loss arises.

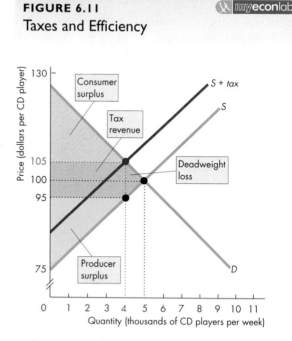

FIGURE 6.11   my econ lab
Taxes and Efficiency

With no tax on CD players, 5,000 a week are bought and sold at $100 each. With a $10 tax on a CD player, the buyer's price rises to $105 a player, the seller's price falls to $95 a player, and the quantity decreases to 4,000 CD players a week. Consumer surplus shrinks to the green area, and the producer surplus shrinks to the blue area. Part of the loss of consumer surplus and producer surplus goes to the government as tax revenue, the purple area. A deadweight loss arises, which is shown by the grey area.

REVIEW QUIZ

1 How does the elasticity of demand influence the effect of a tax on the price paid by buyers, the price received by sellers, the quantity, the tax revenue, and the deadweight loss?
2 How does the elasticity of supply influence the effect of a tax on the price paid by buyers, the price received by sellers, the quantity, the tax revenue, and the deadweight loss?
3 Why does a tax create a deadweight loss?

my econ lab   **Study Plan 6.3**

Your next task is to study intervention in the markets for farm products. These markets have special problems and provide examples of two additional ways of changing market outcomes: subsidies and quotas.

Subsidies and Quotas

AN EARLY OR LATE FROST, A HOT DRY SUMMER, and a wet autumn present just a few of the challenges that fill the lives of farmers with uncertainty and sometimes with economic hardship. Fluctuations in the weather bring big fluctuations in farm output. How do changes in farm output affect farm prices and farm revenues? And how might farmers be helped by intervention in the markets for farm products?

Let's look at some agricultural markets and see how they're affected by the weather and by government interventions.

Harvest Fluctuations

Figure 6.12 shows the market for wheat. In both parts, the demand curve for wheat is D. Once farmers have harvested their crop, they have no control over the quantity supplied and supply is perfectly inelastic along a *momentary supply curve*. With a normal harvest, the momentary supply curve is MS_0, the price is $200 a tonne, the quantity produced is 20 million tonnes, and farm revenue (price multiplied by quantity) is $4 billion.

Poor Harvest In Fig. 6.12(a), a poor harvest decreases the quantity supplied to 15 million tonnes. The momentary supply curve shifts leftward to MS_1, the price rises to $300 a tonne, and farm revenue increases to $4.5 billion. A *decrease* in supply brings a rise in price and an *increase* in farm revenue.

Bumper Harvest In Fig. 6.12(b) a bumper harvest increases the quantity supplied to 25 million tonnes. The momentary supply curve shifts rightward to MS_2, the price falls to $100 a tonne, and farm revenue decreases to $2.5 billion. An *increase* in supply brings a fall in price and a *decrease* in farm revenue.

Elasticity of Demand Farm revenue and the quantity produced fluctuate in opposite directions because the demand for wheat is *inelastic*. The percentage change in the quantity demanded is less than the percentage change in price. In Fig. 6.12(a), the increase in revenue from the higher price ($1.5 billion—the light blue area) exceeds the decrease in revenue from the smaller quantity ($1 billion—the red area). And in Fig. 6.12(b), the decrease in revenue from the lower price ($2 billion—the red area) exceeds the increase in revenue from the increase in the quantity sold ($0.5 billion—the light blue area).

FIGURE 6.12 ⓍⒺ myeconlab
Harvests, Farm Prices, and Farm Revenue

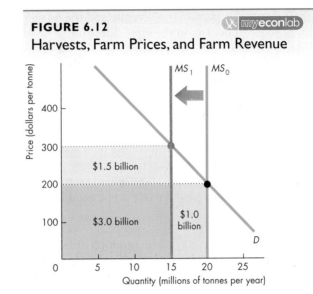

(a) Poor harvest: revenue increases

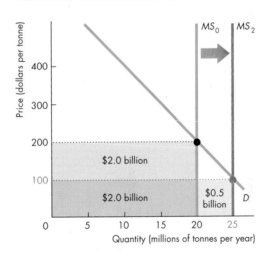

(b) Bumper harvest: revenue decreases

The demand curve for wheat is D. In normal times, the supply curve is MS_0 and 20 million tonnes are sold for $200 a tonne. Farm revenue is $4 billion a year.

In part (a), a poor harvest decreases supply to MS_1. The price rises to $300 a tonne, and farm revenue increases to $4.5 billion—the $1.5 billion increase from the higher price (light blue area) exceeds the $1 billion decrease from the smaller quantity sold (red area).

In part (b), a bumper harvest increases supply to MS_2. The price falls to $100 a tonne, and farm revenue decreases to $2.5 billion—the $2 billion decrease from the lower price (red area) exceeds the $0.5 billion increase from the increase in the quantity sold (light blue area).

If demand is *elastic*, farm revenue and the quantity produced fluctuate in the same direction. Bumper harvests increase revenue, and poor harvests decrease it. But the demand for most agricultural products is inelastic, so the case we've studied is the relevant one.

Avoiding a Fallacy of Composition Although *total* farm revenue increases when there is a poor harvest, the revenue of those *individual* farmers whose entire crop is wiped out decreases. Those whose crop is unaffected gain. So a poor harvest is not good news for all farmers.

Because the markets for farm products often confront farmers with low incomes, government intervention occurs in these markets. In Canada, there are more than 100 farm marketing boards, supported by federal and provincial governments. A **farm marketing board** is a regulatory agency that intervenes in an agricultural market to stabilize the price.

Farm marketing boards might use price floors that work a bit like the minimum wage to stabilize farm prices. You've already seen that a price floor creates a surplus and is inefficient. These same conclusions apply to markets for farm products. But farm marketing boards often use two other methods:

- Subsidies
- Production quotas

Subsidies

A **subsidy** is a payment made by the government to a producer. To see the effects of a subsidy, we'll look at a market for peanuts. Figure 6.13 shows this market. The demand for peanuts is *D* and the supply of peanuts is *S*. With no subsidy, the price is $40 a tonne and 40 million tonnes of peanuts are produced.

Suppose that the government introduces a subsidy of $20 a tonne. A subsidy is like a negative tax. You've seen that a tax is equivalent to an increase in cost. A subsidy is equivalent to a decrease in cost. And a decrease in cost brings an increase in supply.

To determine the position of the new supply curve, we subtract the subsidy from farmers' minimum supply-price. Without a subsidy, farmers are willing to offer 40 million tonnes a year for $40 a tonne. So with a subsidy of $20 a tonne, they will offer 40 million tonnes a year if the price is as low as

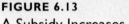

FIGURE 6.13
A Subsidy Increases Production

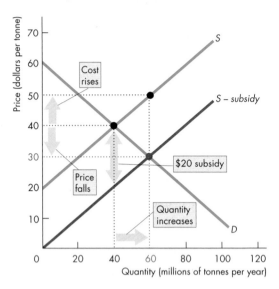

With no subsidy, 40 million tonnes a year are produced at $40 a tonne. A subsidy of $20 a tonne shifts the supply curve rightward to *S – subsidy*. The quantity produced increases to 60 million tonnes a year, the price falls to $30 a tonne, and farmers receive $50 a tonne (the price plus the subsidy). Because marginal cost ($50) exceeds marginal benefit ($30), a deadweight loss arises.

$20 a tonne. The supply curve shifts to the red curve labelled *S – subsidy*.

Equilibrium occurs where the new supply curve intersects the demand curve at 60 million tonnes a year. The price falls to $30 a tonne, but the price plus subsidy received by farmers rises to $50 a tonne.

Because the supply curve *S* is the marginal cost curve, and the demand curve is the marginal benefit curve, a subsidy raises marginal cost above marginal benefit and creates a deadweight loss from overproduction.

The effects of subsidies spill over to the rest of the world. Because they lower the price, subsidized farmers offer some of their output for sale on the world market, which lowers the price in the rest of the world. Faced with lower prices, farmers in other countries decrease production and receive smaller revenues.

Farm subsidies are a major obstacle to achieving an efficient use of resources in the global markets for farm products and are a source of tension between Europe, the United States, and developing nations.

Production Quotas

The markets for milk, eggs, and poultry (among others) have, from time to time, been regulated with production quotas. A **production quota** is an upper limit to the quantity of a good that may be produced in a specified period. To discover the effects of quotas, we'll look at a market for milk in Fig. 6.14. With no quota, the price is $3 a tonne and 16 million tonnes a year are produced.

Suppose that the dairy farmers want to limit total production to get a higher price. They persuade the marketing board to introduce a production quota that limits milk production to a maximum of 14 million tonnes a year.

The effect of a production quota depends on whether it is set below or above the equilibrium quantity. If the government introduced a quota above 16 million tonnes a year, the equilibrium quantity in Fig. 6.14, nothing would change because dairy farmers are already producing less than the quota. But a quota of 14 million is less than the equilibrium quantity. Figure 6.14 shows the effects of the production quota.

To implement the quota, each farmer is assigned a production limit and the total of the production limits equals 14 million tonnes. Production that in total exceeds 14 million tonnes is illegal, so we've shaded the illegal region above the quota. Farmers are no longer permitted to produce the equilibrium quantity because it is in the illegal region. As in the case of price ceilings and floors, market forces and political forces are in conflict.

When the marketing board sets a production quota, it does not regulate the price. Market forces determine it. In the example in Fig. 6.14, with production limited to 14 million tonnes a year, the market price rises to $5 a tonne.

The quota not only raises the price but also *lowers* the marginal cost of producing milk because the farmers slide down their supply (and marginal cost) curves.

A production quota is inefficient because it results in underproduction. At the quota quantity, marginal benefit is equal to the market price and marginal cost is less than the market price, so marginal benefit exceeds marginal cost.

Because of these effects of a quota, such arrangements are often popular with producers and in some cases, producers, not governments, attempt to implement them. But it is hard for quotas to work when they are voluntary. The reason is that each producer has an incentive to cheat and produce a little bit more than the allotted quota. You can see why by comparing the market price and marginal cost. If one producer

could get away with a tiny increase in production, her or his profit would increase. But if all producers cheat by producing above the quota, the market moves back towards the unregulated equilibrium and the gain for producers disappears.

FIGURE 6.14
A Quota Limits Production

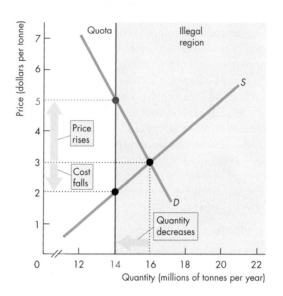

With no quota, 16 million tonnes a year are produced at $3 a tonne. A quota of 14 million tonnes a year reduces the equilibrium quantity to 14 million tonnes a year, the price rises to $5 a tonne, and marginal cost falls to $2 a tonne. Because marginal cost ($2) is less than marginal benefit ($5), a deadweight loss arises from underproduction.

REVIEW QUIZ

1 How do poor harvests and bumper harvests influence farm prices and farm revenues?
2 Explain how a subsidy influences farm prices and output. How does a subsidy affect farm revenues?
3 Explain how a production quota influences farm prices and output. How does a production quota affect farm revenues?

myeconlab Study Plan 6.4

Governments intervene in some markets by making it illegal to trade in a good. Let's now see how these markets work.

Markets for Illegal Goods

THE MARKETS FOR MANY GOODS AND SERVICES are regulated, and buying and selling some goods is illegal. The best-known examples of such goods are drugs, such as marijuana, cocaine, Ecstasy, and heroin.

Despite the fact that these drugs are illegal, trade in them is a multibillion-dollar business. This trade can be understood by using the same economic model and principles that explain trade in legal goods. To study the market for illegal goods, we're first going to examine the prices and quantities that would prevail if these goods were not illegal. Next, we'll see how prohibition works. Then we'll see how a tax might be used to limit the consumption of these goods.

A Free Market for Drugs

Figure 6.15 shows the market for drugs. The demand curve, *D,* shows that, other things remaining the same, the lower the price of drugs, the larger is the quantity of drugs demanded. The supply curve, *S,* shows that, other things remaining the same, the lower the price of drugs, the smaller is the quantity supplied. If drugs were not illegal, the quantity bought and sold would be Q_C and the price would be P_C.

A Market for Illegal Drugs

When a good is illegal, the cost of trading in the good increases. By how much the cost increases and who incurs the cost depend on the penalties for violating the law and the effectiveness with which the law is enforced. The larger the penalties and the more effective the policing, the higher are the costs. Penalties might be imposed on sellers, buyers, or both.

Penalties on Sellers Drug dealers in Canada face large penalties if their activities are detected. For example, a grower of marijuana with 50 plants could be fined and imprisoned for up to 14 years. A heroin trafficker could pay a fine and be imprisoned for life. These penalties are part of the cost of supplying illegal drugs, and they bring a decrease in supply—a leftward shift in the supply curve. To determine the new supply curve, we add the cost of breaking the law to the minimum price that drug dealers are willing to accept. In Fig. 6.15, the cost of breaking the law by selling drugs (*CBL*) is added to the minimum price that dealers will accept and the supply curve shifts

FIGURE 6.15
A Market for an Illegal Good

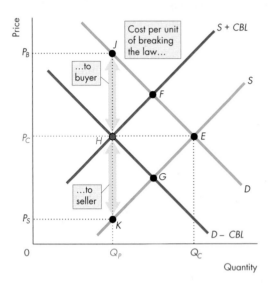

The demand curve for drugs is *D*, and the supply curve is *S*. If drugs are not illegal, the quantity bought and sold is Q_C at a price of P_C—point *E*. If selling drugs is illegal, the cost of breaking the law by selling drugs (*CBL*) is added to the minimum supply-price and supply decreases to *S + CBL*. The market moves to point *F*.

If buying drugs is illegal, the cost of breaking the law is subtracted from the maximum price that buyers are willing to pay, and demand decreases to *D − CBL*. The market moves to point *G*.

With both buying and selling illegal, the supply curve and the demand curve shift and the market moves to point *H*. The market price remains at P_C, but the market price plus the penalty for buying rises—point *J*—and the market price minus the penalty for selling falls—point *K*.

leftward to *S + CBL.* If penalties were imposed only on sellers, the market would move from point *E* to point *F.*

Penalties on Buyers In Canada, it is illegal to *possess* drugs such as marijuana, cocaine, Ecstasy, and heroin. For example, possession of 30 grams of marijuana can bring a one-year prison term and a $2,000 fine and possession of heroin can bring a seven-year prison term. Penalties fall on buyers, and the cost of breaking the law must be subtracted from the value of the good to determine the maximum price buyers are willing to pay for the drugs. Demand decreases, and the demand curve shifts leftward. In Fig. 6.15, the demand curve shifts to $D - CBL$. If penalties were imposed only on buyers, the market would move from point E to point G.

Penalties on Both Sellers and Buyers If penalties are imposed on both sellers *and* buyers, both supply and demand decrease. In Fig. 6.15, the costs of breaking the law are the same for both buyers and sellers, so both curves shift leftward by the same amount. The market moves to point H. The market price remains at the competitive market price P_C, but the quantity bought decreases to Q_P. The buyer pays P_C plus the cost of breaking the law, which is P_B. And the seller receives P_C minus the cost of breaking the law, which is P_S.

The larger the penalties and the greater the degree of law enforcement, the larger is the decrease in demand and/or supply. If the penalties are heavier on sellers, the supply curve shifts farther than the demand curve and the market price rises above P_C. If the penalties are heavier on buyers, the demand curve shifts farther than the supply curve and the market price falls below P_C. In Canada, the penalties on sellers are larger than those on buyers, so the quantity of drugs traded decreases and the market price increases compared with a free market.

With high enough penalties and effective law enforcement, it is possible to decrease demand and/or supply to the point at which the quantity bought is zero. But in reality, such an outcome is unusual. It does not happen in Canada in the case of illegal drugs. The key reason is the high cost of law enforcement and insufficient resources for the police to achieve effective enforcement. Because of this situation, some people suggest that drugs (and other illegal goods) should be legalized and sold openly but should also be taxed at a high rate in the same way that legal drugs such as alcohol are taxed. How would such an arrangement work?

Legalizing and Taxing Drugs

From your study of the effects of taxes, it is easy to see that the quantity of drugs bought could be decreased if drugs were legalized and taxed. A sufficiently high tax could be imposed to decrease supply, raise the price, and achieve the same decrease in the quantity bought as with a prohibition on drugs. The government would collect a large tax revenue.

Illegal Trading to Evade the Tax It is likely that an extremely high tax rate would be needed to cut the quantity of drugs bought to the level prevailing with a prohibition. It is also likely that many drug dealers and consumers would try to cover up their activities to evade the tax. If they did act in this way, they would face the cost of breaking the law—the tax law. If the penalty for tax law violation is as severe and as effectively policed as drug-dealing laws, the analysis we've already conducted applies also to this case. The quantity of drugs bought would depend on the penalties for law breaking and on the way in which the penalties are assigned to buyers and sellers.

Taxes Versus Prohibition: Some Pros and Cons Which is more effective: prohibition or taxes? In favour of taxes and against prohibition is the fact that the tax revenue can be used to make law enforcement more effective. It can also be used to run a more effective education campaign against illegal drug use. In favour of prohibition and against taxes is the fact that prohibition sends a signal that might influence preferences, decreasing the demand for illegal drugs. Also, some people intensely dislike the idea of the government profiting from trade in harmful substances.

REVIEW QUIZ

1 How does the imposition of a penalty for selling an illegal drug influence demand, supply, price, and the quantity of the drug consumed?
2 How does the imposition of a penalty for possessing an illegal drug influence demand, supply, price, and the quantity of the drug consumed?
3 How does the imposition of a penalty for selling *or* possessing an illegal drug influence demand, supply, price, and the quantity of the drug consumed?
4 Is there any case for legalizing drugs?

Ⓧ myeconlab **Study Plan 6.5**

◆ You now know how to use the demand and supply model to predict prices, to study government actions in markets, and to study the sources and costs of inefficiency. Before you leave this topic, take a look at *Reading Between the Lines* on pp. 142–143 about the rise in the minium wage in Alberta.

The Minimum Wage in Action

COCHRANE TIMES, AUGUST 24, 2005

Alberta's minimum wage finally gets boost

As the minimum wage increases in Alberta, consumers may be the ones paying the price.

On Sept. 1, the minimum wage in our province will increase from a measly $5.90 an hour to $7 an hour, putting the minimum wage on par with most other Canadian provinces, a move that unfortunately may mean menu increases at some local restaurants. ...

As a reaction to the minimum wage increase, Taylor last month raised starting wages at McDonald's from $6.50 (part time) and $8 (full time) to $7.50 (part time) and $9 (full time).

And the owner said there's no way the pay increase will not sting a little bit.

"I use about 1,200 hours of labour weekly, so a dollar raise across the board ... it's got to hurt," he said.

"I mean, I can't really see how it won't affect prices eventually."

Across town at Dairy Queen, however, the owner said prices aren't likely to increase. ...

While the wage increase may mean shelling out a few cents more for a Big Mac, 45,000 Albertans in entry-level jobs will benefit from the wage increase.

"Increasing the minimum wage is one way of ensuring Albertans get a better start in the workforce," said Human Resources and Employment Minister Mike Cardinal in a recent news release. "Most Albertans, including employers and employees, agree that the minimum wage should be raised." ...

Essence of the Story

■ The minimum wage in Alberta increased from $5.90 an hour to $7 an hour on September 1, 2005.

■ McDonald's increased its wage rates from $6.50 to $7.50 for part-time workers and from $8 to $9 for full-time workers in August.

■ McDonald's hires 1,200 hours of labour a week.

■ 45,000 Albertans will benefit from the wage increase.

■ Alberta's employment minister said "Increasing the minimum wage is one way of ensuring Albertans get a better start in the workforce."

Economic Analysis

■ Minimum wage rates in Canada range from $6.25 an hour in Newfoundland to $8.50 an hour in Nunavut. Figure 1 shows the data.

■ The minimum wage affects younger low-skilled workers more than older and more skilled workers.

■ A rise in the minimum wage rate in Alberta will decrease employment and increase the unemployment rate of young workers.

■ Figure 2 shows the Alberta labour market for young workers. The demand curve is *LD* and the supply curve is *LS*. (The assumed elasticity of demand is 0.5 and the assumed elasticity of supply is 0.25.)

■ Before September 1, 2005, when the minimum wage rate was $5.90 an hour, 45,000 young people were employed and approximately 5,000 were unemployed.

■ The rise in the minimum wage decreases the quantity of labour demanded, increases the quantity of labour supplied, and increases the unemployment of young workers.

■ With the assumed elasticities of demand and supply, unemployment approximately doubles.

■ If the elasticities are smaller than those assumed, unemployment will increase by a smaller amount.

■ The outcome in Fig. 2 assumes *ceteris paribus*—other things remaining the same.

■ Figure 3 shows that because other things are not the same across the provinces, many factors other than the minimum wage influence the unemployment rate of young workers.

■ The extent of unemployment among young workers, measured here by the ratio of the unemployment rates of the under 25s to the over 25s, is correlated with the minimum wage but the correlation is weak.

You're the Voter

■ Would you support or oppose a rise in the minimum wage in your own province?

■ Can you think of a better way of improving the incomes of young workers who have few skills?

Figure 1 Minimum wage rates across Canada

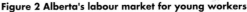

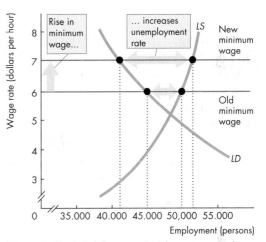

Figure 2 Alberta's labour market for young workers

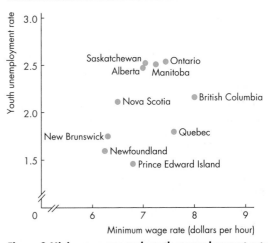

Figure 3 Minimum wage and youth unemployment rates

SUMMARY

KEY POINTS

Housing Markets and Rent Ceilings
(pp. 124–128)

- A decrease in the supply of housing raises rents.
- Higher rents stimulate building, and in the long run, the quantity of housing increases and rents fall.
- A rent ceiling that is set below the equilibrium rent creates a housing shortage, wasteful search, and a black market.

The Labour Market and the Minimum Wage
(pp. 128–131)

- A decrease in the demand for low-skilled labour lowers the wage rate and reduces employment.
- The lower wage rate encourages people with low skill to acquire more skill, which decreases the supply of low-skilled labour and, in the long run, raises their wage rate.
- A minimum wage set above the equilibrium wage rate creates unemployment and increases the amount of time people spend searching for a job.
- A minimum wage hits low-skilled young people hardest.

Taxes (pp. 132–136)

- A tax raises price but usually by less than the tax.
- The shares of a tax paid by buyers and by sellers depend on the elasticity of demand and the elasticity of supply.
- The less elastic the demand and the more elastic the supply, the greater is the price increase, the smaller is the quantity decrease, and the larger is the share of the tax paid by buyers.
- If demand is perfectly elastic or supply is perfectly inelastic, sellers pay the entire tax. And if demand is perfectly inelastic or supply is perfectly elastic, buyers pay the entire tax.

Subsidies and Quotas (pp. 137–139)

- Farm revenues fluctuate because supply fluctuates. Because the demand for most farm products is inelastic, a decrease in supply increases farm revenue, while an increase in supply decreases farm revenue.

- A subsidy is like a negative tax. It lowers the price and leads to inefficient overproduction.
- A quota leads to inefficient underproduction, which raises the price.

Markets for Illegal Goods (pp. 140–141)

- Penalties on sellers of an illegal good increase the cost of selling the good and decrease its supply. Penalties on buyers decrease their willingness to pay and decrease the demand for the good.
- The higher the penalties and the more effective the law enforcement, the smaller is the quantity bought.
- A tax that is set at a sufficiently high rate will decrease the quantity of drug consumed, but there will be a tendency for the tax to be evaded.

KEY FIGURES

Figure 6.2   A Rent Ceiling, 126
Figure 6.3   The Inefficiency of a Rent Ceiling, 127
Figure 6.5   Minimum Wage and Unemployment, 130
Figure 6.6   Inefficiency of a Minimum Wage, 130
Figure 6.11   Taxes and Efficiency, 136
Figure 6.12   Harvests, Farm Prices, and Farm Revenue, 137
Figure 6.13   A Subsidy Increases Production, 138
Figure 6.15   A Market for an Illegal Good, 140

KEY TERMS

Black market, 126
Farm marketing board, 138
Living wage, 131
Minimum wage, 130
Price ceiling, 125
Price floor, 130
Production quota, 139
Rent ceiling, 125
Search activity, 126
Subsidy, 138
Tax incidence, 132

PROBLEMS

Go to **myeconlab** for solutions to odd-numbered problems and additional exercises.

1. The figure shows the demand for and supply of rental housing in the Village.

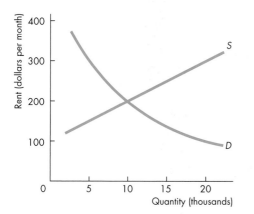

a. What is the market equilibrium?
If a rent ceiling is set at $150 a month, what is
b. The quantity of housing rented?
c. The shortage of housing?
d. The maximum price that someone is willing to pay for the last unit of housing available?

2. The figure shows the demand for and supply of rental housing in Townsville.

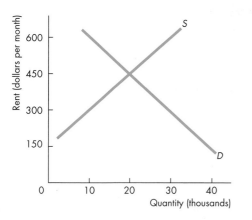

a. What is the market equilibrium?
If a rent ceiling is set at $300 a month, what is
b. The quantity of housing rented?
c. The shortage of housing?
d. The maximum price that someone is willing to pay for the last unit available?

3. The table gives the demand for and supply of teenage labour.

Wage rate (dollars per hour)	Quantity demanded	Quantity supplied
	(hours per month)	
4	3,000	1,000
5	2,500	1,500
6	2,000	2,000
7	1,500	2,500
8	1,000	3,000

a. What are the equilibrium wage rate and level of employment?
b. What is the quantity of unemployment?
c. If a minimum wage of $5 an hour is set for teenagers, how many hours do they work?
d. If a minimum wage of $5 an hour is set for teenagers, how many hours of their labour is unemployed?
e. If a minimum wage is set at $7 an hour for teenagers, what are quantities of employment and unemployment?
f. If a minimum wage is set at $7 an hour and demand increases by 500 hours a month, what is the wage rate paid to teenagers and how many hours of their labour are unemployed?

4. The table gives the demand for and supply of labour of high school graduates.

Wage rate (dollars per hour)	Quantity demanded	Quantity supplied
	(hours per month)	
8	10,000	4,000
9	8,000	6,000
10	6,000	8,000
11	4,000	10,000
12	2,000	12,000

a. On a graph, mark in the equilibrium wage rate and level of employment.
b. What is the level of unemployment?
c. If a minimum wage is set at $9 an hour, how many hours do high school graduates work?
d. If a minimum wage is set at $9 an hour, how many hours of labour are unemployed?
e. If a minimum wage is set at $10 an hour, what are employment and unemployment?
f. If the minimum wage is $10 an hour and demand decreases by 2,000 hours a month, what is the wage rate paid to high school graduates and how many hours of their labour are unemployed?

5. The table gives the demand and supply schedules for chocolate brownies:

Price (cents per brownie)	Quantity demanded	Quantity supplied
	(millions per day)	
50	5	3
60	4	4
70	3	5
80	2	6
90	1	7

a. If brownies are not taxed, what is the price of a brownie and how many are consumed?
b. If brownies are taxed at 20¢ each, what is the price and how many brownies are consumed? Who pays the tax?

6. Demand and supply schedules for roses are

Price (dollars per bunch)	Quantity demanded	Quantity supplied
	(bunches per week)	
10	100	40
12	90	60
14	80	80
16	70	100
18	60	120

a. If there is no tax on roses, what is the price and how many bunches are bought?
b. If a tax of $6 a bunch is introduced, what is the price and how many bunches are bought? Who pays the tax?

7. Demand and supply schedules for rice are

Price (dollars per box)	Quantity demanded	Quantity supplied
	(boxes per week)	
1.00	3,500	500
1.10	3,250	1,000
1.20	3,000	1,500
1.30	2,750	2,000
1.40	2,500	2,500
1.50	2,250	3,000
1.60	2,000	3,500

If the government introduces a subsidy of $0.30 a box on rice, what are the price of rice, the marginal cost of producing rice, and the quantity produced?

8. In problem 7, if instead of a subsidy, the government sets a quota of 2,000 boxes a week, what now are your answers?

CRITICAL THINKING

1. Study *Reading Between the Lines* (pp. 142–143) about the market for young workers in Alberta.
   a. If the minimum wage in Alberta were abolished, what do you predict would happen to the quantity of labour employed and the average wage rate?
   b. With the abolition of the minimum wage in Alberta, who would gain and who would lose? Would *society* gain or lose?
   c. Why do you think a large number of Albertans and the government of Alberta supported an increase in the minimum wage in 2005?

WEB EXERCISES

Use the links on myeconlab to work the following exercise.

1. Find information about living wage campaigns.
   a. What is the campaign for a living wage?
   b. How would you distinguish the minimum wage from a living wage?
   c. If the living wage campaign succeeds in getting wages increased above their equilibrium levels, how would you expect the living wage to affect (i) the quantity of labour demanded, (ii) the quantity of labour supplied and, (iii) the amount of unemployment?
   d. Would a living wage above the equilibrium wage be efficient?
   e. Who would stand to gain from a living wage above the equilibrium wage?
   f. Who would stand to lose from a living wage above the equilibrium wage?
   g. Would a living wage above the equilibrium wage be fair?

2. Find information about sugar quotas in Europe. Why do you think the European nations assign production quotas for sugar? If the European sugar quotas are less than the equilibrium quantities, who benefits from and who pays for the quotas?

UNDERSTANDING HOW MARKETS WORK

The Amazing Market

The four chapters that you've just studied explain how markets work. The market is an amazing instrument. It enables people who have never met and who know nothing about each other to interact and do business. It also enables us to allocate our scarce resources to the uses that we value most highly. Markets can be very simple or highly organized.

A simple market is one that the American historian Daniel J. Boorstin describes in *The Discoverers* (p. 161). In the late fourteenth century,

> *The Muslim caravans that went southward from Morocco across the Atlas Mountains arrived after twenty days at the shores of the Senegal River. There the Moroccan traders laid out separate piles of salt, of beads from Ceutan coral, and cheap manufactured goods. Then they retreated out of sight. The local tribesmen, who lived in the strip mines where they dug their gold, came to the shore and put a heap of gold beside each pile of Moroccan goods. Then they, in turn, went out of view, leaving the Moroccan traders either to take the gold offered for a particular pile or to reduce the pile of their merchandise to suit the offered price in gold. Once again the Moroccan traders withdrew, and the process went on. By this system of commercial etiquette, the Moroccans collected their gold.*

An organized market is the Toronto Stock Exchange, which trades many millions of stocks each day. Another is an auction at which the government sells rights to broadcasters and cellular telephone companies for the use of the airwaves.

All of these markets determine the prices at which exchanges take place and enable both buyers and sellers to benefit.

Everything and anything that can be exchanged is traded in markets. There are markets for goods and services; for resources such as labour, capital, and raw materials; for dollars, pounds, and yen; for goods to be delivered now and for goods to be delivered in the future. Only the imagination places limits on what can be traded in markets.

You began your study of markets in Chapter 3 by learning about the laws of demand and supply. There, you discovered the forces that make prices adjust to coordinate buying plans and selling plans. In Chapter 4, you learned how to calculate and use the concept of elasticity to predict the responsiveness of prices and quantities to changes in supply and demand. In Chapter 5, you studied efficiency and discovered the conditions under which a competitive market sends resources to uses in which they are valued most highly. And finally, in Chapter 6, you studied markets in action. There, you learned how markets cope with change and discovered how they operate when governments intervene to fix prices, impose taxes or quotas, subsidize production, or make some goods illegal.

The laws of demand and supply that you've learned and used in these four chapters were discovered during the nineteenth century by some remarkable economists. We conclude our study of demand and supply and markets by looking at the lives and times of some of these economists and by talking to a leading Canadian economist who studies labour markets.

Discovering the Laws of Demand and Supply

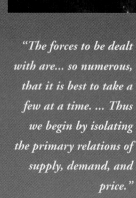

> *"The forces to be dealt with are... so numerous, that it is best to take a few at a time. ... Thus we begin by isolating the primary relations of supply, demand, and price."*
>
> ALFRED
> MARSHALL
> *The Principles
> of Economics*

THE ECONOMIST

Alfred Marshall *(1842–1924) grew up in an England that was being transformed by the railroad and by the expansion of manufacturing. Mary Paley was one of Marshall's students at Cambridge, and when Alfred and Mary married, in 1877, celibacy rules barred Alfred from continuing to teach at Cambridge. By 1884, with more liberal rules, the Marshalls returned to Cambridge, where Alfred became Professor of Political Economy.*

Many others had a hand in refining the theory of demand and supply, but the first thorough and complete statement of the theory as we know it today was set out by Alfred Marshall, with the acknowledged help of Mary Paley Marshall. Published in 1890, this monumental treatise, The Principles of Economics, *became the textbook on economics on both sides of the Atlantic for almost half a century. Marshall was an outstanding mathematician, but he kept mathematics and even diagrams in the background. His supply and demand diagram appears only in a footnote.*

THE ISSUES

The laws of demand and supply that you studied in Chapter 3 were discovered during the 1830s by Antoine-Augustin Cournot (1801–1877), a professor of mathematics at the University of Lyon, France. Although Cournot was the first to use demand and supply, it was the development and expansion of the railroads during the 1850s that gave the newly emerging theory its first practical applications. Railroads then were at the cutting edge of technology just as airlines are today. And as in the airline industry today, competition among the railroads was fierce.

Dionysius Lardner (1793–1859), an Irish professor of philosophy at the University of London, used demand and supply to show railroad companies how they could increase their profits by cutting rates on long-distance business on which competition was fiercest and by raising rates on short-haul business on which they had less to fear from other transportation suppliers.

Today, economists use the principles that Lardner worked out during the 1850s to calculate the freight rates and passenger fares that will give airlines the largest possible profit. And the rates calculated have a lot in common with the railroad rates of the nineteenth century. On local routes on which there is little competition, fares per kilometre are highest, and on long-distance routes on which the airlines compete fiercely, fares per kilometre are lowest.

Known satirically among scientists of the day as "Dionysius Diddler," Lardner worked on an amazing range of problems from astronomy to railway engineering to economics. A colourful character, he would have been a regular guest on late-night talk shows if they had been around in the 1850s. Lardner visited the École des Ponts et Chaussées (School of

Bridges and Roads) in Paris and must have learned a great deal from Jules Dupuit.

In France, Jules Dupuit (1804–1866), a French engineer/economist, used demand to calculate the benefits from building a bridge and, once the bridge was built, for calculating the toll to charge for its use. His work was the forerunner of what is today called *cost-benefit analysis*. Working with the principles invented by Dupuit, economists today calculate the costs and benefits of highways and airports, dams, and power stations.

NOW

Today, using the same principles that Dupuit devised, economists calculate whether the benefits of expanding airports and air-traffic control facilities are sufficient to cover their costs. Airline companies use the principles developed by Lardner to set their prices and to decide when to offer "seat sales." Like the railroads before them, the airlines charge a high price per kilometre on short flights, for which they face little competition, and a low price per kilometre on long flights, for which competition is fierce.

THEN

Dupuit used the law of demand to determine whether a bridge or canal would be valued enough by its users to justify the cost of building it. Lardner first worked out the relationship between the cost of production and supply and used demand and supply theory to explain the costs, prices, and profits of railroad operations. He also used the theory to discover ways of increasing revenue by raising rates on short-haul business and lowering them on long-distance freight.

Markets do an amazing job. The laws of demand and supply help us to understand how markets work. But in some situations, a market must be designed and institutions must be created to enable the market to function well. Also, the item traded often makes a crucial difference to how the market works. One market that has some special features is the labour market, as you will discover in the conversation on the following pages with Paul Beaudry, one of Canada's leading economists.

Paul Beaudry is a Professor of Economics at the University of British Columbia and currently holds the Canada Research Chair in Economics. He is also a Faculty Research Fellow at the National Bureau of Economic Research in the United States. He was born in Québec City in 1960. He obtained a bachelor's degree in Economics at the Université Laval, a master's degree at the University of British Columbia, and a doctoral degree at Princeton University. Professor Beaudry's research is concerned with the functioning of markets, particularly the labour market. Professor Beaudry was granted the Bank of Canada's Research Fellowship for 2005.

Paul Beaudry

Benoît Carmichael and Patrick González (co-authors of our French Canadian edition) talked with Paul Beaudry about his work and the progress economists have made since the time of Alfred Marshall in understanding how markets work.

Professor Beaudry, what attracted you to economics?

Several factors influenced my choice. During my secondary education and at the beginning of the CEGEP, I was mostly interested in mathematics and science. Then, at the university, I was introduced to philosophy and to philosophical questions. Philosophy classes deeply moved me. In fact, they changed my vision of the world. I became passionate about fundamental questions such as: Why do I exist? What is the notion of good and evil? What is a just society?

All these questions started to make me doubt. Initially, I thought that I would follow a career in science or engineering, but all these questions put me in a state of uncertainty. So I decided to stop my studies and travel. I worked in construction, so I could afford a big trip for myself. I travelled through all of Europe, North Africa, and Turkey. While on these trips, I talked a lot about philosophical and social questions with the people that I met. It was a fabulous experience!

During these talks economic questions were often raised: Why are certain countries rich and others poor? What should we do to reduce these inequalities? I quickly realized that the questions I understood the least were those related to the economics, and I thought that these question were important ones. Moreover, I was beginning to believe that several of the fundamental philosophical questions I was thinking about were impossible to solve. But this was not the case for economic questions. So I decided to get back to my studies and to study economics. I found that studies in economics allowed me both to address important social and human questions and to use formal mathematics tools that I liked.

What do we know today about the functioning of markets that Alfred Marshall ignored?

In the classical framework of Alfred Marshall, prices play an important role, but quite a simple one. When the price of a good rises, consumers want to consume less of it, and producers want to produce more of it. In Marshall's world, economic market participants do not try to extract information from prices, they react in a mechanical way.

On the other hand, in several markets, prices play a much more complex role than that envisioned by Marshall. Let's take the example of the stock market. The holder of a share listed on the stock exchange won't necessarily want to sell it when its price increases. Indeed, the increase in the share price can signify that the underlying company is in a good position to make profits; the holder will then want to wait for the share price to increase again. Let's take another example. When we buy a bottle of wine, we often think that its price is an indication of the quality of the wine. The information role of prices did not appear in Marshall's work.

In your research work, you are very interested in labour markets. What are the characteristics of labour markets that make them different from other markets?

When a company hires someone, it must ensure that the person is sufficiently motivated to perform the required tasks diligently and not shirk. In contrast, when a company buys a tonne of steel to build a bridge, it needn't wonder about the steel's motivation to do its work. A labour market is therefore very different from other markets because it is made up of individuals who have their own motivations and objectives. That is why one of the roles of a good employer is to find a way to reconcile the interests of an employee with those of the company.

For most goods, this kind of problem doesn't exist. Buying a good at the lowest possible price often proves to be the best strategy. However, an employer has to recognize that his employees want to be treated fairly and impartially. If he doesn't pay them enough, it is most probable that they won't put in much effort or show very much enthusiasm for their work.

> " ... when a company buys a tonne of steel to build a bridge, it needn't wonder about the steel's motivation to do its work. A labour market is ... different ... because it is made of individuals who have their own motivations and objectives. "

Marshall believed that the market would direct young people towards the jobs they do best. But he believed that taxes should cover the cost of education. Today, some people see education as an investment in human capital that should be paid for by the families who benefit. What is your view on this issue?

Education has two aspects. It increases the skills of an individual in the labour market, and therefore also increases a person's earnings. Also, thanks to education, people are more informed, and that is important for the functioning of a democracy. In the first case, the gain is essentially private, so it seems reasonable to ask young people or their families to contribute to the costs of education. However, in the second case, the gain obtained through education is a social gain, so it seems fair that the state should cover a part of costs of education. This is, in fact, what we now observe. It remains very difficult to make decisions about what percentage of university fees students should pay? 75 percent? 50 percent? 25 percent? This question is open to debate.

Over the past 25 years in North America, we have observed a deterioration in the relative compensation of low-skilled workers. However, in European countries such as Germany, this decrease hasn't been as large. What explains this difference?

It is a very good question, and a topic that still raises lots of discussion. My own research puts forward the important role of demography. In North America, the baby boom of the 1950s and 1960s considerably increased the work force at the end of the 1970s and the beginning of the 1980s. On the other hand, during the same period, neither private savings nor investment in physical capital increased. Thus, the increase in labour supply and the absence of an increase in the supply of physical capital created a relative shortage of physical capital.

The economy reacted to this shortage in several ways. We have observed a strong tendency towards the adoption of new methods of production which use physical capital in an efficient way, as well as an increase in imports of goods that use physical capital in an intensive way. These two changes have resulted in a reduction of the demand for labour, in particular among less-qualified workers. This, in turn, has

> " *What we have to remember is that the labour market is principally a market of long-term relations.* "

resulted in an increase of the gap in income between qualified and less-qualified workers. In Germany, where the baby boom was not so importance, the problem of a relative shortage of physical capital did not occur. The structure of employment remained stable and the income of less-qualified workers did not decrease.

Through your work, you have demonstrated that people who enter the labour market during a time of recession have less interesting career prospects than those who enter it during a period of expansion. Why is this so?

In spite of the fact that the labour market does not function exactly as the apple market does, it still is a market which reflects the strengths of the supply and demand model. In times of recession, the demand for labour is weak and people who enter the labour market in such times receive less attractive job offers.

What we have to remember is that the labour market is principally a market of long-term relations. Thus, if a worker enters the labour market during a good period, he will generally manage to negotiate a job that will offer him promising career prospects. Conversely, a worker who enters the labour market during a time of recession will generally obtain a badly paid job which offers mediocre career prospects. This is in fact what the analytical frame-

152

work of supply and demand predicts in the case of a market based on long-term relations.

How should the government intervene in the labour market when it is undergoing profound structural change? Are the usual policies (such as employment insurance) still appropriate?

First, we have to understand that the labour market is in a state of continuous flux. It is very difficult for a government to make the distinction between a structural change and cyclical change (the latter being more temporary). Government intervention is therefore limited. At best, the state can help individuals absorb the many ups and downs of the labour market without having to determine whether the change is structural or not. This is precisely the role played by employment insurance.

Unfortunately, employment insurance programs are not perfect, and they often do not help people adapt to change. Employment insurance must be flexible and allow people to go back to university or to experiment with new types of jobs. Too often, employment insurance incites people to the status quo and in so doing does not fulfill its primary function: that of helping workers to adapt to a labour market in perpetual flux.

How do you recognize a good economics student? Are there any particular skills that you are looking for?

A good economics student is a student who likes history and politics and who is not afraid of mathematics. A good economic student is one who observes society and who asks why things are the way they are.

A characteristic that I always look for in an economics student is open-mindedness. A student must not have too many preconceived ideas or be too politically committed. If he or she is too involved in a social cause, he or she often loses some sense of objectivity. That said, the student must be passionate about social issues but shouldn't believe that he or she already knows all the answers and risks becoming the champion of a cause instead of an economics researcher.

Emotions and principles have their place, but facts and scientific methods are the very essence of the rigorous economic research that provides answers about the functioning of the economy.

Utility and Demand

CHAPTER 7

Water, Water, Everywhere

We need water to live. We don't need diamonds for much besides decoration. If the benefits of water far outweigh the benefits of diamonds, why does water cost practically nothing while diamonds are expensive?

When a winter storm cuts off the power supply, the prices of alternative sources of heat and light, such as firewood and candles, rise dramatically. But people buy as much firewood and as many candles as they can get their hands on. Our demand for goods that provide heat and light is price inelastic. Why?

When the personal computer (PC) was introduced in 1980, it cost more than $5,000 and consumers didn't buy very many. Since then, the price has tumbled and people are buying PCs in enormous quantities. Our demand for PCs is price elastic. What makes the demand for some things price elastic while the demand for others is price inelastic?

When you buy a monthly transit pass, each additional ride you take is free. What limits the quantity bought when something is "free"?

◆ In the preceding four chapters, we saw that demand has an important effect on the price of a good. But we did not analyze what exactly shapes a person's demand. This chapter examines household behaviour and its influence on demand. It explains why demand for some goods is elastic and the demand for other goods is inelastic. It also explains the paradox that the prices of diamonds and water are so out of proportion to their benefits. And in *Reading Between the Lines* at the end of the chapter, we look at demand when you can buy a monthly pass so the price of an additional unit is zero.

After studying this chapter, you will be able to

- ■ **Explain what limits a household's consumption choices**

- ■ **Describe preferences using the concept of utility and distinguish between total utility and marginal utility**

- ■ **Explain the marginal utility theory of consumer choice**

- ■ **Use marginal utility theory to predict the effects of changing prices and incomes**

- ■ **Explain the paradox of value**

The Household's Budget

A HOUSEHOLD'S BUDGET PLACES A LIMIT ON ITS consumption choices. And a household's preferences determine which of all its possible choices a household makes. We begin by studying the factors that determine the household's budget and its consumption possibilities.[1]

Consumption Possibilities

A household's consumption choices are constrained by the household's income and by the prices of the goods and services it buys. The household has a given amount of income to spend and cannot influence the prices of the goods and services it buys.

A household's *budget line* describes the limits to its consumption choices. Let's consider Lisa's household. Lisa has an income of $30 a month, and she plans to buy only two goods: movies and pop. The price of a movie is $6; the price of pop is $3 a six-pack. If Lisa spends all her income, she will reach the limits to her consumption of movies and pop.

Figure 7.1 illustrates Lisa's possible consumption of movies and pop. Rows *A* through *F* in the table show six possible ways of allocating $30 to these two goods. For example, Lisa can see 2 movies for $12 and buy 6 six-packs of pop for $18 (row *C*). Points *A* through *F* in the graph illustrate the possibilities presented in the table. The line passing through these points is Lisa's budget line.

Lisa's budget line is a constraint on her choices. It marks the boundary between what she can afford and what she cannot afford. She can afford all the points on the line and those inside it. She cannot afford the points outside the line. Lisa's consumption possibilities depend on the price of a movie, the price of pop, and her income. Her consumption possibilities change when the price of a movie, the price of a six-pack of pop, or her income changes.

The budget line can be described by the relative price of the two goods and the consumer's real income.

---

[1] This chapter and Chapter 8 deal with the same topic but explain two different methods of representing a household's preferences. The chapters are written on the assumption that you will most likely study only one of them. If you do study both chapters, you will find that the first sections of each that discuss the household budget constraint are very similar.

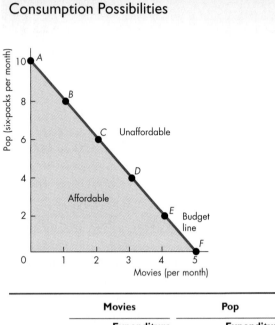

FIGURE 7.1
Consumption Possibilities

	Movies		Pop	
		Expenditure		Expenditure
Possibility	Quantity	(dollars)	Six-packs	(dollars)
A	0	0	10	30
B	1	6	8	24
C	2	12	6	18
D	3	18	4	12
E	4	24	2	6
F	5	30	0	0

Rows *A* through *F* in the table show six possible ways in which Lisa can allocate $30 to movies and pop. For example, Lisa can buy 2 movies and 6 six-packs of pop (row *C*). The combination in each row costs $30. These possibilities are points *A* through *F* in the graph. The line through those points is a boundary between what Lisa can afford and what she cannot afford. Her choices must lie along the line *AF* or inside the orange area.

Relative Price

A **relative price** is the price of one good divided by the price of another good. The price of a movie is $6 and the price of pop is $3 a six-pack, so the relative price of a movie in terms of pop is $6 per movie divided by $3 per six-pack, which equals 2 six-packs per movie. That is, to see one more movie, Lisa must

FIGURE 7.2
Changes in Prices and Income

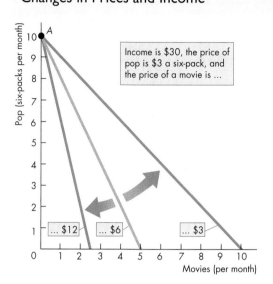

Income is $30, the price of pop is $3 a six-pack, and the price of a movie is ...

... $12   ... $6   ... $3

(a) A change in price

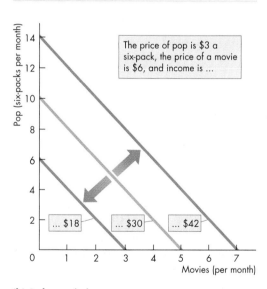

The price of pop is $3 a six-pack, the price of a movie is $6, and income is ...

... $18   ... $30   ... $42

(b) A change in income

In part (a), the price of a movie changes. A fall in the price from $6 to $3 rotates the budget line outward and makes it flatter. A rise in the price from $6 to $12 rotates the budget line inward and makes it steeper.

In part (b), income changes. A rise in income shifts the budget line outward and a fall in income shifts the budget line inward. But its slope does not change.

give up 2 six-packs. The opportunity cost of a movie is 2 six-packs.

A Price Change The relative price is the slope of the budget line. And when a price changes, the relative price changes, so the slope of the budget line changes. Figure 7.2(a) illustrates two changes. When the price of a movie falls from $6 to $3, Lisa's budget line rotates outward and she can afford to consume more of both goods. When the price of a movie rises from $6 to $12, Lisa's budget line rotates inward and she cannot afford as much of either good.

Real Income

A household's **real income** is the household's income expressed as the quantity of goods that the household can afford to buy. Expressed in terms of pop, Lisa's real income is 10 six-packs. This quantity is the maximum number of six-packs that she can buy. It is equal to her money income, $30, divided by the price of pop, $3 a six-pack.

A Change in Income Real income in terms of pop is the point at which the budget line intersects the y-axis. And when money income changes, real income changes, so the budget line shifts. But the slope of the budget line doesn't change. Figure 7.2(b) illustrates two changes in money income. When Lisa's money income rises from $30 to $42, her budget line shifts outward and she can afford to consume more of both goods. When Lisa's money income falls to $18, her budget line shifts inward and she cannot afford as much of either good.

REVIEW QUIZ

1 What does a household's budget line show?
2 How do real income and the relative price influence the budget line?
3 If the price of one good changes, what happens to the relative price and to the slope of the household's budget line?
4 If a household's money income changes and prices do not change, what happens to the household's real income

myeconlab Study Plan 7.1

Preferences and Utility

HOW DOES LISA DIVIDE HER AVAILABLE BUDGET between movies and pop? The answer depends on her likes and dislikes—her *preferences*. Economists use the concept of utility to describe preferences. The benefit or satisfaction that a person gets from the consumption of a good or service is called **utility**. Let's now see how we can use the concept of utility to describe preferences.

Total Utility

Total utility is the total benefit that a person gets from the consumption of goods and services. Total utility depends on the level of consumption—more consumption generally gives more total utility. The units of utility are arbitrary. Suppose we tell Lisa that we want to measure her utility. We're going to call the utility from no consumption zero. And we are going to call the utility she gets from 1 movie a month 50 units. We then ask her to tell us, on the same scale, how much she would like 2, 3, and more movies up to 14 a month. We also ask her to tell us, on the same scale, how much she would like 1 six-pack of pop a month, 2 six-packs, and more up to 14 six-packs a month. Table 7.1 shows Lisa's answers.

Marginal Utility

Marginal utility is the change in total utility that results from a one-unit increase in the quantity of a good consumed. When the number of six-packs Lisa buys increases from 4 to 5 a month, her total utility from pop increases from 181 units to 206 units. So for Lisa, the marginal utility of consuming a fifth six-pack each month is 25 units. The table in Fig. 7.3 shows Lisa's marginal utility from pop. Notice that marginal utility appears midway between the quantities of pop. It does so because it is the change in consumption from 4 to 5 six-packs that produces the marginal utility of 25 units. The table displays calculations of marginal utility for each number of six-packs that Lisa buys from 1 to 5.

Figure 7.3(a) illustrates the total utility that Lisa gets from pop. The more pop Lisa drinks in a month, the more total utility she gets. Figure 7.3(b) illustrates her marginal utility. This graph tells us that as Lisa drinks more pop, the marginal utility that she gets from pop decreases. For example, her marginal utility

TABLE 7.1   Lisa's Total Utility from Movies and Pop

Movies		Pop	
Quantity per month	Total utility	Six-packs per month	Total utility
0	0	0	0
1	50	1	75
2	88	2	117
3	121	3	153
4	150	4	181
5	175	5	206
6	196	6	225
7	214	7	243
8	229	8	260
9	241	9	276
10	250	10	291
11	256	11	305
12	259	12	318
13	261	13	330
14	262	14	341

decreases from 75 units for the first six-pack to 42 units from the second six-pack and to 36 units from the third.

Diminishing Marginal Utility

We call this decrease in marginal utility as the quantity of the good consumed increases the principle of **diminishing marginal utility**.

Marginal utility is positive but diminishes as consumption of a good increases. Why does marginal utility have these two features? In Lisa's case, she likes pop, and the more she drinks the better. That's why marginal utility is positive. The benefit that Lisa gets from the last six-pack consumed is its marginal utility. To see why marginal utility diminishes, think about the following two situations: In one, you've just been studying all through the day and evening and you've been too busy finishing an assignment to go shopping. A friend drops by with a six-pack of pop.

FIGURE 7.3
Total Utility and Marginal Utility

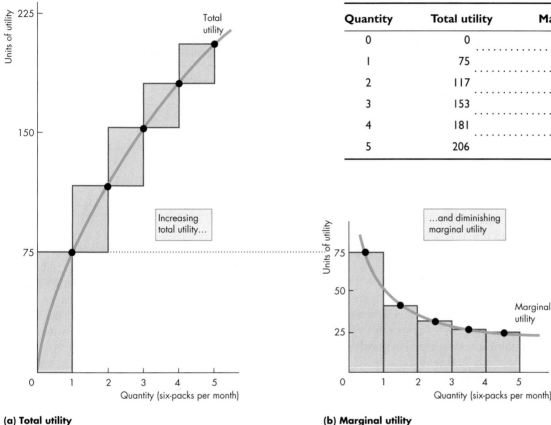

Quantity	Total utility	Marginal utility
0	0	
		75
1	75	
		42
2	117	
		36
3	153	
		28
4	181	
		25
5	206	

(a) Total utility

(b) Marginal utility

The table shows that as Lisa consumes more pop, her total utility from pop increases. The table also shows her marginal utility—the change in total utility resulting from the last six-pack she consumes. Marginal utility declines as consumption increases. The figure graphs Lisa's total utility and marginal utility from pop. Part (a) shows her total utility. It also shows as a bar the extra total utility she gains from each additional six-pack—her marginal utility. Part (b) shows how Lisa's marginal utility from pop diminishes by placing the bars shown in part (a) side by side as a series of declining steps.

The utility you get from that pop is the marginal utility from one six-pack. In the second situation, you've been on a pop binge. You've been working on an assignment all day but you've guzzled three six-packs while doing so. You are up to your eyeballs in pop. You are happy enough to have one more can. But the thrill that you get from it is not very large. It is the marginal utility of the nineteenth can in a day.

We've now described Lisa's budget and preferences. Our next task is to combine these two elements and see how she chooses what to consume.

REVIEW QUIZ

1 What is utility and how do we use the concept of utility to describe a consumer's preferences?
2 What is the distinction between total utility and marginal utility?
3 What is the key assumption about marginal utility?

myeconlab Study Plan 7.2

Maximizing Utility

A HOUSEHOLD'S INCOME AND THE PRICES THAT IT faces limit the household's consumption choices, and the household's preferences determine the utility that it can obtain from each consumption possibility. The key assumption of marginal utility theory is that the household chooses the consumption possibility that maximizes its total utility. This assumption of utility maximization is a way of expressing the fundamental economic problem: scarcity. People's wants exceed the resources available to satisfy those wants, so they must make hard choices. In making choices, they try to get the maximum attainable benefit—that is, to maximize total utility.

Let's see how Lisa allocates $30 a month between movies and pop to maximize her total utility when the price of a movie is $6 and pop is $3 a six-pack.

The Utility-Maximizing Choice

The most direct way of calculating how Lisa spends her income to maximize her total utility is by making a table like Table 7.2. The rows of this table show the affordable combinations of movies and pop that lie along Lisa's budget line in Fig. 7.1. The table records three things: first, the number of movies seen and the total utility derived from them (the left side of the table); second, the number of six-packs consumed and the total utility derived from them (the right side of the table); and third, the total utility derived from both movies and pop (the centre column).

The first row of Table 7.2 records the situation when Lisa watches no movies and buys 10 six-packs. In this case, Lisa gets no utility from movies and 291 units of total utility from pop. Her total utility from movies and pop (the centre column) is 291 units. The rest of the table is constructed in the same way.

The combination of movies and pop that maximizes Lisa's total utility is highlighted in the table. When Lisa sees 2 movies and buys 6 six-packs of pop, she gets 313 units of total utility. This is the best Lisa can do, given that she has only $30 to spend and given the prices of movies and six-packs. If she buys 8 six-packs of pop, she can see only 1 movie. She gets 310 units of total utility, 3 less than the maximum attainable. If she sees 3 movies, she can drink only 4 six-packs. She gets 302 units of total utility, 11 less than the maximum attainable.

TABLE 7.2   Lisa's Utility-Maximizing Combinations

	Movies		Total utility from movies and pop	Pop	
	Quantity per month	Total utility		Total utility	Six-packs per month
A	0	0	291	291	10
B	1	50	310	260	8
C	2	88	313	225	6
D	3	121	302	181	4
E	4	150	267	117	2
F	5	175	175	0	0

We've just described Lisa's consumer equilibrium. A **consumer equilibrium** is a situation in which a consumer has allocated all his or her available income in the way that, given the prices of goods and services, maximizes his or her total utility. Lisa's consumer equilibrium is 2 movies and 6 six-packs.

In finding Lisa's consumer equilibrium, we measured her *total* utility from all the affordable combinations of movies and pop. But there is a better way of determining her consumer equilibrium. It uses the idea that choices are made at the margin—an idea that you first met in Chapter 1. Let's look at this alternative.

Equalizing Marginal Utility per Dollar

A consumer's total utility is maximized by following the rule:

Spend all the available income and equalize the marginal utility per dollar for all goods.

The **marginal utility per dollar** is the marginal utility from a good divided by its price. For example, Lisa's marginal utility from seeing 1 movie a month, MU_M, is 50 units of utility. The price of a movie, P_M, is $6, which means that the marginal utility per dollar from 1 movie a month, MU_M/P_M, is 50 units divided by $6, or 8.33 units of utility per dollar.

You can see why following this rule maximizes total utility by thinking about a situation in which

Lisa has spent all her income but the marginal utilities per dollar is not equal for all goods. Suppose that Lisa's marginal utility per dollar for pop, MU_P/P_P exceeds that for movies. By spending a dollar more on pop and a dollar less on movies, her total utility from pop rises and her total utility from movies falls. But her utility gain from pop exceeds her utility loss from movies, so her total utility increases. Because she consumes more pop, her marginal utility from pop has fallen. And because she sees fewer movies, her marginal utility from movies has risen. Lisa keeps increasing her consumption of pop and decreasing the movies she sees until the two marginal utilities per dollar are equal, or when

$$\frac{MU_M}{P_M} = \frac{MU_P}{P_P}.$$

Table 7.3 calculates Lisa's marginal utility per dollar for each good. Each row exhausts Lisa's income of $30. In row B, Lisa's marginal utility from movies is 50 units (use Table 7.1 to calculate the marginal utilities). Because the price of a movie is $6, Lisa's marginal utility per dollar for movies is 50 units divided by $6, which is 8.33. Marginal utility per dollar for each good, like marginal utility, decreases as more of the good is consumed.

Lisa maximizes her total utility when the marginal utility per dollar for movies is equal to the marginal utility per dollar for pop—possibility C. Lisa consumes 2 movies and 6 six-packs.

Figure 7.4 shows why the rule "equalize marginal utility per dollar for all goods" works. Suppose that instead of seeing 2 movies and consuming 6 six-packs (possibility C), Lisa sees 1 movie and consumes 8 six-packs (possibility B). She then gets 8.33 units of utility per dollar for movies and 5.67 units per dollar for pop. Lisa can increase her total utility by buying less pop and seeing more movies. If she sees one additional movie and spends less on pop, her total utility from movies increases by 8.33 units per dollar and her total utility from pop decreases by 5.67 units per dollar. Her total utility increases by 2.66 units per dollar, as shown by the blue area.

Or suppose that Lisa sees 3 movies and consumes 4 six-packs (possibility D). In this situation, her

---

FIGURE 7.4
Equalizing Marginal Utilities per Dollar

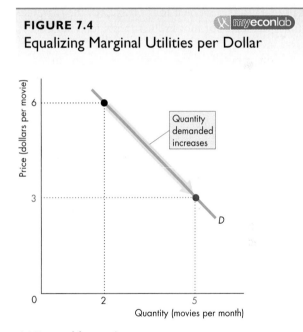

(a) Demand for movies

If Lisa sees 1 movie and consumes 8 six-packs (possibility B), her marginal utility per dollar for movies exceeds that for pop. She can get more total utility by seeing one more movie. If she consumes 4 six-packs and sees 3 movies (possibility D), her marginal utility per dollar for pop exceeds that for movies. She can get more total utility by seeing one less movie and consuming more pop. When Lisa's marginal utility per dollar for both goods is equal, her total utility is maximized.

TABLE 7.3   Equalizing Marginal Utilities per Dollar

	Movies ($6 each)			Pop ($3 per six-pack)		
	Quantity	Marginal utility	Marginal utility per dollar	Six-packs	Marginal utility	Marginal utility per dollar
A	0	0		10	15	5.00
B	1	50	8.33	8	17	5.67
C	2	38	6.33	6	19	6.33
D	3	33	5.50	4	28	9.33
E	4	29	4.83	2	42	14.00
F	5	25	4.17	0	0	

marginal utility per dollar for movies (5.50) is less than her marginal utility per dollar for pop (9.33). Lisa can now increase her total utility by seeing one less movie and consuming more pop, as the green area shows.

The Power of Marginal Analysis The method we've just used to find Lisa's utility-maximizing choice of movies and pop is an example of the power of marginal analysis. By comparing the marginal gain from having more of one good with the marginal loss from having less of another good, Lisa is able to ensure that she gets the maximum attainable utility.

The rule to follow is simple: If the marginal utility per dollar for movies exceeds the marginal utility per dollar for pop, see more movies and buy less pop; if the marginal utility per dollar for pop exceeds the marginal utility per dollar for movies, buy more pop and see fewer movies.

More generally, if the marginal gain from an action exceeds the marginal loss, take the action. You will meet this principle time and again in your study of economics. And you will find yourself using it when you make your own economic choices, especially when you must make a big decision.

Units of Utility In maximizing total utility by making the marginal utility per dollar equal for both goods, the units in which utility is measured do not matter. Any arbitrary units will work. It is in this respect that utility is like temperature. Predictions about the freezing point of water don't depend on the temperature scale; and predictions about a household's consumption choice don't depend on the units of utility.

REVIEW QUIZ

1 What is Lisa's goal when she chooses the quantities of movies and pop to consume?
2 What are the two conditions that are met if a consumer is maximizing utility?
3 Explain why equalizing the marginal utility of each good does *not* maximize utility.
4 Explain why equalizing the marginal utility per dollar for all goods *does* maximize utility.

 myeconlab **Study Plan 7.3**

Predictions of Marginal Utility Theory

WE'RE NOW GOING TO USE MARGINAL UTILITY theory to make some predictions. In Chapter 3, we assumed that a fall in the price of a good, other things remaining the same, brings an increase in the quantity demanded of that good—the law of demand. We also assumed that a fall in the price of a substitute of a good decreases demand for that good and a rise in income increases the demand for a normal good. We're now going to see that these assumptions are predictions of marginal utility theory.

A Fall in the Price of a Movie

A fall in the price of a movie, other things remaining the same, changes the quantity of movies demanded and brings a movement along the demand curve for movies. We've already found one point on Lisa's demand curve for movies. Figure 7.5 shows this point on Lisa's demand curve for movies.

To find another point on her demand curve for movies, we need to work out what Lisa buys when the price of a movie changes. Suppose that the price of a movie falls from $6 to $3 and nothing else changes.

To work out the effect of this change in the price of a movie on Lisa's buying plans, we must first determine the combinations of movies and pop that she can afford at the new prices. Then we calculate the new marginal utilities per dollar. Finally, we determine the combination that makes the marginal utilities per dollar for movies and pop equal.

The rows of Table 7.4 show the combinations of movies and pop that exhaust Lisa's $30 of income when the price of a movie is $3 and the price of a six-pack is $3. Lisa's preferences do not change when prices change, so her marginal utility schedule remains the same as that in Table 7.3. Divide her marginal utility from movies by $3 to get the marginal utility per dollar for movies.

Lisa now sees 5 movies and drinks 5 six-packs. She *substitutes* movies for pop. Figure 7.4 shows both of these effects. In part (a), we've found another point on Lisa's demand curve for movies. And we've discovered that her demand curve obeys the law of demand. In part (b), we see that a fall in the price of a movie decreases the demand for pop. The demand curve for pop shifts leftward. For Lisa, pop and movies are substitutes.

TABLE 7.4   How a Change in Price of a
Movie Affects Lisa's Choices

Movies ($3 each)		Pop ($3 per six-pack)	
Quantity	Marginal utility per dollar	Six-packs	Marginal utility per dollar
0		10	5.00
1	16.67	9	5.33
2	**12.67**	8	5.67
3	11.00	7	6.00
4	9.67	**6**	**6.33**
5	8.33	5	8.33
6	7.00	4	9.33
7	6.00	3	12.00
8	5.00	2	14.00
9	4.00	1	25.00
10	3.00	0	

FIGURE 7.5   myeconlab

A Fall in the Price of a Movie

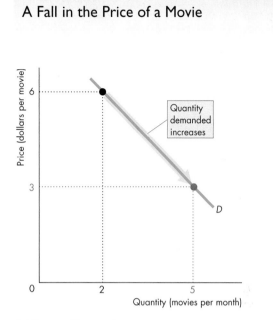

(a) Demand for movies

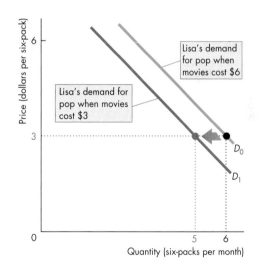

A Rise in the Price of Pop

In Fig. 7.5(b), we know only one point on Lisa's
demand curve for pop when the price of a movie is
$3. To find Lisa's demand curve for pop, we must see
how she responds to a change in the price of pop.
Suppose that the price of pop rises from $3 to $6 a
six-pack. The rows of Table 7.5 show the combinations of movies and pop that exhaust Lisa's $30 of
income when the price of a movie is $3 and the price
of a six-pack is $6. Again, Lisa's preferences don't
change when the price changes. Divide Lisa's marginal
utility from pop by $6 to get her marginal utility per
dollar for pop.

Lisa now drinks 2 six-packs a month and sees 6
movies a month. Lisa *substitutes* movies for pop. Figure
7.6 shows both of these effects. In part (a), we've found
another point on Lisa's demand curve for pop. And
we've confirmed that this demand curve obeys the law
of demand. In part (b), we see that a rise in the price of
pop increases the demand for movies. The demand
curve for movies shifts rightward. This change again
tells us that for Lisa, pop and movies are substitutes.

When the price of a movie falls and the price of pop
remains the same, the quantity of movies demanded by Lisa
increases, and in part (a), Lisa moves along her demand
curve for movies. Also, when the price of a movie falls,
Lisa's demand for pop decreases, and in part (b), her
demand curve for pop shifts leftward. For Lisa, pop and
movies are substitutes.

TABLE 7.5   How a Change in Price of Pop
                 Affects Lisa's Choices

| Movies ($3 each) | | Pop ($6 per six-pack) | |
Quantity	Marginal utility per dollar	Six-packs	Marginal utility per dollar
0		5	4.17
2	12.67	4	4.67
4	9.67	3	6.00
6	7.00	2	7.00
8	5.00	1	12.50
10	3.00	0	

Marginal utility theory predicts these two results:

1. When the price of a good rises, the quantity demanded of that good decreases.
2. When price of one good rises, the demand for another good that can serve as a substitute increases.

These predictions of marginal utility theory sound familiar because they correspond to the assumptions that we made about demand in Chapter 3. There, we assumed that the demand curve for a good slopes downward and that a rise in the price of a substitute for that good increases the demand for the good.

We have now seen that marginal utility theory predicts how the quantities of goods and services that people demand respond to price changes. The theory enables us to derive the consumer's demand curve and predict how the demand curve for one good shifts when the price of another good changes.

Marginal utility theory also helps us to predict how demand changes when income changes. Let's study the effects of a change in income on demand.

FIGURE 7.6
A Rise in the Price of Pop

myeconlab

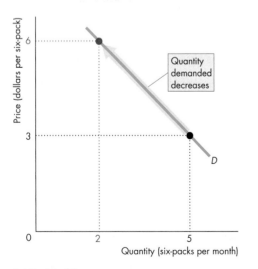

(a) Demand for pop

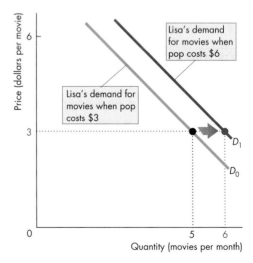

(b) Demand for movies

When the price of pop rises and the price of a movie remains the same, the quantity of pop demanded by Lisa decreases, and in part (a), Lisa moves along her demand curve for pop. Also, when the price of pop rises, Lisa's demand for movies increases, and in part (b), her demand curve for movies shifts rightward.

A Rise in Income

Let's suppose that Lisa's income increases from $30 to $42 a month and that the price of a movie is $3 and the price of a six-pack is $3. We saw in Table 7.4 that with these prices and with an income of $30 a month, Lisa sees 5 movies and drinks 5 six-packs a month. We want to compare this choice of movies and pop with Lisa's choice when her income is $42.

Table 7.6 shows the calculations needed to make the comparison. With $42, Lisa can see 14 movies a month and buy no pop or buy 14 six-packs a month and see no movies or choose any combination of the two goods in the rows of the table. We calculate the marginal utility per dollar in exactly the same way as we did before and find the quantities at which the marginal utility per dollar for movies and the marginal utility per dollar for pop are equal. When Lisa's income

is $42, the marginal utility per dollar is equal for both goods when she sees 7 movies and drinks 7 six-packs of pop a month.

By comparing this situation with that in Table 7.4, we see that with an additional $12 a month, Lisa buys 2 more six-packs and sees 2 more movies a month. Lisa's response arises from her preferences, as described by her marginal utilities. Different preferences would produce different quantitative responses. With a larger income, the consumer always buys more of a *normal* good and less of an *inferior* good. For Lisa, pop and movies are normal goods. When her income increases, Lisa buys more of both goods.

You have now completed your study of the marginal utility theory of a household's consumption choices. Table 7.7 summarizes the key assumptions, implications, and predictions of the theory.

TABLE 7.6   Lisa's Choices with an Income of $42 a Month

Movies ($3 each)		Pop ($3 per six-pack)	
Quantity	Marginal utility per dollar	Six-packs	Marginal utility per dollar
0		14	3.67
1	16.67	13	4.00
2	12.67	12	4.33
3	11.00	11	4.67
4	9.67	10	5.00
5	**8.33**	9	5.33
6	7.00	8	5.67
7	**6.00**	7	**6.00**
8	5.00	6	6.33
9	4.00	**5**	**8.33**
10	3.00	4	9.33
11	2.00	3	12.00
12	1.00	2	14.00
13	0.67	1	25.00
14	0.33	0	

TABLE 7.7   Marginal Utility Theory

Assumptions

■ A consumer derives utility from the goods consumed.

■ Each additional unit of consumption yields additional total utility—marginal utility is positive.

■ As the quantity of a good consumed increases, marginal utility decreases.

■ A consumer's aim is to maximize total utility.

Implication

■ Total utility is maximized when all the available income is spent and when the marginal utility per dollar is equal for all goods.

Predictions

■ Other things remaining the same, the higher the price of a good, the smaller is the quantity bought (the law of demand).

■ The higher the price of a good, the greater is the quantity bought of substitutes for that good.

■ The larger the consumer's income, the greater is the quantity demanded of normal goods.

Temperature: An Analogy

Utility is similar to temperature. Both are abstract concepts, and both have units of measurement that are arbitrary. You can't *observe* temperature. You can observe water turning to steam if it is hot enough or turning to ice if it is cold enough. And you can construct an instrument—a thermometer—that can help you to predict when such changes will occur. We call the scale on the thermometer *temperature* and we call the units of temperature *degrees*. But these degree units are arbitrary. We can use Celsius units or the Fahrenheit units or some other.

The concept of utility helps us make predictions about consumption choices in much the same way that the concept of temperature helps us make predictions about physical phenomena.

Admittedly, marginal utility theory does not enable us to predict how buying plans change with the same precision that a thermometer enables us to predict when water will turn to ice or steam. But the theory provides important insights into buying plans and has some powerful implications, as you are about to discover. It helps us to understand why people buy more of a good or service when its price falls, why people buy more of most goods when their incomes increase. It also resolves the paradox of value, as you are about to see.

REVIEW QUIZ

1 When the price of a good falls and the prices of other goods and a consumer's income remain the same, what happens to the consumption of the good whose price has fallen and to the consumption of other goods?

2 Elaborate on your answer to the previous question by using demand curves. For which good is there a change in demand and for which is there a change in the quantity demanded?

3 If a consumer's income increases and if all goods are normal goods, how does the quantity bought of each good change?

 myeconlab   **Study Plan 7.4**

We're going to end this chapter by returning to a recurring theme throughout your study of economics: the concept of efficiency and the distinction between price and value.

Efficiency, Price, and Value

MARGINAL UTILITY THEORY HELPS US TO DEEPEN our understanding of the concept of efficiency and also helps us to see more clearly the distinction between value and price. Let's find out how.

Consumer Efficiency and Consumer Surplus

When Lisa allocates her limited budget to maximize utility, she is using her resources efficiently. Any other allocation of her budget wastes some resources.

But when Lisa has allocated her limited budget to maximize utility, she is *on* her demand curve for each good. A demand curve is a description of the quantity demanded at each price when utility is maximized. When we studied efficiency in Chapter 5, we learned that value equals marginal benefit and that a demand curve is also a willingness-to-pay curve. It tells us a consumer's *marginal benefit*—the benefit from consuming an additional unit of a good. You can now give the idea of marginal benefit a deeper meaning:

Marginal benefit is the maximum price a consumer is willing to pay for an extra unit of a good or service when utility is maximized.

The Paradox of Value

For centuries, philosophers have been puzzled by a paradox that we raised at the start of this chapter. Water, which is essential to life itself, costs little, but diamonds, which are useless in comparison to water, are expensive. Why? Adam Smith tried to solve this paradox. But not until the theory of marginal utility had been developed could anyone give a satisfactory answer.

You can solve this puzzle by distinguishing between *total* utility and *marginal* utility. The total utility that we get from water is enormous. But remember, the more we consume of something, the smaller is its marginal utility. We use so much water that its marginal utility—the benefit we get from one more glass of water—diminishes to a small value. Diamonds, on the other hand, have a small total utility relative to the total utility from water, but because we buy few diamonds, they have a high marginal utility. When a household has maximized its total utility, it has allocated its budget in the way that makes the

FIGURE 7.7

The Paradox of Value

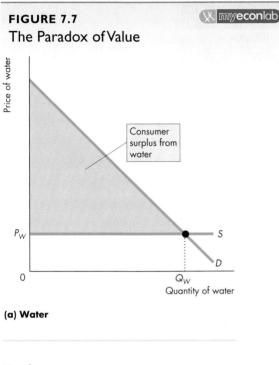

(a) Water

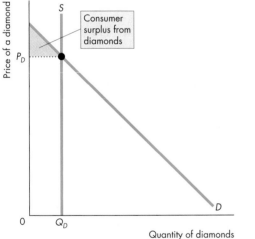

(b) Diamonds

Part (a) shows the demand for water, D, and the supply of water, S. The supply is assumed to be perfectly elastic at the price P_W. At this price, the quantity of water consumed is Q_W and the consumer surplus from water is the large green triangle. Part (b) shows the demand for diamonds, D, and the supply of diamonds, S. The supply is assumed to be perfectly inelastic at the quantity Q_D. At this quantity, the price of a diamond is P_D and the consumer surplus from diamonds is the small green triangle. Water is valuable—has a large consumer surplus—but cheap. Diamonds are less valuable than water—have a smaller consumer surplus—but are expensive.

marginal utility per dollar equal for all goods. That is, the marginal utility from a good divided by the price of the good is equal for all goods.

This equality of marginal utilities per dollar holds true for diamonds and water: Diamonds have a high price and a high marginal utility. Water has a low price and a low marginal utility. When the high marginal utility of diamonds is divided by the high price of diamonds, the result is a number that equals the low marginal utility of water divided by the low price of water. The marginal utility per dollar is the same for diamonds as for water.

Another way to think about the paradox of value uses *consumer surplus*. Figure 7.7 explains the paradox of value by using this idea. The supply of water (part a) is perfectly elastic at price P_W, so the quantity of water consumed is Q_W and the consumer surplus from water is the large green area. The supply of diamonds (part b) is perfectly inelastic at price Q_D, so the price of diamonds is P_D and the consumer surplus from diamonds is the small green area. Water is cheap but brings a large consumer surplus, while diamonds are expensive but bring a small consumer surplus.

◆ You have now completed your study of the marginal utility theory. And you've seen how the theory can be used to explain our real-world consumption choices. You can see the theory in action once again in *Reading Between the Lines* on pp. 166–167, where it is used to interpret how commuters in Winnipeg use the network of water buses along the Assiniboine and Red Rivers.

The next chapter presents an alternative theory of household behaviour. To help you see the connection between the two theories of consumer behaviour, we'll continue with the same example. We'll meet Lisa again and discover another way of understanding how she gets the most out of her $30 a month.

What's the Marginal Utility of a Boat Ride?

WINNIPEG FREE PRESS, JULY 25, 2001

New network of transit boats invite all aboard

With the city skyline behind him, Mayor Glen Murray rode to work yesterday morning, one of the first passengers in the city's new water transit boat.

"This is a fast, hassle-free and affordable way to travel that avoids traffic congestion," Murray said as the system's inaugural ride was filmed and photographed by the media.

The water bus shuttle links six public docks along the Assiniboine and Red Rivers.

Murray boarded the shuttle near his home, a new dock at the foot of Hugo Street, off Wellington Crescent. A 14-minute ride took Murray to the newly constructed dock in Stephen Juba Park at the end of Bannatyne Avenue, where he then walked to city hall.

The new service links the east Exchange area with the Corydon Avenue strip from the Hugo Street dock, with stops in between at The Forks, Tache, the Midtown bridge, and docks at the Legislature and the Osborne Street bridge.

...

For a $2 fee, riders can travel from dock to dock. Passengers are not given life jackets but they will be offered to children. Monthly commuter passes for rush-hour service costs $100. Day passes are $7; $6 for seniors and youths.

The shuttle will operate seven days a week; weekday service has rush-hour departures at eight-minute intervals from 7–9:30 a.m. and 4–6 p.m., with regular 15-minute departures until 11 p.m. On weekends, the service will have departures at 15-minute intervals from 10 a.m.–11 p.m.

The 12-passenger boats travel fully loaded at a maximum speed of about 40 kilometres per hour. ...

Essence of the Story

■ A water bus shuttle links six public docks along the Assiniboine and Red Rivers in Winnipeg.

■ The price of a one-way trip is $2. The price of a one-day pass is $7 ($6 for seniors and youths). The price of a one-month rush-hour pass is $100.

■ The shuttle operates seven days a week. On weekdays boats depart at 15-minute intervals and at eight-minute intervals during rush hours.

■ A boat carries 12 passengers at a maximum speed of 40 kilometres per hour.

Economic Analysis

■ The people who live in the region served by the Winnipeg water bus shuttle choose the method of transportation and number of trips that maximize utility.

■ The price of each trip is $2 (no special passes), so each person takes the number of trips that makes the marginal utility per dollar for boat trips equal to the marginal utility per dollar for other goods.

■ The table illustrates a person's choice if the amount available is $160, the price of a boat ride is $2, and the price of a unit of other goods is $10.

■ The person maximizes utility in this example by taking 20 boat trips and consuming 12 units of other goods.

■ But a Winnipeg commuter must make a more complicated choice because the boat company offers special passes. We'll consider just the $100 monthly pass.

■ Figure 1 shows the consumption possibilities that face the commuter. The commuter can pay $2 a trip or $100 for a month of "free" trips.

■ You can see that the person who takes fewer than 50 trips a month can buy more other goods by paying $2 a trip. The person who takes more than 50 trips a month can buy more other goods by paying $100 for the trips.

■ To decide whether to buy a monthly commuter pass for $100 or pay $2 per trip, the commuter must make two calculations, each similar to the one you've just seen, but with a twist.

■ If the utility-maximizing number of trips at $2 a trip turns out to be greater than 50 a month, the choice is easy: buy a commuter pass and save some money that can be spent on other goods.

■ If the utility-maximizing number of trips at $2 a trip turns out to be less than 50 a month, the commuter needs to reason as follows.

■ If I buy a commuter pass for $100, I can take any number of trips I choose and the cost of one marginal trip is zero. So I will take a trip if its marginal utility is positive.

■ The total utility that I get from these trips is the marginal utility from a commuter pass—it is the change in total utility that results from the decision to buy the pass.

■ So I will buy a commuter pass when the change in total utility that results from the decision to buy the pass divided by $100 is greater than or equal to the marginal utility per dollar for other goods.

■ In this case, I will take boat rides until the marginal utility of a ride is zero.

Winnipeg Traveller's Choices at $2 a Trip

	Boat trips ($2 each)			Other goods ($10 each)		
	Quantity	Marginal utility	Marginal utility per dollar	Quantity	Marginal utility	Marginal utility per dollar
A	0			16	10	1.00
B	10	10	5.00	14	20	2.00
C	**20**	**8**	**4.00**	**12**	**40**	**4.00**
D	30	6	3.00	10	60	6.00
E	40	4	2.00	8	80	8.00
F	50	3	1.50	6	100	10.00
G	60	2	1.00	4	120	12.00
H	70	1	0.50	2	140	14.00
I	80	0	0	0		

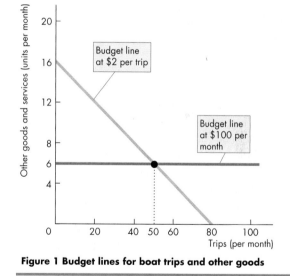

Figure 1 Budget lines for boat trips and other goods

167

SUMMARY

KEY POINTS

The Household's Budget (pp. 154–155)

- A household's budget limits its consumption choices.
- A household's consumption possibilities are constrained by its income and by the prices of goods and services. Some combinations of goods and services are affordable, and some are not affordable.

Preferences and Utility (pp. 156–157)

- A household's preferences can be described by marginal utility.
- The key assumption of marginal utility theory is that the marginal utility of a good or service decreases as consumption of the good or service increases.
- Marginal utility theory assumes that people buy the affordable combination of goods and services that maximizes their total utility.

Maximizing Utility (pp. 158–160)

- Total utility is maximized when all the available income is spent and when the marginal utility per dollar is equal for all goods.
- If the marginal utility per dollar for good *A* exceeds that for good *B*, total utility increases if the quantity purchased of good *A* increases and the quantity purchased of good *B* decreases.

Predictions of Marginal Utility Theory (pp. 160–164)

- Marginal utility theory predicts the law of demand. That is, other things remaining the same, the higher the price of a good, the smaller is the quantity demanded of that good.
- Marginal utility theory also predicts that other things remaining the same, the larger the consumer's income, the larger is the quantity demanded of a normal good.
- The market demand curve is found by summing horizontally all the individual demand curves.

Efficiency, Price, and Value (pp. 164–165)

- When a consumer maximizes utility, he or she is using resources efficiently.
- Marginal utility theory resolves the paradox of value.
- When we talk loosely about value, we are thinking of *total* utility or consumer surplus. But price is related to *marginal* utility.
- Water, which we consume in large amounts, has a high total utility and a large consumer surplus, but the price of water is low and the marginal utility from water is low.
- Diamonds, which we consume in small amounts, have a low total utility and a small consumer surplus, but the price of a diamond is high and the marginal utility from diamonds is high.

KEY FIGURES AND TABLE

Figure 7.1   Consumption Possibilities, 154
Figure 7.2   Changes in Prices and Income, 155
Figure 7.3   Total Utility and Marginal Utility, 157
Figure 7.4   Equalizing Marginal Utilities per Dollar, 159
Figure 7.5   A Fall in the Price of a Movie, 161
Figure 7.6   A Rise in the Price of Pop, 162
Figure 7.7   The Paradox of Value, 165
Table 7.7   Marginal Utility Theory, 163

KEY TERMS

Consumer equilibrium, 158
Diminishing marginal utility, 156
Marginal utility, 156
Marginal utility per dollar, 158
Real income, 155
Relative price, 154
Total utility, 156
Utility, 156

PROBLEMS

Go to ⓧ myeconlab for solutions to odd-numbered problems and additional exercises.

1. Shirley spends all her income on movies and popcorn and the table shows her consumption possibilities.

Movies (number per week)	Popcorn (cartons per week)
0	20
1	15
2	10
3	5
4	0

If Shirley spends $40 a week:
a. What is the price of a carton of popcorn?
b. What is the price of a movie ticket?
c. What is the opportunity cost of a movie in terms of popcorn?
d. What is the Shirley's real income in terms of popcorn?

2. Lou spends all his income on CDs and spy novels. The price of a CD is $10 and the price of a spy novel is $15. Lou's income is $75 a month. Make a graph of Lou's budget to illustrate his consumption possibilities.

3. Jason enjoys rock CDs and spy novels and spends $60 a month on them. The table shows the utility he gets from each good.

Quantity per month	Utility from rock CDs	Utility from spy novels
1	60	20
2	110	38
3	150	53
4	180	64
5	200	70

a. Draw graphs showing Jason's utility from rock CDs and from spy novels and compare the two utility graphs. Can you say anything about Jason's preferences?
b. Draw graphs that show Jason's marginal utility from rock CDs and from spy novels.
c. What do the two marginal utility graphs tell you about Jason's preferences?

d. If the price of a rock CD is $10 and the price of a spy novel is $10, how does Jason spend the $60?

4. Martha enjoys classical CDs and travel books and spends $75 a month on them. The table shows the utility she gets from each good.

Quantity per month	Utility from classical CDs	Utility from travel books
1	90	120
2	110	136
3	126	148
4	138	152
5	146	154

a. Draw graphs showing Martha's utility from classical CDs and from travel books and compare the two utility graphs. Can you say anything about Martha's preferences?
b. Draw graphs that show Martha's marginal utility from classical CDs and from travel books.
c. What do the two marginal utility graphs tell you about Martha's preferences?
d. If the price of a classical CD is $15 and the price of a travel book is $15, how does Martha spend the $75 a month?

5. Max enjoys windsurfing and snorkelling. The table shows the marginal utility he gets from each activity.

Hours per day	Marginal utility from windsurfing	Marginal utility from snorkelling
1	120	40
2	100	36
3	80	30
4	60	22
5	40	12
6	12	10
7	10	8

Max has $35 to spend, and he can spend as much time as he likes on his leisure pursuits. Windsurfing equipment rents for $10 an hour, and snorkelling equipment rents for $5 an hour. How long does Max spend windsurfing and how long does he spend snorkelling?

6. Pete enjoys rock concerts and the opera. The table shows the marginal utility he gets from each activity.

Number per month	Marginal utility from rock concerts	Marginal utility from operas
1	120	200
2	100	160
3	80	120
4	60	80
5	40	40
6	20	0

Pete has $200 a month to spend on concerts. The price of a rock concert ticket is $20, and the price of an opera ticket is $40. How many rock concerts and how many operas does Pete attend?

7. In problem 5, Max's sister gives him $20 to spend on his leisure pursuits, so he now has $55.
   a. Draw a graph that shows Max's consumption possibilities.
   b. How many hours does Max choose to windsurf and how many hours does he choose to snorkel now that he has $55 to spend?

8. In problem 6, Pete's uncle gives him $60 to spend on concert tickets, so he now has $260.
   a. Draw a graph that shows Pete's consumption possibilities.
   b. How many rock concerts and how many operas does Pete now attend?

9. In problem 7, if the rent on windsurfing equipment decreases to $5 an hour, how many hours does Max now windsurf and how many hours does he snorkel?

10. In problem 6, if the price of an opera ticket decreases to $20, how many rock concerts and operas will Pete attend?

11. Max, in problem 5, takes a Club Med vacation, the cost of which includes unlimited sports activities. There is no extra charge for equipment. If Max windsurfs and snorkels for 6 hours a day, how many hours does he windsurf and how many hours does he snorkel?

12. Pete, in problem 6, wins a prize and has more than enough money to satisfy his desires for rock concerts and opera. He decides that he would like to buy a total of 7 tickets each month. How many rock concerts and how many operas does he now attend?

CRITICAL THINKING

1. Study *Reading Between the Lines* (pp. 166–167) on the Winnipeg water transit boats and then answer the following questions:
   a. If price of a ride is $2 and the price of a day pass is $6, how does a person decide whether to buy the pass or pay for each ride?
   b. List the components of the opportunity cost of a ride other than the cost of the ticket.
   c. What does marginal utility theory predict will happen to the demand for public transit as incomes rise?

2. Smoking is banned on most airline flights. Use marginal utility theory to explain
   a. The effect of the ban on the utility of smokers.
   b. How the ban influences the decisions of smokers.
   c. The effects of the ban on the utility of non-smokers.
   d. How the ban influences the decisions of nonsmokers.

WEB EXERCISES

Use the links on (X) **myeconlab to work the following exercises.**

1. Read what Henry Schimberg, former CEO of Coca-Cola, said about the market for bottled water. Use marginal utility theory to explain and interpret his remarks.

2. Obtain information about the prices on the Toronto Transit Commission system.
   a. Show the effects of the different ticket options on the consumer's budget line.
   b. How would a person decide whether to pay for each trip, to buy a day pass, or to buy a pass for a longer period? Use marginal utility theory to answer this question.
   c. How do you think the number of riders would change if the price of a single trip fell and the price of a day pass increased?

Possibilities, Preferences, and Choices

Subterranean Movements

Like the continents floating on the earth's mantle, our spending patterns change steadily over time. On such subterranean movements, business empires rise and fall. We can now choose whether to buy our music on a CD or download it and play it on an iPod or burn our own CD. As the prices of a music download, an iPod, and a CD burner have tumbled, people are increasingly buying downloads and music CD sales have taken a hit.

The prices of electronic textbooks—e-books—have also fallen and these books are now cheaper than printed textbooks. Yet most students continue to buy printed textbooks. Why, when e-books are cheaper than printed books, have e-books not caught on and replaced printed books in the same way that the new music technologies have replaced CDs?

Subterranean movements also govern the way we spend our time. The average workweek has fallen steadily from 70 hours a week in the nineteenth century to 35 hours a week today. While the average workweek is now much shorter than it once was, far more people now have jobs. Why has the average workweek declined?

◆ In this chapter, we're going to study a model of choice that predicts the effects of changes in prices and incomes on what people buy and the effects of changes in wage rates on how people allocate time between leisure and work. At the end of the chapter, in *Reading Between the Lines*, we'll use the model to explain why students buy more printed textbooks than e-books, even though e-books are cheaper.

After studying this chapter, you will be able to

- **Describe a household's budget line and show how it changes when income or prices change**

- **Make a map of preferences by using indifference curves and explain the principle of diminishing marginal rate of substitution**

- **Predict the effects of changes in prices and income on consumption choices**

- **Predict the effects of changes in wage rates on work–leisure choices**

Consumption Possibilities

CONSUMPTION CHOICES ARE LIMITED BY INCOME and by prices. A household has a given amount of income to spend and cannot influence the prices of the goods and services it buys. A household's **budget line** describes the limits to its consumption choices.

Let's look at Lisa's budget line.[1] Lisa has an income of $30 a month to spend. She buys two goods: movies and pop. The price of a movie is $6, and the price of pop is $3 a six-pack. Figure 8.1 shows alternative affordable ways for Lisa to consume movies and pop. Row *A* says that she can buy 10 six-packs of pop and see no movies, a combination of movies and pop that exhausts her monthly income of $30. Row *F* says that Lisa can watch 5 movies and drink no pop—another combination that exhausts the $30 available. Each of the other rows in the table also exhausts Lisa's income. (Check that each of the other rows costs exactly $30.) The numbers in the table define Lisa's consumption possibilities. We can graph Lisa's consumption possibilities as points *A* through *F* in Fig. 8.1.

Divisible and Indivisible Goods Some goods—called divisible goods—can be bought in any quantity desired. Examples are gasoline and electricity. We can best understand household choice if we suppose that all goods and services are divisible. For example, Lisa can consume a half a movie a month on the average by seeing one movie every two months. When we think of goods as being divisible, the consumption possibilities are not just the points *A* through *F* shown in Fig. 8.1, but those points plus all the intermediate points that form the line running from *A* to *F*. Such a line is a budget line.

Lisa's budget line is a constraint on her choices. It marks the boundary between what is affordable and what is unaffordable. She can afford any point on the line and inside it. She cannot afford any point outside the line. The constraint on her consumption depends on prices and her income, and the constraint changes when the price of a good or her income changes. Let's see how by studying the budget equation.

[1] If you have studied Chapter 7 on marginal utility theory, you have already met Lisa. This tale of her thirst for pop and zeal for movies will sound familiar to you—up to a point. But in this chapter, we're going to use a different method for representing preferences—one that does not require us to resort to the idea of utility.

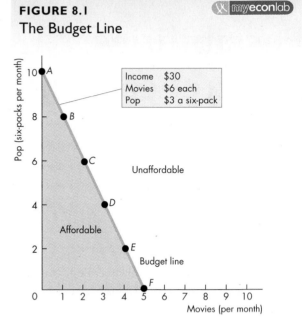

FIGURE 8.1
The Budget Line

Consumption possibility	Movies (per month)	Pop (six-packs per month)
A	0	10
B	1	8
C	2	6
D	3	4
E	4	2
F	5	0

Lisa's budget line shows the boundary between what she can and cannot afford. The rows of the table list Lisa's affordable combinations of movies and pop when her income is $30, the price of pop is $3 a six-pack, and the price of a movie is $6. For example, row A tells us that Lisa spends all of her $30 income when she buys 10 six-packs and sees no movies. The figure graphs Lisa's budget line. Points A through F on the graph represent the rows of the table. For divisible goods, the budget line is the continuous line AF. To calculate the equation for Lisa's budget line, start with expenditure equal to income:

$$\$3Q_P + \$6Q_M = \$30.$$

Divide by $3 to obtain

$$Q_P + 2Q_M = \$10.$$

Subtract $2Q_M$ from both sides to obtain

$$Q_P = 10 - 2Q_M.$$

The Budget Equation

We can describe the budget line by using a *budget equation*. The budget equation starts with the fact that

Expenditure = Income.

Expenditure is equal to the sum of the price of each good multiplied by the quantity bought. For Lisa,

Expenditure = (Price of pop × Quantity of pop) + (Price of a movie × Quantity of a movie)

Call the price of pop P_P, the quantity of pop Q_P, the price of a movie P_M, the quantity of movies Q_M, and income Y. We can now write Lisa's budget equation as

$$P_P Q_P + P_M Q_M = Y.$$

Or, using the prices Lisa faces, $3 for a six-pack and $6 for a movie, and Lisa's income, $30, we get

$$\$3 Q_P + \$6 Q_M = \$30.$$

Lisa can choose any quantities of pop (Q_P) and movies (Q_M) that satisfy this equation. To find the relationship between these quantities, divide both sides of the equation by the price of pop (P_P) to get

$$Q_P + \frac{P_M}{P_P} \times Q_M = \frac{Y}{P_P}.$$

Now subtract the term $P_M/P_P \times Q_M$ from both sides of this equation to get

$$Q_P = \frac{Y}{P_P} - \frac{P_M}{P_P} \times Q_M.$$

For Lisa, income (Y) is $30, the price of a movie (P_M) is $6, and the price of pop (P_P) is $3 a six-pack. So Lisa must choose the quantities of movies and pop to satisfy the equation

$$Q_P = \frac{\$30}{\$3} - \frac{\$6}{\$3} \times Q_M,$$

or

$$Q_P = 10 - 2 Q_M.$$

To interpret the equation, look at the budget line in Fig. 8.1 and check that the equation delivers that budget line. First, set Q_M equal to zero. The budget equation tells us that Q_P, the quantity of pop, is Y/P_P, which is 10 six-packs. This combination of Q_M and Q_P is the one shown in row A of the table in Fig. 8.1. Next set Q_M equal to 5. Q_P now equals zero (row F of the table). Check that you can derive the other rows.

The budget equation contains two variables (Q_M and Q_P) that the household chooses and two variables (Y/P_P and P_M/P_P) that the household takes as given. Let's look more closely at these variables.

Real Income A household's **real income** is the household's income expressed as a quantity of goods the household can afford to buy. Expressed in terms of pop, Lisa's real income is Y/P_P. This quantity is the maximum number of six-packs that she can buy. It is equal to her money income divided by the price of pop. Lisa's income is $30 and the price of pop is $3 a six-pack, so her real income in terms of pop is 10 six-packs, which is shown in Fig. 8.1 as the point at which the budget line intersects the y-axis.

Relative Price A **relative price** is the price of one good divided by the price of another good. In Lisa's budget equation, the variable P_M/P_P is the relative price of a movie in terms of pop. For Lisa, P_M is $6 a movie and P_P is $3 a six-pack, so P_M/P_P is equal to 2 six-packs per movie. That is, to see one more movie, Lisa must give up 2 six-packs.

You've just calculated Lisa's opportunity cost of a movie. Recall that the opportunity cost of an action is the best alternative forgone. For Lisa to see 1 more movie a month, she must forgo 2 six-packs. You've also calculated Lisa's opportunity cost of pop. For Lisa to consume 2 more six-packs a month, she must forgo seeing 1 movie. So her opportunity cost of 2 six-packs is 1 movie.

The relative price of a movie in terms of pop is the magnitude of the slope of Lisa's budget line. To calculate the slope of the budget line, recall the formula for slope (see the Chapter 1 Appendix): Slope equals the change in the variable measured on the y-axis divided by the change in the variable measured on the x-axis as we move along the line. In Lisa's case (Fig. 8.1), the variable measured on the y-axis is the quantity of pop and the variable measured on the x-axis is the quantity of movies. Along Lisa's budget line, as pop decreases from 10 to 0 six-packs, movies increase from 0 to 5. So the magnitude of the slope of the budget line is 10 six-packs divided by 5 movies, or 2 six-packs per movie. The magnitude of this slope is exactly the same as the relative price we've just calculated. It is also the opportunity cost of a movie.

A Change in Prices When prices change, so does the budget line. The lower the price of the good measured on the horizontal axis, other things remaining the same, the flatter is the budget line. For example, if the price of a movie falls from $6 to $3, real

FIGURE 8.2 myeconlab
Changes in Prices and Income

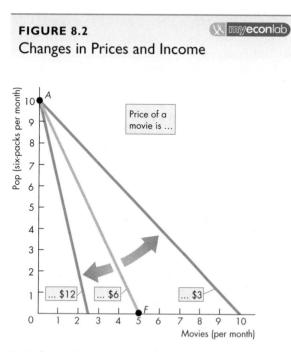

Price of a movie is …

… $12   … $6   … $3

(a) A change in price

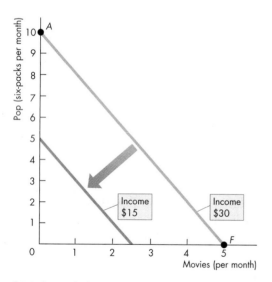

Income $15   Income $30

(b) A change in income

In part (a), the price of a movie changes. A fall in the price from $6 to $3 rotates the budget line outward and makes it flatter. A rise in the price from $6 to $12 rotates the budget line inward and makes it steeper.

In part (b), income falls from $30 to $15 while the prices of movies and pop remain constant. The budget line shifts leftward, but its slope does not change.

income in terms of pop does not change but the relative price of a movie falls. The budget line rotates outward and becomes flatter, as Fig. 8.2(a) illustrates. The higher the price of the good measured on the horizontal axis, other things remaining the same, the steeper is the budget line. For example, if the price of a movie rises from $6 to $12, the relative price of a movie increases. The budget line rotates inward and becomes steeper, as Fig. 8.2(a) illustrates.

A Change in Income A change in money income changes real income but does not change the relative price. The budget line shifts, but its slope does not change. The bigger a household's money income, the bigger is real income and the farther to the right is the budget line. The smaller a household's money income, the smaller is real income and the farther to the left is the budget line. Figure 8.2(b) shows the effect of a change in money income on Lisa's budget line. The initial budget line when Lisa's income is $30 is the same one that we began with in Fig. 8.1. The new budget line shows how much Lisa can consume if her income falls to $15 a month. The two budget lines have the same slope because the relative price is the same. The new budget line is closer to the origin because Lisa's real income has decreased.

REVIEW QUIZ

1 What does a household's budget line show?
2 How does the relative price and a household's real income influence its budget line?
3 If a household has an income of $40 and buys only bus rides at $4 each and magazines at $2 each, what is the equation of the household's budget line?
4 If the price of one good changes, what happens to the relative price and to the slope of the household's budget line?
5 If a household's money income changes and prices do not change, what happens to the household's real income and budget line?

myeconlab **Study Plan 8.1**

We've studied the limits to what a household can consume. Let's now learn how we can describe preferences and make a map that contains a lot of information about a household's preferences.

Preferences and Indifference Curves

YOU ARE GOING TO DISCOVER A VERY NEAT IDEA: that of drawing a map of a person's preferences. A preference map is based on the intuitively appealing idea that people can sort all the possible combinations of goods into three groups: preferred, not preferred, and indifferent. To make this idea more concrete, let's ask Lisa to tell us how she ranks various combinations of movies and pop.

Figure 8.3 shows part of Lisa's answer. She tells us that she currently sees 2 movies and drinks 6 six-packs a month at point C. She then lists all the combinations of movies and pop that she says are just as acceptable to her as her current consumption. When we plot these combinations of movies and pop, we get the green curve in Fig. 8.3(a). This curve is the key element in a map of preferences and is called an indifference curve.

An **indifference curve** is a line that shows combinations of goods among which a consumer is *indifferent*. The indifference curve in Fig. 8.3(a) tells us that Lisa is just as happy to see 2 movies and drink 6 six-packs a month at point C as she is to consume the combination of movies and pop at point G or at any other point along the curve.

Lisa also says that she prefers all the combinations of movies and pop above the indifference curve in Fig. 8.3(a)—the yellow area—to those on the indifference curve. And she prefers any combination on the indifference curve to any combination in the grey area below the indifference curve.

The indifference curve in Fig. 8.3(a) is just one of a whole family of such curves. This indifference curve appears again in Fig. 8.3(b) labelled I_1. The curves labelled I_0 and I_2 are two other indifference curves. Lisa prefers any point on indifference curve I_2 to any point on indifference curve I_1, and she prefers any point on I_1 to any point on I_0. We refer to I_2 as being a higher indifference curve than I_1 and I_1 as being higher than I_0.

A preference map is a series of indifference curves that resemble the contour lines on a map. By looking at the shape of the contour lines on a map, we can draw conclusions about the terrain. Similarly, by looking at the shape of indifference curves, we can draw conclusions about a person's preferences.

Let's learn how to "read" a preference map.

FIGURE 8.3
A Preference Map

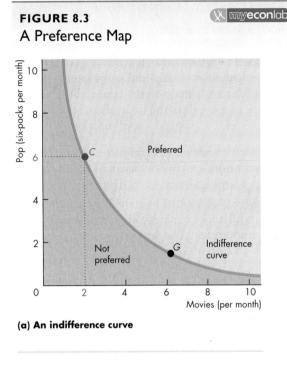

(a) An indifference curve

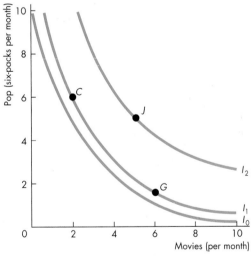

(b) Lisa's preference map

In part (a), Lisa drinks 6 six-packs of pop and sees 2 movies a month at point C. She is indifferent between all the points on the green indifference curve such as C and G. She prefers any point above the indifference curve (the yellow area) to any point on it, and she prefers any point on the indifference curve to any point below it (the grey area). A preference map is a number of indifference curves. Part (b) shows three indifference curves—I_0, I_1, and I_2—that are part of Lisa's preference map. She prefers point J to point C or G, so she prefers any point on I_2 to any point on I_1.

Marginal Rate of Substitution

The **marginal rate of substitution** (*MRS*) is the rate at which a person will give up good *y* (the good measured on the *y*-axis) to get an additional unit of good *x* (the good measured on the *x*-axis) and at the same time remain indifferent (remain on the same indifference curve). The magnitude of the slope of an indifference curve measures the marginal rate of substitution.

- If the indifference curve is *steep*, the marginal rate of substitution is *high*. The person is willing to give up a large quantity of good *y* to get an additional unit of good *x* while remaining indifferent.

- If the indifference curve is *flat*, the marginal rate of substitution is *low*. The person is willing to give up a small amount of good *y* to get an additional unit of good *x* while remaining indifferent.

Figure 8.4 shows you how to calculate the marginal rate of substitution. Suppose that Lisa drinks 6 six-packs and sees 2 movies at point *C* on indifference curve *I*₁. To calculate her marginal rate of substitution we measure the magnitude of the slope of the indifference curve at point *C*. To measure this magnitude, place a straight line against, or tangent to, the indifference curve at point *C*. Along that line, as the quantity of pop decreases by 10 six-packs, the number of movies increases by 5—an average of 2 six-packs per movie. So at point *C*, Lisa is willing to give up pop for movies at the rate of 2 six-packs per movie—a marginal rate of substitution of 2.

Now suppose that Lisa drinks 1.5 six-packs and sees 6 movies at point *G* in Fig. 8.4. Her marginal rate of substitution is now measured by the slope of the indifference curve at point *G*. That slope is the same as the slope of the tangent to the indifference curve at point *G*. Here, as the quantity of pop decreases by 4.5 six-packs, the number of movies increases by 9—an average of 1/2 six-pack per movie. So at point *G*, Lisa is willing to give up pop for movies at the rate of 1/2 six-pack per movie—a marginal rate of substitution of 1/2.

As Lisa sees more movies and drinks less pop, her marginal rate of substitution diminishes. Diminishing marginal rate of substitution is the key assumption of consumer theory. A **diminishing marginal rate of substitution** is a general tendency for a person to be willing to give up less of good *y* to get one more unit of good *x*, and at the same time remain indifferent, as the quantity of *x* increases. In Lisa's case, she is less willing to give up less pop to see one more movie, as the number of movies she sees increases.

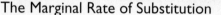

FIGURE 8.4
The Marginal Rate of Substitution

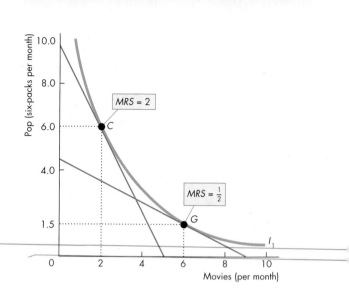

The magnitude of the slope of an indifference curve is called the marginal rate of substitution (*MRS*). The red line at point *C* tells us that Lisa is willing to give up 10 six-packs to see 5 movies. Her marginal rate of substitution at point *C* is 10 divided by 5, which equals 2. The red line at point *G* tells us that Lisa is willing to give up 4.5 six-packs to see 9 movies. Her marginal rate of substitution at point *G* is 4.5 divided by 9, which equals 1/2.

Your Own Diminishing Marginal Rate of Substitution Think about your own diminishing marginal rate of substitution. Imagine that in a week, you drink 10 six-packs of pop and see no movies. Most likely, you are willing to give up a lot of pop so that you can see just 1 movie. But now imagine that in a week, you drink 1 six-pack and see 6 movies. Most likely, you will now not be willing to give up much pop to see a seventh movie. As a general rule, the greater the number of movies you see, the smaller is the quantity of pop you are willing to give up to see one additional movie.

The shape of a person's indifference curves incorporates the principle of the diminishing marginal rate of substitution because the curves are bowed towards the origin. The tightness of the bend of an indifference curve tells us how willing a person is to substitute one good for another while remaining indifferent. Let's look at some examples that make this point clear.

Degree of Substitutability

Most of us would not regard movies and pop as being close substitutes. We probably have some fairly clear ideas about how many movies we want to see each month and how many cans of pop we want to drink. But to some degree, we are willing to substitute between these two goods. No matter how big a pop freak you are, there is surely some increase in the number of movies you can see that will compensate you for being deprived of a can of pop. Similarly, no matter how addicted you are to the movies, surely some number of cans of pop will compensate you for being deprived of seeing one movie. A person's indifference curves for movies and pop might look something like those shown in Fig. 8.5(a).

Close Substitutes Some goods substitute so easily for each other that most of us do not even notice which we are consuming. The different brands of personal computers are an example. As long as it has an "Intel inside" and runs Windows, most of us don't care whether our PC is a Dell, a Sony, or any other brand. The same holds true for marker pens. Most of

us don't care whether we use a marker pen from the campus bookstore or one from the local supermarket. When two goods are perfect substitutes, their indifference curves are straight lines that slope downward, as Fig. 8.5(b) illustrates. The marginal rate of substitution is constant.

Complements Some goods cannot substitute for each other at all. Instead, they are complements. The complements in Fig. 8.5(c) are left and right running shoes. Indifference curves of perfect complements are L-shaped. One left running shoe and one right running shoe are as good as one left shoe and two right ones. Having two of each is preferred to having one of each, but having two of one and one of the other is no better than having one of each.

The extreme cases of perfect substitutes and perfect complements shown here don't often happen in reality. But they do illustrate that the shape of the indifference curve shows the degree of substitutability between two goods. The more perfectly substitutable the two goods, the more nearly are their

FIGURE 8.5
The Degree of Substitutability

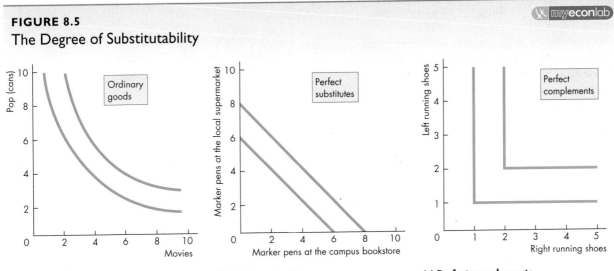

(a) Ordinary goods   **(b) Perfect substitutes**   **(c) Perfect complements**

The shape of the indifference curves reveals the degree of substitutability between two goods. Part (a) shows the indifference curves for two ordinary goods: movies and pop. To drink less pop and remain indifferent, one must see more movies. The number of movies that compensates for a reduction in pop increases as less pop is consumed. Part (b) shows the indifference curves for two perfect substitutes. For the

consumer to remain indifferent, one fewer marker pen from the local supermarket must be replaced by one extra marker pen from the campus bookstore. Part (c) shows two perfect complements—goods that cannot be substituted for each other at all. Having two left running shoes with one right running shoe is no better than having one of each. But having two of each is preferred to having one of each.

"With the pork I'd recommend an Alsatian white or a Coke."

indifference curves straight lines and the less quickly does the marginal rate of substitution diminish. Poor substitutes for each other have tightly curved indifference curves, approaching the shape of those shown in Fig. 8.5(c).

As you can see in the cartoon, according to the waiter's preferences, Coke and Alsatian white wine are perfect substitutes and each is a complement of pork. We hope the customers agree with him.

REVIEW QUIZ

1 What is an indifference curve and how does an indifference map show preferences?
2 Why does an indifference curve slope downward and why is it bowed towards the origin?
3 What do we call the magnitude of the slope of an indifference curve?
4 What is the key assumption about a consumer's marginal rate of substitution?

(X) myeconlab **Study Plan 8.2**

The two components of the model of household choice are now in place: the budget line and the preference map. We will now use these components to work out the household's choice and to predict how choices change when prices and income change.

Predicting Consumer Behaviour

WE ARE NOW GOING TO PREDICT THE QUANTITIES of movies and pop that Lisa chooses to buy. Figure 8.6 shows Lisa's budget line from Fig. 8.1 and her indifference curves from Fig. 8.3(b). We assume that Lisa consumes at her best affordable point, which is 2 movies and 6 six-packs—at point *C*. Here, Lisa

■ Is on her budget line.
■ Is on her highest attainable indifference curve.
■ Has a marginal rate of substitution between movies and pop equal to the relative price of movies and pop.

For every point inside the budget line, such as point *I*, there are points *on* the budget line that Lisa prefers. For example, she prefers all the points on the

FIGURE 8.6   (X) myeconlab
The Best Affordable Point

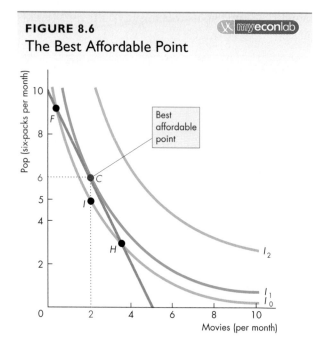

Lisa's best affordable point is *C*. At that point, she is on her budget line and also on the highest attainable indifference curve. At a point such as *H*, Lisa is willing to give up more movies in exchange for pop than she has to. She can move to point *I*, which is just as good as point *H*, and have some unspent income. She can spend that income and move to *C*, a point that she prefers to point *I*.

budget line between *F* and *H* to point *I*. So she chooses a point on the budget line.

Every point on the budget line lies on an indifference curve. For example, point *H* lies on the indifference curve I_0. At point *H*, Lisa's marginal rate of substitution is less than the relative price. Lisa is willing to give up more movies in exchange for pop than the budget line says she must. So she moves along her budget line from *H* towards *C*. As she does so, she passes through a number of indifference curves (not shown in the figure) located between indifference curves I_0 and I_1. All of these indifference curves are higher than I_0, and therefore Lisa prefers any point on them to point *H*. But when Lisa gets to point *C*, she is on the highest attainable indifference curve. If she keeps moving along the budget line, she starts to encounter indifference curves that are lower than I_1. So Lisa chooses point *C*.

At the chosen point, the marginal rate of substitution (the magnitude of the slope of the indifference curve) equals the relative price (the magnitude of the slope of the budget line).

Let's use this model of household choice to predict the effects on consumption of changes in prices and income. We'll begin by studying the effect of a change in price.

A Change in Price

The effect of a change in the price on the quantity of a good consumed is called the **price effect**. We will use Fig. 8.7(a) to work out the price effect of a fall in the price of a movie. We start with the price of a movie at $6, the price of pop at $3 a six-pack, and Lisa's income at $30 a month. In this situation, she drinks 6 six-packs and sees 2 movies a month at point *C*.

Now suppose that the price of a movie falls to $3. With a lower price of a movie, the budget line rotates outward and becomes flatter. (Check back to Fig. 8.2(a) for a refresher on how a price change affects the budget line.) The new budget line is the dark orange one in Fig. 8.7(a).

Lisa's best affordable point is now point *J*, where she sees 5 movies and drinks 5 six-packs of pop. Lisa drinks less pop and watches more movies now that movies are cheaper. She cuts her pop consumption from 6 to 5 six-packs and increases the number of movies she sees from 2 to 5 a month. Lisa substitutes movies for pop when the price of a movie falls and the price of pop and her income remain constant.

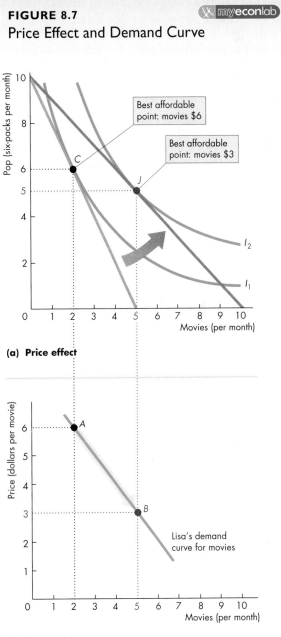

FIGURE 8.7

Price Effect and Demand Curve

(a) Price effect

Best affordable point: movies $6

Best affordable point: movies $3

(b) Demand curve

Lisa's demand curve for movies

Initially, Lisa consumes at point *C* (part a). If the price of a movie falls from $6 to $3, Lisa consumes at point *J*. The move from *C* to *J* is the price effect.

At a price of $6 a movie, Lisa sees 2 movies a month, at point *A* in part (b). At a price of $3 a movie, she sees 5 movies a month, at point *B*. Lisa's demand curve traces out her best affordable quantity of movies as the price of a movie varies, other things remaining the same.

The Demand Curve In Chapter 3, we asserted that the demand curve slopes downward. We can now derive a demand curve from a consumer's budget line and indifference curves. By doing so, we can see that the law of demand and the downward-sloping demand curve are consequences of the consumer's choosing his or her best affordable combination of goods.

To derive Lisa's demand curve for movies, lower the price of a movie and find her best affordable point at different prices. We've just done this for two movie prices in Fig. 8.7(a). Figure 8.7(b) highlights these two prices and two points that lie on Lisa's demand curve for movies. When the price of a movie is $6, Lisa sees 2 movies a month at point A. When the price falls to $3, she increases the number of movies she sees to 5 a month at point B. The demand curve is made up of these two points plus all the other points that tell us Lisa's best affordable consumption of movies at each movie price, given the price of pop and Lisa's income. As you can see, Lisa's demand curve for movies slopes downward—the lower the price of a movie, the more movies she watches each month. This is the law of demand.

Next, let's see how Lisa changes her consumption of movies and pop when her income changes.

A Change in Income

The effect of a change in income on consumption is called the **income effect**. Let's work out the income effect by examining how consumption changes when income changes and prices remain constant. Figure 8.8 shows the income effect when Lisa's income falls. With an income of $30 and with the price of a movie at $3 and the price of pop at $3 a six-pack, she consumes at point J—5 movies and 5 six-packs. If her income falls to $21, she consumes at point K—she sees 4 movies and drinks 3 six-packs. When Lisa's income falls, she consumes less of both goods. Movies and pop are normal goods.

The Demand Curve and the Income Effect A change in income leads to a shift in the demand curve, as shown in Fig. 8.8(b). With an income of $30, Lisa's demand curve is D_0, the same as in Fig. 8.7(b). But when her income falls to $21, she plans to see fewer movies at each price, so her demand curve shifts leftward to D_1.

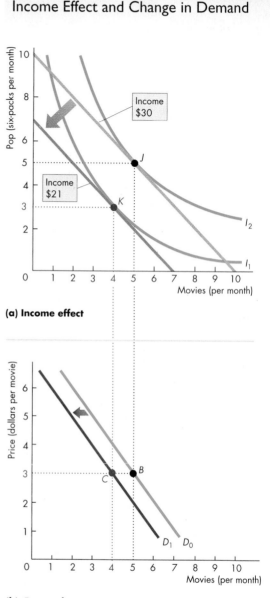

FIGURE 8.8   myeconlab

Income Effect and Change in Demand

(a) Income effect

(b) Demand curve

A change in income shifts the budget line, changes the best affordable point, and changes consumption.

In part (a), when Lisa's income decreases from $30 to $21, she consumes less of both movies and pop.

In part (b), Lisa's demand curve for movies when her income is $30 is D_0. When Lisa's income decreases to $21, her demand curve for movies shifts leftward to D_1. Lisa's demand for movies decreases because she now sees fewer movies at each price.

Substitution Effect and Income Effect

For a normal good, a fall in price *always* increases the quantity bought. We can prove this assertion by dividing the price effect into two parts:

- Substitution effect
- Income effect

Figure 8.9 shows the price effect, and Fig. 8.9(b) divides the price effect into its two parts.

Substitution Effect The **substitution effect** is the effect of a change in price on the quantity bought when the consumer (hypothetically) remains indifferent between the original situation and the new one. To work out Lisa's substitution effect, when the price of a movie falls, we cut her income by enough to leave her on the same indifference curve as before.

When the price of a movie falls from $6 to $3, suppose (hypothetically) that we cut Lisa's income to $21. What's special about $21? It is the income that is just enough, at the new price of a movie, to keep Lisa's best affordable point on the same indifference curve as her original consumption point *C*. Lisa's budget line is now the light orange line in Fig. 8.9(b). With the lower price of a movie and a smaller income, Lisa's best affordable point is *K* on indifference curve I_1. The move from *C* to *K* is the substitution effect of the price change. The substitution effect of the fall in the price of a movie is an increase in the consumption of movies from 2 to 4. The direction of the substitution effect never varies: When the relative price of a good falls, the consumer substitutes more of that good for the other good.

Income Effect To calculate the substitution effect, we gave Lisa a $9 pay cut. To calculate the income effect, we give Lisa her $9 back. The $9 increase in income shifts Lisa's budget line outward, as shown in Fig. 8.9(b). The slope of the budget line does not change because both prices remain constant. This change in Lisa's budget line is similar to the one illustrated in Fig. 8.8. As Lisa's budget line shifts outward, her consumption possibilities expand and her best affordable point becomes *J* on indifference curve I_2. The move from *K* to *J* is the income effect of the price change. In this example, as Lisa's income increases, she increases the number of movies she sees. For Lisa, a movie is a normal good. For a normal good, the income effect reinforces the substitution effect.

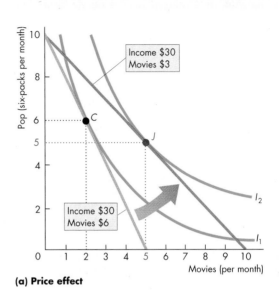

FIGURE 8.9 🅧 myeconlab

Substitution Effect and Income Effect

(a) Price effect

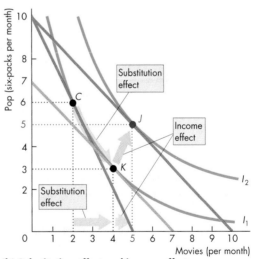

(b) Substitution effect and income effect

The price effect in part (a) can be separated into a substitution effect and an income effect in part (b).

To isolate the substitution effect, we confront Lisa with the new price but keep her on her original indifference curve, I_1. The substitution effect is the move from *C* to *K*.

To isolate the income effect, we confront Lisa with the new price of movies but increase her income so that she can move from the original indifference curve, I_1, to the new one, I_2. The income effect is the move from *K* to *J*.

Inferior Goods The example that we have just studied is that of a change in the price of a normal good. The effect of a change in the price of an inferior good is different. Recall that an inferior good is one whose consumption decreases as income increases. For an inferior good, the income effect is negative. Thus for an inferior good, a lower price does not always lead to an increase in the quantity demanded. The lower price has a substitution effect that increases the quantity demanded. But the lower price also has a negative income effect that reduces the demand for the inferior good. So the income effect offsets the substitution effect to some degree. If the negative income effect exceeded the positive substitution effect, the demand curve would slope upward. This case does not appear to occur in the real world.

Back to the Facts

We started this chapter by observing how consumer spending has changed over the years. The indifference curve model explains those changes. The best affordable choices determine spending patterns. Changes in prices and income change the best affordable choice and change consumption patterns.

REVIEW QUIZ

1 When a consumer chooses the combination of goods and services to buy, what is she or he trying to achieve?
2 Can you explain the conditions that are met when a consumer has found the best affordable combination of goods to buy? (Use the terms budget line, marginal rate of substitution, and relative price in your explanation.)
3 The price of a normal good falls, what happens to the quantity demanded of that good?
4 Into what two effects can we divide the effect of a price change?
5 For a normal good, does the income effect reinforce the substitution effect or does it partly offset the substitution effect?

   myeconlab   **Study Plan 8.3**

The model of household choice can explain many other household choices. Let's look at one of them.

Work–Leisure Choices

HOUSEHOLDS MAKE MANY CHOICES OTHER THAN those about how to spend their income on the various goods and services available. We can use the model of consumer choice to understand many other household choices. Some of these choices are discussed on pp. 192–196. Here we'll study a key choice: how much labour to supply.

Labour Supply

Every week, we allocate our 168 hours between working—called *labour*—and all other activities—called *leisure.* How do we decide how to allocate our time between labour and leisure? We can answer this question by using the theory of household choice.

   The more hours we spend on *leisure,* the smaller is our income. The relationship between leisure and income is described by an *income-time budget line.* Figure 8.10(a) shows Lisa's income-time budget line. If Lisa devotes the entire week to leisure—168 hours—she has no income and is at point Z. By supplying labour in exchange for a wage, she can convert hours into income along the income-time budget line. The slope of that line is determined by the hourly wage rate. If the wage rate is $5 an hour, Lisa faces the flattest budget line. If the wage rate is $10 an hour, she faces the middle budget line. And if the wage rate is $15 an hour, she faces the steepest budget line.

   Lisa buys leisure by not supplying labour and by forgoing income. The opportunity cost of an hour of leisure is the hourly wage rate forgone.

   Figure 8.10(a) also shows Lisa's indifference curves for income and leisure. Lisa chooses her best attainable point. This choice of income and time allocation is just like her choice of movies and pop. She gets onto the highest possible indifference curve by making her marginal rate of substitution between income and leisure equal to her wage rate. Lisa's choice depends on the wage rate she can earn. At a wage rate of $5 an hour, Lisa chooses point A and works 20 hours a week (168 minus 148) for an income of $100 a week. At a wage rate of $10 an hour, she chooses point B and works 35 hours a week (168 minus 133) for an income of $350 a week. And at a wage rate of $15 an hour, she chooses point C and works 30 hours a week (168 minus 138) for an income of $450 a week.

FIGURE 8.10

The Supply of Labour

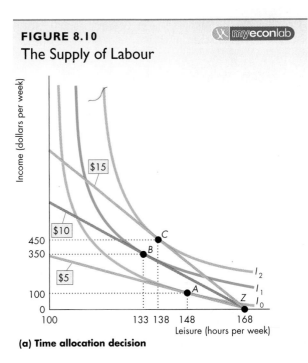

(a) Time allocation decision

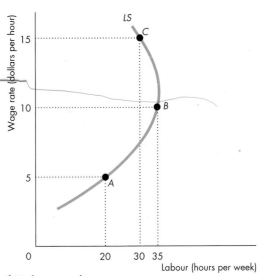

(b) Labour supply curve

In part (a), at a wage rate of $5 an hour, Lisa takes 148 hours of leisure and works 20 hours a week at point A. If the wage rate increases from $5 to $10, she decreases her leisure to 133 hours and increases her work to 35 hours a week at point B. But if the wage rate increases from $10 to $15, Lisa *increases* her leisure to 138 hours and *decreases* her work to 30 hours a week at point C. Part (b) shows Lisa's labour supply curve. Points A, B, and C on the supply curve correspond to Lisa's choices on her income-time budget line in part (a).

The Labour Supply Curve

Figure 8.10(b) shows Lisa's labour supply curve. This curve shows that as the wage rate increases from $5 an hour to $10 an hour, Lisa increases the quantity of labour supplied from 20 hours a week to 35 hours a week. But when the wage rate increases to $15 an hour, she decreases her quantity of labour supplied to 30 hours a week.

Lisa's supply of labour is similar to that described for the economy as a whole at the beginning of this chapter. As wage rates have increased, work hours have decreased. At first, this pattern seems puzzling. We've seen that the hourly wage rate is the opportunity cost of leisure. So a higher wage rate means a higher opportunity cost of leisure. This fact on its own leads to a decrease in leisure and an increase in work hours. But instead, we've cut our work hours. Why? Because our incomes have increased. As the wage rate increases, incomes increase, so people demand more of all normal goods. Leisure is a normal good, so as incomes increase, people demand more leisure.

The higher wage rate has both a *substitution effect* and an *income effect*. The higher wage rate increases the opportunity cost of leisure and so leads to a substitution effect away from leisure. And the higher wage rate increases income and so leads to an income effect towards more leisure. This outcome of rational household choice explains why the average workweek has fallen steadily as wage rates have increased. With higher wage rates, people have decided to use their higher incomes in part to consume more leisure.

REVIEW QUIZ

1 What is the opportunity cost of leisure?
2 Why might a rise in the wage rate lead to an increase in leisure and a decrease in work hours?

myeconlab Study Plan 8.4

◆ *Reading Between the Lines* on pp. 184–185 shows you how the theory of household choice explains why, even though e-books are cheaper than print books, students continue to buy more print books than e-books.

In the chapters that follow, we study firms' choices. We'll see how, in the pursuit of profit, firms make choices that determine the supply of goods and services and the demand for productive resources.

The Marginal Rate of Substitution Between Printed Books and E-Books

THE TORONTO STAR, AUGUST 15, 2005

E-books' latest bid to send paper packing

Move over hardcopies. Starting today, there's a new item on bookstore shelves.

Ten U.S. university bookstores are stocking digital versions of popular textbooks alongside the paper products. The digital version will sell for approximately 33 per cent less than a new, paper copy.

The pilot project will include approximately 200 titles from McGraw-Hill Higher Education, Thomson Learning, Sage Publications and Houghton Mifflin Company.

"We're interested in measuring student demand for digital content," said David Serbun, director of partnerships for Houghton Mifflin's college division. "We're also interested in offering students a choice."

Once a digital textbook has been downloaded to a student's computer, sections can be highlighted and pages can be printed. Students can also search their digital book for keywords.

Downloadable books have been available online for years, but according to Jeff Cohen, advertising and promotions manager for MBS Textbook Exchange Inc., this is the first time that digital books will be featured on stores shelves, right beside the traditional, bound versions.

It was essential to get the digital products into brick and mortar stores, Cohen said, because "the majority of textbook purchases still take place in a physical bookstore."

...

Essence of the Story

■ Ten U.S. university bookstores are stocking electronic versions of textbooks—e-books—alongside the paper products.

■ The price of a digital textbook will be approximately 33 percent less than a new paper copy. One of the publishers says it wants to measure student demand for digital content.

■ E-books have been available online for years but this is the first time that they can be bought alongside print books in a bookstore. The majority of textbook purchases still take place in a physical bookstore.

Economic Analysis

■ Print books and e-books are good substitutes, but not perfect substitutes for most students.

■ When two goods are close substitutes, the marginal rate of substitution doesn't change much as the quantities consumed change, so the indifference curves are relatively straight and a small change in the relative price brings a large change in the quantities bought.

■ Figure 1 shows an example of what a student's indifference curves for print books and e-books might look like.

■ These indifference curves imply that although both print books and e-books have their own unique advantages, on balance, the traditional print book still does a better job than the e-book. It is more convenient and easier to use.

■ The figure also shows two budget lines, the line *AB* and the line *AC*.

■ On these budget lines, the student has a budget for books that enables her to buy 9 print books a year and no e-books.

■ Along the budget line *AB*, the price of a print book is the same as the price of an e-book.

■ Along the budget line *AC*, the price of an e-book is 33 percent lower than the price of a print book.

■ If the two types of book have the same price, the student's best affordable point, where her budget line just touches her indifference curve I_0, is where she buys 9 print books and no e-books.

■ With the price of an e-book 33 percent lower than the price of a print book, the student's best affordable point, where her budget line just touches her indifference curve I_1, is where she buys 7 print books and 3 e-books.

■ If the price of an e-book falls further, relative to the price of a print book, students will substitute more e-books for print books.

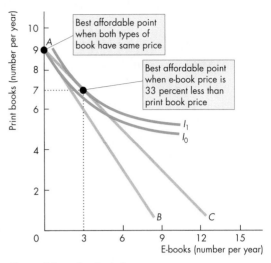

Figure 1 A student's choices

185

KEY POINTS

Consumption Possibilities (pp. 172–174)

- The budget line is the boundary between what the household can and cannot afford given its income and the prices of goods.
- The point at which the budget line intersects the y-axis is the household's real income in terms of the good measured on that axis.
- The magnitude of the slope of the budget line is the relative price of the good measured on the x-axis in terms of the good measured on the y-axis.
- A change in price changes the slope of the budget line. A change in income shifts the budget line but does not change its slope.

Preferences and Indifference Curves (pp. 175–178)

- A consumer's preferences can be represented by indifference curves. An indifference curve joins all the combinations of goods among which the consumer is indifferent.
- A consumer prefers any point above an indifference curve to any point on it and any point on an indifference curve to any point below it.
- The magnitude of the slope of an indifference curve is called the marginal rate of substitution.
- The marginal rate of substitution diminishes as consumption of the good measured on the y-axis decreases and consumption of the good measured on the x-axis increases.

Predicting Consumer Behaviour (pp. 178–182)

- A household consumes at its best affordable point. This point is on the budget line and on the highest attainable indifference curve and has a marginal rate of substitution equal to relative price.
- The effect of a price change (the price effect) can be divided into a substitution effect and an income effect.
- The substitution effect is the effect of a change in price on the quantity bought when the consumer

(hypothetically) remains indifferent between the original situation and the new situation.

- The substitution effect always results in an increase in consumption of the good whose relative price has fallen.
- The income effect is the effect of a change in income on consumption.
- For a normal good, the income effect reinforces the substitution effect. For an inferior good, the income effect works in the opposite direction to the substitution effect.

Work–Leisure Choices (pp. 182–183)

- The indifference curve model of household choice enables us to understand how a household allocates its time between work and leisure.
- Work hours have decreased and leisure hours have increased because the income effect on the demand for leisure has been greater than the substitution effect.

KEY FIGURES

Figure 8.1   The Budget Line, 172
Figure 8.2   Changes in Prices and Income, 174
Figure 8.3   A Preference Map, 175
Figure 8.4   The Marginal Rate of Substitution, 176
Figure 8.6   The Best Affordable Point, 178
Figure 8.7   Price Effect and Demand Curve, 179
Figure 8.8   Income Effect and Change in Demand, 180
Figure 8.9   Substitution Effect and Income Effect, 181

KEY TERMS

Budget line, 172
Diminishing marginal rate of substitution, 176
Income effect, 180
Indifference curve, 175
Marginal rate of substitution, 176
Price effect, 179
Real income, 173
Relative price, 173
Substitution effect, 181

PROBLEMS

Go to **myeconlab** for solutions to odd-numbered problems and additional exercises.

1. Sara's income is $12 a week, popcorn is $3 a bag, and cola is $3 a can.
   a. What is Sara's real income in terms of cola?
   b. What is her real income in terms of popcorn?
   c. What is the relative price of cola in terms of popcorn?
   d. What is the opportunity cost of a can of cola?
   e. What is the equation for Sara's budget line (with popcorn on the left side).
   f. Draw a graph of Sara's budget line with cola on the *x*-axis.
   g. In (f), what is the slope of Sara's budget line? What determines its value?

2. Rashid's income is $100 per week. The price of a CD is $10, and the price of a book is $20.
   a. What is Rashid's real income in terms of CDs?
   b. What is his real income in terms of books?
   c. What is the relative price of a CD in terms of books?
   d. What is the opportunity cost of a book?
   e. What is the equation for Rashid's budget line (with books on the left side).
   f. Draw a graph of Rashid's budget line with CDs on the *x*-axis.
   g. In (f), what is the slope of Rashid's budget line? What determines its value?

3. Sara's income and the prices of popcorn and cola are the same as those in problem 1. The figure illustrates Sara's preferences.

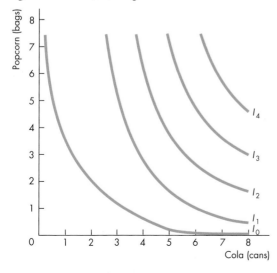

a. What quantities of popcorn and cola does Sara buy?
b. What is Sara's marginal rate of substitution at the point at which she consumes?

4. Rashid's income and the prices of CDs and books are the same as those in problem 2. The figure illustrates his preferences.

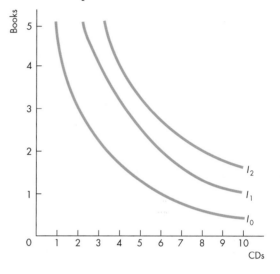

a. What quantities of CDs and books does Rashid buy?
b. What is Rashid's marginal rate of substitution at the point at which he consumes?

5. Now suppose that in problem 3, the price of cola falls to $1.50 a can and the price of popcorn and Sara's income remain the same.
   a. What quantities of cola and popcorn does Sara now buy?
   b. Find two points on Sara's demand curve for cola.
   c. Find the substitution effect of the price change.
   d. Find the income effect of the price change.
   e. Is cola a normal good or an inferior good for Sara?

6. Now suppose that in problem 4, the price of a CD rises to $20 and the price of a book and Rashid's income remain the same.
   a. What quantities of CDs and books does Rashid now buy?
   b. Find two points on Rashid's demand curve for CDs.
   c. Find the substitution effect of the price change.

d. Find the income effect of the price change.

e. Is a CD a normal good or an inferior good for Rashid?

7. Pam buys cookies and comic books. The price of a cookie is $1, and the price of a comic book is $2. Each month, Pam spends all of her income and buys 30 cookies and 5 comic books. Next month, the price of a cookie will fall to 50¢ and the price of a comic book will rise to $5. Assume that Pam's preference map is similar to that in Fig. 8.3(b). Use a graph to answer the following questions.

a. Will Pam be able to buy 30 cookies and 5 comic books next month?

b. Will Pam want to buy 30 cookies and 5 comic books?

c. Which situation does Pam prefer: cookies at $1 and comic books at $2 or cookies at 50¢ and comic books at $5?

d. If Pam changes the quantities that she buys, which good will she buy more of and which will she buy less of?

e. When the prices change next month, will there be an income effect and a substitution effect at work or just one of them?

8. Yangjie buys smoothies and sushi. The price of a smoothie is $5, and the price of sushi is $1 a piece. Each month, Yangjie spends all of her income and buys 10 smoothies and 20 pieces of sushi. Next month, the price of a smoothie will fall to $3 and the price of sushi will rise to $2 a piece. Assume that Yangjie's preference map is similar to that in Fig. 8.3(b). Use a graph to answer the following questions.

a. Will Yangjie be able to buy 10 smoothies and 20 pieces of sushi next month?

b. Will Yangjie want to buy 10 smoothies and 20 pieces of sushi? Explain why.

c. Which situation does Yangjie prefer: smoothies at $5 each and sushi at $1 a piece or smoothies at $3 each and sushi at $2 a piece?

d. If Yangjie changes the quantities that she buys, which good will she buy more of and which will she buy less of?

e. When the prices change next month, will there be an income effect and a substitution effect at work or just one of them? Explain.

CRITICAL THINKING

1. Study *Reading Between the Lines* about print books and e-books on pp. 184–185, and then answer the following questions.

a. Do you buy print books only, or do you buy some e-books as well?

b. Sketch your budget constraint for textbooks and other items.

c. Sketch your indifference curves for textbooks and other goods.

d. What do you predict would happen to the way that you allocate your budget between textbooks and other goods and services if the price of an e-book fell to 10 percent of the price of a current print book?

2. A sales tax is a tax on goods and the GST is a tax on both goods and services. Canadians hate the GST but is a federal sales tax better than the GST? When Canada replaced the federal sales tax with the GST:

a. What happened to the relative price of CD-Rs and haircuts and to a consumer's budget line of CD-Rs and haircuts?

b. How did purchases of CD-Rs and haircuts change?

c. Which tax is better for the consumer? Why?

Use a graph to illustrate your answers and to show the substitution effect and the income effect of the price change.

WEB EXERCISES

Use the links on ⓧ myeconlab **to work the following exercise.**

1. Obtain information about the prices of cell phone service and first-class mail.

a. Sketch the budget constraint for a consumer who spent $50 a month on these two goods in 2002 and 2003.

b. Can you say whether the consumer was better off or worse off in 2002 than in 2003?

c. Sketch some indifference curves for cell phone calls and first-class letters mailed and show the income effect and the substitution effect of the changes in prices that occurred between 2002 and 2003.

APPENDIX

Marginal Utility and Indifference Curves

After studying Chapters 7 and 8 and this appendix, you will be able to

- **Explain the connection between utility and indifference curves**

- **Explain why maximizing utility is the same as choosing the best affordable point**

- **Explain why utility exists**

Two Ways of Describing Preferences

THE MARGINAL UTILITY MODEL DESCRIBES preferences by using the concept of utility. An increase in the quantity consumed of a good brings an increase in the total utility derived from that good and a decrease in its marginal utility (see Table 7.1, p. 155, and Figure 7.2, p. 156).

The indifference curve model describes preferences by using the concepts of preference and indifference to define a map of indifference curves. A higher indifference curve is preferred to a lower one. And along an indifference curve, the marginal rate of substitution diminishes (see Figure 8.3, p. 175, and Figure 8.4, p. 176).

The indifference curve model doesn't need the concept of utility. In fact, it was developed precisely because economists wanted a more objective way of describing preferences. But we can interpret the indifference curve model by using the concept of utility.

Because a consumer is indifferent among the combinations of goods at all the points on an indifference curve, these combinations provide the same amount of total utility. An indifference curve is a constant utility curve.

You can see the connection between utility and an indifference map by looking at Fig. A8.1. Part (a) provides information about the total utility from movies and pop. It is based on Table 7.1, (p. 155), but instead of listing the quantities of the two goods and the total utility arising from each quantity consumed, the numbers are arranged with movies across the bottom and pop down the side. With no pop, the total utility from

FIGURE A8.1
Total Utility and the Indifference Map

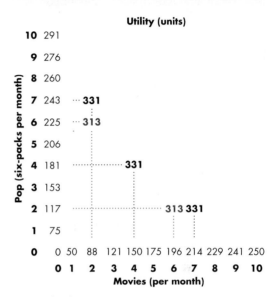

(a) Total utility

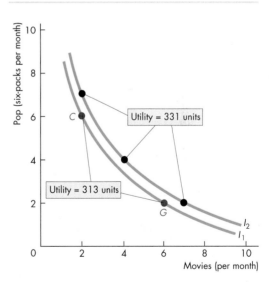

(b) Indifference curves

We can represent preferences by using the concept of utility or indifference curves. In the table, Lisa's total utility depends on the quantities of movies and pop that she consumes. Different combinations yield the same total utility. These combinations lie on an indifference curve. The figure shows two indifference curves: one for 313 units of utility and one for 331 units of utility.

6 movies is 196 units. And with no movies, the total utility from 2 six-packs is 117 units.

Figure A8.1(a) also shows the total utility from some other combinations of movies and pop. For example, the total utility from 6 movies and 2 six-packs is 313 units (196 plus 117). Part (a) shows another combination that delivers 313 units and three combinations that deliver 331 units of utility.

The figure shows the indifference curves associated with these two levels of total utility.

Maximizing Utility Is Choosing the Best Affordable Point

IN THE MARGINAL UTILITY MODEL, LISA maximizes total utility by spending all of her income on the combination of movies and pop that makes the marginal utility per dollar on movies equal to the marginal utility per dollar on pop. That is,

$$MU_M/P_M = MU_P/P_P, \qquad (1)$$

where MU_M is the marginal utility of a movie, P_M is the price of a movie, MU_P is the marginal utility of pop, and P_P is the price of pop.

In the indifference curve model, Lisa chooses the best affordable point by spending all of her income on the combination of movies and pop that makes the marginal rate of substitution (MRS) equal to the relative price of the two goods.

That is,

$$MRS = P_M/P_P. \qquad (2)$$

Maximizing total utility and choosing the best affordable point are the same. To see why, first multiply both sides of equation (1) above by P_M and divide both sides by MU_P to obtain

$$MU_M/MU_P = P_M/P_P. \qquad (3)$$

This equation states that the ratio of the marginal utilities of the two goods is equal to the relative price of the two goods.

Inspect equations (2) and (3) and you can see that if the two ways of describing a consumer's choice are the same, then the marginal rate of substitution must equal the ratio of the marginal utilities of the two goods. That is,

$$MRS = MU_M/MU_P. \qquad (4)$$

To establish that this proposition is true, note that total utility changes when the quantities consumed change in the following way:

$$\Delta U = MU_M \times \Delta Q_M + MU_P \times \Delta Q_P, \qquad (5)$$

where Δ means "change in," U is utility, Q_M is the quantity of movies consumed, and Q_P is the quantity of pop consumed.

Recall that along an indifference curve, total utility is constant so the change in total utility is zero. Then, along an indifference curve, it must be the case that

$$0 = MU_M \times \Delta Q_M + MU_P \times \Delta Q_P, \qquad (6)$$

or

$$MU_M \times \Delta Q_M = -MU_P \times \Delta Q_P. \qquad (7)$$

Divide both sides of equation (7) by MU_P and by ΔQ_M to obtain

$$MU_M/MU_P = -\Delta Q_P/\Delta Q_M. \qquad (8)$$

This equation tells us that along an indifference curve, the change in the quantity of pop consumed divided by the change in the quantity of movies consumed equals the ratio of the marginal utilities of movies and pop.

But $-\Delta Q_P/\Delta Q_M$ (rise over run) is the slope of the indifference curve. And, removing the minus sign, $\Delta Q_P/\Delta Q_M$ is the marginal rate of substitution of movies for pop. So,

$$MRS = \Delta Q_P/\Delta Q_M = MU_M/MU_P. \qquad (9)$$

You've now seen that the two models of consumer choice make identical predictions about the quantities that a consumer chooses. Spending the available budget with the marginal utility per dollar the same for both goods is the same as spending the available budget with the marginal rate of substitution between the two goods equal to their relative price.

Utility Exists!

THE INDIFFERENCE CURVE MODEL IS POWERFUL because its only assumptions are that people can rank alternative combinations of goods as preferred or indifferent and that the marginal rate of substitution diminishes. From these assumptions, we can derive the downward-sloping demand curve. We can also easily visualize the effects of changes in prices and income on a consumer's choice.

The indifference curve model is also powerful because its assumptions imply the existence of utility and of (generally) diminishing marginal utility.

By observing the prices of goods and the quantities consumed, we can infer a consumer's marginal utilities at each quantity.

UNDERSTANDING HOUSEHOLDS' CHOICES

Making the Most of Life

The powerful forces of demand and supply shape the fortunes of families, businesses, nations, and empires in the same unrelenting way that the tides and winds shape rocks and coastlines. You saw in Chapters 3 through 6 how these forces raise and lower prices, increase and decrease quantities bought and sold, cause revenues to fluctuate, and send resources to their most valuable uses.

These powerful forces begin quietly and privately with the choices that each one of us makes.

Chapters 7 and 8 probe these individual choices. Chapter 7 explores the marginal utility theory of human decisions. This theory explains people's consumption plans. It also explains people's consumption of leisure time and its flip side, the supply of work time. Marginal utility theory can even be used to explain "non-economic" choices, such as whether to marry and how many children to have. In a sense, there are no non-economic choices. If there is scarcity, there must be choice. And economics studies all such choices.

Chapter 8 describes a tool that enables us to make a map of people's likes and dislikes, a tool called an *indifference curve*. Indifference curves are considered an advanced topic, so this chapter is *strictly optional*. But the presentation of indifference curves in Chapter 8 is the clearest and most straightforward available, so if you want to learn about this tool, this chapter is the place to do so.

The earliest economists (Adam Smith and his contemporaries) did not have a very deep understanding of households' choices. It was not until the nineteenth century that progress was made in this area. On the following pages, you can spend some time with Jeremy Bentham, the person who pioneered the use of the concept of utility to the study of human choices, and with Steven Levitt of the University of Chicago, who is one of today's most influential students of human behaviour.

PROBING THE IDEAS

People as Rational Decision Makers

THE ECONOMIST

Jeremy Bentham *(1748–1832), who lived in London, was the son and grandson of a lawyer and was himself trained as a barrister. But he rejected the opportunity to maintain the family tradition and, instead, spent his life as a writer, activist, and Member of Parliament in the pursuit of rational laws that would bring the greatest happiness to the greatest number of people.*

Bentham, whose embalmed body is preserved to this day in a glass cabinet in the University of London, was the first person to use the concept of utility to explain human choices. But in Bentham's day, the distinction between explaining and prescribing was not a sharp one, and Bentham was ready to use his ideas to tell people how they ought to behave. He was one of the first to propose pensions for the retired, guaranteed employment, minimum wages, and social benefits such as free education and free medical care.

THE ISSUES

The economic analysis of human behaviour in the family, the workplace, the markets for goods and services, the markets for labour services, and financial markets is based on the idea that our behaviour can be understood as a response to scarcity. Everything we do can be understood as a choice that maximizes total benefit subject to the constraints imposed by our limited resources and technology. If people's preferences are stable in the face of changing constraints, then we have a chance of predicting how they will respond to an evolving environment.

The economic approach explains the incredible change that has occurred during the past 100 years in the way women allocate their time as the consequence of changing constraints, not of changing attitudes. Technological advances have equipped the nation's farms and factories with machines that have increased the productivity of both women and men, thereby raising the wages they can earn. The increasingly technological world has increased the return to education for both women and men and has led to a large increase in high school and university graduates of both sexes. And equipped with an ever-widening array of gadgets and appliances that cut the time taken to do household jobs, an increasing proportion of women have joined the labour force.

The economic explanation might not be correct, but it is a powerful one. And if it is correct, the changing attitudes are a consequence, not a cause, of the economic advancement of women.

NOW

By 2002, more than 60 percent of women were in the labour force, and although many had low-paying jobs, women were increasingly found in the professions and in executive positions. What brought about this dramatic change compared with 100 years earlier? Was it a change in preferences or a change in the constraints that women face?

THEN

Economists explain people's actions as the consequences of choices that maximize total utility subject to constraints. In the 1890s, fewer than 20 percent of women chose market employment, and most of those who did had low-paying and unattractive jobs. The other 80 percent of women chose nonmarket work in the home. What constraints led to these choices?

Steven Levitt, whom you can meet on the following pages, shows us how economic reasoning combined with the data generated by natural experiments deepens our understanding of an astonishing range of human choices.

TALKING WITH

Steven D. Levitt *is Alvin H. Baum Professor of Economics at the University of Chicago. Born in Minneapolis, he was an undergraduate at Harvard and a graduate student at MIT. Among his many honours, he was recently awarded the John Bates Clark Medal given to the best economist under 40.*

Professor Levitt has studied an astonishingly wide range of human choices and their outcomes. He has examined the effects of policing on crime, shown that realtors get a higher price when they sell their own homes than when they sell other people's, devised a test to detect teachers who cheat, and studied the choices of drug dealers and gang members.

The use of natural experiments unifies this apparently diverse body of research. Professor Levitt has an incredible ability to find just the right set of events and the data the events have generated to enable him to isolate the effect he's looking for.

Steven Levitt's research has been made accessible to a wide audience in Freakonomics *(with Stephen J. Dubner), which in August 2005 outsold the new Harry Potter story on Amazon.ca!*

Michael Parkin and Robin Bade talked with Steven Levitt about his career and the progress that economists have made in understanding how people respond to incentives in all aspects of life.

Why did you become an economist?

As a freshman in college, I took introductory economics. All the ideas made perfect sense to me – it was the way I naturally thought. My friends were befuddled. I thought, "This is the field for me!"

The idea of rational choice made at the margin lies at the heart of economics. Would you say that your work generally supports that idea or challenges it? Can you provide some examples?

I don't like the word "rational" in this context. I think economists model agents as being rational just for convenience. What really matters is whether people respond to incentives. My work very much supports the idea that humans in all types of circumstances respond strongly to incentives. I've seen it with drug dealers, auto thieves, sumo wrestlers, real estate agents, and elementary school teachers, just to name a few examples.

Can you elaborate? What are the incentives to which drug dealers respond? And does an understanding of these responses tell us anything about how public policy might influence drug use?

The incentives people face differ depending on their particular circumstances. Drug dealers, for instance, want to make money, but they also want to avoid being arrested or even killed. In the data we have on drug sellers, we see that when the drug trade is more lucrative, dealers are willing to take greater risks of arrest to carve out a share of the market. On the other hand, they also do their best to minimize their risks. For example, crack sellers used to carry the crack with them. When laws were passed imposing stiff penalties on anyone caught with anything more than a minimal amount of crack, drug dealers responded by storing the crack somewhere else, and retrieving only the amount being sold to the current client. Sumo wrestlers, on the other hand, care mostly about their official ranking. Sometimes matches occur where one wrestler has more to lose or gain than the other wrestler. We find that sumo wrestlers make corrupt deals to make sure the wrestler who needs the win is the one who actually wins.

> " *I think of economics as being primarily about a way of looking at the world and a set of tools for thinking clearly.* "

Why is an economist interested in crime and cheating?

I think of economics as being primarily about a way of looking at the world and a set of tools for thinking clearly. The topics you apply these tools to are unlimited. That is why I think economics has been so powerful. If you understand economics and use the tools wisely, you will be a better business person, doctor, public servant, parent.

What is the economic model of crime? And how does it help to design better ways of dealing with criminal activity? Can you illustrate by talking a bit about your work on the behaviour of auto thieves?

The economic model of crime argues that people have a choice of either working for a wage in the legal sector or earning money from illegal activity. The model carefully lays out the set of costs associated with being a criminal (e.g., forgone wages and being punished) and benefits (e.g., the loot) associated with crime and analyzes how a maximizing individual will choose whether to commit crimes and how much crime to commit. One reason the model is useful is because it lays out the various ways in which public policy might influence crime rates. For instance, we can increase the probability of a criminal getting caught, or make the prison sentence

longer for those who are caught. The government might also try to intervene in the labour market to make legal work more attractive—for instance, with a minimum wage.

> " *If you just look at different cities, the places with the most police also have the most crime, but it is not because police cause crime, it is because crime causes police to be hired.* "

What is the problem in figuring out whether more police leads to less crime? How did you find the answer?

We think that when you add more police, crime will fall because the cost of being a criminal goes up because of increased detection. From a public policy perspective, understanding how much crime falls in response to police is an important question. In practice, it is hard to answer this question because we don't randomly hire police. Rather, where crime is bad, there is greater demand for police and thus more police. If you just look at different cities, the places with the most police also have the most crime, but it is not because police cause crime, it is because crime causes police to be hired.

To figure out a causal impact of police on crime, you would like to do a randomized experiment where you added a lot of police at random to some cities and took them away in other cities. That is something you cannot really do in real life. So instead, the economist has to look for "natural experiments" to answer the question.

I used the timing of mayoral elections. It turns out that mayors hire a lot of police before elections to "look tough on crime." If elections do not otherwise affect crime, then the election is kind of like a randomizing device that puts more police in some cities every once in a while. Indeed, I found that crime goes down in the year following elections once the police hired are up and running. It is indirect evidence, but it is an example of how economists use their toolbox to handle difficult questions.

Your work shows that legalized abortion leads to less crime. Can you explain how you reach that conclusion? Can you also explain its implications for the pro-life pro-choice debate?

The theory is simple: unwanted children have hard lives (including being much more likely to be criminals); after legalized abortion, there are fewer unwanted children. Therefore, there should be less crime (with a 15–20 year lag while the babies grow up and reach high crime ages).

We looked at what happened to crime 15–20 years after Roe v. Wade, in states with high and low abortion rates, and in states that legalized abortion a few years earlier than the rest of the country. We could even look at people born immediately before or after abortion became legal.

All the evidence pointed the same way: crime fell a lot because abortion was legalized.

Our results, however, don't have large implications for the abortion debate. If abortion is murder, as pro-life advocates argue, then the changes in crime we see are trivial in comparison. If a woman simply has the right to control her body, as pro-choice advocates argue, then our estimates about crime are likewise irrelevant.

Our results have more to say about unwantedness: There are big benefits to making sure that children who are brought into the world are wanted and well cared for, either through birth control, adoption, abortion, or parental education.

Terrorism is on everyone's minds these days. And presumably, terrorists respond to incentives. Have you thought about how we might be able to use the insights of economics to better understand and perhaps even combat terrorism?

Terrorism is an unusually difficult question to tackle through incentives. The religious terrorists we are most worried about are willing to give up their lives to carry out terrorist acts. So the only punishment we can really offer is preventing them from committing the act by catching them before hand, or maybe minimizing the damage they can do. Unlike typical criminals, the threat of punishing them after the fact will not help deter the crime. Luckily, even among extremists, there are not many people willing to give their lives for a cause.

> " *...every time I observed anything in the world I asked myself, "Is that a natural experiment?"* "

Can a student learn how to use natural experiments or do you have a gift that is hard to teach?

I don't think I have such a gift. Most people who are good at something are good because they have worked hard and practised. That is certainly true with me.

For a while, I just walked around and every time I observed anything in the world I asked myself, "Is that a natural experiment?" Every once in a while I stumbled onto one because I was on the lookout.

What else can a student who wants to become a natural experimenting economist or broader social scientist do to better prepare for that career?

I would say that the best thing students can do is to try to really apply what they are learning to their lives, rather than just memorizing for an exam and quickly forgetting. If you are passionate about economics (or anything else for that matter), you are way ahead of others who are just trying to get by.

Organizing Production

Spinning a Web

In the fall of 1990, a British scientist named Tim Berners-Lee invented the World Wide Web. This remarkable idea paved the way for the creation and growth of thousands of profitable businesses. One of these businesses is McCain Foods Limited, a privately owned multinational frozen food manufacturer with global revenues of almost $6 billion a year. How do McCain Foods and the other 2 million firms in Canada make their business decisions? How do they operate efficiently?

One way in which firms seek to operate efficiently is by establishing incentives for their top executives, managers, and workers. Most of the time, these incentives work well. But sometimes, the people who run big firms spin another web—a web of deceit—and operate outside the law. When this happens, as it did at Enron and WorldCom, spectacular business failures can result. What are the incentive schemes that firms use and why do they sometimes result in catastrophic business failure?

Most of the firms that you know the names of don't make things. They buy and sell things. For example, most of the components of a Dell personal computer are made by other firms. Microsoft creates the operating system, and Intel makes the processor chip. Other firms make the hard drive and modem, and yet others make the CD drive, sound card, and so on. Why doesn't Dell make its own computer components? Why does it leave these activities to other firms and buy from them in markets? How do firms decide what to make themselves and what to buy in the marketplace from other firms?

◆ In this chapter, we are going to learn about firms and the choices they make to cope with scarcity. We begin by studying the economic problems and choices that are common to all firms.

After studying this chapter, you will be able to

- ■ Explain what a firm is and describe the economic problems that *all* firms face

- ■ Distinguish between technological efficiency and economic efficiency

- ■ Define and explain the principal–agent problem and describe how different types of business organizations cope with this problem

- ■ Describe and distinguish between different types of markets in which firms operate

- ■ Explain why markets coordinate some economic activities and firms coordinate others

The Firm and Its Economic Problem

THE 2 MILLION FIRMS IN CANADA DIFFER IN SIZE and in the scope of what they do. But they all perform the same basic economic functions. Each **firm** is an institution that hires and organizes factors of production to produce and sell goods and services.

Our goal is to predict firms' behaviour. To do so, we need to know a firm's goals and the constraints it faces. We begin with the goals.

The Firm's Goal

If you asked a group of entrepreneurs what they are trying to achieve, you would get many different answers. Some would talk about making a high-quality product, others about business growth, others about market share, and others about the job satisfaction of their work force. All of these goals might be pursued, but they are not the fundamental goal. They are means to a deeper goal.

A firm's goal is to maximize profit. A firm that does not seek to maximize profit is either eliminated or bought out by firms that do seek to maximize profit.

What exactly is the profit that a firm seeks to maximize? To answer this question, let's look at Sidney's Sweaters.

Measuring the Firm's Profit

Sidney runs a successful business that makes sweaters. Sidney's Sweaters receives $400,000 a year for the sweaters it sells. Its expenses are $80,000 a year for wool, $20,000 for utilities, $120,000 for wages, and $10,000 in interest on a bank loan. With receipts of $400,000 and expenses of $230,000, Sidney's Sweaters' annual surplus is $170,000.

Sidney's accountant lowers this number by $20,000, which he says is the depreciation (fall in value) of the firm's buildings and knitting machines during the year. (Accountants use Canada Revenue Agency rules based on standards established by the accounting profession to calculate the depreciation.) So the accountant reports that the profit of Sidney's Sweaters is $150,000 a year.

Sidney's accountant measures cost and profit to ensure that the firm pays the correct amount of income tax and to show the bank how its loan has been used. But economists want to predict the decisions that a firm makes. These decisions respond to *opportunity cost* and *economic profit*.

Opportunity Cost

The *opportunity cost* of any action is the highest-valued alternative forgone. The action that you choose not to take—the highest-valued alternative forgone—is the cost of the action that you choose to take. For a firm, the opportunity cost of production is the value of the firm's best alternative use of its resources.

Opportunity cost is a real alternative forgone. But so that we can compare the cost of one action with that of another action, we express opportunity cost in money units. A firm's opportunity cost includes both

- Explicit costs
- Implicit costs

Explicit Costs Explicit costs are paid in money. The amount paid for a resource could have been spent on something else, so it is the opportunity cost of using the resource. For Sidney's Sweaters' expenditures on wool, utilities, wages, and bank interest are explicit costs.

Implicit Costs A firm incurs implicit costs when it forgoes an alternative action but does not make a payment. A firm incurs implicit costs when it

1. Uses its own capital.
2. Uses its owner's time or financial resources.

The cost of using its own capital is an implicit cost—and an opportunity cost—because the firm could rent the capital to another firm. The rental income forgone is the firm's opportunity cost of using its own capital. This opportunity cost is called the **implicit rental rate** of capital.

Firms rent photocopiers, computers, earth-moving equipment, satellite-launching services, and so on. If a firm rents capital, it incurs an explicit cost. If a firm buys the capital it uses, it incurs an implicit cost. The implicit rental rate of capital is made up of

1. Economic depreciation
2. Interest forgone

Economic depreciation is the change in the *market* value of capital over a given period. It is calculated as the market price of the capital at the beginning of the period minus its market price at the end of the period. For example, suppose that Sidney's Sweaters could have sold its buildings and knitting machines on December 31, 2005, for $400,000. If it can sell the same capital on December 31, 2006, for $375,000, its economic depreciation during 2006 is $25,000—the fall in the market value of the capital. This $25,000 is an implicit cost of using the capital during 2006.

The funds used to buy capital could have been used for some other purpose. And in their next best use, they would have yielded a return—an interest income. This forgone interest is part of the opportunity cost of using the capital. For example, Sidney's Sweaters could have bought bonds instead of knitting machines. The interest forgone on the bonds is an implicit cost of using the capital.

Cost of Owner's Resources A firm's owner often supplies entrepreneurial ability—the factor of production that organizes the business, makes business decisions, innovates, and bears the risk of running the business. The return to entrepreneurship is profit, and the return that an entrepreneur can expect to receive on the average is called **normal profit**. Normal profit is part of a firm's opportunity cost because it is the cost of a forgone alternative—running another firm. If normal profit in the textile business is $50,000 a year, this amount is part of the opportunity costs of operating Sidney's Sweaters.

The owner of a firm also can supply labour (in addition to entrepreneurship). The return to labour is a wage. And the opportunity cost of the owner's time spent working for the firm is the wage income forgone by not working in the best alternative job. Suppose that Sidney continues to supply entrepreneurial services to his sweater firm but could at the same time takes another job that pays $40,000 a year. By working for his knitting business, he forgoes $40,000 a year. The amount is part of the opportunity costs of operating Sidney's Sweaters.

Economic Profit

What is the bottom line—the firm's profit or loss? A firm's **economic profit** is equal to its total revenue minus its opportunity cost. The firm's opportunity cost is the sum of its explicit costs and implicit costs. Implicit costs, remember, include *normal profit*. The return to entrepreneurial ability is greater than normal in a firm that makes a positive economic profit. And the return to entrepreneurial ability is less than normal in a firm that makes a negative economic profit—a firm that incurs an economic loss.

Economic Accounting: A Summary

Table 9.1 summarizes the economic accounting concepts that you've just studied. Sidney's Sweaters has total revenue of $400,000 and opportunity cost (explicit costs plus implicit costs) of $365,000. So its economic profit is $35,000.

To achieve the goal of maximum economic profit a firm must make five basic decisions:

1. What goods and services to produce and in what quantities
2. How to produce—the techniques of production to use
3. How to organize and compensate its managers and workers
4. How to market and price its products
5. What to produce itself and what to buy from other firms

In all these decisions, a firm's actions are limited by the constraints that it faces. Our next task is to learn about these constraints.

TABLE 9.1   Economic Accounting

Item		Amount
Total Revenue		**$400,000**
Opportunity Costs		
Wool	$80,000	
Utilities	20,000	
Wages paid	120,000	
Bank interest paid	10,000	
Total Explicit Costs		$230,000
Sidney's wages forgone	40,000	
Sidney's interest forgone	20,000	
Economic depreciation	25,000	
Normal profit	50,000	
Total Implicit Costs		$135,000
Total Cost		**$365,000**
Economic Profit		**$35,000**

The Firm's Constraints

The maximum profit a firm can make is limited by three features of its environment:

- Technology constraints
- Information constraints
- Market constraints

Technology Constraints Economists define technology broadly. A **technology** is any method of producing a good or service. Technology includes the detailed designs of machines. It also includes the layout of the workplace. And it includes the organization of the firm. For example, the shopping mall is a technology for producing retail services. It is a different technology from the catalogue store, which in turn is different from the downtown store.

It might seem surprising that a firm's profits are limited by technology, for it seems that technological advances are constantly increasing profit opportunities. Almost every day, we learn about some new technological advance that amazes us. With computers that speak and recognize our own speech and cars that can find the address we need in a city we've never visited before, we are able to accomplish ever more.

Technology advances over time. But at each point in time, to produce more output and gain more revenue, a firm must hire more resources and incur greater costs. The increase in profit that the firm can achieve is limited by the technology available. For example, by using its current plant and work force, Ford can produce some maximum number of cars per day. To produce more cars per day, Ford must hire more resources, which increases Ford's costs and limits the increase in profit that Ford can make by selling the additional cars.

Information Constraints We never possess all the information we would like to have to make decisions. We lack information about both the future and the present. For example, suppose you plan to buy a new computer. When should you buy it? The answer depends on how the price is going to change in the future. Where should you buy it? The answer depends on the prices at hundreds of different computer shops. To get the best deal, you must compare the quality and prices in every shop. But the opportunity cost of this comparison exceeds the cost of the computer!

Similarly, a firm is constrained by limited information about the quality and effort of its work force, the

current and future buying plans of its customers, and the plans of its competitors. Workers might slacken off when the manager believes they are working hard. Customers might switch to competing suppliers. Firms must compete against competition from a new firm.

Firms try to create incentive systems for workers to ensure that they work hard even when no one is monitoring their efforts. And firms spend millions of dollars on market research. But none of these efforts and expenditures eliminates the problems of incomplete information and uncertainty. And the cost of coping with limited information itself limits profit.

Market Constraints What each firm can sell and the price it can obtain are constrained by its customers' willingness to pay and by the prices and marketing efforts of other firms. Similarly, the resources that a firm can buy and the prices it must pay for them are limited by the willingness of people to work for and invest in the firm. Firms spend billions of dollars a year marketing and selling their products. Some of the most creative minds strive to find the right message that will produce a knockout television advertisement. Market constraints and the expenditures firms make to overcome them limit the profit a firm can make.

REVIEW QUIZ

1 Why do firms seek to maximize profit? What happens to firms that don't pursue this goal?
2 Why do accountants and economists calculate a firm's cost and profit in different ways?
3 What are the items that make opportunity cost differ from the accountant's cost measure?
4 Why is normal profit part of the opportunity cost of operating a firm?
5 What are the constraints that firms face? How does each constraint limit the firm's profit?

myeconlab Study Plan 9.1

In the rest of this chapter and in Chapters 10 through 13, we study the decisions that firms make. We're going to learn how we can predict a firm's behaviour as the response to the constraints that it faces and to changes in those constraints. We begin by taking a closer look at the technology constraints, information constraints, and market constraints that firms face.

Technological and Economic Efficiency

MICROSOFT EMPLOYS A LARGE WORK FORCE, AND most Microsoft workers possess a large amount of human capital. But the firm uses a small amount of physical capital. In contrast, a coal-mining company employs a huge amount of mining equipment (physical capital) and almost no labour. Why? The answer lies in the concept of efficiency. There are two concepts of production efficiency: technological efficiency and economic efficiency. **Technological efficiency** occurs when the firm produces a given output by using the least amount of inputs. **Economic efficiency** occurs when the firm produces a given output at the least cost. Let's explore the two concepts of efficiency by studying an example.

Suppose that there are four alternative techniques for making TV sets:

A. *Robot production.* One person monitors the entire computer-driven process.
B. *Production line.* Workers specialize in a small part of the job as the emerging TV set passes them on a production line.
C. *Bench production.* Workers specialize in a small part of the job but walk from bench to bench to perform their tasks.
D. *Hand-tool production.* A single worker uses a few hand tools to make a TV set.

Table 9.2 sets out the amounts of labour and capital required by each of these four methods to make 10 TV sets a day.

Which of these alternative methods are technologically efficient?

Technological Efficiency

Recall that technological efficiency occurs when the firm produces a given output by using the least inputs. Inspect the numbers in the table and notice that method *A* uses the most capital but the least labour. Method *D* uses the most labour but the least capital. Method *B* and method *C* lie between the two extremes. They use less capital but more labour than method *A* and less labour but more capital than method *D*. Compare methods *B* and *C*. Method *C* requires 100 workers and 10 units of capital to produce 10 TV sets. Those same 10 TV

sets can be produced by method *B* with 10 workers and the same 10 units of capital. Because method *C* uses the same amount of capital and more labour than method *B*, method *C* is not technologically efficient.

Are any of the other methods not technologically efficient? The answer is no. Each of the other three methods is technologically efficient. Method *A* uses more capital but less labour than method *B*, and method *D* uses more labour but less capital than method *B*.

Which of the methods are economically efficient?

Economic Efficiency

Recall that economic efficiency occurs when the firm produces a given output at the least cost. Suppose that labour costs $75 per person-day and that capital costs $250 per machine-day. Table 9.3(a) calculates the costs of using the different methods to make a TV set. By inspecting the table, you can see that method *B* has the lowest cost. Although method *A* uses less labour, it uses too much expensive capital. And although method *D* uses less capital, it uses too much expensive labour.

Method *C*, which is technologically inefficient, is also economically inefficient. It uses the same amount of capital as method *B* but 10 times as much labour. So it costs more. A technologically inefficient method is never economically efficient.

Although *B* is the economically efficient method in this example, method *A* or *D* could be economically efficient with different input prices.

Suppose that labour costs $150 a person-day and capital costs only $1 a machine-day. Table 9.3(b) now shows the costs of making a TV set. In this case,

TABLE 9.2   Four Ways of Making 10 TV Sets a Day

	Method	Quantities of inputs	
		Labour	Capital
A	Robot production	1	1,000
B	Production line	10	10
C	Bench production	100	10
D	Hand-tool production	1,000	1

TABLE 9.3   The Costs of Different Ways of Making 10 TV Sets a Day

(a) Four ways of making TVs

Method	Labour cost ($75 per day)		Capital cost ($250 per day)		Total cost	Cost per TV set
A	$75	+	$250,000	=	$250,075	$25,007.50
B	750	+	2,500	=	3,250	325.00
C	7,500	+	2,500	=	10,000	1,000.00
D	75,000	+	250	=	75,250	7,525.00

(b) Three ways of making TVs: High labour costs

Method	Labour cost ($150 per day)		Capital cost ($1 per day)		Total cost	Cost per TV set
A	$150	+	$1,000	=	$1,150	$115.00
B	1,500	+	10	=	1,510	151.00
D	150,000	+	1	=	150,001	15,000.10

(c) Three ways of making TVs: High capital costs

Method	Labour cost ($1 per day)		Capital cost ($1,000 per day)		Total cost	Cost per TV set
A	$1	+	$1,000,000	=	$1,000,001	$100,000.10
B	10	+	10,000	=	10,010	1,001.00
D	1,000	+	1,000	=	2,000	200.00

method *A* is economically efficient. Capital is now so cheap relative to labour that the method that uses the most capital is the economically efficient method.

Next, suppose that labour costs only $1 a person-day while capital costs $1,000 a machine-day. Table 9.3(c) shows the costs in this case. Method *D*, which uses a lot of labour and little capital, is now the least-cost method and the economically efficient method.

From these examples, you can see that while technological efficiency depends only on what is feasible, economic efficiency depends on the relative costs of resources. The economically efficient method is the one that uses less of a more expensive resource and more of a less expensive resource.

A firm that is not economically efficient does not maximize profit. Natural selection favours efficient firms and opposes inefficient firms. Inefficient firms go out of business or are taken over by firms with lower costs.

REVIEW QUIZ

1 How do we define technological efficiency? Is a firm technologically efficient if it uses the latest technology? Why or why not?

2 How do we define economic efficiency? Is a firm economically inefficient if it can cut costs by producing less? Why or why not?

3 Explain the key distinction between technological efficiency and economic efficiency.

4 Why do some firms use a lot of capital and not much labour, while others use not much capital and lots of labour?

myeconlab **Study Plan 9.2**

Next we study information constraints that firms face and the diversity of organization structures they generate.

Information and Organization

EACH FIRM ORGANIZES THE PRODUCTION OF goods and services by combining and coordinating the productive resources it hires. But there is variety across firms in how they organize production. Firms use a mixture of two systems:

- Command systems
- Incentive systems

Command Systems

A **command system** is a method of organizing production that uses a managerial hierarchy. Commands pass downward through the managerial hierarchy, and information passes upward. Managers spend most of their time collecting and processing information about the performance of the people under their control and making decisions about commands to issue and how best to get those commands implemented.

The military uses the purest form of command system. A commander-in-chief makes the big decisions about strategic objectives. Beneath this highest level, generals organize their military resources. Beneath the generals, successively lower ranks organize smaller and smaller units but pay attention to ever-increasing degrees of detail. At the bottom of the managerial hierarchy are the people who operate weapons systems.

Command systems in firms are not as rigid as those in the military, but they share some similar features. A chief executive officer (CEO) sits at the top of a firm's command system. Senior executives who report to and receive commands from the CEO specialize in managing production, marketing, finance, personnel, and perhaps other aspects of the firm's operations. Beneath these senior managers might be several tiers of middle management ranks that stretch downward to the managers who supervise the day-to-day operations of the business. Beneath these managers are the people who operate the firm's machines and who make and sell the firm's goods and services.

Small firms have one or two layers of managers, while large firms have several layers. As production processes have become ever more complex, management ranks have swollen. Today, more people have management jobs than ever before. But the information revolution of the 1990s slowed the growth of management, and in some industries, it reduced the number of layers of managers and brought a shakeout of middle managers.

Managers make enormous efforts to be well informed. And they try hard to make good decisions and issue commands that end up using resources efficiently. But managers always have incomplete information about what is happening in the divisions of the firm for which they are responsible. It is for this reason that firms use incentive systems as well as command systems to organize production.

Incentive Systems

An **incentive system** is a method of organizing production that uses a market-like mechanism inside the firm. Instead of issuing commands, senior managers create compensation schemes that will induce workers to perform in ways that maximize the firm's profit.

Selling organizations use incentive systems most extensively. Sales representatives who spend most of their working time alone and unsupervised are induced to work hard by being paid a small salary and a large performance-related bonus.

But incentive systems operate at all levels in a firm. CEOs' compensation plans include a share in the firm's profit, and factory floor workers sometimes receive compensation based on the quantity they produce.

Mixing the Systems

Firms use a mixture of commands and incentives. And they choose the mixture that maximizes profit. They use commands when it is easy to monitor performance or when a small deviation from an ideal performance is very costly. They use incentives when monitoring performance is either not possible or too costly to be worth doing.

For example, it is easy to monitor the performance of workers on a production line. If one person works too slowly, the entire line slows. So a production line is organized with a command system.

In contrast, it is costly to monitor a CEO. For example, what did John Roth (former CEO of Nortel) contribute to the initial success and subsequent problems of Nortel? This question can't be answered with certainty, yet Nortel's stockholders had to put someone in charge of the business and provide that person with an incentive to maximize their returns. The performance of Nortel illustrates the nature of this problem, known as the principal–agent problem.

The Principal–Agent Problem

The **principal–agent problem** is the problem of devising compensation rules that induce an *agent* to act in the best interest of a *principal*. For example, the stockholders of Nortel are *principals,* and the firm's managers are *agents*. The stockholders (the principals) must induce the managers (agents) to act in the stockholders' best interest. Similarly, Bill Gates (a principal) must induce the programmers who are working on the next generation of Windows (agents) to work efficiently.

Agents, whether they are managers or workers, pursue their own goals and often impose costs on a principal. For example, the goal of stockholders of CIBC (principals) is to maximize the firm's profit. But the firm's profit depends on the actions of its managers (agents) who have their own goals. Perhaps a manager takes a customer to a ball game on the pretense that she is building customer loyalty, when in fact she is simply enjoying on-the-job leisure. This same manager is also a principal, and her tellers are agents. The manager wants the tellers to work hard and attract new customers so that she can meet her operating targets. But the workers enjoy conversations with each other and take on-the-job leisure. Nonetheless, the firm constantly strives to find ways of improving performance and increasing profits.

Coping with the Principal–Agent Problem

Issuing commands does not address the principal–agent problem. In most firms, the shareholders can't monitor the managers and often the managers can't monitor the workers. Each principal must create incentives that induce each agent to work in the interests of the principal. Three ways of attempting to cope with the principal–agent problem are

- Ownership
- Incentive pay
- Long-term contracts

Ownership By assigning to a manager or worker ownership (or part-ownership) of a business, it is sometimes possible to induce a job performance that increases a firm's profits. Part-ownership schemes for senior managers are quite common, but they are less

common but not unknown for workers. For example, in 1995 Canadian Pacific Ltd. sold off CP Express and Transport, a coast-to-coast trucking operation, to its 3,500 employees.

Incentive Pay Incentive pay schemes—pay related to performance—are very common. They are based on a variety of performance criteria such as profits, production, or sales targets. Promoting an employee for good performance is another example of an incentive pay scheme.

Long-Term Contracts Long-term contracts tie the long-term fortunes of managers and workers (agents) to the success of the principal(s)—the owner(s) of the firm. For example, a multiyear employment contract for a CEO encourages that person to take a long-term view and devise strategies that achieve maximum profit over a sustained period.

These three ways of coping with the principal–agent problem give rise to different types of business organization. Each type of business organization is a different response to the principal–agent problem. Each type uses ownership, incentives, and long-term contracts in different ways. Let's look at the main types of business organization.

Types of Business Organization

The three main types of business organization are

- Sole proprietorship
- Partnership
- Corporation

Sole Proprietorship A *sole proprietorship* is a firm with a single owner—a proprietor—who has unlimited liability. *Unlimited liability* is the legal responsibility for all the debts of a firm up to an amount equal to the entire wealth of the owner. If a sole proprietorship cannot pay its debts, those to whom the firm owes money can claim the personal property of the owner. Some farmers, computer programmers, and artists are examples of sole proprietorships.

The proprietor makes management decisions, receives the firm's profits, and is responsible for its losses. The profits are taxed at the same rate as other sources of the proprietor's personal income.

Partnership A *partnership* is a firm with two or more owners who have unlimited liability. Partners must agree on an appropriate management structure and on how to divide the firm's profits among themselves. The profits of a partnership are taxed as the personal income of the owners. But each partner is legally liable for all the debts of the partnership (limited only by the wealth of that individual partner). Liability for the full debts of the partnership is called *joint unlimited liability*. Most law firms are partnerships.

Corporation A *corporation* is a firm owned by one or more limited liability stockholders. *Limited liability* means that the owners have legal liability only for the value of their initial investment. This limitation of liability means that if the corporation becomes bankrupt, its owners are not required to use their personal wealth to pay the corporation's debts.

Corporations' profits are taxed independently of stockholders' incomes. The stockholders pay tax on dividends and a capital gains tax on the profit they earn when they sell a stock for a higher price than they paid for it. Corporate stocks generate capital gains when a corporation retains some of its profit and reinvests it in profitable activities.

Pros and Cons of Different Types of Firms

The different types of business organization arise as different ways of trying to cope with the principal–agent problem. Each has advantages in particular situations. And because of its special advantages, each type continues to exist. Each type also has its disadvantages, which explains why it has not driven out the other two.

Table 9.4 summarizes these pros and cons of the different types of firms.

TABLE 9.4   The Pros and Cons of Different Types of Firms

Type of Firm	Pros	Cons
Sole proprietorship	■ Easy to set up ■ Simple decision making ■ Profits taxed only once as owner's income	■ Bad decisions not checked by need for consensus ■ Owner's entire wealth at risk ■ Firm dies with owner ■ Capital is expensive ■ Labour is expensive
Partnership	■ Easy to set up ■ Diversified decision making ■ Can survive withdrawal of partner ■ Profits taxed only once as owners' incomes	■ Achieving consensus may be slow and expensive ■ Owners' entire wealth at risk ■ Withdrawal of partner may create capital shortage ■ Capital is expensive
Corporation	■ Owners have limited liability ■ Large-scale, low-cost capital available ■ Professional management not restricted by ability of owners ■ Perpetual life ■ Long-term labour contracts cut labour costs	■ Complex management structure can make decisions slow and expensive ■ Profits taxed twice as company profit and as stockholders' income

FIGURE 9.1   ⓧ myeconlab

Relative Importance of the Three Types of Firms

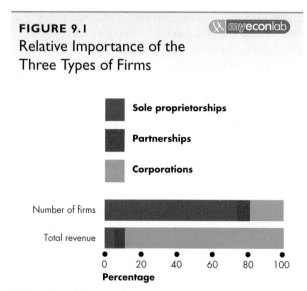

(a) Number of firms and total revenue

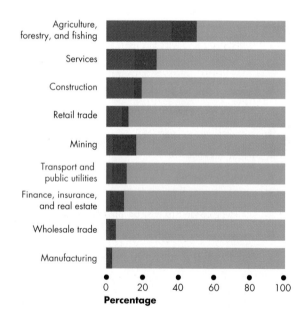

(b) Total revenue in various industries

Three-quarters of all U.S. firms are sole proprietorships, almost one-fifth are corporations, and only a twentieth are partnerships. Corporations account for 86 percent of business revenue (part a). But sole proprietorships and partnerships account for a significant percentage of business revenue in some industries (part b). (We don't have Canadian data on firm types.)

Source of data: U.S. Bureau of the Census, *Statistical Abstract of the United States: 2001.*

The Relative Importance of Different Types of Firms

Figure 9.1(a) shows the relative importance of the three main types of firms in the U.S. economy. The figure also shows that the revenue of corporations is much larger than that of the other types of firms. Although only 18 percent of all firms are corporations, they generate 86 percent of revenue.

Figure 9.1(b) shows the percentage of revenue generated by the different types of firms in various industries. Sole proprietorships in agriculture, forestry, and fishing generate about 40 percent of the total revenue in those sectors. Sole proprietorships in the service sector, construction, and retail trades also generate a large percentage of total revenue. Partnerships in agriculture, forestry, and fishing generate about 15 percent of total revenue. Partnerships are more prominent in services; mining; and finance, insurance, and real estate than in other sectors. Corporations are important in all sectors and have the manufacturing field almost to themselves.

Why do corporations dominate the business scene? Why do the other types of business survive? And why are sole proprietorships and partnerships more prominent in some sectors? The answers to these questions lie in the pros and cons of the different types of business organization that are summarized in Table 9.4. Corporations dominate where a large amount of capital is used. But sole proprietorships dominate where flexibility in decision making is critical.

REVIEW QUIZ

1 Explain the distinction between a command system and an incentive system.
2 What is the principal–agent problem? What are the three ways in which firms try to cope with it?
3 What are the three types of firms? Explain the major advantages and disadvantages of each.
4 Why do all three types of firms survive and in which sectors is each type most prominent?

ⓧ myeconlab   **Study Plan 9.3**

You've now seen how technology constraints influence a firm's use of capital and labour and how information constraints influence a firm's organization. We'll now look at market constraints and see how they influence the environment in which firms compete for business.

Markets and the Competitive Environment

THE MARKETS IN WHICH FIRMS OPERATE VARY A great deal. Some are highly competitive, and profits in these markets are hard to come by. Some appear to be almost free from competition, and firms in these markets earn large profits. Some markets are dominated by fierce advertising campaigns in which each firm seeks to persuade buyers that it has the best products. And some markets display a warlike character.

Economists identify four market types:

1. Perfect competition
2. Monopolistic competition
3. Oligopoly
4. Monopoly

Perfect competition arises when there are many firms, each selling an identical product, many buyers, and no restrictions on the entry of new firms into the industry. The many firms and buyers are all well informed about the prices of the products of each firm in the industry. The worldwide markets for corn, rice, and other grain crops are examples of perfect competition.

Monopolistic competition is a market structure in which a large number of firms compete by making similar but slightly different products. Making a product slightly different from the product of a competing firm is called **product differentiation**. Product differentiation gives the firm in monopolistic competition an element of market power. The firm is the sole producer of the particular version of the good in question. For example, in the market for running shoes, Nike, Reebok, Fila, New Balance, and Asics all make their own version of the perfect shoe. Each of these firms is the sole producer of a particular brand of shoe. Differentiated products are not necessarily different products. What matters is that consumers perceive them to be different. For example, different brands of aspirin are chemically identical (salicylic acid) and differ only in their packaging.

Oligopoly is a market structure in which a small number of firms compete. Computer software, airplane manufacture, and international air transportation are examples of oligopolistic industries. Oligopolies might produce almost identical products, such as the colas produced by Coke and Pepsi. Or they might produce differentiated products such as Chevrolet's Lumina and Ford's Taurus.

Monopoly arises when there is only one firm and it produces a good or service that has no close substitutes and is protected by a barrier preventing the entry of new firms. In some places, the phone, gas, electricity, and water suppliers are local monopolies—monopolies restricted to a given location. Microsoft Corporation, the software developer that created Windows, the operating system used by most PCs, is an example of a global monopoly.

Perfect competition is the most extreme form of competition. Monopoly is the most extreme absence of competition. The other two market types fall between these extremes.

Many factors must be taken into account to determine which market structure describes a particular real-world market. One of these factors is the extent to which the market is dominated by a small number of firms. To measure this feature of markets, economists use indexes called measures of concentration. Let's look at these measures.

Measures of Concentration

Economists use two measures of concentration:

■ The four-firm concentration ratio
■ The Herfindahl–Hirschman Index

The Four-Firm Concentration Ratio The **four-firm concentration ratio** is the percentage of the value of sales accounted for by the four largest firms in an industry. The range of the concentration ratio is from almost zero for perfect competition to 100 percent for monopoly. This ratio is the main measure used to assess market structure.

Table 9.5 shows two calculations of the four-firm concentration ratio: one for tiremakers and one for

printers. In the tiremaking industry with 14 firms, the largest four have 80 percent of the sales, so the four-firm concentration ratio is 80 percent. In the printing industry, with 1,004 firms, the largest four firms have only 0.5 percent of the sales, so the four-firm concentration ratio is 0.5 percent.

A low concentration ratio indicates a high degree of competition, and a high concentration ratio indicates an absence of competition. A monopoly has a concentration ratio of 100 percent—the largest (and only) firm has 100 percent of the sales. A four-firm concentration ratio that exceeds 40 percent is regarded as an indication of a market that is highly concentrated and dominated by a few firms in an oligopoly. A ratio of less than 40 percent is regarded as an indication of a competitive market.

The Herfindahl–Hirschman Index The **Herfindahl–Hirschman Index**—also called the HHI—is the square of the percentage market share of each firm summed over the largest 50 firms (or summed over all the firms if there are fewer than 50) in a market. For example, if there are four firms in a market and the market shares of the firms are 50 percent, 25 percent, 15 percent, and 10 percent, the Herfindahl–Hirschman Index is

$$HHI = 50^2 + 25^2 + 15^2 + 10^2 = 3,450.$$

TABLE 9.5   Concentration Ratio Calculations

Tiremakers Firm	Sales (millions of dollars)	Printers Firm	Sales (millions of dollars)
Top, Inc.	200	Fran's	2.5
ABC, Inc.	250	Ned's	2.0
Big, Inc.	150	Tom's	1.8
XYZ, Inc.	100	Jill's	1.7
Largest 4 firms	700	Largest 4 firms	8.0
Other 10 firms	175	Other 1,000 firms	1,592.0
Industry	875	Industry	**1,600.0**

Four-firm concentration ratios:

Tiremakers: $\frac{700}{875} \times 100 = 80\%$

Printers: $\frac{8}{1,600} \times 100 = 0.5\%$

In perfect competition, the HHI is small. For example, if each of the largest 50 firms in an industry has a market share of 0.1 percent, then the HHI is $0.1^2 \times 50 = 0.5$. In a monopoly, the HHI is 10,000—the firm has 100 percent of the market: $100^2 = 10,000$.

The HHI can be used to classify markets across the spectrum of types. A market in which the HHI is less than 1,000 is regarded as being competitive and the smaller the number, the greater is the degree of competition. A market in which the HHI lies between 1,000 and 1,800 is regarded as being moderately competitive—a form of monopolistic competition. Although the HHI of 10,000 is needed for pure monopoly, a market in which the HHI exceeds 1,800 is regarded as being uncompetitive and a potential matter for concern by competition regulators.

Concentration Measures for the Canadian Economy

Figure 9.2 shows a selection of concentration ratios for Canada that Statistics Canada has calculated.

Industries that produce sugar, tobacco products, beer, tires, and soft drinks and ice have a high degree of concentration and are oligopolies. Industries that produce clothing, bakery items, textiles, and fabrics have low concentration measures and are highly competitive. Industries that produce women's and girl's shirts, pharmaceutical products, and wooden windows and doors are moderately concentrated. These industries are examples of monopolistic competition.

Concentration measures are a useful indicator of the degree of competition in a market. But they must be supplemented by other information to determine a market's structure. Table 9.6 summarizes the range of other information, along with the measures of concentration, that determine which market structure describes a particular real-world market.

Limitations of Concentration Measures

The three main limitations of concentration measures alone as determinants of market structure are their failure to take proper account of

- The geographical scope of the market
- Barriers to entry and firm turnover
- The correspondence between a market and an industry

FIGURE 9.2
Concentration Measures in Canada

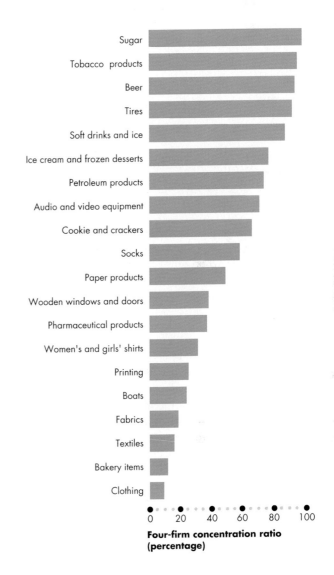

The industries that produce sugar, tobacco products, beer, tires, and soft drinks and ice are highly concentrated, while those that produce clothing, bakery items, textiles, and fabrics are highly competitive. The industries that produce women's and girl's shirts and pharmaceutical products have an intermediate degree of concentration.

Source of data: Adapted from the Statistics Canada publication CANSIM DISC. 10F0007, March 1999.

TABLE 9.6   Market Structure

Characteristics	Perfect competition	Monopolistic competition	Oligopoly	Monopoly
Number of firms in industry	Many	Many	Few	One
Product	Identical	Differentiated	Either identical or differentiated	No close substitutes
Barriers to entry	None	None	Moderate	High
Firm's control over price	None	Some	Considerable	Considerable or regulated
Concentration ratio	0	Low	High	100
HHI (approx. ranges)	Less than 100	101 to 999	More than 1,000	10,000
Examples	Wheat, corn	Food, clothing	Automobiles, cereals	Local water supply

Geographical Scope of Market Concentration measures take a national view of the market. Many goods are sold in a *national* market, but some are sold in a *regional* market and some in a *global* one. The newspaper industry consists of local markets. The concentration measures for newspapers are low, but there is a high degree of concentration in the newspaper industry in most cities. The auto industry has a global market. The three biggest North American car producers don't have much domestic competition, either in Canada or in the United States. But they face tough competition from foreign producers both here and more especially in foreign markets.

Barriers to Entry and Firm Turnover
Concentration measures don't measure barriers to entry. Some industries are highly concentrated but have easy entry and an enormous amount of turnover of firms. For example, many small towns have few restaurants, but there are no restrictions on opening a restaurant and many firms attempt to do so.

Also, an industry might be competitive because of *potential entry*—because a few firms in a market face competition from many firms that can easily enter the market and will do so if economic profits are available.

Market and Industry Correspondence To calculate concentration ratios, Statistics Canada classifies each firm as being in a particular industry. But markets do not always correspond closely to industries for three reasons.

First, markets are often narrower than industries. For example, the pharmaceutical industry, which has a moderate concentration ratio, operates in many separate markets for individual products—for example, measles vaccines and AIDS-fighting drugs. These drugs do not compete with each other, so this industry, which looks competitive, includes firms that are monopolies (or near monopolies) in markets for individual drugs.

Second, most firms make several products. For example, Nortel produces telecommunication equipment and Internet database services, among other things. So this one firm operates in several separate markets. But Statistics Canada classifies Nortel as being in the telecommunication equipment industry. The fact that Nortel competes with other providers of e-commerce database services does not show up in the concentration data for that market.

Third, firms switch from one market to another depending on profit opportunities. For example, Canadian Pacific Ltd., which today produces hotel services, forest products, coal and petroleum products, as well as rail services, has diversified from being just a railroad company. Publishers of newspapers, magazines, and textbooks are today rapidly diversifying into Internet and multimedia products. These switches among industries show that there is much scope for entering and exiting an industry, and so measures of concentration have limited usefulness.

Despite their limitations, concentration measures do provide a basis for determining the degree of competition in an industry when they are combined with information about the geographical scope of the market, barriers to entry, and the extent to which large, multiproduct firms straddle a variety of markets.

Market Structures in the North American Economy

How competitive are the markets of North America? Do most firms operate in competitive markets or in non-competitive markets?

Figure 9.3 provides part of the answer to these questions. It shows the market structure of the U.S. economy and the trends in market structure between 1939 and 1980. (Unfortunately, comparable data for Canada alone and data for the 1980s and 1990s are not available.)

In 1980, three-quarters of the value of goods and services bought and sold in the United States were traded in markets that are essentially competitive—markets that have almost perfect competition or monopolistic competition. Monopoly and the dominance of a single firm accounted for about 5 percent of sales. Oligopoly, which is found mainly in manufacturing, accounted for about 18 percent of sales.

Over the period shown in Fig. 9.3, the U.S. economy became increasingly competitive. You can see that competitive markets have expanded most (blue bars) and oligopoly markets have shrunk most (red bars).

But also during the past decades, the U.S. economy has become much more exposed to competition from the rest of the world. Figure 9.3 does not capture this international competition.

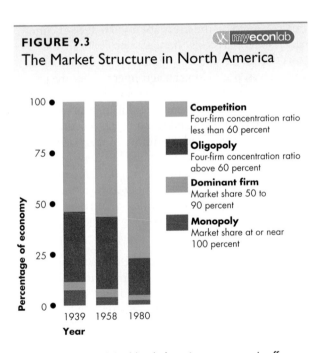

FIGURE 9.3

myeconlab

The Market Structure in North America

Competition
Four-firm concentration ratio less than 60 percent

Oligopoly
Four-firm concentration ratio above 60 percent

Dominant firm
Market share 50 to 90 percent

Monopoly
Market share at or near 100 percent

Three-quarters of the North American economy is effectively competitive (perfect competition or monopolistic competition), one-fifth is oligopoly, and the rest is monopoly. The economy became more competitive between 1939 and 1980. (Professor Shepherd, whose 1982 study remains the latest word on this topic, suspects that although some industries have become more concentrated, others have become less concentrated, so the net picture has probably not changed much since 1980.)

Source of data: William G. Shepherd, "Causes of Increased Competition in the U.S. Economy, 1939–1980," *Review of Economics and Statistics,* November 1982, pp. 613–626.

REVIEW QUIZ

1 What are the four market types? Explain the distinguishing characteristics of each.
2 What are the two measures of concentration? Explain how each measure is calculated.
3 Under what conditions do the measures of concentration give a good indication of the degree of competition in a market?
4 Is the North American economy competitive? Is it becoming more competitive or less competitive?

myeconlab Study Plan 9.4

You now know the variety of market types and the way we classify firms and industries into the different market types. Our final question in this chapter is: What determines the things that firms decide to buy from other firms rather than produce for themselves?

Markets and Firms

AT THE BEGINNING OF THIS CHAPTER, WE defined a firm as an institution that hires productive resources and organizes them to produce and sell goods and services. To organize production, firms coordinate the economic decisions and activities of many individuals. But firms are not the only coordinators of economic decisions. You learned in Chapter 3 that markets coordinate decisions. They do so by adjusting prices and making the decisions of buyers and sellers consistent—making the quantity demanded equal to the quantity supplied for each good and service.

Market Coordination

Markets can coordinate production. For example, markets might coordinate the production of a rock concert. A promoter hires a stadium, some stage equipment, audio and video recording engineers and technicians, some rock groups, a superstar, a publicity agent, and a ticket agent—all market transactions—and sells tickets to thousands of rock fans, audio rights to a recording company, and video and broadcasting rights to a television network—another set of market transactions. Alternatively, if rock concerts were produced like cornflakes, the firm producing them would own all the capital used (stadiums, stage, sound and video equipment) and would employ all the labour needed (singers, engineers, salespeople, and so on).

Outsourcing—buying parts or products from other firms—is another example of market coordination. Dell uses outsourcing for all the components of the computers it produces. The major auto makers use outsourcing for windshields and windows, gearboxes, tires, and many other car parts.

What determines whether a firm or a market coordinates a particular set of activities? How does a firm decide whether to buy from another firm or manufacture an item itself? The answer is cost. Taking account of the opportunity cost of time as well as the costs of the other inputs, a firm uses the method that costs least. In other words, it uses the economically efficient method.

Firms coordinate economic activity when they can perform a task more efficiently than markets can. In such a situation, it is profitable to set up a firm. If markets can perform a task more efficiently than a firm can, people will use markets, and any attempt to set up a firm to replace such market coordination will be doomed to failure.

Why Firms?

There are four key reasons why, in many instances, firms are more efficient than markets as coordinators of economic activity. Firms can achieve

- Lower transactions costs
- Economies of scale
- Economies of scope
- Economies of team production

Transactions Costs The idea that firms exist because there are activities in which they are more efficient than markets was first suggested by University of Chicago economist and Nobel Laureate Ronald Coase. Coase focused on the firm's ability to reduce or eliminate transactions costs. **Transactions costs** are the costs that arise from finding someone with whom to do business, of reaching an agreement about the price and other aspects of the exchange, and of ensuring that the terms of the agreement are fulfilled. Market transactions require buyers and sellers to get together and to negotiate the terms and conditions of their trading. Sometimes lawyers have to be hired to draw up contracts. A broken contract leads to still more expenses. A firm can lower such transactions costs by reducing the number of individual transactions undertaken.

Consider, for example, two ways of getting your creaking car fixed.

1. *Firm coordination:* You take the car to the garage. The garage owner coordinates parts and tools as well as the mechanic's time, and your car gets fixed. You pay one bill for the entire job.
2. *Market coordination:* You hire a mechanic, who diagnoses the problems and makes a list of the parts and tools needed to fix them. You buy the parts from the local wrecker's yard and rent the tools from ABC Rentals. You hire the mechanic again to fix the problems. You return the tools and pay your bills—wages to the mechanic, rental to ABC, and the cost of the parts used to the wrecker.

What determines the method that you use? The answer is cost. Taking account of the opportunity cost of your own time as well as the costs of the other inputs that you would have to buy, you will use the method that costs least. In other words, you will use the economically efficient method.

The first method requires that you undertake only one transaction with one firm. It's true that the firm has to undertake several transactions—hiring the labour and buying the parts and tools required to do the job. But the firm doesn't have to undertake those transactions simply to fix your car. One set of such transactions enables the firm to fix hundreds of cars. Thus there is an enormous reduction in the number of individual transactions that take place if people get their cars fixed at the garage rather than going through an elaborate sequence of market transactions.

Economies of Scale When the cost of producing a unit of a good falls as its output rate increases, **economies of scale** exist. Auto makers, for example, experience economies of scale because as the scale of production increases, the firm can use cost-saving equipment and highly specialized labour. An auto maker that produces only a few cars a year must use hand-tool methods that are costly. Economies of scale arise from specialization and the division of labour that can be reaped more effectively by firm coordination rather than by market coordination.

Economies of Scope A firm experiences **economies of scope** when it uses specialized (and often expensive) resources to produce a *range of goods and services*. For example, Microsoft hires specialist programmers, designers, and marketing experts and uses their skills across a range of software products. As a result, Microsoft coordinates the resources that produce software at a lower cost than can an individual who buys all these services in markets.

Economies of Team Production A production process in which the individuals in a group specialize in mutually supportive tasks is team production. Sport provides the best example of team activity. Some baseball team members specialize in pitching and some in batting, some basketball team members specialize in defence and some in offence. The production of goods and services offers many examples of team activity. For example, production lines in automobile and TV manufacturing plants work most efficiently when individual activity is organized in teams, each specializing in a small task. You can also think of an entire firm as being a team. The team has buyers of raw material and other inputs, production workers, and salespeople. There are even specialists within these various groups. Each individual member of the team specializes, but the value of the output of the team and the profit that it earns depend on the coordinated activities of all the team's

members. The idea that firms arise as a consequence of the economies of team production was first suggested by Armen Alchian and Harold Demsetz of the University of California at Los Angeles.

Because firms can economize on transactions costs, reap economies of scale and economies of scope, and organize efficient team production, it is firms rather than markets that coordinate most of our economic activity. But there are limits to the economic efficiency of firms. If a firm becomes too big or too diversified in the things that it seeks to do, the cost of management and monitoring per unit of output begins to rise, and at some point, the market becomes more efficient at coordinating the use of resources.

Nortel Networks, for example, decided that its corporate business and its wireless business would be handled more efficiently if it split itself into two distinct product divisions.

Sometimes firms enter into long-term relationships with each other that effectively cut out ordinary market transactions and make it difficult to see where one firm ends and another begins. For example, GM has long-term relationships with suppliers of windows, tires, and other parts. Wal-Mart has long-term relationships with suppliers of the goods it sells in its stores. Such relationships make transactions costs lower than they would be if GM or Wal-Mart went shopping on the open market each time it wanted new supplies.

REVIEW QUIZ

1 What are the two ways in which economic activity can be coordinated?
2 What determines whether a firm or a market coordinates production?
3 Why can firms often coordinate production at a lower cost than markets can?

(X) myeconlab   **Study Plan 9.5**

◆ *Reading Between the Lines* on pp. 214–215 explores the challenges and opportunities faced by Nortel Networks. We continue to study firms and their decisions in the next four chapters. In Chapter 10, we learn about the relationships between cost and output at different output levels. These cost–output relationships are common to all types of firms in all types of markets. We then turn to problems that are specific to firms in different types of markets.

Nortel's Challenges and Opportunities

OTTAWASUN.COM SEPTEMBER 7, 2005

Nortel scores major Korean contract

Nortel Networks Corp. and LG Electronics have been chosen by Korea's KTF Corp. cell phone giant to provide equipment for an ultra-high-speed broadband wireless service throughout the country's major metropolitan areas.

Nortel said Wednesday it will provide its high speed downlink packet access wireless equipment, while LGE will provide the core network solution.

"This is the first collaborative win for LGE and Nortel since announcement of the LG-Nortel joint venture in August 2005," Nortel said in a release.

The service will allow KTF subscribers to access new wireless multimedia services such as high-speed music transfers, real-time DVD-quality video, gaming applications, videoconferencing and multimedia collaboration.

The network will be rolled out to 17 cities by December and extended to an additional 45 cities by June 2006.

"We chose the Nortel solution because we believe it will enable us to bring KTF subscribers new and unprecedented levels of wireless speed and functionality and help us to maintain our position as a global leader in mobile broadband," KTF executive vice-president Won-Jin Park said in a statement.

Korea's LGE and Toronto-based Nortel signed a joint venture agreement on Aug. 17 to establish a telecommunication infrastructure company. The company is expected to be established this year.

...

Reprinted by permission of Canadian Press.

Essence of the Story

■ Nortel Networks Corp. and LG Electronics will provide equipment for an ultra-high-speed broadband wireless service in Korea.

■ Nortel will provide high-speed wireless equipment while LGE will provide the core network.

■ The service will allow subscribers to access a wide range of wireless multimedia services including high-speed music transfers and real-time DVD-quality video.

■ Nortel was chosen for its ability to deliver "unprecedented levels of wireless speed and functionality."

Economic Analysis

■ Nortel Networks is a very old Canadian corporation that was in business (under a different name) at the birth of the telephone.

■ Nortel produces a wide range of telecommunications equipment and services to customers in more than 150 countries. During the 1990s, Nortel grew to become the world's second largest telecommunications equipment producer (second to Lucent).

■ Nortel's main customers are telecommunications companies such as Bell, AT&T, Global Crossing, and 360network.

■ Nortel faced a major problem in 2001 as the global market for telecommunications equipment and services collapsed.

■ The collapse came partly from an over expansion as firms scrambled to dominate the $1 trillion global telecommunications market during the 1990s expansion.

■ Faced with a collapse in revenues, Nortel cut back its scale partly by selling assets in businesses outside its core activities and partly by cutting its work force.

■ Nortel also changed its CEO. This move was a change in its entrepreneurial resources.

■ Nortel's goal is to maximize profit, and the news article illustrates one way in which the firm is pursuing this goal.

■ By partnering with other firms, LG in the story, Nortel is able to exploit its own comparative advantage in providieng high-speed wireless technologies.

■ In a world of ever more complex technologies, there is an increasing opportunity for profitable specialization and cooperation between firms.

215

SUMMARY

KEY POINTS

The Firm and Its Economic Problem
(pp. 198–200)

- Firms hire factors of production and organize them to produce and sell goods and services.
- Firms seek to maximize economic profit, which is total revenue minus opportunity cost.
- Technology, information, and market constraints limit a firm's profit.

Technological and Economic Efficiency
(pp. 201–202)

- A method of production is technologically efficient when the firm produces a given output by using the least amount of inputs.
- A method of production is economically efficient when the cost of producing a given output is as low as possible.

Information and Organization (pp. 203–206)

- Firms use a combination of command systems and incentive systems to organize production.
- Faced with incomplete information and uncertainty, firms induce managers and workers to perform in ways that are consistent with the firm's goals.
- Sole proprietorships, partnerships, and corporations use ownership, incentives, and long-term contracts to cope with the principal–agent problem.

Markets and the Competitive Environment
(pp. 207–211)

- Perfect competition occurs when there are many buyers and sellers of an identical product and when new firms can easily enter a market.
- Monopolistic competition occurs when a large number of firms compete with each other by making slightly different products.
- Oligopoly occurs when a small number of producers compete with each other.

- Monopoly occurs when one firm produces a good or service for which there are no close substitutes and the firm is protected by a barrier that prevents the entry of competitors.

Markets and Firms (pp. 212–213)

- Firms coordinate economic activities when they can perform a task more efficiently—at lower cost—than markets can.
- Firms economize on transactions costs and achieve the benefits of economies of scale, economies of scope, and economies of team production.

KEY FIGURE AND TABLES

Figure 9.1   Relative Importance of the Three Types of Firms, 206
Table 9.4   The Pros and Cons of Different Types of Firms, 205
Table 9.5   Concentration Ratio Calculations, 208
Table 9.6   Market Structure, 210

KEY TERMS

Command system, 203
Economic depreciation, 198
Economic efficiency, 201
Economic profit, 199
Economies of scale, 213
Economies of scope, 213
Firm, 198
Four-firm concentration ratio, 208
Herfindahl–Hirschman Index, 208
Implicit rental rate, 198
Incentive system, 203
Monopolistic competition, 207
Monopoly, 207
Normal profit, 199
Oligopoly, 207
Perfect competition, 207
Principal–agent problem, 204
Product differentiation, 207
Technological efficiency, 201
Technology, 200
Transactions costs, 212

PROBLEMS

Go to (X myeconlab) for solutions to odd-numbered problems and additional exercises.

1. One year ago, Jack and Jill set up a vinegar-bottling firm (called JJVB). Use the following information to calculate JJVB's explicit costs and implicit costs during its first year:
   a. Jack and Jill put $50,000 of their own money into the firm.
   b. They bought equipment for $30,000.
   c. They hired one employee to help them for an annual wage of $20,000.
   d. Jack gave up his previous job, at which he earned $30,000, and spent all his time working for JJVB.
   e. Jill kept her old job, which paid $30 an hour, but gave up 10 hours of leisure each week (for 50 weeks) to work for JJVB.
   f. JJVB bought $10,000 of goods and services from other firms.
   g. The market value of the equipment at the end of the year was $28,000.

2. One year ago, Ms. Moffat and Mr. Spieder opened a cheese firm (called MSCF). Use the following information to calculate MSCF's explicit costs and implicit costs during its first year of operation:
   a. Moffat and Spieder put $70,000 of their own money into the firm.
   b. They bought equipment for $40,000.
   c. They hired one employee to help them for an annual wage of $18,000.
   d. Moffat gave up her previous job, at which she earned $22,000, and spent all her time working for MSCF.
   e. Spieder kept his old job, which paid $20 an hour, but gave up 20 hours of leisure each week (for 50 weeks) to work for MSCF.
   f. MSCF bought $5,000 of goods from other firms.
   g. The market value of the equipment at the end of the year was $37,000.

3. Four methods for doing a tax return are with a personal computer, a pocket calculator, a pocket calculator with pencil and paper, and a pencil and paper. With a PC, the job takes an hour; with a pocket calculator, it takes 12 hours; with a pocket calculator and paper and pencil, it takes 12 hours; and with a pencil and paper, it takes 16 hours. The PC and its software cost $1,000, the pocket calculator costs $10, and the pencil and paper cost $1.
   a. Which methods are technologically efficient?
   b. Which method is economically efficient if the wage rate is
      i. $5 an hour?
      ii. $50 an hour?
      iii. $500 an hour?

4. Shawn is a part-time student and he can do his engineering assignment by using a personal computer, a pocket calculator, a pocket calculator and a pencil and paper, or a pencil and paper. With a PC, Shawn completes the job in 1 hour; with a pocket calculator, it takes 15 hours; with a pocket calculator and paper and pencil, it takes 7 hours; and with a pencil and paper, it takes 30 hours. The PC and its software cost $1,000, the pocket calculator costs $20, and the pencil and paper cost $5.
   a. Which methods are technologically efficient?
   b. Which method is economically efficient if the wage rate is
      i. $10 an hour?
      ii. $20 an hour?
      iii. $250 an hour?

5. Alternative ways of laundering 100 shirts are

Method	Labour (hours)	Capital (machines)
A	1	10
B	5	8
C	20	4
D	50	1

   a. Which methods are technologically efficient?
   b. Which method is economically efficient if the hourly wage rate and implicit rental rate of capital are
      i. Wage rate: $1; rental rate: $100?
      ii. Wage rate: $5; rental rate: $50?
      iii. Wage rate: $50; rental rate: $5?

6. Four ways of making 10 surfboards a day are

Method	Labour (hours)	Capital (machines)
A	40	10
B	40	20
C	20	30
D	10	40

   a. Which methods are technologically efficient?

b. Which method is economically efficient if the hourly wage rate and implicit rental rate of capital are

    iv. Wage rate: $1; rental rate: $100?

    v. Wage rate: $5; rental rate: $50?

    vi. Wage rate: $50; rental rate: $5?

7. Sales of the firms in the tattoo industry are

Firm	Sales (dollars)
Bright Spots	4,500
Freckles	3,250
Love Galore	2,500
Native Birds	2,000
Other 15 firms	8,000

a. Calculate the four-firm concentration ratio.

b. What is the structure of the tattoo industry?

8. Sales of the firms in the dry cleaning industry are

Firm	Sales (thousands of dollars)
SqueakyClean, Inc.	15
Village Cleaners, Inc.	25
Plaza Cleaners, Inc.	30
The Cleanery, Inc.	40
Other 20 firms	300

a. Calculate the four-firm concentration ratio.

b. What is the structure of the industry?

9. Market shares of chocolate makers are

Firm	Market Share (percent)
Mayfair, Inc.	15
Bond, Inc.	10
Magic, Inc.	20
All Natural, Inc.	15
Truffles, Inc.	25
Gold, Inc.	15

a. Calculate the Herfindahl–Hirschman Index.

b. What is the structure of the industry?

10. Market shares of orange juice suppliers are

Firm	Market Share (percent)
Natural Fresh, Inc.	75
Fresh Squeezed, Inc.	10
Juice-to-Go, Inc.	8
Juiced-Out, Inc.	7

a. Calculate the Herfindahl–Hirschman Index.

b. What is the structure of the industry?

CRITICAL THINKING

1. Study *Reading Between the Lines* about Nortel Network's challenges and opportunities on pp. 214–215, and then answer the following questions.

    a. What is the deal that Nortel struck with LG Electronics in 2005?

    b. Why did Nortel win this business deal?

    c. Why do you think LG Electronics wanted to enter into a joint venture agreement with Nortel rather than just buying Nortel products?

    d. Why do you think Nortel wanted to enter into a joint venture agreement with LG Electronics rather than just selling its products to LG?

    e. What fundamental economic principle is illustrated and exploited by Nortel's deal with LG?

2. What is the principal–agent problem? Do you think Nortel and LG have such a problem? Describe the problem and explain how Nortel and LG might cope with it.

3. Why are Nortel and LG cooperating to deliver new wireless services in Korea? Why doesn't one of the firms deliver the entire package?

WEB EXERCISES

Use the links on [X myeconlab] to work the following exercise.

1. Read James D. Miller's views on providing airport security services.

    a. What does Mr. Miller argue concerning the best way to organize airport security?

    b. Explain Mr. Miller's views using the principal–agent analysis. Who is the principal and who is the agent?

    c. What exactly is the principal–agent problem in providing airport security services?

    d. Why might a private provider offer better security than a public provider?

    e. Do you think that a private provider would operate at a lower cost than a public provider? Why or why not?

Output and Costs

CHAPTER 10

Technologies Converging

Have you noticed how the traditional phone companies and the cable television companies, as well as Internet portals such as AOL, Yahoo! and MSN, are all getting into each other's lines of business? More and more options become available for everyone and ever more complex plans are on offer that combine cell and fixed phone service with high-speed Internet, cable TV, and other services. Why do we see this proliferation of communication services?

Firms differ in lots of ways—from mom-and-pop convenience stores to multinational giants producing high-tech goods. But regardless of their size or what they produce, all firms must decide how much to produce and how to produce it. How do firms make these decisions?

Most automakers could produce more cars than they can sell. Why do automakers have expensive equipment lying around that isn't fully used? Many electric utilities don't have enough production equipment on hand to meet demand on the coldest and hottest days and must buy power from other producers. Why don't these firms install more equipment so that they can supply the market themselves?

◆ We are going to answer these questions in this chapter. To do so, we are going to study the economic decisions of a small, imaginary firm: Cindy's Sweaters, Inc., a producer of knitted sweaters, which Cindy owns and operates. By studying the economic problems of Cindy's Sweaters and the way Cindy copes with them, we will be able to get a clear view of the problems that face all firms. We're going to begin by setting the scene and describing the time frames in which Cindy makes her business decisions. At the end of the chapter, in *Reading Between the Lines*, we'll return to the telecommunication industry and look at a key feature of its costs.

After studying this chapter, you will be able to

- **Distinguish between the short run and the long run**
- **Explain the relationship between a firm's output and labour employed in the short run**
- **Explain the relationship between a firm's output and costs in the short run and derive a firm's short-run cost curves**
- **Explain the relationship between a firm's output and costs in the long run and derive a firm's long-run average cost curve**

Decision Time Frames

PEOPLE WHO OPERATE FIRMS MAKE MANY
decisions. And all of the decisions are aimed at one
overriding objective: maximum attainable profit. But
the decisions are not all equally critical. Some of the
decisions are big ones. Once made, they are costly (or
impossible) to reverse. If such a decision turns out to
be incorrect, it might lead to the failure of the firm.
Some of the decisions are small ones. They are easily
changed. If one of these decisions turns out to be
incorrect, the firm can change its actions and survive.

The biggest decision that any firm makes is what
industry to enter. For most entrepreneurs, their background knowledge and interests drive this decision.
But the decision also depends on profit prospects. No
one sets up a firm without believing that it will be
profitable—that total revenue will exceed opportunity
cost (see Chapter 9, pp. 198–199).

The firm that we'll study has already chosen the
industry in which to operate. It has also chosen its most
effective method of organization, but it has not decided
the quantity to produce, the quantities of resources to
hire, or the price at which to sell its output.

Decisions about the quantity to produce and the
price to charge depend on the type of market in which
the firm operates. Perfect competition, monopolistic
competition, oligopoly, and monopoly all confront the
firm with their own special problems.

But decisions about how to produce a given output do not depend on the type of market in which the
firm operates. These decisions are similar for *all* types
of firms in *all* types of markets.

The actions that a firm can take to influence the
relationship between output and cost depend on how
soon the firm wants to act. A firm that plans to
change its output rate tomorrow has fewer options
than one that plans to change its output rate six
months from now.

To study the relationship between a firm's output
decision and its costs, we distinguish between two
decision time frames:

- The short run
- The long run

The Short Run

The **short run** is a time frame in which the quantities
of some resources are fixed. For most firms, the fixed
resources are the firm's technology, buildings, and
capital. The management organization is also fixed
in the short run. We call the collection of fixed
resources the firm's *plant*. So in the short run, a
firm's plant is fixed.

For Cindy's Sweaters, the fixed plant is its factory
building and its knitting machines. For an electric
power utility, the fixed plant is its buildings, generators, computers, and control systems.

To increase output in the short run, a firm must
increase the quantity of variable inputs it uses. Labour
is usually the variable input. So to produce more output, Cindy's Sweaters must hire more labour and operate its knitting machines for more hours per day.
Similarly, an electric power utility must hire more
labour and operate its generators for more hours per day.

Short-run decisions are easily reversed. The firm
can increase or decrease its output in the short run by
increasing or decreasing the amount of labour it hires.

The Long Run

The **long run** is a time frame in which the quantities
of *all* resources can be varied. That is, the long run is a
period in which the firm can change its *plant*.

To increase output in the long run, a firm can
choose to change its plant as well as increase the quantity of labour it hires. Cindy's Sweaters can decide to
install some additional knitting machines, use a new
type of machine, and hire more labour. An electric
power utility can decide to install more generators.

Long-run decisions are *not* easily reversed. Once a
plant decision is made, the firm usually must live with
it for some time. To emphasize this fact, we call the
past cost of buying a plant that has no resale value a
sunk cost. A sunk cost is irrelevant to the firm's decisions. The only costs that influence its decisions are the
short-run cost of changing its labour inputs and the
long-run cost of changing its plant.

REVIEW QUIZ

1 Explain the short run and the long run.
2 Why is a sunk cost irrelevant to the decision
   that the firm is making today?

   myeconlab **Study Plan 10.1**

We're going to study costs in the short run and
the long run. We begin with the short run and
describe the technology constraint the firm faces.

Short-Run Technology Constraint

TO INCREASE OUTPUT IN THE SHORT RUN, A FIRM must increase the quantity of labour employed. We describe the relationship between output and the quantity of labour employed by using three related concepts:

1. Total product
2. Marginal product
3. Average product

These product concepts can be illustrated either by product schedules or by product curves. Let's look first at the product schedules.

Product Schedules

Table 10.1 shows some data that describe Cindy's Sweaters' total product, marginal product, and average product. The numbers tell us how Cindy's Sweaters' production increases as more workers are employed. They also tell us about the productivity of Cindy's Sweaters' workers.

Focus first on the columns headed "Labour" and "Total product." **Total product** is the total output produced. You can see from the numbers in these columns that as Cindy's employs more labour, total product increases. For example, when Cindy's employs 1 worker, total product is 4 sweaters a day, and when Cindy's employs 2 workers, total product is 10 sweaters a day. Each increase in employment brings an increase in total product.

The **marginal product** of labour is the increase in total product that results from a one-unit increase in the quantity of labour employed with all other inputs remaining the same. For example, in Table 10.1, when Cindy's increases the number of workers from 2 to 3 and keeps its capital the same, the marginal product of the third worker is 3 sweaters—total product goes from 10 to 13 sweaters.

Average product tells how productive workers are on the average. The **average product** of labour is equal to total product divided by the quantity of labour employed. For example, in Table 10.1, the average product of 3 workers is 4.33 sweaters per worker—13 sweaters a day divided by 3 workers.

If you look closely at the numbers in Table 10.1, you can see some patterns. As the number of workers increases, marginal product at first increases and then begins to decrease. For example, marginal product increases from 4 sweaters a day for the first worker to 6 sweaters a day for the second worker and then decreases to 3 sweaters a day for the third worker. Average product also increases at first and then decreases. You can see the relationships between employment and the three product concepts more clearly by looking at the product curves.

Product Curves

The product curves are graphs of the relationships between employment and the three product concepts you've just studied. They show how total product, marginal product, and average product change as employment changes. They also show the relationships among the three concepts. Let's look at the product curves.

TABLE 10.1	Total Product, Marginal Product, and Average Product			
	Labour (workers per day)	Total product (sweaters per day)	Marginal product (sweaters per additional worker)	Average product (sweaters per worker)
A	0	0		
			4	
B	1	4		4.00
			6	
C	2	10		5.00
			3	
D	3	13		4.33
			2	
E	4	15		3.75
			1	
F	5	16		3.20

Total product is the total amount produced. Marginal product is the change in total product that results from a one-unit increase in labour. For example, when labour increases from 2 to 3 workers a day (row C to row D), total product increases from 10 to 13 sweaters. The marginal product of going from 2 to 3 workers is 3 sweaters. Average product is total product divided by the quantity of labour employed. For example, the average product of 3 workers is 4.33 sweaters per worker (13 sweaters a day divided by 3 workers).

Total Product Curve

Figure 10.1 shows Cindy's Sweaters' total product curve, *TP*. As employment increases, so does the number of sweaters knitted. Points *A* through *F* on the curve correspond to the same rows in Table 10.1.

The total product curve is similar to the *production possibilities frontier* (explained in Chapter 2). It separates the attainable output levels from those that are unattainable. All the points that lie above the curve are unattainable. Points that lie below the curve, in the orange area, are attainable. But they are inefficient—they use more labour than is necessary to produce a given output. Only the points *on* the total product curve are technologically efficient.

Notice especially the shape of the total product curve. As employment increases from zero to 1 to 2 workers per day, the curve becomes steeper. Then, as employment increases to 3, 4, and 5 workers a day, the curve becomes less steep. The steeper the slope of the total product curve, the greater is marginal product, as you are about to see.

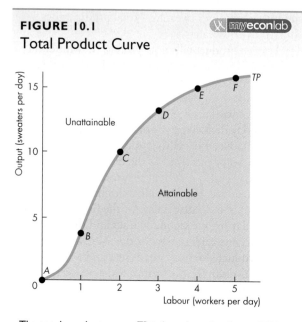

FIGURE 10.1 myeconlab
Total Product Curve

The total product curve, *TP*, is based on the data in Table 10.1. The total product curve shows how the quantity of sweaters changes as the quantity of labour employed changes. For example, 2 workers can produce 10 sweaters a day (point *C*). Points *A* through *F* on the curve correspond to the rows of Table 10.1. The total product curve separates attainable outputs from unattainable outputs. Points below the *TP* curve are inefficient.

Marginal Product Curve

Figure 10.2 shows Cindy's Sweaters' marginal product of labour. Part (a) reproduces the total product curve from Fig. 10.1. Part (b) shows the marginal product curve, *MP*.

In part (a), the orange bars illustrate the marginal product of labour. The height of each bar measures marginal product. Marginal product is also measured by the slope of the total product curve. Recall that the slope of a curve is the change in the value of the variable measured on the *y*-axis—output—divided by the change in the variable measured on the *x*-axis—labour input—as we move along the curve. A one-unit increase in labour input, from 2 to 3 workers, increases output from 10 to 13 sweaters, so the slope from point *C* to point *D* is 3, the same as the marginal product that we've just calculated.

We've calculated the marginal product of labour for a series of unit increases in the quantity of labour. But labour is divisible into smaller units than one person. It is divisible into hours and even minutes. By varying the amount of labour in the smallest units imaginable, we can draw the marginal product curve shown in Fig. 10.2(b). The *height* of this curve measures the *slope* of the total product curve at a point. Part (a) shows that an increase in employment from 2 to 3 workers increases output from 10 to 13 sweaters (an increase of 3). The increase in output of 3 sweaters appears on the vertical axis of part (b) as the marginal product of going from 2 to 3 workers. We plot that marginal product at the midpoint between 2 and 3 workers. Notice that marginal product shown in Fig. 10.2(b) reaches a peak at 1.5 workers, and at that point, marginal product is 6. The peak occurs at 1.5 workers because the total product curve is steepest when employment increases from 1 worker to 2 workers.

The total product and marginal product curves are different for different firms and different types of goods. Ford Motor Company's product curves are different from those of Jim's Burger Stand, which in turn are different from those of Cindy's Sweaters. But the shapes of the product curves are similar because almost every production process has two features:

- Increasing marginal returns initially
- Diminishing marginal returns eventually

Increasing Marginal Returns Increasing marginal returns occur when the marginal product of an additional worker exceeds the marginal product of the

FIGURE 10.2
Marginal Product

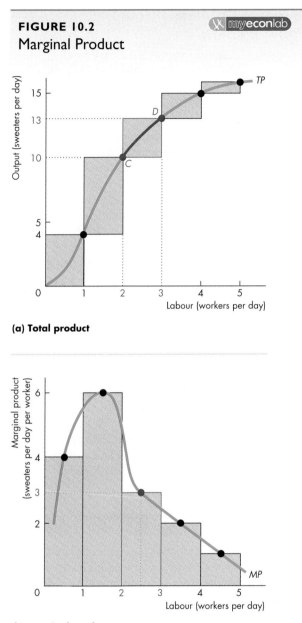

(a) Total product

(b) Marginal product

Marginal product is illustrated by the orange bars. For example, when labour increases from 2 to 3, marginal product is the orange bar whose height is 3 sweaters. (Marginal product is shown midway between the labour inputs to emphasize that it is the result of *changing* inputs.) The steeper the slope of the total product curve (*TP*) in part (a), the larger is marginal product (*MP*) in part (b). Marginal product increases to a maximum (in this example when the second worker is employed) and then declines— diminishing marginal product.

previous worker. Increasing marginal returns arise from increased specialization and division of labour in the production process.

For example, if Cindy employs just one worker, that person must learn all the aspects of sweater production: running the knitting machines, fixing breakdowns, packaging and mailing sweaters, buying and checking the type and colour of the wool. All these tasks must be performed by that one person.

If Cindy hires a second person, the two workers can specialize in different parts of the production process. As a result, two workers produce more than twice as much as one. The marginal product of the second worker is greater than the marginal product of the first worker. Marginal returns are increasing.

Diminishing Marginal Returns   Most production processes experience increasing marginal returns initially. But all production processes eventually reach a point of *diminishing* marginal returns. **Diminishing marginal returns** occur when the marginal product of an additional worker is less than the marginal product of the previous worker.

Diminishing marginal returns arise from the fact that more and more workers are using the same capital and working in the same space. As more workers are added, there is less and less for the additional workers to do that is productive. For example, if Cindy hires a third worker, output increases but not by as much as it did when she hired the second worker. In this case, after two workers are hired, all the gains from specialization and the division of labour have been exhausted. By hiring a third worker, the factory produces more sweaters, but the equipment is being operated at a rate closer to its limits. There are even times when the third worker has nothing to do because the machines are running without the need for further attention. Hiring more and more workers continues to increase output but by successively smaller amounts. Marginal returns are diminishing. This phenomenon is such a pervasive one that it is called a "law"—the law of diminishing returns. The **law of diminishing returns** states that

> As a firm uses more of a variable input, with a given quantity of fixed inputs, the marginal product of the variable input eventually diminishes.

You are going to return to the law of diminishing returns when we study a firm's costs. But before we do that, let's look at the average product of labour and the average product curve.

Average Product Curve

Figure 10.3 illustrates Cindy's Sweaters' average product of labour, *AP*. It also shows the relationship between average product and marginal product. Points *B* through *F* on the average product curve correspond to those same rows in Table 10.1. Average product increases from 1 to 2 workers (its maximum value at point *C*) but then decreases as yet more workers are employed. Notice also that average product is largest when average product and marginal product are equal. That is, the marginal product curve cuts the average product curve at the point of maximum average product. For the numbers of workers at which marginal product exceeds average product, average product is increasing. For the numbers of workers at which marginal product is less than average product, average product is decreasing.

The relationship between the average and marginal product curves is a general feature of the relationship between the average and marginal values of any variable. Let's look at a familiar example.

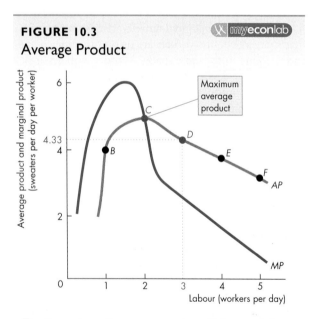

FIGURE 10.3
Average Product   myeconlab

The figure shows the average product of labour and the connection between the average product and marginal product. With 1 worker per day, marginal product exceeds average product, so average product is increasing. With 2 workers per day, marginal product equals average product, so average product is at its maximum. With more than 2 workers per day, marginal product is less than average product, so average product is decreasing.

Marginal Grade and Grade Point Average

To see the relationship between average product and marginal product, think about the similar relationship between Cindy's average grade and marginal grade over five semesters. (Suppose Cindy is a part-time student who takes just one course each semester.) In the first semester, Cindy takes calculus and her grade is a C (2). This grade is her marginal grade. It is also her average grade—her GPA. In the next semester, Cindy takes French and gets a B (3). French is Cindy's marginal course, and her marginal grade is 3. Her GPA rises to 2.5. Because her marginal grade exceeds her average grade, it pulls her average up. In the third semester, Cindy takes economics and gets an A (4)—her new marginal grade. Because her marginal grade exceeds her GPA, it again pulls her average up. Cindy's GPA is now 3, the average of 2, 3, and 4. The fourth semester, she takes history and gets a B (3). Because her marginal grade is equal to her average, her GPA does not change. In the fifth semester, Cindy takes English and gets a D (1). Because her marginal grade, a 1, is below her GPA of 3, her GPA falls.

Cindy's GPA increases when her marginal grade exceeds her GPA. Her GPA falls when her marginal grade is below her GPA. And her GPA is constant when her marginal grade equals her GPA. The relationship between marginal product and average product is exactly the same as that between Cindy's marginal grade and average grade.

REVIEW QUIZ

1 Explain how the marginal product of labour and the average product of labour change as the quantity of labour employed increases (a) initially and (b) eventually.

2 Why does marginal product eventually diminish?

3 Explain the relationship between marginal and average product. How does average product change when marginal product (a) exceeds average product and (b) is less than average product?

   myeconlab   **Study Plan 10.2**

Cindy's Sweaters cares about its product curves because they influence its costs. Let's now look at Cindy's Sweaters' costs.

Short-Run Cost

TO PRODUCE MORE OUTPUT IN THE SHORT RUN, a firm must employ more labour, which means that it must increase its costs. We describe the relationship between output and cost by using three cost concepts:

- Total cost
- Marginal cost
- Average cost

Total Cost

A firm's **total cost** (*TC*) is the cost of the productive resources it uses. Total cost includes the cost of land, capital, and labour. It also includes the cost of entrepreneurship, which is *normal profit* (see Chapter 9, p. 199). We divide total cost into total fixed cost and total variable cost.

Total fixed cost (*TFC*) is the cost of the firm's fixed inputs. Because the quantity of a fixed input does not change as output changes, total fixed cost does not change as output changes.

Total variable cost (*TVC*) is the cost of the firm's variable inputs. Because to change its output a firm must change the quantity of variable inputs, total variable cost changes as output changes.

Total cost is the sum of total fixed cost and total variable cost. That is,

$$TC = TFC + TVC.$$

The table in Fig. 10.4 shows Cindy's total costs. With one knitting machine that Cindy rents for $25 a day, *TFC* is $25. To produce sweaters, Cindy hires labour, which costs $25 a day. *TVC* is the number of workers multiplied by $25. For example, to produce 13 sweaters a day, Cindy hires 3 workers and *TVC* is $75. *TC* is the sum of *TFC* and *TVC*, so to produce 13 sweaters a day, Cindy's total cost, *TC*, is $100. Check the calculation in each row of the table.

Figure 10.4 shows Cindy's total cost curves, which graph total cost against total product. The green total fixed cost curve (*TFC*) is horizontal because total fixed cost does not change when output changes. It is a constant at $25. The purple total variable cost curve (*TVC*) and the blue total cost curve (*TC*) both slope upward because total variable cost increases as output increases. The arrows highlight total fixed cost as the vertical distance between the *TVC* and *TC* curves.

Let's now look at Cindy's marginal cost.

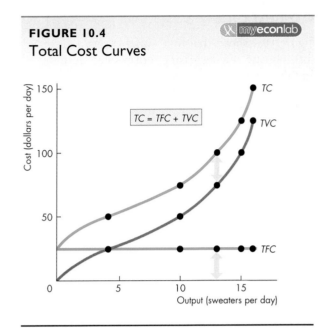

FIGURE 10.4   myeconlab

Total Cost Curves

$$TC = TFC + TVC$$

Labour (workers per day)	Output (sweaters per day)	Total fixed cost (TFC)	Total variable cost (TVC)	Total cost (TC)
		(dollars per day)		
A 0	0	25	0	25
B 1	4	25	25	50
C 2	10	25	50	75
D 3	13	25	75	100
E 4	15	25	100	125
F 5	16	25	125	150

Cindy rents a knitting machine for $25 a day. This amount is Cindy's total fixed cost. Cindy hires workers at a wage rate of $25 a day, and this cost is Cindy's total variable cost. For example, if Cindy employs 3 workers, total variable cost is 3 × $25, which equals $75. Total cost is the sum of total fixed cost and total variable cost. For example, when Cindy employs 3 workers, total cost is $100—total fixed cost of $25 plus total variable cost of $75. The graph shows Cindy's Sweaters' total cost curves. Total fixed cost (*TFC*) is constant—it graphs as a horizontal line—and total variable cost (*TVC*) increases as output increases. Total cost (*TC*) increases as output increases. The vertical distance between the total cost curve and the total variable cost curve is total fixed cost, as illustrated by the two arrows.

Marginal Cost

Figure 10.4 shows that total variable cost and total cost increase at a decreasing rate at small outputs and then begin to increase at an increasing rate as output increases. To understand these patterns in the changes in total cost, we need to use the concept of *marginal cost*.

A firm's **marginal cost** is the increase in total cost that results from a one-unit increase in output. We calculate marginal cost as the increase in total cost divided by the increase in output. The table in Fig. 10.5 shows this calculation. When, for example, output increases from 10 sweaters to 13 sweaters (row *C* to row *D*), total cost increases from $75 to $100. The change in output is 3 sweaters, and the change in total cost is $25. The marginal cost of one of those 3 sweaters is ($25 ÷ 3), which equals $8.33.

Figure 10.5 graphs the marginal cost data in the table as the red marginal cost curve, *MC*. This curve is U-shaped because when Cindy hires a second worker, marginal cost decreases, but when she hires a third, a fourth, and a fifth worker, marginal cost successively increases.

Marginal cost decreases at small outputs because of economies from greater specialization. Marginal cost eventually increases because of *the law of diminishing returns*. The law of diminishing returns means that each additional worker produces a successively smaller addition to output. So to get an additional unit of output, ever more workers are required. Because more workers are required to produce one additional unit of output, the cost of the additional output—marginal cost—must eventually increase.

Marginal cost tells us how total cost changes as output changes. The final cost concept tells us what it costs, on the average, to produce a unit of output. Let's now look at Cindy's Sweaters' average costs.

Average Cost

There are three average costs:

1. Average fixed cost
2. Average variable cost
3. Average total cost

Average fixed cost (*AFC*) is total fixed cost per unit of output. **Average variable cost** (*AVC*) is total variable cost per unit of output. **Average total cost** (*ATC*) is total cost per unit of output. The average

cost concepts are calculated from the total cost concepts as follows:

$$TC = TFC + TVC.$$

Divide each total cost term by the quantity produced, *Q*, to get,

$$\frac{TC}{Q} = \frac{TFC}{Q} + \frac{TVC}{Q}$$

or

$$ATC = AFC + AVC.$$

The table in Fig. 10.5 shows the calculation of average total cost. For example, when output is 10 sweaters (row *C*), average fixed cost is ($25 ÷ 10), which equals $2.50, average variable cost is ($50 ÷ 10), which equals $5.00, and average total cost is ($75 ÷ 10), which equals $7.50. Note that average total cost is equal to average fixed cost ($2.50) plus average variable cost ($5.00).

Figure 10.5 shows the average cost curves. The green average fixed cost curve (*AFC*) slopes downward. As output increases, the same constant fixed cost is spread over a larger output. The blue average total cost curve (*ATC*) and the purple average variable cost curve (*AVC*) are U-shaped. The vertical distance between the average total cost and average variable cost curves is equal to average fixed cost—as indicated by the two arrows. That distance shrinks as output increases because average fixed cost declines with increasing output.

The marginal cost curve (*MC*) intersects the average variable cost curve and the average total cost curve at their minimum points. That is, when marginal cost is less than average cost, average cost is decreasing, and when marginal cost exceeds average cost, average cost is increasing. This relationship holds for both the *ATC* curve and the *AVC* curve and is another example of the relationship you saw in Fig. 10.3 for average product and marginal product and in Cindy's course grades.

Why the Average Total Cost Curve Is U-Shaped

Average total cost, *ATC*, is the sum of average fixed cost, *AFC*, and average variable cost, *AVC*. So the shape of the *ATC* curve combines the shapes of the *AFC* and *AVC* curves. The U shape of the average

FIGURE 10.5
Marginal Cost and Average Costs

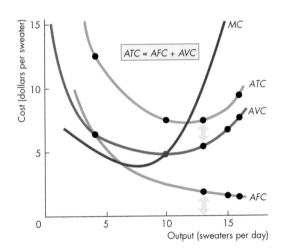

Marginal cost is calculated as the change in total cost divided by the change in output. When output increases from 4 to 10, an increase of 6, total cost increases by $25 and marginal cost is $25 ÷ 6, which equals $4.17. Each average cost concept is calculated by dividing the related total cost by output. When 10 sweaters are produced, AFC is $2.50 ($25 ÷ 10), AVC is $5 ($50 ÷ 10), and ATC is $7.50 ($75 ÷ 10).

The graph shows that the marginal cost curve (MC) is U-shaped and intersects the average variable cost curve and the average total cost curve at their minimum points. Average fixed cost (AFC) decreases as output increases. The average total cost curve (ATC) and average variable cost curve (AVC) are U-shaped. The vertical distance between these two curves is equal to average fixed cost, as illustrated by the two arrows.

	Labour (workers per day)	Output (sweaters per day)	Total fixed cost (TFC)	Total variable cost (TVC)	Total cost (TC)	Marginal cost (MC) (dollars per additional sweater)	Average fixed cost (AFC)	Average variable cost (AVC)	Average total cost (ATC)
A	0	0	25	0	25	.... 6.25	—	—	—
B	1	4	25	25	50	.... 4.17	6.25	6.25	12.50
C	2	10	25	50	75	.... 8.33	2.50	5.00	7.50
D	3	13	25	75	100	.........12.50	1.92	5.77	7.69
E	4	15	25	100	125	.........25.00	1.67	6.67	8.33
F	5	16	25	125	150		1.56	7.81	9.38

total cost curve arises from the influence of two opposing forces:

1. Spreading total fixed cost over a larger output
2. Eventually diminishing returns

When output increases, the firm spreads its total fixed cost over a larger output and so its average fixed cost decreases—its average fixed cost curve slopes downward.

Diminishing returns means that as output increases, ever-larger amounts of labour are needed to produce an additional unit of output. So average vari-

able cost eventually increases, and the AVC curve eventually slopes upward.

The shape of the average total cost curve combines these two effects. Initially, as output increases, both average fixed cost and average variable cost decrease, so average total cost decreases and the ATC curve slopes downward. But as output increases further and diminishing returns set in, average variable cost begins to increase. Eventually, average variable cost increases more quickly than average fixed cost decreases, so average total cost increases and the ATC curve slopes upward.

Cost Curves and Product Curves

The technology that a firm uses determines its costs. Figure 10.6 shows the links between the firm's technology constraint (its product curves) and its cost curves. The upper part of the figure shows the average product curve and the marginal product curve—like those in Fig. 10.3. The lower part of the figure shows the average variable cost curve and the marginal cost curve—like those in Fig. 10.5.

The figure highlights the links between technology and costs. As labour increases initially, marginal product and average product rise and marginal cost and average variable cost fall. Then, at the point of maximum marginal product, marginal cost is a minimum. As labour increases further, marginal product diminishes and marginal cost increases. But average product continues to rise, and average variable cost continues to fall. Then, at the point of maximum average product, average variable cost is a minimum. As labour increases further, average product diminishes and average variable cost increases.

Shifts in the Cost Curves

The position of a firm's short-run cost curves depend on two factors:

- Technology
- Prices of productive resources

Technology A technological change that increases productivity shifts the total product curve upward. It also shifts the marginal product curve and the average product curve upward. With a better technology, the same inputs can produce more output, so technological change lowers costs and shifts the cost curves downward. For example, advances in robot production techniques have increased productivity in the automobile industry. As a result, the product curves of DaimlerChrysler, Ford, and GM have shifted upward, and their cost curves have shifted downward. But the relationships between their product curves and cost curves have not changed. These curves are still linked in the way shown in Fig. 10.6.

Often, a technological advance results in a firm using more capital (a fixed input) and less labour (a variable input). For example, today the telephone companies use computers to provide directory assistance in place of the human operators they used in

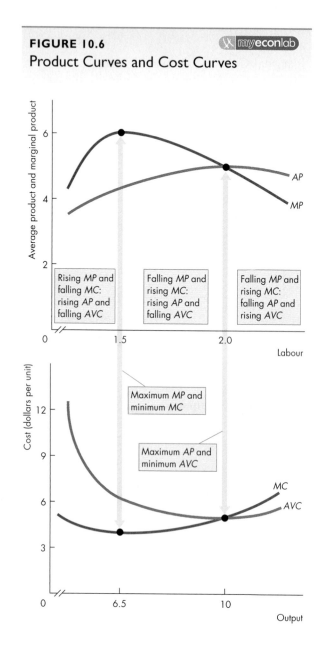

FIGURE 10.6
Product Curves and Cost Curves

A firm's marginal product curve is linked to its marginal cost curve. If marginal product rises, marginal cost falls. If marginal product is a maximum, marginal cost is a minimum. If marginal product diminishes, marginal cost rises. A firm's average product curve is linked to its average variable cost curve. If average product rises, average variable cost falls. If average product is a maximum, average variable cost is a minimum. If average product diminishes, average variable cost rises.

TABLE 10.2   A Compact Glossary of Costs

Term	Symbol	Definition	Equation
Fixed cost		Cost that is independent of the output level; cost of a fixed input	
Variable cost		Cost that varies with the output level; cost of a variable input	
Total fixed cost	TFC	Cost of the fixed inputs	
Total variable cost	TVC	Cost of the variable inputs	
Total cost	TC	Cost of all inputs	$TC = TFC + TVC$
Output (total product)	TP	Total quantity produced (output Q)	
Marginal cost	MC	Change in total cost resulting from a one-unit increase in total product	$MC = \Delta TC \div \Delta Q$
Average fixed cost	AFC	Total fixed cost per unit of output	$AFC = TFC \div Q$
Average variable cost	AVC	Total variable cost per unit of output	$AVC = TVC \div Q$
Average total cost	ATC	Total cost per unit of output	$ATC = AFC + AVC$

the 1980s. When such a technological change occurs, total cost decreases, but fixed costs increase and variable costs decrease. This change in the mix of fixed cost and variable cost means that at small output levels, average total cost might increase, while at large output levels, average total cost decreases.

Prices of Productive Resources An increase in the price of a productive resource increases costs and shifts the cost curves. But how the curves shift depends on which resource price changes. An increase in rent or some other component of *fixed* cost shifts the fixed cost curves (*TFC* and *AFC*) upward and shifts the total cost curve (*TC*) upward but leaves the variable cost curves (*AVC* and *TVC*) and the marginal cost curve (*MC*) unchanged. An increase in wages or some other component of *variable* cost shifts the variable cost curves (*TVC* and *AVC*) upward and shifts the marginal cost curve (*MC*) upward but leaves the fixed cost curves (*AFC* and *TFC*) unchanged. So, for example, if truck drivers' wages increase, the variable cost and marginal

cost of transportation services increase. If the interest expense paid by a trucking company increases, the fixed cost of transportation services increases.

You've now completed your study of short-run costs. All the concepts that you've met are summarized in a compact glossary in Table 10.2.

REVIEW QUIZ

1 What does a firm's short-run cost curves show?
2 How does marginal cost change as output increases (a) initially and (b) eventually?
3 What does the law of diminishing returns imply for the shape of the marginal cost curve?
4 What is the shape of the average fixed cost curve and why?
5 What are the shapes of the average variable cost curve and the average total cost curve and why?

myeconlab Study Plan 10.3

Long-Run Cost

IN THE SHORT RUN, A FIRM CAN VARY THE quantity of labour but the quantity of capital is fixed. So the firm has variable costs of labour and fixed costs of capital. In the long run, a firm can vary both the quantity of labour and the quantity of capital. So in the long run, all the firm's costs are variable. We are now going to study the firm's costs in the long run, when all costs are variable costs and when the quantities of labour and capital vary.

The behaviour of long-run cost depends on the firm's *production function*, which is the relationship between the maximum output attainable and the quantities of both labour and capital.

The Production Function

Table 10.3 shows Cindy's Sweaters' production function. The table lists total product schedules for four different quantities of capital. We identify the quantity of capital by the plant size. The numbers for Plant 1 are for a factory with 1 knitting machine—the case we've just studied. The other three plants have 2, 3, and 4 machines. If Cindy's Sweaters doubles its capital to 2 knitting machines, the various amounts of labour can produce the outputs shown in the second column of the table. The other two columns show the outputs of yet larger quantities of capital. Each column of the table could be graphed as a total product curve for each plant.

Diminishing Returns

Diminishing returns occur at all four quantities of capital as the quantity of labour increases. You can check that fact by calculating the marginal product of labour in plants with 2, 3, and 4 machines. At each plant size, as the quantity of labour increases, the marginal product of labour (eventually) diminishes.

Diminishing Marginal Product of Capital

Diminishing returns also occur as the quantity of capital increases. You can check that fact by calculating the marginal product of capital at a given quantity of labour. The *marginal product of capital* is the change in total product divided by the change in capital when the quantity of labour is constant—equivalently, the change in output resulting from a one-unit increase in the quantity of capital. For example, if Cindy's has 3 workers and increases its capital from

TABLE 10.3   The Production Function

Labour (workers per day)	Output (sweaters per day)			
	Plant I	Plant 2	Plant 3	Plant 4
I	4	10	13	15
2	10	15	18	20
3	13	18	22	24
4	15	20	24	26
5	16	21	25	27
Knitting machines (number)	I	2	3	4

The table shows the total product data for four quantities of capital. The greater the plant size, the larger is the total product for any given quantity of labour. But for a given plant size, the marginal product of labour diminishes. And for a given quantity of labour, the marginal product of capital diminishes.

1 machine to 2 machines, output increases from 13 to 18 sweaters a day. The marginal product of capital is 5 sweaters per day. If Cindy increases the number of machines from 2 to 3, output increases from 18 to 22 sweaters per day. The marginal product of the third machine is 4 sweaters per day, down from 5 sweaters per day for the second machine.

Let's now see what the production function implies for long-run costs.

Short-Run Cost and Long-Run Cost

Continue to assume that Cindy can hire a worker for $25 per day and rent a knitting machine for $25 per machine per day. Using these input prices and the data in Table 10.3, we can calculate and graph the average total cost curves for factories with 1, 2, 3, and 4 knitting machines. We've already studied the costs of a factory with 1 machine in Figs. 10.4 and 10.5. In Fig. 10.7, the average total cost curve for that case is ATC_1. Figure 10.7 also shows the average total cost curve for a factory with 2 machines, ATC_2, with 3 machines, ATC_3, and with 4 machines, ATC_4.

FIGURE 10.7
Short-Run Costs of Four Different Plants

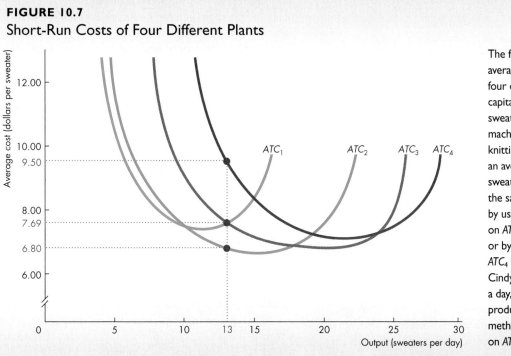

The figure shows short-run average total cost curves for four different quantities of capital. Cindy's can produce 13 sweaters a day with 1 knitting machine on ATC_1 or with 3 knitting machines on ATC_3 for an average cost of $7.69 per sweater. Cindy's can produce the same number of sweaters by using 2 knitting machines on ATC_2 for $6.80 per sweater or by using 4 machines on ATC_4 for $9.50 per sweater. If Cindy's produces 13 sweaters a day, the least-cost method of production—the long-run method—is with 2 machines on ATC_2.

Plant size has a big effect on the firm's average total cost. Two things stand out in Fig. 10.7:

1. Each short-run ATC curve is U-shaped.
2. For each short-run ATC curve, the larger the plant, the greater is the output at which average total cost is a minimum.

Each short-run average total cost curve is U-shaped because, as the quantity of labour increases, its marginal product at first increases and then diminishes. And these patterns in the marginal product of labour, which we examined in some detail for the plant with 1 knitting machine on pp. 222–223, occur at all plant sizes.

The minimum average total cost for a larger plant occurs at a greater output than it does for a smaller plant because the larger plant has a higher total fixed cost and therefore, for any given output level, a higher average fixed cost.

Which short-run average cost curve Cindy's Sweaters operates on depends on its plant size. But in the long run, Cindy chooses the plant size. And which plant size she chooses depends on the output she plans to produce. The reason is that the average total cost of producing a given output depends on the plant size.

To see why, suppose that Cindy plans to produce 13 sweaters a day. With 1 machine, the average total cost curve is ATC_1 (in Fig. 10.7) and the average total cost of 13 sweaters a day is $7.69 per sweater. With 2 machines, on ATC_2, average total cost is $6.80 per sweater. With 3 machines, on ATC_3, average total cost is $7.69 per sweater, the same as with 1 machine. Finally, with 4 machines, on ATC_4, average total cost is $9.50 per sweater.

The economically efficient plant size for producing a given output is the one that has the lowest average total cost. For Cindy's Sweaters, the economically efficient plant to use to produce 13 sweaters a day is the one with 2 machines.

In the long run, Cindy's chooses the plant size that minimizes average total cost. When a firm is producing a given output at the least possible cost, it is operating on its *long-run average cost curve*.

The **long-run average cost curve** is the relationship between the lowest attainable average total cost and output when both plant size and labour change.

The long-run average cost curve is a planning curve. It tells the firm the plant size and the quantity of labour to use at each output to minimize cost. Once the plant size is chosen, the firm operates on the short-run cost curves that apply to that plant size.

The Long-Run Average Cost Curve

Figure 10.8 shows Cindy's Sweaters' long-run average cost curve, *LRAC*. This long-run average cost curve is derived from the short-run average total cost curves in Fig. 10.7. For output rates up to 10 sweaters a day, average total cost is the lowest on ATC_1. For output rates between 10 and 18 sweaters a day, average total cost is the lowest on ATC_2. For output rates between 18 and 24 sweaters a day, average total cost is the lowest on ATC_3. And for output rates in excess of 24 sweaters a day, average total cost is the lowest on ATC_4. The segment of each of the four average total cost curves for which that quantity of capital has the lowest average total cost is highlighted in dark blue in Fig. 10.8. The scallop-shaped curve made up of these four segments is the long-run average cost curve.

Economies and Diseconomies of Scale

Economies of scale are features of a firm's technology that lead to falling long-run average cost as output increases. When economies of scale are present, the *LRAC* curve slopes downward. The *LRAC* curve in Fig. 10.8 shows that Cindy's Sweaters experiences economies of scale for outputs up to 15 sweaters a day.

With given input prices, economies of scale occur if the percentage increase in output exceeds the percentage increase in all inputs. For example, if when a firm increases its labour and capital by 10 percent, output increases by more than 10 percent, its average total cost falls. Economies of scale are present.

The main source of economies of scale is greater specialization of both labour and capital. For example, if GM produces 100 cars a week, each worker must perform many different tasks and the capital must be general-purpose machines and tools. But if GM produces 10,000 cars a week, each worker specializes and becomes highly proficient in a small number of tasks. Also, the capital is specialized and productive.

Diseconomies of scale are features of a firm's technology that lead to rising long-run average cost as output increases. When diseconomies of scale are present, the *LRAC* curve slopes upward. In Fig. 10.8, Cindy's Sweaters experiences diseconomies of scale at outputs greater than 15 sweaters a day.

With given input prices, diseconomies of scale occur if the percentage increase in output is less than the percentage increase in inputs. For example, if when a firm increases its labour and capital by 10 percent, output increases by less than 10 percent,

FIGURE 10.8
Long-Run Average Cost Curve

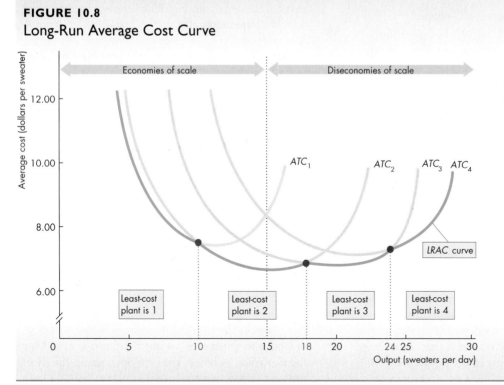

The long-run average cost curve traces the lowest attainable average total cost of production as both the plant size and labour change. Cindy's produces on its long-run average cost curve if it uses 1 machine to produce up to 10 sweaters a day, 2 machines to produce between 10 and 18 sweaters a day, 3 machines to produce between 18 and 24 sweaters a day, and 4 machines to produce more than 24 sweaters a day. Within these ranges, Cindy's varies its output by varying its labour input.

its average total cost rises. Diseconomies of scale are present.

The main source of diseconomies of scale is the difficulty of managing a very large enterprise. The larger the firm, the greater is the challenge of organizing it and the greater is the cost of communicating both up and down the management hierarchy and among managers. Eventually, management complexity brings rising average cost.

Diseconomies of scale occur in all production processes but perhaps only at a very large output rate.

Constant returns to scale are features of a firm's technology that lead to constant long-run average cost as output increases. When constant returns to scale are present, the *LRAC* curve is horizontal.

Constant returns to scale occur if the percentage increase in output equals the percentage increase in inputs. For example, if when a firm increases its labour and capital by 10 percent, output increases by 10 percent, then constant returns to scale are present.

For example, General Motors can double its production of Cavaliers by doubling its production facility for those cars. It can build an identical production line and hire an identical number of workers. With the two identical production lines, GM produces exactly twice as many cars.

Minimum Efficient Scale A firm experiences economies of scale up to some output level. Beyond that level, it moves into constant returns to scale or diseconomies of scale. A firm's **minimum efficient scale** is the smallest quantity of output at which long-run average cost reaches its lowest level.

The minimum efficient scale plays a role in determining market structure, as you will learn in the next three chapters. The minimum efficient scale also helps to answer some questions about real businesses.

Economies of Scale at Cindy's Sweaters The production technology that Cindy's Sweaters uses, shown in Table 10.3 on p. 230, illustrates economies of scale and diseconomies of scale. If Cindy's Sweaters increases its inputs from 1 machine and 1 worker to 2 of each, a 100 percent increase in all inputs, output increases by more than 100 percent, from 4 sweaters to 15 sweaters a day. Cindy's Sweaters experiences economies of scale, and its long-run average cost decreases. But if Cindy's Sweaters increases its inputs to 3 machines and 3 workers, a 50 percent increase, output increases by less than 50 percent, from 15 sweaters to 22 sweaters a day. Now Cindy's Sweaters

experiences diseconomies of scale, and its long-run average cost increases. Its minimum efficient scale is at 15 sweaters a day.

Producing Cars and Generating Electric Power
Why do automakers have expensive equipment lying around that isn't fully used? You can now answer this question. An automaker uses the plant that minimizes the average total cost of producing the output that it can sell. But it operates below the minimum efficient scale. Its short-run average total cost curve looks like ATC_1 in Fig. 10.8. If it could sell more cars, it would produce more cars and its average total cost would fall.

Why do many electric utilities have too little production equipment to meet demand on the coldest and hottest days and have to buy power from other producers? You can now see why this happens and why an electric utility doesn't build more generating capacity. A power producer uses the plant size that minimizes the average total cost of producing the output that it can sell on a normal day. But it produces above the minimum efficient scale and experiences diseconomies of scale. Its short-run average total cost curve looks like ATC_3 in Fig. 10.8. With a larger plant size, its average total costs of producing its normal output would be higher.

REVIEW QUIZ

1 What does a firm's production function show and how is it related to a total product curve?
2 Explain why the law of diminishing returns applies to capital as well as to labour.
3 What does a firm's long-run average cost curve show? How is it related to the firm's short-run average cost curves?
4 What are economies of scale and diseconomies of scale? How do they arise? What do they imply for the the long-run average cost curve?
5 How is a firm's minimum efficient scale determined?

myeconlab **Study Plan 10.4**

◆ *Reading Between the Lines* on pp. 234–235 applies what you've learned about a firm's cost curves. It looks at the key features of the cost curves of firms in the telecommunicatioins industry.

Traditional Phone Versus VoIP

THE GLOBE AND MAIL, AUGUST 22, 2005

Bell targets big business in IP challenge

Talk about a tough sales pitch: Try telling cost-conscious businesses their expensive existing telecommunication networks won't cut it in future, and they should switch to Internet protocol technology because it will lead to productivity improvements and cost savings.

But that's exactly what Bell Canada needs to do. It has a target to develop plans by year-end to move its 1,000 big-business customers to IP-based networks.

The conversion is a key part of Bell's strategy to cut its own expenses and uncover new sources of revenue growth at its business and consumer units amid rising competition from existing and new rivals.

Of course, the transition won't happen overnight. Many clients have poured significant money into their so-called legacy networks, so Bell must consider those investments as it develops timelines for a customer's transition to IP, according to William Bangert, senior vice-president of enterprise business development at Bell.

"If you go in and say I'm going to convert you entirely to IP tomorrow, come what may, without taking into account the investments that they've already made, you may ultimately cost them more money, not less money certainly in the short term," Mr. Bangert said in an interview in his Toronto office.

But when clients make the move to IP, which eliminates the need for separate voice-and-data networks, Bell says it will lower their costs and offer them new applications.

So far, Montreal-based Bell says 111 of its biggest customers have made the move to IP, including Bank of Montreal and Toronto-based Manulife Financial Corp.

It's a big investment. BMO, for example, is paying $84 million over four years to convert 1,100 branches to IP. The bill for Manulife is $140 million over seven years for IP-based voice and data services set up and managed by Bell.

Reprinted with permission from *The Globe and Mail*.

Essence of the Story

■ Bell is trying to get its 1,000 biggest customers to switch to Internet protocol (IP) technology.

■ The conversion is a key part of Bell's strategy to cut its own costs.

■ When Bell customers switch to IP, they too will face lower costs.

■ Bell says that so far 111 of its biggest customers have moved to IP.

■ The Bank of Montreal is spending $84 million and Manulife is spending $140 million to convert to IP.

Economic Analysis

■ Phone companies can choose between two main technologies: traditional telephone or Internet protocol (called VoIP or Voice over the Internet protocol when applied to voice communication).

■ IP technology uses more capital and less labour than does the traditional technology. The cost of the capital is a fixed cost, and the cost of the labour is a variable cost.

■ The total fixed cost of a VoIP system exceeds the total fixed cost of a traditional phone system.

■ The average variable cost of a traditional phone call exceeds the average variable cost of a VoIPcall.

■ Average total cost (ATC) is the sum of average fixed cost and average variable cost. The figure shows the ATC curves for the two technologies.

■ ATC_O is the average total cost curve for a traditional telephone system, and ATC_N is the average total cost curve for a VoIP system.

■ Small firms that make fewer than Q calls a year minimize average total cost by using traditional phone service and avoiding the large cost of installing a VoIP system.

■ Larger firms (like the Bank of Montreal, Manulife, the others of the 111 customers of Bell) that make more than Q calls a year minimize average total cost by using VoIP.

■ The figure shows the long-run average cost curve, LRAC, for voice conversations. Up to Q, the LRAC curve is the highlighted section of ATC_O, and above Q, the LRAC curve is the highlighted section of ATC_N.

■ The large fixed costs of using Internet and more broadly, digital technologies explains why phone companies, cable TV companies, and Internet portal companies are all offering the same array of services. By so doing, they are able to spread this large fixed cost over a greater number of products and services.

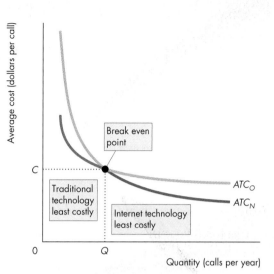

Figure 1 **The cost of a phone call with two technologies**

235

SUMMARY

KEY POINTS

Decision Time Frames (p. 220)

- In the short run, the quantity of some resources are fixed and the quantities of the other resources can be varied.
- In the long run, the quantities of all resources can be varied.

Short-Run Technology Constraint (pp. 221–224)

- A total product curve shows the quantity a firm can produce with a given quantity of capital and different quantities of labour.
- Initially, the marginal product of labour increases as the quantity of labour increases, but eventually, marginal product diminishes—the law of diminishing returns.
- Average product increases initially and eventually diminishes.

Short-Run Cost (pp. 225–229)

- As output increases, total fixed cost is constant, and total variable cost and total cost increase.
- As output increases, average fixed cost decreases and average variable cost, average total cost, and marginal cost decrease at small outputs and increase at large outputs. These cost curves are U-shaped.

Long-Run Cost (pp. 230–233)

- Long-run cost is the cost of production when all inputs—labour and capital—have been adjusted to their economically efficient levels.
- There is a set of short-run cost curves for each different plant size. There is one least-cost plant size for each output. The larger the output, the larger is the plant size that will minimize average total cost.
- The long-run average cost curve traces out the lowest attainable average total cost at each output when both capital and labour inputs can be varied.
- With economies of scale, the long-run average cost curve slopes downward. With diseconomies of scale, the long-run average cost curve slopes upward.

KEY FIGURES AND TABLE

Figure 10.2   Marginal Product, 223
Figure 10.3   Average Product, 224
Figure 10.5   Marginal Cost and Average Costs, 227
Figure 10.6   Product Curves and Cost Curves, 228
Figure 10.7   Short-Run Costs of Four Different Plants, 231
Figure 10.8   Long-Run Average Cost Curve, 232
Table 10.2   A Compact Glossary of Costs, 229

KEY TERMS

Average fixed cost, 226
Average product, 221
Average total cost, 226
Average variable cost, 226
Constant returns to scale, 233
Diminishing marginal returns, 223
Diseconomies of scale, 232
Economies of scale, 232
Law of diminishing returns, 223
Long run, 220
Long-run average cost curve, 231
Marginal cost, 226
Marginal product, 221
Minimum efficient scale, 233
Short run, 220
Sunk cost, 220
Total cost, 225
Total fixed cost, 225
Total product, 221
Total variable cost, 225

PROBLEMS

Go to myeconlab for solutions to odd-numbered problems and additional exercises.

1. Rubber Dinghies' total product schedule is

Labour (workers per week)	Output (dinghies per week)
1	1
2	3
3	6
4	10
5	15
6	21
7	26
8	30
9	33
10	35

   a. Draw the total product curve.
   b. Calculate the average product of labour and draw the average product curve.
   c. Calculate the marginal product of labour and draw the marginal product curve.
   d. What is the relationship between average product and marginal product when Rubber Dinghies produces (i) fewer than 30 dinghies a week and (ii) more than 30 dinghies a week?

2. Sue's SurfBoards' total product schedule is

Labour (workers per week)	Output (surfboards per week)
1	40
2	100
3	140
4	170
5	190
6	200

   a. Draw the total product curve.
   b. Calculate the average product of labour and draw the average product curve.
   c. Calculate the marginal product of labour and draw the marginal product curve.
   d. What is the relationship between the average product and marginal product when Sue's

SurfBoards produces (i) fewer than 100 surfboards a week and (ii) more than 100 surfboards a week?

3. In problem 1, the price of labour is $400 a week and total fixed cost is $1,000 a week.
   a. Calculate total cost, total variable cost, and total fixed cost for each output and draw the short-run total cost curves.
   b. Calculate average total cost, average fixed cost, average variable cost, and marginal cost at each output and draw the short-run average and marginal cost curves.

4. In problem 2, the price of labour is $100 per week and total fixed costs are $200 per week.
   a. Calculate total cost, total variable cost, and total fixed costs for each level of output and draw the short-run total cost curves.
   b. Calculate average total cost, average fixed cost, average variable cost, and marginal cost at each level of output and draw the short-run average and marginal cost curves.

5. In problem 3, suppose that Rubber Dinghies' total fixed cost increases to $1,100 a week. Explain what changes occur in the short-run average and marginal cost curves.

6. In problem 4, suppose that the price of labour increases to $150 per week. Explain what changes occur in the short-run average and marginal cost curves.

7. In problem 3, Rubber Dinghies buys a second plant and the total product of each quantity of labour doubles. The total fixed cost of operating each plant is $1,000 a week. The wage rate is $400 a week.
   a. Set out the average total cost schedule when Rubber Dinghies operates two plants.
   b. Draw the long-run average cost curve.
   c. Over what output ranges is it efficient to operate one plant and two plants?

8. In problem 4, Sue's SurfBoards buys a second plant and the total product of each quantity of labour increases by 50 percent. The total fixed cost of operating each plant is $200 a week. The wage rate is $100 a week.
   a. Set out the average total cost curve when Sue's SurfBoards operates two plants.
   b. Draw the long-run average cost curve.
   c. Over what output ranges is it efficient to operate one plant and two plants?

9. The table shows the production function of Bonnie's Balloon Rides.

Labour	Output (rides per day)			
(workers per day)	Plant 1	Plant 2	Plant 3	Plant 4
10	4	10	13	15
20	10	15	18	20
30	13	18	22	24
40	15	20	24	26
50	16	21	25	27
Balloons (number)	**1**	**2**	**3**	**4**

Bonnie pays $500 a day for each balloon she rents and $25 a day for each worker she hires.

a. Find and graph the average total cost curve for each plant size.
b. Draw Bonnie's long-run average cost curve.
c. What is Bonnie's minimum efficient scale?
d. Explain how Bonnie uses her long-run average cost curve to decide how many balloons to rent.

10. The table shows the production function of Cathy's Cakes.

Labour	Output (cakes per day)			
(workers per day)	Plant 1	Plant 2	Plant 3	Plant 4
1	20	40	55	65
2	40	60	75	85
3	65	75	90	100
4	65	85	100	110
Ovens (number)	**1**	**2**	**3**	**4**

Cathy pays $100 a day for each oven she rents and $50 a day for each kitchen worker she hires.

a. Find and graph the average total cost curve for each plant size.
b. Draw Cathy's long-run average cost curve.
c. Over what output range does Cathy experience economies of scale?
d. Explain how Cathy uses her long-run average cost curve to decide how many ovens to rent.

CRITICAL THINKING

1. Study *Reading Between the Lines* on pp. 234–235 and then answer the following questions:
   a. What is the main difference, from a cost point of view, between traditional telephone service and VoIP?
   b. Why do you think VoIP is becoming more popular?
   c. Would it ever make sense for a firm to use traditional phone service rather than VoIP?
   d. Do you think that VoIP is as common in Africa as it is in Canada? Explain why or why not.
   e. Suppose the government put a tax on VoIP calls but did not put a similar tax on traditional phone calls. How would the tax affect the cost curves of the Bank of Montreal and Manulife? Might these firms want to switch back to traditional phone service?

WEB EXERCISES

Use the links on (X) myeconlab **to work the following exercises.**

1. Obtain information about the cost of producing pumpkins.
   a. List all the costs referred to on the Web page.
   b. For each item, say whether it is a fixed cost or a variable cost.
   c. Make some assumptions and sketch the average cost curves and the marginal cost curve for producing pumpkins.

2. Obtain information about the cost of producing vegetables. For one of the vegetables (your choice):
   a. List all the costs referred to on the Web page.
   b. For each item, say whether it is a fixed cost or a variable cost.
   c. Sketch the average cost curves and the marginal cost curve for producing the vegetable you've chosen.

Perfect Competition

Sweet Competition

Maple syrup is sweet, but producing it and selling it is a tough competitive business. Around 12,000 firms in Canada and the United States produce syrup. In the early 2000s, bumper crops sent the price of maple syrup tumbling. How did producers react to this drop in price? *Reading Between the Lines* at the end of the chapter answers this question. In recent years, new firms have entered the maple syrup business, while others have been squeezed out. Why do some firms enter an industry and others leave it? What are the effects on profits and prices of new firms entering and old firms leaving an industry?

In September 2005, around 150,000 people were unemployed because they had been laid off by the firms that previously employed them. Why do firms lay off workers? Why do firms temporarily shut down?

Over the past few years, there has been a dramatic fall in the prices of personal computers. For example, a slow computer cost almost $4,000 a few years ago, and a fast one costs less than $500 today. What goes on in an industry when the price of its output falls sharply? What happens to the profits of the firms producing such goods? Maple syrup, computers, and most other goods are produced by more than one firm, and these firms compete with each other for sales.

◆ To study competitive markets, we are going to build a model of a market in which competition is as fierce and extreme as possible— more extreme than in the examples we've just considered. We call this situation "perfect competition."

After studying this chapter, you will be able to

- ■ **Define perfect competition**
- ■ **Explain how firms make their supply decisions and why they sometimes shut down temporarily and lay off workers**
- ■ **Explain how price and output are determined and why firms enter and leave an industry**
- ■ **Predict the effects of a change in demand and of a technological advance**
- ■ **Explain why perfect competition is efficient**

Competition

THE FIRMS THAT YOU STUDY IN THIS CHAPTER face the force of raw competition. We call this extreme form of competition perfect competition. **Perfect competition** is an industry in which

- Many firms sell identical products to many buyers.
- There are no restrictions on entry into the industry.
- Established firms have no advantage over new ones.
- Sellers and buyers are well informed about prices.

Farming, fishing, wood pulping and paper milling, the manufacture of paper cups and plastic shopping bags, grocery retailing, photo finishing, lawn service, plumbing, painting, dry cleaning, and the provision of laundry services are all examples of highly competitive industries.

How Perfect Competition Arises

Perfect competition arises if the minimum efficient scale of a single producer is small relative to the demand for the good or service. A firm's *minimum efficient scale* is the smallest quantity of output at which long-run average cost reaches is lowest level. (See Chapter 10, p. 233.) Where the minimum efficient scale of a firm is small relative to demand, there is room for many firms in an industry.

Second, perfect competition arises if each firm is perceived to produce a good or service that has no unique characteristics so that consumers don't care which firm they buy from.

Price Takers

Firms in perfect competition must make many decisions. But one thing they do *not* decide is the price at which to sell their output. Firms in perfect competition are said to be price takers. A **price taker** is a firm that cannot influence the price of a good or service.

The key reason why a perfectly competitive firm is a price taker is that it produces a tiny proportion of the total output of a particular good and buyers are well informed about the prices of other firms.

Imagine that you are a wheat farmer in Saskatchewan. You have 500 hectares under cultivation—which sounds like a lot. But compared to the thousands of hectares across the Canadian prairies and in the Dakotas, Nebraska, Colorado, Oklahoma, and Texas, as well as the thousands more in Argentina, Australia, and Ukraine, your 500 hectares is a drop in the ocean. Nothing makes your wheat any better than any other farmer's, and all the buyers of wheat know the price at which they can do business.

If everybody else sells their wheat for $300 a tonne and you want $310, why would people buy from you? They can go to the next farmer and the next and the one after that and buy all they need for $300 a tonne. This price is determined in the market for wheat, and you are a *price taker*.

A price taker faces a perfectly elastic demand. One farm's wheat is a *perfect substitute* for wheat from the farm next door or from any other farm. Note, though, that the *market* demand for wheat is not perfectly elastic. The market demand curve is downward sloping, and its elasticity depends on the substitutability of wheat for other grains such as barley, rye, corn, and rice.

Economic Profit and Revenue

A firm's goal is to maximize *economic profit*, which is equal to total revenue minus total cost. Total cost is the *opportunity cost* of production, which includes *normal profit*, the return that the entrepreneur can expect to receive on the average in an alternative business. (See Chapter 9, p. 199.)

A firm's **total revenue** equals the price of its output multiplied by the number of units of output sold (price × quantity). **Marginal revenue** is the change in total revenue that results from a one-unit increase in the quantity sold. Marginal revenue is calculated by dividing the change in total revenue by the change in the quantity sold.

Figure 11.1 illustrates these revenue concepts. Cindy's Sweaters is one of a thousand such small firms. Demand and supply in the sweater market determine the price of a sweater. Cindy must take this price. Cindy's Sweaters cannot influence the price by its own actions, so the price remains constant when Cindy changes the quantity of sweaters produced.

The table shows three different quantities of sweaters produced. As the quantity varies, the price remains constant—in this example, at $25 a sweater. Total revenue is equal to the price multiplied by the quantity sold. For example, if Cindy sells 8 sweaters, total revenue is 8 × $25, which equals $200.

Marginal revenue is the change in total revenue resulting from a one-unit change in quantity. For example, when the quantity sold increases from 8 to 9, total revenue increases from $200 to $225, so marginal

FIGURE 11.1

Demand, Price, and Revenue in Perfect Competition

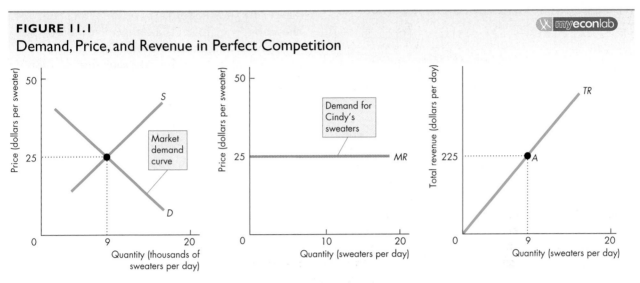

(a) Sweater market

(b) Cindy's marginal revenue

(c) Cindy's total revenue

Quantity sold (Q) (sweaters per day)	Price (P) (dollars per sweater)	Total revenue (TR = P × Q) (dollars)	Marginal revenue (MR = ΔTR/ΔQ) (dollars per additional sweater)
8	25	200	
			25
9	25	225	
			25
10	25	250	

Market demand and supply determine the market price. In part (a), the market price is $25 a sweater and 9,000 sweaters are bought and sold. The demand for Cindy's Sweaters is perfectly elastic at the market price of $25 a sweater. The table calculates total revenue and marginal revenue. Part (b) shows Cindy's Sweaters' marginal revenue curve (MR). This curve is also the demand curve for Cindy's sweaters. Part (c) shows Cindy's total revenue curve (TR). Point A corresponds to the second row of the table.

revenue is $25 a sweater. (Notice that in the table, marginal revenue appears *between* the lines for the quantities sold to remind you that marginal revenue results from the *change* in the quantity sold.)

Because the price remains constant when the quantity sold changes, the change in total revenue resulting from a one-unit increase in the quantity sold equals price. Therefore in perfect competition, marginal revenue equals price.

Figure 11.1(b) shows Cindy's marginal revenue curve (MR). This curve tells us the change in total revenue that results from selling one more sweater. This curve is also the demand curve for Cindy's sweaters. The firm, being a price taker, can sell any quantity it chooses at the market price. The firm faces a perfectly elastic demand for its output.

The total revenue curve (TR) in Fig. 11.1(c) shows the total revenue at each quantity sold. For example, if Cindy sells 9 sweaters, total revenue is $225 (point A).

Because each additional sweater sold brings in a constant amount—$25—the total revenue curve is an upward-sloping straight line.

1 Why is a firm in perfect competition a price taker?

2 In perfect competition, what is the relationship between the demand for the firm's output and the market demand?

3 In perfect competition, why is a firm's marginal revenue curve also the demand curve for the firm's output?

4 Why is the total revenue curve in perfect competition an upward-sloping straight line?

Study Plan 11.1

The Firm's Decisions in Perfect Competition

FIRMS IN A PERFECTLY COMPETITIVE INDUSTRY face a given market price and have the revenue curves that you've studied. These revenue curves summarize the market constraint faced by a perfectly competitive firm.

Firms also face a technology constraint, which is described by the product curves (total product, average product, and marginal product) that you studied in Chapter 10. The technology available to the firm determines its costs, which are described by the cost curves (total cost, average cost, and marginal cost) that you also studied in Chapter 10.

The task of the competitive firm is to make the maximum economic profit possible, given the constraints it faces. To achieve this objective, a firm must make four key decisions: two in the short run and two in the long run.

Short-Run Decisions The *short run* is a time frame in which each firm has a given plant and the number of firms in the industry is fixed. But many things can change in the short run, and the firm must react to these changes. For example, the price for which the firm can sell its output might have a seasonal fluctuation, or it might fluctuate with general business conditions. The firm must react to such short-run price fluctuations and decide

1. Whether to produce or to shut down
2. If the decision is to produce, what quantity to produce

Long-Run Decisions The *long run* is a time frame in which each firm can change the size of its plant and decide whether to leave the industry. Other firms can decide whether to enter the industry. So in the long run, both the plant size of each firm and the number of firms in the industry can change. Also in the long run, the constraints that firms face can change. For example, the demand for the good can permanently fall, or a technological advance can change the industry's costs. The firm must react to such long-run changes and decide

1. Whether to increase or decrease its plant size
2. Whether to stay in an industry or leave it

The Firm and the Industry in the Short Run and the Long Run To study a competitive industry, we begin by looking at an individual firm's short-run decisions. We then see how the short-run decisions of all firms in a competitive industry combine to determine the industry price, output, and economic profit. We then turn to the long run and study the effects of long-run decisions on the industry price, output, and economic profit. All the decisions we study are driven by the pursuit of a single objective: maximization of economic profit.

Profit-Maximizing Output

A perfectly competitive firm maximizes economic profit by choosing its output level. One way of finding the profit-maximizing output is to study a firm's total revenue and total cost curves and find the output level at which total revenue exceeds total cost by the largest amount. Figure 11.2 shows how to do this for Cindy's Sweaters. The table lists Cindy's total revenue and total cost at different outputs, and part (a) of the figure shows Cindy's total revenue and total cost curves. These curves are graphs of the numbers shown in the first three columns of the table. The total revenue curve (*TR*) is the same as that in Fig. 11.1(c). The total cost curve (*TC*) is similar to the one that you met in Chapter 10: As output increases, so does total cost.

Economic profit equals total revenue minus total cost. The fourth column of the table in Fig. 11.2 shows Cindy's economic profit, and part (b) of the figure illustrates these numbers as Cindy's profit curve. This curve shows that Cindy makes an economic profit at outputs between 4 and 12 sweaters a day. At outputs less than 4 sweaters a day, Cindy incurs an economic loss. She also incurs an economic loss if output exceeds 12 sweaters a day. At outputs of 4 sweaters and 12 sweaters a day, total cost equals total revenue and Cindy's economic profit is zero. An output at which total cost equals total revenue is called a *break-even point*. The firm's economic profit at a break-even point is zero. But because normal profit is part of total cost, a firm makes normal profit at a break-even point. That is, at the break-even point, the entrepreneur makes an income equal to the best alternative return forgone.

Notice the relationship between the total revenue, total cost, and profit curves. Economic profit is measured by the vertical distance between the total

FIGURE 11.2

Total Revenue, Total Cost, and Economic Profit

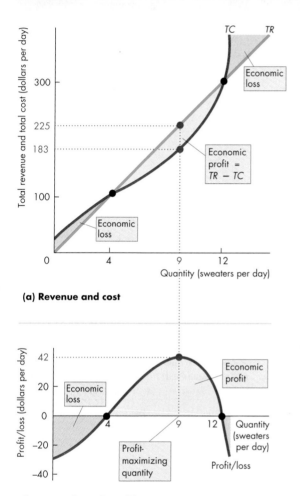

(a) Revenue and cost

Quantity (Q) (sweaters per day)	Total revenue (TR) (dollars)	Total cost (TC) (dollars)	Economic profit (TR – TC) (dollars)
0	0	22	–22
1	25	45	–20
2	50	66	–16
3	75	85	–10
4	100	100	0
5	125	114	11
6	150	126	24
7	175	141	34
8	200	160	40
9	225	183	42
10	250	210	40
11	275	245	30
12	300	300	0
13	325	360	–35

(b) Economic profit and loss

The table lists Cindy's total revenue, total cost, and economic profit. Part (a) graphs the total revenue and total cost curves. The height of the blue area between the total cost and total revenue curves in part (a) is economic profit. Cindy's Sweaters makes maximum economic profit, $42 a day ($225 – $183), when it produces 9 sweaters. At outputs of 4 and 12 sweaters a day, Cindy makes zero economic profit—these are break-even points. At outputs less than 4 and greater than 12 sweaters a day, Cindy incurs an economic loss. In part (b), Cindy's profit curve is at its highest when economic profit is at a maximum and cuts the horizontal axis at the break-even points.

revenue and total cost curves. When the total revenue curve in part (a) is above the total cost curve, between 4 and 12 sweaters, the firm is making an economic profit and the profit curve in Fig. 11.2(b) is above the horizontal axis. At the break-even points, where the total cost and total revenue curves intersect, the profit curve intersects the horizontal axis. The profit curve is at its highest when the distance between TR and TC is greatest. In this example, profit maximization occurs at an output of 9 sweaters a day. At this output, Cindy's economic profit is $42 a day.

Marginal Analysis

Another way of finding the profit-maximizing output is to use *marginal analysis* and compare marginal revenue, *MR,* with marginal cost, *MC.* As output increases, marginal revenue remains constant but marginal cost changes. At small output levels, marginal cost decreases, but it eventually increases. So where the marginal cost curve intersects the marginal revenue curve, marginal cost is rising.

If marginal revenue exceeds marginal cost (if *MR > MC*), the extra revenue from selling one more unit exceeds the extra cost incurred to produce it. The firm makes an economic profit on the marginal unit, so economic profit increases if output *increases*. If marginal revenue is less than marginal cost (if *MR < MC*), the extra revenue from selling one more unit is less than the extra cost incurred to produce it. The firm incurs an economic loss on the marginal unit, so its economic profit decreases if output increases and its economic profit increases if output *decreases.*

If marginal revenue equals marginal cost (if *MR = MC*), economic profit is maximized. The rule *MR = MC* is an example of marginal analysis. Let's check that this rule works to find the profit-maximizing output by returning to Cindy's Sweaters.

Look at Fig. 11.3. The table records Cindy's marginal revenue and marginal cost. Marginal revenue is a constant $25 a sweater. Over the range of outputs shown in the table, marginal cost increases from $19 a sweater to $35 a sweater.

Focus on the highlighted rows of the table. If Cindy increases output from 8 sweaters to 9 sweaters, marginal revenue is $25 and marginal cost is $23. Because marginal revenue exceeds marginal cost, economic profit increases. The last column of the table shows that economic profit increases from $40 to $42, an increase of $2. This economic profit from the ninth sweater is shown as the blue area in the figure.

If Cindy increases output from 9 sweaters to 10 sweaters, marginal revenue is still $25 but marginal cost is $27. Because marginal revenue is less than marginal cost, economic profit decreases. The last column of the table shows that economic profit decreases from $42 to $40. This loss from the tenth sweater is shown as the red area in the figure.

Cindy maximizes economic profit by producing 9 sweaters a day, the quantity at which marginal revenue equals marginal cost.

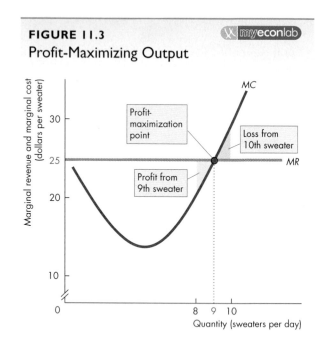

FIGURE 11.3   myeconlab
Profit-Maximizing Output

Quantity (Q) (sweaters per day)	Total revenue (TR) (dollars)	Marginal revenue (MR) (dollars per additional sweater)	Total cost (TC) (dollars)	Marginal cost (MC) (dollars per additional sweater)	Economic profit (TR − TC) (dollars)
7	175		141		34
		 25		 19	
8	200		160		40
		 25		 23	
9	225		183		42
		 25		 27	
10	250		210		40
		 25		 35	
11	275		245		30

Profit is maximized if marginal revenue equals marginal cost. If output increases from 8 to 9 sweaters, marginal cost is $23, which is less than the marginal revenue of $25. If output increases from 9 to 10 sweaters, marginal cost is $27, which exceeds the marginal revenue of $25. Marginal cost and marginal revenue are equal when Cindy produces 9 sweaters a day. If marginal revenue exceeds marginal cost, an increase in output increases economic profit. If marginal revenue is less than marginal cost, an increase in output decreases economic profit. If marginal revenue equals marginal cost, economic profit is maximized.

Profits and Losses in the Short Run

In short-run equilibrium, although the firm produces the profit-maximizing output, it does not necessarily end up making an economic profit. It might do so, but it might alternatively break even (earn a normal profit) or incur an economic loss. To determine which of these outcomes occurs, we compare the firm's total revenue and total cost or, equivalently, we compare price with average total cost. If price equals average total cost, a firm breaks even—makes normal profit. If price exceeds average total cost, a firm makes an economic profit. If price is less than average total cost, a firm incurs an economic loss. Figure 11.4 shows these three possible short-run profit outcomes.

Three Possible Profit Outcomes In Fig. 11.4(a), the price of a sweater is $20. Cindy's profit-maximizing output is 8 sweaters a day. Average total cost is $20 a sweater, so Cindy breaks even and makes normal profit (zero economic profit).

In Fig. 11.4(b), the price of a sweater is $25. Profit is maximized when output is 9 sweaters a day. The average total cost of a sweater is $20.33. Price

exceeds average total cost (ATC), so Cindy makes an economic profit. This economic profit is $42 a day. It is made up of $4.67 per sweater ($25.00 – $20.33) multiplied by the number of sweaters produced ($4.67 × 9 = $42). The blue rectangle shows this economic profit. The height of that rectangle is profit per sweater, $4.67, and the length is the quantity of sweaters produced, 9 a day, so the area of the rectangle is Cindy's economic profit of $42 a day.

In Fig. 11.4(c), the price of a sweater is $17. The average total cost of a sweater is $20.14. Price is less than average total cost, so Cindy incurs an economic loss. Price and marginal revenue are $17 a sweater, and the profit-maximizing (in this case, loss-minimizing) output is 7 sweaters a day. Cindy's total revenue is $119 a day (7 × $17). The economic loss is $3.14 per sweater ($20.14 – $17.00). This loss per sweater multiplied by the number of sweaters produced is $22 ($3.14 × 7 = $22). The red rectangle shows this economic loss. The height of that rectangle is economic loss per sweater, $3.14, and the length is the quantity of sweaters produced, 7 a day, so the area of the rectangle is Cindy's economic loss of $22 a day.

FIGURE 11.4   myeconlab
Three Possible Profit Outcomes in the Short Run

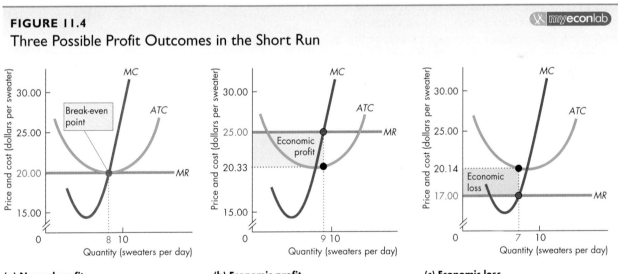

(a) Normal profit   (b) Economic profit   (c) Economic loss

In the short run, the firm might break even (make a normal profit), make an economic profit, or incur an economic loss. If the price equals minimum average total cost, the firm breaks even and makes a normal profit (part a). If the price exceeds the average total cost of producing the profit-

maximizing output, the firm makes an economic profit—the blue rectangle in part (b). If the price is below minimum average total cost, the firm incurs an economic loss—the red rectangle in part (c).

The Firm's Short-Run Supply Curve

A perfectly competitive firm's short-run supply curve shows how the firm's profit-maximizing output varies as the market price varies, other things remaining the same. Figure 11.5 shows how to derive Cindy's supply curve. Part (a) shows Cindy's Sweaters' marginal cost and average variable cost curves, and part (b) shows its supply curve. There is a direct link between the marginal cost and average variable cost curves and the supply curve. Let's see what that link is.

Temporary Plant Shutdown In the short run, a firm cannot avoid incurring its fixed cost. But the firm can avoid variable costs by temporarily laying off its workers and shutting down. If a firm shuts down, it produces no output and it incurs a loss equal to total fixed cost. This loss is the largest that a firm needs to incur. A firm shuts down if the price falls below minimum average variable cost. The **shutdown point** is the output and price at which the firm just covers its total variable cost—point T in Fig. 11.5(a). If the price is $17, the marginal revenue curve is MR_0 and the profit-maximizing output is 7 sweaters a day at point T. But both price and average variable cost equal $17, so Cindy's total revenue equals total variable cost. Cindy incurs an economic loss equal to total fixed cost. At a price below $17, no matter what quantity Cindy produces, average *variable* cost exceeds price and the firm's loss exceeds total fixed cost. At a price below $17, the firm shuts down temporarily.

The Short-Run Supply Curve If the price is above minimum average variable cost, Cindy maximizes profit by producing the output at which marginal cost equals price. We can determine the quantity produced at each price from the marginal cost curve. At a price of $25, the marginal revenue curve is MR_1 and Cindy maximizes profit by producing 9 sweaters. At a price of $31, the marginal revenue curve is MR_2 and Cindy produces 10 sweaters.

Cindy's short-run supply curve, shown in Fig. 11.5(b), has two separate parts: First, at prices that exceed minimum average variable cost, the supply curve is the same as the marginal cost curve above the shutdown point (T). Second, at prices below minimum average variable cost, Cindy shuts down and produces nothing. Its supply curve runs along the vertical axis. At a price of $17, Cindy is indifferent between shutting down and producing 7 sweaters a day. Either way, her loss is the same.

FIGURE 11.5
A Firm's Supply Curve

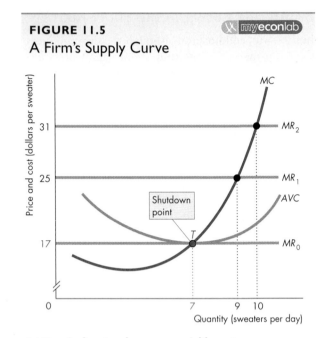

(a) Marginal cost and average variable cost

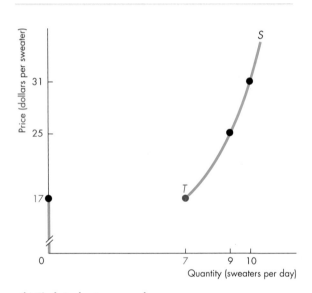

(b) Cindy's short-run supply curve

Part (a) shows Cindy's profit-maximizing output at various market prices. For example, at $25 a sweater, Cindy produces 9 sweaters. Point T is Cindy's shutdown point. At prices below $17, Cindy produces nothing. Part (b) shows Cindy's supply curve. It is made up of the marginal cost curve (part a) at all points above minimum average variable cost and the vertical axis at all prices below minimum average variable cost.

Short-Run Industry Supply Curve

The **short-run industry supply curve** shows the quantity supplied by the industry at each price when the plant size of each firm and the number of firms remain constant. The quantity supplied by the industry at a given price is the sum of the quantities supplied by all firms in the industry at that price.

Figure 11.6 shows the supply curve for the competitive sweater industry. In this example, the industry consists of 1,000 firms exactly like Cindy's Sweaters. At each price, the quantity supplied by the industry is 1,000 times the quantity supplied by a single firm.

The table in Fig. 11.6 shows the firm's and the industry's supply schedule and how the industry supply curve is constructed. At prices below $17, every firm in the industry shuts down; the quantity supplied by the industry is zero. At a price of $17, each firm is indifferent between shutting down and producing nothing or operating and producing 7 sweaters a day. Some firms will shut down, and others will supply 7 sweaters a day. The quantity supplied by each firm is *either* 0 or 7 sweaters, but the quantity supplied by the industry is *between* 0 (all firms shut down) and 7,000 (all firms produce 7 sweaters a day each).

To construct the industry supply curve, we sum the quantities supplied by the individual firms. Each of the 1,000 firms in the industry has a supply schedule like Cindy's. At prices below $17, the industry supply curve runs along the price axis. At a price of $17, the industry supply curve is horizontal—supply is perfectly elastic. As the price rises above $17, each firm increases its quantity supplied and the quantity supplied by the industry increases by 1,000 times that of each firm.

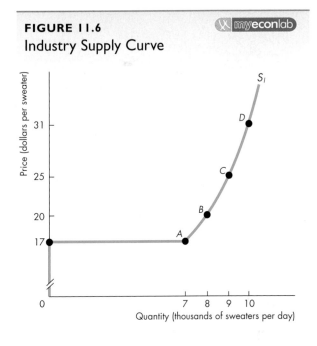

FIGURE 11.6   myeconlab

Industry Supply Curve

	Price (dollars per sweater)	Quantity supplied by Cindy's Sweaters (sweaters per day)	Quantity supplied by industry (sweaters per day)
A	17	0 or 7	0 to 7,000
B	20	8	8,000
C	25	9	9,000
D	31	10	10,000

The industry supply schedule is the sum of the supply schedules of all individual firms. An industry that consists of 1,000 identical firms has a supply schedule similar to that of the individual firm, but the quantity supplied by the industry is 1,000 times as large as that of the individual firm (see the table). The industry supply curve is S_I. Points A, B, C, and D correspond to the rows of the table. At the shutdown price of $17, each firm produces either 0 or 7 sweaters per day. The industry supply is perfectly elastic at the shutdown price.

So far, we have studied a single firm in isolation. We have seen that the firm's actions depend on the market price, which the firm takes as given. But how is the market price determined? Let's find out.

Output, Price, and Profit in Perfect Competition

TO DETERMINE THE MARKET PRICE AND THE quantity bought and sold in a perfectly competitive market, we need to study how market demand and market supply interact. We begin this process by studying a perfectly competitive market in the short run when the number of firms is fixed and each firm has a given plant size.

Short-Run Equilibrium

Industry demand and supply determine the market price and industry output. Figure 11.7(a) shows a short-run equilibrium. The supply curve S is the same as S_I in Fig. 11.6. If demand is shown by the demand curve D_1, the equilibrium price is $20. Each firm takes this price as given and produces its profit-maximizing output, which is 8 sweaters a day. Because the industry has 1,000 firms, industry output is 8,000 sweaters a day.

A Change in Demand

Changes in demand bring changes to short-run industry equilibrium. Figure 11.7(b) shows these changes.

If demand increases, the demand curve shifts rightward to D_2. The price rises to $25. At this price, each firm maximizes profit by increasing output. The new output is 9 sweaters a day for each firm and 9,000 sweaters a day for the industry.

If demand decreases, the demand curve shifts leftward to D_3. The price now falls to $17. At this price, each firm maximizes profit by decreasing its output. The new output is 7 sweaters a day for each firm and 7,000 sweaters a day for the industry.

If the demand curve shifts farther leftward than D_3, the price remains constant at $17 because the industry supply curve is horizontal at that price. Some firms continue to produce 7 sweaters a day, and others temporarily shut down. Firms are indifferent between these two activities, and whichever they choose, they incur an economic loss equal to total fixed cost. The number of firms continuing to produce is just enough to satisfy the market demand at a price of $17.

FIGURE 11.7
Short-Run Equilibrium

myeconlab

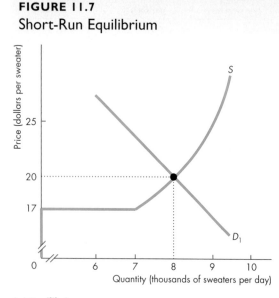

(a) Equilibrium

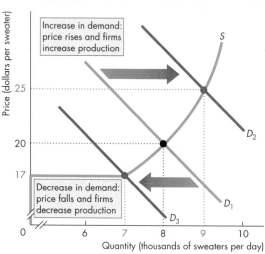

(b) Change in equilibrium

In part (a), the industry supply curve is S. Demand is D_1, and the price is $20. At this price, each firm produces 8 sweaters a day and the industry produces 8,000 sweaters a day. In part (b), when demand increases to D_2, the price rises to $25 and

each firm increases its output to 9 sweaters a day. Industry output is 9,000 sweaters a day. When demand decreases to D_3, the price falls to $17 and each firm decreases its output to 7 sweaters a day. Industry output is 7,000 sweaters a day.

Long-Run Adjustments

In short-run equilibrium, a firm might make an economic profit, incur an economic loss, or break even (make normal profit). Although each of these three situations is a short-run equilibrium, only one of them is a long-run equilibrium. To see why, we need to examine the forces at work in a competitive industry in the long run.

In the long run, an industry adjusts in two ways:

- Entry and exit
- Changes in plant size

Let's look first at entry and exit.

Entry and Exit

In the long run, firms respond to economic profit and economic loss by either entering or exiting an industry. Firms enter an industry in which firms are making an economic profit, and firms exit an industry in which firms are incurring an economic loss. Temporary economic profit and temporary economic loss do not trigger entry and exit. But the prospect of persistent economic profit or loss does.

Entry and exit influence price, the quantity produced, and economic profit. The immediate effect of these decisions is to shift the industry supply curve. If more firms enter an industry, supply increases and the industry supply curve shifts rightward. If firms exit an industry, supply decreases and the industry supply curve shifts leftward.

Let's see what happens when new firms enter an industry.

The Effects of Entry Figure 11.8 shows the effects of entry. Suppose that all the firms in this industry have cost curves like those in Fig. 11.4. At any price greater than $20, firms make an economic profit. At any price less than $20, firms incur an economic loss. And at a price of $20, firms make zero economic profit. Also suppose that the demand curve for sweaters is D. If the industry supply curve is S_1, the market price is $23, and 7,000 sweaters a day are produced. Firms in the industry make an economic profit. This economic profit is a signal for new firms to enter the industry.

As these events unfold, supply increases and the industry supply curve shifts rightward to S_0. With the greater supply and unchanged demand, the market price falls from $23 to $20 a sweater and the quantity

produced by the industry increases from 7,000 to 8,000 sweaters a day.

Industry output increases, but Cindy's Sweaters, like each other firm in the industry, moves down its supply curve and *decreases* output! Because the price falls, each firm produces less. But because the number of firms in the industry increases, the industry as a whole produces more.

Because price falls, each firm's economic profit decreases. When the price falls to $20, economic profit disappears and each firm makes a normal profit.

You have just discovered a key proposition:

As new firms enter an industry, the price falls and the economic profit of each existing firm decreases.

An example of this process occurred during the 1980s in the personal computer industry. When IBM introduced its first PC, there was little competition

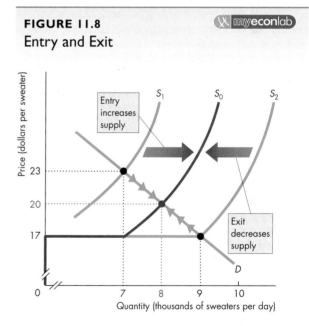

FIGURE 11.8
Entry and Exit

When new firms enter the sweater industry, the industry supply curve shifts rightward, from S_1 to S_0. The equilibrium price falls from $23 to $20, and the quantity produced increases from 7,000 to 8,000 sweaters.

When firms exit the sweater industry, the industry supply curve shifts leftward, from S_2 to S_0. The equilibrium price rises from $17 to $20, and the quantity produced decreases from 9,000 to 8,000 sweaters.

and the price of a PC gave IBM a big profit. But new firms such as Compaq, NEC, Dell, and a host of others entered the industry with machines that were technologically identical to IBM's. In fact, they were so similar that they came to be called "clones." The massive wave of entry into the personal computer industry shifted the supply curve rightward and lowered the price and the economic profit.

Let's now look at the effects of exit.

The Effects of Exit Figure 11.8 also shows the effects of exit. Suppose that firm's costs and market demand are the same as before. But now suppose the supply curve is S_2. The market price is $17, and 9,000 sweaters a day are produced. Firms in the industry now incur an economic loss. This economic loss is a signal for some firms to exit the industry. As firms exit, the industry supply curve shifts leftward to S_0. With the decrease in supply, industry output decreases from 9,000 to 8,000 sweaters and the price rises from $17 to $20.

As the price rises, Cindy's Sweaters, like each other firm in the industry, moves up along its supply curve and increases output. That is, for each firm that remains in the industry, the profit-maximizing output increases. Because the price rises and each firm sells more, economic loss decreases. When the price rises to $20, each firm makes a normal profit.

You've now discovered a second key proposition:

As firms leave an industry, the price rises and the economic loss of each remaining firm decreases.

The same PC industry that saw a large amount of entry during the 1980s and 1990s is now beginning to see some exit. In 2001, IBM, the firm that first launched the PC, announced that it would no longer produce PCs. The intense competition from Compaq, NEC, Dell, and many others that entered the industry following IBM's lead has lowered the price and eliminated the economic profit on PCs. So IBM will now concentrate on servers and other parts of the computer market.

IBM exited the PC market because it was incurring losses on that line of business. Its exit decreased supply and made it possible for the remaining firms in the industry to earn normal profit.

You've now seen how economic profits induce entry, which in turn lowers profits. And you've seen how economic losses induce exit, which in turn eliminates losses. Let's now look at changes in plant size.

Changes in Plant Size

A firm changes its plant size if, by doing so, it can lower its costs and increase its economic profit. You can probably think of lots of examples of firms that have changed their plant size.

One example that has almost certainly happened near your campus in recent years is a change in the plant size of Kinko's or similar copy shops. Another is the number of FedEx vans that you see on the streets and highways. And another is the number of square metres of retail space devoted to selling computers and video games. These are examples of firms increasing their plant size to seek larger profits.

There are also many examples of firms that have decreased their plant size to avoid economic losses. One of these is Country Style Donuts. As competition from other coffee shops became tougher, Country Style Donuts closed 45 shops across Canada in late 2002. Many firms have scaled back in a process called *downsizing* in recent years.

Figure 11.9 shows a situation in which Cindy's Sweaters can increase its profit by increasing its plant size. With its current plant, Cindy's marginal cost curve is MC_0, and its short-run average total cost curve is $SRAC_0$. The market price is $25 a sweater, so Cindy's marginal revenue curve is MR_0, and Cindy maximizes profit by producing 6 sweaters a day.

Cindy's Sweaters' long-run average cost curve is *LRAC*. By increasing its plant size—installing more knitting machines—Cindy's Sweaters can move along its long-run average cost curve. As Cindy's Sweaters increases its plant size, its short-run marginal cost curve shifts rightward.

Recall that a firm's short-run supply curve is linked to its marginal cost curve. As Cindy's marginal cost curve shifts rightward, so does its supply curve. If Cindy's Sweaters and the other firms in the industry increase their plants, the short-run industry supply curve shifts rightward. With a given market demand for sweaters, the market price falls. The fall in the market price limits the extent to which Cindy's can profit from increasing its plant size.

Figure 11.9 also shows Cindy's Sweaters in a long-run competitive equilibrium. This situation arises when the market price has fallen to $20 a sweater. Marginal revenue is MR_1, and Cindy maximizes profit by producing 8 sweaters a day. In this situation, Cindy cannot increase her profit by changing the plant size. Cindy is producing at minimum long-run average cost (point *M* on *LRAC*).

FIGURE 11.9
Plant Size and Long-Run Equilibrium

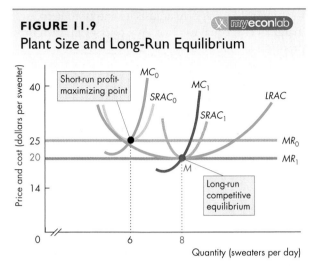

Initially, Cindy's plant has marginal cost curve MC_0 and short-run average total cost curve $SRAC_0$. The market price is $25 a sweater, and Cindy's marginal revenue is MR_0. The short-run profit-maximizing quantity is 6 sweaters a day. Cindy can increase profit by increasing the plant size.

If all firms in the sweater industry increase their plant sizes, the short-run industry supply increases and the market price falls. In long-run equilibrium, a firm operates with the plant size that minimizes its average cost. Here, Cindy's Sweaters operates the plant with short-run marginal cost MC_1 and short-run average cost $SRAC_1$. Cindy's is also on its long-run average cost curve $LRAC$ and produces at point M. Its output is 8 sweaters a day, and its average total cost equals the price of a sweater: $20.

Because Cindy's Sweaters is producing at minimum long-run average cost, it has no incentive to change its plant size. Either a bigger plant or a smaller plant has a higher long-run average cost. If Fig. 11.9 describes the situation of all firms in the sweater industry, the industry is in long-run equilibrium. No firm has an incentive to change its plant size. Also, because each firm is making zero economic profit (normal profit), no firm has an incentive to enter the industry or to leave it.

Long-Run Equilibrium

Long-run equilibrium occurs in a competitive industry when economic profit is zero (when firms earn normal profit). If the firms in a competitive industry are making an economic profit, new firms enter the industry.

If firms can lower their costs by increasing their plant size, they expand. Each of these actions increases the industry supply, shifts the industry supply curve rightward, lowers the price, and decreases economic profit.

Firms continue to enter and profit decreases as long as firms in the industry are making economic profits. When economic profit has been eliminated, firms stop entering the industry. And when firms are operating with the least-cost plant size, they stop expanding.

If the firms in a competitive industry are incurring an economic loss, some firms exit the industry. If firms can lower their costs by decreasing their plant size, they downsize. Each of these actions decreases industry supply, shifts the industry supply curve leftward, raises the price, and decreases economic loss.

Firms continue to exit and economic loss continues to decrease as long as firms in the industry are incurring economic losses. When economic loss has been eliminated, firms stop exiting the industry. And when firms are operating with the least-cost plant size, they stop downsizing.

So in long-run equilibrium in a competitive industry, firms neither enter nor exit the industry and old firms neither expand nor downsize. Each firm earns normal profit.

REVIEW QUIZ

1 When the market demand for the good decreases, explain how the price of the good and the output of each firm in perfect competition changes in the short run.
2 If the firms in a competitive industry earn an economic profit, what happens to supply, price, output, and economic profit in the long run?
3 If the firms in a competitive industry incur an economic loss, what happens to supply, price, output, and economic profit in the long run?

myeconlab **Study Plan 11.3**

You've seen how a competitive industry adjusts towards its long-run equilibrium. But a competitive industry is rarely *in* a state of long-run equilibrium. A competitive industry is constantly and restlessly evolving towards such an equilibrium. But the constraints that firms in an industry face are constantly changing. The two most persistent sources of change are in tastes and technology. Let's see how a competitive industry reacts to such changes.

Changing Tastes and Advancing Technology

INCREASED AWARENESS OF THE HEALTH HAZARDS of smoking has caused a decrease in the demand for tobacco and cigarettes. The development of inexpensive car and air transportation has caused a huge decrease in the demand for long-distance trains and buses. Solid-state electronics have caused a large decrease in the demand for TV and radio repair. The development of good-quality inexpensive clothing has decreased the demand for sewing machines. What happens in a competitive industry when there is a permanent decrease in the demand for its products?

The development of the microwave oven has produced an enormous increase in demand for paper, glass, and plastic cooking utensils and for plastic wrap. The widespread use of the personal computer has brought a huge increase in the demand for CD-Rs. What happens in a competitive industry when the demand for its output increases?

Advances in technology are constantly lowering the costs of production. New bio-technologies have dramatically lowered the costs of producing many food and pharmaceutical products. New electronic technologies have lowered the cost of producing just about every good and service. What happens in a competitive industry when technological change lowers its production costs?

Let's use the theory of perfect competition to answer these questions.

A Permanent Change in Demand

Figure 11.10(a) shows a competitive industry that initially is in long-run equilibrium. The industry demand curve is D_0, the industry supply curve is S_0, the market price is P_0, and industry output is Q_0. Figure 11.10(b) shows a single firm in this initial long-run equilibrium. The firm produces q_0 and makes a normal profit—zero economic profit.

Now suppose that demand decreases and the demand curve shifts leftward to D_1, as shown in Fig. 11.10(a). The price falls to P_1, and the quantity supplied by the industry decreases from Q_0 to Q_1 as the industry slides down its short-run supply curve S_0. Figure 11.10(b) shows the situation facing a firm. Price is now below the firm's minimum average total cost, so the firm incurs an economic loss. But to keep its loss

to a minimum, the firm adjusts its output to keep marginal cost equal to price. At a price of P_1, each firm produces an output of q_1.

The industry is now in short-run equilibrium but not long-run equilibrium. It is in short-run equilibrium because each firm is maximizing profit. But it is not in long-run equilibrium because each firm is incurring an economic loss—its average total cost exceeds the market price.

The economic loss is a signal for some firms to leave the industry. As they do so, short-run industry supply decreases and the supply curve gradually shifts leftward. As industry supply decreases, the price rises. At each higher price, a firm's profit-maximizing output is greater, so the firms remaining in the industry increase their output as the price rises. Each firm slides up its marginal cost or supply curve in Fig. 11.10(b). That is, as firms exit the industry, industry output decreases but the output of the firms that remain in the industry increases.

Eventually, enough firms leave the industry for the industry supply curve to have shifted leftward to S_1 in Fig. 11.10(a). At this time, the price has returned to its original level, P_0. At this price, the firms remaining in the industry produce q_0, the same quantity that they produced before the decrease in demand. Because firms are now making normal profit (zero economic profit), no firm wants to enter or exit the industry. The industry supply curve remains at S_1, and industry output is Q_2. The industry is again in long-run equilibrium.

The difference between the initial long-run equilibrium and the final long-run equilibrium is the number of firms in the industry. A permanent decrease in demand has decreased the number of firms. Each remaining firm produces the same output in the new long-run equilibrium as it did initially and earns a normal profit. In the process of moving from the initial equilibrium to the new one, firms incur economic losses.

We've just worked out how a competitive industry responds to a permanent *decrease* in demand. A permanent increase in demand triggers a similar response, except in the opposite direction. The increase in demand brings a higher price, economic profit, and entry. Entry increases industry supply and eventually the price falls to its original level and economic profit returns to normal profit.

The demand for Internet service increased permanently during the 1990s and huge profit opportunities arose in this industry. The result was

FIGURE 11.10
A Decrease in Demand

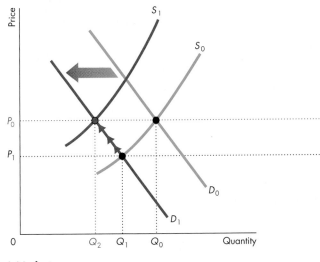

(a) Industry

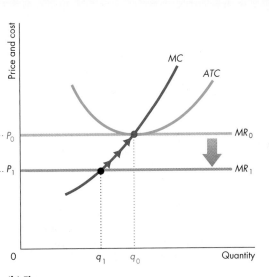

(b) Firm

An industry starts out in long-run competitive equilibrium. Part (a) shows the industry demand curve D_0, the industry supply curve S_0, the equilibrium quantity Q_0, and the market price P_0. Each firm sells its output at price P_0, so its marginal revenue curve is MR_0 in part (b). Each firm produces q_0 and makes a normal profit. Demand decreases permanently from D_0 to D_1 (part a). The equilibrium price falls to P_1, each firm decreases its output to q_1 (part b), and industry output decreases to Q_1 (part a).

In this new situation, firms incur economic losses and some firms leave the industry. As they do so, the industry supply curve gradually shifts leftward, from S_0 to S_1. This shift gradually raises the market price from P_1 back to P_0. Once the price has returned to P_0, each firm makes a normal profit. Firms have no further incentive to leave the industry. Each firm produces q_0, and industry output is Q_2.

a massive rate of entry of Internet service providers. The process of competition and change in the Internet service industry is similar to what we have just studied (but with an increase in demand rather than a decrease in demand).

We've now studied the effects of a permanent change in demand for a good. To study these effects, we began and ended in a long-run equilibrium and examined the process that takes a market from one equilibrium to another. It is this process, not the equilibrium points, that describes the real world.

One feature of the predictions that we have just generated seems odd: In the long run, regardless of whether demand increases or decreases, the price returns to its original level. Is this outcome inevitable? In fact, it is not. It is possible for the long-run equilibrium price to remain the same, rise, or fall.

External Economies and Diseconomies

The change in the long-run equilibrium price depends on external economies and external diseconomies. **External economies** are factors beyond the control of an individual firm that lower the firm's costs as the *industry* output increases. **External diseconomies** are factors outside the control of a firm that raise the firm's costs as industry output increases. With no external economies or external diseconomies, a firm's costs remain constant as the industry output changes.

Figure 11.11 illustrates these three cases and introduces a new supply concept: the long-run industry supply curve.

A **long-run industry supply curve** shows how the quantity supplied by an industry varies as the market price varies after all the possible adjustments have been made, including changes in plant size and the number of firms in the industry.

Figure 11.11(a) shows the case we have just studied—no external economies or diseconomies. The long-run industry supply curve (LS_A) is horizontal. In this case, a permanent increase in demand from D_0 to D_1 has no effect on the price in the long run. The increase in demand brings a temporary increase in price to P_S and in the short run, the quantity increases from Q_0 to Q_S. Entry increases short-run supply from S_0 to S_1, which lowers the price to its original level, P_0, and increases the quantity to Q_1.

Figure 11.11(b) shows the case of external diseconomies. The long-run supply industry curve (LS_B) slopes upward. A permanent increase in demand from D_0 to D_1 increases the price in both the short run and the long run. As in the previous case, the increase in demand brings a temporary increase in price to P_S and in the short run, the quantity increases from Q_0 to Q_S. Entry increases short-run supply from S_0 to S_2, which lowers the price to P_2 and increases the quantity to Q_2.

One source of external diseconomies is congestion. The airline industry provides a good example. With bigger airline industry output, congestion of airports and airspace increases and results in longer delays and extra waiting time for passengers and airplanes. These external diseconomies mean that as the output of air transportation services increases (in the absence of technological advances), average cost increases. As a result, the long-run supply curve is upward sloping. So a permanent increase in demand brings an increase in quantity and a rise in the price. (Industries with external diseconomies might nonetheless have a falling price because technological advances shift the long-run supply curve downward.)

Figure 11.11(c) shows the case of external economies. In this case, the long-run industry supply curve (LS_C) slopes downward. A permanent increase in demand from D_0 to D_1 increases the price in the short run and lowers it in the long run. Again, the increases in demand brings a temporary increase in price to P_S, and in the short run, the quantity increases from Q_0 to Q_S. Entry increases short-run supply from S_0 to S_3, which lowers the price to P_3 and increases the quantity to Q_3.

FIGURE 11.11
Long-Run Changes in Price and Quantity

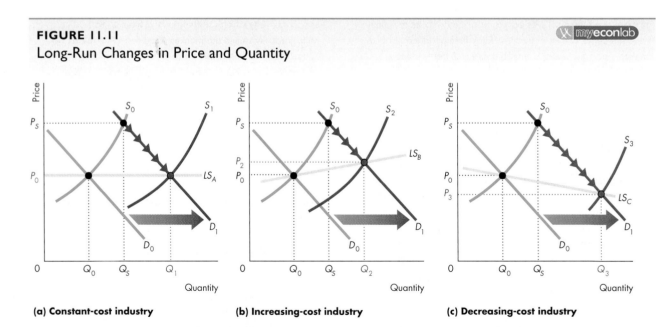

(a) Constant-cost industry   **(b) Increasing-cost industry**   **(c) Decreasing-cost industry**

When demand increases from D_0 to D_1, entry occurs and the industry supply curve gradually shifts rightward from S_0 to S_1. In part (a), the long-run supply curve, LS_A, is horizontal. The quantity increases from Q_0 to Q_1, and the price remains constant at P_0. In part (b), the long-run supply curve is LS_B; the price rises to P_2, and the quantity increases to Q_2. This case occurs in industries with external diseconomies. In part (c), the long-run supply curve is LS_C; the price falls to P_3, and the quantity increases to Q_3. This case occurs in an industry with external economies.

An example of external economies is the growth of specialist support services for an industry as it expands. As farm output increased in the nineteenth and early twentieth centuries, the services available to farmers expanded. New firms specialized in the development and marketing of farm machinery and fertilizers. As a result, average farm costs decreased. Farms enjoyed the benefits of external economies. As a consequence, as the demand for farm products increased, the output increased but the price fell.

Over the long term, the prices of many goods and services have fallen, not because of external economies but because of technological change. Let's now study this influence on a competitive market.

Technological Change

Industries are constantly discovering lower-cost techniques of production. Most cost-saving production techniques cannot be implemented, however, without investing in a new plant and equipment. As a consequence, it takes time for a technological advance to spread through an industry. Some firms whose plants are on the verge of being replaced will be quick to adopt the new technology, while other firms whose plants have recently been replaced will continue to operate with an old technology until they can no longer cover their average variable cost. Once average variable cost cannot be covered, a firm will scrap even a relatively new plant (embodying an old technology) in favour of a plant with a new technology.

New technology allows firms to produce at a lower cost. As a result, as firms adopt a new technology, their cost curves shift downward. With lower costs, firms are willing to supply a given quantity at a lower price or, equivalently, they are willing to supply a larger quantity at a given price. In other words, industry supply increases, and the industry supply curve shifts rightward. With a given demand, the quantity produced increases and the price falls.

Two forces are at work in an industry undergoing technological change. Firms that adopt the new technology make an economic profit. So there is entry by new-technology firms. Firms that stick with the old technology incur economic losses. They either exit the industry or switch to the new technology.

As old-technology firms exit and new-technology firms enter, the price falls and the quantity produced increases. Eventually, the industry arrives at a long-run

equilibrium in which all the firms use the new technology and make a zero economic profit (a normal profit). Because in the long run competition eliminates economic profit, technological change brings only temporary gains to producers. But the lower prices and better products that technological advances bring are permanent gains for consumers.

The process that we've just described is one in which some firms experience economic profits and others experience economic losses. It is a period of dynamic change for an industry. Some firms do well, and others do badly. Often, the process has a geographical dimension—the expanding new-technology firms bring prosperity to what was once the boondocks, and traditional industrial regions decline. Sometimes the new-technology firms are in a foreign country, while the old-technology firms are in the domestic economy. The information revolution of the 1990s produced many examples of changes like these. The computer programming industry, traditionally concentrated in the United States, now flourishes in Canada, the United Kingdom, and India. Television shows and movies, traditionally made in Los Angeles and New York, are now made in large numbers in Toronto and Vancouver.

Technological advances are not confined to the information and entertainment industries. Even milk production is undergoing a major technological change because of genetic engineering.

REVIEW QUIZ

1 Describe the course of events in a competitive industry following a permanent decrease in demand. What happens to output, price, and economic profit in the short run and in the long run?
2 Describe the course of events in a competitive industry following a permanent increase in demand. What happens to output, price, and economic profit in the short run and in the long run?
3 Describe the course of events in a competitive industry following the adoption of a new technology. What happens to output, price, and economic profit in the short run and in the long run?

myeconlab Study Plan 11.4

Competition and Efficiency

A COMPETITIVE INDUSTRY CAN ACHIEVE AN efficient use of resources. You studied efficiency in Chapter 5 using only the concepts of demand, supply, consumer surplus, and producer surplus. But now that you have learned what lies behind the demand and supply curves of a competitive market, you can gain a deeper understanding of how the competitive market achieves efficiency.

Efficient Use of Resources

Recall that resource use is efficient when we produce the goods and services that people value most highly (see Chapter 5, pp. 104–105). If someone can become better off without anyone else becoming worse off, resources are *not* being used efficiently. For example, suppose we produce a computer that no one wants and no one will ever use and at the same time some people are clamouring for more video games. If we produce one computer less and reallocate the unused resources to produce more video games, some people will become better off and no one will be worse off. So the initial resource allocation was inefficient.

In the more technical language that you have learned, resource use is efficient when marginal social benefit equals marginal social cost. In the computer and video games example, the marginal social benefit of video games exceeds the marginal social cost. And the marginal social cost of a computer exceeds its marginal social benefit. So by producing fewer computers and more video games, we move resources towards a higher-valued use.

Choices, Equilibrium, and Efficiency

We can use what you have learned about the decisions made by consumers and competitive firms and market equilibrium to describe an efficient use of resources.

Choices Consumers allocate their budgets to get the most value possible out of them. And we derive a consumer's demand curve by finding how the best budget allocation changes as the price of a good changes. So consumers get the most value out of their resources at all points along the market demand curve, which is also the marginal social benefit curve.

Competitive firms produce the quantity that maximizes profit. And we derive the firm's supply curve by finding the profit-maximizing quantity at each price. So firms get the most value out of their resources at all points along the market supply curve, which is also the marginal social cost curve. (On their supply curves, firms are *technologically efficient*—they get the maximum possible output from given inputs—and *economically efficient*—they combine resources to minimize cost. See Chapter 9, pp. 201–202.)

Equilibrium In competitive equilibrium, the quantity demanded equals the quantity supplied. So the price equals marginal social benefit and marginal social cost. In this situation, the gains from trade between consumers and producers are maximized.

The gains from trade for consumers are measured by *consumer surplus*, which is the area below the demand curve and above the price paid. (See Chapter 5, p. 107.) The gains from trade for producers are measured by *producer surplus*, which is the area above the marginal cost curve and below the price received. (See Chapter 5, p. 109.) The total gains from trade are the sum of consumer surplus and producer surplus.

Efficiency In the absence of external benefits and external costs (see Chapter 5, p. 112 and Chapter 15), when the market for the good or service is in equilibrium resources are being used efficiently. They cannot be reallocated to increase their value.

An Efficient Allocation Figure 11.12 shows an efficient allocation in perfect competition in long-run equilibrium. Part (a) shows the situation of an individual firm and part (b) shows the market. The equilibrium market price is P^*. At that price, each firm earns normal profit (zero economic profit). Each firm has a plant size that enables it to produce at the lowest possible average total cost. In this situation, consumers are as well off as possible because the good cannot be produced at a lower cost and the price equals that least possible cost.

In part (b), consumers are efficient at all points on the market demand curve, $D = MSB$. Producers are efficient at all points on the market supply curve, $S = MSC$. Resources are used efficiently at the quantity Q^* and price P^*. At this point, marginal social benefit equals marginal social cost, and the sum of

FIGURE 11.12
Efficiency of Perfect Competition

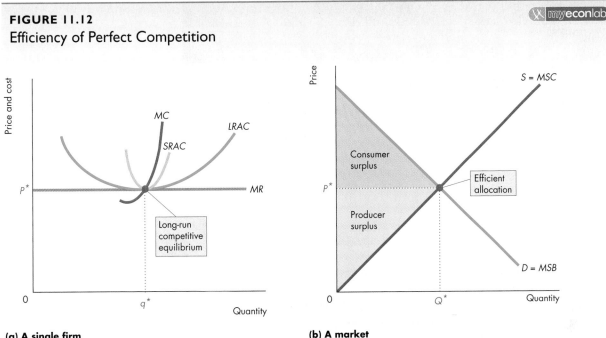

(a) A single firm

(b) A market

In part (a), a firm in perfect competition produces at the lowest possible long-run average total cost at the quantity q^*. In part (b), consumers have made the best available choices and are on the market demand curve and firms are producing at least cost and are on the market supply curve. With no external benefits or external costs, resources are used efficiently at the quantity Q^* and the price P^*. Perfect competition achieves an efficient use of resources.

producer surplus (blue area) and consumer surplus (green area) is maximized.

When firms in perfect competition are away from long-run equilibrium, either entry or exit is taking place and the market is moving towards the situation depicted in Fig. 11.12. But the market is still efficient.

REVIEW QUIZ

1 State the conditions that must be met for resources to be used efficiently.

2 Describe the choices that consumers make and explain why along the market demand curve, consumers are efficient.

3 Describe the choices that producers make and explain why along the market supply curve, producers are efficient.

4 Explain why resources are used efficiently in competitive equilibrium.

myeconlab Study Plan 11.5

As long as marginal social benefit (on the market demand curve) equals marginal social cost (on the market supply curve), the equilibrium in perfect competition is efficient. But it is only in long-run equilibrium that consumers pay the lowest possible price.

◆ You've now completed your study of perfect competition. And *Reading Between the Lines* on pp. 258–259 gives you an opportunity to use what you have learned to understand recent events in the highly competitive maple syrup market.

Although many markets approximate the model of perfect competition, many do not. In Chapter 12, we study markets at the opposite extreme of market power: monopoly. Then, in Chapter 13, we'll study markets that lie between perfect competition and monopoly: monopolistic competition (competition with monopoly elements) and oligopoly (competition among a few producers). When you have completed this study, you'll have a tool kit that will enable you to understand the variety of real-world markets.

Perfect Competition in Maple Syrup

MONTREAL GAZETTE, MARCH 14, 2001

Maple syrup sits unsold in warehouses

A sticky turf war has boiled over in Canada's sugar patch, with farmers and processors feuding over what to do with a glut of maple syrup. . . .

. . . after two bumper crops in a row, producers wonder if it's worth the effort to tap all their trees.

"People naturally aren't encouraged by the prices," said Stanley Holmes, a farmer and maple-syrup producer from Ayer's Cliff who also buys syrup in bulk from neighbouring producers on behalf of Ontario-based processor Delta Foods International.

"Really what they need is less production to get rid of some of this surplus that's hanging over the industry."

Prices alone won't dictate supply, though. Operating conditions, particularly the deep snow still lying in the woods across the province, could also influence the number of trees farmers tap this spring, Holmes said.

"With the snow it's very difficult to get around, and when your prices aren't good, if you have hard conditions like that to overcome, that's another reason not to tackle the job."

Holmes's own sugarbush has a production capacity of 10,000 taps with three-quarters of his trees connected to a pipeline and the rest on buckets. He said he may forego bringing into production those trees that are difficult to reach, especially those not already hooked to a pipeline. . . .

The average floor price for syrup has tumbled from a high of around $2.50 per pound in 1997 and 1998 to $1.56 in 2000 and is not expected to be any higher in 2001.

Reprinted by permission of Dwane Wilkin.

Essence of the Story

■ Two back-to-back bumper maple syrup crops have lowered the price of syrup from $2.50 per pound to $1.56.

■ At this low price, producers are decreasing the number of trees they tap.

■ Supply is influenced by snow, which makes it difficult for producers to tap some of their trees.

■ Stanley Holmes has a production capacity of 10,000 taps. 7,500 of these are connected to a pipeline and the rest on buckets.

■ At today's low price, Stanley Holmes says he may forgo the production on those trees that are difficult to reach and not already hooked to a pipeline.

Economic Analysis

■ Maple syrup—the real kind, not the synthetic syrup such as Aunt Jemima—is produced in Canada and the United States by about 12,000 firms.

■ The market for maple syrup is close to perfectly competitive.

■ Before the bumper crop, the price of maple syrup (in the news article) was $2.50 a pound.

■ After the bumper crop, the price fell to $1.56 a pound.

■ Figure 1 shows why the price fell. The demand curve for maple syrup is D, and before the bumper harvest, the supply curve was S_0. The equilibrium price was $2.50 a pound.

■ The bumper harvest shifted the supply curve rightward to S_1. At the price of $2.50 a pound, there was a surplus of syrup, so the price fell. The new equilibrium price is $1.56 a pound.

■ Figure 2 shows the situation facing Stanley Holmes. Stanley is a price taker and maximizes his profit by producing the quantity at which marginal cost (MC) equals marginal revenue (MR).

■ The figure shows Stanley Holmes' cost curves: average total cost curve, ATC, average variable cost curve, AVC, and marginal cost curve, MC.

■ We don't know the exact position of these curves, and those in the figure are assumed. But we do know from Stanley's description of his supply conditions that his marginal cost curve slopes upward.

■ When Stanley says, "With the snow it's very difficult to get around, and when your prices aren't good, if you have hard conditions like that to overcome, that's another reason not to tackle the job," it means that the marginal cost of tapping all his trees is greater than the market price.

■ Figure 2 also shows Stanley's marginal revenue curves before, MR_0, and after, MR_1, the bumper harvest.

■ At $2.50 a pound, Stanley would tap all his trees (10,000 taps according to the news article). At $1.56 a pound, Stanley doesn't bother to tap the distant trees that are not connected to the pipeline.

■ Although the price is low, Stanley says that he

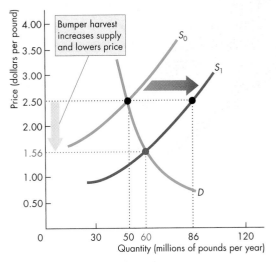

Figure 1 The maple syrup market

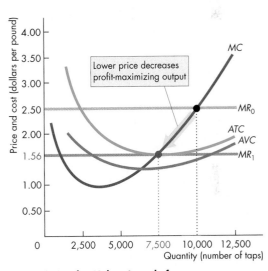

Figure 2 Stanley Holmes' maple farm

will produce from his 7,500 taps that are connected to the pipeline. This fact implies, as Fig. 2 shows, that the price of $1.56 exceeds average variable cost. If it didn't, Stanley would temporarily shut down.

KEY POINTS

Competition (pp. 240–241)

■ A perfectly competitive firm is a price taker.

The Firm's Decisions in Perfect Competition (pp. 242–247)

■ The firm produces the output at which marginal revenue (price) equals marginal cost.

■ In short-run equilibrium, a firm can make an economic profit, incur an economic loss, or make normal profit.

■ If price is less than minimum average variable cost, the firm temporarily shuts down.

■ A firm's supply curve is the upward-sloping part of its marginal cost curve above minimum average variable cost.

■ An industry supply curve shows the sum of the quantities supplied by each firm at each price.

Output, Price, and Profit in Perfect Competition (pp. 248–251)

■ Market demand and market supply determine price.

■ Persistent economic profit induces entry. Persistent economic loss induces exit.

■ Entry and plant expansion increase supply, lower the price, and reduce economic profit. Exit and downsizing decrease supply, raise the price, and reduce economic loss.

■ In long-run equilibrium, economic profit is zero (firms earn normal profit). There is no entry, exit, plant expansion, or downsizing.

Changing Tastes and Advancing Technology (pp. 252–255)

■ A permanent decrease in demand leads to a smaller industry output and a smaller number of firms.

■ A permanent increase in demand leads to a larger industry output and a larger number of firms.

■ The long-run effect of a change in demand on price depends on whether there are external economies (the price falls) or external diseconomies (the price rises) or neither (the price remains constant).

■ New technologies increase supply and in the long run lower the price and increase the quantity.

Competition and Efficiency (pp. 256–257)

■ Resources are used efficiently when we produce goods and services in the quantities that people value most highly.

■ When there are no external benefits and external costs, perfect competition achieves an efficient allocation. Marginal social benefit equals marginal social cost, and the sum of consumer surplus and producer surplus is maximized.

KEY FIGURES

Figure 11.2   Total Revenue, Total Cost, and Economic Profit, 243
Figure 11.3   Profit-Maximizing Output, 244
Figure 11.4   Three Possible Profit Outcomes in the Short Run, 245
Figure 11.5   A Firm's Supply Curve, 246
Figure 11.7   Short-Run Equilibrium, 248
Figure 11.8   Entry and Exit, 249
Figure 11.12   Efficiency of Competition, 257

KEY TERMS

External diseconomies, 253
External economies, 253
Long-run industry supply curve, 253
Marginal revenue, 240
Perfect competition, 240
Price taker, 240
Short-run industry supply curve, 247
Shutdown point, 246
Total revenue, 240

PROBLEMS

Go to **myeconlab** for solutions to odd-numbered problems and additional exercises.

1. The figure shows the cost curves of Quick Copy, one of many copy shops near campus.

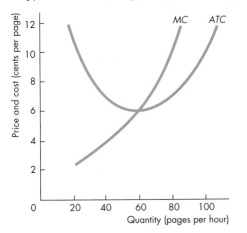

a. If the market price of copying one page is 10 cents, what is Quick Copy's profit-maximizing output?
b. Calculate Quick Copy's profit.
c. With no change in demand or technology, how will the price change in the long run?

2. Jerry's is one of many ice cream stands along the beach. The figure shows Jerry's cost curves.

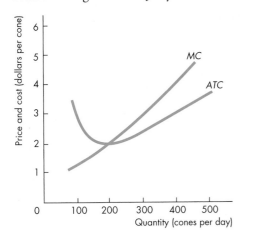

a. If the market price of an ice cream cone is $3, what is Jerry's profit-maximizing output?
b. Calculate Jerry's profit.
c. With no change in demand or technology, how will the price change in the long run?

3. Pat's Pizza Kitchen is a price taker. Its costs are

Output (pizzas per hour)	Total cost (dollars per hour)
0	10
1	21
2	30
3	41
4	54
5	69

a. What is Pat's profit-maximizing output and how much economic profit does Pat make if the market price is (i) $14, (ii) $12, and (iii) $10?
b. What is Pat's shutdown point?
c. Derive Pat's supply curve.
d. At what price will Pat exit the pizza industry?

4. Luigi's Lasagna is a price taker. Its costs are

Output (plates per day)	Total cost (dollars per day)
0	14
1	38
2	48
3	62
4	80
5	102
6	128

a. What is Luigi's profit-maximizing output and how much profit does Luigi make if the market price is (i) $24 a plate, (ii) $20 a plate, and (iii) $12 a plate?
b. What is Luigi's shutdown point?
c. What is Luigi's profit at the shutdown point?
d. At what prices will firms with costs the same as Luigi's enter the lasagna market?

5. The market demand schedule for cassettes is

Price (dollars per cassette)	Quantity demanded (thousands of cassettes per week)
3.65	500
5.20	450
6.80	400
8.40	350
10.00	300
11.60	250
13.20	200
14.80	150

The market is perfectly competitive, and each firm has the following cost structure:

Output (cassettes per week)	Marginal cost (dollars per additional cassette)	Average variable cost	Average total cost
		(dollars per cassette)	
150	6.00	8.80	15.47
200	6.40	7.80	12.80
250	7.00	7.00	11.00
300	7.65	7.10	10.43
350	8.40	7.20	10.06
400	10.00	7.50	10.00
450	12.40	8.00	10.22
500	20.70	9.00	11.00

There are 1,000 firms in the industry.

a. What is the market price?
b. What is the industry's output?
c. What is the output produced by each firm?
d. What is each firm's economic profit?
e. Do firms enter or exit the industry?
f. What is the number of firms in the long run?

6. The same demand conditions as those in problem 5 prevail and there are 1,000 firms in the industry. Firms use the same plant size, but fixed costs increase by $980. What now are your answers to the questions in problem 5?

7. In problem 5, a fall in the price of a compact disc permanently decreases the demand for cassettes and the demand schedule becomes

Price (dollars per cassette)	Quantity demanded (thousands of cassettes per week)
2.95	500
4.13	450
5.30	400
6.48	350
7.65	300
8.83	250
10.00	200
11.18	150

What now are your answers to the questions in problem 5?

8. In problem 6, the fall in the price of a compact disc permanently decreases the demand for cassettes and the demand schedule becomes that given in problem 7. What now are your answers to the questions in problem 6?

CRITICAL THINKING

1. After you have studied *Reading Between the Lines* on pp. 258–259, answer the following questions.
   a. What are the features of the market for maple syrup that make it an example of perfect competition?
   b. During the 1980s, the technology for extracting sap advanced. What effect do you predict that this development had on the price of syrup and the number of firms that produce it?
   c. Suppose that Aunt Jemima invents a syrup that no one can distinguish (in a blind test) from the real thing and can produce it for half the price of real maple syrup. What effect would you expect this development to have on the market for real maple syrup?

2. Why have the prices of pocket calculators and VCRs fallen? What do you think has happened to the costs and economic profits of the firms that make these products?

3. What has been the effect of an increase in world population on the wheat market and the individual wheat farmer?

4. How has the diaper service industry been affected by the decrease in the Canadian birth rate and the development of disposable diapers?

WEB EXERCISES

Use the links on X myeconlab to work the following exercises.

1. Study the *Web Reading Between the Lines* "Dumping Steel." Then answer the following questions:
   a. What is the argument in the news article about limiting steel imports?
   b. Do you agree with the argument? Why or why not?
   c. Why do Canada and the United States claim that foreign steel is being dumped in North America? (Use the links in the *Web Reading Between the Lines* to answer this question.)

Monopoly

Dominating the Internet

eBay and Google are dominant players in the markets they serve. Because most buyers use eBay, most sellers do too. And because most sellers use eBay, so do most buyers. This phenomenon, called a network externality, makes it hard for any other firm to break into the Internet auction business. Because Google is such a good search engine, most people use it to find what they're seeking on the Internet. And because most people use it, most Web site operators advertise with Google.

eBay and Google are obviously not like firms in perfect competition. They don't face a market-determined price. They can choose their own prices. How do firms like these behave? How do they choose the quantity to produce and the price at which to sell it? How does their behaviour compare with that of firms in perfectly competitive industries? Do they charge prices that are too high and that damage the interests of consumers? What benefits do they bring?

As a student, you get lots of discounts: when you get your hair cut, go to a museum, or go to a movie. When you take a trip by air, you almost never pay the full fare. Instead, you buy a discounted ticket. Are the people who operate barbershops, museums, movie theatres, and airlines simply generous folks who don't maximize profit? Aren't they throwing profit away by offering discounts?

◆ In this chapter, we study markets in which the firm can influence the price. We also compare the performance of the firm in such a market with that of a competitive market and examine whether monopoly is as efficient as competition. In *Reading Between the Lines* at the end of the chapter, we'll return to eBay and Google and discover an interesting difference between the market power they enjoy.

After studying this chapter, you will be able to

- ■ **Explain how monopoly arises and distinguish between single-price monopoly and price-discriminating monopoly**

- ■ **Explain how a single-price monopoly determines its output and price**

- ■ **Compare the performance and efficiency of single-price monopoly and competition**

- ■ **Explain how price discrimination increases profit**

- ■ **Explain how monopoly regulation influences output, price, economic profit, and efficiency**

Market Power

MARKET POWER AND COMPETITION ARE THE TWO forces that operate in most markets. **Market power** is the ability to influence the market, and in particular the market price, by influencing the total quantity offered for sale.

The firms in perfect competition that you studied in Chapter 11 have no market power. They face the force of raw competition and are price takers. The firms that we study in this chapter operate at the opposite extreme. They face no competition and exercise raw market power. We call this extreme monopoly. A **monopoly** is an industry that produces a good or service for which no close substitute exists and in which there is one supplier that is protected from competition by a barrier preventing the entry of new firms.

Examples of monopoly include your gas, electricity, and water distributors, as well as De Beers, the South African diamond producer, and Microsoft Corporation, the software developer that created the Windows operating system.

How Monopoly Arises

Monopoly has two key features:

- No close substitutes
- Barriers to entry

No Close Substitutes If a good has a close substitute, even though only one firm produces it, that firm effectively faces competition from the producers of substitutes. Water supplied by a local public utility is an example of a good that does not have close substitutes. While it does have a close substitute for drinking—bottled spring water—it has no effective substitutes for showering or washing a car.

Monopolies are constantly under attack from new products and ideas that substitute for products produced by monopolies. For example, FedEx, Purolator, the fax machine, and e-mail have weakened the monopoly of Canada Post. Similarly, the satellite dish has weakened the monopoly of cable television companies.

But new products also are constantly creating monopolies. An example is Microsoft's monopoly in the DOS operating system during the 1980s and in the Windows operating system today.

Barriers to Entry Legal or natural constraints that protect a firm from potential competitors are called **barriers to entry**. A firm can sometimes create its own barrier to entry by acquiring a significant portion of a key resource. For example, De Beers controls more than 80 percent of the world's supply of natural diamonds. But most monopolies arise from two other types of barriers: legal barriers and natural barriers.

Legal Barriers to Entry Legal barriers to entry create legal monopoly. A **legal monopoly** is a market in which competition and entry are restricted by the granting of a public franchise, government licence, patent, or copyright.

A *public franchise* is an exclusive right granted to a firm to supply a good or service. An example is Canada Post, which has the exclusive right to carry first-class mail. A *government licence* controls entry into particular occupations, professions, and industries. Examples of this type of barrier to entry occur in medicine, law, dentistry, schoolteaching, architecture, and many other professional services. Licensing does not always create monopoly, but it does restrict competition.

A *patent* is an exclusive right granted to the inventor of a product or service. A *copyright* is an exclusive right granted to the author or composer of a literary, musical, dramatic, or artistic work. Patents and copyrights are valid for a limited time period that varies from country to country. In Canada, a patent is valid for 20 years. Patents encourage the *invention* of new products and production methods. They also stimulate *innovation*—the use of new inventions—by encouraging inventors to publicize their discoveries and offer them for use under licence. Patents have stimulated innovations in areas as diverse as soybean seeds, pharmaceuticals, computer memory chips, and video games.

Natural Barriers to Entry Natural barriers to entry create **natural monopoly**, which is an industry in which one firm can supply the entire market at a lower average total cost than two or more firms can.

Figure 12.1 shows a natural monopoly in the distribution of electric power. Here, the market demand curve for electric power is *D*, and the average total cost curve is *ATC*. Because average total cost decreases as output increases, economies of scale prevail over the entire length of the *ATC* curve. One firm can produce 4 million kilowatt-hours at 5 cents a kilowatt-hour. At this price, the quantity demanded is 4 million kilowatt-hours. So if the price were 5 cents, one firm could supply the entire market. If two firms shared the market, it would cost each of them 10 cents a kilowatt-hour to produce a total of 4 million kilowatt-hours. If four firms shared the market, it would cost each of them 15 cents a kilowatt-hour to produce a total of 4 million kilowatt-hours. So in conditions like those shown in Fig. 12.1, one firm can supply the entire market at a lower cost than two or more firms can. The distribution of electric power is an example of natural monopoly. So is the distribution of water and gas.

Most monopolies are regulated in some way by government agencies. We will study such regulation at the end of this chapter. But for two reasons, we'll first study unregulated monopoly. First, we can better understand why governments regulate monopolies and the effects of regulation if we also know how an unregulated monopoly behaves. Second, even in industries with more than one producer, firms often have a degree of monopoly power, and the theory of monopoly sheds light on the behaviour of such firms and industries.

A major difference between monopoly and competition is that a monopoly sets its own price. But in doing so, it faces a market constraint. Let's see how the market limits a monopoly's pricing choices.

Monopoly Price-Setting Strategies

All monopolies face a tradeoff between price and the quantity sold. To sell a larger quantity, the monopoly must charge a lower price. But there are two broad monopoly situations that create different tradeoffs. They are

■ Price discrimination
■ Single price

Price Discrimination Airlines offer a dizzying array of different prices for the same trip. Pizza producers charge one price for a single pizza and almost give away a second pizza. These are examples of *price discrimination*. **Price discrimination** is the practice of selling different units of a good or service for different prices.

When a firm price discriminates, it looks as though it is doing its customers a favour. In fact, it is charging the highest possible price for each unit sold and making the largest possible profit.

Single Price De Beers sells diamonds (of a given size and quality) for the same price to all its customers. If it tried to sell at a low price to some customers and at a higher price to others, only the low-price customers would buy from De Beers. Others would buy from De Beers' low-price customers. De Beers is a *single-price* monopoly. A **single-price monopoly** is a firm that must sell each unit of its output for the same price to all its customers.

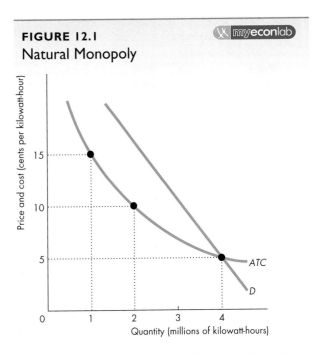

FIGURE 12.1 myeconlab
Natural Monopoly

The market demand curve for electric power is *D*, and the average total cost curve is *ATC*. Economies of scale exist over the entire *ATC* curve. One firm can distribute 4 million kilowatt-hours at a cost of 5 cents a kilowatt-hour. This same total output costs 10 cents a kilowatt-hour with two firms and 15 cents a kilowatt-hour with four firms. So one firm can meet the market demand at a lower cost than two or more firms can, and the market is a natural monopoly.

REVIEW QUIZ

1 How does monopoly arise?
2 How does a natural monopoly differ from a legal monopoly?
3 Distinguish between a price-discriminating and a single-price monopoly.

myeconlab **Study Plan 12.1**

A Single-Price Monopoly's Output and Price Decision

TO UNDERSTAND HOW A SINGLE-PRICE MONOPOLY makes its output and price decision, we must first study the link between price and marginal revenue.

Price and Marginal Revenue

Because in a monopoly there is only one firm, the demand curve facing the firm is the market demand curve. Let's look at Bobbie's Barbershop, the sole supplier of haircuts in Trout River, Newfoundland. The table in Fig. 12.2 shows the market demand schedule. At a price of $20, Bobbie sells no haircuts. The lower the price, the more haircuts per hour Bobbie can sell. For example, at $12, consumers demand 4 haircuts per hour (row *E*).

Total revenue (*TR*) is the price (*P*) multiplied by the quantity sold (*Q*). For example, in row *D*, Bobbie sells 3 haircuts at $14 each, so total revenue is $42. *Marginal revenue* (*MR*) is the change in total revenue (ΔTR) resulting from a one-unit increase in the quantity sold. For example, if the price falls from $16 (row *C*) to $14 (row *D*), the quantity sold increases from 2 to 3 haircuts. Total revenue rises from $32 to $42, so the change in total revenue is $10. Because the quantity sold increases by 1 haircut, marginal revenue equals the change in total revenue and is $10. Marginal revenue is placed between the two rows to emphasize that marginal revenue relates to the *change* in the quantity sold.

Figure 12.2 shows the market demand curve and marginal revenue curve (*MR*) and also illustrates the calculation we've just made. Notice that at each quantity of output, marginal revenue is *less* than price—the marginal revenue curve lies below the demand curve. Why is marginal revenue less than price? It is because when the price is lowered to sell one more unit, two opposing forces affect total revenue. The lower price results in a revenue loss, and the increased quantity sold results in a revenue gain. For example, at a price of $16, Bobbie sells 2 haircuts (point *C*). If she lowers the price to $14, she sells 3 haircuts and has a revenue gain of $14 on the third haircut. But she now receives only $14 on the first two—$2 less than before. As a result, she loses $4 of revenue on the first 2 haircuts. To calculate marginal revenue, she must deduct this amount from the revenue gain of $14. So her marginal revenue is $10, which is less than the price.

FIGURE 12.2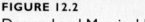

Demand and Marginal Revenue

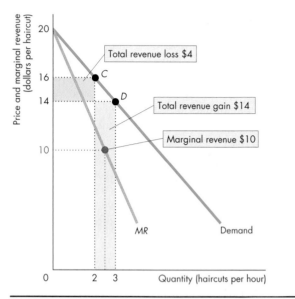

	Price (P) (dollars per haircut)	Quantity demanded (Q) (haircuts per hour)	Total revenue (TR = P × Q) (dollars)	Marginal revenue (MR = ΔTR/ΔQ) (dollars per haircut)
A	20	0	0	
				18
B	18	1	18	
				14
C	16	2	32	
				10
D	14	3	42	
				6
E	12	4	48	
				2
F	10	5	50	

The table shows the demand schedule. Total revenue (*TR*) is price multiplied by quantity sold. For example, in row *C*, the price is $16 a haircut, Bobbie sells 2 haircuts and total revenue is $32. Marginal revenue (*MR*) is the change in total revenue that results from a one-unit increase in the quantity sold. For example, when the price falls from $16 to $14 a haircut, the quantity sold increases by 1 haircut and total revenue increases by $10. Marginal revenue is $10. The demand curve and the marginal revenue curve, *MR*, are based on the numbers in the table and illustrate the calculation of marginal revenue when the price of a haircut falls from $16 to $14.

Marginal Revenue and Elasticity

A single-price monopoly's marginal revenue is related to the *elasticity of demand* for its good. The demand for a good can be *elastic* (the elasticity of demand is greater than 1), *inelastic* (the elasticity of demand is less than 1), or *unit elastic* (the elasticity of demand is equal to 1). Demand is *elastic* if a 1 percent fall in price brings a greater than 1 percent increase in the quantity demanded. Demand is *inelastic* if a 1 percent fall in price brings a less than 1 percent increase in the quantity demanded. And demand is *unit elastic* if a 1 percent fall in price brings a 1 percent increase in the quantity demanded. (See Chapter 4, pp. 86–87.)

If demand is elastic, a fall in price brings an increase in total revenue—the increase in revenue from the increase in quantity sold outweighs the decrease in revenue from the lower price—and marginal revenue is positive. If demand is inelastic, a fall in price brings a decrease in total revenue—the increase in revenue from the increase in quantity sold is outweighed by the decrease in revenue from the lower price—and marginal revenue is negative. If demand is unit elastic, total revenue does not change—the increase in revenue from the increase in quantity sold offsets the decrease in revenue from the lower price—and marginal revenue is zero. (The relationship between total revenue and elasticity is explained in Chapter 4, on p. 88.)

Figure 12.3 illustrates the relationship between marginal revenue, total revenue, and elasticity. As the price of a haircut gradually falls from $20 to $10, the quantity of haircuts demanded increases from 0 to 5 an hour. Over this output range, marginal revenue is positive (part a), total revenue increases (part b), and the demand for haircuts is elastic. As the price falls from $10 to $0 a haircut, the quantity of haircuts demanded increases from 5 to 10 an hour. Over this output range, marginal revenue is negative (part a), total revenue decreases (part b), and the demand for haircuts is inelastic. When the price is $10 a haircut, marginal revenue is zero, total revenue is a maximum, and the demand for haircuts is unit elastic.

In Monopoly, Demand Is Always Elastic

The relationship between marginal revenue and elasticity that you've just discovered implies that a profit-maximizing monopoly never produces an output in the inelastic range of its demand curve. If it did so, it could charge a higher price, produce a smaller quantity, and increase its profit. Let's now look more closely at a monopoly's output and price decision.

FIGURE 12.3

Marginal Revenue and Elasticity

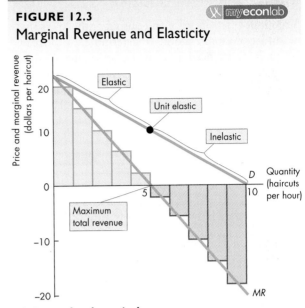

(a) Demand and marginal revenue curves

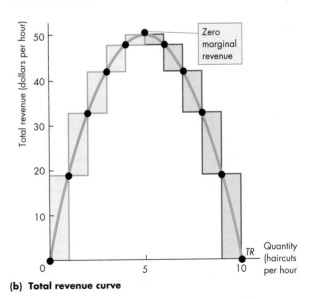

(b) Total revenue curve

In part (a), the demand curve is *D* and the marginal revenue curve is *MR*. In part (b), the total revenue curve is *TR*. Over the range from 0 to 5 haircuts an hour, a price cut increases total revenue, so marginal revenue is positive—as shown by the blue bars. Demand is elastic. Over the range 5 to 10 haircuts an hour, a price cut decreases total revenue, so marginal revenue is negative—as shown by the red bars. Demand is inelastic. At 5 haircuts an hour, total revenue is maximized and marginal revenue is zero. Demand is unit elastic.

Output and Price Decision

A monopoly sets its price and output at the levels that maximize economic profit. To determine this price and output level, we need to study the behaviour of both cost and revenue as output varies. A monopoly faces the same types of technology and cost constraints as a competitive firm. So a monopoly's costs (total cost, average cost, and marginal cost) behave just like those of a firm in perfect competition. And a monopoly's revenues (total revenue, price, and marginal revenue) behave in the way we've just described.

Table 12.1 provides information about Bobbie's costs, revenues, and economic profit and Figure 12.4 shows the same information graphically.

Maximizing Economic Profit You can see in the table and part (a) of the figure that total cost (*TC*) and total revenue (*TR*) both increase as output increases, but *TC* increases at an increasing rate and *TR* increases at a decreasing rate. Economic profit, which equals *TR* minus *TC*, increases at small output levels, reaches a maximum, and then decreases. The maximum profit ($12) occurs when Bobbie sells 3 haircuts for $14 each. If she sells 2 haircuts for $16 each or 4 haircuts for $12 each, her economic profit will be only $8.

Marginal Revenue Equals Marginal Cost You can see in the table and part (b) of the figure Bobbie's marginal revenue (*MR*) and marginal cost (*MC*). When Bobbie increases output from 2 to 3 haircuts, *MR* is $10 and *MC* is $6. *MR* exceeds *MC* by $4 and Bobbie's profit increases by that amount. If Bobbie increases output yet further, from 3 to 4 haircuts, *MR* is $6 and *MC* is $10. In this case, *MC* exceeds *MR* by $4, so profit decreases by that amount.

When *MR* exceeds *MC*, profit increases if output increases. When *MC* exceeds *MR*, profit increases if output *decreases*. When *MC* equals *MR*, profit is maximized.

Figure 12.4(b) shows the maximum profit as price (on the demand curve *D*) minus average total cost (on the *ATC* curve) multiplied by the quantity produced—the blue rectangle.

Maximum Price the Market Will Bear Unlike a firm in perfect competition, a monopoly influences the price of what it sells. But a monopoly doesn't set the price at the maximum *possible* price. At the maximum *possible* price, the firm would be able to sell only one unit of output, which in general is less than the profit-maximizing quantity. Rather, a monopoly produces the profit-maximizing quantity and sells that quantity for the highest price it can get.

TABLE 12.1   A Monopoly's Output and Price Decision

Price (P) (dollars per haircut)	Quantity demanded (Q) (haircuts per hour)	Total revenue (TR = P × Q) (dollars)	Marginal revenue (MR = ΔTR/ΔQ) (dollars per haircut)	Total cost (TC) (dollars)	Marginal cost (MC = ΔTC/ΔQ) (dollars per haircut)	Economic profit (TR – TC) (dollars)
20	0	0		20		−20
			18		1	
18	1	18		21		−3
			14		3	
16	2	32		24		+8
			10		6	
14	3	42		30		+12
			6		10	
12	4	48		40		+8
			2		15	
10	5	50		55		−5

This table gives the information needed to find the profit-maximizing output and price. Total revenue (*TR*) equals price multiplied by the quantity sold. Profit equals total revenue minus total cost (*TC*). Profit is maximized when 3 haircuts are sold at $14 a haircut. Total revenue is $42, total cost is $30, and economic profit is $12 ($42 – $30).

FIGURE 12.4

A Monopoly's Output and Price

myeconlab

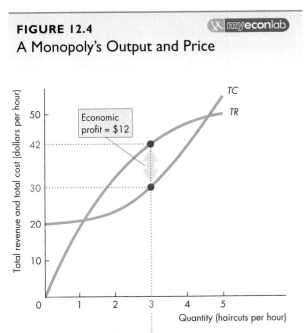

(a) Total revenue and total cost curves

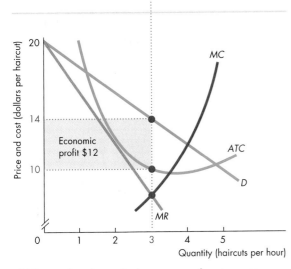

(b) Demand and marginal revenue and cost curves

In part (a), economic profit is the vertical distance equal to total revenue (*TR*) minus total cost (*TC*) and economic profit is maximized at 3 haircuts an hour. In part (b), economic profit is maximized when marginal cost (*MC*) equals marginal revenue (*MR*). The profit-maximizing output is 3 haircuts an hour. The price, determined by the demand curve (*D*), is $14 a haircut. Average total cost is $10 a haircut, so economic profit, the blue rectangle, is $12—the profit per haircut ($4) multiplied by 3 haircuts.

All firms maximize profit by producing the output at which marginal revenue equals marginal cost. For a competitive firm, price equals marginal revenue, so price also equals marginal cost. For a monopoly, price exceeds marginal revenue, so price also exceeds marginal cost.

A monopoly charges a price that exceeds marginal cost, but does it always make an economic profit? In Bobbie's case, when she produces 3 haircuts an hour, her average total cost is $10 (read from the *ATC* curve) and her price is $14 (read from the *D* curve). Her profit per haircut is $4 ($14 minus $10). Bobbie's economic profit is shown by the blue rectangle, which equals the profit per haircut ($4) multiplied by the number of haircuts (3), for a total of $12.

If firms in a perfectly competitive industry make a positive economic profit, new firms enter. That does not happen in monopoly. Barriers to entry prevent new firms from entering an industry in which there is a monopoly. So a monopoly can make a positive economic profit and continue to do so indefinitely. Sometimes that profit is large, as in the international diamond business.

Bobbie makes a positive economic profit. But suppose that the owner of the shop that Bobbie rents increases Bobbie's rent. If Bobbie pays an additional $12 an hour for rent, her fixed cost increases by $12 an hour. Her marginal cost and marginal revenue don't change, so her profit-maximizing output remains at 3 haircuts an hour. Her profit decreases by $12 an hour to zero. If Bobbie pays more than an additional $12 an hour for her shop rent, she incurs an economic loss. If this situation were permanent, Bobbie would go out of business. But entrepreneurs are a hardy lot, and Bobbie might find another shop where the rent is less.

REVIEW QUIZ

1 What is the relationship between marginal cost and marginal revenue when a single-price monopoly maximizes profit?
2 How does a single-price monopoly determine the price it will charge its customers?
3 What is the relationship between price, marginal revenue, and marginal cost when a single-price monopoly is maximizing profit?
4 Why can a monopoly make a positive economic profit even in the long run?

myeconlab **Study Plan 12.2**

Single-Price Monopoly and Competition Compared

IMAGINE AN INDUSTRY THAT IS MADE UP OF MANY small firms operating in perfect competition. Then imagine that a single firm buys out all these small firms and creates a monopoly.

What will happen in this industry? Will the price rise or fall? Will the quantity produced increase or decrease? Will economic profit increase or decrease? Will either the original competitive situation or the new monopoly situation be efficient?

These are the questions we're now going to answer. First, we look at the effects of monopoly on the price and quantity produced. Then we turn to the questions about efficiency.

Comparing Output and Price

Figure 12.5 shows the market we'll study. The market demand curve is D. The demand curve is the same regardless of how the industry is organized. But the supply side and the equilibrium are different in monopoly and competition. First, let's look at the case of perfect competition.

Perfect Competition   Initially, with many small perfectly competitive firms in the market, the market supply curve is S. This supply curve is obtained by summing the supply curves of all the individual firms in the market.

In perfect competition, equilibrium occurs where the supply curve and the demand curve intersect. The quantity produced by the industry is Q_C, and the price is P_C. Each firm takes the price P_C and maximizes its profit by producing the output at which its own marginal cost equals the price. Because each firm is a small part of the total industry, there is no incentive for any firm to try to manipulate the price by varying its output.

Monopoly   Now suppose that this industry is taken over by a single firm. Consumers do not change, so the demand curve remains the same as in the case of perfect competition. But now the monopoly recognizes this demand curve as a constraint on its sales. The monopoly's marginal revenue curve is MR.

The monopoly maximizes profit by producing the quantity at which marginal revenue equals marginal cost. To find the monopoly's marginal cost curve, first

recall that in perfect competition, the industry supply curve is the sum of the supply curves of the firms in the industry. Also recall that each firm's supply curve is its marginal cost curve (see Chapter 11, pp. 246–247). So when the industry is taken over by a single firm, the competitive industry's supply curve becomes the monopoly's marginal cost curve. To remind you of this fact, the supply curve is also labelled MC.

The output at which marginal revenue equals marginal cost is Q_M. This output is smaller than the competitive output Q_C. And the monopoly charges the price P_M, which is higher than P_C. We have established that

Compared to a perfectly competitive industry, a single-price monopoly restricts its output and charges a higher price.

We've seen how the output and price of a monopoly compare with those in a competitive industry. Let's now compare the efficiency of the two types of markets.

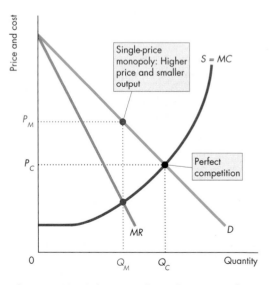

FIGURE 12.5
Monopoly's Smaller Output and Higher Price

A competitive industry produces the quantity Q_C at price P_C. A single-price monopoly produces the quantity Q_M at which marginal revenue equals marginal cost and sells that quantity for the price P_M. Compared to perfect competition, a single-price monopoly restricts output and raises the price.

Efficiency Comparison

You saw in Chapter 11 (pp. 256–257) that (with no external costs and benefits) perfect competition is efficient. Figure 12.6(a), illustrates the efficiency of perfect competition and serves as a benchmark against which to measure the inefficiency of monopoly.

Along the market demand curve ($D = MSB$), consumers are efficient. Along the market supply curve ($S = MSC$), producers are efficient. In competitive equilibrium, the price is P_C, the quantity is Q_C, and marginal social benefit equals marginal social cost.

Consumer surplus is the green triangle under the demand curve and above the equilibrium price (see Chapter 5, p. 107). *Producer surplus* is the blue area above the supply curve and below the equilibrium price (see Chapter 5, p. 109). The sum of the consumer surplus and producer surplus is maximized.

Also, in long-run competitive equilibrium, entry and exit ensure that each firm produces its output at the minimum possible long-run average cost.

To summarize: At the competitive equilibrium, marginal social benefit equals marginal social cost; the sum of consumer surplus and producer surplus is maximized; firms produce at the lowest possible long-run average cost; and resource use is efficient.

Figure 12.6(b) illustrates the inefficiency of monopoly and the sources of that inefficiency. A monopoly restricts output to Q_M and sells its output for P_M. With no external costs ($MC = MSC$) and no external benefits, the smaller output and higher price drive a wedge between marginal social benefit and marginal social cost and create a *deadweight loss*. The grey area shows the deadweight loss and its magnitude is a measure of the inefficiency of monopoly.

Consumer surplus shrinks for two reasons. First, consumers lose by having to pay more for the good. This loss to consumers is a gain for the producer and increases the producer surplus. Second, consumers lose by getting less of the good, and this loss is part of the deadweight loss.

Although the monopoly gains from a higher price, it loses some of the original producer surplus because of the smaller monopoly output. That loss is another part of the deadweight loss.

Because a monopoly produces less than the efficient quantity and faces no competitive threat, it does not produce at the minimum possible long-run average cost. As a result, monopoly damages the social interest in three ways: it produces less, it increases the cost of production, and it increases the price above the increased cost of production.

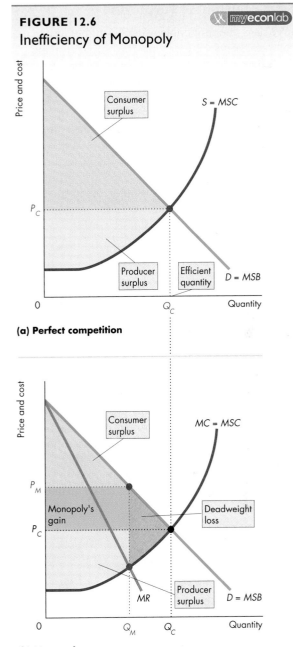

FIGURE 12.6
Inefficiency of Monopoly

(a) Perfect competition

(b) Monopoly

In perfect competition (part a), output is Q_C and the price is P_C. Marginal social benefit (MSB) equals marginal social cost (MSC); consumer surplus (the green triangle) plus producer surplus (the blue area) is maximized; and in the long-run, firms produce at the lowest possible average cost. A monopoly (part b) restricts output to Q_M and raises the price to P_M. Consumer surplus shrinks, the monopoly gains, and a deadweight loss (the grey area) arises.

Redistribution of Surpluses

You've seen that monopoly is inefficient because marginal social benefit exceeds marginal social cost and there is deadweight loss—a social loss. But monopoly also brings a *redistribution* of surpluses.

Some of the lost consumer surplus goes to the monopoly. In Fig. 12.6, the monopoly gets the difference between the higher price, P_M, and the competitive price, P_C, on the quantity sold, Q_M. So the monopoly takes the part of the consumer surplus shown by the darker blue rectangle. This portion of the loss of consumer surplus is not a loss to society. It is redistribution from consumers to the monopoly producer.

Rent Seeking

You've seen that monopoly creates a deadweight loss and so is inefficient. But the social cost of monopoly exceeds the deadweight loss because of an activity called rent seeking. **Rent seeking** is any attempt to capture a consumer surplus, a producer surplus, or an economic profit. The activity is not confined to monopoly. But attempting to capture the economic profit of a monopoly is a major form of rent seeking.

You've seen that a monopoly makes its economic profit by diverting part of consumer surplus to itself. Thus the pursuit of an economic profit by a monopoly is rent seeking. It is the attempt to capture consumer surplus.

Rent seekers pursue their goals in two main ways. They might

- Buy a monopoly
- Create a monopoly

Buy a Monopoly To rent seek by buying a monopoly, a person searches for a monopoly that is for sale at a lower price than the monopoly's economic profit. Trading of taxicab licences is an example of this type of rent seeking. In some cities, taxicabs are regulated. The city restricts both the fares and the number of taxis that can operate so operating a taxi results in economic profit, or rent. A person who wants to operate a taxi must buy a licence from someone who already has one. People rationally devote their time and effort to seeking out profitable monopoly businesses to buy. In the process, they use scarce resources that could otherwise have been employed to produce goods and services. The value of this lost production is part of the social cost of monopoly. The amount

paid for a monopoly is not a social cost because the payment is just a transfer of an existing producer surplus from the buyer to the seller.

Create a Monopoly Rent seeking by creating monopoly is mainly a political activity. It takes the form of lobbying and trying to influence the political process. Such influence might be sought by making campaign contributions in exchange for legislative support or by seeking to influence political outcomes indirectly through publicity in the media or more direct contacts with politicians and bureaucrats. An example of a monopoly right created in this way is the cable television monopoly created and regulated by the Canadian Radio-Television and Telecommunications Commission (CRTC). Another is a regulation that restricts "split-run" magazines. These regulations restrict output and increase price.

This type of rent seeking is a costly activity that uses up scarce resources. Taken together, firms spend billions of dollars lobbying MPs, MPPs, and bureaucrats in the pursuit of licences and laws that create barriers to entry and establish a monopoly right. Everyone has an incentive to rent seek, and because there are no barriers to entry into the rent-seeking activity, there is a great deal of competition for new monopoly rights.

Rent-Seeking Equilibrium

Barriers to entry create monopoly. But there is no barrier to entry into rent seeking. Rent seeking is like perfect competition. If an economic profit is available, a new rent seeker will try to get some of it. And competition among rent seekers pushes up the price that must be paid for a monopoly right to the point at which only a normal profit can be made by operating the monopoly. For example, competition for the right to operate a taxi in Toronto leads to a price of more than $80,000 for a taxi licence, which is sufficiently high to eliminate economic profit for taxi operators and leave them with normal profit.

Figure 12.7 shows a rent-seeking equilibrium. The cost of rent seeking is a fixed cost that must be added to a monopoly's other costs. Rent seeking and rent-seeking costs increase to the point at which no economic profit is made. The average total cost curve, which includes the fixed cost of rent seeking, shifts upward until it just touches the demand curve. Economic profit is zero. It has been lost in rent seeking. Consumer surplus is unaffected. But the dead-

FIGURE 12.7
Rent-Seeking Equilibrium

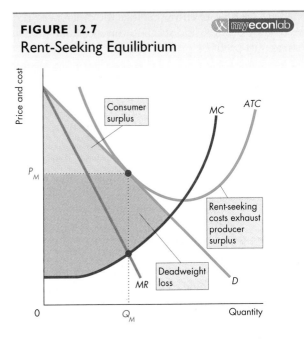

With competitive rent seeking, a monopoly uses all its economic profit to prevent another firm from taking its economic rent. The firm's rent-seeking costs are fixed costs. They shift the ATC curve upward until, at the profit-maximizing price, the firm breaks even.

weight loss of monopoly now includes the original deadweight loss triangle plus the lost producer surplus, shown by the enlarged grey area in the figure.

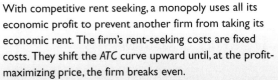

REVIEW QUIZ

1 Why does a single-price monopoly produce a smaller output and charge a higher price than what would prevail if the industry were perfectly competitive?
2 How does a monopoly transfer consumer surplus to itself?
3 Why is a single-price monopoly inefficient?
4 What is rent seeking and how does it influence the inefficiency of monopoly?

Study Plan 12.3

So far, we've considered only a single-price monopoly. But many monopolies do not operate with a single price. Instead, they price discriminate. Let's now see how a price-discriminating monopoly works.

Price Discrimination

PRICE DISCRIMINATION—SELLING A GOOD OR service at a number of different prices—is widespread. You encounter it when you travel, go to the movies, get your hair cut, buy pizza, or visit an art museum. Most price discriminators are not monopolies, but monopolies price discriminate when they can do so.

To be able to price discriminate, a monopoly must

1. Identify and separate different buyer types.
2. Sell a product that cannot be resold.

Price discrimination is charging different prices for a single good or service because of differences in buyers' willingness to pay and not because of differences in production costs. So not all price *differences* are price *discrimination*. Some goods that are similar but not identical have different prices because they have different production costs. For example, the cost of producing electricity depends on the time of day. If an electric power company charges a higher price during the peak consumption periods from 7:00 to 9:00 in the morning and from 4:00 to 7:00 in the evening than it does at other times of the day, it is not price discriminating.

At first sight, it appears that price discrimination contradicts the assumption of profit maximization. Why would a movie theatre allow children to see movies at half price? Why would a hairdresser charge students and senior citizens less? Aren't these firms losing profit by being nice to their customers?

Deeper investigation shows that far from losing profit, price discriminators make a bigger profit than they would otherwise. So a monopoly has an incentive to find ways of discriminating and charging each buyer the highest possible price. Some people pay less with price discrimination, but others pay more.

Price Discrimination and Consumer Surplus

The key idea behind price discrimination is to convert consumer surplus into economic profit. Demand curves slope downward because the value that people place on any good decreases as the quantity consumed of that good increases. When all the units consumed are sold for a single price, consumers benefit. The benefit is the value the consumers get from each unit of the good minus the price actually paid for it. This benefit is *consumer surplus.* Price discrimination is an attempt by a monopoly to capture as much of the consumer surplus as possible for itself.

To extract every dollar of consumer surplus from every buyer, the monopoly would have to offer each individual customer a separate price schedule based on that customer's own willingness to pay. Clearly, such price discrimination cannot be carried out in practice because a firm does not have enough information about each consumer's demand curve.

But firms try to extract as much consumer surplus as possible, and to do so, they discriminate in two broad ways:

- Among units of a good
- Among groups of buyers

Discriminating Among Units of a Good One method of price discrimination charges each buyer a different price on each unit of a good bought. A discount for bulk buying is an example of this type of discrimination. The larger the quantity bought, the larger is the discount—and the lower is the price. (Note that some discounts for bulk arise from lower costs of production for greater bulk. In these cases, such discounts are not price discrimination.)

Discriminating Among Groups of Buyers Price discrimination often takes the form of discriminating between different groups of consumers on the basis of age, employment status, or some other easily distinguished characteristic. This type of price discrimination works when each group has a different average willingness to pay for the good or service.

For example, a face-to-face sales meeting with a customer might bring a large and profitable order. For salespeople and other business travellers, the marginal benefit from a trip is large and the price that such a traveller will pay for a trip is high. In contrast, for a vacation traveller, any of several different trips and even no vacation trip are options. So for vacation travellers, the marginal benefit of a trip is small and the price that such a traveller will pay for a trip is low. Because business travellers are willing to pay more than vacation travellers are, it is possible for an airline to profit by price discriminating between these two groups. Similarly, because students have a lower willingness to pay for a haircut than a working person does, it is possible for a hairdresser to profit by price discriminating between these two groups.

Let's see how an airline exploits the differences in demand by business and vacation travellers and increases its profit by price discriminating.

Profiting by Price Discriminating

Global Air has a monopoly on an exotic route. Figure 12.8 shows the demand curve (*D*) and the marginal revenue curve (*MR*) for travel on this route. It also shows Global Air's marginal cost curve (*MC*) and average total cost curve (*ATC*).

Initially, Global is a single-price monopoly and maximizes its profit by producing 8,000 trips a year (the quantity at which *MR* equals *MC*). The price is $1,200 per trip. The average total cost of producing a trip is $600, so economic profit is $600 a trip. On 8,000 trips, Global's economic profit is $4.8 million a year, shown by the blue rectangle. Global's customers enjoy a consumer surplus shown by the green triangle.

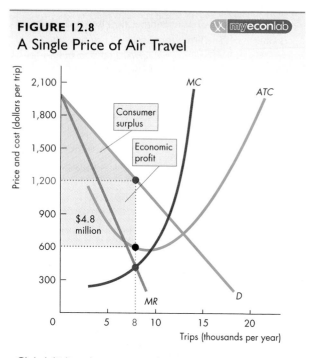

FIGURE 12.8 ⓧ myeconlab
A Single Price of Air Travel

Global Airlines has a monopoly on an air route. The market demand curve is *D* and marginal revenue curve is *MR*. Global Air's marginal cost curve is *MC*, and its average total cost curve is *ATC*. As a single-price monopoly, Global maximizes profit by selling 8,000 trips a year at $1,200 a trip. Its profit is $4.8 million a year—the blue rectangle. Global's customers enjoy a consumer surplus—the green triangle.

Global is struck by the fact that many of its customers are business travellers, and Global suspects that they are willing to pay more than $1,200 a trip. So Global does some market research, which tells Global that some business travellers are willing to pay as much as $1,800 a trip. Also, these customers frequently change their travel plans at the last moment. Another group of business travellers is willing to pay $1,600. These customers know one week ahead when they will travel, and they never want to stay over a weekend. Yet another group would pay up to $1,400. These travellers know two weeks ahead when they will travel and don't want to stay over a weekend.

So Global announces a new fare schedule: no restrictions, $1,800; 7-day advance purchase, non-refundable, $1,600; 14-day advance purchase, non-refundable, $1,400; 14-day advance purchase, must stay over a weekend, $1,200.

Figure 12.9 shows the outcome with this new fare structure and also shows why Global is pleased with

its new fare structure. Global sells 2,000 seats at each of its four new fares. Its economic profit increases by the dark blue steps in Fig. 12.9. Its economic profit is now its original $4.8 million a year plus an additional $2.4 million from its new higher fares. Consumer surplus has shrunk to the smaller green area.

Perfect Price Discrimination

But Global reckons that it can do even better. It plans to achieve **perfect price discrimination**, which extracts the entire consumer surplus. To do so, Global must get creative and come up with a host of additional fares—ranging between $2,000 and $1,200, each of which appeals to a small segment of the business market—that will extract the entire consumer surplus from the business travellers.

With perfect price discrimination, something special happens to marginal revenue. For the perfect price discriminator, the market demand curve becomes the marginal revenue curve. The reason is that when the price is cut to sell a larger quantity, the firm sells only the marginal unit at the lower price. All the other units continue to be sold for the highest price that each buyer is willing to pay. So for the perfect price discriminator, marginal revenue *equals* price and the demand curve becomes the marginal revenue curve.

With marginal revenue equal to price, Global can obtain yet greater profit by increasing output up to the point at which price (and marginal revenue) is equal to marginal cost.

So Global now seeks additional travellers who will not pay as much as $1,200 a trip but who will pay more than marginal cost. More creative pricing comes up with vacation specials and other fares that have combinations of advance reservation, minimum stay, and other restrictions that make these fares unattractive to its existing customers but attractive to a further group of travellers. With all these fares and specials, Global increases sales, extracts the entire consumer surplus, and maximizes economic profit. Figure 12.10 shows the outcome with perfect price discrimination. The dozens of fares paid by the original travellers who are willing to pay between $1,200 and $2,000 have extracted the entire consumer surplus from this group and converted it into economic profit for Global.

The new fares between $900 and $1,200 have attracted 3,000 additional travellers but taken their entire consumer surplus also. Global is earning an economic profit of more than $9 million a year.

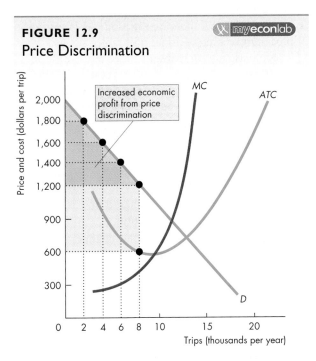

FIGURE 12.9
Price Discrimination

Global revises its fare structure: no restrictions at $1,800, 7-day advance purchase at $1,600, 14-day advance purchase at $1,400, and must stay over a weekend at $1,200. Global sells 2,000 trips at each of its four new fares. Its economic profit increases by $2.4 million a year to $7.2 million a year, which is shown by the original blue rectangle plus the dark blue steps. Global's customers' consumer surplus shrinks.

FIGURE 12.10

Perfect Price Discrimination

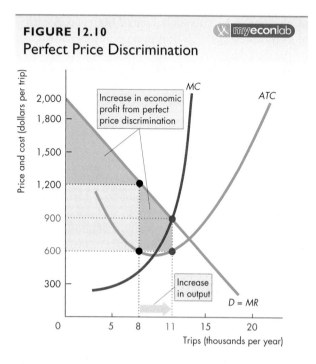

With perfect price discrimination, Global's demand curve becomes its marginal revenue curve. Economic profit is maximized when the lowest price equals marginal cost. Here, Global sells 11,000 trips and makes an economic profit of $9.35 million a year.

Real-world airlines are just as creative as Global, as you can see in the cartoon!

Would it bother you to hear how little I paid for this flight?

From William Hamilton, "Voodoo Economics," © 1992 by Chronicle Books. Published by Chronicle Books LLC, San Francisco. Used with permission. Visit http://www.chroniclebooks.com.

Efficiency and Rent Seeking with Price Discrimination

With perfect price discrimination, output increases to the point at which price equals marginal cost—where the marginal cost curve intersects the demand curve. This output is identical to that of perfect competition. Perfect price discrimination pushes consumer surplus to zero but increases producer surplus to equal the sum of consumer surplus and producer surplus in perfect competition. Deadweight loss with perfect price discrimination is zero. So perfect price discrimination achieves efficiency.

The more perfectly the monopoly can price discriminate, the closer its output gets to the competitive output and the more efficient is the outcome.

But there are two differences between perfect competition and perfect price discrimination. First, the distribution of the total surplus is different. It is shared by consumers and producers in perfect competition, while the producer gets it all with perfect price discrimination. Second, because the producer grabs the surplus, rent seeking becomes profitable.

People use resources in pursuit of rents, and the bigger the rents, the more resources get used in pursuing them. With free entry into rent seeking, the long-run equilibrium outcome is that rent seekers use up the entire producer surplus.

REVIEW QUIZ

1 What is price discrimination and how is it used to increase a monopoly's profit?
2 Explain how consumer surplus changes when a monopoly price discriminates.
3 Explain how consumer surplus, economic profit, and output change when a monopoly perfectly price discriminates.
4 What are some of the ways in which real-world airlines price discriminate?

myeconlab **Study Plan 12.4**

You've seen that monopoly is profitable for the monopolist but costly for other people. It results in inefficiency. Because of these features of monopoly, it is subject to policy debate and regulation. We'll now study the key monopoly policy issues.

Monopoly Policy Issues

MONOPOLY LOOKS BAD WHEN WE COMPARE IT with competition. Monopoly is inefficient, and it captures consumer surplus and converts it into producer surplus or pure waste in the form of rent-seeking costs. If monopoly is so bad, why do we put up with it? Why don't we have laws that crack down on monopoly so hard that it never rears its head? We do indeed have laws that limit monopoly power and regulate the prices that monopolies are permitted to charge. But monopoly also brings some benefits. We begin this review of monopoly policy issues by looking at the benefits of monopoly. We then look at monopoly regulation.

Gains from Monopoly

The main reason why monopoly exists is that it has potential advantages over a competitive alternative. These advantages arise from

- Incentives to innovation
- Economies of scale and economies of scope

Incentives to Innovation Invention leads to a wave of innovation as new knowledge is applied to the production process. Innovation may take the form of developing a new product or a lower-cost way of making an existing product. Controversy has raged over whether large firms with market power or small competitive firms lacking such market power are the most innovative. It is clear that some temporary market power arises from innovation. A firm that develops a new product or process and patents it obtains an exclusive right to that product or process for the term of the patent.

But does the granting of a monopoly, even a temporary one, to an innovator increase the pace of innovation? One line of reasoning suggests that it does. Without protection, an innovator is not able to enjoy the profits from innovation for very long. Thus the incentive to innovate is weakened. A contrary argument is that monopolies can afford to be lazy while competitive firms cannot. Competitive firms must strive to innovate and cut costs even though they know that they cannot hang onto the benefits of their innovation for long. But that knowledge spurs them on to greater and faster innovation.

The evidence on whether monopoly leads to greater innovation than competition is mixed. Large firms do more research and development than do small firms. But research and development are inputs into the process of innovation. What matters is not input but output. Two measures of the output of research and development are the number of patents and the rate of productivity growth. On these measures, it is not clear that bigger is better. But as a new process or product spreads through an industry, the large firms adopt the new process or product more quickly than do small firms. So large firms help to speed the process of diffusion of technological change.

Economies of Scale and Scope Economies of scale and economies of scope can lead to natural monopoly. As you saw at the beginning of this chapter, in a natural monopoly, a single firm can produce at a lower average total cost than can a number of firms.

A firm experiences *economies of scale* when an increase in its output of a good or service brings a decrease in the average total cost of producing it (see Chapter 10, p. 232). A firm experiences *economies of scope* when an increase in the *range of the goods produced* brings a decrease in average total cost (see Chapter 9, p. 213). Economies of scope occur when different goods can share specialized (and usually costly) capital resources. For example, McDonald's can produce both hamburgers and french fries at a lower average total cost than can two separate firms—a burger firm and a french fry firm—because at McDonald's, hamburgers and french fries share the use of specialized food storage and preparation facilities. A firm that produces a wide range of products can hire specialist designers and marketing experts whose skills can be used across the product range, thereby spreading the costs and lowering the average total cost of production of each of the goods.

There are many examples in which a combination of economies of scale and economies of scope arises, but not all of them lead to monopoly. Some examples are the brewing of beer, the manufacture of refrigerators and other household appliances, the manufacture of pharmaceuticals, and the refining of petroleum.

Examples of industries in which economies of scale are so significant that they lead to a natural monopoly are becoming rare. Public utilities such as gas, electric power, local telephone service, and garbage collection once were natural monopolies. But technological advances now enable us to separate the *production* of electric power or natural gas from its *distribution*. The provision of water, though, remains a natural monopoly.

A large-scale firm that has control over supply and can influence price—and therefore behaves like the monopoly firm that you've studied in this chapter—can reap these economies of scale and scope. Small, competitive firms cannot. Consequently, there are situations in which the comparison of monopoly and competition that we made earlier in this chapter is not valid. Recall that we imagined the takeover of a large number of competitive firms by a monopoly firm. But we also assumed that the monopoly would use exactly the same technology as the small firms and have the same costs. If one large firm can reap economies of scale and economies of scope, its marginal cost curve will lie below the supply curve of a competitive industry made up of many small firms. It is possible for such economies of scale and economies of scope to be so large as to result in a larger output and lower price under monopoly than a competitive industry would achieve.

Where significant economies of scale and economies of scope exist, it is usually worth putting up with monopoly and regulating its price.

Regulating Natural Monopoly

Where demand and cost conditions create a natural monopoly, a federal, provincial, or local government agency usually steps in to regulate the prices of the monopoly. By regulating a monopoly, some of the worst aspects of monopoly can be avoided or at least moderated. Let's look at monopoly price regulation.

Figure 12.11 shows the market demand curve *D*, the marginal revenue curve *MR*, the average total cost curve *ATC*, and the marginal cost curve *MC* for a natural gas distribution company that is a natural monopoly.

The firm's marginal cost is constant at 10 cents per cubic metre. But average total cost decreases as output increases. The reason is that the natural gas company has a large investment in pipelines and so has high fixed costs. These fixed costs are part of the company's average total cost and so appear in the *ATC* curve. The average total cost curve slopes downward because as the number of cubic metres sold increases, the fixed cost is spread over a larger number of units. (If you need to refresh your memory on how the average total cost curve is calculated, look back at Chapter 10, pp. 226–227.)

This one firm can supply the entire market at a lower cost than two firms can because average total cost is falling even when the entire market is supplied. (Refer back to pp. 264–265 if you need a quick refresher on natural monopoly.)

Profit Maximization   Suppose the natural gas company is not regulated and instead maximizes profit. Figure 12.11 shows the outcome. The company produces 2 million cubic metres a day, the quantity at which marginal cost equals marginal revenue. It prices the gas at 20 cents a cubic metre and makes an economic profit of 2 cents a cubic metre, or $40,000 a day.

This outcome is fine for the gas company, but it is inefficient. The price of gas is 20 cents a cubic metre when its marginal cost is only 10 cents a cubic metre. Also, the gas company is making a big profit. What can regulation do to improve this outcome?

The Efficient Regulation   If the monopoly regulator wants to achieve an efficient use of resources, it must require the gas monopoly to produce the quantity of gas that brings marginal benefit into equality with marginal cost. Marginal benefit is what the consumer is willing to pay and is shown by the demand curve. Marginal cost is shown by the firm's marginal cost curve. You can see in Fig. 12.11 that this outcome occurs if the price is regulated at 10 cents per cubic metre and if 4 million cubic metres per day are produced. The regulation that produces this outcome is called a marginal cost pricing rule. A **marginal cost pricing rule** sets price equal to marginal cost. It maximizes total surplus in the regulated industry. In this example, that surplus is all consumer surplus and it equals the area of the triangle beneath the demand curve and above the marginal cost curve.

The marginal cost pricing rule is efficient. But it leaves the natural monopoly incurring an economic loss. Because average total cost is falling as output increases, marginal cost is below average total cost. And because price equals marginal cost, price is below average total cost. Average total cost minus price is the loss per unit produced. It's pretty obvious that a natural gas company that is required to use a marginal cost pricing rule will not stay in business for long. How can a company cover its costs and, at the same time, obey a marginal cost pricing rule?

One possibility is price discrimination. The company might charge a higher price to some customers but marginal cost to the customers who pay least. Another possibility is to use a two-part price (called a

FIGURE 12.11

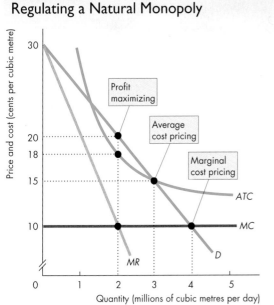

Regulating a Natural Monopoly

A natural monopoly is an industry in which average total cost is falling even when the entire market demand is satisfied. A natural gas producer faces the demand curve D. The firm's marginal cost is constant at 10 cents per cubic metre, as shown by the curve labelled MC. Fixed costs are large, and the average total cost curve, which includes average fixed cost, is shown as ATC. A marginal cost pricing rule sets the price at 10 cents per cubic metre. The monopoly produces 4 million cubic metres per day and incurs an economic loss. An average cost pricing rule sets the price at 15 cents per cubic metre. The monopoly produces 3 million cubic metres per day and makes normal profit.

two-part tariff). For example, the gas company might charge a monthly fixed fee that covers its fixed cost and then charge for gas consumed at marginal cost.

But a natural monopoly cannot always cover its costs in these ways. If a natural monopoly cannot cover its total cost from its customers and if the government wants it to follow a marginal cost pricing rule, then the government must give the firm a subsidy. In such a case, the government raises the revenue for the subsidy by taxing some other activity. But as we saw in Chapter 6, taxes themselves generate deadweight loss. Thus the deadweight loss resulting from additional taxes must be subtracted from the efficiency gained by forcing the natural monopoly to adopt a marginal cost pricing rule.

Average Cost Pricing Regulators almost never impose efficient pricing because of its consequences for the firm's profit. Instead, they compromise by permitting the firm to cover its costs and to earn a normal profit. Recall that normal profit is a cost of production and we include it along with the firm's other fixed costs in the average total cost curve. So pricing to cover cost including normal profit means setting price equal to average total cost—called an **average cost pricing rule**.

Figure 12.11 shows the average cost pricing outcome. The natural gas company charges 15 cents a cubic metre and sells 3 million cubic metres per day. This outcome is better for consumers than the unregulated profit-maximizing outcome. The price is 5 cents a cubic metre lower, and the quantity consumed is 1 million cubic metres per day more. And the outcome is better for the producer than the marginal cost pricing rule outcome. The firm earns normal profit. The outcome is inefficient but less so than the unregulated profit-maximizing outcome.

REVIEW QUIZ

1 What are the two main reasons why monopoly is worth tolerating?
2 Can you provide some examples of economies of scale and economies of scope?
3 Why might the incentive to innovate be greater for a monopoly than for a small competitive firm?
4 What is the price that achieves an efficient outcome for a regulated monopoly? And what is the problem with this price?
5 Compare the consumer surplus, producer surplus, and deadweight loss that arise from average cost pricing with those that arise from profit-maximization and marginal cost pricing.

myeconlab **Study Plan 12.5**

◆ You've now studied perfect competition and monopoly. *Reading Between the Lines* on pp. 280–281 looks at market power in the markets for Internet auctions and search. In the next chapter, we study markets that lie between the extremes of perfect competition and monopoly and that blend elements of the two.

eBay Is a Monopoly But Google Isn't!

THE ECONOMIST, OCTOBER 30, 2002

How Good is Google

... As search engines go... Google has clearly been a runaway success. Not only is its own site the most popular for search on the web, but it also powers the search engines of major portals, such as Yahoo! and AOL. All told, 75% of referrals to websites now originate from Google's algorithms. That is power.

For some time now, Google's board... has been deliberating how to translate that power into money. They appear to have decided to bring Google to the stock market next spring. Bankers have been overheard estimating Google's value at $15 billion or more. That could make Google Silicon Valley's first hot IPO since the dotcom bust, and perhaps its biggest ever.

...To be worth the rumoured $15 billion for longer than it takes a bubble to burst, it will need to raise its profitability substantially. That means matching such internet stars as eBay (market capitalisation $37 billion), but without the natural-monopoly advantages that have made eBay so dominant—the classic network effect of buyers and sellers knowing they do best by all trading in one place. For Google to stay permanently ahead of other search-engine technologies is almost impossible, since it takes so little—only a bright idea by another set of geeks—to lose the lead. In contrast to a portal such as Yahoo!, which also offers customers free e-mail and other services, a pure search engine is always but a click away from losing users.

Essence of the Story

■ Google is the most popular search engine, and 75 percent of referrals to Web sites originate from its searches.

■ Some bankers estimate Google's value at $15 billion or more.

■ It is almost impossible for Google to stay permanently ahead of other search-engine technologies because it takes only a bright idea by another set of programmers to lose its lead.

■ Google does not have the natural-monopoly advantages that have made eBay dominant—network effect of buyers and sellers who know they do best by all trading in one place.

Economic Analysis

■ Almost all the costs of eBay or Google are fixed costs.

■ When all costs are fixed, average fixed cost equals average total cost, and marginal cost is zero. Figure 1 shows eBay's cost curves. (Google's cost curves look just like these.)

■ A natural monopoly has two features:

1) Economies of scale at the output that meets the market demand

2) No close substitutes

■ Both eBay and Google have the first feature but only eBay has the second.

■ If another firm developed a better search engine than Google—a close but better substitute for Google—that firm would take the market for Internet search.

■ Constant vigilance in improving its search engine and keeping it the best available can prevent this outcome for Google.

■ Because eBay enjoys the benefit of a network externality, eBay has no close substitute and is unlikely to be confronted with one.

■ The demand for eBay's services is D in Fig. 1. The firm maximizes profit by setting a price, P, that generates a quantity demanded, Q, where marginal revenue is equal to the zero marginal cost.

■ eBay users enjoy a consumer surplus, eBay earns a large economic profit (capital value at an estimated $37 billion), but there is a deadweight loss.

■ Although as a monopoly eBay is inefficient and creates a deadweight loss, the world is better off with eBay than it would be without it. Figure 2 shows why.

■ In the market for a rarely traded item such as carved bone fishes, the supply including the cost of finding a buyer was S_0 before eBay began to operate. The cost of finding a buyer was so large that this item was not traded.

■ Supply increases to S_1 when eBay lowers the cost of finding a buyer. Now the item is traded. The buyer pays PB and receives a consumer surplus, the seller receives PS and a seller's surplus, and eBay earns an economic profit.

■ A deadweight loss arises because eBay doesn't set price equal to marginal cost. So the market is inefficient. But compared to the situation before eBay existed, a huge consumer surplus and a surplus for the seller arise.

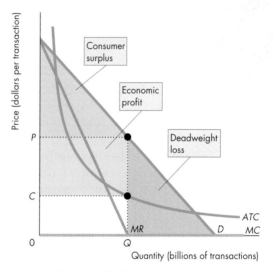

Figure 1 eBay's market for auction services

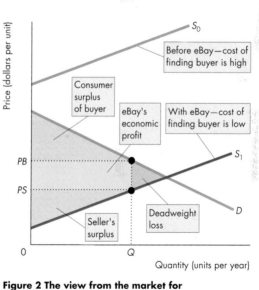

Figure 2 The view from the market for carved bone fishes

You're the Voter

■ Do you think eBay should be regulated and required to set its price equal to its marginal cost? Explain why or why not.

SUMMARY

KEY POINTS

Market Power (pp. 264–265)

- A monopoly is an industry in which there is a single supplier of a good or service that has no close substitutes and in which barriers to entry prevent competition.
- Barriers to entry may be legal (public franchise, licence, patent, copyright) or natural (created by economies of scale) or the firm owns control of a resource.
- A monopoly might be able to price discriminate when there is no resale possibility.
- Where resale is possible, a firm charges one price.

A Single-Price Monopoly's Output and Price Decision (pp. 266–269)

- A monopoly's demand curve is the market demand curve, and a single-price monopoly's marginal revenue is less than price.
- A monopoly maximizes profit by producing the output at which marginal revenue equals marginal cost and by charging the maximum price that consumers are willing to pay for that output.

Single-Price Monopoly and Competition Compared (pp. 270–273)

- A single-price monopoly charges a higher price and produces a smaller quantity than a perfectly competitive industry.
- A single-price monopoly restricts output and creates a deadweight loss.
- The cost of monopoly is the sum of deadweight loss and the resources devoted to rent seeking.

Price Discrimination (pp. 273–276)

- Price discrimination is an attempt by the monopoly to convert consumer surplus into economic profit.
- Perfect price discrimination extracts the entire consumer surplus. Such a monopoly charges a different price for each unit sold and obtains the maximum price that each consumer is willing to pay for each unit bought.

- With perfect price discrimination, the monopoly produces the same output as would a perfectly competitive industry.
- Rent seeking with perfect price discrimination might eliminate the entire consumer surplus and producer surplus.

Monopoly Policy Issues (pp. 277–279)

- A monopoly with large economies of scale and economies of scope can produce a larger quantity at a lower price than a competitive industry can achieve, and a monopoly might be more innovative than small competitive firms.
- Efficient regulation requires a monopoly to charge a price equal to marginal cost, but for a natural monopoly, such a price is less than average total cost.
- Average cost pricing is a compromise pricing rule that covers a firm's costs and provides a normal profit but is not efficient. It is more efficient than unregulated profit maximization.

KEY FIGURES AND TABLE

Figure 12.2   Demand and Marginal Revenue, 266
Figure 12.3   Marginal Revenue and Elasticity, 267
Figure 12.4   A Monopoly's Output and Price, 269
Figure 12.5   Monopoly's Smaller Output and Higher Price, 270
Figure 12.6   Efficiency of Monopoly, 271
Figure 12.9   Price Discrimination, 275
Figure 12.10   Perfect Price Discrimination, 276
Figure 12.11   Regulating a Natural Monopoly, 279
Table 12.1   A Monopoly's Output and Price Decision, 268

KEY TERMS

Average cost pricing rule, 279
Barriers to entry, 264
Legal monopoly, 264
Marginal cost pricing rule, 278
Market power, 264
Monopoly, 264
Natural monopoly, 264
Perfect price discrimination, 275
Price discrimination, 265
Rent seeking, 272
Single-price monopoly, 265

PROBLEMS

Go to myeconlab for solutions to odd-numbered problems and additional exercises.

1. Minnie's Mineral Springs, a single-price monopoly, faces the demand schedule.

Price (dollars per bottle)	Quantity demanded (bottles per hour)
10	0
8	1
6	2
4	3
2	4
0	5

   a. Calculate Minnie's total revenue schedule.
   b. Calculate its marginal revenue schedule.

2. Burma Ruby Mines, a single-price monopoly, faces the demand schedule.

Price (dollars per ruby)	Quantity demanded (rubies per day)
1,100	0
900	1
700	2
500	3
300	4

   a. Calculate Burma's total revenue schedule.
   b. Calculate its marginal revenue schedule.

3. Minnie's Mineral Springs in problem 1 has the following total cost:

Quantity produced (bottles per hour)	Total cost (dollars)
0	1
1	3
2	7
3	13
4	21
5	31

   a. Calculate the marginal cost of producing each output in the table.
   b. Calculate the profit-maximizing output and price.
   c. Calculate the economic profit.

   d. Does Minnie's use resources efficiently? Explain your answer.

4. Burma Ruby Mines in problem 2 has the following total cost:

Quantity produced (rubies per day)	Total cost (dollars)
1	1,220
2	1,300
3	1,400
4	1,520

   a. Calculate the marginal cost of producing each quantity listed in the table.
   b. Calculate the profit-maximizing output and price.
   c. Calculate the economic profit.
   d. Does Burma Ruby Mines use its resources efficiently? Explain your answer.

5. The figure illustrates the situation facing the publisher of the only newspaper containing local news in an isolated community.

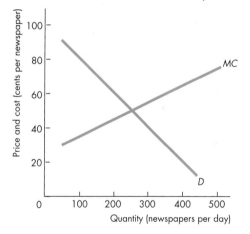

   a. On the graph, draw the publisher's marginal revenue curve.
   b. What are the profit-maximizing quantity and price?
   c. What is the publisher's daily total revenue?
   d. At the price charged, is the demand for newspapers elastic or inelastic? Why?
   e. On the graph, mark in the consumer surplus and deadweight loss.
   f. Might the newspaper try to price discriminate? Explain why or why not.

6. The figure illustrates the situation facing the only coffee shop in an isolated community.

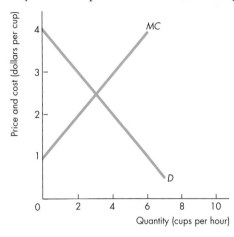

a. What are the profit-maximizing quantity and price of coffee?
b. On the graph, mark the coffee shop's profit.
c. What are consumer surplus and deadweight loss?
d. What is the efficient quantity? Explain your answer.
e. Might the coffee shop try to price discriminate? Explain why or why not.

7. The figure shows the situation facing a natural monopoly that cannot price discriminate.

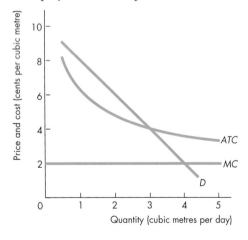

What quantity will be produced and what will be the deadweight loss if the firm is
a. An unregulated profit maximizer?
b. Regulated to earn only normal profit?
c. Regulated to be efficient?

8. In problem 7, marginal cost doubles, what now are your answers?

CRITICAL THINKING

1. After you have studied *Reading Between the Lines* on pp. 280–281, answer the following questions:
   a. Why is eBay a monopoly but Google not a monopoly?
   b. How would you regulate the Internet search engine business to ensure that resources are used efficiently?
   c. How would you regulate the Internet auction business to ensure that resources are used efficiently?
   "Anyone is free to buy stock in eBay, so everyone is free to share in eBay's economic profit, and the bigger that economic profit, the better for all." Evaluate this statement.

WEB EXERCISES

Use the links on ⓧ **myeconlab to work the following exercises.**

1. Read the statement by Ralph Nader about Microsoft.
   a. What are Ralph Nader's main claims about Microsoft?
   b. Do you agree with Ralph Nader? Why or why not?
   c. If some other operating systems are better than Windows, why don't they take off?
   d. Does Ralph Nader identify the main costs to the consumer of Microsoft's practices? Explain why or why not.
2. Study the market for computer chips.
   a. Is it correct to call Intel a monopoly? Why or why not?
   b. How does Intel try to raise barriers to entry in this market?
3. Learn about developments in the Canadian railroad industry of the 1880s.
   a. Was Canadian Pacific a monopoly? Why or why not?
   b. What other elements of market power are discussed on this Web page?
   c. Do you think monopoly was a bigger problem in the 1880s than it is today? Why or why not?

Monopolistic Competition and Oligopoly

CHAPTER 13

Searching the Globe for a Niche

Globalization brings an enormous diversity of products. Canadians enjoy hundreds of varieties of products from around the world. And our entrepreneurs along with others from Europe and the United States search the globe for niche markets in which to sell their products and earn a profit. Paul Rasch, whom you will meet in *Reading Between the Lines* at the end of this chapter, is one of these entrepreneurs. Mr. Rasch sells fruit juice in a fiercely competitive Chinese market. How does he set his price, pick his product line, and choose the quantity to produce? How is Mr. Rasch's profit affected by the actions of other firms in the market?

Two firms make the chips that drive most PCs: Advanced Micro Devices and Intel. How does competition between just two chip makers work? Do they operate in the social interest, like firms in perfect competition? Or do they restrict output to increase profit, like a monopoly?

◆ The theories of perfect competition and monopoly don't predict the behaviour of the firms we've just described. To understand the search for a market niche and the way markets work when only a handful of firms compete, we need the richer models that are explained in this chapter.

After studying this chapter, you will be able to

- **Define and identify monopolistic competition**
- **Explain how price and output are determined in a monopolistically competitive industry**
- **Explain why advertising costs are high in a monopolistically competitive industry**
- **Define and identify oligopoly**
- **Explain two traditional oligopoly models**
- **Use game theory to explain how price and output are determined in oligopoly**
- **Use game theory to explain other strategic decisions**

What Is Monopolistic Competition?

YOU HAVE STUDIED PERFECT COMPETITION, IN which a large number of firms produce at the lowest possible cost, earn no economic profit, and are efficient. And you've studied monopoly, in which a single firm restricts output, produces at a higher cost and price than in perfect competition, and is inefficient.

Most real-world markets are competitive but not perfectly competitive because firms in these markets possess some power to set their prices as monopolies do. We call this type of market *monopolistic competition*.

Monopolistic competition is a market structure in which

- A large number of firms compete.
- Each firm produces a differentiated product.
- Firms compete on product quality, price, and marketing.
- Firms are free to enter and exit.

Large Number of Firms

In monopolistic competition, as in perfect competition, the industry consists of a large number of firms. The presence of a large number of firms has three implications for the firms in the industry.

Small Market Share In monopolistic competition, each firm supplies a small part of the total industry output. Consequently, each firm has only limited power to influence the price of its product. Each firm's price can deviate from the average price of other firms by a relatively small amount.

Ignore Other Firms A firm in monopolistic competition must be sensitive to the average market price of the product. But it does not pay attention to any one individual competitor. Because all the firms are relatively small, no one firm can dictate market conditions, and so no one firm's actions directly affect the actions of the other firms.

Collusion Impossible Firms in monopolistic competition would like to be able to conspire to fix a higher price—called *collusion*. But because there are many firms, collusion is not possible.

Product Differentiation

A firm practises **product differentiation** if it makes a product that is slightly different from the products of competing firms. A differentiated product is one that is a close substitute but not a perfect substitute for the products of the other firms. Some people will pay more for one variety of the product, so when its price rises, the quantity demanded falls but it does not (necessarily) fall to zero. For example, Adidas, Asics, Diadora, Etonic, Fila, New Balance, Nike, Puma, and Reebok all make differentiated running shoes. Other things remaining the same, if the price of Adidas running shoes rises and the prices of the other shoes remain constant, Adidas sells fewer shoes and the other producers sell more. But Adidas shoes don't disappear unless the price rises by a large enough amount.

Competing on Quality, Price, and Marketing

Product differentiation enables a firm to compete with other firms in three areas: product quality, price, and marketing.

Quality The quality of a product is the physical attributes that make it different from the products of other firms. Quality includes design, reliability, the service provided to the buyer, and the buyer's ease of access to the product. Quality lies on a spectrum that runs from high to low. Some firms—such as Dell Computer Corp.—offer high-quality products. They are well designed and reliable, and the customer receives quick and efficient service. Other firms offer a lower-quality product that is less well designed, that might not work perfectly, and that the buyer must travel some distance to obtain.

Price Because of product differentiation, a firm in monopolistic competition faces a downward-sloping demand curve. So, like a monopoly, the firm can set both its price and its output. But there is a tradeoff between the product's quality and price. A firm that makes a high-quality product can charge a higher price than a firm that makes a low-quality product.

Marketing Because of product differentiation, a firm in monopolistic competition must market its product. Marketing takes two main forms: advertising and packaging. A firm that produces a high-quality product wants to sell it for a suitably high price. To be able to do so, it must advertise and package its product in a way that convinces buyers that they are getting the higher quality for which they are paying a higher price. For example, pharmaceutical companies advertise and package their brand-name drugs to persuade buyers that these items are superior to the lower-priced generic alternatives. Similarly, a low-quality producer uses advertising and packaging to persuade buyers that although the quality is low, the low price more than compensates for this fact.

Entry and Exit

In monopolistic competition, there is free entry and free exit. Consequently, a firm cannot make an economic profit in the long run. When firms make an economic profit, new firms enter the industry. This entry lowers prices and eventually eliminates economic profit. When firms incur economic losses, some firms leave the industry. This exit increases prices and profits and eventually eliminates the economic loss. In long-run equilibrium, firms neither enter nor leave the industry and the firms in the industry make zero economic profit.

Examples of Monopolistic Competition

Figure 13.1 shows ten industries that are good examples of monopolistic competition. These industries have a large number of firms (shown in parentheses after the name of the industry). In the most concentrated of these industries, upholstered household furniture, the 4 largest firms produce 30 percent of the industry's total sales and the 20 largest firms produce 69 percent of total sales. The number on the right is the Herfindahl-Hirschman Index. Producers of clothing, bakery items, plastic bags, and boat building operate in monopolistic competition.

FIGURE 13.1
Examples of Monopolistic Competition

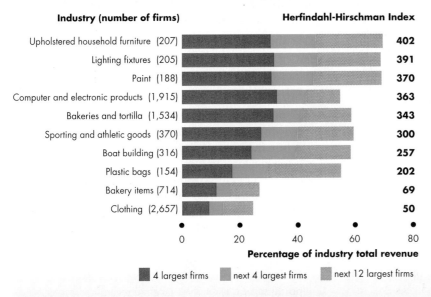

These industries operate in monopolistic competition. The number of firms in the industry is shown in parentheses after the name of the industry. The red bars show the percentage of industry sales by the 4 largest firms. The blue bars show the percentage of industry sales by the next 4 largest firms, and the orange bars show the percentage of industry sales by the next 12 largest firms. So the entire length of the combined red, blue, and orange bars shows the percentage of industry sales by the 20 largest firms. The Herfindahl-Hirschman Index is shown on the right.

Source of data: Adapted from Statistics Canada, Manufacturing, Construction, and Energy Division.

Price and Output in Monopolistic Competition

SUPPOSE YOU'VE BEEN HIRED BY VF CORPORATION, the firm that owns Nautica Clothing Corporation, to manage the production and marketing of Nautica jackets. Think about the decisions that you must make at Nautica. First, you must decide on the design and quality of jackets and on your marketing program. Second, you must decide on the quantity of jackets to produce and the price at which to sell them.

We'll suppose that Nautica has already made its decisions about design, quality, and marketing and now we'll concentrate on the output and pricing decisions. We'll study quality and marketing decisions in the next section.

For a given quality of jackets and marketing activity, Nautica faces given costs and market conditions. How, given its costs and the demand for its jackets, does Nautica decide the quantity of jackets to produce and the price at which to sell them?

The Firm's Short-Run Output and Price Decision

In the short run, a firm in monopolistic competition makes its output and price decision just like a monopoly firm does. Figure 13.2 illustrates this decision for Nautica jackets.

The demand curve for Nautica jackets is *D*. This demand curve tells us the quantity of Nautica jackets demanded at each price, given the prices of other jackets. It is not the demand curve for jackets in general.

The *MR* curve shows the marginal revenue curve associated with the demand curve for Nautica jackets. It is derived just like the marginal revenue curve of a single-price monopoly that you studied in Chapter 12.

The *ATC* curve and the *MC* curve show the average total cost and the marginal cost of producing Nautica jackets.

Nautica's goal is to maximize its economic profit. To do so, it will produce the output at which marginal revenue equals marginal cost. In Fig. 13.2, this output is 125 jackets a day. Nautica charges the highest price that buyers are willing to pay for this quantity, which is determined by the demand curve. This price is $75 per jacket. When Nautica produces 125 jackets a day, its average total cost is $25 per jacket and it makes an economic profit of $6,250 a day ($50 per jacket

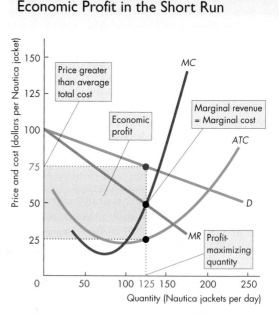

FIGURE 13.2

Economic Profit in the Short Run

Profit is maximized where marginal revenue equals marginal cost. The profit-maximizing quantity is 125 jackets a day. The price of $75 a jacket exceeds the average total cost of $25 a jacket, so the firm makes an economic profit of $50 a jacket. The blue rectangle illustrates economic profit, which equals $6,250 a day ($50 a jacket multiplied by 125 jackets a day).

multiplied by 125 jackets a day). The blue rectangle shows Nautica's economic profit.

Profit Maximizing Might Be Loss Minimizing

Figure 13.2 shows that Nautica is earning a healthy economic profit. But such an outcome is not inevitable. A firm might face a level of demand for its product that is too low for it to earn an economic profit.

Excite@Home was such a firm. Offering high-speed Internet service over the same cable that provides television, Excite@Home hoped to capture a large share of the Internet portal market in competition with AOL, MSN, and a host of other providers.

Figure 13.3 illustrates the situation facing Excite@Home in 2001. The demand curve for its portal service is *D*, the marginal revenue curve is *MR*, the average total cost curve is *ATC*, and the marginal cost curve is *MC*. Excite@Home maximized profit—

FIGURE 13.3

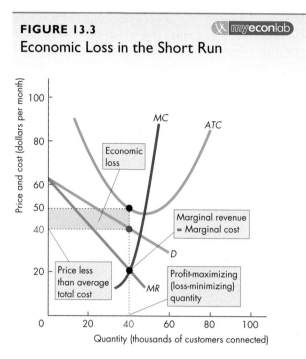

Economic Loss in the Short Run

Profit is maximized where marginal revenue equals marginal cost. The loss-minimizing quantity is 40,000 customers. The price of $40 a month is less than the average total cost of $50 a month, so the firm incurs an economic loss of $10 a customer. The red rectangle illustrates the economic loss, which equals $400,000 a month ($10 a customer multiplied by 40,000 customers).

equivalently, it minimized its loss—by producing the output at which marginal revenue equals marginal cost. In Fig. 13.3, this output is 40,000 customers. Excite@Home charged the price that buyers were willing to pay for this quantity, which was determined by the demand curve and which was $40 a month. With 40,000 customers, Excite@Home's average total cost was $50 per customer, so it incurred an economic loss of $400,000 a month ($10 a customer multiplied by 40,000 customers). The red rectangle shows Excite@Home's economic loss.

So far, the firm in monopolistic competition looks like a single-price monopoly. It produces the quantity at which marginal revenue equals marginal cost and then charges the highest price that buyers are willing to pay for that quantity, determined by the demand curve. The key difference between monopoly and monopolistic competition lies in what happens next when firms either make economic profits or incur economic losses.

Long Run: Zero Economic Profit

A firm like Excite@Home is not going to incur an economic loss for long. Eventually, it goes out of business. Also, there is no restriction on entry into monopolistic competition, so if firms in an industry are making economic profits, other firms have an incentive to enter that industry.

As the Gap and other firms start to make jackets similar to jackets made by Nautica, the demand for Nautica jackets decreases. The demand curve for Nautica jackets and the marginal revenue curve shift leftward. And as these curves shift leftward, the profit-maximizing quantity and price fall.

Figure 13.4 shows the long-run equilibrium. The demand curve for Nautica jackets and the marginal revenue curve have shifted leftward. The firm produces 75 jackets a day and sells them for $50 each. At this output level, average total cost is also $50 per jacket.

FIGURE 13.4

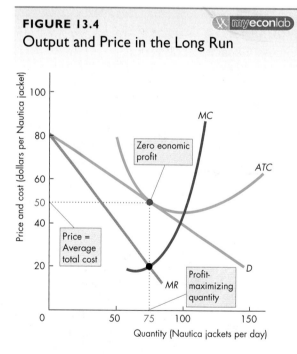

Output and Price in the Long Run

Economic profit encourages entry, which decreases the demand for each firm's product. When the demand curve touches the ATC curve at the quantity at which MR equals MC, the market is in long-run equilibrium. The output that maximizes profit is 75 jackets a day, and the price is $50 per jacket. Average total cost is also $50 per jacket, so economic profit is zero.

So Nautica is making zero economic profit on its jackets. When all the firms in the industry are making zero economic profit, there is no incentive for new firms to enter.

If demand is so low relative to costs that firms incur economic losses, exit will occur. As firms leave an industry, the demand for the products of the remaining firms increases and their demand curves shift rightward. The exit process ends when all the firms in the industry are making zero economic profit.

Monopolistic Competition and Perfect Competition

Figure 13.5 compares monopolistic competition and perfect competition and highlights two key differences between them:

- Excess capacity
- Markup

Excess Capacity A firm has excess capacity if it produces below its efficient scale, which is the quantity at which average total cost is a minimum—the quantity at the bottom of the U-shaped *ATC* curve. In Fig. 13.5, the efficient scale is 100 jackets a day. Nautica (part a) produces 75 Nautica jackets a day and has *excess capacity* of 25 jackets a day. But if all jackets are alike and are produced by firms in perfect competition (part b) each firm produces 100 jackets a day, which is the efficient scale. Average total cost is the lowest possible only in *perfect* competition.

You can see the excess capacity in monopolistic competition all around you. Family restaurants (except for the truly outstanding ones) almost always have some empty tables. You can always get a pizza delivered in less than 30 minutes. It is rare that every pump at a gas station is in use with customers waiting in line. There is always an abundance of realtors ready to help find or sell a home. These industries are examples of monopolistic competition. The firms

---

FIGURE 13.5

Excess Capacity and Markup

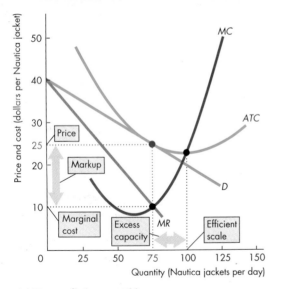

(a) Monopolistic competition

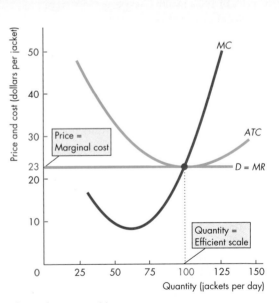

(b) Perfect competition

The efficient scale is 100 jackets a day. In monopolistic competition in the long run, because the firm faces a downward-sloping demand curve for its product, the quantity produced is less than the efficient scale and the firm has excess capacity. Price exceeds marginal cost by the amount of the markup.

In contrast, because in perfect competition the demand for each firm's product is perfectly elastic, the quantity produced equals the efficient scale and price equals marginal cost. The firm produces at the least possible cost and there is no markup.

have excess capacity. They could sell more by cutting their prices, but they would then incur losses.

Markup A firm's markup is the amount by which price exceeds marginal cost. Figure 13.5(a) shows Nautica's markup. In perfect competition, price always equals marginal cost and there is no markup. Figure 13.5(b) shows this case. In monopolistic competition, buyers pay a higher price than in perfect competition and also pay more than marginal cost.

Is Monopolistic Competition Efficient?

You've learned that resources are used efficiently when marginal benefit equals marginal cost. You've also learned that price measures marginal benefit. So if the price of a Nautica jacket exceeds the marginal cost of producing it, the quantity of Nautica jackets produced is less than the efficient quantity. And you've just seen that in long-run equilibrium in monopolistic competition, price *does* exceed marginal cost. So is the quantity produced in monopolistic competition less than the efficient quantity?

Making the Relevant Comparison Two economists meet in the street, and one asks the other how her husband is. "Compared to what?" is the quick reply. This bit of economic wit illustrates a key point: Before we can conclude that something needs fixing, we must check out the available alternatives.

The markup that drives a gap between price and marginal cost in monopolistic competition arises from product differentiation. It is because Nautica jackets are not quite the same as jackets from Banana Republic, CK, Diesel, DKNY, Earl Jackets, Gap, Levi, Ralph Lauren, or any of the other dozens of producers of jackets that the demand for Nautica jackets is not perfectly elastic. The only way in which the demand for jackets from Nautica might be perfectly elastic is if there is only one kind of jacket and all firms make it. In this situation, Nautica jackets are indistinguishable from all other jackets. They don't even have identifying labels.

If there was only one kind of jacket, the marginal benefit of jackets would almost certainly be less than it is with variety. People value variety. And people value variety not only because it enables each person to select what he or she likes best but also because it provides an external benefit. Most of us enjoy seeing variety in the choices of others. Contrast a scene from the China of

the 1960s, when everyone wore a Mao tunic, with the China of today, where everyone wears the clothes of their own choosing. Or contrast a scene from the Germany of the 1930s, when almost everyone who could afford a car owned a first-generation Volkswagen Beetle, with the world of today with its enormous variety of styles and types of automobiles.

If people value variety, why don't we see infinite variety? The answer is that variety is costly. Each different variety of any product must be designed, and then customers must be informed about it. These initial costs of design and marketing—called setup costs—mean that some varieties that are too close to others already available are just not worth creating.

The Bottom Line Product variety is both valued and costly. The efficient degree of product variety is the one for which the marginal benefit of product variety equals its marginal cost. The loss that arises because the marginal benefit of one more unit of a given variety exceeds marginal cost is offset by a gain that arises from having an efficient degree of product variety. So compared to the alternative—complete product uniformity—monopolistic competition is probably efficient.

REVIEW QUIZ

1 How does a firm in monopolistic competition decide how much to produce and at what price to offer its product for sale?
2 Why can a firm in monopolistic competition earn an economic profit only in the short run?
3 Why do firms in monopolistic competition operate with excess capacity?
4 Why is there a price markup over marginal cost in monopolistic competition?
5 Is monopolistic competition efficient?

myeconlab **Study Plan 13.2**

You've seen how the firm in monopolistic competition determines its output and price in both the short run and the long run when the firm produces a given product and undertakes a given marketing effort. But how does the firm *choose* its product quality and marketing effort? We'll now study these decisions.

Product Development and Marketing

WHEN WE STUDIED NAUTICA'S OUTPUT AND price decisions, we assumed that it had already made its product quality and marketing decisions. We're now going to study these decisions and the impact they have on the firm's output, price, and economic profit.

Innovation and Product Development

The prospect of new firms entering the industry keeps firms in monopolistic competition on their toes!

To enjoy economic profits, firms in monopolistic competition must be continually seeking ways of keeping one step ahead of imitators—other firms who imitate the success of the economically profitable firms.

One major way of trying to maintain economic profit is for a firm to seek out new products that will provide it with a competitive edge, even if only temporarily. A firm that introduces a new and differentiated product faces a less elastic demand curve and is able to increase its price and earn an economic profit. Eventually, imitators will make close substitutes for the innovative product and compete away the economic profit arising from an initial advantage. So to restore economic profit, the firm must again innovate.

Cost Versus Benefit of Product Innovation The decision to innovate is based on the same type of profit-maximizing calculation that you've already studied. Innovation and product development are costly activities, but they also bring in additional revenues. The firm must balance the cost and benefit at the margin. At a low level of product development, the marginal revenue from a better product exceeds the marginal cost. When the marginal dollar of product development expenditure (the marginal cost of product development) brings in a dollar of additional revenue (the marginal benefit of product development), the firm is spending the profit-maximizing amount on product development.

For example, when Eidos Interactive released "Lara Croft Tomb Raider: The Angel of Darkness," it was probably not the best game that Eidos could have created. But it was a game with features whose marginal benefit—and consumers' willingness to pay—equalled the marginal cost of those features.

Efficiency and Product Innovation Is product innovation an efficient activity? Does it benefit the consumer? There are two views about the answers to these questions. One view is that monopolistic competition brings to market many improved products that give great benefits to the consumer. Clothing, kitchen and other household appliances, computers, computer programs, cars, and many other products keep getting better every year, and the consumer benefits from these improved products.

But many so-called improvements amount to little more than changing the appearance of a product or giving a different look to the packaging. In these cases, there is little objective benefit to the consumer.

But regardless of whether a product improvement is real or imagined, its value to the consumer is its marginal benefit, which equals the amount the consumer is willing to pay. In other words, the value of product improvements is the increase in price that the consumer is willing to pay. The marginal benefit to the producer is marginal revenue, which in equilibrium equals marginal cost. Because price exceeds marginal cost in monopolistic competition, product improvement is not pushed to its efficient level.

Advertising

Designing and developing products that are actually different from those of its competitors helps a firm achieve some product differentiation. But firms also attempt to create a consumer perception of product differentiation even when actual differences are small. Advertising and packaging are the principal means firms use to achieve this end. An American Express card is a different product from a Visa card. But the actual differences are not the main ones that American Express emphasizes in its marketing. The deeper message is that if you use an American Express card, you can be like Tiger Woods (or some other high-profile successful person).

Advertising Expenditures Firms in monopolistic competition incur huge costs to ensure that buyers appreciate and value the differences between their own products and those of their competitors. So a large proportion of the price we pay for a good covers the cost of selling it. And this proportion is increasing. Advertising in newspapers and magazines and on radio, television, and the Internet is the main selling cost. But it is not the only one. Selling costs include the cost of shopping malls that look like movie sets, glossy catalogues and brochures, and the salaries, air-fares, and hotel bills of salespeople.

The total scale of advertising costs is hard to estimate, but some components can be measured. A survey conducted by a commercial agency suggests that for cleaning supplies and toys, around 15 percent of the price of one of these items is spent on advertising. Figure 13.6 shows estimates for some industries.

For the North American economy as a whole, some 20,000 advertising agencies employ more than 200,000 people and have sales of $45 billion. But these numbers are only part of the total cost of advertising because firms have their own internal advertising departments, the costs of which we can only guess.

Advertising expenditures and other selling costs affect the profits of firms in two ways. They increase costs, and they change demand. Let's look at these effects.

Selling Costs and Total Cost Selling costs such as advertising expenditures increase the costs of a monopolistically competitive firm above those of a

perfectly competitive firm or a monopoly. Advertising costs and other selling costs are fixed costs. They do not vary as total output varies. So, just like fixed production costs, advertising costs per unit decrease as production increases.

Figure 13.7 shows how selling costs and advertising expenditures change a firm's average total cost. The blue curve shows the average total cost of production. The red curve shows the firm's average total cost of production plus advertising. The height of the red area between the two curves shows the average fixed cost of advertising. The *total* cost of advertising is fixed. But the *average* cost of advertising decreases as output increases.

The figure shows that if advertising increases the quantity sold by a large enough amount, it can lower average total cost. For example, if the quantity sold increases from 25 jackets a day with no advertising to 100 jackets a day with advertising, average total cost falls from $60 to $40 a jacket. The reason is that although the *total* fixed cost has increased, the greater fixed cost is spread over a greater output, so average total cost decreases.

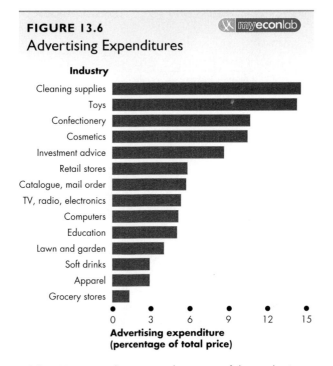

FIGURE 13.6
Advertising Expenditures

Advertising expenditures are a large part of the total price of cleaning supplies, toys, confectionery, and cosmetics.

Source of data: From Schoenfeld & Associates, Lincolnwood, IL. Reported at www.toolkit.cch.com/text/p03_7006.asp.

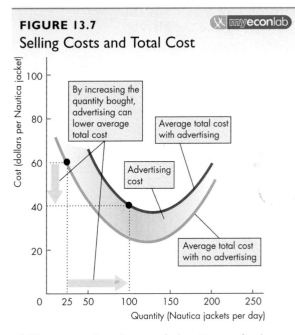

FIGURE 13.7
Selling Costs and Total Cost

Selling costs such as the cost of advertising are fixed costs. When added to the average total cost of production, selling costs increase average total cost by a greater amount at small outputs than at large outputs. If advertising enables sales to increase from 25 jackets a day to 100 jackets a day, average total cost *falls* from $60 to $40 a jacket.

Selling Costs and Demand Advertising and other selling efforts change the demand for a firm's product. But how? Does demand increase or does it decrease? The most natural answer is that advertising increases demand. By informing people about the quality of its products or by persuading people to switch from the products of other firms, a firm might expect to increase the demand for its own products.

But all firms in monopolistic competition advertise. And all seek to persuade customers that they have the best deal. If advertising enables a firm to survive, it might increase the number of firms in the market. And to the extent that it increases the number of firms, it *decreases* the demand for any one firm's product. It also makes the demand for any one firm's product more elastic. So advertising can end up not only lowering average total cost but also lowering the markup and the price.

Figure 13.8 illustrates this possible effect of advertising. In part (a), with no advertising, the demand for Nautica jackets is not very elastic. Profit is maximized at 75 jackets per day, and the markup is large. In part

(b), advertising, which is a fixed cost, increases average total cost from ATC_0 to ATC_1 but leaves marginal cost unchanged at MC. Demand becomes much more elastic, the profit-maximizing quantity increases, and the markup shrinks.

Using Advertising to Signal Quality

Some advertising, such as the Tiger Woods American Express card ads on television and in glossy magazines or the expensive Coke and Pepsi ads, seems hard to understand. There doesn't seem to be any concrete information about a credit card in the glistening smile of a golfer. And surely everyone knows about Coke and Pepsi. What is the gain from pouring millions of dollars a month into advertising these well-known colas?

One answer is that advertising is a signal to the consumer of a high-quality product. A **signal** is an action taken by an informed person (or firm) to send a message to uninformed people. Think about two colas:

FIGURE 13.8
Advertising and the Markup

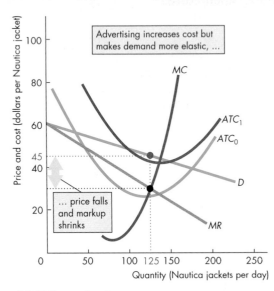

(a) No firms advertise

(b) All firms advertise

With no firms advertising, demand is low and not very elastic. The profit-maximizing output is small, the markup is large, and the price is high.

Advertising increases average total cost and shifts the *ATC* curve upward from ATC_0 to ATC_1. With all firms advertising, the demand for each firm's product becomes more elastic. Output increases, the price falls, and the markup shrinks.

Coke and Oke. Oke knows that its cola is not very good and that its taste varies a lot depending on which cheap batch of unsold cola it happens to buy each week. So Oke knows that while it could get a lot of people to try Oke by advertising, they would all quickly discover what a poor product it is and switch back to the cola they bought before. Coke, in contrast, knows that its product has a high-quality consistent taste and that once consumers have tried it, there is a good chance they'll never drink anything else. On the basis of this reasoning, Oke doesn't advertise but Coke does. And Coke spends a lot of money to make a big splash.

Cola drinkers who see Coke's splashy ads know that the firm would not spend so much money advertising if its product were not truly good. So consumers reason that Coke is indeed a really good product. The flashy expensive ad has signalled that Coke is really good without saying anything about Coke.

Notice that if advertising is a signal, it doesn't need any specific product information. It just needs to be expensive and hard to miss. That's what a lot of advertising looks like. So the signalling theory of advertising predicts much of the advertising that we see.

Brand Names

Many firms create and spend a lot of money promoting a brand name. Why? What benefit does a brand name bring to justify the sometimes high cost of establishing it?

The basic answer is that a brand name provides information about the quality of a product to consumers and an incentive to the producer to achieve a high and consistent quality standard.

To see how a brand name helps the consumer, think about how you use brand names to get information about quality. You're on a road trip, and it is time to find a place to spend the night. You see roadside advertisements for Holiday Inn and Embassy Suites and for Joe's Motel and Annie's Driver Stop. You know about Holiday Inn and Embassy Suites because you've stayed in them before. And you've seen their advertisements. You know what to expect from them. You have no information at all about Joe's and Annie's. They might be better than the lodging you do know about, but without that knowledge, you're not going to chance them. You use the brand name as information and stay at Holiday Inn.

This same story explains why a brand name provides an incentive to achieve high and consistent quality. Because no one would know whether they were

offering a high standard of service, Joe's and Annie's have no incentive to do so. But equally, because everyone expects a given standard of service from Holiday Inn, a failure to meet a customer's expectation would almost surely lose that customer to a competitor. So Holiday Inn has a strong incentive to deliver what it promises in the advertising that creates its brand name.

Efficiency of Advertising and Brand Names

To the extent that advertising and brand names provide consumers with information about the precise nature of product differences and about product quality, they benefit the consumer and enable a better product choice to be made. But the opportunity cost of the additional information must be weighed against the gain to the consumer.

The final verdict on the efficiency of monopolistic competition is ambiguous. In some cases, the gains from extra product variety unquestionably offset the selling costs and the extra cost arising from excess capacity. The tremendous varieties of books and magazines, clothing, food, and drinks are examples of such gains. It is less easy to see the gains from being able to buy a brand-name drug that has a chemical composition identical to that of a cheaper generic alternative. But many people do willingly pay more for the brand-name alternative.

REVIEW QUIZ

1 What are the two main ways, other than by adjusting price, in which a firm in monopolistic competition competes with other firms?
2 Why might product innovation and development be efficient and why might it be inefficient?
3 How does a firm's advertising expenditure influence its cost curves? Does average total cost increase or decrease?
4 How does a firm's advertising expenditure influence the demand for its product? Does demand increase or decrease?
5 Why is it difficult to determine whether monopolistic competition is efficient or inefficient? What is your opinion about the bottom line and why?

myeconlab Study Plan 13.3

What Is Oligopoly?

OLIGOPOLY, LIKE MONOPOLISTIC COMPETITION, lies between perfect competition and monopoly. The firms in oligopoly might produce an identical product and compete only on price, or they might produce a differentiated product and compete on price, product quality, and marketing. **Oligopoly** is a market structure in which

- Natural or legal barriers prevent the entry of new firms.
- A small number of firms compete.

Barriers to Entry

Either natural or legal barriers to entry can create oligopoly. You saw in Chapter 12 how economies of scale and market demand form a natural barrier to entry that can create a *natural monopoly*. These same factors can create a natural oligopoly.

Figure 13.9 illustrates two natural oligopolies. The demand curve, *D* (in both parts of the figure), shows the demand for taxi rides in a town. If the average total cost curve of a taxi company is ATC_1 in part (a), the market is a natural **duopoly**—an oligopoly market with two firms. You can probably see some examples of duopoly where you live. Some cities have only two taxi companies, two car rental firms, two copy centres, or two bookstores.

The lowest price at which the firm would remain in business is $10 a ride. At that price, the quantity of rides demanded is 60 a day, the quantity that can be provided by just two firms. There is no room in this market for three firms. But if there were only one firm, it would earn an economic profit and a second firm would enter to take some of the business and economic profit.

If the average total cost curve of a taxi company is ATC_2 in part (b), the efficient scale of one firm is 20 rides a day. This market is large enough for three firms.

A legal oligopoly arises when a legal barrier to entry protects the small number of firms in a market. A city might license two taxi firms or two bus companies, for example, even though the combination of market demand and economies of scale leaves room for more than two firms.

FIGURE 13.9
Natural Oligopoly

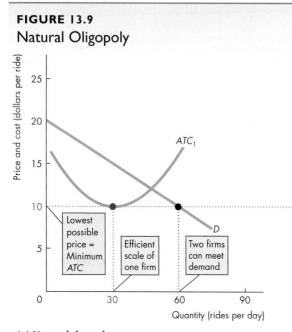

(a) Natural duopoly

The lowest possible price is $10 a ride, which is the minimum average total cost. When a firm produces 30 rides a day, the efficient scale, two firms can satisfy the market demand. This natural oligopoly has two firms—a natural duopoly.

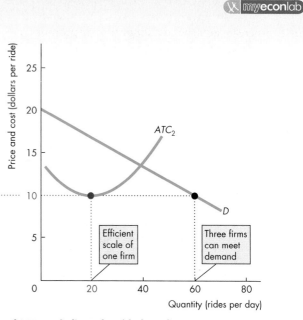

(b) Natural oligopoly with three firms

When the efficient scale of one firm is 20 rides per day, three firms can satisfy the market demand at the lowest possible price. This natural oligopoly has three firms.

Small Number of Firms

Because barriers to entry exist, oligopoly consists of a small number of firms each of which has a large share of the market. Such firms are interdependent and they face a temptation to collude to increase their joint economic profit.

Interdependence With a small number of firms in a market, each firm's actions influence the profits of the other firms. To see how, suppose you run one of the three gas stations in a small town. If you cut your price, your market share increases, and your profits might increase too. But the market share and profits of the other two firms fall, so they most likely cut their prices too. If they do cut their prices, your market share and profit take a tumble. So before deciding to cut your price, you must predict how the other firms will react and take into account the effects of those reactions on your own profit. You are interdependent.

Temptation to Collude When a small number of firms share a market, they can increase their profits by forming a cartel and acting like a monopoly. A **cartel** is a group of firms acting together—colluding—to limit output, raise price, and increase economic profit. Cartels are illegal, but they do operate in some markets. But for reasons that you'll discover in this chapter, cartels tend to break down.

Examples of Oligopoly

Figure 13.10 shows some examples of oligopoly. Identifying oligopoly is the flip side of identifying monopolistic competition. But the borderline between the two market types is hard to pin down. As a practical matter, we try to identify oligopoly by looking at the four-firm concentration ratio and the Herfindahl-Hirschman Index, qualified with other information about the geographical scope of the market and barriers to entry. The HHI that divides oligopoly from monopolistic competition is generally taken to be 1,800. An HHI below 1,800 is usually an example of monopolistic competition, and a market in which the HHI exceeds 1,800 is usually an example of oligopoly.

REVIEW QUIZ

1 What are the two distinguishing features of oligopoly?
2 Why are firms in oligopoly interdependent?
3 Why do firms in oligopoly face a temptation to collude?
4 Think of some examples of oligopolies that you buy from.

myeconlab Study Plan 13.4

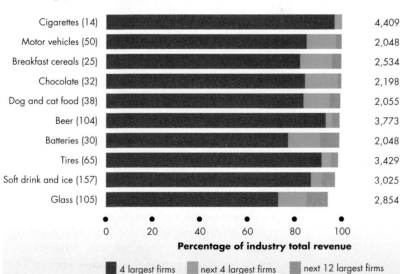

FIGURE 13.10
Examples of Oligopoly

These industries operate in oligopoly. The number of firms in the industry is shown in parentheses after the name of the industry. The red bars show the percentage of industry sales by the 4 largest firms. The blue bars show the percentage of industry sales by the next 4 largest firms, and the orange bars show the percentage of industry sales by the next 12 largest firms. So the entire length of the combined red, blue, and orange bars shows the percentage of industry sales by the 20 largest firms. The Herfindahl-Hirschman Index is shown on the right.

Source of data: Adatped from Statistics Canada, Manufacturing, Construction, and Energy Division.

Two Traditional Oligopoly Models

IN OLIGOPOLY, THE QUANTITY SOLD BY ANY ONE firm depends on that firm's price *and* on the other firms' prices and quantities sold. If you run one of the three gas stations in a small town, you know that you can't ignore the response of your competitor's to your price decisions. But how will your competitors respond? If you cut your price, will they cut their price too? And if you raise your price, will they follow you with their own price rise? Or will they hold their price and leave you to lose market share? Before deciding to raise or lower your price, you must predict how the other firms will react and attempt to calculate the effects of those reactions on your own profit.

Several models have been developed to explain the prices and quantities in oligopoly markets. But no one theory has been found that can explain all the different types of behaviour that we observe in such markets. The models fall into two broad groups: traditional models and game theory models. We'll look at examples of both, starting with two traditional models.

The Kinked Demand Curve Model

The kinked demand curve model of oligopoly is based on the assumption that each firm believes that if it raises its price, others will not follow, but if it cuts its price, other firms will cut theirs.

Figure 13.11 illustrates what the firm believes is the demand for its output. The demand curve (D) has a kink at the current price, P, and quantity, Q. At prices above P, a small price rise brings a big decrease in the quantity sold because other firms do not raise their prices and the firm believes that it loses market share. At prices below P, even a large price cut brings only a small increase in the quantity sold because other firms match the price cut and the firm gets no price advantage over its competitors.

The kink in the demand curve creates a break in the marginal revenue curve (MR). To maximize profit, the firm produces the quantity at which marginal cost equals marginal revenue. That quantity, Q, is where the marginal cost curve passes through the gap AB in the marginal revenue curve. If marginal cost fluctuates between A and B, such as the marginal cost curves MC_0 and MC_1, the firm does not change its price. Only if marginal cost fluctuates outside the range AB does the firm change its price. So the kinked demand curve

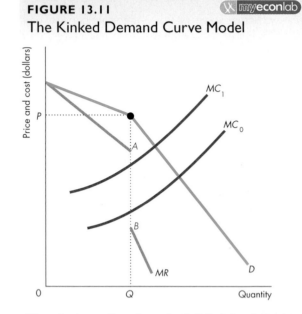

FIGURE 13.11   myeconlab
The Kinked Demand Curve Model

The price in an oligopoly market is *P*. Each firm believes that the demand for its output is the demand curve *D*. At prices above *P*, a small price rise brings a big decrease in the quantity sold because other firms do not raise their prices. At prices below *P*, even a big price cut brings only a small increase in the quantity sold because other firms cut their prices. Because the demand curve is kinked, the marginal revenue curve, *MR*, has a gap *AB*. Profit is maximized by producing *Q*. Marginal cost changes inside the range *AB* leave the price and quantity unchanged.

model predicts that the price is insensitive to small cost changes. A problem with the kinked demand curve model is that the firm's beliefs about the demand for its output are not always correct and the firm can figure that out. If marginal cost increases by enough to cause the firm to increase its price and if all firms experience the same increase in marginal cost, all firms will increase their prices together. The firm's belief that others will not join it in a price rise is incorrect. A firm that bases its actions on beliefs that are wrong does not maximize profit and might even incur an economic loss.

Dominant Firm Oligopoly

A second traditional model explains a dominant firm oligopoly, which arises when one firm—the dominant firm—has a big cost advantage over the other firms and produces a large part of the industry output. The dominant firm sets the market price and the other

FIGURE 13.12
A Dominant Firm Oligopoly

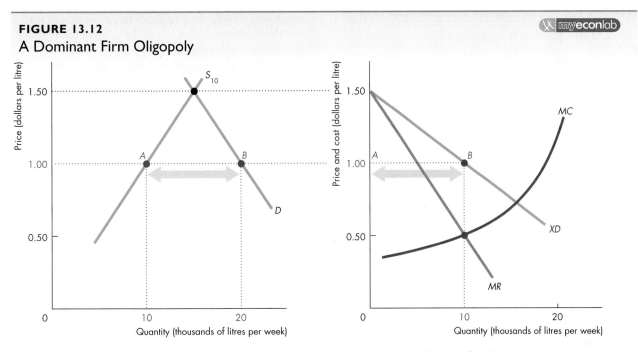

(a) Ten small firms and market demand

The market demand curve for gas in a city is *D* in part (a). There are 10 small competitive firms that together have a supply curve of S_{10}. In addition, there is 1 large firm, Big-G, shown in part (b). Big-G faces the demand curve *XD*, determined as the market demand *D* minus the supply of the 10 small firms S_{10} —the demand that is not satisfied by the small

(b) Big-G's price and output decision

firms. Big-G's marginal revenue is *MR*, and marginal cost is *MC*. Big-G sets its output to maximize profit by equating marginal cost, *MC*, and marginal revenue, *MR*. This output is 10,000 litres per week. The price at which Big-G can sell this quantity is $1 a litre. The 10 small firms take this price, and each firm sells 1,000 litres per week, point *A* in part (a).

firms are price takers. Examples of dominant firm oligopoly are a large gasoline retailer or a big video rental store that dominates its local market.

To see how a dominant firm oligopoly works, suppose that 11 firms operate gas stations in a city. Big-G is the dominant firm. Figure 13.12 shows the market for gas in this city. In part (a), the demand curve *D* tells us the total quantity of gas demanded in the city at each price. The supply curve S_{10} is the supply curve of the 10 small suppliers. Part (b) shows the situation facing Big-G. Its marginal cost curve is *MC*. Big-G faces the demand curve *XD*, and its marginal revenue curve is *MR*. The demand curve *XD* shows the excess demand not met by the 10 small firms. For example, at a price of $1 a litre, the quantity demanded is 20,000 litres, the quantity supplied by the 10 small firms is 10,000 litres, and the excess quantity demanded is 10,000 litres, measured by the distance *AB* in both parts of the figure. To maximize profit, Big-G operates like a monopoly. It sells 10,000 litres a week, where marginal revenue equals marginal

cost, for a price of $1 a litre. The 10 small firms take the price of $1 a litre. They behave just like firms in perfect competition. The quantity of gas demanded in the entire city at $1 a litre is 20,000 litres, as shown in part (a). Of this amount, Big-G sells 10,000 litres and the 10 small firms each sell 1,000 litres.

REVIEW QUIZ

1 What does the kinked demand curve model predict and why must it sometimes make a prediction that contradicts its basic assumption?

2 Do you think a market with a dominant firm is in long-run equilibrium? Explain why or why not.

myeconlab   **Study Plan 13.5**

The traditional models don't enable us to understand all oligopoly markets and we're now going to study some newer models based on game theory.

Oligopoly Games

ECONOMISTS THINK ABOUT OLIGOPOLY AS A GAME, and to study oligopoly markets they use a set of tools called **game theory**. Game theory is a tool for studying *strategic behaviour*—behaviour that takes into account the expected behaviour of others and the recognition of mutual interdependence. Game theory was invented by John von Neumann in 1937 and extended by von Neumann and Oskar Morgenstern in 1944. Today, it is one of the major research fields in economics.

Game theory seeks to understand oligopoly as well as other forms of economic, political, social, and even biological rivalries by using a method of analysis specifically designed to understand games of all types, including the familiar games of everyday life. We will begin our study of game theory and its application to the behaviour of firms by thinking about familiar games.

What Is a Game?

What is a game? At first thought, the question seems silly. After all, there are many different games. There are ball games and parlor games, games of chance and games of skill. But what is it about all these different activities that make them games? What do all these games have in common? All games share four features:

- Rules
- Strategies
- Payoffs
- Outcome

Let's see how these common features of games apply to a game called "the prisoners' dilemma." This game, it turns out, captures some of the essential features of oligopoly, and it gives a good illustration of how game theory works and how it generates predictions.

The Prisoners' Dilemma

Art and Bob have been caught red-handed, stealing a car. Facing airtight cases, they will receive a sentence of two years each for their crime. During his interviews with the two prisoners, the Crown attorney begins to suspect that he has stumbled onto the two people who were responsible for a multimillion-dollar bank robbery some months earlier. But this is just a suspicion. The Crown attorney has no evidence on which he can convict them of the greater crime unless he can get them to confess. The district attorney decides to make the prisoners play a game with the following rules.

Rules Each prisoner (player) is placed in a separate room and cannot communicate with the other prisoner. Each is told that he is suspected of having carried out the bank robbery and that

1. If they both confess to the larger crime, each will receive a sentence of 3 years for both crimes.
2. If he alone confesses and his accomplice does not, he will receive an even shorter sentence of 1 year while his accomplice will receive a 10-year sentence.

Strategies In game theory, **strategies** are all the possible actions of each player. Art and Bob each have two possible actions:

1. Confess to the bank robbery.
2. Deny having committed the bank robbery.

Payoffs Because there are two players, each with two strategies, there are four possible outcomes:

1. Both confess.
2. Both deny.
3. Art confesses and Bob denies.
4. Bob confesses and Art denies.

Each prisoner can work out exactly what happens to him—his *payoff*—in each of these four situations. We can tabulate the four possible payoffs for each of the prisoners in what is called a payoff matrix for the game. A **payoff matrix** is a table that shows the payoffs for every possible action by each player for every possible action by each other player.

Table 13.1 shows a payoff matrix for Art and Bob. The squares show the payoffs for each prisoner—the red triangle in each square shows Art's and the blue triangle shows Bob's. If both prisoners confess (top left), each gets a prison term of 3 years. If Bob confesses but Art denies (top right), Art gets a 10-year sentence and Bob gets a 1-year sentence. If Art confesses and Bob denies (bottom left), Art gets a 1-year sentence and Bob gets a 10-year sentence. Finally, if both of them deny (bottom right), neither can be convicted of the bank robbery charge but both are sentenced for the car theft—a 2-year sentence.

Outcome The choices of both players determine the outcome of the game. To predict that outcome, we use an equilibrium idea proposed by John Nash of Princeton University (who received the Nobel Prize for Economic Science in 1994 and was the subject of the 2001 movie *A Beautiful Mind*). In **Nash equilibrium**, player *A* takes the best possible action given the action of player *B* and player *B* takes the best possible action given the action of player *A*.

In the case of the prisoners' dilemma, the Nash equilibrium occurs when Art makes his best choice given Bob's choice and when Bob makes his best choice given Art's choice.

To find the Nash equilibrium, we compare all the possible outcomes associated with each choice and eliminate those that are dominated—that are not as good as some other choice. Let's find the Nash equilibrium for the prisoners' dilemma game.

Finding the Nash Equilibrium Look at the situation from Art's point of view. If Bob confesses, Art's best action is to confess because in that case, he is sentenced to 3 years rather than 10 years. If Bob does not confess, Art's best action is still to confess because in that case he receives 1 year rather than 2 years. So Art's best action is to confess.

Now look at the situation from Bob's point of view. If Art confesses, Bob's best action is to confess because in that case, he is sentenced to 3 years rather than 10 years. If Art does not confess, Bob's best action is still to confess because in that case, he receives 1 year rather than 2 years. So Bob's best action is to confess.

Because each player's best action is to confess, each does confess, each gets a 3-year prison term, and the Crown attorney has solved the bank robbery. This is the Nash equilibrium of the game.

The Dilemma Now that you have found the solution to the prisoners' dilemma, you can better see the dilemma. The dilemma arises as each prisoner contemplates the consequences of denying. Each prisoner knows that if both of them deny, they will receive only a 2-year sentence for stealing the car. But neither has any way of knowing that his accomplice will deny. Each poses the following questions: Should I deny and rely on my accomplice to deny so that we will both get only 2 years? Or should I confess in the hope of getting just 1 year (provided that my accomplice denies) knowing that if my accomplice does confess, we will both get 3 years in

prison? The dilemma is resolved by finding the equilibrium of the game.

A Bad Outcome For the prisoners, the equilibrium of the game, with each confessing, is not the best outcome. If neither of them confesses, each gets only 2 years for the lesser crime. Isn't there some way in which this better outcome can be achieved? It seems that there is not, because the players cannot communicate with each other. Each player can put himself in the other player's place, and so each player can figure out that there is a best strategy for each of them. The prisoners are indeed in a dilemma. Each knows that he can serve 2 years only if he can trust the other to deny. But each prisoner also knows that it is not in the best interest of the other to deny. So each prisoner knows that he must confess, thereby delivering a bad outcome for both.

The firms in an oligopoly are in a similar situation to Art and Bob in the prisoners' dilemma game. Let's see how we can use this game to understand oligopoly.

TABLE 13.1 Prisoners' Dilemma Payoff Matrix

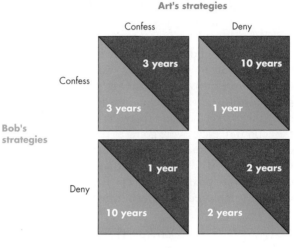

Each square shows the payoffs for the two players, Art and Bob, for each possible pair of actions. In each square, the red triangle shows Art's payoff and the blue triangle shows Bob's. For example, if both confess, the payoffs are in the top left square. The equilibrium of the game is for both players to confess and each gets a 3-year sentence.

An Oligopoly Price-Fixing Game

We can use game theory and a game like the prisoners' dilemma to understand price fixing, price wars, and other aspects of the behaviour of firms in oligopoly. We'll begin with a price-fixing game.

To understand price fixing, we're going to study the special case of duopoly—an oligopoly with two firms. Duopoly is easier to study than oligopoly with three or more firms, and it captures the essence of all oligopoly situations. Somehow, the two firms must share the market. And how they share it depends on the actions of each. We're going to describe the costs of the two firms and the market demand for the item they produce. We're then going to see how game theory helps us to predict the prices charged and the quantities produced by the two firms in a duopoly.

Cost and Demand Conditions Two firms, Trick and Gear, produce switchgears. They have identical costs. Figure 13.13(a) shows their average total cost curve (*ATC*) and marginal cost curve (*MC*). Figure 13.13(b) shows the market demand curve for switchgears (*D*). The two firms produce identical switchgears, so one firm's switchgear is a perfect substitute for the other's. So the market price of each firm's product is identical. The quantity demanded depends on that price—the higher the price, the smaller is the quantity demanded.

This industry is a natural duopoly. Two firms can produce this good at a lower cost than either one firm or three firms can. For each firm, average total cost is at its minimum when production is 3,000 units a week. And when price equals minimum average total cost, the total quantity demanded is 6,000 units a week. So two firms can just produce that quantity.

Collusion We'll suppose that Trick and Gear enter into a collusive agreement. A **collusive agreement** is an agreement between two (or more) producers to form a cartel to restrict output, raise the price, and increase profits. Such an agreement is illegal in Canada and is undertaken in secret. The strategies that firms in a cartel can pursue are to

- Comply
- Cheat

A firm that complies carries out the agreement. A firm that cheats breaks the agreement to its own benefit and to the cost of the other firm.

Because each firm has two strategies, there are four possible combinations of actions for the firms:

1. Both firms comply.
2. Both firms cheat.
3. Trick complies and Gear cheats.
4. Gear complies and Trick cheats.

FIGURE 13.13
Costs and Demand

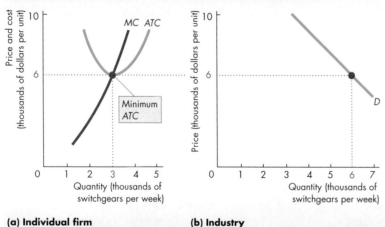

(a) Individual firm

(b) Industry

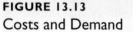

The average total cost curve for each firm is *ATC*, and the marginal cost curve is *MC* (part a). Minimum average total cost is $6,000 a unit, and it occurs at a production of 3,000 units a week.

Part (b) shows the market demand curve. At a price of $6,000, the quantity demanded is 6,000 units per week. The two firms can produce this output at the lowest possible average total cost. If the market had one firm, it would be profitable for another to enter. If the market had three firms, one would exit. There is room for only two firms in this industry. It is a natural duopoly.

Colluding to Maximize Profits Let's work out the payoffs to the two firms if they collude to make the maximum profit for the cartel by acting like a monopoly. The calculations that the two firms perform are the same calculations that a monopoly performs. (You can refresh your memory of these calculations by looking at Chapter 12, pp. 268–269.) The only thing that the duopolists must do beyond what a monopolist does is to agree on how much of the total output each of them will produce.

Figure 13.14 shows the price and quantity that maximize industry profit for the duopolists. Part (a) shows the situation for each firm, and part (b) shows the situation for the industry as a whole. The curve labelled *MR* is the industry marginal revenue curve. This marginal revenue curve is like that of a single-price monopoly (Chapter 12, p. 266). The curve labelled MC_I is the industry marginal cost curve if each firm produces the same level of output. That curve is constructed by adding together the outputs of the two firms at each level of marginal cost. That is, at each level of marginal cost, industry output is twice the output of each individual firm. Thus the curve MC_I in part (b) is twice as far to the right as the curve *MC* in part (a).

To maximize industry profit, the duopolists agree to restrict output to the rate that makes the industry marginal cost and marginal revenue equal. That output rate, as shown in part (b), is 4,000 units a week.

The highest price for which the 4,000 switchgears can be sold is $9,000 each. Trick and Gear agree to charge this price.

To hold the price at $9,000 a unit, production must be not exceed 4,000 units a week. So Trick and Gear must agree on production levels for each of them that total 4,000 units a week. Let's suppose that they agree to split the market equally so that each firm produces 2,000 switchgears a week. Because the firms are identical, this division is the most likely.

The average total cost (*ATC*) of producing 2,000 switchgears a week is $8,000, so the profit per unit is $1,000 and economic profit is $2 million (2,000 units × $1,000 per unit). The economic profit of each firm is represented by the blue rectangle in Fig. 13.14(a).

We have just described one possible outcome for a duopoly game: The two firms collude to produce the monopoly profit-maximizing output and divide that output equally between themselves. From the industry point of view, this solution is identical to a monopoly. A duopoly that operates in this way is indistinguishable from a monopoly. The economic profit that is made by a monopoly is the maximum total profit that can be made by colluding duopolists.

But with price greater than marginal cost, either firm might think of trying to increase profit by cheating on the agreement and producing more than the agreed amount. Let's see what happens if one of the firms does cheat in this way.

FIGURE 13.14

Colluding to Make Monopoly Profits

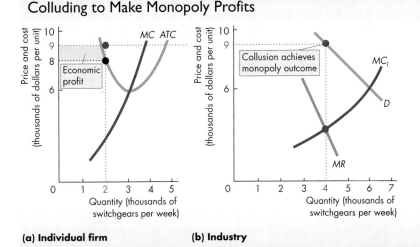

(a) Individual firm

(b) Industry

The industry marginal cost curve, MC_I in part (b), is the horizontal sum of the two firms' marginal cost curves, *MC* in part (a). The industry marginal revenue curve is *MR*. To maximize profit, the firms produce 4,000 units a week (the quantity at which marginal revenue equals marginal cost). They sell that output for $9,000 a unit. Each firm produces 2,000 units a week. Average total cost is $8,000 a unit, so each firm makes an economic profit of $2 million (blue rectangle)—2,000 units multiplied by $1,000 profit a unit.

One Firm Cheats on a Collusive Agreement To set the stage for cheating on their agreement, Trick convinces Gear that demand has decreased and that it cannot sell 2,000 units a week. Trick tells Gear that it plans to cut its price in order to sell the agreed 2,000 units each week. Because the two firms produce an identical product, Gear matches Trick's price cut but continues to produce 2,000 units a week.

In fact, there has been no decrease in demand. Trick plans to increase output, which it knows will lower the price, and Trick wants to ensure that Gear's output remains at the agreed level.

Figure 13.15 illustrates the consequences of Trick's cheating. Part (a) shows Gear (the complier); part (b) shows Trick (the cheat); and part (c) shows the industry as a whole. Suppose that Trick increases output to 3,000 units a week. If Gear sticks to the agreement to produce only 2,000 units a week, total output is 5,000 a week, and given demand in part (c), the price falls to $7,500 a unit.

Gear continues to produce 2,000 units a week at a cost of $8,000 a unit and incurs a loss of $500 a unit, or $1 million a week. This economic loss is represented by the red rectangle in part (a). Trick produces 3,000 units a week at an average total cost of $6,000 each.

With a price of $7,500, Trick makes a profit of $1,500 a unit and therefore an economic profit of $4.5 million. This economic profit is the blue rectangle in part (b).

We've now described a second possible outcome for the duopoly game: One of the firms cheats on the collusive agreement. In this case, the industry output is larger than the monopoly output and the industry price is lower than the monopoly price. The total economic profit made by the industry is also smaller than the monopoly's economic profit. Trick (the cheat) makes an economic profit of $4.5 million, and Gear (the complier) incurs an economic loss of $1 million. The industry makes an economic profit of $3.5 million. Thus the industry profit is $0.5 million less than the economic profit a monopoly would make. But the profit is distributed unevenly. Trick makes a bigger economic profit than it would under the collusive agreement, while Gear incurs an economic loss.

A similar outcome would arise if Gear cheated and Trick complied with the agreement. The industry profit and price would be the same, but in this case, Gear (the cheat) would make an economic profit of $4.5 million and Trick (the complier) would incur an economic loss of $1 million.

Let's next see what happens if both firms cheat.

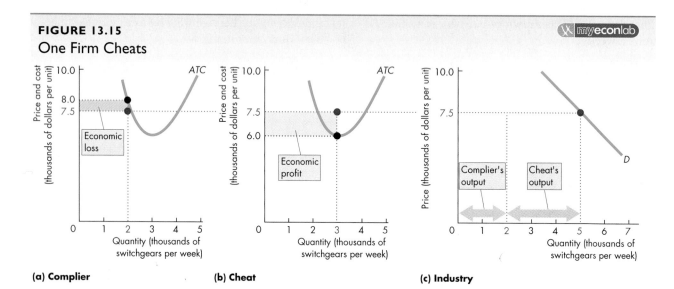

FIGURE 13.15
One Firm Cheats

(a) Complier   (b) Cheat   (c) Industry

One firm, shown in part (a), complies with the agreement and produces 2,000 units. The other firm, shown in part (b), cheats on the agreement and increases its output to 3,000 units. Given the market demand curve, shown in part (c), and with a total production of 5,000 units a week, the price

falls to $7,500. At this price, the complier in part (a) incurs an economic loss of $1 million ($500 per unit × 2,000 units), shown by the red rectangle. In part (b), the cheat makes an economic profit of $4.5 million ($1,500 per unit × 3,000 units), shown by the blue rectangle.

Both Firms Cheat Suppose that both firms cheat and that each firm behaves like the cheating firm that we have just analyzed. Each tells the other that it is unable to sell its output at the going price and that it plans to cut its price. But because both firms cheat, each will propose a successively lower price. As long as price exceeds marginal cost, each firm has an incentive to increase its production—to cheat. Only when price equals marginal cost is there no further incentive to cheat. This situation arises when the price has reached $6,000. At this price, marginal cost equals price. Also, price equals minimum average total cost. At a price less than $6,000, each firm incurs an economic loss. At a price of $6,000, each firm covers all its costs and makes zero economic profit (makes normal profit). Also, at a price of $6,000, each firm wants to produce 3,000 units a week, so the industry output is 6,000 units a week. Given the demand conditions, 6,000 units can be sold at a price of $6,000 each.

Figure 13.16 illustrates the situation just described. Each firm, in part (a), produces 3,000 units a week, and its average total cost is a minimum ($6,000 per unit). The market as a whole, in part (b), operates at the point at which the market demand curve (D) intersects the industry marginal cost curve (MC_I). Each firm has lowered its price and increased its output to try to gain an advantage over the other firm. Each has pushed this process as far as it can without incurring an economic loss.

We have now described a third possible outcome of this duopoly game: Both firms cheat. If both firms

cheat on the collusive agreement, the output of each firm is 3,000 units a week and the price is $6,000. Each firm makes zero economic profit.

The Payoff Matrix Now that we have described the strategies and payoffs in the duopoly game, we can summarize the strategies and the payoffs in the form of the game's payoff matrix. Then we can find the Nash equilibrium.

Table 13.2 sets out the payoff matrix for this game. It is constructed in the same way as the payoff matrix for the prisoners' dilemma in Table 13.1. The squares show the payoffs for the two firms—Gear and Trick. In this case, the payoffs are profits. (For the prisoners' dilemma, the payoffs were losses.)

The table shows that if both firms cheat (top left), they achieve the perfectly competitive outcome—each firm makes zero economic profit. If both firms comply (bottom right), the industry makes the monopoly profit and each firm earns an economic profit of $2 million. The top right and bottom left squares show what happens if one firm cheats while the other complies. The firm that cheats collects an economic profit of $4.5 million, and the one that complies incurs a loss of $1 million.

Nash Equilibrium in the Duopolists' Dilemma
The duopolists have a dilemma like the prisoners' dilemma. Do they comply or cheat? To answer this question, we must find the Nash equilibrium.

FIGURE 13.16
Both Firms Cheat

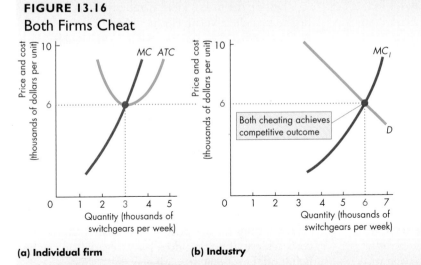

(a) Individual firm   (b) Industry

If both firms cheat by increasing production, the collusive agreement collapses. The limit to the collapse is the competitive equilibrium. Neither firm will cut its price below $6,000 (minimum average total cost) because to do so will result in losses. In part (a), each firm produces 3,000 units a week at an average total cost of $6,000. In part (b), with a total production of 6,000 units, the price falls to $6,000. Each firm now makes zero economic profit. This output and price are the ones that would prevail in a competitive industry.

TABLE 13.2   Duopoly Payoff Matrix

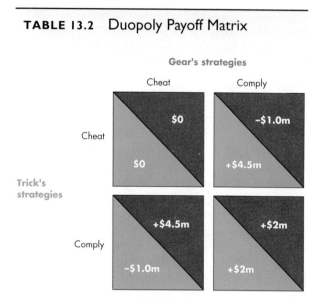

Each square shows the payoffs from a pair of actions. For example, if both firms comply with the collusive agreement, the payoffs are recorded in the bottom right square. The red triangle shows Gear's payoff, and the blue triangle shows Trick's. In Nash equilibrium, both firms cheat.

Look at things from Gear's point of view. Gear reasons as follows: Suppose that Trick cheats. If I comply, I will incur an economic loss of $1 million. If I also cheat, I will make zero economic profit. Zero is better than *minus* $1 million, so I'm better off if I cheat. Now suppose Trick complies. If I cheat, I will make an economic profit of $4.5 million, and if I comply, I will make an economic profit of $2 million. A $4.5 million profit is better than a $2 million profit, so I'm better off if I cheat. So regardless of whether Trick cheats or complies, it pays Gear to cheat. Cheating is Gear's best strategy.

Trick comes to the same conclusion as Gear because the two firms face an identical situation. So both firms cheat. The Nash equilibrium of the duopoly game is that both firms cheat. And although the industry has only two firms, they charge the same price and produce the same quantity as those in a competitive industry. Also, as in perfect competition, each firm makes zero economic profit.

This conclusion is not general and will not always arise. We'll see why not first by looking at some other games that are like the prisoners' dilemma. Then we'll broaden the types of games we consider.

Other Oligopoly Games

Firms in oligopoly must decide whether to mount expensive advertising campaigns; whether to modify their product; whether to make their product more reliable and more durable; whether to price discriminate and, if so, among which groups of customers and to what degree; whether to undertake a large research and development (R&D) effort aimed at lowering production costs; and whether to enter or leave an industry.

All of these choices can be analyzed as games that are similar to the one that we've just studied. Let's look at one example: an R&D game.

An R&D Game

Disposable diapers were first marketed in 1966. The two market leaders from the start of this industry have been Procter & Gamble (the maker of Pampers) and Kimberly-Clark (the maker of Huggies). Procter & Gamble has about 40 percent of the total market, and Kimberly-Clark has about 33 percent. When the disposable diaper was first introduced, it had to be cost-effective in competition with reusable, laundered diapers. A costly research and development effort resulted in the development of machines that could make disposable diapers at a low enough cost to achieve that initial competitive edge. But new firms tried to get into the business and take market share away from the two industry leaders, and the industry leaders themselves battled each other to maintain or increase their own market share.

During the early 1990s, Kimberly-Clark was the first to introduce Velcro closures. And in 1996, Procter & Gamble was the first to introduce "breathable" diapers into the North America market.

The key to success in this industry (as in any other) is to design a product that people value highly relative to the cost of producing them. The firm that creates the most highly valued product and also develops the least-cost technology for producing it gains a competitive edge, undercutting the rest of the market, increasing its market share, and increasing its profit. But the R&D that must be undertaken to achieve product improvements and cost reductions is costly. So the cost of R&D must be deducted from the profit resulting from the increased market share that lower costs achieve. If no firm does R&D, every firm can be better off, but if one firm initiates the R&D activity, all must follow.

Table 13.3 illustrates the dilemma (with hypothetical numbers) for the R&D game that Kimberly-Clark and Procter & Gamble play. Each firm has two strategies: Spend $25 million a year on R&D or spend nothing on R&D. If neither firm spends on R&D, they make a joint profit of $100 million: $30 million for Kimberly-Clark and $70 million for Procter & Gamble (bottom right of the payoff matrix). If each firm conducts R&D, market shares are maintained but each firm's profit is lower by the amount spent on R&D (top left square of the payoff matrix). If Kimberly-Clark pays for R&D but Procter & Gamble does not, Kimberly-Clark gains a large part of Procter & Gamble's market. Kimberly-Clark profits, and Procter & Gamble loses (top right square of the payoff matrix). Finally, if Procter & Gamble conducts R&D and Kimberly-Clark does not, Procter & Gamble gains market share from Kimberly-Clark, increasing its profit, while Kimberly-Clark incurs a loss (bottom left square).

Confronted with the payoff matrix in Table 13.3, the two firms calculate their best strategies. Kimberly-Clark reasons as follows: If Procter & Gamble does not undertake R&D, we will make $85 million if we do and $30 million if we do not; so it pays us to conduct R&D. If Procter & Gamble conducts R&D, we will lose $10 million if we don't and make $5 million if we do. Again, R&D pays off. Thus conducting R&D is the best strategy for Kimberly-Clark. It pays, regardless of Procter & Gamble's decision.

Procter & Gamble reasons similarly: If Kimberly-Clark does not undertake R&D, we will make $70 million if we follow suit and $85 million if we conduct R&D. It therefore pays to conduct R&D. If Kimberly-Clark does undertake R&D, we will make $45 million by doing the same and lose $10 million by not doing R&D. Again, it pays us to conduct R&D. So for Procter & Gamble, R&D is also the best strategy.

Because R&D is the best strategy for both players, it is the Nash equilibrium. The outcome of this game is that both firms conduct R&D. They make less profit than they would if they could collude to achieve the cooperative outcome of no R&D.

The real-world situation has more players than Kimberly-Clark and Procter & Gamble. A large number of other firms share a small portion of the market, all of them ready to eat into the market share of Procter & Gamble and Kimberly-Clark. So the R&D effort by these two firms not only serves the purpose of maintaining shares in their own battle, but also helps to keep barriers to entry high enough to preserve their joint market share.

The Disappearing Invisible Hand

All the games that we've studied are versions of the prisoners' dilemma. The essence of that game lies in the structure of its payoffs. The worst possible outcome for each player arises from cooperating when the other player cheats. The best possible outcome, for each player to cooperate, is not a Nash equilibrium because it is in neither player's *self-interest* to cooperate if the other one cooperates. It is this failure to achieve the best outcome for both players—the best *social outcome* if the two players are the entire economy—that led John Nash to claim (as he was portrayed as doing in the movie *A Beautiful Mind*) that he had challenged Adam Smith's idea that we are always guided, as if by an invisible hand, to promote the social interest when we are pursuing our self-interest.

TABLE 13.3   Pampers Versus Huggies: An R&D Game

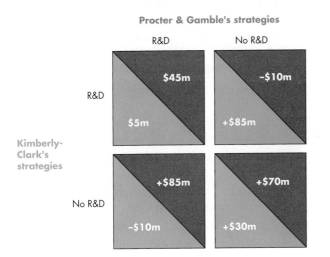

If both firms undertake R&D, their payoffs are those shown in the top left square. If neither firm undertakes R&D, their payoffs are in the bottom right square. When one firm undertakes R&D and the other one does not, their payoffs are in the top right and bottom left squares. The red triangle shows Procter & Gamble's payoff, and the blue triangle shows Kimberly-Clark's. The Nash equilibrium for this game is for both firms to undertake R&D. The structure of this game is the same as that of the prisoners' dilemma.

A Game of Chicken

The Nash equilibrium for the prisoners' dilemma is called a **dominant strategy equilibrium**, which is an equilibrium in which the best strategy of each player is to cheat (deny) *regardless of the strategy of the other player*. Not all games have such an equilibrium, and one that doesn't is a game called "chicken."

In a graphic, if disturbing, version of this game, two cars race towards each other. The first driver to swerve to avoid a crash is "chicken." The payoffs are a big loss for both if no one "chickens," zero for the chicken, and a gain for the player who hangs tough.

If player 1 chickens, player 2's best strategy is to hang tough. And if player 1 hangs tough, player 2's best strategy is to chicken.

For an economic form of this game, suppose the R&D that creates a new diaper technology results in information that cannot be kept secret or patented, so both firms benefit from the R&D of either firm. The chicken in this case is the firm that does the R&D.

Table 13.4 illustrates a payoff matrix for an R&D game of chicken between Kimberly-Clark and Procter & Gamble. Each firm has two strategies: Do the R&D (and "chicken") or do not do the R&D (and hang tough).

If neither "chickens," there is no R&D and each firm earns zero additional profit. If each firm conducts R&D—each "chickens"—each firm earns $5 million (the profit from the new technology minus the cost of the research). If one of the firms does the R&D, the payoffs are $1 million for the chicken and $10 million for the one who hangs tough.

Confronted with the payoff matrix in Table 13.4, the two firms calculate their best strategies. Kimberly-Clark is better off doing R&D if Procter & Gamble does not undertake it. Procter & Gamble is better off doing R&D if Kimberly-Clark doesn't do it. There are two equilibrium outcomes: Only one firm does R&D, but we can't predict which firm it will be.

You can see that it isn't a Nash equilibrium if no firm does the R&D because one firm would then be better off doing it. And you can see that it isn't a Nash equilibrium if both firms do the R&D because then one firm would be better off not doing it.

The firms could toss a coin or use some other random device to make a decision in this game. In some circumstances, such a strategy—called a mixed strategy—is actually better for both firms than choosing any of the strategies we've considered.

TABLE 13.4   An R&D Game of Chicken

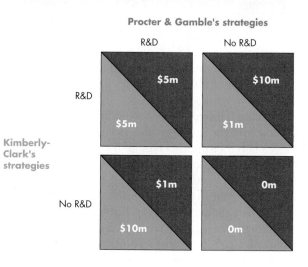

If both firms undertake R&D, their payoffs are those shown in the top left square. If neither firm undertakes R&D, their payoffs are in the bottom right square. When one firm undertakes R&D and the other one does not, their payoffs are in the top right and bottom left squares. The red triangle shows Procter & Gamble's payoff, and the blue triangle shows Kimberly-Clark's. The equilibrium for this R&D game of chicken is for only one firm to undertake R&D. We cannot tell which firm will do the R&D and which will not.

REVIEW QUIZ

1 What are the common features of all games?
2 Describe the prisoners' dilemma game and explain why the Nash equilibrium delivers a bad outcome for both players.
3 Why does a collusive agreement to restrict output and raise price create a game like the prisoners' dilemma?
4 What creates an incentive for firms in a collusive agreement to cheat and increase production?
5 What is the equilibrium strategy for each firm in a duopolists' dilemma and why do the firms not succeed in colluding to raise the price and profits?
6 Describe the payoff matrix for an R&D prisoners' dilemma and chicken game and highlight the difference between the two games.

myeconlab **Study Plan 13.6**

Repeated Games and Sequential Games

THE GAMES THAT WE'VE STUDIED ARE PLAYED just once. In contrast, many real-world games are played repeatedly. This feature of games turns out to enable real-world duopolists to cooperate, collude, and earn a monopoly profit.

Another feature of the game that we've studied is that the players move simultaneously. But in many real-world situations, one player moves first and then the other moves—the play is sequential rather than simultaneous. This feature of real-world games creates a large number of possible outcomes.

We're now going to examine these two aspects of strategic decision-making.

A Repeated Duopoly Game

If two firms play a game repeatedly, one firm has the opportunity to penalize the other for previous "bad" behaviour. If Gear cheats this week, perhaps Trick will cheat next week. Before Gear cheats this week, won't it consider the possibility that Trick will cheat next week? What is the equilibrium of this game?

Actually, there is more than one possibility. One is the Nash equilibrium that we analyzed on p. 306. Both players cheat, and each makes zero economic profit forever. In such a situation, it will never pay one of the players to start complying unilaterally because to do so would result in a loss for that player and a profit for the other. But a **cooperative equilibrium** in which the players make and share the monopoly profit is possible.

A cooperative equilibrium might occur if cheating is punished. There are two extremes of punishment. The smallest penalty is called "tit for tat." A *tit-for-tat strategy* is one in which a player cooperates in the current period if the other player cooperated in the previous period but cheats in the current period if the other player cheated in the previous period. The most severe form of punishment is called a trigger strategy. A *trigger strategy* is one in which a player cooperates if the other player cooperates but plays the Nash equilibrium strategy forever thereafter if the other player cheats.

In the duopoly game between Gear and Trick, a tit-for-tat strategy keeps both players cooperating and earning monopoly profits. Let's see why with an example.

Table 13.5 shows the economic profit that Trick and Gear will make over a number of periods under two alternative sequences of events: colluding and cheating with a tit-for-tat response by the other firm.

If both firms stick to the collusive agreement in period 1, each makes an economic profit of $2 million. Suppose that Trick contemplates cheating in period 1. The cheating produces a quick $4.5 million economic profit and inflicts a $1 million economic loss on Gear. But a cheat in period 1 produces a response from Gear in period 2. If Trick wants to get back into a profit-making situation, it must return to the agreement in period 2 even though it knows that Gear will punish it for cheating in period 1. So in period 2, Gear punishes Trick and Trick cooperates. Gear now makes an economic profit of $4.5 million, and Trick incurs an economic loss of $1 million. Adding up the profits over two periods of play, Trick would have made more profit by cooperating—$4 million compared with $3.5 million.

What is true for Trick is also true for Gear. Because each firm makes a larger profit by sticking with the collusive agreement, both firms do so and the monopoly price, quantity, and profit prevail.

In reality, whether a cartel works like a one-play game or a repeated game depends primarily on the

---

TABLE 13.5   Cheating with Punishment

Period of Play	Collude		Cheat with tit-for-tat	
	Trick's profit	Gear's profit	Trick's profit	Gear's profit
	(millions of dollars)		(millions of dollars)	
1	2	2	4.5	−1.0
2	2	2	−1.0	4.5
3	2	2	2.0	2.0

If duopolists repeatedly collude, each makes an economic profit of $2 million per period of play. If one player cheats in period 1, the other player plays a tit-for-tat strategy and cheats in period 2. The profit from cheating can be made for only one period and must be paid for in the next period by incurring a loss. Over two periods of play, the best that a duopolist can achieve by cheating is an economic profit of $3.5 million, compared to an economic profit of $4 million by colluding.

number of players and the ease of detecting and punishing cheating. The larger the number of players, the harder it is to maintain a cartel.

Games and Price Wars A repeated duopoly game can help us understand real-world behaviour and, in particular, price wars. Some price wars can be interpreted as the implementation of a tit-for-tat strategy. But the game is a bit more complicated than the one we've looked at because the players are uncertain about the demand for the product.

Playing a tit-for-tat strategy, firms have an incentive to stick to the monopoly price. But fluctuations in demand lead to fluctuations in the monopoly price, and sometimes, when the price changes, it might seem to one of the firms that the price has fallen because the other has cheated. In this case, a price war will break out. The price war will end only when each firm is satisfied that the other is ready to cooperate again. There will be cycles of price wars and the restoration of collusive agreements. Fluctuations in the world price of oil might be interpreted in this way.

Some price wars arise from the entry of a small number of firms into an industry that had previously been a monopoly. Although the industry has a small number of firms, the firms are in a prisoners' dilemma and they cannot impose effective penalties for price cutting. The behaviour of prices and outputs in the computer chip industry during 1995 and 1996 can be explained in this way. Until 1995, the market for Pentium chips for IBM-compatible computers was dominated by one firm, Intel Corporation, which was able to make maximum economic profit by producing the quantity of chips at which marginal cost equalled marginal revenue. The price of Intel's chips was set to ensure that the quantity demanded equalled the quantity produced. Then in 1995 and 1996, with the entry of a small number of new firms, the industry became an oligopoly. If the firms had maintained Intel's price and shared the market, together they could have made economic profits equal to Intel's profit. But the firms were in a prisoners' dilemma. So prices fell towards the competitive level.

Let's now study a sequential game. There are many such games, and the one we'll examine is among the simplest. It has an interesting implication and it will give you the flavour of this type of game. The sequential game that we'll study is an entry game in a contestable market.

A Sequential Entry Game in a Contestable Market

If two firms play a sequential game, one firm makes a decision at the first stage of the game and the other makes a decision at the second stage.

We're going to study a sequential game in a **contestable market**—a market in which firms can enter and leave so easily that firms in the market face competition from *potential* entrants. Examples of contestable markets are routes served by airlines and by barge companies that operate on the major waterways. These markets are contestable because firms could enter if an opportunity for economic profit arose and could exit with no penalty if the opportunity for economic profit disappeared.

If the Herfindahl-Hirschman Index (pp. 208–209) is used to determine the degree of competition, a contestable market appears to be uncompetitive. But a contestable market can behave as if it were perfectly competitive. To see why, let's look at an entry game for a contestable air route.

A Contestable Air Route Agile Air is the only firm operating on a particular route. Demand and cost conditions are such that there is room for only one airline to operate. Wanabe, Inc. is another airline that could offer services on the route.

We describe the structure of a sequential game by using a *game tree* like that in Fig. 13.17. At the first stage, Agile Air must set a price. Once the price is set and advertised, Agile can't change it. That is, once set, Agile's price is fixed and Agile can't react to Wanabe's entry decision. Agile can set its price at either the monopoly level or the competitive level.

At the second stage, Wanabe must decide whether to enter or to stay out. Customers have no loyalty (there are no frequent flyer programs) and they buy from the lowest-price firm. So if Wanabe enters, it sets a price just below Agile's and takes all the business.

Figure 13.17 shows the payoffs from the various decisions (Agile's in the red triangles and Wanabe's in the blue triangles).

To decide on its price, Agile's CEO reasons as follows: Suppose that Agile sets the monopoly price. If Wanabe enters, it earns 90 (think of all payoff numbers as thousands of dollars). If Wanabe stays out, it earns nothing. So Wanabe will enter. In this case Agile will lose 50.

FIGURE 13.17

Agile Versus Wanabe: A Sequential Entry Game in a Contestable Market

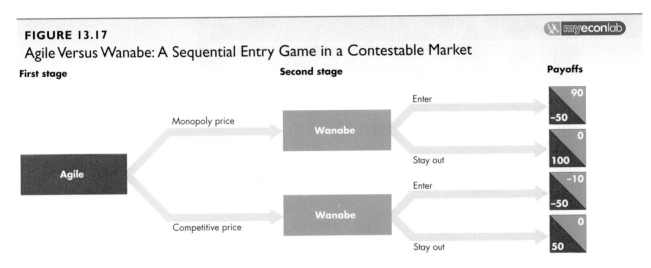

If Agile sets the monopoly price, Wanabe makes 90 (thousand dollars) by entering and earns nothing by staying out. So if Agile sets the monopoly price, Wanabe enters.

If Agile sets the competitive price, Wanabe earns nothing if it stays out and incurs a loss if it enters. So if Agile sets the competitive price, Wanabe stays out.

Now suppose that Agile sets the competitive price. If Wanabe stays out, it earns nothing and if it enters, it loses 10, so Wanabe will stay out. In this case, Agile will earn 50.

Agile's best strategy is to set its price at the competitive level and earn 50 (normal profit). The option of earning 100 by setting the monopoly price with Wanabe staying out is not available to Agile. If Agile sets the monopoly price, Wanabe enters, undercuts Agile, and takes all the business.

In this example, Agile sets its price at the competitive level and earns normal profit. A less costly strategy, called **limit pricing**, sets the price at the highest level that inflicts a loss on the entrant. Any loss is big enough to deter entry, so it is not always necessary to set the price as low as the competitive price. In the example of Agile and Wanabe, at the competitive price, Wanabe incurs a loss of 10 if it enters. A smaller loss would still keep Wanabe out.

This game is interesting because it points to the possibility of a monopoly behaving like a competitive industry and serving the social interest without regulation. But the result is not general and depends on one crucial feature of the setup of the game: At the second stage, Agile is locked into the price set at the first stage.

If Agile could change its price in the second stage, it would want to set the monopoly price if Wanabe stayed out—100 with the monopoly price beats 50

with the competitive price. But Wanabe can figure out what Agile would do, so the price set at the first stage has no effect on Wanabe. Agile sets the monopoly price and Wanabe might either stay out or enter.

We've looked at two of the many possible repeated and sequential games, and you've seen how these types of game can provide insights into the complex forces that determine prices and profits.

REVIEW QUIZ

1 If a prisoners' dilemma game is played repeatedly, what punishment strategies might the players employ and how does playing the game repeatedly change the equilibrium?

2 If a market is contestable, how does the equilibrium differ from that of a monopoly?

myeconlab **Study Plan 13.7**

◆ Monopolistic competition and oligopoly are the most common market structures that you encounter in your daily life. *Reading Between the Lines* on pp. 312–313 looks at monopolistic competition in action in China.

So far, except for a brief look at monopoly policy issues at the end of Chapter 12, we've studied unregulated market power. Your task in the next chapter is to see how Canadian competition policy influences market power.

Monopolistic Competition in China's Juice Market

WALL STREET JOURNAL, OCTOBER 13, 2003

Competition in China Erodes Profit Margins

American businessman Paul Rasch elbows his way through a crowded Carrefour supermarket to the display of Great Lakes fruit juice, the product his family's U.S. company has been selling here for a decade.

It is on sale for $2.30 a bottle, but a Chinese competitor, Huiyuan, is offering a bigger bottle at half the price. Mr. Rasch walks down an aisle teeming with dozens of fruit-juice brands, ...

Selling consumer goods in China is getting harder ... as foreign corporations face brutal competition from Chinese rivals. Veteran foreign executives now describe the mid-1990s as the golden days, when their products were novelties, consumers were impressionable, and domestic competition trailed. ...

... Great Lakes entered China in 1993 to make and sell 100% fruit juice, then a novelty. ...

China today may be the most perfectly efficient demonstration of capitalism in the world. Once a product proves popular, a business will unroll it on a national scale if it can. Rivals latch on to innovations instantly. ... The fruit-juice market took off in 2001 after three companies—Taiwan archrivals Tingyi Holding Corp. and Uni-President Enterprises Corp., and Coca-Cola Co.—launched fruit drinks with 10% juice content. ...

Other juice businesses piled in ... Juice and juice-drink sales hit $1.4 billion last year, a 40% surge from the year earlier ...

... In the fruit-juice market that Great Lakes pioneered, it now does $10 million in annual sales; Mr. Rasch says sales are growing 20% a year and that the business is profitable. But Tingyi, a relative latecomer to the field, now claims a 20% share of a $1 billion-plus market, while Uni-President, which holds the No. 1 spot, has an even larger business. Industry executives estimate that Huiyuan leads the pure-juice category with about $100 million in sales. ...

Essence of the Story

■ Great Lakes, a U.S. company, began selling fruit juice in China in 1993.

■ In the mid-1990s, foreign firms in China could sell products that were new to the Chinese market with little domestic competition.

■ As fruit juice became more popular, new companies, both domestic and foreign, launched new fruit drinks.

■ Now Great Lakes faces competition from dozens of brands.

■ Great Lakes now has an annual revenue of $10 million, and the business is profitable.

Economic Analysis

■ The market for fruit juice in China is an example of monopolistic competition.

■ Figure 1 shows the situation facing Great Lakes when it had little competition in the fruit-juice market in China in 1993.

■ The firm's average total cost curve is ATC_0, the marginal cost curve is MC_0, the demand curve is D_0, and the marginal revenue curve is MR_0.

■ To maximize profit, Great Lakes produces the quantity at which marginal revenue equals marginal cost. It sells 10 million bottles of fruit juice a year at a price of $3.00 a bottle.

■ The blue rectangle shows Great Lakes' economic profit.

■ Since 1993, many firms have entered the fruit-juice market in China.

■ Each firm produces a fruit juice that is slightly different from the fruit juice produced by its competitors.

■ The firms compete on quality, price, and marketing.

■ The entry of the new firms into the market decreases the demand for fruit juice from Great Lakes and makes the demand for Great Lakes fruit juice more elastic.

■ At the same time, Great Lakes' costs increase as Great Lakes increases its expenditures on advertising and marketing.

■ Figure 2 shows the situation facing Great Lakes after the entry of new firms into the market.

■ The firm's average total cost curve is ATC_1, the marginal cost curve is MC_1, the demand curve is D_1, and the marginal revenue curve is MR_1.

■ Now Great Lakes maximizes profit by selling 4.4 million bottles of fruit juice a year for a price of $2.30 a bottle.

■ Great Lakes earns zero economic profit because price is equal to average total cost.

■ Although Great Lakes earns zero economic profit, it does earn a normal profit. Normal profit is included in total cost.

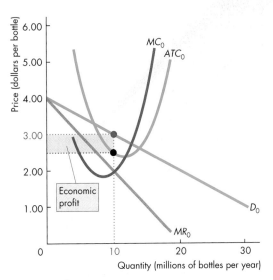

Figure 1 Before entry

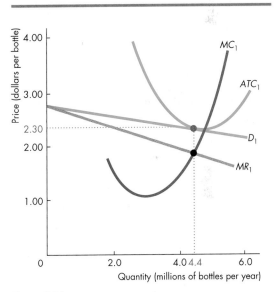

Figure 2 After entry

313

SUMMARY

KEY POINTS

What Is Monopolistic Competition?
(pp. 286–287)

- Monopolistic competition occurs when a large number of firms compete with each other on product quality, price, and marketing.

Price and Output in Monopolistic Competition (pp. 288–291)

- Each firm in monopolistic competition faces a downward-sloping demand curve and produces the quantity at which marginal revenue equals marginal cost.
- Entry and exit result in zero economic profit and excess capacity in long-run equilibrium.

Product Development and Marketing
(pp. 292–295)

- Firms in monopolistic competition innovate and develop new products.
- Advertising expenditures increase total cost, but they might lower average total cost if they increase the quantity sold by enough.
- Advertising expenditures might increase demand, but they might also decrease the demand for a firm's product by increasing competition.
- Whether monopolistic competition is inefficient depends on the value we place on product variety.

What Is Oligopoly? (pp. 296–297)

- Oligopoly is a market in which a small number of firms compete.

Two Traditional Oligopoly Models (pp. 298–299)

- If rivals match price cuts but do not match price hikes, firms face a kinked demand curve and change prices only when large cost changes occur.
- If one firm dominates a market, it acts like a monopoly and the small firms take the price as given and act like perfectly competitive firms.

Oligopoly Games (pp. 300–308)

- Oligopoly is studied by using game theory, which is a method of analyzing strategic behaviour.

- In a prisoners' dilemma game, two prisoners acting in their own self-interest harm their joint interest.
- An oligopoly (duopoly) price-fixing game is a prisoners' dilemma in which the firms might collude or cheat. The Nash equilibrium is that both firms cheat and output and price are the same as in perfect competition.
- Firms' decisions about advertising and R&D can be studied by using game theory.

Repeated Games and Sequential Games (pp. 309–311)

- In a repeated game, a punishment strategy can produce a cooperative equilibrium in which price and output are the same as in a monopoly.
- In a sequential contestable market game, a small number of firms can behave like firms in perfect competition.

KEY FIGURES AND TABLES

Figure 13.2   Economic Profit in the Short Run, 288
Figure 13.4   Output and Price in the Long Run, 289
Figure 13.5   Excess Capacity and Markup, 290
Figure 13.7   Selling Costs and Total Cost, 293
Figure 13.8   Advertising and the Markup, 294
Figure 13.13 Costs and Demand, 302
Figure 13.14 Colluding to Make Monopoly Profits, 303
Figure 13.16 Both Firms Cheat, 305
Table 13.1   Prisoners' Dilemma Payoff Matrix, 301
Table 13.2   Duopoly Payoff Matrix, 306

KEY TERMS

Cartel, 297
Collusive agreement, 302
Contestable market, 310
Cooperative equilibrium, 309
Dominant strategy equilibrium, 308
Duopoly, 296
Game theory, 300
Limit pricing, 311
Monopolistic competition, 286
Nash equilibrium, 301
Oligopoly, 296
Payoff matrix, 300
Product differentiation, 286
Signal, 294
Strategies, 300

PROBLEMS

Go to (X) myeconlab for solutions to odd-numbered problems and additional exercises.

1. The shows the situation facing Lite and Kool, Inc., a producer of running shoes.

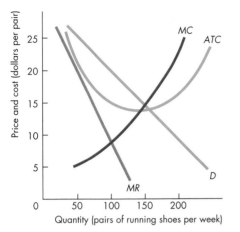

a. What quantity does Lite and Kool produce?
b. What does it charge?
c. How much profit does Lite and Kool make?

2. The figure shows the situation facing The Stiff Shirt, Inc., a producer of shirts.

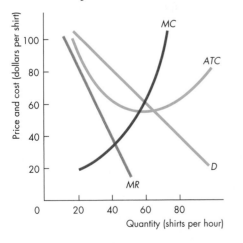

a. What quantity does The Stiff Shirt produce?
b. What does it charge?
c. How much profit does it make?

3. A firm in monopolistic competition produces running shoes. If it spends nothing on advertising, it can sell no shoes at $100 a pair, and for each $10 cut in price, the quantity of shoes it can sell increases by 25 pairs a day, so at $20 a pair, it can sell 200 pairs a day. The firm's total fixed cost is $4,000 a day. Its average variable cost and marginal cost is a constant $20 per pair. If the firm spends $3,000 a day on advertising, it can double the quantity of shoes sold at each price.

a. If the firm doesn't advertise, what is
   i.   The quantity of shoes produced?
   ii. The price per pair?
   iii. The firm's economic profit or loss?
b. If the firm does advertise, what is
   i.   The quantity of shoes produced?
   ii. The price per pair?
   iii. The firm's economic profit or loss?
c. Will the firm advertise or not? Why?

4. The firm in problem 3 has the same demand and costs as before if it does not advertise. The firm undertakes some quality improvements in its shoes that raise its marginal and average cost to $40 a pair. If the firm spends $3,000 a day on advertising with a new agency, it can double the amount that consumers are willing to pay at each quantity demanded.

a. If the firm hires the new agency, what quantity does it produce and what price does it charge?
b. What is the firm's economic profit or loss?
c. What is the firm's profit in the long run?

5. A firm with a kinked demand curve experiences an increase in fixed costs. Explain how the firm's price, output, and profit change.

6. A firm with a kinked demand curve experiences an increase in variable cost. Explain how the firm's price, output, and profit change.

7. An industry with one very large firm and 100 very small firms experiences an increase in the demand for its product. Use the dominant firm model to explain the effects on the price, output, and economic profit of
a. The large firm.
b. The typical small firm.

8. An industry with one very large firm and 100 very small firms experiences an increase in total variable cost. Use the dominant firm model to explain the effects on the price, output, and economic profit of
a. The large firm.
b. The typical small firm.

9. Consider a game with two players and in which each player is asked a question. The players can answer the question honestly or lie. If both answer honestly, each receives $100. If one answers honestly and the other lies, the liar receives $500 and the honest player gets nothing. If both lie, then each receives $50.

   a. Describe this game in terms of its players, strategies, and payoffs.
   b. Construct the payoff matrix.
   c. What is the equilibrium for this game?

10. Describe the game known as the prisoners' dilemma. In describing the game,

   a. Make up a story that motivates the game.
   b. Work out a payoff matrix.
   c. Describe how the equilibrium of the game is arrived at.

11. Soapy and Suddies, Inc. are the only producers of soap powder. They collude and agree to share the market equally. If neither firm cheats, each makes $1 million profit. If either firm cheats, the cheat makes a profit of $1.5 million, while the complier incurs a loss of $0.5 million. Neither firm can police the other's actions.

   a. If the game is played once,
      i.   What is the profit of each firm if both cheat?
      ii. Describe the best strategy for each firm.
      iii. Construct the payoff matrix.
      iv. What is the equilibrium of the game?
   b. If this duopoly game can be played many times, describe some of the strategies that each firm might adopt.

12. Healthy and Energica are the only producers of a new energy drink. The firms collude and agree to share the market equally. If neither firm cheats, each firm makes $4 million profit. If either firm cheats, the cheat makes $6 million profit, while the complier incurs a loss of $1.5 million. Neither firm can police the other's actions.

   a. If the game is played once,
      i.   What is the payoff matrix?
      ii. Describe the best strategy for each firm.
      iii. What is the equilibrium of the game?
   b. If this game can be played many times, what are two strategies that could be adopted?

CRITICAL THINKING

1. Study *Reading Between the Lines* on pp. 312–313 and then answer the following questions.

   a. Why is the juice market in China an example of monopolistic competition?
   b. Why did it become harder to sell fruit juice in China during the 1990s?
   c. How do firms in the fruit-juice market in China try to earn an economic profit?
   d. Do you think the fruit-juice market in China has excess capacity? Explain why or why not.
   e. What must Paul Rasch do to keep earning an economic profit?

2. Suppose that Netscape and Microsoft each develop their own versions of an amazing new Web browser that allows advertisers to target consumers with great precision. Also, the new browser is easier and more fun to use than existing browsers. Each firm is trying to decide whether to sell the browser or to give it away. What are the likely benefits from each action? Which action is likely to occur?

3. Why do Coca-Cola and PepsiCo spend huge amounts on advertising? Do they benefit? Does the consumer benefit? Explain your answer.

WEB EXERCISES

Use the links on (myeconlab) **to work the following exercise.**

1. Obtain information about cell phone plans in your region of Canada.

   a. In what type of market are cell phone plans sold?
   b. Describe the main features of the cell phone plans that companies offer and classify each feature as influencing fixed cost or variable cost of the plans.
   c. Why does each cell phone company offer so many plans?
   d. Who benefits from the choice of so many plans—you the buyer of a plan or the cell phone company?
   e. Are the cell phone companies playing a game? If so, describe the game. Is it a one-shot game or a repeated game? How do you know which type of game it is?

UNDERSTANDING FIRMS AND MARKETS

Managing Change

Our economy is constantly changing. Every year, new goods appear and old ones disappear. New firms are born and old ones die. This process of change is initiated and managed by firms operating in markets. When a new product is invented, just one or two firms sell it initially. For example, when the personal computer first became available, there was an Apple or an IBM. The IBM-PC had just one operating system, DOS, made by Microsoft. One firm, Intel, made the chip that ran the IBM-PC. These are examples of industries in which the producer has market power to determine the price of the product and the quantity produced. The extreme case of a single producer that cannot be challenged by new competitors is *monopoly*, which Chapter 12 explained.

But not all industries with just one producer are monopolies. In many cases, the firm that is first to produce a new good faces severe competition from new rivals. One firm facing potential competition is the case of a *contestable market*. If demand increases and makes space for more than one firm, an industry becomes increasingly competitive. Even with just two rivals, the industry changes its face in a dramatic way. *Duopoly*—the case of just two producers—illustrates this dramatic change. The two firms must play close attention to each other's production and prices and must predict the effects of their own actions on the actions of the other firm. We call this situation one of *strategic interdependence*. As the number of rivals grows, the industry becomes an *oligopoly*, in which a small number of firms devise strategies and pay close attention to the strategies of their competitors.

With the continued arrival of new firms in an industry, the market eventually becomes competitive. Competition might be limited because each firm produces its own special version or brand of a good. This case is called *monopolistic competition* because it has elements of both monopoly and competition. Chapter 13 explored the behaviour of firms in all of these types of markets that lie between monopoly at the one extreme and perfect competition at the other.

When competition is extreme—the case that we call *perfect competition*—the market changes again in a dramatic way. Now the firm is unable to influence price. Chapter 11 explained this case.

Often, an industry that is competitive becomes less so as the bigger and more successful firms in the industry begin to swallow up the smaller firms, either by driving them out of business or by acquiring their assets. Through this process, an industry might return to oligopoly or even monopoly. You can see such a movement in the auto and banking industries today.

By studying firms and markets, we gain a deeper understanding of the forces that allocate scarce resources and begin to see the anatomy of the invisible hand.

Many economists have advanced our understanding of these forces and we'll now meet two of them. John von Neumann pioneered the idea of game theory. And Bengt Holmstrom is one of today's leading students of strategic behaviour.

PROBING THE IDEAS

Market Power

THE ECONOMIST

John Von Neumann *was one of the great minds of the twentieth century. Born in Budapest, Hungary, in 1903, Johnny, as he was known, showed early mathematical brilliance. His first mathematical publication was an article that grew out of a lesson with his tutor, which he wrote at the age of 18! But it was at the age of 25, in 1928, that von Neumann published the article that began a flood of research on game theory— a flood that has still not subsided today. In that article, he proved that in a zero-sum game (like sharing a pie), there exists a best strategy for each player.*

Von Neumann invented the computer and built the first modern practical computer, and he worked on the "Manhattan Project," which developed the atomic bomb at Los Alamos, New Mexico, during World War II.

Von Neumann believed that the social sciences would progress only if they used mathematical tools. But he believed that they needed different tools from those developed from the physical sciences.

THE ISSUES

It is not surprising that firms with market power will charge higher prices than those charged by competitive firms. But how much higher?

This question has puzzled generations of economists. Adam Smith said, "The price of a monopoly is upon every occasion the highest which can be got." But he was wrong. Antoine-Augustin Cournot (see p. 148) first worked out the price a monopoly will charge. It is not the "highest which can be got" but the price that maximizes profit. Cournot's work was not appreciated until almost a century later when Joan Robinson explained how a monopoly sets its price.

Questions about monopoly became urgent and practical during the 1870s, a time when rapid technological change and falling transportation costs enabled huge monopolies to emerge in the United States. These monopolies dominated oil, steel, railroads, tobacco, and even sugar. Industrial empires grew ever larger.

The success of the nineteenth century monopolies led to the creation of our anti-combine laws—laws that limit the use of monopoly power. Those laws have been used to prevent monopolies from being set up and to break up existing monopolies. They were used in the United States during the 1960s to end a conspiracy between General Electric, Westinghouse, and other firms when they colluded to fix their prices instead of competing with each other. The laws were used during the 1980s to bring greater competition to long-distance telecommunication. But in spite of anti-combine laws, near monopolies still exist. Among the most prominent today are those in computer chips and operating systems. Like their forerunners, today's near monopolies make huge profits.

But unlike the situation in the nineteenth century, the technological change taking place today is strengthening the forces of competition. Today's information technologies are creating substitutes for services that previously had none. Direct satellite TV is competing with cable, and new phone companies are competing with the traditional phone monopolies.

THEN

Ruthless greed, exploitation of both workers and customers—these are the traditional images of monopolies and the effects of their power. These images appeared to be an accurate description during the 1880s, when monopolies stood at their peak of power and influence. One monopolist, John D. Rockefeller, Sr., built his giant Standard Oil Company, which by 1879 was refining 90 percent of the nation's oil and controlling its entire pipeline capacity.

NOW

Despite anti-combine laws that regulate monopolies, they still exist. One is the monopoly in cable television. In many cities, one firm decides which channels viewers will receive and the price they will pay. During the 1980s, with the advent of satellite technology and specialist cable program producers such as CNN and HBO, the cable companies expanded their offerings. At the same time, they steadily increased prices and their businesses became very profitable. But the very technologies that made cable television profitable are now challenging its market power. Direct satellite TV services are eroding cable's monopoly and bringing greater competition to this market.

Today, many economists who work on microeconomics use the ideas that John von Neumann pioneered. Game theory is the tool of choice. One economist who has made good use of this tool (and many other tools) is Bengt Holmstrom of MIT, whom you can meet on the following pages.

Bengt Holmstrom *is Paul A. Samuelson Professor of Economics in the department of economics and the Sloan School of Management at the Massachusetts Institute of Technology. Born in 1949 in Helsinki, Finland, he studied mathematics and physics at the University of Helsinki as an undergraduate and then worked as an operations researcher before going to Stanford University as an economics graduate student. Professor Holmstrom's research on the way firms use contracts and incentives is recognized as providing a major advance in our understanding of the mechanisms that operate inside firms. Beyond his academic research, Professor Holmstrom has provided services to a number of major corporations, including Nokia, of which he is currently a director.*

Michael Parkin and Robin Bade talked with Bengt Holmstrom about his work and the progress that economists have made in understanding firms and the markets in which they operate since the pioneering ideas about the nature of the firm by Ronald Coase.

Bengt Holmstrom

Professor Holmstrom, did you study economics as an undergraduate? What drew you to this subject?

No. I was a math and physics major as an undergraduate in Helsinki. I got into economics the way many people do through a side door from mathematics and operations research at Stanford Graduate School of Business.

How did you get interested in the economics of the firm?

I went from my undergraduate degree to work as an operations research analyst at a large conglomerate in Finland. I was hired to implement a company-wide corporate planning model. This was the early 70s, when large optimization models were expected to help firms make better long-term plans and run operations more centrally.

It didn't take me very long to realize that this was a misguided belief. The problem was that the data came from people lower down that had an apparent incentive to misrepresent the numbers. Their minds were focused on outwitting the model. My interest in incentives was entirely driven by this experience.

One of your most profound insights was to view the entire firm as an incentive system. What do you mean when you describe a firm as an incentive system? What implications follow from this view of the firm?

When people talk about incentives, they tend to think about some explicit reward system like a salesperson's commission or a stock option for an executive or something like that.

The key insight has been to understand that incentives are influenced in an enormous number of ways, indirectly and implicitly. For instance, constraints and bureaucratic rules are very important pieces of the overall incentive system. There are many different ways of getting people to do what you think they should be doing.

Sometimes the best incentive is to pay no incentive! Incentives can be terribly damaging if they are poorly designed.

The firm as an incentive system is an expression of the fact that you need to think about *all* the possible ways in which you can influence people's actions and then how you orchestrate the instruments that are available. These instruments include promotion incentives, rewards, or even just praise. The narrow view that it's just a matter of paying a bonus of some sort is very misguided.

> "Sometimes the best incentive is to pay no incentive! Incentives can be terribly damaging if they are poorly designed."

Can you talk about the role of the economist as economic advisor to a firm? One view is that firms are efficient and the task of the economist is to understand why. Another view is that the economist can help firms to become efficient—for example, by devising better incentive mechanisms. Can the economist help firms to become efficient? And are there other roles for the economist as advisor to a firm?

There's a well-known paradox—and tension—in economics. Positive economics deals with figuring out what is optimal—what is the best that can be done—and then using the description of optimal behaviour as a predictive tool—as a way of explaining why things are the way they are in the world.

And yet at the same time, nothing is presumably perfect so there is room for innovation—organizational innovation and economic innovation—which leads to the economic advice you're asking about.

There are many roles an economist can play as advisor to a firm. If we really understand things better, maybe we can actually make improvements in them. If nothing else, we can understand that if the constraints change, then a system that's designed in a particular way would need to adapt itself to the new circumstances. For example, a firm might have a centralized organization that's good in one set of circumstances and then suddenly the circumstances change and innovation becomes very important, as we seem to think it is right now. Then that situation calls for changes towards organizational structures that are more suited for innovation.

So you can explain the tradeoff between central control and more flexible, innovative structures so that a firm's managers understand these forces. They then might decide to move in the direction that better achieves their objectives. Or they might realize that the reason why other firms change organizational structures may not be relevant in their case.

The economist can help people understand the variety of organizations so that they can pick the right one for the right set of circumstances. There isn't one organization that's good for everything—quite the contrary. Some activities require one kind of organization; some activities require another kind of organization. Charities, for instance, would not be well run by for-profit firms because they would run away with the money. That's an extreme example. So, non-profit organizations play a very important role in running charities.

Joint stock companies have proven to be an extremely flexible and robust form of organization both for small- and large-scale activities. Their scalability is one reason for their enormous success.

Are there any examples of serious progress that we've made in understanding which types of organizations work best in which circumstances?

I think there are lots. There's a big debate right now about airport security that's a wonderful illustration of the insight that the firm is an incentive system and an example of the possibility of having incentives that are too strong in the wrong place. One view is that profit-making companies that run the airport security checking are too oriented towards profit and too little oriented towards quality, because the quality checks come so infrequently. The standard argument is that if they make a mistake they must pay for it, so they have a strong incentive to deliver high-quality work. But if accidents happen infrequently, that sort of feedback mechanism is just too weak. This is a logical reason for moving in the direction of taking away profit-making incentives from airport security checking.

The very existence of the firm comes from the fact that it is there to remove and restructure incorrect incentives—excessively high-powered incentives that come from the market—and to get people to cooperate. In the market, it can be harder to cooperate because everyone is working for his or her own benefit. This works very well if there are a lot of alternatives to choose—if there's competition. But when there is a small number of traders, or where quality is hard to assess, bringing the activity inside the firm is quite natural.

One firm, Enron, was big news during 2002. What do models of incentive systems tell us about what went wrong with Enron?

I think Enron, like most of these disaster cases, teaches that misplaced incentives lead to potentially big mistakes. It's almost tautological to say that if wrongdoing was done, it was done because the incentives weren't aligned correctly. Now, how much of it was a design flaw within Enron and how much was a flaw of the overall system, is harder to judge. There were certainly regulatory problems—energy production regulations had changed; the energy market had been opened up and arbitrage opportunities created. Some of the activities of Enron that sought to profit from this new regulatory environment were entirely legal.

Then there was financial innovation. It's an old, old idea that it would be nice to remove debts from the balance sheet of a firm to make it look better to investors. And apparently new financial instruments had been created to make off-balance sheet operations possible. Some of them were clearly questionable and perhaps some of them illegal.

But the other problem—and this is a system problem, not just an Enron problem—is that when things are going well and everybody believes that the world is moving forward, it's very hard to question something. You go further and further out on a limb, and then the limb breaks and you learn that that was too much.

> " *I don't think that a system that rules out everything that can go wrong is the right system.* "

I don't see Enron as catastrophically as most people seem to. I think that we would pay a big price if we never let anybody like Enron try. If you regulate things so that nothing like it ever could have happened, it probably would have also thrown out a lot of good innovations with it. It's part of the system to learn by having certain things like this happen.

I'm not defending Enron's actions. But I'm trying to give a different angle to the possible response. System design is different from trying to correct individual cases. I don't think that a system that rules out everything that can go wrong is the right system.

Is it important for an academic economist to have professional interests in the "real world"?

I think everybody's different. For me it has been important because I got interested in incentives through non-academic work. That's where I started, and I was just lucky that incentives happened to be a topical issue when I entered the field.

I don't think one could, in any sense, say that everybody must have real-world experience. You have to find your own sources of stimulation and discover what makes you curious and what makes you interested. For some people, that's just being exceedingly theoretical and not thinking about much else. Some are very talented that way: Other people desperately need some connection with the real world. For me, that has been very valuable.

Needless to say, the fact that we are all different is extremely important for overall progress.

What advice do you have for a student who is just starting to study economics? Do you think that economics is a good subject in which to major? What other subjects would you urge students to study alongside economics?

I'm a big believer that people do their best work and have their happiest life when they do the things that they are really interested in. With the wonderful undergraduate system that North America has, I would advise students to sample broadly and go in the direction they get most excited about. But I think there are many reasons to like economics. It spans a fascinating range of questions. At its heart, economics is about understanding social systems, current and past, and how these systems could be improved for the welfare of the human race. I'm confident that economics has contributed a great deal to the current levels of welfare in the West. And I'm optimistic that the developing world will also benefit from our intellectual progress. As an economist, you can have a really big impact, even if the results are less visible than in the natural sciences like physics. For me, it has been incredibly inspiring.

Competition Policy

Social Interest or Special Interests?

When you consume water, electric power, cable TV, or local telephone service, you buy from a regulated monopoly. Why do we regulate the industries that produce these goods and services? How do we regulate them? Does regulation work in the interests of consumers—the public interest—or does it serve the interests of producers—special interests?

The government used its anti-combine laws to end Northern Telecom's monopoly on phone equipment and Bell Canada's monopoly on long-distance phone calls as well as the installation of phone lines. This action brought competition into all three markets. Now you can choose where to buy your phone equipment, which long-distance telephone service to use, and the company to install your phone line.

What are the anti-combine laws? How have they evolved over the years? How are they used today? Do they serve the public interest of consumers or the special interests of producers?

◆ This chapter surveys the regulation, public ownership, and anti-combine law that are designed to limit the power of firms in monopoly and oligopoly markets and to protect the interest of the consumer. You will see, in *Reading Between the Lines* at the end of the chapter, how Rogers Commuication Inc. and BCE Inc are pursuing a new natural monopoly in broadband satellite Internet service.

After studying this chapter, you will be able to

- ■ **Explain how government arises from market failure and inequality**

- ■ **Define regulation, public ownership, and anti-combine law and distinguish between the social interest and capture theories of regulation**

- ■ **Explain how regulation affects prices, outputs, profits, and the distribution of the gains from trade between consumers and producers**

- ■ **Explain how public ownership affects prices, outputs, profits, and allocative efficiency**

- ■ **Explain how ant-combine law is used in Canada today**

The Economic Theory of Government

THE ECONOMIC THEORY OF GOVERNMENT explains the economic roles of governments, the economic choices that governments make, and the consequences of those choices.

Governments exist for two major reasons. First, they establish and maintain property rights and set the rules for the redistribution of income and wealth. Property rights are the foundation on which all market activity takes place. They replace stealing with a rule-based and law-enforced system for redistributing income and wealth.

Second, governments provide mechanisms for allocating scarce resources when the market economy results in inefficiency—a situation called **market failure**. When market failure occurs, too many of some things and too few of some other things are produced. Choices made in the pursuit of self-interest have not served the social interest. By reallocating resources, it is possible to make some people better off while making no one worse off.

In this and following chapters, we're going to study five economic problems that governments and public choices address. They are

- Monopoly and oligopoly regulation
- Externalities
- The provision of public goods
- The use of common resources
- Income redistribution

Monopoly and Oligopoly Regulation

Monopoly or oligopoly firms seek maximum profit by restricting output and keeping the price above marginal cost. For example, Microsoft has a (near) monopoly in personal computer operating systems, and the price that Microsoft is able to get for a copy of Windows vastly exceeds the marginal cost of producing it. Other practices, such as forcing consumers to buy an operating system and a Web browser in a single package might be against the social interest, but they also provide Microsoft with a bigger profit.

Governments regulate monopoly and oligopoly and enact anti-combine laws that prevent cartels and other restrictions on competition. We study these regulations and laws in the next parts of this chapter.

Externalities

When a chemical factory (legally) dumps its waste into a river and kills the fish, it imposes a cost—called an *external cost*—on the members of a fishing club who fish downstream. When a homeowner fills her garden with spring bulbs, she generates an external benefit for all the passers-by. External costs and benefits are not usually taken into account by the people whose actions create them. The chemical factory does not take the fishing club's wishes into account when it decides whether to dump waste into the river. The homeowner does not take her neighbours' views into account when she decides to fill her garden with flowers. We study externalities in Chapter 15.

The Provision of Public Goods

Some goods and services are consumed by everyone and no one can be excluded from the benefits that arise from their provision. Examples are national defence, law and order, and sewage and waste disposal services. A national defence system can't isolate individuals and refuse to protect them. Airborne diseases from untreated sewage don't favour some people and hit others. A good or service that is consumed by everyone is called a *public good*.

The market economy fails to deliver the efficient quantity of public goods because of a *free-rider problem*. Everyone tries to free ride on everyone else because the good is available to all whether they pay for it or not.

We'll provide a more thorough description of public goods and the free-rider problem in Chapter 16. We'll also study the factors that influence the scale of provision of public goods in that chapter.

The Use of Common Resources

Some resources are owned by no one and used by everyone. Examples are fish in the ocean, our lakes, and our provincial parks. Every week, hundreds of boats scoop up thousands of tonnes of fish from the Atlantic Ocean. The consequence is that the stocks of some species—Atlantic Cod is one of them—are dangerously depleted. Every summer, people trek over pathways in provincial parks and damage the natural habitat.

The market economy fails to use common resources efficiently because no one has an incentive to conserve what everyone else is free to use.

We'll describe this problem more thoroughly in Chapter 16, where we'll also review some ideas for coping with the problem.

Income Redistribution

The market economy delivers an unequal distribution of income and wealth, and income support systems and progressive income taxes influence the distribution of the gains from economic activity. You've already seen, in Chapter 6, how taxes affect markets and create deadweight losses. We'll look at the role of taxes in redistributing income in Chapter 18 after learning how factor markets operate.

Public Choice and the Political Marketplace

Replacing markets with government regulation is no simple matter. Just as there can be market failure, so also, government failure can arise. **Government failure** is a situation in which government actions result in inefficiency.

Government failure can arise because government is a complex organization made up of millions of individuals, each with his or her own economic objectives. Government policy is the outcome of the choices made by these individuals. To analyze these choices, economists have developed a *public choice theory* of the political marketplace.

Figure 14.1 shows the actors in the political marketplace. They are

- Voters
- Firms
- Politicians
- Bureaucrats

Voters Voters are consumers in the political marketplace. In the markets for goods and services, people express their preferences by their willingness to pay. In the political marketplace, they express their preferences by their votes, campaign contributions, and lobbying activity. Public choice theory assumes that voters support the policies they believe will make them better off and oppose the policies that they believe will make them worse off. It is voters' perceptions rather than reality that guide their choices.

Firms Firms are also consumers in the political marketplace. They express their preferences by their campaign contributions and lobbying activity. Public choice theory assumes that entrepreneurs support the policies that benefit their firms and oppose the policies that damage their interest. Again, it is perceptions rather than reality that guide these choices.

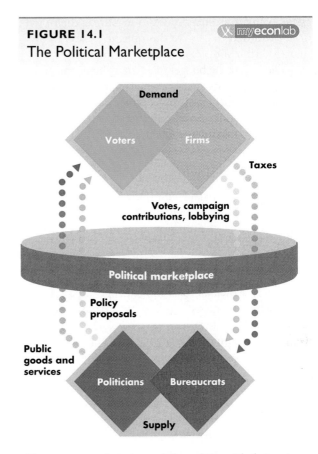

FIGURE 14.1 myeconlab
The Political Marketplace

Voters express their demands for policies with their votes, and voters and firms express demands by making campaign contributions and lobbying. Politicians propose policies that appeal to a majority of voters and to firms whose campaign contributions they seek. Bureaucrats try to maximize the budgets of their departments. A political equilibrium is a situation in which no group can improve its position by making a different choice.

Politicians Politicians are the entrepreneurs of the political marketplace. Public choice theory assumes that the objective of a politician is to get elected and to remain in office. Votes to a politician are like economic profit to a firm. To get enough votes, politicians propose policies that they expect will appeal to a majority of voters. But election campaigns are costly operations. So politicians also pay close attention to the demands of the firms that pay for election campaigns.

Bureaucrats Bureaucrats are the hired officials in government departments. They are the producers in the political marketplace. Public choice theory assumes that bureaucrats aim to maximize their own utility and that to achieve this objective they try to maximize the budgets of their departments.

The bigger the budget of a department, the greater is the prestige of its chief and the larger is the opportunity for promotion for people farther down the bureaucratic ladder. So all bureaucrats at all levels have an interest in maximizing the department's budget.

Political Equilibrium

Voters, firms, politicians, and bureaucrats make choices that best further their own objectives. But each group is constrained by the preferences of the other groups and by what is technologically feasible. The outcome that results from the choices of voters, firms, politicians, and bureaucrats is a **political equilibrium**, which is a situation in which all their choices are compatible and in which no group can improve its position by making a different choice.

Being in a political equilibrium is not the same thing as everyone being in agreement. Some politicians and their supporters devote resources to trying to change existing laws and regulations to their advantage. Other politicians and their supporters devote resources to opposing change. But no politician, bureaucrat, voter, or campaign contributor thinks it worthwhile to change the resources they are devoting to these activities.

REVIEW QUIZ

1 What are the two main reasons why governments exist?

2 What is market failure and what are the major sources of market failure? Can you think of some examples of market failure on the campus of your university?

3 Describe the political marketplace. Who are the demanders and who are the suppliers in the political market? How do the demanders "pay" the suppliers?

myeconlab   **Study Plan 14.1**

The rest of this chapter looks at the public choices that we make in regulating and controlling monopoly and oligopoly.

Monopoly and Oligopoly Regulation

GOVERNMENT INTERVENES IN MONOPOLY AND oligopoly markets to influence prices, quantities produced, and the distribution of the gains from economic activity in three main ways:

- Regulation
- Public ownership
- Anti-combine law

Regulation consists of rules administered by a government agency to influence economic activity by determining prices, product standards and types, and the conditions under which new firms may enter an industry.

Public ownership is the operation of a business as a **Crown corporation**—a corporation owned by the public and operated (in principle) in the social interest.

Anti-combine law is law that regulates and prohibits certain kinds of market behaviour, such as monopoly and monopolistic practices.

Before we describe these methods of influencing the behaviour of firms and markets, we must examine the economic theory of monopoly and oligopoly regulation, which is part of the broader public choice theory that we've just reviewed.

The Economic Theory of Regulation

In the political marketplace in which monopoly and oligopoly are regulated, there is a demand for regulation, a supply of regulation, and an equilibrium amount and type of regulation.

The Demand for Regulation People and firms demand the regulation that makes them better off and they express this demand through political activity: voting, lobbying, and making campaign contributions.

Consumers demand regulation that increases consumer surplus and firms demand regulation that increases producer surplus. The greater the number of people or firms that can benefit from a regulation, the greater is the demand for it. But numbers alone do not always translate into an effective political force because it is costly to organize for political action. A more powerful influence on the demand for regulation is the gain per person or per firm that results from it.

The Supply of Regulation Politicians supply the regulations that increase their campaign funds and that get them enough votes to achieve and maintain office. If a regulation benefits a large number of people and by enough for it to be noticed, that regulation appeals to politicians and is supplied. If a regulation benefits a large number of people but by too small an amount per person to be noticed, that regulation does not appeal to politicians and is not supplied.

If a regulation benefits a small number of people but by a large amount per person, that regulation also appeals to politicians because it helps them to get campaign funds from those who gain.

Equilibrium Regulation In political equilibrium, regulation might be in the social interest or in the self-interest of producers. The **social interest theory** of regulation is that politicians supply the regulation that achieves an efficient allocation of resources. According to this view, the political process works well and eliminates deadweight loss.

The **capture theory** of regulation is that regulation is in the self-interest of producers—a situation of government failure. The key idea of capture theory is that the cost of political organization is high and the political process will supply only those regulations that increase the surplus of small, easily identified groups that have low organization costs. Such regulations are supplied even if they impose costs on others, provided that those costs are spread thinly and widely enough that they do not decrease votes.

Political liberals tend to believe that regulation is in the social interest and that when it is not, greater efforts by politicians and bureaucrats can ensure that it is changed. Political conservatives tend to believe that most regulation is in the self-interest of producers and that no regulation is better for the social interest than the regulation that we have.

REVIEW QUIZ

1 How do consumers and producers express their demand for regulation?
2 What regulation do politicians supply?
3 Distinguish between the social interest and capture theories of regulation.

X myeconlab **Study Plan 14.2**

Let's now look at the regulations that exist in our economy today and see how they work.

Regulation and Deregulation

THE PAST DECADE OR SO HAS SEEN DRAMATIC changes in the way in which the government has regulated the Canadian economy. We're going to examine some of these changes. To begin, we'll look at what the government regulates and also at the scope of regulation. Then we'll turn to the regulatory process itself and examine how regulators control prices and other aspects of market behaviour. Finally, we'll tackle the more difficult and controversial questions: Why does the government regulate some things but not others? Who benefits from the regulation that we have—consumers or producers?

The Scope of Regulation

Regulation in Canada touches a wide range of economic activity. Table 14.1 sets out the major federal regulatory agencies, together with a brief statement of their responsibilities. As you can see by inspecting that table, the predominant sectors subject to regulation are agriculture, energy, transport, and telecommunications.

Provincial and municipal governments also establish regulations covering a wide range of economic activity. Some of these—for example, municipal regulation of the taxicab industry—have important direct effects on the marketplace. Our analysis of the regulatory process and the effects of regulation apply with equal force to price, output, and profit regulation at these other governmental levels.

What exactly do regulatory agencies do? How do they regulate?

The Regulatory Process

Though regulatory agencies vary in size and scope and in the detailed aspects of economic life that they control, there are certain features common to all agencies.

First, the government appoints the senior bureaucrats who are the key decision makers in a regulatory agency. In addition, all agencies have a permanent bureaucracy made up of experts in the industry being regulated and who are often recruited from the regulated firms. Agencies have financial resources, voted by Parliament, to cover the costs of their operations.

TABLE 14.1   Federal Regulatory Agencies

Agency	Responsibility
Atomic Energy Control Board	Administers the Atomic Energy Control Act governing all uses of radioactive material.
Canadian Dairy Commission	Administers national dairy policy, which seeks to give producers an adequate return and keep the price to consumers low.
Canadian Radio-Television and Telecommunications Commission	Regulates all aspects of radio, television, and telecommunications.
Canadian Grain Commission	Regulates grain handling, establishes and maintains quality standards, audits grain stocks, and supervises future trading.
Canadian Wheat Board	Regulates exports of wheat and barley and domestic sales for human consumption.
National Energy Board	Regulates oil, gas, and electrical industries.
National Farm Products Marketing Council	Advises government on the establishment and operation of national agricultural marketing agencies and works with those agencies and provincial governments to promote marketing of farm products. Chicken, egg, and turkey agencies have been established under its aegis.
Canadian Transport Commission	Regulates transports under federal jurisdiction including rail, air, water, and pipeline and some interprovincial commercial motor transport.

Source: Adapted from the Statistics Canada publication *Canada Year Book*, Catalogue 11–402, 1992, pp. 543–558.

Second, each agency adopts a set of practices or operating rules for controlling prices and other aspects of economic performance. These rules and practices are based on well-defined physical and financial accounting procedures that are relatively easy to administer and to monitor.

In a regulated industry, individual firms are usually free to determine the technology that they will use in production. But they are not free to determine the prices at which they will sell their output, the quantities that they will sell, or the markets that they will serve. The regulatory agency grants certification to a company to serve a particular market with a particular line of products. The agency also determines the level and structure of prices that the company can charge. In some cases, the agency also determines the scale of output permitted.

To analyze the way in which regulation works, it is convenient to distinguish between the regulation of a natural monopoly and the regulation of cartels. Let's begin with the regulation of a natural monopoly.

Natural Monopoly

We defined *natural monopoly* in Chapter 12 (p. 264) as an industry in which one firm can supply the entire market at a lower average total cost than two or more firms can. Examples of natural monopoly include local distribution of cable television signals, electricity and gas, and urban rail services. For these activities, most of the costs are fixed and the larger the output, the lower is the monopoly's average total cost. It is much more expensive to have two or more competing sets of wires, pipes, and train lines serving every neighbourhood than it is to have a single set. (What is a natural monopoly changes over time as technology changes. With the introduction of fibre-optic cables, telephone companies and cable TV companies can compete with each other in both markets, so what was once a natural monopoly is becoming a more competitive industry. Direct satellite TV is also beginning to break the cable TV monopoly.)

Let's consider the example of cable TV. Figure 14.2 illustrates. The market demand curve for cable TV is *D*.

FIGURE 14.2

Natural Monopoly: Marginal Cost Pricing

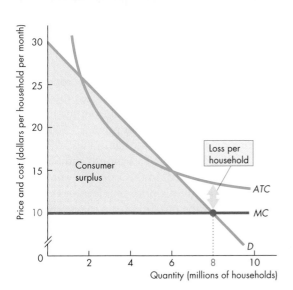

A cable TV operator faces the demand curve D. The firm's marginal cost, MC, is constant at $10 per household per month. Fixed costs are large, and the average total cost curve, which includes average fixed cost, is ATC. A marginal cost pricing rule sets the price at $10 a month, with 8 million households being served. The green area is consumer surplus. The firm incurs a loss on each household, indicated by the red arrow. To remain in business, the firm must price discriminate, use a two-part tariff, or receive a subsidy.

The cable TV company's marginal cost curve is MC. That marginal cost curve is (assumed to be) horizontal at $10 per household per month—that is, the cost of providing each additional household with a month of cable programming is $10. The cable company has a heavy investment in satellite receiving dishes, cables, and control equipment and so has high fixed costs. These fixed costs are part of the company's average total cost curve, shown as ATC. The average total cost curve slopes downward because as the number of households served increases, the fixed cost is spread over a larger number of households. (If you need to refresh your memory on how the average total cost curve is calculated, take a quick look back at Chapter 10, p. 226.)

Regulation in the Social Interest How will cable TV be regulated according to the social interest theory? In social interest theory, regulation maximizes total surplus (the sum of consumer surplus and producer surplus), which occurs if marginal cost equals price. As you can see in Fig. 14.2, that outcome occurs if the price is regulated at $10 per household per month and if 8 million households are served. Such a regulation is called a **marginal cost pricing rule**. A marginal cost pricing rule sets price equal to marginal cost. It maximizes total surplus in the regulated industry.

A natural monopoly that is regulated to set price equal to marginal cost incurs an economic loss. Because its average total cost curve is falling, marginal cost is below average total cost. Because price equals marginal cost, price is below average total cost. Average total cost minus price is the loss per unit produced. It's obvious that a company that is required to use a marginal cost pricing rule will not stay in business for long. How can a company cover its costs and, at the same time, obey a marginal cost pricing rule?

One possibility is price discrimination (see Chapter 12, pp. 273–276). Another possibility is to use a two-part price (called a two-part tariff). For example, local telephone companies can charge consumers a monthly fee for being connected to the telephone system and then charge a price equal to marginal cost for each local call. A cable TV operator can charge a one-time connection fee that covers its fixed cost and then charge a monthly fee equal to marginal cost.

If a natural monopoly cannot cover its total cost from its customers, and if the government wants it to follow a marginal cost pricing rule, the government must give the firm a subsidy. In such a case, the government raises the revenue for the subsidy by taxing some other activity. But as we saw in Chapter 6, taxes themselves generate deadweight loss.

The deadweight loss that results from additional taxes must be subtracted from the efficiency gained by forcing the natural monopoly to adopt a marginal cost pricing rule.

It is possible that deadweight loss will be minimized by permitting the natural monopoly to charge a higher price than marginal cost rather than by taxing some other sector of the economy to subsidize the natural monopoly. Such a pricing arrangement is called an average cost pricing rule. An **average cost pricing rule** sets price equal to average total cost. Figure 14.3 shows the average cost pricing solution.

FIGURE 14.3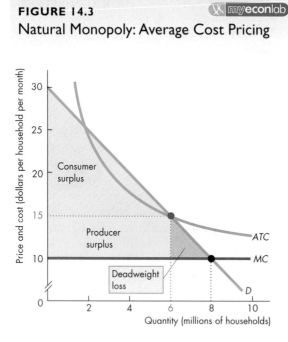

Natural Monopoly: Average Cost Pricing

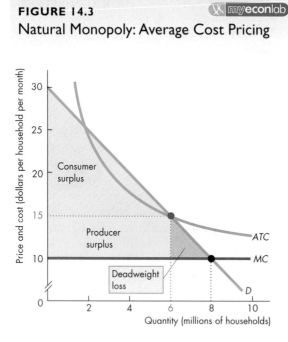

Average cost pricing sets the price equal to average total cost. The cable TV operator charges $15 a month and serves 6 million households. In this situation, the firm breaks even—average total cost equals price. Total surplus (the sum of consumer surplus and producer surplus) is reduced and a deadweight loss, shown by the grey triangle, arises.

With average cost pricing, the cable TV operator charges $15 a month and serves 6 million households. A deadweight loss arises, which is shown by the grey triangle in Fig. 14.3.

The marginal cost pricing rule and the average cost pricing rule that we've just examined are easier to state than to implement. The major obstacle to implementing them is that the regulator knows less than the regulated firm about the cost of production.

The regulator does not directly observe the firm's costs and doesn't know how hard the firm is trying to minimize cost. For this reason, regulators use one of two practical rules:

- Rate of return regulation
- Price cap regulation

Let's see whether these rules deliver an outcome that is in the social interest or the private interest.

Rate of Return Regulation Under **rate of return regulation**, a regulated firm must justify its price by showing that the price enables it to earn a specified target percent return on its capital. The target rate of return is determined with reference to what is normal in competitive industries. This rate of return is part of the opportunity cost of the natural monopoly and part of the firm's average total cost.

If the regulator could observe the firm's total cost and also know that the firm had minimized total cost, it would accept only a price proposal from the firm that was equivalent to average cost pricing.

The outcome would be like that in Fig. 14.3, where the regulated price is $15 a month and 6 million households are served. In this case, rate of return regulation would result in a price that favours the consumer and prevents the producer from maximizing profit. The monopoly will have failed to capture the regulator, and the outcome will be closer to that predicted by the social interest theory of regulation.

But the managers of a regulated firm might not minimize cost. And if the firm is regulated to achieve a target rate of return, the managers have an incentive to inflate costs and raise price. One way to inflate the firm's costs is to spend on inputs that are not strictly required for the production of the good. On-the-job luxury in the form of sumptuous office suites, limousines, free baseball tickets (disguised as public relations expenses), company jets, lavish international travel, and entertainment are all ways in which managers can inflate costs.

Managers also have an incentive to use more capital than the efficient amount because the more capital they use, the larger is the total return they are permitted to earn. And they have an incentive to make larger-than-required charges for depreciation and losses from bad debts.

If the cable TV operator in our example manages to persuade the regulator that its true average total cost curve is that shown as *ATC (inflated)* in Fig. 14.4, then the regulator, applying the normal rate of return principle, will accept the firm's proposed price of $20 a month. At this price, 4 million households buy cable service. So the price and quantity will be the same as those under unregulated monopoly.

Price Cap Regulation For the reason we've just examined, rate of return regulation is increasingly being replaced by price cap regulation. A **price cap regulation** is a price ceiling—a rule that specifies the highest price the firm is permitted to set. This type of

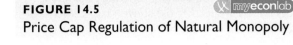

FIGURE 14.4
Natural Monopoly: Inflating Cost

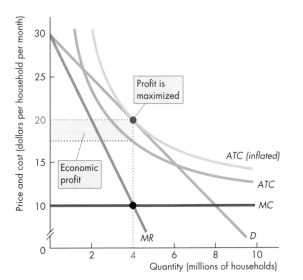

If the cable TV operator is able to inflate its costs to *ATC (inflated)* and persuade the regulator that these are genuine minimum costs of production, rate of return regulation results in a price of $20 a month—the profit-maximizing price. To the extent that the producer can inflate costs above average total cost, the price rises, output decreases, and deadweight loss increases. The profit is captured by the managers, not the shareholders (owners) of the firm.

FIGURE 14.5
Price Cap Regulation of Natural Monopoly

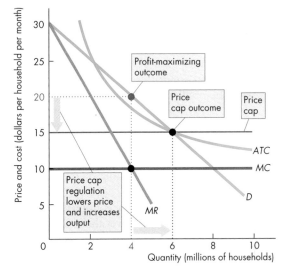

If the cable TV operator is subject to a price cap regulation, the price cap limits the price that may be charged. At all quantities less than 6 million, the firm incurs a loss. At all quantities greater than 6 million, the firm also incurs a loss. Only at an output of 6 million can the firm break even and earn a normal rate of return. The firm has an incentive to keep costs as low as possible and to produce the quantity demanded at the price cap.

regulation gives a firm an incentive to operate efficiently and keep costs under control. Price cap regulation has become common for the electricity and telecommunications industries and is replacing rate of return regulation.

The CRTC has used price cap regulation since the mid-1990s to regulate the prices of telephone services provided by Canada's major telephone companies.

To see how a price cap works, let's suppose that the cable TV operator in our previous example is subject to this type of regulation. Figure 14.5 shows what happens.

Without regulation, the firm maximizes profit by serving 4 million households and charging a price of $20 a month. If a price cap is set at $15 a month, the firm is permitted to sell any quantity it chooses at that price or at a lower price. At 4 million house-

holds, the firm now incurs an economic loss. It can decrease the loss by *increasing* output to 6 million households. But at more than 6 million households, the firm incurs losses. So the profit-maximizing quantity is 6 million households—the same as with average cost pricing.

Notice that a price cap lowers the price and increases output. This outcome is in sharp contrast to the effect of a price ceiling in a competitive market that you studied in Chapter 6 (pp. 124–127). The reason is that in an unregulated monopoly, the equilibrium output is less than the competitive equilibrium output and the price cap regulation replicates the conditions of a competitive market.

In Fig. 14.5, the price cap delivers average cost pricing. In practice, the regulator might set the price cap too high. For this reason, price cap regulation is often combined with **earnings sharing regulation**, under which profits that rise above a target level must be shared with the firm's customers.

Social Interest or Capture in Natural Monopoly Regulation?

It is not clear whether natural monopoly regulation produces prices and quantities that more closely correspond with the predictions of capture theory or with social interest theory. But one thing is clear: Price regulation does not require natural monopolies to use the marginal cost pricing rule. If it did, most natural monopolies would make losses and receive hefty government subsidies to enable them to remain in business.

There is an exception. Many telephone companies use marginal cost pricing. They cover their total cost by charging a flat fee each month for being connected to their system and then permit each call to be made at its marginal cost—zero.

A test of whether natural monopoly regulation is in the social interest or the self-interest of the producer is to examine the rates of return earned by regulated natural monopolies. If those rates of return are significantly higher than those in the rest of the economy, then, to some degree, the regulator might have been captured by the producer. If the rates of return in the regulated monopoly industries are similar to those in the rest of the economy, then we cannot tell for sure if the regulator has been captured because we cannot know the extent to which costs have been inflated by the managers of the regulated firms. There is plenty of empirical evidence that many natural monopolies in Canada do earn higher rates of return than the economy average.

One recent striking example is cable television service; telephone service is another. The rates of return in these two industries exceed 10 percent a year, approaching double the economy average. Perhaps the most dramatic piece of evidence that regulation benefits the regulated firm is the profits of Bell Canada Enterprises (BCE), prior to deregulation of long-distance phone services. BCE is a conglomerate that produced *regulated* long-distance telephone services and *unregulated* phone equipment (Northern Telecom) and financial services (Montreal Trustco). In 1992, BCE made a total profit of $1.4 billion on total assets of $12.3 billion, a profit rate of 11.4 percent. But this total was made up of a profit for the regulated Bell Canada of $0.9 billion on assets of $7 billion—a return of 12.9 percent—and a profit for all of BCE's *unregulated* operations of $0.5 billion on assets of $5.3 billion—9.4 percent.

Until the early 1990s, long-distance telephone service was a natural monopoly, but technological advances in telecommunications have changed the situation. Today, the industry is an oligopoly. But oligopoly is also regulated. Let's examine regulation in oligopolistic industries—the regulation of cartels.

Cartel Regulation

A *cartel* is a collusive agreement among a number of firms that is designed to restrict output and achieve a higher profit for the cartel's members. Cartels are illegal in Canada and in most other countries. But international cartels can sometimes operate legally, such as the international cartel of oil producers known as OPEC (the Organization of Petroleum Exporting Countries).

Illegal cartels can arise in oligopoly industries. An oligopoly is a market structure in which a small number of firms compete with each other. We studied oligopoly (and duopoly—two firms competing for a market) in Chapter 13. There, we saw that if firms manage to collude and behave like a monopoly, they can set the same price and sell the same total quantity as a monopoly firm would. But we also discovered that in such a situation, each firm will be tempted to cheat, increasing its own output and profit at the expense of the other firms. The result of such cheating on the collusive agreement is the unravelling of the monopoly equilibrium and the emergence of a competitive outcome with zero economic profit for producers. Such an outcome benefits consumers at the expense of producers.

How is oligopoly regulated? Does regulation prevent monopoly practices or does it encourage those practices? According to the social interest theory, oligopoly is regulated to ensure a competitive outcome. According to the capture theory, oligopoly regulators are captured by the firms and the regulation enables the firms to earn economic profit and operate against the social interest.

Let's look at these two possible outcomes in the oligopoly market for trucking tomatoes from the fields in southwestern Ontario to a ketchup factory in Leamington, illustrated in Fig. 14.6. The market demand curve for trips is *D*. The industry marginal

FIGURE 14.6

Collusive Oligopoly

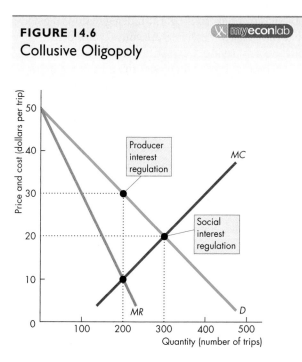

Ten trucking firms transport tomatoes from southwestern Ontario to Leamington. The demand curve is *D*, and the industry marginal cost curve is *MC*. Under competition, the *MC* curve is the industry supply curve. If the industry is competitive, the price of a trip will be $20 and 300 trips will be made each week. Producers will demand regulation that restricts entry and limits output to 200 trips a week, where industry marginal revenue (*MR*) is equal to industry marginal cost (*MC*). This regulation raises the price to $30 a trip and results in each producer making maximum profit—as if it is a monopoly.

cost curve—and the competitive supply curve—is *MC*.

If this industry is regulated in the social interest, the price will be set so that marginal benefit equals marginal cost. The price will be $20 a trip, and there will be 300 trips a week. A price cap regulation at $20 a trip could achieve this outcome.

How would this industry be regulated according to the capture theory? Regulation that is in the self-interest of the producer will maximize profit. To find the outcome in this case, we need to determine the price and quantity when marginal cost equals marginal revenue. The marginal revenue curve is *MR*. So mar-

ginal cost equals marginal revenue at 200 trips a week. The price of a trip is $30.

One way the cartel can achieve this outcome is to have regulations limit the output of each firm in the industry. If there are 10 trucking companies, an output limit of 20 trips per company ensures that the total number of trips in a week is 200. Penalties can be imposed to ensure that no single producer exceeds its output limit.

All the firms in the industry would support this type of regulation because it helps to prevent cheating and to maintain a monopoly outcome. Each firm knows that without effectively enforced production quotas, every firm has an incentive to increase output. (For each firm, price exceeds marginal cost, so a greater output brings a larger profit.) So each firm wants a method of preventing output from rising above the industry profit-maximizing level, and the quotas enforced by regulation achieve this end. With this type of cartel regulation, the regulator enables a cartel to operate legally and in its own best interest.

Social Interest or Capture in Cartel Regulation?

What does cartel regulation do in practice? Although there is disagreement about the matter, the consensus view is that regulation tends to favour the producer. Trucking and airlines (when they were regulated by the Canadian Transport Commission) and taxicabs (regulated by cities) are specific examples in which profits of producers increased as a result of regulation.

The most dramatic examples of regulation favouring the producer are in agriculture. An Economic Council of Canada study, based on the situation prevailing in the early 1980s, estimated that regulation of the egg-producing and broiler chicken industries alone transferred more than $100 million a year to just 4,600 individual producers.[1]

You can see that this situation is a good example of the predictions of capture theory. The 4,600 producers received, on the average, $22,000 a year. In the dollars of 2005, this amount becomes $53,000 a year. Contrast this large gain per producer with the loss of at the most a few pennies per dozen that the consumers of eggs paid.

[1] J.D. Forbes, R.D. Hughes, and T.K. Warley, *Economic Intervention and Regulation in Canadian Agriculture* (Ottawa: Department of Supply and Services, 1982).

The producer's self-interest was much greater than the individual consumer's and the social interest. So the producer's self-interest prevailed, even though, in aggregate, the scheme created deadweight loss.

Further evidence on cartel and oligopoly regulation can be obtained from the performance of prices and profit following deregulation. If, following deregulation, prices and profit fall, then, to some degree, the regulation must have been serving the self-interest of the producer.

In contrast, if, following deregulation, prices and profits remain constant or increase, then the regulation may be presumed to have been serving the social interest. Because there has been a substantial amount of deregulation in recent years, we can use this test of oligopoly regulation to see which of the two theories better fits the facts.

The evidence is mixed, but in the cases of the airline, trucking industries, long-distance phone calls, three main oligopolies that have been deregulated, prices fell and there was a large increase in the volume of business.

Making Predictions

Most industries have a few producers and many consumers. In these cases, public choice theory predicts that regulation will protect producers' self-interest because a small number of people stand to gain a large amount and so they will be fairly easy to organize as a cohesive lobby. Under such circumstances, politicians will be rewarded with campaign contributions rather than votes. But there are situations in which the social interest is sufficiently strong and well organized and thus able to prevail. There are also cases in which the balance switches from self-interest of producers to the social interest, as seen in the deregulation process that began in the late 1970s.

Deregulation raises some hard questions for economists seeking to understand and make predictions about regulation. Why were the transportation and telecommunications sectors deregulated? If producers gained from regulation and if the producer lobby was strong enough to achieve regulation, what happened in the 1970s to change the equilibrium to one in which the social interest prevailed? We do not have a complete answer to this question at the present time. But regulation had become so costly to voters, and the potential benefits to them from deregulation so great, that the cost of organizing the voters' voice became a price worth paying.

One factor that increased the cost of regulation borne by voters and brought deregulation in the transportation sector was the large increase in energy prices in the 1970s. These price hikes made route regulation by the Canadian Transport Commission extremely costly and changed the balance of the political equilibrium to favour voters.

Technological change was the main factor at work in the telecommunications sector. New satellite-based, computer-controlled long-distance technologies enabled smaller producers to offer low-cost services. These producers wanted a share of Bell Canada's business—and profit.

As communications costs fall, it becomes more likely that the social interest will prevail. If this line of reasoning is correct, we will see more regulation and deregulation in the future that is in the social interest.

REVIEW QUIZ

1 What are the main regulatory agencies in Canada? What are their responsibilities?

2 Why does natural monopoly need to be regulated?

3 What pricing rule enables a natural monopoly to operate in the social interest and why is that rule difficult to implement?

4 Why is a marginal cost pricing rule difficult to implement?

5 How does rate of return regulation work and what problems does it create?

6 How does price cap regulation work and what problems is it designed to overcome?

7 How might cartels be regulated in the social interest?

myeconlab   **Study Plan 14.3**

Let's now turn to the second method of intervention in markets: public ownership.

Public Ownership

CROWN CORPORATIONS HAVE A SIGNIFICANT AND historical presence in Canadian society. Before Confederation, Crown corporations were used for building canals and operating ports and harbours.

The establishment of the Canadian nation involved a commitment to build a railroad to link New Brunswick and Nova Scotia to central Canada. Over the years, vast distances, a sparse population, the presence of a powerful neighbour, strong and distinct national interests, and the existence of two main cultural and linguistic groups nurtured the establishment of Crown corporations.

A Crown corporation is a corporation in which the government has 100 percent ownership. There are federal and provincial Crown corporations, and they are involved in many sectors of the economy, including transportation; energy and resources; agriculture and fisheries; development and construction; government services; culture; financial intermediaries; telecommunications and broadcasting; provincial lotteries; housing; and alcoholic beverages.

Examples of Crown corporations include the Business Development Bank of Canada, the Canadian Museum of Nature, and the Ontario Lottery and Gaming Corporation.

Public ownership provides another way in which the government can influence the behaviour of a natural monopoly. And in principle, this method might achieve an efficient use of resources. But does that actually happen? What are the effects of the public ownership of a natural monopoly on the efficient use of resources? How does a publicly owned corporation actually operate?

To explore some alternative patterns of behaviour for public corporations, we'll begin by laying out the benchmark of efficiency.

Efficient Crown Corporation

One possibility is that a Crown corporation is operated in a manner that results in economic efficiency—marginal benefit equals marginal cost and the sum of producer surplus and consumer surplus is maximized.

Consider the example of a publicly owned railroad that has a natural monopoly. Figure 14.7 shows the demand for freight service and the railroad's costs.

FIGURE 14.7
An Efficient Crown Corporation

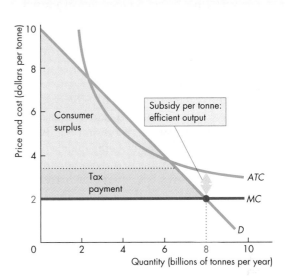

This figure shows a railroad operated by a Crown corporation that produces the output at which price equals marginal cost. Its output is 8 billion tonnes a year and the price is $2 a tonne. The Crown corporation receives a subsidy that enables it to cover its total cost, and that cost is the minimum possible cost of providing the efficient quantity.

The demand curve is *D*. The marginal cost curve is *MC*. Notice that the marginal cost curve is horizontal at $2 a tonne. The railroad has a heavy investment in track, trains, and control equipment, so it has large fixed costs. These fixed costs feature in the company's average total cost curve *ATC*. The average total cost curve slopes downward because as the number of tonnes of freight carried increases, the fixed costs are spread over a larger number of tonnes.

To be efficient, a Crown corporation obeys the rule:

Produce the output at which price equals marginal cost.

In this example, that output level is 8 billion tonnes a year at a price—and marginal cost—of $2 a tonne. To be able to operate in this manner, a publicly owned railroad has to be subsidized; the subsidy on each unit of output must equal the difference between average total cost and marginal cost. And the subsidy has to be collected in a way other than through the price of the good or service produced. In other words, the subsidy has to be collected by taxation. If the government taxes each household a fixed amount, the consumer surplus will shrink to the green triangle shown in Fig. 14.7 but consumer surplus will be at its maximum.

The situation depicted in Fig. 14.7 achieves an efficient outcome because marginal benefit equals marginal cost and consumer surplus is maximized. But it is not an outcome that is necessarily compatible with the interests of the managers of the Crown corporation. Two possible models of the behaviour of managers are bureaucratic budget maximization or profit maximization. What do these alternative models predict about Crown corporation behaviour?

A Bureaucracy Model of Public Enterprise

The basic assumption of the economic theory of bureaucracy is that bureaucrats aim to maximize the budget of their bureau. The equivalent assumption for the managers of a Crown corporation is that they seek to maximize the budget of the Crown corporation. The effect of budget maximization by the managers of a Crown corporation depends on the pricing constraints under which the managers operate. We will consider two alternative cases:

- Budget maximization with marginal cost pricing
- Budget maximization at a zero price

Budget Maximization with Marginal Cost Pricing If the bureau maximizes its budget but obeys the marginal cost pricing rule, it will produce the efficient outcome. It will produce 8 billion tonnes a year and it will sell its output for $2 a tonne, as Fig. 14.8 illustrates. But the corporation will not minimize its production cost. It will inflate its costs and become inefficient. It will hire more workers than the number required to produce 8 billion tonnes a year, and its internal control mechanisms, which would ensure internal efficiency (as in a private profit-maximizing firm), will be weak. As a result, the average total cost of the corporation will rise to *ATC (inflated)*.

What determines the limit on the extent to which the corporation can inflate its costs? The answer is the

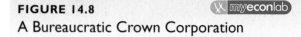

FIGURE 14.8
A Bureaucratic Crown Corporation

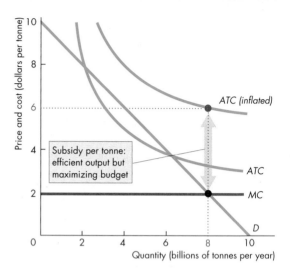

This figure shows what happens if the managers of the Crown corporation pursue their own interest and maximize the Crown corporation's budget by padding costs. Average total cost now increases to *ATC (inflated)*. If the corporation is required to keep price equal to marginal cost, the quantity produced is efficient, but the managers divert the consumer surplus to the Crown corporation.

maximum amount that the users of the output can be made to pay through taxation. That maximum is the total consumer surplus. That maximum consumer surplus is the area beneath the demand curve and above the marginal cost curve. You can work out how big it is by using the usual formula for the area of the triangle. The height of this triangle is $8 and its base is 8 billion tonnes a year, so the consumer surplus is $32 billion a year. Spread over 8 billion tonnes, $32 billion gives a subsidy of $4 a tonne, the amount shown in Fig. 14.8. $32 billion will be the upper limit that any government—in a political democracy—can extract from the taxpayer-consumers of the product of this corporation. If the subsidy were higher, people would vote to shut down the Crown corporation because the subsidy would exceed the consumer surplus.

Budget Maximization at Zero Price What happens if a government bureau provides its goods or services free? Of course, it is improbable that a publicly owned railroad would be able to persuade politicians and taxpayers that its activities should be expanded to the point of providing its services free. But there are several examples of publicly provided goods that are indeed free. Primary and secondary education and health care are two outstanding examples. For the sake of comparison, we'll continue with our railroad, improbable though it is.

If in Fig. 14.8 the bureau increases output to the point at which the price that consumers are willing to pay for the last unit produced is zero, output rises to 10 billion tonnes a year. A deadweight loss is created because the marginal cost of production, $2 a tonne, is higher than the marginal benefit or willingness to pay, $0 per tonne. The bureau will be inefficient in its internal operations and inflate its costs. The subsidy will increase to the highest that the public will be willing to pay. The maximum subsidy will equal the consumer surplus.

A Profit-Maximizing Public Enterprise

If a public enterprise is operated in a similar way to a private natural monopoly, its managers will want to get the maximum profit available and make the largest possible contribution to the government's finances.

To maximize profit, the public enterprise would produce the quantity at which marginal revenue equals marginal cost. This outcome always involves underproduction relative to the efficient quantity unless the firm can price discriminate. A perfectly price discriminating public enterprise would produce the efficient quantity (see Chapter 12, p. 276) and it would maximize the budget of the enterprise.

Compromise Outcome

Crown corporations are unlikely to behave in exactly the way predicted by any of the three models we've considered. There will be a tendency for a public corporation to underproduce and to inflate its budget, but not to the extent shown in Fig. 14.8. There will be a tendency for consumer interest to have some influence, but not to the degree shown in Fig. 14.7. The prediction about the behaviour of a Crown corporation is that it will produce more but at a higher average total cost than a private firm would produce.

Crown Corporations in Reality

How do actual Crown corporations behave? Several studies have been directed to answering this question. One of the most fruitful ways of approaching the question is to compare public and private enterprises in which, as far as possible, other things are equal. There are two well-known and well-studied cases for which other things seemed to be fairly equal. One such comparison is of Canada's public and private railroads—Canadian National (CN) and Canadian Pacific (CP). The other is from Australia, which had two domestic airlines, one private and the other public, that flew almost identical routes at almost identical times every day. Economists studied the costs of these similar enterprises and concluded that each of the publicly owned enterprises operated with a cost structure that was significantly higher than that of the corresponding private firm. In the case of CN and CP, the estimated difference was 14 percent.[2]

Privatization

Largely because of an increasing understanding of how bureaucracies work and of the inefficiency of publicly operated enterprises, there has been a move to sell off publicly owned corporations. Since the mid-1980s, the federal government has sold a dozen companies, including Air Canada and CN.

REVIEW QUIZ

1 How might a Crown corporation operate efficiently?
2 What are the effects of budget maximization by the managers of a Crown corporation?
3 What limits the maximum budget of a Crown corporation?

myeconlab **Study Plan 14.4**

Let's now turn to the third method of market intervention: anti-combine law.

[2] W.S.W. Caves and Lauritis Christensen, "The Relative Efficiency of Public v. Private Firms in a Competitive Environment: The Case of Canada's Railroads," *Journal of Political Economy* 88, 5 (September–October 1980), 958–76.

Anti-Combine Law

ANTI-COMBINE LAW GIVES POWERS TO THE courts and to government agencies to influence markets. Like regulation, anti-combine law can work in the public interest to maximize total surplus or in private interests to maximize the surpluses of particular special interest groups such as producers. We'll describe Canada's anti-combine law and then examine some recent cases.

Canada's Anti-Combine Law

Canada's anti-combine law dates from 1889. At that time, monopoly was a major political issue and people were concerned about the absence of competition in industries as diverse as sugar and groceries, biscuits and confectionery, coal, binder twine, agricultural implements, stoves, coffins, eggs, and fire insurance.

Canada's anti-combine law today is defined in the Competition Act of 1986, which is described in Table 14.6. The Act established a Competition Bureau and a Competition Tribunal. The Competition Act distinguishes between practices that are

1. Criminal
2. Noncriminal

Conspiracy to fix prices, bid-rigging, other anti-competitive price-fixing actions, and false advertising are criminal offences. The courts handle alleged offences, and the standard level of proof beyond a reasonable doubt must be established.

Mergers, abuse of a dominant market position, refusal to deal, and other actions designed to limit competition such as exclusive dealing are noncriminal offences. The Director of the Competition Bureau sends alleged violations of a noncriminal nature to the Competition Tribunal for examination.

Some Major Anti-Combine Cases

Let's see how the Competition Act has been working by looking at some recent cases. The first case we'll examine is important because it confirms the Competition Tribunal's power to enforce its orders.

Chrysler In 1986, Chrysler stopped supplying auto parts to Richard Brunet, a Montreal auto dealer. Chrysler also discouraged other dealers from supplying Brunet. The Competition Tribunal claimed that Chrysler wanted Brunet's business for itself and ordered Chrysler to resume doing business with Brunet. Chrysler did not resume sending supplies and the Tribunal cited Chrysler for contempt. Appeals against this ruling eventually reached the Supreme Court of Canada, which confirmed the Tribunal's power over contempt for its ruling. But the Tribunal subsequently dropped its contempt charge.

The second case we'll look at concerns aspartame, the sweetener in many soft drinks.

NutraSweet NutraSweet, the maker of aspartame, tried to gain a monopoly in aspartame. It did so by licensing the use of its "swirl" only on products for which it had an exclusive deal. The Competition Tribunal ruled that this action unduly limited competition and told NutraSweet that it may not enforce existing contracts, enter into new contracts in which it is the exclusive supplier, or give inducements to encourage the display of its "swirl." The result of this case was an increase in competition and a fall in the price of aspartame in Canada.

The third case we'll examine concerns a publication you use almost every day: the Yellow Pages.

Bell Canada Enterprises Two subsidiaries of Bell Canada Enterprises have a 90 percent share of the market for the publication of telephone directories in their territories. These companies tie the sale of advertising services to the sale of advertising space in the Yellow Pages. If you want to advertise in the Yellow Pages, you must buy the advertising services of one of these two companies. As a result, other advertising agencies cannot effectively compete for business in Yellow Pages advertising. The Director of the Competition Bureau applied for an order prohibiting the tied-sale practice of these two companies.

Other Anti-Competitive Agreements During 1995 and 1996, the Competition Bureau took action against several anti-competitive agreements. Among such cases were driving schools in Sherbrooke, ready-mix concrete in the Saguenay-Lac St-Jean region, real estate dealing in Calgary, the importing of Australian mandarin oranges, wire for baling pulp, and ambulance services in Alberta.

The Competition Bureau is extremely active in reviewing and, in some cases, blocking mergers. The next cases we examine fall into this category.

TABLE 14.2   Canada's Anti-Combine Law: The Competition Act, 1986

Abuse of Dominant Position

79 (1)   Where on application by the Director, the Tribunal finds that:
   (a)   one or more persons substantially or completely control, throughout Canada or any area thereof, a class or species of business,
   (b)   that person or those persons have engaged in or are engaging in a practice of anti-competitive acts, and
   (c)   the practice has had, is having or is likely to have the effect of preventing or lessening competition substantially in a market,
   the Tribunal may make an order prohibiting all or any of those persons from engaging in that practice.

Mergers

92 (1)   Where on application by the Director, the Tribunal finds that a merger or proposed merger prevents or lessens, or is likely to prevent or lessen, competition substantially ... the Tribunal may ... [,]
   in the case of a completed merger, order any party to the merger or any other person
   (i)   to dissolve the merger ...
   (ii)   to dispose of assets and shares ...

   [or]
   in the case of a proposed merger, make an order directed against any party to the proposed merger or any other person
   (i)   ordering the person ... not to proceed with the merger
   (ii)   ordering the person not to proceed with part of the merger

---

Canada Packers and Labatt Canada Packers Inc. and John Labatt Ltd. proposed a merger of their flour milling operations that would have made them the biggest miller in Canada and the fifth biggest in North America. The Competition Tribunal stopped this merger, saying that the Canadian flour milling business had been run too much like a cartel and that more, not less, competition was needed.

Banks Some attempts to merge are so politically sensitive that they are decided at the highest political level. One example is the decision of the federal government to block an attempted merger by the Royal Bank and the Bank of Montreal. If Canada's two major banks eventually merge, the sanction of the federal government will be needed.

Social or Special Interest?

The intent of anti-combine law is to protect the public interest and restrain the profit-seeking and anti-competitive actions of producers. On the whole, the

overall thrust of the law and its enforcement has been in line with its intent and has served the social interest. Further, if the recent cases we have examined are setting a trend, we can expect a continuation of decisions from the courts and the Competition Tribunal in future cases that serve the social interest.

REVIEW QUIZ

1 What is the Act of Parliament that provides our anti-combine law?
2 What actions violate the anti-combine law?
3 Under what circumstances is a merger unlikely to be approved?

myeconlab **Study Plan 14.5**

◆ In this chapter, we've seen how the government intervenes in markets to affect prices, quantities, consumer surplus, and producer surplus. *Reading Between the Lines* on pp. 340–341 looks at a new natural monopoly in broadband Internet service.

Market Power of Broadband Providers

BLOOMBERG.COM, SEPTEMBER 16, 2005

Rogers, BCE Join to Build Canadian Broadband Net

Rogers Communications Inc. and BCE Inc., which compete for telephone and cable customers, plan to build a Canada-wide wireless broadband network together to add customers in areas including those currently without Web access.

The network will cost $200 million to build, No. 1 Canadian phone carrier BCE and Rogers, the biggest cable-television and mobile-phone company, said in a statement today. The system will be equipped to offer high-speed Internet access to more than two-thirds of Canadians in about three years.

The companies partnered on the network because both had purchased stakes in Inukshuk Internet Inc., which owns the rights to the broadband spectrum. The rivals will operate the network and compete to sell services in the 40 cities and about 50 rural and remote areas the network will cover.

. . .

"The economies of scale by a joint venture with Rogers allowed us to build one infrastructure across Canada," BCE Vice President Trevor Anderson said in an interview.

. . .

The Canadian Competition Bureau will examine the proposal to determine whether the venture requires a formal review, merger notification unit chief Daniel Campagna said in an interview. "We are aware of the matter. We have to look at whether we can actually review" the venture under Canadian law, he said.

Essence of the Story

■ BCE, Canada's biggest phone company, and Rogers Communication, the biggest cable-television company jointly own Inukshuk Internet Inc.

■ Inukshuk is building a $200 million high-speed Internet system.

■ The Inukshuk network will serve two-thirds of Canadian households and cover 40 cities and 50 rural and remote areas.

■ The Canadian Competition Bureau will examine the venture but has not yet determined whether is has the power to formally review it.

Economic Analysis

■ The cost of building a broadband Internet service is high—$200 million—and if Rogers Communication and BCE each built their own network, the cost would be double this amount.

■ The marginal cost of operating a broadband Internet service is low.

■ The marginal benefit and demand for broadband Internet services is high. Based on current prices in major cities, it is between $40 and $50 a month.

■ The combination of cost conditions and demand conditions make the market for broadband Internet service a natural monopoly.

■ Figure 1 shows this market in Canada, served by Inukshuk.

■ Inukshuk's average fixed cost curve, AFC, is based the fact that it is spending $200 million to build its network.

■ We'll assume that Inukshuk faces a real interest rate of 5 percent a year, that normal profit is another 5 percent a year, and that the system will operate for 20 years and then need replacing. These assumptions mean that Inukshuk's total fixed cost is $30 million a year—$10 million interest, $10 million normal profit, and $10 million depreciation.

■ The AFC curve is based on this average total cost of $30 million a year.

■ We don't know Inukshuk's variable and marginal cost. But we'll assume that it is a constant $48 per customer served per year. The curve labelled AVC = MC shows this cost.

■ Adding the average fixed cost and average variable cost together give the average total cost curve, ATC.

■ We don't know how much Canadians in remote regions and cities not now served with broadband are willing to pay for this service. But we'll assume that a few are willing to pay $168 a year ($14 a month). We'll also assume that this amount decreases as shown by the demand curve D.

■ Along this demand curve, by the time 10 million customers are buying broadband service, the marginal customer is willing to pay only $48 a year, or $4 a month. (This assumption is probably too low.)

■ On the assumptions we've made, marginal revenue equals marginal cost when 5 million customers are served and the price of the service is $108 a year (or $9 a month).

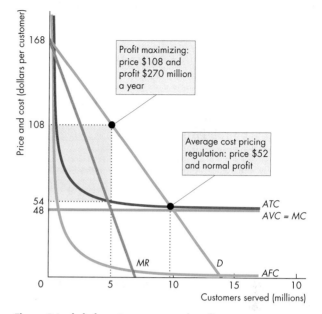

Figure 1 Inukshuk cost, revenue, and profit

■ The average total cost of serving 5 million customers is $54, so this quantity maximized profit. On the assumptions made, profit is $270 million a year.

■ If the Canadian Competition Bureau could regulate this natural monopoly and force it to price at average cost, Inukshuk would serve almost 10 million customers and charge a price (on our assumptions) of about $52 a year.

You're the Voter

■ Do you think that the Canadian Competition Bureau should prevent Inukshuk from creating a natural monopoly?

■ Do you think that the Canadian Competition Bureau should permit Inukshuk to create a natural monopoly and then regulate it?

■ Do you think that the Canadian Competition Bureau should permit Inukshuk to create a natural monopoly and then let the market work without regulation?

341

SUMMARY

KEY POINTS

The Economic Theory of Government (pp. 324–326)

- Government exists to regulate monopoly and oligopoly, cope with externalities, provide public goods, control the use of common resources, and redistribute income.
- Public choice theory explains how voters, firms, politicians, and bureaucrats interact in a political marketplace.

Monopoly and Oligopoly Regulation (pp. 326–327)

- Government uses regulation and anti-combine law to intervene in monopoly and oligopoly markets.
- Consumers demand regulation that increases consumer surplus, and firms demand regulation that increases producer surplus.
- Equilibrium regulation might be in the social interest and eliminate deadweight loss or in the self-interest of producers who capture the regulators.

Regulation and Deregulation (pp. 327–334)

- Natural monopolies and cartels are regulated by agencies controlled by politically appointed bureaucrats and staffed by a permanent bureaucracy of experts.
- Regulated firms must comply with rules about price, product quality, and output levels.
- Regulation has not lowered the profit rates of regulated firms.

Public Ownership (pp. 335–337)

- Crown corporations are 100 percent owned by federal and provincial governments and they produce such items as broadcasting, hydroelectric power, and telecommunications.
- The economic theory of bureaucracy is that managers maximize the bureau's budget subject to political constraints.

- Crown corporations tend to be inefficient: They overproduce and their costs are too high.

Anti-Combine Law (pp. 338–339)

- Anti-combine law provides an alternative way for government to control monopoly and monopolistic practices.
- The Competition Act of 1986 sets out Canada's anti-combine law and places responsibility for enforcement with the Competition Tribunal.

KEY FIGURES AND TABLE

Figure 14.1   The Political Marketplace, 325
Figure 14.2   Natural Monopoly: Marginal Cost Pricing, 329
Figure 14.3   Natural Monopoly: Average Cost Pricing, 330
Figure 14.4   Natural Monopoly: Inflating Cost, 331
Figure 14.5   Price Cap Regulation of Natural Monopoly, 331
Figure 14.6   Collusive Oligopoly, 333
Table 14.2   Canada's Anti-Combine Law: The Competition Act, 1986, 339

KEY TERMS

Anti-combine law, 326
Average cost pricing rule, 329
Capture theory, 327
Crown corporation, 326
Earnings sharing regulation, 332
Government failure, 325
Marginal cost pricing rule, 329
Market failure, 324
Political equilibrium, 326
Price cap regulation, 330
Rate of return regulation, 330
Regulation, 326
Social interest theory, 327

Externalities

Greener and Smarter

We burn huge quantities of fossil fuels—coal, natural gas, and oil—that cause acid rain and possibly global warming. We dump toxic waste into rivers, lakes, and oceans. These environmental issues are simultaneously everybody's problem and nobody's problem. How can we take account of the damage that we cause others every time we turn on our heating or air conditioning systems?

Almost every day, we hear about a new discovery—in medicine, engineering, chemistry, physics, or even economics. The advance of knowledge seems boundless. And more and more people are learning more and more of what is already known. The stock of knowledge is increasing, apparently without bound. We are getting smarter. But are we getting smarter fast enough? Are we spending enough on research and education? Do enough people remain in school for long enough? And do we work hard enough at school? Would we be better off if we spent more on research and education?

◆ In this chapter, we study the problems that arise because many of our actions create externalities. They affect other people, for ill or good, in ways that we do not usually take into account when we make our own economic choices. We study two big areas—pollution and knowledge—in which externalities are especially important. Externalities are a major source of *market failure*. When market failure occurs, we must either live with the inefficiency it creates or try to achieve greater efficiency by making *public choices*. This chapter studies these choices. We close the chapter in *Reading Between the Lines* by looking at air pollution in Ontario today.

After studying this chapter, you will be able to

- Explain how externalities arise

- Explain why negative externalities lead to inefficient overproduction and how property right, emission charges, marketable permits, and taxes can be used to achieve a more efficient outcome

- Explain why positive externalities lead to inefficient underproduction and how public provision, subsidies, vouchers, and patents can increase economic efficiency

Externalities in Our Lives

A COST OR BENEFIT THAT ARISES FROM PRODUCtion and falls on someone other than the producer, or a cost or benefit that arises from consumption and falls on someone other than the consumer is called an **externality**. Let's review the range of externalities, classify them, and look at some everyday examples.

An externality can arise from either *production* or *consumption* and it can be either a **negative externality**, which imposes an external cost, or a **positive externality**, which provides an external benefit. So there are four types of externalities:

- Negative production externalities
- Positive production externalities
- Negative consumption externalities
- Positive consumption externalities

Negative Production Externalities

Every weekday morning and afternoon, Highway 401 that runs across the north of Toronto slows to a crawl as trucks and commuters compete for positions on what looks more like an expensive parking lot than an expressway. A similar situation occurs in every major Canadian city from Vancouver to Halifax and every major city around the world. Each road user imposes a negative production externality on other road users.

Logging and the clearing of forests are the source of another negative production externality. These activities destroy the habitat of wildlife and influence the amount of carbon dioxide in the atmosphere, which has a long-term effect on temperature. Everyone living and future generations bear these external costs. Pollution, which we examine in the next section, is another example of this type of externality.

Positive Production Externalities

When Labonte Honey Inc. moves its bees into a blueberry orchard in the Lac St-Jean area of northern Quebec, the honeybees collect pollen and nectar from the fruit blossoms to make the honey. At the same time, they pollinate the blueberry flowers, which increases the output of blueberries. Two positive production externalities are present in this example: Labonte Honey gets a positive production externality from the owner of the fruit orchard, and the fruit grower gets a positive production externality from Labonte.

Negative Consumption Externalities

Negative consumption externalities are a source of irritation for most of us. Smoking tobacco in a confined space creates fumes that many people find unpleasant and that pose a health risk. So smoking in restaurants and on airplanes generates a negative externality. To avoid this negative externality, many restaurants and all airlines ban smoking. But while a smoking ban avoids a negative consumption externality for most people, it imposes a negative consumption externality on smokers who would prefer to enjoy the consumption of tobacco while dining or taking a plane trip.

Noisy parties and outdoor rock concerts are other examples of negative consumption externalities. They are also examples of the fact that a simple ban on an activity is not a solution. Banning noisy parties avoids the external cost on sleep-seeking neighbours, but it results in the sleepers imposing an external cost on the fun-seeking partygoers.

Permitting dandelions to grow in lawns, not picking up leaves in the fall, and allowing a dog to bark loudly or to foul a neighbour's lawn are other sources of negative consumption externalities.

Positive Consumption Externalities

When you get a flu vaccination, you lower your risk of getting infected this winter. And if you avoid the flu, your neighbour who didn't get vaccinated has a better chance of avoiding it too. Flu vaccination generates positive consumption externalities.

When the owner of a historic building restores it, everyone who sees the building gets pleasure from it. Similarly, when someone erects a spectacular house—such as those built in Montreal's "Golden Square Mile" in the 1800s—or another exciting structure—such as the CN Tower or SkyDome in Toronto—an external consumption benefit flows to everyone who has an opportunity to view it. Education, which we examine in this chapter, is another example of this type of externality.

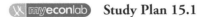 **Study Plan 15.1**

Negative Externalities: Pollution

POLLUTION IS NOT A NEW PROBLEM AND IS NOT restricted to rich industrial countries. Preindustrial towns and cities in Europe had sewage disposal problems that created cholera epidemics and plagues that killed millions. London's air in the Middle Ages was dirtier than that of Los Angeles today. Some of the worst pollution today is found in Russia and China. Nor is the desire to find solutions to pollution new. The development in the fourteenth century of garbage and sewage disposal is an example of early attempts to tackle pollution.

Popular discussions of pollution usually pay little attention to economics. They focus on physical aspects of the problem, not on the costs and benefits. A common assumption is that if people's actions cause *any* pollution, those actions must cease. In contrast, an economic study of pollution emphasizes costs and benefits. An economist talks about the efficient amount of pollution. This emphasis on costs and benefits does not mean that economists, as citizens, do not share the same goals as others and value a healthy environment. Nor does it mean that economists have the right answers and everyone else has the wrong ones (or vice versa). The starting point for an economic analysis of pollution is the demand for a pollution-free environment.

The Demand for a Pollution-Free Environment

The demand for a pollution-free environment is greater today than it has ever been. We express this demand by joining organizations that lobby for antipollution regulations and policies. We vote for politicians who support the policies that we want to see implemented. We buy "green" products, even if we pay a bit more to do so. And we pay higher housing costs and commuting costs to live in pleasant neighbourhoods.

The demand for a pollution-free environment has grown for two main reasons. First, as our incomes increase, we demand a larger range of goods and services, and one of these "goods" is a pollution-free environment. We value clean air, unspoiled natural scenery, and wildlife, and we are willing and able to pay for them.

Second, as our knowledge of the effects of pollution grows, we are able to take measures that reduce those effects. For example, now that we know how sulphur dioxide causes acid rain and how clearing rain forests destroys natural stores of carbon dioxide, we are able, in principle, to design measures that limit these problems.

Let's look at the range of pollution problems that have been identified and the actions that create those problems.

The Sources of Pollution

Economic activity pollutes air, water, and land, and these individual areas of pollution interact through the *ecosystem*.

Air Pollution Sixty percent of our air pollution comes from road transportation and industrial processes. Only 16 percent arises from electric power generation.

A common belief is that air pollution is getting worse. In many developing countries, air pollution *is* getting worse. But air pollution in the richest country, the United States, is getting less severe for most substances. Figure 15.1 shows the trends in the concentrations of six air pollutants. Lead has been almost eliminated from our air. Sulphur dioxide, carbon monoxide, and suspended particulates have been reduced to around a half of their 1980 levels. And even the more stubborn ozone and nitrogen dioxide are at around 70 percent of their 1980 levels.

These reductions in levels of air pollution are even more impressive when they are compared with the level of economic activity. Between 1970 and 2000, total production in North America increased by 158 percent. During this same period, vehicle kilometres travelled increased by 143 percent, energy consumption increased by 45 percent, and the population increased by 36 percent. While all this economic activity was on the increase, air pollution from all sources *decreased* by 29 percent.

While the facts about the sources and trends in air pollution are not in doubt, there is disagreement about the *effects* of air pollution. The least controversial is *acid rain* caused by sulphur dioxide and nitrogen oxide emissions from coal- and oil-fired generators of electric utilities. Acid rain begins with air pollution, and it leads to water pollution and damages vegetation.

More controversial are airborne substances (suspended particulates) such as lead from leaded gasoline. Some scientists believe that in sufficiently large

FIGURE 15.1

Trends in Air Pollution

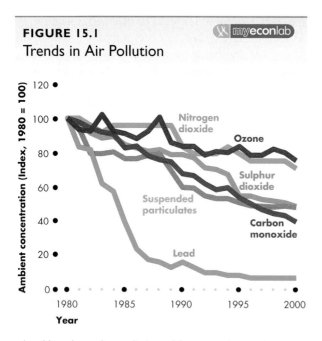

Lead has almost been eliminated from our air; concentrations of carbon monoxide, sulphur dioxide, and suspended particulates have decreased to about 50 percent of their 1980 levels; and nitrogen dioxide and ozone have fallen to about 70 percent of their 1980 levels.

Source: U.S. Environmental Protection Agency, *National Air Quality and Emissions Trends Report,* 1999 and 2000.

concentrations, these substances (189 of which have currently been identified) cause cancer and other life-threatening conditions.

Even more controversial is global warming. The United Nations' International Panel on Climate Change (IPCC), supported by many scientists, believes that the earth's temperature has increased by about 0.6 degrees Celsius over the past 100 years as a result of human generated carbon dioxide emissions. This view led to the adoption of the Kyoto Protocol by most nations, including Canada.

An alternative view is that the earth's temperature has been rising steadily since about 1500 and that human activity might be responsible for a smaller and less dramatic increase than the IPCC believes.

The data are still being debated and pored over and this controversy remains unsettled.

One air pollution problem has almost been eliminated: lead from gasoline. In part, this happened because the cost of living without leaded gasoline, it turns out, is not high. But sulphur dioxide and the so-called greenhouse gases are a much tougher prob-

lem to tackle. The major sources of these pollutants are road vehicles and electric utilities. Their alternatives are costly or have pollution problems of their own. Road vehicles can be made "greener" in a variety of ways. One is with new fuels, and some alternatives being investigated are alcohol, natural gas, propane and butane, and hydrogen. Another way of making cars and trucks "greener" is to change the chemistry of gasoline. Refiners are working on reformulations of gasoline that reduce tailpipe emissions. Similarly, electric power can be generated in cleaner ways by harnessing solar power, tidal power, or geothermal power. While technically possible, these methods are more costly than conventional carbon-fuelled generators. Another alternative is nuclear power. This method is good for air pollution but creates a potential long-term problem for land and water pollution because there is no known entirely safe method of disposing of spent nuclear fuel.

Water Pollution The largest sources of water pollution are the dumping of industrial waste and treated sewage in lakes and rivers and the runoff from fertilizers. A more dramatic source is the accidental spilling of crude oil into the oceans such as the *Exxon Valdez* spill in Alaska in 1989.

There are two main alternatives to polluting the waterways and oceans. One is the chemical processing of waste to render it inert or biodegradable. The other, in wide use for nuclear waste, is to use land sites for storage in secure containers.

Land Pollution Land pollution arises from dumping toxic waste products. Ordinary household garbage does not pose a pollution problem unless contaminants from dumped garbage seep into the water supply. This possibility increases as landfills reach capacity and less suitable landfill sites are used. It is estimated that 80 percent of existing landfills will be full by 2010. Some regions (New York, New Jersey, and other East Coast states) and some countries (Japan and the Netherlands) are seeking less costly alternatives to landfill, such as recycling and incineration. Recycling is an apparently attractive alternative, but it requires an investment in new technologies to be effective. Incineration is a high-cost alternative to landfill, and it produces air pollution. Furthermore, these alternatives are not free, and they become efficient only when the cost of using landfill is high.

Private Costs and Social Costs

A *private cost* of production is a cost that is borne by the producer of a good or service. *Marginal cost* is the cost of producing an *additional unit* of a good or service. So **marginal private cost** (*MC*) is the cost of producing an additional unit of a good or service that is borne by the producer of that good or service.

You've seen that an *external cost* is a cost of producing a good or service that is *not* borne by the producer but borne by other people. A **marginal external cost** is the cost of producing an additional unit of a good or service that falls on people other than the producer.

Marginal social cost (*MSC*) is the marginal cost incurred by the entire society—by the producer and by everyone else on whom the cost falls—and is the sum of marginal private cost and marginal external cost. That is,

$$MSC = MC + \text{Marginal external cost.}$$

We express costs in dollars. But we must always remember that a cost is an opportunity cost—what we give up to get something. A marginal external cost is what someone other than the producer of a good or service must give up when the producer makes one more unit of the item. Something real, such as a clean river or clean air, is given up.

Valuing an External Cost Economists use market prices to put a dollar value on the cost of pollution. For example, suppose that there are two similar rivers, one polluted and the other clean. Five hundred identical homes are built along the side of each river. The homes on the clean river rent for $2,500 a month, and those on the polluted river rent for $1,500 a month. If the pollution is the only detectable difference between the two rivers and the two locations, the rent decrease of $1,000 per month is the cost of the pollution. For the 500 homes on the polluted river, the external cost is $500,000 a month.

External Cost and Output Figure 15.2 shows an example of the relationship between output and cost in a chemical industry that pollutes. The marginal cost curve, *MC*, describes the private marginal cost borne by the firms that produce the chemical. Marginal cost increases as the quantity of chemical produced increases. If the firms dump waste into a river, they impose an external cost that increases with the amount of the chemical produced. The marginal social cost curve, *MSC*, is the sum of marginal private cost and marginal external cost. For example, when output is 4,000 tonnes per month, marginal private cost is $100 a tonne, marginal external cost is $125 a tonne, and marginal social cost is $225 a tonne.

In Fig. 15.2, when the quantity of chemical produced increases, the amount of pollution increases and the external cost of pollution increases.

Figure 15.2 shows the relationship between the quantity of chemical produced and the amount of pollution created, but it doesn't tell us how much pollution gets created. That quantity depends on how the market for the chemical operates. First, we'll see what happens when the industry is free to pollute.

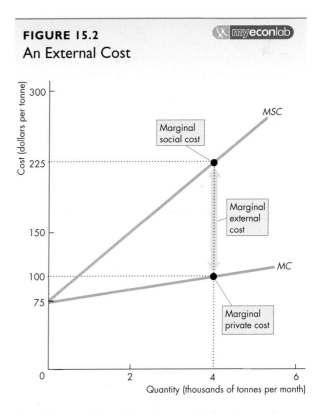

FIGURE 15.2 myeconlab
An External Cost

The *MC* curve shows the private marginal cost borne by the factories that produce a chemical. The *MSC* curve shows the sum of marginal private cost and marginal external cost. When output is 4,000 tonnes of chemical per month, marginal private cost is $100 a tonne, marginal external cost is $125 a tonne, and marginal social cost is $225 a tonne.

Production and Pollution: How Much?

When an industry is unregulated, the amount of pollution it creates depends on the market equilibrium price and quantity of the good produced. In Fig. 15.3, the market demand curve for a pollution-creating chemical is *D*. This curve also measures the marginal social benefit, *MSB*, from the chemical. The supply curve is *S*. This curve also measures the marginal private cost, *MC*, of the producers. The supply curve is the marginal private cost curve because when firms make their production and supply decisions, they consider only the costs that they will bear. Market equilibrium occurs at a price of $100 a tonne and a quantity of 4,000 tonnes a month.

This equilibrium is inefficient. You learned in Chapter 5 that the allocation of resources is efficient when marginal social benefit equals marginal social cost. But we must count *all* the costs—private and external. So with an external cost, the allocation is efficient when marginal social benefit equals marginal *social* cost. This outcome occurs when the quantity of chemical produced is 2,000 tonnes a month. The market equilibrium overproduces and creates a deadweight loss shown by the grey triangle.

How can the people who live by the polluted river get the chemical factories to decrease their output of chemical and create less pollution? If some method can be found to achieve this outcome, everyone—the owners of the chemical factories and the residents of the riverside homes—can gain. Let's explore some solutions.

Property Rights

Sometimes it is possible to reduce the inefficiency arising from an externality by establishing a property right where one does not currently exist. **Property rights** are legally established titles to the ownership, use, and disposal of factors of production and goods and services that are enforceable in the courts.

Suppose that the chemical factories own the river and the 500 homes alongside it. The rent that people are willing to pay depends on the amount of pollution. Using the earlier example, people are willing to pay $2,500 a month to live alongside a pollution-free river but only $1,500 a month to live with the pollution created by 4,000 tonnes of chemical a month. If the factories produce this quantity of chemical, they lose $1,000 a month for each home and a total of $500,000 a month. The chemical factories are now confronted

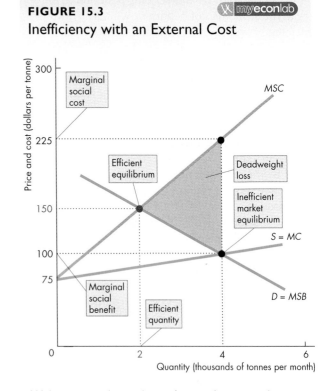

FIGURE 15.3   myeconlab

Inefficiency with an External Cost

With an external cost, the market supply curve is the marginal private cost curve, *S* = *MC*. The market demand curve is the marginal social benefit curve, *D* = *MSB*. Market equilibrium at a price of $100 a tonne and 4,000 tonnes a month is inefficient because marginal social cost exceeds marginal social benefit. The efficient quantity is 2,000 tonnes a month. The grey triangle shows the deadweight loss created by the pollution externality.

with the cost of their pollution—forgone rent from the people who live by the river.

Figure 15.4 illustrates the outcome by using the same example as in Fig. 15.3. With property rights in place, the *MC* curve no longer measures all the costs that the factories face in producing the chemical. It excludes the pollution costs that they must now bear. The *MSC* curve now becomes the marginal private cost curve *MC*. All the costs fall on the factories, so the market supply curve is based on all the marginal costs and is the curve labelled *S* = *MC* = *MSC*.

The market equilibrium price is now $150 a tonne and a quantity of 2,000 tonnes a month. This outcome is efficient. The factories still produce some pollution, but it is the efficient quantity.

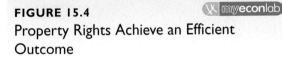

FIGURE 15.4

Property Rights Achieve an Efficient Outcome

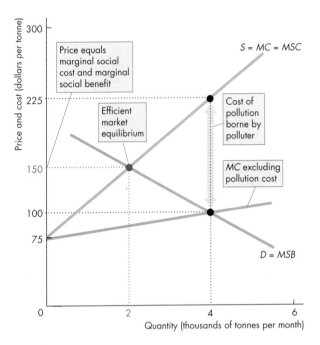

With property rights, the marginal cost curve that excludes pollution costs shows only part of the producers' marginal cost. The marginal private cost curve includes the cost of pollution, and the supply curve is S = MC = MSC. Market equilibrium is at a price of $150 a tonne and a quantity of 2,000 tonnes a month and is efficient because marginal social cost equals marginal social benefit.

The Coase Theorem

Does it matter how property rights are assigned? Does it matter whether the polluter or the victim of the pollution owns the resource that might be polluted? Until 1960, everyone—including economists who had thought long and hard about the problem—thought that it did matter. But in 1960, Ronald Coase had a remarkable insight, now called the Coase theorem.

The **Coase theorem** is the proposition that if property rights exist, if only a small number of parties are involved, and if transactions costs are low, then private transactions are efficient. There are no externalities because the transacting parties take all the costs and benefits into account. Furthermore, it doesn't matter who has the property rights.

Application of the Coase Theorem In the example that we've just studied, the factories own the river and the homes. Suppose that instead, the residents own their homes and the river. Now the factories must pay a fee to the homeowners for the right to dump their waste. The greater the quantity of waste dumped into the river, the more the factories must pay. So again, the factories face the opportunity cost of the pollution they create. The quantity of chemical produced and the amount of waste dumped are the same whoever owns the homes and the river. If the factories own them, they bear the cost of pollution because they receive a lower income from home rents. And if the residents own the homes and the river, the factories bear the cost of pollution because they must pay a fee to the homeowners. In both cases, the factories bear the cost of their pollution and dump the efficient amount of waste into the river.

The Coase solution works only when transactions costs are low. **Transactions costs** are the opportunity costs of conducting a transaction. For example, when you buy a house, you incur a series of transactions costs. You might pay a realtor to help you find the best place and a lawyer to run checks that assure you that the seller owns the property and that after you've paid for it, the ownership has been properly transferred to you.

In the example of the homes alongside a river, the transactions costs that are incurred by a small number of chemical factories and a few homeowners might be low enough to enable them to negotiate the deals that produce an efficient outcome. But in many situations, transactions costs are so high that it would be inefficient to incur them. In these situations, the Coase solution is not available.

Suppose, for example, that everyone owns the airspace above their homes up to, say, 10 kilometres. If someone pollutes your airspace, you can charge a fee. But to collect the fee, you must identify who is polluting your airspace and persuade them to pay you. Imagine the costs of negotiating and enforcing agreements with the 300 million people who live in Canada and the United States and the several thousand factories that emit sulphur dioxide and create acid rain that falls on your property! In this situation, we use public choices to cope with externalities. But the transactions costs that block a market solution are real costs, so attempts by the government to deal with externalities offer no easy solution. Let's look at some of these attempts.

Government Actions in the Face of External Costs

The three main methods that governments use to cope with externalities are

- Taxes
- Emission charges
- Marketable permits

Taxes The government can use taxes as an incentive for producers to cut back on pollution. Taxes used in this way are called **Pigovian taxes**, in honour of Arthur Cecil Pigou, the British economist who first worked out this method of dealing with externalities during the 1920s.

By setting the tax rate equal to the marginal external cost, firms can be made to behave in the same way as they would if they bore the cost of the externality directly. To see how government actions can change market outcomes in the face of externalities, let's return to the example of the chemical factories and the river.

Assume that the government has assessed the marginal external cost accurately and imposes a tax on the factories that exactly equals this cost. Figure 15.5 illustrates the effects of this tax.

The market demand curve and marginal social benefit curve, $D = MSB$, and the firms' marginal cost curve, MC, are the same as in Fig. 15.3. The pollution tax equals the marginal external cost of the pollution. We add this tax to the marginal cost to find the market supply curve. This curve is the one labelled $S = MC + tax = MSC$. This curve is the market supply curve because it tells us the quantity supplied at each price given the firms' marginal cost and the tax they must pay. This curve is also the marginal social cost curve because the pollution tax has been set equal to the marginal external cost.

Demand and supply now determine the market equilibrium price at $150 a tonne and the equilibrium quantity at 2,000 tonnes a month. At this scale of chemical production, the marginal social cost is $150 and the marginal benefit is $150, so the outcome is efficient. The firms incur a marginal cost of $88 a tonne and pay a tax of $62 a tonne. The government collects tax revenue of $124,000 a month.

Emission Charges Emission charges are an alternative to a tax for confronting a polluter with the external cost of pollution. The government sets a price per unit of pollution. The more pollution a firm creates,

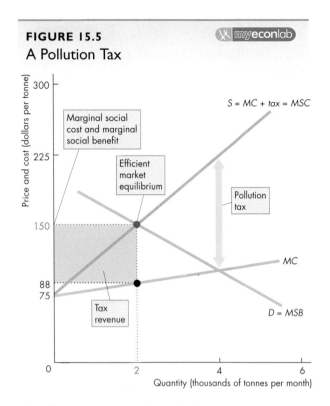

FIGURE 15.5   ⓧ myeconlab
A Pollution Tax

A pollution tax is imposed equal to the marginal external cost of pollution. The supply curve becomes the marginal private cost curve, MC, plus the tax: $S = MC + tax$. Market equilibrium is at a price of $150 a tonne and a quantity of 2,000 tonnes a month and is efficient because marginal social cost equals marginal social benefit. The government collects a tax revenue shown by the purple rectangle.

the more it pays in emission charges. This method of dealing with pollution externalities has been used only modestly in North America but is common in Europe where, for example, France, Germany, and the Netherlands make water polluters pay a waste disposal charge.

To work out the emission charge that achieves efficiency, the government needs a lot of information about the polluting industry that, in practice, is rarely available.

Marketable Permits Instead of taxing or imposing emission charges on polluters, each potential polluter might be assigned a permitted pollution limit. Each firm knows its own costs and benefits of pollution, and making pollution limits marketable is a clever way of using this private information that is unknown to the government. The government issues each firm a permit to emit a certain amount of pollution, and firms can buy and sell these permits. Firms that have a low marginal cost of reducing pollution sell their permits, and firms that have a high marginal cost of reducing pollution buy permits. The market in permits determines the price at which firms trade permits. And firms buy or sell permits until their marginal cost of pollution equals the market price.

This method of dealing with pollution provides an even stronger incentive than do emission charges to find technologies that pollute less because the price of a permit to pollute rises as the demand for permits increases.

A Real-World Market for Emission Permits Environment Canada has not used marketable permits but the Environmental Protection Agency (EPA) in the United States has. The EPA first implemented air quality programs following the passage of the Clean Air Act in 1970.

Trading in lead pollution permits became common during the 1980s, and this marketable permit program has been rated a success. It enabled lead to be virtually eliminated from the atmosphere of the United States (see Fig. 15.1). But this success might not easily translate to other situations because lead pollution has some special features. First, most lead pollution came from a single source: leaded gasoline. Second, lead in gasoline is easily monitored. Third, the objective of the program was clear: to eliminate lead in gasoline. The EPA is now considering using marketable permits to promote efficiency in the control of chlorofluorocarbons, the gases that are believed to damage the ozone layer.

REVIEW QUIZ

1 What is the distinction between a negative production externality and a negative consumption externality?
2 What is the distinction between private cost and social cost?
3 How does an externality prevent a competitive market from allocating resources efficiently?
4 How can an externality be eliminated by assigning property rights? How does this method of coping with an externality work?
5 How do taxes help us to cope with externalities? Can a pollution tax be used to induce firms to produce the efficient quantity of pollution?

(X) myeconlab **Study Plan 15.2**

Positive Externalities: Knowledge

KNOWLEDGE COMES FROM EDUCATION AND research. To study the economics of knowledge, we must distinguish between private and social benefits.

Private Benefits and Social Benefits

A *private benefit* is a benefit that the consumer of a good or service receives. *Marginal benefit* is the benefit from an *additional unit* of a good or service. So a **marginal private benefit** (*MB*) is the benefit from an additional unit of a good or service that the consumer of that good or service receives.

The *external benefit* from a good or service is the benefit that someone other than the consumer receives. A **marginal external benefit** is the benefit from an additional unit of a good or service that people other than the consumer enjoy.

Marginal social benefit (*MSB*) is the marginal benefit enjoyed by society—by the consumer of a good or service (marginal private benefit) plus the marginal benefit enjoyed by others (the marginal external benefit). That is,

$$MSB = MB + \text{Marginal external benefit.}$$

Figure 15.6 shows an example of the relationship between marginal private benefit, marginal external benefit, and marginal social benefit. The marginal benefit curve, *MB*, describes the marginal private benefit—such as expanded job opportunities and higher incomes—enjoyed by university graduates. Marginal private benefit decreases as the quantity of education increases.

But university graduates generate external benefits. On the average, they are better citizens. Their crime rates are lower, and they are more tolerant of the views of others. A society with a large number of university graduates can support activities such as high-quality newspapers and television channels, music, theatre, and other organized social activities.

In the example in Fig. 15.6, the marginal external benefit is $15,000 per student per year when 15 million students enroll in university. The marginal social benefit curve, *MSB*, is the sum of marginal private benefit and marginal external benefit. For example, with 15 million students, the marginal private benefit is $10,000 per student and the marginal

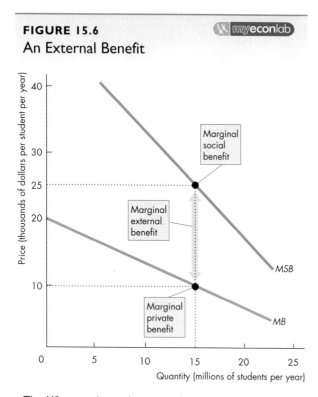

FIGURE 15.6   ⓧ myeconlab
An External Benefit

The *MB* curve shows the marginal private benefit enjoyed by the people who receive a university education. The *MSB* curve shows the sum of marginal private benefit and marginal external benefit. When 15 million students attend university, marginal private benefit is $10,000 per student, marginal external benefit is $15,000 per student, and marginal social benefit is $25,000 per student.

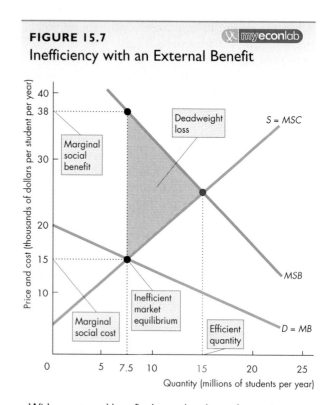

FIGURE 15.7   ⓧ myeconlab
Inefficiency with an External Benefit

With an external benefit, the market demand curve is the marginal private benefit curve, *D = MB*. The market supply curve is the marginal social cost curve, *S = MSC*. Market equilibrium at a tuition of $15,000 a year and 7.5 million students is inefficient. The efficient quantity is 15 million students. The grey triangle shows the deadweight loss created because too few students enroll in university.

external benefit is $15,000 per student, so the marginal social benefit is $25,000 per student.

When people make schooling decisions, they ignore its external benefits and consider only its private benefits. So if education were provided by private schools that charged full-cost tuition, we would produce too few university graduates.

Figure 15.7 illustrates the underproduction if the government left education to the private market. The market supply curve is the marginal social cost curve of the private schools, *S = MSC*. The demand curve is the marginal private benefit curve, *D = MB*. Market equilibrium occurs at a tuition of $15,000 per student per year and 7.5 million students per year. At this equilibrium, marginal social benefit is $38,000 per student, which exceeds marginal social cost by $23,000. There are too few students in university. The efficient number is 15 million, where

marginal social benefit equals marginal social cost. The grey triangle shows the deadweight loss.

Underproduction similar to that in Fig. 15.7 would occur in grade school and high school if an unregulated market produced it. When children learn basic reading, writing, and number skills, they receive the private benefit of increased earning power. But even these basic skills bring the external benefit of developing better citizens.

External benefits also arise from the discovery of new knowledge. When Isaac Newton worked out the formulas for calculating the rate of response of one variable to another—calculus—everyone was free to use his method. When a spreadsheet program called VisiCalc was invented, Lotus Corporation and Microsoft were free to copy the basic idea and create 1-2-3 and Excel. When the first shopping mall was built and found to be a successful way of arranging retailing, everyone was free to copy the idea, and malls spread like mushrooms.

Once someone has discovered how to do something, others can copy the basic idea. They do have to work to copy an idea, so they face an opportunity cost. But they do not usually have to pay a fee to the person who made the discovery to use it. When people make decisions, they ignore the external benefits and consider only the private benefits.

When people make decisions about the quantity of education or the amount of research to undertake, they balance the marginal private cost against the marginal private benefit. They ignore the external benefit. As a result, if we left education and research to unregulated market forces, we would get too little of these activities.

To get closer to producing the efficient quantity of a good or service that generates an external benefit, we make public choices, through governments, to modify the market outcome.

Government Actions in the Face of External Benefits

Four devices that governments can use to achieve a more efficient allocation of resources in the presence of external benefits are

- Public provision
- Private subsidies
- Vouchers
- Patents and copyrights

Public Provision Under **public provision**, a public authority that receives its revenue from the government produces the good or service. The education services produced by the public universities, colleges, and schools are examples of public provision.

Figure 15.8(a) shows how public provision might overcome the underproduction that arises in Fig. 15.7. Public provision cannot lower the cost of production, so marginal social cost is the same as before. Marginal

---

FIGURE 15.8
Public Provision or Private Subsidy to Achieve an Efficient Outcome

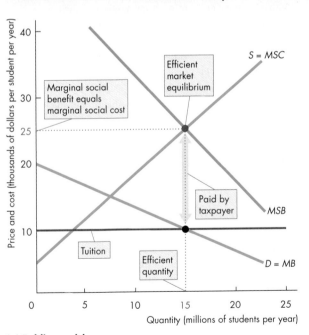

(a) Public provision

In part (a), marginal social benefit equals marginal social cost with 15 million students, the efficient quantity. Tuition is set at $10,000 per student, and the taxpayers cover the other $15,000 of the cost per student.

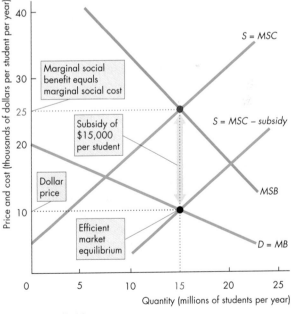

(b) Private subsidy

In part (b), with a subsidy of $15,000 per student, the supply curve is S = MSC – subsidy. The equilibrium price is $10,000, and the market equilibrium is efficient with 15 million students. Marginal social benefit equals marginal social cost.

private benefit and marginal external benefit are also the same as before.

The efficient quantity occurs where marginal social benefit equals marginal social cost. In Fig. 15.8(a), this quantity is 15 million students. Tuition is set to ensure that the efficient number of students enrolls. That is, tuition is set equal to the marginal private benefit at the efficient quantity. In Fig. 15.8(a), tuition is $10,000 a year. The rest of the cost of the public university is borne by the taxpayers and, in this example, is $15,000 per student per year.

Private Subsidies A **subsidy** is a payment that the government makes to private producers. By making the subsidy depend on the level of output, the government can induce private decision makers to consider external benefits when they make their choices.

Figure 15.8(b) shows how a subsidy to private universities works. In the absence of a subsidy, the market supply curve of private university education is the marginal social cost curve, $S = MSC$. If the government provides a subsidy to universities of $15,000 per student, we must subtract the subsidy from the marginal cost of education to find the supply curve. That curve is $S = MSC - subsidy$. The market demand is the marginal benefit curve, $D = MB$. The equilibrium tuition (market price) is $10,000 a year, and the equilibrium quantity is 15 million students. To educate 15 million students the marginal social cost is $25,000 a year. The marginal social benefit is also $25,000 a year. So by setting the subsidy equal to marginal external benefit, marginal social cost is equal to marginal social benefit and the outcome is efficient. The tuition and the subsidy just cover the university's costs.

Vouchers A **voucher** is a token that the government provides to households, which they can use to buy specified goods or services. Milton Friedman, recipient of the 1976 Nobel Prize for Economic Science, has long advocated vouchers as a means of providing parents with greater choice and control over the education of their children. Some people advocate them for college and university so that students can both receive financial help and exercise choice.

A school voucher allows parents to choose the school their children will attend and to use the voucher to pay part of the cost. The school cashes the vouchers to pay its bills. A voucher provided to a university student would work in a similar way. Because vouchers can be spent only on a specified item, they

FIGURE 15.9
Vouchers Achieve an Efficient Outcome

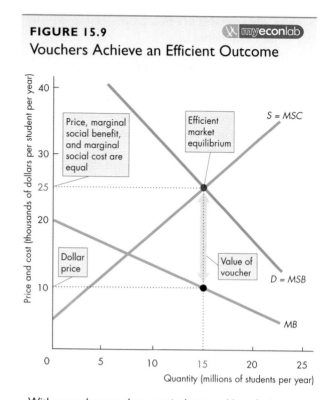

With a voucher equal to marginal external benefit, buyers are willing to pay MB plus the value of the voucher, so the demand curve becomes the marginal social benefit curve, $D = MSB$. Market equilibrium is efficient with 15 million students enrolled in university because price, marginal social benefit, and marginal cost are equal. The tuition consists of the dollar price of $10,000 and the value of the voucher.

increase the willingness to pay for that item and so increase the demand for it.

Figure 15.9 shows how a voucher system works. The government provides a voucher equal to the marginal external benefit. Students use these vouchers to supplement the dollars they pay for university education. The marginal social benefit curve becomes the demand for university education, $D = MSB$. The market equilibrium occurs at a price of $25,000 per student per year, and 15 million students enrol in universities. Each student pays $10,000 tuition, and universities collect an additional $15,000 per student from the voucher.

If the government estimates the value of the external benefit correctly and makes the value of the voucher equal the marginal external benefit, the outcome from the voucher scheme is efficient. Marginal cost equals marginal social benefit, and the dead-weight loss is eliminated.

Vouchers are similar to subsidies, but their advocates say that they are more efficient than subsidies because the consumer can monitor school performance more effectively than the government can.

Patents and Copyrights Knowledge might be an exception to the principle of diminishing marginal benefit. Additional knowledge (about the right things) makes people more productive. And there seems to be no tendency for the additional productivity from additional knowledge to diminish.

For example, in just 15 years, advances in knowledge about microprocessors have given us a sequence of processor chips that has made our personal computers increasingly powerful. Each advance in knowledge about how to design and manufacture a processor chip has brought apparently ever larger increments in performance and productivity. Similarly, each advance in knowledge about how to design and build an airplane has brought apparently ever larger increments in performance: Orville and Wilbur Wright's 1903 Flyer was a one-seat plane that could hop a farmer's field. The Lockheed Constellation, designed in 1949, was an airplane that could fly 120 passengers from New York to London, but with two refueling stops in Newfoundland and Ireland. The latest version of the Airbus 340 can carry 250 people nonstop from Singapore to New York, a flight of 15,325 kilometres that takes 20 hours. Similar examples of dramatic change can be found in agriculture, biogenetics, telecommunications, engineering, entertainment, and medicine.

One reason why the stock of knowledge increases without diminishing returns is the sheer number of different techniques that can in principle be tried. Paul Romer explains this fact. "Suppose that to make a finished good, 20 different parts have to be attached to a frame, one at a time. A worker could proceed in numerical order, attaching part one first, then part two.... Or the worker could proceed in some other order, starting with part 10, then adding part seven.... With 20 parts, . . . there are [more] different sequences . . . than the total number of seconds that have elapsed since the big bang created the universe, so we can be confident that in all activities, only a very small fraction of the possible sequences have ever been tried."[1]

Think about all the processes, all the products, and all the different bits and pieces that go into each, and you can see that we have only begun to scratch around the edges of what is possible.

Because knowledge is productive and generates external benefits, it is necessary to use public policies to ensure that those who develop new ideas have incentives to encourage an efficient level of effort. The main way of providing the right incentives uses the central idea of the Coase theorem and assigns property rights—called **intellectual property rights**—to creators. The legal device for establishing intellectual property rights is the patent or copyright. A **patent** or **copyright** is a government-sanctioned exclusive right granted to the inventor of a good, service, or productive process to produce, use, and sell the invention for a given number of years. A patent enables the developer of a new idea to prevent others from benefiting freely from an invention for a limited number of years.

Although patents encourage invention and innovation, they do so at an economic cost. While a patent is in place, its holder has a monopoly. And monopoly is another source of inefficiency (which is explained in Chapter 12). But without a patent, the effort to develop new goods, services, or processes is diminished and the flow of new inventions is slowed. So the efficient outcome is a compromise that balances the benefits of more inventions against the cost of temporary monopoly in newly invented activities.

REVIEW QUIZ
1 What is special about knowledge that creates external benefits?
2 How might governments use public provision, private subsidies, and vouchers to achieve an efficient amount of education?
3 How might governments use public provision, private subsidies, vouchers, and patents and copyrights to achieve an efficient amount of research and development?
ⓧ myeconlab **Study Plan 15.3**

◆ *Reading Between the Lines* on pp. 358–359 looks at the pollution created by generating electricity and the debate over whether the regulation of power utilities is too lax or too severe.

---

[1] Paul Romer, "Ideas and Things," in *The Future Surveyed*, supplement to *The Economist*, September 11, 1993, pp. 71–72.

The Air Pollution Debate

THE GLOBE AND MAIL, APRIL 16, 2002

Three plants spew bulk of pollutants

Three large coal-fired power plants in Southern Ontario produce 83 per cent of all the harmful air pollutants from the province's electric-power sector, according to documents obtained under the Freedom of Information Act.

In the first full look at air emissions from the province's 143 generating facilities, the coal plants— located near Toronto, Simcoe and Sarnia— stand out because they produced 24 million tonnes of contaminants that cause global warming, acid rain, smog, and heavy-metal poisoning in wildlife.

The bulk of the pollutants, tracked over an eight-month period in 2000, are carbon dioxide, sulphur dioxide and nitrogen oxides, but they also include nerve poisons, such as mercury, that are toxic to humans and wildlife even in small concentrations.

The figures also show that the province's publicly owned utility, Ontario Power Generation, is the worst polluter, producing the lion's share of the emissions, with nearly 91 per cent of the total.

The company that was the next-largest emitter, TransAlta Cogen LP, produced only 1.4 per cent.

Ontario Power is such a big polluter partly because it generates the bulk of the province's electricity, and partly because of its use of coal to carry out this task.

. . .

Reprinted with permission from The Globe and Mail.

Essence of the Story

■ Ontario Power Generation creates 91 per cent of total emissions from Ontario's electric power producing sector.

■ Ontario Power's three largest power plants account for 83 percent of the province's air pollution.

■ These emissions include carbon dioxide, sulfur dioxide, and nitrogen oxides, as well as mercury.

Economic Analysis

■ Producing electricity brings a tradeoff between cost and air quality.

■ The cheapest fuels and technologies are dirty.

■ None of these technologies are used in Canada today. But they are used in China and Russia where air pollution is a serious problem.

■ Canada, in contrast, has achieved a high standard of air quality.

■ But is the standard high enough? Or is it too high?

■ To answer this question, we need to consider the economics of pollution from producing electricity.

■ Figure 1 shows the market demand for electricity and its marginal social benefit as the curve $D = MSB$. The curve MC shows the marginal cost of producing electricity in dirty plants.

■ With an unregulated and competitive market, the quantity produced is 6 megawatt hours.

■ Because the plants are dirty, a pollution problem arises. The curve MSC shows the marginal social cost of producing electricity.

■ The vertical distance between the MC curve and the MSC curve is the marginal external cost.

■ Taking the marginal external cost into account, we can find the efficient quantity of electricity to produce and the efficient amount of pollution.

■ In the example in Fig. 1, the efficient quantity is 4 megawatt hours. Notice that at the efficient quantity, we still have pollution, but a smaller amount than with the unregulated outcome.

■ Figure 2 shows the same demand and cost curves as Fig. 1 but focuses on the overall cost of pollution—its deadweight loss.

■ If production is cut to 4 megawatt hours, the deadweight loss disappears and we have the efficient outcome.

■ If power companies are regulated to use a more costly but cleaner technology, the MC curve shifts upward, the cost of electricity rises, the quantity produced decreases, and the deadweight loss from pollution shrinks.

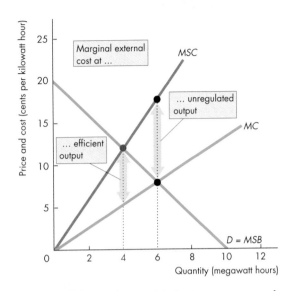

Figure 1 Efficient and unregulated outcomes compared

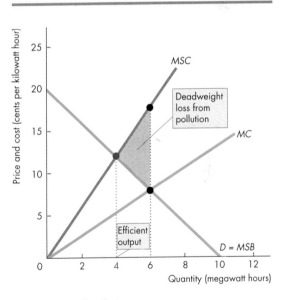

Figure 2 Cost of pollution

■ If the additional private cost is less than the external cost of pollution, production and pollution move towards but remain above their efficient levels.

■ If the additional private cost exceeds the external cost of pollution, production and pollution move below their efficient levels.

359

SUMMARY

KEY POINTS

Externalities in Our Lives (p. 346)

- An externality can arise from either a production activity or a consumption activity.
- A negative externality imposes an external cost.
- A positive externality provides an external benefit.

Negative Externalities: Pollution (pp. 347–353)

- External costs are costs of production that fall on people other than the producer of a good or service. Marginal social cost equals marginal private cost plus marginal external cost.
- Producers take account only of marginal private cost and produce more than the efficient quantity when there is a marginal external cost.
- Sometimes it is possible to overcome a negative externality by assigning a property right.
- When property rights cannot be assigned, governments might overcome externalities by using taxes, emission charges, or marketable permits.

Positive Externalities: Knowledge (pp. 353–357)

- External benefits are benefits that are received by people other than the consumer of a good or service. Marginal social benefit equals marginal private benefit plus marginal external benefit.
- External benefits from education arise because better-educated people tend to be better citizens, commit fewer crimes, and support social activities.
- External benefits from research arise because once someone has worked out a basic idea, others can copy it.
- Vouchers or subsidies to schools or the provision of public education below cost can achieve a more efficient provision of education.

- Patents and copyrights create intellectual property rights and an incentive to innovate. But they do so by creating a temporary monopoly, the cost of which must be balanced against the benefit of more inventive activity.

KEY FIGURES

Figure 15.3   Inefficiency with an External Cost, 350
Figure 15.4   Property Rights Achieve an Efficient Outcome, 351
Figure 15.5   A Pollution Tax, 352
Figure 15.7   Inefficiency with an External Benefit, 354
Figure 15.8   Public Provision or Private Subsidy to Achieve an Efficient Outcome, 355
Figure 15.9   Vouchers Achieve an Efficient Outcome, 356

KEY TERMS

Coase theorem, 351
Copyright, 357
Externality, 346
Intellectual property rights, 357
Marginal external benefit, 353
Marginal external cost, 349
Marginal private benefit, 353
Marginal private cost, 349
Marginal social benefit, 353
Marginal social cost, 349
Negative externality, 346
Patent, 357
Pigovian taxes, 352
Positive externality, 346
Property rights, 350
Public provision, 355
Subsidy, 356
Transactions costs, 351
Voucher, 356

PROBLEMS

Go to [myeconlab] for solutions to odd-numbered problems and additional exercises.

1. The table provides information about costs and benefits arising from the production of pesticide that pollutes a lake used by a trout farmer.

Total product of pesticide (tonnes per week)	Pesticide producer's MC	Marginal external cost	Marginal social benefit of pesticide
	(dollars per tonne)		
0	0	0	250
1	5	33	205
2	15	67	165
3	30	100	130
4	50	133	100
5	75	167	75
6	105	200	55
7	140	233	40

a. If no one owns the lake and there is no regulation of pollution, what is the quantity of pesticide produced and what is the marginal cost of pollution borne by the trout farmer?

b. If the trout farm owns the lake, how much pesticide is produced and what does the pesticide producer pay the farmer per tonne?

c. If the pesticide producer owns the lake, and if a pollution-free lake rents for $1,000 a week, how much pesticide is produced per week and how much rent per week does the farmer pay the factory for the use of the lake?

d. Compare the quantities of pesticide produced in your answers to (b) and (c) and explain the relationship between these quantities.

2. The table at the top of the next column provides information about the costs and benefits of steel smelting that pollutes the air of a city.

a. With no property rights in the city's air and no regulation of pollution, what is the quantity of steel produced per week and what is the marginal cost of pollution borne by the citizens?

b. If the city owns the steel plant, how much steel is produced per week and what does the city charge the steel producer per tonne?

Total product of steel (tonnes per week)	Steel producer's MC	Marginal external cost	Marginal social benefit of steel
	(dollars per tonne)		
0	0	0	1,200
10	100	15	1,100
20	200	25	1,000
30	300	50	900
40	400	100	800
50	500	200	700
60	600	300	600
70	700	400	500
80	800	500	400

c. If the steel firm owns the city, and if the residents of a pollution-free city are willing to pay $15,000 a week in property taxes, how much steel is produced per week and how much are the citizens willing to pay in property taxes to live in the polluted city?

d. Compare the quantities of steel produced in your answers to (b) and (c) and explain the relationship between these quantities.

3. Back at the pesticide plant and trout farm described in problem 1, suppose that no one owns the lake and that the government introduces a pollution tax.

a. What is the tax per tonne of pesticide produced that achieves an efficient outcome?

b. Explain the connection between your answer to (a) and the answer to problem 1.

4. Back at the steel smelter and city in problem 2, suppose that the city government introduces a pollution tax.

a. What is the tax per tonne of steel produced that will achieve an efficient outcome?

b. Explain the connection between your answer to (a) and the answer to problem 2.

5. In problem 1, suppose that no one owns the lake and that the government issues two marketable pollution permits, one to the farmer and one to the factory. Each may pollute the lake by the same amount, and the total amount of pollution is the efficient amount.

a. What is the quantity of pesticide produced?

b. What is the market price of a pollution permit? Who buys and who sells a permit?

c. What is the connection between your answer and the answers to problems 1 and 3?

6. Using the information given in problem 2, suppose that the city government issues two marketable pollution permits, one to the city government and one to the smelter. Each may pollute the air by the same amount, and the total is the efficient amount.
   a. How much steel is produced?
   b. What is the market price of a permit? Who buys and who sells a permit?
   c. What is the connection between your answer and the answers to problems 2 and 4?

7. The marginal social cost of educating a student is $4,000 a year and is constant. The figure shows the marginal private benefit curve.

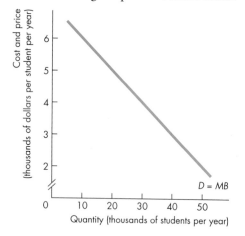

   a. With no government involvement and if the schools are competitive, how many students are enrolled and what is the tuition?
   b. The external benefit from education is $2,000 per student per year and is constant. If the government provides the efficient amount of education, how many school places does it offer and what is the tuition?

8. Technological advances cut the marginal social cost of educating a student to $2,000 a year. The marginal private benefit is the same as that in problem 7. The external benefit from education increases to $4,000 per student per year.
   a. With no government involvement and if the schools are competitive, how many students are enrolled and what is the tuition?
   b. If the government provides the efficient amount of education, how many school places does it offer and what is the tuition?
   c. Compare the outcomes in problem 8 with those in problem 7. Explain the differences.

CRITICAL THINKING

1. After you have studied *Reading Between the Lines* on pp. 358–359, answer the following questions:
   a. Which electric power companies create most of the air pollution in the electricity industry in Ontario?
   b. What are the pros and cons of stiffening the regulations that power utilities face?
   c. If a technological advance lowers the cost of producing electricity but leaves the marginal external pollution cost unchanged, would the adoption of this technology in an unregulated market increase or decrease pollution? Explain using figures like those on p. 359.

WEB EXERCISES

Use the links on (X) myeconlab **to work the following exercises.**

1. Obtain two viewpoints on global warming and then answer these questions:
   a. What are the benefits and costs of greenhouse gas emissions?
   b. Do you think environmentalists are correct in the view that greenhouse gas emissions must be cut or do you think the costs of reducing greenhouse gas emissions exceed the benefits?
   c. If greenhouse gas emissions are to be reduced, should firms be assigned production limits or marketable permits?

2. Visit the Canadian Wind Energy Association and read the pages on Quick Facts and Frequently Asked Questions (FAQs).
   a. What sorts of positive externalities arise in the generation of electricity using wind technologies?
   b. What sorts of negative externalities (external costs) arise in the generation of electricity using wind technologies?
   c. Which do you think are more serious—the external costs of generating electricity from wind or from burning coal and oil?
   d. Can you think of reasons why, despite the lower external costs, a campaign against the use of wind technology might be more successful than a campaign against the use of coal or oil?

Public Goods and Common Resources

CHAPTER 16

Free Riding and Overusing the Commons

Why does government provide some goods and services such as the enforcement of law and order and national defence? Why don't we let private firms produce these items and people buy the quantities that they demand in the marketplace? Is the scale of provision of these government-provided services correct? Or do governments produce either too much or too little of these items?

More and more people with ever-increasing incomes demand ever-greater quantities of most goods and services. One item that we demand more and more of is fish grown wild in the ocean. The fish stocks of the world's oceans are not owned by anyone. They are common resources and everyone is free to use them. Are our fish stocks being overused? Are we in danger of bringing extinction to some species? Must the price of fish inevitably keep rising? What can be done to conserve the world's fish stocks?

These are the questions that we study in this chapter. We begin by classifying goods and resources. We then explain what determines the scale of government provision of public services. Finally, we study the tragedy of the commons. In *Reading Between the Lines* at the end of the chapter, we look at a pressing tragedy of the global commons—the problem of overuse of the world's tropical rainforests.

After studying this chapter, you will be able to

- Distinguish among private goods, public goods, and common resources
- Explain how the free-rider problem arises and how the quantity of public goods is determined
- Explain the tragedy of the commons and its possible solutions

Classifying Goods and Resources

WHAT'S THE DIFFERENCE BETWEEN THE TORONTO Police Department and Brink's Security; between fish in the Pacific Ocean and fish produced by a BC fish farm; and between a live Shania Twain concert and a show on network television? Each pair differs in the extent to which people can be *excluded* from them and in the extent to which one person's consumption *rivals* the consumption of others.

A good or service or a resource is **excludable** if it is possible to prevent someone from enjoying the benefits of it. Brink's security services, BC Seafood's fish, and a Shania Twain concert are examples. You must pay to consume them.

A good or service or a resource is **nonexcludable** if it is impossible (or extremely costly) to prevent someone from benefiting from it. The services of the Toronto police, fish in the Pacific Ocean, and a concert on network television are examples.

A good or service or a resource is **rival** if its use by one person decreases the quantity available for someone else. A Brink's truck can't deliver cash to two banks at the same time. A fish can be consumed only once. And one seat at a concert can hold only one person at a time. These items are rival.

A good or service or a resource is **nonrival** if its use by one person does not decrease the quantity available for someone else. The services of the Toronto police and a concert on network television are nonrival. The arrival of one more person in a neighbourhood doesn't lower the level of police protection enjoyed by the community. And no other viewer is affected when someone switches on the TV.

A Four-Fold Classification

Figure 16.1 classifies goods, services, and resources into four types.

Private Goods A **private good** is both rival and excludable. A can of Coke and a fish on East Point Seafood's farm are examples of private goods.

Public Goods A **public good** is both nonrival and nonexcludable. A public good can be consumed simultaneously by everyone, and no one can be excluded from enjoying its benefits. National defence is the best example of a public good.

FIGURE 16.1   myeconlab
Four-Fold Classification of Goods

	Excludable	Nonexcludable
Rival	**Private goods** Food and drink Car House	**Common resources** Fish in ocean Atmosphere City parks
Nonrival	**Natural monopolies** Internet Cable television Bridge or tunnel	**Public goods** National defence The law Air-traffic control

A private good is one for which consumption is rival and from which consumers can be excluded. A public good is one for which consumption is nonrival and from which it is impossible to exclude a consumer. A common resource is one that is rival but nonexcludable. And a natural monopoly is nonrival but excludable.

Common Resources A **common resource** is rival and nonexcludable. A unit of a common resource can be used only once, but no one can be prevented from using what is available. Ocean fish are a common resource. They are rival because a fish taken by one person isn't available for anyone else, and they are nonexcludable because it is difficult to prevent people from catching them.

Natural Monopolies In a natural monopoly, economies of scale exist over the entire range of output for which there is a demand (see p. 264). A special case of natural monopoly has zero marginal cost. Buyers can be excluded but the good is nonrival. The Internet and cable television are examples.

Two Problems

Public goods create a **free-rider problem**—the absence of an incentive for people to pay for what they consume. *Common resources* create the **tragedy of the commons**—the absence of incentives to prevent the overuse and depletion of a resource.

The rest of this chapter looks more closely at the free-rider problem and the tragedy of the commons and examines public choice solutions to them.

myeconlab   **Study Plan 16.1**

Public Goods and the Free-Rider Problem

SUPPOSE THAT FOR ITS DEFENCE, A COUNTRY must launch some surveillance satellites. The benefit provided by a satellite is the *value* of its services. The *value* of a *private* good is the maximum amount that a person is willing to pay for one more unit, which is shown by the person's demand curve. The *value* of a *public* good is the maximum amount that *all the people* are willing to pay for one more unit of it. To calculate the value placed on a public good, we use the concepts of total benefit and marginal benefit.

The Benefit of a Public Good

Total benefit is the dollar value that a person places on a given level of provision of a good. The greater the quantity of a good, the larger is a person's total benefit. *Marginal benefit* is the increase in total benefit that results from a one-unit increase in the quantity of a good.

Figure 16.2 shows the marginal benefit that arises from defence satellites for a society with only two people, Lisa and Max, whose marginal benefits are graphed as MB_L and MB_M, respectively, in parts (a) and (b) of the figure. The marginal benefit from a public good (like that from a private good) diminishes as the quantity of the good increases. For Lisa, the marginal benefit from the first satellite is $80 and that from the second is $60. By the time five satellites are deployed, Lisa's marginal benefit is zero. For Max, the marginal benefit from the first satellite is $50 and that from the second is $40. By the time five satellites are deployed, Max perceives only $10 worth of marginal benefit.

Part (c) shows the economy's marginal benefit curve, *MB*. The economy's marginal benefit curve for a public good is different from the market demand curve for a *private* good. To obtain the market demand curve for a private good, we sum the quantities demanded by all individuals at each price—we sum the individual demand curves *horizontally* (see Chapter 5, p. 106). But to find the economy's marginal benefit curve of a *public* good, we sum the marginal benefits of each individual at each quantity—we sum the individual marginal benefit curves *vertically*. So the curve *MB* in part (c) is the marginal benefit curve for the economy made up of Lisa and Max. Lisa's marginal benefit from

FIGURE 16.2
Benefits of a Public Good

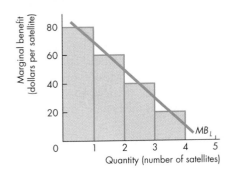

(a) Lisa's marginal benefit

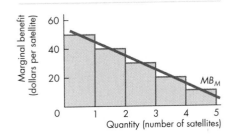

(b) Max's marginal benefit

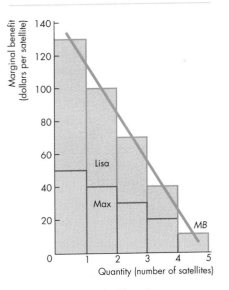

(c) Economy's marginal benefit

The marginal benefit to the economy at each quantity of the public good is the sum of the marginal benefits of all individuals. The marginal benefit curves are MB_L for Lisa, MB_M for Max, and *MB* for the economy.

each satellite gets added to Max's marginal benefit from each satellite because they *both* consume the services of each satellite.

The Efficient Quantity of a Public Good

An economy with two people would not buy any satellites—because the total benefit would fall far short of the cost. But an economy with 30 million people might. To determine the efficient quantity, we need to take the cost as well as the benefit into account.

The cost of a satellite is based on technology and the prices of the resources used to produce it (just like the cost of producing sweaters, which you studied in Chapter 10).

Figure 16.3 sets out the benefits and costs. The second and third columns of the table show the total and marginal benefits. The next two columns show the total and marginal costs of producing satellites. The final column shows net benefit. Total benefit, *TB*, and total cost, *TC*, are graphed in part (a) of the figure.

The efficient quantity is the one that maximizes *net benefit*—total benefit minus total cost—and occurs when 2 satellites are provided.

The fundamental principles of marginal analysis that you have used to explain how consumers maximize utility and how firms maximize profit can also be used to calculate the efficient scale of provision of a public good. Figure 16.3(b) shows this alternative approach. The marginal benefit curve is *MB*, and the marginal cost curve is *MC*. When marginal benefit exceeds marginal cost, net benefit increases if the quantity produced increases. When marginal cost exceeds marginal benefit, net benefit increases if the quantity produced decreases. Marginal benefit equals marginal cost with 2 satellites. So making marginal cost equal to marginal benefit maximizes net benefit and uses resources efficiently.

Private Provision by Market

We have now worked out the quantity of satellites that maximizes net benefit. Would a private firm—North Pole Protection, Inc.—deliver that quantity? It would not. To do so, it would have to collect $15 billion to cover its costs—or $500 from each of the 30 million people in the economy. But no one would have an incentive to buy his or her "share" of the satellite system. Everyone would reason as follows: The number of satellites provided by North Pole Protection, Inc., is not affected by my $500. But my own private consumption is greater if I free ride and do not pay my share of the cost of the satellite system. If I do not pay, I enjoy the same level of security and I can buy more private goods. Therefore I will spend my $500 on other goods and free ride on the public good. This is the free-rider problem.

If everyone reasons the same way, North Pole Protection has zero revenue and so provides no satellites. Because two satellites is the efficient level, private provision is inefficient.

Public Provision by Majority Vote

Suppose that voters agree with each other on all issues except for the quantity of satellites. An equal number of voters want each level of provision from zero to five so 40 percent of voters want zero or one; 40 percent want three or four, and 20 percent want two, the efficient quantity.

There are two political parties, the Hawks represent the 40 percent who would like more than two satellites; the Doves represent the 40 percent who would like fewer than two satellites; and no party represents the 20 percent who want two satellites.

The Hawks realize that if they propose any number of satellites greater than two, the Doves can propose two and win the election. The Doves get 60 percent of the vote. Similarly, the Doves realize that if they propose any number fewer than two, the Hawks can propose two and win the election with 60 percent of the votes.

Contemplating these possible election outcomes, the Hawks realize that they cannot be too hawkish and the Doves realize that they can't be too dovish.

The only proposal that either can make that doesn't guarantee electoral defeat is two. By proposing two satellites, each party gets the support of their 40 percent plus a further 10 percent because the middle group doesn't care which party wins the election.

The result of the politicians' contemplating the alternative possible election outcomes is that each party proposes two satellites, so regardless of who wins the election, this is the quantity of satellites installed. And this quantity is efficient. It maximizes the net benefit of the voters.

Thus in this example, competition in the political marketplace results in the efficient provision of a public good. But for this outcome to occur, the median voter must want the efficient outcome, and voters must be well informed. As you will see below, voters do not always have the incentive to achieve this outcome.

FIGURE 16.3
The Efficient Quantity of a Public Good

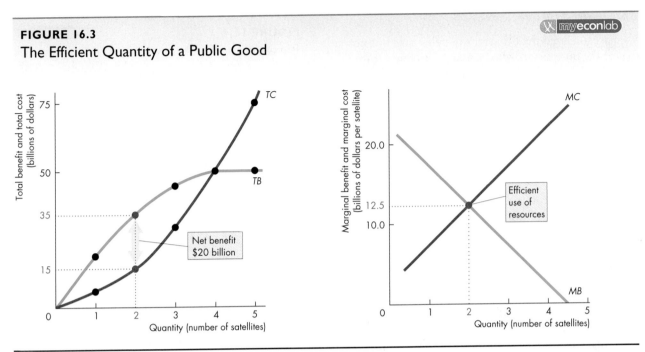

Quantity (number of satellites)	Total benefit (billions of dollars)	Marginal benefit (billions of dollars per satellite)	Total cost (billions of dollars)	Marginal cost (billions of dollars per satellite)	Net benefit (billions of dollars)
0	0		0		0
		20		5	
1	20		5		15
		15		10	
2	35		15		20
		10		15	
3	45		30		15
		5		20	
4	50		50		0
		0		25	
5	50		75		−25

Net benefit—the vertical distance between total benefit, TB, and total cost, TC—is maximized when 2 satellites are installed (part a) and where marginal benefit, MB, equals marginal cost, MC (part b). The Doves would like 1 satellite, and the Hawks would like 4. But each party recognizes that its only hope of being elected is to provide 2 satellites—the quantity that maximizes net benefit and so leaves no room for the other party to improve on.

The Principle of Minimum Differentiation In the example we've just studied, both parties propose identical policies. This tendency towards identical policies is an example of the **principle of minimum differentiation**, which is the tendency for competitors to make themselves similar to appeal to the maximum number of clients or voters. This principle not only describes the behaviour of political parties but also explains why fast-food restaurants cluster in the same block and even why new auto models have similar features. If McDonald's opens a restaurant in a new location, it is likely that Burger King will open next door to McDonald's rather than a mile down the road. If Chrysler designs a new van with a sliding door on the driver's side, most likely Ford will too.

The Role of Bureaucrats

We have analyzed the behaviour of politicians but not that of the bureaucrats who translate the choices of the politicians into programs and who control the day-to-day activities that deliver public goods. Let's now see how the economic choices of bureaucrats influence the political equilibrium.

To do so, we'll stick with the previous example. We've seen that competition between two political parties delivers the efficient quantity of satellites. But will the bureaucrats in the Department of National Defence (DND) cooperate and accept this outcome?

The bureaucrats' objective is to maximize the defence budget—see Chapter 14, pp. 325–326. With 2 satellites being provided at minimum cost, the defence budget is $15 billion (see Fig. 16.4). To increase its budget, the DND might do two things. First, it might try to persuade the politicians that 2 satellites cost more than $15 billion. As Fig. 16.4 shows, if possible, the DND would like to convince Parliament that 2 satellites cost $35 billion—the entire benefit. Second, and pressing its position even more strongly, the DND might argue for more satellites. It might press for 4 satellites and a budget of $50 billion. In this situation, total benefit and total cost are equal and net benefit is zero.

The DND wants to maximize its budget, but won't the politicians prevent it from doing so because the DND's preferred outcome costs votes? They will if voters are well informed and know what is best for them. But voters might be rationally ignorant. In this case, well-informed interest groups might enable the DND to achieve its objective.

Rational Ignorance

A principle of public choice theory is that it is rational for a voter to be ignorant about an issue unless that issue has a perceptible effect on the voter's income. **Rational ignorance** is the decision *not* to acquire information because the cost of doing so exceeds the expected benefit. For example, each voter knows that he or she can make virtually no difference to the defence policy of the government of Canada. Each voter also knows that it would take an enormous amount of time and effort to become even moderately well informed about alternative defence technologies. So voters remain relatively uninformed about the technicalities of defence issues. (Though we are using defence policy as an example, the same applies to all

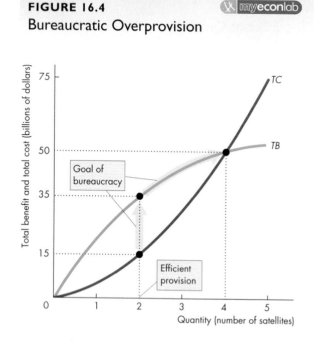

FIGURE 16.4   myeconlab
Bureaucratic Overprovision

The goal of bureaucrats is to maximize the department's budget. A bureaucracy that maximizes the budget will seek to increase the budget until its total cost equals total benefit. Then it will use the budget to expand output and expenditure. Here, the DND tries to get $35 billion to provide 2 satellites. It would like to increase the quantity to 4 satellites with a budget of $50 billion.

aspects of government economic activity.)

All voters are consumers of national defence. But not all voters are producers of national defence. Only a small number are in this latter category. Voters who own or work for firms that produce satellites have a direct personal interest in defence because it affects their incomes. These voters have an incentive to become well informed about defence issues and to operate a political lobby aimed at furthering their own interests. In collaboration with the defence bureaucracy, these voters exert a larger influence than do the relatively uninformed voters who only consume this public good.

When the rationality of the uninformed voter and special interest groups are taken into account, the political equilibrium provides public goods in excess of the efficient quantity. So in the satellite example, 3 or 4 satellites might be installed rather than the efficient quantity, which is 2 satellites.

Two Types of Political Equilibrium

We've seen that two types of political equilibrium are possible: efficient and inefficient. These two types of political equilibrium correspond to two theories of government:

■ Social interest theory
■ Public choice theory

Social Interest Theory Social interest theory predicts that governments make choices that achieve efficiency. This outcome occurs in a perfect political system in which the median voter wants the efficient outcome and voters are fully informed about the benefits and costs of alternative policies.

Public Choice Theory Public choice theory predicts that governments make choices that result in inefficiency. This outcome occurs in political markets in which voters are rationally ignorant and base their votes only on issues that they know affect their own net benefit. Voters pay more attention to their interests as producers than their interests as consumers, and public officials also act in their own best interest. The result is *government failure* that parallels market failure.

Why Government Is Large and Grows

Now that we know how the quantity of public goods is determined, we can explain part of the reason for the growth of government. Government grows in part because the demand for some public goods increases at a faster rate than the demand for private goods. There are two possible reasons for this growth:

■ Voter preferences
■ Inefficient overprovision

Voter Preferences The growth of government can be explained by voter preferences in the following way. As voters' incomes increase (as they do in most years), the demand for many public goods increases more quickly than income. (Technically, the *income elasticity of demand* for many public goods is greater than 1—see Chapter 4, pp. 92–93.) These goods include public health, education, national defence, highways, airports, and air-traffic control systems. If politicians did not support increases in expenditures on these items, they would not get elected.

Inefficient Overprovision Inefficient overprovision might explain the *size* of government but not its *growth rate*. It (possibly) explains why government is *larger* than its efficient scale, but it does not explain why governments use an increasing proportion of total resources.

Voters Strike Back

If government grows too large relative to the value that voters place on public goods, there might be a voter backlash against government programs and a large bureaucracy. Electoral success during the 1990s at the provincial and federal levels required politicians of all parties to embrace smaller, leaner, and more efficient government. The September 11 attacks have led to a greater willingness to pay for security but have probably not lessened the desire for lean government.

Another way in which voters—and politicians—can try to counter the tendency of bureaucrats to expand their budgets is to privatize the production of public goods. Government *provision* of a public good does not automatically imply that a government-operated bureau must *produce* the good. Garbage collection (a public good) is often done by a private firm, and experiments are being conducted with private fire departments and even private prisons.

REVIEW QUIZ

1 What is the free-rider problem and why does it make the private provision of a public good inefficient?
2 Under what conditions will competition for votes among politicians result in an efficient quantity of a public good?
3 How do rationally ignorant voters and budget-maximizing bureaucrats prevent competition in the political marketplace from producing the efficient quantity of a public good? Do they result in too much or too little public provision of public goods?

myeconlab Study Plan 16.2

You've seen how public goods create a free-rider problem that would result in the underprovision of such goods. We're now going to learn about common resources and see why they result in the opposite problem—the overuse of such resources.

Common Resources

ATLANTIC OCEAN COD STOCKS HAVE BEEN declining since the 1950s, and some marine biologists fear that this species is in danger of becoming extinct in some regions. The whale population of the South Pacific and South Atlantic have been declining, and a ban on commercial whaling around Antarctica is now in place to regenerate the population. Since the start of the Industrial Revolution in 1750, the concentration of carbon dioxide in the atmosphere has steadily increased. It is estimated that it is about 30 percent higher today than it was in 1750.

All these situations involve common property, and the problem that we have identified is called the tragedy of the commons.

The Tragedy of the Commons

The *tragedy of the commons* is the absence of incentives to prevent the overuse and depletion of a commonly owned resource. If no one owns a resource, no one considers the effects of her or his use of the resource on others.

The Original Tragedy of the Commons   The term "tragedy of the commons" comes from fourteenth century England where areas of rough grassland surrounded villages. The commons were open to all and used for grazing cows and sheep owned by the villagers.

Because the commons were open to all, no one had an incentive to ensure that the land was not over grazed. The result was a severe overgrazing situation. Because the commons were overgrazed, the quantity of cows and sheep that they could feed kept on falling.

During the sixteenth century, the price of wool increased and England became a wool exporter to the world. Sheep farming became profitable, and sheep owners wanted to gain more effective control of the land they used. So the commons were gradually enclosed and privatized. Overgrazing ended, and land use became more efficient.

A Tragedy of the Commons Today   One of today's pressing tragedies of the commons is overfishing. Several fish species have been seriously overfished, and one of them is Atlantic Cod.

To study the tragedies of the commons, we'll use the Atlantic Cod as an example.

Sustainable Production

Sustainable production is the rate of production that can be maintained indefinitely. In the case of ocean fish, the sustainable rate of production is the quantity of fish (of a given species) that can be caught each year into the indefinite future.

The production rate depends on the existing stock of fish and the number of boats that go fishing. For a given stock of fish, sending more boats to sea increases the quantity of fish caught. But sending too many boats to sea depletes the stock.

So as the number of boats increases, the quantity of fish caught increases as long as the stock is maintained. But above some crucial level, as more boats go fishing, the stock of fish decreases and the number of fish caught also decreases.

Table 16.1 provides some numbers that illustrate the relationship between the number of boats that go fishing and the quantity of fish caught. The numbers in this example are hypothetical.

TABLE 16.1   Sustainable Production: Total, Average, and Marginal Catch

	Boats (thousands)	Total catch (thousands of tonnes)	Average catch (tonnes per boat)	Marginal catch (tonnes per boat)
A	0	0		
				90
B	1	90	90	
				70
C	2	160	80	
				50
D	3	210	70	
				30
E	4	240	60	
				10
F	5	250	50	
				−10
G	6	240	40	
				−30
H	7	210	30	
				−50
I	8	160	20	
				−70
J	9	90	10	
				−90
K	10	0	0	

As the number of fishing boats increases, the quantity of fish caught increases up to the maximum sustainable catch and then decreases. The average catch and marginal catch decrease as the number of boats increases.

Total Catch The total catch is the sustainable rate of production. The numbers in the first two columns of Table 16.1 show the relationship between the number of fishing boats and the total catch, and Fig. 16.5 illustrates this relationship.

You can see that as the number of boats increases from zero to 5,000, the sustainable catch increases to a maximum of 250,000 tonnes a month. As the number of boats increases above 5,000, the sustainable catch begins to decrease. By the time 10,000 boats are fishing, the fish stock is depleted to the point at which no fish can be caught.

With more than 5,000 boats, there is overfishing. Overfishing arises if the number of boats increases to the point at which the fish stock begins to fall and the remaining fish are harder to find and catch.

Average Catch The average catch is the catch per boat and equals the total catch divided by the number of boats. The numbers in the third column of Table 16.1 show the average catch.

One boat catches 100 tonnes a month. With 1,000 boats, the total catch is 90,000 tonnes and the catch per boat is 90 tonnes. With 2,000 boats, the

total catch is 160,000 tonnes, and the catch per boat 80 tonnes. As more boats take to the ocean, the catch per boat decreases. By the time 8,000 boats are fishing, each boat is catching just 20 tonnes a month.

The decreasing average catch is an example of the principle of diminishing returns.

Marginal Catch The marginal catch is the change in the total catch that occurs when one more boat joins the existing number. It is calculated as the change in the total catch divided by the increase in the number of boats. The numbers in the fourth column of Table 16.1 show the marginal catch.

For example, in rows *C* and *D* of the table, when the number of boats increases by 1,000, the catch increases by 50,000 tonnes, so the increase in the catch per boat equals 50 tonnes. In the table, we place this amount midway between the two rows because it is the marginal catch at 2,500 boats, midway between the two levels that we used to calculate it.

Notice that the marginal catch, like the average catch, decreases as the number of boats increases. Also notice that the marginal catch is always less than the average catch.

When the number of boats reaches that at which the sustainable catch is a maximum, the marginal catch is zero. At a larger number of boats, the marginal catch becomes negative—more boats decrease the total catch.

An Overfishing Equilibrium

The tragedy of the commons is that common resources are overused. Why might the fish stock be overused? Why might overfishing occur? Why isn't the maximum number of boats that take to the sea the number that maximizes the sustainable catch—5,000 in this example?

To answer this question, we need to look at the marginal cost and marginal private benefit to an individual fisher.

Suppose that the marginal cost of a fishing boat is the equivalent of 20 tonnes of fish a month. That is, to cover the opportunity cost of maintaining and operating a boat, the boat must catch 20 tonnes of fish a month. This quantity of fish also provides the boat owner with normal profit (part of the cost of operating the boat), so the boat owner is willing to go fishing.

The marginal private benefit of operating a boat is the quantity of fish the boat can catch. This quantity is

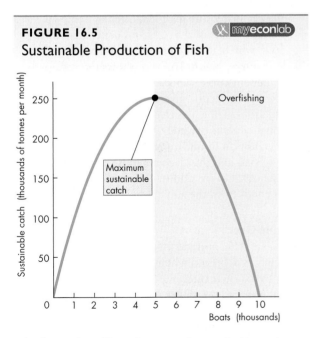

FIGURE 16.5 myeconlab
Sustainable Production of Fish

As the number of boats increases, the sustainable catch increases up to a maximum. Beyond that number, more boats will diminish the fish stock and the sustainable catch decreases. Overfishing occurs when the maximum sustainable catch decreases.

the average catch that we've just calculated. The average catch is the marginal private benefit because that is the quantity of fish that the boat owner gets by taking the boat to sea.

The boat owner will go fishing as long as the average catch (marginal private benefit) exceeds the marginal cost. And the boat owner will maximize profit when marginal private benefit equals marginal cost.

Figure 16.6 shows the marginal cost curve, *MC*, and the marginal private benefit curve, *MPB*. The *MPB* curve is based on the numbers for the average catch in Table 16.1.

You can see in Fig. 16.6 that with fewer than 8,000 boats, each boat catches more fish than it costs to catch them. Because boat owners can gain from fishing, the number of boats is 8,000 and there is an overfishing equilibrium.

If one boat owner stopped fishing, the overfishing would be less severe. But that boat owner would be giving up an opportunity to earn an economic profit.

FIGURE 16.6
Why Overfishing Occurs

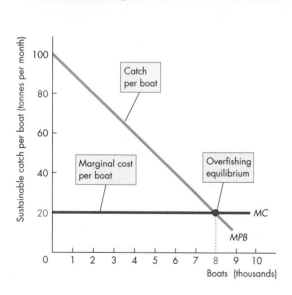

The average catch decreases as the number of boats increases. The average catch per boat is the marginal private benefit, *MPB*, of a boat. The marginal cost of a boat is equivalent to 20 tonnes of fish, shown by the curve *MC*. The equilibrium number of boats is 8,000—an overfishing equilibrium.

The private interest is to fish, but the social interest is to limit fishing. The quantity of fish caught by each boat decreases as additional boats are introduced. But when individual boat owners are deciding whether to fish, they ignore this decrease. They consider only the marginal *private* benefit. The result is an *inefficient* overuse of the resource.

The Efficient Use of the Commons

What is the efficient use of a common resource? It is the use of the resource that makes the marginal cost of using the resource equal to the marginal *social* benefit from its use.

Marginal Social Benefit The marginal *social* benefit of a boat is the boat's marginal catch—the increase in the total catch that results from an additional boat. The reason is that when an additional boat puts to sea, it catches the average catch but it decreases the average catch for itself and for every other boat. The social benefit is the increase in the quantity of fish caught, not the average number of fish caught.

We calculated the marginal catch in Table 16.1 and we repeat part of that table for convenience in Fig. 16.7, which also shows marginal social benefit as the *MSB* curve. Figure 16.7 also shows the marginal private benefit curve, *MPB*.

Notice that at any given number of boats, marginal social benefit is less than marginal private benefit. Each boat benefits privately from the average catch, but the addition of one more boat *decreases* the catch of every boat, and this decrease must be subtracted from the catch of the additional boat to determine the social benefit from the additional boat.

Efficient Use Figure 16.7 also shows the marginal cost curve, *MC*, and the efficient outcome. Efficiency is achieved when *MSB* equals *MC* with 4,000 boats, each catching 60 tonnes of fish a month. You can see in the table that when the number of boats increases from 3,000 to 4,000 (with 3,500 being the midpoint), marginal social benefit is 30 tonnes, which exceeds marginal cost. When the number of boats increases from 4,000 to 5,000 (with 4,500 being the midpoint), marginal social benefit is 10 tonnes, which is less than marginal cost. At 4,000 boats, marginal social benefit is 20 tonnes, which equals marginal cost.

FIGURE 16.7   myeconlab
Efficient Use of a Common Resource

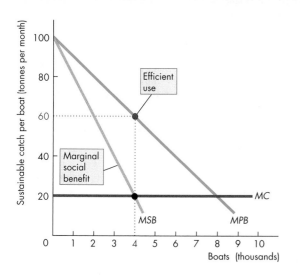

Boats (thousands)	Total catch (thousands of tonnes)	MPB (tonnes per boat)	MSB (tonnes per boat)
A	0	0	
			90
B	1	90	90
			70
C	2	160	80
			50
D	3	210	70
			30
E	4	240	60
			10
F	5	250	50

The marginal social benefit, MSB, of a fishing boat is the change in total benefit that results from an additional boat. The table shows the MSB calculations. When the number of boats increases from 2,000 to 3,000 (from row C to row D), the total catch increases from 160,000 to 210,000 tonnes and the marginal catch and MSB is 50 tonnes. The figure graphs the MSB curve as well as the MPB curve. Marginal social benefit is less than marginal private benefit and decreases as the number of boats increases. The efficient quantity of boats is that at which MSB equals MC and is 4,000. The efficient use of a common resource does not overuse the resource.

Achieving an Efficient Outcome

Defining the conditions under which a common resource is used efficiently is easier than bringing those conditions about. To use a common resource efficiently, it is necessary to design an incentive mechanism that confronts the users of the resource with the marginal social consequences of their actions. The same principles apply to common resources as those that you met when you studied externalities in Chapter 15.

Three main methods might be used to achieve the efficient use of a common resource. They are

- Property rights
- Quotas
- Individual transferable quotas (ITQs)

Property Rights A common resource that no one owns and that anyone is free to use contrasts with *private property*, which is a resource that *someone* owns and has an incentive to use in the way that maximizes its value. One way of overcoming the tragedy of the commons is to remove the commons and make the resource private property. By assigning private property rights, each owner faces the same conditions as society faces. The *MSB* curve of Fig. 16.7 becomes the marginal *private* benefit curve, and the use of the resource is efficient.

The private property solution to the tragedy of the commons *is* available in some cases. It was the solution to the original tragedy of the commons in England's Middle Ages. It is also a solution that has been used to prevent the airwaves that we use to carry our cell phone messages from being overused. The right to use this space—called the frequency spectrum—has been auctioned by governments to the highest bidders, and the owner of a particular part of the spectrum is the only one permitted to use it (or license someone else to use it).

But assigning private property rights is not always feasible. It would be difficult, for example, to assign private property rights to the oceans. It would not be impossible, but the cost of enforcing private property rights over thousands of square kilometres of ocean would be high. And it would be even harder to assign and protect private property rights to the atmosphere.

In some cases, there is an emotional objection to assigning private property rights. When private property rights are too costly to assign and enforce, some form of government intervention is used, and quotas are the simplest.

Quotas You studied the effects of a quota in Chapter 6 (p. 139) and learned that a quota can drive a wedge between marginal benefit and marginal cost and create deadweight loss. But in that earlier example, the market was efficient without a quota. In the case of the use of common property, the market is inefficient and is overproducing. So a quota that limits production can bring a move towards a more efficient outcome.

Figure 16.8 shows a quota that achieves an efficient use of a common resource. A quota is set for total production at the quantity at which marginal social benefit equals marginal cost. Here, that quantity is what 4,000 boats can produce. Individual boat owners are assigned their own share of the total permitted catch. If everyone sticks to the assigned quota, the outcome is efficient.

There are two problems in implementing a quota. First, it is in everyone's self-interest to cheat and use more of a common resource than the amount based on the assigned quota. The reason is that marginal private

benefit exceeds marginal cost. So by catching more than the allocated quota, each boat owner gets a higher income. If everyone breaks the quota, overproduction returns and the tragedy of the commons remains.

Second, marginal cost is not, in general, the same for every producer. Some producers have a comparative advantage in using a resource.

Efficiency requires that producers with the lowest marginal cost are the ones that get the quotas. But the government department that allocates quotas does not possess information about individual marginal cost. Even if the government tried to get this information, producers would have an incentive to lie about their costs in order to get a bigger quota.

So a quota can work, but only if the activities of every producer can be monitored and all producers have the same marginal cost. Where producers are hard or very costly to monitor or where marginal costs vary across producers, a quota cannot achieve an efficient outcome.

Individual Transferable Quotas Where producers are hard to monitor and where marginal costs differ across producers, a more sophisticated quota system can be used. An **individual transferable quota (ITQ)** is a production limit that is assigned to an individual who is free to transfer the quota to someone else. A market in ITQs emerges, and ITQs are transferred at their market price.

Figure 16.9 shows how ITQs work. In the market for ITQs, the price is the highest price that an ITQ is worth. If the number of ITQs issued equals the efficient production level, that price will equal the amount shown in the figure. This price equals the marginal private benefit at the quota quantity minus the private marginal cost of using a boat. The price rises to this level because people who don't have a quota would be willing to pay this amount to acquire the right to fish. And people who do own a quota could sell it for this price, so to not sell it is to incur an opportunity cost. The result is that the marginal cost, which now includes the cost of the ITQ, rises from MC_0 to MC_1. The equilibrium is efficient.

Individual differences in marginal cost do not prevent an ITQ system from delivering the efficient outcome. Producers that have a low marginal cost are willing and able to pay more for a quota than are producers that have a high marginal cost. The market price of a quota will equal the marginal cost of the

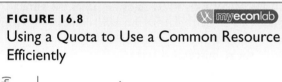

FIGURE 16.8   myeconlab

Using a Quota to Use a Common Resource Efficiently

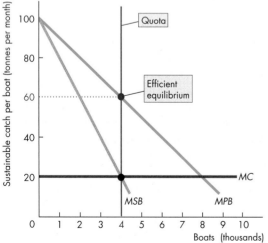

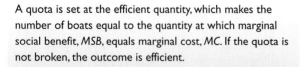

A quota is set at the efficient quantity, which makes the number of boats equal to the quantity at which marginal social benefit, *MSB*, equals marginal cost, *MC*. If the quota is not broken, the outcome is efficient.

FIGURE 16.9   ⓧ myeconlab

Individual Transferable Quotas to Use a Common Resource Efficiently

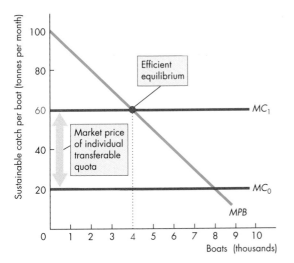

ITQs are issued on a scale that keeps output at the efficient level. The market price of an ITQ equals the marginal private benefit minus marginal cost. Because each user of the common resource faces the opportunity cost of using the resource, self-interest achieves the social interest.

marginal producer at the efficient quantity. Producers with higher marginal costs will not produce.

Public Choice and the Political Equilibrium

You saw in the previous part of this chapter where we studied the provision of public goods that a political equilibrium might be inefficient—that there might be government failure.

This same political outcome might arise in the face of a tragedy of the commons. Defining an efficient allocation of resources and designing an ITQ system to achieve that allocation is not sufficient to ensure that the political process delivers the efficient outcome. In the case of the wild ocean fish stock, some countries have achieved an efficient political equilibrium, but not all have done so.

There is wide agreement among economists that ITQs offer the most effective tool for dealing with overfishing and achieving an efficient use of the stock of ocean fish. So a political commitment to ITQs is an

efficient outcome, and an unwillingness to use ITQs is an inefficient political outcome.

Australia and New Zealand have introduced ITQs to conserve fish stocks in the South Pacific Ocean. The evidence from these examples suggests that ITQs work well. Fishing boat operators have an incentive to cheat and produce more than the amount for which they have a quota. But such cheating seems to be relatively rare. And producers that have paid for a quota have an incentive to monitor and report on cheating by others who have not paid the market price for a quota.

So ITQs do the job they are designed to do: help to maintain fish stocks. But they also reduce the size of the fishing industry. This consequence of ITQs puts them against the self-interest of fishers.

In Canada, the opposition to ITQs has prevented this solution from being adopted. One parliamentary committee even went so far as to argue that evidence from Australia and New Zealand should not be used to justify ITQs in Canada.

In the United States the opposition to ITQs is so strong that the fishing industry managed to persuade Congress to outlaw them, a move that led to the end of attempts to introduce ITQs in the Gulf of Mexico and the Northern Pacific.

REVIEW QUIZ

1   What is the tragedy of the commons?
2   Provide two examples of the tragedy of the commons, including one from your own neighbourhood.
3   Describe the conditions under which a common resource is used efficiently.
4   Review three methods that might achieve the efficient use of a common resource and explain the obstacles to efficiency.

ⓧ myeconlab   **Study Plan 16.3**

◆ *Reading Between the Lines* on pp. 376–377 looks at the overuse of tropical rainforests.

The next chapter begins a new part of your study of microeconomics and examines the third big question—for whom are goods and services produced? We examine the markets for factors of production and discover how wage rates and other incomes are determined.

Rainforests: A Tragedy of the Commons

Malaysia laundering rainforest logs

Environmental campaigners in Malaysia are accusing the government of involvement in the criminal destruction of the endangered forests of Indonesia.

Their concerns come as the United Nations publishes its Global Environment Outlook report, in which it warns that 15% of the earth's land cover has now been degraded by human activity—and nearly a third of that is due to deforestation.

An investigation by the BBC has revealed that Malaysia is importing timber which has been felled illegally in nearby Indonesia, and then disguising its origin by using it for the manufacture of garden furniture or other products which are labelled as of Malaysian origin.

...

Just a few miles south of Malaysia's capital Kuala Lumpur there is a brand new port where boats with Indonesian flags are unloading the banned round logs.

And stacking them on the dockside where they will be turned into Malaysian doors or Malaysian garden furniture.

A junior manager at the Kuala Lumpur-based company Harvest, admitted that some of the timber coming in was from Indonesia and it was being stamped by the state government as an official import. ...

BBC, http://news.bbc.co.uk/2/hi/asia-pacific/2002590.stm.

Essence of the Story

■ A United Nations report says that 15 percent of the earth's land cover has been degraded by human activity, almost a third of which is due to deforestation.

■ Malaysia has been accused of importing timber felled illegally in Indonesia, disguising its origin, and using it to manufacture garden furniture or other products that are labelled as of Malaysian origin.

Economic Analysis

■ The tropical rainforests of Indonesia grow valuable hardwood timber.

■ These forests are also home to many rare species and a carbon-dioxide sink that helps to maintain the earth's atmosphere.

■ The forests are common property, but their use is subject to the laws and international agreements.

■ The private incentive to exploit these forest resources is strong.

■ And because no one owns the forests, there is no incentive to conserve the resources and use them on a sustainable basis.

■ The result is overuse, just like the overuse of the commons of England in the Middle Ages.

■ The figures illustrate the tragedy of the commons in a tropical rainforest.

■ Figure 1 shows the relationship between the sustainable production of wood from a rainforest and the number of lumber producers working the forest.

■ Figure 2 shows the marginal benefit and marginal cost of a producer and the marginal social benefit and marginal social cost.

■ The marginal cost of felling a tree incurred by a producer is assumed to be zero.

■ As a common resource, the marginal benefit received by a producer is MB, and LD producers acting in their self-interest deplete the resource. Sustainable production falls to zero.

■ As a privately owned resource, the marginal social benefit curve, MSB, becomes the marginal private benefit curve. Self-interest results in LP producers who maximize the sustainable output of the rainforest.

■ If the only benefit from the rainforest were its timber, maximum sustainable timber output would be efficient.

■ But external benefits arise from the diversity of the wildlife supported by the forest, so destroying the forest creates an external cost and marginal social cost exceeds the zero marginal private cost.

■ Production in the social interest—the efficient level of production—is achieved with LS producers and is less than the maximum sustainable production.

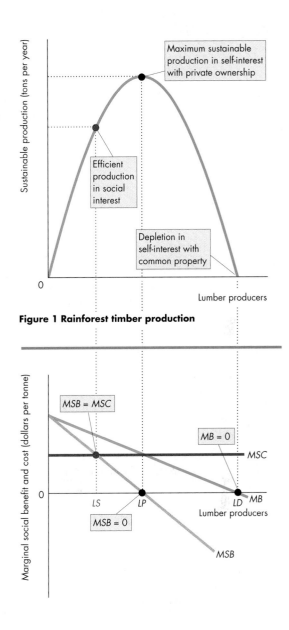

Figure 1 Rainforest timber production

Figure 2 Marginal benefit and marginal cost

You're the Voter

■ Would you support a law that banned the importing of products made from tropical rainforests? Provide your reasons.

SUMMARY

KEY POINTS

Classifying Goods and Resources (p. 364)

- A private good is a good or service that is rival and excludable.
- A public good is a good or service that is nonrival and nonexcludable.
- A common resource is a resource that is rival but nonexcludable.

Public Goods and the Free-Rider Problem (pp. 365–369)

- A public good is a good or service that is consumed by everyone and that is *nonrival* and *nonexcludable.*
- A public good creates a *free-rider* problem: No one has an incentive to pay their share of the cost of providing a public good.
- The efficient level of provision of a public good is that at which net benefit is maximized. Equivalently, it is the level at which marginal benefit equals marginal cost.
- Competition between political parties, each of which tries to appeal to the maximum number of voters, can lead to the efficient scale of provision of a public good and to both parties proposing the same policies—the principle of minimum differentiation.
- Bureaucrats try to maximize their budgets, and if voters are rationally ignorant, producer interests might result in voting to support taxes that provide public goods in quantities that exceed those that maximize net benefit.

Common Resources (pp. 370–375)

- Common resources create the tragedy of the commons—no one has a private incentive to conserve the resources and use it at an efficient rate.
- A common resource is used to the point at which the marginal private benefit equals the marginal cost.
- A common resource might be used efficiently by creating a private property right, setting a quota, or issuing individual transferable quotas.

KEY FIGURES

Figure 16.1   Four-Fold Classification of Goods, 364
Figure 16.2   Benefits of a Public Good, 365
Figure 16.3   The Efficient Quantity of a Public Good, 367
Figure 16.4   Bureaucratic Overprovision, 368
Figure 16.6   Why Overfishing Occurs, 372
Figure 16.7   Efficient Use of a Common Resource, 373

KEY TERMS

Common resource, 364
Excludable, 364
Free-rider problem, 364
Individual transferable quota (ITQ), 374
Nonexcludable, 364
Nonrival, 364
Principle of minimum differentiation, 367
Private good, 364
Public good, 364
Rational ignorance, 368
Rival, 364

PROBLEMS

Go to X myeconlab for solutions to odd-numbered problems and additional exercises.

1. You are provided with the following information about a sewage disposal system that a city of 1 million people is considering installing.

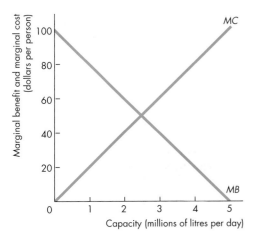

a. What is the capacity that achieves maximum net benefit?
b. How much will each person have to pay in taxes to pay for the efficient capacity level?
c. What is the political equilibrium if the median voter wants the efficient quantity and voters are well informed?
d. What is the political equilibrium if voters are rationally ignorant and bureaucrats achieve the highest attainable budget?

2. You are provided with the following information about a mosquito control program.

Quantity (square miles sprayed per day)	Marginal cost (dollars per day)	Marginal benefit (dollars per day)
0	0	0
1	1,000	5,000
2	2,000	4,000
3	3,000	3,000
4	4,000	2,000
5	5,000	1,000

a. What is the quantity of spraying that achieves maximum net benefit?
b. What is the total tax revenue needed to pay for the efficient quantity of spraying?

c. What is the political equilibrium if the median voter wants the efficient quantity and voters are well informed?
d. What is the political equilibrium if voters are rationally ignorant and bureaucrats achieve the highest attainable budget?

3. The table shows the value of cod caught in the North Atlantic Ocean by Canadian, American, and European fishing boats. It also shows the value that concerned citizens of Canada, the United States, and Europe place on the Atlantic cod stock. The marginal cost of operating a boat is $70,000 a month.

Number of boats	Value of cod caught (thousands of dollars per month)	Value placed on cod stock by concerned citizens (thousands of dollars per month)
0	0	10,000
10	2,000	9,000
20	3,500	8,000
30	4,500	7,000
40	4,800	6,000
50	5,000	5,000
60	4,800	4,000
70	4,200	3,000
80	2,400	2,000

a. What is the marginal private benefit of each fishing boat?
b. What is the marginal social cost of each fishing boat?
c. With no regulation of cod fishing, what is the equilibrium number of boats and the approximate value of cod caught?
d. Is the equilibrium in part (c) an overfishing equilibrium?
e. What is the marginal social benefit of each fishing boat?
f. What is the efficient number of boats?
g. What is the efficient value of the cod catch?
h. Do you you think that the concerned citizens of Canada, the United States, and Europe and the fishing industry will agree about how much cod should be caught?
i. If Canada, the United States, and the European Union issued ITQs to fishing boats to limit the catch to the efficient quantity, what would be the price of an ITQ?

4. The table shows the value of salmon caught in the Pacific Ocean by Canadian, American, and Japanese fishing boats. It also shows the value that concerned citizens of Canada, the United States, and Japan place on the Pacific salmon stock. The marginal cost of operating a boat is $100,000 a month.

Number of boats	Value of salmon caught (thousands of dollars per month)	Value placed on salmon stock by concerned citizens (thousands of dollars per month)
0	0	10,000
5	500	9,500
10	1,000	9,000
15	1,500	8,500
20	2,000	8,000
25	1,750	7,500
30	1,500	7,000
35	1,000	6,500
40	500	6,000

a. What is the marginal private benefit of each fishing boat?
b. What is the marginal social cost of each fishing boat?
c. With no regulation of salmon fishing, what is the equilibrium number of boats and the approximate value of salmon caught?
d. Is the equilibrium in part (c) an overfishing equilibrium?
e. What is the marginal social benefit of each fishing boat?
f. What is the efficient number of boats?
g. What is the efficient value of the salmon catch?
h. Do you think that the concerned citizens of Canada, the United States, and Japan and the fishing industry will agree about how much salmon should be caught?
i. If Canada, the United States, and Japan issued ITQs to fishing boats to limit the catch to the efficient quantity, what would be the price of an ITQ?

CRITICAL THINKING

1. After you have studied *Reading Between the Lines* on pp. 376–377, answer the following questions:
   a. What is happening in Malaysia that is contributing to the depletion of the Indonesian tropical rainforest?
   b. How would the creation of private property rights in Indonesian rainforests change the way in which the forest resources are used?
   c. Would private ownership solve all the problems of resource overuse? If not, why not?

2. Your city council is contemplating upgrading its system for controlling traffic signals. The council believes that by installing computers, it can improve the speed of the traffic flow. The bigger the computer the council buys, the better job it can do. The mayor and the other elected officials who are working on the proposal want to determine the scale of the system that will win them the most votes. The city bureaucrats want to maximize the budget. Suppose that you are an economist who is observing this public choice. Your job is to calculate the quantity of this public good that uses resources efficiently.
   a. What data would you need to reach your own conclusions?
   b. What does the public choice theory predict will be the quantity chosen?
   c. How could you, as an informed voter, attempt to influence the choice?

WEB EXERCISES

Use the links on ⓧmyeconlab to work the following exercises.

1. Read the article on demand revealing processes.
   a. What is a demand revealing process and what is its purpose?
   b. Why might using a demand revealing process deliver a more efficient level of public goods than our current political system?
   c. Why might our current political system deliver a more efficient level of public goods than would a demand revealing process?

Making the Rules

Creating a system of responsible democratic government is a huge enterprise and one that can easily go wrong. Creating a constitution that makes despotic and tyrannical rule impossible is relatively easy. And we achieved such a constitution for Canada by using some sound economic ideas. We've designed a sophisticated system of incentives—of carrots and sticks—to make the government responsive to public opinion and to limit the ability of individual self-interest to gain at the expense of the social interest. But we have not managed to create a constitution that effectively blocks the ability of special interest groups to capture the consumer and producer surpluses that result from specialization and exchange.

We have created a system of government to deal with four economic problems. First, the market economy would produce too small a quantity of those public goods and services that we must consume together, such as national defence and air-traffic control. Second, the market economy enables monopoly to restrict production and charge too high a price. Third, the market economy produces too large a quantity of some goods and services, the production of which creates pollution. And fourth, the market economy generates a distribution of income and wealth that most people believe is too unequal. So we need a government to help cope with these economic problems. But when governments get involved in the economy, people try to steer the government's actions in directions that bring personal gains at the expense of the social interest.

The three chapters in this part explained the problems with which the market has a hard time coping. Chapter 14 overviewed the entire range of problems and studied one of them, competition policy and the regulation of natural monopoly, more deeply. Chapter 15 dealt with externalities. It examined the external costs imposed by pollution and the external benefits that come from education and research. Chapter 15 described some of the ways in which externalities can be dealt with. And it explained that one way of coping with externalities is to strengthen the market and "internalize" the externalities rather than to intervene in the market. Chapter 16 studied the problems created by public goods and common resources.

Many economists have thought long and hard about the problems discussed in this part. But few have had as profound an effect on our ideas in this area as Ronald Coase, whom you can meet on the following page. You can also meet Caroline Hoxby of Harvard University, an economist whose work has shed important light on public choice issues, especially in the field of education.

Externalities and Property Rights

THE ECONOMIST

Ronald Coase *(1910–), was born in England and educated at the London School of Economics, where he was deeply influenced by his teacher, Arnold Plant, and by the issues of his youth: communist central planning versus free markets. Professor Coase has lived in the United States since 1951. He first visited America as a 20-year-old on a travelling scholarship during the depths of the Great Depression. It was on this visit, and before he had completed his bachelor's degree, that he conceived the ideas that 60 years later were to earn him the 1991 Nobel Prize for Economic Science. He discovered and clarified the significance of transactions costs and property rights for the functioning of the economy. Ronald Coase has revolutionized the way we think about property rights and externalities and has opened up the growing field of law and economics.*

"The question to be decided is: Is the value of fish lost greater or less than the value of the product which contamination of the stream makes possible?"

RONALD H.
COASE
*The Problem of
Social Cost*

THE ISSUES

As knowledge accumulates, we are becoming more sensitive to environmental externalities. We are also developing more sensitive methods of dealing with them. But all the methods involve a public choice.

Urban smog, which is both unpleasant and dangerous to breathe, forms when sunlight reacts with emissions from the tailpipes of automobiles. Because of this external cost of auto exhaust, we set emission standards and tax gasoline. Emission standards increase the cost of a car, and gasoline taxes increase the cost of the marginal mile travelled. The higher costs decrease the quantity demanded of road transportation and so decrease the amount of pollution it creates. Is the value of cleaner urban air worth the higher cost of transportation? The public choices of voters, regulators, and lawmakers answer this question.

Acid rain, which imposes a cost on everyone who lives in its path, falls from sulphur-laden clouds produced by electric utility smokestacks. This external cost is being tackled with a market solution. This solution is marketable permits, the price and allocation of which are determined by the forces of supply and demand. Private choices determine the demand for pollution permits, but a public choice determines the supply.

As cars stream onto an urban freeway during the morning rush hour, the highway clogs and becomes an expensive parking lot. Each rush hour traveller imposes external costs on all the others. Today, road users bear private congestion costs but do not face a share of the external congestion costs that they create. But a market solution to this problem is now technologically feasible. It is a solution that charges road users a fee similar to a toll that varies with time of day and degree of congestion. Confronted with the social marginal cost of their actions, each road user makes a choice and the market for highway space is efficient. Here, a public choice to use a market solution leaves the final decision about the degree of congestion to private choices.

THEN

Chester Jackson, a Lake Erie fisherman, recalls that when he began fishing on the lake, boats didn't carry drinking water. Fishermen drank from the lake. Speaking after World War II, Jackson observed, "Can't do that today. Those chemicals in there would kill you." Farmers used chemicals, such as the insecticide DDT that got carried into the lake by runoff. Industrial waste and trash were also dumped in the lake in large quantities. As a result, Lake Erie became badly polluted during the 1940s and became incapable of sustaining a viable fish stock.

NOW

Today, Lake Erie supports a fishing industry, just as it did in the 1930s. No longer treated as a garbage dump for chemicals, the lake is regenerating its ecosystem. Fertilizers and insecticides are now recognized as products that have potential externalities, and their external effects are assessed by Environment Canada before new versions are put into widespread use. Dumping industrial waste into rivers and lakes is now subject to much more stringent regulations and penalties. Lake Erie's externalities have been dealt with by one of the methods available: government regulation.

Caroline Hoxby, whom you can meet on the following pages, has done much to improve our understanding of policy choices in education.

383

TALKING WITH

Caroline M. Hoxby is *Professor of Economics at Harvard University. Born in Cleveland, Ohio, she was an undergraduate at Harvard and a graduate student at Oxford and MIT.*

Professor Hoxby is a leading student of the economics of education. She has written many articles on this topic and has published books entitled The Economics of School Choice *and* College Choices *(both University of Chicago Press, 2003 and 2004). She is Program Director of the Economics of Education Program at the National Bureau of Economic Research, serves on several other national boards that study education issues, and has advised or provided testimony to several state legislatures and the United States Congress.*

Michael Parkin and Robin Bade talked with Caroline Hoxby about her work and the progress that economists have made in understanding how the financing and provision of education influence the quality of education and the equality of access to it.

Although this conversation deals with the experience of the United States, there are some important lessons in it for Canadians, especially Caroline Hoxby's message about public versus private schools and the ability of vouchers to achieve any desired goals.

Caroline M. Hoxby

Why did you decide to become an economist?

I've wanted to be an economist from about the age of 13. That was when I took my first class in economics (an interesting story in itself) and discovered that all of the thoughts swimming around in my head belonged to a "science" and there was an entire body of people who understood this science—a lot better than I did, anyway. I can still recall reading *The Wealth of Nations* for the first time; it was a revelation.

What drew you to study the economics of education?

We all care about education, perhaps because it is the key means by which opportunity is (or should be) extended to all in the United States. Also, nearly everyone now acknowledges that highly developed countries like the United States rely increasingly on education as the engine of economic growth. Thus, one reason I was drawn to education is its importance. However, what primarily drew me was that education issues were so clearly begging for economic analysis and that there was so little of it. I try hard to understand educational institutions and problems, but I insist on bringing economic logic to bear on educational issues.

Why is education different from fast food? Why don't we just let people buy it from private firms that are regulated to maintain quality standards analogous to the safety standards that the FDA imposes on fast-food producers?

The thing that makes education different from fast food is not that we cannot buy it from private institutions that are regulated to maintain quality standards. We do this all the time—think of private schools and colleges. What makes education different is that it is (a) an investment, not consumption, and (b) the capital markets for financing the investments work poorly when left on their own. Essentially, our country has an interest in every person investing optimally in his or her education. To make investments, however, people need funds that allow them to attend good schools and take time away from work. Children don't have these funds and cannot arrange for loans that they may or may not pay off decades later. Therefore, children depend on their families for funds, and families do not necessarily have the funds to invest optimally or the right incentives to do so. Society has a role in filling the gaps in the capital market; it fills this role by public funding of elementary and secondary education, government guaranteed loans, college savings programs, and so on. There is no particular reason, however, why government needs to actually run schools; it can provide the funding without actually providing schooling.

In one of your papers, you posed the question: Does competition among public schools benefit students or taxpayers? What are the issues, what was your answer, and how did you arrive at it?

We are all familiar with the fact that families choose public schools when they choose where to live. This traditional form is by far the most pervasive form of school choice in the United States, and few parents who exercise it would be willing to give it up. Yet, until quite recently, we did not know whether having such traditional school choice was good for students (high achievement) or taxpayers (more efficient schools). It is important to know because some people in the United States, especially poor people who live in central cities, are unable to exercise this form of school choice. Economists hypothesized that this lack of choice might be a reason why many children from poor, central city families receive such a deficient education, especially considering the dollars spent in their schools (which spend significantly more than the median school).

To investigate this hypothesis, I examined all of the metropolitan areas in the United States. They vary a great deal in the degree of traditional choice available to parents. On one extreme, there is a group of metropolitan areas with hundreds of school districts. On the other extreme, there is a group of metropolitan areas with only one school district. Most

are somewhere in between. A family in a metropolitan area with one district may have no easy way of "escaping" a badly run district administration. A family in a metropolitan area with hundreds of districts can choose among several districts that match well with its job location, housing preferences, and so on.

Looking across metropolitan areas with many districts (lots of potential competition from traditional school choice) and few districts (little potential competition), I found that areas with greater competition had substantially higher student achievement for any given level of school spending. This suggests that schools are more efficient producers of achievement when they face competition.

What do we know about the relative productivity of public and private schools?

It is somewhat difficult to say whether achievement is higher at public or private schools in the United States. The best studies use randomly assigned private school scholarships, follow the same children over time, or use "natural experiments" in which some areas accidentally end up with more private schools than others. These studies tend to find that, for the same student, private schools produce achievement that is up to 10 percent higher. However, for understanding which type of school is more productive, we actually do not need private schools to have higher achievement. For the sake of argument, let's "call it a draw" on the achievement question.

In recent studies comparing achievement in public and private schools, the public schools spent an average of $9,662 per student and the private schools spent an average of $2,427 per student. These spending numbers, combined with achievement that we will call equal, suggest that the private schools were 298 percent more productive. I would not claim that this number is precisely correct; we could think of some minor adjustments. But it is difficult not to conclude that the private schools are significantly more productive. They produce equal achievement for a fraction of the cost.

What can economists say about the alternative methods of financing education? Is there a voucher solution that could work?

There is definitely a voucher solution that could work because vouchers are inherently an extremely flexible policy. People often see the word "voucher" and think of, say, a $2,000 voucher being given to a small share of children. But this need not be so. Anything that we can do with public school financing we can do better with a voucher because vouchers can be specific to a student, whereas the government can never ensure that funds get to an individual student by giving those funds to his or her district.

> " *Economists should say to policy makers: "Tell me your goals; I'll design you a voucher."* "

Any well-designed voucher system will give schools an incentive to compete. However, when designing vouchers, we can also build in remedies for a variety of educational problems. Vouchers can be used to ensure that disabled children get the funding they need and the program choices they need. Compared to current school finance programs, vouchers can do a better job of ensuring that low income families have sufficient funds to invest in the child's education. Well-designed vouchers can encourage schools to make their student bodies socio-economically diverse. Economists should say to policy makers: "Tell me your goals; I'll design you a voucher."

Is there a conflict between efficiency and equity in the provision of quality education?

To raise the public funds that allow all families to invest optimally in their children's education, we have to have taxes. Taxes always create some deadweight loss, so we always create some inefficiency when we raise the funds we need to provide equitable educational opportunities. However, if the funds are used successfully and actually induce people to make optimal investments in their education, we have eliminated much more inefficiency than the taxes created. Thus, in an ideal world, there need not be a conflict between efficiency and equity.

In the real world, public funds are often raised with taxes (creating deadweight loss) and then are not successfully used. If we spend twice as much on public schools and do not have higher achievement to show for it, then there are no efficiency gains to overwhelm the efficiency losses from taxation. In other words, to avoid a conflict between equity and efficiency, we must learn how to use public funds productively in education. This is what the economics of education is all about.

What advice do you have for a student who is just starting to study economics? Is economics a good subject in which to major? What other subjects go well alongside it? And do you have anything special to say to women who are making a career choice? What must we do to get more women in our subject?

Students who are just starting to study economics should do two things. First, learn the tools even if they seem abstruse. Once you have mastered the tools, you will be able to "see the forest for the trees." As long as you don't master the tools, you will be in the trees and will find it hard to think about economic problems. Second, think about economic problems! The real world is a great moving textbook of economics, once you have the tools to analyze it.

Economics is a great subject in which to major because it trains you for life, for many careers, and for the thinking that you would need in a leadership position. I think that it is the best training for a future career in business, the law, or policy making. Don't forget non-profits: every year, non-profit organizations try to hire people with economics skills who are also interested in charitable schemes.

Math and statistics courses are complementary to economics because they make it easier for a student to master the tools quickly. Economics goes well with many studies in the arts and sciences, too. It all depends on what you want to use economics for. If you want to do health policy-making, take economics along with pre-medical courses. If you want to be a policy maker in the performing arts, take economics along with music.

I wish that there were more women in economics: Our field loses far too many talented minds. Also, women who need to understand economics for their careers are sometimes without it. To aspiring women economists, I can only say to hang in there. Mastering economics is empowering. You will never have to worry about your opinion not being taken seriously if you are a good economist.

Demand and Supply in Factor Markets

CHAPTER 17

Many Happy Returns

It may not be your birthday, and even if it is, chances are you are spending most of it working. But at the end of the week or month (or, if you're devoting all your time to university, when you graduate), you will receive the *returns* from your labour. Those returns vary a lot. Ed Jones, who spends his days in a small container suspended from the top of Toronto's high-rise buildings cleaning windows, makes a happy return of $12 an hour. Roy Halladay, a Blue Jays pitcher, makes a very happy return of $10.5 million for playing around 80 baseball games. Some differences in earnings might seem surprising. For example, your university football coach might earn much more than your economics professor. Why aren't *all* jobs well paid?

Most of us have little trouble spending our pay. But most of us do manage to save some of what we earn. What determines the amount of saving that people do and the returns they make on that saving?

Some people earn their income by supplying natural resources such as oil. What determines the price of a natural resource?

◆ In this chapter, we study the markets for factors of production—labour, capital, natural resources—and learn how their prices and people's incomes are determined. And we'll see in *Reading Between the Lines* at the end of the chapter how Atlantic storms in the summer of 2005 influenced the price of oil.

After studying this chapter, you will be able to

■ Explain how a market for a factor of production works

■ Explain how firms' demand for labour and households' supply of labour determine the wage rate and employment

■ Explain how firms choose the quantity of capital to use

■ Explain how natural resource prices are determined in competitive resource markets

■ Explain the concept of economic rent and distinguish between economic rent and opportunity cost

Factor Prices and Incomes

GOODS AND SERVICES ARE PRODUCED USING THE four *factors of production—labour, capital, land*, and *entrepreneurship*. We defined these factors of production in Chapter 1, pp. 3–4. Incomes are determined by the quantities of the factors used and by *factor prices*. The factor prices are the *wage* rate earned by labour, the *interest* rate earned by capital, the *rental* rate earned by land, and the *normal* profit rate earned by entrepreneurship.

In addition to the four factor incomes, a residual income *economic profit* (or *economic loss*) is earned (or borne) by the firm's owners, who might be the entrepreneur or the stockholders.

Factors of production, like goods and services, are traded in markets. Some factor markets are competitive and behave similarly to competitive markets for goods and services. Other factor markets have monopoly elements. Our focus in this chapter is on competitive factor markets but an appendix (pp. 413–418) examines monopoly elements in labour markets. Demand and supply is the main tool used to understand a competitive factor market.

Firms demand factors of production and households supply them. The quantity demanded of a factor of production is the quantity that firms plan to hire during a given time period and at a given factor price. The law of demand applies to factors of production just as it does to goods and services. The lower the factor price, other things remaining the same, the greater is the quantity demanded of that factor.

The demand for a factor of production is called a **derived demand** because it is *derived* from the demand for the goods and services produced by the factor.

The quantity supplied of a factor of production also depends on its price. With a possible exception that you'll see later in this chapter, the law of supply applies to factors of production. The higher the price of a factor, other things remaining the same, the greater is the quantity supplied of that factor.

Figure 17.1 shows a factor market. The demand curve for the factor is the curve labelled *D*, and the supply curve of the factor is the curve labelled *S*. The equilibrium factor price is *PF*, and the equilibrium quantity is *QF*. The income earned by the factor is its price multiplied by the quantity used. In Fig. 17.1, the factor income equals the area of the blue rectangle.

A change in demand or supply changes the equilibrium price, quantity, and income. An increase in

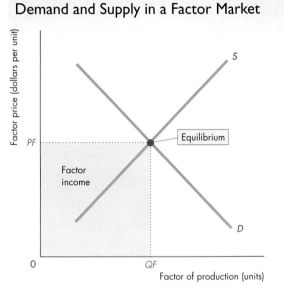

FIGURE 17.1
Demand and Supply in a Factor Market

The demand curve for a factor of production (*D*) slopes downward, and the supply curve (*S*) slopes upward. Where the demand and supply curves intersect, the factor price (*PF*) and the quantity of the factor used (*QF*) are determined. The factor income is the product of the factor price and the quantity of the factor, as represented by the blue rectangle.

demand shifts the demand curve rightward and increases income. An increase in supply shifts the supply curve rightward and income might increase, decrease, or remain constant depending on the elasticity of demand for the factor. If demand is elastic, income rises; if demand is inelastic, income falls; and if demand is unit elastic, income remains constant (see Chapter 4, p. 88).

REVIEW QUIZ

1 Why do we call the demand for a factor of production a *derived demand*? From what is it derived?
2 Why does an increase in the supply of a factor of production have an ambiguous effect on the factor's income?

myeconlab **Study Plan 17.1**

The rest of this chapter explores the influences on the demand for and supply of factors of production. We begin with the market for labour.

Labour Markets

FOR MOST OF US, THE LABOUR MARKET IS OUR only source of income. And in recent years, many people have had a tough time. But over the years, both wages and the quantity of labour have moved steadily upward. Figure 17.2(a) shows the record since 1975. Using 1997 dollars to remove the effects of inflation, the real wage rate (measured as total compensation per hour of work) increased by about 20 percent, from $16 in 1975 to more than $19 in 2004. Over the same period, the quantity of labour employed increased by 60 percent, from 18 billion hours in 1975 to 29 billion hours in 2004.

Figure 17.2(b) shows why these trends occurred. The demand for labour increased from LD_{75} to LD_{04}, and this increase was much larger than the increase in the supply of labour from LS_{75} to LS_{04}.

A lot of diversity lies behind the average wage rate and the aggregate quantity of labour. During the 1980s and 1990s, some wage rates grew much more rapidly than the average and others fell. To understand the trends in the labour market, we must probe the forces that influence the demand for labour and the supply of labour. This chapter studies these forces. We begin on the demand side of the labour market.

The Demand for Labour

The demand for labour is a derived demand. A **derived demand** is a demand for a factor of production that is derived from the demand for the goods and services produced by that factor of production. The derived demand for labour (and for the other factors demanded by firms) is driven by the firm's objective, which is to maximize profit.

You learned in Chapters 11, 12, and 13 that a profit-maximizing firm produces the output at which marginal cost equals marginal revenue. This principle holds true for all firms regardless of whether they operate in perfect competition, monopolistic competition, oligopoly, or monopoly.

A firm that maximizes profit hires the quantity of labour that can produce the profit-maximizing output. What is that quantity of labour? And how does the quantity of labour used change as the real wage rate changes? We can answer these questions by comparing the *marginal revenue* earned by hiring one more worker with the *marginal cost* of that worker. Let's look first at the marginal revenue side of this comparison.

FIGURE 17.2   ⓧ myeconlab

Canadian Labour Market Trends

(a) Labour and wage rate

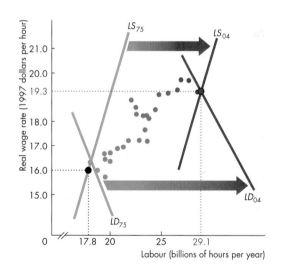

(b) Changes in demand and supply in the labour market

Between 1975 and 2004, the real wage rate increased by 20 percent and the quantity of labour employed increased by 60 percent. Part (a) shows these increases. Each dot in part (b) shows the real wage rate and the quantity of labour in each year from 1975 to 2004. Part (b) also shows the changes in demand and supply that generated these trends. The demand for labour increased from LD_{75} to LD_{04}, and the supply of labour increased from LS_{75} to LS_{04}. Demand increased by more than supply increased, so both the real wage rate and the quantity of labour employed increased.

Source of data: Statistics Canada, CANSIM Tables 282–0002, 282–0022, and 380–0001.

Marginal Revenue Product

The change in total revenue that results from employing one more unit of labour is called the **marginal revenue product** of labour. Table 17.1 shows you how to calculate marginal revenue product for a firm in perfect competition.

The first two columns show the total product schedule for Max's Wash 'n' Wax car wash service. The numbers tell us how the number of car washes per hour varies as the quantity of labour varies. The third column shows the *marginal product of labour*—the change in total product that results from a one-unit increase in the quantity of labour employed. (Look back at p. 221 for a quick refresher.)

The car wash market in which Max operates is perfectly competitive, and he can sell as many washes as he chooses at $4 a wash, the (assumed) market price. So Max's *marginal revenue* is $4 a wash.

Given this information, we can now calculate *marginal revenue product* (the fourth column). It equals marginal product multiplied by marginal revenue. For example, the marginal product of hiring a second worker is 4 car washes, and because marginal revenue is $4 a wash, the marginal revenue product of the second worker is $16 (4 washes at $4 each).

The last two columns of Table 17.1 show an alternative way of calculating the marginal revenue product of labour. Total revenue is equal to total product multiplied by price. For example, 2 workers produce 9 washes per hour and generate a total revenue of $36 (9 washes at $4 each). One worker produce 5 washes per hour and generates a total revenue of $20 (5 washes at $4 each). Marginal revenue product, in the sixth column, is the change in total revenue from hiring one more worker. When the second worker is hired, total revenue increases from $20 to $36, an increase of $16. So the marginal revenue product of the second worker is $16, which agrees with our previous calculation.

Diminishing Marginal Revenue Product As the quantity of labour increases, marginal revenue product diminishes. For a firm in perfect competition, marginal revenue product diminishes because marginal product diminishes. For a monopoly (or in monopolistic competition or oligopoly), marginal revenue product diminishes for a second reason. When more labour is hired and total product increases, the firm must cut its price to sell the extra product. So marginal product *and* marginal revenue decrease, both of which bring decreasing marginal revenue product.

TABLE 17.1   Marginal Revenue Product at Max's Wash 'n' Wax

	Quantity of labour (L) (workers)	Total product (TP) (car washes per hour)	Marginal product (MP = ΔTP/ΔL) (washes per worker)	Marginal revenue product (MRP = MR × MP) (dollars per worker)	Total revenue (TR = P × TP) (dollars)	Marginal revenue product (MRP = ΔTR/ΔL) (dollars per worker)
A	0	0		20	0	
			5			20
B	1	5		16	20	
			4			16
C	2	9		12	36	
			3			12
D	3	12		8	48	
			2			8
E	4	14		4	56	
			1			4
F	5	15			60	

The car wash market is perfectly competitive, and the price is $4 a wash, so marginal revenue is $4 a wash. Marginal revenue product equals marginal product (column 3) multiplied by marginal revenue. For example, the marginal product of the second worker is 4 washes and marginal revenue is $4 a wash, so the marginal revenue product of the second worker (in column 4) is $16. Alternatively, if Max hires 1 worker (row B), total product is 5 washes an hour and total revenue is $20 (column 5). If he hires 2 workers (row C), total product is 9 washes an hour and total revenue is $36. By hiring the second worker, total revenue rises by $16— the marginal revenue product of labour is $16.

The Labour Demand Curve

Figure 17.3 shows how the labour demand curve is derived from the marginal revenue product curve. The *marginal revenue product curve* graphs the marginal revenue product of a factor at each quantity of the factor hired. Figure 17.3(a) illustrates the marginal revenue product curve for workers employed by Max. The horizontal axis measures the number of workers that Max hires, and the vertical axis measures the marginal revenue product of labour. The blue bars show the marginal revenue product of labour as Max employs more workers. These bars correspond to the numbers in Table 17.1. The curve labelled *MRP* is Max's marginal revenue product curve.

A firm's marginal revenue product curve is also its demand for labour curve. Figure 17.3(b) shows Max's demand for labour curve (*D*). The horizontal axis measures the number of workers hired—the same as in Fig. 17.3(a). The vertical axis measures the wage rate in dollars per hour. In Fig. 17.3(a), when Max increases the quantity of labour employed from 2 workers an hour to 3 workers an hour, his marginal revenue product is $12 an hour. In Fig. 17.3(b), at a wage rate of $12 an hour, Max hires 3 workers.

The marginal revenue product curve is also the demand for labour curve because the firm hires the profit-maximizing quantity of labour. If the wage rate is *less* than marginal revenue product, the firm can increase its profit by employing one more worker. Conversely, if the wage rate is *greater* than marginal revenue product, the firm can increase its profit by employing one fewer worker. But if the wage rate *equals* marginal revenue product, then the firm cannot increase its profit by changing the number of workers it employs. The firm is making the maximum possible profit. Thus the quantity of labour demanded by the firm is such that the wage rate equals the marginal revenue product of labour.

The demand for labour curve slopes downward: The lower the wage rate, other things remaining the same, the more workers a firm hires. Why? Because the demand curve is also the marginal revenue product curve and marginal revenue product diminishes as the quantity of labour employed increases.

When we studied firms' output decisions, we discovered that a condition for maximum profit is that marginal revenue equals marginal cost. We've now discovered another condition for maximum profit: Marginal revenue product of a factor equals the factor's price. Let's study the connection between these two conditions.

FIGURE 17.3
The Demand for Labour at Max's Wash 'n' Wax

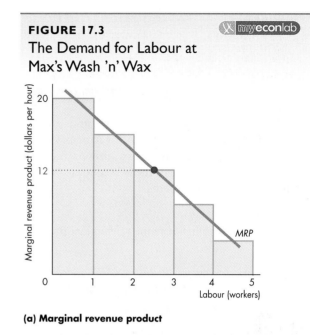

(a) Marginal revenue product

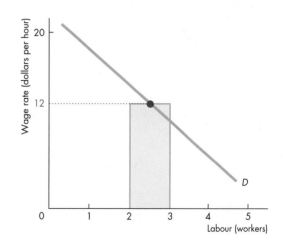

(b) Demand for labour

Max's Wash 'n' Wax operates in a perfectly competitive car wash market and can sell any quantity of washes at $4 a wash. The blue bars in part (a) represent the firm's marginal revenue product of labour. They are based on the numbers in Table 17.1. The orange line is the firm's marginal revenue product of labour curve. Part (b) shows Max's demand for labour curve. This curve is identical to Max's marginal revenue product curve. Max demands the quantity of labour that makes the wage rate equal to the marginal revenue product of labour. The demand for labour curve slopes downward because marginal revenue product diminishes as the quantity of labour employed increases.

Equivalence of Two Conditions for Profit Maximization

Profit is maximized when, at the quantity of labour hired, *marginal revenue product* equals the wage rate and when, at the output produced, *marginal revenue* equals *marginal cost*.

These two conditions for maximum profit are equivalent. The quantity of labour that maximizes profit produces the output that maximizes profit.

To see the equivalence of the two conditions for maximum profit, first recall that

Marginal revenue product = Marginal revenue × Marginal product.

If we call marginal revenue product *MRP*, marginal revenue *MR*, and marginal product *MP*, we have

$$MRP = MR \times MP.$$

If we call the wage rate *W*, the first condition for maximum profit is

$$MRP = W.$$

But $MRP = MR \times MP$, so

$$MR \times MP = W.$$

This equation tells us that when profit is maximized, marginal revenue multiplied by marginal product equals the wage rate.

Divide the last equation by *MP* to obtain

$$MR = W \div MP.$$

This equation states that when profit is maximized, marginal revenue equals the wage rate divided by the marginal product of labour.

The wage rate divided by the marginal product of labour equals marginal cost. It costs the firm *W* to hire one more hour of labour. But the labour produces *MP* units of output. So the cost of producing one of those units of output, which is marginal cost, is *W* divided by *MP*.

If we call marginal cost *MC*, then

$$MR = MC,$$

which is the second condition for maximum profit.

Because the first condition for maximum profit implies the second condition, these two conditions are equivalent. Table 17.2 summarizes the calculations you've just done and shows the equivalence of the two conditions for maximum profit.

TABLE 17.2   Two Conditions for Maximum Profit

Symbols

Marginal product	**MP**
Marginal revenue	**MR**
Marginal cost	**MC**
Marginal revenue product	**MRP**
Wage rate	**W**

Two Conditions for Maximum Profit

1. **MR = MC**   2. **MRP = W**

Equivalence of Conditions

1. *MRP/MP* = **MR**   =   **MC** = *W/MP*

Multiply by MP to give

MRP = MR × MP   *MC × MP = W*

Flipping the equation over

2. *MR × MP* = **MRP**   =   **W** = *MC × MP*

The two conditions for maximum profit are that marginal revenue (*MR*) equals marginal cost (*MC*) and that marginal revenue product (*MRP*) equals the wage rate (*W*). These two conditions are equivalent because marginal revenue product (*MRP*) equals marginal revenue (*MR*) multiplied by marginal product (*MP*) and the wage rate (*W*) equals marginal cost (*MC*) multiplied by marginal product (*MP*).

Max's Numbers Check the numbers for Max's Wash 'n' Wax and confirm that the conditions you've just examined work. Max's profit-maximizing labour decision is to hire 3 workers if the wage rate is $12 an hour. When Max hires 3 workers, marginal product is 3 washes. Max sells the 3 washes for a marginal revenue of $4 a wash. So marginal revenue product is 3 washes multiplied by $4 a wash, which equals $12 per hour. At a wage rate of $12 an hour, Max is maximizing profit.

Equivalently, Max's marginal cost is $12 an hour divided by 3 washes per hour, which equals $4 per wash. At a marginal revenue of $4 a wash, Max is maximizing profit.

You've discovered that the law of demand applies for labour just as it does for goods and services. Other things remaining the same, the lower the wage rate (the price of labour), the greater is the quantity of labour demanded.

Let's now see what changes the demand for labour and shifts the demand for labour curve.

Changes in the Demand for Labour

The demand for labour depends on three factors:

1. The price of the firm's output
2. Other factor prices
3. Production technology

The Price of the Firm's Output The higher the price of the firm's output, the greater is its demand for labour. The price of output affects the demand for labour through its influence on marginal revenue product. A higher price for the firm's output increases marginal revenue, which, in turn, increases the marginal revenue product of labour. A change in the price of a firm's output leads to a shift in the firm's demand for labour curve. If the price of the firm's output increases, the demand for labour increases and the demand for labour curve shifts rightward.

Other Factor Prices If the price of some other factor of production changes, the demand for labour changes, but only in the *long run* when all factors of production can be varied. The effect of a change in some other factor price depends on whether that factor is a *substitute* for or a *complement* of labour. Computers are substitutes for telephone operators but complements of word processor operators. So if computers become less costly to use, the demand for telephone operators decreases but the demand for word processor operators increases.

Production Technology An advance in technology that changes the marginal product of labour changes

the demand for labour. There is a general belief that advances in technology destroy jobs and therefore decrease the demand for labour. In fact, the opposite is true. Advances in technology destroy *some* jobs and create others. But the number of jobs created exceeds the number destroyed.

New technologies are substitutes for some types of labour and complements of other kinds. For example, the electronic telephone exchange is a substitute for telephone operators, so the arrival of this new technology has decreased the demand for telephone operators. This same new technology is a complement of systems managers, programmers, and electronic engineers. So its arrival has increased the demand for these types of labour.

Again, these effects on the demand for labour are long-run effects that occur when a firm adjusts all its resources and incorporates new technologies into its production process.

Table 17.3 summarizes the influences on a firm's demand for labour.

TABLE 17.3   A Firm's Demand for Labour

The Law of Demand

(Movements along the demand curve for labour)

The quantity of labour demanded by a firm

Decreases if:	Increases if:
▪ The wage rate increases	▪ The wage rate decreases

Changes in Demand

(Shifts in the demand curve for labour)

A firm's demand for labour

Decreases if:	Increases if:
▪ The firm's output price decreases	▪ The firm's output price increases
▪ The price of a substitute for the factor falls	▪ The price of a substitute for the factor rises
▪ The price of a complement of the factor rises	▪ The price of a complement of the factor falls
▪ A new technology decreases the marginal product of labour	▪ A new technology increases the marginal product of labour

Market Demand

So far, we've studied the demand for labour by an individual firm. The market demand for labour is the total demand by all firms. The market demand for labour curve is derived (like the market demand curve for any good or service) by adding together the quantities demanded by all firms at each wage rate. Because each firm's demand for labour curve slopes downward, so does the market demand curve.

Elasticity of Demand for Labour

The elasticity of demand for labour measures the responsiveness of the quantity of labour demanded to the wage rate. This elasticity is important because it tells us how labour income changes when the supply of labour changes. An increase in supply (other things remaining the same) brings a lower wage rate. If demand is inelastic, it also brings lower labour income. But if demand is elastic, an increase in supply brings a lower wage rate and an increase in labour income. And if the demand for labour is unit elastic, a change in supply leaves labour income unchanged.

The demand for labour is less elastic in the short run, when only the quantity of labour can be varied, than in the long run, when the quantities of labour and other factors of production can be varied. The elasticity of demand for labour depends on

- The labour intensity of the production process
- The elasticity of demand for the product
- The substitutability of capital for labour

Labour Intensity A labour-intensive production process is one that uses a lot of labour and little capital. Home building is an example. The greater the degree of labour intensity, the more elastic is the demand for labour. To see why, first suppose that wages are 90 percent of total cost. A 10 percent increase in the wage rate increases total cost by 9 percent. Firms will be sensitive to such a large change in total cost, so if the wage rate increases, firms will decrease the quantity of labour demanded by a relatively large amount. But if wages are 10 percent of total cost, a 10 percent increase in the wage rate increases total cost by only 1 percent. Firms will be less sensitive to this increase in cost, so if the wage rate increases in this case, firms will decrease the quantity of labour demanded by a relatively small amount.

The Elasticity of Demand for the Product The greater the elasticity of demand for the good, the larger is the elasticity of demand for the labour used to produce it. An increase in the wage rate increases the marginal cost of producing the good and decreases the supply of it. The decrease in the supply of the good increases the price of the good and decreases the quantity demanded of the good and the quantities of the factors of production used to produce it. The greater the elasticity of demand for the good, the larger is the decrease in the quantity demanded of the good and so the larger is the decrease in the quantities of the factors of production used to produce it.

The Substitutability of Capital for Labour The more easily capital can be used instead of labour in production, the more elastic is the long-run demand for labour. For example, it is easy to use robots rather than assembly-line workers in car factories and grape-picking machines rather than labour in vineyards. So the demand for these types of labour is elastic. At the other extreme, it is difficult (though possible) to substitute computers for newspaper reporters, bank loan officers, and teachers. So the demand for these types of labour is inelastic.

Let's now turn from the demand side of the labour market to the supply side and examine the decisions that people make about how to allocate time between working and other activities.

The Supply of Labour

People can allocate their time to two broad activities: labour supply and leisure. (Leisure is a catch-all term. It includes all activities other than supplying labour.) For most people, leisure is more enjoyable than supplying labour. We'll look at the labour supply decision of Jill, who is like most people. She enjoys her leisure time, and she would be pleased if she didn't have to spend her weekends working a supermarket checkout line.

But Jill has chosen to work weekends. The reason is that she is offered a wage rate that exceeds her *reservation wage*. Jill's reservation wage is the lowest wage at which she is willing to supply labour. If the wage rate exceeds her reservation wage, she supplies some labour. But how much labour does she supply? The quantity of labour that Jill supplies depends on the wage rate.

Substitution Effect Other things remaining the same, the higher the wage rate Jill is offered, at least over a range, the greater is the quantity of labour that she supplies. The reason is that Jill's wage rate is her *opportunity cost of leisure*. If she quits work an hour early to catch a movie, the cost of that extra hour of leisure is the wage rate that Jill forgoes. The higher the wage rate, the less willing Jill is to forgo the income and take the extra leisure time. This tendency for a higher wage rate to induce Jill to work longer hours is a *substitution effect.*

But there is also an *income effect* that works in the opposite direction to the substitution effect.

Income Effect The higher Jill's wage rate, the higher is her income. A higher income, other things remaining the same, induces Jill to increase her demand for most goods. Leisure is one of those goods. Because an increase in income creates an increase in the demand for leisure, it also creates a decrease in the quantity of labour supplied.

Backward-Bending Supply of Labour Curve As the wage rate rises, the substitution effect brings an increase in the quantity of labour supplied while the income effect brings a decrease in the quantity of labour supplied. At low wage rates, the substitution

effect is larger than the income effect, so as the wage rate rises, people supply more labour. But as the wage rate continues to rise, the income effect eventually becomes larger than the substitution effect and the quantity of labour supplied decreases. The labour supply curve is *backward bending*.

Figure 17.4(a) shows the labour supply curves for Jill, Jack, and Kelly. Each labour supply curve is backward bending, but the three people have different reservation wage rates.

Market Supply The market supply of labour curve is the sum of the individual supply curves. Figure 17.4(b) shows the market supply curve (S_M) derived from the supply curves of Jill, Jack, and Kelly (S_A, S_B, and S_C, respectively) in Fig. 17.4(a). At a wage rate of less than $1 an hour, no one supplies any labour. At a wage rate of $1 an hour, Jill works but Jack and Kelly don't. As the wage rate increases and reaches $7 an hour, all three of them are working. The market supply curve S_M eventually bends backward, but it has a long upward-sloping section.

Changes in the Supply of Labour The supply of labour changes when influences other than the wage rate change. The key factors that change the supply of labour and that over the years have increased it are

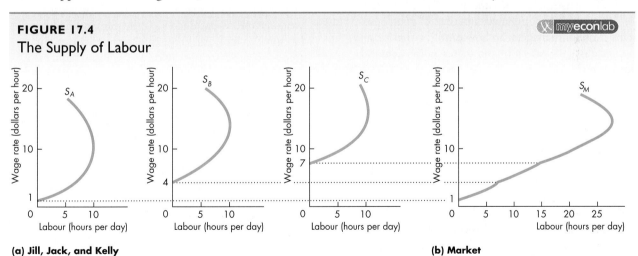

FIGURE 17.4

The Supply of Labour

(a) Jill, Jack, and Kelly

(b) Market

Part (a) shows the labour supply curves of Jill (S_A), Jack (S_B), and Kelly (S_C). Each person has a reservation wage below which she or he will supply no labour. As the wage rises, the quantity of labour supplied increases to a maximum. If the wage continues to rise, the quantity of labour supplied begins to decrease. Each person's supply curve eventually bends backward.

Part (b) shows how, by adding the quantities of labour supplied by each person at each wage rate, we derive the market supply curve of labour (S_M). The market supply curve has a long upward-sloping region before it bends backward.

1. Adult population
2. Technology in the home

An increase in the adult population increases the supply of labour. So does a technological change in home production (of meals, laundry services, and cleaning services). These factors that increase the supply of labour shift the labour supply curve rightward.

Let's now build on what we've learned about the demand for labour and the supply of labour and study labour market equilibrium and the trends in wage rates and employment.

Labour Market Equilibrium

Wages and employment are determined by equilibrium in the labour market, as you saw in Fig. 17.1. Over the years, the equilibrium wage rate and employment level have both increased. You can now explain why.

Trends in the Demand for Labour The demand for labour has *increased* because of advances in production technology, and the demand for labour curve has shifted steadily rightward.

Many people are surprised that advances in production technology *increase* the demand for labour. They see new technologies *destroying jobs*, not creating them. Downsizing has become a catchword as the use of computers has eliminated millions of "good" jobs, even those of managers. So how can it be that technological change *creates* jobs and increases the demand for labour?

Technological change destroys some jobs and creates others. But it creates more jobs than it destroys, and *on the average*, the new jobs pay more than the old ones did. But to benefit from the advances in technology, people must acquire new skills and change their jobs. For example, during the past 20 years, the demand for typists has fallen almost to zero. But the demand for people who can type (on a computer rather than a typewriter) and do other tasks as well has increased. And the output of these people is worth more than that of a typist. So the demand for people with typing (and other) skills has increased.

Trends in the Supply of Labour The supply of labour has increased because of growth in the adult population and technological change in home production. The mechanization of home production of fast-food preparation services (the freezer and the microwave oven) and laundry services (the automatic washer and dryer and wrinkle-free fabrics) has decreased the time spent on activities that once were full-time jobs and have led to a large increase in the supply of labour. As a result, the supply labour curve has shifted steadily rightward, but at a slower pace than the shift in the demand curve.

Trends in Equilibrium Because advances in production technology have increased demand by more than population growth and technological change in home production have increased supply, both wage rates and employment have increased. But not everyone has shared in the increased prosperity that comes from higher wage rates. Some groups have been left behind, and some have even seen their wage rates fall. Why?

Two key reasons can be identified. First, advances in production technology affect the marginal productivity of different groups in different ways. High-skilled computer-literate workers have benefited from the information revolution while low-skilled workers have suffered. The demand for the services of the first group has increased, and the demand for the services of the second group has decreased. (Draw a supply and demand graph, and you will see that these changes widen the wage difference between the two groups.) Second, international competition has lowered the marginal revenue product of low-skilled workers and so has decreased the demand for their labour. We look further at skill differences and at trends in the distribution of income in Chapter 18.

REVIEW QUIZ

1 What links the quantity that a firm produces and the quantity of labour it employs?
2 What is the distinction between marginal revenue product and marginal revenue? Provide an example that illustrates the distinction.
3 When a firm's marginal revenue product equals the wage rate, marginal revenue also equals marginal cost. Why? Provide a numerical example different from that in the text.
4 What determines the amount of labour that households plan to supply?
5 Describe and explain the trends in wage rates and employment.

myeconlab   **Study Plan 17.2**

Capital Markets

CAPITAL MARKETS ARE THE CHANNELS THROUGH which firms obtain *financial* resources to buy *physical* capital resources. These financial resources come from saving. The "price of capital," which adjusts to make the quantity of capital supplied equal to the quantity demanded, is the interest rate.

For most of us, capital markets are where we make our biggest-ticket transactions. We borrow in a capital market to buy a home. And we lend in capital markets to build up a fund on which to live when we retire. Do the rates of return in capital markets increase as wage rates do?

Figure 17.5(a) answers this question by showing the record from 1975 to 2004. Measuring interest rates as *real* interest rates, which means that we subtract the loss in the value of money from inflation, returns have fluctuated. They ranged from close to zero in the late 1970s to a bit more than 10 percent in 1984. Over the same period, the quantity of capital employed increased steadily. In 2004, it stood at $4.6 trillion, twice its 1975 level.

Figure 17.5(b) shows why these trends occurred. Demand increased from KD_{75} to KD_{04}, and this increase was similar to the increase in supply from KS_{75} to KS_{04}. The interest rate in 2004 was almost identical to that of 1975.

To understand the trends in the capital market, we must again probe the forces of demand and supply. Many of the ideas you've already met in your study of the labour market apply to the capital market as well. But there are some special features of capital. Its main special feature is that in the capital market, people must compare *present* costs with *future* benefits. Let's discover how people make these comparisons by studying the demand for capital.

The Demand for Capital

A firm's demand for *financial* capital stems from its demand for *physical* capital, and the amount that a firm plans to borrow in a given time period is determined by its planned investment—purchases of new capital. This decision is driven by the firm's attempt to maximize profit.

As a firm increases the quantity of capital employed, other things remaining the same, the marginal revenue product of capital eventually diminishes. To maximize profit, a firm increases its plant size and

FIGURE 17.5
Canadian Capital Market Trends

(a) Capital stock and interest rate

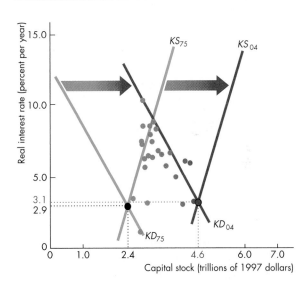

(b) Changes in demand and supply in the capital market

The real interest rate (the interest rate adjusted for inflation) fluctuated between close to zero and 10 percent a year between 1975 and 2004. During the same period, the quantity of capital approximately doubled. Part (a) shows these trends. Part (b) shows the changes in the demand for and supply of capital that generated the trends. The demand for capital increased from KD_{75} to KD_{04}, and the supply of capital increased from KS_{75} to KS_{04}.

Sources of data: Statistics Canada, CANSIM Tables 378–0004 and 176–0043.

uses more capital if the marginal revenue product of capital exceeds the price of capital. But the marginal revenue product comes in the future, and capital must be paid for in the present. So the firm must convert *future* marginal revenue products into a *present value* so that it can be compared with the price of the new equipment. To make this conversion, we use the technique of discounting.

Discounting and Present Value

Discounting is converting a future amount of money to a present value. And the **present value** of a future amount of money is the amount that, if invested today, will grow to be as large as that future amount when the interest that it will earn is taken into account.

The easiest way to understand discounting and present value is to begin with the relationship between an amount invested today, the interest that it earns, and the amount that it will grow to in the future. The future amount is equal to the present amount (present value) plus the interest it will accumulate in the future. That is,

$$\text{Future amount} = \text{Present value} + \text{Interest income.}$$

The interest income is equal to the present value multiplied by the interest rate, r, so

$$\text{Future amount} = \text{Present value} + (r \times \text{Present value})$$

or

$$\text{Future amount} = \text{Present value} \times (1 + r).$$

If you have $100 today and the interest rate is 10 percent a year ($r = 0.1$), one year from today you will have $110—the original $100 plus $10 interest. Check that the above formula delivers that answer: $100 \times 1.1 = \$110$.

The formula that we have just used calculates a future amount one year from today from the present value and an interest rate. To calculate the present value, we just work backward. Instead of multiplying the present value by $(1 + r)$, we divide the future amount by $(1 + r)$. That is,

$$\text{Present value} = \frac{\text{Future value}}{(1 + r)}.$$

You can use this formula to calculate present value. This calculation of present value is called discounting.

Let's check that we can use the present value formula by calculating the present value of $110 one year from now when the interest rate is 10 percent a year. You'll be able to guess that the answer is $100 because we just calculated that $100 invested today at 10 percent a year becomes $110 in one year. So it follows immediately that $100 is the present value of $110 in one year's time. But let's use the formula. Putting the numbers into the above formula, we have

$$\text{Present value} = \frac{\$110}{(1 + 0.1)}$$

$$= \frac{\$110}{1.1} = \$100.$$

Calculating the present value of an amount of money one year from now is the easiest case. But we can also calculate the present value of an amount any number of years in the future. As an example, let's see how we calculate the present value of an amount of money that will be available two years from now.

Suppose that you invest $100 today for two years at an interest rate of 10 percent a year. The money will earn $10 in the first year, which means that by the end of the first year, you will have $110. If the interest of $10 is invested, then the interest earned in the second year will be a further $10 on the original $100 plus $1 on the $10 interest. Thus the total interest earned in the second year will be $11. The total interest earned overall will be $21 ($10 in the first year and $11 in the second year). After two years, you will have $121. From the definition of present value, you can see that $100 is the present value of $121 two years hence. That is, $100 is the present amount that, if invested at an interest rate of 10 percent a year, will grow to $121 two years from now.

To calculate the present value of an amount of money two years in the future, we use the formula:

$$\text{Present value} = \frac{\text{Amount of money two years in future}}{(1 + r)^2}.$$

Use this formula to calculate the present value of $121 two years from now at an interest rate of 10 percent a year. With these numbers, the formula gives

$$\text{Present value} = \frac{\$121}{(1 + 0.1)^2}$$

$$= \frac{\$121}{(1.1)^2}$$

$$= \frac{\$121}{1.21}$$

$$= \$100.$$

We can calculate the present value of an amount of money n years in the future by using a formula similar to the one we've already used. The general formula is

$$\text{Present value} = \frac{\substack{\text{Amount of money} \\ n \text{ years in future}}}{(1 + r)^n}.$$

For example, if the interest rate is 10 percent a year, $100 to be received 10 years from now has a present value of $38.55. That is, if $38.55 is invested today at 10 percent a year it accumulates to $100 in 10 years.

You've seen how to calculate the present value of an amount of money one year in the future, two years in the future, and n years in the future. Most practical applications of present value calculate the present value of a sequence of future amounts of money that spread over several years. To calculate the present value of a sequence of amounts over several years, we use the formula you have learned and apply it to each year. We then sum the present values for each year to find the present value of the sequence of amounts.

For example, suppose that a firm expects to receive $100 a year for each of the next five years. And suppose that the interest rate is 10 percent per year (0.1 per year). The present value of these five payments of $100 each is calculated by using the following formula

$$PV = \frac{\$100}{1.1} + \frac{\$100}{1.1^2} + \frac{\$100}{1.1^3} + \frac{\$100}{1.1^4} + \frac{\$100}{1.1^5},$$

which equals

$$PV = \$90.91 + \$82.64 + \$75.13 + \$68.30 + \$62.09$$

$$= \$379.07.$$

You can see that the firm receives $500 over five years. But because the money arrives in the future, it is not worth $500 today. Its present value is only $379.07. And the farther in the future the money arrives, the smaller is its present value. The $100 received one

year in the future is worth $90.91 today. And the $100 received five years in the future is worth only $62.09 today.

Let's now see how a firm uses the concept of present value to achieve an efficient use of capital.

The Present Value of a Computer We'll see how a firm decides how much capital to buy by calculating the present value of a new computer.

Tina runs Taxfile, Inc., a firm that sells advice to taxpayers. Tina is considering buying a new computer that costs $2,000. The computer has a life of two years, after which it will be worthless. If Tina buys the computer, she will pay $2,000 now and she expects to generate business that will bring in an additional $1,150 at the end of each of the next two years.

To calculate the present value, PV, of the marginal revenue product of a new computer, Tina calculates

$$PV = \frac{MRP_1}{(1 + r)} + \frac{MRP_2}{(1 + r)^2}.$$

Here, MRP_1 is the marginal revenue product received by Tina at the end of the first year. MRP_1 is converted to a present value by dividing it by $(1 + r)$. The term MRP_2 is the marginal revenue product received at the end of the second year. It is converted to a present value by dividing it by $(1 + r)^2$.

If Tina can borrow or lend at an interest rate of 4 percent a year, the present value of her marginal revenue product is given by

$$PV = \frac{\$1,150}{(1 + 0.04)} + \frac{\$1,150}{(1 + 0.04)^2}$$

$$PV = \$1,106 + \$1,063$$

$$PV = \$2,169.$$

The present value (PV) of $1,150 one year in the future is $1,150 divided by 1.04 (4 percent as a proportion is 0.04). The present value of $1,150 two years in the future is $1,150 divided by $(1.04)^2$. Tina works out those two present values and then adds them to get the present value of the future flow of marginal revenue product, which is $2,169.

Parts (a) and (b) of Table 17.4 summarize the data and the calculations we've just made. Review these calculations and make sure you understand them.

TABLE 17.4   Net Present Value of an Investment—Taxfile, Inc.

(a) Data

Price of computer	$2,000
Life of computer	2 years
Marginal revenue product	$1,150 at end of each year
Interest rate	4% a year

(b) Present value of the flow of marginal revenue product

$$PV = \frac{MRP_1}{(1+r)} + \frac{MRP_2}{(1+r)^2}$$

$$= \frac{\$1,150}{1.04} + \frac{\$1,150}{(1.04)^2}$$

$$= \$1,106 + \$1,063$$

$$= \$2,169$$

(c) Net present value of investment

NPV = PV of marginal revenue product − Price of computer
$$= \$2,169 - \$2,000$$
$$= \$169$$

Tina's Decision to Buy Tina decides whether to buy the computer by comparing the present value of its future flow of marginal revenue product with its purchase price. She makes this comparison by calculating the net present value (*NPV*) of the computer. **Net present value** is the present value of the future flow of marginal revenue product generated by the capital minus the price of the capital. If the net present value is positive, the firm buys additional capital. If the net present value is negative, the firm does not buy additional capital. Table 17.4(c) shows the calculation of Tina's net present value of a computer. The net present value is $169—greater than zero—so Tina buys the computer.

Tina can buy any number of computers that cost $2,000 and have a life of two years. But like all other factors of production, capital is subject to diminishing marginal returns. The greater the amount of capital employed, the smaller is its marginal revenue product. So if Tina buys a second computer or a third one, she

gets successively smaller marginal revenue products from the additional machines.

Table 17.5(a) sets out Tina's marginal revenue products for one, two, and three computers. The marginal revenue product of one computer (the case just reviewed) is $1,150 a year. The marginal revenue product of a second computer is $1,100 a year, and the marginal revenue product of a third computer is $1,050 a year. Table 17.5(b) shows the calculations of the present values of the marginal revenue products of the first, second, and third computers.

You've seen that with an interest rate of 4 percent a year, the net present value of one computer is posi-

---

TABLE 17.5   Taxfile's Investment Decision

(a) Data

Price of computer	$2,000
Life of computer	2 years
Marginal revenue product:	
Using 1 computer	$1,150 a year
Using 2 computers	$1,100 a year
Using 3 computers	$1,050 a year

(b) Present value of the flow of marginal revenue product

If $r = 0.04$ (4% a year):

Using 1 computer $PV = \dfrac{\$1,150}{1.04} + \dfrac{\$1,150}{(1.04)^2} = \$2,169$

Using 2 computers $PV = \dfrac{\$1,100}{1.04} + \dfrac{\$1,100}{(1.04)^2} = \$2,075$

Using 3 computers $PV = \dfrac{\$1,050}{1.04} + \dfrac{\$1,050}{(1.04)^2} = \$1,980$

If $r = 0.08$ (8% a year):

Using 1 computer $PV = \dfrac{\$1,150}{1.08} + \dfrac{\$1,150}{(1.08)^2} = \$2,051$

Using 2 computers $PV = \dfrac{\$1,100}{1.08} + \dfrac{\$1,100}{(1.08)^2} = \$1,962$

If $r = 0.12$ (12% a year):

Using 1 computer $PV = \dfrac{\$1,150}{1.12} + \dfrac{\$1,150}{(1.12)^2} = \$1,944$

tive. At an interest rate of 4 percent a year, the present value of the marginal revenue product of a second computer is $2,075, which exceeds its price by $75. So Tina buys a second computer. But at an interest rate of 4 percent a year, the present value of the marginal revenue product of a third computer is $1,980, which is $20 less than the price of the computer. So Tina does not buy a third computer.

A Change in the Interest Rate We've seen that at an interest rate of 4 percent a year, Tina buys two computers. Suppose that the interest rate is 8 percent a year. In this case, the present value of the first computer is $2,051 (see Table 17.5(b)), so Tina still buys one machine because it has a positive net present value. But at an interest rate of 8 percent a year, the present value of the second computer is $1,962, which is less than $2,000, the price of the computer. So at this interest rate, Tina buys only one computer.

Suppose that the interest rate is even higher, 12 percent a year. In this case, the present value of the marginal revenue product of one computer is $1,944 (see Table 17.5(b)). At this interest rate, Tina buys no computers.

These calculations trace Taxfile's demand schedule for capital, which shows the value of computers demanded by Taxfile at each interest rate. Other things remaining the same, as the interest rate rises, the quantity of capital demanded decreases. The higher the interest rate, the smaller is the quantity of *physical* capital demanded. But to finance the purchase of *physical* capital, firms demand *financial* capital. So the higher the interest rate, the smaller is the quantity of *financial* capital demanded.

Demand Curve for Capital

A firm's demand curve for capital shows the relationship between the quantity of financial capital demanded by the firm and the interest rate, other things remaining the same. Figure 17.6(a) shows Tina's demand curve for capital and the four points on it that we've just found. If Tina can buy other capital items so that her demand for capital is divisible into one-dollar units (not restricted to jumping in $2,000 units, her demand curve for capital would look like the entire blue curve in Fig. 17.6(a).

Figure 17.6(b) shows the market demand curve for capital, *KD*, which is the horizontal sum of the demand curves of each firm. In the figure, the quantity of capital demanded in the entire capital market is $1,500 billion when the interest rate is 6 percent a year.

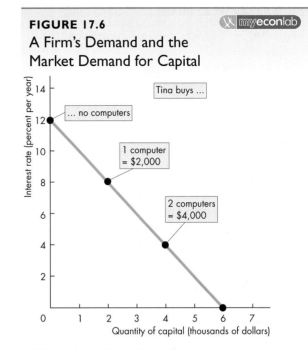

FIGURE 17.6

A Firm's Demand and the Market Demand for Capital

(a) Tina's demand curve for capital

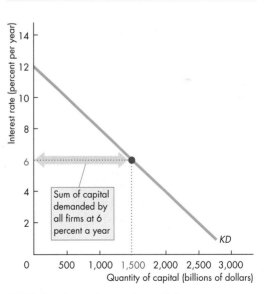

(b) Market demand curve for capital

For each firm, the lower the interest rate, the greater is the quantity of capital demanded. The market demand curve is the (horizontal) sum of the firms' demand curves.

You've seen how the demand for capital is determined. Let's now look at the supply side of the capital market.

The Supply of Capital

The quantity of financial capital supplied results from people's saving decisions. The main factors that determine saving are

- Income
- Expected future income
- Interest rate

Let's see how these factors influence Aaron's saving decisions.

Income Saving is the act of converting *current* income into *future* consumption. When Aaron's income increases, he plans to consume more both now and in the future. But to increase *future* consumption, Aaron must save today. So, other things remaining the same, the higher Aaron's income, the more he saves. The relationship between saving and income is remarkably stable.

Expected Future Income If Aaron's current income is high and his expected future income is low, he will have a high level of saving. But if Aaron's current income is low and his expected future income is high, he will have a low (perhaps even negative) level of saving.

Students have low current incomes compared with expected future incomes so they tend to consume more than they earn. In middle age, most people are earning more than they expect to earn when they retire. So they save for their retirement years.

Interest Rate A dollar saved today grows into a dollar plus interest tomorrow. The higher the interest rate, the greater is the amount that a dollar saved today becomes in the future. Thus the higher the interest rate, the greater is the opportunity cost of current consumption. With a higher opportunity cost of current consumption, Aaron cuts his current consumption and increases his saving.

Supply Curve of Capital

The supply curve of capital shows the relationship between the quantity of financial capital supplied and the interest rate, other things remaining the same. The curve KS_0 in Fig. 17.7 is a supply curve of capital. An increase in the interest rate brings an increase in the quantity of capital supplied and a movement along the supply curve.

Let's now use what we've learned about the demand for and supply of capital and see how the interest rate is determined.

The Interest Rate

Saving plans and investment plans are coordinated through capital markets, and the real interest rate adjusts to make these plans compatible.

Figure 17.7 shows the capital market. The demand for capital is KD_0, and the supply of capital is KS_0. The equilibrium real interest rate is 6 percent a year, and the quantity of capital—the amount of investment by firms and saving by households—is $1,500 billion.

If the interest rate exceeded 6 percent a year, the quantity of capital supplied would exceed the quantity of capital demanded and the interest rate would fall. The interest rate would keep falling until the capital surplus was eliminated.

If the interest rate were less than 6 percent a year, the quantity of capital demanded would exceed the quantity of capital supplied and the interest rate would rise. The interest rate would keep rising until the capital shortage was eliminated.

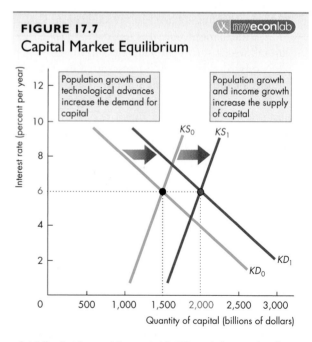

FIGURE 17.7   myeconlab
Capital Market Equilibrium

Initially, the demand for capital is KD_0 and the supply of capital is KS_0. The equilibrium interest rate is 6 percent a year, and the quantity of capital is $1,500 billion. Over time, the demand and supply of capital increase to KD_1 and KS_1. The quantity of capital increases, but the interest rate is constant. The demand and supply of capital are influenced by common and related factors.

Changes in Demand and Supply

Over time, both the demand for capital and the supply of capital increase. The demand curve shifts rightward to KD_1, and the supply curve shifts to KS_1. Both curves shift because the same or related forces influence them. Population growth increases both demand and supply. Technological advances increase demand and bring higher incomes, which in turn increase supply. Because both demand and supply increase over time, the quantity of capital increases but the real interest rate remains constant.

In reality, the real interest rate fluctuates, as you can see in Fig. 17.5(a). The reason is that the demand for capital and the supply of capital do not change in lockstep. Sometimes rapid technological change brings an increase in the demand for capital *before* it brings the higher incomes that increase the supply of capital. When this sequence of events occurs, the real interest rate rises. The first half of the 1980s was such a time, as you can see in Fig. 17.5(a).

At other times, the demand for capital grows slowly or even decreases temporarily. Supply outgrows demand and the real interest rate falls. Figure 17.5(a) shows that the mid-1970s and the period from 1984 through 1991 were two such periods.

REVIEW QUIZ

1 What is the distinction between *physical* capital and *financial* capital and what is the capital market?
2 What is discounting and how is it used to calculate a present value? When might you want to calculate a present value to make a decision?
3 How does a firm compare the future marginal revenue product of capital with the current price of capital?
4 What are the main influences on a firm's demand for capital?
5 What are the main influences on the supply of capital?
6 What have been the main changes in the interest rate and how can we explain those changes by using the demand for and supply of capital?

myeconlab Study Plan 17.3

The lessons that we've just learned about capital markets can be used to understand the prices of nonrenewable natural resources. Let's see how.

Natural Resource Markets

NATURAL RESOURCES, OR WHAT ECONOMISTS CALL *land*, fall into two categories:

■ Renewable
■ Nonrenewable

Renewable natural resources are natural resources that are repeatedly replenished by nature. Examples are land (in its everyday sense), rivers, lakes, rain, and sunshine.

Nonrenewable natural resources are natural resources that nature does not replenish. Once used, they are no longer available. Examples are coal, natural gas, and oil—the so-called hydrocarbon fuels.

The demand for natural resources as inputs into production is based on the same principle of marginal revenue product as the demand for labour (and the demand for capital). But the supply of natural resources is special. Let's look first at the supply of renewable natural resources.

The Supply of a Renewable Natural Resource

The quantity of land and other renewable natural resources is fixed. The quantity supplied cannot be changed by individual decisions. People can vary the amount of land they own. But when one person buys some land, another person sells it. The aggregate quantity of land supplied of any particular type and in any particular location is fixed, regardless of the decisions of any individual. This fact means that the supply of each particular piece of land is perfectly inelastic. Figure 17.8 illustrates such a supply. Regardless of the rent available, the quantity of land supplied on Toronto's Yorkville is a fixed number of square metres.

Because the supply of land is fixed regardless of its price, price is determined by demand. The greater the demand for a specific piece of land, the higher is its price.

Expensive land can be, and is, used more intensively than inexpensive land. For example, high-rise buildings enable land to be used more intensively. However, to use land more intensively, it has to be combined with another factor of production: capital. An increase in the amount of capital per block of land does not change the supply of land itself.

FIGURE 17.8
The Supply of Land

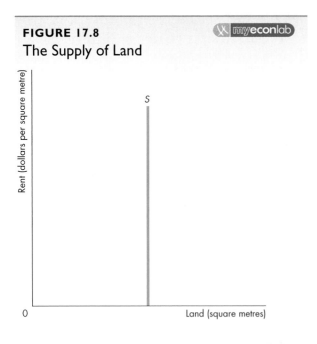

The supply of a given piece of land is perfectly inelastic. No matter what the rent, no more land than the quantity that exists can be supplied.

Although the supply of each type of land is fixed and its supply is perfectly inelastic, each individual firm, operating in competitive land markets, faces an elastic supply of land. For example, Bloor Street in Toronto has a fixed amount of land, but Chapters, the bookstore, could rent some space from The Bay, the department store. Each firm can rent the quantity of land that it demands at the going rent, as determined in the marketplace. Thus, provided that land markets are competitive, firms are price takers in these markets, just as they are in the markets for other productive resources.

The Supply of a Nonrenewable Natural Resource

The *stock* of a natural resource is the quantity in existence at a given time. This quantity is fixed and is independent of the price of the resource. The *known* stock of a natural resource is the quantity that has been discovered. This quantity increases over time because advances in technology enable ever less accessible sources to be discovered. Both of these *stock* concepts influence the price of a nonrenewable natural resource. But the influence is indirect. The direct influence on

price is the rate at which the resource is supplied for use in production—called the *flow* supply.

The flow supply of a nonrenewable natural resource is *perfectly elastic* at a price that equals the present value of the expected price next period.

To see why, think about the economic choices of Saudi Arabia, a country that possesses a large inventory of oil. Saudi Arabia can sell an additional billion barrels of oil right now and use the income it receives to buy U.S. bonds. Or it can keep the billion barrels in the ground and sell them next year. If it sells the oil and buys bonds, it earns the interest rate on the bonds. If it keeps the oil and sells it next year, it earns the amount of the price increase or loses the amount of the price decrease between now and next year.

If Saudi Arabia expects the price of oil to rise next year by a percentage that equals the current interest rate, the price that it expects next year equals $(1 + r)$ multiplied by this year's price. For example, if this year's price is $40 a barrel and the interest rate is 5 percent a year ($r = 0.5$), then next year's expected price is $1.05 \times \$40$, which equals $42 a barrel.

With the price expected to rise to $42 a barrel next year, Saudi Arabia is indifferent between selling now for $40 and not selling now but waiting until next year and selling for $42. Saudi Arabia expects to make the same return either way. So at $40 a barrel, Saudi Arabia will sell whatever quantity is demanded.

But if Saudi Arabia expects the price to rise next year by a percentage that exceeds the current interest rate, then Saudi Arabia expects to make a bigger return by hanging onto the oil than by selling the oil and buying bonds. So it keeps the oil and sells none. And if Saudi Arabia expects the price to rise next year by a percentage that is less than the current interest rate, the bond gives a bigger return than the oil, so Saudi Arabia sells as much oil as it can.

Recall the idea of discounting and present value. The minimum price at which Saudi Arabia is willing to sell oil is the present value of the expected future price. At this price, it will sell as much oil as buyers demand. So its supply is perfectly elastic.

Price and the Hotelling Principle

Figure 17.9 shows the equilibrium in a natural resource market. Because supply is perfectly elastic at the present value of next period's expected price, the actual price of the natural resource equals the present value of next period's expected price. Also, because the current price is the present value of the expected

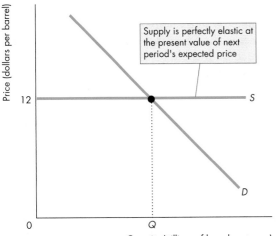

FIGURE 17.9 〔myeconlab〕

A Nonrenewable Natural Resource Market

The supply of a nonrenewable natural resource is perfectly elastic at the *present value* of next period's expected price. The demand for a nonrenewable natural resource is determined by its marginal revenue product. The price is determined by supply and equals the *present value* of next period's expected price.

FIGURE 17.10 〔myeconlab〕

Falling Resource Prices

The prices of metals (here a price index that measures the average of the prices of aluminum, copper, iron ore, lead, manganese, nickel, silver, tin, and zinc) have tended to fall over time, not rise as predicted by the Hotelling Principle. The reason is that unanticipated advances in technology have decreased the cost of extracting resources and greatly increased the exploitable known reserves.

Source of data: International Financial Statistics (various issues), Washington, DC: International Monetary Fund.

future price, the price of the resource is expected to rise at a rate equal to the interest rate.

The proposition that the price of a resource is expected to rise at a rate equal to the interest rate is called the *Hotelling Principle*. It was first realized by Harold Hotelling, a mathematician and economist at Columbia University. But as Fig. 17.10 shows, *actual* prices do not follow the path *predicted* by the Hotelling Principle. Why do the prices of nonrenewable natural resources sometimes fall rather than follow their expected path and increase over time?

The key reason is that the future is unpredictable. Expected technological change is reflected in the price of a natural resource. But a previously unexpected new technology that leads to the discovery or the more efficient use of a nonrenewable natural resource causes its price to fall. Over the years, as technology has advanced, we have become more efficient in our use of nonrenewable natural resources. And we haven't just become more efficient. We've become more efficient than we expected to.

REVIEW QUIZ

1 Why is the supply of a *renewable* natural resource such as land perfectly inelastic?
2 At what price is the flow supply of a nonrenewable natural resource perfectly elastic and why?
3 Why is the price of a nonrenewable natural resource expected to rise at a rate equal to the interest rate?
4 Why do the prices of nonrenewable resources not follow the path predicted by the Hotelling Principle?

〔myeconlab〕 **Study Plan 17.4**

People supply resources to earn an income. But some people earn enormous incomes. Are such incomes necessary to induce people to work and supply other resources? Let's now answer this question.

Income, Economic Rent, and Opportunity Cost

YOU'VE NOW SEEN HOW FACTOR PRICES ARE determined by the interaction of demand and supply. And you've seen that demand is determined by marginal productivity and supply is determined by the resources available and by people's choices about their use. The interaction of demand and supply in factor markets determines who receives a large income and who receives a small income.

Large and Small Incomes

A major-league baseball player earns $12 million a year because he has a high marginal revenue product—reflected in the demand for his services—and the supply of people with the combination of talents needed for this kind of job is small—reflected in the supply. Equilibrium occurs at a high wage rate and a small quantity employed.

People who work at fast-food restaurants earn a low wage rate because they have a low marginal revenue product—reflected in the demand for their services—and many people are able and willing to supply their labour for these jobs. Equilibrium occurs at a low wage rate and a large quantity employed.

If the demand for baseball players increases, their incomes increase by a large amount and the number of baseball players barely changes. If the demand for fast-food workers increases, the number of people doing these jobs increases by a large amount and the wage rate barely changes.

Another difference between a major-league baseball player and a fast-food worker is that if the baseball player were hit with a pay cut, he would probably still supply his services, but if a fast-food worker were hit with a pay cut, he would probably quit. This difference arises from the distinction between economic rent and opportunity cost.

Economic Rent and Opportunity Cost

The total income of a factor of production is made up of its economic rent and its opportunity cost. **Economic rent** is the income received by the owner of a factor of production over and above the amount required to induce that owner to offer the factor for use. Any factor of production can receive an economic rent. The income required to induce the supply of a factor of production is the opportunity cost of using the factor—the value of the factor in its next best use.

Figure 17.11(a) illustrates the way in which a factor income has an economic rent and opportunity cost component. The figure shows the market for a factor of production. It could be *any* factor of production—labour, capital, or land—but we'll suppose that it is labour. The demand curve is D, and the supply curve is S. The wage rate is W, and the quantity employed is C. The income earned is the sum of the yellow and green areas. The yellow area below the supply curve measures opportunity cost, and the green area above the supply curve but below the factor price measures economic rent.

To see why the area below the supply curve measures opportunity cost, recall that a supply curve can be interpreted in two different ways. It shows the quantity supplied at a given price, and it shows the minimum price at which a given quantity is willingly supplied. If suppliers receive only the minimum amount required to induce them to supply each unit of the factor, they will be paid a different price for each unit. The prices will trace the supply curve, and the income received will be entirely opportunity cost—the yellow area in Fig. 17.11(a).

The concept of economic rent is similar to the concept of producer surplus that you met in Chapter 5. Economic rent is the price a person receives for the use of a factor minus the minimum price at which a given quantity of the factor is willingly supplied. Economic rent is *not* the same thing as the "rent" that a farmer pays for the use of some land or the "rent" that you pay for your apartment. Everyday "rent" is a price paid for the services of land or a building. *Economic rent* is a component of the income received by any factor of production.

The portion of the factor income that consists of economic rent depends on the elasticity of the supply of the factor. When the supply of a factor is perfectly inelastic, its entire income is economic rent. Most of the income received by Garth Brooks and Pearl Jam is economic rent. Also, a large part of the income of a major-league baseball player is economic rent. When the supply of a factor of production is perfectly elastic, none of its income is economic rent. Most of the income of a babysitter is opportunity cost. In general, when supply is neither perfectly elastic nor perfectly

FIGURE 17.11

Economic Rent and Opportunity Cost

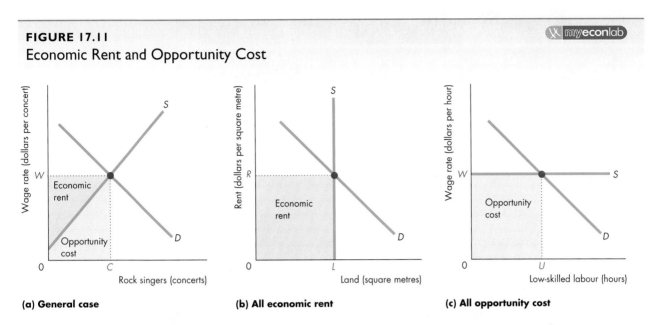

(a) General case   **(b) All economic rent**   **(c) All opportunity cost**

When the supply curve of a factor slopes upward—the general case—as in part (a), part of the factor income is economic rent (the green area) and part is opportunity cost (the yellow area). When the supply of a factor is perfectly

inelastic (the supply curve is vertical), as in part (b), the entire factor income is economic rent. When the supply of the factor is perfectly elastic, as in part (c), the factor's entire income is opportunity cost.

inelastic, like that illustrated in Fig. 17.11(a), some part of the factor income is economic rent and the other part is opportunity cost.

Figures 17.11(b) and 17.11(c) show the other two possibilities. Part (b) shows the market for a particular parcel of land in Vancouver. The quantity of land is fixed in size at L square metres. So the supply curve of the land is vertical—perfectly inelastic. No matter what the rent on the land is, there is no way of increasing the quantity that can be supplied. Suppose that the demand curve in Fig. 17.11(b) shows the marginal revenue product of this block of land. Then it commands a rent of R. The entire income accruing to the owner of the land is the green area in the figure. This income is *economic rent*.

Figure 17.11(c) shows the market for a factor of production that is in perfectly elastic supply. An example of such a market might be that for low-skilled labour in a poor country such as India or China. In those countries, large amounts of labour flock to the cities and are available for work at the going wage rate (in this case, W). In these situations, the supply of labour is almost perfectly elastic. The entire income earned by these workers is opportunity cost. They receive no economic rent.

REVIEW QUIZ

1 Why does a major-league baseball player earn a larger income than a babysitter?
2 What is the distinction between an economic rent and an opportunity cost?
3 Is the income that the Toronto Blue Jays pay to Roy Halliday an economic rent or compensation for his opportunity cost?
4 Is a Big Mac more expensive in Toronto than in Sudbury because land rents are higher in Toronto, or are land rents higher in Toronto because people in Toronto are willing to pay more for a Big Mac?

Study Plan 17.5

◆ *Reading Between the Lines* on pp. 408–409 looks at the market for crude oil and the impact of hurricanes on that market.

The next chapter looks at how the market economy distributes income and explains the trends in the distribution of income. The chapter also looks at the efforts by governments to redistribute income and modify the market outcome.

A Resource Market in Action

GLOBEANDMAIL.COM, SEPTEMBER 21, 2005

Rita fuels oil's rise

Oil prices climbed Wednesday as Hurricane Rita gathered force and approached the Gulf of Mexico, threatening to disrupt production in an area still reeling from the damage inflicted by Katrina.

In the U.S., the National Hurricane Centre said Rita has become a Category 4 storm, and could strengthen further in the coming hours. In a new release, it called Rita an "extremely dangerous hurricane" and warned that it could reach Category 5, the top of the hurricane scale. ...

The news inflamed fears that the storm could damage coastal Texas and Louisiana by week's end. A slew of energy companies, including Exxon Mobil Corp., Chevron Corp. and ConocoPhillips, have evacuated workers from platforms in the Gulf.

In its weekly update, the Energy Department said crude stockpiles fell by 322,000 barrels to 308.1 million in the week ended Sept. 16. Analysts were expecting a rise of 1 million barrels.

Gasoline inventories, however, rose by 3.5 million barrels to 195 million while distillate fuel, a category that includes heating oil and diesel, rose 820,000 barrels to 134 million.

Crude oil for November delivery rose 60 cents to $66.80 a barrel on the New York Mercantile Exchange Wednesday. ...

The U.S. Minerals Management Service said Tuesday that 136 platforms — mostly in the New Orleans area — remain unstaffed from both Katrina and Rita. That is 53 more than Monday.

The industry has lost production of more than 26 million barrels of oil since Aug. 26, when companies first evacuated for Katrina — about 4.7 per cent of the Gulf's yearly oil output, the agency said. ...

Reprinted with permission from *The Globe and Mail*.

Essence of the Story

■ Hurricane Katrina in the U.S oil producing Gulf region cut oil production by 26 million barrels between August 26 and September 21—a cut of 4.7 percent of the region's annual output.

■ On September 21, a second major hurricane, Rita, was expected to bring even more damage, and cut production even more.

■ Energy stockplies fell by 322,000 barrels to 308.1 million barrels in just one week.

■ As Rita continued to build, the price of crude oil rose 60 cents to $66.80 a barrel.

Economic Analysis

■ August and September 2005 were months of unusual hurricane activity in the Atlantic Ocean.

■ Hurricane Katrina (August 24 to 29) wiped out New Orleans and decreased U.S. crude oil production by almost 1 million barrels per day.

■ Hurricane Rita (September 18 to 23) devastated the Texas coast and took yet more oil production off line.

■ The world oil price reacted to these events in a way that is consistent with the theory of resource price determination that you've studied in this chapter.

■ Figure 1 shows the daily price of crude oil from August 1 through September 21.

■ Before Katrina, the price was $65 a barrel. At its peak after Katrina, the price had risen to $68 a barrel.

■ Figure 2 shows why this price rise occurred.

■ The decrease in production in the U.S. gulf region of 0.9 million barrels a day meant that the oil market must allocate a smaller total output among competing uses.

■ The demand for oil, D, is inelastic. In the figure, the elasticity of demand is 0.24.

■ The price at which the new smaller quantity is demanded is $68 a barrel.

■ Anticipating this equilibrium price, rational traders stand ready to buy into inventory or sell from inventory, so the market supply curve is perfectly elastic at this price. The supply curve shifts from S_0 before Katrina to S_1 after Katrina.

■ Even before Rita hit, the price increased in anticipation of a further decrease in the capacity to produce crude oil.

■ Figure 3 puts the events of the summer of 2005 in a longer perspective.

■ The real price of crude oil in 2005 was high by historical standards. But it was not at a record high.

■ That occurred in 1979, when the Organization of Petroleum Exporting Countries, OPEC, cut production by a staggering 8 million barrels a day— approaching 10 times the cut that resulted from the 2005 hurricanes.

■ The words you're reading were written on September 22, 2005. At that date, it seemed unlikely that the price of oil would remain above $60 a barrel into 2006. But you now know whether this prediction was correct.

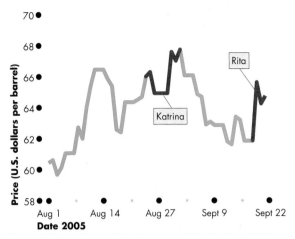

Figure 1 The price of oil in August and September 2005

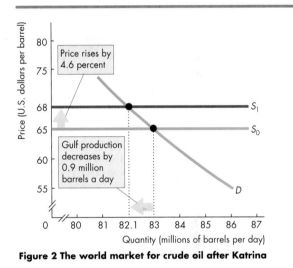

Figure 2 The world market for crude oil after Katrina

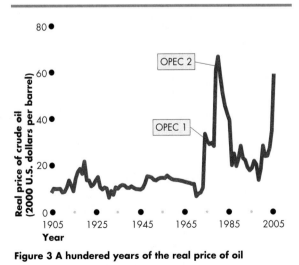

Figure 3 A hundered years of the real price of oil

Sources of data: See page C–1.

409

SUMMARY

KEY POINTS

Factor Prices and Incomes (p. 388)

- An increase in the demand for a factor of production increases the factor's price and total income; a decrease in the demand for a factor of production decreases its price and total income.
- An increase in the supply of a factor of production increases the quantity used but decreases its price and might increase or decrease its total income depending on whether demand is elastic or inelastic.

Labour Markets (pp. 389–396)

- The demand for labour is determined by the marginal revenue product of labour.
- The demand for labour increases if the price of the firm's output rises or if an advance in production technology increases marginal product.
- The elasticity of demand for labour depends on the labour intensity of production, the elasticity of demand for the product, and the ease with which labour can be substituted for capital.
- The quantity of labour supplied increases as the real wage rate increases, but at high wage rates, the supply curve eventually bends backward.
- The supply of labour increases as the adult population increases and with technological change in home production.
- Wage rates increase because demand for labour increases by more than the supply for labour.

Capital Markets (pp. 397–403)

- To make an investment decision, a firm compares the *present value* of the marginal revenue product of capital with the price of capital.
- The higher the interest rate, the greater is the amount of saving and the quantity of capital supplied.
- Capital market equilibrium determines the real interest rate.
- Common and related factors influence both demand and supply so the interest rate fluctuates but doesn't rise or fall over time.

Natural Resource Markets (pp. 403–405)

- The demand for natural resources is determined by marginal revenue product.
- The supply of land is inelastic.
- The supply of nonrenewable natural resources is perfectly elastic at a price equal to the present value of the expected future price.
- The price of nonrenewable natural resources is expected to rise at a rate equal to the interest rate but fluctuates and sometimes falls.

Income, Economic Rent, and Opportunity Cost (pp. 406–407)

- Economic rent is the income received by the owner of a factor of production over and above the amount needed to induce the owner to supply the factor for use.
- The rest of a factor's income is an opportunity cost.
- When the supply of a factor is perfectly inelastic, its entire income is made up of economic rent, and when supply is perfectly elastic, the entire income is made up of opportunity cost.

KEY FIGURES AND TABLES

Figure 17.1   Demand and Supply in a Factor Market, 388
Figure 17.3   The Demand for Labour at Max's Wash 'n' Wax, 391
Figure 17.11 Economic Rent and Opportunity Cost, 407
Table 17.2   Two Conditions for Maximum Profit, 392
Table 17.3   A Firm's Demand for Labour, 393

KEY TERMS

Derived demand, 388
Discounting, 398
Economic rent, 406
Marginal revenue product, 390
Net present value, 400
Nonrenewable natural resource, 403
Present value, 398
Renewable natural resource, 403

PROBLEMS

Go to myeconlab **for solutions to odd-numbered problems and additional exercises.**

1. The figure illustrates the market for blueberry pickers.

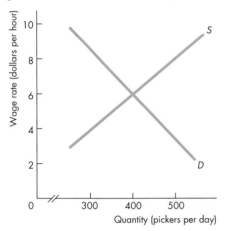

   What is the wage rate paid to blueberry pickers, how many blueberry pickers get hired, and what is the total income received by pickers?

2. In problem 1, if the demand for blueberry pickers decreases by 100 a day, what is the new wage rate paid to the pickers, how many pickers get laid off, and what is the total income paid to pickers?

3. In Wanda's fish shop, students can pack the following amounts of fish in an hour:

Number of students	Quantity of fish (kilograms)
1	20
2	50
3	90
4	120
5	145
6	165
7	180
8	190

   Wanda can sell her fish for 50¢ a kilogram, and the wage rate of packers is $7.50 an hour.

   a. Calculate the marginal product of the students and draw the marginal product curve.
   b. Calculate the marginal revenue product and draw the marginal revenue product curve.

   c. Find Wanda's demand for labour curve.
   d. How many students does Wanda employ?

4. In Larry's gourmet ice cream factory, workers can produce the following quantities in a day:

Number of workers	Quantity of ice cream (batches)
1	4
2	10
3	18
4	24
5	29
6	33
7	36
8	38

   Larry can sell ice cream for $25 a batch, and the wage rate of his workers is $100 a day.

   a. Calculate the marginal product of the workers and draw the marginal product curve.
   b. Calculate the marginal revenue product of the workers and draw the marginal revenue product curve.
   c. Find Larry's demand for labour curve.
   d. How much ice cream does Larry sell?

5. Back at Wanda's fish shop described in problem 3, the price of fish falls to 33.33¢ a kilogram but fish packers' wages remain at $7.50 an hour.

   a. What happens to the students' marginal product?
   b. What happens to Wanda's marginal revenue product?
   c. What happens to her demand for labour curve?
   d. What happens to the number of students that she employs?

6. Back at Larry's ice cream making plant described in problem 4, the price of ice cream falls to $20 a batch but the wage rate remains at $100 a day.

   a. What happens to the workers' marginal product?
   b. What happens to Larry's marginal revenue product?
   c. What happens to his demand for labour curve?
   d. What happens to the number of workers that he employs?

7. Back at Wanda's fish shop described in problem 3, packers' wages increase to $10 an hour but the price of fish remains at 50¢ a kilogram.

  a. What happens to marginal revenue product?

  b. What happens to Wanda's demand for labour curve?

  c. How many students does Wanda employ?

8. Back at Larry's ice cream factory described in problem 4, the wage rate rises to $125 a day but the price of ice cream remains at $25 a batch.

  a. What happens to marginal revenue product?

  b. What happens to Larry's demand for labour curve?

  c. How many workers does Larry employ?

9. Using the information provided in problem 3, calculate Wanda's marginal revenue, marginal cost, and marginal revenue product. Show that when Wanda is making maximum profit, marginal cost equals marginal revenue and marginal revenue product equals the wage rate.

10. Using the information provided in problem 4, calculate Larry's marginal revenue, marginal cost, and marginal revenue product. Show that when Larry is making maximum profit, marginal cost equals marginal revenue and marginal revenue product equals the wage rate.

11. Greg has found an oil well in his backyard. A geologist estimates that a total of 10 million barrels can be pumped for a pumping cost of $2 a barrel. The price of oil is $40 a barrel. How much oil does Greg sell each year? If you can't predict how much he will sell, what extra information would you need to be able to do so?

12. Orley has a wine cellar in which he keeps choice wines from around the world. What does Orley expect to happen to the prices of the wines he keeps in his cellar? Explain your answer. How does Orley decide which wine to drink and when to drink it?

13. Draw a graph to illustrate the situation in problem 1. Show on the graph the blueberry pickers':

  a. Economic rent.

  b. Opportunity cost.

14. Draw a graph to illustrate the situation in problem 2. Show on the graph the blueberry pickers':

  a. Economic rent.

  b. Opportunity cost.

CRITICAL THINKING

1. Study *Reading Between the Lines* on pp. 408–409 and answer the following questions:

  a. What determines the price of a natural resource such as crude oil?

  b. How did hurricane Katrina affect the price of oil in August and September 2005?

  c. What was the elasticity of demand implied by the price and quantity changes that occurred in the crude oil market following hurricane Katrina?

  d. How has the price of oil moved over the past 100 years? Do the movements confirm or contradict the Hotelling Principle?

  e. Do you expect the price of oil to keep rising? Explain why or why not.

2. "We are running out of natural resources and must take urgent action to conserve our precious reserves." "There is no shortage of resources that the market cannot cope with." Debate these two views. List the pros and cons for each.

3. Why do we keep finding new reserves of oil? Why don't we do a once-and-for-all big survey that catalogues the earth's entire inventory of natural resources?

WEB EXERCISES

Use the links on (myeconlab) **to work the following exercise.**

1. Read the article on prize money in the tennis grand slams.

  a. Do women get the same pay as men in professional tennis?

  b. Why might men earn more than women in tennis?

  c. What is the case for equal pay for men and women tennis players?

  d. Can you think of other sports in which there is either equality or a big disparity between the earnings of men and women? How would you explain the rewards in this sport?

APPENDIX

Labour Unions

After studying this appendix you will be able to

■ Explain why union workers earn more than nonunion workers

■ Explain how a labour market works in a monopsony

■ Explain the effects of a minimum wage law in a monopsony

Market Power in the Labour Market

JUST AS A MONOPOLY PRODUCER CAN RESTRICT output and raise price, so a monopoly resource owner can restrict supply and raise the price of the resource.

Labour unions are the main source of market power in the labour market. A **labour union** is an organized group of workers that aims to increase wages and influence other job conditions.

Traditionally, a union was formed by a group of workers who had similar skills but who worked for firms in different industries and regions—for example, the union of electrical workers. The industrial union was created when workers in mass-production industries unionized. These workers had a variety of skills but they worked in the same industry. Today, most unions have members who work in different industries and have a wide range of skills. For example, the members of the United Steelworkers union work in steel mills, factories, bakeries, and offices.

Most unions are members of the Canadian Labour Congress, which was created in 1956 with the merger of the Labour Council of Canada (founded in 1883) and the Canadian Congress of Labour (founded in 1940).

Around one-third of workers are members of a union. Some of these unions are small, but industrial unions are large. Union organization is based on a subdivision known as the *local*. The local can be organized

as a closed shop, a union shop, or an open shop. A *closed shop* is an arrangement in which the firm can hire only union members. Most closed shops are in the construction industry. A *union shop* is an arrangement in which the firm can hire workers who are not union members, but new workers must join the union, usually at the end of their probationary period. Union shops are common in manufacturing industries and the public sector. An *open shop* is an arrangement in which no employee is required to join the union or pay union dues. There is no restriction on who can work in the "shop." A compromise between the union shop and the open shop is the **Rand Formula**: a requirement that all workers represented by a union must pay union dues, whether they join the union or not.

Unions negotiate with employers or their representatives in a process called *collective bargaining*. The main weapons available to the union and the employer in collective bargaining are the strike and the lockout. A *strike* is a group decision by the workers to refuse to work under prevailing conditions. A *lockout* is a firm's refusal to operate its plant and employ its workers. Each party uses the threat of a strike or a lockout to try to get an agreement in its own favour. Sometimes, when the two parties in the collective bargaining process cannot agree on the wage rate or other conditions of employment, they agree to submit their disagreement to binding arbitration. *Binding arbitration* is a process in which a third party—an arbitrator—determines wages and other employment conditions on behalf of the negotiating parties.

Although they are not labour unions in a legal sense, professional associations act in ways similar to labour unions. A *professional association* is an organized group of professional workers such as lawyers or physicians (for example, the Ontario Medical Association). Professional associations control entry into the professions and license practitioners, ensuring the adherence to minimum standards of competence. But they also influence the compensation and other labour market conditions of their members.

Union Objectives and Constraints

A union has three broad objectives that it strives to achieve for its members:

1. To increase compensation
2. To improve working conditions
3. To expand job opportunities

Each of these objectives contains a series of more detailed goals. For example, in seeking to increase members' compensation, a union operates on a variety of fronts: wage rates, fringe benefits, retirement pay, and such things as vacation allowances. In seeking to improve working conditions, a union is concerned with occupational health and safety as well as the environmental quality of the workplace. In seeking to expand job opportunities, a union tries to get greater job security for existing union members and to find ways of creating additional jobs for them.

A union's ability to pursue its objectives is restricted by two sets of constraints—one on the supply side of the labour market and the other on the demand side. On the supply side, the union's activities are limited by how well it can restrict nonunion workers from offering their labour in the same market as union labour. The larger the fraction of the work force controlled by the union, the more effective the union can be in this regard. It is difficult for unions to operate in markets where there is an abundant supply of willing nonunion labour. For example, the market for part-time checkout clerks is very tough for a union to organize because of the enormous rate of turnover of participants in that market. At the other extreme, unions in the construction industry can better pursue their goals because they can influence the number of people who can obtain skills as electricians, plasterers, and carpenters. The professional associations of dentists and physicians are best able to restrict the supply of dentists and physicians. These groups control the number of qualified workers by controlling either the examinations that new entrants must pass or entrance into professional degree programs.

On the demand side of the labour market, the union faces a tradeoff that arises from firms' profit-maximizing decisions. Because labour demand curves slope downward, anything a union does that increases the wage rate or other employment costs decreases the quantity of labour demanded.

Let's see how unions operate in competitive labour markets.

A Union in a Competitive Labour Market

When a union operates in an otherwise competitive labour market, it seeks to increase wages and other compensation and to limit employment reductions by increasing demand for the labour of its members.

That is, the union tries to take actions that shift the demand curve for its members' labour rightward.

Figure A17.1 illustrates a competitive labour market that a union enters. The demand curve is D_C, and the supply curve is S_C. Before the union enters the market, the wage rate is $7 an hour and 100 hours of labour are employed.

Now suppose that a union is formed to organize the workers in this market. The union can attempt to increase wages in this market in two ways. It can try to restrict the supply of labour, or it can try to stimulate the demand for labour. First, look at what happens if the union has sufficient control over the supply of labour to be able to restrict that supply artificially below its competitive level—to S_U. If that is all the union is able to do, employment falls to 85 hours of labour and the wage rate rises to $8 an hour. The

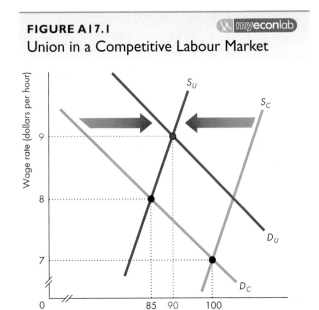

FIGURE A17.1   myeconlab
Union in a Competitive Labour Market

In a competitive labour market, the demand curve is D_C and the supply curve is S_C. Competitive equilibrium occurs at a wage rate of $7 an hour with 100 hours employed. By restricting employment below the competitive level, the union shifts the supply of labour to S_U. If the union can do no more than that, the wage rate will increase to $8 an hour but employment will fall to 85 hours. If the union can increase the demand for labour and shift the demand curve to D_U, then it can increase the wage rate still higher, to $9 an hour, and achieve employment of 90 hours.

union simply picks its preferred position along the demand curve that defines the tradeoff it faces between employment and the wage rate.

You can see that if the union can only restrict the supply of labour, it raises the wage rate but decreases the number of jobs available. Because of this outcome, unions try to increase the demand for labour and shift the demand curve rightward. Let's see what they might do to achieve this outcome.

How Unions Try to Change the Demand for Labour

Unless a union can take actions that change the demand for the labour that it represents, it has to accept the fact that a higher wage rate can be obtained only at the price of lower employment.

The union tries to operate on the demand for labour in two ways. First, it tries to make the demand for union labour inelastic. Second, it tries to increase the demand for union labour. Making the demand for labour less elastic does not eliminate the tradeoff between employment and the wage rate. But it does make the tradeoff less unfavourable. If a union can make the demand for labour less elastic, it can increase the wage rate at a lower cost in terms of lost employment opportunities. But if the union can increase the demand for labour, it might even be able to increase both the wage rate and the employment opportunities of its members. Some of the methods used by the unions to change the demand for the labour of its members are to

- Increase the marginal product of union members
- Encourage import restrictions
- Support minimum wage laws
- Support immigration restrictions
- Increase demand for the good produced

Unions try to increase the marginal product of their members, which in turn increases the demand for their labour, by organizing and sponsoring training schemes, by encouraging apprenticeship and other on-the-job training activities, and by professional certification.

One of the best examples of import restrictions is the support by the Canadian Auto Workers union (CAW) for import restrictions on foreign cars.

Unions support minimum wage laws to increase the cost of employing low-skilled labour. An increase in the wage rate of low-skilled labour leads to a decrease in the quantity demanded of low-skilled labour and to an increase in demand for high-skilled union labour, a substitute for low-skilled labour.

Restrictive immigration laws decrease the supply of low-skilled workers and increase their wage rate. As a result, the demand for high-skilled union labour increases.

Because the demand for labour is a derived demand, an increase in the demand for the good produced by union labour increases the demand for union labour. The garment workers' union urging us to buy union-made clothes and the CAW asking us to buy only North American cars made by union workers are examples of attempts by unions to increase the demand for union labour.

Figure A17.1 illustrates the effects of an increase in the demand for the labour of a union's members. If the union can increase the demand for labour to D_U, it can achieve an even bigger increase in the wage rate with a smaller fall in employment. By maintaining the restricted labour supply at S_U, the union increases the wage rate to \$9 an hour and achieves an employment level of 90 hours of labour.

Because a union restricts the supply of labour in the market in which it operates, its actions increase the supply of labour in nonunion markets. Workers who can't get union jobs must look elsewhere for work. This increase in the supply of labour in nonunion markets lowers the wage rate in those markets and further widens the union–nonunion differential.

The Scale of Union–Nonunion Wage Differentials

We have seen that unions can influence the wage rate by restricting the supply of labour and increasing the demand for labour. How much of a difference to wage rates do unions make in practice?

Union wage rates are, on the average, 30 percent higher than nonunion wage rates. In mining and financial services, union and nonunion wages are similar. In services, manufacturing, and transportation, the differential is between 11 and 19 percent. In wholesale and retail trades, the differential is 28 percent, and in construction, it is 65 percent.

But these union–nonunion wage differentials don't give a true measure of the effects of unions. In some industries, union wages are higher than nonunion wages because union members do jobs that involve greater skill. Even without a union, those workers would receive a higher wage. To calculate the effects of unions, we have to examine the wages of unionized and nonunionized workers who do nearly identical work. The evidence suggests that after allowing for skill differentials, the union–nonunion wage differential lies between 10 percent and 25 percent. For example, airline pilots who belong to the Air Line Pilots' Association earn about 25 percent more than nonunion pilots with the same skill.

Let's now look at monopsony.

Monopsony

A MARKET IN WHICH THERE IS A SINGLE BUYER IS called **monopsony**. This market type is unusual, but it does exist. With the growth of large-scale production over the last century, large manufacturing plants such as coal mines, steel and textile mills, and car manufacturers became the major employer in some regions, and in some places a single firm employed almost all the labour. Today, the provincial health insurance plans are the major employers of health-care professionals. These employers have market power. In monopsony, the employer determines the wage rate and pays the lowest wage at which it can attract the labour it plans to hire. A monopsony makes a bigger profit than a group of firms that compete with each other for their labour. Let's find out how a monopsony achieves this outcome.

Like all firms, a monopsony has a downward-sloping marginal revenue product curve, which is *MRP* in Fig. A17.2. This curve tells us the extra revenue the monopsony receives by selling the output produced by an extra hour of labour. The labour supply curve is *S*. This curve tells us how many hours are supplied at each wage rate. It also tells us the minimum wage for which a given quantity of labour is willing to work.

A monopsony recognizes that to hire more labour, it must pay a higher wage; equivalently, by hiring less labour, it can pay a lower wage. Because a monopsony controls the wage rate, the marginal cost of labour exceeds the wage rate. The marginal cost of labour is shown by the curve *MCL*. The relationship between the marginal cost of labour curve and the supply curve is similar to the relationship between the marginal cost and average cost curves that you studied in Chapter 10. The supply curve is like the average cost of labour curve. In Fig. A17.2, the firm can hire 49 hours of labour for a wage rate of just below $4.90 an hour.

The firm's total labour cost is $240. But suppose that the firm hires 50 hours of labour. It can hire the 50th hour of labour for $5 an hour. The total cost of labour is now $250 an hour. So hiring the 50th hour of labour increases the total cost of labour from $240 to $250, which is a $10 increase. The marginal cost of labour is $10 an hour. The curve *MCL* shows the $10 marginal cost of hiring the 50th hour of labour.

To calculate the profit-maximizing quantity of labour to hire, the firm sets the marginal cost of labour equal to the marginal revenue product of labour. That is, the firm wants the cost of the last worker hired to equal the extra total revenue brought in. In Fig. A17.2, this outcome occurs when the monopsony employs 50 hours of labour. What is the wage rate that the monopsony pays? To hire 50 hours of labour, the firm must pay $5 an hour, as shown by the supply of labour curve. So each worker is paid $5 an hour. But the marginal revenue product of labour is $10 an hour, which means that the firm makes an economic profit of $5 on the last hour of labour that it hires. Compare this outcome with that in a competitive labour market. If

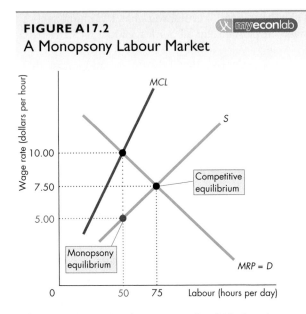

FIGURE A17.2   myeconlab
A Monopsony Labour Market

A monopsony is a market structure in which there is a single buyer. A monopsony in the labour market has the marginal revenue product curve *MRP* and faces a labour supply curve *S*. The marginal cost of labour curve is *MCL*. Making the marginal cost of labour equal to marginal revenue product maximizes profit. The monopsony hires 50 hours of labour and pays the lowest wage for which that labour will work, which is $5 an hour.

the labour market shown in Fig. A17.2 were competitive, equilibrium would occur at the point of intersection of the demand curve and the supply curve. The wage rate would be $7.50 an hour, and 75 hours of labour a day would be employed. So compared with a competitive labour market, a monopsony decreases both the wage rate and employment.

The ability of a monopsony to cut the wage rate and employment to increase its profit depends on the elasticity of labour supply. If the supply of labour is highly elastic, a monopsony has little power to cut the wage rate and employment to boost its profit.

Monopsony Tendencies

Today, monopsony is rare. Workers can commute long distances to a job, so most people have more than one potential employer. But firms that are dominant employers in isolated communities do face an upward-sloping supply of labour curve and so have a marginal cost of labour that exceeds the wage rate. But in such situations, there is also, usually, a union. Let's see how unions and monopsonies interact.

Monopsony and a Union

In Chapter 12, we discovered that in monopoly, a firm can determine the market price. We've now seen that in monopsony—a market with a single buyer— the buyer can determine the price. Suppose that a union operates in a monopsony labour market. A union is like a monopoly. If the union (monopoly seller) faces a monopsony buyer, the situation is called **bilateral monopoly**. In bilateral monopoly, the wage rate is determined by bargaining.

In Fig. A17.2, if the monopsony is free to determine the wage rate and the level of employment, it hires 50 hours of labour for a wage rate of $5 an hour. But suppose that a union represents the workers. The union agrees to maintain employment at 50 hours but seeks the highest wage rate that the employer can be forced to pay. That wage rate is $10 an hour—the wage rate that equals the marginal revenue product of labour. The union might not be able to get the wage rate up to $10 an hour. But it won't accept $5 an hour. The monopsony firm and the union bargain over the wage rate, and the result is an outcome between $10 an hour and $5 an hour.

The outcome of the bargaining depends on the costs that each party can inflict on the other as a result of a failure to agree on the wage rate. The firm can shut down the plant and lock out its workers, and the

workers can shut down the plant by striking. Each party knows the other's strength and knows what it will lose if it does not agree to the other's demands. If the two parties are equally strong and they realize it, they will split the gap between $5 and $10 and agree to a wage rate of $7.50 an hour. If one party is stronger than the other—and both parties know that—the agreed wage will favour the stronger party. Usually, an agreement is reached without a strike or a lockout. The threat is usually enough to bring the bargaining parties to an agreement. When a strike or lockout does occur, it is usually because one party has misjudged the costs each party can inflict on the other.

Minimum wage laws have interesting effects in monopsony labour markets. Let's study these effects.

Monopsony and the Minimum Wage

In a competitive labour market, a minimum wage that exceeds the equilibrium wage decreases employment (see Chapter 6, p. 130). In a monopsony labour market, a minimum wage can *increase* both the wage rate and employment. Let's see how.

Figure A17.3 shows a monopsony labour market in which the wage rate is $5 an hour and 50 hours of labour are employed. A minimum wage law is passed that requires employers to pay at least $7.50 an hour.

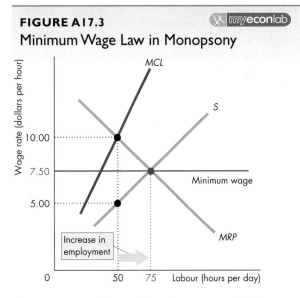

FIGURE A17.3   (X) myeconlab
Minimum Wage Law in Monopsony

In a monopsony labour market, the wage rate is $5 an hour and 50 hours are hired. If a minimum wage law increases the wage rate to $7.50 an hour, employment increases to 75 hours.

The monopsony in Fig. A17.3 now faces a perfectly elastic supply of labour at $7.50 an hour up to 75 hours. Above 75 hours, a wage above $7.50 an hour must be paid to hire additional hours of labour. Because the wage rate is a fixed $7.50 an hour up to 75 hours, the marginal cost of labour is also constant at $7.50 up to 75 hours. Beyond 75 hours, the marginal cost of labour rises above $7.50 an hour. To maximize profit, the monopsony sets the marginal cost of labour equal to the marginal revenue product of labour. That is, the monopsony hires 75 hours of labour at $7.50 an hour. The minimum wage law has made the supply of labour perfectly elastic and made the marginal cost of labour the same as the wage rate up to 75 hours. The law has not affected the supply of labour curve or the marginal cost of labour at employment levels above 75 hours. The minimum wage law has succeeded in raising the wage rate by $2.50 an hour and increasing the amount of labour employed by 25 hours.

SUMMARY

KEY POINTS

Market Power in the Labour Market
(pp. 413–416)

- In a competitive labour market, a union obtains a higher wage rate only at the expense of lower employment but it tries to influence the demand for labour.
- Union workers earn 10 to 25 percent more than comparable nonunion workers.

Monopsony (pp. 416–418)

- A monopsony employs less labour and pays a wage rate below that in a competitive labour market.
- In bilateral monopoly, the wage rate is determined by bargaining.
- In monopsony, a minimum wage law can raise the wage rate and increase employment.

KEY TERMS

Bilateral monopoly, 413
Labour union, 413
Monopsony, 416
Rand Formula, 413

PROBLEMS

Go to myeconlab for solutions to odd-numbered problems and additional exercises.

1. A monopsony gold-mining firm operates in an isolated part of the Amazon basin. The table shows the firm's labour supply schedule (columns 1 and 2) and total product schedule (columns 2 and 3). The price of gold is $1.40 a grain.

Wage rate (dollars per day)	Number of workers	Quantity produced (grains per day)
5	0	0
6	1	10
7	2	25
8	3	45
9	4	60
10	5	70
11	6	75

a. What wage rate does the company pay?
b. How many workers does the gold mine hire?
c. What is the value of marginal product at the quantity of labour employed?

2. A monopsony logging firm operates in an isolated part of the Yukon. The table shows the firm's labour supply schedule (columns 1 and 2) and total product schedule (columns 2 and 3). The price of logs is $2 a tonne.

Wage rate (dollars per day)	Number of workers	Quantity produced (tonnes per day)
5	0	0
6	1	9
7	2	17
8	3	24
9	4	30
10	5	35
11	6	39
12	7	42

a. What wage rate does the company pay?
b. How many workers does the company hire?
c. What is the value of marginal product at the quantity of labour employed?

Economic Inequality

CHAPTER 18

Rags and Riches

Ken Thomson's family fortune, Canada's largest, is estimated at more than $22 billion. The poorest of Canada's richest 100 families is worth a mere $336 million.

In stark contrast to these richest Canadians are the poorest, who can be seen any evening on the park benches of our major cities and in the hostels of the Salvation Army. Here are men and women who have no visible wealth other than their clothes and a few meagre possessions.

Most Canadians are not as poor as those who seek help from the Salvation Army, but there is a large amount of relative poverty in our nation. One in ten families has an income that is so low that it spends close to half of it on rent.

Why are some people exceedingly rich, while others are very poor?

◆ In this chapter, we study economic inequality—its extent, its sources, and the things governments do to make it less extreme. We begin by looking at some facts about economic inequality in Canada today. We end, in *Reading Between the Lines*, by looking at the changing gap between the rich and the poor and the changing scale of redistribution in Canada.

After studying this chapter, you will be able to

- Describe the inequality in income and wealth and the trends in inequality in Canada
- Explain the features of the labour market that contribute to economic inequality
- Describe the methods and scale of government income redistribution

Measuring Economic Inequality

STATISTICS CANADA PROVIDES MEASURES OF economic inequality based on three definitions of income: market income, total income, and after-tax income. **Market income** equals the wages, interest, rent, and profit earned in factor markets before paying income taxes. **Total income** equals *market income* plus cash payments to households by governments. **After-tax income** equals *total income* minus tax payments by households to governments.

The Distribution of After-Tax Income

Figure 18.1 shows the distribution of annual after-tax income across all households in Canada in 2003. Note that the *x*-axis measures income and the *y*-axis measures the percentage of households.

The most common household income, called the *mode* income, was received by the 8.2 percent of the households whose income fell between $15,000 and $19,999.

The income that separated the households into two equal groups, called the *median* income, was $39,700. One-half of Canadian households had an income greater than this amount, and the other half had an income less than this amount. The average household income in 2003, called the *mean* income, was $48,400.

You can see in Fig. 18.1 that the mode income is less than the median income, and the median income is less than the mean income. This feature of the distribution of income tells us that there are more households with low incomes than with high incomes. And some of the high incomes are very high.

The income distribution in Fig. 18.1 is called a *positively skewed* distribution, which means that it has a long tail of high values. This distribution's shape contrasts with a *bell-shaped* distribution like that of people's heights. In a bell-shaped distribution, the mean, median, and mode are all equal.

Another way of looking at the distribution of income is to measure the percentage of after-tax income received by each given percentage of households. Data are reported for five groups—called quintiles or one-fifth shares—each consisting of 20 percent of households.

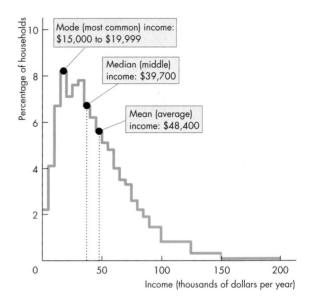

FIGURE 18.1

The Distribution of Income in Canada in 2003

The distribution of income is positively skewed. The mode (most common) income is less than the median (middle) income, which in turn is less than the mean (average) income. A very small percentage of households earn incomes in the range above $150,000 up to several million dollars a year—this part of the distribution is off the scale of this figure.

Source of data: Income Statistics Division, Statistics Canada, Table 202–0601.

Figure 18.2 shows the distribution of after-tax income based on these shares in 2003. The poorest 20 percent of households received 5 percent of after-tax income; the second-poorest 20 percent received 10.8 percent of after-tax income; the middle 20 percent received 16.5 percent of after-tax income; the second-highest 20 percent received 24.1 percent of after-tax income; and the highest 20 percent received 43.6 percent of after-tax income.

The distribution of after-tax income in Fig. 18.1 and the quintile shares in Fig. 18.2 tell us that income is distributed unequally. But we need a way of comparing the distribution of income in different periods and using different measures. A neat graphical tool called the Lorenz curve enables us to make such comparisons.

FIGURE 18.2
Canadian Quintile Shares

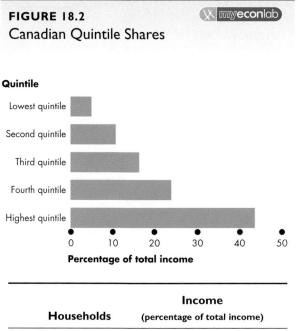

Households	Income (percentage of total income)
Lowest 20 percent	5.0
Second-lowest 20 percent	10.8
Middle 20 percent	16.5
Second-highest 20 percent	24.1
Highest 20 percent	43.6

All households are ranked from those with the lowest income to those with the highest income and then divided into 5 equal groups. Each group is called a quintile (or a one-fifth of the households). The bar chart shows that the distribution of after-tax income in Canada is unequal.

Source of data: Income Statistics Division, Statistics Canada, Table 202–0604.

The Income Lorenz Curve

The income **Lorenz curve** graphs the cumulative percentage of income against the cumulative percentage of households. Figure 18.3 shows the income Lorenz curve using the quintile shares from Fig. 18.2. The table shows the percentage of income in each quintile group. For example, row *A* tells us that the lowest quintile of households receives 5 percent of after-tax income. The table also shows the *cumulative* percentages of households and income. For example, row *B* tells us that the lowest two quintiles (lowest 40 percent) of households receive 15.8 percent of after-tax

FIGURE 18.3
The Income Lorenz Curve

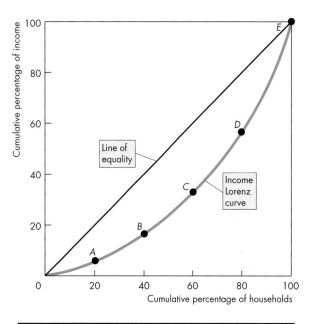

Households		Income	
Percentage	Cumulative percentage	Percentage	Cumulative percentage
A Lowest 20	20	5.0	5.0
B Second-lowest 20	40	10.8	15.8
C Middle 20	60	16.5	32.3
D Second-highest 20	80	24.1	56.4
E Highest 20	100	43.6	100.0

The cumulative percentage of income is graphed against the cumulative percentage of households. Points *A* through *E* on the Lorenz curve correspond to the rows of the table. If incomes were distributed equally, each 20 percent of households would receive 20 percent of income and the Lorenz curve would fall along the line of equality. The Lorenz curve shows that income is unequally distributed.

Source of data: Income Statistics Division, Statistics Canada, Table 202–0604.

income (5 percent for the lowest quintile and 10.8 percent for the second-lowest). The income Lorenz curve graphs the cumulative income shares against the cumulative household percentages.

If income were distributed equally across all the households, each quintile would receive 20 percent of after-tax income and the cumulative percentages of income received by the cumulative percentages of households would fall along the straight line labelled "Line of equality" in Fig. 18.3. The actual distribution of income is shown by the curve labelled "Income Lorenz curve." The closer the Lorenz curve is to the line of equality, the more equal is the distribution.

The Distribution of Wealth

The distribution of wealth provides another way of measuring economic inequality. A household's wealth is the value of the things that it owns at a *point in time*. In contrast, income is the amount that the household receives over a given *period of time*.

Figure 18.4 shows the Lorenz curve for wealth in Canada in 1999. Median household wealth in that year was $64,000. Wealth is extremely unequally distributed, and for this reason, the data are grouped by unequal groups of households. The poorest 40 percent of households owns only 1.1 percent of total wealth (row A' in the table). The next poorest 10 percent owns only 2.8 percent of total wealth (row B') and the next poorest 10 percent owns only 4.7 percent of total wealth (row C'). So the poorest 60 percent of households owns only 8.6 percent of total wealth. At the other end of the wealth distribution, the wealthiest 10 percent of households owns 55.6 percent of total wealth (row G').

Figure 18.4 shows the income Lorenz curve (from Fig. 18.2) alongside the wealth Lorenz curve. You can see that the Lorenz curve for wealth is much farther away from the line of equality than the Lorenz curve for income is, which means that the distribution of wealth is much more unequal than the distribution of income.

Wealth Versus Income

We've seen that wealth is much more unequally distributed than income. Which distribution provides the better description of the degree of inequality? To answer this question, we need to think about the connection between wealth and income.

Wealth is a stock of assets, and income is the flow of earnings that results from the stock of wealth. Suppose that Kate owns assets worth $1 million—has a wealth of $1 million. If the rate of return on assets is

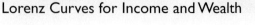

FIGURE 18.4

Lorenz Curves for Income and Wealth

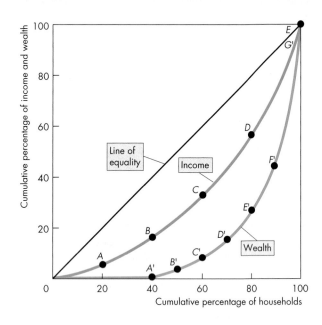

	Households		Wealth	
	Percentage	Cumulative percentage	Percentage	Cumulative percentage
A' Lowest 40	40	1.1	1.1
B' Next 10	50	2.8	3.9
C' Next 10	60	4.7	8.6
D' Next 10	70	7.4	16.0
E' Next 10	80	11.0	27.0
F' Next 10	90	17.4	44.4
G' Next 10	100	55.6	100.0

The cumulative percentage of wealth is graphed against the cumulative percentage of households. Points A' through G' on the Lorenz curve for wealth correspond to the rows of the table. By comparing the Lorenz curves for income and wealth, we can see that wealth is distributed much more unequally than income.

Source of data: Income Statistics Division, Statistics Canada, Table 202–0604 and Catalogue 75–202–XIE.

5 percent a year, then she receives an income of $50,000 a year from those assets. We can describe Kate's economic condition by using either her wealth of $1 million or her income of $50,000 a year. When the rate of return is 5 percent a year, $1 million of wealth equals $50,000 of income in perpetuity. Wealth and income are just different ways of looking at the same thing.

But in Fig. 18.4, the distribution of wealth is more unequal than the distribution of income. Why? It is because the wealth data do not include the value of human capital, while the income data measure income from all forms of wealth, including human capital.

Table 18.1 illustrates the consequence of omitting human capital from the wealth data. Lee has twice the wealth and twice the income of Peter. But Lee's human capital is less than Peter's—$200,000 compared with $499,000. And Lee's income from human capital of $10,000 is less than Peter's income from human capital of $24,950. Lee's nonhuman capital is larger than Peter's—$800,000 compared with $1,000. And Lee's income from nonhuman capital of $40,000 is larger than Peter's income from nonhuman capital of $50.

When Lee and Peter are surveyed by Statistics Canada in a national wealth and income survey, their incomes are recorded as $50,000 and $25,000, respectively, which implies that Lee is twice as well off as Peter. And their tangible assets are recorded as $800,000 and $1,000, respectively, which implies that Lee is 800 times as wealthy as Peter.

Because the national survey of wealth excludes human capital, the income distribution is a more accurate measure of economic inequality than the wealth distribution.

Annual or Lifetime Income and Wealth?

A typical household's income changes over time. It starts out low, grows to a peak when the household's workers reach retirement age, and then falls after retirement. Also, a typical household's wealth changes over time. Like income, wealth starts out low, grows to a peak at the point of retirement, and falls after retirement.

Suppose we look at three households that have identical lifetime incomes. One household is young, one is middle-aged, and one is retired. The middle-aged household has the highest income and wealth, the retired household has the lowest, and the young household falls in the middle. The distributions of annual income and wealth in a given year are unequal, but the

TABLE 18.1	Capital, Wealth, and Income			
	Lee		**Peter**	
	Wealth	**Income**	**Wealth**	**Income**
Human capital	$200,000	$10,000	$499,000	$24,950
Other capital	800,000	40,000	1,000	50
Total	$1,000,000	$50,000	$500,000	$25,000

When wealth is measured to include the value of human capital as well as other forms of capital, the distribution of income and the distribution of wealth display the same degree of inequality.

distributions of lifetime income and wealth are equal. So some of the inequality in annual income arises because different households are at different stages in the life cycle. But we can see *trends* in the income distribution using annual income data.

Trends in Inequality

Figure 18.5 shows how the distribution of income has changed between 1980 and 2003. The trends are

■ The share of total income received by the richest 20 percent of households has increased from 40 percent in 1980 to 43.7 percent in 2003.
■ The share of total income received by the poorest 20 percent of households has remained constant at 5 percent.
■ The shares of total income received by the other three groups have decreased, and the share of the third (the middle) 20 percent of households has decreased most from 18.3 percent in 1980 to 16.5 percent in 2003.

No one knows for sure why these trends have occurred, and a large amount of research has been done to try to explain them.

The most likely explanation is one that we'll explore and explain in the next section: Higher-income groups have gained and lower-income groups have lost because the technological change of the past few decades has increased the productivity of higher skilled workers and decreased the productivity of lower-skilled workers. Increased international mobility and competition is another possible explanation.

FIGURE 18.5 ⓧ myeconlab
Trends in the Distribution of Income

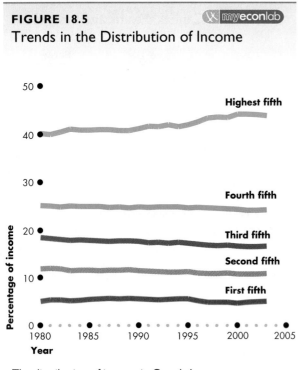

The distribution of income in Canada became more unequal in the 1980s and 1990s. The percentage of total income earned by the highest fifth increased the most, and the third (middle) fifth lost the most.

Source of data: Income Statistics Division, Statistics Canada, Table 202–0604.

FIGURE 18.6 ⓧ myeconlab
The Poverty Rate

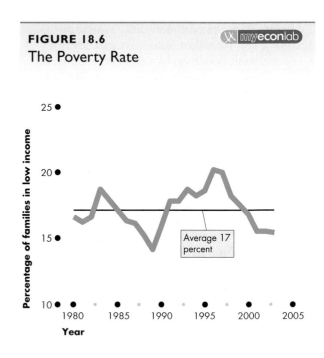

The incidence of poverty in Canada has fluctuated between 14 and 20 percent of families. On the average, 17 percent of families have incomes below the low-income cutoff.

Source of data: Income Statistics Division, Statistics Canada, Table 202–0804.

Poverty

Families at the low end of the income distribution are so poor that they are considered to be living in poverty. **Poverty** is a state in which a family's income is too low to be able to buy the quantities of food, shelter, and clothing that are deemed necessary. Poverty is a relative concept. Millions of people in Africa and Asia survive on less than $400 a year.

In Canada, poverty is measured in terms of a low-income cutoff. The **low-income cutoff** is the income level, determined separately for different types of families (for example, single persons, couples, one parent), that is selected such that families with incomes below that limit normally spend 55 percent or more of their income on food, shelter, and clothing.

How much poverty (defined as incomes below the low-income cutoff) is there in Canada, and is the problem getting worse or better? Figure 18.6 answers this question.

The incidence of poverty has fluctuated between a low of 14 percent in 1989 and a high of 20 percent in 1996 and 1997. But there has been no trend in poverty and on the average, 17 percent of Canadian families have incomes below the low-income cutoff.

Who Are the Poor?

The lowest incomes are earned by people who scratch out a living doing seasonal work on farms. But the poorest Canadians are people who earn nothing and rely on handouts to survive. The incidence of poverty varies systematically depending on family characteristics and six characteristics stand out:

- Source of income
- Household type
- Age of householder
- Number of children
- Education
- Labour force status

Source of Income Not surprisingly, a household that earns its income either by working or from investments is unlikely to be poor and a household that receives its income in the form of a transfer payment from the government is more likely to be poor.

Household Type Households with two parents present are unlikely to be poor. The most likely to be poor are households with a single female parent, almost 50 percent of whom live in poverty.

Age of Householder The youngest and the oldest households have lower incomes and a greater incidence of poverty than middle-aged households.

Number of Children On the average, the greater the number of children in a household, the smaller is the income per person. And the greater the number of children, the more likely is the household to be living below the poverty level.

Education Education makes a huge difference to a household's income and to the risk of poverty. A person who has not completed high school earns a fraction of a high school graduate's earnings and has the highest poverty risk. University graduates and those with a post-graduate or professional degree have the lowest risk of poverty.

Labour Force Status Households that are in the labour force, even if unemployed, tend to have higher incomes than those not in the labour force—either because they've retired or because they have become discouraged by a persistent failure to find a suitable job.

How Long Does Poverty Last?

Most poverty is temporary and short-lived. Figure 18.7 shows the numbers: 75 percent of those in poverty remain in that state for less than a year and another 8 percent of those in poverty remain so for 1 year. Poverty rates for people who are in that state for 2 years or more are very low.

Given that the average poverty rate is 17 percent of families, you can see that around 2 percent of Canadian families experience poverty that persists for more than 2 years.

The duration of poverty, like its level, depends on household characteristics, and education is the key

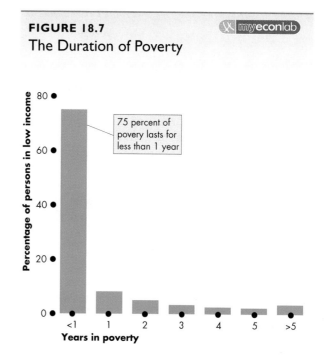

FIGURE 18.7

The Duration of Poverty

> 75 percent of poverty lasts for less than 1 year

Most people in poverty do not remain in that state for long. The poverty rate falls off as the duration of poverty increases. Poverty spells that last for 4 and 5 years are extremely rare. But poverty spells that last for 1 year are quite common.

Source of data: Income Statistics Division, Statistics Canada, Table 202–0807.

characteristic. The least well educated tend to be those who experience the most persistent poverty.

The Sources of Economic Inequality

WE'VE DESCRIBED ECONOMIC INEQUALITY IN Canada. Our task now is to explain it. We began this task in Chapter 17 by learning about the forces that influence demand and supply in the markets for labour, capital, and land. We're now going to deepen our understanding of these forces.

Inequality arises from unequal labour market outcomes and from unequal ownership of capital. We'll begin by looking at labour markets and two of their features that contribute to differences in incomes:

- Human capital
- Discrimination

Human Capital

A clerk in a law firm earns less than a tenth of the amount earned by the lawyer he assists. An operating room assistant earns less than a tenth of the amount earned by the surgeon with whom she works. A bank teller earns less than a tenth of the amount earned by the bank's CEO. These differences in earnings arise from differences in human capital. We can explain these differences by using a model of competitive labour markets.

We'll study a model economy with two levels of human capital, which we'll call high-skilled labour and low-skilled labour. The low-skilled labour might represent the law clerk, the operating room assistant, or the bank teller, and the high-skilled labour might represent the lawyer, the surgeon, or the bank's CEO. We'll first look at the demand side of the markets for these two types of labour.

The Demand for High-Skilled and Low-Skilled Labour High-skilled workers can perform tasks that low-skilled labour would perform badly or perhaps could not perform at all. Imagine an untrained person doing open-heart surgery. High-skilled labour has a higher marginal revenue product than low-skilled labour. As we learned in Chapter 14, a firm's demand for labour curve is the same as the marginal revenue product of labour curve.

Figure 18.8(a) shows the demand curves for high-skilled and low-skilled labour. The demand curve for high-skilled labour is D_H, and that for low-skilled labour is D_L. At any given level of employment, firms are willing to pay a higher wage rate to a high-skilled worker than to a low-skilled worker. The gap between the two wage rates measures the marginal revenue product of skill. For example, at an employment level of 2,000 hours, firms are willing to pay $12.50 for a high-skilled worker and only $5 for a low-skilled worker, a difference of $7.50 an hour. Thus the marginal revenue product of skill is $7.50 an hour.

The Supply of High-Skilled and Low-Skilled Labour High-skilled labour has more human capital than low-skilled labour, and human capital is costly to acquire. The opportunity cost of acquiring human capital includes actual expenditures on such things as tuition and room and board and also costs in the form of lost or reduced earnings while the skill is being acquired. When a person goes to school full-time, that cost is the total earnings forgone. But some people acquire skills on the job—on-the-job training. Usually, a worker undergoing on-the-job training is paid a lower wage than one doing a comparable job but not undergoing training. In such a case, the cost of acquiring the skill is the difference between the wage paid to a person not being trained and that paid to a person being trained.

The position of the supply curve of high-skilled labour reflects the cost of acquiring human capital. Figure 18.8(b) shows two supply curves: one for high-skilled labour and the other for low-skilled labour. The supply curve for high-skilled labour is S_H, and that for low-skilled labour is S_L.

The high-skilled labour supply curve lies above the low-skilled labour supply curve. The vertical distance between the two supply curves is the compensation that high-skilled labour requires for the cost of acquiring the skill. For example, suppose that the quantity of low-skilled labour supplied is 2,000 hours at a wage rate of $5 an hour. This wage rate compensates the low-skilled workers mainly for their time on the job. Consider next the supply of high-skilled labour. To induce 2,000 hours of high-skilled labour to be supplied, firms must pay a wage rate of $8.50 an hour. This wage rate for high-skilled labour is higher than that for low-skilled labour because high-skilled workers must be compensated not only for the time on the job but also for the time and other costs of acquiring the skill.

Wage Rates of High-Skilled and Low-Skilled Labour To work out the wage rates of high-skilled and low-skilled labour, we have to bring together the effects of skill on the demand for and supply of labour.

FIGURE 18.8
Skill Differentials

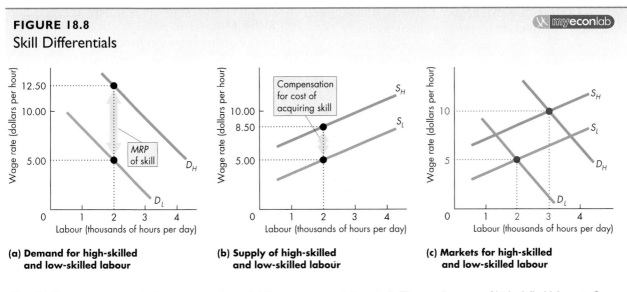

(a) Demand for high-skilled and low-skilled labour

(b) Supply of high-skilled and low-skilled labour

(c) Markets for high-skilled and low-skilled labour

Part (a) illustrates the marginal revenue product of skill. Low-skilled workers have a marginal revenue product that gives rise to the demand curve D_L. High-skilled workers have a higher marginal revenue product than low-skilled labour, so the demand curve for high-skilled labour, D_H, lies to the right of D_L. The vertical distance between these two curves is the marginal revenue product of the skill.

Part (b) shows the effects of the cost of acquiring skills on the supply of labour. The supply curve of low-skilled labour is S_L. The supply curve of high-skilled labour is S_H. The vertical distance between these two curves is the required compensation for the cost of acquiring a skill.

Part (c) shows the equilibrium employment and the wage differential. Low-skilled workers earn $5 an hour, and 2,000 hours of low-skilled labour are employed. High-skilled workers earn $10 an hour, and 3,000 hours of high-skilled labour are employed. The wage rate for high-skilled labour always exceeds that for low-skilled labour.

Figure 18.8(c) shows the demand curves and the supply curves for high-skilled and low-skilled labour. These curves are the same as those plotted in parts (a) and (b). Equilibrium occurs in the market for low-skilled labour where the supply and demand curves for low-skilled labour intersect. The equilibrium wage rate is $5 an hour, and the quantity of low-skilled labour employed is 2,000 hours. Equilibrium in the market for high-skilled labour occurs where the supply and demand curves for high-skilled labour intersect. The equilibrium wage rate is $10 an hour, and the quantity of high-skilled labour employed is 3,000 hours.

As you can see in part (c), the equilibrium wage rate of high-skilled labour is higher than that of low-skilled labour. There are two reasons why this occurs: First, high-skilled labour has a higher marginal revenue product than low-skilled labour, so at a given wage rate, the quantity of high-skilled labour demanded exceeds that of low-skilled labour. Second, skills are costly to acquire, so at a given wage rate, the quantity of high-skilled labour supplied is less than that of low-skilled labour. The wage differential (in this case, $5 an

hour) depends on both the marginal revenue product of the skill and the cost of acquiring it. The higher the marginal revenue product of the skill, the larger is the vertical distance between the demand curves. The more costly it is to acquire a skill, the larger is the vertical distance between the supply curves. The higher the marginal revenue product of the skill and the more costly it is to acquire, the larger is the wage differential between high-skilled and low-skilled labour.

Do Education and Training Pay? Rates of return on high school and college education have been estimated to be in the range of 5 to 10 percent a year after allowing for inflation, which suggests that a university or college degree is a better investment than almost any other that a person can undertake.

Inequality Explained by Human Capital Differences Human capital differences help to explain some of the inequality that we've described. They also help to explain some of the trends in the distribution of income that occurred during the past 20 years.

You saw on p. 425 that better educated, middle-aged, two-parent households are more likely to have a high income than other household types. Human capital differences are correlated with these household characteristics. Education contributes directly to human capital. Age contributes indirectly to human capital because older workers have more experience than younger workers. Human capital differences can also explain a small part of the inequality associated with sex. A larger proportion of men than women have completed a college or university degree. These differences in education levels have disappeared in the current generation and for the population as a whole they are becoming smaller. But they have not yet been eliminated.

Interruptions to a career reduce the effectiveness of job experience in contributing to human capital. Historically, job interruptions have been more common for women than for men because women's careers have been interrupted for bearing and raising children. This factor is a possible source of lower wages, on the average, for women. Although maternity leave and day-care facilities are making career interruptions for women less common, job interruptions remain a problem for many women.

Trends in Inequality Explained by Human Capital Trends   You saw in Fig. 18.5 that high-income households have earned an increasing share of after-tax income while low-income households have earned a decreasing share. Human capital differences are a possible explanation for this trend, and Fig. 18.9 illustrates this explanation. The supply of low-skilled labour (part a) and that of high-skilled labour (part b) are S, and initially, the demand in each market is D_0. The low-skilled wage rate is $5 an hour, and the high-skilled wage rate is $10 an hour.

Information technologies such as computers and laser scanners are *substitutes* for low-skilled labour: They perform tasks that previously were performed by low-skilled labour. The introduction of these technologies has decreased the demand for low-skilled labour (part a), decreased the number of low-skilled jobs, and lowered the wage rate of low-skilled workers.

These same technologies require high-skilled labour to design, program, and run them. High-skilled labour and the information technologies are *complements*. So the introduction of these technologies has increased the demand for high-skilled labour (part b), increased the number of high-skilled jobs, and raised the wage rate of high-skilled workers.

FIGURE 18.9

Explaining the Trend in Income Distribution

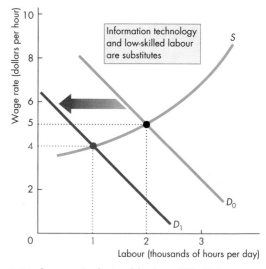

(a) A decrease in demand for low-skilled labour

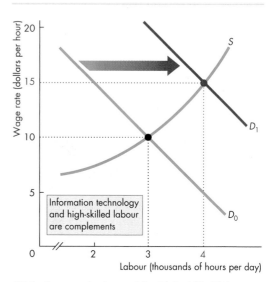

(b) An increase in demand for high-skilled labour

Low-skilled labour in part (a) and information technologies are substitutes. When these technologies were introduced, the demand for low-skilled labour decreased and the quantity of this type of labour and its wage rate decreased. High-skilled labour in part (b) and information technologies are complements. When these technologies were introduced, the demand for high-skilled labour increased and the quantity of this type of labour and its wage rate increased.

Discrimination

Human capital differences can explain some of the economic inequality that we observe. But it can't explain all of it. Discrimination is another possible source of inequality.

Suppose that females and males have identical abilities as investment advisors. Figure 18.10 shows the supply curves of females, S_F (in part a), and of males, S_M (in part b). The marginal revenue product of investment advisors shown by the two curves labelled *MRP* in parts (a) and (b) is the same for both groups.

If everyone is free of sex-based prejudice, the market determines a wage rate of $40,000 a year for investment advisors. But if the customers are prejudiced against women, this prejudice is reflected in the wage rate and employment.

Suppose that the perceived marginal revenue product of the females, when discriminated against, is MRP_{DA}. Suppose that the perceived marginal revenue product for males, the group discriminated in favour of, is MRP_{DF}. With these *MRP* curves, females earn $20,000 a year and only 1,000 females work as investment advisors. Males earn $60,000 a year, and 3,000 of them work as investment advisors.

Counteracting Forces Economists disagree about whether prejudice actually causes wage differentials, and one line of reasoning implies that it does not. In the example you've just studied, customers who buy from men pay a higher service charge for investment advice than do the customers who buy from women. This price difference acts as an incentive to encourage people who are prejudiced to buy from the people against whom they are prejudiced. This force could be strong enough to eliminate the effects of discrimination altogether.

Suppose, as is true in manufacturing, that a firm's customers never meet its workers. If such a firm discriminates against women (or against visible minorities), it can't compete with firms who hire these groups because its costs are higher than those of the unprejudiced firms. Only firms that do not discriminate survive in a competitive industry.

Whether because of discrimination or for some other reason, women on average do earn lower incomes than men. Another possible source of women's lower wage rates arises from differences in the relative degree of specialization of women and men.

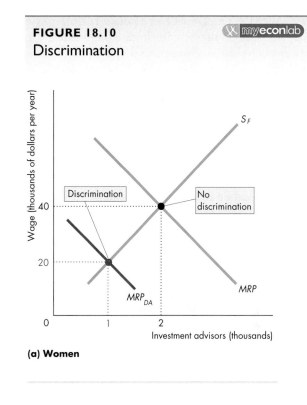

FIGURE 18.10
Discrimination

(a) Women

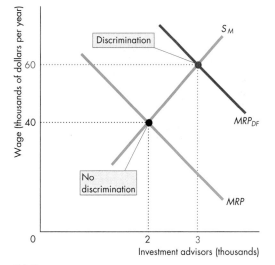

(b) Men

With no discrimination, the wage rate is $40,000 a year and 2,000 of each group are hired. With discrimination against women, the marginal revenue product curve in part (a) is MRP_{DA} and that in part (b) is MRP_{DF}. The wage rate for women falls to $20,000 a year, and only 1,000 are employed. The wage rate for men rises to $60,000 a year, and 3,000 are employed.

Differences in the Degree of Specialization
Couples must choose how to allocate their time between working for a wage and doing jobs in the home, such as cooking, cleaning, shopping, organizing vacations, and, most important, bearing and raising children. Let's look at the choices of Bob and Sue.

Bob might specialize in earning an income and Sue in taking care of the home. Or Sue might specialize in earning an income and Bob in taking care of the home. Or both of them might earn an income and share home production jobs.

The allocation they choose depends on their preferences and on the earning potential of each of them. The choice of an increasing number of households is for each person to diversify between earning an income and doing some home chores. But in most households, Bob will specialize in earning an income and Sue will both earn an income and bear a larger share of the task of running the home. With this allocation, Bob will probably earn more than Sue. If Sue devotes time and effort to ensuring Bob's mental and physical well-being, the quality of Bob's market labour will be higher than it would be if he were diversified. If the roles were reversed, Sue would be able to supply market labour that earns more than Bob.

To test whether the degree of specialization accounts for earnings differences between the sexes, economists have compared the incomes of men and women who never married. They have found that, on the average, with equal amounts of human capital, the wages of these two groups are the same.

We've examined some sources of inequality in the labour market. Let's now look at the way inequality arises from unequal ownership of capital.

Unequal Ownership of Capital

You've seen that inequality in wealth (excluding human capital) is much greater than inequality in income. This inequality arises from saving and transfers of wealth from one generation to the next.

The higher a household's income, the more that household tends to save and pass on to the next generation. Saving is not always a source of increased inequality. If a household saves to redistribute an uneven income over its life cycle and enable consumption to fluctuate less than income, saving decreases inequality. If a lucky generation that has a high income saves a large part of that income and leaves capital to a succeeding generation that is unlucky, this act of saving also decreases the degree of inequality. But two fea-

tures of intergenerational transfers of wealth lead to increased inequality: People can't inherit debt, and marriage tends to concentrate wealth.

Can't Inherit Debt Although a person may die in debt—with negative wealth—a debt can't be forced onto the next generation of a family. So inheritance only adds to a future generation's wealth; inheritance cannot decrease wealth.

Most people inherit nothing or a very small amount. A few people inherit an enormous fortune. As a result, intergenerational transfers make the distribution of income persistently more unequal than the distribution of ability and job skills. A household that is poor in one generation is more likely to be poor in the next. A household that is wealthy in one generation is more likely to be wealthy in the next. And marriage reinforces this tendency.

Marriage and Wealth Concentration People tend to marry within their own socioeconomic class—a phenomenon called *assortative mating*. In everyday language, "like attracts like." Although there is a good deal of folklore that "opposites attract," perhaps such Cinderella tales appeal to us because they are so rare in reality. Wealthy people seek wealthy partners.

Because of assortative mating, wealth becomes more concentrated in a small number of families and the distribution of wealth becomes more unequal.

REVIEW QUIZ

1 What role does human capital play in accounting for income inequality?
2 What role might discrimination play in accounting for income inequality?
3 What are the possible reasons for income inequality by sex and race?
4 What are the possible reasons for income inequality by age group?
5 Does inherited wealth make the distribution of income less equal or more equal?
6 Why does wealth inequality persist across generations?

myeconlab   **Study Plan 18.2**

Next, we're going to see how taxes and government programs redistribute income and decrease the degree of economic inequality.

Income Redistribution

THE THREE MAIN WAYS IN WHICH GOVERNMENTS in Canada redistribute income are

- Income taxes
- Income maintenance programs
- Subsidized services

Income Taxes

Income taxes may be progressive, regressive, or proportional. A **progressive income tax** is one that taxes income at an average rate that increases with the level of income. The **average tax rate** is the percentage of income paid in taxes. A **regressive income tax** is one that taxes income at an average rate that decreases with the level of income. A **proportional income tax** (also called a *flat-rate income tax*) is one that taxes income at a constant rate, regardless of the level of income.

The income tax rates that apply in Canada are composed of two parts: federal and provincial taxes. The highest income tax rates are in Quebec and the lowest are in Alberta. There is variety in the detailed tax arrangements in the individual provinces but the tax system, at both the federal and provincial levels, is progressive.

The poorest Canadians pay no income tax. Even those who earn $30,000 a year pay a very low rate of income tax. Those whose incomes are $50,000 a year pay about 21 percent of their income in income taxes; those whose incomes are $100,000 a year pay about 28 percent in income tax; and as incomes increase, the average tax rate increases to 45 percent or higher.

Income Maintenance Programs

Three main types of programs redistribute income by making direct payments (in cash, services, or vouchers) to people in the lower part of the income distribution. They are

- Social security programs
- Employment Insurance program
- Welfare programs

Social Security Programs Four programs—Old Age Security (OAS), Guaranteed Income Supplement (GIS), the Allowance (for spouses of low-income OAS pensioners), and the Allowance for the Survivor (AS)—ensure a minimum level of income for senior citizens. Cash payments to retired or disabled workers or their surviving spouses are paid for by compulsory payroll taxes on both employers and employees. In 2005, the maximum OAS was $476.97 a month, the maximum GIS for a single person was $566.87, the maximum Allowance was $846.21, and the maximum AS was $934.24.

Employment Insurance Program To provide an income to unemployed workers, the federal government has established an unemployment compensation program. The Employment Insurance program is funded by employee and employer contributions, and after a qualifying period the worker is entitled to receive a benefit if he or she becomes unemployed. In 2005, the maximum unemployment benefit was $413 a week or 55 percent of gross weekly earnings over the previous 20 weeks.

Welfare Programs Other welfare programs provide income maintenance for families and persons. They are

1. Canada Assistance Plan, a plan shared equally by the federal and provincial governments that gives financial assistance to families and individuals who are in need, regardless of the cause; the assistance includes food, shelter, fuel, utilities, family supplies, items required to carry on a trade, certain welfare services, and health and social services
2. Family Supplement and Canada Child Tax Benefit programs, designed to help families who have inadequate financial support
3. Canada/Quebec Pension Plans, funded equally by employee and employer contributions, provide retirement benefits, survivor benefits, disability benefits, and death benefits
4. Workers' Compensation, a provincial program funded by employers, designed to provide financial assistance as well as medical care and rehabilitation of workers injured at work

Subsidized Services

A great deal of redistribution takes place in Canada through the provision of subsidized services, which is the provision of goods and services by the government at prices below the cost of production. The taxpayers who consume these goods and services receive a transfer in kind from the taxpayers who do not consume them. The two most important areas in which this form of redistribution takes place are education—both kindergarten through Grade 12 and college and university—and health care.

Canadian students enrolled in the universities in Ontario pay annual tuition fees of around $5,000. The cost of one year's education at one of these universities is about $20,000. Thus families with a member enrolled in these institutions receive a benefit from the government of about $15,000 a year. Those with several college or university students receive proportionately higher benefits.

Government provision of health care to all residents has brought high-quality and high-cost health care to millions of people who earn too little to buy such services themselves. As a result, this program has contributed to reducing inequality.

The Scale of Income Redistribution

To determine the scale of income redistribution, we need to compare the distribution of *market income* with the distribution of *after-tax income*. The data available on benefits exclude the value of subsidized services (such as the value of university education and health care services), so the resulting distribution might understate the total amount of redistribution from the rich to the poor.

Figure 18.11 shows the scale of redistribution based on the calculations just described. In part (a), the blue Lorenz curve describes the market distribution of income and the green Lorenz curve shows the distribution of income after all taxes and benefits. (The Lorenz curve based on *total income*—market income plus transfer payments from governments—lies between these two curves.)

The distribution after taxes and benefits is much less unequal than the market distribution. In 2003, the lowest 20 percent of households received only 1.1 percent of market income but 5 percent of after-tax income. The highest 20 percent of households received 51.6 percent of market income but only 43.7 percent of after-tax income.

Figure 18.11(b) highlights the percentage of total income redistributed among the five groups. The share of total income received by the lowest three quintiles (60 percent) of households increased. The share of total income received by the fourth quintile fell slightly. And the share of total income received by the highest quintile fell by almost 8 percent of total income.

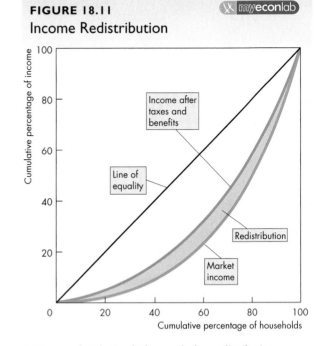

FIGURE 18.11

Income Redistribution

(a) Income distribution before and after redistribution

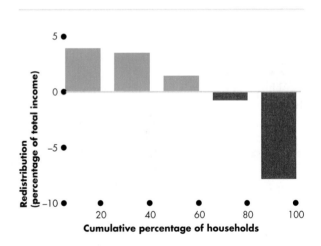

(b) The scale of redistribution

Redistribution reduces the degree of inequality that the market generates. In 2003, the 20 percent of households with the lowest incomes received net benefits that increased their share from 1.1 percent of market income to 5 percent of income after redistribution. The 20 percent of households with the highest incomes paid taxes that decreased their share from 51.6 percent of market income to 43.7 percent of income after redistribution.

Source of data: Income Statistics Division, Statistics Canada, Table 202–0701.

The Big Tradeoff

The redistribution of income creates what has been called the **big tradeoff**, a tradeoff between equity and efficiency. The big tradeoff arises because redistribution uses scarce resources and weakens incentives.

A dollar collected from a rich person does not translate into a dollar received by a poor person. Some of the dollar collected gets used up in the process of redistribution. Tax-collecting agencies such as the Canada Revenue Agency and welfare-administering agencies (as well as tax accountants and lawyers) use skilled labour, computers, and other scarce resources to do their work. The bigger the scale of redistribution, the greater is the opportunity cost of administering it.

But the cost of collecting taxes and making welfare payments is a small part of the total cost of redistribution. A bigger cost arises from the inefficiency—deadweight loss—of taxes and benefits. Greater equality can be achieved only by taxing productive activities such as work and saving. Taxing people's income from their work and saving lowers the after-tax income they receive. This lower after-tax income makes them work and save less, which in turn results in smaller output and less consumption not only for the rich who pay the taxes but also for the poor who receive the benefits.

It is not only taxpayers who face weaker incentives to work. Benefit recipients also face weaker incentives. In fact, under the welfare arrangements that prevail in Canada today, the weakest incentives to work are those faced by households that benefit most from welfare. When a welfare recipient gets a job, benefits are withdrawn and eligibility for support is withdrawn. In effect, these households face a marginal tax rate of more than 100 percent on their earnings. This arrangement locks poor households in a welfare trap.

So the scale and methods of income redistribution must pay close attention to the incentive effects of taxes and benefits.

A Major Welfare Challenge The poorest people in Canada are women who have not completed high school, have a child (or children), and live without a partner. But all single mothers present a major welfare challenge. First, their numbers are large. There are approximately one million single mothers in Canada today. Second, their economic plight and the economic prospects for their children are serious.

Janet Peterson and her four children aged 3 to 13 are one example. Janet has a serious physical disability.

She receives a social assistance cheque each month for $1,286, or $15,432 a year. The low-income cutoff for a family of five is $30,910. So Janet and her children live in severe poverty. She spends $625 a month on rent, $400 on food, and the rest on gas, hydro, the phone, and transportation. To provide Janet Peterson (and the other million single mothers) with an income that matches the low-income cutoff would cost more than $10 billion a year.

Janet Peterson has a physical disability that makes it unlikely that she could work. Many other single mothers are in this situation. But this is not the typical case. Most single mothers are physically fit and are capable of working. And some of them are well educated and therefore can earn a high wage rate. Even those single mothers who have not completed high school are capable of either attending school or getting a job.

For physically fit single mothers, the long-term solution to their problem is education and on-the-job training—acquiring human capital. The short-term solution is welfare. But welfare must be designed to minimize the disincentive to pursue the long-term goal. This is the challenge in designing an adequate welfare program.

REVIEW QUIZ

1 How do governments in Canada redistribute income?

2 How large is the scale of redistribution in Canada?

3 What is one of the major welfare challenges today and how is it being tackled in Canada?

myeconlab   **Study Plan 18.3**

We've examined economic inequality in Canada, and we've seen how inequality arises. And we've seen that inequality has increased since 1980. *Reading Between the Lines* on pp. 434–435 looks at Canada's changing inequality and redistribution through taxes.

You've now completed your study of microeconomics. You've seen how markets work and do a remarkable job of reconciling self-interest and the social interest. You've also seen that in situations in which market failure occurs government action might improve the allocation of resources. But you've seen too that failure can occur in the political marketplace.

Changing Inequality and Redistribution

CALGARY HERALD, 23 APRIL 2005

Rich Canadians pay half of all federal income tax

More than half the taxes the federal government collected in 2002 came from the top 10 per cent of the country's income earners, according to a study released Friday by Statistics Canada.

People in the highest income bracket saw the smallest drop in their effective tax rate between 1990 and 2002, a time when rates fell for all Canadians, the study said. Moreover, the share of federal income taxes paid by this group of high-income earners rose in the decade covered by the report.

By comparison, the share of federal taxes paid by people in the bottom half of Canada's tax scale diminished significantly, the study showed. ...

"We do know that top income tax rates in this country are still high, they're among the highest in the world, particularly if you combine them with provincial rates," said Derek Burleton, senior economist with TD Bank Financial Group. ...

Jim Stanford, an economist with the Canadian Auto Workers, looked at the study results differently, suggesting they painted only a partial picture of the economic well-being of low-income earners and pointing to the last decade as a time of growing income inequality.

The tax cuts implemented in this period favoured the rich more than the poor, Stanford said, though he acknowledged that measures such as the child tax credit helped low-income earners.

"The progressivity of the system has actually diminished somewhat since 1990," he added.

"Some people who support a progressive system could say (such a system) is good, but the actual driving force is a regressive force, namely that pre-tax income is becoming more unequal."

The impact of taxes such as the GST, not considered in the study, hit low-income earners harder than they did richer Canadians, Stanford said.

"If you were to measure the total taxes—not just income taxes—paid by the lower-income people, it wouldn't look as positive as this study which focused only on the income tax," he said.

"The overall tax burden borne by lower-income people is much higher than just their share of income taxes."

Reprinted by permission of Joe Paraskevas.

Essence of the Story

■ A Statistics Canada report says that more than 50 percent of federal income tax came from the country's top 10 percent of earners.

■ The share of income tax paid by the bottom 50 percent of earners decreased.

■ Jim Stanford of the Canadian Auto Workers says the study is misleading and that the tax cuts of the 1990s favoured the rich.

■ Also, says Stanford, taking account of the GST further favours the rich against the poor.

■ The overall burden of the tax system borne by lower income groups is much larger than the report says.

Economic Analysis

■ In this chapter, we described the degree of income redistribution by examining the Lorenz curve for after-tax income with that for market income.

■ We analyzed the shift in the Lorenz curve that arises from taxes and benefits by calculating the percentage of total income that is transferred across the quintiles.

■ We made this comparison for 2003 only and didn't examine how redistribution has changed.

■ The news article compares 1990 and 2002. We will do some further analysis and compare 1990 and 2003.

■ Figure 1 shows the quintile shares of after-tax income in 1990 and 2003. The blue bars show the data for 1990 and the red bars for 2003.

■ You can see that the share of after-tax income received by the highest quintile increased while the shares of the other four quintiles decreased—after-tax income inequality increased.

■ Was the amount of redistribution from taxes and benefits responsible for this increase in inequality?

■ Figure 2 answers this question and shows that it was not.

■ Figure 2 shows the percentage of total after-tax income transferred across the quintiles in 1990 (blue bars) and 2003 (red bars).

■ You can see that the highest quintile paid a larger percentage of its income to the lower quintiles.

■ But you can also see that the fourth quintle paid less and the third (middle) quintile received more. The two lowest quintiles received less.

■ So the changes in taxes and benefits hurt the richest and the poorest Canadians and benefitted the middle income and upper middle income groups.

■ This change in redistribution is consistent with the idea that the political process favours the median voter—the voter needed to gain a majority in an election.

■ Jim Stanford of the Canadian Auto Workers says that taking account of the GST would change the picture and show that the poorer Canadians pay a much bigger share of taxes.

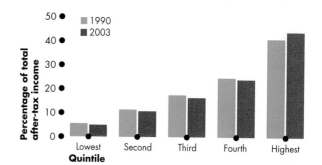

Figure 1 Quintile shares of after-tax income

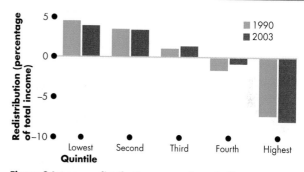

Figure 2 Income redistribution across the quintiles

■ He is correct in saying that the GST makes a difference to the calculation of who pays the taxes and how much redistribution comes from the tax system.

■ But the GST doesn't change the picture radically because the higher quintiles also pay most of the GST.

■ Remember that the GST is a flat percentage of expenditure on items covered by the tax. Some of the items on which the lower quintiles spend a large proportion

of their incomes are exempt from the GST. So the higher quintiles, who spend much more than the lower quintiles, end up paying the bulk of the GST.

■ Whether the tax system in Canada redistributes too much or too little is a difficult question and one that will always be on the political agenda.

SUMMARY

KEY POINTS

Measuring Economic Inequality (pp. 420–425)

- In 2003, the mode after-tax income was in the range between $15,000 and $19,999 a year, the median after-tax income was $39,700, and the mean after-tax income was $48,400.
- The income distribution is positively skewed.
- The poorest 20 percent of households received 5 percent of total income, and the wealthiest 20 percent received 43.6 percent of total income.
- Wealth is distributed more unequally than income because the wealth data exclude the value of human capital.
- Since 1980, the share of income received by the richest 20 percent of households has increased, the share of the poorest 20 percent has remained constant, and the shares of income received by the other three groups of households have decreased.
- Source of income, household type, age of householder, number of children, education, and labour market status all influence household income.

The Sources of Economic Inequality (pp. 426–430)

- Inequality arises from differences in human capital.
- Inequality might arise from discrimination.
- Inequality between men and women might arise from differences in the degree of specialization.
- Intergenerational transfers of wealth lead to increased inequality because people can't inherit debt, and assortative mating tends to concentrate wealth.

Income Redistribution (pp. 431–433)

- Governments redistribute income through progressive income taxes, income maintenance programs, and subsidized services.
- Redistribution increases the share of total income received by the lowest three quintiles (60 percent) of households and decreases the share of total income received by the highest quintile. The share of the fourth quintile falls slightly.

- Because the redistribution of income weakens incentives, it creates a tradeoff between equity and efficiency.
- Effective redistribution seeks to support the long-term solution to low income, which is education and job training—acquiring human capital.

KEY FIGURES

Figure 18.1   The Distribution of Income in Canada in 2003, 420
Figure 18.4   Lorenz Curves for Income and Wealth, 422
Figure 18.5   Trends in the Distribution of Income, 424
Figure 18.6   The Poverty Rate, 424
Figure 18.8   Skill Differentials, 427
Figure 18.9   Explaining the Trend in Income Distribution, 428
Figure 18.10   Descrimination, 429
Figure 18.11   Income Redistribution, 432

KEY TERMS

After-tax income, 420
Average tax rate, 431
Big tradeoff, 433
Lorenz curve, 421
Low-income cutoff, 424
Market income, 420
Poverty, 424
Progressive income tax, 431
Proportional income tax, 431
Regressive income tax, 431
Total income, 420

PROBLEMS

Go to (X)myeconlab for solutions to odd-numbered problems and additional exercises.

1. The table shows income shares in the United States in 2000.

Households	Income (percent of total)
Lowest 20 percent	4.8
Second-lowest 20 percent	10.5
Third-lowest 20 percent	15.8
Fourth-lowest 20 percent	22.8
Highest 20 percent	46.1

a. Draw a Lorenz curve for the United States in 2000 and compare it with that for Canada in 2003 shown in Fig. 18.3.
b. Was Canadian income distributed more equally or less equally than that in the United States?
c. Can you think of some reasons for the differences in the distribution of income in Canada and the United States?

2. The table shows income shares in Sweden in 1992.

Households	Income (percent of total)
Lowest 20 percent	6.7
Second-lowest 20 percent	12.2
Third-lowest 20 percent	17.6
Fourth-lowest 20 percent	24.5
Highest 20 percent	39.0

a. Draw the Lorenz curve for income in Sweden in 1992.
b. Was income distributed more equally or less equally in Canada in 2003 than in Sweden in 1992?
c. Use the information provided in problem 1 on the distribution of income in the United States in 2000. Was income distributed more equally or less equally in the United States in 2000 than in Sweden in 1992?
d. Can you think of some reasons for the differences in the distribution of income in Canada and Sweden?

3. The following figure shows the demand for and supply of low-skilled labour.

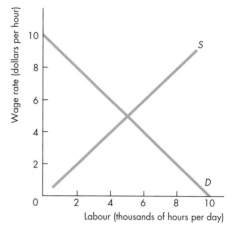

High-skilled workers have twice the marginal revenue product of low-skilled workers. (The marginal revenue product at each employment level is twice the marginal revenue product of a low-skilled worker.) But the cost of acquiring the skill adds $2 an hour to the wage that must be offered to attract high-skilled labour. What is

a. The wage rate of low-skilled labour?
b. The quantity of low-skilled labour employed?
c. The wage rate of high-skilled labour?
d. The quantity of high-skilled labour employed?

4. The following figure shows the demand for and supply of low-skilled labour.

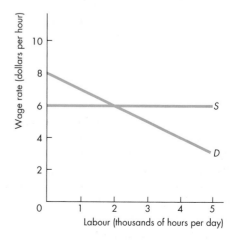

The marginal revenue product of a high-skilled worker is $10 an hour greater than that of a low-skilled worker. (The marginal revenue product at each employment level is $10 greater than that of a low-skilled worker.) The cost of acquiring the skill adds $6 an hour to the wage that must be offered to attract high-skilled labour.

a. What is the wage rate of low-skilled labour?
b. What is the quantity of low-skilled labour employed?
c. What is the wage rate of high-skilled labour?
d. What is the quantity of high-skilled labour employed?
e. Why does the wage rate of a high-skilled worker exceed that of a low-skilled worker by exactly the cost of acquiring the skill?

5. The table shows the distribution of market income in Canada in 2003.

Households	Market income (percent of total)
Lowest 20 percent	1.1
Second-lowest 20 percent	7.3
Third-lowest 20 percent	15.1
Fourth-lowest 20 percent	24.9
Highest 20 percent	51.6

a. What is market income?
b. Draw the Lorenz curve for the distribution of market income.
c. Compare the distribution of market income with the distribution of after-tax income shown in Fig. 18.3. Which distribution is more unequal and why?

6. Use the information provided in problem 5 and in Fig. 18.3.
a. What is the percentage of market income that is redistributed from the highest income group?
b. What are the percentages of market income that are redistributed to the lower income groups?
c. Describe the effects of increasing the amount of income redistribution in Canada to the point at which the lowest income group receives 15 percent of after-tax income and the highest income group receives 30 percent of after-tax income.

CRITICAL THINKING

1. Study *Reading Between the Lines* on pp. 434–435 and then
a. Describe the main facts about the changes in the distribution of after-tax income in Canada.
b. Describe the main facts about changes in the distribution of the burden of the federal income tax reported in the news article.
c. Why might it be argued that the rich pay too much tax?
d. Why might it be argued that the rich pay too little tax?
e. What policy issues are raised by the news article?
f. How do you think the tax system and the welfare system should be changed to influence the distribution of after-tax income in Canada today?

WEB EXERCISES

Use the links on (X)myeconlab to work the following exercises.

1. Obtain data on income distribution among major league baseball players. Then
a. Describe the main facts about the income distribution of major league players.
b. Compare the income distribution of these players with the income distribution of Canada.
c. Which is more unequal?
d. What is the problem with inequality?

2. Download the World Bank's Deininger and Squire Data Set on income distribution in a large number of countries.
a. Which country in the data set has the most unequal distribution?
b. Which country in the data set has the most equal distribution?
c. Can you think of reasons that might explain the differences in income distribution in the two countries you've identified?

UNDERSTANDING FACTOR MARKETS

For Whom?

During the past 40 years, the rich have been getting richer at a faster pace than the poor. This trend is new. From the end of World War II until 1965, the poor got richer at a faster pace than the rich and the gap between rich and poor narrowed a bit. What are the forces that generate these trends? The answer to this question is the forces of demand and supply in factor markets. These forces determine wages, interest rates, and the prices of land and natural resources. These forces also determine people's incomes.

The three categories of resources are human, capital, and natural. Human resources include labour, human capital, and entrepreneurship. The income of labour and human capital depends on wage rates and employment levels, which are determined in labour markets. The income from capital depends on interest rates and the amount of capital, which are determined in capital markets. The income from natural resources depends on prices and quantities that are determined in natural resource markets. Only the return to entrepreneurship is not determined directly in a market. That return is normal profit plus economic profit, and it depends on how successful each entrepreneur is in the business that he or she runs.

The chapters in this part study the forces at play in factor markets and explain how those forces have led to changes in the distribution of income.

The overview of all the factor markets in Chapter 17 explained how the demand for factors of production results from the profit-maximizing decisions of firms. You studied these decisions from a different angle in Chapters 9–13, where you learned how firms choose their profit-maximizing output and price. Chapter 17 explained how a firm's profit-maximizing decisions determine its demand for productive factors. It also explained how factor supply decisions are made and how equilibrium in factor markets determines factor prices and the incomes of owners of factors of production.

Some of the biggest incomes earned by superstars are a surplus that we call *economic rent*.

Chapter 17 used labour resources and the labour market as its main example. But it also looked at some special features of capital markets and natural resource markets.

Chapter 18 studied the distribution of income. This chapter took you right back to the fundamentals of economics and answered one of the big economic questions: Who gets to consume the goods and services that are produced?

Many outstanding economists have advanced our understanding of factor markets and the role they play in helping to resolve the conflict between the demands of humans and the resources available. One of them is Thomas Robert Malthus, whom you can meet on the following page. You can also enjoy the insights of Janet Currie, a Canadian professor of economics at UCLA and a prominent contemporary labour economist.

Running Out of Resources

THE ECONOMIST

Thomas Robert Malthus

(1766–1834), an English clergyman and economist, was an extremely influential social scientist. In his best-selling Essay on the Principle of Population, *published in 1798, he predicted that population growth would outstrip food production and said that wars, famine, and disease were inevitable unless population growth was held in check by what he called "moral restraint." By "moral restraint," he meant marrying at a late age and living a celibate life. He married at the age of 38 a wife of 27, marriage ages that he recommended for others. Malthus's ideas were regarded as too radical in their day. And they led Thomas Carlyle, a contemporary thinker, to dub economics the "dismal science." But the ideas of Malthus had a profound influence on Charles Darwin, who got the key idea that led him to the theory of natural selection from reading the* Essay on the Principle of Population. *And David Ricardo and the classical economists were strongly influenced by Malthus's ideas.*

THE ISSUES

Is there a limit to economic growth, or can we expand production and population without effective limit? Thomas Malthus gave one of the most influential answers to these questions in 1798. He reasoned that population, unchecked, would grow at a geometric rate—1, 2, 4, 8, 16 . . . —while the food supply would grow at an arithmetic rate—1, 2, 3, 4, 5. . . . To prevent the population from outstripping the available food supply, there would be periodic wars, famines, and plagues. In Malthus's view, only what he called moral restraint could prevent such periodic disasters.

As industrialization proceeded through the nineteenth century, Malthus's idea came to be applied to all natural resources, especially those that are exhaustible.

Modern-day Malthusians believe that his basic idea is correct and that it applies not only to food but also to every natural resource. In time, these prophets of doom believe, we will be reduced to the subsistence level that Malthus predicted. He was a few centuries out in his predictions but not dead wrong.

One modern-day Malthusian is ecologist Paul Ehrlich, who believes that we are sitting on a "population bomb." Governments must, says Ehrlich, limit both population growth and the resources that may be used each year.

In 1931, Harold Hotelling developed a theory of natural resources with different predictions from those of Malthus. The Hotelling Principle is that the relative price of an exhaustible natural resource will steadily rise, bringing a decline in the quantity used and an increase in the use of substitute resources.

Julian Simon (who died in 1998) challenged both the Malthusian gloom and the Hotelling Principle. He believed that people are the "ultimate resource" and predicted that an increasing population lessens the pressure on natural resources. A bigger population provides a larger number of resourceful people who can work out more efficient ways of using scarce resources. As these solutions are found, the prices of exhaustible resources actually fall. To demonstrate his point, in 1980, Simon bet Ehrlich that the prices of five metals—copper, chrome, nickel, tin, and tungsten—would fall during the 1980s. Simon won the bet!

THEN

No matter whether it is agricultural land, an exhaustible natural resource, or the space in the centre of Winnipeg and no matter whether it is 2006 or, as shown here, 1913, there is a limit to what is available, and we persistently push against that limit. Economists see urban congestion as a consequence of the value of doing business in the city centre relative to the cost. They see the price mechanism, bringing ever-higher rents and prices of raw materials, as the means of allocating and rationing scarce natural resources. Malthusians, in contrast, explain congestion as the consequence of population pressure, and they see population control as the solution.

NOW

In Tokyo, the pressure on space is so great that in some residential neighbourhoods, a parking space costs $1,700 a month. To economize on this expensive space—and to lower the cost of car ownership and hence boost the sale of new cars—Honda, Nissan, and Toyota, three of Japan's big car producers, have developed a parking machine that enables two cars to occupy the space of one. The most basic of these machines costs a mere $10,000— less than six months' parking fees.

Malthus developed his ideas about population growth in a world in which women played a limited role in the economy. Malthus did not consider the opportunity cost of women's time a factor to be considered in predicting trends in the birth rate and population growth. But today, the opportunity cost of women's time is a crucial factor because women play an expanded role in the labour force. One woman who has made significant contributions to our knowledge of labour markets is Janet Currie of UCLA. You can meet Professor Currie on the following pages.

TALKING WITH

Janet Currie is a professor of economics at the University of California, Los Angeles. Born in 1960 in Kingston, Canada, she attended the University of Toronto, where she received her B.A. and M.A. in economics before moving to Princeton University, where she completed her Ph.D. in 1988. Professor Currie's research examines a wide range of public programs—medical, nutritional, educational, and housing—on (mainly) poor families. She has provided valuable assessments of the short-term and long-term effects of the Head Start program (enriched preschool for children in poor households) and Medicaid (government provided health insurance for poor mothers and their children).

Janet Currie

Michael Parkin and Robin Bade talked with Janet Currie about her work and the progress that economists have made in understanding how public policies can influence the distribution of income and economic well-being as well as the supply of labour and human capital.

Professor Currie, what attracted you to economics?

I was attracted to economics because it addresses questions of broad human interest (such as poverty and inequality) with intellectual rigour. Some may view the economic paradigm as restrictive (does everyone really maximize utility all the time?), but it provides a set of tools that yield powerful predictions about human behaviour, and it can be tested. For example, the "Law of Demand" (people consume less of a good when the price goes up) can be adopted to think about why many eligible people do not participate in social programs that might benefit them.

Why are there still relatively few women in our field?

Like other scientific careers, that of an economist requires an initial investment in mathematical skills. Mathematics is the language of science, and it is difficult to become a scientist if you don't speak the language. Undergraduate programs in economics may be partially to blame for not preparing students adequately for graduate work in the field. Many programs are aimed more at preparing students for careers in law or business. While this may be what the majority of undergraduate economics students want, we should also serve those who may go on to study economics in graduate school.

Difficulties in combining work and family are also an issue, but economics is not unique in requiring women to devote a lot of time to their careers at precisely the point when traditionally women would spend most time with their families. However, supports such as maternity leave and child care are improving, and making it easier for younger women to "do it all."

Could you briefly describe Head Start and summarize your main conclusions about its effects?

Head Start is a preschool program for disadvantaged three- to five-year-old children. In a series of studies comparing Head Start children to siblings who did not attend, I find evidence of lasting effects of Head Start in terms of schooling attainment and reductions in criminal activity. These findings are important because, while everyone would like to believe that investments in children pay off, there was little prior evidence of longer-term effects of Head Start.

You asked in a recent paper "Are public housing projects good for kids?" What's the answer?

The title of this paper is intentionally provocative. Given all the negative publicity about some housing projects, most people assume that public housing must be bad for children. However, the key question is not whether kids in public housing do worse than other kids (they do) but whether they do better than they would have done in the absence of the program. For example, without the program, some children might have become homeless or had to move many times. It turns out that on average, public housing programs do improve the housing available to poor families and have some positive effects in terms of schooling attainments.

In another paper, published in 1998, you summarized what we know and need to know about the effects of welfare programs on children. What, in a nutshell, do we know? What do we still need to know? And how would we set about finding the needed answers?

One striking conclusion from this review of welfare programs is that the available evidence suggests that in-kind programs are more effective than traditional welfare programs, which give cash to parents. This might account for the growing proportion of aid to poor families that is given in the form of specific in-kind benefits (e.g., Head Start, medical insurance, housing assistance). However, the evidence is far from complete. We need a lot more information about effects of programs on children, since antipoverty programs are often justified in terms of their possible beneficial effects on children. We also need more information about longer-term effects of programs. For example, does it matter at what age the benefits are received?

In terms of how to find out what we need to know, I am a big supporter of social experiments, since a real random-assignment, treatment-control design provides more convincing answers than most statistical studies. On the other hand, it isn't possible to mount an experiment for every question. Much more could be done with existing data if more of it was made available to researchers, and if governments were more willing to allow linkages of different data sources.

What are some of the social experiments that have provided convincing answers? And how could economists do better work if governments were more willing to allow linkages of different data sources?

The great thing about a well-designed experiment is that anyone can understand the results. For example, in a drug trial, we randomly assign people to a treatment group that gets the drug and to a control group that gets a placebo. Because of the random assignment, the two groups are the same on average, so that any *ex poste* differences in how they do can be attributed to the treatment.

> " *The great thing about a well-designed experiment is that anyone can understand the results.* "

Social experiments like the "Moving to Opportunity" project also rely on random assignment. In this experiment, the treatment consisted of giving a voucher to families in public housing projects that allowed the families to move into a low-poverty neighbourhood and gave them some assistance in relocating. The initial results indicate that the experiment had an effect on youth crime, as well as on criminal victimization. So far, there are no positive effects on schooling attainment or parental employment, but it is possible that these will emerge in the followup that is currently being conducted.

Another interesting experiment involves Early Head Start, a program that extends Head Start benefits to infants and toddlers. This program has demonstrated short-term effects of the program on cognitive test scores. Again, it will be necessary to do some long-term followup in order to see whether these benefits are retained.

The downside of experiments is that they are very expensive, relative to a statistical study, and cannot be used to answer questions other than those they were designed to address. Some of my work on the effects of Medicaid expansions provides an example of what can be done by linking various types of data. The U.S. government collects a good deal of survey data about health insurance and health-care utilization. Because my co-author, Jon Gruber, was working in Washington, we were able to get state identifiers so that we could link information about Medicaid income cutoffs in each state to the individual-level records. This enabled us to ask how changing the income cutoffs affected health-care utilization. In recent years, the government has been unwilling to release geographic identifiers, so that it is not possible to do a similar study of more recent health insurance expansions.

A few years ago, you stuck out your neck on the never-to-end minimum wage issue. What, according to your work, is the effect of the minimum wage on youth employment?

We found compelling evidence that youths affected by minimum wage legislation were less likely to be employed than those who were not (because they had wages either above or below the affected group). There are some obvious methodological flaws with some of the work arguing that minimum wages actually increase employment (such as failures to properly control for increases in demand, which might be driving increases in employment even at the higher minimum wages). However, much of the work (my own included) ignores an important question, which is whether we actually want to increase employment among youths. If higher minimum wages reduced employment but increased schooling, perhaps this would be a good outcome.

You've studied the effects of restrictions on the use of public funds for abortion. What did you discover?

Many people have argued that restrictions on abortion may cause more unwanted children to be born

and hence worsen infant and child outcomes. The basic idea of my paper was that if this were true, then one ought to be able to see the effect in the distribution of birthweights. That is, if children who would have been aborted are more likely to be of low birthweight (because their mothers did not take care of themselves), then one should see more low birthweight infants in areas that adopt abortion restrictions. We did not, however, find this effect. In hindsight, it is not obvious that children who are born as a result of abortion restrictions ought to be less healthy than average, since the majority of women seeking abortions are young and non-poor.

> " ... *economists are increasingly contributing to debate (and frequently having the last word) on questions that used to be considered far outside their scope.* "

What advice do you have for a student who is just starting to study economics? Do you think that economics is a good subject in which to major? What other subjects would you urge students to study alongside economics?

I have never regretted choosing economics as a major. Economics gives one the tools to study a vast array of social issues in a rigorous manner. Not surprisingly, economists are increasingly contributing to debate (and frequently having the last word) on questions that used to be considered far outside their scope. Economic concepts such as "opportunity cost," "selection bias," and "cost-benefit analysis" are central to the discussion of a vast array of policy issues.

Students who want to leave open the option of graduate work in economics should make sure they take enough mathematics courses to get them through a good graduate program.

A First Look at Macroeconomics

CHAPTER 19

What Will Your World Be Like?

During the past 100 years, the quantity of goods and services produced in Canada's farms, factories, shops, and offices has expanded more than twentyfold. As a result, we have a much higher standard of living than our grandparents had. Will production always expand?

For most of us, a high standard of living means finding a good job. What kind of job will you find when you graduate? Will you have lots of choice, or will you face a labour market with a high unemployment rate in which jobs are hard to find?

A high standard of living means being able to afford to buy life's necessities and have some fun. If prices rise too quickly, some people get left behind and must trim what they buy. What will the dollar buy next year; in ten years when you are paying off your student loan; and in 50 years when you are spending your life's savings in retirement?

Since 1997, the federal government has collected more in taxes than it has spent on public services. But for the 26 years before 1997, the government ran a deficit. How will government budget deficits and surpluses affect your future?

To keep production expanding and prevent an economic slowdown, the federal government and the Bank of Canada—the nation's financial managers—take policy actions. How do their actions influence production, jobs, prices, and the ability of Canadians to compete in the global marketplace?

◆ These are the questions of macroeconomics that you are about to study. In *Reading Between the Lines* at the end of the chapter, we'll take a quick look at Canada's macroeconomic performance in 2005.

After studying this chapter, you will be able to

■ Describe the origins and issues of macroeconomics

■ Describe the trends and fluctuations in economic growth

■ Describe the trends and fluctuations in jobs and unemployment

■ Describe the trends and fluctuations in inflation

■ Describe the trends and fluctuations in government and international deficits

■ Identify the macroeconomic policy challenges and describe the tools available for meeting them

Origins and Issues of Macroeconomics

ECONOMISTS BEGAN TO STUDY ECONOMIC growth, inflation, and international payments as long ago as the 1750s, and this work was the origin of macroeconomics. But modern macroeconomics did not emerge until the **Great Depression**, a decade (1929–1939) of high unemployment and stagnant production throughout the world economy. In the Depression's worst year, 1933, the production of Canada's farms, factories, shops, and offices was only 70 percent of its 1929 level and 20 percent of the labour force was unemployed. These were years of human misery on a scale that is hard to imagine today. They were also years of extreme pessimism about the ability of the market economy to work properly. Many people believed that private ownership, free markets, and democratic political institutions could not survive.

The science of economics had no solutions to the Great Depression. The major alternative system of central planning and socialism seemed increasingly attractive to many people. It was in this climate of economic depression and political and intellectual turmoil that modern macroeconomics emerged with the publication in 1936 of John Maynard Keynes' *The General Theory of Employment, Interest, and Money* (see pp. 530–531).

Short-Term Versus Long-Term Goals

Keynes' theory was that depression and high unemployment result from insufficient private spending and that to cure these problems, the government must increase its spending. Keynes focused primarily on the *short term*. He wanted to cure an immediate problem almost regardless of the *long-term* consequences of the cure. "In the long run," said Keynes, "we're all dead."

But Keynes believed that after his cure for depression had restored the economy to a normal condition, the long-term problems of inflation and slow economic growth would return. And he suspected that his cure for depression, increased government spending, might trigger inflation and might lower the long-term growth rate of production. With a lower long-term growth rate, the economy would create fewer jobs. If this outcome did occur, a policy aimed at lowering unemployment in the short run might end up increasing it in the long run.

By the late 1960s and through the 1970s, Keynes' predictions became a reality. Inflation increased, economic growth slowed, and in some countries unemployment became persistently high. The causes of these developments are complex. But they point to an inescapable conclusion: The long-term problems of inflation, slow growth, and persistent unemployment and the short-term problems of economic fluctuations intertwine and are most usefully studied together. So although macroeconomics was reborn during the Great Depression, it has now returned to its older tradition. Today, macroeconomics is a subject that tries to understand long-term economic growth and inflation as well as short-term business fluctuations and unemployment.

The Road Ahead

There is no unique way to study macroeconomics. Because its rebirth was a product of depression, the common practice for many years was to pay most attention to short-term output fluctuations and unemployment, but never to completely lose sight of the long-term issues. When a rapid inflation emerged during the 1970s, this topic returned to prominence. During the 1980s, when long-term growth slowed in Canada and other rich industrial countries but exploded in East Asia, economists redirected their energy towards economic growth. During the 1990s, as information technologies further shrank the globe, the international dimension of macroeconomics became more prominent. The result of these developments is that modern macroeconomics is a broad subject that studies all the issues we've just identified: economic growth and fluctuations, unemployment, inflation, and government and international deficits.

Over the past 40 years, economists have developed a clearer understanding of the forces that determine macroeconomic performance and have devised policies that they hope will improve this performance. Your main goal is to become familiar with the theories of macroeconomics and the policies that they make possible. To set you on your path towards this goal, we're going to take a first look at economic growth, jobs and unemployment, inflation, and surpluses and deficits, and learn why these macroeconomic phenomena merit our attention.

myeconlab   **Study Plan 19.1**

Growth and Fluctuations

YOUR PARENTS ARE RICHER THAN YOUR GRAND-parents were when they were young. But are you going to be richer than your parents are? And are your children going to be richer than you? The answers depend on the rate of economic growth.

Economic growth is the expansion of the economy's production possibilities. It can be pictured as an outward shift of the production possibilities frontier (*PPF*)—see Chapter 2, pp. 40–41.

We measure economic growth by the increase in real gross domestic product. **Real gross domestic product** (also called **real GDP**) is the value of the total production of all the nation's farms, factories, shops, and offices measured in the prices of a single year. Real GDP in Canada is currently measured in the prices of 1997 (called 1997 dollars). We use the dollar prices of a single year to eliminate the influence of *inflation*—the increase in the average level of prices—and determine how much production has grown from one year to another. (Real GDP is explained more fully in Chapter 20 on pp. 466–470.)

Real GDP is not a perfect measure of total production because it does not include everything that is produced. It excludes the things we produce for ourselves at home (preparing meals, doing laundry, house painting, gardening, and so on). It also excludes production that people hide to avoid taxes or because the activity is illegal—the underground economy. But despite its shortcomings, real GDP is the best measure of total production available. Let's see what it tells us about economic growth.

Growth and Fluctuations in Canada

Figure 19.1 shows real GDP in Canada since 1961 and highlights two features of economic growth:

- The growth of potential GDP
- Fluctuations of real GDP around potential GDP

The Growth of Potential GDP When all the economy's labour, capital, land, and entrepreneurial ability are fully employed, the value of production is called **potential GDP**. Real GDP fluctuates around potential GDP and the rate of long-term economic growth is measured by the growth rate of potential GDP. It is shown by the steepness of the potential GDP line (the black line) in Fig. 19.1.

From 1960 through 1973, potential GDP grew at an unusually rapid rate of 5.1 percent a year. But the growth rate slowed from the mid-1970s to the mid-1990s. The growth rate of output per person sagged during these years in a phenomenon called the **productivity growth slowdown**. The growth rate of potential GDP increased during the late 1990s and 2000s, but it is too soon to tell whether this increase is the beginning of a new phase of more rapid growth.

Why did the productivity growth slowdown occur? This question is controversial. We explore the causes of the productivity growth slowdown in Chapter 31. Whatever its cause, the slowdown means that we all have smaller incomes today than we would have had if the economy had continued to grow at its 1960s rate.

Let's now look at real GDP fluctuations around potential GDP.

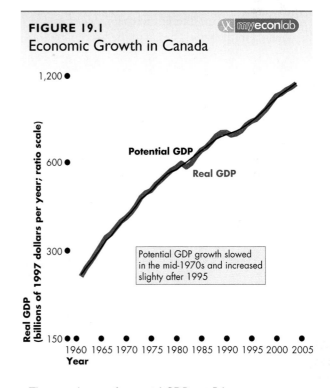

FIGURE 19.1
Economic Growth in Canada

The growth rate of potential GDP was 5.1 percent a year from 1960 through 1973. Growth slowed from the mid-1970s to the mid-1990s but sped up slightly after 1995. Real GDP fluctuates around potential GDP.

Sources of data: Real GDP, Statistics Canada, Table 380–0017. Potential GDP, calculated from Bank of Canada and International Monetary Fund estimates of the gap between actual real GDP and potential GDP.

Fluctuations of Real GDP Around Potential GDP
Real GDP fluctuates around potential GDP in a business cycle. A **business cycle** is the periodic but irregular up-and-down movement in production.

Business cycles are not regular, predictable, or repeating cycles like the phases of the moon. Their timing changes unpredictably. But cycles do have some things in common. Every business cycle has two phases:

1. A recession
2. An expansion

and two turning points:

1. A peak
2. A trough

Figure 19.2 shows these features of the most recent business cycle in Canada. A **recession** is a period during which real GDP decreases—the growth rate of real GDP is negative—for at least two successive quarters. The most recent recession, which is highlighted in the figure, began in the first quarter of

1990 and ended in the first quarter of 1991. This recession lasted for four quarters. An **expansion** is a period during which real GDP increases. The most recent expansion began in the second quarter of 1991. This expansion is the longest expansion on record. An earlier expansion ended in the first quarter of 1990.

When a business cycle expansion ends and a recession begins, the turning point is called a *peak*. The most recent peak occurred in the first quarter of 1990. When a business cycle recession ends and an expansion begins, the turning point is called a *trough*. The most recent trough occurred in the first quarter of 1991.

Recessions are rare. But real GDP sometimes sinks below potential GDP without a recession, when the growth rate remains positive. A **growth recession** occurs when the real GDP growth rate remains positive but slows so that real GDP falls below potential GDP. Three growth recessions occurred during the long expansion of the 1990s and 2000s: from the beginning of 1995 to the first quarter of 1996, from mid-2000 to mid-2001, and for most of 2003.

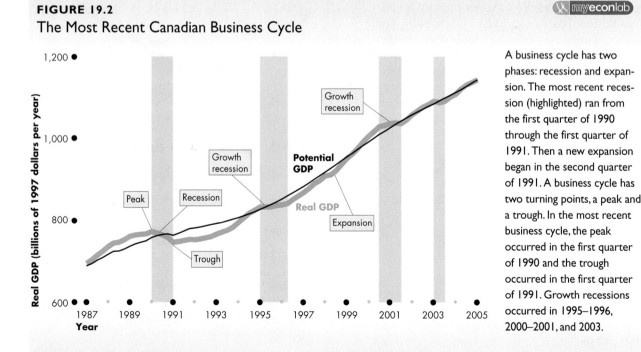

FIGURE 19.2
The Most Recent Canadian Business Cycle

A business cycle has two phases: recession and expansion. The most recent recession (highlighted) ran from the first quarter of 1990 through the first quarter of 1991. Then a new expansion began in the second quarter of 1991. A business cycle has two turning points, a peak and a trough. In the most recent business cycle, the peak occurred in the first quarter of 1990 and the trough occurred in the first quarter of 1991. Growth recessions occurred in 1995–1996, 2000–2001, and 2003.

Sources of data: Real GDP, Statistics Canada, Table 380–0017. Potential GDP, calculated from Bank of Canada and International Monetary Fund estimates of the gap between real GDP and potential GDP.

The Most Recent Recession in Historical Perspective Compared with earlier recessions, the 1991 recession was mild. You can see how mild by looking at Fig. 19.3, which shows a longer history of Canadian economic growth. The biggest decrease in real GDP occurred during the Great Depression of the 1930s. A decrease also occurred in 1946 and 1947, after a huge World War II expansion. A serious recession also occurred during the early 1980s, when the Bank of Canada and the Federal Reserve Board in the United States hiked interest rates to previously unimagined levels.

Each of these economic downturns was more severe than that in 1991. But you can see that the Great Depression was much more severe than anything that followed it. This episode was so extreme that we call it a *depression*.

This last truly great depression occurred before governments started taking policy actions to stabilize the economy. It also occurred before the birth of modern macroeconomics. Is the absence of another great depression a sign that macroeconomics has contributed to economic stability? Some people believe it is. Others doubt it. We'll

evaluate these opinions on a number of occasions in this book.

We've looked at real GDP growth and fluctuations in Canada. But is the Canadian experience typical? Do other countries share our experience? Let's see whether they do.

Economic Growth Around the World

All countries experience economic growth, but the growth rate varies both over time and across countries. The fluctuations in economic growth rates over time tend to be correlated across countries, but some countries experience greater volatility in growth rates than others. And some growth rate differences across countries persist over a number of years.

We'll compare Canada's economic growth over time with that in other countries. And we'll look at longer term differences in economic growth rates among countries and groups of countries.

Growth Rates over Time First, we'll compare the growth rate of real GDP per person in Canada with that in the three largest economies: the United States, Japan, and Germany.

FIGURE 19.3

Long-Term Economic Growth in Canada

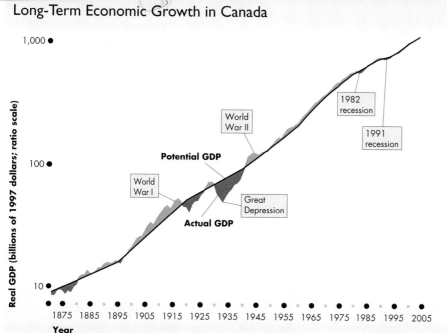

The thin black line shows potential GDP. Along this line, real GDP grew at an average rate of 3.7 percent a year between 1870 and 2004. The blue areas show when real GDP was above potential GDP, and the red areas show when it was below potential GDP. During some periods, such as World War II, real GDP expanded quickly. During other periods, such as the Great Depression and more recently in 1982 (following interest rate hikes) and 1991, real GDP declined.

Sources of data: 1870–1925, Angus Maddison, Dynamic Forces in Capitalist Development, Oxford University Press, New York, 1991. 1926–2001, and Statistics Canada, Historical Statistics of Canada, series F 55 and CANSIM series v1992292.

Figure 19.4(a) shows these four growth rates from 1960 to 2000 (from 1970 for Germany). You can see three striking facts in the figure. First, during the 1960s Japan's growth rate was much faster than that in the other countries. Second, after 1970 all four growth rates were similar. And third, Canada's growth rate has been a bit less that that of the United States so the gap between Canada and the United States has widened slightly.

Persistent Differences in Growth Rates Second, we'll look at longer term persistent differences across countries. Figure 19.4(b) compares the growth of the Canadian economy with that of several other countries and regions from 1980 through 2004. Among the advanced economies (the red bars), the European Union has grown the slowest and the U.S. economy has grown fastest. Canada is just behind the United States.

Among the developing economies (the green bars) the most rapid growth has occurred in Asia, where the average growth rate was more than 7 percent a year. The slowest growing developing countries are in the Western Hemisphere (Central and South America) and Africa.

The transition economies (purple bar) include those of Russia and the countries of Central and Eastern Europe that are making a transition from a state-managed economy to a market economy. Growth in Central and Eastern Europe averaged 2 percent a year. But production in Russia has shrunk.

World average growth (the blue bar) has been 3.4 percent a year, somewhat greater than the Canadian growth rate.

Consequences of Persistent Differences The persistent differences in growth rates are bringing dramatic change in how world real GDP is shared across economies. Because Canada and the United States are growing more slowly than the world, the North American economy's share of world real GDP is falling. But some fast-growing nations such as China and India are becoming significantly bigger parts of the global economy. China's share of world real GDP increased from 4 percent in 1980 to 13 percent in 2004 and India increased from 2 percent in 1980 to 6 percent in 2004. And the share of these large Asian economies continues to expand. If the current trends persist, the Asian economy will be larger than that of North America by around 2020.

FIGURE 19.4
Economic Growth Around the World

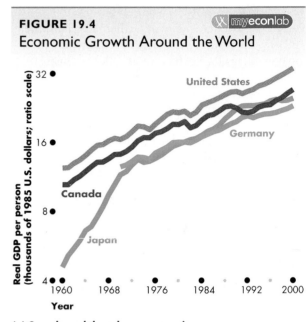

(a) Canada and three large economies

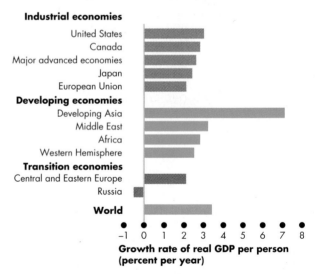

(b) Average growth rates: 1980–2004

In part (a), Japan grew fastest during the 1960s. Canadian economic growth has been a bit slower than that of the United States. In part (b), growth rate differences persist. Between 1980 and 2004, Asian economies grew fastest and the Russian economy shrank. The Canadian growth rate is a bit lower than the world average growth rate.

Source of data: Alan Heston, Robert Summers, and Bettina Aten, Penn World Table Version 6.1, Center for International Comparisons at the University of Pennsylvania (CICUP), October 2002. and International Monetary Fund, *World Economic Outlook*, September 2005, Washington, D.C.

The Lucas Wedge and the Okun Gap

You've seen that productivity growth slowed during the 1970s. And you've seen that real GDP growth fluctuates so that real GDP falls below potential GDP from time to time. How costly are the growth slowdown and lost output over the business cycle?

The answers are provided by two measures:

- The Lucas wedge
- The Okun gap

The Lucas Wedge The **Lucas wedge** is the accumulated loss of output that results from a slowdown in the growth rate of real GDP per person. It is given this name because Robert E. Lucas Jr., a leading macroeconomist, drew attention to it and remarked that once you begin to think about the benefits of faster economic growth, it is hard to think about anything else!

Figure 19.5(a) shows the Lucas wedge that arises from the productivity growth slowdown of the 1970s. The black line in the figure tracks the path that potential GDP would have followed if its 1960s growth rate had been maintained through the next 35 years to 2005.

The Lucas wedge is a staggering $11.5 trillion—10 years' real GDP at the 2005 level. This incredibly large number is a measure of the cost of slower productivity growth.

The Okun Gap Real GDP minus potential GDP is called the **output gap**. The output gap can be positive (real GDP exceeds potential GDP) or negative (potential GDP exceeds real GDP). When the output gap is negative, it is sometimes called the *Okun gap* because Arthur M. Okun, an economic adviser to President Lyndon Johnson, drew attention to it as a source of loss from economic fluctuations.

Figure 19.5(b) shows the Okun gap from the recessions that occurred over the same years as those for which we've just calculated the Lucas wedge.

The Okun gap is $173 billion—about two months of real GDP in 2005. This number is a measure of the cost of business cycle fluctuations.

You can see that the Lucas wedge is a much bigger deal than the Okun gap—*66 times* as big a deal! Smoothing the business cycle saves spells of high unemployment and lost output. But maintaining a high rate of productivity growth makes a dramatic difference to the standard of living.

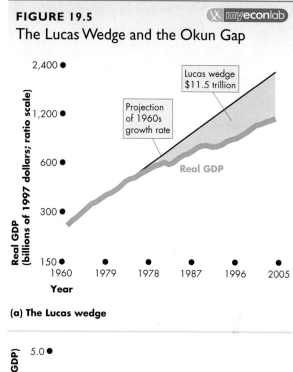

FIGURE 19.5

The Lucas Wedge and the Okun Gap

(a) The Lucas wedge

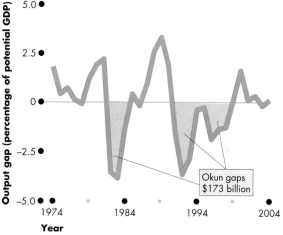

(b) The Okun gap

In part (a), the Lucas wedge that arises from the productivity growth slowdown of the 1970s is a staggering $11.5 trillion or ten times the real GDP of 2005.

In part (b), the Okun gap that arises from the lost production in recessions since the early 1970s amount to $173 billion or about two months of real GDP in 2005.

Over this 35-year period, the Lucas wedge is 66 times as large as the Okun gap.

Sources of data: Real GDP, Statistics Canada, Table 380–0017. Potential GDP calculated from Bank of Canada and International Monetary Fund estimates of the gap between actual and potential GDP. Growth projections are authors' calculations.

Benefits and Costs of Economic Growth

The Lucas wedge is a measure of the dollar value of lost real GDP if the growth rate slows. But this cost translates into real goods and services. It is a cost in terms of an inferior Canadian health-care system, fewer child-care services, worse roads, and less housing. We even have less to spend on cleaner lakes, more trees, and cleaner air.

But fast growth is also costly. Its main cost is forgone *current* consumption. To sustain a high growth rate, resources must be devoted to advancing technology and accumulating capital rather than to *current* consumption. This cost cannot be avoided. But it brings the benefit of greater consumption in the future. (See Chapter 2, p. 38.)

Two other possible costs of faster growth are a more rapid depletion of exhaustible natural resources such as oil and natural gas and increased pollution of the air, rivers, and oceans. But neither of these two costs is inevitable. The technological advances that bring economic growth help us to economize on natural resources and to clean up the environment. For example, more efficient auto engines cut gasoline use and tailpipe emissions.

REVIEW QUIZ

1 What is economic growth and how is the long-term economic growth rate measured?

2 What is the distinction between real GDP and potential GDP?

3 What is a business cycle and what are its phases?

4 What is a recession?

5 In what phase of the business cycle was the Canadian economy during 2005?

6 What happened to economic growth in Canada and other countries during the 1970s?

7 What are the benefits and the costs of long-term economic growth?

ⓧ myeconlab Study Plan 19.2

We've seen that real GDP grows and that it fluctuates over the business cycle. The business cycle brings fluctuations in the number of jobs available and in unemployment. Let's now examine these macroeconomic problems.

Jobs and Unemployment

WHAT KIND OF LABOUR MARKET WILL YOU ENTER when you graduate? Will there be plenty of good jobs to choose from, or will there be so much unemployment that you will be forced to take a low-paying job that doesn't use your education? The answer depends, to a large degree, on the total number of jobs available and on the unemployment rate.

Jobs

The Canadian economy is an incredible job-creating machine. In 2005, 16 million Canadians or 62 percent of those aged 15 years and older had jobs. That number is 2.7 million more than in 1995 and 4.4 million more than in 1985. Every year, on the average, since the mid-1970s, the Canadian economy has created about 220,000 *additional* jobs. Since 2000, it has created 1.6 million additional jobs.

The pace of job creation and destruction fluctuates over the business cycle. More jobs are destroyed than created during a recession, so the number of jobs decreases. For example, during the 1991 recession, Canadian production shrank and 260,000 jobs disappeared. But through the expansion that followed, the number of jobs created expanded quickly and many more jobs were created during the expansion than the number destroyed in the recession. By the beginning of 1995, there were more people at work than before the recession began.

Unemployment

Not everyone who wants a job can find one. On any one day in a normal or average year, more than 1 million people are unemployed, and during a recession or depression, unemployment rises above this level. For example, in November 1992, the worst month for unemployment in recent times, 1,740,000 people were looking for jobs.

Unemployment is defined as a state in which a person does not have a job but is available for work, willing to work, and has made some effort to find work within the previous four weeks. The total number of people who are employed and unemployed is called the **labour force**. The **unemployment rate** is the percentage of the people in the labour force who are unemployed. (The concepts of the labour force and unemployment are explained more fully in Chapter 21 on pp. 488–489.)

The unemployment rate is not a perfect measure of the underutilization of labour for several reasons. We'll review two of the main ones.

First, the unemployment rate excludes discouraged workers. A **discouraged worker** is a person who does not have a job, is available for work, and is willing to work but who has given up the effort to find work. Many people switch between the unemployed and discouraged worker categories in both directions every month. Second, the unemployment rate measures unemployed people rather than unemployed labour hours. As a result, the unemployment rate excludes part-time workers who want full-time jobs.

These limitations of unemployment tend to underestimate the amount of labour market slack. But despite them, the unemployment rate is the best available measure of underused labour resources. Let's look at some facts about unemployment.

Unemployment in Canada

Figure 19.6 shows the unemployment rate in Canada from 1926 through 2005. Three features stand out. First, during the Great Depression of the 1930s, the unemployment rate climbed to an all-time high of almost 20 percent during 1933 and remained high throughout the 1930s.

Second, the unemployment rate reached an all-time low of 1.2 percent during World War II.

Third, although in recent years we have not experienced anything as devastating as the Great Depression, we have seen some high unemployment rates during recessions. The figure highlights two of them—the 1982 recession and the 1991 recession.

Fourth, the unemployment rate never falls to zero. In the period since World War II, the average unemployment rate has been 6.7 percent.

How does Canadian unemployment compare with unemployment in other countries?

FIGURE 19.6
Unemployment in Canada

Unemployment is a persistent feature of economic life, but its rate varies. At its worst—during the Great Depression—20 percent of the labour force was unemployed. Even in recent recessions, the unemployment rate climbed towards 12 percent. Between the late 1960s and 1982, there was a general tendency for the unemployment rate to increase. Since 1982, the unemployment rate has remained below its 1982 peak and fell during the 1990s.

Sources of data: Statistics Canada, *Historical Statistics of Canada,* 2nd edition, 1983 and CANSIM Table 282–0002.

Unemployment Around the World

Figure 19.7 compares the unemployment rate in Canada with those in Western Europe, Japan, and the United States. Over the period shown in this figure, Canadian unemployment averaged 9 percent, much higher than Japanese unemployment (which averaged 3.3 percent), and higher than U.S. unemployment (which averaged 6.2 percent) and UK unemployment (which averaged 7.8 percent). Only the average of France, Italy, and Germany (9.2 percent) exceeded that of Canada.

Unemployment rates in all the countries fluctuate over the business cycle, increasing during a recession and decreasing during an expansion. The cycles in Canadian unemployment are similar to those in U.S. unemployment, but the European cycle is out of phase with the North American cycle.

During the past 25 years, the trend in U.S. unemployment has been downward and during the past 15 years, the trend in Japanese unemployment has been upward. The unemployment rates of Canada and Western Europe display no trends.

Let's now look at some of the consequences of unemployment that make it the serious problem that it is.

Why Unemployment Is a Problem

Unemployment is a serious economic, social, and personal problem for two main reasons:

- Lost production and incomes
- Lost human capital

Lost Production and Incomes The loss of a job brings an immediate loss of income and production. These losses are devastating for the people who bear them and make unemployment a frightening prospect for everyone. Employment insurance creates a safety net, but it does not provide the same living standard that having a job provides.

Lost Human Capital Prolonged unemployment can permanently damage a person's job prospects. For example, a manager loses his job when his employer downsizes. Short of income, he becomes a taxi driver. After a year in this work, he discovers that he can't compete with new MBA graduates. He eventually gets hired as a manager but in a small firm and at a low wage. He has lost some of his human capital.

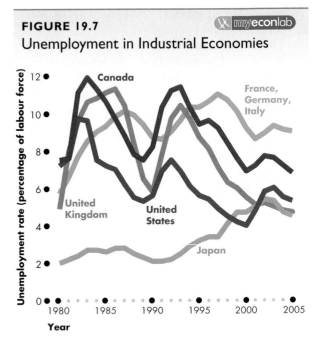

FIGURE 19.7
Unemployment in Industrial Economies

The unemployment rate in Canada has been higher, on the average, than the unemployment rates of the United States, the United Kingdom, and Japan. Only France, Italy, and Germany have higher average unemployment rates than Canada. The cycle in Canadian unemployment is similar to that in U.S. unemployment but out of phase with that in Western Europe.

Source of data: International Monetary Fund, *World Economic Outlook,* September 2005, Washington, D.C.

The costs of unemployment are spread unequally, which makes unemployment a highly charged political problem as well as a serious economic problem.

REVIEW QUIZ

1 What have been the main trends and cycles in the unemployment rate in Canada since 1926?
2 Compare unemployment in Canada, the United States, Western Europe, and Japan.
3 What are the main costs of unemployment that make it a serious problem?

myeconlab Study Plan 19.3

Let's now turn to the third major macroeconomic issue: inflation.

Inflation

PRICES ON THE AVERAGE CAN BE RISING, FALLING, or stable. **Inflation** is a process of rising prices. We measure the *inflation rate* as the percentage change in the *average* level of prices or the **price level**. A common measure of the price level is the *Consumer Price Index* (CPI). The CPI tells us how the average price of all the goods and services bought by a typical urban household changes from month to month. (The CPI is explained in Chapter 21, p. 498.)

So that you can see how the inflation rate is measured, let's do a calculation. In December 2003, the CPI was 122.3, and in December 2004, it was 124.6, so the inflation rate during 2004 was

$$\text{Inflation rate} = \frac{124.6 - 122.3}{122.3} \times 100$$

$$= 1.9 \text{ percent.}$$

Inflation in Canada

Figure 19.8 shows the Canadian inflation rate from 1960 through 2005. During the early 1960s, the inflation rate was low. It began to increase during the late 1960s at the time of the Vietnam War. But the largest increases occurred in 1974 and 1980, years in which the actions of the Organization of Petroleum Exporting Countries (OPEC) resulted in exceptionally large increases in the price of oil. Inflation was brought under control in the early 1980s when Bank of Canada Governor Gerald Bouey and U.S. Federal Reserve Chairman Paul Volcker pushed interest rates up and people cut back on their spending. Since the early 1990s, inflation has been kept inside an announced target range of between 1 percent and 3 percent a year.

The inflation rate rises and falls over the years, but it rarely becomes negative. If the inflation rate is negative, the price *level* is falling and we have **deflation**. Since the 1930s, the price level has generally increased—the inflation rate has been positive.

FIGURE 19.8
Inflation in Canada

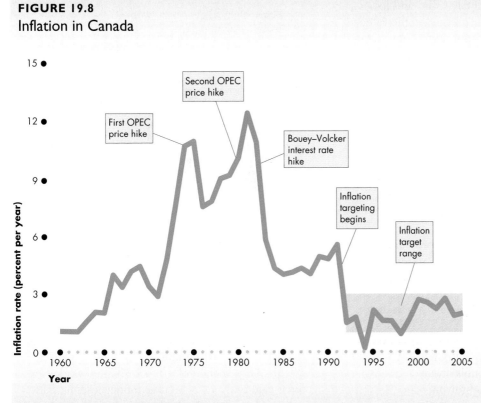

Inflation is a persistent feature of economic life in Canada. The inflation rate was low in the first half of the 1960s, but it increased during the late 1960s at the time of the Vietnam War. The inflation rate increased further with the OPEC oil price hikes but eventually declined in the early 1980s because of policy actions taken by the Bank of Canada. Since the early 1990s the Bank of Canada has kept the inflation rate inside a target range of 1 to 3 percent a year.

Source of data: Statistics Canada, CANSIM Table 326–0002.

Inflation Around the World

Figure 19.9 shows inflation around the world since 1970. It also shows the Canadian inflation rate in a broader perspective. Part (a) shows that the other industrial countries shared Canada's burst of double-digit inflation during the 1970s and the decline in inflation during the 1980s and 1990s. But Canada has achieved a lower inflation rate than most countries. Part (b) shows that the average inflation rate of industrial countries has been very low compared with that of developing counties. Among the developing countries, the most extreme inflation in recent times occurred in the Democratic Republic of Congo, where the inflation rate was 23,773 percent a year in 1994!

Is Inflation a Problem?

A very low inflation rate is not a problem. But a high inflation rate is a serious problem. It makes inflation hard to predict, and unpredictable inflation makes the economy behave a bit like a casino in which some people gain and some lose and no one can predict where the gains and losses will fall. Gains and losses occur because of unpredictable changes in the value of money. Money is used as a measuring rod of value in the transactions that we undertake. Borrowers and lenders, workers and employers, all make contracts in terms of money. If the value of money varies unpredictably over time, then the amounts *really* paid and received—the quantity of goods that the money will buy—also fluctuate unpredictably. Measuring value with a measuring rod whose units vary is a bit like trying to measure a piece of cloth with an elastic ruler. The size of the cloth depends on how tightly the ruler is stretched.

In a period of rapid, unpredictable inflation, resources get diverted from productive activities to forecasting inflation. It becomes more profitable to forecast the inflation rate correctly than to invent a new product. Doctors, lawyers, accountants, farmers—just about everyone—can make themselves better off, not by specializing in the profession for which they have been trained but by spending more of their time dabbling as amateur economists and inflation forecasters and managing their investment portfolios.

From a social perspective, this diversion of talent resulting from inflation is like throwing scarce resources onto the garbage heap. This waste of resources is a cost of inflation.

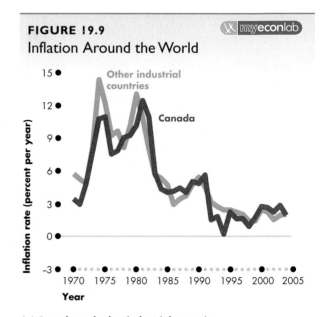

FIGURE 19.9

Inflation Around the World

(a) Canada and other industrial countries

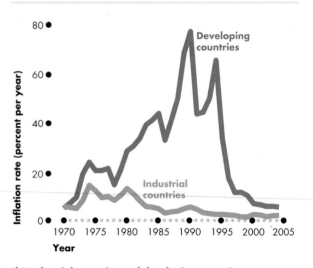

(b) Industrial countries and developing countries

Inflation in Canada is similar to that in other industrial countries. Compared with developing countries, inflation in Canada and the other industrial countries is low.

Sources of data: International Monetary Fund, *International Financial Statistics Yearbook*, Washington, D.C., 2004.

The most serious type of inflation is called *hyperinflation*—an inflation rate that exceeds 50 percent a month. At the height of a hyperinflation, workers are often paid twice a day because money loses its value so quickly. As soon as workers are paid, they rush out to spend their wages before they lose too much value.

Hyperinflation is rare but there have been some spectacular examples of it. Several European countries experienced hyperinflation during the 1920s after World War I and again during the 1940s after World War II. During these episodes, money became utterly worthless and the financial system collapsed.

But hyperinflation is more than just a historical curiosity. It can occur at any time. In 1994, when the Democratic Republic of Congo had an inflation rate of 23,773 percent a year, its price level was rising by 58 percent a month! Bolivia, Nicaragua, and Peru have had inflation rates in exess of 10,000 percent a year—close to 50 percent a month—during the past 20 years.

Inflation imposes costs, but getting rid of inflation is also costly. Policies that lower the inflation rate increase the unemployment rate. Most economists think the increase in the unemployment rate that accompanies a fall in the inflation rate is temporary. But some economists say that higher unemployment is a permanent cost of low inflation. The cost of lowering inflation must be evaluated when an anti-inflation policy is pursued. You will learn more about inflation and the costs of curing it in Chapter 28.

REVIEW QUIZ

1 What is inflation and how does it influence the value of money?
2 How is inflation measured?
3 What has been Canada's inflation record since 1961?
4 How does inflation in Canada compare with inflation in other industrial countries and in developing countries?
5 What are some of the costs of inflation that make it a serious economic problem?

myeconlab Study Plan 19.4

Now that you've studied economic growth and fluctuations, unemployment, and inflation, let's turn to the fourth macroeconomic issue: surpluses and deficits. What happens when a government spends more than it collects in taxes? And what happens when a nation buys more from other countries than it sells to them? Do governments and nations face the problem that you and I would face if we spent more than we earned? Do they run out of funds? Let's look at these questions.

Surpluses and Deficits

IN 1998, FOR THE FIRST TIME IN ALMOST 30 YEARS, the federal government had a budget surplus. For 26 years, it had a deficit. And most years, Canada has an international deficit. What is the government budget surplus and deficit? What is an international deficit?

Government Budget Surplus and Deficit

If a government collects more in taxes than it spends, it has a surplus—a **government budget surplus**. If a government spends more than it collects in taxes, it has a deficit—a **government budget deficit**. The federal government had a surplus in 2004.

Figure 19.10(a) shows the federal government and total government budget surplus and deficit from 1960 to 2005. (Total government is federal, provincial, and local governments.) So that we can compare the surplus or deficit in one year with that in another year, we measure the surplus or deficit as a percentage of GDP. (The concept of GDP, which is explained more fully in Chapter 20, pp. 466–470, equals total income in the economy.) You can think of this measure as the number of cents of surplus or deficit per dollar of income earned by an average Canadian.

The total government had a budget deficit every year from 1975 through 1996. The government deficit fluctuated and swelled during recessions. From 1982 through 1996, the deficit was never less than 2 percent of GDP.

Since 1993, the federal government deficit has shrunk, and in 1998, a surplus emerged. Since 1998, the federal budget surplus has become larger. In 2004, the federal government surplus was 1.5 percent of GDP.

International Surplus and Deficit

When we import goods and services from the rest of the world, we make payments to foreigners. When we export goods and services to the rest of the world, we receive payments from foreigners. If our imports exceed our exports, we have an international deficit.

Figure 19.10(b) shows the history of Canada's international balance from 1960 to 2004. The figure shows the balance on the **current account**, which includes our exports minus our imports but also takes into account interest payments paid to and received from the rest of the world. To compare

FIGURE 19.10
Government Budget and International Surpluses and Deficits

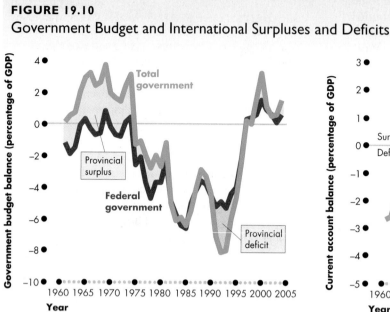

(a) Canadian government budget balance

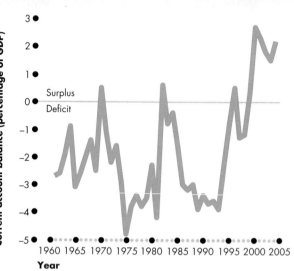

(b) Canadian international balance

In part (a), the federal government had a large and persistent deficit from 1970 to1996. The provincial governments
had a large deficit during the early 1990s.

In part (b), the Canadian current account shows the balance
of our exports minus our imports. In most years since

1970, Canada has had an international deficit. The deficit
became large during the mid-1970s and early 1980s. It per-
sisted at around 3 to 4 percent of GDP through the mid-
1990s. From 1999 to 2004, Canada had an international
surplus.

Source of data: Statistics Canada, CANSIM Tables 376–0001, 380–0002, and 380–0007.

one year with another, the figure shows the current
account as a percentage of GDP. In 2001, Canada
had a current account surplus of 2.8 percent of
GDP. But in most years, Canada has had a current
account deficit and it has fluctuated. From 1986 to
1995, the deficit was persistently around 3 percent
to 4 percent of GDP. Our imports have exceeded
our exports during these years. In 1996 and
between 1999 and 2004, Canada had a current
account surplus.

Do Surpluses and Deficits Matter?

Why do deficits cause anxiety? What happens when a
government cannot cover its spending with taxes, or
when a country buys more from other countries than
it sells to them?

If you spend more than you earn, you have a
deficit. And to cover your deficit, you go into debt.
But when you borrow, you must pay interest on your

debt. Just like you, if a government or a nation has a
deficit, it must borrow. And like you, the government
and the nation must pay interest on their debts.

Whether borrowing and paying out huge
amounts of interest is a good idea depends on what
the borrowed funds are used for. If you borrow to
finance a vacation, you must eventually tighten your
belt, cut spending, and repay your debt as well as pay
interest on the debt. But if you borrow to invest in a
business that earns a large profit, you might be able
to repay your debt and pay the interest on it while
continuing to increase your spending. It is the same
with a government and a nation. A government or a
nation that borrows to increase its consumption
might be heading for trouble later. But a government
or a nation that borrows to buy assets that earn a
profit might be making a sound investment.

You will learn more about the government's
budget surplus in Chapter 24 and about the international current account in Chapter 32.

1 What determines a government's budget deficit or budget surplus?
2 How have the budgets of the federal government and the provincial governments evolved since 1971?
3 What is a country's international deficit?
4 How has the Canadian international deficit changed since 1971?

myeconlab Study Plan 19.5

Macroeconomic Policy Challenges and Tools

FROM THE TIME OF ADAM SMITH'S *Wealth of Nations* in 1776 until the publication of Keynes' *General Theory of Employment, Interest, and Money* in 1936, it was widely believed that the only economic role for government was to enforce property rights. The economy behaved best, it was believed, if the government left people free to pursue their own best interests. The macroeconomics of Keynes challenged this view. Keynes' central point was that the economy will not fix itself and that government actions are needed to achieve and maintain full employment. The Canadian government declared full employment as a policy goal soon after World War II ended.

Policy Challenges and Tools

Today, the five widely agreed challenges for macroeconomic policy are to

1. Reduce unemployment
2. Boost economic growth
3. Stabilize the business cycle
4. Keep inflation low
5. Reduce government and international deficits

But how can we do all these things? What are the tools available to pursue the macroeconomic policy challenges? Macroeconomic policy tools are divided into two broad categories:

■ Fiscal policy
■ Monetary policy

Fiscal Policy Making changes in tax rates and in government spending programs is called **fiscal policy**. This range of actions is under the control of the federal government. Fiscal policy can be used to try to boost long-term growth by creating incentives that encourage saving, investment, and technological change. Fiscal policy can also be used to try to smooth out the business cycle. When the economy is in a recession, the government might cut taxes or increase its spending. Conversely, when the economy is in a rapid expansion, the government might increase taxes or cut its spending in an attempt to slow real GDP growth and prevent inflation from increasing. Fiscal policy is discussed in Chapter 24.

Monetary Policy Changing interest rates and changing the amount of money in the economy is called **monetary policy**. These actions are under the control of the Bank of Canada. The principal aim of monetary policy is to keep inflation in check. To achieve this objective, the Bank prevents the quantity of money from expanding too rapidly. Monetary policy can also be used to smooth the business cycle. When the economy is in recession, the Bank might lower interest rates and inject money into the economy. And when the economy is in a rapid expansion, the Bank might increase interest rates in an attempt to slow real GDP growth and prevent inflation from increasing. We study monetary policy in Chapter 28.

1 What are the main challenges of macroeconomic policy?
2 What are the main tools of macroeconomic policy?
3 Can you distinguish between fiscal policy and monetary policy?

myeconlab Study Plan 19.6

In your study of macroeconomics, you will learn what is currently known about the causes of unemployment, economic growth, business cycles, inflation, and government and international surpluses and deficits. You will also learn more about the policy choices and challenges that the government and the Bank of Canada face. *Reading Between the Lines* on pp. 460–461 examines unemployment, inflation, and economic growth in Canada in 2005.

Unemployment, Inflation, and Growth

THE GLOBE AND MAIL, OCTOBER 8, 2005

As unemployment rate declines, spectre of worker shortage raised

Canada's unemployment rate dropped back to a three-decade low in September, and a survey suggests companies are having increasing difficulty finding the right kinds of workers to support their growing businesses.

The unemployment rate fell 0.1 percentage points to 6.7 per cent last month, tying with June, 2005, for the lowest rate since March, 1976.

"There just isn't a huge supply of available and qualified workers," said Douglas Porter, deputy chief economist at BMO Nesbitt Burns. ...

About 19,200 full-time jobs were added to the economy in September, offset by a loss of about 21,400 part-time jobs, Statscan said.

While its report suggests companies weren't hiring much in September, firms told the Bank of Canada that they had strong intentions of hiring in the future.

In the central bank's quarterly Business Outlook Survey, 50 per cent of the companies surveyed said they intended to hire more people in the next 12 months.

And a whopping 51 per cent said they are facing labour shortages that restrict their ability to meet demand. That's up from 36 per cent in the bank's summer survey.

Regional differences in the Canadian economy are becoming more pronounced, the central bank said, with energy-rich Western Canada very optimistic about sales growth over the next year. About three-quarters of Western companies said they expect to hire more workers in the next year. ...

The central bank survey also pointed to signs of rising inflation expectations.

About one-quarter of the companies said they expect inflation to rise above the 3-per-cent ceiling on the bank's target band. And 60 per cent expect annual inflation to be in the top end of the target range.

The Statistics Canada jobs report also revealed some signs of inflation, with average hourly earnings rising 3.5 per cent from a year earlier — higher than in August, and higher than the national inflation rate of 2.6 per cent. ...

Essence of the Story

■ In September 2005, Canada's unemployment rate was 6.7 percent.

■ This unemployment rate was the lowest since 1976.

■ Full-time jobs replaced part-time jobs.

■ Surveys showed that businesses were expected serious labour shortages in the near future.

■ A survey by the Bank of Canada revealed that more people were expecting the inflation rate to rise.

■ Regional differences existed with the strongest growth occurring in the energy sector of Western Canada.

Economic Analysis

■ The Canadian economy experienced a falling unemployment rate throughout 2004 and 2005.

■ Figure 1 shows this unemployment record.

■ When the unemployment rate falls too low, labour shortages arise that might make wage rates rise more rapidly.

■ If wage rates do rise more rapidly, inflation might increase.

■ The Bank of Canada survey of inflation expectations reported in the news article found some signs that people were beginning to think a higher inflation rate was coming.

■ There was little evidence in the actual inflation performance of 2004 and 2005 to support the expectation of higher inflation.

■ Figure 2 shows the inflation rate in 2004 and 2005. Despite a rising inflation rate during 2005, the rate remained firmly inside the Bank of Canada's target range of 1 percent to 3 percent a year.

■ The news article says that the Canadian economy is experiencing differnt rates of growth in different sectors.

■ In particular, it points to more rapid growth in the energy sectors of Western Canada.

■ Figure 3 provides some perspective on this observation.

■ The figure shows the growth rates of production in various industries in the year from July 2004 to July 2005 (the most recent data available at the time of writing.)

■ The sectors that are growing fastest are *not* those associated with energy. Mining and oil and gas extraction expanded more slowly than the national average.

■ It was retail trade, wholesale trade, information and cultural industries, utilities, education services, construction, finance, insurance and real estate, administrative and waste management services, transportation and warehousing—all services, that expanded the most quickly.

■ It is because sectors expand at different rates with some sectors shrinking that labour is reallocated and that unemployment arises.

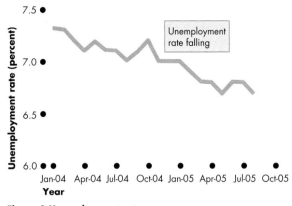

Figure 1 Unemployment rate

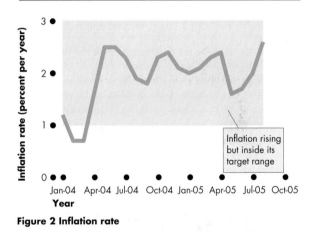
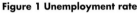

Figure 2 Inflation rate

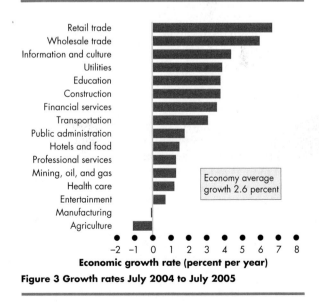

Figure 3 Growth rates July 2004 to July 2005

461

SUMMARY

KEY POINTS

Origins and Issues of Macroeconomics (p. 446)

- Macroeconomics studies economic growth and fluctuations, jobs and unemployment, inflation, and surpluses and deficits.

Growth and Fluctuations (pp. 447–452)

- Economic growth is the expansion of potential GDP. Real GDP fluctuates around potential GDP in a business cycle.
- The main benefit of long-term economic growth is higher future consumption, and the main cost is lower current consumption.
- Slow productivity growth (the Lucas wedge) is more costly than the business cycle (the Okun gap).

Jobs and Unemployment (pp. 452–454)

- The Canadian economy creates about 200,000 jobs a year but unemployment persists.
- Canadian unemployment increases during a recession and decreases during an expansion.
- The Canadian unemployment rate is higher than that in the United States and Japan.
- Unemployment can permanently damage a person's job prospects.

Inflation (pp. 455–457)

- Inflation, a process of rising prices, is measured by the percentage change in the CPI.
- Inflation is a problem because it lowers the value of money and makes money less useful as a measuring rod of value.

Surpluses and Deficits (pp. 457–459)

- When the government collects more in taxes than it spends, the government has a budget surplus. When the government spends more than it collects in taxes, the government has a budget deficit.

- When imports exceed exports, a nation has an international deficit.
- Deficits are financed by borrowing.

Macroeconomic Policy Challenges and Tools (p. 459)

- The macroeconomic policy challenge is to use fiscal policy and monetary policy to boost long-term growth, stabilize the business cycle, lower unemployment, tame inflation, and prevent large deficits.

KEY FIGURES

Figure 19.1   Economic Growth in Canada, 447
Figure 19.2   The Most Recent Canadian Business Cycle, 448
Figure 19.3   Long-Term Economic Growth in Canada, 449
Figure 19.6   Unemployment in Canada, 453
Figure 19.8   Inflation in Canada, 455
Figure 19.10 Government Budget and International Surpluses and Deficits, 458

KEY TERMS

Business cycle, 448
Current account, 457
Deflation, 455
Discouraged worker, 453
Economic growth, 447
Expansion, 448
Fiscal policy, 459
Government budget deficit, 457
Government budget surplus, 457
Great Depression, 446
Growth recession, 448
Inflation, 455
Labour force, 452
Lucas wedge, 451
Monetary policy, 459
Output gap, 451
Potential GDP, 447
Price level, 455
Productivity growth slowdown, 447
Real gross domestic product (real GDP), 447
Recession, 448
Unemployment, 452
Unemployment rate, 452

PROBLEMS

Go to [X myeconlab] for solutions to odd-
numbered problems and additional exercises.

1. In which country in 1992 was
   a. The growth rate of real GDP highest: Canada, Japan, or the United States?
   b. The unemployment rate highest: Canada, Japan, the United Kingdom, or the United States?
   c. The inflation rate lowest: Canada, Germany, the United Kingdom, or the United States?
   d. The government budget deficit (as a percentage of GDP) largest: Canada, Japan, the United Kingdom, or the United States?

2. In which country in 2000 was
   a. The growth rate of real GDP highest: Canada, Japan, or the United States?
   b. The unemployment rate lowest: Canada, Japan, the United Kingdom, or the United States?
   c. The inflation rate lowest: Canada, the United Kingdom, Japan, or the United States?
   d. The government budget surplus (as a percentage of GDP) smallest: Canada, the United Kingdom, or the United States?
   e. Is it possible to say in which country consumption possibilities are growing fastest? Why or why not?

3. The figure shows the real GDP growth rates in India and Pakistan from 1989 to 1996.

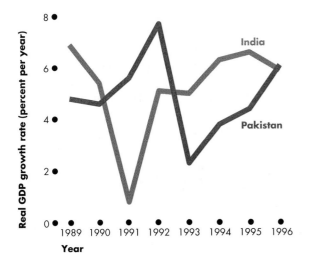

   a. In which years did economic growth in
      i. India increase? And in which year was growth the fastest?
      ii. Pakistan decrease? And in which year was growth the slowest?
   b. Compare the paths of economic growth in India and Pakistan during this period.

4. The figure shows the growth rate of real GDP per person in Australia and Japan from 1989 to 1996.

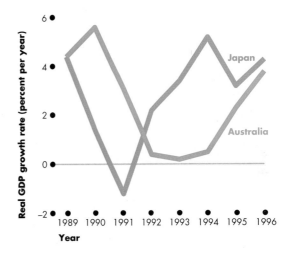

   a. In which years did economic growth in
      i. Australia increase? And in which year was growth the fastest?
      ii. Japan decrease? And in which year was growth the slowest?
   b. Compare the paths of economic growth in Australia and Japan during this period.

5. The figure shows real GDP in Germany from the first quarter of 1991 to the second quarter of 1994.

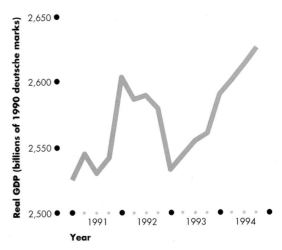

a. How many recessions did Germany experience during this period?

b. In which quarters, if any, did Germany experience a business cycle peak?

c. In which quarters, if any, did Germany experience a business cycle trough?

d. In which quarters, if any, did Germany experience an expansion?

6. The table shows Canada's rate of economic growth during 2004 and the first two quarters of 2005.

	2004	2005
First quarter	0.6	0.5
Second quarter	1.2	0.8
Third quarter	0.9	
Fourth quarter	0.5	

a. Did Canada experience a recession during this period?

b. Did the economic growth rate speed up or slow down during 2004 and 2005?

c. Which of the two years had the highest average economic growth rate?

7. Use Data Graphing on **MyEconLab** to answer the following questions. In 1998, which country—Canada, Japan, the United Kingdom, or the United States—had

a. The largest budget deficit?

b. A current account surplus?

8. Use Data Graphing on **MyEconLab** to answer the following questions. In 2002, which country—Canada, Japan, the United Kingdom, or the United States—had

a. The largest budget surplus?

b. The largest current account deficit?

9. Use Data Graphing on **MyEconLab** to make a scatter diagram of the inflation rate and the unemployment rate in Canada.

a. Describe the relationship.

b. Do you think that low unemployment brings an increase in the inflation rate?

10. Use Data Graphing on **MyEconLab** to make a scatter diagram of the government budget deficit as a percentage of GDP and the unemployment rate in Canada.

a. Describe the relationship.

b Do you think that low unemployment brings a decrease in the budget deficit?

CRITICAL THINKING

1. Study *Reading Between the Lines* on pp. 460–461 and then answer the following questions

a. What happened to Canada's unemployment rate during 2004 and 2005?

b. What happened to Canada's inflation rate during 2004 and 2005?

c. Which sectors of the Canadian economy experienced the fastest growth during 2004 and 2005?

d. Which sectors of the Canadian economy experienced the slowest growth or even shrank during 2004 and 2005?

WEB EXERCISES

Use the links on (X) myeconlab to work the following exercises.

1. Get the latest data on real GDP, unemployment, and inflation in Canada.

a. Update Figs. 19.2, 19.6, and 19.8.

b. What dangers does the Canadian economy face today?

c. What actions, if any, do you think might be needed to keep the economy strong?

2. Get data on the unemployment rate in your home province.

a. Compare unemployment in your home province with that in Canada as a whole.

b. Why do you think your province might have a higher or a lower unemployment rate than the Canadian average?

3. Get data on the Consumer Price Index for the capital city in your home province.

a. Compare the inflation rate in the capital city of your home province with that in Canada as a whole.

b. Compare the inflation rate in the capital city of your home province with that of the capital cities in neighbouring provinces.

4. Get data on the following variables for Canada for the most recent period. Describe how the following variables have changed over the last year.

a. The unemployment rate

b. The inflation rate

c. The government budget surplus or deficit

d. The international deficit

Measuring GDP and Economic Growth

CHAPTER 20

An Economic Barometer

Will our economy keep expanding through 2006 and 2007? And will the expansion be rapid or slow? Or are we going to slip into recession? Many Canadian companies wanted to know the answer to this question. Nortel wanted to know whether to hire more workers or delay the hirings for a while. Bombardier wanted to know whether to expand its capacity to build railroad engines. To assess the state of the economy and to make big decisions about business expansion and contraction, firms such as Nortel and Bombardier use forecasts of GDP. What exactly *is* GDP and how can we use it to tell us how rapidly our economy is expanding or if we are headed towards recession?

To reveal the growth or shrinkage of GDP, we must remove the effects of inflation and assess how *real* GDP is changing. How do we remove the inflation component of GDP to reveal *real* GDP?

Some countries are rich while others are poor. How do we compare economic well-being in one country with that in another? How can we make international comparisons of GDP?

◆ In this chapter, you will find out how economic statisticians measure GDP, real GDP, and the economic growth rate. You will also learn about the limitations of these measures. In *Reading Between the Lines* at the end of the chapter, we'll look at Canadian real GDP during 2005.

After studying this chapter, you will be able to

- **Define GDP and use the circular flow model to explain why GDP equals aggregate expenditure and aggregate income**

- **Explain the two ways of measuring GDP**

- **Explain how we measure *real* GDP and the GDP deflator**

- **Explain how we use real GDP to measure economic growth and describe the limitations of our measure**

Gross Domestic Product

WHAT EXACTLY IS GDP, HOW IS IT CALCULATED, what does it mean, and why do we care about it? You are going to discover the answers to these questions in this chapter. First, what *is* GDP?

GDP Defined

GDP, or **gross domestic product**, is the market value of all the final goods and services produced within a country in a given time period. This definition has four parts:

- Market value
- Final goods and services
- Produced within a country
- In a given time period

We'll examine each in turn.

Market Value To measure total production, we must add together the production of apples and oranges, computers and popcorn. Just counting the items doesn't get us very far. For example, which is the greater total production: 100 apples and 50 oranges, or 50 apples and 100 oranges?

GDP answers this question by valuing items at their *market values*—at the prices at which each item is traded in markets. If the price of an apple is 10¢, the market value of 50 apples is $5. If the price of an orange is 20¢, the market value of 100 oranges is $20. By using market prices to value production, we can add the apples and oranges together. The market value of 50 apples and 100 oranges is $5 plus $20, or $25.

Final Goods and Services To calculate GDP, we value the *final goods and services* produced. A **final good** (or service) is an item that is bought by its final user during a specified time period. It contrasts with an **intermediate good** (or service), which is an item that is produced by one firm, bought by another firm, and used as a component of a final good or service.

For example, a Ford SUV is a final good, but a Firestone tire on the SUV is an intermediate good. A Dell computer is a final good, but an Intel Pentium chip inside the computer is an intermediate good.

If we were to add the value of intermediate goods and services produced to the value of final goods and services, we would count the same thing many times—a problem called *double counting*. The value of an SUV already includes the value of the tires, and the value of a Dell PC already includes the value of the Pentium chip inside it.

Some goods can be an intermediate good in some situations and a final good in other situations. For example, the ice cream that you buy on a hot summer day is a final good, but the ice cream that a café buys and uses to make sundaes is an intermediate good. The sundae is the final good. So whether a good is an intermediate good or a final good depends on what it is used for, not on what it is.

Some items that people buy are neither final goods nor intermediate goods. Examples of such items include financial assets—stocks and bonds—and second-hand goods—used cars and existing homes. These items are not part of GDP. But a used car and an existing home were part of GDP in the year in which they were produced.

Produced Within a Country Only goods and services that are produced *within a country* count as part of that country's GDP. Roots Canada Limited, a Canadian firm, produces T-shirts in Taiwan, and the market value of those T-shirts is part of Taiwan's GDP, not part of Canada's GDP. Toyota, a Japanese firm, produces automobiles in Cambridge, Ontario, and the value of this production is part of Canada's GDP, not part of Japan's GDP.

In a Given Time Period GDP measures the value of production *in a given time period*—normally either a quarter of a year (called the quarterly GDP data) or a year (called the annual GDP data).

GDP measures not only the value of total production but also total income and total expenditure. The equality between the value of total production and total income is important because it shows the direct link between productivity and living standards. Our standard of living rises when our incomes rise and we can afford to buy more goods and services. But we must produce more goods and services if we are to be able to buy more goods and services.

Rising incomes and a rising value of production go together. They are two aspects of the same phenomenon—increasing productivity. To see why, we study the circular flow of expenditure and income.

GDP and the Circular Flow of Expenditure and Income

Figure 20.1 illustrates the circular flow of expenditure and income. The economy consists of households, firms, governments, and the rest of the world (the diamonds), which trade in factor markets, goods (and services) markets, and financial markets. We focus first on households and firms.

Households and Firms Households sell and firms buy the services of labour, capital, and land in factor markets. For these factor services, firms pay income to households: wages for labour services, interest for the use of capital, and rent for the use of land. A fourth factor of production, entrepreneurship, receives profit.

Firms' retained earnings—profits that are not distributed to households—are part of the household sector's income. You can think of retained earnings as

being income that households save and lend back to firms. Figure 20.1 shows the total income—*aggregate income*—received by households, including retained earnings, by the blue dots labelled *Y*.

Firms sell and households buy consumer goods and services—such as inline skates and haircuts—in the markets for goods and services. The total payment for these goods and services is **consumption expenditure**, shown by the red dots labelled *C*.

Firms buy and sell new capital equipment—such as computer systems, airplanes, trucks, and assembly line equipment—in the goods market. Some of what firms produce is not sold but is added to inventory. For example, if GM produces 1,000 cars and sells 950 of them, the other 50 cars remain in GM's inventory of unsold cars, which increases by 50 cars. When a firm adds unsold output to inventory, we can think of the firm as buying goods from itself. The purchase of new plant, equipment, and buildings and

---

FIGURE 20.1

The Circular Flow of Expenditure and Income

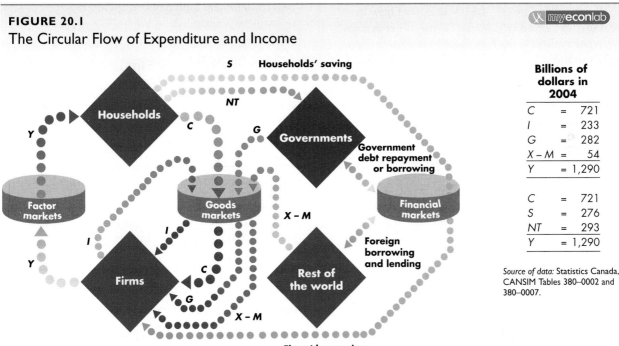

Billions of dollars in 2004		
C	=	721
I	=	233
G	=	282
X – M	=	54
Y	=	1,290
C	=	721
S	=	276
NT	=	293
Y	=	1,290

Source of data: Statistics Canada, CANSIM Tables 380–0002 and 380–0007.

In the circular flow of expenditure and income, households make consumption expenditures (*C*); firms make investment expenditures (*I*); governments purchase goods and services (*G*); and the rest of the world purchases net exports (*X – M*)—(red flows). Households receive incomes (*Y*) from firms (blue flow).

Aggregate income (blue flow) equals aggregate expenditure (red flows). Households use their income to consume (*C*), save (*S*), and pay net taxes (*NT*). Firms borrow to finance their investment expenditures, and governments and the rest of the world borrow to finance their deficits or lend their surpluses (green flows).

the additions to inventories are **investment**, shown by the red dots labelled *I*.

Governments Governments buy goods and services, called **government expenditures**, from firms. In Fig. 20.1, government expenditures on goods and services are shown as the red flow *G*. Governments use taxes to pay for their purchases. Figure 20.1 shows taxes as net taxes by the green dots labelled *NT*. **Net taxes** are equal to taxes paid to governments minus transfer payments received from governments. *Transfer payments* are cash transfers from governments to households and firms, such as social security benefits, unemployment compensation, and subsidies, and interest payments on the governments' debt.

Rest of the World Firms sell goods and services to the rest of the world, **exports**, and buy goods and services from the rest of the world, **imports**. The value of exports minus the value of imports is called **net exports**, which Fig. 20.1 shows by the red flow *X* – M.

If net exports are positive, there is a net flow from the rest of the world to Canadian firms. If net exports are negative, there is net flow from Canadian firms to the rest of the world.

GDP Equals Expenditure Equals Income Gross domestic product can be determined in two ways: by the total expenditure on goods and services or by the total income earned producing goods and services.

The total expenditure—*aggregate expenditure*—is the sum of the red flows in Fig. 20.1. Aggregate expenditure equals consumption expenditure plus investment plus government expenditures plus net exports.

Aggregate income earned producing goods and services is equal to the total amount paid for the factors used—wages, interest, rent, and profit. This amount is shown by the blue flow in Fig. 20.1. Because firms pay out as incomes (including retained profits) everything they receive from the sale of their output, income (the blue flow) equals expenditure (the sum of the red flows). That is,

$$Y = C + I + G + X - M.$$

The table in Fig. 20.1 shows the numbers for 2004. You can see that the sum of the expenditures is $1,290 billion, which also equals aggregate income.

Because aggregate expenditure equals aggregate income, these two methods of valuing GDP give the same answer. So

GDP equals aggregate expenditure and equals aggregate income.

The circular flow model is the foundation on which the national economic accounts are built.

Financial Flows

The circular flow model also enables us to see the connection between the expenditure and income flows and flows through the financial markets that finance deficits and pay for investment. These flows are shown in green in Fig. 20.1. Household **saving** (*S*) is the amount that households have left after they have paid their net taxes and bought their consumption goods and services. Government borrowing finances a government budget deficit. (Government lending arises when the government has a budget surplus.) And foreign borrowing pays for a deficit with the rest of the world. These financial flows are the sources of the funds that firms use to pay for their investment in new capital. Let's look a bit more closely at how investment is financed.

How Investment Is Financed

Investment adds to the stock of capital and is one of the determinants of the rate at which production grows. Investment is financed from three sources:

1. Private saving
2. Government budget surplus
3. Borrowing from the rest of the world

Private saving is the green flow labelled *S* in Fig. 20.1. Notice that households' income is consumed, saved, or paid in net taxes. That is,

$$Y = C + S + NT.$$

But you've seen that *Y* also equals the sum of the components of aggregate expenditure. That is,

$$Y = C + I + G + X - M.$$

By using these two equations, you can see that

$$I + G + X - M = S + NT$$

Now subtract *G* and *X* from both sides of the last equation and add *M* to both sides to obtain

$$I = S + (NT - G) + (M - X).$$

In the last equation, $(NT - G)$ is the government budget surplus and $(M - X)$ is borrowing from the rest of the world.

If net taxes (NT) exceed government expenditures (G), the government has a budget surplus equal to $(NT - G)$, and this surplus contributes towards paying for investment. If net taxes are less than government expenditures, the government has a budget deficit equal to $(NT - G)$, which is now negative. This deficit subtracts from the sources that finance investment.

If we import more than we export, we borrow an amount equal to $(M - X)$ from the rest of the world. So part of the rest of the world's saving finances investment in Canada. If we export more than we import, we lend an amount equal to $(X - M)$ to the rest of the world. So part of Canadian saving is used to finance investment in other countries.

The sum of private saving (S) and government saving $(NT - G)$ is called **national saving**. So investment is financed by national saving and foreign borrowing. In 2004, Canadian investment was $233 billion. National saving was $287 billion and $X - M$ was $54 billion. Canada lent $54 billion to the rest of the world.

Gross and Net Domestic Product

What does the "gross" in GDP mean? *Gross* means *before* accounting for the depreciation of capital. The opposite of gross is *net*, which means *after* accounting for the depreciation of capital. To understand what the depreciation of capital is and how it affects aggregate expenditure and income, we need to expand the accounting framework that we use and distinguish between flows and stocks.

Flows and Stocks in Macroeconomics A **flow** is a quantity per unit of time. The water that is running from an open faucet into a bathtub is a flow. So is the number of CDs you buy during a month and the amount of income that you earn during a month. GDP is a flow—the value of the final goods and services produced in a country *during a given time period*. Saving and investment are also flows.

A **stock** is a quantity that exists at a point in time. The water in a bathtub is a stock. So are the number of CDs that you own and the amount of money in your savings account. The two key stocks in macroeconomics are wealth and capital. And the flows of saving and investment change these stocks.

Wealth and Saving The value of all the things that people own is called **wealth**. What people own (a stock) is related to what they earn (a flow). People earn an income, which is the amount they receive during a given time period from supplying the services of factors of production. Income that is left after paying net taxes is either consumed or saved. *Consumption expenditure* is the amount spent on consumption goods and services. *Saving* is the amount of after-tax income remaining after consumption expenditures are met. So saving adds to wealth.

For example, suppose that at the end of the school year, you have $250 in a savings account and some textbooks that are worth $300. That's all you own. Your wealth is $550. Suppose that you take a summer job and earn an income after taxes of $5,000. You are extremely careful and spend only $1,000 through the summer on consumption goods and services. At the end of the summer, when school starts again, you have $4,250 in your savings account. Your wealth is now $4,550. Your wealth has increased by $4,000, which equals your saving of $4,000. Your saving of $4,000 equals your income after taxes of $5,000 minus your consumption expenditure of $1,000.

National wealth and national saving work just like this personal example. The wealth of a nation at the start of a year equals its wealth at the start of the previous year plus its saving during the year. Its saving equals its income after taxes minus its consumption expenditure.

Capital and Investment *Capital* is the plant, equipment, buildings, and inventories of raw materials and semi-finished goods that are used to produce other goods and services. The amount of capital in the economy exerts a big influence on GDP.

Two flows change the stock of capital: investment and depreciation. *Investment*, the purchase of new capital, increases the stock of capital. (Investment includes additions to inventories.) **Depreciation** is the decrease in the stock of capital that results from wear and tear and obsolescence. Another name for depreciation is **capital consumption**. The total amount spent on purchases of new capital and on replacing depreciated capital is called **gross investment**. The amount by which the stock of capital increases is called **net investment**.

Net investment = Gross investment − Depreciation.

Figure 20.2 illustrates these concepts. On January 1, 2006, Cindy's CDs, Inc., had 3 machines. This quantity was its initial capital. During 2006, Cindy's scrapped an older machine. This quantity is its depreciation. After depreciation, Cindy's stock of capital was down to 2 machines. But also during 2006, Cindy's bought 2 new machines. This amount is its gross investment. By December 31, 2006, Cindy's CDs had 4 machines, so its capital had increased by 1 machine. This amount is Cindy's net investment. Cindy's net investment equals its gross investment (the purchase of 2 new machines) minus its depreciation (1 machine scrapped).

The example of Cindy's CDs can be applied to the economy as a whole. The nation's capital stock decreases because capital depreciates and increases because of gross investment. The change in the nation's capital equals its net investment.

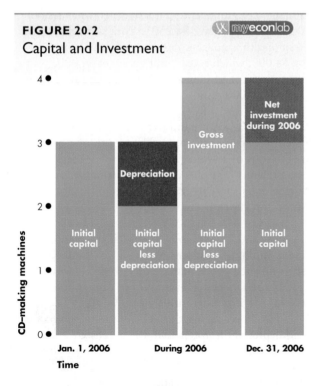

FIGURE 20.2

Capital and Investment

Cindy's CDs has a capital stock at Dec. 31, 2006 that equals its capital stock at Jan. 1, 2006 plus its net investment during 2006. Net investment is equal to gross investment less depreciation. Cindy's gross investment is the 2 new machines bought during the year, and its depreciation is the 1 machine that Cindy's scrapped during the year. Cindy's net investment is 1 machine.

Back to the Gross in GDP We can now see the distinction between gross domestic product and net domestic product. On the income side of the flows that measure GDP, a firm's *gross* profit is its profit *before* subtracting *depreciation*. A firm's gross profit is part of aggregate income, so depreciation is counted as part of gross income and GDP. Similarly, on the expenditure side of the flows that measure GDP, *gross investment* includes depreciation, so depreciation is counted as part of aggregate expenditure, and total expenditure is a gross measure.

Net domestic product excludes depreciation. Like GDP, net domestic product can be viewed as the sum of incomes or expenditures. Net income includes firms' *net* profits—profits *after* subtracting depreciation. And net expenditure includes *net* investment, which also excludes depreciation.

The Short Term Meets the Long Term The flows and stocks that you've just studied influence GDP growth and fluctuations. One of the reasons why GDP grows is that the capital stock grows. Investment adds to capital, so investment leads to GDP growth. But investment fluctuates, which brings fluctuations to GDP. So capital and investment along with wealth and saving are part of the key to understanding both GDP growth and fluctuations.

Investment and saving interact with income and consumption expenditure in a circular flow of expenditure and income. In this circular flow, income equals expenditure, which also equals the value of production. This equality is the foundation on which a nation's economic accounts are built and from which its GDP is measured.

REVIEW QUIZ

1 Define GDP. Distinguish between a final good and an intermediate good. Provide examples.
2 Why does GDP equal aggregate income and also equal aggregate expenditure?
3 How is Canadian investment financed? What determines national saving?
4 What is the distinction between gross and net?

myeconlab   **Study Plan 20.1**

Let's now see how the ideas that you've just studied are used in practice. We'll see how GDP and its components are measured in Canada today.

Measuring Canada's GDP

STATISTICS CANADA USES THE CONCEPTS THAT YOU met in the circular flow model to measure GDP and its components in the *National Income and Expenditure Accounts.* Because the value of aggregate output equals aggregate expenditure and aggregate income, there are two approaches available for measuring GDP, and both are used. They are

- The expenditure approach
- The income approach

The Expenditure Approach

The *expenditure approach* measures GDP as the sum of consumption expenditure (C), investment (I), government expenditures on goods and services (G), and net exports of goods and services ($X - M$), corresponding to the red flows in the circular flow model in Fig. 20.1. Table 20.1 shows the result of this approach for 2004. The table uses the terms in the *National Income and Expenditure Accounts.*

Personal expenditures on consumer goods and services are the expenditures by households on goods and services produced in Canada and in the rest of the world. They include goods such as CDs and books and services such as banking and legal advice. They do *not* include the purchase of new homes, which Statistics Canada counts as part of investment. But they do include the purchase of other consumer durable goods such as cars and microwave ovens.

Business investment is expenditure on capital equipment and buildings by firms and expenditure on new homes by households. It also includes the change in business inventories.

Government expenditures on goods and services are the purchases of goods and services by all levels of government. This item includes expenditures on national defence and garbage collection. But it does *not* include *transfer payments* because they are not purchases of goods and services.

Net exports of goods and services are the value of exports minus the value of imports. This item includes telephone equipment that Nortel sells to AT&T in the United States (a Canadian export), and Japanese DVD players that Sears buys from Sony (a Canadian import).

Table 20.1 shows the relative magnitudes of the four items of aggregate expenditure.

TABLE 20.1   GDP: The Expenditure Approach

Item	Symbol	Amount in 2004 (billions of dollars)	Percentage of GDP
Personal expenditures on consumer goods and services	C	721	56.0
Business investment	I	233	18.0
Government expenditures on goods and services	G	282	21.8
Net exports of goods and services	X – M	54	4.2
Gross domestic product	Y	1,209	100.0

The expenditure approach measures GDP as the sum of personal expenditures on consumer goods and services (C), business investment (I), government expenditures on goods and services (G), and net exports ($X - M$). In 2004, GDP measured by the expenditure approach was $1,290 billion. Personal expenditures on consumer goods and services is the largest expenditure item.

Source of data: Statistics Canada, CANSIM Table 380–0002.

The Income Approach

The *income approach* measures GDP by summing the incomes that firms pay households for the factors of production they hire—wages for labour, interest for capital, rent for land, and profits for entrepreneurship. Let's see how the income approach works.

The *National Income and Expenditure Accounts* divide incomes into five categories:

1. Wages, salaries, and supplementary labour income
2. Corporate profits
3. Interest and miscellaneous investment income
4. Farmers' income
5. Income from non-farm unincorporated businesses

Wages, salaries, and supplementary labour income is the payment for labour services. It includes net wages and salaries (called "take-home pay") plus taxes withheld plus benefits such as pension contributions.

Corporate profits are the profits of corporations, some of which are paid to households in the form of dividends and some of which are retained by corporations as undistributed profits. They are all income.

Interest and miscellaneous investment income is the interest households receive on loans they make minus the interest households pay on their own borrowing.

Farmers' income and *income from non-farm unincorporated businesses* are a mixture of the previous three items. They include compensation for labour, payment for the use of capital, and profit, lumped together in these two catch-all categories.

Table 20.2 shows these five incomes and their relative magnitudes.

The sum of the incomes is called *net domestic income at factor cost*. The term *factor cost* is used because it is the cost of the *factors of production* used to produce final goods and services. When we sum all the expenditures on final goods and services, we arrive at a total called *domestic product at market prices*. Market prices and factor cost would be the same except for indirect taxes and subsidies.

An *indirect tax* is a tax paid by consumers when they buy goods and services. (In contrast, a *direct tax* is a tax on income.) Provincial sales taxes, GST, and taxes on alcohol, gasoline, and tobacco products are indirect taxes. Because of indirect taxes, consumers pay more for some goods and services than producers receive. Market price exceeds factor cost. For example, if the sales tax is 7 percent, when you buy a $1 chocolate bar you pay $1.07. The factor cost of the chocolate bar including profit is $1. The market price is $1.07.

A *subsidy* is a payment by the government to a producer. Payments made to grain growers and dairy farmers are subsidies. Because of subsidies, consumers pay less for some goods and services than producers receive. Factor cost exceeds market price.

To get from factor cost to market price, we add indirect taxes and subtract subsidies. Making this adjustment brings us one step closer to GDP, but it does not quite get us there.

The final step is to add depreciation (or capital consumption). You can see the reason for this adjustment by recalling the distinction between gross and net profit and between gross and net investment. Total income is a net number because it includes firms' net profits, which exclude depreciation. Total expenditure is a gross number because it includes gross investment. So to get from total income to GDP, we must add depreciation to total income.

TABLE 20.2   GDP: The Income Approach

Item	Amount in 2004 (billions of dollars)	Percentage of GDP
Wages, salaries, and supplementary labour income	644	49.9
Corporate profits	187	14.5
Interest and miscellaneous investment income	55	4.3
Farmers' income	3	0.2
Income from non-farm unincorporated businesses	81	6.3
Indirect taxes *less* subsidies	148	11.5
Capital consumption (depreciation)	172	13.3
Gross domestic product	1,290	100.0

The sum of all incomes equals net domestic income at factor cost. GDP equals net domestic income at factor cost plus indirect taxes less subsidies plus capital consumption (depreciation). In 2004, GDP measured by the income approach was $1,290 billion. Wages, salaries, and supplementary labour income was by far the largest part of aggregate income.

Source of data: Statistics Canada, CANSIM Table 380–0001.

REVIEW QUIZ

1 What is the expenditure approach to measuring GDP?
2 What is the income approach to measuring GDP?
3 What adjustments must be made to total income to make it equal GDP?

myeconlab Study Plan 20.2

You now know how GDP is defined and measured. The dollar value of GDP can change because either prices change or the volume of goods and services produced changes. You are next going to learn how we unscramble these two sources of change in GDP to reveal changes in the volume of goods and services produced—changes in what we call *real* GDP.

Real GDP and the Price Level

YOU'VE SEEN THAT GDP MEASURES TOTAL expenditure on final goods and services in a given period. In 2004, GDP was $1,290 billion. The year before, in 2003, GDP was $1,216 billion. Because GDP in 2004 was greater than in 2003, we know that one or two things must have happened during 2004:

- We produced more goods and services in 2004 than in 2003.
- We paid higher prices for our goods and services in 2004 than we paid in 2003.

Producing more goods and services contributes to an improvement in our standard of living. Paying higher prices means that our cost of living has increased but our standard of living has not. So it matters a great deal why GDP has increased.

You're now going to learn how economists at Statistics Canada split GDP into two parts. One part tells us the change in production, and the other part tells us the change in prices. The method that is used has changed in recent years, and you are going to learn about the new method.

We measure the change in production by using a number that we call real GDP. **Real GDP** is the value of final goods and services produced in a given year when valued at constant prices. By comparing the value of the goods and services produced at constant prices, we can measure the change in the volume of production.

Calculating Real GDP

Table 20.3 shows the quantities produced and the prices in 2005 for an economy that produces only two goods: balls and bats. The first step towards calculating real GDP is to calculate **nominal GDP**, which is the value of the final goods and services produced in a given year valued at the prices that prevailed in that same year. Nominal GDP is just a more precise name for GDP that we use when we want to be emphatic that we are not talking about real GDP.

Nominal GDP Calculation To calculate nominal GDP in 2005, sum the expenditures on balls and bats in 2005 as follows:

Expenditure on balls = 100 balls × $1 = $100.

Expenditure on bats = 20 bats × $5 = $100.

Nominal GDP in 2005 = $100 + $100 = $200.

Table 20.4 shows the quantities produced and the prices in 2006. The quantity of balls produced increased to 160, and the quantity of bats produced increased to 22. The price of a ball fell to 50¢, and the price of a bat increased to $22.50. To calculate nominal GDP in 2006, we sum the expenditures on balls and bats in 2006 as follows:

Expenditure on balls = 160 balls × $0.50 = $80.

Expenditure on bats = 22 bats × $22.50 = $495.

Nominal GDP in 2006 = $80 + $495 = $575.

To calculate real GDP, we choose one year, called the *base year*, against which to compare the other years. In Canada today, the base year is 1997. The choice of the base year is not important. It is just a common reference point. We'll use 2005 as the base year. By definition, real GDP equals nominal GDP in the base year. So real GDP in 2005 is $200.

Base-Year Prices Value of Real GDP The base-year prices method of calculating real GDP, which is the traditional method, values the quantities produced in each year at the prices of the base year. Table 20.5 shows the prices in 2005 and the quantities in 2006 (based on the information in Tables 20.3 and

TABLE 20.3 GDP Data for 2005

Item	Quantity	Price
Balls	100	$1.00
Bats	20	$5.00

TABLE 20.4 GDP Data for 2006

Item	Quantity	Price
Balls	160	$ 0.50
Bats	22	$22.50

TABLE 20.5   2006 Quantities and 2005 Prices

Item	Quantity	Price
Balls	160	$1.00
Bats	22	$5.00

20.4). The value of the 2006 quantities at the 2005 prices is calculated as follows:

Expenditure on balls = 160 balls × $1.00 = $160.

Expenditure on bats = 22 bats × $5.00 = $110.

Value of the 2006 quantities at 2005 prices = $270.

Using the traditional base-year prices method, $270 would be recorded as real GDP in 2006.

Chain-Weighted Output Index Calculation The **chain-weighted output index** method, which is the new method of calculating real GDP, uses the prices of two adjacent years to calculate the real GDP growth rate. So to find the real GDP growth rate in 2006, we compare the quantities produced in 2005 and 2006 by using both the 2005 prices and the 2006 prices. We then average the two sets of numbers in a special way that we'll now describe.

To compare the quantities produced in 2005 and 2006 at 2006 prices, we need to calculate the value of 2005 quantities at 2006 prices. Table 20.6 summarizes these quantities and prices. The value of the 2005 quantities at the 2006 prices is calculated as follows:

Expenditure on balls = 100 balls × $0.50 = $50.

Expenditure on bats = 20 bats × $22.50 = $450.

Value of the 2005 quantities at 2006 prices = $500.

We now have two comparisons between 2005 and 2006. At the 2005 prices, the value of production increased from $200 in 2005 to $270 in 2006.

TABLE 20.6   2005 Quantities and 2006 Prices

Item	Quantity	Price
Balls	100	$ 0.50
Bats	20	$22.50

The increase in value is $70, and the percentage increase is ($70 ÷ $200) × 100, which is 35 percent.

At the 2006 prices, the value of production increased from $500 in 2005 to $575 in 2006. The increase in value is $75, and the percentage increase is ($75 ÷ $500) × 100, which is 15 percent.

The new method of calculating real GDP uses the average of these two percentage increases. The average of 35 percent and 15 percent is (35 + 15) ÷ 2, which equals 25 percent. Real GDP is 25 percent greater in 2006 than in 2005. Real GDP in 2005 is $200, so real GDP in 2006 is $250.

Chain Linking The calculation that we've just described is repeated each year. Each year is compared with its preceding year. So in 2007, the calculations are repeated but using the prices and quantities of 2006 and 2007. Real GDP in 2007 equals real GDP in 2006 increased by the calculated percentage change in real GDP for 2007. For example, suppose that real GDP for 2007 is calculated to be 20 percent greater than that in 2006. You know that real GDP in 2006 is $250. So real GDP in 2007 is 20 percent greater and is $300. In every year, real GDP is valued in base-year dollars (in this example, 2005 dollars).

By applying the calculated percentage change to the real GDP of the preceding real GDP, each year is linked back to the dollars of the base year like the links in a chain.

Calculating the Price Level

You've seen how real GDP is used to reveal the change in the quantity of goods and services produced. We're now going to see how we can find the change in prices that increases our cost of living.

The average level of prices is called the **price level**. One measure of the price level is the **GDP deflator**, which is an average of current-year prices expressed as a percentage of base-year prices. We calculate the GDP deflator by using nominal GDP and real GDP in the formula:

GDP deflator = (Nominal GDP ÷ Real GDP) × 100.

You can see why the GDP deflator is a measure of the price level. If nominal GDP rises but real GDP remains unchanged, it must be that the price level has risen. The formula gives a higher value for the GDP deflator. The larger the nominal GDP for a given real GDP, the higher is the price level and the larger is the GDP deflator.

TABLE 20.7   Calculating the GDP Deflator

Year	Nominal GDP	Real GDP	GDP deflator
2005	$200	$200	100
2006	$575	$250	230

Table 20.7 shows how the GDP deflator is calculated. In 2005, the base year, the deflator is 100. In 2006, it is 230, which equals nominal GDP of $575 divided by real GDP of $250 and then multiplied by 100.

Deflating the GDP Balloon

You can think of GDP as a balloon that is blown up by growing production and rising prices. In Fig. 20.3, the GDP deflator lets the inflation air out of the nominal GDP balloon—the contribution of rising prices—so that we can see what has happened to *real* GDP. The red balloon for 1984 shows real GDP in that year. The green balloon shows *nominal* GDP in

2004. The red balloon for 2004 shows real GDP for that year. To see real GDP in 2004, we *deflate* nominal GDP using the GDP deflator.

REVIEW QUIZ

1 What is the distinction between nominal GDP and real GDP?
2 What is the traditional method of calculating real GDP?
3 What is the new method of calculating real GDP?
4 How is the GDP deflator calculated?

myeconlab   **Study Plan 20.3**

You now know how to calculate real GDP and the GDP deflator. Your next task is to learn how to use real GDP to calculate economic growth and to make economic welfare comparisons. We also look at some limitations of real GDP as a measure of economic welfare and as a tool for comparing living standards across countries.

FIGURE 20.3
The Canadian GDP Balloon

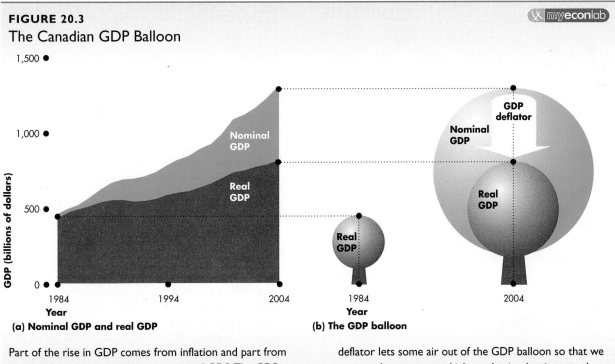

(a) Nominal GDP and real GDP

(b) The GDP balloon

Part of the rise in GDP comes from inflation and part from increased production—an increase in real GDP. The GDP deflator lets some air out of the GDP balloon so that we can see the extent to which production has increased.

Source of data: Statistics Canada, CANSIM Table 380–0002.

Measuring Economic Growth

WE USE ESTIMATES OF REAL GDP TO CALCULATE the economic growth rate. The **economic growth rate** is the percentage change in the quantity of goods and services produced from one year to the next. To calculate the economic growth rate, we use the formula:

$$\text{Economic growth rate} = \frac{\text{Real GDP this year} - \text{Real GDP last year}}{\text{Real GDP last year}} \times 100.$$

For example, real GDP was $1,124 billion in 2004 and $1,092 billion in 2003. So the economic growth rate (percent per year) during 2004 was

$$\text{Economic growth rate} = \frac{\$1,124 - \$1,092}{\$1,092} \times 100$$

$$= 2.93 \text{ percent.}$$

We want to measure the economic growth rate so that we can make

- Economic welfare comparisons
- International comparisons
- Business cycle forecasts

Although the real GDP growth rate is used for these three purposes, it is not a perfect measure for any of them. Nor is it a totally misleading measure. We'll evaluate the limitations of real GDP and its growth rate in each of the three cases.

Economic Welfare Comparisons

Economic welfare is a comprehensive measure of the general state of economic well-being. Economic welfare improves when the production per person of *all* the goods and services grows. The goods and services that make up real GDP growth are only a part of all the items that influence economic welfare.

Today, because of real GDP growth, real GDP per person in Canada of $33,000 is 80 percent higher that it was in 1971. But are we 80 percent better off? Does this growth of real GDP provide a full and accurate measure of the change in economic welfare?

It does not. The reason is that economic welfare depends on many factors that are not measured by real GDP or that are not measured accurately by real GDP. Some of these factors are

- Overadjustment for inflation
- Household production
- Underground economic activity
- Health and life expectancy
- Leisure time
- Environment quality
- Political freedom and social justice

Overadjustment for Inflation The price indexes that are used to measure inflation give an upward-biased estimate of true inflation. (You will learn about the sources of this bias on p. 501.) If we overestimate the rise in prices, we underestimate the growth of real GDP. When car prices rise because cars have gotten better (safer, more fuel efficient, more comfortable), the GDP deflator counts the price increase as inflation. So what is really an increase in production is counted as an increase in price rather than an increase in real GDP. It is deflated away by the wrongly measured higher price level. The magnitude of this bias is probably less than 1 percentage point a year, but its exact magnitude is not known.

Household Production An enormous amount of production takes place every day in our homes. Preparing meals, cleaning the kitchen, changing a light bulb, cutting the grass, washing the car, doing the laundry, and helping a high school student with homework are all examples of productive activities that do not involve market transactions and are not counted as part of GDP.

If all these activities grew at the same rate as real GDP, then not measuring them would not be a problem. But it is likely that market production, which is part of GDP, is increasingly replacing household production, which is not part of GDP. Two trends point in this direction. One is the number of people who have jobs, which has increased from 58 percent in 1970 to 65 percent in 2001. The other is the trend in the purchase of traditionally home-produced goods and services in the market. For example, more and more families now eat in fast-food restaurants—one of the fastest-growing industries in Canada today—and use day-care services. This trend means that an increasing proportion of food preparation and child care that were part of household production are now measured as part of GDP. So real GDP grows more rapidly than does real GDP plus home production.

Underground Economic Activity The *underground economy* is the part of the economy that is purposely hidden from the view of the government to avoid taxes and regulations or because the goods and services being produced are illegal. Because underground economic activity is unreported, it is omitted from GDP.

The underground economy is easy to describe, even if it is hard to measure. It includes the production and distribution of illegal drugs, production that uses illegal labour that is paid less than the minimum wage, and jobs done for cash to avoid paying income taxes. This last category might be quite large and includes tips earned by cab drivers, hairdressers, and hotel and restaurant workers.

Estimates of the scale of the underground economy range between 5 and 15 percent of GDP ($60 billion to $180 billion) in Canada and much more in some countries. It is particularly large in some Eastern European countries that are making a transition from communist economic planning to a market economy.

If the underground economy is a constant proportion of the total economy, the growth rate of real GDP provides a useful estimate of *changes* in economic welfare. But production can shift from the underground economy to the rest of the economy, and can shift the other way. The underground economy expands relative to the rest of the economy if taxes rise sharply or if regulations become especially restrictive. And the underground economy shrinks relative to the rest of the economy if the burdens of taxes and regulations ease.

During the 1980s, when tax rates were cut, there was an increase in the reporting of previously hidden income and tax revenues increased. So some part (but probably a small part) of the expansion of real GDP during the 1980s represented a shift from the underground economy rather than an increase in production.

Health and Life Expectancy Good health and a long life—the hopes of everyone—do not show up in real GDP, at least not directly. A larger real GDP does enable us to spend more on medical research, health care, a good diet, and exercise equipment. And as real GDP has increased, our life expectancy has lengthened—from 70 years at the end of World War II to approaching 80 years today. Infant deaths and death in childbirth, two fearful scourges of the nineteenth century, have almost been eliminated.

But we face new health and life expectancy problems every year. AIDS and drug abuse are taking young lives at a rate that causes serious concern. When we take these negative influences into account, we see that real GDP growth overstates the improvements in economic welfare.

Leisure Time Leisure time is an economic good that adds to our economic welfare. Other things remaining the same, the more leisure we have, the better off we are. Our working time is valued as part of GDP, but our leisure time is not. Yet from the point of view of economic welfare, leisure time must be at least as valuable to us as the wage that we earn for the last hour worked. If it were not, we would work instead of taking the leisure. Over the years, leisure time has steadily increased. The workweek has become shorter, more people take early retirement, and the number of vacation days has increased. These improvements in economic well-being are not reflected in real GDP.

Environmental Quality Economic activity directly influences the quality of the environment. The burning of hydrocarbon fuels is the most visible activity that damages our environment. But it is not the only example. The depletion of exhaustible resources, the mass clearing of forests, and the pollution of lakes and rivers are other major environmental consequences of industrial production.

Resources that are used to protect the environment are valued as part of GDP. For example, the value of catalytic converters that help to protect the atmosphere from automobile emissions are part of GDP. But if we did not use such pieces of equipment and instead polluted the atmosphere, we would not count the deteriorating air that we were breathing as a negative part of GDP.

An industrial society possibly produces more atmospheric pollution than an agricultural society does. But pollution does not always increase as we become wealthier. Wealthy people value a clean environment and are willing to pay for one. Compare the pollution in East Germany in the late 1980s with pollution in Canada. East Germany, a poor country, polluted its rivers, lakes, and atmosphere in a way that is unimaginable in Canada or in wealthy West Germany.

Political Freedom and Social Justice Most people value political freedoms such as those provided by the Canadian Charter of Rights and Freedoms and the

Constitution of Canada. And they value social justice or fairness—equality of opportunity and social security safety nets that protect people from the extremes of misfortune.

A country might have a very large real GDP per person but have limited political freedom and equity. For example, an elite might enjoy political liberty and extreme wealth while the vast majority are effectively enslaved and live in abject poverty. Such an economy would generally be regarded as having less economic welfare than one that had the same amount of real GDP but in which political freedoms were enjoyed by everyone. Today, China has rapid real GDP growth but limited political freedoms, while Russia has slow real GDP growth and an emerging democratic political system. Economists have no easy way to determine which of these countries is better off.

The Bottom Line Do we get the wrong message about the growth in economic welfare by looking at the growth of real GDP? The influences that are omitted from real GDP are probably important and could be large. Developing countries have a larger underground economy and a larger amount of household production than do developed countries. So as an economy develops and grows, part of the apparent growth might reflect a switch from underground to regular production and from home production to market production. This measurement error overstates the rate of economic growth and the improvement in economic welfare.

Other influences on living standards include the amount of leisure time available, the quality of the environment, the security of jobs and homes, and the safety of city streets. It is possible to construct broader measures that combine the many influences that contribute to human happiness. Real GDP will be one element in those broader measures but by no means the whole of them.

International Comparisons

All the problems we've just reviewed affect the economic welfare of every country, so to make international comparisons of economic welfare, factors additional to real GDP must be used. But real GDP comparisons are major components of international welfare comparisons, and two special problems arise in making these comparisons. First, the real GDP of one country must be converted into the same currency units as the real GDP of the other country.

Second, the same prices must be used to value the goods and services in the two countries. Let's look at these two problems by using a striking example: a comparison of China and the United States.

In 2003, real GDP per person in the United States was $39,000. The official Chinese statistics published in the International Monetary Fund's (IMF) World Economic Outlook (WEO) say that real GDP per person in China in 2003 was 9,500 yuan. (The yuan is the currency of China.) On the average, during 2003, $US1 was worth 8.276 yuan.

If we use this exchange rate to convert Chinese yuan into U.S. dollars, we get a value of $1,150. This comparison of China and the United States makes China look extremely poor. In 2003, GDP per person in the United States was 34 times that in China.

Figure 20.4 shows the story of real GDP in China from 1983 to 2003 based on converting the yuan to the U.S. dollar at the market exchange rate

Figure 20.4 also shows another story based on an estimate of real GDP per person that is much larger than the official measure. Let's see how this alternative measurement is made. GDP in the United States is measured by using prices that prevail in the United States. China's GDP is measured by using prices that prevail in China. But the relative prices in the two countries are very different. Some goods that are expensive in the United States cost very little in China. These items have a small weight in China's real GDP. If, instead of using China's prices, all the goods and services produced in China are valued at the prices prevailing in the United States, then a more valid comparison can be made of GDP in the two countries. Such a comparison uses prices called *purchasing power parity prices* or PPP.

Alan Heston, Robert Summers, and Bettina Aten, economists in the Center for International Comparisons at the University of Pennsylvania, have used PPP prices to construct real GDP data for more than 100 countries. The IMF now uses methods similar to those of Heston, Summers, and Aten to calculate PPP estimates of GDP in all countries. The PPP comparisons tell a remarkable story about China.

According to the PPP comparisons, GDP per person in the United States in 2003 was 6 times that of China, not the 34 times shown at the market exchange rate. Figure 20.4 shows the PPP view of China's real GDP and compares it with the market exchange rate view.

A prominent China scholar, Thomas Rawski of the University of Pittsburgh, doubts both sets of data

FIGURE 20.4

myeconlab

Two Views of Real GDP in China

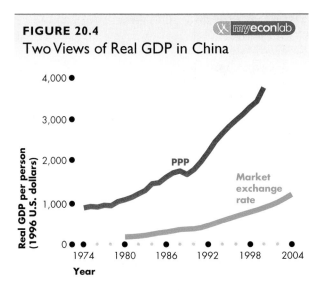

Valuing GDP at the market exchange rate (MER), China is a poor developing country in which income per person is less than 3 percent of the U.S. level. But valuing GDP at purchasing power parity (PPP) prices, China's real GDP is 16 percent of the U.S. level. Some China scholars think that even the market exchange rate numbers are too big. So there is much uncertainty about China's real GDP.

Sources of data: International Monetary Fund, World Economic Outlook database, April, 2005, and Alan Heston, Robert Summers, and Bettina Aten, Penn World Table Version 6.1, Center for International Comparisons at the University of Pennsylvania (CICUP), October 2002.

shown in Fig. 20.4. He believes that the growth rate of China's real GDP has been exaggerated for some years and that even the market exchange rate data overstate real GDP in China.

U.S. real GDP is measured pretty reliably. But China's is not. The alternative measures of China's real GDP are unreliable, and the truth about real GDP in China is not known. But China is growing, and many businesses are paying close attention to the prospects of expanding their activities in China and other fast-growing Asian economies.

Business Cycle Forecasts

If policymakers plan to raise interest rates to slow an expansion that they believe is too strong, they look at the latest estimates of real GDP. But suppose that for the reasons we've just discussed, real GDP is mismeasured. Does this mismeasurement hamper our ability to identify the phases of the business cycle? It does

not. The reason is that although the omissions from real GDP do change over time, they probably do not change in a systematic way with the business cycle. So inaccurate measurement of real GDP does not necessarily cause a wrong assessment of the phase of the business cycle.

The fluctuations in economic activity measured by real GDP tell a reasonably accurate story about the phase of the business cycle that the economy is in. When real GDP grows, the economy is in a business cycle expansion; when real GDP shrinks (for two successive quarters), the economy is in a recession. Also, as real GDP fluctuates, so do production and jobs.

But real GDP fluctuations probably exaggerate or overstate the fluctuations in total production and economic welfare. The reason is that when business activity slows in a recession, household production increases and so does leisure time. When business activity speeds up in an expansion, household production and leisure time decrease. Because household production and leisure time increase in a recession and decrease in an expansion, real GDP fluctuations tend to overstate the fluctuations in total production and in economic welfare. But the directions of change of real GDP, total production, and economic welfare are probably the same.

REVIEW QUIZ

1 Does real GDP measure economic welfare? If not, why not?
2 Does real GDP measure total production of goods and services? If not, what are the main omissions?
3 How can we make valid international comparisons of real GDP?
4 Does the growth of real GDP measure the economic growth rate accurately?
5 Do the fluctuations in real GDP measure the business cycle accurately?

myeconlab **Study Plan 20.4**

◆ You've now studied the methods used to measure GDP, economic growth, and the price level. And you've learned about some of the limitations of these measures. *Reading Between the Lines* on pp. 480–481 looks at Canadian real GDP during 2005.

Your next task is to learn how we measure employment and unemployment and inflation.

The Quarterly GDP Report

GLOBE AND MAIL, 1 SEPTEMBER 2005

Economy on a roll in second quarter

The Canadian economy picked up steam in the second quarter, expanding at a greater-than-expected 3.2-per-cent annual pace, and economists say that makes an interest rate rise next week a done deal.

Strong retail sales and home building, combined with a decline in imports, underpinned second-quarter activity, Statistics Canada said yesterday. The number was well above economists' expectations of a 2.7-per-cent gain and surpassed the Bank of Canada's 2.3-per-cent forecast. Growth in the first quarter, meantime, was revised down to 2.1 per cent.

The report reinforced the view that interest rates will rise next week. The central bank meets on Wednesday and is widely expected to raise its key rate for the first time in 11 months, to 2.75 per cent from 2.5 per cent, to keep inflation in check as the economy grows. ...

Yesterday's Statscan report showed imports fell 0.9 per cent while exports edged up 0.2 per cent. Retail trade rose 1.1 per cent in the quarter, while wholesale trade gained 2.3 per cent, boosted by strong demand for durable and semi-durable goods. Personal expenditures grew 0.6 per cent. Investment in housing rose 1.9 per cent, after declining in the first quarter. As a result, the finance and insurance and the real estate sectors gained 0.9 per cent. The output of real estate agents and brokers jumped 4.4 per cent in the quarter amid a strong home resale market.

Reprinted with permission from *The Globe and Mail.*

Essence of the Story

■ Statistics Canada reported that real GDP grew at an annual rate of 3.2 percent in the second quarter of 2005.

■ Real GDP had grown at an annual rate of 2.1 percent in the first quarter of 2005, so the growth rate sped up in the second quarter.

■ The component of aggregate expenditure that grew quickly during the second quarter of 2005 was consumer expenditure.

■ Imports decreased, which also helped speed growth of domestic production during the second quarter.

Economic Analysis

■ Statistics Canada reports the nation's GDP numbers every three months.

■ To make the quarterly numbers easy to compare with annual numbers, growth rates are reported at annual rates.

■ An annual growth rate is calculated from quarterly data by using the formula:

$$g = [(x_t/x_{t-1})^4 - 1] \times 100,$$

where g is the annualized growth rate, x_t is the value of the variable in the current quarter, and x_{t-1} is the value of the variable in the preceding quarter.

■ The change in real GDP in a quarter is equal to

$$\Delta C + \Delta I + \Delta G + \Delta X - \Delta M$$

■ Figure 1 shows the composition of the increase in real GDP in the second quarter of 2005 with the change in inventories, a component of investment, shown separately from the rest of investment.

■ You can see in the left column of Fig. 1 that the increase in consumption expenditure and the decrease in imports made larger contributions to the change in real GDP than did the other components.

■ You can also see that the increase in real GDP coming from the decrease in imports was almost offset by the decrease in inventories.

■ The news article compares the second quarter with the first quarter, and Fig. 2 shows the composition of the increase in real GDP in the first quarter of 2005.

■ You can see in the right column of Fig. 2 that in the first quarter, the increase in imports and the decrease in inventories offset most of the increases in the other components of real GDP and made the increase in real GDP small.

■ So real GDP increased by more in the second quarter of 2005 than it did in the first quarter because imports fell and inventories fell less in the second quarter than in the first quarter.

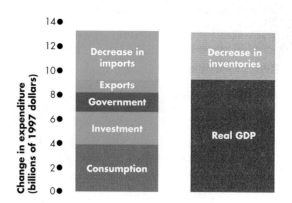

Figure 1 Changes in second quarter of 2005

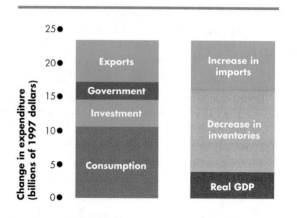

Figure 2 Changes in first quarter of 2005

SUMMARY

KEY POINTS

Gross Domestic Product (pp. 466–470)

- GDP, or gross domestic product, is the market value of all the final goods and services produced in a country during a given period.
- A final good is an item that is bought by its final user during a specified time period, and contrasts with an intermediate good, which is a component of a final good.
- GDP is calculated by using the expenditure and income totals in the circular flow of expenditure and income.
- Aggregate expenditure on goods and services equals aggregate income and GDP.

Measuring Canada's GDP (pp. 471–472)

- Because aggregate expenditure, aggregate income, and the value of aggregate production are equal, we can measure GDP by using the expenditure approach or the income approach.
- The expenditure approach sums consumption expenditure, investment, government expenditures on goods and services, and net exports.
- The income approach sums wages, interest, rent, and profit (and indirect taxes and depreciation).

Real GDP and the Price Level (pp. 473–475)

- Real GDP is measured by a chain-weighted output index that compares the value of production each year with its value at the previous year's prices.
- The GDP deflator measures the price level based on the prices of the items that make up GDP.

Measuring Economic Growth (pp. 476–479)

- We measure the economic growth rate as the percentage change in real GDP.

- Real GDP growth is not a perfect measure of economic growth because it excludes quality improvements, household production, the underground economy, environmental damage, health and life expectancy, leisure time, political freedom, and social justice.
- The growth rate of real GDP gives a good indication of the phases of the business cycle.

KEY FIGURES AND TABLES

Figure 20.1   The Circular Flow of Expenditure and Income, 467
Figure 20.2   Capital and Investment, 470
Table 20.1   GDP: The Expenditure Approach, 471
Table 20.2   GDP: The Income Approach, 472

KEY TERMS

Capital consumption, 469
Chain-weighted output index, 474
Consumption expenditure, 467
Depreciation, 469
Economic growth rate, 476
Economic welfare, 476
Exports, 468
Final good, 466
Flow, 469
GDP deflator, 474
Government expenditures, 468
Gross domestic product (GDP), 466
Gross investment, 469
Imports, 468
Intermediate good, 466
Investment, 468
National saving, 469
Net exports, 468
Net investment, 469
Net taxes, 468
Nominal GDP, 473
Price level, 474
Real GDP, 473
Saving, 468
Stock, 469
Wealth, 469

PROBLEMS

Go to **myeconlab** for solutions to odd-numbered problems and additional exercises.

1. The figure at the bottom of the page shows the flows of expenditure and income on Lotus Island. During 2005, *A* was $20 million, *B* was $60 million, *C* was $24 million, *D* was $30 million, and *E* was $6 million. Calculate
   a. Aggregate expenditure.
   b. Aggregate income.
   c. GDP.
   d. Government budget deficit.
   e. Household saving.
   f. Government saving.
   g. National saving.
   h. Borrowing from the rest of the world.

2. In problem 1, during 2006, *A* was $25 million, *B* was $450 million, *C* was $30 million, *D* was $30 million, and *E* was –$10 million. Calculate the quantities in problem 1 during 2006.

3. Martha owns a copy shop that has 10 copiers. One copier wears out each year and is replaced. In addition, this year Martha will expand her business to 14 copiers. Calculate Martha's initial capital stock, depreciation, gross investment, net investment, and final capital stock.

4. Wendy operates a weaving shop with 20 looms. One loom wears out each year and is replaced. But this year, Wendy will expand her business to 24 looms. Calculate Wendy's initial capital stock, depreciation, gross investment, net investment, and final capital stock.

5. The transactions in Ecoland last year were

Item	Dollars
Wages paid to labour	800,000
Consumption expenditure	600,000
Taxes	250,000
Transfer payments	50,000
Profits	200,000
Investment	250,000
Government expenditures	200,000
Exports	300,000
Saving	300,000
Imports	250,000

   a. Calculate Ecoland's GDP.
   b. Did you use the expenditure approach or the income approach to make this calculation?
   c. How is investment financed?

6. The transactions in Highland last year were

Item	Dollars
Wages paid to labour	400,000
Consumption expenditure	350,000
Net taxes	125,000
Profits	140,000
Investment	150,000
Government expenditures	130,000
Exports	120,000
Saving	135,000
Imports	140,000

   a. Calculate Highland's GDP.
   b. What extra information do you need to calculate net domestic product at factor cost?
   c. Where does Highland get the funds to finance its investment?

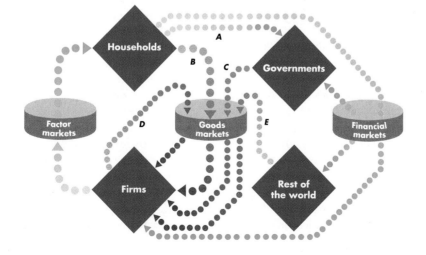

7. Bananaland produces only bananas and sunscreen. The base year is 2005, and the tables give the quantities produced and prices.

	Quantity	
Good	2005	2006
Bananas	1,000 bunches	1,100 bunches
Sunscreen	500 bottles	525 bottles

	Price	
Good	2005	2006
Bananas	$2 a bunch	$3 a bunch
Sunscreen	$10 a bottle	$8 a bottle

   a. Calculate nominal GDP in 2005 and 2006.
   b. Calculate real GDP in 2006 using the base-year prices method.

8. Sea Island produces only lobsters and crabs. The base year is 2006, and the tables give the quantities produced and the prices.

	Quantity	
Good	2006	2007
Lobsters	1,000	1,450
Crabs	500	525

	Price	
Good	2006	2007
Lobsters	$20 each	$25 each
Crabs	$10 each	$12 each

   a. Calculate nominal GDP in 2006 and 2007.
   b. Calculate real GDP in 2007 using the base-year prices method.

9. Bananaland (in problem 7) decides to use the chain-weighted output index method to calculate real GDP. Using this method,
   a. Calculate the growth rate of real GDP in 2006.
   b. Calculate the GDP deflator in 2006.
   c. Compare and comment on the differences in real GDP using the base-year prices and chain-weighted output index methods.

10. Sea Island (in problem 8) decides to use the chain-weighted output index method to calculate real GDP. Using this method,
    a. Calculate the growth rate of real GDP in 2007.
    b. Calculate the GDP deflator in 2007.
    c. Compare and comment on the differences in real GDP using the base-year prices and chain-weighted output index methods.

CRITICAL THINKING

1. Study *Reading Between the Lines* on pp. 480–481 and then answer the following questions:
   a. In the first and second quarters of 2005, which components of aggregate expenditure increased most?
   b. According to the news article, which components of aggregate income increased most during the first and second quarters of 2005?
   c. What happened to net exports during the first two quarters of 2005? Did they increase or decrease? Did Canada increase or decrease its net lending to the rest of the world during those two quarters?
   d. Was Canada in a recession, growth recession, or expansion during the first half of 2005?
   e. What happened to total investment during the first two quarters of 2005?
   f. Where, in the circular flow model, do changes in business inventories appear?

WEB EXERCISES

Use the links on (X myeconlab) **to work the following exercise.**

1. Visit Statistics Canada. There you can obtain all the available data on GDP and the components of aggregate expenditure and aggregate income. You will find data in current prices (nominal GDP) and constant prices (real GDP).
   a. What is the value of nominal GDP in the current quarter?
   b. What is the value of real GDP in the current quarter using the chain-weighted index method?
   c. What is the GDP deflator in the current quarter?
   d. What was the value of real GDP in the same quarter of the previous year?
   e. By how much has real GDP changed over the past year? (Express your answer as a percentage.)
   f. Did real GDP increase or decrease and what does the change tell you about the state of the economy over the past year?

Monitoring Cycles, Jobs, and the Price Level

CHAPTER 21

Vital Signs

Our economy ebbs and flows like a tide between strong expansion, slow down, and recession. What exactly is a recession, who decides when one begins and ends, and what criteria are used to make these decisions?

Each month, we chart the unemployment rate as a measure of Canadian economic health. How do we measure the unemployment rate? What does it tell us? Is it a reliable vital sign for the economy?

Every month, we also chart the number of people working, the number of hours they work, and the wages they receive. Are most new jobs full time or part time? And are they high-wage jobs or low-wage jobs?

As the Canadian economy has expanded over the past few years, the unemployment rate has trended downward. But even in the boom times of 2005, more than 1 million Canadians were unemployed. Questions about the health of the labour market are of vital importance to these unemployed workers and to the millions of others who fear the risk of unemployment.

Having a good job that pays a decent wage is only half of the equation that translates into a good standard of living. The other half is the cost of living. We track the cost of the items that we buy with another number that is published every month—the Consumer Price Index, or CPI. What is the CPI? How is it calculated? And does it provide a reliable guide to the changes in our cost of living?

◆ These are the questions we study in this chapter. We begin by looking at the way in which a recession is identified and dated. And we end, in *Reading Between the Lines,* by putting the spotlight on the CPI in 2005.

After studying this chapter, you will be able to

- ■ **Explain how we date the business cycle**
- ■ **Define the unemployment rate, the labour force participation rate, the employment-to-population ratio, and aggregate hours**
- ■ **Describe the sources and types of unemployment and define full employment and the natural rate of unemployment**
- ■ **Explain how we measure the price level and the inflation rate using the CPI**

The Business Cycle

THE BUSINESS CYCLE IS A PERIODIC BUT IRREGU-lar up-and-down movement in production and jobs (see p. 448). There is no official, government-sponsored record of the dating of business cycles. Instead, business cycles are identified by two private agencies: the Economic Cycle Research Institute (ECRI) and the National Bureau of Economic Research (NBER). The ECRI identifies and dates the business cycles in Canada and 17 other countries and the NBER dates the U.S. business cycle. The working definition of the business cycle used by the ECRI is as follows:

> ... pronounced, pervasive and persistent advances and declines in aggregate economic activity, which cannot be defined by any single variable, but by the consensus of key measures of output, income, employment and sales.[1]

A business cycle has two phases—expansion and recession—and two turning points—peak and trough. The NBER, whose methods the ECRI uses, defines the phases and turning points of the cycle as follows.

> A *recession* is a significant decline in activity spread across the economy, lasting more than a few months, visible in industrial production, employment, real income, and wholesale-retail trade. A recession begins just after the economy reaches a *peak* of activity and ends as the economy reaches its *trough*. Between trough and peak, the economy is in an *expansion*.[2]

Real GDP is the broadest measure of economic activity, and another popular working definition of a recession is a decrease in real GDP that lasts for at least two quarters. But we don't measure real GDP each month, so the ECRI and NBER do not use the real GDP numbers. Instead, they look at employment, which is the broadest *monthly* indicator of economic activity, along with other monthly measures that include personal income, sales of goods, and industrial production.

Business Cycle Dates

Figure 21.1(a) provides a quick summary of the Canadian business cycle since 1926. The figure shows the percentage deviation of real GDP from potential GDP.

The Great Depression, which began with a recession that ran from August 1929 to March 1933, was the most severe contraction of economic activity ever experienced. Over a 43-month period, real GDP shrank by 33 percent. Canada has had only four other recessions: at the end of World War II, 1954, 1982, and 1990–1991. The ECRI identified one other recession during 1957, but it was so mild that it doesn't show up in the real GDP data.

Expansion is the normal state of the economy, and the biggest expansion occurred during World War II. But the longest expansion ran from 1954 to 1982 (except for a mild stop in 1957). There is no correlation between the length of an expansion and the length of the preceding recession.

Growth Rate Cycles

Because recessions are rare, just looking at expansions and recessions misses a lot of the volatility in our economy. An alternative and more sensitive approach is to examine growth rate cycle downturns. A **growth rate cycle downturn** is a

> ... pronounced, pervasive and persistent decline in the *growth rate* of aggregate economic activity. The procedures used to identify peaks and troughs in the growth rate cycle are analogous to those used to identify business cycle turning points, except that they are applied to the growth rates of the same time series, rather than their levels.[3]

Figure 21.1(b) shows the growth rate cycles since 1961 (the first year for which we have quarterly real GDP data).

REVIEW QUIZ
1 What are the phases of the business cycle?
2 Have recessions been getting worse?
myeconlab Study Plan 21.1

---

[1] You can find this definition and the dates of the business cycles in 18 countries at the ECRI Web site (www.businesscycle.com).

[2] "The NBER's Business Cycle Dating Procedure," January 10, 2002, NBER Web site (www.nber.org). (Italics added.)

[3] This definition is from the ECRI Web site (with small changes).

FIGURE 21.1

Two Views of Canadian Business Cycles

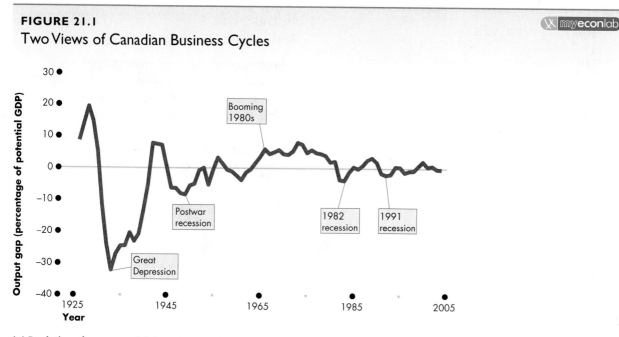

(a) Deviations from potential GDP since 1926

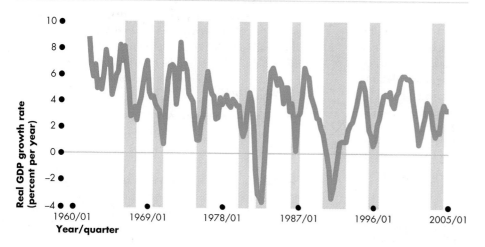

(b) Growth rate cycles since 1961

Part (a) shows the patterns of recession and expansion since the mid-1920s using real GDP as the measuring rod. Recessions have lasted from almost four years during the Great Depression, when real GDP fell by 33 percent, to a year in 1953–1954, when real GDP fell by 1.2 percent. Canada has had only four recessions since World War II.

Part (b) shows the higher frequency growth rate cycles since 1961, again using real GDP as the measuring rod of economic activity. The two deepest growth rate recessions occurred during 1982 and 1991, the periods in which real GDP shrank and the economy was in recession in part (a). The other growth rate recessions identified by the shading in the figure were milder and did not take real GDP growth into negative territory.

Sources of data: Business cycle dates and growth rate cycle dates: The Economic Cycle Research Institute. Real GDP: Statistics Canada, Historical Statistics of Canada, Catalogue 11-516-XIE (1926–1960) and Table 380–0002 (1961–2004).

Jobs and Wages

YOU HAVE SEEN THAT EMPLOYMENT IS ONE OF THE key features of the economy that helps the ECRI and NBER to determine the onset of recession. The state of the labour market has a large impact on our incomes and our lives. We become concerned when jobs are hard to find and more relaxed when they are plentiful. But we want a good job, which means that we want a well-paid and interesting job.

You are now going to learn how economists track the health of the labour market.

Population Survey

Every month, Statistics Canada surveys 54,000 households and asks a series of questions about the age and job market status of their members. This survey is called the Labour Force Survey. Statistics Canada uses the answers to describe the anatomy of the labour force.

Figure 21.2 shows the population categories used by Statistics Canada and the relationships among the categories in 2004. It divides the population into two groups: the working-age population and others who are too young to work. The **working-age population** is the total number of people aged 15 years and over. Statistics Canada divides the working-age population into two groups: those in the labour force and those not in the labour force. It also divides the labour force into two groups: the employed and the unemployed. So the **labour force** is the sum of the employed and the unemployed.

To be counted as employed in the Labour Force Survey, a person must have either a full-time job or a part-time job. To be counted as *un*employed, a person must be available for work and must be in one of three categories:

1. Without work but has made specific efforts to find a job within the previous four weeks
2. Laid off from a job and waiting to be called back to work
3. Waiting to start a new job within four weeks

Anyone surveyed who satisfies one of these three criteria is counted as unemployed. People in the working-age population who are neither employed nor unemployed are classified as not in the labour force.

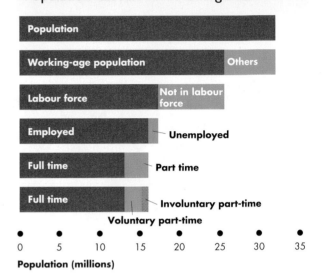

FIGURE 21.2

Population Labour Force Categories

The population is divided into the working-age population and others. The working-age population is divided into those in the labour force and those not in the labour force. The labour force is divided into those employed and those unemployed. The people employed are divided into full-time and part-time workers. And part-time workers are divided into those who are voluntary and involuntary part-time workers.

Source of data: Statistics Canada, CANSIM Tables 282–0002 and 051–0001.

In 2004, the population of Canada was 31.95 million of which 6.52 million were under 15 years of age. The working-age population was 25.43 million and of these 8.25 million were not in the labour force. Most of them were either in school full time or retired. The remaining 17.18 million people made up the Canadian labour force. Of these, 15.95 million were employed and 1.23 million were unemployed.

Four Labour Market Indicators

Statistics Canada calculates four indicators of the state of the labour market:

- The unemployment rate
- The involuntary part-time rate
- The labour force participation rate
- The employment-to-population ratio

The Unemployment Rate The amount of unemployment is an indicator of the extent to which people who want jobs can't find them. The **unemployment rate** is the percentage of the people in the labour force who are unemployed. That is,

$$\text{Unemployment rate} = \frac{\text{Number of people unemployed}}{\text{Labour force}} \times 100$$

and

$$\text{Labour force} = \text{Number of people employed} + \text{Number of people unemployed.}$$

In 2004, the number of people employed was 15.95 million and the number unemployed was 1.23 million. So the labour force was 17.18 million (15.95 million plus 1.23 million) and the unemployment rate was 7.2 percent (1.23 million ÷ 17.18 million × 100).

Figure 21.3 shows the unemployment rate (the orange line and plotted on the right-hand scale) and three other labour market indicators between 1961 and 2004. The average unemployment rate has been 7.8 percent, and it reached peak values at the ends of the 1982 and 1990–1991 recessions.

The Involuntary Part-Time Rate Part-time workers who want full-time work do not get counted as being unemployed. To measure this type of underemployment, Statistics Canada counts the number of involuntary part-time workers—part-time workers who want full-time jobs. The *involuntary part-time rate* is the percentage of the people in the labour force who work part time but want full-time jobs.

$$\text{Involuntary part-time rate} = \frac{\text{Number of involuntary part-time workers}}{\text{Labour force}} \times 100.$$

In 2004, the number of involuntary part-time workers was 922,000, the labour force was 17.18 million, and the involuntary part-time rate was 5.4 percent.

Figure 21.3 shows the involuntary part-time rate (plotted on the right-hand scale). (The break occurs because the criterion for involuntary changed in 1997.) You can see that an increasing percentage of the labour force wants full-time work but is not able to get full-time work. You can also see that the fluctuations in the involuntary part-time rate are like those in the unemployment rate.

FIGURE 21.3

Employment, Unemployment, and the Labour Force: 1960–2004

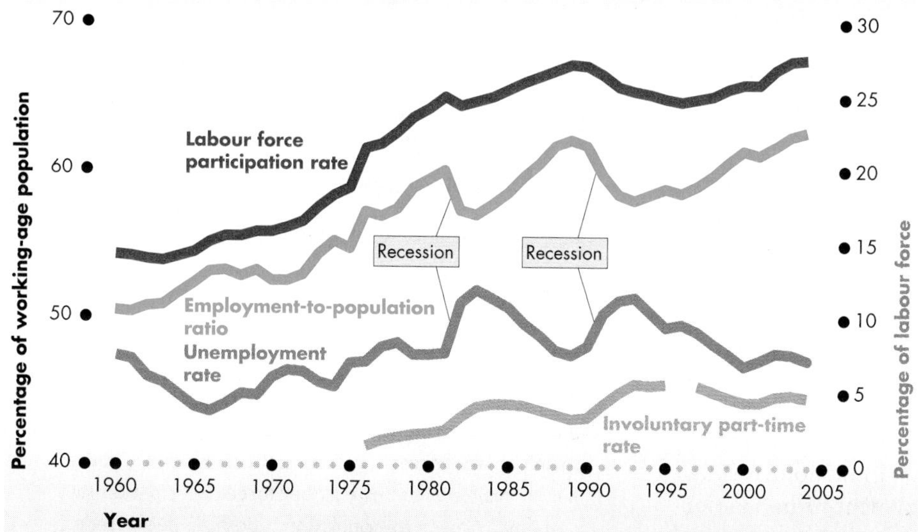

The unemployment rate and the involuntary part-time rate increase in recessions and decrease in expansions. The labour force participation rate and the employment-to-population ratio have upward trends and fluctuate with the business cycle. The employment-to-population ratio fluctuates more than the labour force participation rate and reflects cyclical fluctuations in the unemployment rate. Fluctuations in the labour force participation rate arise mainly because of discouraged workers.

Source of data: Statistics Canada, *Labour Force Historical Review,* CD-ROM, 2005 and CANSIM Table 282–0002.

The Labour Force Participation Rate The number of people of working age who join the labour force is an indicator of the willingness of people to take jobs. The **labour force participation rate** is the percentage of the working-age population who are members of the labour force. That is,

$$\text{Labour force participation rate} = \frac{\text{Labour force}}{\text{Working-age population}} \times 100.$$

In 2004, the labour force was 17.18 million and the working-age population was 25.43 million. By using the above equation, you can calculate the labour force participation rate. It was 67.6 percent (17.18 million ÷ 25.43 million × 100).

Figure 21.3 shows the labour force participation rate (graphed in red and plotted on the left-hand scale). It has followed an upward trend and has increased from 54.1 percent during the early 1960s to 67.6 percent in 2004. It has also had some mild fluctuations. They result from unsuccessful job seekers becoming discouraged workers. **Discouraged workers** are people who are available and willing to work but have not made specific efforts to find a job within the previous four weeks. These workers often temporarily leave the labour force during a recession and re-enter during an expansion and become active job seekers.

The Employment-to-Population Ratio The number of people of working age who have jobs is an indicator of both the availability of jobs and the degree of match between people's skills and jobs. The **employment-to-population ratio** is the percentage of people of working age who have jobs. That is,

$$\text{Employment-to-population ratio} = \frac{\text{Number of people employed}}{\text{Working-age population}} \times 100.$$

In 2004, the number of people employed was 15.95 million and the working-age population was 25.43 million. By using the above equation, you can calculate the employment-to-population ratio. It was 62.7 percent (15.95 million ÷ 25.43 million × 100).

Figure 21.3 shows the employment-to-population ratio (graphed in blue and plotted against the left-hand scale). It increased from 50 percent during the early 1960s to 62.7 percent in 2004. The increase in the

employment-to-population ratio means that the Canadian economy has created jobs at a faster rate than the working-age population has grown. This labour market indicator also fluctuates, and its fluctuations coincide with but are opposite to those in the unemployment rate. The employment-to-population ratio falls during a recession and increases during an expansion.

Why have the labour force participation rate and the employment-to-population ratio increased? The main reason is an increase in the number of women in the labour force. Figure 21.4 shows this increase. Shorter work hours, higher productivity, and an increased emphasis on white-collar jobs have expanded the job opportunities and wages available to women. At the same time, technological advances have increased productivity in the home and freed up women's time to take jobs outside the home.

Figure 21.4 also shows another remarkable trend in the Canadian labour force: The labour force par-

FIGURE 21.4

The Changing Face of the Labour Market

The upward trends in the labour force participation rate and the employment-to-population ratio are accounted for mainly by the increasing participation of women in the labour market. The male labour force participation rate and employment-to-population ratio have decreased.

Source of data: Statistics Canada, CANSIM Table 282–0002.

ticipation rate and the employment-to-population ratio for men have *decreased*. These indicators decreased because increasing numbers of men were remaining in school longer and because some were retiring earlier.

Aggregate Hours

The four labour market indicators that we've just examined are useful signs of the health of the economy and directly measure what matters to most people: jobs. But these four indicators don't tell us the quantity of labour used to produce real GDP, and we cannot use them to calculate the productivity of labour. The productivity of labour is significant because it influences the wages people earn.

The reason why the number of people employed does not measure the quantity of labour employed is that jobs are not all the same. People in part-time jobs might work just a few hours a week. People in full-time jobs work around 35 to 40 hours a week. And some people regularly work overtime. For example, a 7-11 store might hire six students who work for 3 hours a day each. Another 7-11 store might hire two full-time workers who work 9 hours a day each. The number of people employed in these two stores is eight, but the total hours worked by six of the eight is the same as the total hours worked by the other two. To determine the total amount of labour used to produce real GDP, we measure labour in hours rather than in jobs. **Aggregate hours** are the total number of hours worked by all the people employed, both full time and part time, during a year.

Figure 21.5(a) shows aggregate hours in the Canadian economy from 1960 to 2004. Like the employment-to-population ratio, aggregate hours have an upward trend. But aggregate hours have not grown as quickly as has the number of people employed. Between 1960 and 2004, the number of people employed in Canada increased by 163 percent. During that same period, aggregate hours increased by a bit more than 118 percent. Why the difference? Because average hours per worker decreased.

Figure 21.5(b) shows average hours per worker. After hovering at a bit more than 40 hours a week during the early 1960s, average hours per worker decreased to about 33 hours a week during the 2000s. This shortening of the average workweek arose partly because of a decrease in the average hours worked by full-time workers, but mainly because the number of

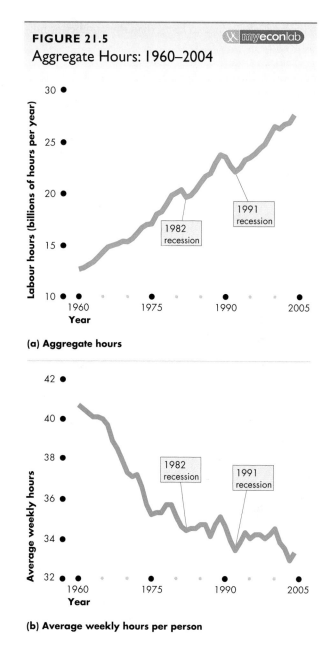

FIGURE 21.5
Aggregate Hours: 1960–2004

(a) Aggregate hours

(b) Average weekly hours per person

Aggregate hours (part a) measure the total labour used to produce real GDP more accurately than does the number of people employed because an increasing proportion of jobs are part time. Between 1960 and 2004, aggregate hours increased by an average of 1.8 percent a year. Fluctuations in aggregate hours coincide with the business cycle. Aggregate hours have increased at a slower rate than the number of jobs because the average workweek has shortened (part b).

Source of data: Statistics Canada, CANSIM Tables 282–0002 and 282–0022.

part-time jobs increased faster than the number of full-time jobs.

Fluctuations in aggregate hours and average hours per worker line up with the business cycle. Figure 21.5 highlights the past two recessions, during which aggregate hours decreased and average hours per worker decreased more quickly than the trend.

Real Wage Rate

The **real wage rate** is the quantity of goods and services that an hour's work can buy. It is equal to the money wage rate (dollars per hour) divided by the price level. If we use the GDP deflator to measure the price level, the real wage rate is expressed in 1997 dollars because the GDP deflator is 100 in 1997. The real wage rate is a significant economic variable because it measures the reward for labour.

What has happened to the real wage rate in Canada? Figure 21.6 answers this question. Figure 21.6 shows the broadest measure of the average hourly real wage rate in the Canadian economy.

The money wage rate is calculated from the national income accounts and aggregate hours. We know from the income side of the national income accounts the total amount of labour income. This total includes wages and salaries and all supplementary labour income such as health and insurance benefits. It includes all labour income, not just that of people who are paid by the hour. If we divide this total by aggregate hours, we arrive at an estimate of the economy-wide average money wage rate. This average includes all types of labour in all parts of the economy.

The real wage rate follows an upward path. But the trend growth rate slowed during the 1970s and early 1980s in the *productivity growth slowdown*. This productivity growth slowdown is the main reason for this behaviour of the average real wage rate.

The average real wage rate usually increases but you can see in Fig. 21.6 that it sometimes decreases. The real wage rate decreased during the late 1970s, the 1990s, and the early 2000s.

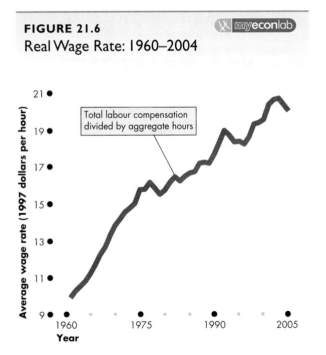

FIGURE 21.6

Real Wage Rate: 1960–2004

[myeconlab]

The average hourly real wage rate follows an upward trend. But the trend growth rate of the real wage rate slowed during the 1970s and early 1980s. Occasionally, the real wage rate falls, as it did in the late 1970s, the 1990s, and the early 2000s.

Source of data: Statistics Canada, CANSIM Tables 282–0002, 282–0022, and 380–0001.

REVIEW QUIZ

1 What are the trends in the unemployment rate, the labour force participation rate, and the employment-to-population ratio?

2 How do the unemployment rate, the labour force participation rate, and the employment-to-population ratio fluctuate over the business cycle?

3 Has the female labour force participation rate been similar to or different from the male labour force participation rate?

4 How have aggregate hours changed since 1960?

5 How did the average hourly real wage rate change during the 1990s?

[myeconlab] **Study Plan 21.2**

You've now seen how we measure employment, unemployment, and the real wage rate. Your next task is to study the anatomy of unemployment and see why it never disappears, even at full employment.

Unemployment and Full Employment

HOW DO PEOPLE BECOME UNEMPLOYED, AND how does a period of unemployment end? How long do people remain unemployed on the average? Who is at greatest risk of becoming unemployed? Let's answer these questions by looking at the anatomy of unemployment.

The Anatomy of Unemployment

People become unemployed if they

1. Lose their jobs and search for another job.
2. Leave their jobs and search for another job.
3. Enter or re-enter the labour force to search for a job.

People end a spell of unemployment if they

1. Are hired or recalled.
2. Withdraw from the labour force.

People who are laid off from their jobs, either permanently or temporarily, are called *job losers*. Some job losers become unemployed, but some immediately withdraw from the labour force. People who voluntarily quit their jobs are called *job leavers*. Like job losers, some job leavers become unemployed and search for a better job, while others withdraw from the labour force temporarily or permanently retire from work. People who enter or re-enter the labour force are called *entrants* and *re-entrants*. Entrants are mainly people who have just left school. Some entrants get a job right away and are never unemployed, but many spend time searching for their first job, and during this period, they are unemployed. Re-entrants are people who have previously withdrawn from the labour force. Most of these people are formerly discouraged workers. Figure 21.7 shows these labour market flows.

The Sources of Unemployment Figure 21.8 shows unemployment by reason for becoming unemployed. Job losers are the biggest source of unemployment. On the average, they account for around half of total unemployment. Also, their number fluctuates a great deal. At the trough of the recession of 1990–1991, on any given day, almost 1 million of

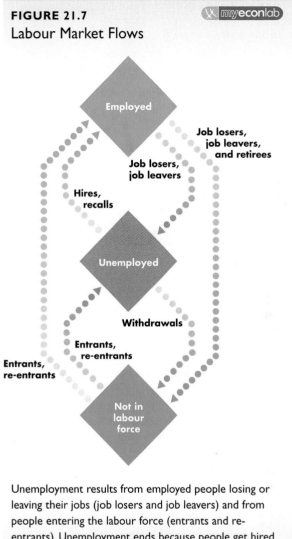

FIGURE 21.7
Labour Market Flows   myeconlab

Unemployment results from employed people losing or leaving their jobs (job losers and job leavers) and from people entering the labour force (entrants and re-entrants). Unemployment ends because people get hired or recalled or because they withdraw from the labour force.

the 1.6 million people unemployed were job losers. In contrast, at the business cycle peak year of 1989, fewer than 600,000 of the 1 million people unemployed were job losers.

Entrants and re-entrants also make up a large component of the unemployed, and their number fluctuates but more mildly than the fluctuations in the number of job losers.

Job leavers are the smallest and most stable source of unemployment. On any given day, less than 200,000 people are unemployed because they are job leavers. The number of job leavers is remarkably

FIGURE 21.8
Unemployment by Reason

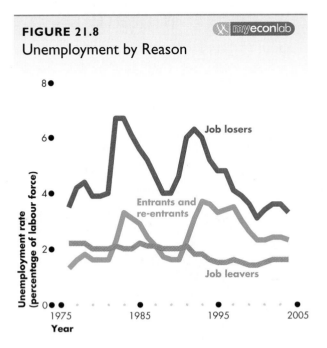

Everyone who is unemployed is a job loser, a job leaver, or an entrant or re-entrant into the labour force. Most unemployment results from job loss. The number of job losers fluctuates more closely with the business cycle than do the numbers of job leavers and entrants and re-entrants. Entrants and re-entrants are the second most common type of unemployed people. Their number fluctuates with the business cycle because of discouraged workers. Job leavers are the least common type of unemployed people.

Source of data: Statistics Canada, *Labour Force Historical Review* CD-ROM, 2005.

FIGURE 21.9
Unemployment by Duration

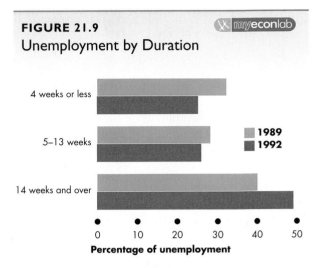

Close to a business cycle peak in 1989, when the unemployment rate was 7.5 percent, 32 percent of unemployment lasted for 4 weeks or less, 28 percent lasted for 5 to 13 weeks, and less than 40 percent lasted for 14 weeks or more. In a business cycle trough in 1992, when the unemployment rate was 11 percent, 25 percent of unemployment lasted for 4 weeks or less, 26 percent lasted for 5 to 13 weeks, and 49 percent lasted for 14 weeks or more.

Source of data: Statistics Canada, *Labour Force Historical Review* CD-ROM, 2001.

constant, although to the extent that it fluctuates, it does so in line with the business cycle: A slightly larger number of people leave their jobs in good times than in bad times.

The Duration of Unemployment Some people are unemployed for a week or two, and others are unemployed for periods of a year or more. The longer the spell of unemployment, the greater the personal cost to the unemployed. The average duration of unemployment varies over the business cycle.

Figure 21.9 compares the duration of unemployment at a business cycle peak in 1989, when the unemployment rate was low, with that at a business cycle trough in 1992, when the unemployment rate

was high. In 1989 when the unemployment rate hit a low of 7.5 percent, 32 percent of the unemployed were in that situation for less than 4 weeks and less than 40 percent of the unemployed were jobless for longer than 13 weeks. In 1992 when the unemployment rate reached a high of 11 percent, only 25 percent of the unemployed found a new job in 4 weeks or less and 49 percent were unemployed for more than 13 weeks. At both low and high unemployment rates, about 27 percent of the unemployed take between 4 weeks and 13 weeks to find a job.

The Demographics of Unemployment Figure 21.10 shows unemployment for different demographic groups. The figure shows that high unemployment rates occur among young workers. In the business cycle trough in 1992, the teenage unemployment rate was 20 percent. Even in 1989, when the national unemployment rate was 7.5 percent, the teenage unemployment rate was 13 percent.

FIGURE 21.10 myeconlab
Unemployment by Demographic Group

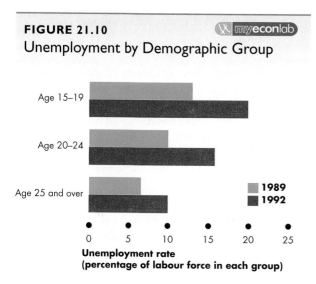

Teenagers experience the highest unemployment rates. In the 1992 business cycle trough (when unemployment was at its highest rate, 11 percent), the teenage unemployment rate was 20 percent. Even at the 1989 business cycle peak (when the unemployment rate was at its lowest, 7.5 percent), the teenage unemployment rate was 13 percent.

Source of data: Statistics Canada, CANSIM Table 282–0002.

Why is the unemployment rate of young people so high? There are three reasons. First, young people are still in the process of discovering what they are good at and trying different lines of work. So they leave their jobs more frequently than do older workers. Second, firms sometimes hire teenagers on a short-term trial basis. So the rate of job loss is higher for teenagers than for other people. Third, most young persons are not in the labour force but are in school. This fact means that the percentage of the young adult population that is unemployed is much lower than the percentage of the young labour force that is unemployed. In 2001, for example, 340,000 15-to-24 year olds were unemployed and 2.3 million were employed. So the 15-to-24 year olds' unemployment rate was 12.9 percent. But 4 million were enrolled in post-secondary education. If we considered being in school as the equivalent of having a job and measured the unemployment rate as the percentage of the labour force plus the school population, we would record a 5.1 percent unemployment rate among 15-to-24 year olds.

Types of Unemployment

Unemployment is classified into four types that are based on its origins. They are

- Frictional
- Structural
- Seasonal
- Cyclical

Frictional Unemployment The unemployment that arises from normal labour turnover—from people entering and leaving the labour force and from the ongoing creation and destruction of jobs—is called **frictional unemployment**. This type of unemployment is a permanent and healthy phenomenon in a dynamic, growing economy.

The unending flow of people into and out of the labour force and the processes of job creation and job destruction create the need for people to search for jobs and for businesses to search for workers. Always, there are businesses with unfilled jobs and people seeking jobs. Look in your local newspaper, and you will see that there are always some jobs being advertised. Businesses don't usually hire the first person who applies for a job, and unemployed people don't usually take the first job that comes their way. Instead, both firms and workers spend time searching out what they believe will be the best match available. By this search process, people can match their own skills and interests with the available jobs and find a satisfying job and income. While these unemployed people are searching, they are frictionally unemployed.

The amount of frictional unemployment depends on the rate at which people enter and re-enter the labour force and on the rate at which jobs are created and destroyed. During the 1970s, the amount of frictional unemployment increased as a consequence of the post-war baby boom that began during the 1940s. By the late 1970s, the baby boom created a bulge in the number of people leaving school. As these people entered the labour force, the amount of frictional unemployment increased.

The amount of frictional unemployment is influenced by unemployment compensation. The greater the number of unemployed people covered by employment insurance and the more generous the unemployment benefits they receive, the longer is the average time taken in job search and the greater is the amount of frictional unemployment. Canadian employment insurance is among the most comprehensive and generous in the world. It is much more comprehensive than that in the United States. This factor is one reason why the Canadian unemployment rate has exceeded the U.S. unemployment rate since the early 1980s. But there are other reasons. Canadian workers, especially young workers who make up the so-called Generation X, have shorter spells of employment and more frequent intervening spells of unemployment, supported by employment insurance, than do young U.S. workers.[4]

Structural Unemployment The unemployment that arises when changes in technology or international competition change the skills needed to perform jobs or change the locations of jobs is called **structural unemployment**. This type of unemployment usually lasts longer than frictional unemployment because workers must retrain and possibly relocate to find a job. For example, when a steel plant in Hamilton, Ontario, is automated, some jobs in that city are destroyed. Meanwhile, in the Ottawa valley and Vancouver, new jobs for security guards, life-insurance salespeople, and retail clerks are created. The unemployed former steelworkers remain unemployed for several months until they move, retrain, and get one of these jobs. Structural unemployment is painful, especially for older workers for whom the best available option might be to retire early but with a lower income than they had expected.

At some times the amount of structural unemployment is modest. At other times it is large, and at such times, structural unemployment can become a serious long-term problem. It was especially large during the late 1970s and early 1980s. During those years, oil price hikes and an increasingly competitive international environment destroyed jobs in traditional Canadian industries, such as auto and steel, and created jobs in new industries, such as electronics and bioengineering, as well as in banking and insurance. Structural unemployment was also present dur-

ing the early 1990s as many businesses and governments "downsized."

Seasonal Unemployment Many jobs are available only at certain times of the year. **Seasonal unemployment** is the unemployment that arises because the number of jobs available has decreased because of the season. Most seasonal unemployment in Canada occurs in the winter because construction and outdoor farming essentially close down for several months.

Cyclical Unemployment The unemployment that fluctuates over the business cycle is called **cyclical unemployment**. This type of unemployment increases during a recession and decreases during an expansion. An auto worker who is laid off because the economy is in a recession and who gets rehired some months later when the expansion begins has experienced cyclical unemployment.

Full Employment

There is always *some* unemployment. So what do we mean by *full employment*? **Full employment** occurs when there is no cyclical unemployment or, equivalently, when all the unemployment is frictional, structural, and seasonal. The unemployment rate at full employment is called the **natural rate of unemployment**. The divergence of the unemployment rate from the natural rate of unemployment is cyclical unemployment.

There can be a lot of unemployment at full employment, and the term "full employment" is an example of a technical economic term that does not correspond with everyday language. The term "natural rate of unemployment" is another technical economic term whose meaning does not correspond with everyday language. For most people—especially for unemployed workers—there is nothing *natural* about unemployment.

So why do economists call a situation with a lot of unemployment "full employment"? And why is the unemployment at full employment called "natural"?

The reason is that the economy is a complex mechanism that is always changing. Every day, some people retire, new workers enter the labour force, some businesses downsize or fail and others expand or start up. This process of change creates unavoidable frictions and dislocations, which create unemployment. Economists don't agree about the size of the natural rate of unemployment or the extent to which it fluctuates.

---

[4] These conclusions are based on the work of David Card and Craig W. Riddell, "A Comparative Analysis of Unemployment in Canada and the United States," *Small Differences that Matter: Labour Markets and Income Maintenance in Canada and the United States*, edited by Richard Freeman and David Card, Chicago: University of Chicago Press and NBER, 1993, pp. 149–189; and Audra J. Bowlus, "What Generation X Can Tell Us About the U.S.–Canadian Unemployment Rate Gap," University of Western Ontario, 1996.

FIGURE 21.11

Unemployment and Real GDP   myeconlab

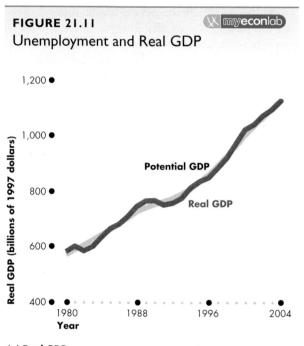

(a) Real GDP

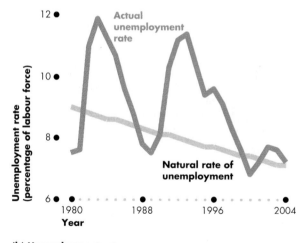

(b) Unemployment rate

As real GDP fluctuates around potential GDP (part a), the unemployment rate fluctuates around the natural rate of unemployment (part b). In the deep 1982 recession, the unemployment rate reached almost 12 percent. In the milder 1990–1991 recession, the unemployment rate peaked at about 11 percent. The natural rate of unemployment has gradually decreased since 1980.

Sources of data: Statistics Canada, CANSIM Tables 282–0002 and 380–0002, and International Monetary Fund, *World Economic Outlook*, Output gap series.

Real GDP and Unemployment Over the Cycle

The quantity of real GDP at full employment is called **potential GDP**. You will study the forces that determine potential GDP in Chapter 30 (pp. 712–713). Over the business cycle, real GDP fluctuates around potential GDP and the unemployment rate fluctuates around the natural rate of unemployment. Figure 21.11 illustrates these fluctuations in Canada between 1980 and 2004—real GDP in part (a) and the unemployment rate in part (b).

When the economy is at full employment, the unemployment rate equals the natural rate of unemployment and real GDP equals potential GDP. When the unemployment rate is less than the natural rate of unemployment, real GDP is greater than potential GDP. And when the unemployment rate is greater than the natural rate of unemployment, real GDP is less than potential GDP.

Figure 21.11(b) shows one view of the natural rate of unemployment. Keep in mind that economists do not know the magnitude of the natural rate of unemployment, so the natural rate shown in the figure is only one estimate. In Fig. 21.11(b), the natural rate of unemployment has gradually fallen from about 9 percent in 1980 to about 7 percent in 2004. This estimate of the natural rate of unemployment in Canada is one that many, but not all, economists would accept.

REVIEW QUIZ

1 What are the categories of people who become unemployed?
2 Define frictional unemployment, structural unemployment, seasonal unemployment, and cyclical unemployment and provide an example of each type of unemployment.
3 What is the natural rate of unemployment?
4 How might the natural rate of unemployment change and what factors might make it change?
5 How does the unemployment rate fluctuate over the business cycle?

myeconlab **Study Plan 21.3**

Your final task in this chapter is to learn about another vital sign that gets monitored every month: the Consumer Price Index (CPI). What is the CPI, how do we measure it, and what does it mean?

The Consumer Price Index

STATISTICS CANADA CALCULATES THE CONSUMER Price Index every month. The **Consumer Price Index (CPI)** is a measure of the average of the prices paid by urban consumers for a fixed "basket" of consumer goods and services. What you learn in this section will help you to make sense of the CPI and relate it to your own economic life. The CPI tells you what has happened to the value of the money in your pocket.

Reading the CPI Numbers

The CPI is defined to equal 100 for a period called the **base period**. Currently, the base period is 1992. That is, for the average of the 12 months of 1992, the CPI equals 100.

In August 2005, the CPI was 128. This number tells us that the average of the prices paid by urban consumers for a fixed market basket of consumer goods and services was 28 percent higher in August 2005 than it was on the average during 1992.

In August 2004, the CPI was 124.8. Comparing the August 2005 CPI with the August 2004 CPI tells us that the index of the prices paid by urban consumers for a fixed basket of consumer goods and services increased during the year ended August 2005 by 3.2—from 124.8 to 128.0—or 2.6 percent.

Constructing the CPI

Constructing the CPI is a huge operation that costs millions of dollars and involves three stages:

■ Selecting the CPI basket
■ Conducting the monthly price survey
■ Calculating the CPI

Selecting the CPI Basket The first stage in constructing the CPI is to select what is called the CPI basket. This "basket" contains the goods and services represented in the index and the relative importance attached to each of them. The idea is to make the relative importance of the items in the CPI basket the same as that in the budget of an average urban household. For example, because people spend more on housing than on bus rides, the CPI places more weight on the price of housing than on the price of bus rides.

Statistics Canada uses several baskets and calculates several alternative CPIs. The goal of the alternatives is to omit items that are highly volatile and that mask the deeper changes in the index. Here, we'll look only at the main "All-Items" index.

To determine the spending patterns of households and to select the CPI basket, Statistics Canada conducts a survey of consumer's expenditure. This survey is costly and so is undertaken only once every few years. Today's CPI basket is based on data gathered in a Consumer Expenditure Survey of 1996.

Figure 21.12 shows the CPI basket at the end of 2001. The basket contains thousands of individual goods and services arranged in the eight large groups shown in the figure. The most important item in a household's budget is shelter, which accounts for 26.8 percent of total expenditure. Transportation comes next at 19.8 percent. Third in relative importance is food at 16.9 percent. These three groups account for almost two-thirds of the average household budget.

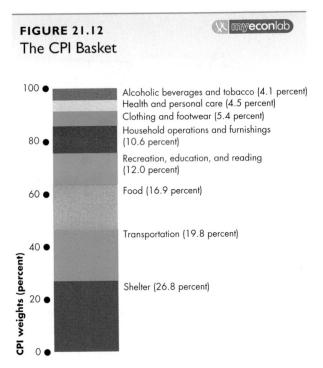

FIGURE 21.12
The CPI Basket

The CPI basket consists of the items that an average urban household buys. It consists mainly of shelter (26.8 percent), transportation (19.8 percent), and food (16.9 percent). All other items add up to 36.5 percent of the total.

Source of data: Statistics Canada, Catalogue 62-001-XIB.

Statistics Canada breaks down each of these categories into smaller ones. For example, the recreation, education, and reading category breaks down into textbooks and supplies, tuition, telephone services, and personal computer services.

As you look at the relative importance of the items in the CPI basket, remember that they apply to the *average* household. *Individual* households are spread around the average. Think about your own expenditure and compare the basket of goods and services you buy with the CPI basket.

Conducting the Monthly Price Survey Each month, Statistics Canada employees check the prices of the goods and services in the CPI basket in 64 urban centres. Because the CPI aims to measure price *changes*, it is important that the prices recorded each month refer to exactly the same item. For example, suppose that the price of a box of jellybeans has increased, but a box now contains more beans. Has the price of jellybeans increased? Statistics Canada employees must record the details of changes in quality or packaging so that price changes can be isolated from other changes.

Once the raw price data are in hand, the next task is to calculate the CPI.

Calculating the CPI The CPI calculation has three steps:

1. Find the cost of the CPI basket at base period prices.
2. Find the cost of the CPI basket at current period prices.
3. Calculate the CPI for the base period and the current period.

We'll work through these three steps for a simple example. Suppose the CPI basket contains only 10 oranges and 5 haircuts. We'll construct an annual CPI rather than a monthly CPI with the base period 2004 and the current period 2005.

Table 21.1 shows the quantities in the CPI basket and the prices in the base period and current period.

Part (a) contains the data for the base period. In that period, the price of an orange was $1 and the price of a haircut was $8. To find the cost of the CPI basket at base period prices, multiply the quantities in the CPI basket by the base period prices. The cost of oranges is $10 (10 at $1 each), and the cost of haircuts is $40 (5 at $8 each). So the total cost of the CPI basket at base period prices was $50 ($10 + $40).

Part (b) contains the price data for the current period. The price of an orange increased from $1 to $2, which is a 100 percent increase ($1 ÷ $1 × 100 = 100). The price of a haircut increased from $8 to $10, which is a 25 percent increase ($2 ÷ $8 × 100 = 25).

The CPI provides a way of averaging these price increases by comparing the costs of the CPI basket rather than the prices of the items. To find the cost of the CPI basket at the current period prices multiply the quantities in the CPI basket by their 2005 prices. The cost of oranges is $20 (10 at $2 each), and the cost of haircuts is $50 (5 at $10 each). So the total cost of the fixed CPI basket at current period prices is $70 ($20 + $50).

You've now taken the first two steps towards calculating the CPI: calculating the cost of the CPI basket in the base period and the cost in the current period. The third step uses the numbers you've just calculated to find the CPI for 2004 and 2005.

The formula for the CPI is

$$\text{CPI} = \frac{\text{Cost of CPI basket at current period prices}}{\text{Cost of CPI basket at base period prices}} \times 100.$$

Table 21.1   The CPI: A Simplified Calculation

(a) The cost of the CPI basket at base period prices: 2004

Item	CPI basket Quantity	Price	Cost of CPI basket
Oranges	10	$1	$10
Haircuts	5	$8	$40
Cost of CPI basket at base period prices			$50

(b) The cost of the CPI basket at current period prices: 2005

Item	CPI basket Quantity	Price	Cost of CPI basket
Oranges	10	$ 2	$20
Haircuts	5	$10	$50
Cost of CPI basket at current period prices			$70

In Table 21.1, you have established that in 2004, the cost of the CPI basket was $50 and in 2005, it was $70. You also know that the base period is 2004. So the cost of the CPI basket at base period prices is $50. If we use these numbers in the CPI formula, we can find the CPI for 2004 and 2005.

$$\text{CPI in 2004} = \frac{\$50}{\$50} \times 100 = 100.$$

$$\text{CPI in 2005} = \frac{\$70}{\$50} \times 100 = 140.$$

The principles that you've applied in this simplified CPI calculation apply to the calculations performed every month by Statistics Canada.

Measuring Inflation

A major purpose of the CPI is to measure *changes* in the cost of living and in the value of money. To measure these changes, we calculate the **inflation rate**—the percentage change in the price level from one year to the next. To calculate the inflation rate, we use the formula:

$$\frac{\text{Inflation}}{\text{rate}} = \frac{(\text{CPI this year} - \text{CPI last year})}{\text{CPI last year}} \times 100.$$

We can use this formula to calculate the inflation rate. The CPI in August 2005 was 128.0, and the CPI in August 2004 was 124.8. So the inflation rate during the year to August 2005 was

$$\text{Inflation rate} = \frac{(128.0 - 124.8)}{124.8} \times 100 = 2.6.$$

Figure 21.13 shows the CPI and the inflation rate in Canada during the 34 years from 1970 and 2004. The two parts of the figure are related.

Figure 21.13 shows that when the price *level* in part (a) rises rapidly, the inflation rate in part (b) is high, and when the price level in part (a) rises slowly, the inflation rate in part (b) is low. Notice in part (a) that the CPI increased every year during this period. During the late 1970s and early 1980s, the CPI increased rapidly, but its rate of increase slowed after 1985 to an average of 2.9 percent a year.

The CPI is not a perfect measure of the price level, and changes in the CPI probably overstate the inflation rate. Let's look at the sources of bias.

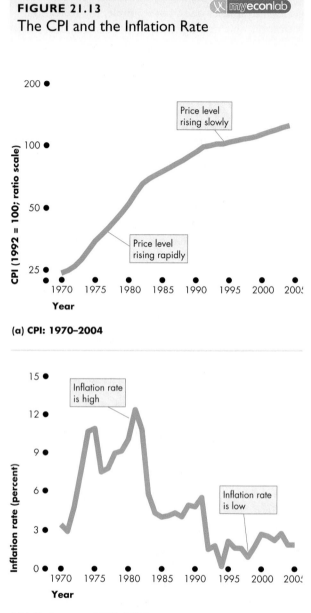

FIGURE 21.13   [X] myeconlab

The CPI and the Inflation Rate

(a) CPI: 1970–2004

(b) Inflation rate: 1970–2004

In part (a), the CPI (the price level) has increased every year. In part (b), the inflation rate has averaged 5.25 percent a year. When the price level increased rapidly during the 1970s and early 1980s, the inflation rate was high and sometimes exceeded 10 percent a year. But after 1985, the price level increased slowly and the inflation rate fell to an average of 2.9 percent a year.

Source of data: Statistics Canada, CANSIM Table 326–0002.

The Biased CPI

The main sources of bias in the CPI are

- New goods bias
- Quality change bias
- Commodity substitution bias
- Outlet substitution bias

New Goods Bias If you want to compare the price level in 2005 with that in 1975, you must somehow compare the price of a computer today with that of a typewriter in 1975. Because a PC is more expensive than a typewriter was, the arrival of the PC puts an upward bias into the CPI and its inflation rate.

Quality Change Bias Cars, CD players, television sets and many other items get better every year. Part of the rise in the prices of these items is a payment for improved quality and is not inflation. But the CPI counts the entire price rise as inflation and so overstates inflation.

Commodity Substitution Bias Changes in relative prices lead consumers to change the items they buy. For example, if the price of beef rises and the price of chicken remains unchanged, people buy more chicken and less beef. Suppose they switch from beef to chicken on a scale that provides the same amount of protein and the same enjoyment as before and their expenditure is the same as before. The price of protein has not changed. But because it ignores the substitution of chicken for beef, the CPI says the price of protein has increased.

Outlet Substitution Bias When confronted with higher prices, people use discount stores more frequently and convenience stores less frequently. This phenomenon is called *outlet substitution*. The CPI surveys do not monitor outlet substitutions.

The Magnitude of the Bias

How big is the bias in the measurement of the CPI? The answer varies from country to country. In the United States, the bias is believed to range between 1 percent and 2 percent a year. But in Canada, it is believed to be at most 1 percent a year and probably less than this amount.

To reduce the bias problems, Statistics Canada revises the basket used for calculating the CPI about every 10 years. Also, Statistics Canada tries to estimate the quantitative effects of the various sources of bias and eliminate them by statistical adjustments. It is these adjustments that make Canada's CPI a more reliable measure of the price level than the CPI in the United States is of the U.S. price level.

Some Consequences of the Bias

The bias in the CPI has three main consequences. It

- Distorts private contracts.
- Increases government outlays.
- Biases estimates of real earnings.

Many private agreements, such as wage contracts, are linked to the CPI. For example, a firm and its workers might agree to a three-year wage deal that increases the wage rate by 2 percent a year *plus* the percentage increase in the CPI. Such a deal ends up giving the workers more *real* income than the firm intended.

Close to a third of federal government outlays are linked directly to the CPI. And while a bias of 1 percent a year seems small, accumulated over a decade, it adds up to billions of dollars of additional expenditures.

Trade unions and businesses bargain over wages based in part on changes in the CPI. If the CPI is biased upwards, businesses might agree to wage increases that are larger than they would accept if the CPI were measured accurately.

REVIEW QUIZ

1 What is the CPI and how is it calculated?
2 How do we calculate the inflation rate and what is the relationship between the CPI and the inflation rate?
3 What are the four main ways in which the CPI is an upward-biased measure of the price level?
4 What problems arise from the CPI bias?

myeconlab **Study Plan 21.4**

◆ *Readings Between the Lines* on pp. 502–503 looks at the CPI in 2005. You've now completed your study of the measurement of macroeconomic performance. Your task in the following chapters is to learn what determines that performance and how policy actions might improve it.

The Monthly CPI Report

THE DAILY, 22 SEPTEMBER 2005

August 2005 CPI Report

... In August, consumers paid 2.6% more than in August 2004 for the goods and services included in the Consumer Price Index (CPI) basket, up strongly from the 2.0% increase recorded in July. However, the 12-month change in the All-items index excluding energy rose more moderately from 1.4% in July to 1.6% in August.

Gasoline prices were the primary reason for the jump in the 12-month change in the All-items index. After rising 12.3% between July 2004 and July 2005, gasoline prices soared 20.1% between August 2004 and August 2005. ...

The main contributors towards moderating these increases were lower prices for computer equipment and supplies and for traveller accommodation. ...

Prices for restaurant meals were up 2.9% compared with August 2004. Higher operating costs were the main reason behind the higher prices. This increase was similar to those observed in recent months. ...

All major components of the CPI posted 12-month increases with the exception of recreation, education and reading, which edged down 0.2% due to lower prices for computer equipment and supplies. Transportation (+5.8%), shelter (+2.9%), and food (+2.6%) exerted the strongest upward pressure on the All-items index.

Alcoholic beverages and tobacco products (+2.3%), health and personal care (+1.9%), household operations and furnishings (+0.7%), and clothing and footwear (+0.4%) also rose, but to a lesser extent.

The substantial increase in gasoline prices pushed up the CPI monthly index. With strong upward pressure from gasoline prices, the CPI rose by 0.4% in August to 128.0 (1992=100). To a lesser extent, prices for the purchase and leasing of automotive vehicles also contributed to the rise in the All-items index. Lower prices for fresh vegetables, natural gas and fresh fruit nonetheless moderated this increase.

Excerpt: "August 2005 CPI Report," adapted from the Statistics Canada publication *The Daily*, Catalogue 11–001, September 22, 2005, available at www.statcan.ca/Daily/English/050922/d050922a.htm.

Essence of the Story

■ Statistics Canada reported that the inflation rate between August 2004 and August 2005 was 2.6 percent.

■ Gasoline prices increased by 20.1 percent between August 2004 and August 2005, and this increase was reported as the primary reason for the jump in the inflation rate.

■ Lower prices for computer equipment and traveller accommodation moderated the overall rise in consumer prices.

Economic Analysis

■ Statistics Canada reports the nation's Consumer Price Index (CPI) numbers every month.

■ The CPI is an indicator of the changes in consumer prices experienced by Canadians.

■ The CPI is obtained by comparing the price of a fixed basket of commodities purchased by Canadians over different time periods—the CPI basket.

■ The CPI basket includes food, shelter, household operations and furnishings, clothing and footwear, transportation, health and personal care, recreation, education and reading, and alcoholic beverages and tobacco products.

■ Figure 1 shows the CPI for each month from January 2002 through August 2005.

■ In January 2002, the CPI was 116.2 and in August 2005, it was 128.

■ Figure 2 shows the annual inflation rate for each month between January 2002 and August 2005. You can see that the inflation rate was on a rising trend through 2002 and on a falling through 2003.

■ Through 2004 and 2005, the inflation rate was in the middle of its target range of 1 percent to 3 percent a year.

■ In addition to reporting the CPI, Statistics Canada also reports a monthly index for each component of the CPI basket.

■ Figure 3 shows the percentage changes in each component of the CPI basket between July and August 2005 expressed as annualized percentage changes.

■ These price changes tell us about the changes in *relative prices*. They do not tell us anything about inflation. Nor do they tell us *why* the inflation rate changed.

■ It is a common mistake in the media to say that the inflation rate increased (or decreased) *because* a particular price increased (or decreased).

■ The price of gasoline increased, which increased the relative price of transportation. But this change in relative prices provides no information about why the inflation rate changed. Lots of relative prices changed, as Fig. 3 shows.

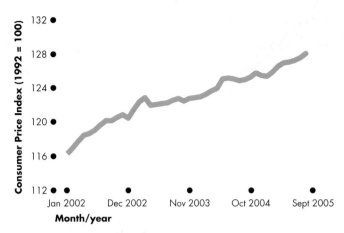

Figure 1 Consumer Price Index

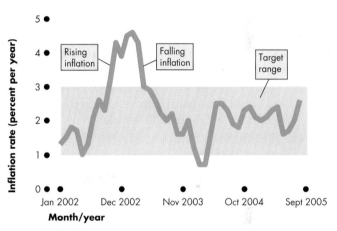

Figure 2 Inflation rate

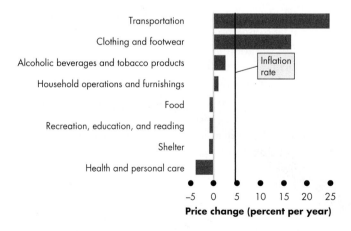

Figure 3 Relative price changes between July and August 2005

503

SUMMARY

KEY POINTS

The Business Cycle (pp. 486–487)

- A recession is a significant decline in activity spread across the economy and lasting more than a few months.
- Another definition of recession is a decrease in real GDP that lasts for at least two quarters.
- The ECRI has identified only four recessions and expansions in Canada since World War II.

Jobs and Wages (pp. 488–492)

- The unemployment rate averaged 7.8 percent between 1960 and 2004. It increases in recessions and decreases in expansions.
- The labour force participation rate and the employment-to-population ratio have an upward trend and fluctuate with the business cycle.
- The labour force participation rate has increased for females and decreased for males.
- Aggregate hours have an upward trend, and they fluctuate with the business cycle.
- Average hourly real wage rate grows but the growth rate slowed during the 1970s.

Unemployment and Full Employment (pp. 493–497)

- People are constantly entering and leaving the state of unemployment.
- The duration of unemployment fluctuates over the business cycle. But the demographic patterns of unemployment are constant.
- Unemployment can be frictional, structural, seasonal, and cyclical.
- When all unemployment is frictional, structural, and seasonal, the economy is at full employment, the unemployment rate equals the natural rate of unemployment, and real GDP equals potential GDP.
- Over the business cycle, real GDP fluctuates around potential GDP and the unemployment rate fluctuates around the natural rate of unemployment.

The Consumer Price Index (pp. 498–501)

- The Consumer Price Index (CPI) measures the average of the prices paid by urban consumers for a fixed basket of consumer goods and services.
- The CPI is defined to equal 100 for the base period—currently 1992.
- The inflation rate is the percentage change in the CPI from one year to the next.
- Changes in the CPI probably overstate the inflation rate slightly.
- The bias in the CPI distorts private contracts and increases government outlays.

KEY FIGURES

Figure 21.1   Two Views of Canadian Business Cycles, 487
Figure 21.2   Population Labour Force Categories, 488
Figure 21.7   Labour Market Flows, 493
Figure 21.11   Unemployment and Real GDP, 497
Figure 21.12   The CPI Basket, 498

KEY TERMS

Aggregate hours, 491
Base period, 498
Consumer Price Index (CPI), 498
Cyclical unemployment, 496
Discouraged workers, 490
Employment-to-population ratio, 490
Frictional unemployment, 495
Full employment, 496
Growth rate cycle downturn, 486
Inflation rate, 500
Labour force, 488
Labour force participation rate, 490
Natural rate of unemployment, 496
Potential GDP, 497
Real wage rate, 492
Seasonal unemployment, 496
Structural unemployment, 496
Unemployment rate, 489
Working-age population, 488

PROBLEMS

Go to ⓧ myeconlab **for solutions to odd-numbered problems and additional exercises.**

1. Statistics Canada reported the following data for January 2000: Labour force: 15,537,700 Employment: 14,339,200 Working-age population: 24,137,100. Calculate the
   a. Unemployment rate.
   b. Labour force participation rate.
   c. Employment-to-population ratio.

2. Statistics Canada reported the following data for January 2001: Labour force: 16,219,800 Employment: 14,990,400 Working-age population: 24,764,100. Calculate the
   a. Unemployment rate.
   b. Labour force participation rate.
   c. Employment-to-population ratio.

3. During 2000, the working-age population in Canada increased by 327,100, employment increased by 280,900, and the labour force increased by 330,400. Use these numbers and the data in problem 1 to calculate the change in unemployment and the change in the number of people not in the labour force in 2000.

4. During 2001, the working-age population in Canada increased by 299,900, employment decreased by 16,600, and the labour force increased by 329,200. Use these data and the data in problem 2 to calculate the change in unemployment and the change in the number of people not in the labour force in 2001.

5. In August 2000, the unemployment rate was 7.2 percent. In August 2001, the unemployment rate was 7.5 percent. Use this information to predict what happened between August 2000 and August 2001 to the numbers of
   a. Job losers and job leavers.
   b. Labour force entrants and re-entrants.

6. In January 2001, the unemployment rate was 7.5 percent. In January 2002, the unemployment rate was 8.6 percent. Use these data to predict what happened between January 2001 and January 2002 to the numbers of
   a. Job losers and job leavers.
   b. Labour force entrants and re-entrants.

7. In July 2005, on Sandy Island, 10,000 people were employed, 1,000 were unemployed, and 5,000 were not in the labour force. During August 2005, 80 people lost their jobs, 20 quit their jobs, 150 were hired or recalled, 50 withdrew from the labour force, and 40 entered or re-entered the labour force. Calculate for July 2005
   a. The labour force.
   b. The unemployment rate.
   c. The working-age population.
   d. The employment-to-population ratio.
   And calculate for the end of August 2005
   e. The number of people unemployed.
   f. The number of people employed.
   g. The labour force.
   h. The unemployment rate.

8. In July 2006 on Sandy Island, 11,000 people were employed, 900 were unemployed, and 5,000 were not in the labour force. During August 2006, 40 people lost their jobs, 10 quit their jobs, 180 were hired, 20 withdrew from the labour force, and 60 entered or re-entered the labour force. Calculate for July 2006
   a. The labour force.
   b. The unemployment rate.
   c. The working-age population.
   d. The employment-to-population ratio.
   And calculate for the end of August 2006
   e. The number of people unemployed.
   f. The number of people employed.
   g. The labour force.
   h. The unemployment rate.

9. A typical family on Sandy Island buys only juice and cloth. The cost of the CPI basket at base year prices was $65 ($40 for juice at $4 a bottle and $25 for cloth at $5 a length). In the current year, juice is $4 a bottle and cloth is $6 a length. Calculate
   a. The CPI basket.
   b. The CPI in the current year.
   c. The inflation rate in the current year.

10. A typical family on Lizard Island buys only mangoes and nuts. The cost of the CPI basket at base year prices was $70 ($60 on nuts at $3 a bag and $10 on mangoes at $1 each). In the current year, mangoes are $1.50 each and nuts are $4 a bag. Calculate
    a. The CPI basket.
    b. The CPI in the current year.
    c. The inflation rate in the current year.

CRITICAL THINKING

1. Study *Reading Between the Lines* on pp. 502–503 and then answer the following questions:
   a. Describe the changes in the CPI that occurred during 2005.
   b. Explain the difference between a change in a relative price and inflation. Which relative prices increased most in August 2005 and which increased least or fell?
   c. Do you think the news article did a good job reporting the August CPI numbers? Write a brief report that does a better job and explain why it is better.

2. Thinking about the economy of Sandy Island in problems 7 and 8:
   a. In what phase of its business cycle was Sandy Island during 2006?
   b. What do you predict would be happening to real GDP on Sandy Island? Why?
   c. What do you predict would be happening to real GDP per person on Sandy Island? Why?

3. Describe the main features of the labour market at the peak of the business cycle.

4. Describe the main features of the labour market at the trough of the business cycle.

5. You've seen in this chapter that the average workweek has shortened over the years. Do you think that shorter work hours are a problem or a benefit? Do you expect the average workweek to keep getting shorter? Why or why not?

6. An increasing number of jobs are part-time jobs. Can you think of some reasons for this trend? Who benefits from part-time jobs: the employer, the worker, or both? Explain with examples.

7. You've seen that the CPI is biased and over-states the true inflation rate. It would be a simple matter to adjust the CPI for the known average bias. Yet we continue to keep a flawed measure of inflation in place. Why do you think we don't adjust the CPI for the known average bias so that its measure of the inflation rate is more accurate? Explain who gains from the biased measure and who loses from it. Try to think of reasons why those who lose have not persuaded those who win to adopt a more accurate measure.

WEB EXERCISES

Use the links on   myeconlab   to work the following exercise.

1. Visit the Web site of the Bank of Canada and review the latest Monetary Policy Report of the Bank of Canada. In which phase of the business cycle is the economy in your region? How does your region compare to the nation as a whole?

2. Visit the Web site of Statistics Canada and find labour market data for your own province.
   a. What have been the trends in employment, unemployment, and labour force participation in your province during the past two years?
   b. On the basis of what you know about your own province, how would you set about explaining these trends?
   c. Try to identify those industries that have expanded most and those that have shrunk.
   d. What are the problems with your own provincial labour market that you think need provincial government action to resolve?
   e. What actions do you think your provincial government must take to resolve these problems? Answer this question by using the demand and supply model of the labour market and predict the effects of the actions you prescribe.
   f. Compare the labour market performance of your own province with that of Canada.
   g. If your province is performing better than the national average, to what do you attribute the success? If your province is performing worse than the national average, to what do you attribute its problems? What federal actions are needed in your provincial labour market?

3. Visit the Web site of Statistics Canada and find CPI data for your own province.
   a. What have been the trends in the CPI in your province during the past two years?
   b. Compare the CPI performance of your own province with that of Canada as a whole.
   c. On the basis of what you know about your own province, how would you set about explaining its deviation from the Canadian average?

Aggregate Supply and Aggregate Demand

CHAPTER 22

Production and Prices

During the ten years from 1995 to 2005, Canadian real GDP increased by 40 percent. Expanding at this pace, real GDP doubles every 21 years. What forces bring persistent and rapid expansion of real GDP?

Expanding real GDP brings a rising standard of living. Inflation brings a rising cost of living. Because of inflation, you need $2 today to buy what $1 bought in 1980. What causes inflation?

You saw in the previous chapter that our economy doesn't expand at a constant pace. Instead, it ebbs and flows over the business cycle. You also saw that we had a recession during 1990 and early 1991. For half a year, real GDP decreased. Since that time, our economy has expanded, but at a variable rate. Why do we have a business cycle?

Because our economy fluctuates, the government and the Bank of Canada try to smooth its path. How do the policy actions of the government and the Bank of Canada affect production and prices?

◆ To answer questions like these, we need a *model* of real GDP and the price level. Our main task in this chapter is to study such a model: the *aggregate supply–aggregate demand model*. Our second task is to use the aggregate supply–aggregate demand (or *AS–AD*) model to answer the questions we've just posed. You'll discover that this model enables us to understand the forces that make our economy expand, that bring inflation, and that cause business cycle fluctuations. At the end of the chapter, in *Reading Between the Lines*, we'll put the *AS–AD* model to work to understand the macroeconomic effects of implementing the Kyoto agreement on climate control.

After studying this chapter, you will be able to

- ■ **Define and explain what determines aggregate supply**
- ■ **Define and explain what determines aggregate demand**
- ■ **Explain macroeconomic equilibrium and the effects of fluctuations in aggregate supply and aggregate demand**
- ■ **Explain Canadian economic growth, inflation, and the business cycle by using the *AS–AD* model**

Aggregate Supply

THE AGGREGATE SUPPLY–AGGREGATE DEMAND model enables us to understand three features of macroeconomic performance:

- Growth of potential GDP
- Inflation
- Business cycle fluctuations

The model uses the concepts of *aggregate* supply and *aggregate* demand to determine *real GDP* and the *price level* (the GDP deflator). We begin by looking at the limits to production that influence aggregate supply.

Aggregate Supply Fundamentals

The *quantity of real GDP supplied* (Y) depends on

1. The quantity of labour (*L*)
2. The quantity of capital (*K*)
3. The state of technology (*T*)

The influence of these three factors on the quantity of real GDP supplied is described by the **aggregate production function**, which is written as the equation:

$$Y = F(L, K, T).$$

In words, the quantity of real GDP supplied is determined by (is a function *F* of) the quantities of labour and capital and the state of technology. The larger is *L*, *K*, or *T*, the greater is *Y*.

At any given time, the quantity of capital and the state of technology are fixed. They depend on decisions that were made in the past. The population is also fixed. But the quantity of labour is not fixed. It depends on decisions made by people and firms about the supply of and demand for labour.

The labour market can be in any one of three states: at full employment, above full employment, or below full employment.

Even at full employment, there are always some people looking for jobs and some firms looking for people to hire. The reason is that there is a constant churning of the labour market. Every day, some jobs are destroyed as businesses reorganize or fail. Some jobs are created as new businesses start up or existing ones expand. Some workers decide, for any of a thousand personal reasons, to quit their jobs. And other people decide to start looking for a job. This constant churning in the labour market prevents unemploy-ment from ever disappearing. The unemployment rate at full employment is called the **natural rate of unem-ployment**.

Another way to think about full employment is as a state of the labour market in which the quantity of labour demanded equals the quantity supplied. Firms demand labour only if it is profitable to do so. And the lower the wage rate, which is the cost of labour, the greater is the quantity of labour demanded. People supply labour only if doing so is the most valuable use of their time. And the higher the wage rate, which is the return to labour, the greater is the quantity of labour supplied. The wage rate that makes the quantity of labour demanded equal to the quantity of labour supplied is the equilibrium wage rate. At this wage rate, there is full employment. (You can study the labour market at full employment in Chapter 30 on pp. 712–713.)

The quantity of real GDP at full employment is *potential GDP*, which depends on the full-employment quantity of labour, the quantity of capital, and the state of technology. Over the business cycle, employment fluctuates around full employment and real GDP fluctuates around potential GDP.

To study aggregate supply in different states of the labour market, we distinguish between

- Long-run aggregate supply
- Short-run aggregate supply

Long-Run Aggregate Supply

The economy is constantly bombarded by events that move real GDP away from potential GDP and, equivalently, that move employment away from full employment. Following such an event, forces operate to take real GDP back towards potential GDP and restore full employment. The **macroeconomic long run** is a time frame that is sufficiently long for these forces to have done their work so that real GDP equals potential GDP and full employment prevails.

The **long-run aggregate supply curve** is the relationship between the quantity of real GDP supplied and the price level in the long run when real GDP equals potential GDP. Figure 22.1 shows this relationship as the vertical line labelled *LAS*. Along the long-run aggregate supply curve, as the price level changes, real GDP remains at potential GDP, which in Fig. 22.1 is $1,000 billion. The long-run aggregate supply curve is always vertical and is located at potential GDP.

FIGURE 22.1
Long-Run Aggregate Supply

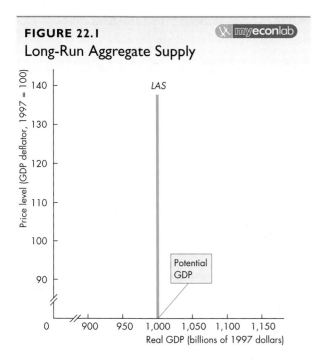

The long-run aggregate supply curve (*LAS*) shows the relationship between potential GDP and the price level. Potential GDP is independent of the price level, so the *LAS* curve is vertical at potential GDP.

The long-run aggregate supply curve is vertical because potential GDP is independent of the price level. The reason for this independence is that a movement along the *LAS* curve is accompanied by a change in *two* sets of prices: the prices of goods and services—the price level—and the prices of productive resources. A 10 percent increase in the prices of goods and services is matched by a 10 percent increase in the money wage rate and other resource prices. That is, the price level, money wage rate, and other resource prices all change by the same percentage, and *relative prices* and the *real wage rate* remain constant. When the price level changes but relative prices and the real wage rate remain constant, real GDP also remains constant.

Production at a Pepsi Plant You can see why real GDP remains constant when all prices change by the same percentage if you think about production decisions at a Pepsi bottling plant. The plant is producing the quantity of Pepsi that maximizes profit. The plant

can increase production but only by incurring a higher *marginal cost* (see Chapter 2, p. 37). So the firm has no incentive to change production.

Short-Run Aggregate Supply

The **macroeconomic short run** is a period during which real GDP has fallen below or risen above potential GDP. At the same time, the unemployment rate has risen above or fallen below the natural rate of unemployment.

The **short-run aggregate supply curve** is the relationship between the quantity of real GDP supplied and the price level in the short run when the money wage rate, the prices of other resources, and potential GDP remain constant. Figure 22.2 shows a short-run aggregate supply curve as the upward-sloping curve labelled *SAS*. This curve is based on the short-run aggregate supply schedule, and each point on the *SAS* curve corresponds to a row of the aggregate supply schedule. For example, point *A* on the *SAS* curve and row A of the schedule tell us that if the price level is 100, the quantity of real GDP supplied is $900 billion.

At point *C*, the price level is 110 and the quantity of real GDP supplied is $1,000 billion, which equals potential GDP. If the price level is higher than 110, real GDP exceeds potential GDP; if the price level is below 110, real GDP is less than potential GDP.

Back at the Pepsi Plant You can see why the short-run aggregate supply curve slopes upward by returning to the Pepsi bottling plant. The plant produces the quantity that maximizes profit. If the price of Pepsi rises and the money wage rate and other costs don't change, the *relative price* of Pepsi rises and the firm has an incentive to increase its production. The higher relative price of Pepsi covers the higher marginal cost of producing more Pepsi, so the firm increases production.

Similarly, if the price of Pepsi falls and the money wage rate and other costs don't change, the lower relative price is not sufficient to cover the marginal cost of Pepsi, so the firm decreases production.

Again, what's true for Pepsi bottlers is true for the producers of all goods and services. So when the price level rises and the money wage rate and other resource prices remain constant, the quantity of real GDP supplied increases.

FIGURE 22.2

Short-Run Aggregate Supply

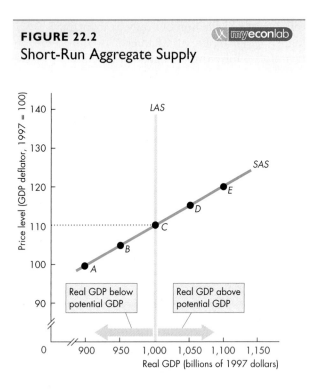

	Price level (GDP deflator)	Real GDP (billions of 1997 dollars)
A	100	900
B	105	950
C	110	1,000
D	115	1,050
E	120	1,100

The short-run aggregate supply curve shows the relationship between the quantity of real GDP supplied and the price level when the money wage rate, other resource prices, and potential GDP remain the same. The short-run aggregate supply curve, SAS, is based on the schedule in the table. This curve is upward-sloping because firms' marginal costs increase as output increases, so a higher price is needed, relative to the prices of productive resources, to bring forth an increase in the quantity produced. On the SAS curve, when the price level is 110, real GDP equals potential GDP. If the price level is greater than 110, real GDP exceeds potential GDP; if the price level is below 110, real GDP is less than potential GDP.

Movements Along the *LAS* and *SAS* Curves

Figure 22.3 summarizes what you've just learned about the *LAS* and *SAS* curves. When the price level, the money wage rate, and other resource prices rise by the same percentage, relative price remains constant and real GDP remains at potential GDP. There is a *movement along* the *LAS* curve.

When the price level rises but the money wage rate and other resource prices remain the same, the quantity of real GDP supplied increases and there is a *movement along* the *SAS* curve.

Let's next study the influences that bring changes in aggregate supply.

FIGURE 22.3

Movements Along the Aggregate Supply Curves

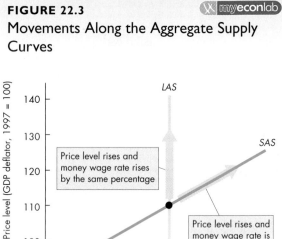

A rise in the price level with no change in the money wage rate and other resource prices brings an increase in the quantity of real GDP supplied and a movement along the short-run aggregate supply curve, SAS.

A rise in the price level with equal percentage increases in the money wage rate and other resource prices keeps the quantity of real GDP supplied constant at potential GDP and brings a movement along the long-run aggregate supply curve, LAS.

Changes in Aggregate Supply

You've just seen that a change in the price level brings a movement along the aggregate supply curves but does not change aggregate supply. Aggregate supply changes when influences on production plans other than the price level change. Let's begin by looking at factors that change potential GDP.

Changes in Potential GDP When potential GDP changes, both long-run aggregate supply and short-run aggregate supply change. Potential GDP changes for three reasons:

1. A change in the full-employment quantity of labour
2. A change in the quantity of capital
3. An advance in technology

An increase in the full-employment quantity of labour, an increase in the quantity of capital, or an advance in technology increases potential GDP. And an increase in potential GDP changes both the long-run aggregate supply and short-run aggregate supply.

Figure 22.4 shows these effects of a change in potential GDP. Initially, the long-run aggregate supply curve is LAS_0 and the short-run aggregate supply curve is SAS_0. If an increase in the quantity of capital or a technological advance increases potential GDP to $1,100 billion, long-run aggregate supply increases and the long-run aggregate supply curve shifts rightward to LAS_1. Short-run aggregate supply also increases, and the short-run aggregate supply curve shifts rightward to SAS_1.

Let's look more closely at the influences on potential GDP and the aggregate supply curves.

A Change in the Full-Employment Quantity of Labour

A Pepsi bottling plant that employs 100 workers bottles more Pepsi than an otherwise identical plant that employs ten workers. The same is true for the economy as a whole. The larger the quantity of labour employed, the greater is GDP.

Over time, potential GDP increases because the labour force increases. But (with constant capital and technology) *potential* GDP increases only if the full-employment quantity of labour increases. Fluctuations in employment over the business cycle bring fluctuations in real GDP. But these changes in real GDP are fluctuations around potential GDP. They are not changes in potential GDP and long-run aggregate supply.

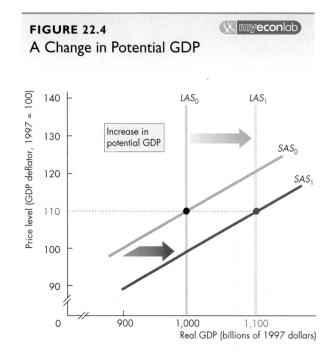

FIGURE 22.4   myeconlab
A Change in Potential GDP

An increase in potential GDP increases both long-run aggregate supply and short-run aggregate supply and shifts both aggregate supply curves rightward, from LAS_0 to LAS_1 and from SAS_0 to SAS_1.

A Change in the Quantity of Capital

A Pepsi bottling plant with two production lines bottles more Pepsi than an otherwise identical plant that has only one production line. For the economy, the larger the quantity of capital, the more productive is the labour force and the greater is its potential GDP. Potential GDP per person in capital-rich Canada is vastly greater than that in capital-poor China and Russia.

Capital includes *human capital*. One Pepsi plant is managed by an economics major with an MBA and has a labour force with an average of ten years of experience. This plant produces a much larger output than an otherwise identical plant that is managed by someone with no business training or experience and that has a young labour force that is new to bottling. The first plant has a greater amount of human capital than the second. For the economy as a whole, the larger the quantity of *human capital*—the skills that people have acquired in school and through on-the-job training—the greater is potential GDP.

An Advance in Technology A Pepsi plant that has pre-computer age machines produces less than one that uses the latest robot technology. Technological change enables firms to produce more from any given amount of inputs. So even with fixed quantities of labour and capital, improvements in technology increase potential GDP.

Technological advances are by far the most important source of increased production over the past two centuries. Because of technological advances, one farmer in Canada today can feed 100 people and one auto worker can produce almost 14 cars and trucks in a year.

Let's now look at the effects of changes in the money wage rate.

Changes in the Money Wage Rate and Other Resource Prices

When the money wage rate or the money prices of other resources (such as the price of oil) change, short-run aggregate supply changes but long-run aggregate supply does not change.

Figure 22.5 shows the effect on aggregate supply of an increase in the money wage rate. Initially, the short-run aggregate supply curve is SAS_0. A rise in the money wage rate *decreases* short-run aggregate supply and shifts the short-run aggregate supply curve leftward to SAS_2.

The money wage rate (and resource prices) affect short-run aggregate supply because they influence firms' costs. The higher the money wage rate, the higher are firms' costs and the smaller is the quantity that firms are willing to supply at each price level. So an increase in the money wage rate decreases short-run aggregate supply.

A change in the money wage rate does *not* change long-run aggregate supply because on the *LAS* curve, a change in the money wage rate is accompanied by an equal percentage change in the price level. With no change in *relative* prices, firms have no incentive to change production and real GDP remains constant at potential GDP.

In Fig. 22.5, the vertical distance between the original *SAS* curve and the new *SAS* curve is determined by the percentage change in the money wage rate. That is, the percentage increase in the price level between point *A* and point *B* equals the percentage increase in the money wage rate.

Because potential GDP does not change when the money wage rate changes, long-run aggregate supply does not change. The long-run aggregate supply curve remains at *LAS*.

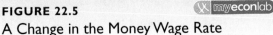

FIGURE 22.5

A Change in the Money Wage Rate

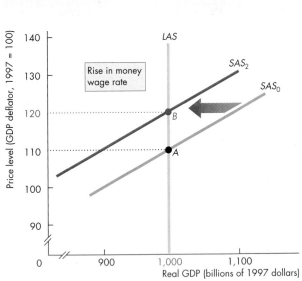

A rise in the money wage rate decreases short-run aggregate supply and shifts the short-run aggregate supply curve leftward from SAS_0 to SAS_2. A rise in the money wage rate does not change potential GDP, so the long-run aggregate supply curve does not shift.

Aggregate Demand

THE QUANTITY OF REAL GDP DEMANDED IS THE sum of the real consumption expenditure (C), investment (I), government expenditures (G), and exports (X) minus imports (M). That is,

$$Y = C + I + G + X - M.$$

The *quantity of real GDP demanded* is the total amount of final goods and services produced in Canada that people, businesses, governments, and foreigners plan to buy.

These buying plans depend on many factors. Some of the main ones are

- The price level
- Expectations
- Fiscal policy and monetary policy
- The world economy

We first focus on the relationship between the quantity of real GDP demanded and the price level. To study this relationship, we keep all other influences on buying plans the same and ask: How does the quantity of real GDP demanded vary as the price level varies?

The Aggregate Demand Curve

Other things remaining the same, the higher the price level, the smaller is the quantity of real GDP demanded. This relationship between the quantity of real GDP demanded and the price level is called **aggregate demand**. Aggregate demand is described by an aggregate demand schedule and an aggregate demand curve.

Figure 22.6 shows an aggregate demand curve (AD) and an aggregate demand schedule. Each point on the AD curve corresponds to a row of the table. For example, point C' on the AD curve and row C' of the table tell us that if the price level is 110, the quantity of real GDP demanded is $1,000 billion.

The aggregate demand curve slopes downward for two reasons:

- Wealth effect
- Substitution effects

Wealth Effect When the price level rises but other things remain the same, *real* wealth decreases. Real

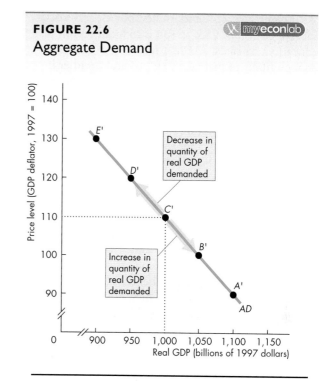

FIGURE 22.6
Aggregate Demand

	Price level (GDP deflator)	Real GDP (billions of 1997 dollars)
A'	90	1,100
B'	100	1,050
C'	110	1,000
D'	120	950
E'	130	900

The aggregate demand curve (*AD*) shows the relationship between the quantity of real GDP demanded and the price level. The aggregate demand curve is based on the aggregate demand schedule in the table. Each point A' through E' on the curve corresponds to the row in the table identified by the same letter. When the price level is 110, the quantity of real GDP demanded is $1,000 billion, shown by point C'. A change in the price level with all other influences on aggregate buying plans remaining the same brings a change in the quantity of real GDP demanded and a movement along the AD curve.

wealth is the amount of money in the bank, bonds, stocks, and other assets that people own, measured not in dollars but in terms of the goods and services that this money, bonds, and stocks will buy.

People save and hold money, bonds, and stocks for many reasons. One reason is to build up funds for education expenses. Another reason is to build up enough funds to meet possible medical or other big bills. But the biggest reason is to build up enough funds to provide a retirement income.

If the price level rises, real wealth decreases. People then try to restore their wealth. To do so, they must increase saving and, equivalently, decrease current consumption. Such a decrease in consumption is a decrease in the quantity of real GDP demanded.

Maria's Wealth Effect You can see how the wealth effect works by thinking about Maria's buying plans. Maria lives in Moscow, Russia. She has worked hard all summer and saved 20,000 rubles (the currency of Russia), which she plans to spend attending graduate school when she has finished her economics degree. So Maria's wealth is 20,000 rubles. Maria has a part-time job, and her income from this job pays her current expenses. The price level in Russia rises by 100 percent, and now Maria needs 40,000 rubles to buy what 20,000 rubles once bought. To try to make up some of the fall in value of her savings, Maria saves even more and cuts her current spending to the bare minimum.

Substitution Effects When the price level rises and other things remain the same, interest rates rise. The reason is related to the wealth effect that you've just studied. A rise in the price level decreases the real value of the money in people's pockets and bank accounts. With a smaller amount of real money around, banks and other lenders can get a higher interest rate on loans. But faced with higher interest rates, people and businesses delay plans to buy new capital and consumer durable goods and cut back on spending.

This substitution effect involves substituting goods in the future for goods today and is called an *intertemporal* substitution effect—a substitution across time. To increase future consumption, consumption today must decrease and saving increase.

To see this intertemporal substitution effect more clearly, think about your own plan to buy a new computer. At an interest rate of 5 percent a year, you might borrow $2,000 and buy the new machine you've been researching. But at an interest rate of 10 percent a year, you might decide that the payments would be too high. You don't abandon your plan to buy the computer, but you decide to delay your purchase.

A second substitution effect works through international prices. When the Canadian price level rises and other things remain the same, Canadian-made goods and services become more expensive relative to foreign-made goods and services. This change in *relative prices* encourages people to spend less on Canadian-made items and more on foreign-made items. For example, if the Canadian price level rises relative to the U.S. price level, Americans buy fewer Canadian-made cars (Canadian exports decrease) and Canadians buy more U.S.-made cars (Canadian imports increase). Canadian GDP decreases.

Maria's Substitution Effects In Moscow, Russia, Maria makes some substitutions. She was planning to trade in her old motor scooter and get a new one. But with a higher price level and faced with higher interest rates, she decides to make her old scooter last one more year. Also, with the prices of Russian goods sharply increasing, Maria substitutes a low-cost dress made in Malaysia for the Russian-made dress she had originally planned to buy.

Changes in the Quantity of Real GDP Demanded When the price level rises and other things remain the same, the quantity of real GDP demanded decreases—a movement up the *AD* curve as shown by the arrow in Fig. 22.6. When the price level falls and other things remain the same, the quantity of real GDP demanded increases—a movement down the *AD* curve.

We've now seen how the quantity of real GDP demanded changes when the price level changes. How do other influences on buying plans affect aggregate demand?

Changes in Aggregate Demand

A change in any factor that influences buying plans other than the price level brings a change in aggregate demand. The main factors are

- Expectations
- Fiscal policy and monetary policy
- The world economy

Expectations An increase in expected future income, other things remaining the same, increases the quantity of consumption goods (especially big-ticket items such as cars) that people plan to buy today and increases aggregate demand today.

An increase in the expected future inflation rate increases aggregate demand today because people decide to buy more goods and services at today's relatively lower prices. An increase in expected future profit increases the investment that firms plan to undertake today and increases aggregate demand today.

Fiscal Policy and Monetary Policy The government's attempt to influence the economy by setting and changing taxes, making transfer payments, and purchasing goods and services is called **fiscal policy**. A tax cut or an increase in transfer payments—for example, unemployment benefits or welfare payments—increases aggregate demand. Both of these influences operate by increasing households' disposable income. **Disposable income** is aggregate income minus taxes plus transfer payments. The greater the disposable income, the greater is the quantity of consumption goods and services that households plan to buy and the greater is aggregate demand.

Government expenditures on goods and services are one component of aggregate demand. So if the government spends more on hospitals, schools, and highways, aggregate demand increases.

Monetary policy consists of changes in interest rates and in the quantity of money in the economy. Interest rates and the quantity of money are determined by the Bank of Canada (described in Chapters 25 and 28). An increase in the quantity of money in the economy increases aggregate demand. To see why money affects aggregate demand, imagine that the Bank of Canada borrows the army's helicopters, loads them with millions of new $10 bills, and sprinkles these bills like confetti across the nation. People gather the newly available money and plan to spend some of it. So the quantity of goods and services demanded increases. But people don't plan to spend all the new money. They plan to save some of it and lend it to others through the banks. Interest rates fall, and with lower interest rates, people plan to buy more consumer durables and firms plan to increase their investment.

The World Economy Two main influences that the world economy has on aggregate demand are the foreign exchange rate and foreign income. The *foreign exchange rate* is the amount of a foreign currency that you can buy with a Canadian dollar. Other things remaining the same, a rise in the foreign exchange rate decreases aggregate demand. To see how the foreign exchange rate influences aggregate demand, suppose

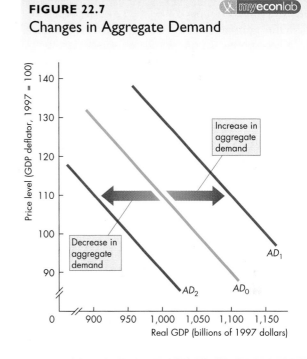

FIGURE 22.7 myeconlab
Changes in Aggregate Demand

Aggregate demand

Decreases if:

■ Expected future income, inflation, or profits decrease

■ Fiscal policy decreases government expenditures, increases taxes, or decreases transfer payments

■ Monetary policy increases interest rates and decreases the quantity of money

■ The foreign exchange rate increases or foreign income decreases

Increases if:

■ Expected future income, inflation, or profits increase

■ Fiscal policy increases government expenditures, decreases taxes, or increases transfer payments

■ Monetary policy decreases interest rates and increases the quantity of money

■ The foreign exchange rate decreases or foreign income increases

that $1 exchanges for 100 Japanese yen. A Fujitsu phone (made in Japan) costs 12,500 yen, and an equivalent Nortel phone (made in Canada) costs $110. In Canadian dollars, the Fujitsu phone costs $125, so people around the world buy the cheaper

Canadian phone. Now suppose the foreign exchange rate rises to 125 yen per dollar. At 125 yen per dollar, the Fujitsu phone costs $100 and is now cheaper than the Nortel phone. People will switch from the Canadian phone to the Japanese phone. Canadian exports will decrease and Canadian imports will increase, so Canadian aggregate demand will decrease.

An increase in foreign income increases Canadian exports and increases Canadian aggregate demand. For example, an increase in income in Japan and Germany increases Japanese and German consumers' and producers' planned expenditures on Canadian-made goods and services.

Shifts of the Aggregate Demand Curve When aggregate demand changes, the aggregate demand curve shifts. Figure 22.7 shows two changes in aggregate demand and summarizes the factors that bring about such changes.

Aggregate demand increases and the aggregate demand curve shifts rightward from AD_0 to AD_1 when expected future income, inflation, or profit increases; government expenditures on goods and services increase; taxes are cut; transfer payments increase; the quantity of money increases and interest rates fall; the foreign exchange rate falls; or foreign income increases.

Aggregate demand decreases and the aggregate demand curve shifts leftward from AD_0 to AD_2 when expected future income, inflation, or profit decreases; government expenditures on goods and services decrease; taxes increase; transfer payments decrease; the quantity of money decreases and interest rates rise; the foreign exchange rate rises; or foreign income decreases.

REVIEW QUIZ

1 What does the aggregate demand curve show? What factors change and what factors remain the same when there is a movement along the aggregate demand curve?

2 Why does the aggregate demand curve slope downward?

3 How do changes in expectations, fiscal policy and monetary policy, and the world economy change aggregate demand and shift the aggregate demand curve?

   (X) myeconlab **Study Plan 22.2**

Macroeconomic Equilibrium

THE PURPOSE OF THE AGGREGATE SUPPLY– aggregate demand model is to explain changes in real GDP and the price level. To achieve this purpose, we combine aggregate supply and aggregate demand and determine macroeconomic equilibrium. There is a macroeconomic equilibrium for each of the time frames for aggregate supply: a long-run equilibrium and a short-run equilibrium. Long-run equilibrium is the state towards which the economy is heading. Short-run equilibrium is the normal state of the economy as it fluctuates around potential GDP.

We'll begin our study of macroeconomic equilibrium by looking first at the short run.

Short-Run Macroeconomic Equilibrium

The aggregate demand curve tells us the quantity of real GDP demanded at each price level, and the short-run aggregate supply curve tells us the quantity of real GDP supplied at each price level. **Short-run macroeconomic equilibrium** occurs when the quantity of real GDP demanded equals the quantity of real GDP supplied. That is, short-run equilibrium occurs at the point of intersection of the AD curve and the SAS curve. Figure 22.8 shows such an equilibrium at a price level of 110 and real GDP of $1,000 billion (points C and C').

To see why this position is the equilibrium, think about what happens if the price level is something other than 110. Suppose, for example, that the price level is 120 and that real GDP is $1,100 billion (at point E on the SAS curve). The quantity of real GDP demanded is less than $1,100 billion, so firms are unable to sell all their output. Unwanted inventories pile up, and firms cut both production and prices. Production and prices are cut until firms can sell all their output. This situation occurs only when real GDP is $1,000 billion and the price level is 110.

Now suppose the price level is 100 and real GDP is $900 billion (at point A on the SAS curve). The quantity of real GDP demanded exceeds $900 billion, so firms are unable to meet the demand for their output. Inventories decrease, and customers clamour for goods and services. So firms increase production and raise prices. Production and prices increase until firms can meet demand. This situation

FIGURE 22.8
Short-Run Equilibrium

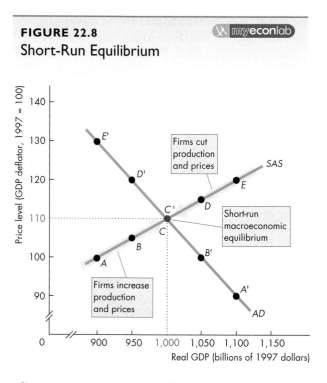

Short-run macroeconomic equilibrium occurs when real GDP demanded equals real GDP supplied—at the intersection of the aggregate demand curve (AD) and the short-run aggregate supply curve (SAS). Here, such an equilibrium occurs at points C and C', where the price level is 110 and real GDP is $1,000 billion. If the price level is 120 and real GDP is $1,100 billion (point E), firms will not be able to sell all their output. They will decrease production and cut prices. If the price level is 100 and real GDP is $900 billion (point A), people will not be able to buy all the goods and services they demand. Firms will increase production and raise their prices. Only when the price level is 110 and real GDP is $1,000 billion can firms sell all that they produce and can people buy all that they demand. This is the short-run macroeconomic equilibrium.

occurs only when real GDP is $1,000 billion and the price level is 110.

In short-run equilibrium, the money wage rate is fixed. It does not adjust to bring full employment. So in the short run, real GDP can be greater than or less than potential GDP. But in the long run, the money wage rate does adjust and real GDP moves towards potential GDP. We are going to study this adjustment process. But first, let's look at the economy in long-run equilibrium.

Long-Run Macroeconomic Equilibrium

Long-run macroeconomic equilibrium occurs when real GDP equals potential GDP—equivalently, when the economy is on its *long-run* aggregate supply curve. Figure 22.9 shows *long-run* equilibrium, which occurs at the intersection of the aggregate demand curve and the long-run aggregate supply curve (the blue curves). Long-run equilibrium comes about because the money wage rate adjusts. Potential GDP and aggregate demand determine the price level, and the price level influences the money wage rate. In long-run equilibrium, the money wage rate has adjusted to put the (green) short-run aggregate supply curve through the long-run equilibrium point.

We'll look at this money wage adjustment process later in this chapter. But first, let's see how the AS–AD model helps us to understand economic growth and inflation.

FIGURE 22.9
Long-Run Equilibrium

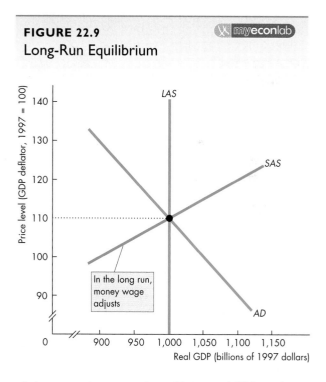

In long-run macroeconomic equilibrium, real GDP equals potential GDP. So long-run equilibrium occurs where the aggregate demand curve intersects the long-run aggregate supply curve. In the long run, aggregate demand determines the price level and has no effect on real GDP. The money wage rate adjusts in the long run, so the SAS curve intersects the LAS curve at the long-run equilibrium price level.

Economic Growth and Inflation

Economic growth occurs because over time, the quantity of labour grows, capital is accumulated, and technology advances. These changes increase potential GDP and shift the long-run aggregate supply curve rightward. Figure 22.10 shows such a shift. The growth rate of potential GDP is determined by the pace at which labour grows, capital is accumulated, and technology advances.

Inflation occurs when, over time, aggregate demand increases by more than long-run aggregate supply increases. That is, inflation occurs if the aggregate demand curve shifts rightward by more than the rightward shift in the long-run aggregate supply curve. Figure 22.10 shows such shifts.

If aggregate demand increased at the same pace as long-run aggregate supply, we would experience real GDP growth with no inflation.

In the long run, the main influence on aggregate demand is the growth rate of the quantity of money. At times when the quantity of money is growing quickly, aggregate demand also grows quickly and the inflation rate is high. When the growth rate of the quantity of money slows, other things remaining the same, the inflation rate eventually decreases.

Our economy experiences growth and inflation, like that shown in Fig. 22.10. But it does not experience *steady* economic growth and *steady* inflation. Real GDP fluctuates around potential GDP in a business cycle, and inflation also fluctuates. When we study the business cycle, we ignore economic growth. By doing so, we can see the business cycle more clearly.

The Business Cycle

The business cycle occurs because aggregate demand and short-run aggregate supply fluctuate but the money wage rate does not adjust quickly enough to keep real GDP at potential GDP. Figure 22.11 shows three types of short-run equilibrium.

In part (a), there is a below full-employment equilibrium. A **below full-employment equilibrium** is a macroeconomic equilibrium in which potential GDP exceeds real GDP. When potential GDP exceeds real GDP, the *output gap* is negative[1] and is called a **recessionary gap**. This name reminds us that a gap has opened up between potential GDP and real GDP either because the economy has experienced a recession or because real GDP, while growing, has grown more slowly than potential GDP.

The below full-employment equilibrium shown in Fig. 22.11(a) occurs where the aggregate demand curve AD_0 intersects the short-run aggregate supply curve SAS_0 at a real GDP of $980 billion and a price level of 110. The recessionary gap is $20 billion. The Canadian economy was in a situation similar to that shown in Fig. 22.11(a) during the early 1980s, and again during the early 1990s. In those years, real GDP was less than potential GDP.

Figure 22.11(b) is an example of *long-run equilibrium*, in which real GDP equals potential GDP. In this example, the equilibrium occurs where the aggregate demand curve AD_1 intersects the short-run aggregate supply curve SAS_1 at an actual and potential GDP of $1,000 billion. The Canadian economy was in a situation such as that shown in Fig. 22.11(b) in 1999.

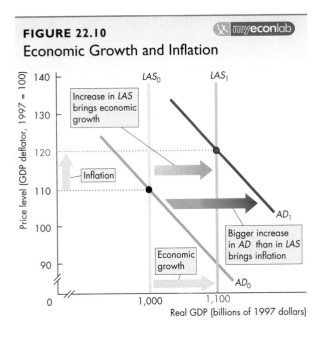

FIGURE 22.10
Economic Growth and Inflation

Economic growth is the persistent increase in potential GDP. Economic growth is shown as an ongoing rightward shift of the *LAS* curve. Inflation is the persistent rise in the price level. Inflation occurs when aggregate demand increases by more than the increase in long-run aggregate supply.

---

[1] A negative output gap is also sometimes called an Okun gap (see p. 451). An Okun gap and a recessionary gap are alternative names for the same phenomenon.

Figure 22.11(c) shows an above full-employment equilibrium. An **above full-employment equilibrium** is a macroeconomic equilibrium in which real GDP exceeds potential GDP. When real GDP exceeds potential GDP, the *output gap* is positive and is called an **inflationary gap**. This name reminds us that a gap has opened up between real GDP and potential GDP and that this gap creates inflationary pressure.

The above full-employment equilibrium shown in Fig. 22.11(c) occurs where the aggregate demand curve AD_2 intersects the short-run aggregate supply curve SAS_2 at a real GDP of $1,020 billion and a price

level of 110. Real GDP exceeds potential GDP and the inflationary gap is $20 billion. The Canadian economy was last in a situation similar to that depicted in Fig. 22.11(c) in 2000.

The economy moves from one type of equilibrium to another as a result of fluctuations in aggregate demand and in short-run aggregate supply. These fluctuations produce fluctuations in real GDP and the price level. Figure 22.11(d) shows how real GDP fluctuates around potential GDP.

Let's now look at some of the sources of these fluctuations around potential GDP.

FIGURE 22.11
The Business Cycle

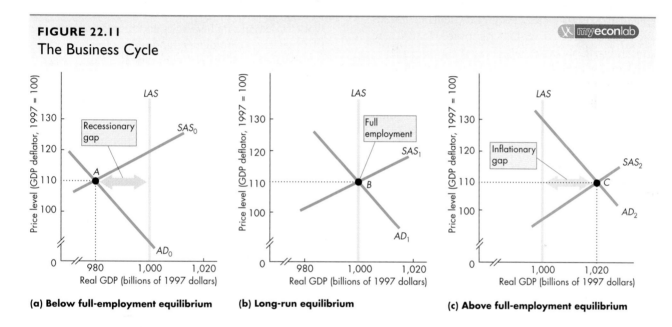

(a) Below full-employment equilibrium (b) Long-run equilibrium (c) Above full-employment equilibrium

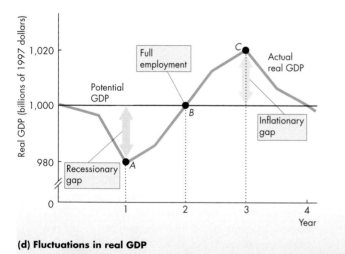

(d) Fluctuations in real GDP

Part (a) shows a below full-employment equilibrium in year 1; part (b) shows a long-run equilibrium in year 2; and part (c) shows an above full-employment equilibrium in year 3. Part (d) shows how real GDP fluctuates around potential GDP in a business cycle.

In year 1, a recessionary gap exists and the economy is at point *A* (in parts a and d). In year 2, the economy is in long-run equilibrium and the economy is at point *B* (in parts b and d). In year 3, an inflationary gap exists and the economy is at point *C* (in parts c and d).

Fluctuations in Aggregate Demand

One reason real GDP fluctuates around potential GDP is that aggregate demand fluctuates. Let's see what happens when aggregate demand increases.

Figure 22.12(a) shows an economy in long-run equilibrium. The aggregate demand curve is AD_0, the short-run aggregate supply curve is SAS_0, and the long-run aggregate supply curve is LAS. Real GDP equals potential GDP at $1,000 billion, and the price level is 110.

Now suppose that the world economy expands and that the demand for Canadian-made goods increases in Japan and Europe. The increase in Canadian exports increases aggregate demand, and the aggregate demand curve shifts rightward from AD_0 to AD_1 in Fig. 22.12(a).

Faced with an increase in demand, firms increase production and raise prices. Real GDP increases to $1,050 billion, and the price level rises to 115. The economy is now in an above full-employment equilibrium. Real GDP exceeds potential GDP, and there is an inflationary gap.

The increase in aggregate demand has increased the prices of all goods and services. Faced with higher prices, firms have increased their output rates. At this stage, prices of goods and services have increased but the money wage rate has not changed. (Recall that as we move along a short-run aggregate supply curve, the money wage rate is constant.)

The economy cannot produce in excess of potential GDP forever. Why not? What are the forces at work that bring real GDP back to potential GDP?

Because the price level has increased and the money wage rate is unchanged, workers have experienced a fall in the buying power of their wages and firms' profits have increased. In these circumstances, workers demand higher wages and firms, anxious to maintain their employment and output levels, meet those demands. If firms do not raise the money wage rate, they will either lose workers or have to hire less productive ones.

As the money wage rate rises, the short-run aggregate supply curve begins to shift leftward. In Fig. 22.12(b), the short-run aggregate supply curve moves

FIGURE 22.12
An Increase in Aggregate Demand

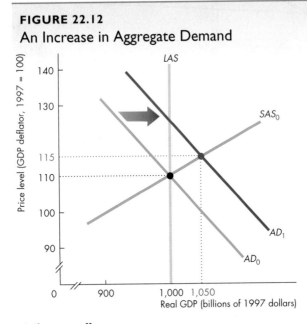

(a) Short-run effect

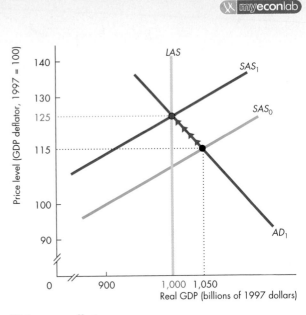

(b) Long-run effect

An increase in aggregate demand shifts the aggregate demand curve from AD_0 to AD_1. In short-run equilibrium, real GDP increases to $1,050 billion and the price level rises to 115. In this situation, an inflationary gap exists. In the long run, the money wage rate rises and the short-run aggregate

supply curve shifts leftward from SAS_0 to SAS_1 in part (b). As the SAS curve shifts leftward, it intersects the aggregate demand curve AD_1 at higher price levels and real GDP decreases. Eventually, the price level rises to 125 and real GDP decreases to $1,000 billion—potential GDP.

from SAS_0 towards SAS_1. The rise in the money wage rate and the shift in the SAS curve produce a sequence of new equilibrium positions. Along the adjustment path, real GDP decreases and the price level rises. The economy moves up along its aggregate demand curve as the arrowheads show.

Eventually, the money wage rate rises by the same percentage as the price level. At this time, the aggregate demand curve AD_1 intersects SAS_1 at a new long-run equilibrium. The price level has risen to 125, and real GDP is back where it started, at potential GDP.

A decrease in aggregate demand has similar but opposite effects to those of an increase in aggregate demand. That is, a decrease in aggregate demand shifts the aggregate demand curve leftward. Real GDP decreases to less than potential GDP, and a recessionary gap emerges. Firms cut prices. The lower price level increases the purchasing power of wages and increases firms' costs relative to their output prices because the money wage rate remains unchanged. Eventually, the money wage rate falls and the short-run aggregate supply curve shifts rightward. But the money wage rate changes slowly, so real GDP slowly returns to potential GDP and the price level falls slowly.

Let's now work out how real GDP and the price level change when aggregate supply changes.

Fluctuations in Aggregate Supply

Fluctuations in short-run aggregate supply can bring fluctuations in real GDP around potential GDP. Suppose that initially real GDP equals potential GDP. Then there is a large but temporary rise in the price of oil. What happens to real GDP and the price level?

Figure 22.13 answers this question. The aggregate demand curve is AD_0, the short-run aggregate supply curve is SAS_0, and the long-run aggregate supply curve is LAS. Real GDP is $1,000 billion, which equals potential GDP, and the price level is 110. Then the price of oil rises. Faced with higher energy and transportation costs, firms decrease production. Short-run aggregate supply decreases, and the short-run aggregate supply curve shifts leftward to SAS_1. The price level rises to 120, and real GDP decreases to $950 billion. Because real GDP decreases, the economy experiences recession. Because the price level increases, the economy experiences inflation. A combination of recession and inflation, called *stagflation*, actually occurred in the United States in the mid-1970s. But events like this are not common and Canada escaped the worst of that recession.

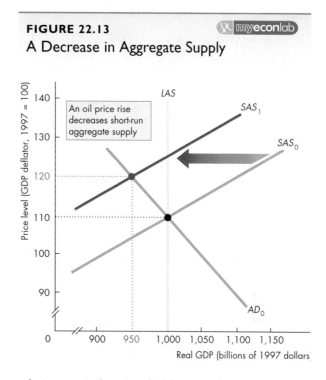

FIGURE 22.13   (X) myeconlab

A Decrease in Aggregate Supply

An increase in the price of oil decreases short-run aggregate supply and shifts the short-run aggregate supply curve from SAS_0 to SAS_1. Real GDP decreases from $1,000 billion to $950 billion, and the price level increases from 110 to 120. The economy experiences both recession and inflation—a situation known as stagflation.

REVIEW QUIZ

1 Does economic growth result from increases in aggregate demand, short-run aggregate supply, or long-run aggregate supply?

2 Does inflation result from increases in aggregate demand, short-run aggregate supply, or long-run aggregate supply?

3 Describe three types of short-run macroeconomic equilibrium.

4 How do fluctuations in aggregate demand and short-run aggregate supply bring fluctuations in real GDP around potential GDP?

(X) myeconlab   **Study Plan 22.3**

Let's put our new knowledge of aggregate supply and aggregate demand to work and see how we can explain recent Canadian macroeconomic performance.

Canadian Economic Growth, Inflation, and Cycles

THE ECONOMY IS CONTINUALLY CHANGING. IF you imagine the economy as a video, then an aggregate supply–aggregate demand figure such as Fig. 22.13 is a freeze-frame. We're going to run the video—an instant replay—but keep our finger on the freeze-frame button and look at some important parts of the previous action. Let's run the video from 1961.

Figure 22.14 shows the state of the economy in 1961 at the point of intersection of its aggregate demand curve, AD_{61}, and short-run aggregate supply curve, SAS_{61}. Real GDP was $240 billion, and the GDP deflator was 17 (less than one-fifth of its 2004 level). In 1961, real GDP equalled potential GDP—the economy was on its long-run aggregate supply curve, LAS_{61}.

By 2004, the economy had reached the point marked by the intersection of aggregate demand curve AD_{04} and short-run aggregate supply curve SAS_{04}. Real

GDP was $1,124 billion, and the GDP deflator was 115. Potential GDP in 2004 was also $1,124 billion.

The path traced by the blue and red dots in Fig. 22.14 shows three key features:

- Economic growth
- Inflation
- Business cycles

Economic Growth

Over the years, real GDP grows—shown in Fig. 22.14 by the rightward movement of the points. The faster real GDP grows, the larger is the horizontal distance between successive dots in the figure. The forces that generate economic growth are those that increase potential GDP. Potential GDP grows because the quantity of labour grows, we accumulate physical capital and human capital, and our technologies advance.

These forces that bring economic growth were strongest during the 1960s and late 1990s through 2002.

FIGURE 22.14
Aggregate Supply and Aggregate Demand: 1961–2004

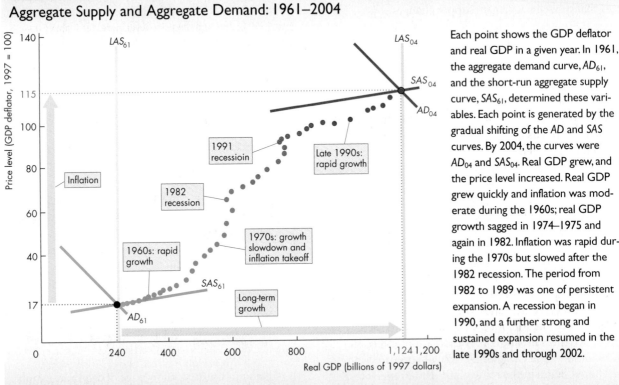

Each point shows the GDP deflator and real GDP in a given year. In 1961, the aggregate demand curve, AD_{61}, and the short-run aggregate supply curve, SAS_{61}, determined these variables. Each point is generated by the gradual shifting of the AD and SAS curves. By 2004, the curves were AD_{04} and SAS_{04}. Real GDP grew, and the price level increased. Real GDP grew quickly and inflation was moderate during the 1960s; real GDP growth sagged in 1974–1975 and again in 1982. Inflation was rapid during the 1970s but slowed after the 1982 recession. The period from 1982 to 1989 was one of persistent expansion. A recession began in 1990, and a further strong and sustained expansion resumed in the late 1990s and through 2002.

Source of data: Statistics Canada, CANSIM Tables 326–0002 and 380–0003.

Inflation

The price level rises over the years—shown in Fig. 22.14 by the upward movement of the points. The larger the rise in the price level, the larger is the vertical distance between successive dots in the figure. The main force generating the persistent increase in the price level is a tendency for aggregate demand to increase at a faster pace than the increase in long-run aggregate supply. All of the factors that increase aggregate demand and shift the aggregate demand curve influence the pace of inflation. But one factor—the growth of the quantity of money—is the main source of *persistent* increases in aggregate demand and persistent inflation.

Business Cycles

Over the years, the economy grows and shrinks in cycles—shown in Fig. 22.14 by the wavelike pattern made by the points, with the recessions highlighted. The cycles arise because the expansion of short-run aggregate supply and the growth of aggregate demand do not proceed at a fixed, steady pace. Although the economy has cycles, recessions do not usually follow quickly on the heels of their predecessors; "double-dip" recessions like the one in the cartoon are rare.

The Evolving Economy: 1961–2004

During the 1960s, real GDP growth was rapid and inflation was low. This was a period of rapid increases in aggregate supply and of moderate increases in aggregate demand.

The mid-1970s were years of rapid inflation and slow growth. The major source of these developments was a series of massive oil price increases that slowed the rightward shift of the aggregate supply curve and rapid increases in the quantity of money that speeded the rightward shift of the aggregate demand curve. The short-run aggregate supply curve shifted rightward at a slower pace than the aggregate demand curve shifted rightward.

The rest of the 1970s saw high inflation—the price level increased quickly—and only moderate growth in real GDP. By 1980, inflation was a major problem and the Bank of Canada decided to take strong action against it. The Bank permitted interest rates to rise to previously unknown levels. Consequently, aggregate demand decreased. By 1982, the decrease in aggregate demand put the economy into a deep recession.

"Please stand by for a series of tones. The first indicates the official end of the recession, the second indicates prosperity, and the third the return of the recession."

During the years 1983–1990, capital accumulation and steady technological advance resulted in a sustained rightward shift of the *LAS* curve. Wage growth was moderate, and the *SAS* curve shifted rightward. Aggregate demand growth kept pace with the growth of aggregate supply. Sustained but steady growth in aggregate supply and aggregate demand kept real GDP growing and inflation steady. The economy moved from a recession with real GDP less than potential GDP in 1982 to above full employment in 1990. It was in this condition when a decrease in aggregate demand led to the 1990–1991 recession. The economy stagnated for a year and then began to expand again, expanding rapidly during the late 1990s. Growth slowed in 2001 before expanding again.

◆ The *AS–AD* model explains economic growth, inflation, and the business cycle. The model is a useful one because it enables us to keep our eye on the big picture. But it lacks detail. It does not tell us as much as we need to know about the deeper forces that lie behind aggregate supply and aggregate demand. The chapters that follow begin to fill in the details on aggregate demand. But before you embark on this next stage, take a look at *Reading Between the Lines* on pp. 524–525, which looks at the effects of implementing the Kyoto agreement on climate control on aggregate supply and aggregate demand in the Canadian economy in 2010.

Kyoto in the AS–AD Model

FINANCIAL POST, OCTOBER 12, 2002

Kyoto could cost 244,000 jobs

The federal government conceded yesterday that implementing the Kyoto Protocol on climate change could cost the Canadian economy as many as a quarter of a million jobs, and $21-billion in output, by the end of the decade.

In a long awaited impact study of Kyoto, federal officials predicted the accord could mean between 61,000 and 244,000 fewer jobs by 2010. They also forecast the accord could mean gross domestic product would be between 0.4% ($5-billion) and 1.6% ($21-billion) lower than expected by the same year.

The federal document argued that the 244,000 job figure and 1.6% drop in GDP growth was a worst-case scenario. Officials said the lower figures were more likely. ...

Private-sector estimates place the cost of implementing Kyoto at 450,000 jobs by 2010, and $4.5-billion annually.

Pierre Alvarez, president of the Canadian Association of Petroleum Producers, called the federal calculations "empty numbers," adding that Ottawa's Kyoto plan remains a mystery.

"This is a model based on hypothetical assumptions, assumptions no one else has ever seen," he said.

"To extrapolate from that, they are simply empty numbers that are of little value to the current debate."

He added: "The assumptions are based on estimates we don't necessarily agree ..."

Nancy Hughes Anthony, president of the Canadian Chamber of Commerce, charged yesterday the government's economic model leaves a "false impression" about the impact of the Kyoto Protocol by presenting optimistic projections.

But she said it is even clear from the best and worst-case scenarios in the federal analysis that the prosperity of Canadians will suffer if Jean Chrétien, the Prime Minister, pushes ahead with ratification of Kyoto by the end of the year. ...

Reprinted by permission of the *National Post*.

Essence of the Story

■ The federal government predicts that ratifying the Kyoto accord will lower employment by between 61,000 and 244,000 jobs by 2010.

■ The government also predicts that ratifying the Kyoto accord will lower real GDP by between 0.4 percent ($5 billion) and 1.6 percent ($21 billion) by 2010.

■ The government regards the higher numbers —244,000 jobs and $21 billion real GDP—as the worst-case scenario.

■ Private-sector estimates place the cost of implementing Kyoto at 450,000 jobs by 2010 and $4.5 billion annually.

Economic Analysis

■ Implementing the Kyoto accord requires Canada to cut its emissions of "greenhouse" gases, measured as carbon dioxide equivalent, from more than 700 million tonnes a year in 2002 to 540 million tonnes a year by 2010.

■ To achieve this large cut in emissions, we must generate electricity more cleanly and use technologies that are more costly and less productive.

■ We must also increase the fuel efficiency of automobiles and trucks.

■ These activities decrease the productivity of labour, slow the accumulation of productive capital, and slow the pace of productivity-enhancing technological change.

■ The overall consequence of this slowdown in productivity growth is a slower growth rate of potential GDP.

■ By not implementing the Kyoto accord and maintaining recent trends, real GDP will grow by 3 percent a year.

■ Maintaining the recent inflation trends (and the Bank of Canada's target for inflation), the inflation rate will be 2 percent a year.

■ Figure 1 shows that if these trends persist, by 2010 real GDP will be $1,240 billion, up by 27 percent from its 2002 level; and the price level will be 125, up by 17 percent from its 2002 level.

■ Figure 2 shows the difference that implementing Kyoto will make, using the government's worst-case scenario.

■ Relative to the base line case, long-run aggregate supply will be lower at LAS_1, and real GDP will be $21 billion lower.

■ If the Bank of Canada continues to pursue an inflation target of 2 percent a year, aggregate demand growth will slow to match the growth of potential GDP. The AD curve and SAS curve will be at AD_1 and SAS_1, and the price level will be unaffected by Kyoto.

■ If aggregate demand growth does not slow to match the slower growth rate of potential GDP, Kyoto will bring increased inflation.

■ The decrease in employment that results from Kyoto will either decrease the labour force or increase the natural rate of unemployment. It will not affect cyclical unemployment.

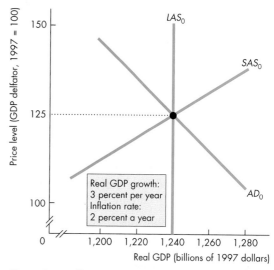

Figure 1 Base line case—no Kyoto

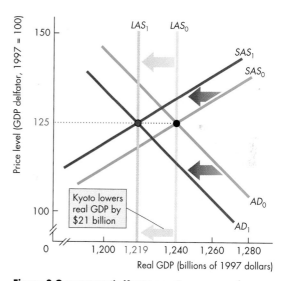

Figure 2 Government's Kyoto worst-case scenario

You're the Voter

■ Based just on its macroeconomic consequences, do you think that implementing Kyoto is a big deal?

■ What macroeconomic reasons would you give for supporting or opposing the implementation of Kyoto?

525

SUMMARY

KEY POINTS

Aggregate Supply (pp. 508–512)

- In the long run, the quantity of real GDP supplied is potential GDP, which is independent of the price level. The long-run aggregate supply curve is vertical.
- In the short run, the money wage rate is constant, so a rise in the price level increases the quantity of real GDP supplied. The short-run aggregate supply curve is upward sloping.
- A change in potential GDP changes both long-run and short-run aggregate supply. A change in the money wage rate or other resource prices changes only short-run aggregate supply.

Aggregate Demand (pp. 513–516)

- A rise in the price level decreases the quantity of real GDP demanded, other things remaining the same.
- The reason is that the higher price level decreases the quantity of *real* money, raises the interest rate, and raises the price of domestic goods compared with foreign-made goods.
- Changes in expected future income, inflation, and profit; changes in fiscal policy and monetary policy; and changes in world real GDP and the foreign exchange rate change aggregate demand.

Macroeconomic Equilibrium (pp. 516–521)

- In the short run, real GDP and the price level are determined by aggregate demand and short-run aggregate supply.
- In the long run, real GDP equals potential GDP and aggregate demand determines the price level and the money wage rate.
- Economic growth occurs because potential GDP increases.
- Inflation occurs because aggregate demand grows more quickly than potential GDP grows.
- Business cycles occur because aggregate demand and aggregate supply fluctuate.

Canadian Economic Growth, Inflation, and Cycles (pp. 522–523)

- Potential GDP grew fastest during the 1960s and late 1990s through 2002 and slowest during the late 1970s and early 1990s.
- Inflation persists because aggregate demand grows faster than potential GDP.
- Business cycles occur because aggregate supply and aggregate demand change at an uneven pace.

KEY FIGURES

Figure 22.2   Short-Run Aggregate Supply, 510
Figure 22.3   Movements Along the Aggregate Supply Curves, 510
Figure 22.4   A Change in Potential GDP, 511
Figure 22.5   A Change in the Money Wage Rate, 512
Figure 22.6   Aggregate Demand, 513
Figure 22.7   Changes in Aggregate Demand, 515
Figure 22.8   Short-Run Equilibrium, 517
Figure 22.9   Long-Run Equilibrium, 517
Figure 22.10   Economic Growth and Inflation, 518
Figure 22.11   The Business Cycle, 519
Figure 22.12   An Increase in Aggregate Demand, 520
Figure 22.14   Aggregate Supply and Aggregate Demand: 1961–2004, 522

KEY TERMS

Above full-employment equilibrium, 519
Aggregate demand, 513
Aggregate production function, 508
Below full-employment equilibrium, 518
Disposable income, 515
Fiscal policy, 515
Inflationary gap, 519
Long-run aggregate supply curve, 508
Long-run macroeconomic equilibrium, 517
Macroeconomic long run, 508
Macroeconomic short run, 509
Monetary policy, 515
Natural rate of unemployment, 508
Recessionary gap, 518
Short-run aggregate supply curve, 509
Short-run macroeconomic equilibrium, 516

PROBLEMS

Go to ⓧ **myeconlab** **for solutions to odd-numbered problems and additional exercises.**

1. The following events occur that influence the economy of Toughtimes:
   - A deep recession hits the world economy.
   - Oil prices rise sharply.
   - Businesses expect huge losses in the near future.
   a. Explain the separate effects of each of these events on real GDP and the price level, starting from a position of long-run equilibrium.
   b. Explain the combined effects of these events on real GDP and the price level, starting from a position of long-run equilibrium.
   c. Explain what the Toughtimes government and the Bank of Toughtimes can do to overcome the problems faced by the economy.

2. The following events occur that influence the economy of Coolland:
   - There is a strong expansion in the world economy.
   - Businesses expect huge profits in the near future.
   - The Coolland government cuts its expenditure.
   a. Explain the separate effects of each of these events on real GDP and the price level, starting from a position of long-run equilibrium.
   b. Explain the combined effects of these events on real GDP and the price level, starting from a position of long-run equilibrium.
   c. Explain why the Coolland government or the Bank of Coolland might want to take action to influence the Coolland economy.

3. The economy of Mainland has the following aggregate demand and supply schedules:

Price level	Real GDP demanded	Real GDP supplied in the short run
	(billions of 1997 dollars)	
90	450	350
100	400	400
110	350	450
120	300	500
130	250	550
140	200	600

a. In a figure, plot the aggregate demand curve and the short-run aggregate supply curve.
b. What are the values of real GDP and the price level in Mainland in a short-run macroeconomic equilibrium?
c. Mainland's potential GDP is $500 billion. Plot the long-run aggregate supply curve in the same figure in which you answered part (a).

4. The economy of Miniland has the following aggregate demand and supply schedules:

Price level	Real GDP demanded	Real GDP supplied in the short run
	(billions of 1997 dollars)	
90	600	150
100	500	200
110	400	250
120	300	300
130	200	350
140	100	400

a. In a figure, plot the aggregate demand curve and the short-run aggregate supply curve.
b. What are the values of real GDP and the price level in Miniland in a short-run macroeconomic equilibrium?
c. Miniland's potential GDP is $250 billion. Plot the long-run aggregate supply curve in the same figure in which you answered part (a).

5. In problem 3, aggregate demand increases by $100 billion. How do real GDP and the price level change in the short run?

6. In problem 4, aggregate demand decreases by $150 billion. How do real GDP and the price level change in the short run?

7. In problem 3, aggregate supply decreases by $100 billion. What now is the short-run macroeconomic equilibrium?

8. In problem 4, aggregate supply increases by $150 billion. What now is the short-run macroeconomic equilibrium?

9. In the economy shown in the figure on the next page, initially the short-run aggregate supply is SAS_0 and aggregate demand is AD_0. Then some events change aggregate demand, and the aggregate demand curve shifts rightward to AD_1. Later, some other events change aggregate supply, and the short-run aggregate supply curve shifts leftward to SAS_1.

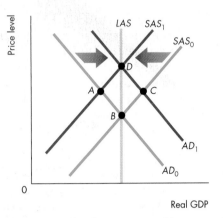

a. What is the short-run equilibrium point after the change in aggregate demand?
b. What is the equilibrium point after the change in aggregate supply?
c. What events could have changed aggregate demand from AD_0 to AD_1?
d. What events could have changed aggregate supply from SAS_0 to SAS_1?

10. In the economy shown in the figure, initially long-run aggregate supply is LAS_0, short-run aggregate supply is SAS_0, and aggregate demand is AD. Then some events change aggregate supply, and the aggregate supply curves shift rightward to LAS_1 and SAS_1.

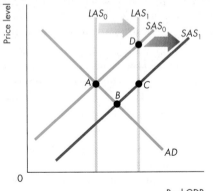

a. What is the short-run equilibrium point after the change in aggregate supply?
b. What events could have changed long-run aggregate supply from LAS_0 to LAS_1?
c. What events could have changed short-run aggregate supply from SAS_0 to SAS_1?
d. After the increase in aggregate supply, is real GDP greater than or less than potential GDP?
e. What change in aggregate demand will make real GDP equal to potential GDP?

CRITICAL THINKING

1. After you have studied the effects of implementing the Kyoto agreement on aggregate supply and aggregate demand in the Canadian economy in *Reading Between the Lines* on pp. 524–525:
   a. List the factors that influence long-run aggregate supply and explain how Kyoto might impact each of these factors.
   b. List the factors that influence short-run aggregate supply and explain how Kyoto might impact each of these factors.
   c. List the factors that influence aggregate demand and explain how Kyoto might impact each of these factors.
   d. Use the *AS–AD* model to illustrate and to explain why Kyoto need not increase the inflation rate, even if it brings a large decrease in potential GDP.

WEB EXERCISES

Use the links on myeconlab **to work the following exercise.**

1. Find data on recent changes in and forecasts of real GDP and the price level in Canada.
   a. What is your forecast of next year's real GDP?
   b. What is your forecast of next year's price level?
   c. What is your forecast of the inflation rate?
   d. What is your forecast of the growth rate of real GDP?
   e. Do you think there will be a recessionary gap or an inflationary gap next year?

2. Find data on recent changes in and forecasts of real GDP and the price level in Japan.
   a. What is your forecast of next year's real GDP?
   b. What is your forecast of next year's price level?
   c. What is your forecast of the inflation rate?
   d. What is your forecast of the growth rate of real GDP?
   e. Compare and contrast the performance of the Canadian and Japanese economies.

UNDERSTANDING THE THEMES OF MACROECONOMICS

The Big Picture

Macroeconomics is a large and controversial subject that is interlaced with political ideological disputes. And it is a field in which charlatans as well as serious thinkers have much to say. This page is a map that looks back at the road you've just travelled and forward at the path you will take from here.

You began your study of macroeconomics with the core questions of the subject. What are the causes of

- Economic growth?
- Business cycles?
- Unemployment?
- Inflation?

In Chapter 19, you took your first look at each of these questions. You learned some facts about economic growth, business cycles, unemployment, and inflation. In Chapter 20, you learned how we measure the economy's output and the price level. These measures are used to calculate the economic growth rate, business cycle fluctuations, and inflation. You discovered that making these measurements is not straightforward and that small measurement errors can have a big effect on our perceptions about how we are doing.

In Chapter 21, you learned how we measure the state of the labour market—the levels of employment and unemployment and wages. And in Chapter 22, you studied the macroeconomic version of supply and demand—*aggregate supply* and *aggregate*

demand. You saw that the aggregate supply–aggregate demand model is the big picture model. It explains both the long-term trends in economic growth and inflation and the short-term business cycle fluctuations in production, jobs, and inflation.

The chapters that lie ahead of you look behind aggregate supply and aggregate demand, beginning on the aggregate demand side. In Chapters 23 through 29, you will study aggregate demand, inflation, and recession and learn about the macroeconomics that Keynes developed as a response to the Great Depression. And you will learn about money and the banking system and the effects of monetary policy and fiscal policy on aggregate demand.

Then, in Chapters 30 through 32, you will study aggregate supply, economic growth, and international trade. In Chapter 30, you study the economy at full employment and the forces that change potential GDP. In Chapter 31, you study the process of economic growth. Here, you learn today's answer to the question posed by Adam Smith—what are the causes of differences in the wealth of nations? In Chapter 32 you will study the globalization of economic activity and international trade.

Before continuing your study of macroeconomics, spend a few minutes with John Maynard Keynes and Jean-Baptiste Say, the leading scholars who developed this subject. And spend a few minutes with one of today's leading Canadian macroeconomists, Peter Howitt of Brown University.

Macroeconomic Revolutions

THE ECONOMIST

John Maynard Keynes, *born in England in 1883, was one of the outstanding minds of the twentieth century. He wrote on probability as well as economics, represented Britain at the Versailles peace conference at the end of World War I, was a master speculator on international financial markets (an activity he conducted from bed every morning and which made and lost him several fortunes), and played a prominent role in creating the International Monetary Fund. He was a member of the Bloomsbury Group, a circle of outstanding artists and writers that included E. M. Forster, Bertrand Russell, and Virginia Woolf. Keynes was a controversial and quick-witted figure. A critic once complained that Keynes had changed his opinion on some matters, to which Keynes retorted: "When I discover I am wrong, I change my mind. What do you do?"*

"The ideas of economists and political philosophers, both when they are right and when they are wrong, are more powerful than is commonly understood. Indeed the world is ruled by little else."

JOHN MAYNARD KEYNES *The General Theory of Employment, Interest, and Money*

THE ISSUES

During the Industrial Revolution, as technological change created new jobs and destroyed old ones, people began to wonder whether the economy could create enough jobs and sufficient demand to buy all the things that the new industrial economy could produce.

Jean-Baptiste Say argues that production creates incomes that are sufficient to buy everything that is produced—supply creates its own demand—an idea that came to be called Say's Law.

Say and Keynes would have had a lot to disagree about. Jean-Baptiste Say, born in Lyon, France, in 1767 (he was 9 years old when Adam Smith's *Wealth of Nations* was published), suffered the wrath of Napoleon for his views on government and the economy. In today's world, Say would be leading a radical conservative charge for a smaller and leaner government. Say was the most famous economist of his era on both sides of the Atlantic. His book, *Traité d'économie politique (A Treatise in Political Economy)*, published in 1803, became a best-selling university economics textbook in both Europe and North America.

As the Great Depression of the 1930s became more severe and more prolonged, Say's Law looked less and less relevant. John Maynard Keynes revolutionized macroeconomics thinking by turning Say's Law on its head, arguing that production does not depend on supply. Instead, it depends on what people are willing to buy—on demand. Or as Keynes put it, production depends on effective demand. It is possible, argued Keynes, for people to refuse to spend all of their incomes. If businesses fail to spend on new capital the amount that people plan to save, demand might be less than supply. In this situation, resources might go unemployed and remain unemployed indefinitely.

The influence of Keynes persists even today, more than 60 years after the publication of his main work. But during the past 20 years, Nobel Laureate Robert E. Lucas, Jr., with significant contributions from a list of outstanding macroeconomists too long to name, has further revolutionized macroeconomics. Today, we know a lot about economic growth, unemployment, inflation, and business cycles. And we know how to use fiscal policy and monetary policy to improve macroeconomic performance. But we don't yet have all the answers. Macroeconomics remains a field of lively controversy and exciting research.

THEN

In 1776, James Hargreaves, an English weaver and carpenter, developed a simple hand-operated machine called a spinning jenny (pictured here). Using this machine, a person could spin 80 threads at once. Thousands of hand-wheel spinners, operators of machines that could spin only one thread, lost their jobs. They protested by wrecking spinning jennies. In the long run, the displaced hand-wheel spinners found work, often in factories that manufactured the machines that had destroyed their previous jobs. From the earliest days of the Industrial Revolution to the present day, people have lost their jobs as new technologies have automated what human effort had previously been needed to accomplish.

NOW

Advances in computer technology have made it possible for us to dial our own telephone calls to any part of the world and get connected in a flash. A task that was once performed by telephone operators, who made connections along copper wires, is now performed faster and more reliably by computers along fibre-optic cables. Just as the Industrial Revolution transformed the textile industry, so today's Information Revolution is transforming the telecommunications industry. In the process, the mix of jobs is changing. There are fewer jobs for telephone operators but more jobs for telephone systems designers, builders, managers, and marketers. In the long run, as people spend the income they earn in their changing jobs, supply creates its own demand, just as Say predicted. But does supply create its own demand in the short run, when displaced workers are unemployed?

Peter Howitt, whom you can meet on the following pages, is one of the most distinguished macroeconomists. He has contributed much to our understanding of economic growth and the business cycle and played a significant role in the contemporary macroeconomic revolution.

TALKING WITH

Peter Howitt is Lyn Crost Professor of Social Sciences in the Department of Economics at Brown University. Born in 1946 in Toronto, he was an undergraduate at McGill University and a graduate student at Northwestern University. He began his research and teaching career at the University of Western Ontario in 1972, where he spent many productive years before moving to the United States in 1996. Professor Howitt is a past president of the Canadian Economics Association and is one of the world's leading macroeconomists. He has done research on all aspect of macroeconomics, with a focus in recent years on economic growth.

Micheal Parkin and Robin Bade talked with Peter Howitt about his work and the major macroeconomic problems facing Canada today.

Peter Howitt

What attracted you to economics?

When I was in high school I had a part-time job as office boy with a small company that imported wool from around the world and sold it to textile mills in Ontario and Quebec. I was fascinated by the way wool prices went up and down all the time, and this curiosity led me to enroll in an honours economics course. My interests soon switched to macroeconomics, but I was always driven by curiosity to find out more about the workings of the human anthill.

You have made outstanding contributions to our understanding of all the major problems of macroeconomics, notably unemployment, economic growth, and inflation. Which of these issues do you believe is the most serious one for Canada today? Can they be separated?

Right now [near the end of 1996] growth and unemployment are the most important. Inflation has been under control for several years. We still have what was once called "creeping inflation," as the price level is rising by about 2 percent per year, but that's a less serious problem than the fact that over 10 percent of the labour force is unemployed and that the economy appears no longer to be growing at the high rates we experienced in the 1950s and 1960s.

Of course, all of these problems are interrelated. Learning about all the interrelationships is one of the things that makes economics so interesting. Take the relationship between growth and unemployment, for example. If you take a short-run perspective, then these two variables would appear to be negatively related. If the economy grows faster, there will be more jobs, and better paying jobs, which will draw people out of unemployment. But in the long run it looks quite different. You can't maintain a high growth rate indefinitely by continuing to put idle people to work, because at some point you will have everyone in the economy working. Instead, to keep the economy growing at a high rate you have to keep finding ways to make people more productive. You get this from having technological progress, from innovations that improve the efficiency of production processes and that allow people to produce new goods that contribute to our material welfare in ways that previous generations never have imagined.

Now the industrial innovations that underlie economic growth in the long run usually come at a cost. This is what Schumpeter meant by the term "creative destruction." For example, if I invent a new good this will create new jobs for people to produce the good, but it will also destroy the jobs of people who produce the goods that mine will replace. So an economy that is going through a period of rapid technological change is likely to have good growth prospects, but it may also have a high rate of unemployment. The people whose jobs are destroyed may eventually find even better jobs but it will take time, so there will be a lot of people in a temporary situation of unemployment. To make a long story short, even though a short burst of growth from one quarter to the next is likely to reduce the rate of unemployment, a sustained rise in the rate of growth from one decade to the next will create a rise in the rate of unemployment.

> " *... industrial innovations that underlie economic growth in the long run usually come at a cost. This is what Schumpeter meant by the term "creative destruction."* "

What does your research tell us about the main sources of Canada's persistently high unemployment rate during the 1980s and 1990s?

I think a lot of what has taken place in Canada is an example of the effects of creative destruction that I talked about. A lot of technological change destroys low-skill jobs, and also destroys the value of old skills. In particular, a lot of clerical and middle management jobs have been made redundant by computers. Computers open up new jobs for people able to master the technology, but a lot of people don't have the skills or the knowledge to profit from these opportunities. This is a global phenomenon, not just limited to Canada. Computers are having a revolutionary effect on economic life all over the world. In the United States it hasn't appeared to produce much unemployment. Instead what you see is a growing gap between the wages of skilled and unskilled workers. In Canada that gap isn't as visible, largely because we have more generous minimum wages and unemployment insurance benefits, which means that a fall in the demand for low-skill workers shows up more in a rise in unemployment and less in a fall in their wages than in the United States.

Why did our economic growth rate slow during the 1980s?

The short answer is that no one knows. But I think the answer probably lies in the computer revolution that I have talked about. Ultimately I think this revolution is going to give us a higher growth rate. But we have to accumulate a lot of knowledge in order to profit from it. We have been going through a collective learning experience that has been enormously costly, and this has been a continual drag on productivity, even though in the end I expect it will greatly enhance productivity.

Also, I think we are underestimating growth rates nowadays. This is because we are investing a lot in knowledge—knowledge of how to harness the power of the computer and to exploit the opportunities that it presents. Investment in knowledge is like investment in machinery in that it entails the sacrifice of resources now in return for the promise of more income sometime in the future. But while the national income accountant measures investment in machines as part of the economy's output of final goods and services, investment in knowledge is just treated as wasted resources.

Was the pursuit of low inflation worthwhile? Have we now got too low an inflation rate?

I think the pursuit of low inflation was definitely worthwhile, although in retrospect we maybe should have been more patient. Inflation impairs one of the most useful devices in the economic system—the conventional measure of value. Now that we have almost eliminated inflation we have a much healthier economic system. I don't think we should go much further, however, because you may have to raise unemployment even higher in order to get inflation all the way down to zero, and once you have it down to 2 percent you have little more to gain by reducing it even further. Also, further reductions in inflation may impair the working of the labour market. That is, people whose real wages are falling for whatever reason may be more inclined to continue working if they can at least avoid having to submit to a nominal wage cut, but can instead take the real-wage cut through the back door of inflation. With 2 percent inflation there is still lots of room for this sort of real-wage flexibility, but with no inflation there is none at all.

> " *... one of the great things about economics is that you can be paid well for spending your time satisfying your curiosity.* "

Some economists say that the Bank of Canada can speed up the economic growth rate by forgetting about low inflation and keeping interest rates low. Others say the best hope for increasing the growth rate is low inflation. Who is right?

The first group is certainly not right, except perhaps in a very short-run sense. You can't sustain a high growth rate for long by printing more money. Before long you'll end up with a higher rate of inflation and even higher interest rates as lenders seek compensation for the fall in the value of money. A lot of recent econometric evidence has been produced by various writers studying the experience of different countries that shows over long periods of time that inflation and growth are negatively correlated. More inflation from one decade to the next is likely to produce a fall in the growth rate rather than a rise. The effect doesn't appear to be numerically very large, but even a small drop in the growth rate can have a significant depressing effect on the level of real income if sustained for a decade or two.

What advice would you give to a student who wants to become a professional economist today?

My first advice for anyone interested in doing economics is to give full reign to your curiosity. The greatest satisfaction that I have received as an economist has been from discovering things about how the world works, from seeing a little more clearly some of the complex interactions between the different parts of the economy. I can still remember the excitement I felt when I started to see how demand and supply work, and when I learned about the circular flow of economic activity and how it can be affected by saving and investment decisions. I am happy to say that this sense of excitement has never left me. Furthermore, one of the great things about economics is that you can be paid well for spending your time satisfying your curiosity. Satisfying your curiosity is enjoyable, but if you want to accomplish something you can't let yourself be satisfied easily. You have to keep asking questions, and trying to answer them. It's easy to think you have solved a problem when you haven't explored things deeply enough. The best way for a student to do this is to do lots of exercises, and to discuss what you are doing with others. The same applies throughout one's career.

Expenditure Multipliers

Economic Amplifier or Shock Absorber?

Céline Dion sings into a microphone in a barely audible whisper. Increasing in volume, through the magic of electronic amplification, her voice fills Toronto's Molson Amphitheatre.

Ralph Klein, the premier of Alberta, and his secretary are being driven to a business meeting along one of Edmonton's less well-repaired streets. The car's wheels bounce and vibrate over some of the worst potholes in the nation, but its passengers are completely undisturbed and the secretary's notes are written without a ripple, thanks to the car's efficient shock absorbers.

Investment and exports fluctuate like the volume of Céline Dion's voice and the uneven surface of an Edmonton street. How does the economy react to those fluctuations? Does it react like a limousine, absorbing the shocks and providing a smooth ride for the economy's passengers? Or does it behave like an amplifier, blowing up the fluctuations and spreading them out to affect the many millions of participants in an economic rock concert?

◆ You will explore these questions in this chapter. You will learn how a recession or an expansion begins when a change in investment or exports induces an amplified change in aggregate expenditure and real GDP. And you'll learn the crucial role played by business inventories in the transition from expansion to recession and back to expansion. *Reading Between the Lines* at the end of the chapter looks at the multiplier at work during the first half of 2005, when real GDP was expanding quickly.

After studying this chapter, you will be able to

■ Explain how expenditure plans and real GDP are determined when the price level is fixed

■ Explain equilibrium expenditure at a fixed price level

■ Explain the expenditure multiplier and how recessions and expansions begin

■ Explain the relationship between aggregate expenditure and aggregate demand and how the multiplier gets smaller as the price level changes

535

Expenditure Plans and GDP

THE COMPONENTS OF AGGREGATE EXPENDITURE are consumption expenditure (C), investment (I), government expenditures on goods and services (G), and net exports—exports (X) minus imports (M). The sum of these components is real GDP (Y). (See Chapter 20, p. 468). That is,

$$Y = C + I + G + X - M.$$

Two of these components—consumption expenditure and imports—depend on the level of real GDP. Because real GDP influences consumption expenditure and imports, and because consumption expenditure and imports are components of aggregate expenditure, there is a two-way link between aggregate expenditure and GDP. You are going to learn how this two-way link determines real GDP at a given price level.

The starting point is to consider the first piece of the two-way link: the influence of real GDP on planned consumption expenditure and saving.

Consumption and Saving Plans

Several factors influence consumption expenditure and saving. The most direct influence, especially in the short term, is disposable income. **Disposable income** is real GDP or aggregate income (Y) minus net taxes (NT)—taxes minus transfer payments. And aggregate income equals real GDP. The equation for disposable income (YD) is

$$YD = Y - NT.$$

Disposable income is either spent on consumption goods and services—consumption expenditure (C)—or saved (S). So planned consumption expenditure plus planned saving equals disposable income. That is,

$$YD = C + S.$$

The table in Fig. 23.1 shows some examples of planned consumption expenditure and planned saving at different levels of disposable income. The greater the disposable income, the greater is consumption expenditure and the greater is saving. Also, at each amount of disposable income, consumption expenditure plus saving equals disposable income.

The relationship between consumption expenditure and disposable income, with other things remaining the same, is called the **consumption function**. The relationship between saving and disposable income, with other things remaining the same, is called the **saving function**. Let's look at the consumption function and saving function in Fig. 23.1.

Consumption Function Figure 23.1(a) shows a consumption function. The y-axis measures consumption expenditure and the x-axis measures disposable income. Along the consumption function, the points labelled A through F correspond to the rows of the table. For example, point E shows that when disposable income is $800 billion, consumption expenditure is $750 billion. Along the consumption function, as disposable income increases, consumption expenditure also increases.

At point A on the consumption function, consumption expenditure is $150 billion even though disposable income is zero. This consumption expenditure is called *autonomous consumption*, and it is the amount of consumption expenditure that would take place in the short run even if people had no current income. You can think of this amount as the expenditure on the vital necessities of life.

When consumption expenditure exceeds disposable income, past savings are used to pay for current consumption. Such a situation cannot last forever, but it can occur temporarily.

Consumption expenditure in excess of autonomous consumption is called *induced consumption*—expenditure that is induced by an increase in disposable income.

45° Line Figure 23.1(a) also contains a 45° line, the height of which measures disposable income. At each point on this line, consumption expenditure equals disposable income. In the range over which the consumption function lies above the 45° line—between A and D—consumption expenditure exceeds disposable income. In the range over which the consumption function lies below the 45° line—between D and F—consumption expenditure is less than disposable income. And at the point at which the consumption function intersects the 45° line—at point D—consumption expenditure equals disposable income.

Saving Function Figure 23.1(b) shows a saving function. The x-axis is exactly the same as that in part (a). The y-axis measures saving. Again, the points marked A through F correspond to the rows of the table. For example, point *E* shows that when disposable income is $800 billion, saving is $50 billion. Along the saving function, as disposable income increases, saving also increases. At disposable incomes less than $600 billion (point *D*), saving is negative. Negative saving is called *dissaving*. At disposable incomes greater than $600 billion, saving is positive, and at $600 billion, saving is zero.

Notice the connection between the two parts of Fig. 23.1. When consumption expenditure exceeds

disposable income in part (a), saving is negative in part (b). When consumption expenditure is less than disposable income in part (a), saving is positive in part (b). And when consumption expenditure equals disposable income in part (a), saving is zero in part (b).

When saving is negative (when consumption expenditure exceeds disposable income), past savings are used to pay for current consumption. Such a situation cannot last forever, but it can occur if disposable income falls temporarily.

FIGURE 23.1
Consumption Function and Saving Function

myeconlab

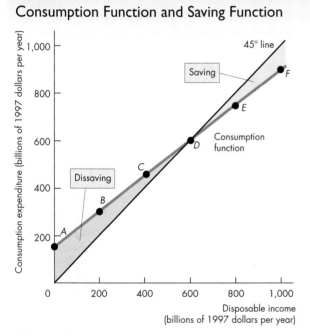

(a) Consumption function

	Disposable income	Planned consumption expenditure	Planned saving
		(billions of 1997 dollars per year)	
A	0	150	−150
B	200	300	−100
C	400	450	−50
D	600	600	0
E	800	750	50
F	1,000	900	100

The table shows consumption expenditure and saving plans at various levels of disposable income. Part (a) of the figure shows the relationship between consumption expenditure and disposable income (the consumption function). The height of the consumption function measures consumption expenditure at each level of disposable income. Part (b) shows the relationship between saving and disposable income (the saving function). The height of the saving function measures saving at each level of disposable income. Points A through F on the consumption and saving functions correspond to the rows in the table. The height of the 45° line in part (a) measures disposable income. So along the 45° line, consumption expenditure equals disposable income. Consumption expenditure plus saving equals disposable income. When the consumption function is above the 45° line, saving is negative (dissaving occurs). When the consumption function is below the 45° line, saving is positive. At the point where the consumption function intersects the 45° line, all disposable income is consumed and saving is zero.

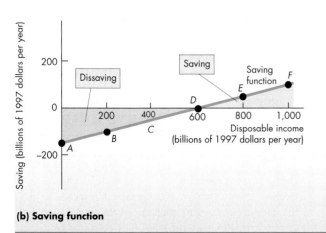

(b) Saving function

Marginal Propensity to Consume

The amount by which consumption expenditure changes when disposable income changes depends on the marginal propensity to consume. The **marginal propensity to consume** (*MPC*) is the fraction of a *change* in disposable income that is consumed. It is calculated as the *change* in consumption expenditure (Δ*C*) divided by the *change* in disposable income (Δ*YD*) that brought it about. That is,

$$MPC = \frac{\Delta C}{\Delta YD}.$$

In the table in Fig. 23.1, when disposable income increases from $600 billion to $800 billion, consumption expenditure increases from $600 billion to $750 billion. The $200 billion increase in disposable income increases consumption expenditure by $150 billion. The *MPC* is $150 billion divided by $200 billion, which equals 0.75.

    The marginal propensity to consume is the slope of the consumption function. You can check this fact out in Fig. 23.2(a). Here, a $200 billion increase in disposable income from $600 billion to $800 billion is the base of the red triangle. The increase in consumption expenditure that results from this increase in disposable income is $150 billion and is the height of the triangle. The slope of the consumption function is given by the formula "slope equals rise over run" and is $150 billion divided by $200 billion, which equals 0.75—the *MPC*.

Marginal Propensity to Save

The amount by which saving changes when disposable income changes depends on the marginal propensity to save. The **marginal propensity to save** (*MPS*) is the fraction of a *change* in disposable income that is saved. It is calculated as the *change* in saving (Δ*S*) divided by the *change* in disposable income (Δ*YD*) that brought it about. That is,

$$MPS = \frac{\Delta S}{\Delta YD}.$$

In the table in Fig. 23.1, an increase in disposable income from $600 billion to $800 billion increases saving from zero to $50 billion. The $200 billion increase in disposable income increases saving by $50 billion. The *MPS* is $50 billion divided by $200 billion, which equals 0.25.

FIGURE 23.2   my**econ**lab

Marginal Propensities to Consume and Save

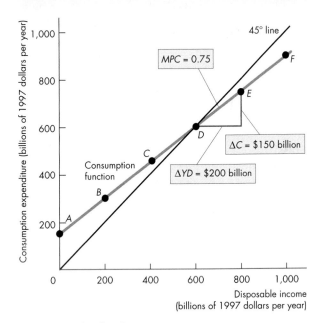

(a) Consumption function

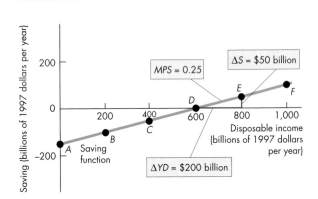

(b) Saving function

The marginal propensity to consume, *MPC*, is equal to the change in consumption expenditure divided by the change in disposable income, other things remaining the same. It is measured by the slope of the consumption function. In part (a), the *MPC* is 0.75.

    The marginal propensity to save, *MPS*, is equal to the change in saving divided by the change in disposable income, other things remaining the same. It is measured by the slope of the saving function. In part (b), the *MPS* is 0.25.

The marginal propensity to save is the slope of the saving function. You can check this fact out in Fig. 23.2(b). Here, a $200 billion increase in disposable income from $600 billion to $800 billion (the base of the red triangle) increases saving by $50 billion (the height of the triangle). The slope of the saving function is $50 billion divided by $200 billion, which equals 0.25—the *MPS*.

The marginal propensity to consume plus the marginal propensity to save always equals 1. They sum to 1 because consumption expenditure and saving exhaust disposable income. Part of each dollar increase in disposable income is consumed, and the remaining part is saved. You can see that these two marginal propensities sum to 1 by using the equation:

$$\Delta C + \Delta S = \Delta YD.$$

Divide both sides of the equation by the change in disposable income to obtain

$$\frac{\Delta C}{\Delta YD} + \frac{\Delta S}{\Delta YD} = 1.$$

$\Delta C/\Delta YD$ is the marginal propensity to consume (*MPC*), and $\Delta S/\Delta YD$ is the marginal propensity to save (*MPS*), so

$$MPC + MPS = 1.$$

Other Influences on Consumption Expenditure and Saving

You've seen that a change in disposable income leads to changes in consumption expenditure and saving. A change in disposable income brings movements along the consumption function and saving function. A change in any other influence on consumption expenditure and saving shifts the consumption function and the saving function as shown in Fig. 23.3.

The main other influences are

1. Expected future disposable income
2. The real interest rate
3. Wealth

An increase in expected future disposable income makes people feel better off and leads to an increase in current consumption expenditure and a decrease in current saving. A fall in the real interest rate, other things remaining the same, encourages an increase in

FIGURE 23.3   myeconlab

Shifts in the Consumption and Saving Functions

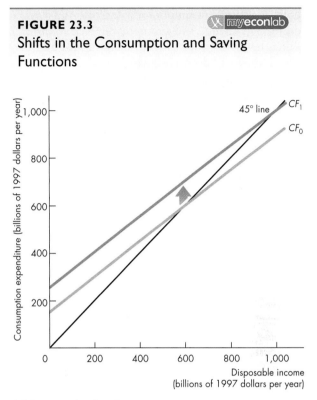

(a) Consumption function

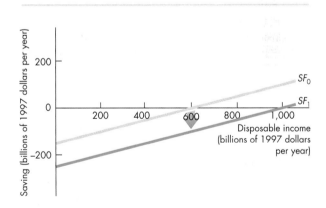

(b) Saving function

An increase in expected future disposable income, a fall in the real interest rate, or an increase in wealth shifts the consumption function upward from CF_0 to CF_1 and the saving function downward from SF_0 to SF_1.

A decrease in expected future disposable income, a rise in the real interest rate, or a decrease in wealth shifts the consumption function downward and shifts the saving function upward.

borrowing and consumption expenditure and a decrease in saving. And an increase in wealth, other things remaining the same, stimulates consumption expenditure and decreases saving.

When expected future disposable income increases, the real interest rate falls, or when wealth increases, consumption expenditure increases and saving decreases. In Fig. 23.3 the consumption function shifts upward from CF_0 to CF_1, and the saving function shifts downward from SF_0 to SF_1.

When expected future disposable income decreases, the real interest rate rises, or when wealth decreases, consumption expenditure decreases and saving increases. The consumption function shifts downward and the saving function shifts upward. Such shifts often occur when a recession begins because at such a time, expected future disposable income decreases.

We've studied the theory of the consumption function. Let's now see how that theory applies to the Canadian economy.

The Canadian Consumption Function

Figure 23.4 shows the Canadian consumption function. Each point identified by a blue dot represents consumption expenditure and disposable income for a particular year. (The dots are for the years 1961 to 2004. Five of the years are identified in the figure.) The line labelled CF_{61} is an estimate of the Canadian consumption function in 1961, and the line labelled CF_{04} is an estimate of the Canadian consumption function in 2004.

The slope of the consumption function in Fig. 23.4 is 0.85, which means that a $100 billion increase in disposable income brings a $85 billion increase in consumption expenditure. This slope, which is an estimate of the marginal propensity to consume, is an assumption that is at the middle of the range of values that economists have estimated for the marginal propensity to consume.

The consumption function shifts upward over time as other influences on consumption expenditure change. Of these other influences, expected future disposable income, the real interest rate, and wealth fluctuate and so bring upward *and* downward shifts in the consumption function. A low real interest rate and rise in wealth that came from a real estate boom brought a strong increase in autonomous consumption expenditure and an upward shift of the consumption function in 2003 and 2004.

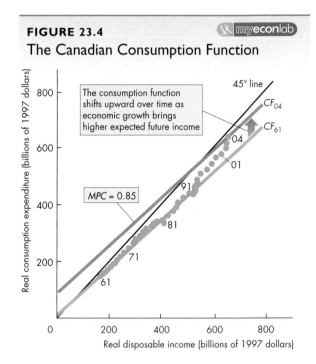

FIGURE 23.4
myeconlab

The Canadian Consumption Function

Each blue dot shows consumption expenditure and disposable income for a particular year. The lines CF_{61} and CF_{04} are estimates of the Canadian consumption function in 1961 and 2004, respectively. Here, the (assumed) marginal propensity to consume is 0.85.

Source of data: Statistics Canada, CANSIM Tables 380–0002, 384–0013, and 384–0035.

Consumption as a Function of Real GDP

You've seen that consumption expenditure changes when disposable income changes. And you've seen that disposable income is equal to real GDP minus net taxes. So consumption expenditure is a function of real GDP. An increase in real GDP increases disposable income, which increases consumption expenditure. But an increase in real GDP also increases net taxes. So when real GDP increases, consumption expenditure increases but by less than it would if net taxes were unchanged. We're going to use this link between consumption expenditure and real GDP to determine equilibrium expenditure. But before we do so, we need to look at one other component of aggregate expenditure: imports. Like consumption expenditure, imports are influenced by real GDP.

Import Function

Canadian imports are determined by many factors, but in the short run, one factor dominates: Canadian real GDP. Other things remaining the same, the greater the Canadian real GDP, the larger is the quantity of Canadian imports.

The relationship between imports and real GDP is determined by the marginal propensity to import. The **marginal propensity to import** is the fraction of an increase in real GDP that is spent on imports. It is calculated as the change in imports divided by the change in real GDP that brought it about, other things remaining the same. For example, if a $100 billion increase in real GDP increases imports by $25 billion, the marginal propensity to import is 0.25.

In recent years, since the North American Free Trade Agreement (NAFTA) was implemented, Canadian imports have surged. For example, between 1991 and 2005, real GDP increased by $398 billion and imports increased by $262 billion. If no factors other than real GDP influenced imports during this period, these numbers would imply a marginal propensity to import of 0.66 ($262 billion divided by $398 billion). But NAFTA and other factors (such as lower communication costs) increased imports. If one half of the increase in imports resulted from other factors and the other half from the increase in real GDP, the marginal propensity to import is 0.33.

REVIEW QUIZ

1 Which components of aggregate expenditure are influenced by real GDP?
2 Define the marginal propensity to consume. What is your estimate of your own marginal propensity to consume? After you graduate, will it change? Why or why not?
3 How do we calculate the effects of real GDP on consumption expenditure and imports?

myeconlab Study Plan 23.1

Real GDP influences consumption expenditure and imports. But consumption expenditure and imports—along with investment, government expenditures, and exports—influence real GDP. Your next task is to study this second piece of the two-way link between aggregate expenditure and real GDP and see how all the components of aggregate planned expenditure interact to determine real GDP.

Equilibrium Expenditure at a Fixed Price Level

MOST FIRMS ARE LIKE YOUR LOCAL SUPERMARKET. They set their prices, advertise their products and services, and sell the quantities their customers are willing to buy. If they persistently sell a greater quantity than they plan to and are constantly running out of inventory, they eventually raise their prices. And if they persistently sell a smaller quantity than they plan to and have inventories piling up, they eventually cut their prices. But in the very short term, their prices are fixed. They hold the prices they have set, and the quantities they sell depend on demand, not supply.

The Aggregate Implications of Fixed Prices

Fixed prices have two immediate implications for the economy as a whole:

1. Because each firm's price is fixed, the *price level* is fixed.
2. Because demand determines the quantities that each firm sells, *aggregate demand* determines the aggregate quantity of goods and services sold, which equals real GDP.

So to understand how real GDP is determined when the price level is fixed, we must understand how aggregate demand is determined. Aggregate demand is determined by aggregate expenditure plans. We define **aggregate planned expenditure** as *planned* consumption expenditure plus *planned* investment plus *planned* government expenditures plus *planned* exports minus *planned* imports.

You've just studied planned consumption expenditure and planned imports and seen that these two components of aggregate planned expenditure are influenced by real GDP. The other components of aggregate expenditure—investment, government expenditures, and exports—are not influenced by real GDP. They fluctuate for many reasons but not because real GDP fluctuates.

You are now going to study a model called the *aggregate expenditure model*, which explains how consumption expenditure, imports, and real GDP are *simultaneously* determined by a two-way link between expenditure plans and real GDP.

The Aggregate Expenditure Model

You are now going to discover how aggregate expenditure plans interact to determine real GDP when the price level is fixed. First, we will study the relationship between aggregate planned expenditure and real GDP. Second, we'll learn about the key distinction between *planned* expenditure and *actual* expenditure. And third, we'll study equilibrium expenditure, a situation in which aggregate planned expenditure and actual expenditure are equal.

The relationship between aggregate planned expenditure and real GDP can be described by either an aggregate expenditure schedule or an aggregate expenditure curve. The *aggregate expenditure schedule* lists aggregate planned expenditure generated at each level of real GDP. The *aggregate expenditure curve* is a graph of the aggregate expenditure schedule.

FIGURE 23.5
Aggregate Expenditure

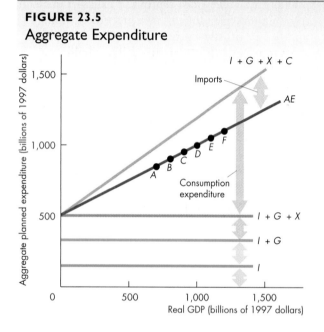

The aggregate expenditure schedule shows the relationship between aggregate planned expenditure and real GDP. Aggregate planned expenditure is the sum of planned consumption expenditure, investment, government expenditures, and exports minus imports. For example, in row B of the table, when real GDP is $800 billion, planned consumption expenditure is $560 billion, planned investment is $150 billion, planned government expenditures on goods and services are $180 billion, planned exports are $170 billion, and planned imports are $160 billion. So when real GDP is $800 billion, aggregate planned expenditure is $900 billion ($560 + $150 + $180 + $170 − $160). The schedule shows that aggregate planned expenditure increases as real GDP increases.

This relationship is graphed as the aggregate expenditure curve AE. The components of aggregate expenditure that increase with real GDP are consumption expenditure and imports. The other components—investment, government expenditures, and exports—do not vary with real GDP.

	Real GDP (Y)	Consumption expenditure (C)	Investment (I)	Government expenditures (G)	Exports (X)	Imports (M)	Aggregate planned expenditure (AE = C + I + G + X − M)
				(billions of 1997 dollars)			
	0	0	150	180	170	0	500
A	700	490	150	180	170	140	850
B	800	560	150	180	170	160	900
C	900	630	150	180	170	180	950
D	1,000	700	150	180	170	200	1,000
E	1,100	770	150	180	170	220	1,050
F	1,200	840	150	180	170	240	1,100

Aggregate Planned Expenditure and Real GDP

The table in Fig. 23.5 sets out an aggregate expenditure schedule together with the components of aggregate planned expenditure. To calculate aggregate planned expenditure at a given real GDP, we add the various components together. The first column of the table shows real GDP, and the second column shows the consumption expenditure generated by each level of real GDP. A $100 billion increase in real GDP generates a $70 billion increase in consumption expenditure—the *MPC* is 0.7.

The next two columns show investment and government expenditures on goods and services. Investment depends on such factors as the real interest rate and the expected future profit. But at a given point in time, these factors generate a particular level of investment. Suppose this level of investment is $150 billion. Also, suppose that government expenditures on goods and services is $180 billion.

The next two columns show exports and imports. Exports are influenced by income in the rest of the world, prices of foreign-made goods and services relative to the prices of similar Canadian-made goods and services, and foreign exchange rates. But exports are not directly affected by real GDP in Canada. Exports are a constant $170 billion no matter what real GDP in Canada is. Imports increase as real GDP increases. A $100 billion increase in real GDP generates a $20 billion increase in imports—the marginal propensity to import is 0.2.

The final column shows aggregate planned expenditure—the sum of planned consumption expenditure, investment, government expenditures on goods and services, and exports minus imports.

Figure 23.5 plots an aggregate expenditure curve. Real GDP is shown on the *x*-axis, and aggregate planned expenditure is shown on the *y*-axis. The aggregate expenditure curve is the red line *AE*. Points *A* through *F* on that curve correspond to the rows of the table. The *AE* curve is a graph of aggregate planned expenditure (the last column) plotted against real GDP (the first column).

Figure 23.5 also shows the components of aggregate expenditure. The constant components—investment (*I*), government expenditures on goods and services (*G*), and exports (*X*)—are shown by the horizontal lines in the figure. Consumption expenditure (*C*) is the vertical gap between the lines labelled *I* + *G* + *X* and *I* + *G* + *X* + *C*.

To construct the *AE* curve, subtract imports (*M*) from the line labelled *I* + *G* + *X* + *C*. Aggregate expenditure is expenditure on Canadian-made goods and services. But the components of aggregate expenditure—*C*, *I*, and *G*—include expenditure on imported goods and services. For example, if you buy a new cell phone, your expenditure is part of consumption expenditure. But if the cell phone is a Nokia made in Finland, your expenditure on it must be subtracted from consumption expenditure to find out how much is spent on goods and services produced in Canada—on Canadian real GDP. Money paid to Nokia for cell phone imports from Finland does not add to aggregate expenditure in Canada.

Because imports are only a part of aggregate expenditure, when we subtract imports from the other components of aggregate expenditure, aggregate planned expenditure still increases as real GDP increases, as you can see in Fig. 23.5.

Consumption expenditure minus imports, which varies with real GDP, is called **induced expenditure**. The sum of investment, government expenditures, and exports, which does not vary with real GDP, is called **autonomous expenditure**. Consumption expenditure and imports can also have an autonomous component—a component that does not vary with real GDP. Another way of thinking about autonomous expenditure is that it would be the amount of aggregate planned expenditure if real GDP were zero.

In Fig. 23.5, autonomous expenditure is $500 billion—aggregate planned expenditure when real GDP is zero. For each $100 billion increase in real GDP, induced expenditure increases by $50 billion.

The aggregate expenditure curve summarizes the relationship between aggregate *planned* expenditure and real GDP. But what determines the point on the aggregate expenditure curve at which the economy operates? What determines *actual* aggregate expenditure?

Actual Expenditure, Planned Expenditure, and Real GDP

Actual aggregate expenditure is always equal to real GDP, as we saw in Chapter 20 (p. 468). But aggregate *planned* expenditure is not necessarily equal to actual aggregate expenditure and therefore is not necessarily equal to real GDP. How can actual expenditure and planned expenditure differ from each other? Why don't expenditure plans get implemented? The main reason is that firms might end up with greater inventories than planned or with smaller inventories than planned. People carry out their consumption expenditure plans, the government implements its planned purchases of goods and services, and net exports are as planned. Firms carry out their plans to purchase new buildings, plant, and equipment. But one component of investment is the change in firms' inventories. If aggregate planned expenditure is less than real GDP, firms don't sell all the goods they produce and they

end up with inventories they hadn't planned. If aggregate planned expenditure exceeds real GDP, firms sell more than they produce and inventories decrease below the level that firms had planned.

Equilibrium Expenditure

Equilibrium expenditure is the level of aggregate expenditure that occurs when aggregate *planned* expenditure equals real GDP. It is the level of aggregate

FIGURE 23.6
Equilibrium Expenditure

myeconlab

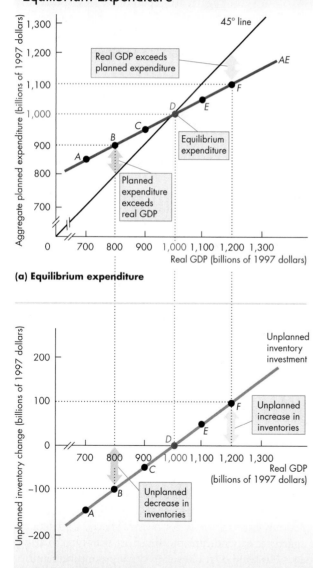

(a) Equilibrium expenditure

(b) Unplanned inventory changes

	Real GDP (Y)	Aggregate planned expenditure (AE)	Unplanned inventory change (Y – AE)
		(billions of 1997 dollars)	
A	700	850	–150
B	800	900	–100
C	900	950	–50
D	1,000	1,000	0
E	1,100	1,050	50
F	1,200	1,100	100

The table shows expenditure plans at different levels of real GDP. When real GDP is $1,000 billion, aggregate planned expenditure equals real GDP.

Part (a) of the figure illustrates equilibrium expenditure, which occurs when aggregate planned expenditure equals real GDP at the intersection of the 45° line and the AE curve. Part (b) of the figure shows the forces that bring about equilibrium expenditure. When aggregate planned expenditure exceeds real GDP, inventories decrease—for example, at point B in both parts of the figure. Firms increase production, and real GDP increases.

When aggregate planned expenditure is less than real GDP, inventories increase—for example, at point F in both parts of the figure. Firms decrease production, and real GDP decreases. When aggregate planned expenditure equals real GDP, there are no unplanned inventory changes and real GDP remains constant at equilibrium expenditure.

expenditure and real GDP at which everyone's spending plans are fulfilled. When the price level is fixed, equilibrium expenditure determines real GDP. When aggregate planned expenditure and actual aggregate expenditure are unequal, a process of convergence towards equilibrium expenditure occurs. And throughout this convergence process, real GDP adjusts. Let's examine equilibrium expenditure and the process that brings it about.

Figure 23.6(a) illustrates equilibrium expenditure. The table sets out aggregate planned expenditure at various levels of real GDP. These values are plotted as points A through F along the AE curve. The 45° line shows all the points at which aggregate planned expenditure equals real GDP. Thus where the AE curve lies above the 45° line, aggregate planned expenditure exceeds real GDP; where the AE curve lies below the 45° line, aggregate planned expenditure is less than real GDP; and where the AE curve intersects the 45° line, aggregate planned expenditure equals real GDP. Point D illustrates equilibrium expenditure. At this point, real GDP is $1,000 billion.

Convergence to Equilibrium

What are the forces that move aggregate expenditure towards its equilibrium level? To answer this question, we must look at a situation in which aggregate expenditure is away from its equilibrium level. Suppose that in Fig. 23.6, real GDP is $800 billion. With real GDP at $800 billion, actual aggregate expenditure is also $800 billion. But aggregate *planned* expenditure is $900 billion (point B in Fig. 23.6a). Aggregate planned expenditure exceeds real GDP. When people spend $900 billion and firms produce goods and services worth $800 billion, firms' inventories fall by $100 billion (point B in Fig. 23.6b). Recall that *investment* is the purchase of new plant, equipment and buildings and *additions to inventories*. Because the change in inventories is part of investment, *actual* investment is $100 billion less than *planned* investment.

Real GDP doesn't remain at $800 billion for very long. Firms have inventory targets based on their sales. When inventories fall below target, firms increase production to restore inventories to the target level. To increase inventories, firms hire additional labour and increase production. Suppose that they increase production in the next period by $100 billion. Real GDP increases by $100 billion to $900 billion. But again, aggregate planned expenditure

exceeds real GDP. When real GDP is $900 billion, aggregate planned expenditure is $950 billion (point C in Fig. 23.6a). Again, inventories decrease, but this time by less than before. With real GDP of $900 billion and aggregate planned expenditure of $950 billion, inventories decrease by $50 billion (point C in Fig. 23.6b). Again, firms hire additional labour, and production increases; real GDP increases yet further.

The process that we've just described—planned expenditure exceeds real GDP, inventories decrease, and production increases—ends when real GDP has reached $1,000 billion. At this real GDP, there is equilibrium. Unplanned inventory changes are zero. Firms do not change their production.

You can do an experiment similar to the one we've just done but starting with a level of real GDP greater than equilibrium expenditure. In this case, aggregate planned expenditure is less than real GDP, inventories pile up, and firms cut production. As before, real GDP keeps on changing (decreasing this time) until it reaches its equilibrium level of $1,000 billion.

REVIEW QUIZ

1 What is the relationship between aggregate planned expenditure and real GDP in expenditure equilibrium?
2 How does equilibrium expenditure come about? What adjusts to achieve equilibrium?
3 If real GDP and aggregate expenditure are less than their equilibrium levels, what happens to firms' inventories? How do firms change their production? And what happens to real GDP?
4 If real GDP and aggregate expenditure are greater than their equilibrium levels, what happens to firms' inventories? How do firms change their production? And what happens to real GDP?

myeconlab   **Study Plan 23.2**

We've learned that when the price level is fixed, real GDP is determined by equilibrium expenditure. And you have seen how unplanned changes in inventories and the production response that they generate brings a convergence towards equilibrium expenditure. We're now going to study *changes* in equilibrium expenditure and discover an economic amplifier called the *multiplier*.

The Multiplier

INVESTMENT AND EXPORTS CAN CHANGE FOR many reasons. A fall in the real interest rate might induce firms to increase their planned investment. A wave of innovation, such as occurred with the spread of multimedia computers in the 1990s, might increase expected future profits and lead firms to increase their planned investment. An economic boom in the United States and Western Europe might lead to a large increase in their expenditure on Canadian-produced goods and services—on Canadian exports. These are all examples of increases in autonomous expenditure.

When autonomous expenditure increases, aggregate expenditure increases, and so do equilibrium expenditure and real GDP. But the increase in real GDP is *larger* than the change in autonomous expenditure. The **multiplier** is the amount by which a change in autonomous expenditure is magnified or multiplied to determine the change in equilibrium expenditure and real GDP.

To get the basic idea of the multiplier we'll work with an economy in which there are no income taxes and no imports. So we'll first assume that these factors are absent. Then, when you understand the basic idea, we'll bring these factors back into play and see what difference they make to the multiplier.

The Basic Idea of the Multiplier

Suppose that investment increases. The additional expenditure by businesses means that aggregate expenditure and real GDP increase. The increase in real GDP increases disposable income, and with no income taxes, real GDP and disposable income increase by the same amount. The increase in disposable income brings an increase in consumption expenditure, which in turn adds even more to aggregate expenditure. Real GDP and disposable income increase further, and so does consumption expenditure. The initial increase in investment brings an even bigger increase in aggregate expenditure because it induces an increase in consumption expenditure. The magnitude of the increase in aggregate expenditure that results from an increase in autonomous expenditure is determined by the *multiplier*.

The table in Fig. 23.7 sets out aggregate planned expenditure. When real GDP is $900 billion, aggregate planned expenditure is $925 billion. For each

$100 billion increase in real GDP, aggregate planned expenditure increases by $75 billion. This aggregate expenditure schedule is shown in the figure as the aggregate expenditure curve AE_0. Initially, equilibrium expenditure is $1,000 billion. You can see this equilibrium in row B of the table and in the figure where the curve AE_0 intersects the 45° line at the point marked B.

Now suppose that autonomous expenditure increases by $50 billion. What happens to equilibrium expenditure? You can see the answer in Fig. 23.7. When this increase in autonomous expenditure is added to the original aggregate planned expenditure, aggregate planned expenditure increases by $50 billion at each level of real GDP. The new aggregate expenditure curve is AE_1. The new equilibrium expenditure, highlighted in the table (row D'), occurs where AE_1 intersects the 45° line and is $1,200 billion (point D'). At this real GDP, aggregate planned expenditure equals real GDP.

The Multiplier Effect

In Fig. 23.7, the increase in autonomous expenditure of $50 billion increases equilibrium expenditure by $200 billion. That is, the change in autonomous expenditure leads, like Céline Dion's electronic equipment, to an amplified change in equilibrium expenditure. This amplified change is the *multiplier effect*—equilibrium expenditure increases by *more than* the increase in autonomous expenditure. The multiplier is greater than 1.

Initially, when autonomous expenditure increases, aggregate planned expenditure exceeds real GDP. As a result, inventories decrease. Firms respond by increasing production so as to restore their inventories to the target level. As production increases, so does real GDP. With a higher level of real GDP, *induced expenditure* increases. Thus equilibrium expenditure increases by the sum of the initial increase in autonomous expenditure and the increase in induced expenditure. In this example, induced expenditure increases by $150 billion, so equilibrium expenditure increases by $200 billion.

Although we have just analyzed the effects of an *increase* in autonomous expenditure, the same analysis applies to a decrease in autonomous expenditure. If initially the aggregate expenditure curve is AE_1, equilibrium expenditure and real GDP are $1,200 billion. A decrease in autonomous expenditure of $50 billion shifts the aggregate expenditure

FIGURE 23.7
The Multiplier

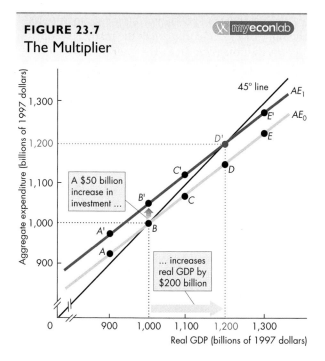

Real GDP	Aggregate planned expenditure			
(Y)	Original (AE₀)		New (AE₁)	
	(billions of 1997 dollars)			
900	A	925	A'	975
1,000	B	1,000	B'	1,050
1,100	C	1,075	C'	1,125
1,200	D	1,150	D'	1,200
1,300	E	1,225	E'	1,275

A \$50 billion increase in autonomous expenditure shifts the AE curve upward by \$50 billion from AE_0 to AE_1. Equilibrium expenditure increases by \$200 billion from \$1,000 billion to \$1,200 billion. The increase in equilibrium expenditure is 4 times the increase in autonomous expenditure, so the multiplier is 4.

curve downward by \$50 billion to AE_0. Equilibrium expenditure decreases from \$1,200 billion to \$1,000 billion. The decrease in equilibrium expenditure (\$200 billion) is larger than the decrease in autonomous expenditure that brought it about (\$50 billion).

Why Is the Multiplier Greater Than 1?

We've seen that equilibrium expenditure increases by more than the increase in autonomous expenditure. This makes the multiplier greater than 1.

How come? Why does equilibrium expenditure increase by more than the increase in autonomous expenditure?

The multiplier is greater than 1 because of induced expenditure—an increase in autonomous expenditure *induces* further increases in expenditure. If Rogers Cablesystems spends \$10 million on a new pay-per-view system, aggregate expenditure and real GDP immediately increase by \$10 million. But that is not the end of the story. Video system designers and computer producers now have more income, and they spend part of the extra income on cars, microwave ovens, vacations, and a host of other goods and services. Real GDP now increases by the initial \$10 million plus the extra consumption expenditure induced by the \$10 million increase in income. The producers of cars, microwave ovens, vacations, and other goods and services now have increased incomes, and they, in turn, spend part of the increase in their incomes on consumption goods and services. Additional income induces additional expenditure, which creates additional income.

We have seen that a change in autonomous expenditure has a multiplier effect on real GDP. But how big is the multiplier effect?

The Size of the Multiplier

The *multiplier* is the amount by which a change in autonomous expenditure is multiplied to determine the change in equilibrium expenditure that it generates. To calculate the multiplier, we divide the change in equilibrium expenditure by the change in autonomous expenditure. Let's calculate the multiplier for the example in Fig. 23.7. Initially, equilibrium expenditure is \$1,000 billion. Then autonomous expenditure increases by \$50 billion, and equilibrium expenditure increases by \$200 billion, to \$1,200 billion. So

$$\text{Multiplier} = \frac{\text{Change in equilibrium expenditure}}{\text{Change in autonomous expenditure}}$$
$$= \frac{\$200 \text{ billion}}{\$50 \text{ billion}} = 4.$$

The Multiplier and the Slope of the *AE* Curve

What determines the magnitude of the multiplier? The answer is the slope of the *AE* curve. The steeper the slope of the *AE* curve, the larger is the multiplier. To see why, think about what the slope of the *AE* curve tells you. It tells you by how much induced expenditure increases when real GDP increases. The steeper the *AE* curve, the greater is the increase in induced expenditure that results from a given increase in real GDP. Let's do a calculation to show the relationship between the slope of the *AE* curve and the multiplier.

The change in real GDP (ΔY) equals the change in induced expenditure (ΔN) plus the change in autonomous expenditure (ΔA). That is,

$$\Delta Y = \Delta N + \Delta A.$$

The slope of the *AE* curve equals the "rise," ΔN, divided by the "run," ΔY. That is,

$$\text{Slope of } AE \text{ curve} = \Delta N \div \Delta Y.$$

So

$$\Delta N = \text{Slope of } AE \text{ curve} \times \Delta Y.$$

Now use this equation to replace ΔN in the first equation above to give

$$\Delta Y = (\text{Slope of } AE \text{ curve} \times \Delta Y) + \Delta A.$$

Now, solve for ΔY as

$$(1 - \text{Slope of } AE \text{ curve}) \times \Delta Y = \Delta A$$

and rearrange to give

$$\Delta Y = \frac{\Delta A}{1 - \text{Slope of the } AE \text{ curve}}.$$

Finally, divide both sides of the previous equation by ΔA to give

$$\text{Multiplier} = \frac{\Delta Y}{\Delta A} = \frac{1}{1 - \text{Slope of } AE \text{ curve}}.$$

Using the numbers for Fig. 23.7, the slope of the *AE* curve is 0.75, so the multiplier is

$$\text{Multiplier} = \frac{1}{1 - 0.75} = \frac{1}{0.25} = 4.$$

When there are no income taxes and no imports, the slope of the *AE* curve equals the marginal propensity to consume (*MPC*). So the multiplier is

$$\text{Multiplier} = \frac{1}{1 - MPC}.$$

There is another formula for the multiplier in this special case. Because the marginal propensity to consume (*MPC*) plus the marginal propensity to save (*MPS*) sum to 1, the term ($1 - MPC$) equals *MPS*. Therefore, another formula for the multiplier is

$$\text{Multiplier} = \frac{1}{MPS}.$$

Because the marginal propensity to save (*MPS*) is a number between 0 and 1, the multiplier is greater than 1.

Figure 23.8 illustrates the multiplier process. In round 1, autonomous expenditure increases by $50 billion (shown by the green bar). At this time, induced expenditure does not change, so aggregate expenditure and real GDP increase by $50 billion. In round 2, the larger real GDP induces more consumption expenditure. Induced expenditure increases by 0.75 times the increase in real GDP, so the increase in real GDP of $50 billion induces a further increase in expenditure of $37.5 billion. This change in induced expenditure (the green bar in round 2), when added to the previous increase in expenditure (the blue bar in round 2), increases aggregate expenditure and real GDP by $87.5 billion. The round 2 increase in real GDP induces a round 3 increase in expenditure. The process repeats through successive rounds. Each increase in real GDP is 0.75 times the previous increase. The cumulative increase in real GDP gradually approaches $200 billion.

So far, we've ignored imports and income taxes. Let's now see how these two factors influence the multiplier.

Imports and Income Taxes

The multiplier is determined, in general, not only by the marginal propensity to consume but also by the marginal propensity to import and by the marginal tax rate.

Imports make the multiplier smaller than it otherwise would be. To see why, think about what happens following an increase in investment. An increase in

FIGURE 23.8

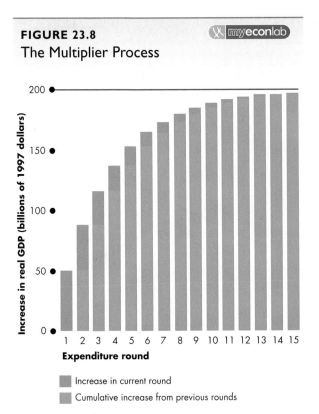

The Multiplier Process

Autonomous expenditure increases in round 1 by $50 billion. As a result, real GDP increases by the same amount. With a marginal propensity to consume of 0.75, each additional dollar of real GDP induces an additional 0.75 of a dollar of aggregate expenditure. The round 1 increase in real GDP induces an increase in consumption expenditure of $37.5 billion in round 2. At the end of round 2, real GDP has increased by $87.5 billion. The extra $37.5 billion of real GDP in round 2 induces a further increase in consumption expenditure of $28.1 billion in round 3. Real GDP increases yet further to $115.6 billion. This process continues with real GDP increasing by ever-smaller amounts. When the process comes to an end, real GDP has increased by a total of $200 billion.

investment increases real GDP, which in turn increases consumption expenditure. But part of the increase in consumption expenditure is expenditure on imported goods and services, not Canadian-produced goods and services. Only expenditure on Canadian-produced goods and services increases Canadian real GDP. The larger is the marginal propensity to import, the smaller is the change in Canadian real GDP.

Income taxes also make the multiplier smaller than it otherwise would be. Again, think about what happens following an increase in investment. Real GDP increases. But because income taxes increase, disposable income increases by less than the increase in real GDP. Consequently, consumption expenditure increases by less than it would if taxes had not changed. The larger the marginal tax rate, the smaller is the change in disposable income and real GDP.

The marginal propensity to import and the marginal tax rate together with the marginal propensity to consume determine the multiplier. And their combined influence determines the slope of the *AE* curve. The multiplier is equal to 1 divided by (1 minus the slope of the *AE* curve).

Figure 23.9 compares two situations. In Fig. 23.9(a), there are no imports and no taxes. The slope of the *AE* curve equals the marginal propensity to consume, which is 0.75, and the multiplier is 4. In Fig. 23.9(b), imports and income taxes decrease the slope of the *AE* curve to 0.5. In this case, the multiplier is 2.

Over time, the value of the multiplier changes as tax rates change and as the marginal propensity to consume and the marginal propensity to import change. These ongoing changes make the multiplier hard to predict. But they do not change the fundamental fact that an initial change in autonomous expenditure leads to a magnified change in aggregate expenditure and real GDP.

The math note on pp. 558–559 shows the effects of taxes, imports, and the *MPC* on the multiplier.

Now that we've studied the multiplier and the factors that influence its magnitude, let's use what we've learned to gain some insights into business cycle turning points.

Business Cycle Turning Points

At business cycle turning points, the economy moves from expansion to recession or from recession to expansion. Economists understand these turning points as seismologists understand earthquakes. They know quite a lot about the forces and mechanisms that produce them, but they can't predict them. The forces that bring business cycle turning points are the swings in autonomous expenditure such as investment and exports. The mechanism that gives momentum to the economy's new direction is the multiplier. Let's use what we've now learned to examine these turning points.

FIGURE 23.9

The Multiplier and the Slope of the *AE* Curve

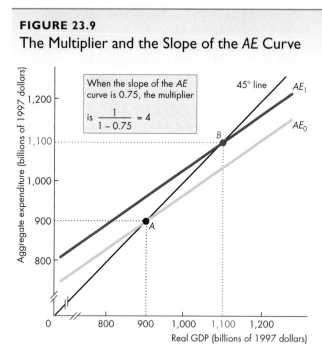

(a) Multiplier is 4

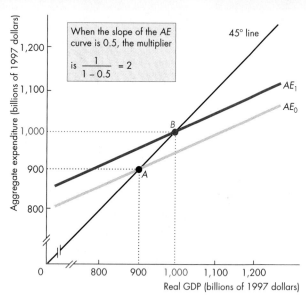

(b) Multiplier is 2

Imports and income taxes make the *AE* curve less steep and reduce the value of the multiplier. In part (a), with no imports and income taxes, the slope of the *AE* curve is 0.75 (the marginal propensity to consume) and the multiplier is 4.

But with imports and income taxes, the slope of the *AE* curve is less than the marginal propensity to consume. In part (b), the slope of the *AE* curve is 0.5. In this case, the multiplier is 2.

An Expansion Begins An expansion is triggered by an increase in autonomous expenditure that increases aggregate planned expenditure. At the moment the economy turns the corner into expansion, aggregate planned expenditure exceeds real GDP. In this situation, firms see their inventories taking an unplanned dive. The expansion now begins. To meet their inventory targets, firms increase production, and real GDP begins to increase. This initial increase in real GDP brings higher incomes that increase disposable income and stimulate consumption expenditure. The multiplier process kicks in, and the expansion picks up speed.

A Recession Begins The process we've just described works in reverse at a business cycle peak. A recession is triggered by a decrease in autonomous expenditure that decreases aggregate planned expenditure. At the moment the economy turns the corner into recession, real GDP exceeds aggregate planned

expenditure. In this situation, firms see unplanned inventories piling up. The recession now begins. To lower their inventories, firms cut production, and real GDP begins to decrease. This initial decrease in real GDP brings lower incomes that cut consumption expenditure. The multiplier process reinforces the initial cut in autonomous expenditure, and the recession takes hold.

The Next Canadian Recession? Since 1991, the Canadian economy has been in a business cycle expansion. The last real GDP trough was in the first quarter of 1991. The science of macroeconomics cannot predict when the next recession will begin. A recession seemed possible in 1998 following a rapid buildup of inventories during 1997. But firms had planned that inventory buildup. In late 2005, there was still no immediate prospect of the next recession. But it will surely come. And when it does, the mechanism you've just studied will operate.

The economy's potholes are changes in investment and exports. The economy does not operate like the shock absorbers on Ralph Klein's car. While the price level is fixed, the effects of the economic potholes are not smoothed out. Instead, they are amplified like Céline Dion's voice. But we've considered only the adjustments in spending that occur when the price level is fixed. What happens after a long enough time lapse for the price level to change? Let's answer this question.

The Multiplier and the Price Level

WHEN FIRMS CAN'T KEEP UP WITH SALES AND THEIR inventories fall below target, they increase production, but at some point, they raise their prices. Similarly, when firms find unwanted inventories piling up, they decrease production, but eventually they cut their prices. So far, we've studied the macroeconomic consequences of firms changing their production levels when their sales change, but we haven't looked at the effects of price changes. When individual firms change their prices, the economy's price level changes.

To study the simultaneous determination of real GDP and the price level, we use the *aggregate supply–aggregate demand model*, which is explained in Chapter 22. But to understand how aggregate demand adjusts, we need to work out the connection between the aggregate supply–aggregate demand model and the equilibrium expenditure model that we've used in this chapter. The key to understanding the relationship between these two models is the distinction between the aggregate *expenditure* and aggregate *demand* and the related distinction between the aggregate *expenditure curve* and the aggregate *demand curve*.

Aggregate Expenditure and Aggregate Demand

The aggregate expenditure curve is the relationship between aggregate planned expenditure and real GDP when all other influences on aggregate planned expenditure remain the same. The aggregate demand curve is the relationship between the aggregate quantity of goods and services demanded and the price level when all other influences on aggregate demand remain the same. Let's explore the links between these two relationships.

Aggregate Expenditure and the Price Level

When the price level changes, aggregate planned expenditure changes and the quantity of real GDP demanded changes. The aggregate demand curve slopes downward. Why? There are two main reasons:

■ Wealth effect
■ Substitution effects

Wealth Effect Other things remaining the same, the higher the price level, the smaller is the purchasing power of people's real wealth. For example suppose you have $100 in the bank and the price level is 110. If the price level rises to 130, your $100 buys fewer goods and services. You are less wealthy. With less wealth, you will probably want to try to spend a bit less and save a bit more. The higher the price level, other things remaining the same, the lower is aggregate planned expenditure.

Substitution Effects A rise in the price level today, other things remaining the same, makes current goods and services more costly relative to future goods and services and people delay making their purchases—an *intertemporal substitution*. A rise in the price level, other things remaining the same, makes Canadian-produced goods more expensive relative to foreign-produced goods and services and increases imports and decreases exports—an *international substitution*.

When the price level rises, each of these effects reduces aggregate planned expenditure at each level of real GDP. As a result, when the price level *rises*, the *AE* curve shifts *downward*. A fall in the price level has the opposite effect. When the price level *falls*, the *AE* curve shifts *upward*.

Figure 23.10(a) shows the shifts of the *AE* curve. When the price level is 110, the aggregate expenditure curve is AE_0, which intersects the 45° line at point *B*. Equilibrium expenditure is $1,000 billion. If the price level increases to 130, the aggregate expenditure curve shifts downward to AE_1, which intersects the 45° line at point *A*. Equilibrium expenditure is $900 billion. If the price level decreases to 90, the aggregate expenditure curve shifts upward to AE_2, which intersects the 45° line at point *C*. Equilibrium expenditure is $1,100 billion.

We've just seen that when the price level changes, other things remaining the same, the *AE* curve shifts and the equilibrium expenditure changes. And when the price level changes, other things remaining the same, there is a movement along the *AD* curve. Figure 23.10(b) shows these movements along the *AD* curve. At a price level of 110, the aggregate quantity of goods and services demanded is $1,000 billion—point *B* on the *AD* curve. If the price level rises to 130, the aggregate quantity of goods and services demanded decreases to $900 billion. There is a movement along the *AD* curve to point *A*. If the price level falls to 90, the aggregate quantity of goods and services demanded increases to $1,100 billion. There is a movement along the *AD* curve to point *C*.

Each point on the *AD* curve corresponds to a point of equilibrium expenditure. The equilibrium expenditure points *A, B,* and *C* in Fig. 23.10(a) correspond to the points *A, B,* and *C* on the *AD* curve in Fig. 23.10(b).

A change in the price level, other things remaining the same, shifts the *AE* curve and brings a movement along the *AD* curve. A change in any other influence on aggregate planned expenditure shifts *both* the *AE* curve and the *AD* curve. For example, an increase in investment or in exports increases both aggregate planned expenditure and aggregate demand and shifts both the *AE* curve and the *AD* curve. Figure 23.11 illustrates the effect of such an increase.

Initially, the aggregate expenditure curve is AE_0 in part (a) and the aggregate demand curve is AD_0 in part (b). The price level is 110, real GDP is $1,000 billion, and the economy is at point *A* in both parts of the figure. Now suppose that investment increases by $100 billion. At a constant price level of 110, the aggregate expenditure curve shifts upward by $100 billion to AE_1. This curve intersects the 45° line at an equilibrium expenditure of $1,200 billion (point *B*).

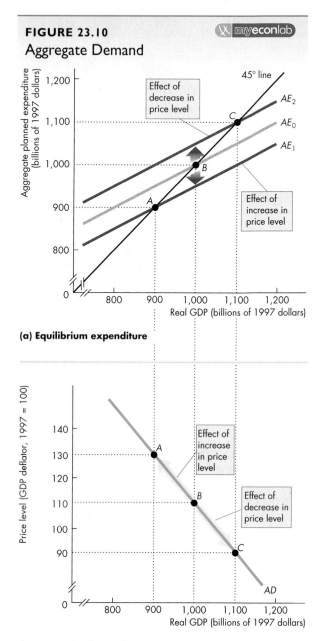

FIGURE 23.10
Aggregate Demand

(a) Equilibrium expenditure

(b) Aggregate demand

A change in the price level *shifts* the *AE* curve and results in a *movement along* the *AD* curve. When the price level is 110, the *AE* curve is AE_0 and equilibrium expenditure is $1,000 billion at point *B*. When the price level rises to 130, the *AE* curve is AE_1 and equilibrium expenditure is $900 billion at point *A*. When the price level falls to 90, the *AE* curve is AE_2 and equilibrium expenditure is $1,100 billion at point *C*. Points *A, B,* and *C* on the *AD* curve in part (b) correspond to the equilibrium expenditure points *A, B,* and *C* in part (a).

FIGURE 23.11

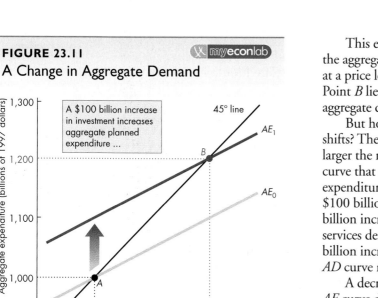

A Change in Aggregate Demand

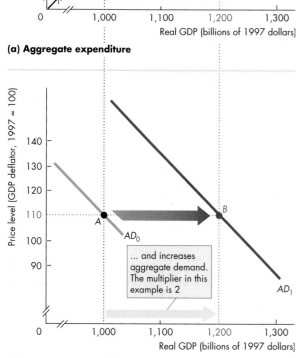

A $100 billion increase in investment increases aggregate planned expenditure ...

(a) Aggregate expenditure

... and increases aggregate demand. The multiplier in this example is 2.

(b) Aggregate demand

The price level is 110. When the aggregate expenditure curve is AE_0 (part a), the aggregate demand curve is AD_0 (part b). An increase in autonomous expenditure shifts the AE curve upward to AE_1. In the new equilibrium, real GDP is $1,200 billion (at point B). Because the quantity of real GDP demanded at a price level of 110 increases to $1,200 billion, the AD curve shifts rightward to AD_1.

This equilibrium expenditure of $1,200 billion is the aggregate quantity of goods and services demanded at a price level of 110, as shown by point B in part (b). Point B lies on a new aggregate demand curve. The aggregate demand curve has shifted rightward to AD_1.

But how do we know by how much the AD curve shifts? The multiplier determines the answer. The larger the multiplier, the larger is the shift in the AD curve that results from a given change in autonomous expenditure. In this example, the multiplier is 2. A $100 billion increase in investment produces a $200 billion increase in the aggregate quantity of goods and services demanded at each price level. That is, a $100 billion increase in autonomous expenditure shifts the AD curve rightward by $200 billion.

A decrease in autonomous expenditure shifts the AE curve downward and shifts the AD curve leftward. You can see these effects by reversing the change that we've just described. If the economy is initially at point B on the aggregate expenditure curve AE_1, the aggregate demand curve is AD_1. A decrease in autonomous expenditure shifts the aggregate planned expenditure curve downward to AE_0. The aggregate quantity of goods and services demanded decreases from $1,200 billion to $1,000 billion, and the aggregate demand curve shifts leftward to AD_0.

Let's summarize what we have just discovered:

If some factor other than a change in the price level increases autonomous expenditure, the AE curve shifts upward and the AD curve shifts rightward.

The size of the AD curve shift depends on the change in autonomous expenditure and the multiplier.

Equilibrium GDP and the Price Level

In Chapter 22, we learned that aggregate demand and short-run aggregate supply determine equilibrium real GDP and the price level. We've now put aggregate demand under a more powerful microscope and have discovered that a change in investment (or in any component of autonomous expenditure) changes aggregate demand and shifts the aggregate demand curve. The magnitude of the shift depends on the multiplier. But whether a change in autonomous expenditure results ultimately in a change in real GDP, a change in the price level, or a combination of the two depends on aggregate supply. There are two time frames to consider: the short run and the long run. First we'll see what happens in the short run.

An Increase in Aggregate Demand in the Short Run Figure 23.12 describes the economy. In part (a), the aggregate expenditure curve is AE_0 and equilibrium expenditure is $1,000 billion—point A. In part (b), aggregate demand is AD_0 and the short-run aggregate supply curve is SAS. (Chapter 22, pp. 509–510 explains the SAS curve.) Equilibrium is at point A, where the aggregate demand and short-run aggregate supply curves intersect. The price level is 110, and real GDP is $1,000 billion.

Now suppose that investment increases by $100 billion. With the price level fixed at 110, the aggregate expenditure curve shifts upward to AE_1. Equilibrium expenditure increases to $1,200 billion—point B in part (a). In part (b), the aggregate demand curve shifts rightward by $200 billion, from AD_0 to AD_1. How far the aggregate demand curve shifts is determined by the multiplier when the price level is fixed.

But with this new aggregate demand curve, the price level does not remain fixed. The price level rises, and as it does so, the aggregate expenditure curve shifts downward. The short-run equilibrium occurs when the aggregate expenditure curve has shifted downward to AE_2 and the new aggregate demand curve, AD_1, intersects the short-run aggregate supply curve. Real GDP is $1,130 billion, and the price level is 123 (at point C).

When price level effects are taken into account, the increase in investment still has a multiplier effect on real GDP, but the multiplier effect is smaller than it would be if the price level were fixed. The steeper the slope of the SAS curve, the larger is the increase in the price level and the smaller is the multiplier effect on real GDP.

An Increase in Aggregate Demand in the Long Run Figure 23.13 illustrates the long-run effect of an increase in aggregate demand. In the long run, real GDP equals potential GDP and the economy is at full employment. Potential GDP is $1,000 billion, and the long-run aggregate supply curve is LAS. Initially, the economy is at point A (parts a and b).

Investment increases by $100 billion. The aggregate expenditure curve shifts to AE_1, and the aggregate demand curve shifts to AD_1. With no change in the price level, the economy would move to point B and real GDP would increase to $1,200 billion. But in the short run, the price level rises to 123 and real GDP increases to only $1,130 billion. With the higher price level, the AE curve shifts from AE_1 to AE_2. The econ-

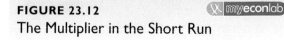

FIGURE 23.12

The Multiplier in the Short Run

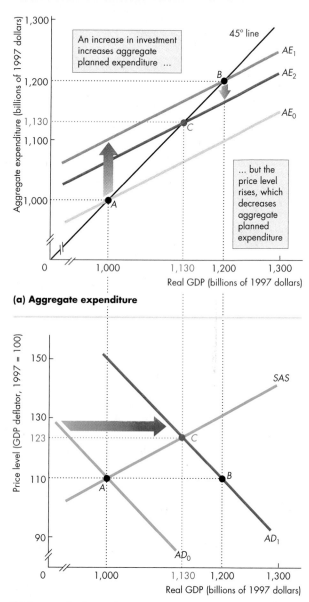

(a) Aggregate expenditure

(b) Aggregate demand

An increase in investment shifts the AE curve from AE_0 to AE_1 (part a) and shifts the AD curve from AD_0 to AD_1 (part b). The price level does not remain at 110 but rises, and the higher price level shifts the AE curve downward from AE_1 to AE_2. The economy moves to point C in both parts. In the short run, when prices are flexible, the multiplier effect is smaller than when the price level is fixed.

FIGURE 23.13

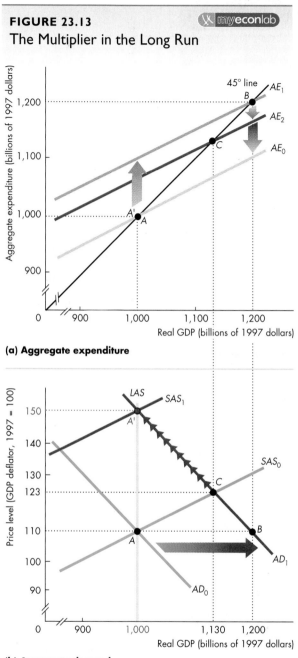

The Multiplier in the Long Run

(a) Aggregate expenditure

(b) Aggregate demand

Starting from point A, an increase in investment shifts the AE curve to AE_1 and shifts the AD curve to AD_1. In the short run, the economy moves to point C. In the long run, the money wage rate rises, which shifts the SAS curve to SAS_1. The price level rises, the AE curve shifts back to AE_0, and real GDP decreases. The economy moves to point A'. In the long run, the multiplier is zero.

omy is now in a short-run equilibrium at point C.

Real GDP is now above potential GDP. The labour force is more than fully employed, and shortages of labour increase the money wage rate. The higher money wage rate increases costs, which decreases short-run aggregate supply and shifts the SAS curve leftward to SAS_1. The price level rises further, and real GDP decreases. There is a movement along AD_1, and the AE curve shifts downward from AE_2 towards AE_0. When the money wage rate and the price level have increased by the same percentage, real GDP is again equal to potential GDP and the economy is at point A'. In the long run, the multiplier is zero.

REVIEW QUIZ

1 How does a change in the price level influence the AE curve and the AD curve?

2 If autonomous expenditure increases with no change in the price level, what happens to the AE curve and the AD curve? Which curve shifts by an amount that is determined by the multiplier and why?

3 How does real GDP change in the short run when there is an increase in autonomous expenditure? Does real GDP change by the same amount as the change in aggregate demand? Why or why not?

4 How does real GDP change in the long run when there is an increase in autonomous expenditure? Does real GDP change by the same amount as the change in aggregate demand? Why or why not?

myeconlab **Study Plan 23.4**

◆ You are now ready to apply what you've learned about aggregate expenditure fluctuations and study the role of fiscal policy in smoothing the business cycle. That is the topic of Chapter 24, in which we study the effects of government expenditures, taxes, and the government deficit.

But before you leave the current topic, look at *Reading Between the Lines* on pp. 556–557, which looks at the rapid expansion of real GDP that occurred in Canada during the first half of 2005.

The Aggregate Expenditure Multiplier in Action

CALGARY HERALD, 1 JULY 2005

Spring economic rebound stronger than expected: Increased oilsand production boosts activity

The Canadian economy was off to a hot start this spring, with a stronger than expected rebound in growth in April and a record surge in homes sales in May. Economic activity bounced back 0.4 per cent in April after declining 0.1 per cent in March, boosted by increased oilsands production, an end to a student strike in Quebec, and strong auto sales, Statistics Canada reported Thursday.

... Meanwhile, in its report on economic growth, Statistics Canada noted milder than usual weather in April in most parts of the country and in the northern U.S. lowered the demand for natural gas and reduced the output of related activities. Mining activity increased on the strength of higher output by copper, nickel, lead and zinc ore mines, while a strike brought iron ore mining. Retail and wholesale sales, meanwhile, were boosted by new car sales, although the gain in retail sales gains was widespread. Manufacturing output increased slightly, regaining some of the ground lost in February and March although auto production continued to decline. While sales of existing homes were strong in May, residential construction in April fell for the fourth straight month. "Since the beginning of the year, residential construction activity has decreased 3.3 percent," Statistics Canada noted. Non-residential building construction also dipped by 0.1 percent.

Essence of the Story

■ In 2005, Canada had record household spending, a 30-year low in its unemployment rate, and the highest ever company profits.

■ Real GDP was expected to grow by 3 percent—up from 2.6 percent a year earlier.

■ Canada had the second-best performing economy in the G7.

■ Oil production has brought a burst of investment.

■ A government budget surplus, low inflation, and low interest rates are boosting confidence and stimulating growth.

Economic Analysis

- During the first half of 2005, real GDP increased by $15 billion.

- The table shows the amounts by which the components of aggregate expenditure increased.

- On the average, an additional dollar of real GDP brings about 66 cents of additional consumption expenditure and about 33 cents of additional imports.

- Using these two values, the slope of the AE curve is 0.33 and we can calculate the multiplier: $1/(1 - \text{Slope of } AE \text{ curve})$ $= 1/(1 - 0.33)$ $= 1/0.67 = 1.5$.

- The increase in consumption expenditure was $14 billion. Of this, $10 billion was induced by the increase in real GDP. The rest was an increase in autonomous consumption—the consumption function shifted upward during the first half of 2005 by $4 billion.

- The increase in autonomous consumption most likely resulted from low real interest rates that made consumers willing to borrow to finance large purchases of durable goods.

- The increase in imports was $8 billion and about $5 billion was in-

duced by the $15 billion increase in real GDP and the rest came from an increase in autonomous imports—an upward shift in the import function of $3 billion.

- The increases in fixed investment, government expenditures, exports, and investment in inventories sum to $9 billion.

- Adding the increase in autonomous consumption, $4 billion, and subtracting the increase in autonomous imports, $3 billion, gives an increase in autonomous expenditure of $10 billion.

- Based on the assumptions just described, Fig. 1 shows the AE curve in the fourth quarter of 2004, AE_0, and in the second quarter of 2005, AE_1.

- The AE curve shifted upward by $10 billion (the assumed increase in autonomous expenditure), and real GDP increased from $1,037 billion to $1,052 billion, an increase of $15 billion.

- Check that the increase in real GDP equals the increase in autonomous expenditure, $10 billion, multiplied by 1.5, the multiplier.

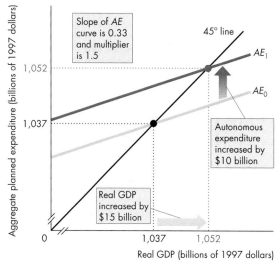

Figure 1 Increase in autonomous expenditure and multiplier

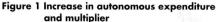

Item	Increase (billions of 1997 dollars)
Consumption expenditure	+14
Fixed investment	+8
Government expenditure	+4
Exports	+7
minus Imports	−8
Investment in inventories	−10
Real GDP	+15

Mathematical Note
The Algebra of the Multiplier

THIS NOTE EXPLAINS THE MULTIPLIER IN GREATER detail than that presented on p. 548. We begin by defining the symbols we need:

- Aggregate planned expenditure, AE
- Real GDP, Y
- Consumption expenditure, C
- Investment, I
- Government expenditures, G
- Exports, X
- Imports, M
- Net taxes, NT
- Disposable income, YD
- Autonomous consumption expenditure, a
- Marginal propensity to consume, b
- Marginal propensity to import, m
- Marginal tax rate, t
- Autonomous expenditure, A

Aggregate Expenditure

Aggregate planned expenditure (AE) is the sum of the planned amounts of consumption expenditure (C), investment (I), government expenditures (G), and exports (X) minus the planned amount of imports (M). That is,

$$AE = C + I + G + X - M.$$

Consumption Function Consumption expenditure (C) depends on disposable income (YD), and we write the consumption function as

$$C = a + bYD.$$

Disposable income (YD) equals real GDP minus net taxes ($Y - NT$). So if we replace YD with ($Y - NT$), the consumption function becomes

$$C = a + b(Y - NT).$$

Net taxes equal real GDP (Y) multiplied by the marginal tax rate (t). That is,

$$NT = tY.$$

Use this equation in the previous one to obtain

$$C = a + b(1 - t)Y.$$

This equation describes consumption expenditure as a function of real GDP.

Import Function Imports depend on real GDP, and the import function is

$$M = mY.$$

Aggregate Expenditure Curve Use the consumption function and the import function to replace C and M in the aggregate planned expenditure equation. That is,

$$AE = a + b(1 - t)Y + I + G + X - mY.$$

Collect the terms on the right side of the equation that involve Y to obtain

$$AE = (a + I + G + X) + [b(1 - t) - m]Y.$$

Autonomous expenditure (A) is ($a + I + G + X$), and the slope of the AE curve is $[b(1 - t) - m]$. So the equation for the AE curve, which is shown in Fig. 1, is

$$AE = A + [b(1 - t) - m]Y.$$

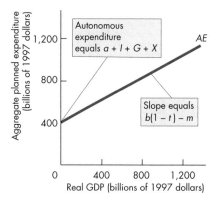

Figure 1 The AE curve

Equilibrium Expenditure

Equilibrium expenditure occurs when aggregate planned expenditure (AE) equals real GDP (Y). That is,

$$AE = Y.$$

In Fig. 2, the scales of the x-axis (real GDP) and the y-axis (aggregate planned expenditure) are identical, so the 45° line shows the points at which aggregate planned expenditure equals real GDP.

Figure 2 shows the point of equilibrium expenditure at the intersection of the AE curve and the 45° line.

To calculate equilibrium expenditure and real GDP, we solve the equations for the AE curve and the 45° line for the quantity Y. So starting with

$$AE = A + [b(1 - t) - m]Y$$

$$AE = Y,$$

replace AE with Y in the AE equation to obtain

$$Y = A + [b(1 - t) - m]Y.$$

The solution for Y is

$$Y = \frac{1}{1 - [b(1 - t) - m]} A.$$

The Multiplier

The multiplier equals the change in equilibrium expenditure and real GDP (Y) that results from a change in autonomous expenditure (A) divided by the change in autonomous expenditure.

A change in autonomous expenditure (ΔA) changes equilibrium expenditure and real GDP (ΔY) by

$$\Delta Y = \frac{1}{1 - [b(1 - t) - m]} \Delta A.$$

So

$$\text{Multiplier} = \frac{1}{1 - [b(1 - t) - m]}.$$

The size of the multiplier depends on the slope of the AE curve, $b(1 - t) - m$. The larger the slope, the larger is the multiplier. So the multiplier is larger,

- The greater the marginal propensity to consume (b)
- The smaller the marginal tax rate (t)
- The smaller the marginal propensity to import (m)

An economy with no imports and no marginal taxes has $m = 0$ and $t = 0$. In this special case, the multiplier equals $1/(1 - b)$. If b is 0.75, then the multiplier is 4, as shown in Fig. 3.

In an economy with taxes and imports, if $t = 0.2$, $m = 0.1$, and $b = 0.75$, the multiplier is $1 \div [1 - 0.75(1 - 0.2) - 0.1]$, which equals 2.

Make up some more examples to show the effects of b, t, and m on the multiplier.

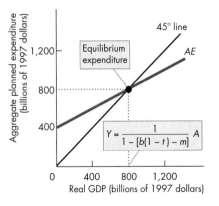

Figure 2 Equilibrium expenditure

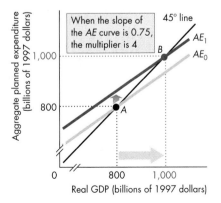

Figure 3 The multiplier

SUMMARY

KEY POINTS

Expenditure Plans and GDP (pp. 536–541)

- When the price level is fixed, expenditure plans determine real GDP.
- Consumption expenditure is determined by disposable income, and the marginal propensity to consume (*MPC*) determines the change in consumption expenditure brought about by a change in disposable income. Real GDP is the main influence on disposable income.
- Imports are determined by real GDP, and the marginal propensity to import determines the change in imports brought about by a change in real GDP.

Equilibrium Expenditure at a Fixed Price Level (pp. 541–545)

- Aggregate *planned* expenditure depends on real GDP.
- Equilibrium expenditure occurs when aggregate planned expenditure equals actual expenditure and real GDP.

The Multiplier (pp. 546–551)

- The multiplier is the magnified effect of a change in autonomous expenditure on real GDP.
- The multiplier equals 1 divided by (1 minus the slope of the *AE* curve).
- The multiplier is influenced by the marginal propensity to consume, the marginal propensity to import, and the marginal tax rate.

The Multiplier and the Price Level (pp. 551–555)

- The *AD* curve is the relationship between the quantity of real GDP demanded and the price level, other things remaining the same.
- The *AE* curve is the relationship between aggregate planned expenditure and real GDP, other things remaining the same.

- At a given price level, there is a given *AE* curve. A change in the price level changes aggregate planned expenditure and shifts the *AE* curve. A change in the price level also creates a movement along the *AD* curve.
- A change in autonomous expenditure that is not caused by a change in the price level shifts the *AE* curve and shifts the *AD* curve. The magnitude of the shift of the *AD* curve depends on the multiplier and on the change in autonomous expenditure.
- The multiplier decreases as the price level changes and the multiplier in the long run is zero.

KEY FIGURES

Figure 23.1   Consumption Function and Saving Function, 537
Figure 23.2   Marginal Propensities to Consume and Save, 538
Figure 23.5   Aggregate Expenditure, 542
Figure 23.6   Equilibrium Expenditure, 544
Figure 23.7   The Multiplier, 547
Figure 23.8   The Multiplier Process, 549
Figure 23.9   The Multiplier and the Slope of the *AE* Curve, 550
Figure 23.10   Aggregate Demand, 552
Figure 23.11   A Change in Aggregate Demand, 553
Figure 23.12   The Multiplier in the Short Run, 554
Figure 23.13   The Multiplier in the Long Run, 555

KEY TERMS

Aggregate planned expenditure, 541
Autonomous expenditure, 543
Consumption function, 536
Disposable income, 536
Equilibrium expenditure, 544
Induced expenditure, 543
Marginal propensity to consume, 538
Marginal propensity to import, 541
Marginal propensity to save, 538
Multiplier, 546
Saving function, 536

PROBLEMS

Go to **myeconlab** for solutions to odd-numbered problems and additional exercises.

1. You are given the following information about the economy of Heron Island:

Disposable income (millions of dollars per year)	Consumption expenditure (millions of dollars per year)
0	5
10	10
20	15
30	20

Calculate Heron Island's
   a. Marginal propensity to consume.
   b. Saving at each level of disposable income.
   c. Marginal propensity to save.

2. You are given the following information about the economy of Spendthrift Island:

Disposable income (millions of dollars per year)	Saving (millions of dollars per year)
0	−10
50	−5
100	0
150	5
200	10

   a. Calculate the marginal propensity to save.
   b. Calculate consumption at each level of disposable income.
   c. Calculate the marginal propensity to consume.
   d. Why is the island called "Spendthrift"?

3. Turtle Island has no imports, exports, or taxes, and the price level is fixed. The figure shows the components of aggregate planned expenditure.
   a. What is autonomous expenditure?
   b. What is the marginal propensity to consume?
   c. What is aggregate planned expenditure when real GDP is $6 billion?
   d. If real GDP is $2 billion, what is happening to inventories?
   e. If real GDP is $6 billion, what is happening to inventories?
   f. What is the multiplier?

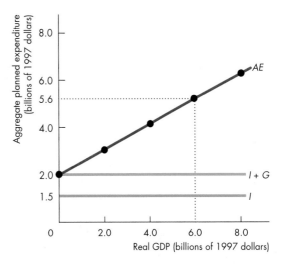

4. The spreadsheet lists the components of aggregate planned expenditure in Spice Bay. The numbers are in billions of cloves, the currency of Spice Bay.

	A	B	C	D	E	F	G
1		Y	C	I	G	X	M
2	A	100	110	50	60	60	15
3	B	200	170	50	60	60	30
4	C	300	230	50	60	60	45
5	D	400	290	50	60	60	60
6	E	500	350	50	60	60	75
7	F	600	410	50	60	60	90

In Spice Bay,
   a. What is autonomous expenditure?
   b. What is the marginal propensity to consume?
   c. What is aggregate planned expenditure when real GDP is 200 billion cloves?
   d. If real GDP is 200 billion cloves, what is happening to inventories?
   e. If real GDP is 500 billion cloves, what is happening to inventories?
   f. What is the multiplier in Spice Bay?

5. You are given the following information about the economy of Zeeland: Autonomous consumption expenditure is $100 billion, and the marginal propensity to consume is 0.9. Investment is $460 billion, government expenditures on goods and services are $400 billion, and net taxes are a constant $400 billion—they do not vary with income.

a. What is the consumption function?
b. What is the equation that describes the
   AE curve?
c. Calculate equilibrium expenditure.
d. If investment falls to $360 billion, what is
   the change in equilibrium expenditure and
   what is the size of the multiplier?

6. You are given the following information about
   the economy of Antarctica: Autonomous consumption expenditure is $1 billion, and the
   marginal propensity to consume is 0.8.
   Investment is $5 billion, government expendi-
   tures on goods and services are $4 billion, and
   net taxes are a constant $4 billion—they do not
   vary with income.
   a. What is the consumption function?
   b. What is the equation that describes the
      AE curve?
   c. Calculate equilibrium expenditure.
   d. If investment falls to $3 billion, what is the
      change in equilibrium expenditure and what
      is the size of the multiplier?

7. Suppose that in problem 5, the price level is
   100 and real GDP equals potential GDP.
   a. If investment increases by $100 billion, what
      happens to the quantity of real GDP
      demanded?
   b. In the short run, does equilibrium real GDP
      increase by more than, less than, or the same
      amount as the increase in the quantity of real
      GDP demanded?
   c. In the long run, does equilibrium real GDP
      increase by more than, less than, or the same
      amount as the increase in the quantity of real
      GDP demanded?
   d. In the short run, does the price level in
      Zeeland rise, fall, or remain unchanged?
   e. In the long run, does the price level in
      Zeeland rise, fall, or remain unchanged?

8. Suppose that in problem 6, the price level is
   100 and real GDP equals potential GDP.
   a. If investment increases by $1 billion, what
      happens to the quantity of real GDP
      demanded?
   b. In the long run, does equilibrium real GDP
      increase by more than, less than, or the same
      amount as the increase in the quantity of real
      GDP demanded?
   c. In the short run, does the price level in
      Antarctica rise, fall, or remain unchanged?

CRITICAL THINKING

1. Study *Reading Between the Lines* on pp. 556–557
   and then:
   a. Describe the changes in the components of
      aggregate expenditure during the first half of
      2005.
   b. Suppose that the assumptions about the
      extent to which a change in real GDP
      induces a change in consumption expendi-
      ture and imports on p. 557 are incorrect and
      that the slope of the *AE* curve is 0.3, not
      0.33. What does this imply about the change
      in autonomous expenditure during the first
      half of 2005? What does it imply about the
      magnitude of the multiplier?
   c. Draw the *AE* curves for the fourth quarter
      of 2004 and second quarter of 2005 on the
      assumption that the slope of the *AE* curve
      is 0.3.

WEB EXERCISES

Use the links on (X) **myeconlab** **to work the
following exercise.**

1. Obtain data on real GDP per person and consumption as a percentage of real GDP for
   Canada, China, South Africa, and Mexico since
   1960.
   a. In a spreadsheet, multiply your real GDP
      data by the consumption percentage and di-
      vide by 100 to obtain data on real consump-
      tion expenditure per person.
   b. Make graphs like Fig. 23.4 that show the re-
      lationship between consumption and real
      GDP for these four countries.
   c. On the basis of the numbers you've obtained,
      in which country do you expect the multipli-
      er to be largest (other things being equal)?
   d. What other data would you need to be able to
      calculate the multipliers for these countries?

2. You are a research assistant in the office of the
   Prime Minister. Draft a note for the Prime
   Minister that explains the power and limitations
   of the multiplier. The Prime Minister wants
   only 250 words of crisp, clear, jargon-free explanation together with a lively example.

Fiscal Policy

CHAPTER 24

Balancing Acts on Parliament Hill

In 2004, the federal government spent 15.5 cents of every dollar that Canadians earned and collected 16 cents of every dollar earned in taxes. What are the effects of government spending and taxes on the economy? Does a dollar spent by the government have the same effect as a dollar spent by someone else? Does it create jobs, or does it destroy them?

Do taxes harm employment and economic growth?

For many years during the 1980s and 1990s, the government had a large budget deficit and ran up a debt. During the late 1990s, spending cuts brought the deficit under control and created a surplus. But in 2004, your share of government debt stood at $16,500. Does it matter if the government doesn't balance its books? What are the effects of an ongoing government deficit and accumulating debt? Do they slow economic growth? Do they impose a burden on future generations—on you and your children? Was the deficit-cutting exercise of the late 1990s beneficial to our economy?

◆ These are the fiscal policy issues that you will study in this chapter. We'll begin by describing the federal budget and the process of creating it. We'll also look at the recent history of the budget. We'll then use the multiplier analysis of Chapter 23 and the *AS–AD* model of Chapter 22 to study the effects of the budget on the economy. At the end of the chapter, in *Reading Between the Lines*, we'll look at the federal government's winter heating budget measures.

After studying this chapter, you will be able to

- **Describe how federal and provincial budgets are created and describe their recent history**

- **Distinguish between automatic and discretionary fiscal policy and define and explain the fiscal policy multipliers**

- **Explain the effects of fiscal policy in both the short run and the long run**

- **Distinguish between and explain the demand-side and supply-side effects of fiscal policy**

Government Budgets

THE ANNUAL STATEMENT OF THE OUTLAYS AND revenues of the government of Canada, together with the laws and regulations that approve and support those outlays and revenues, make up the **federal budget**. Similarly, a **provincial budget** is an annual statement of the revenues and outlays of a provincial government, together with the laws and regulations that approve or support those revenues and outlays.

Before World War II, the federal budget had no purpose other than to finance the business of government. But since the late 1940s, the federal budget has assumed a second purpose, which is to pursue the government's fiscal policy. **Fiscal policy** is the use of the federal budget to achieve macroeconomic objectives such as full employment, sustained long-term economic growth, and price level stability. Our focus is this second purpose.

Budget Making

The federal government and Parliament make fiscal policy. The process begins with long drawn-out consultations between the Minister of Finance and Department of Finance officials and their counterparts in the provincial governments. These discussions deal with programs that are funded and operated jointly by the two levels of government. The Minister also consults with business and consumer groups on a wide range of issues.

After all these consultations, and using economic projections made by Department of Finance economists, the Minister develops a set of proposals, which are discussed in Cabinet and which become government policy. The Minister finally presents a budget plan to Parliament, which debates the plan and enacts the laws necessary to implement it.

Highlights of the 2005 Budget

Table 24.1 shows the main items in the federal budget. The numbers are projected amounts for the fiscal year beginning on April 1, 2005. The three main items shown are

- Revenues
- Outlays
- Budget balance

TABLE 24.1   The Federal Budget in 2005–06

Item	Projections (billions of dollars)	
Revenues	**200**	
Personal income taxes		94
Corporate income taxes		29
Indirect taxes		66
Investment income		11
Outlays	**196**	
Transfer payments		119
Expenditures on goods and services		42
Debt interest		35
Budget balance	**+4**	

Sources of data: Department of Finance *Budget Plan* 2005 and Statistics Canada, CANSIM Table 183–0004.

Revenues Revenues are the federal government's receipts, which in the 2005–06 budget were projected at $200 billion. These revenues come from four sources:

1. Personal income taxes
2. Corporate income taxes
3. Indirect taxes
4. Investment income

The largest revenue source is *personal income taxes*, which in 2005–06 were projected to be $94 billion. These are the taxes paid by individuals on their incomes. The second largest source of revenue is *indirect taxes*, which in 2005–06 were projected to be $66 billion. These taxes include the Goods and Services Tax (the GST) and taxes on the sale of gasoline, alcoholic drinks, and a few other items. The smallest revenue sources are *corporate income taxes*, which are the taxes paid by companies on their profits, and *investment income*, which is the income from government enterprises and investments.

In 2005–06, corporate income taxes were projected to raise $29 billion and investment income was projected at $11 billion. Total federal government revenue in 2005–06 was projected at $200 billion.

Outlays Outlays are classified in three categories:

1. Transfer payments
2. Expenditures on goods and services
3. Debt interest

The largest outlay, and by a big margin, is *transfer payments*. Transfer payments are payments to individuals, businesses, other levels of government, and the rest of the world. In 2005–06, this item was $119 billion. It includes unemployment cheques and welfare payments to individuals, farm subsidies, grants to provincial and local governments, aid to developing countries, and dues to international organizations such as the United Nations.

Expenditures on goods and services are expenditures on final goods and services, and in 2005–06 this item totalled $42 billion. These expenditures include those on national defence, computers for Canada Revenue Agency, government cars, and highways. This component of the federal budget is *government expenditures on goods and services* that appears in the circular flow of expenditure and income and in the national income and product accounts (see Chapter 20, pp. 467–468).

Debt interest is the interest on the government debt. In 2005–06, this item was $35 billion—almost as much as government expenditures on goods and

services. This interest payment is large because the government has a large debt—$524 billion. This large debt has arisen because, until recently, the federal government has had a large and persistent budget deficit.

Budget Balance The government's budget balance is equal to its revenues minus its outlays. That is,

Budget balance = Revenues – Outlays.

If revenues exceed outlays, the government has a **budget surplus**. If outlays exceed revenues, the government has a **budget deficit**. If revenues equal outlays, the government has a **balanced budget**. In 2005–06, with projected outlays of $196 billion and revenues of $200 billion, the government projected a budget surplus of $4 billion.

How typical is the federal budget of 2005–06? Let's look at its recent history.

The Budget in Historical Perspective

Figure 24.1 shows the government's revenues, outlays, and budget balance since 1961. To get a better sense of the magnitudes of these items, they are shown as percentages of GDP. Expressing them in this way lets us see how large the government is

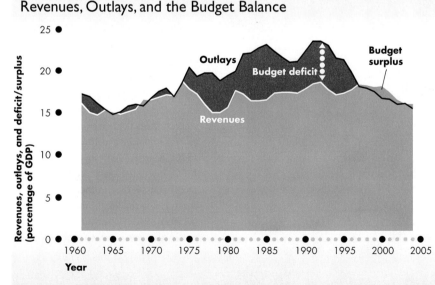

FIGURE 24.1

Revenues, Outlays, and the Budget Balance

The figure records the federal government's revenues, outlays, and budget balance as percentages of GDP from 1961 to 2004. During the 1960s, outlays and revenues increased. During the late 1970s and through the 1980s, outlays continued to rise but revenues fell, so a budget deficit arose. During the 1990s, spending cuts eliminated the budget deficit and after 1997, the federal government had a budget surplus.

Source of data: Statistics Canada, CANSIM Tables 380–0002 and 380–0007.

relative to the size of the economy, and also helps us to study *changes* in the scale of government over time. You can think of the percentages of GDP as telling you how many cents of each dollar that Canadians earn get paid to and spent by the government.

During the 1960s, government expanded but outlays and revenues kept pace with each other. But from 1971 through 1996, the federal budget was in deficit, and the average deficit over these years was 4.2 percent of GDP. The deficit climbed to a peak of 6.6 percent of GDP in 1985. It then decreased through the rest of the 1980s. During the recession of 1990–1991, the deficit increased again. The deficit remained above 4 percent of GDP for most of the 1980s and early 1990s.

Only in 1997 did the federal government finally eradicate its deficit. And it did so by cutting outlays, especially transfer payments to provincial governments.

Why did the government deficit grow during the early 1980s and remain high through the early 1990s? The immediate answer is that outlays increased while revenues remained relatively constant. But which components of outlays increased? And did all the sources of revenues remain constant?

To answer these questions, we need to examine each of the sources of revenues and outlays in detail. We'll begin by looking at the sources of revenues.

Revenues Figure 24.2 shows the components of government revenues since 1961. Total revenues have no strong trend. They increased through the 1960s and again through the 1980s. But they decreased during the 1970s and the first-half of the 2000s. The main source of the fluctuations in revenues was personal income taxes. Indirect taxes also fluctuated but corporate income taxes and investment income were more stable than the other two revenue components.

The increase in personal income taxes during the 1980s resulted from increases in tax rates in successive budgets.

Indirect taxes decreased during the 1990s mainly because an old Federal Sales Tax was replaced by the Goods and Services Tax or GST. Initially, this switch maintained revenues at a constant level, but gradually, the revenue from indirect taxes (as a percentage of GDP) fell.

Outlays Figure 24.3 shows the components of government outlays since 1961. Total outlays increased steadily from 1971 through 1985, were relatively flat through 1993, and then decreased sharply after 1993. The main source of the changing trend in outlays is transfer payments to provincial governments. These payments swelled during the 1980s and were cut drastically during the late 1990s.

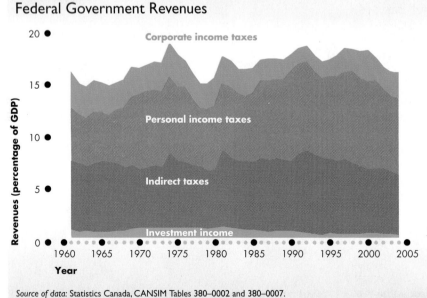

FIGURE 24.2
Federal Government Revenues

The figure shows four main components of government revenues (as percentages of GDP): personal income taxes, corporate income taxes, indirect taxes, and investment income. Revenues from personal income taxes fluctuated most. They increased during the 1960s and early 1970s, decreased during the late 1970s, increased again during the 1980s and 1990s, and then decreased again during the 2000s. Indirect taxes fell after 1990. The other two components of revenues remained steady.

Source of data: Statistics Canada, CANSIM Tables 380–0002 and 380–0007.

FIGURE 24.3
Federal Government Outlays

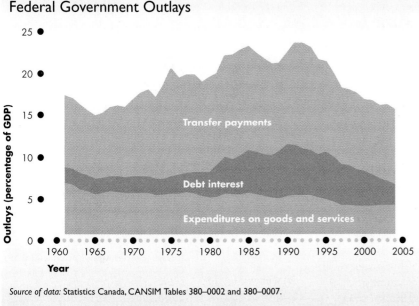

The figure shows three components of government outlays (as percentages of GDP): expenditures on goods and services, debt interest, and transfer payments. Expenditures on goods and services have had a downward trend. Transfer payments increased from 1965 to 1990 but decreased sharply during the 1990s. Debt interest increased steadily during the 1980s as the budget deficit fed on itself, but decreased during the late 1990s as surpluses began to lower the government's debt.

Source of data: Statistics Canada, CANSIM Tables 380–0002 and 380–0007.

To understand the changes in debt interest, we need to see the connection between the budget deficit and government debt.

Deficit and Debt The government borrows to finance its deficit. And **government debt** is the total amount of government borrowing. It is the sum of past deficits minus the sum of past surpluses. When the government has a deficit, its debt increases. Once a persistent deficit emerged during the 1980s, the deficit began to feed on itself. The deficit led to increased borrowing; increased borrowing led to larger debt and larger interest payments; and larger interest payments led to a larger deficit and yet larger debt. That is the story of the increasing deficit of the 1980s.

Figure 24.4 shows the history of government debt since 1940. By the end of World War II, debt (as a percentage of GDP) was at an all-time high of 113 percent. Huge wartime deficits had increased debt to the point that it exceeded GDP. Post-war budget surpluses lowered the debt to GDP ratio through 1974, by which time it stood at 18 percent, its lowest point since World War II. Small deficits increased the debt to GDP ratio slightly through the 1970s, and large deficits increased it dramatically between 1981 and 1986. During the late 1980s, the

FIGURE 24.4
Federal Government Debt

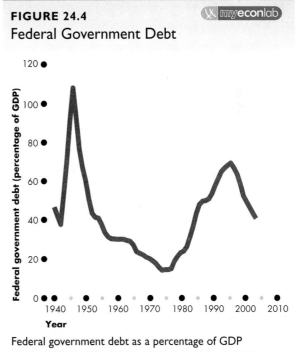

Federal government debt as a percentage of GDP increased during World War II, decreased from 1946 through 1974, increased through 1997, and then began to decrease again.

Source of data: Statistics Canada, CANSIM Tables 380–0002 and 385–0010.

ratio continued to increase but at a more moderate rate. It grew quickly again during the 1990–1991 recession, but its growth rate slowed after 1995 and debt interest decreased as a percentage of GDP.

Debt and Capital When individuals and businesses incur debts, they usually do so to buy capital—assets that yield a return. In fact, the main point of debt is to enable people to buy assets that will earn a return that exceeds the interest paid on the debt. The government is similar to individuals and businesses in this regard. Some government expenditure is investment—the purchase of public capital that yields a return. Highways, major irrigation schemes, public schools and universities, public libraries, and the stock of national defence capital all yield a social rate of return that probably far exceeds the interest rate the government pays on its debt.

But government debt, which is $524 billion, is much larger than the value of the public capital stock. This fact means that some government debt has been incurred to finance public consumption expenditure.

Provincial and Local Government Budgets

The *total government* sector of Canada includes provincial and local governments as well as the federal government. In 2004, when federal government outlays were $196 billion, provincial and local government outlays were $246 billion and total government outlays were $442 billion. Most provincial and local government outlays are on public hospitals and public schools, colleges, and universities.

Provincial government outlays and revenue sources vary a great deal across the provinces. Figure 24.5 shows the range of variation. Part (a) shows outlays as a percentage of provincial GDP. You can see that outlays of Northern and Atlantic governments are greatest, and government outlays of Ontario, Alberta, British Columbia, and Saskatchewan are the least. Part (b) shows the sources of provincial revenues as a percentage of total outlays. The Northern and Atlantic provinces receive the largest transfers from the federal government, while Alberta, Ontario, Quebec, and British Columbia receive the least.

Figure 24.6 shows the revenues, outlays, and deficits of the federal government and of total government between 1961 and 2004.

You can see that federal government outlays and revenues and total government outlays and revenues

FIGURE 24.5

Provincial Government Budgets

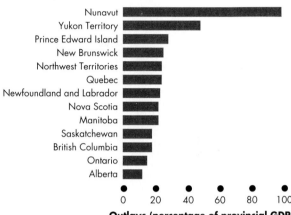

Outlays (percentage of provincial GDP)

(a) Outlays

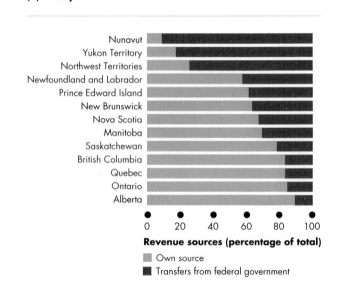

Revenue sources (percentage of total)

☐ Own source
■ Transfers from federal government

(b) Revenues

Provincial government budgets vary a lot across the provinces. As a percentage of provincial GDP, outlays (part a) are highest in Northern and Atlantic Canada and lowest in Ontario, Alberta, British Columbia, and Saskatchewan. The Northern and Atlantic regions receive the largest share of revenues from the federal government (part b) while Alberta, Ontario, Quebec, and British Columbia receive the least.

Source of data: Statistics Canada, CANSIM Tables 384–0002 and 385–0002.

FIGURE 24.6

Total Government Budgets

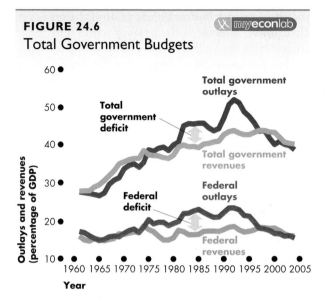

Total government is the sum of the federal, provincial, and local governments. Total government expanded from 1961 through the early 1990s and then shrank rapidly. Both the federal government and the provincial governments had large deficits during the 1980s but these deficits decreased after 1995 and then turned to surpluses.

Source of data: Statistics Canada, CANSIM Tables 380–0002 and 380–0007.

FIGURE 24.7

Government Deficits Around the World in 2005

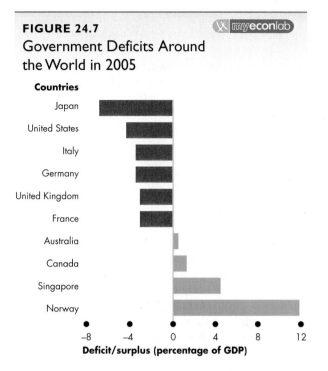

Governments in most countries had budget deficits in 2005. The largest ones were in Japan, the United States, Italy, and Germany. Australia, Canada, Singapore, and Norway had budget surpluses. As a percentage of GDP, Norways' surplus is huge.

Source of data: International Monetary Fund, *World Economic Outlook*, April 2005.

fluctuate in similar ways, but the total government is much larger than the federal government. In other words, the provincial and local governments are a large component of total government. You can also see that total government outlays fluctuate more than federal government outlays.

How does the Canadian government budget balance compare with budgets in other countries?

The Canadian Government Budget in Global Perspective

Is Canada unusual in having eliminated its budget deficit and now to be running a budget surplus? Do other countries have budget surpluses, or do they have budget deficits? Figure 24.7 answers these questions. In today's world, most countries have budget deficits. To compare countries, we measure the budget surplus or deficit as a percentage of GDP. The biggest deficit relative to GDP is found in Japan, where the deficit is almost 7 percent of GDP. The United States along with France, Italy, Germany, and

the United Kingdom also have budget deficits. Only a handful of countries, with Canada, have budget surpluses. But Norway has a huge surplus.

REVIEW QUIZ

1 What are the main items of government revenues and outlays?
2 Under what circumstances does the government have a budget surplus?
3 Explain the connection between a government budget deficit and a government debt.

Study Plan 24.1

Your next task is to study the effects of the government's budget on the economy and learn about fiscal policy multipliers.

Fiscal Policy Multipliers

FISCAL POLICY ACTIONS CAN BE EITHER AUTOmatic or discretionary. **Automatic fiscal policy** is a change in fiscal policy that is triggered by the state of the economy. For example, an increase in unemployment triggers an automatic increase in payments to the unemployed. A fall in incomes triggers an automatic decrease in tax revenues. That is, this type of fiscal policy adjusts automatically. **Discretionary fiscal policy** is a policy action that is initiated by an act of Parliament. It requires a change in tax laws or in some spending program. For example, a cut in income tax rates and an increase in defence spending are discretionary fiscal policy actions. That is, discretionary fiscal policy is a deliberate policy action.

We begin by studying the effects of *discretionary* changes in government expenditures and taxes. To focus on the essentials, we'll initially study a model economy that is simpler than the one in which we live. In our model economy, there is no international trade and the taxes are autonomous. **Autonomous taxes** are taxes that do not vary with real GDP. The government fixes them, and they change when the government changes them. But they do not vary automatically with the state of the economy.

The main example of an autonomous tax is the *property tax*. This tax varies across individuals and depends on the value of the property a person occupies. But unlike the income tax, it does not change simply because a person's income changes.

We use autonomous taxes in our model economy because they make the principles we are studying easier to understand. Once we've grasped the principles, we'll explore our real economy with its international trade and income taxes—taxes that *do* vary with real GDP.

Like our real economy, the model economy we study is bombarded by spending fluctuations. Business investment in new buildings, plant and equipment, and inventories fluctuates because of swings in profit expectations and interest rates. These fluctuations set up multiplier effects that begin a recession or an expansion. If a recession takes hold, unemployment increases and incomes fall. If an expansion becomes too strong, inflationary pressures build up. To minimize the effects of these swings in spending, the government might change either its expenditures on goods and services or taxes. By changing either of these items, the government can influence aggregate expenditure and real GDP, but

the government's budget deficit or surplus also changes. An alternative fiscal policy action is to change both expenditures and taxes together so that the budget balance does not change. We are going to study the initial effects of these discretionary fiscal policy actions in the very short run when the price level is fixed. Each of these actions creates a multiplier effect on real GDP. These multipliers are the

- Government expenditures multiplier
- Autonomous tax multiplier

Government Expenditures Multiplier

The **government expenditures multiplier** is the magnification effect of a change in government expenditures on goods and services on equilibrium expenditure and real GDP.

Government expenditures are a component of aggregate expenditure. So when government expenditures on goods and services change, aggregate expenditure and real GDP change. The change in real GDP induces a change in consumption expenditure, which brings a further change in aggregate expenditure. A multiplier process ensues. This multiplier process is like the one described in Chapter 23 (pp. 546–549). Let's look at an example.

A Mackenzie Valley Pipeline Multiplier Canada's Arctic region is rich in natural gas. But to get that gas to Canadian and U.S. markets, a huge $6 billion pipeline would have to be built. Although it is a controversial project because of its potential impact on the environment, building a pipeline in this region would have a large multiplier effect. Construction workers would be hired who would spend much of their income in the Arctic region. Retail stores, schools, health-care centres, hotels and motels, and recreational facilities would open and hire yet more people. Some of the income earned by this second wave of workers would also be spent in the region. The Arctic economy would expand until aggregate planned expenditure again equalled aggregate income.

The Size of the Multiplier Our task is to find equilibrium expenditure and the change in real GDP when government expenditures change. Table 24.2 illustrates the government expenditures multiplier with a numerical example. The first data column lists various possible levels of real GDP. The second column shows *induced expenditures*—induced consump-

TABLE 24.2   The Government Expenditures Multiplier

	Real GDP (Y)	Induced expenditure (N)	Initial autonomous expenditure (A)	Initial aggregate planned expenditure (AE = N + A)	New autonomous expenditures (A')	New aggregate planned expenditure (AE' = N + A')
				(billions of dollars)		
A	900	525	400	925	450	975
B	1,000	600	400	1,000	450	1,050
C	1,100	675	400	1,075	450	1,125
D	1,200	750	400	1,150	450	1,200
E	1,300	825	400	1,225	450	1,275

tion expenditure minus imports. In this example, a $100 billion increase in real GDP induces a $75 billion increase in aggregate planned expenditure. For example when real GDP increases from $900 billion (row A) to $1,000 billion, (row B), induced expenditure increases from $525 billion to $600 billion. This relationship between real GDP and induced expenditure means that the *slope of the aggregate expenditure (AE) curve* is 0.75.

The third column shows the initial level of autonomous expenditure—investment plus government expenditures plus exports plus the autonomous component of consumption expenditure. In this example, autonomous expenditure is initially equal to $400 billion.

The next column shows the initial level of aggregate planned expenditure, which is the sum of induced expenditure and the initial level of autonomous expenditure.

Equilibrium expenditure and real GDP occur when aggregate planned expenditure equals actual expenditure. In this example, equilibrium expenditure is $1,000 billion (highlighted in row B of the table.)

The final two columns of the table show what happens when government expenditures increase by $50 billion. The new level of autonomous expenditure is $450 billion. And at each level of real GDP the new level of aggregate planned expenditure is $50 billion higher than the initial level. For example, at the initial real GDP of $1,000 billion (row B), aggregate planned expenditure increases to $1,050 billion.

Because at the initial equilibrium real GDP, aggregate planned expenditure exceeds real GDP, inventories decrease. So firms increase production. Output, incomes, and expenditure increase. Increased incomes bring a further increase in induced expenditure, which is less than the increase in income. Aggregate planned expenditure increases and eventually, a new equilibrium is reached. The new equilibrium is at a real GDP of $1,200 billion (highlighted in row D).

A $50 billion increase in government expenditures has increased equilibrium expenditure and real GDP by $200 billion. So the government expenditures multiplier is 4.

Just as in the case of the investment multiplier, the size of the multiplier depends on the slope of the AE curve and is

$$\text{Government expenditures multiplier} = \frac{1}{1 - \text{Slope of } AE \text{ curve}}.$$

Let's use this formula with the numbers in the above example and confirm that the multiplier is 4. You've seen that the slope of the AE curve is 0.75. So the government expenditures multiplier is

$$\text{Government expenditures multiplier} = \frac{1}{1 - 0.75} = \frac{1}{0.25} = 4.$$

Figure 24.8 illustrates the government expenditures multiplier. Initially, aggregate planned expenditure is shown by the curve labelled AE_0. The points on this curve, labelled A through E, correspond with

FIGURE 24.8

Government Expenditures Multiplier

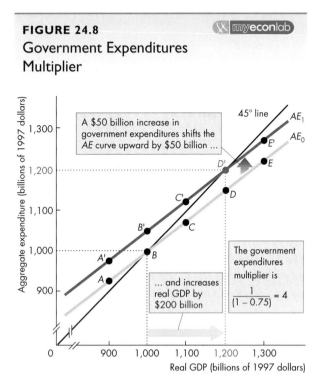

A \$50 billion increase in government expenditures shifts the AE curve upward by \$50 billion ...

... and increases real GDP by \$200 billion

The government expenditures multiplier is

$$\frac{1}{(1 - 0.75)} = 4$$

Initially, the aggregate expenditure curve is AE_0, and real GDP is \$1,000 billion (at point B). An increase in government expenditures of \$50 billion increases aggregate planned expenditure at each level of real GDP by \$50 billion. The aggregate expenditure curve shifts upward from AE_0 to AE_1—a parallel shift.

At the initial real GDP of \$1,000 billion, aggregate planned expenditure is now \$1,050 billion. Because aggregate planned expenditure is greater than real GDP, real GDP increases. The new equilibrium is reached when real GDP is \$1,200 billion—the point at which the AE_1 curve intersects the 45° line (at point D'). In this example, the government expenditures multiplier is 4.

the rows of Table 24.2. This AE curve intersects the 45° line at point B. Equilibrium expenditure and real GDP are \$1,000 billion.

When government expenditures increase by \$50 billion, the AE curve shifts upward by that amount to AE_1. With this new AE curve, equilibrium expenditure and real GDP increase by \$200 billion to \$1,200 billion. The increase in real GDP is 4 times the increase in government expenditures. The government expenditures multiplier is 4.

You've seen that in the very short term, when the price level is fixed, an increase in government expenditures increases real GDP. But to produce more output, more people must be employed, so in the short term, an increase in government expenditures can create jobs.

A second way in which the government might act to increase real GDP in the very short run is by cutting taxes or increasing transfer payments. And the government might change autonomous taxes (or transfer payments) or induced taxes (or transfer payments.) Let's see how these actions work.

Autonomous Tax Multiplier

The **autonomous tax multiplier** is the magnification effect of a change in autonomous taxes on equilibrium aggregate expenditure and real GDP. An *increase* in taxes *decreases* disposable income, which *decreases* consumption expenditure. The amount by which consumption expenditure initially changes is determined by the marginal propensity to consume. Suppose that the marginal propensity to consume is 0.9, so a \$1 tax cut increases disposable income by \$1 and increases aggregate expenditure initially by 90¢.

This initial change in aggregate expenditure has a multiplier just like the government expenditures multiplier. We've seen that the government expenditures multiplier is 1/(1– Slope of the AE curve). Because a tax *increase* leads to a *decrease* in expenditure, the autonomous tax multiplier is *negative*. And because a change in autonomous taxes changes aggregate expenditure initially by only *MPC* multiplied by the tax change, the autonomous tax multiplier is

$$\frac{\text{Autonomous}}{\text{tax multiplier}} = \frac{-MPC}{1 - \text{Slope of } AE \text{ curve}}.$$

Figure 24.9 illustrates the autonomous tax multiplier. Initially, the aggregate expenditure curve is AE_0 and equilibrium expenditure is \$1,000 billion. Taxes increase by \$50 billion, and disposable income falls by that amount. With a marginal propensity to consume of 0.9, aggregate expenditure decreases initially by \$45 billion and the AE curve shifts downward by that amount to AE_1. Equilibrium expenditure and real GDP decrease by \$180 billion, to \$820 billion. The autonomous tax multiplier is

$$\frac{\text{Autonomous}}{\text{tax multiplier}} = \frac{-0.9}{1 - 0.75} = -3.6.$$

FIGURE 24.9
Autonomous Tax Multiplier

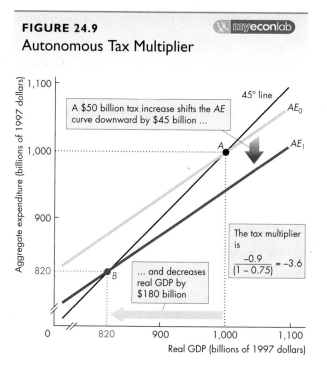

A $50 billion tax increase shifts the *AE* curve downward by $45 billion ...

... and decreases real GDP by $180 billion

The tax multiplier is

$$\frac{-0.9}{(1-0.75)} = -3.6$$

Initially, the aggregate expenditure curve is AE_0 and equilibrium expenditure is $1,000 billion. The marginal propensity to consume is 0.9. Autonomous taxes increase by $50 billion, so disposable income falls by $50 billion. The decrease in aggregate expenditure is found by multiplying this change in disposable income by the marginal propensity to consume and is $50 billion × 0.9 = $45 billion. The aggregate expenditure curve shifts *downward* by this amount to AE_1. Equilibrium expenditure decreases by $180 billion, from $1,000 billion to $820 billion. The autonomous tax multiplier is –3.6.

Autonomous Transfer Payments The autonomous tax multiplier also tells us the effects of a change in autonomous transfer payments. Transfer payments are like negative taxes, so an increase in transfer payments works like a decrease in taxes. Because the tax multiplier is negative, a decrease in taxes increases expenditure. An increase in transfer payments also increases expenditure. So the autonomous transfer payments multiplier is positive. It is

$$\frac{\text{Autonomous transfer}}{\text{payments multiplier}} = \frac{MPC}{1 - \text{Slope of } AE \text{ curve}}.$$

Induced Taxes and Transfer Payments

In the examples we've studied so far, we've changed only autonomous taxes and transfer payments. We're now going to look at induced taxes and transfer payments.

The tax laws define tax *rates* to be paid, not tax *dollars* to be paid. Tax *dollars* paid depend on tax *rates* and incomes. But incomes vary with real GDP, so tax *revenues* depend on real GDP. When the economy expands, tax revenues increase because real GDP increases. When the economy is in a recession, tax revenues decrease because real GDP decreases.

On the outlay side of the budget, the government creates programs that entitle suitably qualified people and businesses to receive benefits. The spending on such programs is not fixed in dollars and it results in transfer payments that depend on the economic state of individual citizens and businesses. When the economy is in a recession, unemployment is high, the number of people experiencing economic hardship increases, and a larger number of firms and farms experience hard times. Transfer payments increase. When the economy expands, transfer payments decrease.

Net taxes (taxes minus transfer payments) that vary with real GDP are called **induced taxes**. And the change in induced taxes equals the change in real GDP multiplied by the marginal tax rate. The *marginal tax rate* is the proportion of an additional dollar of real GDP that flows to the government in net taxes. The higher the marginal tax rate, the larger is the proportion of an additional dollar of real GDP that is paid to the government and the smaller is the induced change in aggregate expenditure.

An increase in the marginal tax rate decreases disposable income, decreases consumption expenditure, and has a multiplier effect on real GDP.

But an increase in the marginal tax rate also decreases the magnitude of the autonomous expenditure multipliers (the investment, government expenditures, autonomous tax and autonomous transfer payments multipliers). It does so by decreasing the slope of the *AE* curve. With a high marginal tax rate, when real GDP increases, induced taxes increase by more and disposable income and consumption expenditure by less than they do with a low marginal tax rate. So aggregate expenditure increases by less than it otherwise would have. The *AE* curve is flatter, its slope is smaller, and the multipliers are smaller.

International Trade and Fiscal Policy Multipliers

Not all expenditure in Canada is on Canadian-produced goods and services. Some of it is on imports—on foreign-produced goods and services. Imports affect the fiscal policy multipliers in the same way that they influence the investment multiplier, as explained in Chapter 23 (see pp. 548–549). The extent to which an additional dollar of real GDP is spent on imports is determined by the *marginal propensity to import*. Expenditure on imports does not generate Canadian real GDP and does not lead to an increase in Canadian consumption expenditure. The larger the marginal propensity to import, the smaller are the government expenditures and autonomous tax and transfer payments multipliers.

The math note on pp. 584–585 explains the details of the effects of induced taxes and transfer payments and imports on the fiscal policy multipliers.

So far, we've studied *discretionary* fiscal policy. Let's now look at *automatic* stabilizers.

Automatic Stabilizers

Automatic stabilizers are mechanisms that stabilize real GDP without explicit action by the government. Their name is borrowed from engineering and conjures up images of shock absorbers, thermostats, and sophisticated devices that keep airplanes and ships steady in turbulent air and seas. But automatic fiscal stabilizers do not actually stabilize. They just make the fluctuations less severe. These stabilizers operate because income taxes and transfer payments fluctuate with real GDP. If real GDP begins to decrease, tax revenues fall and transfer payments rise and the government's budget deficit increases. Let's look at the budget deficit over the business cycle.

Budget Deficit Over the Business Cycle Figure 24.10 shows the business cycle and fluctuations in the budget deficit between 1980 and 2004. Part (a) shows the fluctuations of real GDP around potential GDP. Part (b) shows the federal budget deficit (as a percentage of GDP). Both parts highlight recessions by shading those periods. By comparing the two parts of the figure, you can see the relationship between the business cycle and the budget deficit. As a rule, when the economy is in an expansion, the budget deficit declines. (In the figure, a declining deficit means a deficit that is getting closer to zero.) As the expansion slows before the recession begins, the

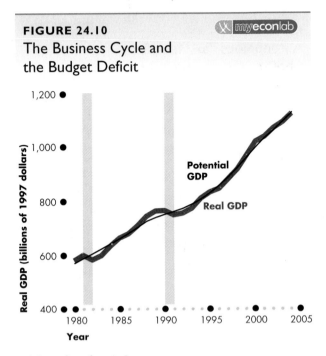

FIGURE 24.10

The Business Cycle and the Budget Deficit

(a) Growth and recessions

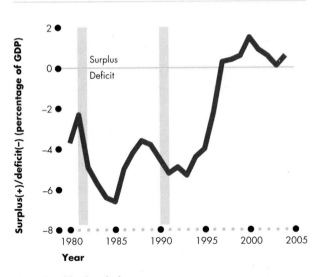

(b) Federal budget balance

As real GDP fluctuates around potential GDP (part a), the budget deficit fluctuates (part b). During a recession (shaded years), tax revenues decrease, transfer payments increase, and the budget deficit increases. The deficit also increases *before* a recession as real GDP growth slows and *after* a recession before real GDP growth speeds up.

Source of data: Statistics Canada, CANSIM Tables 380–0002 and 380–0007.

budget deficit increases. It continues to increase during the recession and for a further period after the recession is over. Then, when the expansion is well underway, the budget deficit declines again.

The budget deficit fluctuates with the business cycle because tax revenues and transfer payments fluctuate with real GDP. As real GDP increases in an expansion, tax revenues increase and transfer payments decrease, so the budget deficit automatically decreases. As real GDP decreases in a recession, tax revenues decrease and transfer payments increase, so the budget deficit automatically increases.

Fluctuations in investment and exports have a multiplier effect on real GDP. But fluctuations in tax revenues (and the budget deficit) act as an automatic stabilizer. They decrease the swings in disposable income and make the multiplier effect smaller. They dampen both expansions and recessions.

Cyclical and Structural Balances Because the government budget balance fluctuates with the business cycle, we need a method of measuring the budget surplus or deficit as a temporary cyclical phenomenon or a persistent structural phenomenon. A temporary cyclical surplus or deficit vanishes when full employment returns. A persistent structural surplus or deficit requires government action to remove it.

To determine whether the budget balance is persistent or temporary, economists have developed the concepts of the structural budget balance and the cyclical budget balance. The **structural surplus or deficit** is the budget balance that would occur if the economy were at full employment and real GDP were equal to potential GDP. The **cyclical surplus or deficit** is the actual surplus or deficit minus the structural surplus or deficit. That is, the cyclical surplus or deficit is the part of the budget balance that arises purely because real GDP does not equal potential GDP. For example, suppose that the budget deficit is $10 billion. And suppose that economists have determined that there is a structural deficit of $2.5 billion. Then there is a cyclical deficit of $7.5 billion.

Figure 24.11 illustrates the concepts of the cyclical surplus or deficit and the structural surplus or deficit. The blue curve shows government outlays. The outlays curve slopes downward because transfer payments, a component of government outlays, decrease as real GDP increases. The green curve shows revenues. The revenues curve slopes upward because most components of tax revenues increase as incomes and real GDP increase.

FIGURE 24.11   myeconlab

Cyclical and Structural Deficits and Surpluses

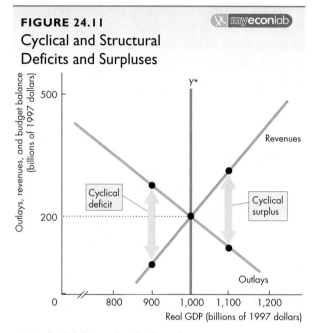

(a) Cyclical deficit and cyclical surplus

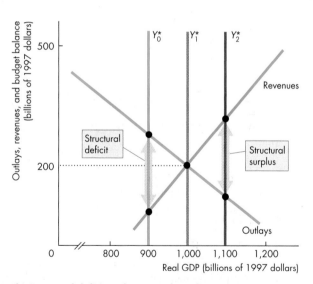

(b) Structural deficit and structural surplus

In part (a), potential GDP is $1,000 billion. If real GDP equals potential GDP, the government has a *balanced budget*. There is no *structural deficit*. If real GDP is less than potential GDP, the budget deficit is in a *cyclical deficit*. If real GDP exceeds potential GDP, the budget surplus is in a *cyclical surplus*. In part (b), if real GDP and potential GDP are $900 billion, there is a *structural deficit*. But if real GDP and potential GDP are $1,100 billion, there is a *structural surplus*.

In Fig. 24.11(a), potential GDP is $1,000 billion. If real GDP is $1,000 billion, outlays and revenues each equal $200 billion. Real GDP equals potential GDP, so the government has a *balanced budget*. If real GDP is $900 billion (below potential GDP), the government has a budget deficit and this deficit is a *cyclical deficit*. If real GDP is $1,100 billion (above potential GDP) the government has a budget surplus and this surplus is a *cyclical surplus*.

In Fig. 24.11(b), if both real GDP and potential GDP are $900 billion, the budget deficit is a structural deficit. If both real GDP and potential GDP are $1,000 billion, the budget is balanced—a structural balance of zero. When both real GDP and potential GDP are $1,100 billion, the budget surplus is a structural surplus.

The Canadian federal government had a structural budget deficit starting in the mid-1970s and continuing through the mid-1990s. That is, even if the economy had been at full employment with real GDP equal to potential GDP, the budget would have been in deficit. Worse, the structural deficit was so large that even at the peak of a business cycle, the budget was in deficit. At the end of the 1990s, a budget surplus emerged. It is probable that this surplus was a structural surplus because the economy was close to full employment.

REVIEW QUIZ

1 What are the government expenditures multiplier and the autonomous tax multiplier? How do these multiplier effects work?

2 Which has the larger multiplier effect: a change in government expenditures or a change in autonomous taxes? Why is one larger than the other?

3 How do income taxes and imports influence the size of the fiscal policy multipliers?

4 How do income taxes and transfer payments work as automatic stabilizers to dampen the business cycle?

5 How do we tell whether a budget deficit needs government action to remove it?

myeconlab **Study Plan 24.2**

Your next task is to see how, with the passage of more time and with some price level adjustments, these multiplier effects change.

Fiscal Policy Multipliers and the Price Level

WE'VE SEEN HOW REAL GDP RESPONDS TO changes in fiscal policy when the price level is fixed and all the adjustments that take place are in spending, income, and production. The period over which this response occurs is very short. Once production starts to change, regardless of whether it increases or decreases, prices also start to change. The price level and real GDP change together, and the economy moves to a new short-run equilibrium.

To study the simultaneous changes in real GDP and the price level, we use the *AS–AD* model of Chapter 22. In the long run, both the price level and the money wage rate respond to fiscal policy. As these further changes take place, the economy gradually moves towards a new long-run equilibrium. We also use the *AS–AD* model to study these adjustments.

We begin by looking at the effects of fiscal policy on aggregate demand and the aggregate demand curve.

Fiscal Policy and Aggregate Demand

You learned about the relationship between aggregate demand, aggregate expenditure, and equilibrium expenditure in Chapter 23 (pp. 551–553). You are now going to use what you learned there to work out what happens to aggregate demand, the price level, and real GDP when fiscal policy changes. We'll start by looking at the effects of a change in fiscal policy on aggregate demand.

Figure 24.12 shows the effects of an increase in government expenditures on aggregate demand. Initially, the aggregate expenditure curve is AE_0 in part (a), and the aggregate demand curve is AD_0 in part (b). The price level is 110, real GDP is $1,000 billion, and the economy is at point *A* in both parts of the figure. Now suppose that the government increases its expenditures by $50 billion. At a constant price level of 110, the aggregate expenditure curve shifts upward to AE_1. This curve intersects the 45° line at an equilibrium expenditure of $1,200 billion at point *B*. This amount is the aggregate quantity of goods and services demanded at a price level of 110, as shown by point *B* in part (b). Point *B* lies on a new aggregate demand curve. The aggregate demand curve has shifted rightward to AD_1.

The government expenditures multiplier determines the distance by which the aggregate demand

FIGURE 24.12

Government Expenditures and Aggregate Demand

myeconlab

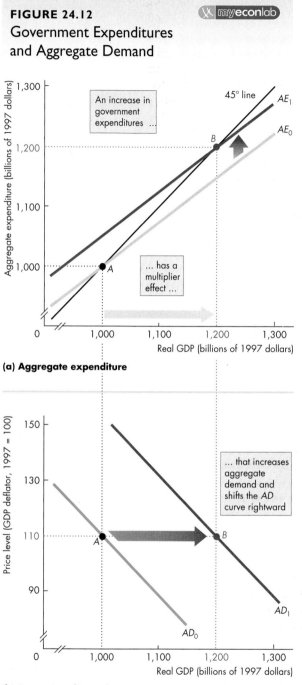

(a) Aggregate expenditure

(b) Aggregate demand

The price level is 110, the aggregate planned expenditure curve is AE_0 (part a), and the aggregate demand curve is AD_0 (part b). An increase in government expenditures shifts the AE curve to AE_1 and increases equilibrium real GDP to $1,200 billion. The AD curve shifts rightward to AD_1.

curve shifts rightward. The larger the multiplier, the larger is the shift in the aggregate demand curve resulting from a given change in government expenditures. In this example, a $50 billion increase in government expenditures produces a $200 billion increase in the aggregate quantity of goods and services demanded at each price level. The multiplier is 4. So the $50 billion increase in government expenditures shifts the aggregate demand curve rightward by $200 billion.

Figure 24.12 shows the effects of an increase in government expenditures. But a similar effect occurs for *any* expansionary fiscal policy. An **expansionary fiscal policy** is an increase in government expenditures or a decrease in taxes. But the distance that the aggregate demand curve shifts is smaller for a decrease in taxes than for an increase in government expenditures of the same size.

Figure 24.12 can also be used to illustrate the effects of a **contractionary fiscal policy**—a decrease in government expenditures or an increase in taxes. In this case, start at point *B* in each part of the figure and decrease government expenditures or increase taxes. Aggregate demand decreases and the aggregate demand curve shifts leftward from AD_1 to AD_0.

Equilibrium GDP and the Price Level in the Short Run We've seen how an increase in government expenditures increases aggregate demand. Let's now see how it changes real GDP and the price level. Figure 24.13(a) describes the economy. Aggregate demand is AD_0, and the short-run aggregate supply curve is *SAS*. (Check back to Chapter 22, pp. 509–510, to refresh your understanding of the *SAS* curve.) Equilibrium is at point *A*, where the aggregate demand and short-run aggregate supply curves intersect. The price level is 110, and real GDP is $1,000 billion.

An increase in government expenditures of $50 billion shifts the aggregate demand curve rightward from AD_0 to AD_1. While the price level is fixed at 110, the economy moves towards point *B* and real GDP increases towards $1,200 billion. But during the adjustment process, the price level does not remain constant. It gradually rises, and the economy moves along the short-run aggregate supply curve to the point of intersection of the short-run aggregate supply curve and the new aggregate demand curve—point *C*. The price level rises to 123, and real GDP increases to only $1,130 billion.

FIGURE 24.13

Fiscal Policy, Real GDP, and the Price Level

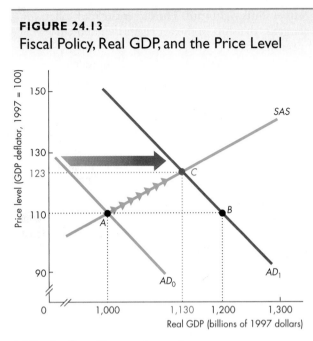

(a) Fiscal policy with unemployment

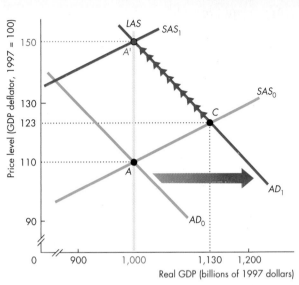

(b) Fiscal policy at full employment

An increase in government expenditures shifts the AD curve from AD_0 to AD_1 (part a). With a fixed price level, the economy would have moved to point B. But the price level rises, and in the short run, the economy moves along the SAS curve to point C. The price level increases to 123, and real GDP increases to $1,130 billion.

At point C, real GDP exceeds potential GDP and unemployment is below the natural rate (part b). The money wage rate rises, and short-run aggregate supply decreases. The SAS curve shifts leftward to SAS_1, and in the long run, the economy moves to point A'. The price level rises to 150, and real GDP returns to $1,000 billion.

When we take the price level effect into account, the increase in government expenditures still has a multiplier effect on real GDP, but the effect is smaller than it would be if the price level remained constant. Also, the steeper the slope of the SAS curve, the larger is the increase in the price level, the smaller is the increase in real GDP, and the smaller is the government expenditures multiplier. But the multiplier is not zero.

In the long run, real GDP equals potential GDP—the economy is at full-employment equilibrium. When real GDP equals potential GDP, an increase in aggregate demand has the same short-run effect as we've just worked out, but its long-run effect is different. The increase in aggregate demand raises the price level but leaves real GDP unchanged at potential GDP.

To study this case, let's see what happens if the government embarks on an expansionary fiscal policy when real GDP equals potential GDP.

Fiscal Expansion at Potential GDP

Suppose that real GDP is equal to potential GDP, which means that unemployment is equal to the natural rate of unemployment. But suppose also that the unemployment rate is high and that most people, including the government, mistakenly think that unemployment must be above the natural rate. In this situation, the government tries to lower the unemployment rate by using an expansionary fiscal policy.

Figure 24.13(b) shows the effect of an expansionary fiscal policy when real GDP equals potential GDP. In this example, potential GDP is $1,000 billion. Aggregate demand increases, and the aggregate demand curve shifts rightward from AD_0 to AD_1. The short-run equilibrium, point C, is an above full-employment equilibrium. Now the money wage rate begins to increase and short-run aggregate supply decreases. The SAS curve shifts leftward from SAS_0 to

SAS_1. The economy moves up the aggregate demand curve AD_1 towards point A'.

When all the wage and price adjustments have occurred, the price level is 150 and real GDP is again at potential GDP of $1,000 billion. The multiplier is zero. There has been only a temporary increase in real GDP but a permanent rise in the price level.

Limitations of Fiscal Policy

Because the short-run fiscal policy multipliers are not zero, expansionary fiscal policy can be used to increase real GDP and decrease the unemployment rate in a recession. Contractionary fiscal policy can also be used, if the economy is overheating, to decrease real GDP and help to keep inflation in check. But two factors limit the use of fiscal policy.

First, the legislative process is slow, which means that it is difficult to take fiscal policy actions in a timely way. The economy might be able to benefit from fiscal stimulation right now, but it will take Parliament many months, perhaps more than a year, to act. By the time the action is taken, the economy might need an entirely different fiscal medicine.

Second, it is not always easy to tell whether real GDP is below (or above) potential GDP. A change in aggregate demand can move real GDP away from potential GDP, or a change in aggregate supply can change real GDP and change potential GDP. This difficulty is a serious one because, as you've seen, fiscal stimulation might occur too close to full employment, in which case it will increase the price level and have no long-run effect on real GDP.

REVIEW QUIZ

1 How do changes in the price level influence the multiplier effects of fiscal policy on real GDP?
2 What are the long-run effects of fiscal policy on real GDP and the price level when real GDP equals potential GDP?

myeconlab Study Plan 24.3

So far, we've ignored any potential effects of fiscal policy on aggregate supply. Yet many economists believe that the supply-side effects of fiscal policy are the biggest. Let's now look at these effects.

Supply-Side Effects of Fiscal Policy

TAX CUTS INCREASE DISPOSABLE INCOME AND increase aggregate demand. But tax cuts also strengthen incentives to work and save, which increase aggregate supply. The strength of the supply-side effects of tax cuts is not known with certainty. Some economists believe that the supply-side effects are large and exceed the demand-side effects. Other economists, while agreeing that supply-side effects are present, believe that they are relatively small.

The controversy over the magnitude of the effects of taxes on aggregate supply is a political controversy. Generally speaking, people on the conservative or right wing of the political spectrum believe that supply-side effects are powerful, and people on the liberal or left wing of the political spectrum view supply-side effects as being small.

Regardless of which view is correct, we can study the supply-side effects of tax cuts by using the AS–AD model. Let's study the effects of taxes on potential GDP and then see how the supply-side effects and demand-side effects together influence real GDP and the price level.

Fiscal Policy and Potential GDP

Potential GDP depends on the full-employment quantity of labour, the quantity of capital, and the state of technology. Taxes can influence all three of these factors. The main tax to consider is the income tax. By taxing the incomes people earn when they work or save, the government weakens the incentives to work and save. The result is a smaller quantity of labour and capital and a smaller potential GDP. Also, the income tax weakens the incentive to develop new technologies that increase income. So the pace of technological change might be slowed, which slows the growth rate of potential GDP. Let's look at the effect of the income tax on both the quantity of labour and the quantity of capital.

Labour Market Taxes The quantity of labour is determined by demand and supply in the labour market. Figure 24.14(a) shows a labour market. The demand for labour is LD and the supply is LS. The equilibrium real wage rate is $15 an hour and 30 billion hours of labour per year are employed.

FIGURE 24.14

 myeconlab

Supply-Side Effects of the Income Tax

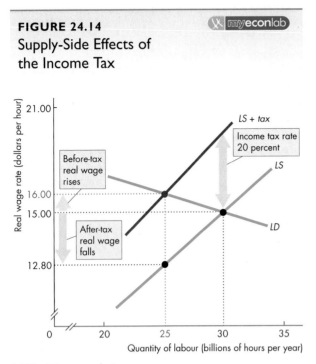

(a) The labour market

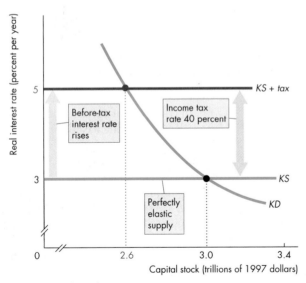

(b) The capital market

In part (a), an income tax decreases the supply of labour and shifts the supply curve from *LS* to *LS* + *tax*. The quantity of labour decreases. In part (b), the income tax decreases the supply of capital and shifts the supply curve from *KS* to *KS* + *tax*. The quantity of capital decreases. With less labour and less capital, potential GDP decreases.

Now suppose that an income tax is introduced. An income tax weakens the incentive to work and decreases the supply of labour. With a 20 percent income tax, the labor supply curve shifts to *LS* + *tax*. If workers are willing to supply the 30 billionth hour a year for $15.00 with no tax, then with a 20 percent tax, they are willing to supply the 30 billionth hour only if the wage rate is $18.75 an hour. The quantity of labour employed decreases to 25 billion hours a year. The *before-tax* real wage rate rises to $16 an hour and the *after-tax* real wage rate falls to $12.80 an hour.

Capital and the Income Tax The quantity of capital is determined by demand and supply in the capital market. Figure 24.14(b) shows the capital market. The demand for capital is *KD* and the supply is *KS*. Because capital is internationally mobile, its supply is highly elastic. In this example, with no income tax, quantity of capital is $3 trillion and the interest rate is 3 percent a year.

A tax on the income from capital weakens the incentive to save and decreases the supply of capital. The supply curve shifts to *KS* + *tax*. With the new supply of capital curve, the quantity of capital decreases to $2.6 trillion. With a 40 percent income tax, the *before-tax* interest rate rises to 5 percent a year and the *after-tax* interest rate remains at 3 percent a year.

Potential GDP and *LAS* Because the income tax decreases the equilibrium quantities of labour and capital, it also decreases potential GDP. But potential GDP determines long-run aggregate supply. So the income tax decreases long-run aggregate supply and shifts the *LAS* curve leftward.

Supply Effects and Demand Effects

Let's now bring the supply-side effects and demand-side effects of fiscal policy together. Figure 24.15(a) shows the most likely effects of a tax cut. The tax cut increases aggregate demand and shifts the *AD* curve rightward, just as before. But a tax cut that increases the incentive to work and save also increases aggregate supply. It shifts the long-run and short-run aggregate supply curves rightward. Here we focus on the short run and show the effect on the *SAS* curve, which shifts rightward to *SAS*₁. In this example, the tax cut has a large effect on aggregate demand and a small effect on aggregate supply. The *AD* curve shifts rightward by a larger amount than the rightward shift

FIGURE 24.15

Two Views of the Supply-Side Effects of Fiscal Policy

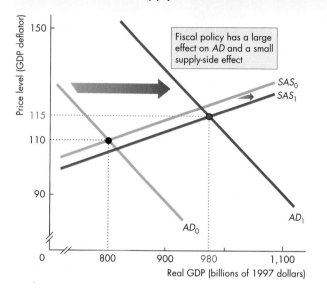

(a) The traditional view

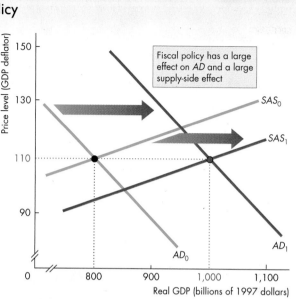

(b) The supply-side view

A tax cut increases aggregate demand and shifts the *AD* curve rightward from AD_0 to AD_1 (both parts). Such a policy change also has a supply-side effect. If the supply-side effect is small, the *SAS* curve shifts rightward from SAS_0 to SAS_1 in part (a). The demand-side effect dominates the supply-side effect, real GDP increases, and the price level rises.

If the supply-side effect of a tax cut is large, the *SAS* curve shifts to SAS_1 in part (b). Here, the supply-side effect is the same as the demand-side effect—an increase of $200 billion. Real GDP increases, and the price level remains constant. But if the supply-side effect were larger than the demand-side effect, the price level would actually fall.

in the *SAS* curve. The outcome is a rise in the price level and an increase in real GDP. But notice that the price level rises by *less* and real GDP increases by *more* than would occur if there were no supply-side effects.

Figure 24.15(b) shows the effects that supply-siders believe occur. A tax cut still has a large effect on aggregate demand, but it has a similarly large effect on aggregate supply. Both the *AD* curve and the *SAS* curve shift rightward by $200 billion. In this particular case, the price level remains constant and real GDP increases by $200 billion. A slightly larger increase in aggregate supply would have brought a fall in the price level, a possibility that some supply-siders believe could occur.

The general point, with which everyone agrees, is that a tax cut that strengthens the incentives to work and save increases real GDP by more and is less inflationary than an equal-size expansionary fiscal policy that does not change or that weakens incentives.

REVIEW QUIZ

1 How do income taxes and payroll taxes influence the labour market, and how would a cut in these taxes influence real GDP?

2 How would an income tax cut influence aggregate supply and aggregate demand?

3 How would an income tax cut influence real GDP and the price level?

myeconlab **Study Plan 24.4**

◆ You've seen how fiscal policy influences real GDP and potential GDP. *Reading Between the Lines* on pp. 582–583 looks at Finance Minister Goodale's plan to spend $2 billion helping low-income families cope with the high cost of winter heating.

Your next task is to study the other main arm of macroeconomic policy: monetary policy.

A Winter Heating Multiplier

NATIONAL POST, OCTOBER 5, 2005

Ottawa to announce $2-billion program to help poor with high heating bills

The federal government is set to commit more than $2 billion to a five-year plan that will help Canadians cope with high heating costs, The Canadian Press has learned.

Most of the money will be used to make low-income housing more energy efficient, a federal official said on condition of anonymity.

But some will be distributed to low-income families directly in rebate cheques, the source said.

The cheques will go to recipients of Guaranteed Income Supplement and the National Child Benefit Tax Supplement. ...

Earlier Tuesday, Finance Minister Ralph Goodale said legislation will be introduced Friday to provide assistance to "the most vulnerable in society."

It was not clear how much of the $2 billion will be "new" money. The sum might include funds from the

Finance minister Ralph Goodale.
(CP PHOTO/Tom Hanson)

Kyoto implementation plan. It could also include $100 million for energy efficiency that was added to the budget last year. ...

Reprinted by permission of The Canadian Press.

Essence of the Story

■ The federal government plans to spend $2 billion to help low-income families cope with high heating costs.

■ Most of this money will be spent on high-efficiency furnaces for low-income housing.

■ Some of this money will be spent by sending cheques to families who receive income support and child benefits from the government.

■ Some (but a small part) of the money might come from funds already committed to implementing the Kyoto agreement.

Economic Analysis

■ In mid-2005, real GDP was $1,152 billion (1997 dollars) and the GDP deflator was 115.

■ The economy was close to full employment with an estimated output gap of 0.1 percent of real GDP or a bit more than $1 billion.

■ The government planned to increase expdenditures on home heating for low-income families by $2 billion over a 5-year period.

■ You can see why the government needed to be cautious about how quickly it injected these expenditures into the economy. If the entire $2 billion were spent in a single year, real GDP would go above potential GDP and inflationary pressure would arise.

■ Figure 1 shows the aggregate expenditure curve in mid-2005 as AE_0. Equilibrium expenditure was $1,152 billion.

■ If the government increased expenditure by $2 billion, the AE curve would shift upward by that amount. The reason is that although some of the expenditure is a transfer payment, because it is a transfer to the poor, it is likely that all of it would be spent

(and none saved)—the marginal propensity to consume of poor people is 1.

■ Assuming a slope for the AE curve of 0.33, the multiplier is 1.5 (see p. 557) and an increase in autonomous expenditure of $2 billion increases equilibrium expenditure by $3 billion.

■ So, in Figure 1, when the AE curve shifts upward to AE_1, equilibrium expenditure increases to $1,155 billion.

■ In Figure 2, the aggregate demand curve shifts rightward by $3 billion from AD_0 to AD_1.

■ The increase in aggregate demand turns a recessionary gap into an inflationary gap and the price level rises.

■ The inflationary gap brings a rise in the money wage rate and a decrease in short-run aggregate supply. The SAS curve shifts from SAS_0 to SAS_1 and the price level rises further.

■ By spreading its help to low-income families over a number of years, the government will avoid the inflationary consequences illustrated here.

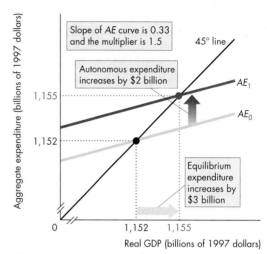

Figure 1 **Aggregate expenditure**

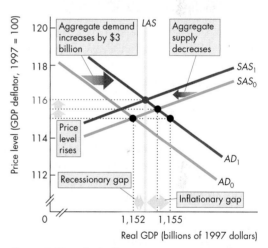

Figure 2 *AD and AS effects*

You're the Voter

■ Do you think the federal government's method of helping low-income families is sound?

■ Do you think the federal government should finance its help to low-income families with a tax increase? Explain why or why not.

583

Mathematical Note
The Algebra of the Fiscal Policy Multipliers

THIS MATHEMATICAL NOTE DERIVES FORMULAS FOR the fiscal policy multipliers. We begin by defining the symbols we need:

- Aggregate planned expenditure, AE
- Real GDP, Y
- Consumption expenditure, C
- Investment, I
- Government expenditures, G
- Exports, X
- Imports, M
- Net taxes, NT
- Autonomous consumption expenditure, a
- Autonomous taxes, T_a
- Autonomous transfer payments, T_r
- Marginal propensity to consume, b
- Marginal propensity to import, m
- Marginal tax rate, t
- Autonomous expenditure, A

Equilibrium Expenditure

Aggregate planned expenditure is

$$AE = C + I + G + X - M.$$

The consumption function is

$$C = a + b(Y - NT).$$

Net taxes equals autonomous taxes minus autonomous transfer payments plus induced taxes, which is

$$NT = T_a - T_r + tY.$$

Use the last equation in the consumption function to give consumption expenditure as a function of GDP:

$$C = a - bT_a + bT_r + b(1 - t)Y.$$

The import function is

$$M = mY.$$

Use the consumption function and the import function to replace C and M in the aggregate planned expenditure equation to obtain

$$AE = a - bT_a + bT_r + b(1 - t)Y + I + G + X - mY.$$

Collect the terms that involve Y on the right side of the equation to obtain

$$AE = (a - bT_a + bT_r + I + G + X) + [b(1 - t) - m]Y.$$

Autonomous expenditure (A) is given by

$$A = a - bT_a + bT_r + I + G + X$$

and the slope of the AE curve is $[b(1 - t) - m]$, so

$$AE = A + [b(1 - t) - m]Y.$$

Equilibrium expenditure occurs when aggregate planned expenditure (AE) equals real GDP (Y). That is,

$$AE = Y.$$

To calculate equilibrium expenditure, we solve the equation:

$$Y = A + [b(1 - t) - m]Y$$

to obtain

$$Y = \frac{1}{1 - [b(1 - t) - m]}A.$$

Government Expenditures Multiplier

The government expenditures multiplier equals the change in equilibrium expenditure (Y) that results from a change in government expenditures (G) divided by the change in government expenditures. Because autonomous expenditure is equal to

$$A = a - bT_a + bT_r + I + G + X,$$

the change in autonomous expenditure equals the change in government expenditures. That is,

$$\Delta A = \Delta G.$$

The government expenditures multiplier is found by working out the change in Y that results from the change in A. You can see from the solution for Y that

$$\Delta Y = \frac{1}{1 - [b(1 - t) - m]}\Delta G.$$

The government expenditures multiplier equals

$$\frac{1}{1 - [b(1 - t) - m]}.$$

In an economy in which $t = 0$ and $m = 0$, the government expenditures multiplier is $1/(1 - b)$. With $b = 0.75$, the government expenditures multiplier equals 4, as part (a) of the figure below shows. Make up some examples and use the above formula to show how b, m, and t influence the government expenditures multiplier.

Autonomous Tax Multiplier

The autonomous tax multiplier equals the change in equilibrium expenditure (Y) that results from a change in autonomous taxes (T_a) divided by the change in autonomous taxes. Because autonomous expenditure is equal to

$$A = a - bT_a + bT_r + I + G + X,$$

the change in autonomous expenditure equals *minus* b multiplied by the change in autonomous taxes. That is,

$$\Delta A = -b\Delta T_a.$$

You can see from the solution for equilibrium expenditure Y that

$$\Delta Y = \frac{-b}{1 - [b(1 - t) - m]}\Delta T_a.$$

The autonomous tax multiplier equals

$$\frac{-b}{1 - [b(1 - t) - m]}.$$

In an economy in which $t = 0$ and $m = 0$, the autonomous tax multiplier is $-b/(1 - b)$. With $b = 0.75$, the autonomous tax multiplier equals -3, as part (b) of the figure shows. Make up some exam-

ples and use the above formula to show how b, m, and t influence the autonomous tax multiplier.

Autonomous Transfer Payments Multiplier

The autonomous transfer payments multiplier equals the change in equilibrium expenditure (Y) that results from a change in autonomous transfer payments (T_r) divided by the change in autonomous transfer payments. Because autonomous expenditure is equal to

$$A = a - bT_a + bT_r + I + G + X,$$

the change in autonomous transfer payments changes autonomous expenditure such that

$$\Delta A = b\Delta T_r.$$

Because transfer payments are like negative taxes, the autonomous transfer payments multiplier equals minus the autonomous tax multiplier. The autonomous transfer payments multiplier equals

$$\frac{b}{1 - [b(1 - t) - m]}.$$

In an economy in which $t = 0$ and $m = 0$, the autonomous transfer payments multiplier is $b/(1 - b)$. With $b = 0.75$, the autonomous transfer payments multiplier equals 3, as part (c) of the figure shows. Make up some examples and use the above formula to show how b, m, and t influence the autonomous transfer payments multiplier.

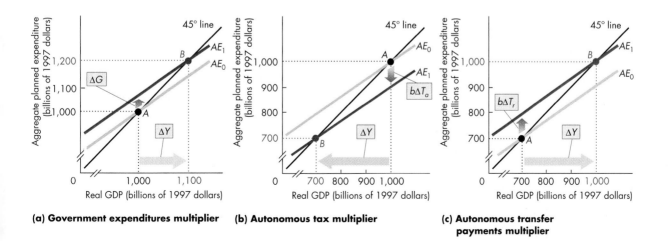

(a) Government expenditures multiplier   (b) Autonomous tax multiplier   (c) Autonomous transfer payments multiplier

SUMMARY

KEY POINTS

Government Budgets (pp. 564–569)

- The federal budget finances the activities of the government and is used to stabilize real GDP.
- Federal revenues come from personal income taxes, corporate income taxes, indirect taxes, and investment income. Federal outlays include transfer payments, expenditures on goods and services, and debt interest.
- When government revenues exceed outlays, the government has a budget surplus.

Fiscal Policy Multipliers (pp. 570–576)

- Fiscal policy actions are discretionary or automatic.
- Government expenditures, taxes, and transfer payments have multiplier effects on real GDP.
- The government expenditures multiplier equals (1 – Slope of AE curve). The autonomous tax multiplier equals $-MPC /(1 - \text{Slope of } AE \text{ curve})$.
- The transfer payments multiplier is equal to the magnitude of autonomous tax multiplier but is positive.
- Induced taxes and transfer payments and imports make the fiscal policy multipliers smaller.
- Income taxes and transfer payments act as automatic stabilizers.

Fiscal Policy Multipliers and the Price Level (pp. 576–579)

- An expansionary fiscal policy increases aggregate demand and shifts the aggregate demand curve rightward. It increases real GDP and raises the price level. (A contractionary fiscal policy has the opposite effects.)
- Price level changes dampen fiscal policy multiplier effects.
- At potential GDP, an expansionary fiscal policy raises the price level but leaves real GDP unchanged. The fiscal policy multipliers are zero.

Supply-Side Effects of Fiscal Policy (pp. 579–581)

- Fiscal policy has supply-side effects because increases in taxes weaken the incentives to work and save.
- A tax cut increases both aggregate demand and aggregate supply and increases real GDP, but the tax cut has an ambiguous effect on the price level.

KEY FIGURES

Figure 24.8   Government Expenditures Multiplier, 572
Figure 24.9   Autonomous Tax Multiplier, 573
Figure 24.10   The Business Cycle and the Budget Deficit, 574
Figure 24.11   Cyclical and Structural Deficits and Surpluses, 575
Figure 24.12   Government Expenditures and Aggregate Demand, 577
Figure 24.13   Fiscal Policy, Real GDP, and the Price Level, 578
Figure 24.15   Two Views of the Supply-Side Effects of Fiscal Policy, 581

KEY TERMS

Automatic fiscal policy, 570
Automatic stabilizers, 574
Autonomous taxes, 570
Autonomous tax multiplier, 572
Balanced budget, 565
Budget deficit, 565
Budget surplus, 565
Contractionary fiscal policy, 577
Cyclical surplus or deficit, 575
Discretionary fiscal policy, 570
Expansionary fiscal policy, 577
Federal budget, 564
Fiscal policy, 564
Government debt, 567
Government expenditures multiplier, 570
Induced taxes, 573
Provincial budget, 564
Structural surplus or deficit, 575

PROBLEMS

Go to [X myeconlab] for solutions to odd-numbered problems and additional exercises.

1. In the economy of Zap, the marginal propensity to consume is 0.9. Investment is $50 billion, government expenditures on goods and services are $40 billion, and autonomous taxes are $40 billion. Zap has no exports and no imports.

   a. The government cuts its expenditures on goods and services to $30 billion. What is the change in equilibrium expenditure?

   b. What is the value of the government expenditures multiplier?

   c. The government continues to buy $40 billion worth of goods and services and cuts autonomous taxes to $30 billion. What is the change in equilibrium expenditure?

   d. What is the value of the autonomous tax multiplier?

   e. The government simultaneously cuts both its expenditures on goods and services and taxes to $30 billion. What is the change in equilibrium expenditure? Why does equilibrium expenditure decrease?

2. In the economy of Zip, the marginal propensity to consume is 0.8. Investment is $60 billion, government expenditures on goods and services are $50 billion, and autonomous taxes are $60 billion. Zip has no exports and no imports.

   a. The government increases its expenditures on goods and services to $60 billion. What is the change in equilibrium expenditure?

   b. What is the value of the government expenditures multiplier?

   c. The government continues to buy $60 billion worth of goods and services and increases autonomous taxes to $70 billion. What is the change in equilibrium expenditure?

   d. What is the value of the autonomous tax multiplier?

   e. The government simultaneously increases both its expenditures on goods and services and taxes by $10 billion. What is the change in equilibrium expenditure? Why does equilibrium expenditure increase?

3. Suppose that the price level in the economy of Zap as described in problem 1 is 100. The economy is also at full employment.

   a. If the government of Zap increases its expenditures on goods and services by $10 billion, what happens to the quantity of real GDP demanded?

   b. How does Zap's aggregate demand curve change? Draw a two-part figure that is similar to Fig. 24.12 to illustrate the change in both the *AE* curve and the *AD* curve.

   c. In the short run, does equilibrium real GDP increase by more than, less than, or the same amount as the increase in the quantity of real GDP demanded?

   d. In the long run, does equilibrium real GDP increase by more than, less than, or the same amount as the increase in the quantity of real GDP demanded?

   e. In the short run, does the price level in Zap rise, fall, or remain unchanged?

   f. In the long run, does the price level in Zap rise, fall, or remain unchanged?

4. Suppose that the price level in the economy of Zip as described in problem 2 is 100. The economy is also at full employment.

   a. If the government of Zip decreases its expenditures on goods and services by $5 billion, what happens to the quantity of real GDP demanded?

   b. How does Zip's aggregate demand curve change? Draw a two-part figure that is similar to Fig. 24.12 to illustrate the change in both the *AE* curve and the *AD* curve.

   c. In the short run, does equilibrium real GDP decrease by more than, less than, or the same amount as the increase in the quantity of real GDP demanded?

   d. In the short run, does the price level in Zip rise, fall, or remain unchanged?

   e. Why does real GDP decrease by a smaller amount than the decrease in aggregate demand?

5. The figure shows outlays and revenues of the government of Dreamland. Potential GDP is $40 million.

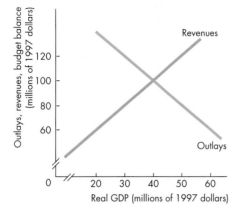

a. What is the government's budget balance if real GDP equals potential GDP?
b. Does Dreamland have a structural surplus or deficit if its real GDP is $40 million? What is the size of the structural surplus or deficit? Explain why.
c. What is the government's budget balance if real GDP is $30 million?
d. If Dreamland's real GDP is $30 million, does Dreamland have a structural surplus or deficit? What is its size? Explain why.
e. If Dreamland's real GDP is $50 million, does Dreamland have a structural surplus or deficit? What is its size? Explain why.

6. In problem 5, if Dreamland's real GDP is $50 million,
a. What is the government's budget balance?
b. Does Dreamland have a structural surplus? What is its size? Explain why.
c. What is the government's budget balance if potential GDP is $30 million?
d. If Dreamland's potential GDP is $30 million, does Dreamland have a structural surplus or deficit? What is its size? Explain why.
e. What would Dreamland's real GDP have to be for it to have neither a structural deficit or surplus nor a cyclical deficit or surplus if its potential GDP is $40 million?

1. Study *Reading Between the Lines* on pp. 582–583 and then
a. Describe the federal government's plan to help low-income Canadians with the high cost of winter heating.
b. Do you think the government is planning to finance this expenditure in an appropriate manner?
c. What do you predict would happen to aggregate demand if instead of spreading this expenditure over five years, the government spent the money in a single year?
d. Suppose the economy went into a recession in 2006. Would such an event change your answer to parts b and c? If so, how? If not, why not?
2. Thinking about the supply-side effects of the 2006 budget,
a. What would be the main effects of lower income tax rates on the level of potential GDP?
b. How would lower income taxes influence the real wage rate and the real interest rate?
c. What are the main costs of lower income taxes?

Use the links on [myeconlab] **to work the following exercises.**

1. Visit the Department of Finance and obtain data on the current federal budget. Use the information that you find, together with the fiscal policy multiplier analysis that you've learned about in this chapter, to predict the effects of the Canadian budget on real GDP and the price level. Explain reasons for your predictions.
2. Visit Statistics Canada and obtain the most recent data you can find on the revenues, outlays, and budget surplus or deficit for Canada and for the province in which you live.
a. What are the main features of the two sets of budget data?
b. What are the main trends in the budget data?
c. Predict the effects of your province's budget on provincial GDP.

Money, Banking, and Interest Rates

CHAPTER 25

Money Makes the World Go Around

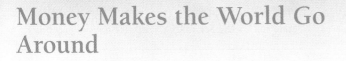

Money, like fire and the wheel, has been around for a long time. Wampum (beads made from shells) was used as money by the First Nations of North America, and tobacco was used by early American colonists. Today, we use coins, bank notes, cheques, debit cards, and credit cards. Tomorrow, we'll use "smart cards" that keep track of spending. Are all these things money?

When we deposit some coins or notes into a bank, are they still money?

There are enough coins and Bank of Canada notes circulating today for every Canadian to have a wallet stuffed with more than $1,300. In addition, there is enough money deposited in banks and other financial institutions for every Canadian to have a deposit of more than $27,000. Why do we hold all this money?

During 2004, interest rates fell to historically low levels and then, in 2005, they began to edge upward. What determines interest rates and what makes them fall or rise?

◆ In this chapter, you'll study the functions of money, the functions of banks and other financial institutions, and the Bank of Canada. You will learn how banks create money, and how interest rates are determined. At the end of the chapter, in *Reading Between the Lines*, we look at the growth in the use of debit cards and credit cards and the surprisingly small effect these electronic payment methods are having on the amount of cash we use.

After studying this chapter, you will be able to

- **Define money and describe its functions**

- **Describe the banking system and explain the economic functions of banks, the Bank of Canada, and the payments system**

- **Explain how banks create money**

- **Explain what determines the demand for money**

- **Explain what determines the supply of money and the interest rate**

What Is Money?

WHAT DO WAMPUM, TOBACCO, AND NICKELS AND dimes have in common? Why are they all examples of money? To answer these questions, we need a definition of money. **Money** is any commodity or token that is generally acceptable as the means of payment. A **means of payment** is a method of paying for goods and services or of settling a debt. When a payment has been made, there is no remaining obligation between the parties to a transaction. So what wampum, tobacco, and nickels and dimes have in common is that they have served (or still do serve) as the means of payment. But money performs three other functions:

- Medium of exchange
- Unit of account
- Store of value

Medium of Exchange

A *medium of exchange* is an object that is generally accepted in exchange for goods and services. Money acts as such a medium. Without a medium of exchange, we would exchange one good or service directly for another in an exchange called **barter**. For example, if you want to buy a hamburger, you offer the paperback novel you've just finished reading in exchange for it. Barter requires a *double coincidence* of wants, a situation that occurs when Joe wants to buy what Ann wants to sell and Ann wants to buy what Joe wants to sell. To get your hamburger, you must find someone who's selling hamburgers and who wants your paperback novel. Money ensures that there is a double coincidence of wants because people with something to sell will always accept money in exchange for it.

Unit of Account

A *unit of account* is an agreed measure for stating the prices of goods and services. To get the most out of your budget, you have to figure out whether seeing one more movie is worth its opportunity cost. But that cost is not dollars and cents. It is the number of ice-cream cones, cans of pop, or phone calls that you must give up. It's easy to do such calculations when all these goods have prices in terms of dollars and cents (see Table 25.1). If the price of a movie is $6 and the price of a six-pack of pop is $3, you know right away that seeing one movie costs you 2 six-packs of pop. If

---

TABLE 25.1   A Unit of Account Simplifies Price Comparisons

Good	Price in money units	Price in units of another good
Movie	$6.00 each	2 six-packs of pop
Pop	$3.00 per six-pack	2 ice-cream cones
Ice cream	$1.50 per cone	3 packs of jelly beans
Jelly beans	50¢ per pack	2 local phone calls
Phone call	25¢ per call	1/2 pack of jelly beans

Money as a unit of account: The price of a movie is $6 and the price of a local phone call is 25¢, so the opportunity cost of a movie is 24 local phone calls ($6.00 ÷ 25¢ = 24).

No unit of account: You go to a movie theatre and learn that the price of a movie is 2 six-packs of pop. You go to a candy store and learn that a pack of jelly beans costs 2 local phone calls. But how many phone calls does seeing a movie cost you? To answer that question, you go to the convenience store and find that a six-pack of pop costs 2 ice-cream cones. Now you head for the ice-cream shop, where an ice-cream cone costs 3 packs of jelly beans. Now you get out your pocket calculator: 1 movie costs 2 six-packs of pop, or 4 ice-cream cones, or 12 packs of jelly beans, or 24 phone calls!

---

jelly beans are 50¢ a pack, one movie costs 12 packs of jelly beans. You need only one calculation to figure out the opportunity cost of any pair of goods and services.

But imagine how troublesome it would be if your local movie theatre posted its price as 2 six-packs of pop, and if the convenience store posted the price of a six-pack of pop as 2 ice-cream cones, and if the ice-cream shop posted the price of a cone as 3 packs of jelly beans, and if the candy store priced a pack of jelly beans as 2 local phone calls! Now how much running around and calculating would you have to do to figure out how much that movie is going to cost you in terms of the pop, ice cream, jelly beans, or phone calls that you must give up to see it?

You get the answer for pop right away from the sign posted at the movie theatre. But for all the other goods you'd have to visit many different stores to establish the price of each commodity in terms of another and then calculate prices in units that are relevant for your own decision. Cover up the column labelled "price in money units" in Table 25.1 and see how hard it is to figure out the number of local phone calls it costs to see one movie. It's enough to make a person swear off movies! How much simpler it is if all the prices are expressed in dollars and cents.

Store of Value

Anything that can be held and exchanged later for goods and services is a *store of value*. Money acts as a store of value. If it did not, it would not be acceptable in exchange for goods and services.

No store of value is completely safe. The value of a physical object—such as a house, a car, or a work of art—fluctuates over time. The value of money fluctuates, and when there is inflation, its value persistently falls. The more stable the value of money, the better it can act as a store of value and the more useful it is as a means of payment.

Money in Canada Today

In Canada today, money consists of

- Currency
- Deposits at banks and other financial institutions

Currency The coins and Bank of Canada notes that we use today are known as **currency**. Currency is money because the government declares it to be so. Look at a Bank of Canada note and notice the words

> "CE BILLET A COURS LÉGAL—THIS NOTE IS LEGAL TENDER."

Currency is the most convenient type of money for settling small debts and buying low-priced items.

Deposits Deposits at banks and other financial institutions are also money. Deposits are money because they can be converted into currency and because they are used to settle debts. When you write a cheque or use a debit card, you are telling your bank to transfer money from your account to the account of the person from whom you are buying. Bank deposits are the most convenient type of money for settling large debts and buying big-ticket items.

Official Measures of Money There is no unique measure of money. The two main measures used in Canada today are M1 and M2+. Figure 25.1 shows the items that make up these two measures.

M1 consists of currency held outside the banks plus demand deposits at chartered banks that are owned by individuals and businesses. M1 does *not* include currency held by banks, and it does not include currency and bank deposits owned by the government of Canada. **M2+** consists of M1 plus personal savings deposits and nonpersonal notice deposits at chartered banks plus all types of deposits at trust and mortgage loan companies, credit unions, caisses populaires, and other financial institutions.

FIGURE 25.1
Two Measures of Money

$ billions
in June 2005

M2+		911
Comprises all in M1, plus...		
Deposits at other financial institutions		99
Deposits at credit unions and caisses populaires		148
Deposits at trust and mortgage loan companies		11
Nonpersonal notice deposits at chartered banks		65
Personal savings deposits at chartered banks		410
M1		**178**
Demand deposits		134
Currency outside banks		44

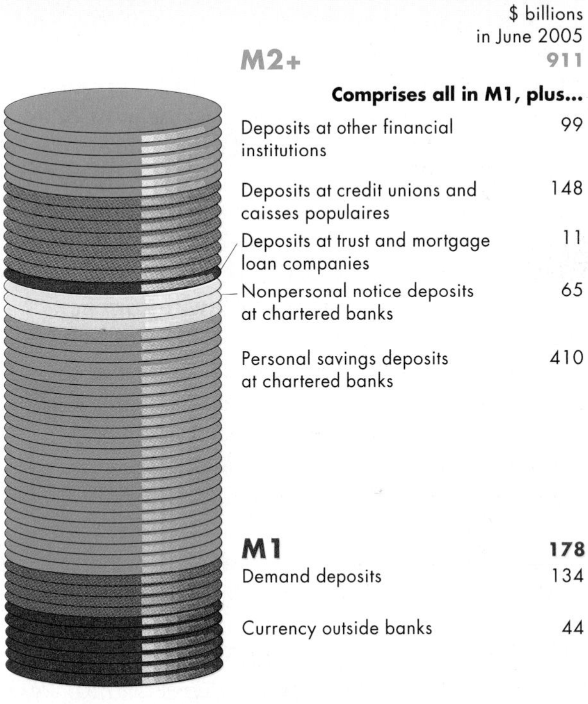

M1
- Currency held outside banks
- Demand deposits at chartered banks that are owned by individuals and businesses

M2+
- M1
- Personal savings deposits at chartered banks
- Nonpersonal notice deposits at chartered banks
- Deposits at trust and mortgage loan companies
- Deposits at credit unions and caisses populaires
- Deposits at other financial institutions

Source of data: Bank of Canada, *Banking and Financial Statistics*, Table E1.

Are M1 and M2+ Really Money? The test of whether something is money is whether it serves as a means of payment. Currency passes the test. But what about deposits? Deposit accounts on which cheques can be written are money because they can be transferred directly from one person to another in a transaction that is equivalent to handing over currency. Because M1 consists of currency plus demand deposits and each of these is a means of payment, M1 *is money.*

But what about M2+? Some of the savings deposits in M2+ are just as much a means of payment as the demand deposits in M1. You can use the automated teller machine (ATM) at the grocery store checkout or gas station and transfer funds directly from your savings account to pay for your purchase. But other savings deposits are not means of payment. They are known as *liquid assets.* **Liquidity** is the property of being instantly convertible into a means of payment with little loss in value. Because most of the deposits in M2+ are quickly and easily converted into currency or demand deposits, they are operationally similar to M1, but they are not means of payment.

Deposits Are Money but Cheques Are Not In defining money, we include, along with currency, deposits at banks and other financial institutions. But we do not count the cheques that people write as money. Why are deposits money and cheques not?

To see why deposits are money but cheques are not, think about what happens when Colleen buys some roller blades for $200 from Rocky's Rollers. When Colleen goes to Rocky's shop, she has $500 in her deposit account at the Laser Bank. Rocky has $1,000 in his deposit account—at the same bank, as it happens. The total deposits of these two people are $1,500. Colleen writes a cheque for $200. Rocky takes the cheque to the bank and deposits it. Rocky's bank balance rises from $1,000 to $1,200 and Colleen's balance falls from $500 to $300. The total deposits of Colleen and Rocky are still the same as before: $1,500. Rocky now has $200 more and Colleen has $200 less.

This transaction has transferred money from Colleen to Rocky. The cheque itself was never money. There wasn't an extra $200 worth of money while the cheque was in circulation. The cheque instructs the bank to transfer money from Colleen to Rocky.

If Colleen and Rocky use different banks, there is an extra transaction. Rocky's bank needs to collect the $200 that it has put in Rocky's account from Colleen's bank. So when Colleen's bank takes the $200 from her account, it pays that amount to Rocky's bank.

We describe this process of interbank payments in the next section (see pp. 595–596).

Debit Cards Are Not Money So cheques are not money. But what about debit cards? Isn't presenting a debit card to pay for your roller blades the same thing as using money? Why aren't debit cards counted as part of the quantity of money?

A debit card enables you to pay with an electronic cheque. When you use a debit card, money leaves your bank account and is deposited into the account of the person from whom you are buying at the instant of the transaction.

Credit Cards Are Not Money Sometimes you need ID and you pull out your driver's licence. Your credit card is another type of ID card—a special ID card that enables you to take a loan at the instant you buy something. When you sign a credit card sales slip, you are saying: "I agree to pay for these goods when the credit card company bills me." Once you get your statement from the credit card company, you must make the minimum payment due (or clear your balance). To make that payment you need money—you need to have currency or a bank deposit to pay the credit card company. So although you use a credit card when you buy something, the credit card is not the *means of payment* and it is not money.

REVIEW QUIZ

1 What makes something money? What functions does money perform? Why do you think packs of chewing gum don't serve as money?
2 What problems arise when a commodity is used as money?
3 What are the main components of money in Canada today?
4 What are two official measures of money in Canada? Are all the measures really money?
5 Why are cheques, debit cards, and credit cards not money?

myeconlab **Study Plan 25.1**

We've seen that the main component of money in Canada is deposits at banks and other financial firms. Let's take a closer look at the banking system.

The Banking System

THE BANKING SYSTEM CONSISTS OF PRIVATE AND public institutions that create money and manage the nation's monetary and payments systems. These institutions play a crucial role in financial markets and have profound effects on overall economic performance. We're going to describe these institutions and explain their economic funtions. To so so, we'll divide the institutions into three groups:

- Depository institutions
- The Bank of Canada
- The payments system

Depository Institutions

A **depository institution** is a private firm that takes deposits from households and firms and makes loans to other households and firms. The deposits of three types of depository institution are included in the nation's money. They are

- Chartered banks
- Credit unions and caisses populaires
- Trust and mortgage loan companies

Chartered Banks A **chartered bank** is a private firm, chartered under the Bank Act of 1992 to receive deposits and make loans. The chartered banks are by far the largest institutions in the banking system and conduct all types of banking and financial business. In 2005, 14 Canadian-owned banks (including the Royal Bank of Canada, CIBC, Bank of Montreal, Bank of Nova Scotia, National Bank of Canada, and TD Canada Trust) and 33 foreign-owned banks had deposits that are included in M2+ of $609 billion.

Credit Unions and Caisses Populaires A **credit union** is a cooperative organization that operates under the Co-operative Credit Association Act of 1992 and that receives deposits from and makes loans to its members. A caisse populaire is a similar type of institution that operates in Quebec. In 2005, the deposits in these institutions were $148 billion.

Trust and Mortgage Loan Companies A **trust and mortgage loan company** is a privately owned deposi-tory institution that operates under the Trust and Loan Companies Act of 1992. These institutions receive deposits, make loans, and act as trustee for pension funds and for estates. In 2005, they had deposits that are included in M2+ of $11 billion.

All Banks Now Historically, Canada made a sharp legal distinction between banks and other depository institutions. But the economic functions of all depository institutions have grown increasingly similar. This fact is recognized in laws governing these institutions that became effective in 1992. Because they all perform the same essential economic functions, we'll call all these institutions banks unless we need to distinguish among them.

Profit and Prudence: A Balancing Act The aim of any bank is to maximize the wealth of its owners. To achieve this objective, the interest rate at which a bank lends exceeds the interest rate at which it borrows. But a bank must perform a delicate balancing act. Lending is risky, and the more a bank ties up its deposits in high-risk, high-interest-rate loans, the bigger is its chance of not being able to repay its depositors. And if depositors perceive a high risk of not being repaid, they withdraw their funds and create a crisis for the bank. So a bank must be prudent in the way it uses its deposits, balancing security against profit.

Reserves and Loans To achieve security for its depositors, a bank divides its funds into two parts: reserves and loans. **Reserves** are currency in a bank's vault plus its deposit at the Bank of Canada. The currency in a bank's vaults is a reserve to meet depositors' demand for cash. The bank replenishes the ATM every time you and your friends raid it for cash for a midnight pizza. The account of a bank at the Bank of Canada is similar to your own bank account. Banks use these accounts to receive and make payments. A bank deposits cash into or draws cash out of its account at the Bank of Canada and writes cheques on that account to settle debts with other banks.

If a bank kept all its deposits as reserves, it wouldn't make any profit. In fact, it keeps only a small fraction of its funds in reserves and lends the rest. A bank has four types of assets:

1. *Overnight loans* are loans that one bank makes to another for one night only. The loan is repaid at

the start of the next business day. A bank that has surplus reserves makes overnight loans to banks that have a shortage of reserves.

2. *Liquid assets* are Canadian government Treasury bills and commercial bills. These assets are the banks' first line of defence if they need cash. They can be sold and instantly converted into cash with virtually no risk of loss. Because liquid assets are virtually risk-free, they have a low interest rate.

3. *Investment securities* are longer-term Canadian government bonds and other bonds. These assets can be sold quickly and converted into cash but at prices that fluctuate. Because their prices fluctuate, these assets are riskier than liquid assets but they have a higher interest rate.

4. *Loans* are commitments of fixed amounts of money for agreed-upon periods of time. Most banks' loans are made to corporations to finance the purchase of capital equipment and inventories and to households—personal loans—to finance purchases of consumer durable goods, such as cars or boats. The outstanding balances on credit card accounts are also bank loans. Loans are the riskiest assets of a bank because they cannot be converted into cash until they are due to be repaid. And some borrowers default and never repay. Because they are the riskiest of a bank's assets, loans also carry the highest interest rate.

The Economic Functions of Banks Banks make a profit from the spread between the interest rate they pay on deposits and the interest rate at which they lend. What services do banks perform that make depositors willing to accept a low interest rate and borrowers willing to pay a higher one? Banks provide four services for which people are willing to pay:

1. *Create liquidity*. Most of the liabilities of banks are money; others are highly liquid assets that are easily convertible into money.

    Banks create liquidity by borrowing short and lending long. Borrowing short means taking deposits but standing ready to repay them on short notice (and even on no notice in the case of demand deposits). Lending long means making loan commitments for a prearranged, and often long period. For example, when a person makes a deposit with a trust company, that deposit can be withdrawn at any time. But the trust company

makes a lending commitment to a homebuyer for 5 years.

2. *Minimize the cost of borrowing* by bringing borrowers and lenders together. Imagine how troublesome it would be if there were no banks. A firm that was looking for $1 million to buy a new production plant would probably have to hunt around for several dozen people from whom to borrow in order to acquire enough funds for its capital project. Banks lower those costs. The firm that needs $1 million can go to a single bank to obtain those funds. The bank has to borrow from a large number of people, but it's not doing that just for this one firm and the $1 million that it wants to borrow. The bank can establish an organization that is capable of raising funds from a large number of depositors and can spread the cost of this activity over a large number of borrowers.

3. *Minimize the cost of monitoring borrowers*. Lending money is a risky business. There is always a danger that the borrower may not repay. Firms are the biggest borrowers. They borrow to invest in projects that they hope will return a profit but sometimes those hopes are not fulfilled. Monitoring the activities of a borrower and ensuring that the best possible decisions are being taken to make a profit and to avoid a loss are costly and specialized activities. Imagine how costly it would be if each household that lent money to a firm had to incur the costs of monitoring that firm directly. By depositing funds with a bank, households avoid those costs. The bank performs the monitoring activity by using specialized resources that have a much lower cost than what each household would incur if it had to undertake the activity individually.

4. *Pool risk*. There is always a chance of a loan not being repaid—of default. Lending to a large number of individuals reduces the risk of default—if one person defaults on a loan, it is a nuisance but not a disaster. But if only one person borrows and that person defaults on the loan, the entire loan is a write-off. Banks enable people to pool risk in an efficient way. Thousands of people lend money to any one bank, and, in turn, the bank re-lends the money to hundreds, perhaps thousands, of individuals and firms. If any one firm defaults on its loan, that default is spread across all the depositors and no individual depositor is left exposed to a high degree of risk.

The Bank of Canada

The Bank of Canada is Canada's **central bank**, a public authority that supervises other banks and financial institutions, financial markets, and the payments system and conducts monetary policy.

You will learn much more about the Bank of Canada when we study monetary policy in Chapter 27. For now, all we need to understand is the bare outlines of what the Bank of Canada does and its place in the banking system.

The Bank of Canada is a bank. And like all banks, it accepts deposits, make loans, and holds investment securities. But the Bank of Canada is special in three important ways. It is the

- Banker to banks and government
- Lender of last resort
- Sole issuer of bank notes

Banker to Banks and Government The Bank of Canada has a restricted list of customers. They are the chartered banks, credit unions and caisses populaires, and trust and morgage loan companies that make up the banking system; the government of Canada; and the central banks of other countries. The Bank of Canada accepts deposits from these customers. And the deposits of the banks are part of their reserves.

Lender of Last Resort The Bank of Canada makes loans to banks. But it is the **lender of last resort**, which means that it stands ready to make loans when the banking system as a whole is short of reserves. If some banks are short of reserves while others have surplus reserves, the overnight loan market moves the funds from one bank to another.

Sole Issuer of Bank Notes The Bank of Canada is the only bank that is permitted to issues bank notes. You might think that such a monopoly is natural, but it isn't. In some banking systems—those of Ireland and Scotland are examples—private banks also issue bank notes. But in Canada and most other countries, the central bank has a monopoly on this activity.

The Bank of Canada's Balance Sheet The balance sheet of the Bank of Canada summarizes the activities that we've just described. The Bank of Canada's assets are government of Canada securities and last-resort loans to banks. Much of the time, there are no last-resort loans outstanding, so the Bank's only assets are its government of Canada securities.

The Bank of Canada's liabilities are Bank of Canada notes and deposits of banks and the government. The bank notes are what we use in our daily transactions. Some of these bank notes are held by households and firms and others are in the tills and vaults of banks and in ATM machines. The total value of Bank of Canada notes in 2005 was $44 billion.

The deposits of banks at the Bank of Canada are small in magnitude but large in importance. On any given day these deposits are around $50 million. To see how tiny this amount is, compare it to the total deposits in M2+. Those deposits were $867 billion in 2005. So the $50 million of reserves on deposit at the Bank of Canada represents about one penny for every $2,000 of deposits in M2+.

How can the banks manage with such a small amount of reserves at the Bank of Canada? The answer is that Canada has an amazingly efficient payments system—one of the most efficient in the world.

The Payments System

The **payments system** is the system through which banks make payments to each other to settle transactions by their customers. You saw why we need such a system when you thought about Colleen buying some new roller blades from Rocky. If Colleen banks at TD Canada Trust and Rocky's bank is CIBC, when Colleen writes her cheque to buy the blades, TD Canada Trust must take $200 from Colleen and pay that amount to CIBC; and CIBC must put the $200 into Rocky's account.

Most transactions between two parties involve two banks and so require one bank to pay another. Think about what happens when Jack, who banks at CIBC, gets $50 cash from an Interac Automated Banking Machine. Interac gives Jack the $50 in cash and his CIBC deposit balance goes down by $50. But now, CIBC owes Interac $50.

The payments system enables banks to make payments to each other. This system in Canada is operated by the Canadian Payments Association or CPA, a not-for-profit organization created by parliament in 2000. The CPA owns and operates the two national payments systems:

- Large Value Transfer System
- Automated Clearing Settlement System

Large Value Transfer System The **Large Value Transfer System (LVTS)** is an electronic payments system that enables financial institutions and their customers to make large payments instantly and with the sure knowledge that the payment has been made. It was launched in 1999. The Bank of Canada along with 14 of the largest banks have access to the LVTS, and on an average day, it handles more than 18,000 payments worth an astonishing $140 billion.

Throughout any given day, the LVTS members send payments back and forth to each other. When the transactions are added up at the end of the day, some of these financial institutions may end up needing money, while others may have funds left over.

Every day, LVTS members borrow and lend money to each other on a one-day basis, to cover their net LVTS positions. The interest rate paid on these and other overnight loans is called the *overnight rate*. This interest rate plays a central role in the Bank of Canada's monetary policy, as you will learn in Chapter 28.

Automated Clearing Settlement System The **Automated Clearing Settlement System (ACSS)** is the system through which all payments not processed by the LVTS are handled. These payments include cheques and small-value electronic payments, such as point-of-sale debit card or ABM transactions. Unlike the LVTS, which operates continuously through the day, the ACSS settles the net amounts owed just once a day. On an average day, the ACSS handles more than 20 million payments worth around $17 billion.

REVIEW QUIZ

1 What are Canada's main depository institutions?
2 Why don't banks keep all the money that people place on deposit in their vaults?
3 What are the economic functions of banks?
4 How do banks create liquidity and pool risk?
5 How does the Bank of Canada differ from all other banks?
6 What is the payments sytem?

myeconlab Study Plan 25.2

We've described the functions of banks and other depository institutions. We're now going to see how these firms have the ability to create money.

How Banks Create Money

BANKS CREATE MONEY. BUT THIS DOESN'T MEAN that they have smoke-filled back rooms in which counterfeiters are busily working. Remember, most money is deposits, not currency. What banks create is deposits, and they do so by making loans.

Creating Deposits by Making Loans

The easiest way to see that banks create deposits is to think about what happens when Jack, who has a Visa card issued by CIBC, uses his card to buy a tank of gas from PetroCan. When Jack signs the card pay slip, he takes a loan from CIBC and obligates himself to repay the loan at a later date. At the end of the business day, a PetroCan clerk takes a pile of signed credit card sales slips, including Jack's, to PetroCan's bank. For now, let's assume that PetroCan also banks at CIBC. The bank immediately credits PetroCan's account with the value of the slips (minus the bank's commission).

You can see that these transactions have created a bank deposit and a loan. Jack has increased the size of his loan (his credit card balance) and PetroCan has increased the size of its bank deposit. And because deposits are money, CIBC has created money.

If as we've just assumed, Jack and PetroCan use the same bank, no further transactions take place. CIBC has an increase in deposits and loans. But the outcome is essentially the same when two banks are involved in the transactions. If PetroCan's bank is the Royal Bank, then CIBC pays the Royal Bank using its reserves. CIBC has an increase in loans and a decrease in reserves; the Royal Bank has an increase in reserves and an increase in deposits. And the banking system as a whole has an increase in deposits and loans and no change in reserves.

If Jack had swiped his card at an automatic payment pump, all these transactions would have occurred at the time he filled his tank, and the quantity of money would have increased by the amount of his purchase (minus the bank's commission for conducting the transactions).

The quantity of deposits that banks can create is limited by three factors:

■ The monetary base
■ Desired reserves
■ Desired currency holding

The Monetary Base The liabilities of the Bank of Canada (plus coins issued by the Canadian Mint) form the **monetary base**—the sum of Bank of Canada notes outside the Bank of Canada, banks' deposits at the Bank of Canada, and coins held by households, firms, and banks. The size of the monetary base limits the total quantity of money that the banking system can create because banks have a desired level of reserves and households and firms have a desired level of currency holding and both of these desired holdings of the monetary base depend on the quantity of money.

Desired Reserves A bank's *actual reserves* consist of the currency in its vaults and its deposit at the Bank of Canada. A bank uses its reserves to meet depositors' demand for currency and to make payments to other banks.

You've also seen that banks don't have $100 of reserves for every $100 that people have deposited with them. If the banks did behave that way, they wouldn't earn any profit.

Banks today have reserves of $3 for every $100 of M1 deposits and 40¢ for every $100 of M2+ deposits. Most of these reserves are currency. You saw in the previous section that reserves in the form of deposits at the Bank of Canada are tiny. No need for panic. These reserve levels are adequate for ordinary business needs.

The fraction of a bank's total deposits that are held in reserves is called the **reserve ratio**. So, with reserves of $3 for every $100 of M1 deposits, that reserve ratio is 0.3 or 3 pecent, and with reserves of 40¢ for every $100 of M2+ deposits, that reserve ratio is 0.004 or 0.4 percent.

A bank's *desired reserves* are the reserves that it wishes to hold. In most banking systems, banks are *required* to hold a level of reserves that does not fall below some specifed percentage of total deposits. This percentage is called the *required reserve ratio*. In Canada, the required reserve ratio was lowered during the 1990s and by the mid-1990s it was lowered to zero.

The **desired reserve ratio** is the ratio of reserves to deposits that a bank wants to hold. Because there are no required reserves, banks in Canada are free to determine the prudent level of reserves—and the desired reserve ratio—based on their daily business requirments.

A bank's reserve ratio changes when its customers make a deposit or a withdrawal. If a bank's customer makes a deposit, reserves and deposits increase by the same amount, so the bank's reserve ratio increases. Similarly, if a bank's customer makes a withdrawal, reserves and deposits decrease by the same amount, so the bank's reserve ratio decreases.

A bank's **excess reserves** are its actual reserves minus its desired reserves. Whenever the banking system as a whole has excess reserves, the banks are able to create money. Banks increase their loans and deposits when they have excess reserves and they decrease their loans and deposits when they are short of reserves—when desired reserves exceed actual reserves.

But the greater the desired reserve ratio, the smaller is the quantity of deposits and money that the banking system can create from a given amount of monetary base.

Desired Currency Holding We hold our money in the form of currency and bank deposits. The proportion of money held as currency isn't constant but at any given time, people have a definite view as to how much they want to hold in each form of money.

In 2004, for every dollar of M1 deposits held, we held 35¢ of currency and for every dollar of M2+ deposits, we held 5¢ of currency.

Because people want to hold some proportion of their money in the form of currency, when the total quantity of bank deposits increases, so does the quantity of currency that people want to hold. Because desired currency holding increases when deposits increase, currency leaves the banks when loans are made and deposits increase. We call the leakage of currency from the banking system the *currency drain*. And we call the ratio of currency to deposits the **currency drain ratio**.

The greater the currency drain ratio, the smaller is the quantity of deposits and the smaller is the quantity of money that the banking system can create from a given amount of monetary base.

The Money Creation Process

The money creation process begins when the banks have excess reserves. A sequence of events then plays out. The sequence, which keeps repeating until all the reserves are desired and no excess reserves are being held, has nine steps. They are

1. Banks have excess reserves.
2. Banks lend excess reserves.
3. Bank deposits increase.

4. The quantity of money increases.

5. New money is used to make payments.

6. Some of the new money remains on deposit.

7. Some of the new money is a *currency drain*.

8. Desired reserves increase because deposits have increased.

9. Excess reserves decrease, but remain positive.

Figure 25.2 illustrates this process.

To make the process of money creation more concrete, let's work through an example for a banking system in which each bank has a desired reserve ratio of 10 percent and the currency drain ratio is 50 percent. (Although these ratios are larger than the ones in the Canadian economy, they make the process end more quickly and enable you to see more clearly the principles at work.)

Figure 25.3 will keep track of the numbers. The process begins when all the banks have zero excess reserves except one bank, and it has excess reserves of $100,000. You can see these numbers in the first row of the "running tally" in Fig. 25.3.

The bank lends the $100,000 to Amy, who writes a cheque for $66,667 to buy a copy-shop franchise from Barb and withdraws $33,333 in currency to make some cash transactions. At this point, currency has increased by $33,333, bank deposits have increased by $66,667, and the quantity of money has increased by $100,000. You can see these numbers in Fig. 25.3 as the second row of the running tally.

For Amy's bank, that is the end of the story. But Barb's bank has now got some excess reserves. Barb's deposit has increased by $66,667 and so have the reserves of Barb's bank. With a 10 percent desired reserve ratio, Barb's bank now wants to hold an additional $6,667 in reserves and to loan the other $60,000. The bank loans $60,000 to Bob, who writes a cheque for $40,000 to buy a luxury car from Carl and withdraws $20,000 in currency.

Now currency has increased by $53,333, bank deposits have increased by $106,667, and the quantity of money has increased by $160,000. You can see these numbers in the running tally in Fig. 25.3.

FIGURE 25.2

How the Banking System Creates Money by Making Loans

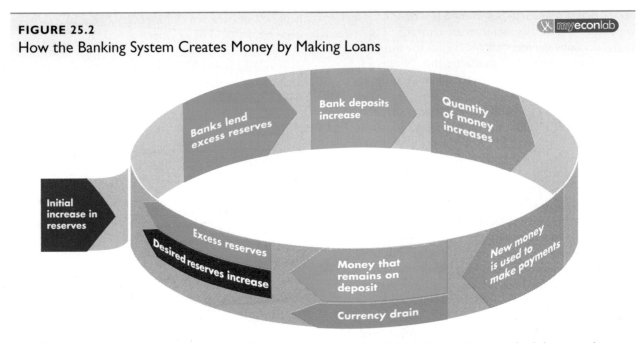

Initially, the banking system has excess reserves. Banks lend the excess reserves, new bank deposits are created, and the quantity of money increases. New money is used to make payments. Households and firms receiving payments keep some of the receipts as currency—a currency drain—and place the rest on deposit in banks. The increase in bank deposits increases banks' reserves but also increases banks' desired reserves. Desired reserves increase by less than the increase in actual reserves, so the banks still have some excess reserves, though less than before. The process repeats until excess reserves have been eliminated.

Barb's bank now has no excess reserves. But Carl's bank has now got some excess reserves. Carl's deposit has increased by $40,000 and so have the reserves of Carl's bank. With a 10 percent desired reserve ratio, Carl's bank now wants to hold an additional $4,000 in reserves and to loan the other $36,000. The bank loans $36,000 to Chuck, who writes a cheque for $24,000 to buy a boat and withdraws $12,000 in currency.

By now, currency has increased by $65,333, bank deposits have increased by $130,667, and the quantity of money has increased by $196,000. You can see these numbers in the running tally in Fig. 25.3.

Figure 25.3 shows one additional round in the process and also shows the final tallies. When the

process ends, reserves have increased by $16,667, currency has increased by $83,333, deposits have increased by $166,667, and the quantity of money has increased by $250,000.

The Money Multiplier

The sequence in Fig. 25.3 is the first four stages of the process that finally reaches the totals shown in the final row of the running tally. To figure out the entire process, look closely at the numbers in the figure. The initial increase in reserves is $100,000 (call it A). At each stage, the loan is 60 percent (0.6) of the previous loan and the quantity of money increases by 0.6 of the previous increase. Call that proportion L ($L = 0.6$). We can write down the complete sequence as an

FIGURE 25.3
The Money Creation Process: An Example

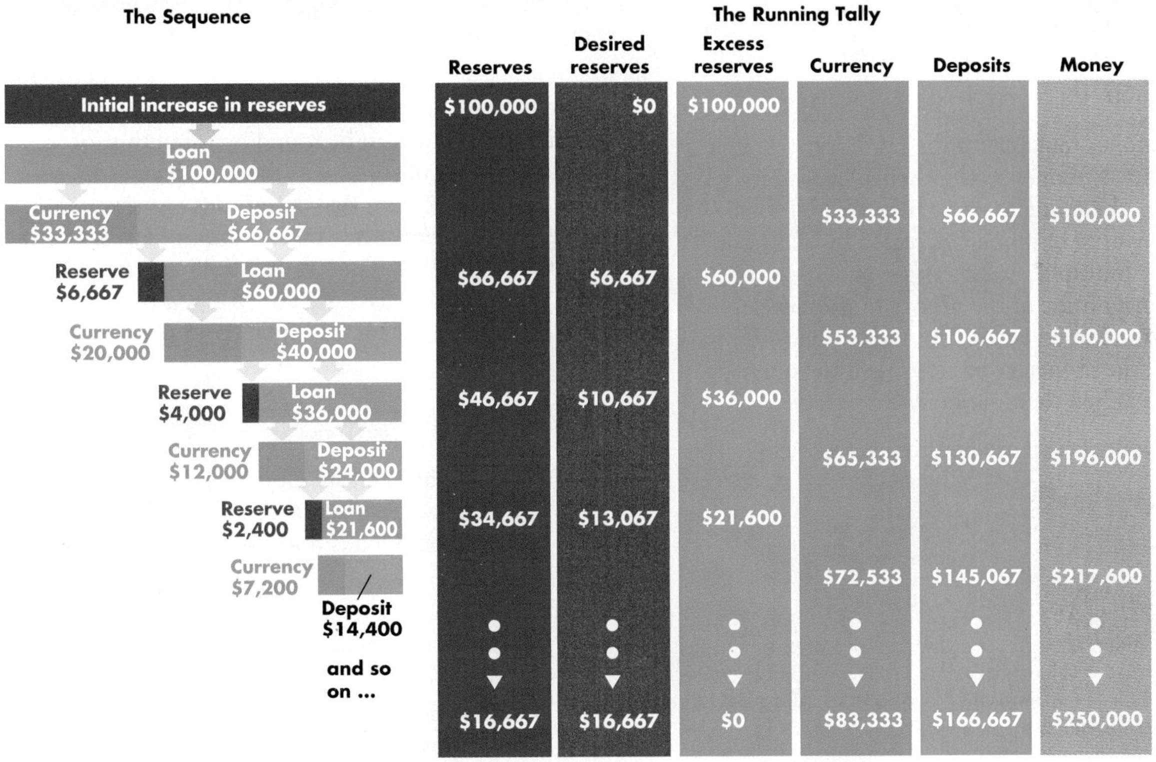

	Reserves	Desired reserves	Excess reserves	Currency	Deposits	Money
Initial increase in reserves	$100,000	$0	$100,000			
Loan $100,000						
Currency $33,333 / Deposit $66,667				$33,333	$66,667	$100,000
Reserve $6,667 / Loan $60,000	$66,667	$6,667	$60,000			
Currency $20,000 / Deposit $40,000				$53,333	$106,667	$160,000
Reserve $4,000 / Loan $36,000	$46,667	$10,667	$36,000			
Currency $12,000 / Deposit $24,000				$65,333	$130,667	$196,000
Reserve $2,400 / Loan $21,600	$34,667	$13,067	$21,600			
Currency $7,200 / Deposit $14,400				$72,533	$145,067	$217,600
and so on ...	$16,667	$16,667	$0	$83,333	$166,667	$250,000

A bank has excess reserves of $100,000. It loans those reserves. Of the amount loaned, $33,333 (50 percent of deposits) leaves the banks in a currency drain and $66,667 remains on deposit. Desired reserves increase by $6,667 (10 percent of the deposit) and the banks loan $60,000.

Of this amount, $20,000 leaves the banks in a currency drain and $40,000 remains on deposit. The process repeats until the banks have created enough deposits to eliminate their excess reserves. $100,000 of excess reserves creates $250,000 of money.

equation as follows:

$$A + AL + AL^2 + AL^3 + AL^4 + AL^5 \ldots$$

Remember, L is a fraction, so at each stage in this sequence the amount of new loans and new money gets smaller. The total value of loans made and money created at the end of the process is the above sum, which is[1]

$$A/(1 - L).$$

If we use the numbers from the example, the total increase in the quantity of money is

$$\$100{,}000 + 60{,}000 + 36{,}000 + 21{,}600 + \ldots$$

$$= \$100{,}000 \, (1 + 0.6 + 0.36 + 0.216 + \ldots)$$

$$= \$100{,}000 \, (1 + 0.6 + 0.6^2 + 0.6^3 + \ldots)$$

$$= \$100{,}000 \times 1/(1 - 0.6)$$

$$= \$100{,}000 \times 1/(0.4)$$

$$= \$100{,}000 \times 2.5$$

$$= \$250{,}000.$$

The **money multiplier** is the ratio of the change in the quantity of money to the change in monetary base. Here, the monetary base increased by \$100,000 and the quantity of money increased by \$250,000 so the money multiplier is 2.5.

The magnitude of the money multiplier depends on the desired reserve ratio and the currency drain ratio. Call the monetary base MB and the quantity of money M. When there are no excess reserves,

$$MB = \text{Desired currency holding} + \text{Desired reserves}$$

Also,

$$M = \text{Deposits} + \text{Desired currency holding}$$

Call the currency drain ratio a and the desired reserve ratio b. Then,

$$\text{Desired currency holding} = a \times \text{Deposits}$$

$$\text{Desired reserves} = b \times \text{Deposits}$$

We can now rewrite the equations for MB and M as

$$MB = (a + b) \times \text{Deposits}$$

$$M = (1 + a) \times \text{Deposits}.$$

Divide the above equation for M by the one for MB and you see that

$$M = (1 + a)/(a + b) \times MB.$$

Use the values $a = 0.5$ and $b = 0.1$ and you will see that $(1 + a)/(a + b) = 1.5/0.6 = 2.5$.

The Money Multiplier in Canada The money multiplier in Canada can be found by using this formula and the values of a and b in the Canadian economy.

Because we have two definitions of money, M1 and M2+, we have two money multipliers. Using the numbers for 2004: For M1, a is 0.35 and b is 0.03 so the M1 multiplier is 3.55. For M2+, a is 0.004 and b is 0.05 so the M2+ multiplier is 18.6.

REVIEW QUIZ

1 How do banks create money by making loans, and what are the factors that limit the amount of money and loans that banks can create?
2 A bank manager tells you that she doesn't create money. She just lends the money that people deposit in the bank. How do you explain to her that she's wrong and that she does create money?
3 If people decided to hold less currency and more deposits, how would the quantity of money change?

   myeconlab Study Plan 25.3

---

[1] Both here and in the expenditure multiplier process in Chapter 23, the sequence of values is called a convergent geometric series. To find the sum of a series such as this, begin by calling the sum S. Then write the sum as

$$S = A + AL + AL^2 + AL^3 + AL^4 + AL^5 + \ldots$$

Multiply by L to get,

$$LS = AL + AL^2 + AL^3 + AL^4 + AL^5 + \ldots$$

and then subtract the second equation from the first to get

$$S(1 - L) = A$$

or

$$S = A/(1 - L).$$

You now know how money gets created. Your next task is to study the demand for money.

The Demand for Money

THE AMOUNT OF MONEY WE RECEIVE EACH WEEK in payment for our labour is income—a *flow*. The amount of money that we hold in our wallet or in a deposit account at the bank is an inventory—a *stock*. There is no limit to how much income we would like to *receive* each week. But there is a limit to how big an inventory of money each of us would like to *hold* and not spend.

The Influences on Money Holding

The quantity of money that people choose to hold depends on four main factors:

- The price level
- The interest rate
- Real GDP
- Financial innovation

The Price Level The quantity of money measured in dollars is *nominal money*. The quantity of nominal money demanded is proportional to the price level, other things remaining the same. That is, if the price level rises by 10 percent, people hold 10 percent more nominal money than before, other things remaining the same. If you hold $20 to buy your weekly movies and pop, you will increase your money holding to $22 if the prices of movies and pop—and your wage rate—increase by 10 percent.

The quantity of money measured in constant dollars (for example, in 1997 dollars) is called *real money*. Real money is equal to nominal money divided by the price level. It is the quantity of money measured in terms of what it will buy. In the above example, when the price level rises by 10 percent and you increase the amount of money that you hold by 10 percent, you keep your *real* money constant. Your $22 at the new price level buys the same quantity of goods and is the same quantity of *real money* as your $20 at the original price level. The quantity of real money held does not depend on the price level.

The Interest Rate A fundamental principle of economics is that as the opportunity cost of something increases, people try to find substitutes for it. Money is no exception. The higher the opportunity cost of holding money, other things remaining the same, the smaller is the quantity of real money demanded. But what is the opportunity cost of holding money? It is the interest rate that you must forgo on other assets that you could hold instead of money minus the interest rate that you can earn by holding money.

The interest rate that you earn on currency and demand deposits is zero. So the opportunity cost of holding these items is the interest rate on other assets such as a savings bond or Treasury bill. By holding money instead, you forgo the interest that you otherwise would have received. This forgone interest is the opportunity cost of holding money.

Money loses value because of inflation. So why isn't the inflation rate part of the cost of holding money? It is: Other things remaining the same, the higher the expected inflation rate, the higher are all interest rates and the higher, therefore, is the opportunity cost of holding money. The forces that make the interest rate change to reflect changes in the expected inflation rate are described in Chapter 27, pp. 648–649.)

Real GDP The quantity of money that households and firms plan to hold depends on the amount they are spending, and the quantity of money demanded in the economy as a whole depends on aggregate expenditure—real GDP.

Again, suppose that you hold an average of $20 to finance your weekly purchases of movies and pop. Now imagine that the prices of these goods and of all other goods remain constant but that your income increases. As a consequence you now spend more, and you keep a larger amount of money on hand to finance your higher volume of expenditure.

Financial Innovation Technological change and the arrival of new financial products—called **financial innovation**—change the quantity of money held. The major financial innovations are the widespread use of

1. Daily interest deposits
2. Automatic transfers between demand deposits and savings deposits
3. Automatic teller machines
4. Credit cards and debit cards

These innovations have occurred because the development of computing power has lowered the cost of calculations and record keeping.

We summarize the effects of the influences on money holding by using a demand for money curve.

The Demand for Money Curve

The **demand for money curve** is the relationship between the quantity of real money demanded and the interest rate when all other influences on the amount of money that people wish to hold remain the same.

Figure 25.4 shows a demand for money curve, *MD*. When the interest rate rises, other things remaining the same, the opportunity cost of holding money rises and the quantity of real money demanded decreases—there is a movement along the demand for money curve. Similarly, when the interest rate falls, the opportunity cost of holding money falls, and the quantity of real money demanded increases—there is a movement down along the demand for money curve.

When any other influence on the amount of money that people plan to hold changes, there is a change in the demand for money and the demand for money curve shifts. Let's study these shifts.

Shifts in the Demand for Money Curve

A change in real GDP or financial innovation changes the demand for money and shifts the demand for money curve.

Figure 25.5 illustrates the change in the demand for money. A decrease in real GDP decreases the demand for money and shifts the demand curve leftward from MD_0 to MD_1. An increase in real GDP has the opposite effect. It increases the demand for money and shifts the demand curve rightward from MD_0 to MD_2.

The influence of financial innovation on the demand for money curve is more complicated. It might increase the demand for some types of deposits, decrease the demand for others, and decrease the demand for currency.

We'll look at the effects of changes in real GDP and financial innovation by studying the demand for money in Canada.

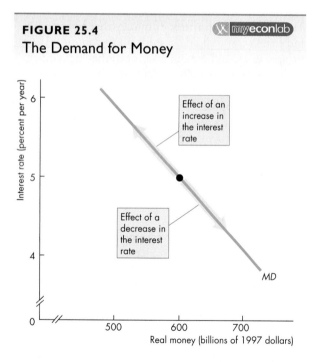

FIGURE 25.4
The Demand for Money

The demand for money curve, *MD*, shows the relationship between the quantity of real money that people plan to hold and the interest rate, other things remaining the same. The interest rate is the opportunity cost of holding money. A change in the interest rate brings a movement along the demand curve.

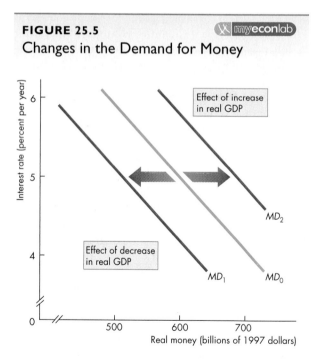

FIGURE 25.5
Changes in the Demand for Money

A decrease in real GDP decreases the demand for money and shifts the demand curve leftward from MD_0 to MD_1. An increase in real GDP increases the demand for money and shifts the demand curve rightward from MD_0 to MD_2. Financial innovation decreases the demand for some forms of money and increases the demand for other forms.

The Demand for Money in Canada

Figure 25.6 shows the relationship between the interest rate and the quantity of real money demanded in Canada between 1968 and 2004. Each dot shows the interest rate and the quantity of money held as a percentage of GDP in a given year. We've measured money as a percentage of GDP to remove the effects of rising incomes and a rising price level in order to reveal the relationship between money holding and the interest rate. In part (a), the measure of money is M1 and in part (b), it is M2+.

In 1968, the demand for M1 (in part a) was MD_0. During the 1980s, the demand for M1 decreased and the demand curve for M1 shifted leftward and by 1991, it had become MD_1. During the late 1990s and early 2000s, the demand for M1 increased and the demand curve for M1 shifted rightward. By 2004, the demand curve for M1 has shifted to MD_2.

In 1968, the demand curve for M2+ (in part b) was MD_0. During the 1970s, the demand for M2+ increased and the demand curve for M2+ shifted rightward. By 1981, it had shifted to MD_1. During the 1990s, the demand for M2+ decreased and by 2004, the demand curve for M2+ had shifted leftward to MD_2.

Why did the demand curves shift? Financial innovation is the main reason. During the 1970s, the arrival of automatic transfers between demand deposits and savings deposits made M2+ deposits increasingly attractive, so the demand for these

---

FIGURE 25.6
The Demand for Money in Canada

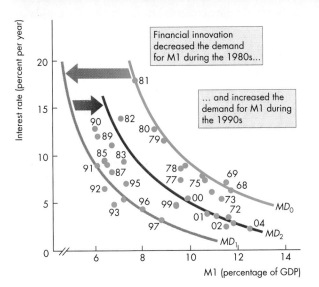

(a) Demand for M1

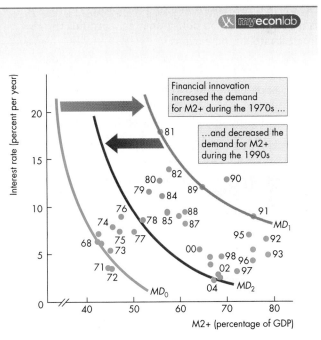

(b) Demand for M2+

The dots show the quantity of real money and the interest rate in each year between 1968 and 2004. Between 1968 and 1981, the demand for M1 was MD_0 in part (a). The demand for M1 decreased during the 1980s and the demand curve shifted leftward to MD_1. The demand for M1 increased during the late 1990s and early 2000s and the demand curve shifted rightward to MD_2.

Source of data: Bank of Canada, *Banking and Financial Statistics*, tables E1 and F1.

In 1968, the demand curve for M2+ was MD_0 in part (b). During the 1970s, the demand for M2+ increased and by 1981 the demand curve had shifted rightward to MD_1. During the 1990s, the demand for M2+ decreased and the demand curve shifted leftward to MD_2. Financial innovation is the main reason for the shifts in the demand for money curves.

deposits increased. Later, daily interest on chequing accounts increased the demand for M1 deposits.

You can see by comparing the two parts of Fig. 25.6 that the financial innovation that increased the demand for M2+ during the 1970s did not decrease the demand for M1. But rising interest rates during the 1970s decreased the quantity of M1 demanded—shown by a movement along the demand for M1 curve, MD_0, in part (a).

The opportunity cost of holding money is the interest forgone by not holding some other type of asset. But what is forgone depends partly on the interest rate that is paid on money itself. The interest rate on currency and demand deposits is zero. So for these components of money, the opportunity cost of holding money is the interest rate on non-money assets. But savings deposits and other types of deposits that are included in M2+ earn interest. So the opportunity cost of holding these forms of money is the interest rate on non-money assets minus the interest rate on these deposits.

At one time, economists believed that the quantity of money was a good indicator of the state of aggregate demand and that too rapid a growth in the quantity of money indicated that aggregate demand was growing too quickly. But the shifts in the demand for money curve have changed that belief.

REVIEW QUIZ

1 What are the main influences on the quantity of real money that people and businesses plan to hold?

2 What does the demand for money curve show?

3 How does an increase in the interest rate change the quantity of money demanded, and how would you use the demand for money curve to show the effects?

4 How does an increase in real GDP change the demand for money, and how would you use the demand for money curve to show the effects?

5 How have financial innovations changed the demand for M1 and the demand for M2+?

myeconlab **Study Plan 25.4**

Your final task in this chapter is to see how the interest rate is determined by demand and supply in the market for money.

Interest Rate Determination

AN INTEREST RATE IS THE PERCENTAGE YIELD ON a financial security such as a *bond* or a *stock*. The **interest rate** is the amount received by a lender and paid by a borrower expressed as a percentage of the amount of the loan.

A bond is a promise to make a sequence of future payments. There are many different possible sequences but the simplest one is the case of a bond called a perpetuity. A *perpetuity* is a bond that promises to pay a specified fixed amount of money each year forever. The issuer of such a bond will never buy the bond back (redeem it); the bond will remain outstanding forever and will earn a fixed dollar payment each year. Because the payment each year is a fixed dollar amount, the interest rate on a bond varies as the price of the bond varies. In the case of a perpetuity, the formula that links the interest rate to the price of the bond is a particularly simple one. That formula is

$$\text{Interest rate} = \frac{\text{Dollar payment per year}}{\text{Price of bond}} \times 100.$$

This formula states that the higher the price of a bond, other things remaining the same, the lower is the interest rate. An example will make this relationship clear. Suppose the government of Canada sells a bond that promises to pay $10 a year. If the price of the bond is $100, the interest rate is 10 percent a year—$10 is 10 percent of $100. If the price of the bond is $50, the interest rate is 20 percent a year—$10 is 20 percent of $50. If the price of the bond is $200, the interest rate is 5 percent a year—$10 is 5 percent of $200.

You've just seen the link between the price of a bond and the interest rate. Because of this link, fluctuations in the interest rate bring fluctuations in the price of a bond. People try to anticipate these fluctuations and avoid holding bonds when they expect the price of a bond to fall. But they spread their risks. To do so, they divide their wealth between bonds (and other interest-bearing financial assets) and money, and the amount they hold as money depends on the interest rate. We can study the forces that determine the interest rate either in the market for bonds or the market for money. Because the Bank of Canada can influence the supply of *money* (which we study in Chapter 27), we focus on the market for money.

Money Market Equilibrium

The supply of and the demand for money determine the interest rate. The actions of the Bank of Canada and the banking system determine the supply of money. The Bank of Canada is the sole supplier of monetary base and it can choose the terms on which currency and reserves for the banks are supplied. Two extreme cases span the range of possibilities. The Bank of Canada can either:

■ Target the quantity of money
■ Target the interest rate

Quantity of Money Target If the Bank of Canada targets the quantity of money, then the quantity of money supplied is fixed and the money supply curve is the vertical *MS* in Fig. 25.7.

On any given day, all the influences on the demand for money except for the interest rate are constant. But the lower the interest rate, the greater is the quantity of money demanded along the demand for money curve, *MD*.

When the quantity of money supplied equals the quantity of money demanded, the money market is in equilibrium. Equilibrium is achieved by changes in the interest rate. If the interest rate is above equilibrium, people demand a smaller quantity of money than the quantity supplied. They are holding too much money so they buy bonds. This action raises the price of a bond and lowers the interest rate. Conversely, if the interest rate is below equilibrium, people are holding too little money so they sell bonds. This action lowers the price of a bond and raises the interest rate. Only when the interest rate is at the level at which people are holding the quantity of money supplied do they willingly hold the money and take no actions that change the interest rate.

Interest Rate Target If the Bank of Canada targets the interest rate, then the quantity of monetary base supplied and the quantity of money supplied is the quantity demanded at the Bank's chosen interest rate.

In Fig. 25.7, if the Bank wants to set the interest rate at 5 percent a year, then the quantity of money demanded will equal $600 billion, so that will be the quantity of money in the economy. But if the Bank of Canada wants an interest rate of 4 percent a year, it must allow the monetary base and quantity of money to increase to equal the larger quantity demanded at 4 percent a year.

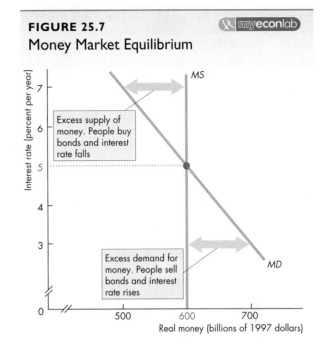

FIGURE 25.7
Money Market Equilibrium

If the Bank of Canada targets the quantity of money, equilibrium occurs when the interest rate has adjusted to make the quantity of money demanded equal to the quantity supplied. If the Bank of Canada targets the interest rate, the quantity of money adjusts to equal the quantity demanded.

◆ You now know what money is, how the banking system creates it, and how its quantity influences or might be influenced by the interest rate. The next three chapters build on this one and explain how the Bank of Canada conducts its monetary policy. In the next chapter, you will see how the exchange rate is determined and how Canada's flexible exchange rate enables the Bank of Canada to target the inflation rate. In Chapter 27, you will study the inflation process. And then, in Chapter 28, you will study monetary policy.

Canada's Changing Demand for Money

Essence of the Story

■ The use of paper money is decreasing, and the use of electronic credit and debit charges is increasing.

■ Joseph D'Cruz, a professor of strategy at the Rotman School of Management at the University of Toronto, says that cash is an inefficient system and because Canadians trust their banks, electronic systems will continue to decrease the use of cash.

■ Some retailers refuse to accept $50 bills or $100 bills because they fear counterfeiting, and some even put $5 bills through a security scan.

■ A survey shows that cash payments decreased from more than 50 percent of transactions in 1995 to 30 percent in 2001.

■ Because each transaction is small, the fast-food sector has been the most resistant to electronic transactions—but even in this sector, the use of cash is decreasing.

FINANCIAL POST, DECEMBER 3, 2002

Odds stacked against cash

From consumer demands for speed and convenience to banks' hunger for fatter returns, a collusion of forces is ensuring that the use of paper money is sliding into decline.

"Cash is a very inefficient system, physical bills don't last very long before they need replacing, if you lose it there is no recourse and it costs a lot to count and process," says Joseph D'Cruz a professor of strategy at the Rotman School of Management at the University of Toronto. "Couple that with the very high level of trust Canadians place in their national banks and the rise of electronic banking is sure to drive down the use of cash."

If Canadians have trust in their banks, they seem to have less trust in their national currency. Retailers from Dominion to Tim Hortons and Shoppers Drug Mart have refused to accept bills in $50 or $100 denominations out of counterfeiting fears. Some stores, including Loblaws, have even started to put lowly $5 bills through a security scan. It's just one more reason that cash and other paper transactions, including cheques, are giving way to debit and credit charges. ...

... Interac Direct Payment—which polls Canadians annually to establish their preferred mode of payment for goods and services—says the use of electronic payment outstripped cash transactions in 1999. ... In 1995 well over half of all transactions were made in cash, by last year cash accounted for roughly 30% of transactions, according to Interac. ...

One of the last industries to resist accepting credit and debit has been fast food—because consumers spend roughly $5 each and the merchant pays a fee for customers to pay electronically. In Canada, however, fast food joints including McDonald's, Burger King, and Wendy's introduced debit payment several years ago.

Reprinted by permission of the *National Post*.

Economic Analysis

■ Figure 1 shows the amount of currency in Canada as a percentage of GDP since 1970. This percentage decreased during the 1970s and 1980s but increased during the early 1990s and was steady after 1994.

■ The news article emphasizes reasons why the amount of currency might have *decreased*. But why did currency increase during the 1990s?

■ Currency is one component of money, and the demand for money increases when real GDP increases.

■ In Fig. 1, we graph currency *as a percentage of GDP* to remove the influence of GDP on the amount of currency held.

■ So Fig. 1 tells us that even holding real GDP constant, currency increased during the early 1990s and did not decrease in the early 2000s.

■ The reason for the increase in currency is that the interest rate, which is the opportunity cost of holding currency, decreased during the 1990s.

■ Figure 2 shows the relationship between the amount of currency (as a percentage of GDP) against the interest rate on savings accounts at chartered banks.

■ You can see that, just as predicted by the theory of the demand for money, the lower the interest rate, the greater is the quantity of currency held.

■ As the opportunity cost of holding currency increased during the 1970s, the amount of currency held (as a percentage of GDP) decreased.

■ And as the opportunity cost of holding currency decreased during the 1990s, the amount of currency held (as a percentage of GDP) increased.

■ A change in the interest rate changes the quantity of currency demanded, but it does not change the demand for currency.

■ The demand for currency changes when some other influence on payment methods changes.

■ So what is left of the message in the news article? As we increasingly use debit cards, are we using less currency?

■ Figure 2 provides part of the answer. The demand for currency has decreased. The demand curve of the 1990s is to the left of the demand curve of the 1970s.

■ But the demand for currency decreased during the early 1980s, not during the late 1990s when electronic payments technologies spread.

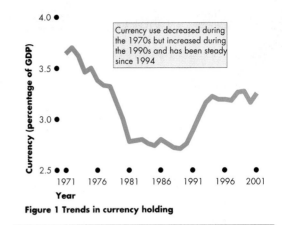

Figure 1 Trends in currency holding

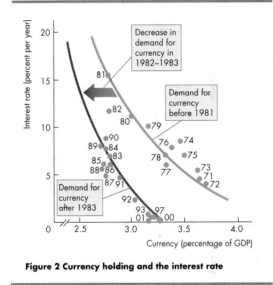

Figure 2 Currency holding and the interest rate

■ Most likely, the very high interest rate of 1981 made people think harder about how to be more economical in their use of currency, and the lesson was a permanent one.

■ Debit cards, which enable us to pay for purchases directly from our bank accounts, and credit cards, which enable us to buy on credit through the month and pay when we receive our own pay cheques, decrease our demand for currency.

■ As more and more businesses accept debit cards and credit cards and as more and more transactions are done by debit cards and credit cards, people will hold less cash.

■ But these changes are not visible in the aggregate data. Some other changes are working in the opposite direction to maintain the overall popularity of currency.

607

SUMMARY

KEY POINTS

What Is Money? (pp. 590–592)

- Money is the means of payment, a medium of exchange, a unit of account, and a store of value.
- M1 consists of currency and households' and businesses' demand deposits at chartered banks; M2+ consists of M1 plus savings deposits and other deposits at all types of depository institutions.

The Banking System (pp. 593–596)

- The banking system consists of depository institutions (the chartered banks, credit unions and caisses populaires, and trust and mortgage loan companies), the Bank of Canada, and the payments system.
- Banks provide four main economic services: They create liquidity, minimize the cost of obtaining funds, minimize the cost of monitoring borrowers, and pool risks.

How Banks Create Money (pp. 596–600)

- Banks create money by making loans.
- The total quantity of money that can be created depends on the monetary base, the desired reserves ratio, and the currency drain ratio.

The Demand for Money (pp. 601–604)

- The quantity of money demanded is the amount of money that people plan to hold.
- The quantity of real money equals the quantity of nominal money divided by the price level.
- The quantity of real money demanded depends on the interest rate, real GDP, and financial innovation. As the interest rate rises, the quantity of real money demanded decreases.

Interest Rate Determination (pp. 604–605)

- The Bank of Canada can set the quantity of money or the interest rate.
- If the quantity of money is fixed, the interest rate (and an asset price) adjusts to make the quantity of money demanded equal the quantity supplied.

- If the Bank of Canada wants to achieve a given interest rate, it must permit the monetary base and the quantity of money to adjust to equal the quantity of money demanded at that interest rate.

KEY FIGURES

Figure 25.1   Two Measures of Money, 591
Figure 25.2   How the Banking System Creates Money by Making Loans, 598
Figure 25.3   The Money Creation Process: An Example, 599
Figure 25.4   The Demand for Money, 602
Figure 25.5   Changes in the Demand for Money, 602
Figure 25.7   Money Market Equilibrium, 605

KEY TERMS

Automated Clearing Settlement System (ACSS), 596
Barter, 590
Central bank, 595
Chartered bank, 593
Credit union, 593
Currency, 591
Currency drain ratio, 597
Demand for money curve, 602
Depository institution, 593
Desired reserve ratio, 597
Excess reserves, 597
Financial innovation, 601
Interest rate, 604
Large Value Transfer System (LVTS), 596
Lender of last resort, 595
Liquidity, 592
M1, 591
M2+, 591
Means of payment, 590
Monetary base, 597
Money, 590
Money multiplier, 600
Payments system, 595
Reserve ratio, 597
Reserves, 593
Trust and mortgage loan company, 593

PROBLEMS

Go to ⓧ myeconlab for solutions to odd-numbered problems and additional exercises.

1. In Canada today, money includes which of the following items?
   a. Bank of Canada notes in the Bank of Montreal's cash machines
   b. Your Visa card
   c. The quarters inside public phones
   d. Canadian dollar coins in your pocket
   e. The cheque you have just written to pay for your rent
   f. The loan you took out last August to pay for your school fees

2. Which of the following items are money? Explain why.
   a. Demand deposits at CIBC
   b. Bell Canada stock held by individuals
   c. A "loonie"
   d. Canadian government securities

3. Sara withdraws $1,000 from her savings account at the Lucky Trust and Mortgage Company, keeps $50 in cash, and deposits the balance in her demand deposit account at the Bank of Montreal. What is the immediate change in M1 and M2+?

4. Monica takes $10,000 from her savings account at Happy Credit Union and puts the funds into her demand deposit account at the Royal Bank. What is the immediate change in M1 and M2+?

5. The banks in Zap have:

Reserves	$250 million
Loans	$1,000 million
Deposits	$2,000 million
Total assets	$2,500 million

   a. Construct the banks' balance sheet. If you are missing any assets, call them "other assets"; if you are missing any liabilities, call them "other liabilities."
   b. Calculate the banks' reserve ratio.
   c. If banks hold no excess reserves and the currency drain ratio is 10 percent, calculate the money multiplier.

6. The banks in Zip have:

Reserves	$205 million
Loans	$3,750 million
Deposits	$4,000 million
Total assets	$4,200 million

   a. Construct the banks' balance sheet. If you are missing any assets, call them "other assets"; if you are missing any liabilities, call them "other liabilities."
   b. Calculate the banks' reserve ratio.
   c. If banks hold no excess reserves and the currency drain ratio is 20 percent, calculate the money multiplier.

7. The spreadsheet provides information about the demand for money in Minland. Column A is the interest rate, R. Columns B, C, and D show the quantity of money demanded at three different levels of real GDP: Y_0 is $10 billion, Y_1 is $20 billion, and Y_2 is $30 billion. The quantity of money supplied by the Minland central bank is $3.0 billion. Initially, real GDP is $20 billion.

	A	B	C	D
1	R	Y_0	Y_1	Y_2
2	7	1.0	1.5	2.0
3	6	1.5	2.0	2.5
4	5	2.0	2.5	3.0
5	4	2.5	3.0	3.5
6	3	3.0	3.5	4.0
7	2	3.5	4.0	4.5
8	1	4.0	4.5	5.0

   What happens in Minland if
   a. The interest rate exceeds 4 percent a year?
   b. The interest rate is less than 4 percent a year?
   c. The interest rate equals 4 percent a year?

8. The Minland economy in problem 7 experiences a severe recession. Real GDP falls to $10 billion. The Minland central bank takes no action to change the quantity of money.
   a. What happens in Minland if the interest rate is 4 percent a year?
   b. What is the equilibrium interest rate?
   c. Compared with the situation in problem 7, does the interest rate in Minland rise or fall? Why?

9. The Minland economy in problem 7 experiences a severe business cycle. Real GDP rises to $30 billion and then falls to $10 billion. The Minland central bank takes no action to change the quantity of money. What happens to the interest rate in Minland

   a. During the expansion phase of the cycle?
   b. During the recession phase of the cycle?

10. Financial innovation in Minland changes the demand for money. People plan to hold $0.5 billion less than the numbers in the spreadsheet.

   a. What happens to the interest rate if the Minland central bank takes no actions?
   b. What happens to the interest rate if the Minland central bank decreases the quantity of money by $0.5 billion? Explain.

11. The figure shows the demand for real money curve in Upland.

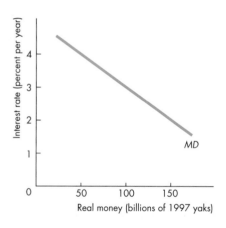

   a. In the figure, draw the supply of money curve if the interest rate is 3 percent a year.
   b. If the Upland central bank wants to lower the interest rate by 1 percentage point, by how much must it change the quantity of real money?

12. In problem 11, a new smart card replaces currency and the demand for money changes. Also, the new smart card causes business to boom and real GDP increases.

   a. Use the figure for problem 11 and draw a new demand for real money curve.
   b. If the Upland central bank wants to prevent the interest rate from changing, what must it do to the quantity of money?

CRITICAL THINKING

1. Study *Reading Between the Lines* on pp. 606–607 and then answer the following questions.

   a. What changes in the payments technology are described in the news article?
   b. What does the news article imply has happened to the amount of currency held?
   c. What are the trends in currency use?
   d. Why did the use of currency increase during the 1990s?
   e. Does the increased use of currency during the 1990s contradict the news article?
   f. What do you expect the future trends in the use of currency to be and why?

2. Rapid inflation in Brazil during the early 1990s caused the cruzeiro, the currency of Brazil, to lose its ability to function as money. People were unwilling to accept it because it lost value too fast. Which of the following items do you think would be most likely to take the place of the cruzeiro and act as money in the Brazilian economy? Why?

   a. Tractor parts
   b. Packs of cigarettes
   c. Loaves of bread
   d. Impressionist paintings
   e. Baseball trading cards

WEB EXERCISES

Use the links on (myeconlab) to work the following exercises.

1. Visit Mark Bernkopf's Central Banking Resource Centre and read the article on Electronic Cash. Also read "The End of Cash" by James Gleick (first published in the *New York Times Magazine* on June 16, 1996). Then answer the following questions.

   a. What is e-cash?
   b. Mark Bernkopf asks: "Will 'e-cash' enable private currencies to overturn the ability of governments to make monetary policy?" Will it?
   c. When you buy an item on the Internet and pay by using a form of e-cash, are you using money? Explain why or why not.
   c. In your opinion, is the concern about e-cash a real concern or hype?

The Exchange Rate

CHAPTER 26

Many Monies!

The Canadian dollar—or loonie—is just one of more than a hundred kinds of money that circulate in the global economy. The loonie is an important money, but it isn't in the truly big league. The world's four big monies are the U.S dollar (the money of the United States), the yen (of Japan), the pound (of the United Kingdom), and the euro (of the European Union). The first three have been around for a long time, and the euro is new. But although it was launched in 1999, the euro is already an international currency. Most of the world's international trade and finance is conducted using these four currencies.

In 1976, the Canadian dollar was worth a bit more than a U.S. dollar. But in 2002, the Canadian dollar fell to 63 U.S. cents before climbing back to 85 U.S. cents in 2005.

Why does the Canadian dollar fluctuate against the U.S. dollar? Is there anything we can do or should do to stabilize the value of the dollar? And why do we have a Canadian dollar? Why doesn't North America do what Europe has done and have just one money?

◆ In this chapter, you're going to learn what determines the exchange rate and why the Canadian dollar fluctuates against other currencies. You're going to see that the Bank of Canada could intervene in the foreign exchange market to peg the value of the dollar. But you're also going to see why the Bank of Canada choses to *not* intervene in this market. You will also see why we don't scrap the Canadian dollar and use the same money as the Americans. At the end of the chapter, in *Reading Between the Lines*, we'll look at the day-to-day and longer term fluctuations in the Canadian dollar.

After studying this chapter, you will be able to

- ■ **Describe the foreign exchange market and define the exchange rate**
- ■ **Explain how the exchange rate is determined**
- ■ **Explain why the exchange rate fluctuates and explain interest rate parity and purchasing power parity**
- ■ **Describe and assess the benefits and costs of a flexible exchange rate, managed exchange rate, fixed exchange rate, and monetary union**

Currencies and Exchange Rates

WHEN WE BUY FOREIGN GOODS OR INVEST IN another country, we have to obtain some of that country's money to make the transaction. When foreigners buy Canadian-produced goods or invest in Canada, they have to obtain some Canadian dollars. We get foreign money and foreigners get Canadian dollars in the foreign exchange market.

Foreign money, like Canadian money, consists of notes and coins plus bank deposits. When we described Canadian money in Chapter 25, we distinguished between currency (notes and coins) and bank deposits. But when we talk about foreign money, we usually refer to it as foreign currency and don't make the distinction between notes, coins, and bank deposits—foreign notes, coins, and bank deposits are called **foreign currency**.

Figure 26.1 shows the maginitudes of our use of the Canadian dollar and foreign currency in our international trading activities in markets for goods and services. Beyond these markets, we also use foreign currency extensively in asset markets when we borrow and lend internationally.

The figure shows the not very surprising fact that the most important foreign currency for Canada is the U.S. dollar. The European euro comes second, followed by the Japanese yen and the U.K. pound. Dozens of other currencies make up the "others" category.

The Foreign Exchange Market

We get foreign currency in the **foreign exchange market**, which is the market in which the currency of one country is exchanged for the currency of another.

The foreign exchange market is not a place like a downtown flea market or produce market. The market is made up of thousands of people—importers and exporters, banks, and specialists in the buying and selling of foreign currency—called foreign exchange brokers.

The foreign exchange market opens on Monday morning in Hong Kong, which is still Sunday evening in Montreal and Toronto. As the day advances, markets open in Singapore, Tokyo, Bahrain, Frankfurt, London, New York, Montreal, Toronto, and Vancouver. As the West Coast markets

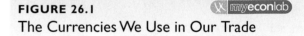

FIGURE 26.1
The Currencies We Use in Our Trade

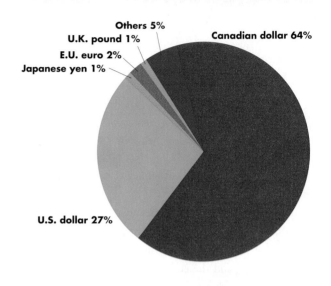

Our trade in goods and services is paid for using the Canadian dollar, the U.S. dollar, the U.K. pound, the E.U. euro, the Japanese yen, and dozens of other currencies.

Source of data: Statistics Canada, CANSIM Table 376–001 and authors' assumptions.

close, Hong Kong is only an hour away from opening for the next day of business. The sun barely sets on the foreign exchange market. Dealers around the world are in continual contact by telephone, and on a typical day in 2005, 50 billion Canadian dollars changed hands on the foreign exchange market and more than $2 trillion of all currencies were traded.

Foreign Exchange Rates

The price at which one currency exchanges for another is called a **foreign exchange rate**. For example, in October 2005, one Canadian dollar bought 85 U.S. cents. The exchange rate was 85 U.S. cents per Canadian dollar.

Figure 26.2 shows the annual average exchange rate of the Canadian dollar in terms of the U.S. dollar between 1951 and 2005. You can see that the exchange rate fluctuates. Sometimes it rises, but in most years the Canadian dollar has fallen in value against the U.S. dollar.

FIGURE 26.2

The Canadian Dollar–U.S. Dollar Exchange Rate

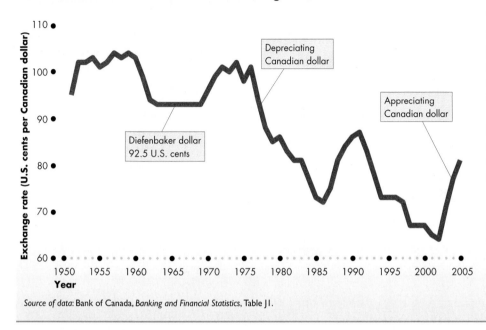

The Canadian dollar exchange rate, expressed as U.S. cents per Canadian dollar, was fixed at 92.5 U.S. cents in May 1962 (when John G. Diefenbaker was Prime Minister) until June 1970. But most of the time, the Canadian dollar fluctuates against the U.S. dollar. The Canadian dollar depreciated against the U.S. dollar from 1976 through 1986 and from 1991 through 2001. It appreciated from 1986 through 1991 and from 2002 through 2005.

Source of data: Bank of Canada, *Banking and Financial Statistics*, Table J1.

When a currency falls in value, we say that it depreciates. **Currency depreciation** is a fall in the value of one currency in terms of another currency. For example, when the Canadian dollar fell from 101 U.S. cents in 1976 to 94 U.S. cents in 1977, the Canadian dollar depreciated by 7 percent. When a currency rises in value, we say that it appreciates. **Currency appreciation** is the rise in the value of one currency in terms of another currency. From 1986 to 1991, the Canadian dollar appreciated against the U.S. dollar.

In some periods, the value of the dollar remains steady. From May 1962 to June 1970, the value of the Canadian dollar was pegged by the Bank of Canada at 92.5 U.S. cents. When the decision to peg the dollar was made, John G. Diefenbaker was the Prime Minister and the 92.5 cent dollar came to be known as the Diefenbaker dollar.

Cross Exchange Rates

We've just expressed the value of the Canadian dollar in terms of the U.S. dollar. But we can express the value of the Canadian dollar in terms of any currency—called cross exchange rates. Figure 26.3 shows some cross exchange rates in October 2005. These numbers tell us that when one Canadian dollar

FIGURE 26.3

The Cross Exchange Rates in 2005

	USD	EUR	GBP	JPY*	CAD
USD		1.20	1.76	0.87	0.85
EUR	0.83		1.47	0.72	0.71
GBP	0.57	0.68		0.49	0.48
JPY*	1.15	1.38	2.04		0.98
CAD	1.18	1.41	2.08	1.02	

The table shows cross exchange rates on October 19, 2005. USD is the U.S. dollar; EUR is the European Union euro; GBP is the U.K. pound; JPY* is 100 Japanese yen; CAD is the Canadian dollar.

Read the table vertically to see how much each currency buys. The CAD column shows how many USD, EUR, GBP, and 100s of JPY you get for 1 CAD.

Read the table horizontally to find the prices of the other currencies. The CAD row shows how many CADs you must pay for 1 USD, 1 EUR, 1 GBP or 100 JPY.

Source of data: Sauder School of Business, University of British Columbia, PACIFIC Exchange Rate Services (http://fx.sauder.ubc.ca/).

FIGURE 26.4

The Canadian Dollar Exchange Rate Against the U.K. Pound, E.U. Euro, and Japanese Yen

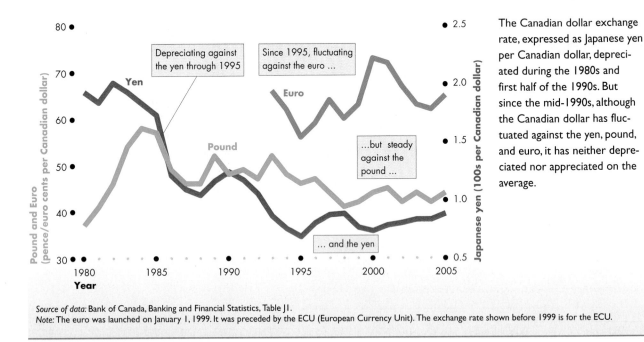

Depreciating against the yen through 1995

Since 1995, fluctuating against the euro ...

...but steady against the pound ...

... and the yen

The Canadian dollar exchange rate, expressed as Japanese yen per Canadian dollar, depreciated during the 1980s and first half of the 1990s. But since the mid-1990s, although the Canadian dollar has fluctuated against the yen, pound, and euro, it has neither depreciated nor appreciated on the average.

Source of data: Bank of Canada, Banking and Financial Statistics, Table J1.
Note: The euro was launched on January 1, 1999. It was preceded by the ECU (European Currency Unit). The exchange rate shown before 1999 is for the ECU.

bought 85 U.S. cents, it also bought 71 euro cents, 98 Japanese yen, or 48 U.K pence.

In the table in Fig. 26.3, we use the standard 3-letter names for the major currencies: CAD for the Canadian dollar, USD for the U.S. dollar, EUR for the euro, GBP for the U.K. (or Great Britain) pound, and JPY for the Japanese yen. Because the yen has a tiny value relative to the other currencies, it is common to measure the yen in 100s.

Figure 26.4 shows the longer history of the Canadian dollar against the other three major currencies—the pound, the euro and the yen—since 1980. You can see that the Canadian dollar depreciated against the yen through the 1980s and early 1990s. But since 1995, the Canadian dollar–yen exchange rate has seen only slight fluctuations and no tendency to either depreciate or appreciate.

Similarly, there has been no trend either up or down in the exchange rates between the Canadian dollar and the pound or the euro.

The performance of the Canadian dollar in the foreign exchange market raises a number of questions that we address in the rest of this chapter. First, how is the exchange rate determined? Second, why has the

Canadian dollar depreciated against the U.S. dollar and the yen? Third, how does a central bank control the exchange rate, as the Bank of Canada did during the 1960s? Fourth, how does the Bank of Canada operate in the foreign exchange market today? And fifth, why do we have our own currency? Why don't we just use the U.S. dollar and avoid currency fluctuations altogether?

REVIEW QUIZ

1 What is the foreign exchange market and what prices get determined in this market?
2 Distinguish between currency appreciation and currency depreciation.
3 When was the value of the Canadian dollar last pegged against the U.S. dollar?
4 What are the world's major currencies?
5 Against which major currencies has the Canadian dollar depreciated on the average over the past 25 years?

Study Plan 26.1

The Foreign Exchange Market

AN EXCHANGE RATE IS A PRICE—THE PRICE OF one currency in terms of another. And like all prices, an exchange rate is determined in a market—the foreign exchange market.

The Canadian dollar trades in the foreign exchange market and is supplied and demanded by tens of thousands of traders every hour of every business day. Because it has many traders and no restrictions on who may trade, the foreign exchange market is a competitive market.

In a competitive market, demand and supply determine the price. So to understand the forces that determine the exchange rate, we need to study the factors that influence demand and supply in the foreign exchange market. But there is a feature of the foreign exchange market that makes it special.

The Demand for One Money Is the Supply of Another Money

When people who are holding the money of some other country want to exchange it for Canadian dollars, they demand Canadian dollars and supply that other country's money. And when people who are holding Canadian dollars want to exchange them for

Dealers in the foreign exchange market

the money of some other country, they supply Canadian dollars and demand that other country's money.

So the factors that influence the demand for Canadian dollars also influence the supply of U.S. dollars, E.U. euros, U.K. pounds, and Japanese yen. And the factors that influence the demand for those other country's money also influence the supply of Canadian dollars.

We'll first look at the influences on the demand for Canadian dollars in the foreign exchange market.

Demand in the Foreign Exchange Market

People buy Canadian dollars in the foreign exchange market so that they can buy Canadian-made goods and services—Canadian exports. They also buy Canadian dollars so they can buy Canadian assets such as bonds, stocks, businesses, and real estate, or so that they can keep part of their money holding in a Canadian dollar bank account.

The quantity of Canadian dollars demanded in the foreign exchange market is the amount that traders plan to buy during a given time period at a given exchange rate. This quantity depends on many factors but the main ones are

1. The exchange rate
2. World demand for Canadian exports
3. Interest rates in Canada and other countries
4. The expected future exchange rate

So that we can first isolate the exchange rate and see how it is determined, we'll look first at the relationship between the quantity of Canadian dollars demanded in the foreign exchange market and the exchange rate when the other three influences remain the same—the law of demand in the foreign exchange market. In the next section, we'll consider what happens when these other influences change.

The Law of Demand for Foreign Exchange

The law of demand applies to dollars just as it does to anything else that people value. Other things remaining the same, the higher the exchange rate, the smaller is the quantity of Canadian dollars demanded in the foreign exchange market. For example, if the price of the Canadian dollar rose from 80 U.S. cents to 90 U.S. cents but nothing else changed, the quantity of Canadian dollars that people plan to buy in the foreign exchange market would decrease. The exchange rate influences the quantity of dollars demanded for two reasons:

- Exports effect
- Expected profit effect

Exports Effect The larger the value of Canadian exports, the larger is the quantity of Canadian dollars demanded on the foreign exchange market. But the value of Canadian exports depends on the prices of Canadian-made goods and services *expressed in the currency of the foreign buyer*. But these prices depend on the exchange rate. The lower the exchange rate, with other things remaining the same, the lower are the prices of Canadian-produced goods and services to foreigners and the greater is the volume of Canadian exports. So if the exchange rate falls (and other influences remain the same), the quantity of Canadian dollars demanded on the foreign exchange market increases.

To see this effect at work, think about Bombardier, a Montreal firm, that produces a popular airplane called the Canada Regional Jet or CRJ. If the price of a CRJ is $C1 million and the exchange rate is 90 U.S. cents per dollar, the price of this airplane to American Airlines is $US900,000. American Airlines decides that this price is too high, so it doesn't by a CRJ. If the exchange rate falls to 80 U.S. cents per Canadian dollar and nothing else changes, the price of a CRJ now falls to $US800,000. American Airlines now decides to buy a CRJ and buys Canadian dollars on the foreign exchange market.

Expected Profit Effect The larger the expected profit from holding Canadian dollars, the greater is the quantity of Canadian dollars demanded today. But expected profit depends on the exchange rate. The lower today's exchange rate, other things remaining the same, the larger is the expected profit from buying Canadian dollars and the greater is the quantity of Canadian dollars demanded today.

To see this effect at work, suppose that American Express expects the Canadian dollar exchange rate to be 90 U.S. cents at the end of the year. If today's exchange rate is also 90 U.S. cents, there is no gain from buying Canadian dollars now and selling them

at the end of the year. But if the Canadian dollar falls to 80 U.S. cents, and other things remain the same, there is now a 10 cents per dollar profit to be earned.

The lower today's exchange rate, other things remaining the same, the greater is the expected profit from holding Canadian dollars and the greater is the quantity of Canadian dollars demanded today on the foreign exchange market.

Demand Curve for Canadian Dollars

Figure 26.5 shows the demand curve for Canadian dollars in the foreign exchange market. A change in the exchange rate, other things remaining the same, brings a change in the quantity of Canadian dollars demanded and a movement along the demand curve as shown by the arrows.

We will look at the factors that change demand in the next section of this chapter. But first, let's see what determines the supply of Canadian dollars.

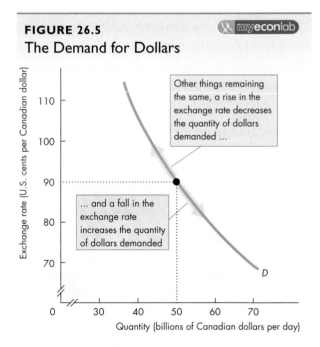

FIGURE 26.5   myeconlab
The Demand for Dollars

Other things remaining the same, a rise in the exchange rate decreases the quantity of dollars demanded ...

... and a fall in the exchange rate increases the quantity of dollars demanded

Exchange rate (U.S. cents per Canadian dollar)

Quantity (billions of Canadian dollars per day)

The quantity of Canadian dollars that people plan to buy depends on the exchange rate. Other things remaining the same, if the exchange rate rises, the quantity of dollars demanded decreases and there is a movement up along the demand curve for dollars. If the exchange rate falls, the quantity of dollars demanded increases and there is a movement down along the demand curve for dollars.

Supply in the Foreign Exchange Market

People sell Canadian dollars and buy other currencies so that they can buy foreign-made goods and services—Canadian imports. People also sell Canadian dollars and buy foreign currencies so that they can buy foreign assets such as bonds, stocks, businesses, and real estate, or so that they can hold part of their money in bank deposits denominated in a foreign currency.

The quantity of Canadian dollars supplied in the foreign exchange market is the amount that traders plan to sell during a given time period at a given exchange rate. This quantity depends on many factors but the main ones are

1. The exchange rate
2. Canadian demand for imports
3. Interest rates in Canada and other countries
4. The expected future exchange rate

Let's look at the relationship between the quantity of Canadian dollars supplied in the foreign exchange market and the exchange rate when the other three influences remain the same—the law of supply in the foreign exchange market.

The Law of Supply of Foreign Exchange

Other things remaining the same, the higher the exchange rate, the greater is the quantity of dollars supplied in the foreign exchange market. For example, if the price of the Canadian dollar rose from 80 U.S. cents to 90 U.S. cents but nothing else changed, the quantity of Canadian dollars that people plan to sell in the foreign exchange market would increase.

The exchange rate influences the quantity of dollars supplied for two reasons:

■ Imports effect
■ Expected profit effect

Imports Effect The larger the value of Canadian imports, the larger is the quantity of Canadian dollars supplied on the foreign exchange market. But the value of Canadian imports depends on the prices of foreign-made goods and services *expressed in Canadian dollars*. So these prices depend on the exchange rate. The higher the exchange rate, with other things remaining the same, the lower are the prices of foreign-produced goods and services to Canadians and the greater is the volume of Canadian imports. So if the exchange rate rises (and other

influences remain the same), the quantity of Canadian dollars supplied on the foreign exchange market increases.

Expected Profit Effect This effect works just like that on the demand for the Canadian dollar but in the opposite direction. The higher the exchange rate, other things remaining the same, the larger is the expected profit from selling Canadian dollars and the greater is the quantity of Canadian dollars supplied.

Supply Curve for Canadian Dollars

Figure 26.6 shows the supply curve of Canadian dollars in the foreign exchange market. A change in the exchange rate, other things remaining the same, brings a change in the quantity of Canadian dollars supplied and a movement along the supply curve as shown by the arrows.

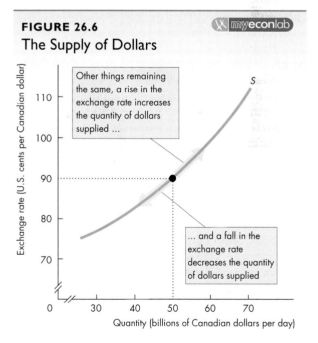

FIGURE 26.6 myeconlab
The Supply of Dollars

Other things remaining the same, a rise in the exchange rate increases the quantity of dollars supplied ...

... and a fall in the exchange rate decreases the quantity of dollars supplied

The quantity of Canadian dollars that people plan to sell depends on the exchange rate. Other things remaining the same, if the exchange rate rises, the quantity of Canadian dollars supplied increases and there is a movement up along the supply curve of dollars. If the exchange rate falls, the quantity of Canadian dollars supplied decreases and there is a movement down along the supply curve of dollars.

Market Equilibrium

Equilibrium in the foreign exchange market depends on how the Bank of Canada operates. Here, we will study equilibrium when the Bank keeps out of this market. In a later section (on pp. 623–625), we examine the effects of alternative actions that the Bank of Canada might take in the foreign exchange market.

Figure 26.7 shows the demand curve for Canadian dollars, *D*, from Fig. 26.5 and the supply curve of Canadian dollars, *S*, from Fig. 26.6, and the equilibrium exchange rate.

The exchange rate acts as a regulator of the quantities demanded and supplied. If the exchange rate is too high, there is a surplus—the quantity supplied exceeds the quantity demanded. For example, in Fig. 26.7, if the exchange rate is 100 U.S. cents per Canadian dollar, there is a surplus of Canadian dollars. If the exchange rate is too low, there is a shortage—the quantity supplied is less than the quantity demanded. For example, in Fig. 26.7, if the exchange rate is 80 U.S. cents per Canadian dollar, there is a shortage of Canadian dollars.

At the equilibrium exchange rate, there is neither a shortage nor a surplus. The quantity supplied equals the quantity demanded. In Fig. 26.7, the equilibrium exchange rate is 90 U.S. cents per Canadian dollar. At this exchange rate, the quantity demanded and the quantity supplied are each $50 billion a day.

The foreign exchange market is constantly pulled to its equilibrium by the forces of supply and demand. Foreign exchange dealers are constantly looking for the best price they can get. If they are selling, they want the highest price available. If they are buying, they want the lowest price available. Information flows from dealer to dealer through the worldwide computer network and the price adjusts second by second to keep buying plans and selling plans in balance. That is, price adjusts minute by minute to keep the market at its equilibrium.

Equilibrium Cross Exchange Rates

In Fig. 26.7, we look only at the exchange rate between the Canadian dollar and the U.S. dollar. The exchange rates between the Canadian dollar and all other currencies are determined in a similar way. But all the cross exchange rates (see Fig 26.3, p. 613) line up so that no profit can be made by buying one currency, selling it for a second one, and then buying back the first one.

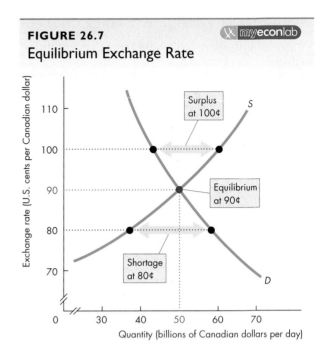

FIGURE 26.7 myeconlab
Equilibrium Exchange Rate

The demand curve for dollars is *D* and the supply curve is *S*. If the exchange rate is 100 U.S. cents per dollar, there is a surplus of dollars and the exchange rate falls. If the exchange rate is 80 U.S. cents per dollar, there is a shortage of dollars and the exchange rate rises. If the exchange rate is 90 U.S. cents per dollar, there is neither a shortage nor a surplus of dollars and the exchange rate remains constant. The foreign exchange market is in equilibrium.

REVIEW QUIZ

1 What are the influences on the demand for Canadian dollars in the foreign exchange market?
2 Provide an example of the exports effect on the demand for Canadian dollars.
3 What are the influences on the supply of Canadian dollars in the foreign exchange market?
4 Provide an example of the imports effect on the supply of Canadian dollars.
5 How is the equilibrium exchange rate determined?

myeconlab **Study Plan 26.2**

Changes in Demand and Supply: Exchange Rate Fluctuations

WHEN THE DEMAND FOR DOLLARS OR THE SUPPLY of dollars changes, the exchange rate changes. We'll now look at the factors that make demand and supply change, starting with the demand side of the market.

Changes in the Demand for Dollars

The demand for dollars on the foreign exchange market changes when any of the following influences change:

- World demand for Canadian exports
- Interest rates in Canada and other countries
- The expected future exchange rate

World Demand for Canadian Exports An increase in world demand for Canadian exports increases the demand for Canadian dollars. To see this effect, think further about Bombardier's sales of CRJ aircraft. An increase in demand for air travel in the United States sends U.S. airlines on a global shopping spree. They decide that the CRJ is the ideal product for them so they order 50 airplanes from Bombardier. The demand for Canadian dollars now increases.

Interest Rates in Canada and Other Countries The higher the interest rate that people can make on Canadian assets compared with foreign assets, the more Canadian assets they buy and the more Canadian dollars they demand on the foreign exchange market.

What matters is not the *level* of Canadian interest rates, but the Canadian interest rate minus the foreign interest rate—a gap called the **Canadian interest rate differential**.

If the Canadian interest rate differential increases by 1 percentage point and other things remain the same, people can earn an extra 1 percent by borrowing in the United States and lending in Canada. As people take advantage of this profit opportunity, the demand for Canadian dollars increases.

The Expected Future Exchange Rate For a given current exchange rate, and all other things remaining the same, a rise in the expected future exchange rate increases the profit that people expect to earn by

holding Canadian dollars and increases the demand for Canadian dollars today.

Figure 26.8 summarizes the influences on the demand for dollars. If the demand for Canadian dollars increases, the demand curve shifts rightward from D_0 to D_1. And if the demand for Canadian dollars decreases, the demand curve shifts leftward from D_0 to D_2.

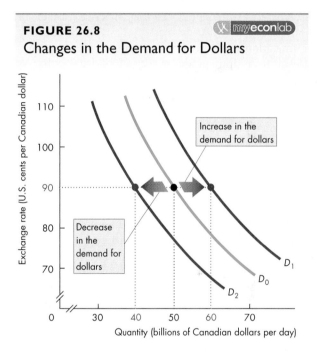

FIGURE 26.8   myeconlab

Changes in the Demand for Dollars

A change in any influence on the quantity of Canadian dollars that people plan to buy, other than today's exchange rate, brings a change in the demand for Canadian dollars.

The demand for Canadian dollars

Increases if:	*Decreases if:*
World demand for Canadian exports increases	World demand for Canadian exports decreases
The Canadian interest rate differential increases	The Canadian interest rate differential decreases
The expected future exchange rate rises	The expected future exchange rate falls

Changes in the Supply of Dollars

The supply of dollars in the foreign exchange market changes when any of the following influences change:

- Canadian demand for imports
- Interest rates in Canada and other countries
- The expected future exchange rate

Canadian Demand for Imports An increase in Canadian demand for imports increases the supply of the Canadian dollar on the foreign exchange market. To see why, think about Bell Canada's purchase of database systems. An increase in demand for telecommunication services sends Bell Canada out shopping for more equipment and services. Bell decides that Oracle's database system produced in the United States is just what it needs, so it increases its purchases from Oracle. The supply of Canadian dollars now increases as Bell goes to the foreign exchange market to get more U.S. dollars.

Interest Rates in Canada and Other Countries The effect of the Canadian interest rate differential on the supply of Canadian dollars is the opposite of its effect on the demand for Canadian dollars. The larger the Canadian interest rate differential, the *smaller* is the supply of Canadian dollars on the foreign exchange market. The supply is smaller because the demand for *foreign* assets is smaller. If people spend less on foreign assets, they supply a smaller quantity of Canadian dollars on the foreign exchange market. So, a rise in the Canadian interest rate, other things remaining the same, decreases the supply of Canadian dollars.

The Expected Future Exchange Rate For a given current exchange rate, and all other things remaining the same, a fall in the expected future exchange rate decreases the profit that people expect to earn by holding Canadian dollars and decreases the quantity of Canadian dollars that people want to hold. To lower their holdings of Canadian dollar assets, people must sell dollars. When they do so, the supply of Canadian dollars on the foreign exchange market increases.

Figure 26.9 summarizes the influences on the supply of dollars. If the supply of Canadian dollars decreases, the supply curve shifts leftward from S_0 to S_1. And if the supply of Canadian dollars increases, the supply curve shifts rightward from S_0 to S_2.

Changes in the Exchange Rate

If the demand for dollars increases and the supply of dollars does not change, the exchange rate rises. If the demand for dollars decreases and the supply of dollars does not change, the exchange rate falls. Similarly, if the supply of dollars decreases and the demand for dollars does not change, the exchange rate rises. If the supply of dollars increases and the demand for dollars does not change, the exchange rate falls. Let's look at two episodes in the life of the Canadian dollar.

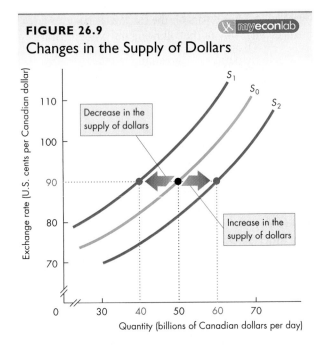

FIGURE 26.9
Changes in the Supply of Dollars

A change in any influence on the quantity of Canadian dollars that people plan to sell, other than today's exchange rate, brings a change in the supply of Canadian dollars.

The supply of Canadian dollars

Increases if:
- Canadian import demand increases
- The Canadian interest rate differential decreases
- The expected future exchange rate falls

Decreases if:
- Canadian import demand decreases
- The Canadian interest rate differential increases
- The expected future exchange rate rises

A Depreciating Dollar: 1991–2002 Between 1991 and 2002, the Canadian dollar fell from 87 U.S. cents to 64 U.S. cents per dollar. Figure 26.10(a) provides a possible explanation for this fall.

In 1991, the demand and supply curves were those labelled D and S_{91}. The exchange rate was 87 U.S. cents per dollar and $30 billion a day were traded.

During the 1990s, the North American Free Trade Agreement (NAFTA) came into effect and the volume of trade between Canada and the United States increased. The supply of Canadian dollars increased. The demand for Canadian dollars would have increased but traders expected the Canadian dollar to depreciate, which offset the factors leading to an increase in demand. Figure 26.10 assumes no change in demand and an increase in supply to S_{02}. The increase in supply with no change in demand lowered the exchange rate and increased the quantity of dollars traded.

An Appreciating Dollar: 2002–2005 Between 2002 and 2005 the Canadian dollar appreciated. It rose from 64 U.S. cents in 2002 to 81 U.S. cents per dollar in 2005. Figure 26.10(b) provides a possible explanation for this rise.

In 2002, the demand and supply curves were those labelled D_{02} and S_{02}—the same curves that Fig. 26.10(a) ends with.

During 2004 and 2005, the world demand for resources increased, driven mainly by rapid economic growth in China and India. The result was a large increase in the world demand for Canadian exports and an increase in the demand for the Canadian dollar. The demand curve shifted from D_{02} to D_{05}. This increase in demand and rise in the Canadian dollar was expected and, as a result, the supply of dollars decreased. The supply curve shifted from S_{02} to S_{05}. The increase in demand and decrease in supply raised the exchange rate from 64 U.S. cents to 81 U.S. cents but left the quantity traded unchanged.

FIGURE 26.10
Exchange Rate Fluctuations

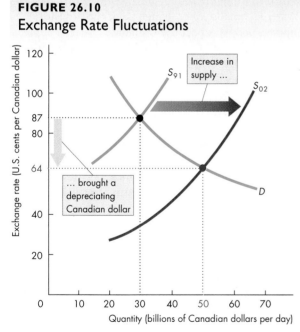

(a) 1991 to 2002

Between 1991 and 2002 in part (a), the Canadian dollar fell from 87 U.S. cents to 64 U.S. cents per dollar. This depreciation occurred because as NAFTA came into effect, the volume of trade increased, which increased both the supply and demand for dollars. But traders expected this depreciation, which offset the increase in demand.

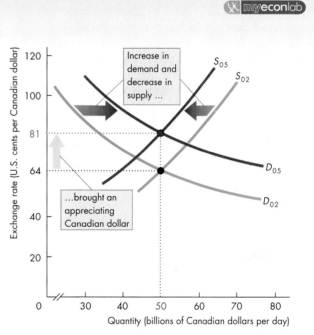

(b) 2002 to 2005

Between 2001 and 2005 in part (b), the exchange rate rose from 64 U.S. cents to 81 U.S. cents per dollar. This appreciation occurred because the world demand for resources increased Canadian exports and increased the demand for dollars. Traders' expected this appreciation, which decreased the supply of dollars.

Exchange Rate Expectations

The changes in the exchange rate that we've just examined occurred in part because the exchange rate was *expected to change.* Explaining a change as arising because it was expected sounds a bit like a self-fulfilling forecast. What makes expectations change? The answer is new information about the deeper forces that influence the value of money. Two such forces are

- Purchasing power parity
- Interest rate parity

Purchasing Power Parity Money is worth what it will buy. But two kinds of money, Canadian dollars and U.S. dollars, for example, might buy different amounts of goods and services. Suppose a Big Mac costs $C4 in Toronto and $US3 in New York. If the Canadian dollar exchange rate is 75 U.S. cents per Canadian dollar, the two monies have the same value. You can buy a Big Mac in either Toronto or New York for either $C4 or $US3.

The situation we've just described is called **purchasing power parity**, which means *equal value of money.* If purchasing power parity does not prevail, some powerful forces go to work. To understand these forces, let's suppose that the price of a Big Mac in New York rises to $US4 but in Toronto it remains at $C4. Suppose the exchange rate remains at 75 U.S. cents per Canadian dollar. In this case, a Big Mac in Toronto still costs $C4 or $US3. But in New York, it costs $US4 or $C5.33. Money buys more in Canada than in the United States. Money is not of equal value in the two countries.

If all (or most) prices have increased in the United States and have not increased in Canada, then people will generally expect that the value of the Canadian dollar on the foreign exchange market must rise. In this situation, the exchange rate is expected to rise. The demand for Canadian dollars increases and the supply of Canadian dollars decreases. The exchange rate rises, as expected. If the exchange rate rises to $US1.00 per Canadian dollar and there are no further price changes, purchasing power parity is restored. A Big Mac now costs $4 in either Canadian or U.S. dollars in New York and in Toronto.

If prices increase in Canada but remain constant in other countries, then people will generally expect that the value of the Canadian dollar on the foreign exchange market is too high and that it is going to

fall. In this situation, the exchange rate is expected to fall. The demand for Canadian dollars decreases and the supply of Canadian dollars increases. The exchange rate falls, as expected.

Ultimately, the value of money is determined by the price level, which in turn is determined by aggregate supply and aggregate demand (see Chapter 22). So the deeper forces that influence the exchange rate have tentacles that spread throughout the economy. If the price level rises more quickly in Canada than in other countries, the exchange rate falls. And if the price level rises more slowly in Canada than in other countries, the exchange rate rises.

Interest Rate Parity Money is worth what it can earn. Again two kinds of money, Canadian dollars and U.S. dollars, might earn different amounts. For example, suppose a Canadian dollar bank deposit in Toronto earns 4 percent a year and a U.S. dollar bank deposit in New York earns 5 percent a year. In this situation, why does anyone deposit money in Toronto? Why doesn't all the money flow to New York? The answer is: because of exchange rate expectations. Suppose people expect the Canadian dollar to appreciate by 1 percent a year. This 1 percent appreciation must be added to the 4 percent interest to obtain a return of 5 percent a year that an American can earn by depositing funds in a Toronto bank. The two returns are equal. This situation is one of **interest rate parity**, which means *equal interest rates* when exchange rate changes are taken into account.

Adjusted for risk, interest rate parity always prevails. Funds move to get the highest return available. If for a few seconds a higher return is available in Toronto than in New York, the demand for Canadian dollars rises and the exchange rate rises until the expected returns are equal.

REVIEW QUIZ

1 Why does the demand for dollars change?
2 Why does the supply of dollars change?
3 What makes the dollar fluctuate?
4 What is purchasing power parity and what happens when this condition doesn't hold?
5 What is interest rate parity and what happens if this condition doesn't hold?

 myeconlab   **Study Plan 26.3**

Exchange Rate Policy

BECAUSE THE EXCHANGE RATE IS THE PRICE OF A country's money in terms of another country's money, governments and central banks must have a policy towards the exchange rate. Four distinctly different exchange rate policies are

- Flexible exchange rate
- Fixed exchange rate
- Crawling peg
- Currency union

Flexible Exchange Rate

A **flexible exchange rate** policy is one that permits the exchange rate to be determined by demand and supply with no direct intervention in the foreign exchange market by the central bank. The Bank of Canada operates a flexible exchange rate.

But even a flexible exchange rate is influenced by central bank actions. If the Bank of Canada raises the Canadian interest rate and other countries keep their interest rates unchanged, the demand for Canadian dollars increases, the supply of Canadian dollars decreases, and the exchange rate rises. (Similarly, if the Bank of Canada lowers the Canadian interest rate, the demand for Canadian dollars decreases, the supply increases, and the exchange rate falls.)

In a flexible exchange rate regime, when the central bank changes the interest rate, its purpose is *not* to influence the exchange rate. Its purpose is to achieve some other monetary policy objective. (We return to this topic at length in Chapter 28.)

Fixed Exchange Rate

A **fixed exchange rate** policy is one that pegs the exchange rate at a value decided by the government or central bank and that blocks the unregulated forces of demand and supply by direct intervention in the foreign exchange market. The Bank of Canada operated a fixed exchange rate during the 1960s when the dollar was pegged at 92.5 U.S. cents.

To maintain a fixed exchange rate, the Bank of Canada would buy dollars to prevent the exchange rate from falling below the target value and sell dollars to prevent the exchange rate from rising above the target value. There is no limit to the quantity of dollars that the Bank of Canada can sell. But there is a

limit to the quantity of dollars the Bank of Canada can buy. That limit is set by the Bank's and the government of Canada's holdings of foreign currency reserves.

Let's look at the foreign exchange interventions that the Bank of Canada can make.

Suppose the Bank of Canada wants the exchange rate to be steady at 90 U.S. cents per dollar. If the exchange rate rises above 90 U.S. cents, the Bank sells dollars. If the exchange rate falls below 90 U.S. cents, the Bank buys dollars. By these actions, it changes the supply of dollars and keeps the exchange rate close to its target rate of 90 U.S. cents per Canadian dollar.

Figure 26.11 shows the Bank of Canada's intervention in the foreign exchange market. The supply of dollars is S and initially the demand for dollars is D_0. The equilibrium exchange rate is 90 U.S. cents

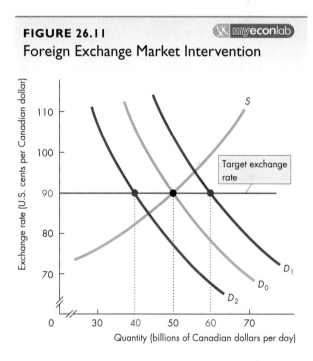

FIGURE 26.11
Foreign Exchange Market Intervention

Initially, the demand for dollars is D_0, the supply of dollars is S, and the exchange rate is 90 U.S. cents per dollar. The Bank of Canada can intervene in the foreign exchange market to keep the exchange rate close to its target rate (90 U.S. cents per dollar in this example). If demand increases from D_0 to D_1, the Bank sells dollars to increase supply. If demand decreases from D_0 to D_2, the Bank buys dollars to decrease supply. Persistent intervention on one side of the foreign exchange market cannot be sustained.

per dollar. This exchange rate is the Bank's target rate, shown by the horizontal red line.

When the demand for dollars increases and the demand curve shifts rightward to D_1, the Bank of Canada sells $10 billion. This action increases the supply of dollars by $10 billion and prevents the exchange rate from rising. When the demand for dollars decreases and the demand curve shifts leftward to D_2, the Bank buys $10 billion. This action decreases the supply of dollars by $10 billion and prevents the exchange rate from falling.

If the demand for dollars fluctuates between D_1 and D_2 and on the average is D_0, the Bank of Canada can repeatedly intervene in the way we've just seen. Sometimes the Bank buys and sometimes it sells but, on the average, it neither buys nor sells.

But suppose the demand for dollars increases permanently from D_0 to D_1. The Bank cannot now maintain the exchange rate at 90 U.S. cents indefinitely. For to do so, the Bank would have to sell dollars every day. When the Bank sells dollars in the foreign exchange market, it buys foreign currency. So the Bank would be piling up foreign currency.

Now suppose the demand for dollars decreases permanently from D_0 to D_2. Again the Bank cannot maintain the exchange rate at 90 U.S. cents indefinitely. In this situation, to hold the exchange rate at 90 U.S. cents per dollar the Bank would have to buy dollars every day. When the Bank buys dollars in the foreign exchange market, it uses its holdings of foreign currency. So the Bank would be losing foreign currency. Eventually, it would run out of foreign currency and would then have to abandon its attempt to fix the exchange rate.

Crawling Peg

A **crawling peg** exchange rate policy is one that selects a target path for the exchange rate with intervention in the foreign exchange market to achieve that path. The Bank of Canada has never operated a crawling peg. But some prominent countries do use this system. China is one of the most recent to do so.

A crawling peg works like a fixed exchange rate except that the target value changes. Sometimes the target changes once a month and sometimes it changes every day.

The idea behind a crawling peg is to avoid wild swings in the exchange rate that might happen if expectations became volatile and to avoid the prob-

lem of running out of reserves, which can happen with a fixed exchange rate.

Currency Union

A **currency union** is a merger of the currencies of a number of countries to form a single money and avoid foreign exchange transactions. The most recently formed currency union is that of the European Union, which has replaced the national monies of France, Germany, Italy, and several other countries with the euro.

Although a currency union is not on the Canadian political agenda, two well-respected Canadian economists, Thomas J. Courchene of Queen's University and Richard Harris of Simon Fraser University, have advocated a currency union between Canada and the United States. What are the benefits and costs of a currency union?

The benefits of a currency union are

- Transparency and competition improve
- Transactions costs fall
- Foreign exchange risk is eliminated
- The real interest rate falls

Transparency and Competition Improve A single currency provides a single unit of account, so prices are easily compared across all the members of the currency union. A country might gain a competitive advantage by becoming more efficient, but it cannot gain an advantage by artificially lowering the prices of its exports through currency depreciation.

Transactions Costs Fall A single currency eliminates foreign exchange transactions costs—the costs of converting Canadian dollars to U.S. dollars or the reverse conversion. To see how big these costs are, take a look at the price you would pay for some U.S. dollars and then look at the price you could get in Canadian dollars if you had some U.S. dollars to sell. You will be shocked at the size of the margin that the banks take when they do a foreign exchange transaction for an ordinary person or small business.

For the European Union, it has been estimated that eliminating foreign exchange transactions has saved 0.4 percent of GDP each year. If Canada saved 0.4 percent of its GDP, it would gain more than $4 billion a year.

Foreign Exchange Risk Eliminated With a single currency, exporters and importers no longer face foreign exchange risk. For example, Focus, a Canadian firm that makes snowboards, sells a consignment of boards to Big5, a U.S. sporting goods retailer. The boards are sold for $US400,000, which, on the day they are shipped is $C500,000. When Big5 gets around to paying for the boards six weeks later, Focus will get $C500,000 only if the exchange rate hasn't changed. But the exchange rate might increase or decrease, exposing Focus to unwanted risk. Focus can avoid this risk by buying Canadian dollars for U.S. dollars in the forward exchange market but only by paying a commission.

The elimination of this exchange risk greatly simplifies the life of Focus and thousands of firms like it.

Real Interest Rates Fall The real interest rate is the cost of capital and the return to saving. It includes a premium for risk. One type of risk is that of default: a borrower not repaying a lender. This type of risk is not affected by currency arrangements. But another type of risk arises from currency fluctuations and inflation fluctuations. If a single currency can eliminate or at least lower these risks, it can lower the real interest rate and stimulate saving and investment.

A currency union also has costs. The two major ones are:

- Shocks that need national monetary policy
- Loss of sovereignty

Shocks that Need National Monetary Policy A single currency means a single monetary policy—in the North American context, one monetary policy for the United States and Canada. But many economic shocks call for a monetary policy response that is specific to the economy receiving the shock. For example, a global energy boom increases aggregate demand in Canada by a bigger percentage than in the United States. So if Canada wants to avoid inflation, it needs to take greater offsetting actions when such a shock occurs than the United States needs to take. Similarly, faster productivity growth in the United States means that aggregate demand can grow faster there than in Canada while avoiding inflation. So to allow for this difference, Canada would want aggregate demand to grow more slowly.

A single common monetary policy is inadequate to deal with differences of these types.

Loss of Sovereignty If a country joins with another or group of other countries to form a currency union, each country surrenders some sovereignty. No longer can each government decide what its monetary policy will be. In principle, national fiscal policy might be used to pursue national economic policy goals where monetary policy is not available. But usually, before a currency union can be agreed upon, some limits must also be agreed for the use of fiscal policy. In Europe, for example, the nations that use the euro have entered into a *Stability and Growth Pact* that places limits on the use of fiscal policy and replaces national freedom of action with a common regional policy.

It is very unlikely that Canada will abandon the Canadian dollar in favour of the U.S. dollar and equally unlikely that the Americans would want to abandon their dollar and join with Canada (and Mexico) in creating a North American dollar equivalent to the euro. In fact, many people are holding their breath waiting for the euro to vanish!

It is also unlikely that Canada will want to abandon its flexible exchange rate policy in favour of a fixed rate or a sliding peg. We'll see in Chapter 28 how Canada takes advantage of the freedom and flexibility that its foreign exchange market policy permits.

REVIEW QUIZ

1 What is a flexible exchange rate and how does it work?
2 What is a fixed exchange rate and how does it get fixed?
3 What is a crawling peg and how does it work?
4 What is a currency union and what are its benefits and costs?

myeconlab Study Plan 26.4

Reading Between the Lines on pages 626–627 looks at the strengthening of the Canadian dollar in 2005. In the next chapter, we look at the constraint on monetary policy imposed by the short-run output inflation tradeoff. Then in Chapter 28, we see how the Bank of Canada conducts its monetary policy.

The Strengthening Canadian Dolar

RESOURCE NEWS INTERNATIONAL, NOVEMBER 23, 2005

Canadian Dollar and Business Outlook

The Canadian dollar continued to show some strength Wednesday morning as favorable domestic data and a generally weaker tone for the US dollar supported the Canadian currency. Strong natural gas and crude oil prices also helped support the Canadian dollar.

Canada's leading indicator was up 0.5% in October compared to the previous month, reported Statistics Canada. The increase came in above analyst expectations for a 0.3% rise, and provided some support for the Canadian dollar.

In addition, recent news out of the US suggests that the US Fed may slow down their pace of interest rate hikes. Meanwhile, the Bank of Canada is still expected to continue raising rates into the new year.

Currently the Bank of Canada's overnight rate of 3.00% compares with the US rate of 4.00%.

Activity was light in the currency markets, as some participants start to back away ahead of the US Thanksgiving holiday on Thursday.

The Canadian dollar was trading at 85.27 US cents (C$1.1728) early in the day, up from Tuesday's North American closing level of 85.13 US cents (C$1.1747). ...

Reprinted by permission of Resource News International.

Essence of the Story

■ The Canadian dollar exchange rate rose slightly on November 23, 2005.

■ The identified sources of the rise were rising energy prices, a stronger than expected economy, and the prospect of rising Canadian interest rates and constant U.S. interest rates.

■ The volume of activity on the foreign exchange market was light as traders began to head for the U.S. Thanksgiving holiday.

■ The exchange rate was 85.27 U.S. cents, up from 85.13 U.S. cents during the day.

Economic Analysis

■ This news article is an example of a similar article that appears every business day.

■ Notice how small movements in the exchange rate (down to 100ths of a cent) are regarded as significant and in need of explanation.

■ Much of the daily movement in the exchange rate is random noise.

■ Figure 1 shows the daily, weekly, and monthly changes in the Canadian dollar exchange rate (all expressed at monthly percentage rates.)

■ The grey line is the daily change, the blue line is the weekly change, and the red line is the monthly change.

■ You can see that most of the daily changes reverse themselves a day or two later.

■ The weekly changes are also noisy and tend to reverse themselves.

■ The monthly changes reveal the more permanent movements and the general direction of change in the exchange rate.

■ Figure 2 shows the monthly changes since 2000, this time expressed as annual rates of change.

■ You can see that the dollar appreciated strongly during 2003 and again, more slowly but persistently during 2005.

■ Changes in world prices of energy and other commodity resources of which Canada has a comparative abundance, are one of the major influences on these broader trends in the exchange rate.

■ The Canadian-U.S. inflation difference and interest rate differential are two other factors.

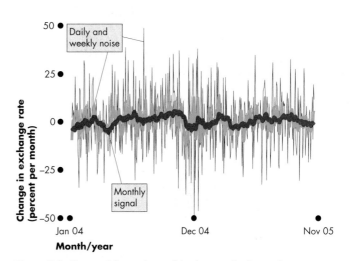

Figure 1 Daily, weekly, and monthly changes in the exchange rate

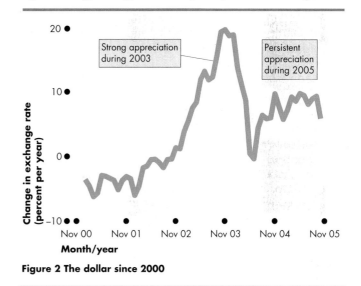

Figure 2 The dollar since 2000

627

SUMMARY

KEY POINTS

Currencies and Exchange Rates (pp. 612–614)

- Foreign currency is obtained in exchange for domestic currency in the foreign exchange market.
- The exchange rate is the price of one currency in terms of another.
- Exchange rates fluctuate and a currency might depreciate or appreciate against other currencies.

The Foreign Exchange Market (pp. 615–618)

- Demand and supply in the foreign exchange market determine the exchange rate.
- The higher the exchange rate, the smaller is the quantity of dollars demanded and the greater is the quantity of dollars supplied.
- The equilibrium exchange rate makes the quantity of dollars demanded equal the quantity of dollars supplied.

Changes in Demand and Supply: Exchange Rate Fluctuations (pp. 619–622)

- Changes in the world demand for Canadian exports, the expected future exchange rate, or the Canadian interest rate differential change the demand for Canadian dollars and shift the demand curve.
- Changes in Canadian demand for imports, the expected future exchange rate, or the Canadian interest rate differential change the supply of Canadian dollars and shift the supply curve.
- Fluctuations in the demand for and supply of dollars bring fluctuations in the exchange rate.
- Exchange rate expectations are influenced by interest rate parity and purchasing power parity.

Exchange Rate Policy (pp. 623–625)

- The government of Canada and the Bank of Canada can adopt any of four alternative exchange rate policies: a flexible exchange rate, a fixed exchange rate, a crawling peg, or a currency union.

- Canada had a fixed exchange rate during the 1960s but now has a flexible exchange rate.
- Some economists advocate a currency union between Canada and the United States, but such a union is not on the political agenda.

KEY FIGURES

Figure 26.2   The Exchange Rate, 613
Figure 26.5   The Demand for Dollars, 616
Figure 26.6   The Supply of Dollars, 617
Figure 26.7   Equilibrium Exchange Rate, 618
Figure 26.8   Changes in the Demand for Dollars, 623
Figure 26.9   Changes in the Supply of Dollars, 620
Figure 26.10   Exchange Rate Fluctuations, 621
Figure 26.11   Foreign Exchange Market Intervention, 623

KEY TERMS

Canadian interest rate differential, 619
Crawling peg, 624
Currency appreciation, 613
Currency depreciation, 613
Currency union, 624
Fixed exchange rate, 623
Flexible exchange rate, 623
Foreign currency, 612
Foreign exchange market, 612
Foreign exchange rate, 612
Interest rate parity, 622
Purchasing power parity, 622

PROBLEMS

Go to (X)myeconlab for solutions to odd-numbered problems and additional exercises.

1. The Canadian dollar exchange rate increased from 80 U.S. cents in 2004 to 85 U.S. cents in 2005.
   a. Did the Canadian dollar appreciate or depreciate against the U.S. dollar?
   b. What was the value of the U.S. dollar in terms of Canadian dollars in 2004?
   c. What was the value of the U.S. dollar in terms of Canadian dollars in 2005?
   d. Did the U.S. dollar appreciate or depreciate in terms of the Canadian dollar?

2. The Canadian dollar exchange rate decreased from 73 euro cents in 2000 to 65 euro cents in 2005.
   a. Did the Canadian dollar appreciate or depreciate in terms of the euro?
   b. What was the value of the euro in terms of Canadian dollars in 2000?
   c. What was the value of the euro in terms of Canadian dollars in 2005?
   d. Did the euro appreciate or depreciate against the Canadian dollar?

3. The table sets out some cross exchange rates. Use the table to answer the following questions.

	USD	EUR	GBP	JPY*	CAD
USD					
EUR	0.80				
GBP	0.60				
JPY*	1.18				
CAD	1.22				

   a. What do the numbers in the first column tell you?
   b. What are the numbers that go in the first row of the table and what do those numbers tell you?
   c. What are the numbers that go in the second row of the table and what do those numbers tell you?
   d. What are the numbers that go in the third row of the table and what do those numbers tell you?
   e. What are the numbers that go in the fourth row of the table and what do those numbers tell you?

   f. What are the numbers that go in the last row of the table and what do those numbers tell you?
   g. What do the numbers in the second through last columns of the table tell you?

4. The table sets out some cross exchange rates. Use the table to answer the following questions.

	USD	EUR	GBP	JPY*	CAD
USD		1.25	1.80	0.95	0.90
EUR					
GBP					
JPY*					
CAD					

   a. What do the numbers in the first row tell you?
   b. What are the numbers that go in the first column of the table and what do those numbers tell you?
   c. What are the numbers that go in the second column of the table and what do those numbers tell you?
   d. What are the numbers that go in the third column of the table and what do those numbers tell you?
   e. What are the numbers that go in the fourth column of the table and what do those numbers tell you?
   f. What are the numbers that go in the last column of the table and what do those numbers tell you?
   g. What do the numbers in the second through last rows of the table tell you?

5. There is a large increase in the global demand for roses and Colombia is the biggest producer of roses. At the same time, the central bank of Colombia increases the interest rate. What happens in the foreign exchange market for Colombian pesos to:
   a. The demand for pesos?
   b. The supply of pesos?
   c. The quantity of pesos demanded?
   d. The quantity of pesos supplied?
   e. The exchange rate of the pesos against the U.S. dollar?

6. There is a large increase in the global demand for diamonds and South Africa is the biggest producer of diamonds. At the same time, the central bank of South Africa cuts the interest

rate. What happens in the foreign exchange market for South African rand to:

a. The demand for rand?
b. The supply of rand?
c. The quantity of rand demanded?
d. The quantity of rand supplied?
f. The exchange rate of the rand against the U.S. dollar?

7. The Canadian dollar appreciates, and Canada's official reserves increase. What can you say about

a. Intervention in the foreign exchange market by the Bank of Canada?
b. The possible Bank of Canada sources of the currency appreciation?
c. The possible private actions behind the appreciation?

8. Canada has a lower inflation rate than the United States. Canada also has more rapid economic growth. The Bank of Canada does not intervene in the foreign exchange market. What can you say about each of the following (and why)?

a. The exchange rate
b. The expected exchange rate
c. The interest rate differential
d. Interest rate parity
d. Purchasing power parity

9. The Canadian dollar is trading at 85 U.S. cents per Canadian dollar. There is purchasing power parity at this exchange rate. The interest rate in Canada is 5 percent a year and the interest rate in the United States is 4 percent a year.

a. Calculate the Canadian interest rate differential?
b. What is the Canadian dollar expected to be worth one year from now?
c. Which country most likely has the lower inflation rate? How can you tell?

10. The Canadian dollar is trading at 90 U.S. cents per Canadian dollar and it is overvalued relative to purchasing power parity. The interest rate in Canada is 5 percent a year and the interest rate in the United States is 4 percent a year.

a. Calculate the Canadian interest rate differential?
b. Is the Canadian dollar expected to appreciate or depreciate?
c. Which country most likely has the lower inflation rate? How can you tell?

CRITICAL THINKING

1. Study *Reading Between the Lines* on pp. 626–627 and then answer the following questions:

a. What do the daily, weekly, and monthly changes in the exchange rate tell us?
b. What, according to the news article, caused the change in the exchange rate on November 22, 2005?
c. Is the explanation given in the news article consistent with interest rate parity?
d. If Canada has an inflation rate persistently below that of the United States, what will happen to the Canadian dollar over the longer term (other things remaining the same)?

2. Why do some economists think we should have a currency union with the United States? What do you think about this idea? Prepare an executive summary of your ideas for the governor of the Bank of Canada.

WEB EXERCISES

Use the links on myeconlab **to work the following exercises.**

1. Visit Statistics Canada and find data on the exchange rate.

a. When did the Canadian dollar appreciate most recently?
b. When did the Canadian dollar depreciate most recently?
c. When was the last time the Canadian dollar had a fixed exchange rate?

2. Visit PACIFIC (an exchange rate service) and read the page on purchasing power parity.

a. What is purchasing power parity?
b. Which currencies are the most overvalued relative to the U.S. dollar today?
c. Which currencies are the most undervalued relative to the U.S. dollar today?
d. Can you offer some suggestions as to why some currencies are overvalued and some are undervalued?
d. Do you think that the information on overvaluation and undervaluation is useful to currency speculators? Why or why not?

Inflation

From Rome to Rio de Janeiro

At the end of the third century, Roman Emperor Diocletian struggled to contain an inflation that raised prices by more than 300 percent a year. At the end of the twentieth century, Brazil's president, Fernando Henrique Cardoso, struggled to contain an inflation that hit a rate of 40 percent per month—or 5,600 percent a year.

Today, the Bank of Canada targets the inflation rate and Canada has remarkable price stability. But during the 1970s, the Canadian price level more than doubled—an inflation of more than 100 percent over the decade. Why do inflation rates vary? And why do serious inflations break out from time to time?

Can we be confident that the Bank of Canada will keep inflation in check? Or might inflation increase so our savings buy less? Or might inflation decrease so our debts are harder to repay? To make good decisions, we need good forecasts of inflation, and not for just next year but for many years into the future. How do people try to forecast inflation? And how do expectations of inflation influence the economy?

In targeting inflation, does the Bank of Canada face a tradeoff between inflation and unemployment? And does a low unemployment rate signal a rising inflation rate? How does inflation affect the interest rate?

◆ We'll answer these questions in this chapter and in doing so, we'll set the stage for the next chapter in which we study the Bank of Canada's inflation-targeting monetary policy. We'll begin by reviewing what inflation is and how it is measured. And we'll end, in *Reading Between the Lines*, by looking at the views of Nobel Laureate George Akerlof on the links between inflation and unemployment in Canada.

After studying this chapter, you will be able to

■ **Distinguish between inflation and a change in the price level and between demand-pull inflation and cost-push inflation**

■ **Explain the quantity theory of money**

■ **Describe the effects of inflation**

■ **Explain the short-run and long-run relationships between inflation and unemployment**

■ **Explain the short-run and long-run relationships between inflation and interest rates**

Inflation: Demand-Pull and Cost-Push

THE MAIN TASK OF THE BANK OF CANADA IS TO keep inflation under control. You will learn about the tools and strategies that the Bank uses in the next chapter. Here, we explain what causes inflation and explore the short-run tradeoffs between inflation and output and between inflation and unemployment. We begin by distinguishing between inflation and a change in the price level.

Inflation and a Change in the Price Level

Inflation is a process in which the *price level is rising* and *money is losing value.*

A change in *one price* is not inflation. For example, if the price of a hot dog jumps to $25 and all other money prices fall slightly so that the price level remains constant, there is no inflation. Instead, the relative price of a hot dog has increased. But if the price of a hot dog and all other prices rise by a similar percentage, then there is inflation.

Inflation is an *ongoing process*, so a one-time jump in the price level is not inflation. Figure 27.1 illustrates this distinction. The red line shows the price level rising continuously. That is inflation. The blue line shows a one-time jump in the price level. That is not inflation.

To measure the inflation *rate,* we calculate the annual percentage change in the price level. For

"Three hundred dollars' of regular."

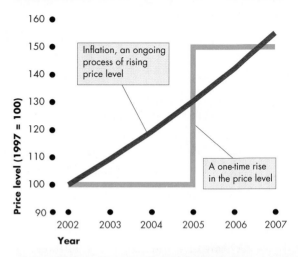

FIGURE 27.1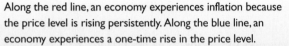

Inflation Versus a One-Time Rise in the Price Level

Along the red line, an economy experiences inflation because the price level is rising persistently. Along the blue line, an economy experiences a one-time rise in the price level.

example, if this year's price level is 126 and last year's price level was 120, the inflation rate is 5 percent per year. That is,

$$\text{Inflation rate} = \frac{126 - 120}{120} \times 100$$

$$= 5 \text{ percent per year.}$$

This equation shows the connection between the *inflation rate* and the *price level.* A high price level isn't the same as a high inflation rate. For a *given price level last year,* the higher the price level in the current year, the higher is the inflation rate.

If the price level is *rising,* the inflation rate is *positive.* And if the price level is *falling,* the inflation rate is *negative.* If the price level rises at a *faster* rate, the inflation rate *increases.* And if the price level rises at a *slower* rate, the inflation rate *decreases.*

Inflation can result from either an aggregate demand shock or an aggregate supply shock. These two sources of impulses are called

■ Demand-pull inflation
■ Cost-push inflation

We'll first study demand-pull inflation.

Demand-Pull Inflation

An inflation that results from an initial increase in aggregate demand is called **demand-pull inflation**. Demand-pull inflation can arise from *any* factor that increases aggregate demand, such as an

1. Increase in the quantity of money
2. Increase in government expenditures
3. Increase in exports

Initial Effect of an Increase in Aggregate Demand
Suppose that last year the price level was 110 and real GDP was $1,000 billion. Potential GDP was also $1,000 billion. Figure 27.2(a) illustrates this situation. The aggregate demand curve is AD_0, the short-run aggregate supply curve is SAS_0, and the long-run aggregate supply curve is LAS.

In the current year, aggregate demand increases to AD_1. Such a situation arises if, for example, the Bank of Canada loosens its grip on the quantity of

money, or the government increases its expenditures on goods and services, or exports increase.

With no change in potential GDP, and with no change in the money wage rate, the long-run aggregate supply curve and the short-run aggregate supply curve remain at LAS and SAS_0, respectively.

The price level and real GDP are determined at the point where the aggregate demand curve AD_1 intersects the short-run aggregate supply curve. The price level rises to 113, and real GDP increases above potential GDP to $1,050 billion. The economy experiences a 2.7 percent rise in the price level (a price level of 113 compared with 110 in the previous year) and a rapid expansion of real GDP. Unemployment falls below its natural rate. The next step in the unfolding story is a rise in the money wage rate.

Money Wage Rate Response Real GDP cannot remain above potential GDP forever. With unemployment below its natural rate, there is a shortage of labour. In this situation, the money wage rate begins

---

FIGURE 27.2
A Demand-Pull Rise in the Price Level

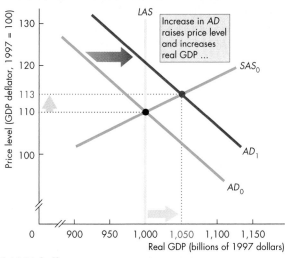

(a) Initial effect

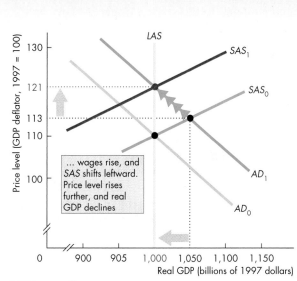

(b) Wages adjust

In part (a), the aggregate demand curve is AD_0, the short-run aggregate supply curve is SAS_0, and the long-run aggregate supply curve is LAS. The price level is 110, and real GDP is $1,000 billion, which equals potential GDP. Aggregate demand increases to AD_1. The price level rises to

113, and real GDP increases to $1,050 billion. In part (b), starting from above full employment, the money wage rate begins to rise and the short-run aggregate supply curve shifts leftward towards SAS_1. The price level rises further, and real GDP returns to potential GDP.

to rise. As it does so, short-run aggregate supply decreases and the *SAS* curve starts to shift leftward. The price level rises further, and real GDP begins to decrease.

With no further change in aggregate demand—that is, the aggregate demand curve remains at AD_1—this process ends when the short-run aggregate supply curve has shifted to SAS_1 in Fig. 27.2(b). At this time, the price level has increased to 121 and real GDP has returned to potential GDP of $1,000 billion, the level from which it started.

A Demand-Pull Inflation Process The process we've just studied eventually ends when, for a given increase in aggregate demand, the money wage rate has adjusted enough to restore the real wage rate to its full-employment level. We've studied a one-time rise in the price level like that described in Fig. 27.1. For inflation to proceed, aggregate demand must persistently increase.

The only way in which aggregate demand can persistently increase is if the quantity of money persistently increases. Suppose the government has a budget deficit that it finances by selling bonds. Also suppose that the Bank of Canada buys some of these bonds. When the Bank of Canada buys bonds, it creates more money. In this situation, aggregate demand increases year after year. The aggregate demand curve keeps shifting rightward. This persistent increase in aggregate demand puts continual upward pressure on the price level. The economy now experiences demand-pull inflation.

Figure 27.3 illustrates the process of demand-pull inflation. The starting point is the same as that shown in Fig. 27.2. The aggregate demand curve is AD_0, the short-run aggregate supply curve is SAS_0, and the long-run aggregate supply curve is *LAS*. Real GDP is $1,000 billion, and the price level is 110. Aggregate demand increases, shifting the aggregate demand curve to AD_1. Real GDP increases to $1,050 billion, and the price level rises to 113. The economy is at an above full-employment equilibrium. There is a shortage of labour, and the money wage rate rises. The short-run aggregate supply curve shifts to SAS_1. The price level rises to 121, and real GDP returns to potential GDP.

But the Bank of Canada increases the quantity of money again, and aggregate demand continues to increase. The aggregate demand curve shifts rightward to AD_2. The price level rises further to 125, and real GDP again exceeds potential GDP at $1,050 bil-

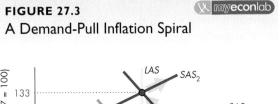

FIGURE 27.3
A Demand-Pull Inflation Spiral

Each time the quantity of money increases, aggregate demand increases, and the aggregate demand curve shifts rightward from AD_0 to AD_1 to AD_2, and so on. Each time real GDP goes above potential GDP, the money wage rate rises and the short-run aggregate supply curve shifts leftward from SAS_0 to SAS_1 to SAS_2, and so on. The price level rises from 110 to 113, 121, 125, 133, and so on. There is a perpetual demand-pull inflation. Real GDP fluctuates between $1,000 billion and $1,050 billion.

lion. Yet again, the money wage rate rises and decreases short-run aggregate supply. The *SAS* curve shifts to SAS_2, and the price level rises further, to 133. As the quantity of money continues to grow, aggregate demand increases and the price level rises in an ongoing demand-pull inflation process.

The process you have just studied generates inflation—an ongoing process of a rising price level.

Demand-Pull Inflation in Chatham You may better understand the inflation process that we've just described by considering what is going on in an individual part of the economy, such as a Chatham ketchup-bottling plant. Initially, when aggregate demand increases, the demand for ketchup increases and the price of ketchup rises. Faced with a higher price, the ketchup plant works overtime and increases production. Conditions are good for workers in Chatham, and the ketchup factory finds it hard to hang onto its best people. To do so, it has to offer a higher money wage rate. As the wage rate rises, so do the ketchup factory's costs.

What happens next depends on what happens to aggregate demand. If aggregate demand remains constant (as in Fig. 27.2b), the firm's costs are increasing, but the price of ketchup is not increasing as quickly as its costs. Production is scaled back. Eventually, the money wage rate and costs increase by the same percentage as the rise in the price of ketchup. In real terms, the ketchup factory is in the same situation as it was initially—before the increase in aggregate demand. The plant produces the same amount of ketchup and employs the same amount of labour as before the increase in demand for ketchup.

But if aggregate demand continues to increase, so does the demand for ketchup and the price of ketchup rises at the same rate as wages. The ketchup factory continues to operate above full employment, and there is a persistent shortage of labour. Prices and wages chase each other upward in an unending spiral.

Demand-Pull Inflation in Canada A demand-pull inflation like the one you've just studied occurred in Canada during the late 1960s and early 1970s. In 1960, inflation was a moderate 2 percent a year, but its rate increased slowly through the mid-1960s. Then, between 1966 and 1969, the inflation rate surged upward. Inflation then decreased slightly during 1970 and 1971, but it took off again in 1972. By 1973, the inflation rate was approaching 10 percent a year.

These increases in inflation resulted from increases in aggregate demand that had two main sources. The first was from the United States, where large increases in government expenditures and in the quantity of money increased aggregate demand in the entire world economy. The second source was an increase in Canadian government expenditures and an increase in the quantity of money.

With the economy above full employment, the money wage rate started to rise more quickly and the *SAS* curve shifted leftward. The Bank of Canada responded with a further increase in the money growth rate, and a demand-pull inflation spiral unfolded. By 1974, the inflation rate had reached double digits.

Next, let's see how shocks to aggregate supply can create cost-push inflation.

Cost-Push Inflation

An inflation that results from an initial increase in costs is called **cost-push inflation**. The two main sources of increases in costs are

1. An increase in money wage rates
2. An increase in the money prices of raw materials

At a given price level, the higher the cost of production, the smaller is the amount that firms are willing to produce. So if money wage rates rise or if the prices of raw materials (for example, oil) rise, firms decrease their supply of goods and services. Aggregate supply decreases, and the short-run aggregate supply curve shifts leftward.[1] Let's trace the effects of such a decrease in short-run aggregate supply on the price level and real GDP.

Initial Effect of a Decrease in Aggregate Supply Suppose that last year the price level was 110 and real GDP was $1,000 billion. Potential real GDP was also $1,000 billion. Figure 27.4 illustrates this situation. The aggregate demand curve was AD_0, the short-run aggregate supply curve was SAS_0, and the long-run aggregate supply curve was *LAS*. In the current year, the world's oil producers form a price-fixing organization that strengthens their market power and increases the relative price of oil. They raise the price of oil, and this action decreases short-run aggregate supply. The short-run aggregate supply curve shifts leftward to SAS_1. The price level rises to 117, and real GDP decreases to $950 billion. The combination of a rise in the price level and a fall in real GDP is called *stagflation*.

This event is a one-time rise in the price level, like that in Fig. 27.1. It is not inflation. In fact, a supply shock on its own cannot cause inflation. Something more must happen to enable a one-time supply shock, which causes a one-time rise in the price level, to be converted into a process of money growth and ongoing inflation. The quantity of money must persistently increase. And it often does increase, as you will now see.

---

[1] Some cost-push forces, such as an increase in the price of oil accompanied by a decrease in the availability of oil, can also decrease long-run aggregate supply. We'll ignore such effects here and examine cost-push factors that change only short-run aggregate supply.

FIGURE 27.4

myeconlab

A Cost-Push Rise in the Price Level

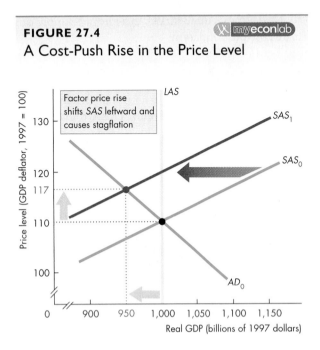

Initially, the aggregate demand curve is AD_0, the short-run aggregate supply curve is SAS_0, and the long-run aggregate supply curve is LAS. A decrease in aggregate supply (for example, resulting from a rise in the world price of oil) shifts the short-run aggregate supply curve to SAS_1. The economy moves to the point where the short-run aggregate supply curve SAS_1 intersects the aggregate demand curve AD_0. The price level rises to 117, and real GDP decreases to $950 billion.

Aggregate Demand Response When real GDP falls, the unemployment rate rises above its natural rate. In such a situation, there is usually an outcry of concern and a call for action to restore full employment. Suppose that the Bank of Canada increases the quantity of money. Aggregate demand increases. In Fig. 27.5, the aggregate demand curve shifts rightward to AD_1. The increase in aggregate demand has restored full employment. But the price level rises to 121, a 10 percent increase over the initial price level.

A Cost-Push Inflation Process The oil producers now see the prices of everything that they buy increase by 10 percent. So they increase the price of oil again to restore its new high relative price. Figure 27.6 continues the story.

The short-run aggregate supply curve now shifts to SAS_2, and another bout of stagflation ensues. The price level rises further, to 129, and real GDP falls to $950 billion. Unemployment increases above its natural rate. If the Bank of Canada responds yet again with an increase in the quantity of money, aggregate demand increases and the aggregate demand curve shifts to AD_2. The price level rises even higher—to 133—and full employment is again restored. A cost-push inflation spiral results. But if the Bank of Canada does not respond, the economy remains below full employment until the price of oil falls.

You can see that the Bank of Canada has a dilemma. If it increases the quantity of money to restore full employment, the Bank invites another oil price hike that will call forth yet a further increase in the quantity of money. Inflation will rage along at a rate decided by the oil-exporting nations. If the Bank of Canada keeps the lid on money growth, the economy operates with a high level of unemployment.

FIGURE 27.5

myeconlab

Aggregate Demand Response to Cost Push

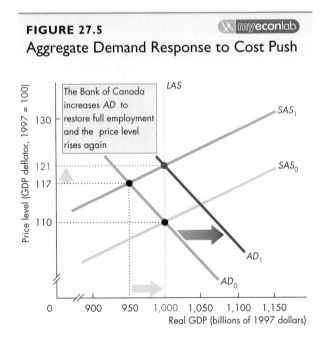

Following a cost-push increase in the price level, real GDP is below potential GDP and unemployment is above its natural rate. If the Bank of Canada responds by increasing aggregate demand to restore full employment, the aggregate demand curve shifts rightward to AD_1. The economy returns to full employment but the price level rises to 121.

Cost-Push Inflation in Chatham What is going on in the Chatham ketchup-bottling plant when the economy is experiencing cost-push inflation? When the oil price increases, so do the costs of bottling ketchup. These higher costs decrease the supply of ketchup, increasing its price and decreasing the quantity produced. The ketchup plant lays off some workers. This situation will persist until either the Bank of Canada increases aggregate demand or the price of oil falls. If the Bank of Canada increases aggregate demand, as it did in the mid-1970s, the demand for ketchup increases and so does its price. The higher price of ketchup brings higher profits, and the bottling plant increases its production. The ketchup factory rehires the laid-off workers.

Cost-Push Inflation in Canada A cost-push inflation like the one you've just studied occurred in Canada during the 1970s. It began in 1974 when the Organization of the Petroleum Exporting Countries (OPEC) raised the price of oil fourfold. The higher oil price decreased aggregate supply, which caused the price level to rise more quickly and real GDP to shrink. The Bank of Canada then faced a dilemma: Would it increase the quantity of money and accommodate the cost-push forces, or would it keep aggregate demand growth in check by limiting money growth? In 1975, 1976, and 1977, the Bank of Canada repeatedly allowed the quantity of money to grow quickly and inflation proceeded at a rapid rate. In 1979 and 1980, OPEC was again able to push oil prices higher. On that occasion, the Bank of Canada decided not to respond to the oil price hike with an increase in the quantity of money. The result was a recession but also, eventually, a fall in inflation.

FIGURE 27.6   myeconlab
A Cost-Push Inflation Spiral

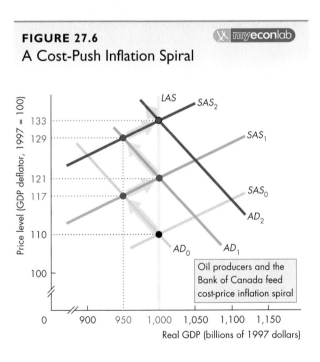

When a cost increase decreases short-run aggregate supply from SAS_0 to SAS_1, the price level rises to 117 and real GDP decreases to $950 billion. The Bank of Canada responds with an increase in the quantity of money. The aggregate demand curve shifts from AD_0 to AD_1, the price level rises to 121, and real GDP returns to $1,000 billion. A further cost increase occurs, which shifts the short-run aggregate supply curve again, this time to SAS_2. Stagflation is repeated, and the price level rises to 129. The Bank of Canada responds again, and the cost-push inflation spiral continues.

REVIEW QUIZ

1 How does demand-pull inflation begin? What are the initial effects of demand-pull inflation on real GDP?
2 When real GDP moves above potential GDP, what happens to the money wage rate and short-run aggregate supply? How do real GDP and the price level respond?
3 What must happen to create a demand-pull inflation spiral?
4 How does cost-push inflation begin? What are the initial effects of a cost-push rise in the price level?
5 What is *stagflation* and why does cost-push inflation cause stagflation?
6 What must the Bank of Canada do to convert a one-time rise in the price level into a freewheeling cost-push inflation?

myeconlab **Study Plan 27.1**

Inflation requires an ongoing increase in the quantity of money. The quantity theory of money explains the link between money growth and inflation.

The Quantity Theory of Money

YOU'VE SEEN THAT REGARDLESS OF WHETHER inflation originates in a demand-pull or a cost-push, to convert a one-time rise in the price level into an ongoing inflation, aggregate demand must increase. And although many factors can and do influence aggregate demand, only one factor can persistently increase in the long run: the quantity of money. This special place of money gives rise to a special long-run theory of inflation: the quantity theory of money.

The **quantity theory of money** is the proposition that in the long run, an increase in the quantity of money brings an equal percentage increase in the price level. To explain the quantity theory of money, we first need to define *the velocity of circulation* and *the equation of exchange*.

The **velocity of circulation** is the average number of times a dollar of money is used annually to buy GDP. But GDP equals the price level (P) multiplied by *real* GDP (Y). That is,

$$GDP = PY.$$

Call the quantity of money M. The velocity of circulation, V, is determined by the equation

$$V = PY/M.$$

For example, if GDP is $1,000 billion ($PY$ = $1,000 billion) and the quantity of money is $250 billion, the velocity of circulation is 4. ($1,000 billion divided by $250 billion equals 4.)

The **equation of exchange** states that the quantity of money (M) multiplied by the velocity of circulation (V) equals GDP, or

$$MV = PY.$$

Given the definition of the velocity of circulation, this equation is always true—it is true by definition. With M equal to $250 billion and V equal to 4, MV is equal to $1,000 billion, the value of GDP.

The equation of exchange becomes the quantity theory of money if the quantity of money does not influence

1. The velocity of circulation
2. Potential GDP

In this case, the equation of exchange tells us that a change in the quantity of money brings about an equal proportional change in the price level. You can see why by solving the equation of exchange for the price level. Divide both sides of the equation by real GDP (Y) to give

$$P = (V/Y) \times M.$$

In the long run, real GDP equals potential GDP, so if potential GDP and velocity are not influenced by the quantity of money, then the relationship between the change in the price level (ΔP) and the change in the quantity of money (ΔM) is

$$\Delta P = (V/Y) \times \Delta M.$$

Divide this equation by $P = (V/Y) \times M$, and multiply by 100 to get

$$(\Delta P/P) \times 100 = (\Delta M/M) \times 100.$$

$(\Delta P/P) \times 100$ is the inflation rate and $(\Delta M/M) \times 100$ is the growth rate of the quantity of money. So this equation is the quantity theory of money: The percentage increase in the price level and the percentage increase in the quantity of money are equal.

Evidence on the Quantity Theory

Figure 27.7 summarizes some Canadian evidence on the quantity theory of money. The figure reveals that

1. On the average, the money growth rate exceeds the inflation rate.
2. The money growth rate is correlated with the inflation rate.

Money growth exceeds inflation because real GDP grows. Money growth that matches real GDP growth does not create inflation. But money growth in excess of real GDP growth does create inflation.

Money growth and inflation are correlated—move up and down together. For example, the rise in the inflation rate during the 1970s was accompanied by a rise in the money growth rate. And the decrease in the inflation rate during the 1980s and 1990s was accompanied by a decrease in the money growth rate. But the correlation is not perfect. Nor does a correlation tell us that money growth *causes* inflation.

Money growth might cause inflation; inflation might cause money growth; or some third variable might simultaneously cause inflation and money growth.

Figure 27.8 shows two scatter diagrams of the inflation rate and the money growth rate for 134 countries in part(a) and for those countries with inflation rates below 20 percent a year in part (b).

FIGURE 27.7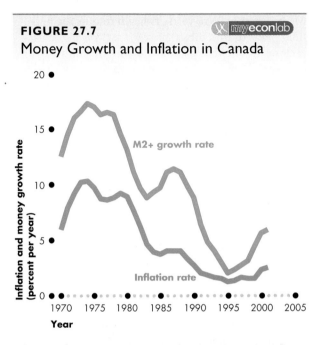

Money Growth and Inflation in Canada

On the average, the money growth rate exceeds the inflation rate because real GDP grows. Money growth and
inflation are correlated—they rise and fall together.

Source of data: Statistics Canada, CANSIM Tables 176–0020, 380–0056.

FIGURE 27.8

Money Growth and Inflation in the World

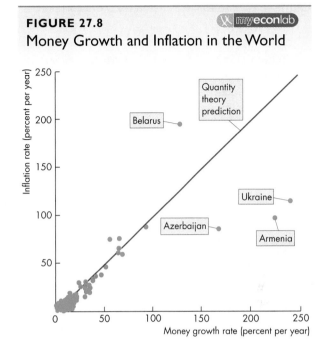

(a) 134 Countries: 1990–2004

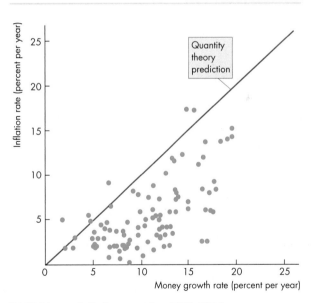

(b) 104 Lower-inflation countries: 1990–2004

Inflation and money growth in 134 countries in part (a)
and 104 low-inflation countries in part (b) show a positive
relationship between money growth and inflation.

Sources of data: International Financial Statistics Yearbook, 2004 and
International Monetary Fund, World Economic Outlook Database,
September 2005.

You can see a general tendency for money growth and
inflation to be correlated but the quantity theory
(shown by the red lines) does not enable us to predict
inflation very precisely from the money growth rate.

REVIEW QUIZ

1 What is the quantity theory of money?
2 What is the velocity of circulation of money
  and how is it calculated?
3 What is the equation of exchange? Can the
  equation of exchange be wrong?
4 What does the long-run historical evidence and
  international evidence on the relationship
  between money growth and inflation tell us
  about the quantity theory of money?

   myeconlab **Study Plan 27.2**

We next turn to an examination of the effects of
inflation.

Effects of Inflation

REGARDLESS OF WHETHER INFLATION IS DEMAND pull or cost push, the failure to correctly *anticipate* it results in unintended consequences. These unintended consequences impose costs in both labour markets and capital markets. Let's examine these costs.

Unanticipated Inflation in the Labour Market

Unanticipated inflation has two main consequences for the operation of the labour market:

- Redistribution of income
- Departure from full employment

Redistribution of Income Unanticipated inflation redistributes income between employers and workers. Sometimes employers gain at the expense of workers, and sometimes they lose. If an unexpected increase in aggregate demand increases the inflation rate, then the money wage rate will not have been set high enough. Profits will be higher than expected, and real wages will buy fewer goods than expected. In this case, employers gain at the expense of workers. But if aggregate demand is expected to increase at a rapid rate and it fails to do so, workers gain at the expense of employers. With a high inflation rate anticipated, the money wage rate is set too high and profits are squeezed. Redistribution between employers and workers creates an incentive for both firms and workers to try to forecast inflation correctly.

Departure from Full Employment Redistribution brings gains to some and losses to others. But a departure from full employment imposes costs on everyone. To see why, let's return to the ketchup-bottling plant in Chatham.

If the bottling plant and its workers do not anticipate inflation but inflation occurs, the money wage rate does not rise to keep up with inflation. The real wage rate falls, and the firm tries to hire more labour and increase production. But because the real wage rate has fallen, the firm has a hard time attracting the labour it wants to employ. It pays overtime rates to its existing work force, and because it runs its plant at a faster pace, it incurs higher plant maintenance and parts replacement costs. But also, because the real wage rate has fallen, workers begin to quit the bottling plant to find jobs that pay a real wage rate that is closer to one that prevailed before the outbreak of inflation. This labour turnover imposes additional costs on the firm. So even though its production increases, the firm incurs additional costs and its profits do not increase as much as they otherwise would. The workers incur additional costs of job search, and those who remain at the bottling plant wind up feeling cheated. They've worked overtime to produce the extra output, and when they come to spend their wages, they discover that prices have increased so their wages buy a smaller quantity of goods and services than expected.

If the bottling plant and its workers anticipate a high inflation rate but it does not occur, the money wage rate increases by too much and the real wage rate rises. At the higher real wage rate, the firm lays off some workers and the unemployment rate increases. The workers who keep their jobs gain, but those who become unemployed lose. Also, the bottling plant loses because its output and profits fall.

Unanticipated Inflation in the Market for Financial Capital

Unanticipated inflation has two consequences for the operation of the market for financial capital:

- Redistribution of income
- Too much or too little lending and borrowing

Redistribution of Income Unanticipated inflation redistributes income between borrowers and lenders. Sometimes borrowers gain at the expense of lenders, and sometimes they lose. When inflation is unexpected, interest rates are not set high enough to compensate lenders for the falling value of money. In this case, borrowers gain at the expense of lenders. But if inflation is expected and then fails to occur, interest rates are set too high. In this case, lenders gain at the expense of borrowers. Redistributions of income between borrowers and lenders create an incentive for both groups to try to forecast inflation correctly.

Too Much or Too Little Lending and Borrowing If the inflation rate turns out to be either higher or lower than expected, the interest rate does not incorporate a correct allowance for the falling value of money and the real interest rate is either lower or higher than it otherwise would be. When the real interest rate turns out to be too low, which occurs when inflation is *higher* than expected, borrowers wish they had borrowed more and lenders wish they had lent less. Both groups would have made different lending and borrowing decisions with greater foresight about the inflation rate. When the real interest rate turns out to be too high, which occurs when inflation is lower than expected, borrowers wish they had borrowed less and lenders wish they had lent more. Again, both groups would have made different lending and borrowing decisions with greater foresight about the inflation rate.

So unanticipated inflation imposes costs regardless of whether the inflation turns out to be higher or lower than anticipated. The presence of these costs gives everyone an incentive to forecast inflation correctly. Let's see how people go about this task.

Forecasting Inflation

Inflation is difficult to forecast for two reasons. First, there are several sources of inflation—the demand-pull and cost-push sources you've just studied. Second, the speed with which a change in either aggregate demand or aggregate supply translates into a change in the price level varies. This speed of response also depends, as you will see below, on the extent to which the inflation is anticipated.

Because inflation is costly and difficult to forecast, people devote considerable resources to improving inflation forecasts. Some people specialize in forecasting, and others buy forecasts from specialists. The specialist forecasters are economists who work for public and private macroeconomic forecasting agencies and for banks, insurance companies, labour unions, and large corporations. The returns these specialists make depend on the quality of their forecasts, so they have a strong incentive to forecast as accurately as possible. The most accurate forecast possible is the one that is based on all the relevant information available and is called a **rational expectation.**

A rational expectation is not necessarily a correct forecast. It is simply the best forecast available. It will often turn out to be wrong, but it was the best forecast that could have been made with the information available.

You've seen the effects of inflation when people fail to anticipate it. And you've seen why it pays to try to anticipate inflation. Let's now see what happens if inflation is correctly anticipated.

Anticipated Inflation

In the demand-pull and cost-push inflations that we studied in this chapter, the money wage rate is sticky. When aggregate demand increases, either to set off a demand-pull inflation or to accommodate a cost-push inflation, the money wage rate does not change immediately. But if people correctly anticipate increases in aggregate demand, they will adjust the money wage rate so that it keeps up with anticipated inflation.

In this case, inflation proceeds with real GDP equal to potential GDP and unemployment equal to its natural rate. Figure 27.9 explains why. Suppose that last year the price level was 110 and real GDP was $1,000 billion, which is also potential GDP. The aggregate demand curve was AD_0, the aggregate supply curve was SAS_0, and the long-run aggregate supply curve was LAS.

Suppose that potential GDP does not change, so the LAS curve does not shift. Also suppose that aggregate demand is expected to increase and that the expected aggregate demand curve for this year is AD_1. In anticipation of this increase in aggregate demand, the money wage rate rises and the short-run aggregate supply curve shifts leftward. If the money wage rate rises by the same percentage as the price level rises, the short-run aggregate supply curve for next year is SAS_1.

If aggregate demand turns out to be the same as expected, the aggregate demand curve is AD_1. The short-run aggregate supply curve SAS_1 and AD_1 determine the actual price level at 121. Between last year and this year, the price level increased from 110 to 121 and the economy experienced an inflation rate of 10 percent, the same as the inflation rate that was anticipated. If this anticipated inflation is ongoing, in the following year aggregate demand increases (as anticipated) and the aggregate demand curve shifts to AD_2. The money wage rate rises to reflect the anticipated inflation, and the short-run aggregate supply curve shifts to SAS_2. The price level rises by a further 10 percent to 133.

What has caused this inflation? The immediate answer is that because people expected inflation, the money wage rate increased and the price level increased. But the expectation was correct. Aggregate demand was expected to increase, and it did increase. Because aggregate demand was *expected* to increase from AD_0 to AD_1, the short-run aggregate supply curve shifted from SAS_0 to SAS_1. Because aggregate demand actually did increase by the amount that was expected, the actual aggregate demand curve shifted from AD_0 to AD_1. The combination of the anticipated and actual shifts of the aggregate demand curve rightward produced an increase in the price level that was anticipated.

Only if aggregate demand growth is correctly forecasted does the economy follow the course described in Fig. 27.9. If the expected growth rate of aggregate demand is different from its actual growth rate, the expected aggregate demand curve shifts by an amount that is different from the actual aggregate demand curve. The inflation rate departs from its expected level, and to some extent, there is unanticipated inflation.

FIGURE 27.9   ⓧ myeconlab
Anticipated Inflation

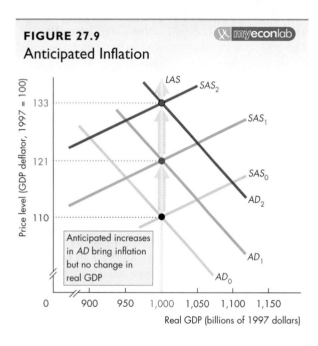

Potential real GDP is $1,000 billion. Last year, the aggregate demand curve was AD_0, and the short-run aggregate supply curve was SAS_0. The actual price level was the same as the expected price level—110. This year, aggregate demand is expected to increase to AD_1. The rational expectation of the price level changes from 110 to 121. As a result, the money wage rate rises and the short-run aggregate supply curve shifts to SAS_1. If aggregate demand actually increases as expected, the actual aggregate demand curve AD_1 is the same as the expected aggregate demand curve. Real GDP is $1,000 billion and the actual price level is 121. The inflation is correctly anticipated. Next year, the process continues with aggregate demand increasing as expected to AD_2 and the money wage rate rising to shift the short-run aggregate supply curve to SAS_2. Again, real GDP remains at $1,000 billion, and the price level rises, as anticipated, to 133.

Unanticipated Inflation

When aggregate demand increases by *more* than expected, there is some unanticipated inflation that looks just like the demand-pull inflation that you studied earlier. Some inflation is expected, and the money wage rate is set to reflect that expectation. The SAS curve intersects the LAS curve at the expected price level. Aggregate demand then increases but by more than expected. So the AD curve intersects the SAS curve at a level of real GDP that exceeds potential GDP. With real GDP above potential GDP and unemployment below its natural rate, the money wage rate rises. So the price level rises further. If aggregate demand increases again, a demand-pull inflation spiral unwinds.

When aggregate demand increases by *less* than expected, there is some unanticipated inflation that looks like the cost-push inflation that you studied earlier. Again, some inflation is expected, and the money wage rate is set to reflect that expectation. The SAS curve intersects the LAS curve at the expected price level. Aggregate demand then increases but by less than expected. So the AD curve intersects the SAS curve at a level of real GDP below potential GDP. Aggregate demand increases to restore full employment. But if aggregate demand is expected to increase by more than it actually does, the money wage rate again rises, short-run aggregate supply again decreases, and a cost-push spiral unwinds.

We've seen that only when inflation is unanticipated does real GDP depart from potential GDP. When inflation is anticipated, real GDP remains at potential GDP. Does this mean that an anticipated inflation has no costs?

The Costs of Anticipated Inflation

The costs of an anticipated inflation depend on its rate. At a moderate rate of 2 or 3 percent a year, the cost is probably small. But as the anticipated inflation rate rises, so does its cost, and an anticipated inflation at a rapid rate can be extremely costly.

Anticipated inflation decreases potential GDP and slows economic growth. These adverse consequences arise for three major reasons:

■ Transactions costs
■ Tax effects
■ Increased uncertainty

Transactions Costs The first transactions costs are known as the "boot leather costs." These are costs that arise from an increase in the velocity of circulation of money and an increase in the amount of running around that people do to try to avoid incurring losses from the falling value of money.

When money loses value at a rapid anticipated rate, it does not function well as a store of value and people try to avoid holding money. They spend their incomes as soon as they receive them, and firms pay out incomes—wages and dividends—as soon as they receive revenue from their sales. The velocity of circulation increases. During the 1920s in Germany, when inflation reached *hyperinflation* levels (rates more than 50 percent a month), wages were paid and spent twice in a single day!

The range of estimates of the boot leather costs is large. Some economists put them at close to zero. Others estimate them to be as much as 2 percent of GDP for a 10 percent inflation. For a rapid inflation, these costs are much more.

The boot leather costs of inflation are just one of several transactions costs that are influenced by the inflation rate. At high anticipated inflation rates, people seek alternatives to money as means of payment and use tokens and commodities or even barter, all of which are less efficient than money as a means of payment. For example, in Russia during the 1990s, when inflation reached 1,000 percent a year, the U.S. dollar started to replace the increasingly worthless Russian ruble. Consequently, people had to keep track of the exchange rate between the ruble and the dollar hour by hour and had to engage in many additional and costly transactions in the foreign exchange market.

Because anticipated inflation increases transactions costs, it diverts resources from producing goods and services and it decreases potential GDP. The faster the anticipated inflation rate, the greater is the decrease in potential GDP and the farther leftward does the *LAS* curve shift.

Tax Effects Anticipated inflation interacts with the tax system and creates serious distortions in incentives. Its major effect is on real interest rates.

Anticipated inflation swells the dollar returns on investments. But dollar returns are taxed, so the effective tax rate rises. This effect becomes serious at even modest inflation rates. Let's consider an example.

Suppose the real interest rate is 4 percent a year and the tax rate is 50 percent. With no inflation, the nominal interest rate is also 4 percent a year and 50 percent of this rate is taxable. The real *after-tax* interest rate is 2 percent a year (50 percent of 4 percent). Now suppose the inflation rate is 4 percent a year, and the nominal interest rate is 8 percent a year. The *after-tax* nominal rate is 4 percent a year (50 percent of 8 percent). Now subtract the 4 percent inflation rate from this amount, and you see that the *after-tax real interest rate* is zero! The true tax rate on interest income is 100 percent.

The higher the inflation rate, the higher is the effective tax rate on income from capital. And the higher the tax rate, the higher is the interest rate paid by borrowers and the lower is the after-tax interest rate received by lenders.

With a low after-tax real interest rate, the incentive to save is weakened and the saving rate falls. With a high cost of borrowing, the amount of investment decreases. And with a fall in saving and investment, the pace of capital accumulation slows and so does the long-term growth rate of real GDP.

Increased Uncertainty When the inflation rate is high, there is increased uncertainty about the long-term inflation rate. Will inflation remain high for a long time, or will price stability be restored? This increased uncertainty makes long-term planning difficult and gives people a shorter-term focus. Investment falls, and the economic growth rate slows.

But this increased uncertainty also misallocates resources. Instead of concentrating on the activities at which they have a comparative advantage, people find it more profitable to search for ways of avoiding the losses that inflation inflicts. As a result, inventive talent that might otherwise work on productive innovations works on finding ways of profiting from the inflation instead.

The implications of inflation for economic growth have been estimated to be enormous. Peter Howitt of Brown University, building on work by Robert Barro of Harvard University, has estimated that if inflation is lowered from 3 percent a year to zero, the growth rate of real GDP will rise by between 0.06 and 0.09 percentage points a year. These numbers might seem small, but they are growth rates. After 30 years, real GDP would be 2.3 percent higher and the present value of all the future output would be 85 percent of current GDP—$850 billion! In the rapid anticipated inflations of Brazil and Russia, the costs are much greater than the numbers given here.

You've seen that an increase in aggregate demand that is not fully anticipated increases both the price level and real GDP. It also decreases unemployment. Similarly, a decrease in aggregate demand that is not fully anticipated decreases the price level and real GDP. It also increases unemployment. Do these relationships mean that there is a tradeoff between inflation and unemployment? Does low unemployment always bring inflation and does low inflation bring high unemployment? We explore these questions.

Inflation and Unemployment: The Phillips Curve

THE *AS–AD* MODEL FOCUSES ON THE PRICE LEVEL and real GDP. Knowing how these two variables change, we can work out what happens to the inflation rate and the unemployment rate. But the *AS–AD* model does not place inflation and unemployment at the centre of the stage.

A more direct way of studying inflation and unemployment uses a relationship called the Phillips curve. The Phillips curve approach uses the same basic ideas as the *AS–AD* model, but it focuses directly on inflation and unemployment. The Phillips curve is so named because New Zealand economist A.W. Phillips popularized it. A **Phillips curve** is a curve that shows a relationship between inflation and unemployment. There are two time frames for Phillips curves:

- The short-run Phillips curve
- The long-run Phillips curve

The Short-Run Phillips Curve

The **short-run Phillips curve** is a curve that shows the tradeoff between inflation and unemployment, holding constant

1. The expected inflation rate
2. The natural rate of unemployment

You've just seen what determines the expected inflation rate. The natural rate of unemployment and the factors that influence it are explained in Chapter 21, pp. 496–497 and Chapter 30, pp. 719–721.

Figure 27.10 shows a short-run Phillips curve, *SRPC*. Suppose that the expected inflation rate is 10 percent a year and the natural rate of unemployment is 6 percent, point *A* in the figure. A short-run Phillips curve passes through this point. If inflation

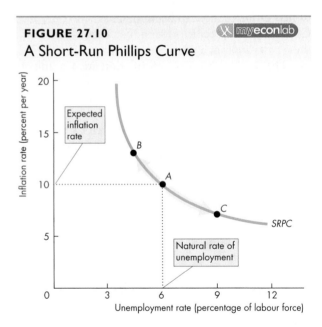

FIGURE 27.10   myeconlab
A Short-Run Phillips Curve

The short-run Phillips curve (*SRPC*) shows the relationship between inflation and unemployment at a given expected inflation rate and a given natural rate of unemployment. With an expected inflation rate of 10 percent a year and a natural rate of unemployment of 6 percent, the short-run Phillips curve passes through point *A*. An unanticipated increase in aggregate demand lowers unemployment and increases inflation—a movement up along the short-run Phillips curve. An unanticipated decrease in aggregate demand increases unemployment and lowers inflation—a movement down along the short-run Phillips curve.

rises above its expected rate, unemployment falls below its expected rate. This joint movement in the inflation rate and the unemployment rate is illustrated as a movement up along the short-run Phillips curve from point *A* to point *B* in the figure. Similarly, if inflation falls below its expected rate, unemployment rises above its natural rate. In this case, there is movement down along the short-run Phillips curve from point *A* to point *C*.

This negative relationship between inflation and unemployment along the short-run Phillips curve is explained by the *AS–AD* model. Figure 27.11 shows the connection between the two approaches. Initially, the aggregate demand curve is AD_0, the short-run aggregate supply curve is SAS_0, and the long-run aggregate supply curve is *LAS*. Real GDP is $1,000 billion, and the price level is 100. Aggregate demand is expected to increase, and the aggregate demand curve is expected to shift rightward to AD_1. Anticipating this increase in aggregate demand, the money wage rate rises, which shifts the short-run aggregate supply curve to SAS_1. What happens to actual inflation and real GDP depends on the *actual* change in aggregate demand.

First, suppose that aggregate demand actually increases by the amount expected, so the aggregate demand curve shifts to AD_1. The price level rises from 100 to 110, and the inflation rate is an anticipated 10 percent a year. Real GDP remains at potential GDP, and unemployment remains at its natural rate—6 percent. The economy moves to point *A* in Fig. 27.11, and it can equivalently be described as being at point *A* on the short-run Phillips curve in Fig. 27.10.

Alternatively, suppose that aggregate demand is expected to increase to AD_1 but actually increases by more than expected, to AD_2. The price level now rises to 113, a 13 percent inflation rate. Real GDP increases above potential GDP, and unemployment falls below its natural rate. We can now describe the economy as moving to point *B* in Fig. 27.11 or as being at point *B* on the short-run Phillips curve in Fig. 27.10.

Finally, suppose that aggregate demand is expected to increase to AD_1 but actually remains at AD_0. The price level now rises to 107, a 7 percent inflation rate. Real GDP falls below potential GDP, and unemployment rises above its natural rate. We can now describe the economy as moving to point *C* in Fig. 27.11 or as being at point *C* on the short-run Phillips curve in Fig. 27.10.

FIGURE 27.11

AS–AD and the Short-Run Phillips Curve

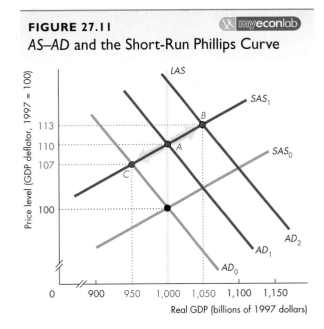

If aggregate demand is expected to increase and shift the aggregate demand curve from AD_0 to AD_1, then the money wage rate rises by an amount that shifts the short-run aggregate supply curve from SAS_0 to SAS_1. If aggregate demand increases as expected, the price level rises to 110, a 10 percent rise, and the economy is at point *A* in this figure and at point *A* on the short-run Phillips curve in Fig. 27.10. If, with the same expectations, aggregate demand increases and shifts the aggregate demand curve from AD_0 to AD_2, the price level rises to 113, a 13 percent rise, and the economy is at point *B* in this figure and at point *B* on the short-run Phillips curve in Fig. 27.10. If, with the same expectations, aggregate demand does not change, the price level rises to 107, a 7 percent rise, and the economy is at point *C* in this figure and at point *C* on the short-run Phillips curve in Fig. 27.10.

The short-run Phillips curve is like the short-run aggregate supply curve. A movement along the *SAS* curve that brings a price level above that expected and an increase in real GDP is equivalent to a movement along the short-run Phillips curve that brings an increase in the inflation rate and a decrease in the unemployment rate. (Similarly, a movement along the *SAS* curve that brings a price level below that expected and a decrease in real GDP is equivalent to a movement along the short-run Phillips curve that brings a decrease in the inflation rate and an increase in the unemployment rate.)

The Long-Run Phillips Curve

The **long-run Phillips curve** shows the relationship between inflation and unemployment when the actual inflation rate equals the expected inflation rate. The long-run Phillips curve is vertical at the natural rate of unemployment. In Fig. 27.12, it is the vertical line *LRPC*. The long-run Phillips curve tells us that any anticipated inflation rate is possible at the natural rate of unemployment. This proposition is consistent with the *AS–AD* model, which predicts that when inflation is anticipated, real GDP equals potential GDP and unemployment is at its natural rate.

When the expected inflation rate changes, the short-run Phillips curve shifts but the long-run Phillips curve does not shift. If the expected inflation rate is 10 percent a year, the short-run Phillips curve is $SRPC_0$. If the expected inflation rate falls to 7 per-cent a year, the short-run Phillips curve shifts down-ward to $SRPC_1$. The distance by which the short-run Phillips curve shifts downward when the expected inflation rate falls is equal to the change in the expected inflation rate.

To see why the short-run Phillips curve shifts when the expected inflation rate changes, let's do a thought experiment. There is full employment, and a 10 percent a year anticipated inflation is raging. The Bank of Canada now begins an attack on inflation by slowing money growth. Aggregate demand growth slows, and the inflation rate falls to 7 percent a year. At first, this decrease in inflation is *un*anticipated, so the money wage rate continues to rise at its original rate. The short-run aggregate supply curve shifts left-ward at the same pace as before. Real GDP decreases, and unemployment increases. In Fig. 27.12, the economy moves from point *A* to point *C* on $SRPC_0$.

If the actual inflation rate remains steady at 7 per-cent a year, this rate eventually comes to be expected. As this happens, wage growth slows and the short-run aggregate supply curve shifts leftward less quickly. Eventually, it shifts leftward at the same pace at which the aggregate demand curve is shifting rightward. The actual inflation rate equals the expected inflation rate, and full employment is restored. Unemployment is back at its natural rate. In Fig. 27.12, the short-run Phillips curve has shifted from $SRPC_0$ to $SRPC_1$ and the economy is at point *D*.

An increase in the expected inflation rate has the opposite effect to that shown in Fig. 27.12. Another important source of shifts in the Phillips curve is a change in the natural rate of unemployment.

Changes in the Natural Rate of Unemployment

The natural rate of unemployment changes for many reasons (see Chapter 30, pp. 719–721). A change in the natural rate of unemployment shifts both the short-run and long-run Phillips curves. Figure 27.13 illustrates such shifts. If the natural rate of unemploy-ment increases from 6 percent to 9 percent, the long-run Phillips curve shifts from $LRPC_0$ to $LRPC_1$, and if expected inflation is constant at 10 percent a year, the short-run Phillips curve shifts from $SRPC_0$ to $SRPC_1$. Because the expected inflation rate is constant, the short-run Phillips curve $SRPC_1$ intersects the long-run curve $LRPC_1$ (point *E*) at the same inflation rate at which the short-run Phillips curve $SRPC_0$ intersects the long-run curve $LRPC_0$ (point *A*).

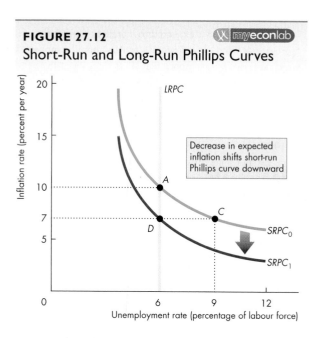

FIGURE 27.12   myeconlab

Short-Run and Long-Run Phillips Curves

The long-run Phillips curve is *LRPC*. A fall in the expected inflation rate from 10 percent a year to 7 percent a year shifts the short-run Phillips curve downward from $SRPC_0$ to $SRPC_1$. The new short-run Phillips curve intersects the long-run Phillips curve at the new expected inflation rate—point *D*. With the original expected inflation rate (of 10 per-cent), a fall in the actual inflation rate to 7 percent a year increases the unemployment rate from 6 percent to 9 per-cent, at point *C*.

FIGURE 27.13

A Change in the Natural Rate of Unemployment

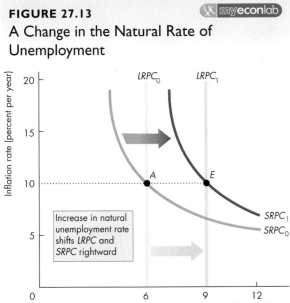

A change in the natural rate of unemployment shifts both the short-run and long-run Phillips curves. Here, the natural rate of unemployment increases from 6 percent to 9 percent, and the two Phillips curves shift right to $SRPC_1$ and $LRPC_1$. The new long-run Phillips curve intersects the new short-run Phillips curve at the expected inflation rate—point E.

The Canadian Phillips Curve

Figure 27.14(a) is a scatter diagram of inflation and unemployment since 1962. The data follow a course like a Formula 1 race track with 2004 almost at the same spot as 1962. Figure 27.14(b) interprets the data in terms of the Phillips curve. In 1962, the natural rate of unemployment was 5 percent so the long-run Phillips curve was $LRPC_1$. The expected inflation rate was 3 percent a year so the short-run Phillips curve, $SRPC_1$, intersects $LRPC_1$ at point A. During the 1970s and through 1982, the expected inflation rate and the natural rate of unemployment increased. The long-run curve shifted to $LRPC_2$ and the short-run curve shifted to $SRPC_2$. During the 1980s and 1990s, the expected inflation rate and the natural rate of unemployment decreased. The long-run curve shifted to $LRPC_3$ and the short-run curve shifted back to $SRPC_1$. The $SRPC$ of 2004 is the same as that of 1962, but in 2004, the natural rate of unemployment is higher and the expected inflation rate is lower than in 1962.

FIGURE 27.14

Phillips Curves in Canada

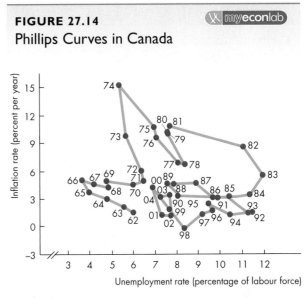

(a) The time sequence

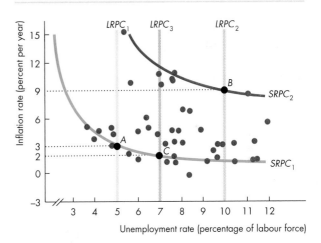

(b) Shifting Phillips curves

In part (a), each dot represents the combination of inflation and unemployment for a particular year in Canada. Part (b) interprets the data with a shifting short-run Phillips curve. The black dots A, B, and C show the combination of the natural rate of unemployment and the expected inflation rate in different periods. The short-run Phillips curve was $SRPC_1$ during the 1960s and the late 1990s and early 2000s. It was $SRPC_2$ during the early 1970s and early 1980s. The long-run Phillips curve was $LRPC_1$ during the 1960s, $LRPC_2$ during the 1970s and early 1980s, and $LRPC_3$ during the 1990s.

Source of data: Statistics Canada, CANSIM Tables 380–0002 and 380–0056.

REVIEW QUIZ

1 How would you use the Phillips curve to illustrate an unanticipated change in the inflation rate?

2 What are the effects of an unanticipated increase in the inflation rate on the unemployment rate?

3 If the expected inflation rate increases by 10 percentage points, how do the short-run Phillips curve and the long-run Phillips curve change?

4 If the natural rate of unemployment increases, what happens to the short-run Phillips curve and the long-run Phillips curve?

5 Does Canada have a stable short-run Phillips curve? Explain why or why not.

6 Does Canada have a stable long-run Phillips curve? Explain why or why not.

myeconlab Study Plan 27.4

So far, we've studied the effects of inflation on real GDP, real wages, employment, and unemployment. But inflation lowers the value of money and changes the real value of the amounts borrowed and repaid. As a result, interest rates are influenced by inflation. Let's see how.

Interest Rates and Inflation

TODAY, BUSINESSES IN CANADA CAN BORROW AT interest rates of around 6 percent a year. Businesses in Russia pay interest rates of 13 percent a year, those in Turkey pay 16 percent a year, and those in Brazil pay 20 percent a year. Canadian businesses also faced interest rates of 20 percent during the early 1980s. Why do interest rates vary so much both across countries and over time? Part of the answer is because risk differences make *real interest rates* vary across countries. Borrowers in high-risk countries pay higher interest rates than do those in low-risk countries. But another part of the answer is that the inflation rate varies.

Figure 27.15 shows that the higher the inflation rate, the higher is the nominal interest rate. This proposition is true for Canada over time in part (a) and the world in 2005 in part (b).

FIGURE 27.15   myeconlab
Inflation and the Interest Rate

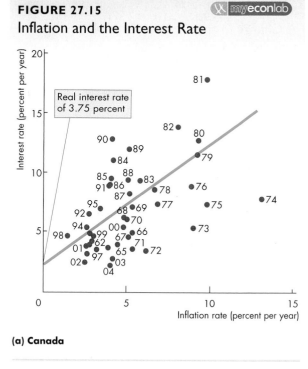

(a) Canada

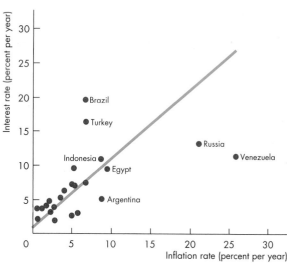

(b) Around the world

Other things remaining the same, the higher the inflation rate, the higher is the nominal interest rate. Part (a) shows this relationship between nominal interest rates and the inflation rate in Canada, and part (b) shows the relationship across a number of countries in 2005.

Sources of data: Statistics Canada, Tables 176–0043 and 380–0056, World Economic Outlook Database, International Monetary Fund, and *The Economist*, Sep. 2005

How Interest Rates Are Determined

The *real* interest rate is determined by investment demand and saving supply in the global market for financial capital. Investment demand and saving supply depend on the real interest rate. And the real interest rate adjusts to make investment plans and saving plans equal. You can think of the forces that determine the equilibrium real interest rate by using the standard demand and supply model. National real interest rates vary around the world-average real interest rate because of national differences in risk.

A *nominal* interest rate is determined by the demand for money and the quantity of money in each nation's money market. The demand for money depends on the nominal interest rate, and the quantity of money is determined by the central bank's monetary policy—the Bank of Canada's monetary policy in Canada. The nominal interest rate adjusts to make the quantity of money demanded equal to the quantity supplied. (Chapter 25, p. 604–605, explains the forces that determine the equilibrium nominal interest rate.)

Why Inflation Influences the Nominal Interest Rate

Because the real interest rate is determined in the global capital market and nominal interest rates are determined in each nation's money market, there is no tight and mechanical link between the two interest rates. But on the average, and other things remaining the same, a 1 percentage point rise in the inflation rate leads to a 1 percentage point rise in the nominal interest rate. Why? The answer is that the financial capital market and the money market are closely interconnected. The investment, saving, and demand for money decisions that people make are connected and the result is that the equilibrium nominal interest rate approximately equals the real interest rate plus the expected inflation rate.

To see why this relationship between the real interest rate and the nominal interest rate arises, think about the investment, saving, and demand for money decisions that people make. Imagine first that there is no inflation. Investment equals saving at a real interest rate of 6 percent a year. The demand for money equals the supply of money at a nominal interest rate of 6 percent a year. Teleglobe Canada is willing to pay an interest rate of 6 percent a year to get the funds it needs to pay for its global investment in new satellites. Sue and thousands of people like her are willing to save and lend Teleglobe Canada the amount it needs for its satellites if

they can get a *real* return of 6 percent a year. (Sue is saving to buy a new car.) And Teleglobe Canada, Sue, and everyone else are willingly holding the quantity of (real) money supplied by the Bank of Canada.

Now imagine that the inflation rate is steady at 4 percent a year and is expected to remain at 4 percent a year. All dollar amounts, including satellite service profits and car prices, are rising by 4 percent a year. If Teleglobe Canada was willing to pay a 6 percent interest rate when there was no inflation, it is now willing to pay 10 percent interest. Its profits are rising by 4 percent a year, so it is *really* paying only 6 percent. Similarly, if Sue was willing to lend at a 6 percent interest rate when there was no inflation, she is now willing to lend only if she gets 10 percent interest. The price of the car Sue is planning to buy is rising by 4 percent a year, so she is *really* getting only a 6 percent interest rate.

Because borrowers are willing to pay the higher rate and lenders are willing to lend only if they get the higher rate when inflation is anticipated, the *nominal interest rate* increases by an amount equal to the expected inflation rate. The *real interest rate* remains constant.

At a nominal interest rate of 10 percent a year, people are willingly holding the quantity of (real) money supplied by the Bank of Canada. This quantity is less than that with zero inflation.

REVIEW QUIZ

1 What is the relationship between the real interest rate, the nominal interest rate, and the expected inflation rate?
2 Why does inflation change the nominal interest rate?

myeconlab Study Plan 27.5

Reading Between the Lines on pp. 650–651 looks at the views of an economist who believes there is a long-run tradeoff between inflation and unemployment.

Your task in the next chapter is to see how the Bank of Canada uses the tools of monetary policy to influence the inflation rate and to try to keep its rate inside a target range.

Inflation–Unemployment Tradeoff

THE VANCOUVER SUN, JUNE 18, 2002

High jobless rate avoidable

Canada could have done more to stimulate employment through the 1990s without risking inflation, the winner of the 2001 Nobel Prize in Economics said Monday.

Dr. George Akerlof said during a meeting of the Canadian Institute for Advanced Research that the chairman of the U.S. Federal Reserve Board, Alan Greenspan, went against the advice of his staff and traditional economic theory and kept stimulating the economy with low interest rates as unemployment hit historic lows.

Canada took a more conservative and ideological approach.

The result was Canada had an unemployment rate much higher than that in the United States, where inflation stayed low even when unemployment fell below five per cent as a result of the investment generated by the economic stimulus program.

"The Canadian economy serves up a sober lesson," said Akerlof, who is a professor of economics at the University of California at Berkeley.

As the economy stalled in the past couple of years, the Bank of Canada lowered interest rates, but unemployment rates have been held high by the global recession, Akerlof said.

"You can't expect that Canada wouldn't have the same repercussions that are happening in the rest of the world," he said.

Akerlof recommended that in future, Canada adopt a policy similar to that employed in the U.S.

"I sincerely hope the Canadian unemployment of the 1990s is not going to repeat itself," he said.

...

Akerlof won the Nobel Prize for work he did more than 30 years ago, describing how markets break down when buyers and sellers have conflicting needs and expectations.

Craig McInnes/*The Vancouver Sun.*

Essence of the Story

■ George Akerlof, a professor of economics at the University of California at Berkeley and a Nobel Laureate, says that Canada could have had higher employment (lower unemployment) with no higher inflation rate during the 1990s.

■ He contrasted Canada with the United States and said that as the unemployment rate hit historic lows, the U.S. kept stimulating the economy with low interest rates.

■ U.S. inflation stayed low even when unemployment fell below 5 percent because of the investment generated by the economic stimulus program.

■ Canada took a more conservative and ideological approach and had an unemployment rate much higher than that in the United States.

Economic Analysis

■ It is difficult to recognize the Canada portrayed by George Akerlof.

■ Canada's unemployment rate was indeed higher than the U.S. unemployment rate.

■ But the gap between the Canadian and U.S. unemployment rates, which opened up during the early 1980s (not the 1990s), was persistent and not cyclical. And the gap narrowed during the early 2000s.

■ Figure 1 shows the unemployment rates in the two countries.

■ Because the unemployment gap was persistent, it is likely that it represents an increase in the natural rate of unemployment in Canada.

■ If Canada's natural rate of unemployment is higher than the U.S. rate, stimulating aggregate demand will bring no improvement in the unemployment situation, but will bring greater inflation.

■ Canada had a more severe inflation problem than the United States during the early 1980s.

■ But Canada brought its inflation under control and had lower inflation than the United States during the 1990s and the early 2000s.

■ Figure 2 shows the inflation records in the two countries.

■ George Akerlof says that U.S. unemployment fell because of a high investment rate.

■ He implies that Canada's investment rate was too low and could have been boosted.

■ Figure 3 shows that generally Canada has invested a larger percentage of its GDP than the United States has invested.

■ It is true that U.S. investment increased during the 1990s. But it increased from a very low level and began to catch up to Canada's higher investment rate.

■ Canada chose to fight inflation and accept a temporarily higher unemployment rate. But the persistently higher unemployment rate in Canada is a natural phenomenon that cannot be changed with demand stimulation.

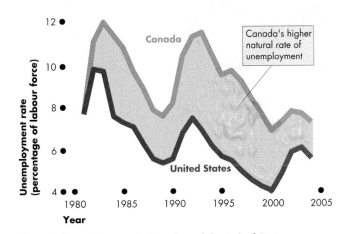

Figure 1 Unemployment in Canada and the United States

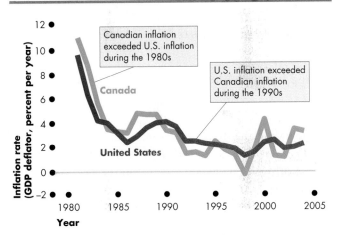

Figure 2 Inflation in Canada and the United States

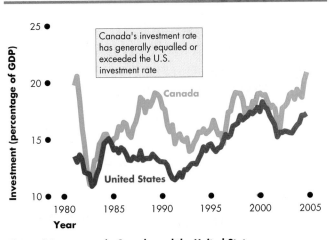

Figure 3 Investment in Canada and the United States

SUMMARY

KEY POINTS

Inflation: Demand-Pull and Cost-Push
(p. 632–637)

- Inflation is a process of persistently rising prices and falling value of money
- Demand-pull inflation arises from increasing aggregate demand.
- The main sources of increases in aggregate demand are increases in the quantity of money, government expenditures, or exports.
- Cost-push inflation can result from any factor that decreases aggregate supply.
- The main sources of decreases in aggregate supply are increasing money wage rates and increasing prices of key raw materials.

The Quantity Theory of Money (pp. 638–639)

- The quantity theory of money is the proposition that money growth and inflation move up and down together in the long run.
- The Canadian and international evidence is consistent with the quantity theory on the average.

Effects of Inflation (pp. 640–644)

- Inflation is costly when it is unanticipated because it creates inefficiencies and redistributes income and wealth.
- People try to anticipate inflation to avoid its costs.
- Forecasts of inflation based on all the available relevant information are called rational expectations.
- A moderate anticipated inflation has a small cost. A rapid anticipated inflation is costly because it decreases potential GDP and slows economic growth.

Inflation and Unemployment: The Phillips Curve (pp. 644–648)

- The short-run Phillips curve shows the tradeoff between inflation and unemployment when the expected inflation rate and the natural rate of unemployment are constant.

- The long-run Phillips curve, which is vertical, shows that when the actual inflation rate equals the expected inflation rate, the unemployment rate equals the natural rate of unemployment.
- Unexpected changes in the inflation rate bring movements along the short-run Phillips curve.
- Changes in expected inflation shift the short-run Phillips curve.
- Changes in the natural rate of unemployment shift both the short-run and long-run Phillips curves.

Interest Rates and Inflation (pp. 648–649)

- The higher the expected inflation rate, the higher is the nominal interest rate.
- As the expected inflation rate rises, borrowers willingly pay a higher interest rate and lenders successfully demand a higher interest rate.
- The nominal interest rate adjusts to equal the real interest rate plus the expected inflation rate.

KEY FIGURES

Figure 27.2   A Demand-Pull Rise in the Price Level, 633
Figure 27.3   A Demand-Pull Inflation Spiral, 634
Figure 27.4   A Cost-Push Rise in the Price Level, 636
Figure 27.6   A Cost-Push Inflation Spiral, 637
Figure 27.9   Anticipated Inflation, 642
Figure 27.10 A Short-Run Phillips Curve, 644
Figure 27.12 Short-Run and Long-Run Phillips Curves, 646

KEY TERMS

Cost-push inflation, 635
Demand-pull inflation, 633
Equation of exchange, 638
Long-run Phillips curve, 646
Phillips curve, 644
Quantity theory of money, 638
Rational expectation, 641
Short-run Phillips curve, 644
Velocity of circulation, 638

PROBLEMS

Go to ⓧ myeconlab for solutions to odd-
numbered problems and additional exercises.

1. The figure shows an economy's long-run aggregate supply curve *LAS*; three aggregate demand
   curves AD_0, AD_1, and AD_2; and three short-run
   aggregate supply curves SAS_0, SAS_1, and SAS_2.
   The economy starts out on the curves AD_0 and
   SAS_0.

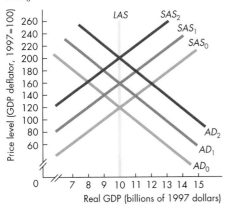

   Some events occur that generate a demand-pull
   inflation.
   a. List the events that might cause a demand-
      pull inflation.
   b. Using the figure, describe the initial effects
      of a demand-pull inflation.
   c. Using the figure, describe what happens as a
      demand-pull inflation spiral unwinds.

2. In the economy described in problem 1, some
   events then occur that generate a cost-push
   inflation.
   a. List the events that might cause a cost-push
      inflation.
   b. Using the figure, describe the initial effects
      of a cost-push inflation.
   c. Using the figure, describe what happens as a
      cost-push inflation spiral unwinds.

3. Quantecon is a country in which the quantity
   theory of money operates. The country has a
   constant population, capital stock, and technology. In year 1, real GDP was $400 million, the
   price level was 200, and the velocity of circulation of money was 20. In year 2, the quantity of
   money was 20 percent higher than in year 1.
   a. What was the quantity of money in year 1?

   b. What was the quantity of money in year 2?
   c. What was the price level in year 2?
   d. What was the level of real GDP in year 2?
   e. What was the velocity of circulation in year 2?

4. In Quantecon described in problem 3, in year
   3, the quantity of money falls to one-fifth of its
   year 2 level.
   a. What is the quantity of money in year 3?
   b. What is the price level in year 3?
   c. What is the level of real GDP in year 3?
   d. What is the velocity of circulation in year 3?
   e. If it takes more than one year for the full
      quantity theory effect to occur, what do you
      predict happens to real GDP in Quantecon
      in year 3? Why?

5. The economy described in problem 1 starts out
   on the curves AD_0 and SAS_0. Some events now
   occur that generate a perfectly anticipated inflation.
   a. List the events that might cause a perfectly
      anticipated inflation.
   b. Using the figure, describe the initial effects
      of an anticipated inflation.
   c. Using the figure, describe what happens as
      an anticipated inflation proceeds.

6. In the economy described in problem 1, suppose that people anticipate deflation (a falling
   price level) but aggregate demand turns out not
   to change.
   a. What happens to the short-run and long-run
      aggregate supply curves? (Draw some new
      curves if you need to.)
   b. Using the figure, describe the initial effects
      of an anticipated deflation.
   c. Using the figure, describe what happens as it
      becomes obvious to everyone that the antici-
      pated deflation is not going to occur.

7. An economy has an unemployment rate of 4 percent and an inflation rate of 5 percent at point *A*
   in the figure. Some events then occur that move
   the economy to point *D*.
   a. Describe the events that could move the econ-
      omy from point *A* to point *D*.
   b. Draw in the figure the economy's short-run
      and long-run Phillips curves when the econ-
      omy is at point *A*.
   c. Draw in the figure the economy's short-run
      and long-run Phillips curves when the econ-
      omy is at point *D*.

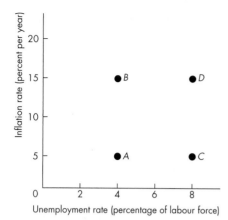

8. In the economy described in problem 7, some events occur that move the economy from point *B* to point *C*.

   a. Describe the events that could move the economy from point *B* to point *C*.
   b. Draw in the diagram the economy's short-run and long-run Phillips curves when the economy is at point *B*.
   c. Draw in the diagram the economy's short-run and long-run Phillips curves when the economy is at point *C*.

9. An economy with a natural rate of unemployment of 4 percent and an expected inflation rate of 6 percent a year has the following inflation and unemployment history:

Year	Inflation rate (percent per year)	Unemployment rate (percentage of labour force)
2001	10	2
2002	8	3
2003	6	4
2004	4	5
2005	2	6

   a. Draw a graph of the economy's short-run and long-run Phillips curves.
   b. If the actual inflation rate rises from 6 percent a year to 8 percent a year, what is the change in the unemployment rate? Explain why it occurs.

10. For the economy described in problem 9, the natural rate of unemployment increases to 5 percent and the expected inflation rate falls to 5 percent a year. Draw the new short-run and long-run Phillips curves in the graph.

CRITICAL THINKING

1. Study *Reading Between the Lines* on pp. 650–651 and then answer the following questions:

   a. What does George Akerlof believe about the tradeoff between inflation and unemployment?
   b. Why, according to Akerlof, did the United States have a better unemployment performance than Canada?
   c. Do you think the data on inflation and unemployment are consistent with the view that the natural rate of unemployment is 7 percent? Explain why or why not.

WEB EXERCISES

Use the links on ⓧ myeconlab to work the following exercises.

1. Obtain data on the growth rate of the quantity of money and the inflation rate in Canada since 2000.

   a. Calculate the average growth rate of the quantity of money since 2000.
   b. Calculate the average inflation rate since 2000.
   c. Make a graph of the growth rate of the quantity of money and the inflation rate since 2000.
   d. Interpret your graph and explain what it tells you about the forces that generate inflation and the relationship between money growth and inflation.

2. Obtain data on the inflation rate and the unemployment rate in the United States during the 1990s and 2000s.

   a. Make a graph using the data you've obtained that is similar to Fig. 27.14.
   b. Describe the similarities and the differences in relationship between inflation and unemployment found in the United States and in Canada.

Monetary Policy

CHAPTER 28

Fiddling with the Knobs

On eight pre-set dates a year, the Bank of Canada announces whether the interest rate will rise, fall, or remain constant until the next decision date. Financial market traders and economic journalists watch the economy for clues about what the Bank will decide. Then, every business day, the Bank of Canada operates in financial markets to implement its decision and ensure that its target interest rate is achieved.

How does the Bank of Canada make its interest rate decision? What exactly does the Bank do every day to keep interest rates where it wants them? And do the Bank's interest rate changes influence the economy in the way the Bank wants and with enough precision? Can the Bank speed up economic growth and reduce unemployment by lowering interest rates and keep inflation in check by raising interest rates?

The Bank of Canada's current monetary policy strategy is relatively new. And it is not the only strategy that might be used. Is the current monetary policy strategy the best one? What are the benefits and what are the risks associated with the strategy?

◆ You learned about the functions of the Bank of Canada and its role in the payments system in Chapter 25. In this chapter, you will learn about the Bank of Canada's monetary policy. You will learn how the Bank influences interest rates and how interest rates influence the economy. You will also review the alternative ways in which monetary policy might be conducted. In *Reading Between the Lines* at the end of the chapter, you will see the dilemma that the Bank of Canada sometimes faces as it tries to steer a steady course between inflation and recession.

After studying this chapter, you will be able to

- **Describe Canada's monetary policy objectives and the framework for setting and achieving them**
- **Explain how the Bank of Canada makes its interest rate decision and achieves it interest rate target**
- **Explain the transmission channels through which the Bank of Canada influences the inflation rate**
- **Explain and compare alternative monetary policy strategies**

Monetary Policy Objective and Framework

CANADA'S MONETARY POLICY OBJECTIVE AND the framework for setting and achieving that objective stem from the relationship between the Bank of Canada and the government of Canada.

We'll first discuss the objective of monetary policy and then describe the framework and assignment of responsibility for achieving the objective.

Monetary Policy Objective

The objective of monetary policy is ultimately political, and it stems from the mandate of the Bank that is set out in the Bank of Canada Act.

Bank of Canada Act The objective of monetary policy as set out in the preamble to the Bank of Canada Act of 1935 is to

regulate credit and currency in the best interests of the economic life of the nation ... and to mitigate by its influence fluctuations in the general level of production, trade, prices and employment, so far as may be possible within the scope of monetary action ...

In simple language, these words have come to mean that the Bank's job is to control the quantity of money and interest rates in order to avoid inflation and, when possible, prevent excessive swings in real GDP growth and unemployment.

This emphasis on inflation has been made concrete by an agreement between the Bank and government.

Joint Statement of the Government of Canada and the Bank of Canada In a joint statement (the most recent of which was made in 2001), the government of Canada and the Bank of Canada have agreed that

- The inflation control target range will be 1 to 3 percent a year.
- Policy will aim at keeping the trend of inflation at the 2 percent target midpoint.
- The agreement will run for five years and be reviewed before the end of 2006.

Interpretation of the Agreement The inflation-control target uses the Consumer Price Index (or CPI) as the measure of inflation. So it is the CPI inflation rate that the Bank has agreed to keep on a 2 percent target trend.

But the Bank also pays close attention to **core inflation**, which is the CPI excluding the eight most volatile prices—the prices of fruit, vegetables, gasoline, fuel oil, natural gas, mortgage interest, intercity transportation, and tobacco—and also excluding changes in indirect taxes—taxes such as GST, HST, and provincial sales taxes.

The Bank believes that the core inflation rate provides a better measure of the underlying inflation trend and a better prediction of future CPI inflation.

Although the Bank watches the core inflation rate closely, it must take into account the possibility that the eight volatile elements that it excludes have a different *trend* inflation rate from the remaining items. As it turns out, between 1995 and 2000, the core and overall CPI trends were the same. But between 2000 and 2005, the core inflation rate ran at about 0.5 percent a year below the overall CPI inflation rate.

Actual Inflation The performance of Canada's inflation since the mid-1990s, when the current target was set, has been close to target. Figure 28.1 shows just how close.

In Fig. 28.1(a), you can see the target range of 1 to 3 percent a year. And you can see that the actual inflation rate has only rarely gone outside the target range. You can also see that the inflation rate has been both above target and below target on occasion, so there is no bias or tendency for inflation to be persistently above or below target.

In Fig. 28.1(b), you can see the trend of inflation at the 2 percent target midpoint. The actual path of the CPI was on trend from 1995 through 1998 and again from 2001 into 2005. But between 1999 and 2001, the CPI moved *below* the 2 percent trend line.

The general message of Fig. 28.1 is that the Bank of Canada has done a remarkable job of holding inflation to its 2 percent target with only small and temporary deviations from that goal.

Rationale for an Inflation-Control Target Two main benefits flow from adopting an inflation-control target. The first benefit is that the purpose of the Bank of Canada's policy actions is more clearly

FIGURE 28.1

myeconlab

Inflation-Control Targets and Outcome

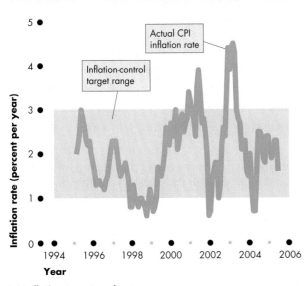

(a) Inflation target and outcome

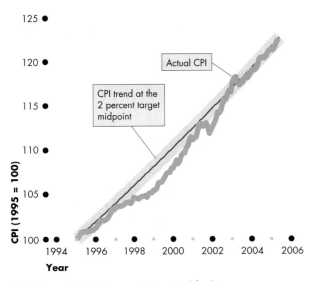

(b) CPI trend at the 2 percent target midpoint

The Bank of Canada and the government of Canada agreed that the inflation-control target range will be 1 percent to 3 percent (part a) and that policy will aim at keeping the trend of inflation at the 2 percent target midpoint (part b).

Sources of data: Statistics Canada, Table 326–0016 and Bank of Canada, Joint Statement of the Government of Canada and the Bank of Canada on the Renewal of the Inflation-Control Target, 17 May, 2001.

understood by financial market traders. A clearer understanding leads to fewer surprises and mistakes on the part of savers and investors.

The second benefit is that the target provides an anchor for expectations about future inflation. Firmly held expectations of low inflation make the short-run output-inflation (or unemployment-inflation) trade-off as favourable as possible. (see Chapter 27, pp. 644–648). Firmly held (and correct) inflation expectations help people make better economic decisions, which in turn helps to achieve a more efficient allocation of resources and a more stable economic growth.

Controversy About the Inflation-Control Target
Not everyone agrees that the adoption of an inflation-control target brings benefits. Critics argue that by focusing on inflation, the Bank of Canada sometimes permits the unemployment rate or real GDP growth rate to suffer.

The fear of these critics is that if the inflation rate begins to edge upward towards and perhaps beyond the upper limit of the target range, the Bank of Canada might reign in aggregate demand and push the economy into recession. The Bank might also end up permitting the dollar to appreciate on the foreign exchange market and making exports suffer.

One response of supporters of inflation targeting is that by keeping inflation low and stable, monetary policy makes its maximum possible contribution towards achieving full employment and sustained economic growth.

Another response is, "look at the record." The last time the Bank of Canada created a recession was at the beginning of the 1990s when it was faced with the threat of ongoing double-digit inflation. Since that time, monetary policy has been sensitive to the state of employment while maintaining its focus on achieving its inflation target.

Responsibility for Monetary Policy

The government of Canada and the Bank of Canada jointly agree on the monetary policy target but the Bank of Canada Act places responsibility for the conduct of monetary policy on the Bank's Governing Council.

Governing Council of the Bank of Canada The members of the Bank's Governing Council are the Governor, Senior Deputy Governor, and four Deputy

Governors. All the members of the Governing Council are experts in monetary economics and monetary policymaking and, normally, they are people who have been promoted from withing the ranks of economists working in the Bank's research and policy departments.

The current Governor (appointed in 2001) is David Dodge, an economist who has had wide experience both in government departments and the Bank.

Bank of Canada Economists The Bank of Canada employs research economists who write papers on monetary policy and the state of the Canadian and international economies. These economists provide the Governing Council with extensive briefings that guide monetary policy.

Consultations with the Government The Bank of Canada Act requires regular consultations on monetary policy between the Governor and the Minister of Finance. The Act also lays out what must happen if the Governor and the Minister disagree in a profound way.

In such an event, the Minister would direct the Bank in writing to follow a specified course and the Bank would be obliged to accept the directive. The Governor would most likely resign in such a situation. While in the past there have been disagreements between the government and the Bank, no formal directive has ever been issued.

You now know the objective of monetary policy and can describe the framework and assignment of responsibility for achieving that objective. Your next task is to see how the Bank of Canada conducts its monetary policy.

REVIEW QUIZ

1 What is the objective of monetary policy?
2 What are the two parts of the inflation-control target?
3 What is core inflation and how does it differ from overall CPI inflation?
4 What is the Bank of Canada's record in achieving its inflation-control target?

myeconlab **Study Plan 28.1**

The Conduct of Monetary Policy

IN THIS SECTION, WE DESCRIBE THE WAY IN which the Bank of Canada conducts its monetary policy. We follow this description in the next section with an account of alternative approaches to monetary policy and an evaluation of the Bank's approach.

Choosing a Policy Instrument

As the sole issuer of Canadian money, the Bank of Canada can decide to control the quantity of money (the monetary base), the price of Canadian money on the foreign exchange market (the exchange rate), or the opportunity cost of holding money (the short-term interest rate). If you need a quick refresher, check back to Chapter 25, pp 604–605 to see how the quantity of money affects the interest rate and to Chapter 26, pp. 623–624 to see how the interest rate or direct intervention in the foreign exchange market affects the exchange rate.

While the Bank of Canada can set any *one* of these three variables, it cannot set all three. The values of two of them are the consequence of the value at which the third one is set. If the Bank decided to decrease the quantity of money, both the interest rate and the exchange rate would rise. If the Bank decided to raise the interest rate, the quantity of money would decrease and the exchange rate would rise. And if the Bank decided to lower the exchange rate, the quantity of money would increase and the interest rate would fall.

So the Bank must decide which of these three instruments to use. It might decide to select one and stick with it. Or it might switch among them.

The Overnight Rate

The Bank of Canada's choice of policy instrument (which is the same choice as that made by most other major central banks) is a short-term interest rate. Given this choice, the Bank permits the exchange rate and the quantity of money to find their own equilibrium values and has no preset views about what those values should be.

The specific interest rate that the Bank of Canada targets is the **overnight loans rate**, which is the interest rate on overnight loans that members of the Large Value Transfer System or LVTS (the big banks) make to each other. (For a refresher about the LVTS, see p. 596.)

Figure 28.2 shows the overnight loans rate since 1995. You can see that the overnight loans rate was a bit more than 8 percent a year in 1995 and it was increased to around 6 percent a year on two occasions. All of these periods of a high overnight loans rate are ones in which inflation was a concern.

In recent years, the overnight rate has been at historically low levels. The reason is that with inflation well anchored inside its target range, the Bank wanted to lean in the direction of avoiding recession.

Since late 2000, the Bank has established eight fixed dates on which it announces its overnight rate target for the coming period of approximately six weeks. Before 2000, the Bank announced changes in the overnight rate whenever it thought a change was required.

Although the Bank can change the overnight rate by any (reasonable) amount that it chooses, it normally changes the rate by only a quarter of a percentage point.[2]

How does the Bank decide the appropriate level for the overnight rate? And how, having made that decision, does the Bank get the overnight rate to move to the target level? We'll now answer these two questions.

The Bank's Decision-Making Process

Two alternative decision-making processes might be used. They are summarized by the terms:

- Instrument rule
- Targeting rule

Instrument Rule An **instrument rule** is a decision rule for monetary policy that sets the policy instrument at a level that is based on the current state of the economy. The best known instrument rule is the *Taylor rule*, which sets the interest rate at a level that depends on the deviation of the inflation rate from target and the size and direction of the output gap. For each percentage point by which inflation is above target the interest rate is set one percentage point higher. And for each percentage point by which real GDP exceeds potential GDP (the percentage size of the output gap), the interest rate is set another percentage point higher. (We examine the Taylor rule later in this chapter—see p. 670.)

Targeting Rule A **targeting rule** is a decision rule for monetary policy that sets the policy instrument at a level that makes the forecast of the ultimate policy target equal to the target. Where the ultimate policy target is the inflation rate and the instrument is the overnight rate, the targeting rule sets the overnight rate at a level that makes the forecast of the inflation rate equal to the inflation target.

To implement such a targeting rule, a central bank must gather and process a large amount of information about the economy, the way it responds to shocks, and the way it responds to policy. It must then process all this data and come to a judgement about the best setting for the policy instrument.

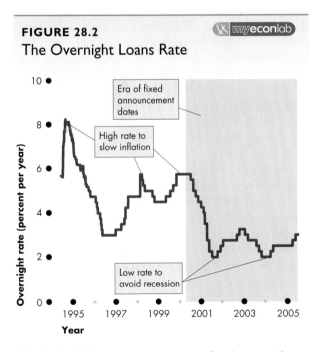

FIGURE 28.2

The Overnight Loans Rate

The Bank of Canada sets a target range for the overnight loans rate and then takes actions to keep the rate inside its target range. When the Bank wants to slow inflation, it takes actions that raise the overnight loans rate. When the Bank wants to avoid recession and inflation is low, it takes actions that lower the overnight loans rate.

Source of data: Bank of Canada, Banking and Financial Statistics, Table F1.

___
[2] A quarter of a percentage point is also called 25 *basis points*. A basis point is one-hundredth of one percentage point.

The Bank of Canada (along with most other central banks) follows a process that uses a targeting rule. For the Bank of Canada, the process begins with an exercise that uses a model of the Canadian economy that you can think of as a sophisticated version of the *AS–AD* model (see Chapter 22). The Bank's economists provide the Governor and Governing Council with a base line forecast that has the overnight rate set at a level that hits the inflation target two years in the future.

All the available regional, national, and international data on macroeconomic performance, financial markets, and inflation expectations are reviewed, discussed, and weighed in a careful deliberative process that ends with the Governing Council finding a consensus on the interest rate level to set.

After announcing an interest rate decision, the Bank engages in a public communication to explain the reasons for the Bank's decision.

Hitting the Overnight Rate Target

Once an interest rate decision is made, the Bank of Canada achieves its target by using two tools:

■ Operating band
■ Open market operations

Operating Band The **operating band** is the target overnight rate plus or minus 0.25 percentage points. So the operating band is 0.5 percentage points wide. The Bank of Canada creates the operating band by setting two other interest rates: bank rate and the interest rate on reserves.

Bank rate is the interest rate that the Bank of Canada charges big (LVTS participating) banks on loans. If a bank is short of reserves, it can always obtain reserves from the Bank of Canada but it must pay bank rate on the amount of borrowed reserves.

The Bank of Canada sets bank rate at the target overnight rate plus 0.25 percentage points. So, for example, when the target overnight rate is 4 percent a year, bank rate is 4.25 percent a year.

Because the Bank of Canada is willing to lend funds to banks at this interest rate, bank rate acts as a cap on the overnight loans rate. If a bank can borrow from the Bank of Canada at bank rate, it will not borrow from another bank unless the overnight loans rate is lower than or equal to bank rate.

The Bank of Canada pays banks interest on their reserves at the Bank of Canada. The Bank calls these reserves "settlement balances" and the interest rate that they earn is the **settlement balances rate**. The Bank of Canada sets the settlement balances rate at the target overnight rate minus 0.25 percentage point, which also equals the low end of the Bank's target range for the overnight loans rate. If banks can earn the settlement balances rate from the Bank of Canada, they will not make overnight loans to other banks unless they earn a higher interest rate than what the Bank of Canada is paying.

You can see now that the Bank of Canada can always make the overnight loans rate remain within 0.25 percentage points of its target. But the Bank wants to do better than that. It wants to keep the overnight loans rate at its target and not at one end of the range or the other. The second policy tool is used to move the overnight loans rate to its target.

Open Market Operations An **open market operation** is the purchase or sale of government of Canada securities—Treasury bills and government bonds—by the Bank of Canada from or to a chartered bank or the public. When the Bank of Canada buys securities, it pays for them with newly created reserves that are held by banks. When the Bank of Canada sells securities, it is paid for them with reserves held by banks. So open market operations directly influence the reserves of banks.

During the morning of each business day, banks trade loans with each other. And just before noon, the Bank of Canada conducts open market operations if they are needed.

If the overnight rate is above target, the Bank buys securities to increase the reserves of the banking system and increase the supply of overnight funds. If the overnight rate is below target, the Bank sells securities to decrease the reserves of the banking system and decrease the supply of overnight funds. If the overnight rate is at the target level, the Bank neither buys nor sells securities.

How an Open Market Operation Works

When the Bank of Canada conducts an open market operation, the reserves of the banking system change. To see why this outcome occurs, we'll trace the effects of an open market operation in which the Bank of Canada *buys* $100 million of government securities in the open market from CIBC.

When the Bank of Canada makes this transaction:

1. CIBC has $100 million less securities, and the Bank of Canada has $100 million more securities.
2. The Bank of Canada pays for the securities by placing $100 million in CIBC's deposit account at the Bank of Canada.

Figure 28.3 shows the effects of these actions on the balance sheets of the Bank of Canada and the CIBC. Ownership of the securities passes from CIBC to the Bank of Canada, so CIBC's assets decrease by $100 million and the Bank of Canada's assets increase by $100 million, as shown by the blue arrow running from CIBC to the Bank of Canada.

The Bank of Canada pays for the securities by placing $100 million in CIBC's deposit account at the Bank of Canada, as shown by the green arrow running from the Bank of Canada to CIBC.

The Bank of Canada's assets increase by $100 million, and its liabilities also increase by $100 million. CIBC's total assets are unchanged. It has sold securities in exchange for reserves.

If the Bank of Canada *sells* $100 million of government securities in the open market, the events that you've just seen occur in reverse.

When the Bank of Canada sells securities:

1. CIBC has $100 million more securities, and the Bank of Canada has $100 million less securities.
2. CIBC pays for the securities by using $100 million of its deposit account at the Bank of Canada. CIBC's reserves decrease by $100 million.

Figure 28.4 shows the effects of these actions on the balance sheets of the Bank of Canada and CIBC. Ownership of the securities passes from the Bank of Canada to CIBC, so CIBC's assets increase by $100 million and the Bank of Canada's assets decrease by $100 million, as shown by the blue arrow running from the Bank of Canada to CIBC.

CIBC uses $100 million of its deposit account at the Bank of Canada to pay for the securities, as the green arrow running from CIBC to the Bank of Canada shows.

The Bank of Canada's assets decrease by $100 million, and its liabilities also decrease by $100 million. CIBC's total assets are unchanged. It has used reserves to buy securities.

An increase or a decrease in reserves changes the overnight loans rate by changing the demand for and supply of overnight loans.

FIGURE 28.3   myeconlab

The Bank of Canada Buys Securities in the Open Market

The Bank of Canada

Assets		Liabilities	
Securities	+$100	Reserves of CIBC	+$100

The Bank of Canada buys securities from a bank ...   ... and pays for the securities by increasing the reserves of the bank

CIBC

Assets		Liabilities
Securities	–$100	
Reserves	+$100	

When the Bank of Canada buys securities in the open market, it creates reserves. Bank of Canada assets and liabilities increase and the selling bank exchanges securities for reserves.

FIGURE 28.4   myeconlab

The Bank of Canada Sells Securities in the Open Market

The Bank of Canada

Assets		Liabilities	
Securities	–$100	Reserves of CIBC	–$100

The Bank of Canada sells securities to a bank ...   ... and the bank uses its reserves to pay for the securities

CIBC

Assets		Liabilities
Securities	+$100	
Reserves	–$100	

When the Bank of Canada sells securities in the open market, it reduces reserves. Bank of Canada assets and liabilities decrease and the buying bank exchanges reserves for securities.

Equilibrium in the Market for Reserves

To see how an open market operation changes the overnight loans rate, we must see what happens in the market for the reserves of the banks.

Banks hold reserves so they can make payments. The amount that a bank will be called on to pay at any given moment fluctuates and cannot be forecast accurately. If a bank runs out of reserves and is obliged to make a payment, reserves must be borrowed from the Bank of Canada. So bank rate is the opportunity cost of borrowed reserves.

The more reserves a bank holds, the less likely it will need to borrow at bank rate. But reserves are costly to hold. The alternative to holding reserves is to lend them to someone else. The higher the interest rate at which reserves can be loaned, the higher is the opportunity cost of holding reserves. And the higher the opportunity cost, the greater is the incentive to economize on the quantity of reserves.

So the quantity of reserves demanded by banks depends on the overnight loans rate. The higher the overnight rate, other things remaining the same, the smaller is the quantity of reserves demanded.

Figure 28.5 shows the demand curve for reserves as the curve labelled *RD*. The *x*-axis measures the quantity of reserves held. If the entire banking system is borrowing from the Bank of Canada, reserves are negative. The *y*-axis measures the overnight rate. You can see that the overnight rate always lies inside the operating band. Why?

The overnight rate cannot exceed bank rate because, if it did, a bank could earn a profit by borrowing from the Bank of Canada and lending to another bank. But all banks can borrow from the Bank of Canada at bank rate, so no bank is willing to pay more than bank rate to borrow reserves.

The overnight rate cannot fall below the settlement balances rate because, if it did, a bank could earn a profit by borrowing from another bank and increasing its reserves at the Bank of Canada. But all banks can earn the settlement balances rate at the Bank of Canada, so no bank is willing to lend reserves at a rate below the settlements balances rate.

The Bank of Canada's open market operations determine the quantity of reserves in the banking system. Equilibrium in the market for reserves—where the quantity of reserves demanded equals the quantity supplied—determines the overnight rate. So by using the open market operations, the Bank of Canada can keep the overnight rate on target.

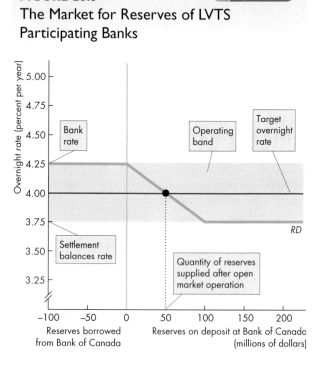

FIGURE 28.5   myeconlab

The Market for Reserves of LVTS Participating Banks

The demand curve for reserves is *RD*. If the overnight rate equals bank rate, banks are indifferent between borrowing reserves and lending reserves. The demand curve is horizontal at bank rate. If the overnight rate equals the settlement balances rate, banks are indifferent between holding reserves and lending reserves. The demand curve is horizontal at the settlement balances rate. Equilibrium, where the quantity of reserves demanded equals the quantity supplied, determines the overnight rate.

REVIEW QUIZ

1 What is the Bank of Canada's monetary policy instrument?
2 Summarize the Bank of Canada's monetary policy decision-making process.
3 What is the operating band? What does it do?
4 What happens when the Bank of Canada buys or sells securities in the open market?
5 How is the overnight rate determined in the market for reserves?

myeconlab   **Study Plan 28.2**

Monetary Policy Transmission

YOU'VE SEEN THAT THE BANK OF CANADA'S GOAL is to keep the inflation rate as close as possible to 2 percent a year. And you've seen how the Bank of Canada can use its power in the market for bank reserves to set the overnight rate at its desired level. We're now going to trace the events that follow a change in the overnight rate and see how those events lead to the ultimate goal of keeping inflation in check. We'll begin with a quick overview of the transmission process and then look at each step a bit more closely.

Quick Overview

When the Bank of Canada lowers the overnight rate, other interest rates and the exchange rate also decrease. The quantity of money increases, and the amount of credit and loans that people and businesses take increases. The lower interest rate increases consumption expenditure and investment. And the lower exchange rate makes Canadian exports cheaper and imports more costly. So net exports increase. Easier bank credit brings an expansion of loans, which reinforces the effects of lower interest rates on consumption expenditure and investment. Aggregate demand increases, which increases real GDP and the price level relative to what they would have been. So real GDP growth and inflation increase.

Similarly, when the Bank of Canada raises the overnight rate, other interest rates and the exchange rate also increase. The quantity of money decreases, and the amount of credit and loans that people and businesses take decreases. The higher interest rate decreases consumption expenditure and investment. And the higher exchange rate makes Canadian exports more expensive and imports cheaper. So net exports decrease. Tighter bank credit brings a contraction of loans, which reinforces the effects of higher interest rates on consumption expenditure and investment. Aggregate demand decreases, which decreases real GDP and the price level relative to what they would have been. So real GDP growth and inflation decrease.

Figure 28.6 provides a schematic summary of these ripple effects, which stretch out over a period of between one and two years. The interest rate and

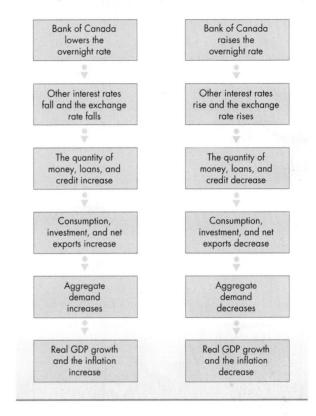

FIGURE 28.6

The Channels for the Ripple Effects of a Change in the Overnight Rate

exchange rate effects are immediate. The effects on money, loans, and credit follow in a few weeks and run for a few months. Spending plans change and real GDP growth changes after about one year. And the inflation rate changes between one year and two years after the change in the overnight rate.

We're going to look at each stage in the transmission process, starting with the interest rate effects.

Interest Rate Fluctuations

The first effect of monetary policy is a change in the interest rate. This effect occurs quickly and relatively predictably. Figure 28.7 shows the fluctuations in four interest rates: the overnight loans rate, the 3-month Treasury bill rate, the 10-year government bond rate, and the long-term corporate bond rate. We've run this graph back to the mid-1970s so that you can see the relationships among the interest rates through turbulent as well as calmer periods.

You know that the Bank of Canada sets the target for the overnight rate and hits that target directly with its open market operations. So there is no doubt about where these interest rate changes are generated. They are driven by monetary policy.

The Treasury Bill Rate The 3-month Treasury bill rate is the rate paid by the government of Canada on short-term debt. It is also similar to the interest rate paid by Canadian businesses on short-term funds. Notice how closely the 3-month Treasury bill rate follows the overnight loans rate. Figure 28.7 shows that these two rates are almost identical.

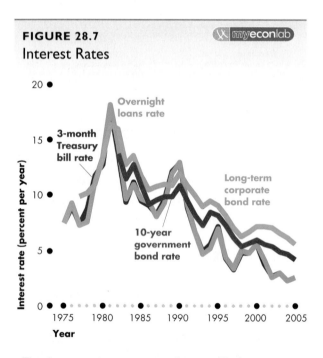

FIGURE 28.7
Interest Rates

The short-term interest rates—the overnight loans rate and the 3-month Treasury bill rate—move closely together. The long-term interest rates—the 10-year government bond rate and the long-term corporate bond rate—also move closely together. But the short-term rates fluctuate more than the long-term rates, although both move in the same general direction. The overnight loans rate peaked at 18 percent a year in 1981. It fell during the 1980s but increased again to 13 percent a year in 1990. It fell again through the 1990s and remained low during the early 2000s.

Source of data: Bank of Canada, *Banking and Financial Statistics*, Table F1.

A powerful substitution effect keep these two interest rates close. The big banks have a choice about how to hold their short-term liquid assets. And an overnight loan to another big bank is a close substitute for short-term securities such as Treasury bills. If the interest rate on Treasury bills is higher than the overnight loans rate, the supply of overnight loans decreases and the demand for Treasury bills increases. The price of Treasury bills rises and their interest rate falls.

Similarly, if the interest rate on Treasury bills is lower than the overnight loans rate, the supply of overnight loans increases and the demand for Treasury bills decreases. The price of Treasury bills falls and their interest rate rises.

When the interest rate on Treasury bill is close to the overnight loans rate, there is no incentive for banks to switch between overnight loans and Treasury bills and the two markets are in equilibrium.

The Long-Term Rates The 10-year government bond rate is the interest rate paid by the government of Canada on longer term loans and the long-term corporate bond rate is the interest rate that large businesses pay to finance investment.

Notice that the fluctuations in the two long-term interest rates are similar but the corporate rate is a bit higher than the government rate. The reason is that corporations are riskier than the government. Notice also how the long-term rates move with the short-term rates. The long-term rates don't fluctuate as much as the short-term rates but they move in similar general directions.

Substitution effects are again responsible for these interest rate movements. Long-term government bonds and long-term corporate bonds are close substitutes, so the interest rates on these bonds move up and down in close harmony.

Short-term loans and long-term loans are substitutes but not close substitutes. So when the Bank of Canada changes the overnight loans rate, its action has a powerful and immediate effect on the other short-term interest rates but a less powerful and less predictable effect on the long-term interest rates.

You can see, for example, that when the Bank of Canada raised the overnight loans rate in 1995, the long-term rates kept falling. A similar thing happened in 1998.

But generally, the long-term rates do move in the same direction as the overnight loans rate.

Exchange Rate Fluctuations

The exchange rate responds to changes in the interest rate in Canada relative to the interest rates in other countries. But other factors are also at work, which make the exchange rate hard to predict. The red line in Fig. 28.8 shows the gap between the Canadian and U.S. overnight loans rates—the Canadian-U.S. interest rate differential. And the blue line shows the exchange rate of the Canadian dollar against the U.S. dollar. You can see that sometimes when the interest rate differential widens (when the Canadian interest rate rises relative to the U.S. rate), the Canadian dollar appreciates. Also, sometimes, when the interest rate differential narrows (when the Canadian interest rate falls relative to the U.S. rate), the Canadian dollar

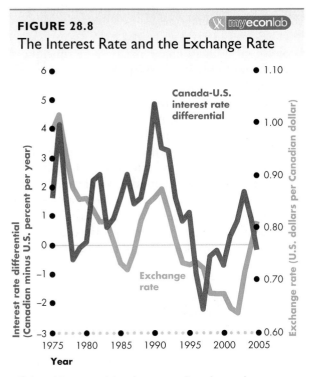

FIGURE 28.8
The Interest Rate and the Exchange Rate

Other things remaining the same, when the gap between Canadian and U.S. short-term interest rates widens, the Canadian dollar rises in value or its value falls less quickly, and when the gap between Canadian and U.S. short-term interest rates narrows, the Canadian dollar falls in value or its value rises less quickly. Most of the time, other things do not remain the same, so the relationship between the interest rate differential and the exchange rate is weak.

Sources of data: Bank of Canada, *Banking and Financial Statistics*, Tables F1 and I1.

depreciates. But the relationship between the interest rate gap and the exchange rate is weak. The exchange rate often changes independently of the interest rate differential.

So, while monetary policy influences the exchange rate, many other factors also make the exchange rate change.

Money and Loans

You saw in Chapter 25 that the quantity of money demanded depends on the interest rate. The lower the interest rate, the greater is the quantity of money demanded, other things remaining the same. Because most money is in the form of bank deposits, a lower interest rate increases the volume of bank deposits and bank loans. And a higher interest rate decreases the volume of bank deposits and bank loans.

So, when the Bank of Canada lowers the overnight loans rate, the quantity of money and the quantity of loans increase.

The Interest Rate and Expenditure Plans

The interest rate influences people's spending decisions. But the interest rate that is relevant for a spending decision is the real interest rate.

Nominal Interest and Real Interest The **nominal interest rate** is the percentage return on an asset such as a bond expressed in terms of money. It is the interest rate that is quoted in everyday transactions and news reports. The **real interest rate** is the percentage return on an asset expressed in terms of what money will buy. It is the nominal interest rate adjusted for inflation and is approximately equal to the nominal interest rate minus the inflation rate.

Suppose that the nominal interest rate is 10 percent a year and the inflation rate is 4 percent a year. The real interest rate is 6 percent a year—10 percent minus 4 percent.[3]

To see why the real interest rate is 6 percent, think about the following example. Jackie lends Joe $1,000 for one year. At the end of the year, Joe repays Jackie

---

[3] The exact calculation allows for the change in the purchasing power of the interest as well as the amount of the loan. To calculate the *exact* real interest rate, use the formula: *real interest rate* = (*nominal interest rate* − *inflation rate*) divided by (1 + *inflation rate*/100). If the nominal interest rate is 10 percent and the inflation rate is 4 percent, the real interest rate is (10 − 4) ÷ (1 + 0.04) = 5.77 percent.

the $1,000 plus interest. At 10 percent a year, the interest is $100, so Jackie receives $1,100 from Joe.

Because of inflation, the money that Joe uses to repay Jackie is worth less than the money that Jackie originally lent to Joe. At an inflation rate of 4 percent a year, Jackie needs an extra $40 a year to compensate her for the fall in the value of money. So when Joe repays the loan, Jackie needs $1,040 to buy the same items that she could have bought for $1,000 when she made the loan. Because Joe pays Jackie $1,100, the interest that she *really* earns is $60, which is 6 percent of the $1,000 that she lent to Joe.

Interest Rate and Opportunity Cost Now that you understand the distinction between the nominal interest rate and the real interest rate, let's think about the effects of interest rates on decisions.

The interest rate influences decisions because it is an opportunity cost. *The nominal interest rate is the opportunity cost of holding money.* And it is the nominal interest rate that is determined by the demand for real money and the supply of real money in the money market. To see why the nominal interest rate is the opportunity cost of holding money, think about the *real* interest rate on money compared with the real interest rate on other financial assets. Money loses value at the inflation rate. So the real interest rate on money equals *minus* the inflation rate. The real interest rate on other financial assets equals the nominal interest rate minus the inflation rate. So the difference between the real interest rate on money and the real interest rate on other financial assets is the nominal interest rate. By holding money rather than some other financial asset, we incur a *real* opportunity cost equal to the nominal interest rate.

The real interest rate is the opportunity cost of spending. Spending more today means spending less in the future. But spending one additional dollar today means cutting future spending by more than a dollar. And the real amount by which future spending must be cut is determined by the *real* interest rate.

A change in the real interest rate changes the opportunity cost of two components of aggregate expenditure:

- Consumption expenditure
- Investment

Consumption Expenditure Other things remaining the same, the lower the real interest rate, the greater is the amount of consumption expenditure and the smaller is the amount of saving.

You can see why the real interest rate influences consumption expenditure and saving by thinking about the effect of the interest rate on a student loan. If the real interest rate on a student loan fell to 1 percent a year, students would be happy to take larger loans and spend more. But if the real interest rate on a student loan jumped to 20 percent a year, students would cut their expenditure—buy cheaper food and find lower-rent accommodation, for example—to pay off their loans as quickly as possible.

The effect of the real interest rate on consumption expenditure is probably not large. It is certainly not as powerful as the effect of disposable income that we studied in Chapter 23 (pp. 536–540). You can think of the real interest rate as influencing *autonomous consumption expenditure* (p. 536). The lower the real interest rate, the greater is autonomous consumption expenditure.

Investment Other things remaining the same, the lower the real interest rate, the greater is the amount of investment.

The funds used to finance investment might be borrowed, or they might be the financial resources of the firm's owners (the firm's retained earnings). But regardless of the source of the funds, the opportunity cost of the funds is the real interest rate. The real interest paid on borrowed funds is an obvious cost. The real interest rate is also the cost of using retained earnings because these funds could be lent to another firm. The real interest rate forgone is the opportunity cost of using retained earnings to finance an investment project.

To decide whether to invest in new capital, firms compare the real interest rate with the expected profit rate from the investment. For example, suppose that Ford expects to earn 20 percent a year from a new car assembly plant. It is profitable for Ford to invest in this new plant as long as the real interest rate is less than 20 percent a year. That is, at a real interest rate below 20 percent a year, Ford will build this assembly plant; at a real interest rate in excess of 20 percent a year, Ford will not. Some projects are profitable at a high real interest rate, but other projects are profitable only at a low real interest rate. So the higher the real interest rate, the smaller is the number of projects that are worth undertaking and the smaller is the amount of investment.

The interest rate has another effect on expenditure plans—it changes net exports.

Net Exports and the Interest Rate A change in the interest rate changes the exchange rate. And a change in the exchange rate changes exports and imports. (See Chapter 26, pp. 616–617).

Interest-Sensitive Expenditure Curve Figure 28.9 illustrates the effects of the real interest rate on aggregate expenditure plans and summarizes those effects in the interest-sensitive expenditure curve. The **interest-sensitive expenditure curve** (the *IE* curve) shows the relationship between interest-sensitive expenditure and the real interest rate when all other influences on expenditure plans remain the same.

Figure 28.9(a) shows the components of interest-sensitive expenditure: autonomous consumption expenditure, investment, and net exports (*NX*). When the real interest rate is 5 percent a year, autonomous consumption expenditure is $20 billion on the curve *CD*. Investment is $50 billion, so when we add investment and autonomous consumption expenditure together, we get $70 billion on the curve

CD + ID. Net exports are $30 billion, so when we add this amount to $70 billion, we obtain the sum of all the interest-sensitive components of aggregate expenditure, which is $100 billion on the *IE* curve.

In Fig. 28.9(b), as the real interest rate changes, interest-sensitive expenditure changes along the *IE* curve. Other things remaining the same, when the real interest rate falls to 3 percent a year, interest-sensitive expenditure increases to $150 billion. And when the real interest rate rises to 7 percent a year, interest-sensitive expenditure decreases to $50 billion.

Loose Link from Overnight Rate to Spending You've seen that long-term interest rates that influence spending plans are linked only loosely to the overnight rate. Also, the response of the *real* long-term interest rate to a change in the nominal rate depends on how inflation expectations change. And the response of expenditure plans to changes in the real interest rate depend on many factors that make the response hard to predict.

FIGURE 28.9

The Interest Rate and Expenditure Plans

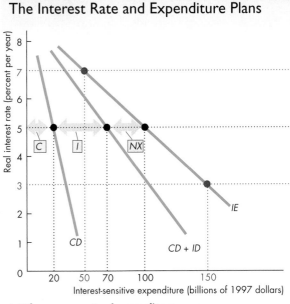

(a) The components of expenditure

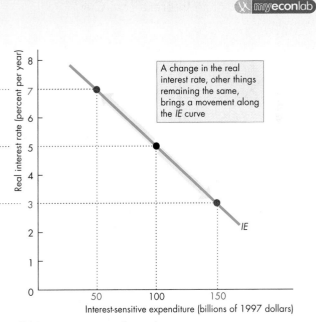

(b) Aggregate expenditure plans

In part (a), when the interest rate is 5 percent a year, autonomous consumption expenditure is $20 billion, investment is $50 billion, net exports are $30 billion, and interest-sensitive expenditure is $100 billion. In part (b), when the real interest rate is 5 percent a year, interest-sensitive expendi-

ture is $100 billion a year on the *IE* curve. Other things remaining the same, when the interest rate falls to 3 percent a year, interest-sensitive expenditure increases to $150 billion a year and when the interest rate rises to 7 percent a year, interest-sensitive expenditure decreases to $50 billion a year.

The Change in Aggregate Demand, Real GDP, and the Price Level

The final link in the transmission chain is a change in aggregate demand and a resulting change in real GDP and the price level. By changing real GDP and the price level relative to what they would have been without a change in the overnight rate, the Bank of Canada influences its ultimate goal, the inflation rate.

If the Bank believes that inflation is at (or heading below) the bottom of the target range because real GDP is below potential GDP, it believes that the economy is in the state shown in Fig. 28.10 at the intersection of aggregate demand curve AD_0 and short-run aggregate supply curve SAS. Real GDP is only $950 billion and the price level is 105.

The Bank of Canada lowers the overnight rate and the transmission process that we've just described unfolds. Eventually, aggregate demand increases and the aggregate demand curve shifts rightward to AD_1.

In the new equilibrium, full employment is restored and the price level rises by more than it would have done in the absence of the overnight rate cut. If the Bank of Canada got everything right, the inflation rate associated with the new price level will be in the middle of the target range.

If the Bank believes that inflation is at (or heading above) the top of the target range because real GDP is above potential GDP, it believes that the economy is in the state shown in Fig. 28.11 at the intersection of aggregate demand curve AD_0 and short-run aggregate supply curve SAS. Real GDP is $1,050 billion and the price level is 115.

The Bank of Canada raises the overnight rate and the transmission process that we've just described unfolds. Eventually, aggregate demand decreases and the aggregate demand curve shifts leftward to AD_1.

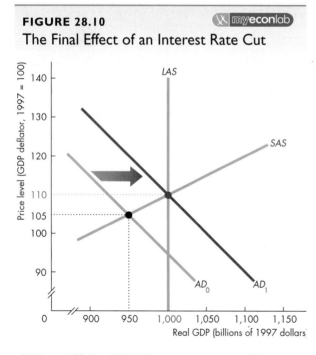

FIGURE 28.10   myeconlab
The Final Effect of an Interest Rate Cut

With real GDP at $950 billion, below potential GDP of $1,000, inflation is low, unemployment is high, and the overnight rate is decreased. Eventually, aggregate demand increases and the AD curve shifts rightward from AD_0 to AD_1. Real GDP increases to potential GDP. The price level rises above what it would otherwise have been but not by so much that it sends the inflation rate above its target.

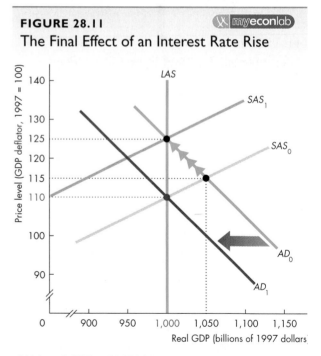

FIGURE 28.11   myeconlab
The Final Effect of an Interest Rate Rise

With real GDP at $1,050 billion, above potential GDP of $1,000, inflation is rising, unemployment is low, and the overnight rate is increased. Eventually, aggregate demand decreases and the AD curve shifts leftward from AD_0 to AD_1. Real GDP decreases to potential GDP and the price level falls below what it would otherwise have been. The inflation rate is held inside its target range.

In the new equilibrium, the inflation threat is eliminated, full employment is restored, and the price level rises by less than it would have done in the absence of the overnight rate rise. Again, if the Bank of Canada got everything right, the inflation rate associated with the new price level will be in the middle of the target range.

Time Lags in the Adjustment Process To achieve its goal of 2 percent inflation, the Bank of Canada needs a combination of good judgment and good luck. Too large a cut in the overnight rate in an underemployed economy can bring inflation, as it did during the 1970s. And too large an increase in the overnight rate in an inflationary economy can create unemployment, as it did in 1981 and again in 1991.

The Bank is especially handicapped by the fact that the monetary policy transmission process is long drawn out. Also, the economy does not always respond in exactly the same way to policy. Further, many factors other than policy are constantly changing and bringing a new situation for policy to respond to.

But monetary policy actions do have a powerful influence. We can see this influence on real GDP growth in Fig. 28.12. A change in the overnight rate feeds through to change real GDP after about a year.

In Fig.28.12, the blue line shows the overnight rate that the Bank of Canada targets minus the long-term bond rate. Changes in the overnight rate have some effect on the long-term bond rate, but this effect is small. The long-term bond rate is also influenced by saving and investment plans and by inflation expectations.

The red line in Fig. 28.12 is the real GDP growth rate *one year later.* You can see that when the overnight rate rises or the long-term bond rate falls, the real GDP growth rate slows down in the following year. The long-term bond rate fluctuates less than the overnight rate, so when the overnight rate rises above the long-term bond rate, it is because the Bank of Canada has pushed the overnight rate up. And when the overnight rate falls below the long-term bond rate, it is because the Bank of Canada has pushed the overnight rate down. So when the Bank of Canada stimulates aggregate demand (pushes the overnight rate down), the real GDP growth rate speeds up, and when the Bank of Canada lowers aggregate demand (pushes the overnight rate up), the real GDP growth rate slows. The inflation rate increases and decreases in sympathy with these fluctuations in the real GDP growth rate. But the effects on the inflation rate take even longer.

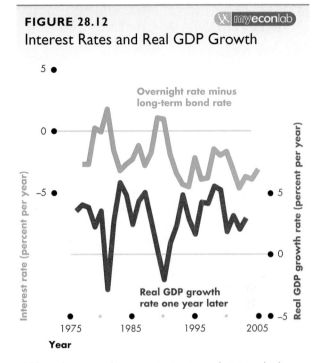

FIGURE 28.12
Interest Rates and Real GDP Growth

When the overnight interest rate rises relative to the long-term bond rate, the real GDP growth rate usually slows about one year later. Similarly, when the overnight rate falls relative to the long-term bond rate, the real GDP growth rate speeds up about one year later.

Sources of data: Interest Rates, see Fig. 28.7; Real GDP Growth, Statistics Canada, CANSIM Table 380–0002.

REVIEW QUIZ

1 Describe the channels by which monetary policy ripples through the economy and explain why each channel operates.
2 Do interest rates fluctuate in response to the Bank of Canada's actions?
3 How do the Bank of Canada's actions influence the exchange rate?
4 How do the Bank of Canada's actions influence real GDP and how long does it take for real GDP to respond to the Bank's policy actions?
5 How do the Bank of Canada's actions influence inflation and how long does it take for inflation to respond to the Bank's policy actions?

myeconlab Study Plan 28.3

Alternative Monetary Policy Strategies

SO FAR IN THIS CHAPTER, WE'VE DESCRIBED AND analyzed the Bank of Canada's method of conducting monetary policy. But the Bank does have choices among alternative monetary policy strategies. We're going to end our discussion of monetary policy by examining the alternatives and explains why the Bank of Canada has rejected them in favour of the interest rate strategy that we've described.

You've seen that we can summarize monetary policy strategies in two broad categories, *instrument rules* and *targeting rules.* And you've seen that the Bank of Canada uses a *targeting rule* approach. So the Bank has rejected instrument rules. It has also rejected other possible targeting rules.

The Bank of Canada might have chosen any of four alternative monetary policy strategies: Two of them are instrument rules and two are alternative targeting rules. The four alternatives are

■ Overnight rate instrument rule
■ Monetary base instrument rule
■ Exchange rate targeting rule
■ Money targeting rule

Overnight Rate Instrument Rule

The idea of setting the overnight rate based on a rule was suggested by Stanford University economist John B. Taylor, and the rule bears his name.

The **Taylor rule** sets the overnight rate in response to only the current inflation rate and the current estimate of the output gap. Calling the overnight rate R, the neutral real overnight rate R^*, the inflation rate π, the target inflation rate $\pi*$, and the output gap (as a percentage of potential GDP), G, the Taylor rule says, set the overnight rate to equal

$$R = R^* + \pi + 0.5(\pi - \pi^*) + 0.5G.$$

Taylor suggests that the neutral real overnight rate is 2 percent a year. So if inflation was on target and the output gap was zero (full employment) and with a 2 percent inflation target, the overnight rate would be 4 percent. It would be less than 4 percent if the economy were below full employment and above 4 percent if the economy were above full employment.

If the Bank of Canada had followed the Taylor rule, the overnight rate would have fluctuated much more than it did. And on some occasions, it would have been much higher than the Bank wanted. For example, during 2005 when the overnight rate was 2.5 percent, the Taylor rule would have put it at 4.5 percent. And in 2003, when the inflation rate temporarily increased to more than 4 percent, the Taylor rule would have raised the overnight rate to more than 8 percent. The overnight rate was actually raised to only 3.25 percent.

The Bank believes that because it uses much more information than just the current inflation rate and the output gap, it is able to set the overnight rate more intelligently than any simple rule can set.

Monetary Base Instrument Rule

Although the Bank of Canada uses open market operations to hit its overnight loans rate target, it could, instead, shoot for a monetary base target.

The idea of setting the monetary base using a rule has been suggested by Carnegie-Mellon University economist Bennet T. McCallum, and a monetary base rule bears his name.

The **McCallum rule** makes the growth rate of the monetary base respond to the long-term average growth rate of real GDP and medium-term changes in the velocity of circulation of the monetary base.

The rule is based on the *quantity theory of money* (see Chapter 27, pp 638–639). McCallum's idea is that by making the monetary base grow at a rate equal to the target inflation rate plus the long-term real GDP growth rate minus the medium-term velocity growth rate, inflation will be kept close to target.

An advantage of the McCallum rule over the Taylor rule is that the Bank does not need to estimate either the neutral real overnight rate or the output gap. Both of these inputs to the Taylor rule are impossible to know exactly and are subject to estimation errors that could send the inflation rate badly off course.

A disadvantage of the McCallum rule compared to the Taylor rule is that it relies on the velocity of circulation being reasonably stable.

The Bank of Canada believes that the velocity of circulation is in fact too unstable and that the Bank does better than it would by following the McCallum rule because the Bank isolates the inflation rate from volatile changes in the velocity of circulation.

Exchange Rate Targeting Rule

The Bank of Canada could, if it wished to do so, intervene in the foreign exchange market to target the exchange rate. A fixed exchange rate is one possible exchange rate target.

But with a fixed exchange rate, a country has no control over its inflation rate. The reason is that for internationally traded goods, *purchasing power parity* (see p. 622) moves domestic prices in line with foreign prices. If a computer chip costs $US100 in Detroit, and if the exchange rate is $C1.20 per $US1.00, then the computer chip will sell for $120 (ignoring local taxes) in Windsor, Ontario. If this purchasing power parity didn't prevail, it would be possible to earn a profit by buying at the lower price and selling at the higher price. This trading would compete away the profit and price difference.

So under a fixed exchange rate, prices of traded goods (and in the long-run the prices of all goods and services) must rise at the same rate in Canada as they do in the United States.

But the Bank of Canada could use a *crawling peg* (see p. 624) as a means of achieving an inflation target. To do so, the Bank would make the exchange rate change at a rate equal to the U.S. inflation rate minus the target inflation rate. If the U.S. inflation rate is 3 percent a year and Canada wants an inflation rate of 2 percent a year, the Bank of Canada would make the Canadian dollar appreciate at a rate of 1 percent a year.

Some developing countries that have an inflation problem use this monetary policy strategy to lower the inflation rate. The main reason for choosing this method is that these countries don't have well-functioning markets for bonds and overnight loans, so they cannot use the policy approach that relies on these features of a banking system.

A major disadvantage of a crawling peg to target the inflation rate is that the real exchange rate often changes in unpredictable ways. Canada's **real exchange rate** with the United States is the relative price of the GDP baskets of goods and services in the two countries. Canadian GDP contains a larger proportion of natural resource products (minerals, oil, and natural gas) than U.S. GDP contains. So when the prices of natural resources change, our real exchange rate changes. To use a crawling peg to target the inflation rate, we would need to be able to identify changes in the real exchange rate and offset them. This task is difficult to accomplish.

Money Targeting Rule

As long ago as 1948, Nobel Laureate Milton Friedman proposed a targeting rule for the quantity of money. Friedman's ***k*-percent rule** makes the quantity of money grow at a rate of *k* percent a year, where *k* equals the growth rate of potential GDP.

Friedman's idea remained just that until the 1970s, when inflation increased to more than 10 percent a year in Canada and several other major countries. In 1976, in a bid to end the inflation, the Bank of Canada adopted the *k*-percent rule for the growth rate of M1. The inflation rate fell, but the policy was abandoned in 1982. (The period from 1982 to 1991 when the first inflation target was adopted were years of evolution towards the policy approach of today).

Money targeting works when the demand for money curve is stable and predictable. But in the world of the 1980s, and of today, technological change in the banking system leads to large and unpredictable shifts in the demand for money curve, which make the use of monetary targeting unreliable.

Why Rules?

You might be wondering why all monetary policy strategies involve *rules*. Why doesn't the Bank of Canada just do what seems best every day, month, and year, at its *discretion*? The answer is that monetary policy is about managing inflation expectations. In both financial markets and labour markets, people must make long-term commitments. So these markets work best when plans are based on correctly anticipated inflation outcomes. A well-understood monetary policy rule helps to create an environment in which inflation is easier to forecast and manage.

REVIEW QUIZ

1 What are the four main alternative rules for conducting monetary policy (other than the one used by the Bank of Canada)?
2 Explain, briefly, why does the Bank of Canada reject each of these alternatives?

myeconlab **Study Plan 28.4**

◆ As you complete your study of monetary policy, take a look at *Reading Between the Lines* on pages 672–673 and see the Bank of Canada's challenge in 2005.

Monetary Policy in Action

GLOBE AND MAIL, NOVEMBER 9, 2005

The great Canadian interest rate paradox

The Bank of Canada is at risk of making a serious error in monetary policy because research shows Ontario and Quebec are extra-sensitive to the effects of rising interest rates, while Alberta is almost immune.

It's well-known that the Bank of Canada already faces a conundrum in setting interest rates as oil and gas power Alberta's economy while the struggling manufacturing sector drags down Central Canada.

But the issues facing bank Governor David Dodge are not just cyclical. They're structural too, argues Benjamin Tal, economist at CIBC World Markets.

Ontario and Quebec are sensitive to rate hikes because their economies are dominated by interest-sensitive sectors, such as construction, manufacturing and utilities, he said. Alberta, on the other hand, is dominated by oil and gas —not very sensitive to interest rates and far more sensitive to global supply and demand.

...

Central bank officials have also argued that they can only base monetary policy decisions on national eco-nomic trends, and can't focus on region-al diversions.

That's obviously true, Mr. Tal responded, but he warns that the bank needs to take into account that, in Central Canada, "the Bank of Canada is probably more powerful than at any time," while in Alberta, "I'm not sure how much higher interest rates will change the momentum.

"The cost of making a mistake here can be significant," he said. For him, rais-ing rates another 50 basis points (or half a percentage point) over the next year would be fine, but 150 points (or 1.5 per-centage points) would be too much.

But economist Carl Gomez sees lit-tle chance of a major mistake by the central bank. Numerous indicators point to the need to raise rates, and yet the Bank of Canada has been very cau-tious and moved slowly, he said in an interview.

If higher rates have an adverse effect on Ontario and Quebec, their weakness will show up in the national numbers that the bank uses to make its decisions on monetary policy, said Mr. Gomez, an economist at Toronto-Dominion Bank.

Reprinted by permission of *The Globe and Mail.*

Essence of the Story

■ The Bank of Canada risks a serious monetary policy error.

■ Strong demand points to the need for a higher interest rate. But the strongest demand is in Alberta and a higher interest rate will have a limited effect there and a big effect in Ontario and Quebec.

■ An interest rate increase of half a per-centage point will not do any harm, but an increase of 1.5 percent-age points will be too much, according to a CIBC economist.

■ The Bank of Canada says that it must respond to national trends, not regional ones.

Economic Analysis

■ In the fall of 2005, the Canadian economy was operating at or perhaps a bit above full employment.

■ The CPI inflation rate for September 2005 was 3.4 percent, a rate that exceeded the upper limit of the inflation-control target range.

■ In line with this underlying economic condition, the Bank of Canada was slowly but surely increasing the overnight rate.

■ The rate was increased in October and was set for a further increase in December (a week before these words were written).

■ This news article is concerned about an issue that is often raised: the difficulty of addressing regional variation with monetary policy.

■ The figures illustrate the regional problem by showing a key part of the monetary transmission mechanism broken into two parts: one for Alberta (in Fig. 1) and one for the rest of Canada (in Fig. 2). Figure 3 shows Canada as a whole.

■ Suppose that initially there is full employment and no inflationary pressure. Then, world demand for oil and gas exports increases and in Alberta, the interest-sensitive expenditure curve shifts rightward from IE_0 to IE_1.

■ In Fig. 3 the Canadian interest-sensitive expenditure curve shifts rightward.

■ But expenditure plans in the rest of Canada (Fig. 2) do not change.

■ The Bank of Canada now sees inflationary pressure and raises the interest rate to 4 percent a year to bring total spending back to the level from which it increased.

■ Expenditure decreases by a small amount in Alberta. Even in Alberta, contrary to the news article, spending plans are sensitive to the interest rate.

■ But the decrease in Alberta spending from the higher interest rate is not as great as the initial increase. So Alberta continues to run at a hot pace.

■ The higher interest rate decreases spending in the rest of Canada, and for Canada as a whole (Fig. 3) expenditure returns to its initial level.

■ Monetary policy has removed the threat of inflation, but it has not addressed the regional imbalance. Market forces (and perhaps fiscal actions) will do that.

You're the Voter

■ Do you think the Bank of Canada can influence regional differences in economic performance?

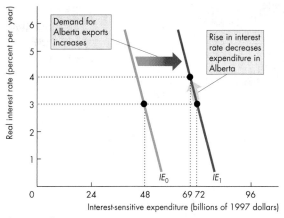

Figure 1 Alberta

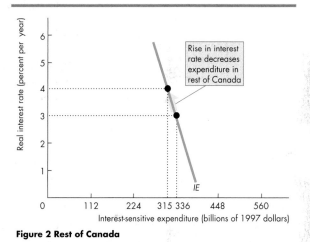

Figure 2 Rest of Canada

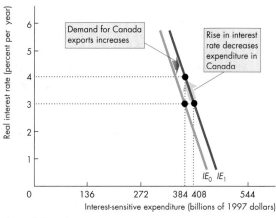

Figure 3 Canada

SUMMARY

KEY POINTS

Monetary Policy Objective and Framework (pp. 656–658)

- The Bank of Canada Act requires the Bank to use monetary policy to avoid inflation and moderate cycles in real GDP and employment.
- The government of Canada and the Bank of Canada have jointly agreed that the Bank will seek to keep CPI inflation between 1 percent and 3 percent a year and will aim for the 2 percent midpoint.
- The Bank has successfully achieved its inflation-control targets.
- The Bank's Governing Council has the responsibility for the conduct of monetary policy, but the Bank and government must consult regularly.

The Conduct of Monetary Policy (pp. 658–662)

- The Bank of Canada's monetary policy instrument is the overnight loans rate.
- The Bank sets the overnight rate target and announces changes on eight fixed dates each year.
- An *instrument rule* for monetary policy makes the instrument respond predictably to the state of the economy. The Bank does *not* use such a rule.
- A *targeting rule* for monetary policy sets the instrument to make the forecast of the inflation rate equal to the target inflation rate. The Bank *does* use such a rule.
- The Bank hits its overnight rate target by setting an operating band and using open market operations.
- By buying or selling government securities in the open market, the Bank of Canada is able to change the reserves of the banking system and change the overnight rate.

Monetary Policy Transmission (pp. 663–669)

- A change in the overnight rate changes other interest rates, the exchange rate, the quantity of money, credit, and loans, aggregate demand, and eventually real GDP and the price level.

- A change in the overnight rate changes real GDP about one year later and changes the inflation rate with an even longer time lag.

Alternative Monetary Policy Strategies (pp. 670–671)

- The main alternatives are the rule for setting the overnight rate, a monetary base rule, exchange rate targeting, or money targeting.
- Rules dominate discretion in monetary policy because they better enable the central bank to manage inflation expectations.

KEY FIGURES

Figure 28.1   Inflation-Control Targets and Outcome, 657

Figure 28.2   The Overnight Loans Rate, 659

Figure 28.5   The Market for Reserves of LVTS Participating Banks, 662

Figure 28.6   The Channels for the Ripple Effects of a Change in the Overnight Rate, 663

Figure 28.9   The Interest Rate and Expenditure Plans, 667

Figure 28.10   The Final Effect of an Interest Rate Cut, 668

Figure 28.11   The Final Effect of an Interest Rate Rise, 668

KEY TERMS

Bank rate, 660

Core inflation, 656

Instrument rule, 659

Interest-sensitive expenditure curve, 667

k-percent rule, 671

McCallum rule, 670

Nominal interest rate, 665

Open market operation, 660

Operating band, 660

Overnight loans rate, 658

Real exchange rate, 671

Real interest rate, 665

Settlement balances rate, 660

Targeting rule, 659

Taylor rule, 670

PROBLEMS

Go to **myeconlab** for solutions to odd-numbered problems and additional exercises.

1. Suppose that the Bank of Canada had an inflation-control target expressed as keeping inflation between 1 percent and 3 percent a year but with no requirement to keep trend inflation at the midpoint of the range.
   a. Starting from a price level of 100 and the Bank achieves its target,
      i   Calculate the highest price level that might occur after 10 years.
      ii. Calculate the lowest price level that might occur after 10 years.
      iii. What is the range of uncertainty about the price level after 10 years?
   b. Would this type of inflation-control target serve the financial markets well and provide an anchor for inflation expectations?

2. Suppose the Bank of Canada had an inflation-control target expressed as keeping inflation between 0 percent and 4 percent a year but was also required to keep trend inflation at the midpoint of the range.
   a. Starting from a price level of 100, what is the likely price level after 10 years if the bank achieves its target?
   b. Comparing this economy with the one in problem 1. Which economy has the greater certainty about inflation over the longer term? Which has the greater short-term certainty?

3. The overnight rate target is 4 percent and the Bank of Canada wants to increase it by 0.25 percentage points.
   a. What bank rate does the Bank of Canada set?
   b. What settlement balances rate does the Bank of Canada set?
   c. Does the Bank buy or sell securities in the open market to raise the overnight rate?
   d. Describe the changes in the balance sheets of the Bank of Canada and a chartered bank following the open market operation in part (c).
   e. Draw a graph like Fig. 28.5 to illustrate the effects of the Bank of Canada's actions in the market for reserves of LVTS participating banks.

4. The target for the overnight rate is 4 percent a year and the Bank of Canada wants to decrease it by 0.25 percentage points.
   a. What bank rate does the Bank of Canada set?
   b. What settlement balances rate does the Bank of Canada set?
   c. Does the Bank of Canada buy or sell securities in the open market to lower the overnight rate?
   d. Describe the changes in the balance sheets of the Bank of Canada and a chartered bank following the open market operation in part (c).
   e. Draw a graph like Fig. 28.5 to illustrate the effects of the Bank of Canada's actions in the market for reserves of LVTS participating banks.

5. The figure shows the economy of Freezone. The aggregate demand curve is AD and the short-run aggregate supply curve is SAS_A. Potential GDP is $300 billion.

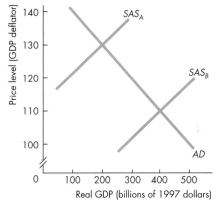

   a. What is the price level and real GDP?
   b. Does Freezone have an unemployment problem or an inflation problem? Why?
   c. What do you predict will happen in Freezone if the central bank takes no monetary policy actions?
   d. What monetary policy action would you advise the central bank to take, and what do you predict will be the effect of that action?

6. Suppose that in Freezone, shown in problem 5, the aggregate demand curve is AD and potential GDP is $300 billion, but the short-run aggregate supply curve is SAS_B.
   a. What is the price level and real GDP?
   b. Does Freezone have an unemployment problem or an inflation problem? Why?

c. What do you predict will happen in Freezone if the central bank takes no monetary policy actions?

d. What monetary policy action would you advise the central bank to take and what do you predict the effect of that action will be?

7. Suppose that in Freezone, shown in problem 5, the short-run aggregate supply curve is SAS_B and potential GDP increases to $350 billion.

a. What happens in Freezone if the central bank lowers the overnight interest rate and buys securities on the open market?

b. What happens in Freezone if the central bank increases the overnight interest rate and sells securities on the open market?

c. Do you recommend that the central bank lower the interest rate and buy securities or increase the interest rate and sell securities? Why?

8. Suppose that in Freezone, shown in problem 5, the short-run aggregate supply curve is SAS_A and a drought decreases potential GDP to $250 billion.

a. What happens in Freezone if the central bank lowers the overnight interest rate and buys securities on the open market?

b. What happens in Freezone if the central bank increases the overnight interest rate and sells securities on the open market?

c. Do you recommend that the central bank lower the interest rate and buy securities or increase the interest rate and sell securities?

CRITICAL THINKING

1. Study *Reading Between the Lines* on pp. 672–673 and then answer the following questions:

a. Why does the CIBC economist say the Bank of Canada risks increasing the overnight rate by too much?

b. What does the Bank of Canada say in response?

c. With which view do you agree and why?

d. Do you think the Bank of Canada went on to get its monetary policy right during 2006, or would you have raised or lowered the interest rate relative to what the Bank set? Provide reasons.

2. When the Bank of Canada brought inflation under control during the early 1990s, it created a recession. Do you think a recession could have been avoided while still lowering the inflation rate? Explain why or why not.

WEB EXERCISES

Use the links on (myeconlab) to work the following exercises.

1. Visit the Bank of Canada and obtain the latest data on the core inflation rate and the overall CPI inflation rate as well as the overnight interest rate. Then answer the following questions.

a. Is the Bank of Canada trying to slow the economy or speed it up? How can you tell?

b. What open market operations do you think the Bank of Canada has undertaken during the past few months?

c. In the light of the Bank of Canada's recent actions, what ripple effects do you expect over the coming months?

d. What do you think the effects of the Bank of Canada's recent actions will be on bond prices, stock prices, and the exchange rate?

2. Visit Statistics Canada and look at the current economic conditions.

a. On the basis of the current state of the Canadian economy, do you predict that the Bank of Canada will raise interest rates, lower interest rates, or hold interest rates steady?

b. Write a brief summary of your predictions and reasons.

Fiscal and Monetary Interactions

Sparks Fly in Ottawa

In 2005, the Parliament of Canada approved a federal government budget that showed a large surplus. Not far from Parliament Hill, on Sparks Street, the Bank of Canada pulls the nation's monetary policy levers that directly target the overnight interest rate and indirectly influence other interest rates, the exchange rate, and the quantity of money and loans. How does the government's fiscal policy interact with the Bank of Canada's monetary policy to influence real GDP, the price level, and the inflation rate?

Does it matter if fiscal and monetary policy come into conflict—creating sparks on Sparks Street?

If a recession is looming on the horizon, is an interest rate cut by the Bank of Canada just as good as a tax cut by Parliament? If the economy is overheating, is an interest rate hike by the Bank of Canada just as good as a tax increase by Parliament?

◆ You already know a lot about the effects of fiscal policy and monetary policy. And you know that their ultimate effects work through their influences on both aggregate demand and aggregate supply. This chapter gives you a deeper understanding of the aggregate demand side of the economy and how the combined actions of the federal government and the Bank of Canada affect aggregate demand. In *Reading Between the Lines* at the end of the chapter, we look at what David Dodge, governor of the Bank of Canada, thinks about the appropriate roles for monetary policy and fiscal policy.

After studying this chapter, you will be able to

■ **Explain macroeconomic equilibrium**

■ **Explain how fiscal policy influences real GDP and the price level**

■ **Explain how monetary policy influences real GDP and the price level**

■ **Explain the Keynesian–monetarist debate**

■ **Explain the effects of fiscal and monetary policies at full employment**

■ **Explain how fiscal and monetary policies might be coordinated or in conflict**

Macroeconomic Equilibrium

YOUR GOAL IN THIS CHAPTER IS TO LEARN HOW fiscal policy and monetary policy interact to influence real GDP, the price level, and the inflation rate. You studied fiscal policy in Chapter 24 and monetary policy in Chapter 28. But these two accounts of the effects of policy didn't explain how fiscal and monetary policy interact. We need to know how they interact because we want to know whether we can use either on its own to achieve the same goals or whether they must be used in the correct combination.

You know that the Bank of Canada targets the inflation rate by influencing the overnight interest rate. The quantity of money is a consequence of the Bank's interest rate decision. Despite the Bank of Canada's approach, we will explore fiscal and monetary policy interactions when the central bank targets the quantity of money. By doing so, we are able to review a long-running debate about policy between Keynesians and monetarists. And we are able to see the potential benefits and risks of the interest rate targeting approach favoured by the Bank of Canada.

To study policy effects, we ask how a given policy action changes the equilibrium. So we begin by describing macroeconomic equilibrium with a fixed target for the quantity of money.

Two Markets in Short-Run Equilibrium

In a short-run equilibrium, the interest rate adjusts to make the quantity of money demanded equal to the quantity of money supplied (Chapter 25, p. 605). And the price level adjusts to make the quantity of real GDP demanded equal to the quantity of real GDP supplied (Chapter 22, pp. 516–517).

But real GDP and the price level influence the demand for money. And the interest rate influences aggregate demand. So the money market and the market for goods and services (for real GDP) are linked together.

Other things remaining the same, the greater the level of aggregate demand, the higher are real GDP and the price level. A higher real GDP means a greater demand for money; a higher price level means a smaller supply of real money; so a greater level of aggregate demand means a higher interest rate.

Aggregate demand depends on the interest rate because consumption expenditure, investment, and net exports are influenced by the interest rate (see Chapter 28, pp. 666–667). So, other things remaining the same, the lower the interest rate, the greater is aggregate demand.

Only one level of aggregate demand and one interest rate are consistent with each other in macroeconomic equilibrium. Figure 29.1 describes this unique equilibrium.

In Fig. 29.1(a), the intersection of the aggregate demand curve, AD, and the short-run aggregate supply curve, SAS, determines real GDP at $1,000 billion and the price level at 110. In Fig. 29.1(b), the intersection of the demand for money curve, MD, and the supply of money curve, MS, determines the interest rate at 5 percent a year. In Fig. 29.1(c) at an interest rate of 5 percent a year, the interest-sensitive expenditure curve, IE, determines the amount of interest-sensitive expenditure at $100 billion.

The position of the AD curve depends on the quantity of money, and the demand for and supply of real money depend on the AD and SAS curves.

Simultaneous Equilibrium

The AS–AD equilibrium in Fig. 29.1(a), the money market equilibrium in Fig. 29.1(b), and interest-sensitive expenditure in Fig. 29.1(c) are consistent with each other. There is no other equilibrium.

To check this claim, assume that aggregate demand is less than AD in Fig. 29.1(a) so that real GDP is less than $1,000 billion. If this assumption is correct, the demand for money curve lies to the left of MD in Fig. 29.1(b) and the equilibrium interest rate is less than 5 percent a year. With an interest rate less than 5 percent a year, interest-sensitive expenditure exceeds the $100 billion in Fig. 29.1(c). If interest-sensitive expenditure exceeds $100 billion, the AD curve lies to the right of the one we assumed and equilibrium real GDP exceeds $1,000 billion. So if we assume a real GDP of less than $1,000 billion, equilibrium real GDP is greater than $1,000 billion. There is an inconsistency. The assumed equilibrium real GDP is too small.

Now assume that aggregate demand is greater than AD in Fig. 29.1(a) so that real GDP exceeds $1,000 billion. If this assumption is correct, the demand for money curve lies to the right of MD in Fig. 29.1(b) and the equilibrium interest rate exceeds 5 percent a year. With an interest rate above 5 percent a year, interest-sensitive expenditure is less than the $100 billion in Fig. 29.1(c), in which case the

FIGURE 29.1

Equilibrium Real GDP, Price Level, Interest Rate, and Expenditure

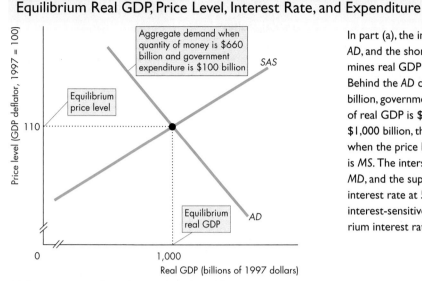

(a) Aggregate supply and aggregate demand

In part (a), the intersection of the aggregate demand curve, AD, and the short-run aggregate supply curve, SAS, determines real GDP at $1,000 billion and the price level at 110. Behind the AD curve, interest-sensitive expenditure is $100 billion, government expenditure is $100 billion, and the rest of real GDP is $800 billion. In part (b), when real GDP is $1,000 billion, the demand for money curve is MD and when the price level is 110, the supply of real money curve is MS. The intersection of the demand for money curve, MD, and the supply of money curve, MS, determines the interest rate at 5 percent a year. In part (c), on the IE curve, interest-sensitive expenditure is $100 billion at the equilibrium interest rate of 5 percent a year.

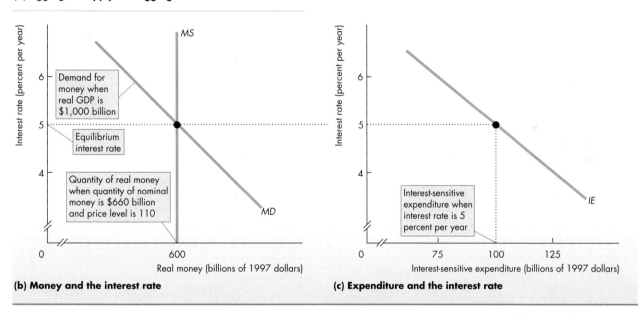

(b) Money and the interest rate

(c) Expenditure and the interest rate

AD curve must lie to the left of the one we assumed and equilibrium real GDP must be smaller than $1,000 billion. So if we assume that real GDP exceeds $1,000 billion, equilibrium real GDP is less than $1,000 billion. There is another inconsistency. The assumed equilibrium real GDP is too large.

Only one level of aggregate demand delivers the same money market equilibrium and AS–AD equilibrium. In this example, it is the aggregate demand curve AD in Fig. 29.1(a). Assuming this level of

aggregate demand implies this level of aggregate demand. Assuming a lower level of aggregate demand implies a higher level. And assuming a higher level of aggregate demand implies a lower level.

Now that you understand how aggregate demand and the interest rate are simultaneously determined, let's study the effects of a change in government expenditures.

Study Plan 29.1

Fiscal Policy in the Short Run

REAL GDP GROWTH IS SLOWING, AND THE finance minister is concerned that a recession is likely. So the government decides to try to head off the recession by using fiscal policy to stimulate aggregate demand. A fiscal policy that increases aggregate demand is called an *expansionary fiscal policy*.

The effects of an expansionary fiscal policy are similar to those of throwing a pebble into a pond. There's an initial splash followed by a series of ripples that become ever smaller. The initial splash is the "first round effect" of the fiscal policy action. The ripples are the "second round effects." You've already met the first round effects in Chapter 24, so here is a refresher.

First Round Effects of Fiscal Policy

The economy starts out in the position shown in Fig. 29.1. Real GDP is $1,000 billion, the price level is 110, the interest rate is 5 percent a year, and interest-sensitive expenditure is $100 billion. The government now increases its expenditures on goods and services by $100 billion.

Figure 29.2 shows the first round effects of this action. The increase in government expenditures has a multiplier effect because it brings an increase in induced expenditure. (You can refresh your memory about the government expenditures multiplier on pp. 570–572.) Let's assume that the multiplier is 2, so a $100 billion increase in government expenditures increases aggregate demand at a given price level by $200 billion. The aggregate demand curve shifts rightward from AD_0 to AD_1. At a price level of 110, the quantity of real GDP demanded increases from $1,000 billion to $1,200 billion.

Real GDP now starts to increase and the price level starts to rise. These are the first round effects of expansionary fiscal policy.

Second Round Effects of Fiscal Policy

Through the second round, real GDP increases and the price level rises until a new macroeconomic equilibrium is reached. But to find that equilibrium and to describe the changes that result from the initial increase in government expenditures, we must keep

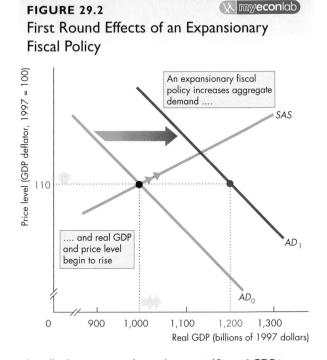

FIGURE 29.2   myeconlab

First Round Effects of an Expansionary Fiscal Policy

Initially, the aggregate demand curve is AD_0, real GDP is $1,000 billion, and the price level is 110. A $100 billion increase in government expenditures on goods and services has a multiplier effect and increases aggregate demand by $200 billion. The aggregate demand curve shifts rightward to AD_1. Real GDP begins to increase and the price level begins to rise. These are the first round effects of an expansionary fiscal policy.

track of further changes in the money market and in expenditure plans.

It is easier to keep track of the second round effects if we split them into two parts: one that results from the increasing real GDP, and the other that results from the rising price level. We follow these effects in Fig. 29.3.

First, the increasing real GDP increases the demand for money. In Fig. 29.3(b), the demand for money curve shifts rightward. Eventually, it shifts to MD_1 and the interest rate rises to 6 percent a year. At this interest rate, interest-sensitive expenditure decreases to $75 billion in Fig. 29.3(c). The decrease in planned expenditure decreases aggregate demand and the aggregate demand curve shifts leftward to AD_2 in Fig. 29.3(a).

FIGURE 29.3
Second Round Effects of an Expansionary Fiscal Policy

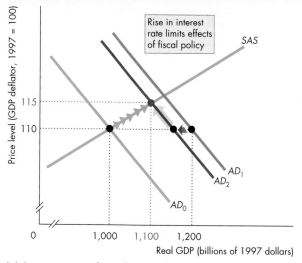

(a) Aggregate supply and aggregate demand

Initially in part (b), the money demand curve is MD_0, the real money supply curve is MS_0, and the interest rate is 5 percent a year. With an interest rate of 5 percent a year, interest-sensitive expenditure is $100 billion on the curve IE (part c). With increased government expenditures, the aggregate demand curve is AD_1 in part (a). Real GDP is increasing, and the price level is rising. The increasing real GDP increases the demand for money and the money demand curve shifts rightward to MD_1. The higher interest rate decreases interest-sensitive expenditure, which decreases aggregate demand to AD_2. The rising price level brings a movement along the new AD curve. It does so because it decreases the quantity of real money. The money supply curve shifts leftward to MS_1, which in turn raises the interest rate further and decreases expenditure. The new equilibrium occurs when real GDP has increased to $1,100 billion and the price level has risen to 115.

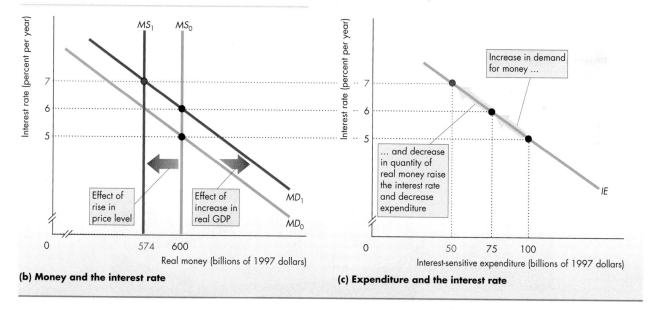

(b) Money and the interest rate

(c) Expenditure and the interest rate

Second, with a given quantity of nominal money, the rising price level decreases the quantity of real money. In Fig. 29.3(b), the money supply curve shifts leftward to MS_1. The decrease in the quantity of real money raises the interest rate further to 7 percent a year. In Fig. 29.3(c), the higher interest rate decreases interest-sensitive expenditure to $50 billion. Because this decrease in spending plans is induced by a rise in the price level, it decreases the quantity of real GDP

demanded and is shown as a movement up along the aggregate demand curve AD_2 in Fig. 29.3(a).

During this second round process, real GDP is increasing and the price level is rising in a gradual movement up along the short-run aggregate supply curve as indicated by the arrows. In the new equilibrium, real GDP is $1,100 billion, the price level is 115, the interest rate is 7 percent a year, and interest-sensitive expenditure is $50 billion.

FIGURE 29.4

How the Economy Adjusts to an Expansionary Fiscal Policy

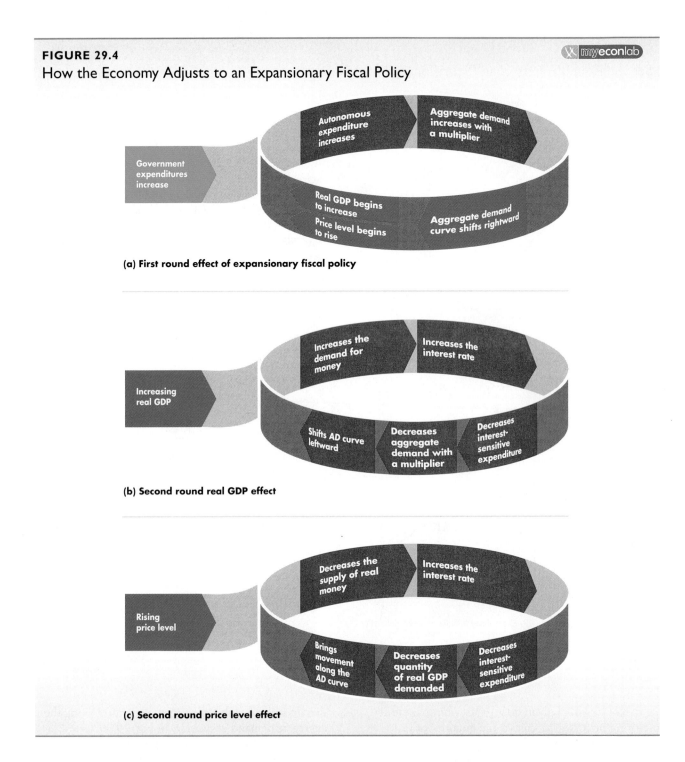

(a) First round effect of expansionary fiscal policy

(b) Second round real GDP effect

(c) Second round price level effect

Just as the initial equilibrium in Fig. 29.1 was consistent, so the new equilibrium is consistent. The *AS–AD* equilibrium in Fig. 29.3(a), the money market equilibrium in Fig. 29.3(b), and interest-sensitive expenditure in Fig. 29.3(c) are all consistent with each other. And there is no other equilibrium.

Figure 29.4(a) summarizes the first round effect of an expansionary fiscal policy action. Figures 29.4(b) and 29.4(c) summarize the two parts of the second round adjustment as the economy responds.

Other Fiscal Policies

Other fiscal policies include a change in transfer payments, such as an increase in unemployment compensation or an increase in social benefits and a change in taxes. All fiscal policy actions work by changing expenditure. But the magnitude of the initial change in expenditure differs for different fiscal actions. For example, changes in taxes and transfer payments change expenditure by smaller amounts than does a change in government expenditures on goods and services. But fiscal policies that change autonomous expenditure by a given amount and in a given direction have similar effects on equilibrium real GDP, the price level, and the interest rate regardless of the initial fiscal action. Let's take a closer look at the effect of the rise in the interest rate.

Crowding Out and Crowding In

Because an expansionary fiscal policy increases the interest rate, it decreases all the interest-sensitive components of aggregate expenditure. One of these components is investment, and the decrease in investment that results from an expansionary fiscal action is called **crowding out.**

Crowding out may be partial or complete. Partial crowding out occurs when the decrease in investment is less than the increase in government expenditures. This is the normal case—and the case we've just seen.

Complete crowding out occurs if the decrease in investment equals the initial increase in government expenditures. For complete crowding out to occur, a small change in the demand for real money must lead to a large change in the interest rate, and the change in the interest rate must lead to a large change in investment.

But another potential influence of government expenditures on investment works in the opposite direction to the crowding-out effect and is called "crowding in." **Crowding in** is the tendency for expansionary fiscal policy to *increase* investment. This effect works in three ways.

First, in a recession, an expansionary fiscal policy might create expectations of a more speedy recovery and bring an increase in expected profits. Higher expected profits might increase investment despite a higher interest rate.

Second, government expenditures might be productive and lead to more profitable business opportunities. For example, a new government-built highway might cut the cost of transporting a farmer's produce to a market and induce the farmer to invest in a new fleet of refrigerated trucks.

Third, if an expansionary fiscal policy takes the form of a cut in taxes on business profits, firms' after-tax profits increase and investment might increase.

The Exchange Rate and International Crowding Out

We've seen that an expansionary fiscal policy leads to higher interest rates. But a change in interest rates also affects the exchange rate. Higher interest rates make the dollar appreciate against other currencies. With interest rates higher in Canada than in the rest of the world, funds flow into Canada and people around the world demand more Canadian dollars. As the dollar appreciates, foreigners find Canadian-produced goods and services more expensive and Canadians find imports less expensive. Exports decrease and imports increase—net exports decrease. The tendency for an expansionary fiscal policy to decrease net exports is called **international crowding out.** The decrease in net exports offsets, to some degree, the initial increase in aggregate expenditure brought about by an expansionary fiscal policy.

REVIEW QUIZ

1 Describe macroeconomic equilibrium. What conditions are met in such an equilibrium? What are the links between aggregate demand, the money market, and interest-sensitive expenditure?
2 What is an expansionary fiscal policy and what are its first round effects? What is happening at the end of the first round?
3 What are the second round effects of an expansionary fiscal policy action? Describe the forces at work and the changes that occur in the interest rate, interest-sensitive expenditure, real GDP, and the price level.
4 What is crowding out? What is crowding in? How do they influence the outcome of a fiscal policy action?
5 How does an expansionary fiscal policy affect the exchange rate? What happens to imports and exports?

myeconlab **Study Plan 29.2**

Monetary Policy in the Short Run

TO STUDY THE EFFECTS OF AN EXPANSIONARY monetary policy, we look at the first round effects and the second round effects, just as we did for fiscal policy. Figure 29.5 describes the economy. The quantity of real money is $600 billion, the interest rate is 5 percent a year, interest-sensitive expenditure is

$100 billion, real GDP is $1,000 billion, and the price level is 110. With a price level of 110, the quantity of money is $660 billion.

The Bank of Canada now increases the quantity of money to $1,155 billion. With a price level of 110, the quantity of real money increases to $1,050 billion. Figure 29.5(a) shows the immediate effect. The real money supply curve shifts rightward from MS_0 to MS_1, and the interest rate falls from 5 percent to 1 percent a year. The lower interest rate increases

FIGURE 29.5
First Round Effects of an Expansionary Monetary Policy

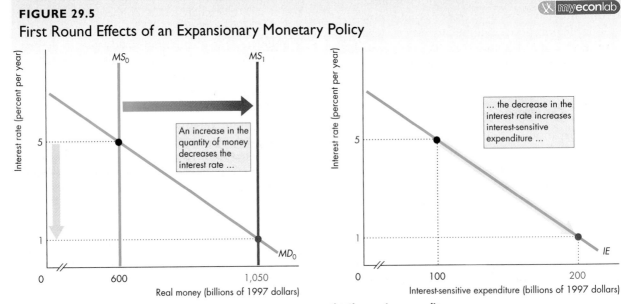

An increase in the quantity of money decreases the interest rate ...

(a) Change in quantity of money

... the decrease in the interest rate increases interest-sensitive expenditure ...

(b) Change in expenditure

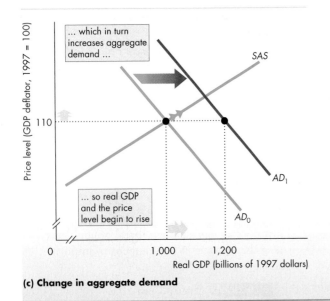

... which in turn increases aggregate demand ...

... so real GDP and the price level begin to rise

(c) Change in aggregate demand

Initially, the real money demand curve is MD_0, the real money supply curve is MS_0, and the interest rate is 5 percent a year (part a). With an interest rate of 5 percent a year, interest-sensitive expenditure is $100 billion on the IE curve (part b). The aggregate demand curve is AD_0. Equilibrium real GDP is $1,000 billion, and the price level is 110 (part c).

An increase in the quantity of money shifts the money supply curve rightward to MS_1 (part a). The interest rate falls to 1 percent a year and interest-sensitive expenditure increases to $200 billion (part b). The increase in expenditure increases aggregate demand and shifts the aggregate demand curve to AD_1 (in part c). Real GDP begins to increase and the price level begins to rise.

interest-sensitive expenditure to $200 billion in part (b). The increase in interest-sensitive expenditure increases aggregate demand and shifts the AD curve rightward from AD_0 to AD_1 (part c). The increase in aggregate demand sets off a multiplier process in which real GDP and the price level begin to increase.

These are the first round effects of an expansionary monetary policy. An increase in the quantity of money lowers the interest rate and increases aggregate demand. Real GDP and the price level begin to increase.

Let's now look at the second round effects.

Second Round Effects

The increasing real GDP and rising price level set off the second round, which Fig. 29.6 illustrates. And as in the case of fiscal policy, it is best to break the second round into two parts: the consequence of increasing real GDP, and the consequence of the rising price level.

The increasing real GDP increases the demand for money from MD_0 to MD_1 in Fig. 29.6(a). The increased demand for money raises the interest rate

---

FIGURE 29.6

Second Round Effects of an Expansionary Monetary Policy

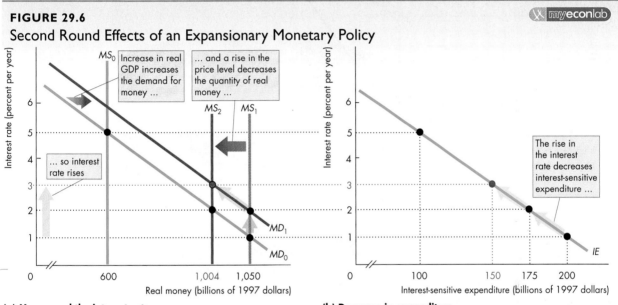

(a) Money and the interest rate

(b) Decrease in expenditure

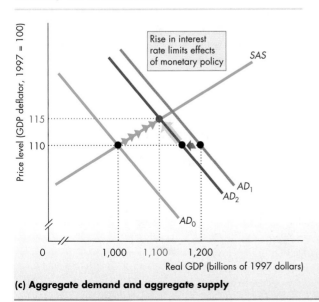

(c) Aggregate demand and aggregate supply

At the start of the second round, the money demand curve is still MD_0 in part (a), the real money supply curve is MS_1, and the interest rate is 1 percent a year. With an interest rate of 1 percent a year, interest-sensitive expenditure is $200 billion on the curve IE in part (b). With the increased quantity of money and interest-sensitive expenditure, the aggregate demand curve is AD_1 in part (c). Real GDP is increasing, and the price level is rising. The increasing real GDP increases the demand for money and the money demand curve shifts rightward to MD_1. The higher interest rate decreases interest-sensitive expenditure, which decreases aggregate demand to AD_2. The rising price level brings a movement along the new AD curve. It does so because the rising price level decreases the quantity of real money and the money supply curve shifts to MS_2. The interest rate rises further and expenditure decreases. The new equilibrium occurs when real GDP has increased to $1,100 billion and the price level has risen to 115.

from 1 percent a year to 2 percent a year. The higher interest rate brings a decrease in interest-sensitive expenditure from $200 billion to $175 billion in Fig. 29.6(b). And the lower level of expenditure decreases aggregate demand and shifts the aggregate demand curve leftward from AD_1 to AD_2 in Fig. 29.6(c).

The rising price level brings a movement along the new aggregate demand curve in Fig. 29.6(c). This movement occurs because the rising price level decreases the quantity of real money. As the price

level rises, the quantity of real money decreases to $1,004 billion and the money supply curve shifts leftward from MS_1 to MS_2 (part a). The interest rate rises further to 3 percent a year. And interest-sensitive expenditure decreases to $150 billion (part b).

In the new short-run equilibrium, real GDP has increased to $1,100 billion, and the price level has risen to 115, where aggregate demand curve AD_2 intersects the short-run aggregate supply curve SAS.

FIGURE 29.7

How the Economy Adjusts to an Expansionary Monetary Policy

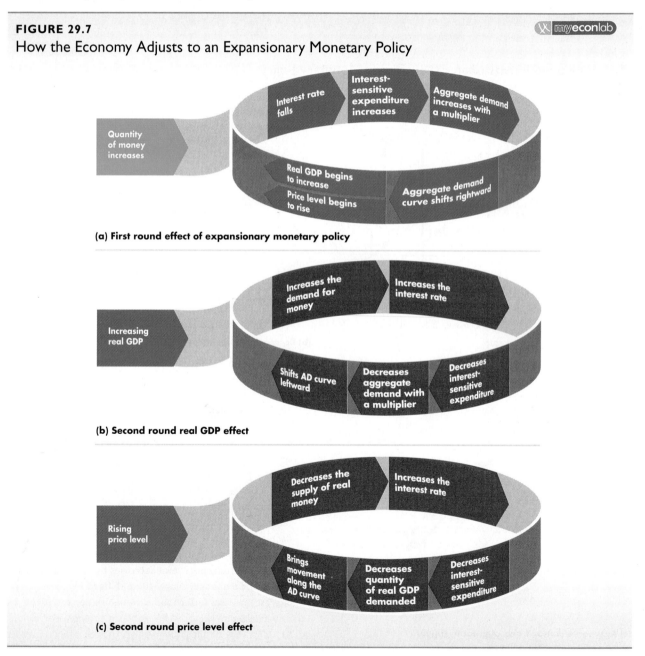

(a) First round effect of expansionary monetary policy

(b) Second round real GDP effect

(c) Second round price level effect

The money demand curve is MD_1, the money supply curve is MS_2, and the interest rate is 3 percent a year in part (a). With an interest rate of 3 percent a year, interest-sensitive expenditure is $150 billion in part (b).

The new equilibrium is the only consistent one and is like that of Fig. 29.1. Figure 29.7 summarizes the adjustments that occur to bring the economy to this new equilibrium.

Money and the Exchange Rate

An increase in the money supply lowers the interest rate. If the interest rate falls in Canada but does not fall in the United States, Japan, and Western Europe, international investors buy the now higher-yielding foreign assets and sell the relatively lower-yielding Canadian assets. As they make these transactions, they sell Canadian dollars. So the dollar depreciates against other currencies. (This mechanism is explained in greater detail in Chapter 26, pp. 615–621.)

With a cheaper Canadian dollar, foreigners face lower prices for Canadian-produced goods and services and Canadians face higher prices for foreign-produced goods and services. Foreigners increase their imports from Canada, and Canadians decrease their imports from the rest of the world. Canadian net exports increase, and real GDP and the price level increase further.

REVIEW QUIZ

1 What are the first round effects of an expansionary monetary policy? What happens to the interest rate, investment and other components of interest-sensitive expenditure, aggregate demand, the demand for money, real GDP, and the price level in the first round?

2 What are the second round effects of an expansionary monetary policy? What happens to the interest rate, investment and other components of interest-sensitive expenditure, aggregate demand, the demand for money, real GDP, and the price level in the second round?

3 How does an expansionary monetary policy influence the exchange rate, imports, and exports?

ⓧ myeconlab   Study Plan 29.3

Relative Effectiveness of Policies

WE'VE SEEN THAT AGGREGATE DEMAND AND REAL GDP are influenced by both fiscal policy and monetary policy. But which policy is the more potent? This question was once at the centre of a controversy among macroeconomists. Later in this section we'll look at that controversy and see how it was settled. But we begin by discovering what determines the effectiveness of fiscal policy.

Effectiveness of Fiscal Policy

The effectiveness of fiscal policy is measured by the magnitude of the increase in aggregate demand that results from a given increase in government expenditures (or decrease in taxes). The effectiveness of fiscal policy depends on the strength of the crowding-out effect. Fiscal policy is most powerful if no crowding out occurs. Fiscal policy is impotent if there is complete crowding out. And the strength of the crowding-out effect depends on two things:

1. The responsiveness of expenditure to the interest rate
2. The responsiveness of the quantity of money demanded to the interest rate

If expenditure is not very responsive to a change in the interest rate, the crowding-out effect is small. But if expenditure is highly responsive to a change in the interest rate, the crowding-out effect is large. Other things remaining the same, the smaller the responsiveness of expenditure to the interest rate, the smaller is the crowding-out effect and the more effective is fiscal policy.

The responsiveness of the quantity of money demanded to the interest rate also affects the size of the crowding-out effect. An increase in real GDP increases the demand for money and with no change in the quantity of money, the interest rate rises. But the extent to which the interest rate rises depends on the responsiveness of the quantity of money demanded to the interest rate. Other things remaining the same, the greater the responsiveness of the quantity of money demanded to the interest rate, the smaller is the rise in the interest rate, the smaller is the crowding-out effect, and the more effective is fiscal policy.

Effectiveness of Monetary Policy

The effectiveness of monetary policy is measured by the magnitude of the increase in aggregate demand that results from a given increase in the quantity of money. Like fiscal policy, the effectiveness of monetary policy depends on two things:

1. The responsiveness of the quantity of money demanded to the interest rate
2. The responsiveness of expenditure to the interest rate

The starting point for monetary policy is a change in the quantity of money that changes the interest rate. A given change in the quantity of money might bring a small change or a large change in the interest rate. The less responsive the quantity of money demanded to the interest rate, the greater is the change in the interest rate. So other things remaining the same, the larger the initial change in the interest rate, the more effective is monetary policy.

But effectiveness of monetary policy also depends on how much expenditure changes. If expenditure is not very responsive to a change in the interest rate, monetary actions do not have much effect on expenditure. But if expenditure is highly responsive to a change in the interest rate, monetary actions have a large effect on aggregate expenditure. The greater responsiveness of expenditure to the interest rate, the more effective is monetary policy.

The effectiveness of fiscal policy and monetary policy that you've just studied was once controversial. During the 1950s and 1960s, this issue lay at the heart of what was called the Keynesian–monetarist controversy. Let's look at the dispute and see how it was resolved.

Keynesian–Monetarist Controversy

The Keynesian–monetarist controversy was an ongoing dispute in macroeconomics between two broad groups of economists. A **Keynesian** is a macroeconomist who regards the economy as being inherently unstable and as requiring active government intervention to achieve stability. Keynesian views about the functioning of the economy are based on the theories of John Maynard Keynes, published in Keynes' *General Theory* (see pp. 530–531). Traditionally, Keynesians assigned a low degree of importance to monetary policy and a high degree of importance to fiscal policy. Modern Keynesians

assign a high degree of importance to both types of policy. A **monetarist** is a macroeconomist who believes that most macroeconomic fluctuations are caused by fluctuations in the quantity of money and that the economy is inherently stable and requires no active government intervention. Monetarist views about the functioning of the economy are based on theories most forcefully set forth by Milton Friedman (see pp. 700–701). Traditionally monetarists assigned a low degree of importance to fiscal policy. But modern monetarists, like modern Keynesians, assign a high degree of importance to both types of policy.

The nature of the Keynesian–monetarist debate has changed over the years. During the 1950s and 1960s, it was a debate about the relative effectiveness of fiscal policy and monetary policy in changing aggregate demand. We can see the essence of that debate by distinguishing three views:

- Extreme Keynesianism
- Extreme monetarism
- The intermediate position

Extreme Keynesianism The extreme Keynesian hypothesis is that a change in the quantity of money has no effect on aggregate demand and a change in government expenditures on goods and services or in taxes has a large effect on aggregate demand. The two circumstances in which a change in the quantity of money has no effect on aggregate demand are when

1. Expenditure is completely insensitive to the interest rate
2. The quantity of money demanded is highly sensitive to the interest rate

If expenditure is completely insensitive to the interest rate (if the *IE* curve is vertical), a change in the quantity of money changes the interest rate, but the change does not affect aggregate expenditure. Monetary policy is impotent.

If the quantity of money demanded is highly sensitive to the interest rate (if the *MD* curve is horizontal), people are willing to hold any amount of money at a given interest rate—a situation called a *liquidity trap*. With a liquidity trap, a change in the quantity of money affects only the amount of money held. It does not affect the interest rate. With an unchanged interest rate, expenditure remains constant. Monetary policy is impotent. Some people believe that Japan was in a liquidity trap during the late 1990s.

Extreme Monetarism The extreme monetarist hypothesis is that a change in government expenditures on goods and services or in taxes has no effect on aggregate demand and that a change in the quantity of money has a large effect on aggregate demand. Two circumstances give rise to these predictions:

1. Expenditure is highly sensitive to the interest rate
2. The quantity of money demanded is completely insensitive to the interest rate

If an increase in government expenditures on goods and services induces an increase in the interest rate that is sufficiently large to reduce expenditure by the same amount as the initial increase in government expenditures, then fiscal policy has no effect on aggregate demand. This outcome is complete crowding out. For this result to occur, either the quantity of money demanded must be insensitive to the interest rate—a fixed amount of money is held regardless of the interest rate—or expenditure must be highly sensitive to the interest rate—any amount of expenditure will be undertaken at a given interest rate.

The Intermediate Position The intermediate position is that both fiscal policy and monetary policy affect aggregate demand. Crowding out is not complete, so fiscal policy does have an effect. There is no liquidity trap and expenditure responds to the interest rate, so monetary policy does indeed affect aggregate demand. This position is the one that now appears to be correct and is the one that we've explored in most of this chapter. Let's see how economists came to this conclusion.

Sorting Out the Competing Claims

The dispute between monetarists, Keynesians, and those taking an intermediate position was essentially a disagreement about the magnitudes of two economic parameters:

1. The responsiveness of expenditure to the interest rate
2. The responsiveness of the demand for real money to the interest rate

If expenditure is highly sensitive to the interest rate or the demand for real money is barely sensitive to the interest rate, then monetary policy is powerful and fiscal policy relatively ineffective. In this case, the world looks similar to the claims of extreme mone-

tarists. If expenditure is very insensitive to the interest rate, or the demand for real money is highly sensitive, then fiscal policy is powerful and monetary policy is relatively ineffective. In this case, the world looks similar to the claims of the extreme Keynesians.

By using statistical methods to study the demand for real money and expenditure and by using data from a wide variety of historical and national experiences, economists were able to settle this dispute. Neither extreme position turned out to be supported by the evidence, and the intermediate position won. The demand curve for real money slopes downward. And expenditure *is* interest sensitive. Neither the money demand curve nor the interest-sensitive expenditure curve is vertical or horizontal, so the extreme Keynesian and extreme monetarist hypotheses are rejected.

Interest Rate and Exchange Rate Effectiveness

Although fiscal policy and monetary policy are alternative ways of changing aggregate demand, they have opposing effects on the interest rate and the exchange rate. A fiscal policy action that increases aggregate demand raises the interest rate and increases the exchange rate. A monetary policy action that increases aggregate demand lowers the interest rate and decreases the exchange rate. Because of these opposing effects on interest rates and the exchange rate, if the two policies are combined to increase aggregate demand, their separate effects on the interest rate and the exchange rate can be minimized.

REVIEW QUIZ

1 What two macroeconomic parameters influence the relative effectiveness of fiscal policy and monetary policy?
2 Under what circumstances is the Keynesian view correct and under what circumstances is the monetarist view correct?
3 How can fiscal policy and monetary policy be combined to increase aggregate demand yet at the same time keep the interest rate constant?

Ⓧ myeconlab **Study Plan 29.4**

We're now going to look at expansionary fiscal and monetary policy at full employment.

Policy Actions at Full Employment

AN EXPANSIONARY FISCAL POLICY OR MONETARY policy can bring the economy to full employment. But it is often difficult to determine whether the economy is below full employment. So an expansionary fiscal policy or monetary policy might be undertaken when the economy is at full employment. What happens then? Let's answer this question starting with an expansionary fiscal policy.

Expansionary Fiscal Policy at Full Employment

Suppose the economy is at full employment and the government increases its expenditures. All the effects that we worked out earlier in this chapter occur. But these effects determine only a *short-run equilibrium*. That is, the first round and second round effects of policy both occur in the short run. There is a third round, which is the long-run adjustment.

Starting out at full employment, an expansionary fiscal policy will create an above full-employment equilibrium in which there is an *inflationary gap*. The money wage rate begins to rise, short-run aggregate supply decreases, and a long-run adjustment occurs in which real GDP decreases to potential GDP and the price level rises.

Figure 29.8 illustrates the combined first and second round short-run effects and the third round long-run adjustment.

In Fig. 29.8, potential GDP is $1,000 billion. Real GDP equals potential GDP on aggregate demand curve AD_0 and short-run aggregate supply curve SAS_0. An expansionary fiscal action increases aggregate demand. The combined first round and second round effect increases aggregate demand to AD_1. Real GDP increases to $1,100 billion and the price level rises to 115. There is an inflationary gap of $100 billion.

With the economy above full employment, a shortage of labour puts upward pressure on the money wage rate, which now begins to rise. And a third round of adjustment begins. The rising money wage rate decreases short-run aggregate supply and the *SAS* curve starts moving leftward towards SAS_1.

As short-run aggregate supply decreases, real GDP decreases and the price level rises. This process

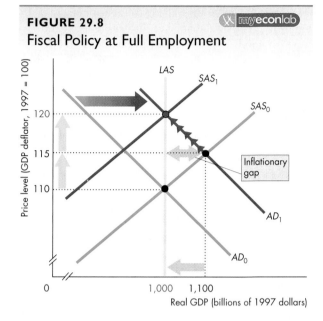

FIGURE 29.8 myeconlab

Fiscal Policy at Full Employment

The long-run aggregate supply curve is *LAS* and initially the aggregate demand curve is AD_0 and the short-run aggregate supply curve is SAS_0. Real GDP is $1,000 billion and the GDP deflator is 110. Fiscal policy changes shift the aggregate demand curve to AD_1. At the new short-run equilibrium, real GDP is $1,100 billion and the GDP deflator is 115. Because real GDP exceeds potential GDP, the money wage rate begins to rise and the short-run aggregate supply curve begins to shift leftward to SAS_1. At the new long-run equilibrium, the GDP deflator is 120 and real GDP is back at its original level.

continues until the inflationary gap has been eliminated and the economy returns to full employment. At long-run equilibrium, real GDP is $1,000, which is potential GDP, and the price level is 120.

Crowding Out at Full Employment

You've just seen that when government expenditures increase at full employment, the long-run change in real GDP is zero. The entire effect of the increase in aggregate demand is to increase the price level. This outcome implies that at full employment, an increase in government expenditures *completely crowds out private expenditure* or *creates an international (net exports) deficit*, or results in a combination of the two.

The easiest way to see why is to recall that aggregate expenditure, which equals consumption expenditure, *C*, plus investment, *I*, plus government expenditures, *G*, plus net exports, *NX*, equals real GDP. That is,

$$Y = C + I + G + NX.$$

Comparing the initial situation with the final outcome, real GDP has not changed. So aggregate expenditure, $C + I + G + NX$, is constant between the two situations.

But government expenditures have increased, so the sum of consumption, investment, and net exports must have decreased. If net exports don't change, consumption plus investment decreases by the full amount of the increase in government expenditures. If consumption and investment don't change, net exports decrease by an amount equal to the increase in government expenditures. A decrease in net exports is an increase in our international deficit.

You've now seen that the effects of expansionary fiscal policy are extremely sensitive to the state of the economy when the policy action is taken. At less than full employment, an expansionary fiscal policy can move the economy towards full employment. At full employment, an expansionary fiscal policy raises the price level and crowds out private expenditure or creates an international deficit.

Expansionary Monetary Policy at Full Employment

Now suppose the economy is at full employment and the Bank of Canada increases the quantity of money. Again, all the effects that we worked out earlier in this chapter occur. But again, these effects determine only a *short-run equilibrium*. That is, the first round and second round effects of monetary policy both occur in the short run. And again, there is a third round, which is the long-run adjustment.

Starting out at full employment, an expansionary monetary policy will create an above full-employment equilibrium in which there is an *inflationary gap*. The money wage rate begins to rise, short-run aggregate supply decreases, and a long-run adjustment occurs in which real GDP decreases to potential GDP and the price level rises.

To illustrate the effects of monetary policy at full employment, look back at Fig. 29.8 but now think of the increase in aggregate demand as resulting from an increase in the quantity of money. You can see that in the short run, an expansionary monetary policy increases real GDP and the price level. But in the long run, expansionary monetary policy increases only the price level and leaves real GDP unchanged at potential GDP.

Long-Run Neutrality

In the long run, a change in the quantity of money changes only the price level and leaves real GDP unchanged. The independence of real GDP from the quantity of money is an example of the long-run neutrality of money.

But long-run neutrality applies not only to real GDP but also to all real variables. The so-called **long-run neutrality** proposition is that in the long run, a change in the quantity of money changes the price level and leaves all real variables unchanged.

You can see this outcome in the case of real GDP in Fig. 29.8. With no change in real GDP, the demand for money does not change. The price level rises by the same percentage as the increase in the quantity of money, so the quantity of real money does not change. With no change in the demand for money and no change in the quantity of real money, the interest rate does not change. And with no change in the interest rate, expenditure remains the same.

Finally, with no change in real GDP or the real interest rate, consumption expenditure, investment, government expenditures, and net exports are unchanged.

Policy Coordination, Conflict, and Risk

SO FAR, WE'VE STUDIED THE INTERACTION OF fiscal policy and monetary policy with each conducted in isolation from the other. We are now going to consider what happens if the two branches of policy are coordinated and if they come into conflict.

Policy coordination occurs when the government and the Bank of Canada work together to achieve a common set of goals.

Policy conflict occurs when the government and the Bank of Canada pursue different goals and the actions of one make it harder (perhaps impossible) for the other to achieve its goals.

Policy Coordination

The basis for policy coordination is the fact that either fiscal policy or monetary policy can be used to influence aggregate demand. Starting from a *below full-employment equilibrium*, an increase in aggregate demand increases real GDP and decreases unemployment. If the size and timing of the policy action is well judged, it can restore full employment. Similarly, starting from an *above full-employment equilibrium*, a decrease in aggregate demand decreases real GDP and can, again if the timing and size of the action is well judged, eliminate an *inflationary gap*. Because either a fiscal policy or a monetary policy action can achieve these objectives, the two policies can (in principle) be combined to also achieve the same outcome.

If either or both policies can restore full employment and eliminate inflation, why does it matter which policy is used? It matters because the two policies have different side effects—different effects on other variables about which people care. These side effects arise because policy influences two key variables:

■ The interest rate
■ The exchange rate

Interest Rate Effects An expansionary fiscal policy *raises* the interest rate, while an expansionary monetary policy *lowers* the interest rate. When the interest rate changes, investment changes, so an expansionary fiscal policy lowers investment (crowding out) while an expansionary monetary policy increases investment. So if an expansionary fiscal policy increases

aggregate demand, consumption expenditure increases and investment decreases. But if an expansionary monetary policy increases aggregate demand, consumption expenditure and investment increase.

By coordinating fiscal policy and monetary policy and increasing aggregate demand with an appropriate combination of the two, it is possible to increase real GDP and lower unemployment with either no change in the interest rate or any desired change in the interest rate. A big dose of fiscal expansion and a small dose of monetary expansion raises the interest rate and decreases investment, while a small dose of fiscal expansion and a big dose of monetary expansion lowers the interest rate and increases investment.

The interest rate affects our long-term growth prospects because the growth rate of potential GDP depends on the level of investment. The connection between investment, capital, and economic growth is explained in Chapter 31.

Exchange Rate Effects An expansionary fiscal policy raises not only the interest rate but also the exchange rate. In contrast, an expansionary monetary policy *lowers* the exchange rate. When the exchange rate changes, net exports change. An expansionary fiscal policy lowers net exports (international crowding out) while an expansionary monetary policy increases net exports. So if full employment is restored by expansionary policy, net exports decrease with fiscal expansion and increase with monetary expansion.

Policy Conflict

Policy conflicts are not planned. But they sometimes happen. When they arise, it is usually because there is a divergence of the political priorities of the government and the objectives of the Bank of Canada.

Governments (both federal and provincial) pay a lot of attention to employment and production over a short time horizon. They look for policies that make their re-election chances high. The Bank of Canada pays a lot of attention to price level stability and has a long time horizon. It doesn't have an election to worry about.

So a situation might arise in which the government wants the Bank to pursue an expansionary monetary policy but the Bank wants to keep its foot on the monetary brake. The government says that an increase in the quantity of money is essential to lower interest rates and the exchange rate and to boost investment and exports. The Bank says that the problem is with fiscal policy. Spending is too high and revenues too low. With fiscal policy too expansionary, interest rates and the exchange rate are high and they cannot be lowered permanently by monetary policy. To lower interest rates and give investment and exports a boost, fiscal policy must become contractionary. Only then can an expansionary monetary policy be pursued.

A Policy Interaction Risk

In the standard analysis of policy interaction that we've studied in this chapter, the central bank targets the quantity of money and money market equilibrium determines the interest rate. But as you learned in Chapter 28, the Bank of Canada conducts monetary policy by targeting the overnight interest rate and money market equilibrium determines the quantity of money.

When a central bank targets the quantity of money, an expansionary fiscal policy action automatically raises the interest rate. It does so by increasing the demand for money. The higher interest rate moderates the effects of the expansionary fiscal policy. Aggregate demand increases and real GDP and the price level rise, but by less than they would if the interest rate were unchanged.

So when a central bank targets the interest rate rather than the quantity of money, an expansionary fiscal policy raises the interest rate only if the central bank takes an explicit action. If the central bank raises the interest rate by the amount that the market would have raised it with a given quantity of money, the outcome will be identical under the two alternative monetary policies.

But if the central bank is slow to change the interest rate, an expansionary fiscal policy might increase aggregate demand by too much. And if the central bank reacts to expansionary fiscal policy with a more aggressive increase in the interest rate, aggregate demand might increase by too little.

The key problem for monetary policy is to make a correct determination of the appropriate interest rate to accompany a change in fiscal policy. The problem is more acute at full employment than in a recession but it is a problem in either situation.

In a recession, if the central bank raises the interest rate too little and too late, an expansionary fiscal policy could overshoot full employment and create an inflationary gap. If the central bank raises the interest rate too much and too soon, an expansionary fiscal policy could undershoot full employment and leave an unwanted recessionary gap.

At full employment, if the central bank raises the interest rate too little and too late, an expansionary fiscal policy would create an inflationary gap that would bring faster inflation, a fall in the real interest rate and a further increase in the inflationary gap. A cumulative inflation would take hold until the central bank moved the interest rate high enough to eliminate the inflationary gap. And if at full employment the central bank raises the interest rate too much and too soon in response to an expansionary fiscal policy, real GDP would fall below full employment and a recessionary gap would emerge. The gap would persist until the central bank lowered the interest rate.

REVIEW QUIZ

1 What are the main things that can be achieved by coordinating fiscal policy and monetary policy?

2 What are the main sources of conflict in policy between the Bank of Canada and the government of Canada?

3 What are the main consequences of the government and the Bank of Canada pursuing conflicting policies? Are all the consequences bad?

myeconlab Study Plan 29.6

◆ You have now studied the interaction of fiscal policy and monetary policy. *Reading Between the Lines* on pp. 694–695 examines the views of David Dodge, governor of the Bank of Canada, on the appropriate roles for monetary policy and fiscal policy today.

You've seen that monetary and fiscal policies are alternative ways of changing aggregate demand and real GDP. But they have different effects on the interest rate and the exchange rate. You've seen what determines the relative effectiveness of fiscal and monetary policies and how the mix of these policies can influence the composition of aggregate expenditure. But you've also seen that the ultimate effects of these policies on real GDP and the price level depend not only on the behaviour of aggregate demand but also on aggregate supply and the state of the labour market.

We next turn to the aggregate supply side of the economy and learn about the factors that determine potential GDP and the economic growth rate.

Monetary and Fiscal Tensions

CALGARY HERALD, SEPTEMBER 4, 2002

Central bank boss warns against big spending

The head of the Bank of Canada has warned the Chrétien government against eroding the country's hard-earned anti-inflation credibility.

The not-so-veiled warning by governor David Dodge came amid rising speculation that the prime minister is about to go on a social policy spending spree in advance of his retirement in 18 months.

It also came on the eve of what many analysts expect will be another interest rate increase aimed at reducing the stimulus that is already in the economy. Earlier this year, the bank rate was the lowest in more than four decades.

In a speech to other central bankers in Jackson Hole, Wyo., last weekend Dodge stressed the importance of the credibility that the bank and government have earned with "joint agreements on inflation-control targets" and "a framework that greatly reduces the probability of running a fiscal deficit and thus puts the debt-to-GDP ratio on a clear downward track."

"Fiscal and monetary credibility is high," Dodge said, noting that markets, businesses and individuals "trust" that the central bank will meet its inflation target and that the government will not start spending more than it takes in.

"Initially, the credibility of these policies was not high," Dodge noted. "So it was essential to demonstrate clearly our resolve to achieve greater fiscal prudence and lower inflation until credibility was gained."

To do that, he said, it meant that the bank at times had to keep interest rates higher, and that the government had to keep a tighter rein on spending than otherwise necessary.

Dodge also said it was fortunate the government in its last budget did not inject a lot of new spending into the economy.

"I say fortunately because ... there was more underlying strength in the economy than we expected," Dodge explained.

He went on to note that the bank had already injected a lot of stimulus into the economy by cutting interest rates.

"Therefore, added fiscal stimulus was not necessary to get the economy going and the monetary stimulus provided is proving much easier to turn around."

Essence of the Story

■ In a speech at a conference of central bankers, Bank of Canada governor David Dodge said that the joint agreements on inflation-control targets between the Bank and government have created a high degree of trust that inflation targets will be met.

■ He warned against increasing government spending and said it was fortunate that in its last budget, the government did not inject a lot of new spending into the economy because the economy was already expanding strongly.

■ He noted that the Bank of Canada had injected a lot of stimulus into the economy by cutting interest rates and that added fiscal stimulus was neither necessary nor as easy to reverse as monetary policy actions.

Economic Analysis

■ Today, Canada's fiscal policy is not in conflict with monetary policy goals. But David Dodge's 2002 speech makes a timeless point.

■ The Governor of the Bank of Canada wants to maintain the Bank's credibility and keep the inflation rate close to 2 percent a year.

■ He thinks that macroeconomic stability —low inflation *and* full employment—is best achieved by using monetary policy alone and fears that if fiscal policy were to become expansionary, inflation would take off.

■ Figure 1 illustrates David Dodge's concern.

■ In Fig. 1, potential GDP is $1,084, but aggregate demand, AD_0, and short-run aggregate supply, SAS_0, intersect at a below full-employment equilibrium so there is a recessionary gap.

■ If to stimulate aggregate demand the Bank of Canada cuts the interest rate and at the same time the government increases its expenditure, the AD curve shifts rightward to AD_1.

■ These expansionary fiscal and monetary policies bring an inflationary gap.

■ With an inflationary gap, the money wage rate begins to rise and the SAS curve starts to shift leftward towards SAS_1.

■ Real GDP decreases towards potential GDP, but inflation takes off as the price level rises to 127.

■ Figure 2 shows what David Dodge would like to achieve.

■ With the same initial recessionary gap, the Bank of Canada takes action to stimulate aggregate demand by cutting the interest rate.

■ The government holds expenditure steady so that fiscal policy does not increase aggregate demand.

■ The AD curve shifts rightward to AD_2 and full employment is achieved while the inflation rate remains low.

■ If the Bank of Canada sees an inflationary gap, it can take quick action in the opposite direction—raise the interest rate—to decrease aggregate demand.

■ In contrast, if increased government spending brings an inflationary gap, it is difficult to cut spending.

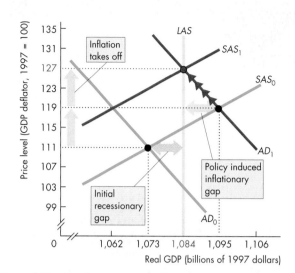

Figure 1 Fiscal and monetary stimulus

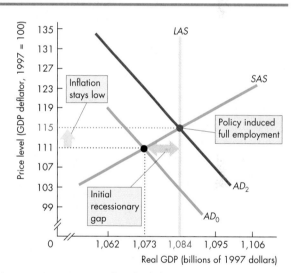

Figure 2 Monetary stimulus alone

You're the Voter

■ Do you agree with David Dodge that monetary policy alone is the appropriate tool for achieving low inflation and full employment?

■ Do you think there is ever a role for fiscal policy?

■ Would you vote for an expansionary fiscal policy today? Explain why or why not.

SUMMARY

KEY POINTS

Macroeconomic Equilibrium (pp. 678–679)

- Equilibrium real GDP, the price level, and the interest rate are determined simultaneously by money market equilibrium and *AS–AD* equilibrium.

Fiscal Policy in the Short Run (pp. 680–683)

- The first round effects of an expansionary fiscal policy are an increase in aggregate demand, an increasing real GDP, and a rising price level.
- The second round effects are an increasing demand for money and a decreasing quantity of real money that increase the interest rate and limit the increase in real GDP and the rise in the price level.
- Interest-sensitive expenditure, which includes investment and net exports, decreases.

Monetary Policy in the Short Run (pp. 684–687)

- The first round effects of an expansionary monetary policy are a fall in the interest rate, an increase in aggregate demand, an increasing real GDP, and a rising price level.
- The second round effects are an increasing demand for money and a decreasing quantity of real money that increase the interest rate and limit the increase in real GDP and the rise in the price level.
- Interest-sensitive expenditure, which includes investment and net exports, increases.

Relative Effectiveness of Policies (pp. 687–689)

- The relative effectiveness of fiscal and monetary policy depends on the interest-sensitivity of both expenditure and the quantity of money demanded.
- The extreme Keynesian position is that only fiscal policy affects aggregate demand. The extreme monetarist position is that only monetary policy affects aggregate demand. Neither extreme is correct.
- The mix of fiscal policy and monetary policy influences the composition of aggregate demand.

Policy Actions at Full Employment (pp. 690–691)

- An expansionary fiscal policy at full employment increases real GDP and the price level in the short run but increases only the price level in the long run. Complete crowding out of investment occurs or the international deficit increases.
- An expansionary monetary policy at full employment increases real GDP and the price level in the short run but increases only the price level in the long run. Money is neutral—has no real effects—in the long run.

Policy Coordination, Conflict, and Risk (pp. 692–693)

- Policy coordination can make changes in the interest rate and the exchange rate small.
- Policy conflict can avoid inflation in the face of a government deficit.

KEY FIGURES

Figure 29.1   Equilibrium Real GDP, Price Level, Interest Rate, and Expenditure, 679
Figure 29.2   First Round Effects of an Expansionary Fiscal Policy, 680
Figure 29.3   Second Round Effects of an Expansionary Fiscal Policy, 681
Figure 29.5   First Round Effects of an Expansionary Monetary Policy, 684
Figure 29.6   Second Round Effects of an Expansionary Monetary Policy, 685
Figure 29.8   Fiscal Policy at Full Employment, 690

KEY TERMS

Crowding in, 683
Crowding out, 683
International crowding out, 683
Keynesian, 688
Long-run neutrality, 691
Monetarist, 688
Policy conflict, 692
Policy coordination, 692

PROBLEMS

Go to ⓧ myeconlab for solutions to odd-numbered problems and additional exercises.

1. In the economy described in Fig. 29.1, suppose the government decreases its expenditures on goods and services.
   a. Work out the first round effects.
   b. Explain how real GDP and the interest rate change.
   c. Explain the second round effects that take the economy to a new equilibrium.

2. In the economy described in Fig. 29.1, suppose the government increases its expenditures on goods and services by $25 billion.
   a. Work out the first round effects.
   b. Explain how real GDP and the interest rate change.
   c. Explain the second round effects that take the economy to a new equilibrium.
   d. Compare the equilibrium in part (c) with the one described on pp. 680–682. In which case is the change in real GDP larger? In which case is the change in the interest rate larger? Why?

3. In the economy described in Fig. 29.1, suppose the Bank of Canada decreases the quantity of money.
   a. Work out the first round effects.
   b. Explain how real GDP and the interest rate change.
   c. Explain the second round effects that take the economy to a new equilibrium.

4. In the economy described in Fig. 29.1, suppose the Bank of Canada increases the quantity of money by $250 billion.
   a. Work out the first round effects.
   b. Explain how real GDP and the interest rate change.
   c. Explain the second round effects that take the economy to a new equilibrium.
   d. Compare the equilibrium in part (c) with the one described on pp. 684–686. In which case is the change in real GDP larger? In which case is the change in the interest rate larger? Why?

5. The economies of two countries, Alpha and Beta, are identical in every way except the following: in Alpha, a change in the interest rate of 1 percentage point (for example, from 5 percent to 6 percent) results in a $1 billion change in the quantity of real money demanded. In Beta, a change in the interest rate of 1 percentage point results in a $0.1 billion change in the quantity of real money demanded.
   a. In which economy does an increase in government expenditures on goods and services have a larger effect on real GDP?
   b. In which economy is the crowding-out effect weaker?
   c. In which economy does a change in the quantity of money have a larger effect on equilibrium real GDP?
   d. Which economy, if either, is closer to the Keynesian extreme and which is closer to the monetarist extreme?

6. The economies of two countries, Gamma and Delta, are identical except: In Gamma, a change in the interest rate of 1 percentage point (for example, from 5 percent to 6 percent) results in a $0.1 billion change in interest-sensitive expenditure. In Delta, a change in the interest rate of 1 percentage point results in a $10 billion change in interest-sensitive expenditure.
   a. In which economy does an increase in government expenditures on goods and services have a larger effect on real GDP?
   b. In which economy is the crowding-out effect weaker?
   c. In which economy does a change in the quantity of money have a larger effect on equilibrium real GDP?
   d. Which economy, if either, is closer to the Keynesian extreme and which is closer to the monetarist extreme?

7. The economy is in a recession and the government wants to increase aggregate demand, stimulate exports, and increase investment. It has three policy options: increase government expenditures on goods and services, decrease taxes, and increase the quantity of money.
   a. Explain the mechanisms at work under each alternative policy.
   b. What is the effect of each policy on the composition of aggregate demand?
   c. What are the short-run effects of each policy on real GDP and the price level?
   d. Which policy would you recommend that the government adopt? Why?

8. The economy has an inflationary gap and the government wants to decrease aggregate demand, cut exports, and decrease investment. It has three policy options: decrease government expenditures on goods and services, increase taxes, and decrease the quantity of money.
   a. Explain the mechanisms at work under each alternative policy.
   b. What is the effect of each policy on the composition of aggregate demand?
   c. What are the short-run effects of each policy on real GDP and the price level?
   d. Which policy would you recommend that the government adopt? Why?

9. The economy is at full employment, but the government is disappointed with the growth rate of real GDP. It wants to increase real GDP growth by stimulating investment. At the same time, it wants to avoid an increase in the price level.
   a. Suggest a combination of fiscal and monetary policies that will achieve the government's objective.
   b. Which policy would you recommend that the government adopt?
   c. Explain the mechanisms at work under your recommended policy.
   d. What is the effect of your recommended policy on the composition of aggregate demand?
   e. What are the short-run and long-run effects of your recommended policy on real GDP and the price level?

10. The economy is at full employment, and the government is worried that the growth rate of real GDP is too high because it is depleting the country's natural resources. The government wants to lower real GDP growth by lowering investment. At the same time it wants to avoid a fall in the price level.
   a. Suggest a combination of fiscal and monetary policies that will achieve the government's objective.
   b. Which policy would you recommend that the government adopt?
   c. Explain the mechanisms at work under your recommended policy.
   d. What is the effect of your recommended policy on the composition of aggregate demand?
   e. What are the short-run and long-run effects of your recommended policy on real GDP and the price level?

CRITICAL THINKING

1. Study *Reading Between the Lines* on pp. 694–695 and then answer the following questions:
   a. What does David Dodge think the government's fiscal policy should be?
   b. What are your predictions about the effects of a large increase in government expenditure on real GDP, the price level, interest rates, investment, the exchange rate, and net exports?
   c. What actions do you think that the Bank of Canada would need to take to ensure that an increase in government expenditure doesn't bring an increase in the inflation rate?
   d. What would happen if the Bank of Canada decided to raise interest rates at the same time that the government increased its expenditure? Explain the likely effects on real GDP, the price level, investment, the exchange rate, and net exports.

WEB EXERCISES

Use the links on myeconlab **to work the following exercises.**

1. Visit the Web sites of the Department of Finance, the Bank of Canada, and Statistics Canada to find information on the current condition of the Canadian economy and current fiscal and monetary policy. On the basis of the current state of the Canadian economy, and in light of what you now know about fiscal and monetary policy interaction, what do you predict would happen to real GDP and the price level
   a. If the Bank of Canada conducted an expansionary monetary policy?
   b. If the Bank of Canada conducted a contractionary monetary policy?
   c. If the government of Canada conducted an expansionary fiscal policy?
   d. If the government of Canada conducted a contractionary fiscal policy?
   e. If the Bank of Canada conducted an expansionary monetary policy and the government of Canada conducted a contractionary fiscal policy?
   f. If the Bank of Canada conducted a contractionary monetary policy and the government of Canada conducted an expansionary fiscal policy?

Money Chasing Goods

Aggregate demand fluctuations bring recessions and expansions. If aggregate demand expands more rapidly than long-run aggregate supply, we get inflation. So understanding the forces that determine aggregate demand helps us to understand both the business cycle and inflation.

It took economists a long time to achieve this knowledge, and we still don't know enough about aggregate demand to be able to forecast it more than a few months ahead. But we do know the basic factors that influence aggregate demand. And we know a lot about how those factors interact to send shock waves rippling through the economy.

Fundamentally, aggregate demand is a monetary phenomenon. The quantity of money is the single most significant influence on aggregate demand. This insight was first outlined more than 200 years ago by David Hume, a Scottish philosopher and close friend of Adam Smith. Said Hume, "In every Kingdom into which money begins to flow in greater abundance than formerly, everything takes a new face: labour and industry gain life; the merchant becomes more enterprising, the manufacturer more diligent and skilful, and even the farmer follows his plough with greater alacrity and attention." Milton Friedman and other economists known as monetarists also emphasize the central role of money. Money lies at the centre of Keynes' theory of aggregate demand as well. But Keynes also called attention to the power of independent changes in government expenditures, taxes, and business investment to influence aggregate demand.

In the modern world, we also recognize the effect of changes in exports on aggregate demand.

The chapters in this part explain the factors that influence aggregate demand and help you to understand how they interact to bring multiplier effects on aggregate expenditure. Chapter 23 explained the effects of changes in business investment and the multiplier effect they have on consumption expenditure and aggregate expenditure. Chapter 24 looked at fiscal policy and applied the model of Chapter 23 to study the effects of changes in government expenditures and taxes. Chapter 25 brought money into the picture and explained what money is, how banks create it, and how the interest rate is determined. Chapter 26 examined the foreign exchange market and the determination of the exchange rate between currencies. Chapter 27 explained inflation and showed how the trend in money growth determines the trend in inflation and how fluctuations in aggregate demand bring fluctuations in inflation, employment, and unemployment. Chapter 28 returned to the Bank of Canada and studied the way the Bank seeks to control inflation by targeting the overnight loans rate. Then, Chapter 29 examined the interactions of fiscal policy and monetary policy.

Many economists have developed the insights you've learned in these chapters. One of the truly outstanding ones is Milton Friedman, whom you can meet on the next page. You can also meet one of today's leading monetary economists, Michael Woodford of Princeton University.

Understanding Inflation

"Inflation is always and everywhere a monetary phenomenon."

MILTON
FRIEDMAN
*The Counter-
Revolution in
Monetary
Theory*

THE ECONOMIST

Milton Friedman *was born into a poor immigrant family in New York City in 1912. He was an undergraduate at Rutgers and graduate student at Columbia University during the Great Depression. Today, Professor Friedman is a Senior Fellow at the Hoover Institution at Stanford University. But his reputation was built between 1946 and 1983, when he was a leading member of the "Chicago School," an approach to economics developed at the University of Chicago and based on the views that free markets allocate resources efficiently and that stable and low money supply growth delivers macroeconomic stability.*

Friedman has advanced our understanding of the forces that determine aggregate demand and clarified the effects of the quantity of money. And for this work, he was awarded the (much overdue, in the opinion of his many admirers) 1977 Nobel Prize for Economic Science.

By reasoning from basic economic principles, Friedman predicted that persistent demand stimulation would not increase output but would cause inflation. When output growth slowed and inflation broke out in the 1970s, Friedman seemed like a prophet, and for a time, his policy prescription, known as monetarism, was embraced around the world.

700

THE ISSUES

The combination of history and economics has taught us a lot about the causes of inflation. Severe inflation—hyperinflation—arises from a breakdown of the normal fiscal policy processes at times of war or political upheaval. Tax revenues fall short of government spending, and newly printed money fills the gap between them. As inflation increases, the quantity of money that is needed to make payments increases, and a shortage of money can even result. So the rate of money growth increases yet further, and prices rise yet faster. Eventually, the monetary system collapses. Such was the experience of Germany during the 1920s and Brazil during the 1990s.

In earlier times, when commodities were used as money, inflation resulted from the discovery of new sources of money. The most recent occurrence of this type of inflation was at the end of the nineteenth century when gold, then used as money, was discovered in Australia, the Klondike, and South Africa.

In modern times, inflation has resulted from keeping the interest rate low so that increases in aggregate demand accommodate increases in costs. The most dramatic such inflations occurred during the 1970s when the Bank of Canada, the Federal Reserve, and other central banks around the world accommodated oil price increases.

To avoid inflation, the interest rate must be set high enough to keep the growth rate of money and aggregate demand in check. But at times of severe cost pressure, central banks feel a strong tug in the direction of avoiding recession and accommodating the cost pressure.

Yet in recent years, the central banks of most of the advanced economies have avoided inflation. They have done so by establishing inflation-control targets, a clearly explained and understood policy process, and a careful public reporting system. The Bank of Canada (along with the Bank of England, the European Central Bank, and the Reserve Banks of Australia and New Zealand) has been a leader in this move towards greater stablity, clarity, and accountability.

But there are risks in the monetary policy strategy favoured by central banks today. The inflation rate that they target is only loosely under their control. And when tested with a large enough shock, inflation could again break loose.

THEN

When inflation is especially rapid, as it was in Germany in 1923, money becomes almost worthless. In Germany at that time, bank notes were more valuable as fire kindling than as money, and the sight of people burning Reichmarks was a common one. To avoid having to hold money for too long, wages were paid and spent twice a day. Banks took deposits and made loans, but at interest rates that compensated both depositors and the bank for the falling value of money—interest rates that could exceed 100 percent a month. The price of a dinner would increase during the course of an evening, making lingering over coffee a very expensive pastime.

NOW

In 1994, Brazil had a computer-age hyperinflation, an inflation rate that was close to 50 percent a month. Banks installed ATMs on almost every street corner and refilled them several times an hour. Brazilians tried to avoid holding currency. As soon as they were paid, they went shopping and bought enough food to get them through to the next payday. Some shoppers filled as many as six carts on a single monthly trip to the supermarket. Also, instead of using currency, Brazilians used credit cards whenever possible. But they paid their card balances off quickly because the interest rate on unpaid balances was 50 percent a month. Only at such a high interest rate did it pay banks to lend to cardholders, because banks themselves were paying interest rates of 40 percent a month to induce depositors to keep their money in the bank.

Many economists today are working on aggregate demand and inflation. One distinguished contributor, whom you can meet on the following pages, is Michael Woodford of Princeton University.

701

TALKING WITH

Michael Woodford

Michael Woodford is Harold H. Helm '20 Professor of Economics and Banking at Princeton University. Born in 1955 in Chicopee, Massachusetts, he was an undergraduate at the University of Chicago and a doctoral student at the Yale Law School before pursuing his doctorate in economics at the Massachusetts Institute of Technology. Professor Woodford's research on money and monetary policy has challenged much traditional thinking, and his ideas about a (future) world without money are attracting a great deal of interest. His advanced text, Interest and Prices: Foundations of a Theory of Monetary Policy, *is published by Princeton University Press.*

Michael Parkin and Robin Bade talked with Michael Woodford about his work and the progress that economists have made in designing effective monetary policy rules.

Why, after completing law school, did you decide to become an economist?

Almost every class in law school was full of economic reasoning. I became fascinated by economic analysis, and thought that I would have to get a better foundation in economics in order to think clearly about legal issues. In the end I found that I liked economics enough to become an economist.

I am able to address questions of public policy, which is what had originally drawn me to law, but in a way that also allows me to indulge a taste for thinking about what the world might be like or should be like, and not simply the way that it already is.

In a world as rapidly changing as ours is, I think that the perspective provided by economics is essential for understanding which kinds of laws and rules make sense.

You are a supporter of rules for monetary policy. Why are rules so important?

In my view, rules are important not because central bankers can't be relied upon to take the public interest to heart, or because they don't know what they're doing, but because the effects of monetary policy depend critically upon what the private sector expects about future policy, and hence about the future course of the economy. Thus effective monetary policy depends more on the successful *management of expectations* than on any direct consequences of the current level of interest rates.

In order to steer people's expectations about future monetary policy in the way that it would like, a central bank needs to communicate details about how policy will be conducted in the future. The best way to do this is by being explicit about the rule that guides its decision making. The central bank also needs to establish a reputation for actually following the rule.

Following the rule means *not* always doing what might seem best in given current conditions. What is best for the economy now will be independent of what people may have expected in the past. But if the central bank doesn't feel bound to follow through on its prior commitments, people will learn that they don't mean anything. Then those commitments will not shape people's expectations in the desired way.

There is actually a strong parallel between monetary policy rules and the law, and the desirability of rules is an example of the per-

702

spective that I gained from the study of law. A judge doesn't simply seek to determine, in each individual case, what outcomes would do the most good, given the individual circumstances. Instead, the judge makes a decision based on rules established either by precedent or by statute. Because the law is rule-based, people are able to forecast more accurately the consequences of their contemplated actions.

A central banker is often portrayed as the captain of the economic ship, steering it skillfully between the rocks of inflation and unemployment in a choppy sea. But a ship's captain doesn't need to care about how the ocean will interpret his actions. So the parallel isn't a good one. In my view, the role of a central banker is more similar to that of a judge than to that of a ship's captain. Both central bankers and judges care enormously about the effects of their decisions on the expectations of people whose behaviour depends on expected future decisions.

> " *Following the rule means not always doing what might seem best in given current conditions.* "

The rule that you favour is different from that suggested by Milton Friedman. What is wrong with the Friedman rule?

Friedman's rule involves a target for the growth rate of some definition of the quantity of money. I don't think that the best monetary rule involves a target of any kind for the growth rate of a monetary aggregate. Friedman's rule is not the worst sort of rule, as simple rules go, but we can do better.

Just a century ago, no one had any idea how to establish a reasonably predictable monetary standard except by guaranteeing the convertibility of money into a precious metal such as gold. We didn't have the surprisingly modern concept of index numbers and today's routinely calculated price indexes like the CPI that enable us to measure, to a decent approximation, the purchasing power of the dollar.

We now understand that pegging the value of money to something like gold is a cruder solution to the problem than is necessary. We don't need to leave the value of money hostage to the vagaries of the gold market simply in order to maintain confidence that a dollar means *something*.

Friedman recognizes the value of a well-managed fiat currency, but supposes that there is unlikely to be much predictability to the value of money unless the central bank is committed to a fixed target growth path for the quantity of money. But that again is a more indirect solution to the problem of maintaining a stable and predictable value for money than is necessary.

And there is a potentially large cost of such a crude approach when the relation between one's favourite monetary aggregate and the value of money shifts over time. A focus on stabilizing a monetary aggregate means less stability than would otherwise have been possible in the purchasing power of money.

So what would be a good monetary rule?

First, there should be a clearly defined target in terms of variables that policymakers actually care about, such as the inflation rate, rather than an "intermediate target" such as a monetary aggregate. Second, the central bank should be as clear as possible about the decision making process through which it determines the level of interest rates that is believed to be consistent with achieving the target.

"Inflation targeting," as currently practised in the United Kingdom, Canada, and New Zealand, is an example of the general approach that I would advocate. But I think that central banks of the inflation-targeting countries could do a better job of explaining the procedures used to determine the interest rate that is judged to be consistent with the inflation target—they could be more transparent.

And all of these countries could better explain to the public the ways in which variables other than inflation are also taken into consideration. I'm not sure that inflation targeting needs to be *stricter*, in the sense that considerations other than inflation should be more scrupulously ruled out. But I think that it is desirable to make it more of a *rule*.

One of the most intriguing issues that you've worked on is the question of what determines the price level in a "cashless economy." How would we control inflation in such a world?

One advantage of the approach to monetary policy that I've just mentioned is that the form of the policy rule that is appropriate need not change much at all if we were to progress to a "cashless economy." As long as the central bank can still control the overnight interest rate—the overnight loans rate in Canada—the *rule* for adjusting the interest rate need not change. Yet there might no longer be any meaning to a target path for a monetary aggregate in such a world.

The critical question is whether a central bank would still be able to control the overnight interest rate in such a world. Some argue that central banks only control interest rates in the interbank market for reserves because the private sector cannot supply a good substitute for reserves and the central bank is therefore a monopoly supplier. They then worry that if private substitutes for reserves were available, central banks would lose control of the interest rate.

But this line of reasoning assumes, as do most textbooks (even the good ones!), that central banks can change the interest rate *only* by changing the *opportunity cost* of holding reserves, which should only be possible in the presence of market power. But central banks can change the overnight interest rate *without* changing the opportunity cost of holding reserves. Indeed, the Bank of Canada already does so. It pays interest on reserves and maintains a fixed difference between the interest rate on reserves and the discount rate—the rate at which it stands willing to lend reserves to the banks. The overnight rate fluctuates inside the range of these two rates, so by changing the interest rate on reserves, the Bank of Canada controls the overnight rate but doesn't change the opportunity cost of holding reserves.

Every central bank, including the Federal Reserve, would have to adjust the interest rate in a way similar to this in a "cashless economy."

Where do you stand on the sources of aggregate fluctuations? Are they primarily an efficient response to the uneven pace of technical change, or are they primarily the consequence of market failure and demand fluctuations?

I don't think that they are primarily an *efficient* response to variations in technical progress or to other real disturbances of that kind. I think that there are important distortions that often result in *inefficient* responses of the economy to real disturbances, and this is why monetary policy matters. But I do think

that real disturbances are important—for example, I don't think that exogenous variations in monetary policy have been responsible for too much of the economic instability in the U.S. economy in recent decades—and I think that their supply-side effects are important, too.

The important issue, to my mind, is not whether the disturbances are thought to have more to do with supply or demand factors; it is whether the economy can be relied upon to respond efficiently to them, regardless of the nature of monetary policy. I don't think that that occurs automatically. The goal of good monetary policy is to bring about such a world: one in which monetary policy is not itself a source of disturbances, and in which the responses to real disturbances are efficient ones. The first part simply requires that monetary policy be systematic, but the second part depends upon the choice of a monetary policy rule of the right sort.

What advice do you have for a student who is just starting to study economics? Is it a good subject in which to major? What other subjects would you urge students to study alongside economics?

I think economics is an excellent major for students with many different interests. Most people who study economics are probably looking for an edge in the business world, and economics is valuable for that. But it's also all extremely valuable background for people interested in careers in law, government, or public policy. And of course, to some of us, the subject is interesting in its own right. I find that the challenges just get deeper the farther I get into the subject.

Probably the most important other subject for someone thinking of actually becoming an economist is mathematics. This is often the determining factor as to how well a student will do in graduate study, because the research literature is a good deal more mathematical than many people suspect from their undergraduate economics courses. But economics is not a branch of mathematics. It's a subject that seeks to understand people and social institutions, and so all sorts of other subjects—history, politics, sociology, psychology, moral and political philosophy—are useful background for an economist, too. I don't at all regret the amount of time I spent in liberal arts courses as an undergraduate.

The Economy at Full Employment

CHAPTER

30

Production and Jobs

Over time, we become more productive and our incomes grow. For each hour we worked in 2004, we earned twice what we earned in 1964. What makes production and incomes grow? Why did productivity grow during a recession?

Our population also grows every year. How does population size influence employment, wage rates, and potential GDP?

We hear a lot about the need to increase our national saving to invest in new capital, the importance of education, and the need to support science and technology. How do capital accumulation, education, and advances in technology influence employment, wage rates, and potential GDP?

You know that when we talk about full employment, we don't mean there is no unemployment. But what determines the amount of unemployment when the economy is at full employment?

◆ We'll answer these questions in this chapter. We'll discover how changes in population, capital, and technology influence production, jobs, and incomes over long periods of time. We'll learn about the forces that create unemployment when the economy is at full employment. And in *Reading Between the Lines* at the end of this chapter, we'll compare productivity in Canada with that in the United States.

After studying this chapter, you will be able to

- **Describe the relationship between the quantity of labour employed and real GDP**

- **Explain what determines the demand for labour and the supply of labour and how labour market equilibrium determines employment, the real wage rate, and potential GDP**

- **Explain how an increase in the population, an increase in capital, and an advance in technology change employment, the real wage rate, and potential GDP**

- **Explain what determines unemployment when the economy is at full employment**

Real GDP and Employment

TO PRODUCE MORE OUTPUT, WE MUST USE MORE inputs. We can increase real GDP by employing more labour, increasing the quantity of capital, or developing technologies that are more productive. In the short term, the quantity of capital and the state of technology are fixed. So to increase real GDP in the short term, we must increase the quantity of labour employed. Let's look at the relationship between real GDP and the quantity of labour employed.

Production Possibilities

When you studied the limits to production in Chapter 2 (see p. 34), you learned about the *production possibilities frontier*, which is the boundary between those combinations of goods and services that can be produced and those that cannot. We can think about the production possibilities frontier for any pair of goods or services when we hold the quantities of all other goods and services constant. Let's think about the production possibilities frontier for two special items: real GDP and leisure time.

Real GDP is a measure of the final goods and services produced in the economy in a given time period valued at constant prices. We measure real GDP as a number of 1997 dollars, but the measure is a *real* one. Real GDP is not a pile of dollars. It is a pile of goods and services. Think of it as a number of big shopping carts filled with goods and services. Each cart contains some of each kind of different goods and services produced, and one cartload of items costs $100 billion. To say that real GDP is $1,000 billion means that real GDP is 10 very big shopping carts of goods and services.

The quantity of leisure time is the number of hours we spend not working. It is the time we spend playing or watching sports, seeing movies, and hanging out with friends. Leisure time is a special type of good or service.

Each hour that we spent pursuing fun could have been an hour that we spent working. So when the quantity of leisure time increases by one hour, the quantity of labour employed decreases by one hour. If we spent all our time having fun rather than working, we would not produce anything. Real GDP would be zero. The more leisure time we forgo to work, the greater is the quantity of labour employed and the greater is real GDP.

The relationship between leisure time and real GDP is a *production possibilities frontier (PPF)*. Figure 30.1(a) shows an example of this frontier. The economy has 45 billion hours of leisure time available. If people use all these hours to pursue leisure, no labour is employed and real GDP is zero. As people forgo leisure and work more, real GDP increases. If people spent 20 billion hours working and took 25 billion hours in leisure, real GDP would be $1,000 billion at point *A*. If people spent all the available hours working, real GDP would be $1,500 billion.

The bowed-out *PPF* displays increasing opportunity cost. The opportunity cost of a given amount of real GDP is the amount of leisure time forgone to produce it. As real GDP increases, each additional unit of real GDP costs an increasing amount of forgone leisure. The reason is that we use the most productive labour first, and as we use more labour, we use increasingly less productive labour.

The Production Function

The **production function** is the relationship between real GDP and the quantity of labour employed when all other influences on production remain the same: It shows how real GDP varies as the quantity of labour employed varies.

Because one more hour of labour employed means one less hour of leisure, the production function is like a mirror image of the leisure time–real GDP *PPF*. Figure 30.1(b) shows the production function (*PF*) for the economy whose *PPF* is shown in Fig. 30.1(a). You can see that when the quantity of labour employed is zero, real GDP is also zero. And as the quantity of labour employed increases, so does real GDP. When 20 billion labour hours are employed, real GDP is $1,000 billion (at point *A*).

A decrease in leisure hours and the corresponding increases in the quantity of labour employed and real GDP bring a movement along the production possibilities frontier and along the production function. The arrows along the *PPF* and the *PF* in Fig. 30.1 show these movements. Such movements occurred when employment and real GDP surged during World War II.

But the increase in real GDP during World War II changed for an additional reason. Labour became more productive. Let's study the influences on the productivity of labour.

FIGURE 30.1

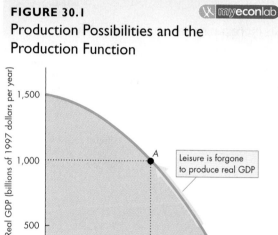

Production Possibilities and the Production Function

(a) Production possibility frontier

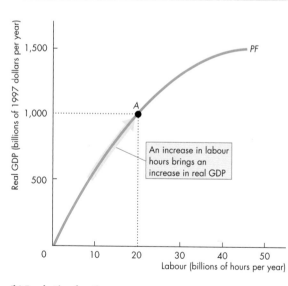

(b) Production function

On the production possibilities frontier in part (a), if we enjoy 45 billion hours of leisure, we produce no real GDP. If we forgo 20 billion hours of leisure time to work and spend 25 billion hours of leisure time, we produce a real GDP of $1,000 billion, at point A. At point A on the production function in part (b), we use 20 billion hours of labour to produce $1,000 billion of real GDP.

Changes in Productivity

When we talk about *productivity*, we usually mean labour productivity. **Labour productivity** is real GDP per hour of labour. Three factors influence labour productivity:

- Physical capital
- Human capital
- Technology

Physical Capital A farm worker equipped with only a stick and primitive tools can cultivate almost no land and grow barely enough food to feed a single family. A farmer equipped with a steel plow pulled by an animal can cultivate more land and produce enough food to feed a small village. A farmer equipped with a modern tractor, plow, and harvester can cultivate thousands of hectares and produce enough food to feed hundreds of people.

By using physical capital on our farms and in our factories, shops, and offices, we get an enormous increase labour productivity. And the more physical capital we use, the greater is labour productivity, other things remaining the same.

Human Capital An economy's **human capital** is the knowledge and skill that people have obtained from education and on-the-job training.

The average university graduate has a greater amount of human capital than the average high school graduate possesses. Consequently, the university graduate is able to perform some tasks that are beyond the ability of the high school graduate. The university graduate is more productive. For the nation as a whole, the greater the amount of schooling its citizens complete, the greater is its real GDP, other things remaining the same.

Regardless of how much schooling a person has completed, not much production is accomplished on the first day at work. Learning about the new work environment consumes the newly hired worker. But as time passes and experience accumulates, the worker becomes more productive. We call this on-the-job education activity **learning-by-doing**.

Learning-by-doing increases labour productivity. The more experienced the labour force, the greater is its labour productivity, and other things remaining the same, the greater is real GDP.

World War II provides a carefully documented example of the importance of this source of increase in labour productivity. In the shipyards that produced the transport vessels called Liberty ships, labour productivity increased by an astonishing 30 percent purely as a result of learning-by-doing.

Technology A student equipped with a pen can complete a readable page of writing in perhaps 10 minutes. This same task takes 5 minutes with a typewriter and 2 minutes with a computer. Travelling on foot from Toronto to Vancouver takes a person (a fit person!) more than 100 days. In a car, the trip takes a comfortable 5 days. And in an airplane, the trip takes 5 hours. These are examples of the impact of technology on productivity. Imagine the profound effect of these advances in technology on the productivity of a movie director who works in Toronto and Vancouver!

Shifts in the Production Function

Any influence on production that increases labour productivity shifts the production function upward. Real GDP increases at each level of labour hours. In Fig. 30.2(a), the production function is initially PF_0. Then an increase in physical capital and human capital or an advance in technology occurs. The production function shifts upward to PF_1.

At each quantity of labour employed, real GDP is greater on the new production function than it was on the original one. For example, at 20 billion hours, real GDP increases from $1,000 billion (point A) to $1,100 billion (point B).

Figure 30.2(b) shows how the production function in Canada shifted upward between 1980 and 2004. Along the production function PF_{04}, labour productivity is 60 percent greater than that on PF_{80}—an increase of 1.9 percent a year.

REVIEW QUIZ

1 What is the relationship between the leisure hours–real GDP *PPF* and the production function?

2 What does the outward-bowed shape of the leisure hours–real GDP *PPF* imply about the opportunity cost of real GDP and why is the *PPF* bowed outward?

3 Why does the production function shift upward when capital increases and/or technology advances?

   ⓧ myeconlab **Study Plan 30.1**

FIGURE 30.2   ⓧ myeconlab

An Increase in Labour Productivity

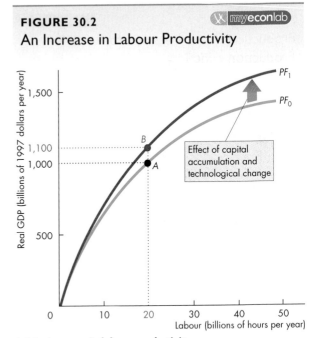

(a) An increase in labour productivity

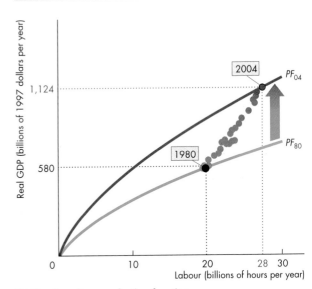

(b) The Canadian production function

On PF_0 in part (a), 20 billion labour hours produce a real GDP of $1,000 billion (point A). An increase in capital or an advance in technology shifts the production function upward to PF_1. Now, 20 billion labour hours produce a real GDP of $1,100 billion (point B). Canadian real GDP has increased (part b) because labour has become more productive and the quantity of labour has increased.

The Labour Market and Aggregate Supply

YOU'VE SEEN THAT IN A GIVEN YEAR, WITH A given amount of physical and human capital and given technology, real GDP depends on the quantity of labour hours employed. To produce more real GDP, we must employ more labour hours. The labour market determines the quantity of labour hours employed. We'll learn how by studying

- The demand for labour
- The supply of labour
- Labour market equilibrium

The Demand for Labour

The **quantity of labour demanded** is the number of labour hours hired by all the firms in the economy. The **demand for labour** is the relationship between the quantity of labour demanded and the real wage rate when all other influences on firms' hiring plans remain the same. The **real wage rate** is the quantity of goods and services that an hour of labour earns. In contrast, the **money wage rate** is the number of dollars that an hour of labour earns. A real wage rate is equal to a money wage rate divided by the price of a good. For the economy as a whole, the average real wage rate equals the average money wage rate divided by the price level. So we express the real wage rate in constant dollars. (Today, we express this real wage rate in 1997 dollars.)

The *real* wage rate influences the quantity of labour demanded because what matters to firms is how much output they must sell to earn the number of dollars they pay for labour (the money wage rate).

We can represent the demand for labour as either a demand schedule or a demand curve. The table in Fig. 30.3 shows part of a demand for labour schedule. It tells us the quantity of labour demanded at three different real wage rates. For example, if the real wage rate falls from $40 an hour to $35 an hour, the quantity of labour demanded increases from 15 billion hours a year to 20 billion hours a year. (You can find these numbers in rows *A* and *B* of the table.) The demand for labour curve is *LD*. Points *A*, *B*, and *C* on the curve correspond to rows *A*, *B*, and *C* of the demand schedule.

Why does the quantity of labour demanded *increase* as the real wage rate *decreases*? That is, why

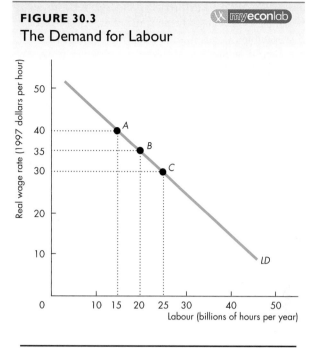

FIGURE 30.3 myeconlab

The Demand for Labour

	Real wage rate (1997 dollars per hour)	Quantity of labour demanded (billions of hours per year)
A	40	15
B	35	20
C	30	25

The table shows part of a demand for labour schedule. Points A, B, and C on the demand for labour curve correspond to the rows of the table. The lower the real wage rate, the greater is the quantity of labour demanded.

does the demand for labour curve slope downward? To answer these questions, we must learn about the marginal product of labour.

The Marginal Product of Labour The **marginal product of labour** is the additional real GDP produced by an additional hour of labour when all other influences on production remain the same. The marginal product of labour is governed by the **law of diminishing returns**, which states that as the quantity of labour increases, other things remaining the same, the marginal product of labour decreases.

The Law of Diminishing Returns Diminishing returns arise because the amount of capital is fixed. Two people operating one machine are not twice as productive as one person operating one machine. Eventually, as more labour hours are hired, workers get in each other's way and output barely increases.

Marginal Product Calculation We calculate the marginal product of labour as the change in real GDP divided by the change in the quantity of labour employed. Figure 30.4(a) shows some calculations, and Fig. 30.4(b) shows the marginal product curve.

In Fig. 30.4(a), when the quantity of labour employed increases from 10 billion hours to 20 billion hours, an increase of 10 billion hours, real GDP increases from $600 billion to $1,000 billion, an increase of $400 billion. The marginal product of labour equals the increase in real GDP ($400 billion) divided by the increase in the quantity of labour employed (10 billion hours), which is $40 an hour.

When the quantity of labour employed increases from 20 billion hours to 30 billion hours, an increase of 10 billion hours, real GDP increases from $1,000 billion to $1,300 billion, an increase of $300 billion. The marginal product of labour equals $300 billion divided by 10 billion hours, which is $30 an hour.

In Fig. 30.4(b), as the quantity of labour employed increases, the marginal product of labour diminishes. Between 10 billion and 20 billion hours (at 15 billion hours), marginal product is $40 an hour. And between 20 billion and 30 billion hours (at 25 billion hours), marginal product is $30 an hour.

Diminishing Marginal Product and the Demand for Labour Firms are in business to maximize profits. Each hour of labour that a firm hires increases output and adds to costs. Initially, an extra hour of labour produces more output than the real wage that the labour costs. Marginal product exceeds the real wage rate. But each additional hour of labour produces less additional output than the previous hour—the marginal product of labour diminishes.

As a firm hires more labour, eventually the extra output from an extra hour of labour is exactly what that hour of labour costs. At this point, marginal product equals the real wage rate. Hire one less hour and marginal product exceeds the real wage rate. Hire one more hour and the real wage rate exceeds marginal product. In either case, profit is less.

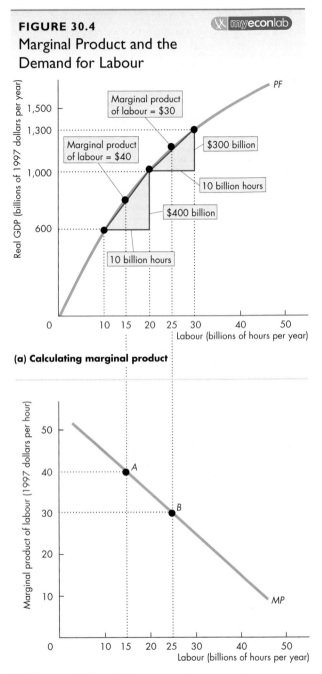

FIGURE 30.4   myeconlab

Marginal Product and the Demand for Labour

(a) Calculating marginal product

(b) The marginal product curve

In part (a), between 10 billion and 20 billion hours, the marginal product of labour is $40 an hour. Between 20 billion and 30 billion hours, the marginal product of labour is $30 an hour. In part (b), at 15 billion hours (midway between 10 billion and 20 billion), the marginal product of labour is $40 an hour at point A on the MP curve. The MP curve is the demand for labour curve.

Because marginal product diminishes as the quantity of labour employed increases, the lower the real wage rate, the greater is the quantity of labour that a firm can profitably hire. The marginal product curve is the same as the demand for labour curve.

You might gain a clearer understanding of the demand for labour by looking at an example.

Demand for Labour in a Ketchup Factory

Suppose that when a ketchup factory employs one additional hour of labour, output increases by 11 bottles. Marginal product is 11 bottles an hour. If the money wage rate is $5.50 an hour and ketchup sells for 50¢ a bottle, the real wage rate is 11 bottles an hour. (We calculate the factory's real wage rate as the money wage rate of $5.50 an hour divided by a price of 50¢ a bottle, which equals a real wage rate of 11 bottles an hour.) Because marginal product diminishes, we know that if the firm did not hire this hour of labour, marginal product would exceed 11 bottles. Because the firm can hire the hour of labour for a real wage rate of 11 bottles, it just pays it to do so.

If the price of ketchup remains at 50¢ a bottle and the money wage rate falls to $5.00 an hour, the real wage rate falls to 10 bottles an hour and the firm increases the quantity of labour demanded.

Similarly, if the money wage rate remains at $5.50 an hour and the price of ketchup rises to 55¢ a bottle, the real wage rate falls to 10 bottles an hour and the firm increases the quantity of labour demanded.

When the firm pays a real wage rate equal to the marginal product of labour, it is maximizing profit.

Changes in the Demand for Labour When the marginal product of labour changes, the demand for labour changes and the demand for labour curve shifts. You've seen that an increase in capital (both physical and human) and an advance in technology that increases labour productivity shift the production function upward. These same forces increase the demand for labour and shift the demand for labour curve rightward.

The Supply of Labour

The **quantity of labour supplied** is the number of labour hours that all the households in the economy plan to work. The **supply of labour** is the relationship between the quantity of labour supplied and the real wage rate when all other influences on work plans remain the same.

We can represent the supply of labour as either a supply schedule or a supply curve. The table in Fig. 30.5 shows a supply of labour schedule. It tells us the quantity of labour supplied at three different real wage rates. For example, if the real wage rate rises from $15 an hour (row *A*) to $35 an hour (row *B*), the quantity of labour supplied increases from 15 billion hours a year to 20 billion hours a year. The curve *LS* is a supply of labour curve. Points *A*, *B*, and *C* on the curve correspond to rows *A*, *B*, and *C* of the supply schedule.

The *real* wage rate influences the quantity of labour supplied because what matters to people is not the number of dollars they earn (the money wage rate) but what those dollars will buy.

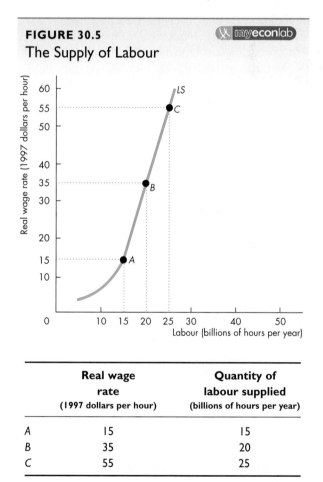

FIGURE 30.5
The Supply of Labour

	Real wage rate (1997 dollars per hour)	Quantity of labour supplied (billions of hours per year)
A	15	15
B	35	20
C	55	25

The table shows part of a supply of labour schedule. Points A, B, and C on the supply of labour curve correspond to the rows of the table. The higher the real wage rate, the greater is the quantity of labour supplied.

The quantity of labour supplied increases as the real wage rate increases for two reasons:

■ Hours per person increase
■ Labour force participation increases

Hours per Person In choosing how many hours to work, a household considers the opportunity cost of not working. This opportunity cost is the real wage rate. The higher the real wage rate, the greater is the opportunity cost of taking leisure and not working. And as the opportunity cost of taking leisure rises, the more the household chooses to work, other things remaining the same.

But other things don't remain the same. The higher the real wage rate, the greater is the household's income. And the higher the household's income, the more it wants to consume. One item that it wants to consume more of is leisure.

So a rise in the real wage rate has two opposing effects. By increasing the opportunity cost of leisure, it makes the household want to consume less leisure and to work more. And by increasing the household's income, it makes the household want to consume more leisure and to work fewer hours. For most households, the opportunity cost effect is stronger than the income effect. So the higher the real wage rate, the greater is the amount of work that the household chooses to do.

Labour Force Participation Some people have productive opportunities outside the labour force. These people choose to work only if the real wage rate exceeds the value of these other productive activities. For example, a parent might spend time caring for her or his child. The alternative is day care. The parent will choose to work only if he or she can earn enough per hour to pay the cost of child care and have enough left to make the work effort worthwhile. The higher the real wage rate, the more likely it is that a parent will choose to work and so the greater is the labour force participation rate.

Labour Supply Response The quantity of labour supplied increases as the real wage rate rises. But the quantity of labour supplied is not highly responsive to the real wage rate. A large percentage change in the real wage rate brings a small percentage change in the quantity of labour supplied.

Let's now see how the labour market determines employment and the real wage rate.

Labour Market Equilibrium

The forces of supply and demand operate in labour markets just as they do in the markets for goods and services. The price of labour is the real wage rate. A rise in the real wage rate eliminates a shortage of labour by decreasing the quantity demanded and increasing the quantity supplied. A fall in the real wage rate eliminates a surplus of labour by increasing the quantity demanded and decreasing the quantity supplied. If there is neither a shortage nor a surplus, the labour market is in equilibrium.

In macroeconomics, we study the economy-wide labour market to determine the total quantity of labour employed and the average real wage rate.

Figure 30.6(a) shows a labour market in equilibrium. The demand curve LD and the supply curve LS are the same as those in Fig. 30.3 and Fig. 30.5, respectively.

If the real wage rate exceeds $35 an hour, the quantity of labour supplied exceeds the quantity demanded and there is a surplus of labour. In this situation, the real wage rate falls.

If the real wage rate is less than $35 an hour, the quantity of labour demanded exceeds the quantity supplied and there is a shortage of labour. In this situation, the real wage rate rises.

If the real wage rate is $35 an hour, the quantity of labour demanded equals the quantity supplied and there is neither a shortage nor a surplus of labour. The labour market is in equilibrium, the real wage rate remains constant, and the equilibrium quantity of labour is 20 billion hours a year. This labour market equilibrium is a *full-employment equilibrium*. The full-employment real wage rate is $35 an hour and the full-employment quantity of labour is 20 billion hours a year.

Potential GDP

You've seen that the production function tells us how much real GDP a given amount of employment can produce. When the economy is at full employment, real GDP produced is potential GDP. So the full-employment quantity of labour produces potential GDP.

Figure 30.6(b) shows potential GDP. The full-employment quantity of labour in Fig. 30.6(a) is 20 billion hours. The production function in Fig. 30.6(b) tells us that 20 billion hours of labour can produce a real GDP of $1,000 billion. This amount is potential GDP.

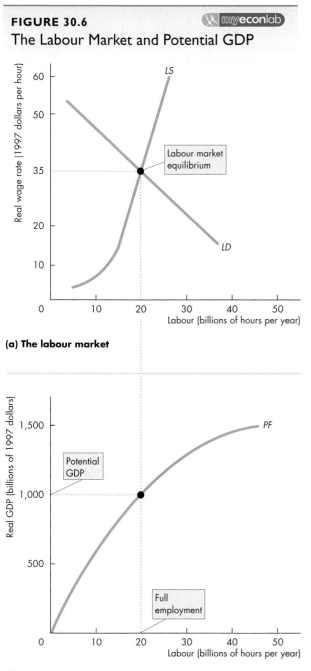

FIGURE 30.6 🅧 myeconlab
The Labour Market and Potential GDP

(a) The labour market

(b) Potential GDP

The economy is at full employment in part (a) when the quantity of labour demanded equals the quantity of labour supplied. The real wage rate is $35 an hour, and 20 billion labour hours are employed. In part (b), potential GDP is the quantity of real GDP determined by the production function and the full-employment quantity of labour.

Aggregate Supply

The **long-run aggregate supply curve** is the relationship between the quantity of real GDP supplied and the price level when real GDP equals potential GDP. Figure 30.7 shows this relationship as the vertical *LAS* curve. Along the long-run aggregate supply curve, as the price level changes, the money wage rate also changes to keep the real wage rate at the full-employment equilibrium level in Fig. 30.6(a). With no change in the real wage rate and no change in employment, real GDP remains at potential GDP.

The **short-run aggregate supply curve** is the relationship between the quantity of real GDP supplied and the price level when the money wage rate and potential GDP remain constant. Figure 30.7 shows a short-run aggregate supply curve as the upward-sloping *SAS* curve. Along the short-run aggregate supply curve, as the price level rises, the money wage rate remains fixed, so the real wage rate *falls*. In Fig. 30.6,

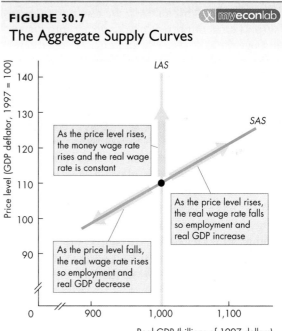

FIGURE 30.7 🅧 myeconlab
The Aggregate Supply Curves

When the price level and the money wage rate change by the same percentage, the real wage rate and the quantity of real GDP supplied are constant. There is a movement along the *LAS* curve. When the price level changes with no change in the money wage rate, the real wage rate changes and employment and the quantity of real GDP supplied change. There is a movement along the *SAS* curve.

when the real wage rate falls, the quantity of labour demanded increases and real GDP increases.

When the economy is at a point on the *SAS* curve and real GDP is above potential GDP, the real wage rate is below the full-employment equilibrium level. And when the economy is at a point on the *SAS* curve and real GDP is below potential GDP, the real wage rate is above the full-employment equilibrium level. In both cases, the quantity of labour that firms employ departs from the quantity that households would like to supply.

Production is efficient in the sense that the economy operates on its production possibilities frontier. But production is inefficient in the sense that the economy operates at the wrong point on the frontier. When the real wage rate is below the full-employment equilibrium, people do too much work and produce too much real GDP. When the real wage rate is above the full-employment equilibrium, people do too little work and produce too little real GDP.

When the real wage rate departs from its full-employment equilibrium level, the resulting shortage or surplus of labour brings market forces into play that move the real wage rate and quantity of labour employed back towards their full-employment levels.

The appendix on pp. 724–729 explains in detail how to derive the *LAS* and *SAS* curves.

REVIEW QUIZ

1 Why does a rise in the real wage rate bring a decrease in the quantity of labour demanded, other things remaining the same?

2 Why does a rise in the real wage rate bring an increase in the quantity of labour supplied, other things remaining the same?

3 What happens in the labour market if the real wage rate is above or below the full-employment level?

4 How is potential GDP determined?

5 What is the relationship between full-employment equilibrium in the labour market and long-run aggregate supply?

6 What is the relationship between the labour market and short-run aggregate supply?

myeconlab **Study Plan 30.2**

Let's now look at *changes* in full-employment equilibrium and potential GDP.

Changes in Potential GDP

REAL GDP WILL INCREASE IF

1. The economy recovers from recession.
2. Potential GDP increases.

Recovery from recession means that the economy moves along the real GDP–leisure *PPF* from a point at which real GDP and employment are too low relative to the full-employment equilibrium point. Equivalently, the economy moves along the short-run aggregate supply curve. Economists have a lot to say about such a move and Chapter 22 explains this type of short-term change in real GDP.

Increasing *potential* GDP means expanding production possibilities. We're going to study the expansion of production possibilities in two steps. First, we look at the factors that change potential GDP. Then, in Chapter 31, we study the process and pace of economic growth.

Potential GDP increases following:

■ An increase in population

■ An increase in labour productivity

An Increase in Population

As the population increases and the additional people reach working age, the supply of labour increases. With more labour available, the economy's production possibilities expand. But does the expansion of production possibilities mean that potential GDP increases? And does it mean that potential GDP *per person* increases?

The answers to these questions have intrigued economists for many years. And they cause heated political debate today. In China, for example, families are under enormous pressure to limit the number of children they have. In some other countries, such as France, the government encourages large families.

We can study the effects of an increase in population by using the model of the full-employment economy in Fig. 30.8. In Fig. 30.8(a), the demand for labour is *LD* and initially the supply of labour is LS_0. At full employment, the real wage rate is $35 an hour and the level of employment is 20 billion hours a year. In Fig. 30.8(b), the production function (*PF*) shows that with 20 billion hours of labour employed, potential GDP is $1,000 billion.

FIGURE 30.8

The Effects of an Increase in Population

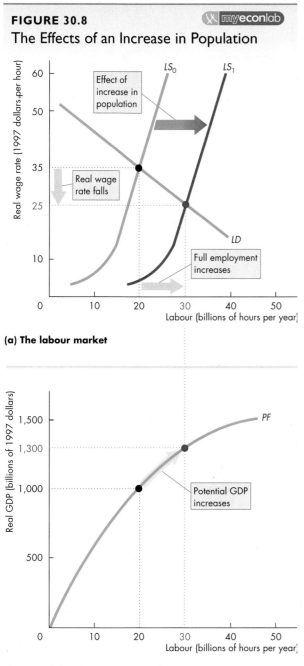

(a) The labour market

(b) Potential GDP

An increase in population increases the supply of labour. In part (a), the real wage rate falls, and the full-employment quantity of labour increases. In part (b), the increase in full employment increases potential GDP. Because the marginal product of labour diminishes, the increased population increases potential GDP but potential GDP per hour of work decreases.

An increase in the population increases the number of people of working age, and the supply of labour increases. The labour supply curve shifts rightward to LS_1. At a real wage rate of $35 an hour, there is now a surplus of labour. So the real wage rate falls. In this example, it falls until it reaches $25 an hour. At $25 an hour, the quantity of labour demanded equals the quantity of labour supplied. Equilibrium employment increases to 30 billion hours a year.

Figure 30.8(b) shows the effect of the increase in equilibrium employment on real GDP. As the full-employment quantity of labour increases from 20 billion hours to 30 billion hours, potential GDP increases from $1,000 billion to $1,300 billion.

So at full employment, an increase in population increases full employment, increases potential GDP, and lowers the real wage rate.

An increase in population also decreases potential GDP per hour of work. You can see this decrease by dividing potential GDP by total labour hours. Initially, with potential GDP at $1,000 billion and labour hours at 20 billion, potential GDP per hour of work was $50. With the increase in population, potential GDP is $1,300 billion and labour hours are 30 billion. Potential GDP per hour of work is $43.33. Diminishing returns are the source of the decrease in potential GDP per hour of work.

You've seen that an increase in population increases potential GDP and decreases potential GDP per work hour. Some people challenge this conclusion and argue that people are the ultimate economic resource. They claim that a larger population brings forth a greater amount of scientific discovery and technological advance. Consequently, they argue that an increase in population never takes place in isolation. It is always accompanied by an increase in labour productivity. Let's now look at the effects of this influence on potential GDP.

An Increase in Labour Productivity

We've seen that three factors increase labour productivity:

- An increase in physical capital
- An increase in human capital
- An advance in technology

Saving and investment increase the quantity of physical capital over time. Education and on-the-job training and experience increase human capital.

Research and development efforts bring advances in technology. In Chapter 31, we study how all these forces interact to determine the growth rate of potential GDP.

Here, we study the *effects* of an increase in physical capital, an increase in human capital, or an advance in technology on the labour market and potential GDP. We'll see how potential GDP, employment, and the real wage rate change when any of these three influences on labour productivity changes.

An Increase in Physical Capital If the quantity of physical capital increases, labour productivity increases. With labour being more productive, the economy's production possibilities expand. How does such an expansion of production possibilities change the real wage rate, employment, and potential GDP?

The additional capital increases the real GDP that each quantity of labour can produce. It also increases the marginal product of labour and so increases the demand for labour. Some physical capital replaces some types of labour, so the demand for those types of labour decreases when capital increases. But an increase in physical capital creates a demand for the types of labour that build, sell, and maintain the additional capital. The increases in demand for labour are always larger than the decreases in demand, and the economy-wide demand for labour increases.

With an increase in the economy-wide demand for labour, the real wage rate rises and the quantity of labour supplied increases. Equilibrium employment increases.

Potential GDP now increases for two reasons. First, a given level of employment produces more real GDP. Second, full employment increases.

An Increase in Human Capital If the quantity of human capital increases, labour productivity increases. Again, with labour being more productive, the economy's production possibilities expand. And this expansion of production possibilities changes the equilibrium real wage rate, full employment, and potential GDP in a similar manner to the effects of a change in physical capital.

An Advance in Technology As technology advances, labour productivity increases. And exactly as in the case of an increase in capital, the economy's production possibilities expand. Again, just as in the case of

an increase in capital, the new technology increases the real GDP that each quantity of labour can produce and increases the marginal product of labour and the demand for labour.

With an increase in the demand for labour, the real wage rate rises, the quantity of labour supplied increases, and equilibrium employment increases. And again, potential GDP increases because a given level of employment produces more real GDP and because full employment increases.

Illustrating the Effects of an Increase in Labour Productivity Figure 30.9 shows the effects of an increase in labour productivity that results from an increase in capital or an advance in technology. In part (a), the demand for labour initially is LD_0 and the supply of labour is LS. The real wage rate is $35 an hour, and full employment is 20 billion hours a year.

In part (b), the production function initially is PF_0. With 20 billion hours of labour employed, potential GDP is $1,000 billion.

Now an increase in capital or an advance in technology increases labour productivity. In Fig. 30.9(a), the demand for labour increases and the demand curve shifts rightward to LD_1. In Fig. 30.9(b), labour productivity increases and the production function shifts upward to PF_1.

In Fig. 30.9(a), at the original real wage rate of $35 an hour, there is now a shortage of labour. So the real wage rate rises. In this example, it keeps rising until it reaches $45 an hour. At $45 an hour, the quantity of labour demanded equals the quantity of labour supplied and full employment increases to 22.5 billion hours a year.

Figure 30.9(b) shows the effects of the increase in full employment combined with the new production function on potential GDP. As full employment increases from 20 billion hours to 22.5 billion hours, potential GDP increases from $1,000 billion to $1,500 billion.

Potential GDP per hour of work also increases. You can see this increase by dividing potential GDP by total labour hours. Initially, with potential GDP at $1,000 billion and labour hours at 20 billion, potential GDP per hour of work was $50. With the increase in labour productivity, potential GDP is $1,500 billion and labour hours are 22.5 billion, so potential GDP per hour of work is $66.67.

Let's use what you've just learned to examine an episode in the life of the Canadian economy.

FIGURE 30.9

The Effects of an Increase in Labour Productivity

myeconlab

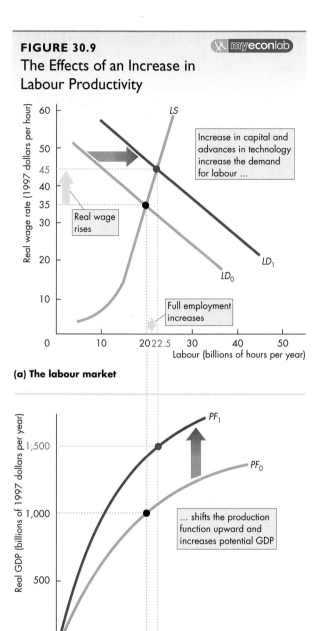

(a) The labour market

(b) Potential GDP

An increase in labour productivity shifts the demand for labour curve rightward from LD_0 to LD_1 in part (a) and the production function upward from PF_0 to PF_1 in part (b). The real wage rate rises from $35 to $45 an hour, and full employment increases from 20 billion to 22.5 billion hours. Potential GDP increases from $1,000 billion to $1,500 billion. Potential GDP increases because labour becomes more productive and full employment increases.

Population and Productivity in Canada

The Canadian economy was close to full employment in 2004. It was also close to full employment in 1980. We're going to compare these two years and look at the forces that moved the economy from one full-employment equilibrium to another.

In 1980, real GDP in Canada was $580 billion, employment was 20 billion hours, and the real wage rate was $15.77 an hour. (We are using 1997 dollars.)

By 2004, real GDP had increased to $1,124 billion, labour hours had increased to 28 billion, and the real wage rate had risen to $20.35 an hour. (Again, we are using 1997 dollars.)

The factors that you've just studied—an increase in population, increases in physical and human capital, and advances in technology—brought these changes.

Population Increase In 1980, the working-age population of Canada was 18.7 million. By 2004, this number had increased to 25.4 million. The 2004 working-age population was 36 percent larger than the 1980 working-age population. Recall that labour hours were 20 billion in 1980. A 36 percent increase would take labour hours in 2004 to 27.2 billion. But labour hours actually increased to 28 billion. Why? The increased labour productivity increased the real wage rate, which increased the quantity of labour supplied by increasing the labour force participation rate.

Capital Increase In 1980, the capital stock in Canada was estimated to be $2.5 trillion (in 1997 dollars). By 2004, the capital stock had increased to $4.9 trillion. This increase in capital increased labour productivity. But the increase in capital was not the only influence on labour productivity. Technological advances also occurred.

Technological Advances In 1980, we were just getting into the information revolution. Personal computers had just arrived. They were slow, had little memory, and had no hard drive, much less the CD-ROM and DVD drives of today. The Internet existed as a tool used by academic researchers for e-mail and file transfers, but no one had imagined the World Wide Web. Telephones couldn't remember numbers or record messages. Communication was slower and more costly than it was to become by 2004.

Production processes were beginning to be computerized but on a limited scale. Banks equipped with ATMs were in the future. Supermarkets with

FIGURE 30.10   myeconlab

Full Employment in Canada: 1980 and 2004

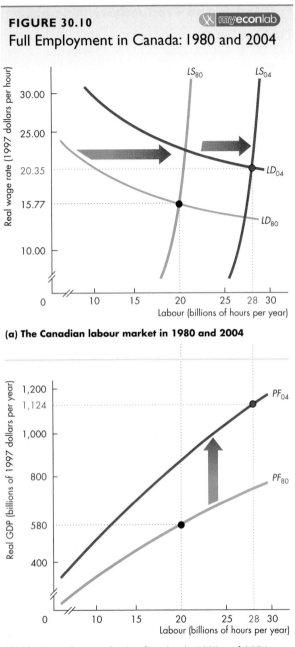

(a) The Canadian labour market in 1980 and 2004

(b) The Canadian production function in 1980 and 2004

In 1980, the real wage rate was $15.77 an hour and the quantity of labour employed was 20 billion hours at the intersection of LD_{80} and LS_{80} in part (a). Potential GDP was $580 billion on PF_{80} in part (b). By 2004, the real wage rate had increased to $20.35 an hour and the quantity of labour employed had increased to 28 billion hours at the intersection of LD_{04} and LS_{04} in part (a). Potential GDP had increased to $1,124 billion on PF_{04} in part (b).

laser scanners were only a dream. Robots in car factories and coal mines were still unknown. The biotechnology sector had yet to be developed. The combined effects of capital accumulation and technological advance have made the workers on our farms and in our factories, shops and offices more productive.

Figure 30.10 shows these effects along with the effects of the increase in population that occurred. In 1980, the demand for labour curve was LD_{80}, the supply of labour curve was LS_{80}, the full-employment real wage rate was $15.77 an hour, and 20 billion hours of labour were employed. The production function in 1980 was PF_{80}. With 20 billion hours of labour employed, real GDP (and potential GDP) was $580 billion.

By 2004, the increase in population had increased the working-age population by 36 percent. This increase in population increased the supply of labour and shifted the labour supply curve rightward to LS_{04}.

The accumulation of capital and advances in technology increased labour productivity. The demand for labour increased, and the demand for labour curve shifted rightward to LD_{04}. And the production function shifted upward to PF_{04}.

The real wage rate increased to $20.35 an hour, and employment increased to 28 billion hours. At this quantity of labour, real GDP (and potential GDP) increased to $1,124 billion.

So in Canada, the effects of an increase in capital and advances in technology have been larger than the effects of increases in population. The forces that increase labour productivity have been strong enough to overcome the effects of an increase in population.

REVIEW QUIZ

1 When the population increases but nothing else changes, why does real GDP per hour of work decrease?

2 How does an increase in capital change the real wage rate, full employment, and potential GDP?

3 How do advances in technology change the real wage rate, full employment, and potential GDP?

4 If, as some people suggest, capital accumulation and technological change always accompany an increase in population, is it possible for potential GDP per hour of work to decrease?

myeconlab   **Study Plan 30.3**

Unemployment at Full Employment

SO FAR, WE'VE FOCUSED ON THE FORCES THAT determine the real wage rate, the quantity of labour employed, and potential GDP. And we've studied the effects of changes in population, capital, and technology on these variables. We're now going to bring unemployment into the picture.

In Chapter 21, we learned how unemployment is measured. We described how people become unemployed—they lose jobs, leave jobs, and enter or re-enter the labour force—and we classified unemployment—it can be frictional, structural, seasonal, and cyclical. We also learned that we call the unemployment rate at full employment the *natural rate of unemployment.*

But measuring, describing, and classifying unemployment do not *explain* it. Why is there always some unemployment? Why does the unemployment rate fluctuate? Why was the unemployment rate lower during the 1960s and the early 2000s than during the 1980s and early 1990s?

We studied the forces that make the unemployment rate fluctuate around the natural rate in Chapter 22. Here, we look at the churning economy and the reasons why we have unemployment, even when the economy is at full employment.

Unemployment is ever present for two broad reasons:

- Job search
- Job rationing

Job Search

Job search is the activity of looking for an acceptable vacant job. There are always some people who have not yet found a suitable job and who are actively searching for one. The reason is that the labour market is in a constant state of change. The failure of existing businesses destroys jobs. The expansion of existing businesses and the startup of new businesses that use new technologies and develop new markets create jobs. As people pass through different stages of life, some enter or re-enter the labour market. Others leave their jobs to look for better ones, and still others retire. This constant churning in the labour market means that there are always some people looking for jobs, and these people are the unemployed.

The amount of job search depends on a number of factors, one of which is the real wage rate. In Fig. 30.11, when the real wage rate is $35 an hour, the economy is at a full-employment equilibrium. The amount of job search that takes place at this wage rate generates unemployment at the natural rate. If the real wage rate is above the full-employment equilibrium—for example, at $45 an hour—there is a surplus of labour. At this higher real wage rate, more job search takes place and the unemployment rate rises above the natural rate. If the real wage rate is below the full-employment equilibrium—for example, at $25 an hour—there is a shortage of labour. At this real wage rate, less job search takes place and the unemployment rate falls below the natural rate.

The market forces of supply and demand move the real wage rate towards the full-employment

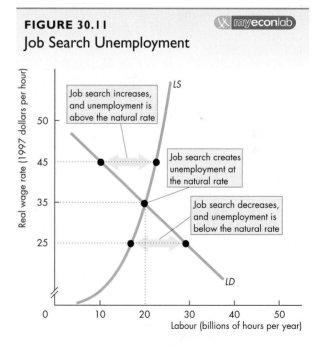

FIGURE 30.11
Job Search Unemployment

When the real wage rate is at its full-employment level—$35 an hour in this example—job search puts unemployment at the natural rate. If the real wage rate is above the full-employment level, there is a surplus of labour. Job search increases, and unemployment rises above the natural rate. If the real wage rate is below the full-employment level, there is a shortage of labour. Job search decreases, and unemployment falls below the natural rate.

equilibrium. And these same forces move the amount of job search towards the level that creates unemployment at the natural rate.

But other influences on the amount of job search bring changes, over time, in the natural rate of unemployment. The main sources of these changes are

- Demographic change
- Unemployment compensation
- Structural change

Demographic Change An increase in the proportion of the population that is of working age brings an increase in the entry rate into the labour force and an increase in the unemployment rate. This factor has been important in the Canadian labour market in recent years. The bulge in the birth rate that occurred from the late 1940s through the late 1950s increased the proportion of new entrants into the labour force during the 1970s and brought an increase in the natural rate of unemployment.

As the birth rate declined, the bulge moved into higher age groups, and the proportion of new entrants declined during the 1980s. During this period, the natural rate of unemployment decreased.

Another demographic trend is an increase in the number of households with two paid workers. When one of these workers becomes unemployed, it is possible, with income still flowing in, to take longer to find a new job. This factor might have increased frictional unemployment.

Unemployment Compensation The length of time that an unemployed person spends searching for a job depends, in part, on the opportunity cost of job search. An unemployed person who receives no unemployment compensation faces a high opportunity cost of job search. In this situation, search is likely to be short and the person is likely to accept a less attractive job rather than continue a costly search process. An unemployed person who receives generous unemployment compensation faces a low opportunity cost of job search. In this situation, search is likely to be prolonged. The unemployed worker will continue to search for an ideal job.

The extension of unemployment compensation to larger groups of workers during the late 1960s and 1970s lowered the opportunity cost of job search. Consequently, the amount of job search and the natural rate of unemployment increased during those years.

Structural Change Labour market flows and unemployment are influenced by the pace and direction of technological change. Sometimes, technological change brings a *structural slump*, a condition in which some industries die and some regions suffer while other industries are born and other regions flourish. When these events occur, labour turnover is high—the flows between employment and unemployment increase and the number of unemployed people increases. The decline of industries in the Maritimes and the rapid expansion of industries in the Ottawa Valley illustrate the effects of technological change and were a source of the increase in unemployment during the 1970s and early 1980s. While these changes were taking place, the natural rate of unemployment increased.

Job Rationing

You've learned that markets *allocate* scarce resources by adjusting the market price to make buying plans and selling plans agree. Another word that has a meaning similar to "allocate" is "ration." Markets *ration* scarce resources by adjusting prices. In the labour market, the real wage rate rations employment and therefore rations jobs. Changes in the real wage rate keep the number of people seeking work and the number of jobs available in balance.

But the real wage rate is not the only possible instrument for rationing jobs. And in some industries, the real wage rate is set above the market equilibrium level. **Job rationing** is the practice of paying a real wage rate above the equilibrium level and then rationing jobs by some method.

Two reasons why the real wage rate might be set above the equilibrium level are

- Efficiency wage
- Minimum wage

Efficiency Wage It is costly for a firm to pay its workers more than the market wage rate. But doing so also brings benefits. An **efficiency wage** is a real wage rate that is set above the full-employment equilibrium wage rate that balances the costs and benefits of this higher wage rate to maximize the firm's profit.

The cost of paying a higher wage is direct. It is the addition to the firm's wage bill. The benefits of paying a higher wage rate are indirect.

First, a firm that pays a high wage rate can attract the most productive workers. Second, the firm can get greater productivity from its work force if it threatens to fire those who do not perform at the desired standard. The threat of losing a well-paid job stimulates greater work effort. Third, workers are less likely to quit their jobs, so the firm faces a lower rate of labour turnover and lower training costs. Fourth, the firm's recruiting costs are lower. The firm always faces a steady stream of available new workers.

Faced with benefits and costs, a firm offers a wage rate that balances productivity gains from the higher wage rate against its additional cost. This wage rate maximizes the firm's profit and is the efficiency wage.

Minimum Wage A **minimum wage** law determines the lowest wage rate at which a firm may legally hire labour. If the minimum wage is set *below* the equilibrium wage, the minimum wage has no effect. The minimum wage law and market forces are not in conflict. But if a minimum wage is set *above* the equilibrium wage, the minimum wage is in conflict with the market forces and does have some effects on the labour market.

In Canada, provincial governments set the minimum wages. In 2005, the minimum wage ranged from a low of $6.25 an hour in Newfoundland to highs of $7.25 an hour in Manitoba, $7.45 an hour in Ontario, and $8.00 an hour in British Columbia. The minimum wage increases from time to time and has fluctuated relative to the average wage of all workers.

Job Rationing and Unemployment Regardless of the reason, if the real wage rate is set above the equilibrium level, the natural rate of unemployment increases. The above-equilibrium real wage rate decreases the quantity of labour demanded and increases the quantity of labour supplied. So even at full employment, the quantity of labour supplied exceeds the quantity of labour demanded.

The surplus of labour is an addition to the amount of unemployment. The unemployment that results from a non-market wage rate and job rationing increases the natural rate of unemployment because it is added to the job search that takes place at full-employment equilibrium.

Economists broadly agree that efficiency wages can create persistent unemployment. And most economists believe that the minimum wage contributes to unemployment, especially among low-skilled young

workers. But David Card of the University of California at Berkeley and Alan Krueger of Princeton University have challenged this view. And the challenge has been rebutted.

Card and Krueger say that an increase in the minimum wage works like an efficiency wage. It makes workers more productive and less likely to quit. Most economists remain skeptical about this suggestion. If higher wages make workers more productive and reduce labour turnover, why don't firms freely pay the wage rates that encourage the correct work habits? Daniel Hamermesh of the University of Texas at Austin says that firms anticipate increases in the minimum wage and cut employment before they occur. Looking for the effects of an increase in the minimum wage after it has occurred misses its effects. Finis Welch of Texas A&M University and Kevin Murphy of the University of Chicago say that regional differences in economic growth and not changes in the minimum wage explain the facts that Card and Krueger found.

REVIEW QUIZ

1 Why does the economy experience unemployment at full employment?
2 Why does the natural rate of unemployment fluctuate?
3 What is job rationing and why does it occur?
4 How does an efficiency wage influence the real wage rate, employment, and unemployment?
5 How does the minimum wage create unemployment?

❌ myeconlab   **Study Plan 30.4**

◆ In this chapter, you've seen how the economy operates at full employment. *Reading Between the Lines* on pp. 722–723 uses what you have learned to compare labour productivity in Canada with that in the United States.

In this chapter, we've studied the real factors that influence potential GDP in a given year. And we've compared potential GDP in different times and places. Your next task is the study the process of economic growth—the interaction of capital accumulation, technological change, and population growth—that brings ever expanding potential GDP.

Canada–U.S. Productivity Gap

WINNIPEG FREE PRESS, OCTOBER 25, 2005

Taxes blamed for lagging Canadian productivity

Over-taxed Canadians are less productive than Americans and, as a result earn more than $9,000 a year less, says a group of accountants which yesterday joined the chorus of business and taxpayer groups calling for more tax relief in the next budget.

Canadian productivity has fallen off dramatically this decade leaving Canadians earning nearly 20 per cent less than Americans, an annual income gap of $9,242 per Canadian, the Certified Management Accountants of Canada told the House of Commons finance committee's pre-budget hearings.

Bank of Canada governor David Dodge, who also appeared before the committee, warned Canadians' living standards can't rise without an improvement in their productivity, commonly measured as output per hour worked.

"Over the longer haul, unless we can get higher productivity growth ... the standard of living can't rise," Dodge told the committee. ...

The accountants, as well as the Canadian Taxpayers Federation, argued in the briefs to the committee lower taxes would also boost productivity and in turn prosperity. ...

But not all groups are calling for tax cuts.

A major public-sector union today will tell the committee a better way to boost productivity is to invest more in public services. "Public services, along with full employment and fairer taxation policies, will increase productivity, improve our quality of life and lead to greater social inclusion," the Canadian Union of Public Employees says in a summary of its brief to the committee.

Essence of the Story

■ A group of accountants believes that the widening gap between Canadian and U.S. productivity is the result of high Canadian taxes.

■ The accountants say that Canadians earn almost 20 percent less than Americans and the annual income gap is $9,242 per person.

■ The accountants call for tax cuts, which they say will boost Canadian productivity.

■ A labour union disagrees with the accountants and says that greater investment in public services and other measures, not tax cuts, will boost Canadian productivity.

Economic Analysis

■ Comparisons of Canada and the United States reveal a widening gap in production per person and incomes.

■ Different methods of making the comparison lead to slightly different numbers, but the picture that Fig. 1 presents is reasonably accurate.

■ Figure 1 shows the ratio of real GDP per person in Canada to real GDP per person in the United States, with the values converted to a common currency using the purchasing power parity (*PPP*) exchange rate between the Canadian and U.S. dollars.

■ Figure 1 illustrates the accountant's concerns. The productivity gap widened between 1984 and 2004 when relative productivity fell from 90 percent to 80 percent.

■ Because income per person equals the value of production per person, the income gap between Canada and the United States has widened in the same way as the productivity gap has widened.

■ Figure 2 illustrates the production functions in Canada and the United States. With more productive capital and technologies, the U.S. production function, PF_{US}, is above the Canadian production function, PF_C.

■ Figure 3 illustrates the implications of the greater productivity for the labour market.

■ The U.S. demand for labour curve, LD_{US}, is above the Canadian demand for labour curve, LD_C.

■ The supply of labour (per person) is LS_{US} in the United States and LS_C in Canada.

■ The equilibrium real wage rate is higher in the United States than in Canada.

■ The accountants base their argument for tax cuts on a comparison of taxes in Canada and the United States.

■ There is no evidence that the labour union's idea of spending more on social services and other government programs would increase Canadian productivity.

You're the Voter

■ Do you agree with the accountants that Canada's low productivity is caused by high taxes? How might you test this view?

■ Do you agree with the labour union that Canada's low productivity is caused low social spending? How might you test this view?

■ Would you vote for lower taxes or more spending on social programs? Why?

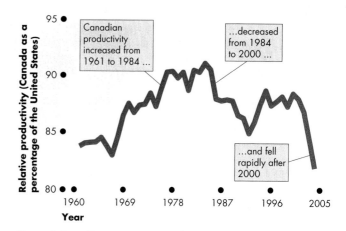

Figure 1 Canadian versus U.S. productivity

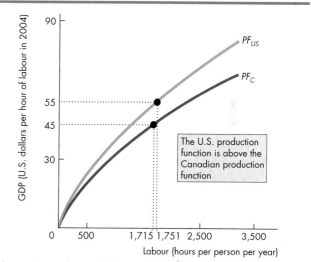

Figure 2 Canadian and U.S. production functions

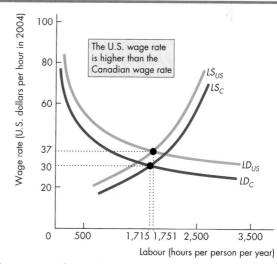

Figure 3 Canadian and U.S. labour markets

Deriving the Long-Run and Short-Run Aggregate Supply Curves

After studying this appendix, you will be able to

■ Derive the long-run aggregate supply curve, explain why it is vertical, and explain the factors that make it shift

■ Describe and explain short-run equilibrium in the labour market

■ Derive the short-run aggregate supply curve, explain the factors that make it shift, and explain what determines its shape

The Aggregate Supply Curves

THIS APPENDIX EXPLAINS HOW TO DERIVE THE long-run aggregate supply curve and the short-run aggregate supply curve. It shows the link between the labour market, the production function, and the long-run aggregate supply curve when prices and the money wage rate are fully adjusted. And it shows the link between the labour market, the production function, and the short-run aggregate supply curve when the money wage rate is sticky. You can think of this appendix as filling in the steps between Fig. 30.6 and Fig. 30.7 on p. 713 of this chapter.

This appendix also explains the factors that change aggregate supply and shift the aggregate supply curves. Finally, the appendix explains why the long-run aggregate supply curve is vertical and why the short-run aggregate supply curve slopes upward.

For many years, economists neglected aggregate supply and placed almost all their attention on aggregate demand. This neglect of aggregate supply was unfortunate because even in the short run, aggregate supply plays a role in determining real GDP. And in the long run, aggregate supply alone determines real GDP.

Deriving the Long-Run Aggregate Supply Curve

FIGURE A30.1 SHOWS HOW TO DERIVE THE LONG-run aggregate supply curve. Part (a) shows the labour market. The demand and supply curves shown are similar to those in Fig. 30.6(a) on p. 713. The equilibrium, a real wage of $35 an hour and employment of 20 billion hours, is exactly the same equilibrium that was determined in that figure.

Figure A30.1(b) shows the production function. This production function is similar to that in Fig. 30.1(b) on p. 707. We know from the labour market (part a) that 20 billion hours of labour are employed. Part (b) tells us that when 20 million hours of labour are employed, real GDP is $1,000 billion.

Figure A30.1(c) shows the long-run aggregate supply curve. That curve tells us that real GDP is $1,000 billion regardless of the price level. To see why, look at what happens when the price level changes.

Start with the economy is at point J in part (c) of the figure. The GDP deflator is 100 and real GDP is $1,000 billion. We've determined, in part (a), that the real wage rate is $35 an hour. With a GDP deflator of 100, the money wage rate (the wage rate in current dollars) is also $35 an hour.

What happens to real GDP if the GDP deflator falls from 100 to 80 (a 20 percent decrease in the price level)? If the money wage rate remains at $35 an hour, the real wage rate rises and the quantity of labour supplied exceeds the quantity demanded. In the long run, the money wage rate will fall. It falls to $28 an hour. With a money wage rate of $28 an hour and a GDP deflator of 80, the real wage rate is still $35 an hour ($28 divided by 80 and multiplied by 100 equals $35). With the lower money wage rate but a constant real wage rate, employment remains at 20 billion hours and real GDP remains at $1,000 billion. The economy is at point K in Fig. A30.1(c).

What happens to real GDP if the GDP deflator rises from 100 to 120 (a 20 percent increase in the price level)? If the money wage rate stays at $35 an hour, the real wage rate falls and the quantity of labour demanded exceeds the quantity supplied. In the long run, the money wage rate rises. It keeps rising until it reaches $42 an hour. At that money wage rate, the real wage rate is $35 an hour ($42 divided by 120 and multiplied by 100 equals $35) and the quantity of labour demanded equals the quantity supplied. Employment remains at 20 billion hours and real GDP remains at $1,000 billion. The economy is at point *I* in Fig. A30.1(c).

Points *J*, *K*, and *I* in part (c) all lie on the long-run aggregate supply curve. We have considered only three price levels. We can consider any price level and we will reach the same conclusion: A change in the price level generates a proportionate change in the money

wage rate and leaves the real wage rate unchanged. Employment and real GDP are also unchanged.

Because in the long run the price level *and the money wage rate* adjust to achieve full employment, the real wage rate, employment, and real GDP remain constant as the price level changes. In the long run, one level of real GDP—potential GDP—occurs at any price level and the *LAS* curve is vertical.

FIGURE A30.1

The Labour Market and Long-Run Aggregate Supply

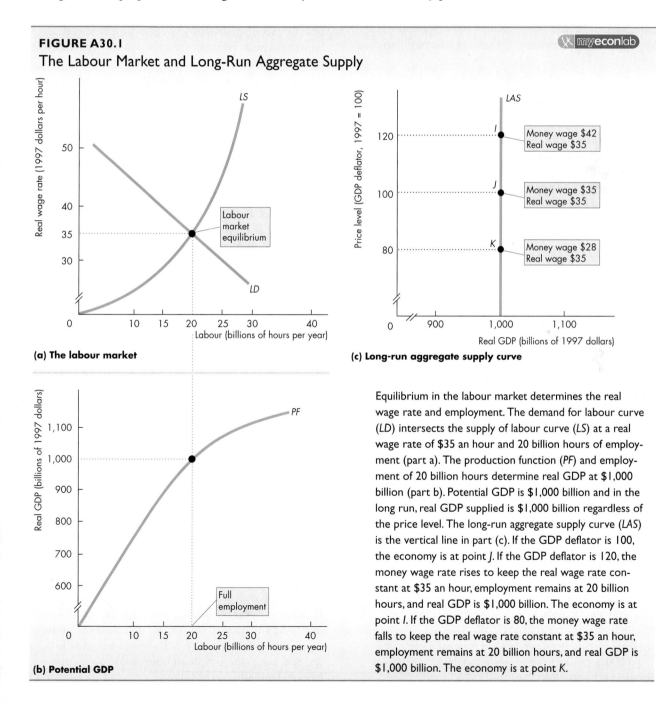

(a) The labour market

(c) Long-run aggregate supply curve

(b) Potential GDP

Equilibrium in the labour market determines the real wage rate and employment. The demand for labour curve (*LD*) intersects the supply of labour curve (*LS*) at a real wage rate of $35 an hour and 20 billion hours of employment (part a). The production function (*PF*) and employment of 20 billion hours determine real GDP at $1,000 billion (part b). Potential GDP is $1,000 billion and in the long run, real GDP supplied is $1,000 billion regardless of the price level. The long-run aggregate supply curve (*LAS*) is the vertical line in part (c). If the GDP deflator is 100, the economy is at point *J*. If the GDP deflator is 120, the money wage rate rises to keep the real wage rate constant at $35 an hour, employment remains at 20 billion hours, and real GDP is $1,000 billion. The economy is at point *I*. If the GDP deflator is 80, the money wage rate falls to keep the real wage rate constant at $35 an hour, employment remains at 20 billion hours, and real GDP is $1,000 billion. The economy is at point *K*.

Changes in Long-Run Aggregate Supply

Long-run aggregate supply can change for two reasons:

- Change in labour supply
- Change in labour productivity

Change in Labour Supply The supply of labour can change for many reasons, but the biggest one is a change in the population. Over time, the population grows and the supply of labour increases.

We study and illustrate the effects of an increase in the supply of labour on potential GDP on pp. 714–715. An increase in the supply of labour means the supply of labour curve shifts rightward. The real wage rate falls and full employment increases. Potential GDP increases.

Now that we've derived the long-run aggregate supply curve, you can see that when potential GDP changes, long-run aggregate supply also changes and the long-run aggregate supply curve shifts. Because an increase in the supply of labour increases potential GDP, it also increases long-run aggregate supply and shifts the long-run aggregate supply curve rightward. The new (vertical) long-run aggregate supply curve is located at the increased level of potential GDP.

Change in Labour Productivity An increase in labour productivity means that a given amount of labour can produce a larger quantity of real GDP. The production function shifts upward and the demand for labour curve shifts rightward. The real wage rate rises, full employment increases. Potential GDP increases.

We study and illustrate the effects of an increase in productivity on the quantity of labour, the real wage rate, and potential GDP on pp. 715–717.

Again, because an increase in labour productivity increases potential GDP, it also increases long-run aggregate supply and shifts the long-run aggregate supply curve rightward. The new (vertical) long-run aggregate supply curve is located at the increased level of potential GDP.

Whether the real wage rate increases when long-run aggregate supply increases depends on the source of the increase in potential GDP. If the source is an increase in the supply of labour, the real wage rate falls. If the source is an increase in labour productivity, the real wage rate rises.

Short-Run Aggregate Supply

SHORT-RUN AGGREGATE SUPPLY IS THE RELATIONship between the quantity of real GDP supplied and the price level when the money wage rate and all other influences on production plans remain the same. We are now going to learn about the connection between short-run aggregate supply and the labour market. But before we can derive the short-run aggregate supply curve, we must understand how the labour market works when the money wage rate is fixed.

Short-Run Equilibrium in the Labour Market

When the money wage rate is fixed, a change in the price level changes the real wage rate. Suppose the money wage rate is $35 an hour and the GDP deflator is 100. Then the real wage rate is also $35 an hour.

Now suppose that the money wage rate remains at $35 an hour but the GDP deflator rises to 116.7. In this case, the real wage rate falls to $30 an hour. A money wage rate of $35 an hour and a GDP deflator of 116.3 enables people to buy the same goods and services that a money wage rate of $30 an hour buys when the GDP deflator is 100.

Alternatively, suppose that the GDP deflator falls to 87.5. In this case, the real wage rate rises to $40 an hour. A money wage rate of $35 an hour with a GDP deflator of 87.5 buys the same quantity of goods and services that a money wage rate of $40 an hour buys when the GDP deflator is 100.

Figure A30.2 shows the labour market in the short run at the three price levels we've just considered. As before, the demand for labour is LD and the supply of labour is LS. The money wage rate is constant at $35 an hour and the higher the price level, the lower is the real wage rate. The three points B, C, and D tell us the quantities of labour demanded at the three real wage rates. If the price level is 87.5, the real wage rate is $40 an hour and the quantity of labour demanded is 15 billion hours a year (point B). If the price level is 100, the real wage rate is $35 an hour and the quantity of labour demanded is 20 billion hours a year (point C). If the price level is 116.7, the real wage rate is $30 an hour and the quantity of labour demanded is 25 billion hours a year (point D).

FIGURE A30.2

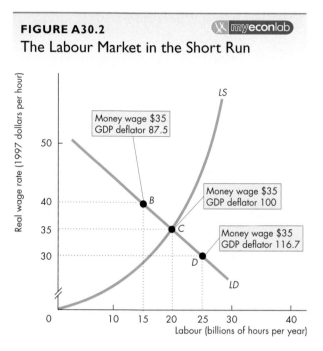

The Labour Market in the Short Run

The labour demand curve is LD and the labour supply curve is LS. The money wage rate is fixed at $35 an hour. If the GDP deflator is 100, the *real* wage rate is $35 an hour and 20 billion hours of labour are employed. The economy operates at point C. If the GDP deflator is 87.5, the real wage rate is $40 an hour and 15 billion hours of labour are employed. The economy operates at point B. If the GDP deflator is 116.7, the real wage rate is $30 an hour and 25 billion hours of labour are employed. The economy operates at point D.

You can see that when the money wage rate is fixed and the price level rises, the real wage rate falls, and the quantity of labour *demanded* increases. But what determines the quantity of labour *employed*?

Employment with Sticky Wages When the real wage rate is not at its full-employment equilibrium level, there are many possible ways in which employment could be determined. It is assumed that when the labour market is not at full employment, firms decide the level of employment and provided that firms pay the agreed money wage rate, households supply whatever quantity of labour firms demand. In the short run, households are willing to be "off" their labour supply curves.

In Fig. A30.2, with a money wage rate of $35 an hour and a price level of 87.5 (point *B*) employment is 15 billion hours. The real wage rate is $40 an hour and in this situation, people supply less labour than they would like to. If the GDP deflator is 116.7, the real wage rate is $30 an hour and employment is 25 billion hours (point *D*). The real wage rate is $30 an hour and in this case, people supply more labour than they would like to.

It is easy to understand why people might supply less labour than they would like to. But why would people supply *more* labour than they would like to? In the long run, they would not. But in the short run, during the life of an existing wage contract, it is quite likely that people will agree to supply whatever quantity of labour their employer demands. The employer gives the employee an "all-or-nothing" choice. The employee must either work the hours requested or find another job.

Deriving the Short-Run Aggregate Supply Curve

The short-run aggregate supply curve is the relationship between the quantity of real GDP supplied and the price level when the money wage rate and all other influences on production plans remain the same. Along the short-run aggregate supply curve, the money wage rate is fixed, so when the price level changes, the *real wage rate changes*. With a change in the real wage rate, employment and real GDP change. The short-run aggregate supply curve is upward sloping.

Figure A30.3 shows the derivation of the short-run aggregate supply curve. Part (a) shows the aggregate labour market. The demand and supply curves are the same as those in Fig. A30.2. The long-run equilibrium, a real wage of $35 an hour and employment of 20 billion hours, is exactly the same equilibrium that was determined in that figure.

Focus first on part (a). It shows the three short-run equilibrium levels of the real wage rate and employment that we discovered in Fig. A30.2. The money wage rate is fixed at $35 an hour. If the price level is 100, the real wage rate is also $35 an hour and 20 billion hours of labour are employed—point *C*. If the price level is 87.5, the real wage rate is $40 an hour and employment is 15 billion hours—point *B*. If the price level is 116.7, the real wage rate is $30 an hour and employment is 25 billion hours—point *D*.

FIGURE A30.3

The Labour Market and Short-Run Aggregate Supply

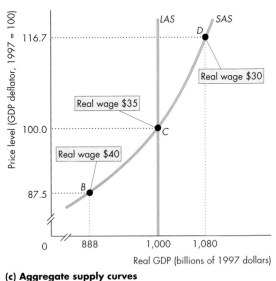

(c) **Aggregate supply curves**

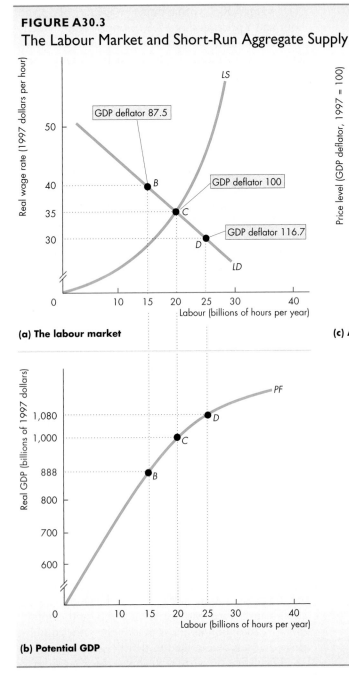

(a) **The labour market**

(b) **Potential GDP**

The money wage rate is fixed at $35 an hour. In part (a), the demand for labour curve (LD) intersects the supply of labour curve (LS) at a real wage rate of $35 an hour and 20 billion hours of employment. If the GDP deflator is 100, the economy operates at point C. In part (b), the production function (PF) determines real GDP at $1,000 billion. The economy is at point C on its long-run aggregate supply curve (LAS), in part (c). If the GDP deflator is 87.5, the real wage rate is $40 an hour and the economy is at point B. Employment is 15 billion hours (part a) and real GDP is $888 billion (part b). The economy is at point B on its short-run aggregate supply curve (SAS) in part (c). If the GDP deflator is 116.7, the real wage rate is $30 an hour and the economy is at point D. Employment is 25 billion hours (part a) and real GDP is $1,080 billion (part b). The economy is at point D on its short-run aggregate supply curve in part (c).

Figure A30.3(b) shows the production function. We know from the labour market (part a) that at different price levels, different quantities of labour are employed. Part (b) shows the real GDP produced by these employment levels. For example, when employment is 15 billion hours, real GDP is $888 billion—point B. When employment is 20 billion hours, real GDP is $1,000 billion—point C. And when employ-

ment is 25 billion hours, real GDP is $1,080 billion—point D.

Figure A30.3(c) shows the short-run aggregate supply curve. It also shows the long-run aggregate supply curve, *LAS*, that we derived in Fig. A30.1. The short-run aggregate supply curve, *SAS*, is derived from the labour market and production function. To see how, first focus on point *B* in all three parts of the figure. At point *B*, the price level is 87.5. From the labour market (part a) we know that when the price level is 87.5, the real wage is $40 an hour, and 15 billion hours of labour are employed. At this employment level, we know from the production function (part b) that real GDP is $888 billion. That's what point *B* on the *SAS* curve in part (c) tells us—when the price level is 87.5, the quantity of real GDP supplied is $888 billion. The other two points on the *SAS* curve, *C* and *D*, are derived in the same way. At point *D*, the price level is 116.7 so the real wage rate is $30 an hour and 25 billion hours of labour are employed (part a). This employment level produces a real GDP of $1,080 billion (part b).

The short-run aggregate supply curve intersects the long-run aggregate supply curve at the price level that delivers the equilibrium real wage rate in the labour market. In this example, that price level is 100. At labour market equilibrium, the economy is at full employment and real GDP equals potential GDP. At price levels above 100, the quantity of real GDP supplied in the short run exceeds potential GDP; at price levels below 100, the quantity of real GDP supplied in the short run falls short of potential GDP.

Changes in Short-Run Aggregate Supply

Short-run aggregate supply can change for two reasons:

- Change in long-run aggregate supply
- Change in money wage rate

Change in Long-Run Aggregate Supply Anything that changes long-run aggregate supply also changes short-run aggregate supply. That is, anything that increases potential GDP increases the quantity of real GDP supplied at each and every price level. Both long-run aggregate supply and short-run aggregate supply increase and both curves shift rightward.

A key feature of the *SAS* curve is that it intersects the *LAS* curve at the price level that puts the real wage rate at its full-employment level—that is, the real wage rate at which the labour market is in equilibrium. So if long-run aggregate supply changes and the *LAS* curve shifts, the short-run aggregate supply curve also shifts. And the new *SAS* curve intersects the new *LAS* curve at the price level that makes the real wage rate equal to its *new* full-employment level.

Change in Money Wage Rate Short-run aggregate supply changes and long-run aggregate supply remains unchanged if the money wage rate changes and all other influences on production plans remain the same. A rise in the money wage rate with a given price level means that the real wage rate has increased. Faced with a higher real wage rate, firms decrease the quantity of labour demanded. Employment decreases and firms produce less output, so the quantity of real GDP supplied decreases.

But the changes that we've just described would occur at any given price level. So short-run aggregate supply decreases. The *SAS* curve shifts leftward.

Short-Run Changes in the Quantity of Real GDP Supplied

Even if short-run aggregate supply does not change, real GDP can change in the short run. The reason is that there can be a *change in the quantity of real GDP supplied*, which appears as a *movement along the SAS curve*. These changes in real GDP are brought about by changes in aggregate demand. All the factors that can change aggregate demand result in a shift of the aggregate demand curve and movement along the *SAS* curve. Real GDP changes and so does the price level. They both change in the same direction. An increase in aggregate demand brings an increase in real GDP and a rise in the price level; a decrease in aggregate demand brings a decrease in real GDP and a fall in the price level.

The Shape of the Short-Run Aggregate Supply Curve

The short-run aggregate supply curve that we've derived in Fig. A30.3(c) is *curved*. Along this *SAS* curve, as the price level rises, real GDP increases. But for given increments in the price level, the increments in real GDP become successively smaller. In contrast, the *SAS* curve in Fig. 30.7 on p. 713, like that in Chapter 22, is linear—a curve that graphs as a straight line. Along a linear *SAS* curve, as the price level rises, real GDP increases. You can regard the linear *SAS* curve as an approximation over a small range of real GDP in the neighbourhood of potential GDP. The farther the economy moves away from potential GDP, the less close is the approximation.

SUMMARY

KEY POINTS

Real GDP and Employment (pp. 706–708)

- To produce real GDP, we must forgo leisure time.
- As the quantity of labour increases, real GDP increases.
- Labour productivity increases if the amount of physical capital or human capital increases or if technology advances.

The Labour Market and Aggregate Supply (pp. 709–714)

- The quantity of labour demanded increases as the real wage rate falls, other things remaining the same.
- The diminishing marginal product of labour is the reason the quantity of labour demanded increases as the real wage rate falls.
- The quantity of labour supplied increases as the real wage rate rises, other things remaining the same.
- At full-employment equilibrium, the quantity of labour demanded equals the quantity of labour supplied.
- Potential GDP is real GDP produced by the full-employment quantity of labour.
- Along the *LAS* curve, the real wage rate is constant at its full-employment level. Along the *SAS* curve, the real wage rate, employment, and real GDP change.

Changes in Potential GDP (pp. 714–718)

- An increase in population increases the supply of labour, lowers the real wage rate, increases the full-employment quantity of labour, and increases potential GDP. It decreases potential GDP per hour of work.
- An increase in capital or an advance in technology increases labour productivity. It shifts the production function upward and the demand for labour curve rightward. The real wage rate rises, the full-employment quantity of labour increases, and potential GDP increases.

Unemployment at Full Employment (pp. 719–721)

- The unemployment rate at full employment is the natural rate of unemployment.
- Unemployment is ever present because of job search and job rationing.
- Job-search unemployment is influenced by demographic change, unemployment compensation, and structural change.
- Job-rationing unemployment arises from efficiency wages and the minimum wage.

KEY FIGURES

Figure 30.1   Production Possibilities and the Production Function, 707
Figure 30.3   The Demand for Labour, 709
Figure 30.4   Marginal Product and the Demand for Labour, 710
Figure 30.5   The Supply of Labour, 711
Figure 30.6   The Labour Market and Potential GDP, 713
Figure 30.7   The Aggregate Supply Curves, 713
Figure 30.8   The Effects of an Increase in Population, 715
Figure 30.9   The Effects of an Increase in Labour Productivity, 717
Figure 30.11   Job Search Unemployment, 719

KEY TERMS

Demand for labour, 709
Efficiency wage, 720
Human capital, 707
Job rationing, 720
Job search, 719
Labour productivity, 707
Law of diminishing returns, 709
Learning-by-doing, 707
Long-run aggregate supply curve, 713
Marginal product of labour, 709
Minimum wage, 721
Money wage rate, 709
Production function, 706
Quantity of labour demanded, 709
Quantity of labour supplied, 711
Real wage rate, 709
Short-run aggregate supply curve, 713
Supply of labour, 711

PROBLEMS

Go to **myeconlab** for solutions to odd-numbered problems and additional exercises.

1. Robinson Crusoe lives on a desert island on the equator. He has 12 hours of daylight every day to allocate between leisure and work. The table shows seven alternative combinations of leisure and real GDP in Crusoe's economy:

Possibility	Leisure (hours per day)	Real GDP (dollars per day)
A	12	0
B	10	10
C	8	18
D	6	24
E	4	28
F	2	30
G	0	30

a. Make a table and a graph of Crusoe's production function.
b. Find the marginal product of labour for Crusoe at different quantities of labour.

2. The people of Nautica have a total of 100 hours every day to allocate between leisure and work. The table shows the combinations of real GDP and leisure in the economy of Nautica:

Possibility	Leisure (hours per day)	Real GDP (dollars per day)
A	0	75
B	20	70
C	40	60
D	60	45
E	80	25
F	100	0

a. Make a table and a graph of Nautica's production function.
b. Find the marginal product of labour for Nautica at different quantities of labour.

3. Use the information provided in problem 1 about Robinson Crusoe's economy. Also, use the information that at a real wage rate of $4.50 an hour, Crusoe is willing to work any number of hours between zero and the total available to him.

a. Make a table that shows Crusoe's demand for labour schedule and draw Crusoe's demand for labour curve.
b. Make a table that shows Crusoe's supply of labour schedule and draw Crusoe's supply of labour curve.
c. What are the full-employment equilibrium real wage rate and quantity of labour in Crusoe's economy?
d. Find Crusoe's potential GDP.

4. Use the information provided in problem 2 about the economy of Nautica. Also, use the information that the people of Nautica are willing to work 10 hours a day for a real wage rate of $10 an hour. And for each 50¢ an hour *increase* in the real wage, they are willing to work an *additional* hour a day.

a. Make a table that shows Nautica's demand for labour schedule and draw Nautica's demand for labour curve.
b. Make a table that shows Nautica's supply of labour schedule and draw Nautica's supply of labour curve.
c. Find the full-employment equilibrium real wage rate and quantity of labour in Nautica's economy.
d. Find Nautica's potential GDP.

5. Robinson Crusoe, whose economy is described in problems 1 and 3, gets a bright idea. He diverts a stream and increases his food production by 50 percent. That is, each hour that he works produces 50 percent more real GDP than before.

a. Make a table that shows Crusoe's new production function and new demand for labour schedule.
b. Find the new full-employment equilibrium real wage rate and quantity of labour in Crusoe's economy.
c. Find Crusoe's new potential GDP.
d. Explain and interpret the results you obtained in parts (a), (b), and (c).

6. Nautica's economy, described in problems 2 and 4, experiences a surge in its population. The supply of labour increases, and 50 percent more hours are supplied at each real wage rate.

a. Make a table that shows Nautica's new supply of labour schedule.
b. Find the new full-employment equilibrium real wage rate and quantity of labour in Nautica's economy.

c. Find Nautica's new potential GDP.
d. Explain and interpret the results you obtained parts in (a), (b), and (c).

7. The figure describes the labour market on Cocoa Island. In addition (not shown in the figure), a survey tells us that when Cocoa Island is at full employment, people spend 1,000 hours a day in job search.

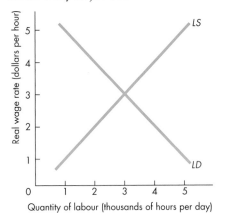

a. Find the full-employment equilibrium real wage rate and quantity of labour employed.
b. Find potential GDP on Cocoa Island. (*Hint*: The demand for labour curve tells you the *marginal* product of labour. How do we calculate the marginal product of labour?)
c. Calculate the natural rate of unemployment on Cocoa Island.

8. On Cocoa Island described in the figure and in problem 7, the government introduces a minimum wage of $4 an hour.
a. Find the new equilibrium real wage rate and quantity of labour employed.
b. What now is potential GDP on Cocoa Island?
c. Calculate the new natural rate of unemployment on Cocoa Island.
d. How much of the unemployment results from the minimum wage?

CRITICAL THINKING

1. Study *Reading Between the Lines* on pp. 722–723 and then answer the following questions:
a. Describe the labour productivity difference between Canada and the United States.
b. List the factors that influence a nation's production function that might explain why there is a gap between U.S. and Canadian labour productivity.
c. List the factors that influence a nation's supply of labour that might explain why the gap between U.S. and Canadian labour productivity has widened.
d. List the factors that influence a nation's production function that might be manipulated by Canadian economic policy to narrow the gap between U.S. and Canadian labour productivity.

2. You are working for the Finance Minister and must write a memo for the minister that provides a checklist of policy initiatives that will increase potential GDP. Be as imaginative as possible, but justify each of your suggestions with reference to the concepts and tools that you have learned about in this chapter.

WEB EXERCISES

Use the links on (X)(myeconlab) **to work the following exercises.**

1. Obtain information about the economy of Russia during the 1990s. Try to figure out what happened to the production possibilities frontier and production function and to the demand for labour and supply of labour in Russia during the 1990s. Tell a story about the Russian economy during those years using only the concepts and tools that you have learned about in this chapter.

2. Obtain information about the economy of China during the period since 2000. Try to figure out what happened to the production possibilities frontier and production function and to the demand for labour and supply of labour in China since 2000. Tell a story about the Chinese economy during those years using only the concepts and tools that you have learned in this chapter.

Economic Growth

CHAPTER 31

Transforming People's Lives

Real GDP per person in Canada more than doubled between 1961 and 2005. If you live in a dorm that was built during the 1960s it is equipped with two electrical outlets: one for a desk lamp and one for a bedside lamp. Today, with the help of a power bar (or two), your room bulges with a personal computer, television and DVD player, stereo system, microwave, refrigerator, coffee maker, and toaster—the list goes on. What has brought about this growth in living standards?

We see even greater change if we look at modern Asia. On the banks of the Li River in Southern China, Songman Yang breeds cormorants, amazing birds that he trains to fish and deliver their catch to a basket on his simple bamboo raft. Songman's work, the capital equipment and technology he uses, and the income he earns are similar to those of his ancestors going back some 2,000 years. Yet all around Songman, in China's bustling cities, people are participating in an economic miracle. They are creating businesses, investing in new technologies, developing local and global markets, and transforming their lives. Why are incomes in China growing so rapidly?

◆ In this chapter, we study the forces that make real GDP grow, that make some countries grow faster than others, and that make our own growth rate sometimes slow down and sometimes speed up. And at the end of the chapter, in *Reading Between the Lines*, we examine Canada's recent productivity growth and find that it has been falling further behind that of the United States.

After studying this chapter, you will be able to

- Describe the long-term growth trends in Canada and other countries and regions
- Identify the main sources of long-term real GDP growth
- Explain the productivity growth slowdown in Canada during the 1970s and the speedup during the 1990s
- Explain the theories of economic growth

Long-Term Growth Trends

THE LONG-TERM GROWTH TRENDS THAT WE study in this chapter are the trends in *potential GDP*. We are interested in long-term growth primarily because it brings rising incomes *per person*. So we begin by looking at some facts about the level and the growth rate of real GDP per person in Canada and around the world. Let's look first at real GDP per person in Canada over the past 75 years.

Growth in the Canadian Economy

Figure 31.1 shows real GDP *per person* in Canada for the 78 years from 1926 to 2004. The average growth rate over this period is 2.2 percent a year.

The earliest years in the graph are dominated by two extraordinary events: the Great Depression of the 1930s and World War II of the 1940s. The fall in real GDP during the depression and the bulge during the war obscure the changes in the long-term growth trend that occurred within these years. Averaging out the depression and the war, the long-term growth rate was close to its 75-year average of 2.2 percent a year.

The 1950s had slow growth but then, during the 1960s, the growth rate speeded up and averaged 3.6 percent a year. The 1970s growth slowed to 2.8 percent a year and in the 1980s the growth rate slowed to a crawl of 1.0 percent a year. After 1996, the growth rate increased again and for the eight years between 1996 and 2004, the growth rate was back at its 75-year average.

A major goal of this chapter is to explain why our economy grows and why the long-term growth rate varies. Why did growth speed up during the 1960s, slow through the 1970s and 1980s, and then speed up again during the late 1990s and early 2000s? Another goal is to explain variations in the growth rate across countries. Let's look at some facts about the growth rates of other nations and compare them with Canada's growth rate.

FIGURE 31.1
Economic Growth in Canada: 1926–2004

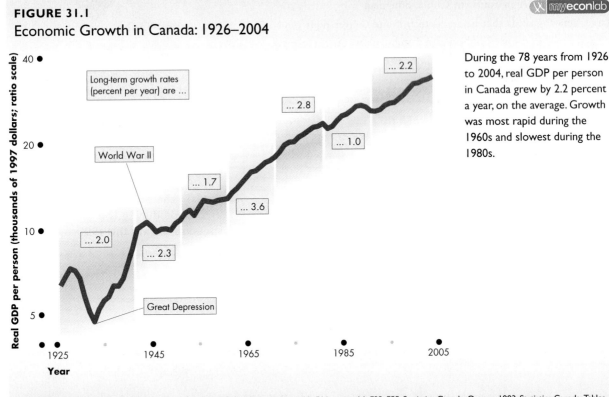

During the 78 years from 1926 to 2004, real GDP per person in Canada grew by 2.2 percent a year, on the average. Growth was most rapid during the 1960s and slowest during the 1980s.

Sources of data: F.H. Leacy (ed.), *Historical Statistics of Canada*, 2nd ed., catalogue 11–516, series A1, F32, F55, Statistics Canada, Ottawa, 1983; Statistics Canada, Tables 380–0002 and 051–0005.

Real GDP Growth in the World Economy

Figure 31.2 shows real GDP per person in Canada and in other countries between 1960 and 2005. (The data shown in this figure are in 2000 U.S. dollars.) Part (a) looks at the seven richest countries—known as the G7 nations. Among these nations, the United States has the highest real GDP per person.

In 2005, Canada had the second-highest real GDP per person and Japan the third. Before the 1990s, Japan grew faster than the United States and was catching up. Japan also grew faster than the Europe Big 4 (France, Germany, Italy, and the United Kingdom) and overtook Europe in the mid-1980s. But during the 1990s, the Japanese economy stagnated while Europe's continued to expand, so by 2005, these nations had similar levels of real GDP per person.

Across a broader group of poorer countries, economic growth has been slower than in Canada and income gaps have widened.

In Fig. 31.2(b), you can see that Africa and Central and South America have grown more slowly than Canada. Real GDP per person in Central and South America slipped from 33 percent of the Canadian level of real GDP per person in 1960 to 28 percent in 2005. Africa slipped from 14 percent of the Canadian level of real GDP per person in 1960 to 9 percent in 2005.

Figure 31.2(b) also shows that after growing during the 1970s and 1980s, the former communist countries of Central Europe stagnated and fell increasingly behind Canada. But by the late 1990s,

---

FIGURE 31.2

Economic Growth Around the World

(a) Growth in the rich G7

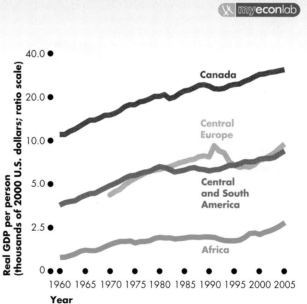

(b) Persistent gaps between rich and poor

Real GDP per person has grown throughout the world economy. Among the rich industrial countries (part a), real GDP growth has been similar in Canada, the Europe Big 4 (France, Germany, Italy, and the United Kingdom), and the United States. Growth in Japan was very rapid during the 1960s, slower during the 1980s, and even slower during the 1990s.

Part (b) shows income per person in a wider range of groups of countries. Central Europe was growing more quickly than Canada during the 1970s and 1980s, but slumped during the 1990s transition to a market economy. Growth in Central and South America and in Africa has been slower than in Canada, so the income gaps between Canada and these countries have widened.

Sources of data: 1960–2000: Alan Heston, Robert Summers and Bettina Aten, Penn World Table Version 6.1, Center for International Comparisons at the University of Pennsylvania (CICUP), October 2002. 2001–2005: *World Economic Outlook,* Washington, DC: International Monetary Fund, October 2005.

these countries were expanding more quickly again. But they remain a long way behind Canada.

The persistent gaps both among the G7 and the richer and poorer groups of countries in Fig. 31.2 is not a universal global phenomenon. Some economies have grown spectacularly and closed the income gap.

Figure 31.3 shows these economies. They are Hong Kong, Korea, Singapore, and Taiwan. During the 1960s, real GDP per person in these economies ranged from 10 to 25 percent of that in Canada. But by 2005, two of them, Hong Kong and Singapore, had overtaken Canada and the other two were close behind.

Figure 31.3 also shows China catching up, but more slowly and from a very long way behind. China's real GDP per person increased from 7 percent of Canada's level in 1960 to 19 percent in 2005.

The four small Asian economies shown in Fig. 31.3 are like fast trains running on the same track at similar speeds and with a roughly constant gap between them. Hong Kong is the lead train and runs about 17 years in front of Korea, which is the last train. Real GDP per person in Korea in 2005 was similar to that of Hong Kong in 1988, 17 years earlier. Between 1960 and 2005, Hong Kong transformed itself from a poor developing economy into one of the world's richest economies.

China is now doing what Hong Kong has done. If China continues its rapid growth, the world economy will become a dramatically different place, because China is equivalent to more than 200 countries of the size of Hong Kong. Whether China will continue on its current path of rapid growth is impossible to predict.

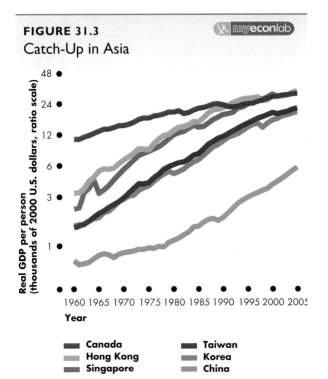

FIGURE 31.3   myeconlab

Catch-Up in Asia

Legend:
- Canada
- Hong Kong
- Singapore
- Taiwan
- Korea
- China

Catch-up has occurred in five economies in Asia. After starting out in 1960 with real GDP per person as low as 10 percent of that in Canada, Hong Kong, Korea, Singapore, and Taiwan have substantially narrowed the gap between them and Canada. And from being a very poor developing country in 1960, China now has a real GDP per person that equals that of Hong Kong in 1960. China is growing at a rate that is enabling it to continue to catch up with Canada.

Sources of data: See Fig. 31.2.

REVIEW QUIZ

1 What has been the average economic growth rate in Canada over the past 75 years? In which periods was growth most rapid and in which periods was it the slowest?

2 Describe the gaps between the levels of real GDP per person in Canada and other countries. For which countries are the gaps narrowing? For which countries are the gaps widening? And for which countries are the gaps remaining unchanged?

3 Compare the growth rates and levels of real GDP per person in Hong Kong, Korea, Singapore, Taiwan, China, and Canada. How far is China behind the other Asian economies?

myeconlab   **Study Plan 31.1**

The facts about economic growth in Canada and around the world raise some big questions that we're now going to answer. We'll study the causes of economic growth in three stages. First, we'll look at the preconditions for growth and the activities that sustain it. Second, we'll learn how economists measure the relative contributions of the sources of growth—an activity called *growth accounting*. And third, we'll study three theories of economic growth that seek to explain how the influences on growth interact to determine the growth rate. Let's take our first look at the causes of economic growth.

The Causes of Economic Growth: A First Look

MOST HUMAN SOCIETIES HAVE LIVED FOR centuries and even thousands of years, like Songman Yang and his ancestors, with no economic growth. The key reason is that they have lacked some fundamental social institutions and arrangements that are essential preconditions for economic growth. Let's see what these preconditions are.

Preconditions for Economic Growth

The most basic precondition for economic growth is an appropriate *incentive* system. Three institutions are crucial to the creation of incentives:

1. Markets
2. Property rights
3. Monetary exchange

Markets enable buyers and sellers to get information and to do business with each other, and market prices send signals to buyers and sellers that create incentives to increase or decrease the quantities demanded and supplied. Markets enable people to specialize and trade and to save and invest. But markets need property rights and monetary exchange.

Property rights are the social arrangements that govern the ownership, use, and disposal of factors of production and goods and services. They include the rights to physical property (land, buildings, and capital equipment), to financial property (claims by one person against another), and to intellectual property (such as inventions). Clearly established and enforced property rights give people an assurance that a capricious government will not confiscate their income or savings.

Monetary exchange facilitates transactions of all kinds, including the orderly transfer of private property from one person to another. Property rights and monetary exchange create incentives for people to specialize and trade, to save and invest, and to discover new technologies.

No unique political system is necessary to deliver the preconditions for economic growth. Liberal democracy, founded on the fundamental principle of the rule of law, is the system that does the best job. It provides a solid base on which property rights can be established and enforced. But authoritarian political systems have sometimes provided an environment in which economic growth has occurred.

Early human societies, based on hunting and gathering, did not experience economic growth because they lacked these preconditions. Economic growth began when societies evolved the three key institutions that create incentives. But the presence of an incentive system and the institutions that create it does not guarantee that economic growth will occur. It permits economic growth but does not make that growth inevitable.

The simplest way in which growth happens when the appropriate incentive system exists is that people begin to specialize in the activities at which they have a comparative advantage and trade with each other. You saw in Chapter 2 how everyone can gain from such activity. By specializing and trading, everyone can acquire goods and services at the lowest possible cost. Equivalently, people can obtain a greater volume of goods and services from their labour.

As an economy moves from one with little specialization to one that reaps the gains from specialization and exchange, its production and consumption grow. Real GDP per person increases, and the standard of living rises.

But for growth to be persistent, people must face incentives that encourage them to pursue three activities that generate ongoing economic growth:

- Saving and investment in new capital
- Investment in human capital
- Discovery of new technologies

These three sources of growth, which interact with each other, are the primary sources of the extraordinary growth in productivity during the past 200 years. Let's look at each in turn.

Saving and Investment in New Capital

Saving and investment in new capital increase the amount of capital per worker and increase real GDP per hour of labour—labour productivity. Labour productivity took the most dramatic upturn when the amount of capital per worker increased during the Industrial Revolution. Production processes that use hand tools can create beautiful objects, but production methods that use large amounts of capital per worker, such as auto plant assembly lines, are much more productive. The accumulation of capital on farms, in textile factories, in iron foundries and steel mills, in coal mines, on building sites, in chemical plants, in auto plants, in banks and insurance companies, and in shopping malls has added incredibly to the productivity of our economy. The next time you see a movie set in the Old West or colonial times, look carefully at the small amount of capital around. Try to imagine how productive you would be in such circumstances compared with your productivity today.

Investment in Human Capital

Human capital—the accumulated skill and knowledge of human beings—is the most fundamental source of economic growth. It is a source of both increased productivity and technological advance.

The development of one of the most basic human skills—writing—was the source of some of the earliest major gains in productivity. The ability to keep written records made it possible to reap ever-larger gains from specialization and exchange. Imagine how hard it would be to do any kind of business if all the accounts, invoices, and agreements existed only in people's memories.

Later, the development of mathematics laid the foundation for the eventual extension of knowledge about physical forces and chemical and biological processes. This base of scientific knowledge was the foundation for the technological advances of the Industrial Revolution 200 years ago and of today's information revolution.

But much human capital that is extremely productive is more humble. It takes the form of millions of individuals learning and repetitively doing simple production tasks and becoming remarkably more productive in the tasks.

One carefully studied example illustrates the importance of this kind of human capital. Between 1941 and 1944 (during World War II), U.S. shipyards produced some 2,500 units of a cargo ship, called the Liberty Ship, to a standardized design. In 1941, it took 1.2 million person-hours to build one ship. By 1942, it took 600,000 person-hours, and by 1943, it took only 500,000. Not much change occurred in the capital employed during these years. But an enormous amount of human capital was accumulated. Thousands of workers and managers learned from experience and accumulated human capital that more than doubled their productivity in two years.

Discovery of New Technologies

Saving and investment in new capital and the accumulation of human capital have made a large contribution to economic growth. But technological change—the discovery and the application of new technologies and new goods—has made an even greater contribution.

People are many times more productive today than they were a hundred years ago. We are not more productive because we have more steam engines per person and more horse-drawn carriages per person. Rather, it is because we have engines and transportation equipment that use technologies that were unknown a hundred years ago and that are more productive than the old technologies were. Technological change makes an enormous contribution to our increased productivity. It arises from formal research and development programs and from informal trial and error, and it involves discovering new ways of getting more out of our resources.

To reap the benefits of technological change, capital must increase. Some of the most powerful and far-reaching fundamental technologies are embodied in human capital—for example, language, writing, and mathematics. But most technologies are embodied in physical capital. For example, to reap the benefits of the internal combustion engine, millions of horse-drawn carriages and horses had to be replaced by automobiles; more recently, to reap the benefits of computerized word processing, millions of typewriters had to be replaced by PCs and printers.

REVIEW QUIZ

1 What economic activities that lead to economic growth do markets, property rights, and monetary exchange facilitate?
2 What are the roles of saving and investment in new capital, the growth of human capital, and the discovery of new technologies in economic growth?
3 Provide some examples of how human capital has created new technologies that are embodied in both human and physical capital.

myeconlab Study Plan 31.2

What is the quantitative contribution of the sources of economic growth? To answer this question, economists use growth accounting.

Growth Accounting

THE QUANTITY OF REAL GDP SUPPLIED (Y) depends on three factors:

1. The quantity of labour (L)
2. The quantity of capital (K)
3. The state of technology (T)

The purpose of **growth accounting** is to calculate how much real GDP growth results from growth of labour and capital and how much is attributable to technological change. The key tool of growth accounting is the **aggregate production function**, which we write as

$$Y = F(L, K, T).$$

In words, the quantity of real GDP supplied is determined by (is a function F of) the quantities of labour and capital and of the state of technology. The larger is L, K, or T, the greater is Y. And the faster L and K grow and T advances, the faster Y grows.

So understanding what makes labour and capital grow and technology advance is the key to understanding economic growth. Labour growth depends primarily on population growth. And the growth rate of capital and the pace of technological advance determine the growth rate of labour productivity.

Labour Productivity

Labour productivity is real GDP per hour of labour. Labour productivity is calculated by dividing real GDP, Y, by aggregate labour hours, L.

Labour productivity determines how much income an hour of labour generates. Figure 31.4 shows labour productivity for the period 1960–2005. Productivity growth was most rapid during the 1960s. It slowed down in 1973 to only one half of its 1960s rate, where it remained for 10 years. Productivity growth slowed even more during the late 1980s. It then speeded up in the new economy of the 1990s. But productivity growth ground to a near halt after 2002.

Growth accounting explains fluctuations in productivity growth by measuring separately the contribution of two components of productivity growth:

- Growth in capital per hour of labour
- Technological change

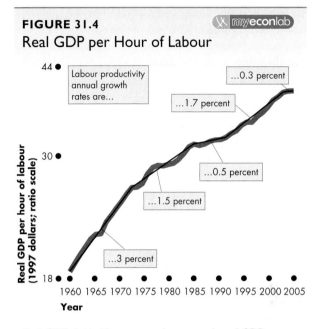

FIGURE 31.4

Real GDP per Hour of Labour

Labour productivity annual growth rates are...

...0.3 percent

...1.7 percent

...0.5 percent

...1.5 percent

...3 percent

Real GDP per hour of labour (1997 dollars; ratio scale)

1960 1965 1970 1975 1980 1985 1990 1995 2000 2005

Year

Real GDP divided by aggregate hours equals real GDP per hour of labour, which is a broad measure of productivity. During the 1960s the productivity growth rate was high. It slowed after 1973 and has fluctuated but been low since then.

Source of data: Centre for the Study of Living Standards, Aggregate Income and Productivity Trends: Canada vs United States, 1961–2004. (Updated June 14, 2005) www.csls.ca.

Capital is physical capital. Technological change includes everything that contributes to labour productivity growth that is not included in the growth in capital per hour. In particular, it includes human capital growth. Human capital growth and technological change are intimately related. Technology advances because knowledge advances. And knowledge is part of human capital. So "technological change" is a broad catchall concept.

The analytical engine of growth accounting is a relationship called the productivity curve. Let's learn about this relationship and see how it is used.

The Productivity Curve

The **productivity curve** is a relationship that shows how real GDP per hour of labour changes as the amount of capital per hour of labour changes with a given state of technology. Figure 31.5 illustrates the productivity curve. Capital per hour of labour is measured on the *x*-axis, and real GDP per hour of labour is measured on the *y*-axis. The figure shows two productivity curves. One is the curve labelled PC_0, and the other is the curve labelled PC_1.

An increase in the quantity of capital per hour of labour increases real GDP per hour of labour, which is shown by a movement along a productivity curve. For example, on PC_0, when capital per hour of labour is $30, real GDP per hour of labour is $20. If capital per hour of labour increases to $60, real GDP per hour of labour increases to $25.

Technological change increases the amount of GDP per hour of labour that can be produced by a given amount of capital per hour of labour. Technological change shifts the productivity curve upward. For example, if capital per hour of labour is $30 and a technological change increases real GDP per hour of labour from $20 to $25, the productivity curve shifts upward from PC_0 to PC_1 in Fig. 31.5. Similarly, if capital per hour of labour is $60, the same technological change increases real GDP per hour of labour from $25 to $32 and shifts the productivity curve upward from PC_0 to PC_1.

To calculate the contributions of capital growth and technological change to productivity growth, we need to know the shape of the productivity curve. The shape of the productivity curve reflects a fundamental economic law—the law of diminishing returns. The **law of diminishing returns** states that as the quantity of one input increases with the quantities of all other inputs remaining the same, output increases but by ever smaller increments. For example, in a factory that has a given amount of capital, as more labour is hired, production increases. But each *additional* hour of labour produces less *additional* output than the previous hour produced. For example, two typists working with one computer type fewer than twice as many pages per day as one typist working with one computer.

Applied to capital, the law of diminishing returns states that if a given number of hours of labour use more capital (with the same technology), the *additional* output that results from the *additional* capital gets smaller as the amount of capital increases. For example, one typist working with two computers types fewer than twice as many pages per day as one typist working with one computer. More generally, one hour of labour working with $40 of capital produces less than twice the output of one hour of labour working with $20 of capital. But how much less? The answer is given by the *one-third rule*.

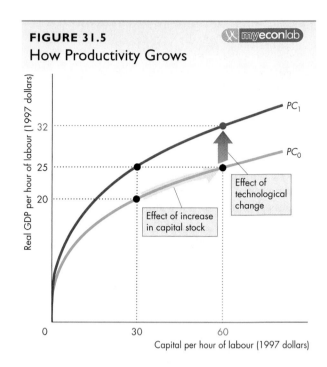

FIGURE 31.5   myeconlab
How Productivity Grows

Productivity is measured by real GDP per hour of labour, and it can grow for two reasons: (1) Capital per hour of labour increases, and (2) technological advances occur. The productivity curve, PC_0, shows the effects of an increase in capital per hour of labour on productivity. Here, when capital per hour of labour increases from $30 to $60, real GDP per hour of labour increases from $20 to $25 along the productivity curve PC_0. Technological advance shifts the productivity curve upward. Here, an advance in technology shifts the productivity curve from PC_0 to PC_1. When capital per hour of labour is $60, real GDP per hour of labour increases from $25 to $32.

The One-Third Rule   Robert Solow of MIT estimated a U.S. productivity curve and discovered the **one-third rule** that, on the average, with no change in technology, a 1 percent increase in capital per hour of labour brings a *one-third of 1 percent* increase in real GDP per hour of labour. This one-third rule is used to calculate the contributions of an increase in capital per hour of labour and technological change to the growth of real GDP. Let's do such a calculation.

Suppose that capital per hour of labour grows by 3 percent a year and real GDP per hour of labour grows by 2.5 percent a year. The one-third rule tells us that capital growth has contributed one-third of

3 percent, which is 1 percent, to the growth of real GDP per hour of labour. The rest of the 2.5 percent growth of real GDP per hour of labour comes from technological change. That is, technological change has contributed 1.5 percent, which is the 2.5 percent growth of real GDP per hour of labour minus the estimated 1 percent contribution of capital growth.

Accounting for the Productivity Growth Slowdown and Speedup

We can use the one-third rule to study Canadian productivity growth and the productivity growth slowdown. Figure 31.6 tells the story, starting in 1961.

Booming Sixties and Early Seventies In 1961, capital per hour of labour was $29 and real GDP per hour of labour was $18 on PC_{61} in Fig. 31.6. By 1973, capital per hour of labour had increased by 34 percent, to $39. With no change in technology, the economy would have moved to point A on PC_{61}, where real GDP per hour of labour has increased by 11.3 percent (1/3 of 34 percent). But rapid technological change shifted the productivity curve upward to PC_{73}.

Slowdown: 1973–1985 From 1973 to 1985, capital per hour of labour increased by 36 percent, to $53. With no change in technology, the economy would have moved to point B on PC_{73} in Fig. 31.6, where real GDP per hour of labour has increased by 12 percent (1/3 of 36 percent). But a small amount of technological change shifted the productivity curve upward to PC_{85}. So the productivity growth slowdown occurred because the contribution of technological change to real GDP growth slowed.

Stagnation: 1985–1991 From 1985 to 1991, capital per hour of labour increased by 9 percent and real GDP per hour of labour expanded by 3 percent (1/3 of 9 percent). The productivity curve remained stuck at its 1985 level.

The New Economy: 1991–2004 From 1991 to 2002, capital per hour of labour increased by 10 percent so with no change in technology, the economy would have moved to point C on PC_{85} in Fig. 31.6, where real GDP per hour of labour has increased by 3.3 percent (1/3 of 10 percent). But a speedup in the pace of technological change shifted the productivity curve upward to PC_{02}. But from 2002 to 2004, the

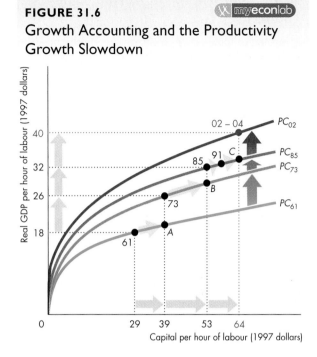

FIGURE 31.6 myeconlab

Growth Accounting and the Productivity Growth Slowdown

Between 1961 and 1973, capital per hour of labour increased from $29 to $39 and rapid technological change shifted the productivity curve upward from PC_{61} to PC_{73}. Between 1973 and 1985, capital per hour of labour increased from $39 to $53 and slower technological change shifted the productivity curve upward from PC_{73} to PC_{85}. Between 1985 and 1991, capital per hour of labour increased but with no technological change the economy moved along PC_{85}. From 1991 to 2002, capital per hour of labour increased to $64 and a speedup in technological change shifted the productivity curve upward from PC_{85} to PC_{02}. From 2002 and 2004, capital per hour of labour and productivity remained constant.

Sources of data: Centre for the Study of Living Standards, Aggregate Income and Productivity Trends: Canada vs United States, 1961–2004. (Updated June 14, 2005), www.csls.ca.

economy had no change in either capital or real GDP per hour of labour.

The growth accounting exercise that we've just worked through shows that although technological change speeded during the 1990s, its pace was slower than that during the 1960s and the so-called new economy was not such a spectacular or unusual growth phenomenon.

Technological Change During the Productivity Growth Slowdown

Technological change did not stop during the productivity growth slowdown. But its focus changed from increasing productivity to coping with

- Energy price shocks
- The environment

Energy Price Shocks Energy price increases that occurred in 1973–1974 and in 1979–1980 diverted research efforts towards saving energy rather than increasing productivity. Airplanes became more fuel efficient, but they didn't operate with smaller crews. Real GDP per litre of fuel increased faster, but real GDP per hour of labour increased more slowly.

The Environment The 1970s saw an expansion of laws and resources devoted to protecting the environment and improving the quality of the workplace. The benefits of these actions—cleaner air and water and safer factories—are not counted as part of real GDP. So the growth of these benefits is not measured as part of productivity growth.

Achieving Faster Growth

Growth accounting tells us that to achieve faster economic growth, we must either increase the growth rate of capital per hour of labour or increase the pace of technological advance (which includes improving human capital). The main suggestions for achieving these objectives are

- Stimulate saving
- Stimulate research and development
- Target high-technology industries
- Encourage international trade
- Improve the quality of education

Stimulate Saving Saving finances investment, which brings capital accumulation. So stimulating saving can stimulate economic growth. The East Asian economies have the highest growth rates and the highest saving rates. Some African economies have the lowest growth rates and the lowest saving rates.

Tax incentives can increase saving. Registered Retirement Savings Plans (RRSPs) are a tax incentive to save. Economists claim that a tax on consumption rather than income provides the best saving incentive.

Stimulate Research and Development Everyone can use the fruits of *basic* research and development efforts. For example, all biotechnology firms can use advances in gene-splicing technology. Because basic inventions can be copied, the inventor's profit is limited, and the market allocates too few resources to this activity.

Governments can use public funds to finance basic research, but this solution is not foolproof. It requires a mechanism for allocating the public funds to their highest-valued use. The National Science and Engineering Research Council of Canada is one possibly efficient channel for allocating public funds to universities to finance and stimulate basic research.

Target High-Technology Industries Some people say that by providing public funds to firms in high-technology industries, a country can become the first to exploit a new technology and can earn above-average profits for a period while others are busy catching up. This strategy is risky and just as likely to use resources inefficiently as to speed growth.

Encourage International Trade Free international trade stimulates growth by extracting all the available gains from specialization and exchange. The fastest-growing nations today are those with the fastest-growing exports and imports.

Improve the Quality of Education A free market in education would produce too few educated people because education brings benefits beyond those valued by the people who receive the education. By funding basic education and by ensuring high standards in basic skills such as language, mathematics, and science, governments can contribute to a nation's growth potential. Education can also be stimulated and improved by using tax incentives to encourage improved private provision.

REVIEW QUIZ

1   Explain how the one-third rule isolates the contributions of capital growth and technological change to productivity growth.

2   Explain how growth accounting gives us information about the factors that contributed to the productivity growth slowdown of the 1970s. Why did the slowdown occur?

myeconlab   **Study Plan 31.3**

Growth Theories

WE'VE SEEN THAT REAL GDP GROWS WHEN THE quantities of labour and capital (which includes human capital) grow and when technology advances. Does this mean that the growth of labour and capital and technological advances *cause* economic growth? It might mean that. But there are other possibilities: *One* of these factors might be the cause of real GDP growth, and the others might be the *effect*. We must try to discover how the influences on economic growth interact with each other to make some economies grow quickly and others grow slowly. And we must probe the reasons why a country's long-term growth rate sometimes speeds up and sometimes slows down.

Growth theories are designed to study the interactions among the several factors that contribute to growth and to disentangle cause and effect. They are also designed to enable us to study the way the different factors influence each other.

Growth theories are also designed to be universal. They are not theories about the growth of poor countries only or rich countries only. They are theories about why and how poor countries become rich and rich countries continue to get richer.

We're going to study three theories of economic growth, each one of which gives some insights into the process of economic growth. But none provides a definite answer to the basic questions: What causes economic growth and why do growth rates vary? Economics has some way to go before it can provide a definite answer to these most important of questions. The three growth theories we study are

- Classical growth theory
- Neoclassical growth theory
- New growth theory

Classical Growth Theory

Classical growth theory is the view that real GDP growth is temporary and that when real GDP per person rises above the subsistence level, a population explosion eventually brings real GDP per person back to the subsistence level. Adam Smith, Thomas Robert Malthus, and David Ricardo, the leading economists of the late eighteenth century and early nineteenth century, proposed this theory, but the view is most closely associated with the name of Malthus and is sometimes called the *Malthusian theory*.

Many people today are Malthusians! They say that if today's global population of 6.2 billion explodes to 11 billion by 2200, we will run out of resources and return to a primitive standard of living. We must act, say the Malthusians, to contain the population growth.

The Basic Classical Idea To understand classical growth theory, let's transport ourselves back to the world of 1776, when Adam Smith is first explaining the idea. Most of the 2.5 million people who live in the newly emerging nations of North America work on farms or on their own land and perform their tasks using simple tools and animal power. They earn an average of 2 shillings (a bit less than $12 in today's money) for working a 10-hour day.

Then advances in farming technology bring new types of plows and seeds that increase farm productivity. As farm productivity increases, farm production increases and some farm workers move from the land to the cities, where they get work producing and selling the expanding range of farm equipment. Incomes rise, and the people seem to be prospering. But will the prosperity last? Classical growth theory says it will not.

Advances in technology—in both agriculture and industry—lead to an investment in new capital, which makes labour more productive. More and more businesses start up and hire the now more productive labour. The greater demand for labour raises the real wage rate and increases employment. At this stage, economic growth has occurred and everyone has benefited from it. Real GDP has increased, and the real wage rate has increased. But the classical economists believe that this new situation can't last because it will induce a population explosion.

Classical Theory of Population Growth When the classical economists were developing their ideas about population growth, an unprecedented population explosion was underway. In Britain and other Western European countries, improvements in diet and hygiene had lowered the death rate while the birth rate remained high. For several decades, population growth was extremely rapid. For example, after being relatively stable for several centuries, the population of Britain increased by 40 percent between 1750 and 1800 and by a further 50 percent between 1800 and 1830. Meanwhile, an estimated 1 million people (about 20 percent of the 1750 population) left Britain for North

America and Australia before 1800, and outward migration continued on a similar scale through the nineteenth century. These facts are the empirical basis for the classical theory of population growth.

To explain the high rate of population growth, the classical economists used the idea of a **subsistence real wage rate**, which is the minimum real wage rate needed to maintain life. If the actual real wage rate is less than the subsistence real wage rate, some people cannot survive and the population decreases. In classical theory, when the real wage rate exceeds the subsistence real wage rate, the population grows. But a rising population brings diminishing returns to labour. So labour productivity eventually decreases. This implication led to economics being called the *dismal science*. The dismal implication is that no matter how much technological change occurs, real wage rates are always pushed back towards the subsistence level.

Classical Theory and the Productivity Curve

Figure 31.7 illustrates the classical growth theory using the productivity curve. Initially, the productivity curve is PC_0. Subsistence real GDP per hour of labour (real wage rate) is $20, shown by the horizontal line. The economy starts out at point A, with $60 of capital per hour of labour and $20 of real GDP per hour of labour, the subsistence level. Because the real wage rate is at the subsistence level, the population is constant.

Then a technological advance occurs, which shifts the productivity curve upward to PC_1. The economy now moves to point B on PC_1, and real GDP per hour of labour rises to $30. Now earning more than the subsistence real wage rate, people have more children and live longer. The population grows.

A growing population means that labour hours grow, so capital per hour of labour falls. As capital per hour of labour falls, there is a movement down along the productivity curve PC_1. Capital per hour of labour and real GDP per hour of labour fall and keep falling as long as the population grows.

This process ends when real GDP per hour of labour is back at the subsistence level at point C on productivity curve PC_1. The population stops growing and capital per hour of labour stops falling.

Repeated advances in technology play out in the same way as the advance that we've just studied. No matter how productive our economy becomes, population growth lowers capital per hour of labour and drives real GDP per hour of labour towards the sub-

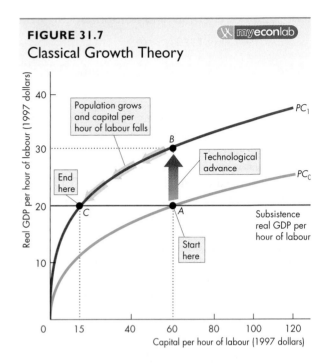

FIGURE 31.7
Classical Growth Theory

The economy starts out at point A with capital per hour of labour of $60 and real GDP per hour of labour of $20—the subsistence level—on productivity curve PC_0. A technological advance shifts the productivity curve upward to PC_1 and the economy moves to point B. The population grows, and both capital and real GDP per hour of labour decrease. The process ends at point C when real GDP per hour of labour is back at its subsistence level.

sistence level. Living standards temporarily improve while the population is expanding, but when the population expansion ends, the standard of living is back at the subsistence level.

Classical Theory and Capital Accumulation

In the story you've just worked through, the total quantity of capital didn't change. Suppose that people save and invest, so capital grows. Doesn't a growing quantity of capital prevent the dismal conclusion of classical theory? It does not. *Anything* that raises real GDP per hour of labour above the subsistence level triggers a population explosion that eventually wipes out the gains from greater productivity.

The dismal conclusion of classical growth theory is a direct consequence of the assumption that the population explodes if real GDP per hour of labour exceeds the subsistence level. To avoid this conclusion, we need a different view of population growth.

The neoclassical growth theory that we'll now study provides a different view.

Neoclassical Growth Theory

Neoclassical growth theory is the proposition that real GDP per person grows because technological change induces a level of saving and investment that makes capital per hour of labour grow. Growth ends only if technological change stops.

Robert Solow of MIT suggested the most popular version of neoclassical growth theory in the 1950s. But Frank Ramsey of Cambridge University in England first developed this theory in the 1920s.

Neoclassical theory's big break with its classical predecessor is its view about population growth. So we'll begin our account of neoclassical theory by examining its views about population growth.

The Neoclassical Economics of Population Growth The population explosion of eighteenth-century Europe that created the classical theory of population eventually ended. The birth rate fell, and while the population continued to increase, its rate of increase became moderate. This slowdown in population growth seemed to make the classical theory less relevant. It also eventually led to the development of a modern economic theory of population growth.

The modern view is that although the population growth rate is influenced by economic factors, the influence is not a simple and mechanical one like that proposed by the classical economists. Key among the economic influences on population growth is the opportunity cost of a woman's time. As women's wage rates increase and their job opportunities expand, the opportunity cost of having children increases. Faced with a higher opportunity cost, families choose to have fewer children and the birth rate falls.

A second economic influence works on the death rate. The technological advance that brings increased productivity and increased incomes brings advances in health care that extend lives.

These two opposing economic forces influence the population growth rate. As incomes increase, both the birth rate and the death rate decrease. It turns out that these opposing forces almost offset each other, so the rate of population growth is independent of the rate of economic growth.

This modern view of population growth and the historical trends that support it contradict the views of the classical economists and call into question the modern doomsday conclusion that the planet will one day be swamped with too many people to feed.

Neoclassical growth theory adopts this modern view of population growth. Forces other than real GDP and its growth rate determine population growth.

Technological Change In the neoclassical theory, the rate of technological change influences the rate of economic growth but economic growth does not influence the pace of technological change. It is assumed that technological change results from chance. When we get lucky, we have rapid technological change, and when bad luck strikes, the pace of technological advance slows.

Target Rate of Return and Saving The key assumption in the neoclassical growth theory concerns saving. Other things remaining the same, the higher the real interest rate, the greater is the amount that people save. To decide how much to save, people compare the real interest rate with a *target rate of return*. If the real interest rate exceeds the target rate of return, saving is sufficient to make capital per hour of labour grow. If the target rate of return exceeds the real interest rate, saving is not sufficient to maintain the current level of capital per hour of labour, so capital per hour of labour shrinks. And if the real interest rate equals a target rate of return, saving is just sufficient to maintain the quantity of capital per hour of labour at its current level.

The Basic Neoclassical Idea To understand neoclassical growth theory, imagine the world of the mid-1950s, when Robert Solow is explaining his idea. Canadians are enjoying post–World War II prosperity. Income per person is around $12,000 a year in today's money. The population is growing at about 1 percent a year. People are saving and investing about 20 percent of their incomes, enough to keep the quantity of capital per hour of labour constant. Income per person is growing, but not by much.

Then technology begins to advance at a more rapid pace across a range of activities. The transistor revolutionizes an emerging electronics industry. New plastics revolutionize the manufacture of household appliances. The national highway system revolutionizes road transportation. Jet airliners start to replace piston-engine airplanes and speed air transportation.

These technological advances bring new profit opportunities. Businesses expand, and new businesses are created to exploit the newly available profitable technologies. Investment and saving increase. The economy enjoys new levels of prosperity and growth. But will the prosperity last? And will the growth last? Neoclassical growth theory says that the *prosperity* will last but the *growth* will not last unless technology keeps advancing.

According to the neoclassical growth theory, the prosperity will persist because there is no classical population growth to induce lower wages.

But growth will stop if technology stops advancing, for two related reasons. First, high profit rates that result from technological change bring increased saving and capital accumulation. But second, capital accumulation eventually results in diminishing returns that lower the rate of return, and that eventually decrease saving and slow the rate of capital accumulation.

Neoclassical Theory and the Productivity Curve

Figure 31.8 illustrates the neoclassical growth theory using the productivity curve. Initially, the productivity curve is PC_0 and the economy is at point A, with $60 of capital per hour of labour and real GDP per hour of labour of $20.

The slope of the productivity curve measures the additional output that results from an additional unit of capital—the marginal product of capital or real interest rate. People have a target rate of return that can be illustrated by a straight line with a slope equal to the target rate of return.

At point A on productivity curve PC_0, the slope of the PC curve equals the slope of the target rate of return line. If the quantity of capital per hour of labour were less than $60, the real interest rate would exceed the target rate of return and capital per hour of labour would grow. If the quantity of capital per hour of labour were greater than $60, the real interest rate would be less than the target rate of return and capital per hour of labour would shrink. But when the quantity of capital per hour of labour is $60, the real interest rate equals the target rate of return and capital per hour of labour is constant.

Now a technological advance occurs that shifts the productivity curve upward to PC_1. The economy now moves to point B on PC_1, and real GDP per hour of labour rises to $30. It is at this point in the classical theory that forces kick in to drive real GDP per hour of labour back to the subsistence level. But in the neoclassical theory, no such forces operate. Instead, at point B, the real interest rate exceeds the target rate of return. (You can see why by comparing

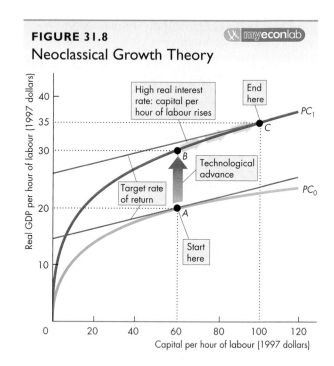

FIGURE 31.8   (X) myeconlab

Neoclassical Growth Theory

The economy starts on productivity curve PC_0 at point A. The slope of the productivity curve measures the rate of return, so at point A the rate of return equals the target rate of return. A technological advance shifts the productivity curve upward to PC_1 and the economy moves to point B. The rate of return exceeds the target rate of return, and the quantity of capital per hour of labour increases—a movement up along the productivity curve PC_1. Growth ends when the rate of return again equals the target rate of return at point C.

the slopes of PC_1 at point B and the target rate of return line.)

With a high real interest rate available, saving and investment increase and the quantity of capital per hour of labour increases. There is a movement up along the productivity curve PC_1, and real GDP per hour of labour increases.

This growth process eventually ends because, as the quantity of capital per hour of labour increases, the real interest rate falls. At point C, where the process ends, the real interest rate again equals the target rate of return.

Throughout the process you've just studied, real GDP per hour of labour grows but the growth rate gradually decreases and eventually growth ends.

But if another advance in technology occurs, the process you've just seen repeats. Ongoing advances in technology constantly increase the rate of return, inducing the saving that increases capital per hour of labour. The growth process persists as long as technology advances. And the growth rate fluctuates because technological progress occurs at a variable rate.

A Problem with Neoclassical Growth Theory All economies have access to the same technologies, and capital is free to roam the globe seeking the highest available rate of return. Given these facts, neoclassical growth theory implies that growth rates and income levels per person around the globe will converge. While there is some sign of convergence among the rich countries, as Fig. 31.2(a) shows, convergence is slow, and it does not appear to be imminent for all countries, as Fig. 31.2(b) shows.

New growth theory attempts to overcome this shortcoming of neoclassical growth theory. It also attempts to explain how the rate of technological change is determined.

New Growth Theory

New growth theory holds that real GDP per person grows because of the choices people make in the pursuit of profit and that growth can persist indefinitely. Paul Romer of Stanford University developed this theory during the 1980s, but the ideas go back to the work by Joseph Schumpeter during the 1930s and 1940s.

The theory begins with two facts about market economies:

- Discoveries result from choices.
- Discoveries bring profit and competition destroys profit.

Discoveries and Choices When people discover a new product or technique, they think of themselves as being lucky. They are right. But the pace at which new discoveries are made—and at which technology advances—is not determined by chance. It depends on how many people are looking for a new technology and how intensively they are looking.

Discoveries and Profits Profit is the spur to technological change. The forces of competition squeeze profits, so to increase profit, people constantly seek either lower-cost methods of production or new and better

products for which people are willing to pay a higher price. Inventors can maintain a profit for several years by taking out a patent or copyright. But eventually, a new discovery is copied, and profits disappear.

Two further facts play a key role in the new growth theory:

- Discoveries are a public capital good.
- Knowledge is capital that is not subject to the law of diminishing returns.

Discoveries Are a Public Capital Good Economists call a good a *public good* when no one can be excluded from using it and when one person's use does not prevent others from using it. National defence is one example of a public good. Knowledge is another.

When in 1992, Marc Andreesen and his friend Eric Bina developed a browser they called Mosaic, they laid the foundation for Netscape Navigator and Internet Explorer, two pieces of capital that have increased productivity unimaginably.

While patents and copyrights protect the inventors or creators of new products and production processes and enable them to reap the returns from their innovative ideas, once a new discovery has been made, everyone can benefit from its use. And one person's use of a new discovery does not prevent others from using it. Your use of a Web browser doesn't prevent someone else from using that same browser simultaneously.

Because knowledge is a public good, as the benefits of a new discovery spread, free resources become available. These resources are free because nothing is given up when they are used. They have a zero opportunity cost. Knowledge is even more special because it is not subject to diminishing returns.

Knowledge Capital Is Not Subject to Diminishing Returns Production is subject to diminishing returns when one resource is fixed and the quantity of another resource changes. Adding labour to a fixed amount of equipment or adding equipment to a fixed amount of labour both bring diminishing marginal product—diminishing returns.

But increasing the stock of knowledge makes labour and machines more productive. Knowledge capital does not bring diminishing returns.

The fact that knowledge capital does *not* experience diminishing returns is the central novel proposition of the new growth theory. And the implication of this simple and appealing idea is astonishing. The new growth theory has no growth-stopping mechanism like those of the other two theories. As physical capital accumulates, the rate of return falls. But the incentive to innovate and earn a higher profit becomes stronger. So innovation occurs, which increases the rate of return. Real GDP per hour of labour grows indefinitely as people find new technologies that yield a higher rate of return.

The growth rate depends on people's ability to innovate and the rate of return. Over the years, the ability to innovate has changed. The invention of language and writing (the two most basic human capital tools) and later the development of the scientific method and the establishment of universities and research institutions brought huge increases in the rate of return. Today, a deeper understanding of genes is bringing profit in a growing biotechnology industry. And astonishing advances in computer technology are creating an explosion of profit opportunities in a wide range of information-age industries.

New Growth Theory and the Productivity Curve

Figure 31.9 illustrates new growth theory. Like Fig. 31.8, which illustrates neoclassical growth theory, Fig. 31.9 contains a productivity curve and a target rate of return line.

But unlike in neoclassical theory, the productivity curve in the new growth theory never stands still. The pursuit of profit means that technology is always advancing and human capital is always growing. The result is an ever upward-shifting PC curve. As physical capital is accumulated, diminishing returns lower its rate of return. But ever-advancing productivity counteracts this tendency and keeps the rate of return above the target rate of return curve.

Advancing technology and human capital growth keep the PC curve shifting upward in Fig. 31.9 from PC_0 to PC_1 to PC_2 and beyond. As the productivity curve shifts upward, capital per hour of labour and real GDP per hour of labour increase together along the line labelled "Ak line."

The new growth theory implies that although the productivity curve shows diminishing returns, if capital is interpreted more broadly as physical capital, human capital, and the technologies they embody, then real GDP per hour of labour grows at the same rate as the growth in capital per hour of labour. Real GDP per hour of labour is proportional to capital per hour of labour.

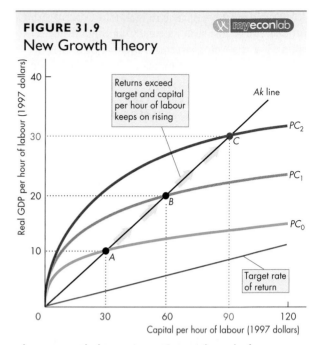

FIGURE 31.9
New Growth Theory

In new growth theory, economic growth results from incentives to innovate and from capital that does not experience diminishing returns. The productivity curve, PC, keeps shifting upward, and real GDP per hour of labour and capital per hour of labour grow along the Ak line.

Real GDP per hour of labour y is related to capital per hour of labour k by the equation:

$$y = Ak.$$

In Fig 31.9, $A = (1/3)$. When capital per hour of labour is $30, real GDP per hour of labour is $10 at point A. People look for yet more profit and accumulate yet more capital. The economy expands to point B, with capital per hour of labour of $60 and real GDP per hour of labour of $20. In pursuit of further profit, technology keeps advancing and capital per hour of labour rises to $90 with real GDP per hour of labour of $30, at point C. Real GDP per hour of labour and capital per hour of labour increase without limit.

A Perpetual Motion Economy The new growth theory sees the economy as a perpetual motion machine, which Fig. 31.10 illustrates. Insatiable wants lead us to pursue profit, innovate, and create new and better products. New firms start up and old firms go out of business. As firms start up and die, jobs are created and destroyed. New and better jobs

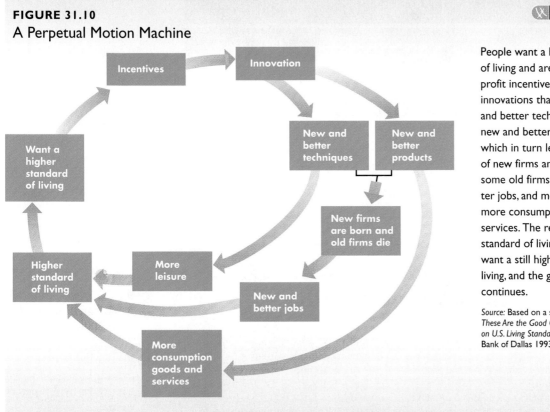

FIGURE 31.10

A Perpetual Motion Machine

People want a higher standard of living and are spurred by profit incentives to make the innovations that lead to new and better techniques and new and better products, which in turn lead to the birth of new firms and the death of some old firms, new and better jobs, and more leisure and more consumption goods and services. The result is a higher standard of living. But people want a still higher standard of living, and the growth process continues.

Source: Based on a similar figure in *These Are the Good Old Days: A Report on U.S. Living Standards*, Federal Reserve Bank of Dallas 1993 Annual Report.

lead to more leisure and more consumption. But our insatiable wants are still there, so the process continues, going around and around a circle of wants, profits, innovation, and new products.

Sorting Out the Theories

Which theory is correct? Probably none, but they all teach us something of value. The classical theory reminds us that our physical resources are limited and that with no advances in technology, we must eventually hit diminishing returns. Neoclassical theory reaches essentially the same conclusion, but not because of a population explosion. Instead, it emphasizes diminishing returns to capital and reminds us that we cannot keep growth going just by accumulating physical capital. We must also advance technology and accumulate human capital. We must become more creative in our use of scarce resources. New growth theory emphasizes the possible capacity of human resources to innovate at a pace that offsets diminishing returns.

REVIEW QUIZ

1 What is the key idea of classical growth theory that leads to the dismal outcome?
2 What, according to the neoclassical growth theory, is the fundamental cause of economic growth?
3 What is the key proposition of the new growth theory that makes growth persist?

myeconlab **Study Plan 31.4**

◆ Economic growth is the single most decisive factor influencing a country's living standard. Another is the extent to which the country exploits its comparative advantage in international trade. We study this topic in the next chapter. Before embarking on this topic, take a look at *Reading Between the Lines* on pp. 750–751 and compare Canada's recent productivity growth with that of the United States.

Forecasting Economic Growth

THE GLOBE AND MAIL, NOVEMBER 14, 2005

Not everyone's pessimistic about productivity

Ottawa economist Stephen Poloz lives in a city where people are tearing their hair out over Canada's abysmal productivity record.

The country's prosperity is at stake, they argue, because for years, companies and workers have found few new ways to improve their efficiency, while the rest of the world — notably, the United States — zooms ahead.

Canada's standard of living will deteriorate, they say, unless the government cuts taxes and invests millions in new investment incentives, and unless the private sector becomes much more imaginative. They will be watching Finance Minister Ralph Goodale closely today when he delivers his mini-budget, to see whether he can give business what it needs to reverse the trend.

But Mr. Poloz, chief economist at Export Development Canada, isn't the least bit worried. He believes Canada's productivity is on the verge of a recovery, with or without the federal government's help.

"We believe it's happening," Mr. Poloz said in a recent interview.

Mr. Poloz is in a small but growing camp of experts who believe a turnaround in productivity is at hand, as Canadian companies discover the benefits of cheap imports, new technology, and low wages on the other side of the world.

But their arguments are met with skepticism from others who are as pessimistic as ever about Canada's prospects.

"I don't think we're about to see 3-per-cent productivity growth," said Andrew Sharpe, executive director of the Centre for the Study of Living Standards.

No one would disagree that Canada's productivity, defined as output as a percentage of hours, has been embarrassing these past few years. On average, Canada's productivity growth has hovered just above zero since 2000. The U.S., on the other hand, has seen productivity grow by an average of 3.8 per cent since the start of the decade.

But according to Mr. Poloz, this is about to change. ... he says, Canadian companies of all sizes are discovering how to cut costs and increase output by doing more business offshore.

Reprinted with permission of *The Globe and Mail*.

Essence of the Story

■ Canadian productivity has barely changed since 2000.

■ During that same period, U.S. productivity has grown by 3.8 percent a year.

■ Economist Stephen Poloz believes that things are about to change and that Canadian productivity growth is starting to increase.

■ Economist Andrew Sharp doesn't think we'll see 3 percent a year productivity growth.

Economic Analysis

■ Canadian real GDP per person has never been as high as that of the United States.

■ During the last 45 years (since 1961), Canadian real GDP per person has fluctuated between a low of 81 percent and a high of 92 percent of U.S. real GDP per person.

■ Figure 1 shows the data. Relative to U.S. real GDP per person, Canadian real GDP per person was steady at 85 percent during the 1960s, climbed through the 1970s, fell during the 1980s to a low in 1993, increased through 2002, and fell through 2004.

■ What explains these changes in Canadian real GDP per person relative to the U.S. level?

■ Three broad possible answers are:
(1) Canadians work fewer hours than Americans.
(2) Canadians have less capital per unit of output than Americans.
(3) Canadians have lower overall productivity—total factor productivity—than Americans.

■ Figure 2 shows that the first two possibilities do not explain the trends.

■ Hour worked per Canadian have fluctuated relative to U.S. labour hours per person, and Canadian work hours did fall during the late 1980s and much of the 1990s. But Canadian work hours increased after 1997 and by 2004 exceeded U.S. hours.

■ Capital per unit of output (the capital output ratio) increased in Canada from 80 percent of the U.S. level in 1961 to 100 percent during the 2000s.

■ Figure 2 shows growth during the decade 1992–2002. Over this period, Canada tops the table and the United States places second. But the United States was top until 2000.

■ Figure 3 shows the source of Canada's problem. Total factor productivity in Canada collapsed from 99 percent of the U.S. level in 1974 to 88 percent in 1992. It increased somewhat through 2000 but then decreased again.

■ The reasons for Canada's poor growth of total factor productivity are complex and controversial.

■ If Stephen Poloz is to be proved correct, it is Canada's total factor productivity that must improve.

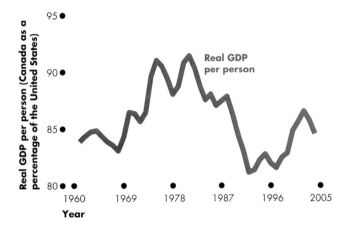

Figure 1 Real GDP compared

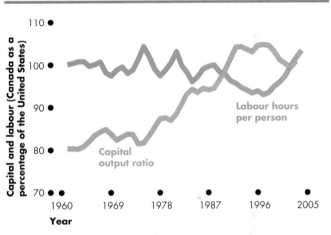

Figure 2 Factor inputs compared

Figure 3 Productivity compared

SUMMARY

KEY POINTS

Long-Term Growth Trends (pp. 734–736)

- Between 1926 and 2004, real GDP per person in Canada grew at an average rate of 2.2 percent a year. Growth was most rapid during the 1960s and slowest during the 1980s.
- The real GDP per person gaps between Canada and Hong Kong, Korea, Taiwan, and China have narrowed. The gaps between Canada and Central and South America, Africa, and Central Europe have widened.

The Causes of Economic Growth: A First Look (pp. 737–738)

- Economic growth requires an *incentive* system created by markets, property rights, and monetary exchange.
- Economic growth occurs when people save, invest in physical and human capital, and discover new technologies.

Growth Accounting (pp. 739–742)

- Growth accounting measures the contributions of capital accumulation and technological change to productivity growth.
- Growth accounting uses the productivity curve and the one-third rule: A 1 percent increase in capital per hour of labour brings an increase in real GDP per hour of labour of one-third of 1 percent.
- During the productivity growth slowdown of the 1970s, technological change made no contribution to real GDP growth.
- It might be possible to achieve faster growth by stimulating saving, stimulating research and development, targeting high-technology industries, encouraging more international trade, and improving the quality of education.

Growth Theories (pp. 743–749)

- In classical theory, when technological advances increase real GDP per person above the *subsistence* level, a population explosion brings diminishing returns to labour and real GDP per person returns to the subsistence level.
- In neoclassical growth theory, when technological advances increase saving and investment, an increase in the capital stock brings diminishing returns to capital and eventually, without further technological change, the capital stock and real GDP per person stop growing.
- In new growth theory, when technological advances increase saving and investment, an increase in the capital stock *does not* bring diminishing returns to capital and growth persists indefinitely.

KEY FIGURES

Figure 31.1   Economic Growth in Canada: 1926–2004, 734
Figure 31.5   How Productivity Grows, 740
Figure 31.6   Growth Accounting and the Productivity Growth Slowdown, 741
Figure 31.7   Classical Growth Theory, 744
Figure 31.8   Neoclassical Growth Theory, 746
Figure 31.9   New Growth Theory, 748

KEY TERMS

Aggregate production function, 739
Classical growth theory, 743
Growth accounting, 739
Labour productivity, 739
Law of diminishing returns, 740
Neoclassical growth theory, 745
New growth theory, 747
One-third rule, 740
Productivity curve, 739
Subsistence real wage rate, 744

PROBLEMS

Go to ⓧ myeconlab for solutions to odd-numbered problems and additional exercises.

1. The following information has been discovered about the economy of Longland. The economy's productivity curve is

Capital per hour of labour (1997 dollars per hour)	Real GDP per hour of labour (1997 dollars per hour)
10	3.80
20	5.70
30	7.13
40	8.31
50	9.35
60	10.29
70	11.14
80	11.94

Does this economy conform to the one-third rule? If so, explain why. If not, explain why not and explain what rule, if any, it does conform to. Explain how you would do the growth accounting for this economy.

2. The following information has been discovered about the economy of Flatland. The economy's productivity curve is

Capital per hour of labour (1997 dollars per hour)	Real GDP per hour of labour (1997 dollars per hour)
20	6.00
40	7.50
60	8.44
80	9.14
100	9.72
120	10.20
140	10.62
160	11.00

Does this economy conform to the one-third rule? If so, explain why. If not, explain why not and explain what rule, if any, it does conform to. Explain how you would do the growth accounting for this economy.

3. In Longland, described in problem 1, capital per hour of labour in 2003 was $40 and real GDP per hour of labour was $8.31. In 2005, capital per hour of labour was $50 and real GDP per hour of labour was $10.29 an hour.

a. Does Longland experience diminishing returns? Explain why or why not.
b. Use growth accounting to find the contribution of the change in capital between 2003 and 2005 to the growth of productivity in Longland.
c. Use growth accounting to find the contribution of technological change between 2003 and 2005 to the growth of productivity in Longland.

4. In Flatland, described in problem 2, capital per hour of labour in 2003 was $60 and real GDP per hour of labour was $8.44. In 2005, capital per hour of labour was $120 and real GDP per hour of labour was $12.74 an hour.

a. Does Flatland experience diminishing returns? Explain why or why not.
b. Use growth accounting to find the contribution of the change in capital between 2003 and 2005 to the growth of productivity in Flatland.
c. Use growth accounting to find the contribution of technological change between 2003 and 2005 to the growth of productivity in Flatland.

5. The following information has been discovered about the economy of Cape Despair. Subsistence real GDP per hour of labour is $15. Whenever real GDP per hour rises above this level, the population grows, and when real GDP per hour of labour falls below this level, the population falls. The productivity curve in Cape Despair is as follows:

Capital per hour of labour (1997 dollars per hour)	Real GDP per hour of labour (1997 dollars per hour)
20	8
40	15
60	21
80	26
100	30
120	33
140	35
160	36

Initially, the population of Cape Despair is constant, and real GDP per hour of labour is at its subsistence level. Then a technological advance shifts the productivity curve upward by $7 at each level of capital per hour of labour.

a. What are the initial capital per hour of labour and real GDP per hour of labour?

b. What happens to real GDP per hour of labour immediately following the technological advance?

c. What happens to the population growth rate following the technological advance?

d. What is the eventual quantity of capital per hour of labour in Cape Despair?

6. Martha's Island is an economy that behaves according to the neoclassical growth model. The economy has no growth, a target rate of return of 10 percent a year, and the following productivity curve:

Capital per hour of labour (1997 dollars per hour)	Real GDP per hour of labour (1997 dollars per hour)
40	16
80	30
120	42
160	52
200	60
240	66
280	70
320	72

A technological advance shifts the productivity curve upward.

a. What is the initial capital per hour of labour on Martha's Island?

b. What is the initial real GDP per hour of labour?

c. What happens to the real interest rate immediately following the technological advance?

d. What happens to the return on capital and the quantity of capital per hour of labour?

7. Romeria is a country that behaves according to the predictions of new growth theory. The target rate is 3 percent a year. A technological advance increases the demand for capital and raises the rate of return to 5 percent a year. Describe the events that happen in Romeria and contrast them with the events in Martha's Island in problem 6.

8. Suppose that in Romeria, described in problem 7, technological advance slows and the rate of return falls to 3 percent a year. Describe what happens in Romeria.

CRITICAL THINKING

1. Study *Reading Between the Lines* on pp. 750–751 and then answer the following questions:

a. How does the growth rate of real GDP per person in Canada compare with that of the United States?

b. What is the source of Canada's slower growth of real GDP per person. Distinguish among the contrubutions of labour, capital, and total factor productivity.

c. Suppose someone argued that Canada's growth of real GDP per person appears to be slower than that of the United States because Canada has moved from above full employment to below full employment. Explain why that argument is wrong.

2. Is faster economic growth always a good thing? Argue the case for faster growth and the case for slower growth and then reach a conclusion on whether Canadian growth should be increased or decreased.

WEB EXERCISES

Use the links on (X myeconlab) **to work the following exercises.**

1. Go to the Penn World Table Web site and obtain data on real GDP per person for Canada, China, South Africa, and Mexico since 1960.

a. Draw a graph of the data.

b. Which country has the lowest real GDP per person and which has the highest?

c. Which country has experienced the fastest growth rate since 1960 and which the slowest?

d. Explain why the growth rates in these four countries are ranked in the order you have discovered.

e. Obtain data for any four other countries that interest you. Describe and explain the patterns that you find for these countries.

2. Write a memo to your member of Parliament in which you set out the policies you believe the Canadian government must follow to speed up the growth rate of real GDP in Canada.

Trading with the World

Silk Routes and Sucking Sounds

Since ancient times, people have expanded their trading as far as technology allowed. Marco Polo opened up the silk route between Europe and China in the thirteenth century. Today, container ships laden with cars and electronics and Boeing 747s stuffed with farm-fresh foods ply sea and air routes, carrying billions of dollars' worth of goods. Why do people go to such great lengths to trade with those in other nations?

In 1994, Canada entered into a free trade agreement with the United States and Mexico—the North American Free Trade Agreement, or NAFTA. Some people predicted a "giant sucking sound" as jobs were transferred from high-wage Michigan and Ontario to low-wage Mexico. Can we compete with a country that pays its workers a fraction of Canadian wages? Are there any industries, besides perhaps the software and movie industries, in which we have an advantage?

Canada exports lumber to the United States for home building. But U.S. lumber producers say that Canadian producers receive an unfair subsidy from their government, so the United States has imposed a tariff on Canadian lumber imports. Do tariffs benefit the importing country? We examine this question in *Reading Between the Lines*.

◆ In this chapter, we're going to learn about international trade and discover how *all* nations can gain from trading with other nations. We'll discover that all nations can compete, no matter how high their wages. We'll also explain why, despite the fact that international trade brings benefits to all, governments restrict trade.

After studying this chapter, you will be able to

- Describe the trends and patterns in international trade

- Explain comparative advantage and explain why all countries can gain from international trade

- Explain the effects of international trade restrictions

- Explain the arguments for trade restrictions and why they are flawed

- Describe a country's balance of payments accounts and explain what determines the current account balance

- Describe the North American Free Trade Agreement

Patterns and Trends in International Trade

THE GOODS AND SERVICES THAT WE BUY FROM people in other countries are called **imports**. The goods and services that we sell to people in other countries are called **exports**. What are the most important things that we import and export? Most people would probably guess that a rich nation such as Canada imports raw materials and exports manufactured goods. Although that is one feature of Canadian international trade, it is not its most important feature. The vast bulk of our exports *and* imports is manufactured goods. We sell foreigners earth-moving equipment, airplanes, telecommunications equipment, and scientific equipment. We buy televisions, DVDs, blue jeans, and T-shirts from foreigners. Also, we are a major exporter of agricultural products and raw materials. We also import and export a huge volume of services.

Trade in Goods

Of the goods that we trade, manufactured goods account for 74 percent of our exports and 84 percent of our imports. Industrial materials (raw materials and semimanufactured items) account for 44 percent of our exports and 28 percent of our imports, and agricultural products account for only 7 percent of our exports and 5 percent of our imports. Our largest individual export and import items are capital goods and automobiles.

But goods account for only 87 percent of our exports and 83 percent of our imports. The rest of our international trade is in services.

Trade in Services

You may be wondering how a country can "export" and "import" services. Here are some examples.

If you take a vacation in France and travel there on an Air France flight from Montreal, you import transportation services from France. The money you spend in France on hotel bills and restaurant meals is also classified as the import of services. Similarly, the money spent by a French student on vacation in Canada is a Canadian export of services to France.

When we import TV sets from South Korea, the owner of the ship that transports them might be Greek and the company that insures them might be British. The payments that we make for the transportation and insurance are Canadian imports of services. Similarly, when a Canadian shipping company transports timber from British Columbia to Tokyo, the transportation cost is a Canadian export of a service to Japan. Our international trade in these types of services is large and growing.

Geographical Patterns of International Trade

Canada has trading links with every part of the world, but the United States is our biggest trading partner. In 2004, 82 percent of our exports went to the United States and 69 percent of our imports came from the United States. Our trade with the European Union is also large—6 percent of our exports and 10 percent of our imports in 2004. Other trading partners include the countries of Latin America and Japan. But our trade with Japan is only 2 percent of exports and 3 percent of imports.

Trends in the Volume of Trade

In 1978, we exported 25 percent of total output and imported 25 percent of the goods and services that we bought. In 2004, we exported 44 percent of total output and imported 39 percent of the goods and services that we bought.

On the export side, capital goods, automobiles, food, and raw materials have remained large items and held a roughly constant share of total exports. But the composition of imports has changed. Food and raw material imports have fallen steadily. Imports of fuel increased during the 1970s but decreased during the 1980s. Imports of machinery have grown and today approach 30 percent of total imports.

Net Exports and International Borrowing

The value of exports minus the value of imports is called **net exports**. In 2004, Canadian net exports were $54 billion. Our exports were $54 billion more than our imports. When we export more than we import, as we did in 2004, we lend to foreigners or buy some of their assets. When we import more than we export, we borrow from foreigners or sell some of our assets to them.

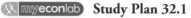 **Study Plan 32.1**

The Gains from International Trade

THE FUNDAMENTAL FORCE THAT GENERATES international trade is *comparative advantage*. And the basis of comparative advantage is divergent *opportunity costs*. You met these ideas in Chapter 2, when we learned about comparative advantages and the gains from specialization and trade between Liz and Joe.

Joe specializes in producing just one good, but most nations, like Liz, do not go to the extreme of specializing in a single good and importing everything else. Like Liz and Joe, nations can increase the consumption of all goods if they redirect their scarce resources towards the production of those goods and services in which they have a comparative advantage.

To see how this outcome occurs, we'll apply the same basic ideas that we learned in the case of Liz and Joe to trade among nations. We'll begin by recalling how we can use the production possibilities frontier to measure opportunity cost. Then we'll see how divergent opportunity costs bring comparative advantage and how by moving resources to increase production of the good in which each country has a comparative advantage countries can gain from international trade, just as Liz and Joe did.

Opportunity Cost in Farmland

Farmland (a fictitious country) can produce grain and cars at any point inside or along its production possibilities frontier, *PPF*, shown in Fig. 32.1. (We're holding constant the output of all the other goods that Farmland produces.) The Farmers (the people of Farmland) are consuming all the grain and cars that they produce, and they are operating at point *A* in the figure. That is, Farmland is producing and consuming 15 million tonnes of grain and 8 million cars each year. What is the opportunity cost of a car in Farmland?

We can answer that question by calculating the slope of the production possibilities frontier at point *A*. The magnitude of the slope of the frontier measures the opportunity cost of one good in terms of the other. To measure the slope of the frontier at point *A*, place a straight line tangential to the frontier at point *A* and calculate the slope of that straight line. Recall that the formula for the slope of a line is the change in the value of the variable measured on the *y*-axis divided by the change in the value of the variable

measured on the *x*-axis as we move along the line. Here, the variable measured on the *y*-axis is millions of tonnes of grain, and the variable measured on the *x*-axis is millions of cars. So the slope is the change in the number of tonnes of grain divided by the change in the number of cars.

As you can see from the red triangle at point *A* in the figure, if the number of cars produced increases by 2 million, grain production decreases by 18 million tonnes. So the magnitude of the slope is 18 million divided by 2 million, which equals 9. That is, to get 1 more car, the people of Farmland must give up 9 tonnes of grain. So the opportunity cost of 1 car is 9 tonnes of grain. Equivalently, 9 tonnes of grain cost 1 car. For the people of Farmland, these opportunity costs are the prices they face. The price of a car is 9 tonnes of grain, and the price of 9 tonnes of grain is 1 car.

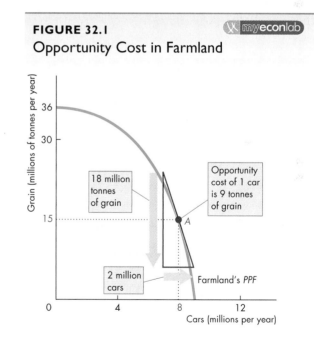

FIGURE 32.1   myeconlab
Opportunity Cost in Farmland

Farmland produces and consumes 15 million tonnes of grain and 8 million cars a year. That is, it produces and consumes at point A on its production possibilities frontier. Opportunity cost is equal to the magnitude of the slope of the production possibilities frontier. The red triangle tells us that at point A, 18 million tonnes of grain must be forgone to get 2 million cars. That is, at point A, 2 million cars cost 18 million tonnes of grain. Equivalently, 1 car costs 9 tonnes of grain or 9 tonnes of grain cost 1 car.

Opportunity Cost in Mobilia

Figure 32.2 shows the production possibilities frontier of Mobilia (another fictitious country). Like the Farmers, the Mobilians consume all the grain and cars that they produce. Mobilia consumes 18 million tonnes of grain a year and 4 million cars, at point A'.

Let's calculate the opportunity costs in Mobilia. At point A', the opportunity cost of a car is equal to the magnitude of the slope of the red line tangential to the production possibilities frontier, *PPF*. You can see from the red triangle that the magnitude of the slope of Mobilia's production possibilities frontier is 6 million tonnes of grain divided by 6 million cars, which equals 1 tonne of grain per car. To get 1 more car, the Mobilians must give up 1 tonne of grain. So the opportunity cost of 1 car is 1 tonne of grain, or equivalently, the opportunity cost of 1 tonne of grain is 1 car. These are the prices faced in Mobilia.

Comparative Advantage

Cars are cheaper in Mobilia than in Farmland. One car costs 9 tonnes of grain in Farmland but only

1 tonne of grain in Mobilia. But grain is cheaper in Farmland than in Mobilia—9 tonnes of grain cost only 1 car in Farmland, while that same amount of grain costs 9 cars in Mobilia.

Mobilia has a comparative advantage in car production. Farmland has a comparative advantage in grain production. A country has a comparative advantage in producing a good if it can produce that good at a lower opportunity cost than any other country. Let's see how opportunity cost differences and comparative advantage generate gains from international trade.

The Gains from Trade: Cheaper to Buy Than to Produce

If Mobilia bought grain for what it costs Farmland to produce it, then Mobilia could buy 9 tonnes of grain for 1 car. That is much lower than the cost of growing grain in Mobilia, for there it costs 9 cars to produce 9 tonnes of grain. If the Mobilians can buy grain at the low Farmland price, they will reap some gains.

If the Farmers can buy cars for what it costs Mobilia to produce them, they will be able to obtain a car for 1 tonne of grain. Because it costs 9 tonnes of grain to produce a car in Farmland, the Farmers would gain from such an opportunity.

In this situation, it makes sense for Mobilians to buy their grain from Farmers and for Farmers to buy their cars from Mobilians. But at what price will Farmland and Mobilia engage in mutually beneficial international trade?

The Terms of Trade

The quantity of grain that Farmland must pay Mobilia for a car is Farmland's **terms of trade** with Mobilia. Because Canada exports and imports many different goods and services, we measure the terms of trade in the real world as an index number that averages the terms of trade over all the items we trade.

The forces of international supply and demand determine the terms of trade. Figure 32.3 illustrates these forces in the Farmland–Mobilia international car market. The quantity of cars *traded internationally* is measured on the *x*-axis. On the *y*-axis, we measure the price of a car. This price is expressed as the *terms of trade*: tonnes of grain per car. If no international trade takes place, the price of a car in Farmland is 9 tonnes of grain, its opportunity cost, indicated by

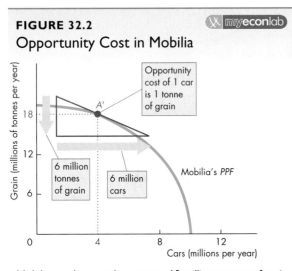

FIGURE 32.2
Opportunity Cost in Mobilia

Mobilia produces and consumes 18 million tonnes of grain and 4 million cars a year. That is, it produces and consumes at point A' on its production possibilities frontier. Opportunity cost is equal to the magnitude of the slope of the production possibilities frontier. The red triangle tells us that at point A', 6 million tonnes of grain must be forgone to get 6 million cars. That is, at point A', 6 million cars cost 6 million tonnes of grain. Equivalently, 1 car costs 1 tonne of grain or 1 tonne of grain costs 1 car.

FIGURE 32.3

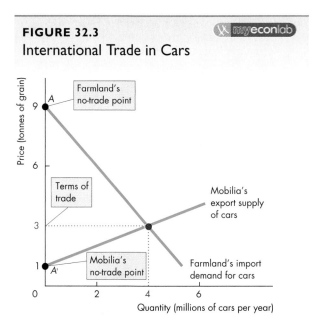

International Trade in Cars

myeconlab

Farmland's import demand curve for cars is downward sloping, and Mobilia's export supply curve of cars is upward sloping. Without international trade, the price of a car is 9 tonnes of grain in Farmland (point A) and 1 tonne of grain in Mobilia (point A').

With free international trade, the price (terms of trade) is determined where the export supply curve intersects the import demand curve: 3 tonnes of grain per car. At that price, 4 million cars a year are imported by Farmland and exported by Mobilia. The value of grain exported by Farmland and imported by Mobilia is 12 million tonnes a year, the quantity required to pay for the cars imported.

point A in the figure. Again, if no trade takes place, the price of a car in Mobilia is 1 tonne of grain, its opportunity cost, indicated by point A' in the figure. The no-trade points A and A' in Fig. 32.3 correspond to the points identified by those same letters in Figs. 32.1 and 32.2. The lower price of a car (terms of trade), the greater is the quantity of cars that the Farmers are willing to import from the Mobilians. This fact is illustrated by the downward-sloping curve, which shows Farmland's import demand for cars.

The Mobilians respond in the opposite direction. The higher the price of a car (terms of trade), the greater is the quantity of cars that Mobilians are willing to export to Farmers. This fact is reflected in Mobilia's export supply of cars—the upward-sloping line in Fig. 32.3.

The international market in cars determines the equilibrium terms of trade (price) and quantity traded. This equilibrium occurs where the import demand curve intersects the export supply curve. In this case, the equilibrium terms of trade are 3 tonnes of grain per car. Mobilia exports and Farmland imports 4 million cars a year. Notice that the terms of trade are lower than the initial price in Farmland but higher than the initial price in Mobilia.

Balanced Trade

The number of cars exported by Mobilia—4 million a year—is exactly equal to the number of cars imported by Farmland. How does Farmland pay for its cars? The answer is by exporting grain. How much grain does Farmland export? You can find the answer by noticing that for 1 car, Farmland must pay 3 tonnes of grain. So for 4 million cars, Farmland pays 12 million tonnes of grain. Farmland's exports of grain are 12 million tonnes a year, and Mobilia imports this same quantity of grain.

Mobilia is exchanging 4 million cars for 12 million tonnes of grain each year, and Farmland is doing the opposite: exchanging 12 million tonnes of grain for 4 million cars. Trade is balanced between these two countries. The value received from exports equals the value paid out for imports.

Changes in Production and Consumption

We've seen that international trade makes it possible for Farmers to buy cars at a lower price than they can produce them and sell their grain for a higher price. International trade also enables Mobilians to sell their cars for a higher price and buy grain for a lower price. Both countries gain. How is it possible for *both* countries to gain? What are the changes in production and consumption that accompany these gains?

An economy that does not trade with other economies has identical production and consumption possibilities. Without trade, the economy can consume only what it produces. But with international trade, an economy can consume different quantities of goods from those that it produces. The production possibilities frontier describes the limit of what a country can produce, but it does not describe the limits to what it can consume. Figure 32.4 will help you to see the distinction between production possibilities and consumption possibilities when a country trades with other countries.

FIGURE 32.4

Expanding Consumption Possibilities

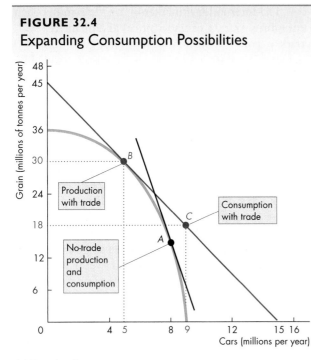

(a) Farmland

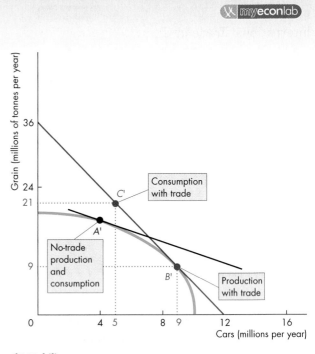

(b) Mobilia

With no international trade, the Farmers produce and consume at point *A* and the opportunity cost of a car is 9 tonnes of grain (the slope of the black line in part a). Also, with no international trade, the Mobilians produce and consume at point *A'* and the opportunity cost of 1 tonne of grain is 1 car (the slope of the black line in part b).

Goods can be exchanged internationally at a price of 3 tonnes of grain for 1 car along the red line in each part of the figure. In part (a), Farmland decreases its production of cars and increases its production of grain, moving from

A to *B*. It exports grain and imports cars, and it consumes at point *C*. The Farmers have more of both cars and grain than they would if they produced all their own consumption goods—at point *A*. In part (b), Mobilia increases car production and decreases grain production, moving from *A'* to *B'*. Mobilia exports cars and imports grain, and it consumes at point *C'*. The Mobilians have more of both cars and grain than they would if they produced all their own consumption goods—at point *A'*.

First of all, notice that the figure has two parts: part (a) for Farmland and part (b) for Mobilia. The production possibilities frontiers that you saw in Figs. 32.1 and 32.2 are reproduced here. The slopes of the two black lines in the figure represent the opportunity costs in the two countries when there is no international trade. Farmland produces and consumes at point *A*, and Mobilia produces and consumes at *A'*. Cars cost 9 tonnes of grain in Farmland and 1 tonne of grain in Mobilia.

Consumption Possibilities The red line in each part of Fig. 32.4 shows the country's consumption possibilities with international trade. These two red

lines have the same slope, and the magnitude of that slope is the opportunity cost of a car in terms of grain on the world market: 3 tonnes per car. The *slope* of the consumption possibilities line is common to both countries because its magnitude equals the *world* price. But the position of a country's consumption possibilities line depends on the country's production possibilities. A country cannot produce outside its production possibilities curve, so its consumption possibilities curve touches its production possibilities curve. Farmland could choose to consume at point *B* with no international trade or, with international trade, at any point on its red consumption possibilities line.

Free Trade Equilibrium With international trade, the producers of cars in Mobilia can get a higher price for their output. As a result, they increase car production. At the same time, grain producers in Mobilia get a lower price for their grain, and so they reduce grain production. Producers in Mobilia adjust their output by moving along their production possibilities frontier until the opportunity cost in Mobilia equals the world price (the opportunity cost in the world market). This situation arises when Mobilia is producing at point B' in Fig. 32.4(b).

But the Mobilians do not consume at point B'. That is, they do not increase their consumption of cars and decrease their consumption of grain. Instead, they sell some of their car production to Farmland in exchange for some of Farmland's grain. They trade internationally. But to see how that works out, we first need to check in with Farmland to see what's happening there.

In Farmland, producers of cars now get a lower price and producers of grain get a higher price. As a consequence, producers in Farmland decrease car production and increase grain production. They adjust their outputs by moving along the production possibilities frontier until the opportunity cost of a car in terms of grain equals the world price (the opportunity cost on the world market). They move to point B in part (a). But the Farmers do not consume at point B. Instead, they trade some of their additional grain production for the now cheaper cars from Mobilia.

The figure shows us the quantities consumed in the two countries. We saw in Fig. 32.3 that Mobilia exports 4 million cars a year and Farmland imports those cars. We also saw that Farmland exports 12 million tonnes of grain a year and Mobilia imports that grain. So Farmland's consumption of grain is 12 million tonnes a year less than it produces, and its consumption of cars is 4 million a year more than it produces. Farmland consumes at point C in Fig. 32.4(a).

Similarly, we know that Mobilia consumes 12 million tonnes of grain more than it produces and 4 million cars fewer than it produces. Mobilia consumes at point C' in Fig. 32.4(b).

Calculating the Gains from Trade

You can now literally see the gains from trade in Fig. 32.4. Without trade, Farmers produce and consume at A (part a)—a point on Farmland's production possibilities frontier. With international trade, Farmers

consume at point C in part (a)—a point *outside* the production possibilities frontier. At point C, Farmers are consuming 3 million tonnes of grain a year and 1 million cars a year more than before. These increases in consumption of both cars and grain, beyond the limits of the production possibilities frontier, are the Farmers' gains from international trade.

Mobilians also gain. Without trade, they consume at point A' in part (b)—a point on Mobilia's production possibilities frontier. With international trade, they consume at point C'—a point outside their production possibilities frontier. With international trade, Mobilia consumes 3 million tonnes of grain a year and 1 million cars a year more than it would without trade. These are the gains from international trade for Mobilia.

Gains for Both Countries

Trade between the Farmers and the Mobilians does not create a winner and a loser. Both countries gain. Farmers selling grain and Mobilians selling cars face an increased demand for their products because the net demand by foreigners is added to domestic demand. With an increase in demand, the price rises.

Farmers buying cars and Mobilians buying grain face an increased supply of these products because the net foreign supply is added to domestic supply. With an increase in supply, the price falls.

Gains from Trade in Reality

The gains from trade that we have just studied between Farmland and Mobilia in grain and cars occur in a model economy—in a world economy that we have imagined. But these same phenomena occur every day in the real global economy.

Comparative Advantage in the Global Economy
We buy TVs and DVD players from Korea, machinery from Europe, and fashion goods from Hong Kong. In exchange, we sell machinery, grain and lumber, airplanes, computers, and financial services. All this international trade is generated by comparative advantage, just like the international trade between Farmland and Mobilia in our model economy. All international trade arises from comparative advantage, even when trade is in similar goods such as tools and machines. At first thought, it seems puzzling that countries exchange manufactured goods. Why doesn't each developed country produce all the manufactured goods its citizens want to buy?

Trade in Similar Goods Why does Canada produce airplanes for export at the same time that Air Canada and our other airlines buy airplanes from the United States and Europe? Wouldn't it make more sense to produce all the airplanes that Air Canada and other Canadian airlines want to buy here in Canada? After all, we have access to the best technology available for producing planes. Aerospace workers in Canada are surely as productive as their fellow workers in the United States and Europe. So why does Canada have a comparative advantage in some types of airplanes and the United States and Europe in others?

Diversity of Taste and Economies of Scale The first part of the answer is that buyers have a large diversity of wants. Let's stick with the example of airplanes. Some airline operators sell time-share services in small executive jets, some airlines fly short routes in sparsely populated areas, some fly short routes in densely populated areas, some serve long-haul intercontinental routes that have heavy traffic, some serve long-haul intercontinental routes that have light traffic, some carry people and some specialize in cargo.

Because they face such highly varied markets, the airlines and other firms that offer air transportation services look for the types of airplanes that most closely match their wants. The large diversity in the characteristics of air transportation services means that airlines are willing to pay more for an airplane that matches their needs than they would be willing to pay for a single one-type-all-purpose airplane.

The second part of the answer to the puzzle is economies of scale—the tendency for the average cost to be lower, the larger the scale of production. In such situations, larger and larger production runs lead to ever lower average costs. Production of many goods, including airplanes, involves economies of scale. For example, if Bombardier makes only a handful of planes of a particular type and design, it must use production techniques that are much more labour-intensive and much less automated than those employed to make a hundred planes of a particular model. With short production runs and labour-intensive production techniques, costs are high. With very large production runs and automated assembly lines, production costs are much lower. But to obtain lower costs, the automated assembly lines have to produce a large number of planes.

It is the combination of diversity of wants and economies of scale that determines opportunity cost, produces comparative advantages, and generates such a large amount of international trade in similar commodities. With international trade, each airplane maker has the whole world market to serve. Each producer can specialize in a limited range of products and then sell its output to the entire world market.

This arrangement enables large production runs on the most popular planes to achieve economies of scale and low production costs.

The situation in the market for airplanes is also present in many other industries, especially those producing specialized equipment and parts. For example, Canada exports illustration software but imports database software, exports telecommunications systems but imports PCs, exports specialized video equipment but imports DVD players. International trade in similar but slightly different manufactured products is profitable.

REVIEW QUIZ

1 What is the fundamental source of the gains from international trade?
2 In what circumstances can countries gain from international trade?
3 What determines the goods and services that a country will export?
4 What determines the goods and services that a country will import?
5 What is comparative advantage and what role does it play in determining the amount and type of international trade that occurs?
6 How can it be that all countries gain from international trade and that there are no losers?
7 Provide some examples of comparative advantage in today's world.
8 Why does Canada both export and import automobiles?

myeconlab Study Plan 32.2

You've now seen how free trade brings gains for all countries. But trade is not free in our world. We'll now take a brief look at the history of trade restrictions and work out their effects. We'll see that free trade brings the greatest possible benefits and that international trade restrictions are costly.

International Trade Restrictions

GOVERNMENTS RESTRICT INTERNATIONAL TRADE to protect domestic industries from foreign competition by using two main tools:

1. Tariffs
2. Nontariff barriers

A **tariff** is a tax that is imposed by the importing country when an imported good crosses its international boundary. A **nontariff barrier** is any action other than a tariff that restricts international trade. Examples of nontariff barriers are quantitative restrictions and licensing regulations limiting imports. First, let's look at tariffs.

The History of Tariffs

The Canadian economy has always been protected by a tariff. Figure 32.5 shows the history of that tariff, from Confederation through 2004. The figure shows tariffs as a percentage of total imports—the average tariff rate. As you can see, the average tariff rate climbed from the early 1870s to exceed 20 percent by the late 1880s. The rate fluctuated but gradually decreased through the early 1920s. It increased again

during the Great Depression years of the early 1930s. During these years, most countries increased their tariff rates in what became a "beggar-thy-neighbour" policy. The average tariff then decreased through the late 1930s and continued its decrease throughout the years after World War II. Today, the average tariff rate is less than 1 percent.

The reduction in tariffs after World War II followed the signing in 1947 of the **General Agreement on Tariffs and Trade** (GATT). From its formation, GATT organized a series of "rounds" of negotiations that resulted in a steady process of tariff reduction. One of these, the Kennedy Round that began in the early 1960s, resulted in large tariff cuts starting in 1967. Another, the Tokyo Round, resulted in further tariff cuts in 1979. The final round, the Uruguay Round, started in 1986 and was completed in 1994.

The Uruguay Round was the most ambitious and comprehensive of the rounds and led to the creation of the **World Trade Organization** (WTO). Membership of the WTO brings greater obligations for countries to observe the GATT rules. Canada signed the Uruguay Round agreements, and Parliament ratified them in 1994.

In 2005, the WTO embarked on the Doha Round, which aimed to further liberalize world trade. But at the end of 2005, this round was stalled by disagreement on U.S. and E.U. agricultural subsidies.

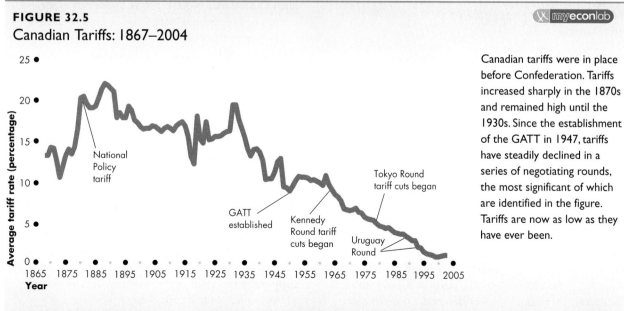

FIGURE 32.5
Canadian Tariffs: 1867–2004

Canadian tariffs were in place before Confederation. Tariffs increased sharply in the 1870s and remained high until the 1930s. Since the establishment of the GATT in 1947, tariffs have steadily declined in a series of negotiating rounds, the most significant of which are identified in the figure. Tariffs are now as low as they have ever been.

Sources of data: Statistics Canada, *Historial Statistics of Canada*, Series G485, CANSIM Tables 380–0002 and 380–0034.

In addition to the agreements under the GATT and the WTO, Canada is a party to the **North American Free Trade Agreement** (NAFTA), which became effective on January 1, 1994, and under which barriers to international trade among the United States, Canada, and Mexico will be virtually eliminated after a 15-year phasing-in period.

In other parts of the world, trade barriers have virtually been eliminated among the member countries of the European Union, which has created the largest unified tariff-free market in the world. In 1994, discussions among the Asia-Pacific Economic Cooperation (APEC) led to an agreement in principle to work towards a free-trade area that embraces China, all the economies of East Asia and the South Pacific, and the United States and Canada. These countries include the fastest-growing economies and hold the promise of heralding a global free-trade area.

The effort to achieve freer trade underlines the fact that trade in some goods is still subject to a high tariff. Textiles and footwear are among the goods that face the highest tariffs, and rates on these items average more than 10 percent. Some individual items face a tariff much higher than the average. For example, when you buy a pair of blue jeans for $20, you pay about $5 more than you would if there were no tariffs on textiles. Other goods that are protected by tariffs are agricultural products, energy and chemicals, minerals, and metals. The meat, cheese, milk, and eggs that you consume cost significantly more because of protection than they would with free international trade.

The temptation for governments to impose tariffs is a strong one. First, tariffs provide revenue to the government. Second, they enable the government to satisfy special interest groups in import-competing industries. But, as we'll see, free international trade brings enormous benefits that are reduced when tariffs are imposed. Let's see how.

How Tariffs Work

To see how tariffs work, let's return to the example of trade between Farmland and Mobilia. Figure 32.6 shows the international market for cars in which these two countries are the only traders. The volume of trade and the price of a car are determined at the point of intersection of Mobilia's export supply curve of cars and Farmland's import demand curve for cars.

In Fig. 32.6, these two countries trade cars and grain in exactly the same way that we saw in Fig. 32.3.

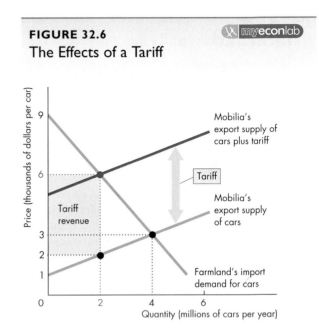

FIGURE 32.6
The Effects of a Tariff

Farmland imposes a tariff on car imports from Mobilia. The tariff increases the price that Farmers have to pay for cars. It shifts the supply curve of cars in Farmland leftward. The vertical distance between the original supply curve and the new one is the amount of the tariff, $4,000 per car. The price of a car in Farmland increases, and the quantity of cars imported decreases. The government of Farmland collects a tariff revenue of $4,000 per car—a total of $8 billion on the 2 million cars imported. Farmland's exports of grain decrease because Mobilia now has a lower income from its exports of cars.

Mobilia exports cars, and Farmland exports grain. The volume of car imports into Farmland is 4 million a year, and the world market price of a car is 3 tonnes of grain. Figure 32.6 expresses prices in dollars rather than in units of grain and is based on a money price of grain of $1,000 a tonne. With grain costing $1,000 a tonne, the money price of a car is $3,000.

Now suppose that the government of Farmland, perhaps under pressure from car producers, decides to impose a tariff on imported cars. In particular, suppose that a tariff of $4,000 per car is imposed. (This is a huge tariff, but the car producers of Farmland are pretty fed up with competition from Mobilia.) What happens?

- The supply of cars in Farmland decreases.
- The price of a car in Farmland rises.
- The quantity of cars imported by Farmland decreases.
- The government of Farmland collects the tariff revenue.
- Resource use is inefficient.
- The *value* of exports changes by the same amount as the *value* of imports, and trade remains balanced.

Change in the Supply of Cars Farmland cannot buy cars at Mobilia's export supply price. It must pay that price plus the $4,000 tariff. So the supply curve in Farmland shifts leftward. The new supply curve is that labelled "Mobilia's export supply of cars plus tariff." The vertical distance between Mobilia's original export supply curve and the new supply curve is the tariff of $4,000 a car.

Rise in Price of a Car A new equilibrium occurs where the new supply curve intersects Farmland's import demand curve for cars. That equilibrium is at a price of $6,000 a car, up from $3,000 with free trade.

Fall in Imports Car imports fall from 4 million to 2 million cars a year. At the higher price of $6,000 a car, domestic car producers increase their production. Domestic grain production decreases as resources are moved into the expanding car industry.

Tariff Revenue Total expenditure on imported cars by the Farmers is $6,000 a car multiplied by the 2 million cars imported ($12 billion). But not all of that money goes to the Mobilians. They receive $2,000 a car, or $4 billion for the 2 million cars. The difference—$4,000 a car, or a total of $8 billion for the 2 million cars—is collected by the government of Farmland as tariff revenue.

Inefficiency The people of Farmland are willing to pay $6,000 for the marginal car imported. But the opportunity cost of that car is $2,000. So there is a gain from trading an extra car. In fact, there are gains—willingness to pay exceeds opportunity cost—all the way up to 4 million cars a year. Only when 4 million cars are being traded is the maximum price that a Farmer is willing to pay equal to the minimum price that is acceptable to a Mobilian. Restricting trade reduces the gains from trade.

Trade Remains Balanced With free trade, Farmland was paying $3,000 a car and buying 4 million cars a year from Mobilia. The total amount paid to Mobilia for imports was $12 billion a year. With a tariff, Farmland's imports have been cut to 2 million cars a year and the price paid to Mobilia has also been cut to only $2,000 a car. The total amount paid to Mobilia for imports has been cut to $4 billion a year. Doesn't this fact mean that Farmland now has a balance of trade surplus? It does not.

The price of a car in Mobilia has fallen. But the price of grain remains at $1 a tonne. So the relative price of a car has fallen, and the relative price of grain has increased. With free trade, the Mobilians could buy 3,000 tonnes of grain for the price of one car. Now they can buy only 2,000 tonnes for the price of a car. With a higher relative price of grain, the quantity demanded by the Mobilians decreases and Mobilia imports less grain. But because Mobilia imports less grain, Farmland exports less grain. In fact, Farmland's grain industry suffers from two sources. First, there is a decrease in the quantity of grain sold to Mobilia. Second, there is increased competition for inputs from the now-expanded car industry. The tariff leads to a contraction in the scale of the grain industry in Farmland.

It seems paradoxical at first that a country imposing a tariff on cars hurts its own export industry, lowering its exports of grain. It may help to think of it this way: Mobilians buy grain with the money they make from exporting cars to Farmland. If they export fewer cars, they cannot afford to buy as much grain. In fact, in the absence of any international borrowing and lending, Mobilia must cut its imports of grain by exactly the same amount as the loss in revenue from its export of cars. Grain imports into Mobilia are cut back to a value of $4 billion, the amount that can be paid for by the new lower revenue from Mobilia's car exports. Trade is still balanced. The tariff cuts imports and exports by the same amount. The tariff has no effect on the *balance* of trade, but it reduces the *volume* of trade.

The result that we have just derived is perhaps one of the most misunderstood aspects of international economics. On countless occasions, politicians and others call for tariffs to lower a balance of trade deficit or argue that lowering tariffs will create a balance of trade deficit. The balance of international trade is not caused by a lack of competitiveness. Its cause lies in a nation's saving as you'll see later in this chapter (on pp. 774–775).

Nontariff Barriers

The two main forms of nontariff barriers are

1. Quotas
2. Voluntary export restraints

A **quota** is a quantitative restriction on the import of a particular good, which specifies the maximum amount of the good that may be imported in a given period of time. A **voluntary export restraint** (VER) is an agreement between two governments in which the government of the exporting country agrees to restrain the volume of its own exports.

Quotas are especially prominent in agriculture. Voluntary export restraints are used to regulate trade between Japan and Canada.

How Quotas and VERs Work

To see how a quota works, suppose that Farmland imposes a quota that restricts its car imports to 2 million cars a year. Figure 32.7 shows the effects of this action. The quota is shown by the vertical red line at 2 million cars a year. Because it is illegal to exceed the quota, car importers buy only that quantity from Mobilia, for which they pay $2,000 a car. But because the import supply of cars is restricted to 2 million cars a year, people are willing to pay $6,000 per car. This is the price of a car in Farmland.

The value of imports falls to $4 billion, exactly the same as in the case of the tariff in Fig. 32.6. So with lower incomes from car exports and with a higher relative price of grain, Mobilians cut back on their imports of grain in exactly the same way that they did under a tariff.

The key difference between a quota and a tariff lies in who collects the gap between the import supply price and the domestic price. In the case of a tariff, it is the government of the importing country. In the case of a quota, it goes to the person who has the right to import under the import quota regulations.

A VER is like a quota arrangement in which quotas are allocated to each exporting country. The effects of a VER are similar to those of a quota but differ from them in that the gap between the domestic price and the export price is captured not by domestic importers but by the foreign exporter. The government of the exporting country has to establish procedures for allocating the restricted volume of exports among its producers.

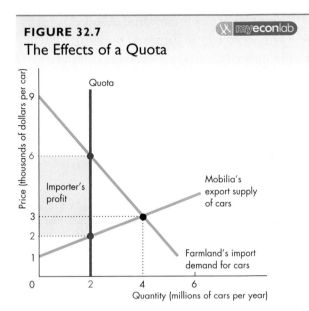

FIGURE 32.7 myeconlab
The Effects of a Quota

Farmland imposes a quota of 2 million cars a year on car imports from Mobilia. That quantity appears as the vertical line labelled Quota. Because the quantity of cars supplied by Mobilia is restricted to 2 million, the price of a car in Farmland increases to $6,000. Importing cars is profitable because Mobilia is willing to supply cars at $2,000 each. There is competition for import quotas.

REVIEW QUIZ

1 What are the tools that a country can use to restrict international trade?
2 What do international trade restrictions do to the gains from international trade?
3 Which is best for a country: restricted trade, no trade, or free trade? Why?
4 What does a tariff on imports do to the volume of imports and the volume of exports?
5 In the absence of international borrowing and lending, how do tariffs and other international trade restrictions influence the total value of imports and exports and the balance of trade—the value of exports minus the value of imports?

myeconlab **Study Plan 32.3**

We're now going to look at some commonly heard arguments for restricting international trade and see why they are almost never correct.

The Case Against Protection

FOR AS LONG AS NATIONS AND INTERNATIONAL trade have existed, people have debated whether a country is better off with free international trade or with protection from foreign competition. The debate continues, but for most economists, a verdict has been delivered and is the one you have just seen. Free trade promotes prosperity for all; protection is inefficient. We've seen the most powerful case for free trade in the example of how Farmland and Mobilia both benefit from their comparative advantage. But there is a broader range of issues in the free trade versus protection debate. Let's review these issues.

Three arguments for restricting international trade are

- The employment argument
- The infant-industry argument
- The dumping argument

Let's look at each in turn.

The Employment Argument

The argument that protection saves jobs goes as follows: When we buy shoes from Brazil or shirts from Taiwan, Canadian workers in these industries lose their jobs. With no earnings and poor prospects, these workers become a drain on welfare and spend less, causing a ripple effect of further job losses. The proposed solution to this problem is to ban imports of cheap foreign goods and protect Canadian jobs. This argument for protection does not withstand scrutiny for three reasons.

First, free trade does cost some jobs, but it also creates other jobs. It brings about a global rationalization of labour and allocates labour resources to their highest-valued activities. Because of international trade in textiles, tens of thousands of workers in Canada have lost their jobs because textile mills and other factories have closed. But tens of thousands of workers in other countries have gotten jobs because textile mills have opened there. And tens of thousands of Canadian workers have gotten better-paying jobs than those of textile workers because other export industries have expanded and created more jobs than have been destroyed.

Second, imports create jobs. They create jobs for retailers that sell imported goods and firms that service those goods. They also create jobs by creating incomes in the rest of the world, some of which are spent on imports of Canadian-made goods and services.

Although protection does save particular jobs, it does so at inordinate cost. A striking example of the cost of quotas is that of the quotas on the import of textiles. Quotas imposed under an international agreement called the Multifibre Arrangement (which ended in 2005) protected textile jobs, especially in the United States. The U.S. International Trade Commission (ITC) estimated that because of quotas, 72,000 jobs existed in textiles that would otherwise have disappeared and the annual clothing expenditure in the United States was $US 15.9 billion or $U.S. 160 per family higher than it will be with free trade. Equivalently, the ITC estimated that each textile job saved cost $US 221,000 a year.

The Infant-Industry Argument

The so-called **infant-industry argument** for protection is that it is necessary to protect a new industry to enable it to grow into a mature industry that can compete in world markets. The argument is based on the idea of *dynamic comparative advantage*, which can arise from learning-by-doing (see Chapter 2).

Learning-by-doing is a powerful engine of productivity growth, and comparative advantage does evolve and change because of on-the-job experience. But these facts do not justify protection.

First, the infant-industry argument is valid only if the benefits of learning-by-doing *not only* accrue to the owners and workers of the firms in the infant industry but also *spill over* to other industries and parts of the economy. For example, there are huge productivity gains from learning-by-doing in the manufacture of aircraft. But almost all of these gains benefit the stockholders and workers of Bombardier. Because the people making the decisions, bearing the risk, and doing the work are the ones who benefit, they take the dynamic gains into account when they decide on the scale of their activities. In this case, almost no benefits spill over to other parts of the economy, so there is no need for government assistance to achieve an efficient outcome.

Second, even if the case is made for protecting an infant industry, it is more efficient to do so by subsidizing the firms in the industry, with the subsidy paid out of taxes.

The Dumping Argument

Dumping occurs when a foreign firm sells its exports at a price below its cost of production. Dumping might be used by a firm that wants to gain a global monopoly. In this case, the foreign firm sells its output at a price below its cost to drive domestic firms out of business. When the domestic firms have gone, the foreign firm takes advantage of its monopoly position and charges a higher price for its product. Dumping is usually regarded as a justification for temporary countervailing tariffs.

But there are powerful reasons to resist the dumping argument for protection. First, it is virtually impossible to detect dumping because it is hard to determine a firm's costs. As a result, the test for dumping is whether a firm's export price is below its domestic price. But this test is a weak one because it can be rational for a firm to charge a low price in markets in which the quantity demanded is highly sensitive to price and a higher price in a market in which demand is less price-sensitive.

Second, it is hard to think of a good that is produced by a natural *global* monopoly. So even if all the domestic firms were driven out of business in some industry, it would always be possible to find several and usually many alternative foreign sources of supply and to buy at prices determined in competitive markets.

Third, if a good or service were a truly global natural monopoly, the best way of dealing with it would be by regulation—just as in the case of domestic monopolies. Such regulation would require international cooperation.

The three arguments for protection that we've just examined have an element of credibility. The counterarguments are in general stronger, however, so these arguments do not make the case for protection. But they are not the only arguments that you might encounter. There are many other newer arguments against globalization and for protection. The most common of them are that protection

- Maintains national security
- Allows us to compete with cheap foreign labour
- Brings diversity and stability
- Penalizes lax environmental standards
- Protects national culture
- Prevents rich countries from exploiting developing countries

Maintains National Security

The national security argument for protection is that a country must protect industries that produce defence equipment and armaments and industries on which the defence industries rely for their raw materials and other intermediate inputs. This argument for protection does not withstand close scrutiny.

First, it is an argument for international isolation, for in a time of war, there is no industry that does not contribute to national defence. Second, if the case is made for boosting the output of a strategic industry, it is more efficient to achieve this outcome with a subsidy to the firms in the industry that is financed out of taxes. Such a subsidy would keep the industry operating at the scale judged appropriate, and free international trade would keep the prices faced by consumers at their world market levels.

Allows Us to Compete with Cheap Foreign Labour

With the removal of tariffs in Canadian trade with Mexico, people said we would hear a "giant sucking sound" as jobs rushed to Mexico. Let's see what's wrong with this view.

The labour cost of a unit of output equals the wage rate divided by labour productivity. For example, if a Canadian auto worker earns $30 an hour and produces 15 units of output an hour, the average labour cost of a unit of output is $2. If a Mexican auto assembly worker earns $3 an hour and produces 1 unit of output an hour, the average labour cost of a unit of output is $3. Other things remaining the same, the higher a worker's productivity, the higher is the worker's wage rate. High-wage workers have high productivity. Low-wage workers have low productivity.

Although high-wage Canadian workers are more productive, on the average, than low-wage Mexican workers, there are differences across industries. Canadian labour is relatively more productive in some activities than in others. For example, the productivity of Canadian workers in producing financial services and telephone systems is relatively higher than their productivity in the production of metals and some standardized machine parts. The activities in which Canadian workers are relatively more productive than their Mexican counterparts are those in which Canada has a *comparative advantage*. By engaging in free trade, increasing our production and exports of the goods and services in which we have a comparative advantage and decreasing our production and increasing our imports of the goods and services in which our trading partners have a comparative advantage, we can make ourselves and the citizens of other countries better off.

Brings Diversity and Stability

A diversified investment portfolio is less risky than one that has all the eggs in one basket. The same is true for an economy's production. A diversified economy fluctuates less than an economy that produces only one or two goods.

But big, rich, diversified economies such as those of Canada, the United States, Japan, and Europe do not have this type of stability problem. Even a country such as Saudi Arabia that produces only one good (in this case, oil) can benefit from specializing in the activity at which it has a comparative advantage and then investing in a wide range of other countries to bring greater stability to its income and consumption.

Penalizes Lax Environmental Standards

Another argument for protection is that many poorer countries, such as Mexico, do not have the same environmental policies that we have and, because they are willing to pollute and we are not, we cannot compete with them without tariffs. So if they want free trade with the richer and "greener" countries, they must clean up their environments to our standards.

This argument for trade restrictions is not entirely convincing. A poor country is less able than a rich one to devote resources to achieving high environmental standards. So if free trade helps a poor country to become richer, it will also help that country to develop the means to improve its environment.

But there probably is a case for using the negotiation of free trade agreements such as NAFTA to hold member countries to higher environmental standards. There is an especially large payoff from using such bargaining to try to avoid irreversible damage to resources such as tropical rainforests.

Protects National Culture

The national culture argument is that free trade in books, magazines, movies, and television programs means U.S. domination and the end of local culture. So, the reasoning continues, it is necessary to protect domestic "culture" industries from free international trade to ensure the survival of a national cultural identity.

Protection of these industries is common and takes the form of nontariff barriers. For example, local content regulations on radio and television broadcasting and in magazines is often required.

The cultural identity argument for protection has no merit. Writers, publishers, and broadcasters want to limit foreign competition so that they can earn larger economic profits. But many of the creators of so-called American cultural products are not Americans but the talented citizens of other countries, ensuring the survival of their national cultural identities in Hollywood! Also, if national culture is in danger, it isn't clear that preventing competition is the best way of restoring it to health. Competition among cultures might be a source of strength.

Prevents Rich Countries from Exploiting Developing Countries

Wage rates in some developing countries are indeed very low. Do we, by trading with these countries, exploit them and their workers?

By trading with developing countries, we increase the demand for the goods that these countries produce and, more significantly, we increase the demand for their labour. When the demand for labour in developing countries increases, the wage rate also increases. So, rather than exploiting people in developing countries, international trade improves their opportunities and increases their incomes.

We have reviewed five arguments in favour of protection and seen that they all have flaws and leave the case for free international trade a strong one.

Why Is International Trade Restricted?

Why, despite all the arguments against protection, is trade restricted? There are two key reasons:

- Tariff revenue
- Rent seeking

Tariff Revenue Government revenue is costly to collect. In the developed countries such as Canada, a well-organized tax collection system is in place that can generate billions of dollars of income tax and sales tax revenues. This tax collection system is made possible by the fact that most economic transactions are done by firms that must keep properly audited financial records. Without such records, the revenue collection agencies (for example, Canada Revenue Agency) would be severely hampered in the work. Even with audited financial accounts, some proportion of potential tax revenue is lost. Nonetheless, for the industrialized countries, income taxes and sales taxes are the major sources of revenue and the tariff plays a very small role.

But governments in developing countries have a difficult time collecting taxes from their citizens. Much economic activity takes place in an informal economy with few financial records. So only a small amount of revenue is collected from income taxes and sales taxes in these countries. The one area in which economic transactions are well recorded and audited is in international trade. So this activity is an attractive base for tax collection in these countries and is used much more extensively than in the developed countries.

Rent Seeking Rent seeking is the major reason why international trade is restricted. Rent seeking is lobbying and other political activity that seeks to capture the gains from trade. Free trade increases consumption possibilities *on the average*, but not everyone shares in the gain and some people even lose. Free trade brings benefits to some and imposes costs on others, with total benefits exceeding total costs. It is the uneven distribution of costs and benefits that is the principal source of impediment to achieving more liberal international trade.

Think about our example of trade in cars and grain between Farmland and Mobilia. In Farmland, the benefits from free trade accrue to all the producers of grain and to those producers of cars who would not have to bear the costs of adjusting to a smaller car industry. Those costs are transition costs, not permanent costs. The costs of moving to free trade are borne by those car producers and their employees who have to become grain producers.

The number of people who gain will, in general, be enormous in comparison with the number who lose. The gain per person will therefore be rather small. But the loss per person to those who bear the loss will be large. Because the losses that fall on those who bear them are large, it pays those people to incur considerable expense to lobby against free trade. On the other hand, it does not

pay those who gain to organize to achieve free trade. The gain from trade for any one individual is too small for that individual to spend much time or money on a political organization whose goal is to achieve free trade.

Winners—free traders—and losers–anti-free traders—each in pursuit of their self-interest, weigh benefits against costs and choose their best actions. But because only the anti-free traders have enough at stake, they will do more political lobbying than the free traders.

Compensating Losers

If, in total, the gains from free international trade exceed the losses, why don't those who stand to gain from free trade offer to compensate those who stand to lose so that everyone votes for free trade?

The main answer is that there are serious obstacles to providing direct and correctly calculated compensation. First, the cost of identifying the losers from free trade and of estimating the value of their losses would be enormous.

Second, it would never be clear whether a person who has fallen on hard times is suffering because of free trade or for other reasons, perhaps reasons that are largely under the control of the individual. Third, some people who look like losers at one point in time may, in fact, end up gaining. The young auto worker that loses her job in Windsor and becomes a computer assembly worker in Ottawa resents the loss of work and the need to move. But a year or two later, looking back on events, she counts herself fortunate. She has made a move that has increased her income and given her greater job security.

Despite the absence of explicit compensation, those who lose from a change in protection do receive some compensation. But compensation is not restricted to the losers from changes in trade policy. In Canada (and in all the other rich industrial countries) elaborate schemes are in place to ensure that people who suffer from economic change receive help during their transition to new activities.

Two major forms of compensation in Canada arise from interprovincial fiscal transfers and employment insurance. Interprovincial fiscal transfers result in tax dollars collected in the rich and expanding regions of the country being spent in the

When the United States and Canada negotiated the Canada–U.S. Free Trade Agreement (the predecessor of NAFTA), U.S. President Ronald Reagan (hand outstretched on the right) and Prime Minister Brian Mulroney (maple-leafed figure on the left), were able to go only as far as their national self-interested rent seekers would allow them to go in dismantling tariffs and other barriers to free trade between the world's two largest trading partners.

Cartoon by Alan King, *The Ottawa Citizen*, Canwest News Service. Reprinted by permission of Alan King/*The Ottawa Citizen*.

poorer regions. Employment insurance provides compensation for workers who lose their jobs regardless of the reason for the job loss. Jobs lost because of changes in international protection are included among those for which benefits are paid.

But because we do not explicitly compensate the losers from free international trade, protectionism remains a popular and permanent feature of our national economic and political life.

Protection to Avoid a Trade Deficit

In our review of the arguments for protection, we did not consider the idea of limiting imports to help a country to achieve an international trade surplus or avoid a deficit. But this argument is sometimes heard.

Today, Canada has a surplus in its international trade. But many countries have deficits and the United States is the largest deficit nation. Some people say that because China floods the United States with cheap goods, China is a major source of the U.S. deficit. So limiting imports from China is justified as a way of limiting the deficit. In the next section, you will see what determines a country's international trade balance and why a deficit doesn't justify protection.

REVIEW QUIZ

1 Can we save jobs, develop new industries, or restrain foreign monopoly by restricting international trade?

2 Can trade protection help to achieve national security goals, or better protect the environmental and national culture?

3 What is the main argument against international trade restrictions?

4 What are the two main reasons for imposing tariffs on imports?

5 What type of country benefits most from the revenue from tariffs? Provide some examples of such countries.

6 If international trade restrictions are costly, why do we use them? Why don't the people who gain from trade organize a political force that is strong enough to ensure that their interests are protected?

7 Why don't we have free trade and compensate the people who lose from it?

myeconlab **Study Plan 32.4**

The Balance of International Payments

SO FAR IN THIS CHAPTER, WE'VE LOOKED AT balanced trade between countries. We're now going to see what makes trade unbalanced—why countries have international deficits and surpluses. When a country has an international deficit, it must borrow from the rest of the world. And when a country has an international surplus, it must lend to the rest of the world. Let's look at the scale of Canada's international trading and borrowing and lending and at the way in which we keep our records of these transactions. These records are called the balance of payments accounts.

Balance of Payments Accounts

A country's *balance of payments accounts* record its international trading, borrowing, and lending. There are in fact three balance of payments accounts:

1. Current account
2. Capital account
3. Official settlements account

The *current account* records payments for imports of goods and services from abroad, receipts from exports of goods and services sold abroad, net interest paid abroad, and net transfers (such as foreign aid payments). The *current account balance* equals exports minus imports, net interest payments, and net transfers. The *capital account* records foreign investment in Canada minus Canadian investment abroad. The *official settlements account* records the change in official Canadian reserves. *Official Canadian reserves* are the government's holdings of foreign currency. If Canadian official reserves increase, the official settlements account balance is *negative*. The reason is that holding foreign money is like investing abroad. Canadian investment abroad is a minus item in the capital account and in the official settlements account. (By the same reasoning, if official Canadian reserves decrease, the official settlements account balance is *positive*.)

The sum of the balances on the three accounts always equals zero. That is, to pay for a current account deficit, we must either borrow more from abroad than we lend abroad or use our official reserves to cover the shortfall.

Table 32.1 shows the Canadian balance of payments accounts in 2004. Items in the current account and capital account that provide foreign currency to Canada have a plus sign; items that cost Canada foreign currency have a minus sign. The table shows that in 2004, exports plus net transfers exceeded imports plus net interest payments and the current account had a surplus of $29 billion.

What do we do with our current account surplus? We lend it to the rest of the world. The capital account tells us by how much. We borrowed $62 billion (foreign investment in Canada) but made loans of $88 billion (Canadian investment abroad). Thus our net foreign lending was $26 billion. A statistical discrepancy arises because of illegal and hidden transactions, which in 2004 was –$6 billion.

The sum of our current account balance, capital account balance and statistical discrepancy is the change in our official reserves. In 2004, reserves decreased because our current account balance of $29 billion plus the capital account balance of –$26 billion and the statistical discrepancy of –$6 billion was –$3 billion. When our reserves decrease, we record

---

TABLE 32.1   Canadian Balance of Payments Accounts in 2004

Current account	Billions of dollars
Imports of goods and services	–437
Exports of goods and services	+491
Net interest payments	–50
Net transfers	+25
Current account balance	+29

Capital account	
Foreign investment in Canada	+62
Canadian investment abroad	–88
Capital account balance	–26
Statistical discrepancy	–6

Official settlements account	
Official settlements account balance	+3

Source: Statistics Canada, CANSIM tables 376–0001 and 376–0002.

the official settlements balance as a positive number. Why? Because a decrease in our reserves is like borrowing from the rest of the world.

The numbers in Table 34.1 give a snapshot of the balance of payments accounts in 2004. Figure 32.8 puts that snapshot into perspective by showing the balance of payments between 1984 and 2004. Because the economy grows and the price level rises, changes in the dollar value of the balance of payments do not convey much information. To remove the influences of growth and inflation, Fig. 32.8 shows the balance of payments as a percentage of nominal GDP.

As you can see, the capital account balance is almost a mirror image of the current account balance. The official settlements balance is very small in comparison with the balances of these other two accounts. A large current account deficit (and capital account surplus) emerged during the 1980s but declined after 1993. By 1996 we had a small surplus and after two more years of deficit, the early 2000s saw an increasing current account surplus.

You can understand the balance of payments and the way the accounts are linked together if you think about the income and expenditure, borrowing and lending, and bank account of an individual.

Individual Analogy Joanne's income from her job in 2005 was $25,000 and she has $10,000 worth of investments that earned her an interest income of $1,000 in that year. Joanne's current account shows an income of $26,000. Joanne spent $18,000 on consumption goods and services. She also bought a new house, which cost her $60,000. So Joanne's total expenditure was $78,000. Her income minus her expenditure is –$52,000 ($26,000 minus $78,000). This amount is Joanne's current account deficit.

To cover her $52,000 deficit, Joanne has to use the money that she has in the bank or take a loan. Joanne took a mortgage of $50,000 to help buy her house so her capital account surplus was $50,000. With a current account deficit of $52,000 and a capital account surplus of $50,000, Joanne is still $2,000 short. She got that $2,000 from her bank account. Her cash holdings decreased by $2,000.

Joanne's income from work is like a country's income from exports. Her income from investments is like a country's interest income from foreigners. Her purchases of goods and services, are like a country's imports. Joanne's mortgage—borrowing from someone else—is like a country's borrowing from the rest of the world. The change in her bank account is like the change in the country's official reserves.

FIGURE 32.8
The Balance of Payments: 1984–2004

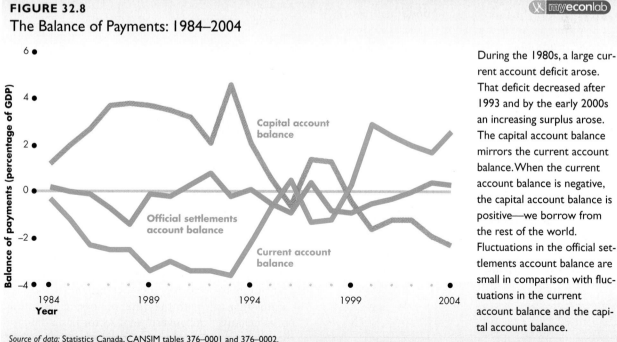

During the 1980s, a large current account deficit arose. That deficit decreased after 1993 and by the early 2000s an increasing surplus arose. The capital account balance mirrors the current account balance. When the current account balance is negative, the capital account balance is positive—we borrow from the rest of the world. Fluctuations in the official settlements account balance are small in comparison with fluctuations in the current account balance and the capital account balance.

Source of data: Statistics Canada, CANSIM tables 376–0001 and 376–0002.

Borrowers and Lenders, Debtors and Creditors

A country that has a current account deficit and that borrows more from the rest of the world than it lends to it is called a *net borrower*. Similarly, a *net lender* is a country that lends more to the rest of the world than it borrows from it.

From 1999 through 2004, Canada was a net lender. But most years, Canada has been a net borrower. And most countries are net borrowers.

A net borrower might be going deeper into debt or might simply be reducing its net assets held in the rest of the world. The total stock of foreign investment determines whether a country is a debtor or creditor. A *debtor nation* is a country that during its entire history has borrowed more from the rest of the world than it has lent to it. It has a stock of outstanding debt to the rest of the world that exceeds the stock of its own claims on the rest of the world. A *creditor nation* is a country that has invested more in the rest of the world than other countries have invested in it.

Canada is a debtor nation. Should we be concerned that Canada is a net borrower and debtor nation? The answer to this question depends on what we do with the funds that we borrow. If borrowing finances investment that in turn generates economic growth and higher income, borrowing is not a problem. If borrowing finances consumption, then higher interest payments are being incurred, and as a consequence, consumption will eventually have to be reduced. In this case, the more the borrowing and the longer it goes on, the greater is the reduction in consumption that will eventually be necessary.

Current Account Balance

The current account balance (in Table 32.1) is the sum of exports minus imports, net interest income, and net transfers. Exports minus imports equals net exports and fluctuations in net exports are the main source of fluctuations in the current account balance.

You are about to discover that net exports do not depend on our competitiveness in international markets. Instead, they depend on the government budget and private saving and investment. To see how, look at Table 32.2[1].

---

[1]If you've studied macroeconomics, you learned about the National Income Accounts in Chapter 20.

TABLE 32.2   Net Exports, the Government Budget, Saving, and Investment

	Symbols and equations	Canada in 2004 (billions of dollars)
(a) Variables		
Exports*	X	493
Imports*	M	438
Government expenditures	G	282
Net taxes	NT	302
Investment	I	234
Saving	S	269
(b) Balances		
Net exports	$X - M$	$493 - 438 = 55$
Government sector	$NT - G$	$302 - 282 = 20$
Private sector	$S - I$	$269 - 234 = 35$
(c) Relationship among balances		
National accounts	$Y = C + I + G + X - M$	
	$= C + S + NT$	
Rearranging:	$X - M = S - I + NT - G$	
Net exports	$X - M$	55
Equals:		
Government sector	$NT - G$	20
Plus		
Private sector	$S - I$	35

Source of data: Statistics Canada, CANSIM tables 380–0002 and 380–0022.

* The national income accounts' measures of exports and imports are different from the balance of payments' accounts measures by small amounts.

Part (a) lists the national income variables that we need, with their symbols. Part (b) defines three balances. We've just defined net exports. The *government sector balance* is equal to net taxes minus government expenditures on goods and services. If that number is positive, the government sector has a surplus that is lent to the other sectors; if that number is negative, the government sector has a deficit that must be financed by borrowing from the other sectors. The government sector balance is the sum of the balances of the federal, provincial, and municipal governments. The *private sector balance* is equal to saving minus investment. If saving exceeds investment, a private sector has a surplus and it is lent to other sectors. If investment exceeds saving, borrowing from other sectors finances a private sector deficit.

Part (b) shows the values of these balances for Canada in 2004. Net exports were a surplus of $55 billion. The government sector had a surplus of $20 billion. And the private sector had a surplus of $35 billion.

Part (c) shows the relationship among the three balances. From the national income accounts, we know that real GDP (Y) is the sum of consumption expenditure (C), investment (I), government expenditures (G), and net exports ($X - M$). It also equals the sum of consumption expenditure (C), saving (S), and net taxes (NT). Rearranging these equations tells us that net exports ($X - M$) is the sum of the government sector surplus ($NT - G$) and the private sector surplus ($S - I$). In Canada in 2004, the government sector had a surplus of $20 billion and the private sector had a surplus of $35 billion. The government sector surplus plus the private sector surplus equals net exports of $55 billion.

The Twin Deficits

You've seen that net exports equals the sum of the government surplus and the private surplus. And net exports plus debt interest (and other small transfers) equals the current account balance. What is the relationship over time between the current account balance and the government budget balance? How do these balances fluctuate over time? Figure 32.9 answers this question. It shows the government budget (the red line) and the current account balance (the blue line).

You can see that, with an important exception during the early 1980s, there is a tendency for the current account to go into a deeper deficit when the government budget goes into a deeper deficit. Because of the tendency for the government budget deficit and the current account deficit to move in the same direction they have been called the *twin deficits*.

Why are the two deficits linked? They are linked because capital is highly mobile in today's world. If the Canadian government increases expenditures or lowers taxes, total spending in Canada rises. But with the economy at or near full employment, the extra

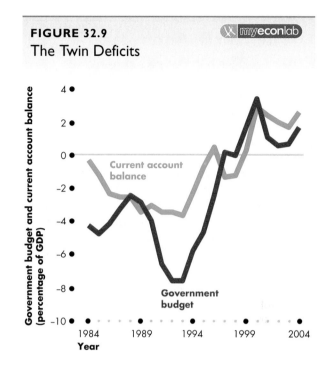

FIGURE 32.9
The Twin Deficits

The current account balance and the government budget balance move in similar ways and look like twin deficits. But this relationship broke down during the early 1980s when the private sector surplus swelled.

Source of data: Statistics Canada, CANSIM tables 376–0001 and 380–0007.

goods and services demanded are sucked in from the rest of the world. Imports increase. Capital flows in to pay for those imports. Saving and investment don't change. This relationship broke down during the early 1980s because Canada was in recession and investment decreased relative to saving.

REVIEW QUIZ

1   What types of transactions do we record in the balance of payments accounts?
2   What transactions does the current account record? What transactions does the capital account record? What transactions does the official settlements account record?
3   What determines the current account balance?

myeconlab   **Study Plan 32.5**

The North American Free Trade Agreement

THE NORTH AMERICAN FREE TRADE AGGREEMENT came into effect on January 1, 1994. It was the outgrowth of an earlier Canada–United States Free Trade Agreement, which was signed in 1988 and came into effect on January 1, 1989. Both agreements were struck only after years of intense negotiations and, on the Canadian side of the border, an intense political debate. First, let's look at the terms of the Canada–United States Free Trade Agreement and at the progress made in achieving freer trade between two of the world's largest trading partners.

The Terms of the Canada–United States Agreement

The main terms of the Canada–United States Free Trade Agreement are:

- Tariffs to be phased out through 1999
- Nontariff barriers to be reduced
- Free trade in energy products, with energy re-source sharing in times of national shortage
- More freedom of trade in services
- Future negotiations to eliminate subsidies
- Creation of dispute-settling mechanisms

Removal of Tariffs Scheduled tariff cuts began on January 1, 1989 and were completed on January 1, 1998. But tariff protection remains in place and an atmosphere of tension prevails in many areas. Agriculture remains effectively protected with new tariffs that have replaced old quotas. And a series of *countervailing duties* has been introduced to offset the effects of domestic subsidies. Further, several *antidumping duties* have also been introduced in cases in which it is alleged that products are being exported at a price below the cost of production.

Nontariff Barriers Nontariff barriers such as government procurement policies of buying local products are removed by the agreement. Subsequent to entering into the free trade agreement, Canada and the United States took on additional obligations as members of the WTO that require the removal of agricultural quotas. Many agricultural quotas have been removed but they have been replaced with tar-

iffs. So despite the free trade agreement, we remain a long way from achieving free trade in agricultural products.

Energy Products Free trade in energy products existed before the free trade agreement but the agreement ratified the intent to maintain that arrangement. The agreement that scarce energy resources will be shared in times of national shortage became a controversial one. In effect, what the energy sharing clause amounts to is an agreement that governments will not intervene in energy markets to prevent firms from selling their energy to the other country.

Trade in Services International trade in services has expanded more quickly than trade in manufactured goods in recent years. The free trade agreement, recognizing this factor and seeking to facilitate further expansion of trade in services between the United States and Canada, incorporates two principles: the *right of establishment* and *national treatment*. The right of establishment means that American firms have the right to set up branches in Canada and Canadian firms have the right to set up operations in the United States. National treatment means that each country will treat the goods and firms and investors of the other country as if they were operating within its own borders.

Future Negotiations on Subsidies In both the United States and Canada, there are many subsidies, especially on agricultural products. The presence of subsidies causes problems and makes it legitimate under the agreement for the country importing subsidized goods to impose countervailing duties. As we have just noted, several such duties have been imposed.

Dispute-Settling Mechanisms The Free Trade Agreement included two dispute-settling mechanisms: one to settle disputes relating to all aspects of the agreement, and the other to deal with applications of countervailing duties and antidumping laws in either country. For example, the United States has applied for and received permission to impose countervailing duties on Canadian exports of durum wheat, lumber products, poultry, and live hogs. In each case, the United States accuses Canada of subsidizing these industries unfairly so that Canadian exports are cheaper than the prices at which U.S. producers can supply these goods.

The Extension of the Agreement: NAFTA

The North American Free Trade Agreement (NAFTA) is an agreement among Canada, the United States, and Mexico that has six objectives. They are to

1. Eliminate trade barriers
2. Promote conditions of fair competition
3. Increase investment opportunities
4. Protect intellectual property rights
5. Create an effective dispute resolution mechanism
6. Establish a framework for the expansion of the agreement to include other nations in the hemisphere

Effects of the Free Trade Agreement

Working out the effects of an agreement as complex as NAFTA is difficult, and there is no general consensus on what the effects have been. The theory that you have studied in this chapter predicts that the removal of tariffs will produce an increase in the *volume* of international trade. That is, the theory predicts that Canadians will increasingly specialize in those activities at which they have a comparative advantage and Mexicans and Americans will specialize in a different range of activities and that the three countries will exchange a larger volume of goods and services.

As predicted, trade among the three countries has increased. During the first five years of NAFTA, Canada's trade with the United States increased by 80 percent and Canada's trade with Mexico doubled.

The trade expansion that followed the entry of Mexico in 1995 was especially dramatic. Mexico's exports increased by 31 percent (in U.S. dollar value) in 1995 and by 21 percent in 1996, compared with increases that averaged less than 15 percent a year during the two years before the agreement. But trade expansion with Mexico has not been in one direction. Mexico's imports also increased following the agreement by 23 percent in both 1996 and 1997.

During the 1990s, Canada's exports expanded from less than 30 percent of total production to 36 percent, and Canada's imports have increased from 27 percent to 34 percent of total expenditure.

Canada greatly increased its exports of advertising services, office and telecommunications equipment, paper, and transportation services. And its imports of meat and dairy products, communications services, clothing, furniture, and processed foods and beverages also increased by a large percentage.

These huge changes in exports and imports brought gains from increased specialization and exchange. But they also brought a heavy toll of adjustment. Thousands of jobs were lost in the declining sectors and new jobs were created in the expanding sectors. The amount of job destruction in the years following the free trade agreement was historically high and the unemployment rate rose for three successive years. Only during the Great Depression did the rate of job destruction exceed that of the late 1980s and early 1990s. To what extent a high rate of labour market turnover was caused by the free trade agreement is unclear and controversial. But the net outcome of NAFTA appears to be strongly positive. More than a million new Canadian jobs were created between 1994 and 1999.

REVIEW QUIZ

1 Describe the main features of the Canada–U.S. Free Trade Agreement of 1988.
2 What effect has NAFTA had on nontariff barriers?
3 What effect has NAFTA had on trade in services?
4 How has the volume of trade among Canada, the United States, and Mexico changed during the period since NAFTA was established?

myeconlab   **Study Plan 32.6**

◆ You've now seen how free international trade enables all nations to gain from trade. By producing goods in which we have a comparative advantage and trading some of our production for that of others, we expand our consumption possibilities. Placing impediments on that trade decreases the gains from trade. By opening our country up to free international trade, the market for the things that we sell expands and their relative prices rise. The market for the things that we buy also expands, and their relative prices fall.

Reading Between the Lines on pp. 778–779 looks at the softwood lumber dispute between the United States and Canada. This dispute provides a clear example of the economic cost of restricting international trade.

Tariffs in Action: Lumber

TELEGRAPH–JOURNAL, OCTOBER 20, 2005

Retaliation in softwood lumber dispute not advised

Retaliating against the United States over its refusal to accept legal defeat in the softwood lumber dispute would hurt Canada more than the Americans, a Canadian forest industry spokesman says.

Instead, Canada should get more active in U.S. politics by advancing the interests of the mass of American homeowners and other lumber consumers against a small group of protectionist corporations, Carl Grenier, general manager of the Free Trade Lumber Council, said Wednesday.

"Sabre-rattling makes some people feel good, especially when it's against the U.S.," Mr. Grenier, whose group represents companies accounting for about 40 per cent of Canadian lumber shipments to America, told the Economic Club of Toronto. ...

A better approach is to "transform what has been a fight between U.S. producers and Canadian producers of softwood lumber into a fight between U.S. producers and consumers."

And although it might seem attractive to find new markets for Canadian exports—especially oil and gas for which "other customers are lining up at the pump"—Mr. Grenier noted that the North American Free Trade Agreement originated from the failure of the Trudeau government's 1970s Third Option strategy of trade diversification.

"For the foreseeable future, most of our trade eggs will stay firmly in the U.S. basket."...

Reprinted with permission from The Canadian Press.

Essence of the Story

■ It is not in Canada's interest to retaliate against the United States for the U.S. tariff on softwood imports from Canada.

■ Instead, Canada should appeal to the self-interest of American homeowners and other lumber consumers.

■ While it might seem attractive to find new markets for Canadian oil and gas exports, we must remember that NAFTA had its origin in the failure to diversify trade when Pierre Trudeau was prime minister.

■ The reality is that our trading future is with the United States.

Economic Analysis

■ The United States has imposed a 27 percent tariff on imports of Canadian lumber.

■ The tariff damages Canada, but it also damages the United States.

■ Figure 1 shows the U.S. market for lumber.

■ The demand curve of U.S. buyers of lumber is D.

■ There are two supply curves: the supply curve of the Canadian producers, S_C, and the supply curve of U.S. producers, S_{US}. We'll assume that Canada can supply any quantity at a price of $100 per load.

■ With no tariff, the quantity of lumber bought in the United States is QC_0. Of this amount, QP_0 is produced in the United States and the rest is imported from Canada, as shown by the arrow in Fig. 1.

■ Now the United States puts a 27 percent tariff on the import of lumber. Canadian lumber is now supplied to the U.S. market at the original supply price, $100, plus the tariff, $27, so the supply curve of lumber from Canada shifts to become S_C + *tariff*.

■ With the tariff, the quantity of lumber bought in the United States is QC_1. Of this amount, QP_1 is produced in the United States and the rest is imported from Canada, as shown by the arrow in Fig. 1.

■ The tariff decreases U.S. consumption and imports and increases U.S. production.

■ Figure 2 shows the winners and the losers in the United States.

■ The winners include U.S lumber producers, who gain additional producer surplus, which is shown by the blue area in Fig. 2.

■ Another winner is the U.S. government, which collects additional revenue, shown by the purple area in Fig. 2.

■ The sum of the blue, purple, and grey areas is the loss of consumer surplus that results from the tariff.

■ A deadweight loss arises—the decrease in consumer surplus exceeds the increase in producer surplus plus the tariff revenue—regardless of whether Canadian lumber producers receive a subsidy.

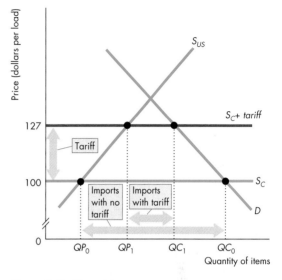

Figure 1 Tariffs and imports

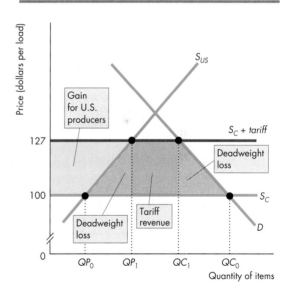

Figure 2 Winners and losers

SUMMARY

KEY POINTS

Patterns and Trends in International Trade
(p. 756)

- Large flows of trade take place between countries, most of which is in manufactured goods exchanged among rich industrialized countries.
- The volume of Canadian international trade is about 40 percent of total production.

The Gains from International Trade (pp. 757–762)

- When opportunity costs diverge, comparative advantage brings gains from trade.
- By increasing its production of goods in which it has a comparative advantage and then trading some of the increased output, a country can consume at points outside its production possibilities frontier.
- In the absence of international borrowing and lending, trade is balanced as prices adjust to reflect the international supply of and demand for goods.
- The world price balances the production and consumption plans of the trading parties. At the equilibrium price, trade is balanced.

International Trade Restrictions (pp. 763–766)

- Countries restrict international trade by imposing tariffs and nontariff barriers, such as quotas and VERS.
- International trade restrictions raise the domestic price of imported goods, lower the volume of imports, and reduce the total value of imports and exports by the same amount.

The Case Against Protection (pp. 767–771)

- Arguments that protection is necessary to save jobs, to protect infant industries, and to prevent dumping are weak.
- Arguments that protection is necessary for national security, allows us to compete with cheap foreign labour, makes the economy diversified and stable, penalizes lax environmental standards, protects national culture, and prevents exploitation of developing countries are flawed.

- Trade is restricted because tariffs raise government revenue and because protection brings a small loss to a large number of people and a large gain per person to a small number of people.

The Balance of International Payments
(pp. 772–775)

- A country's international transactions are recorded in its balance of payments accounts.
- The net exports surplus is equal to the government sector surplus plus the private sector surplus.

The North American Free Trade Agreement
(pp. 776–777)

- NAFTA is an agreement among Canada, the United States, and Mexico, which began in 1994 and grew from a previous Canada–U.S. agreement.
- Under NAFTA, trade has expanded more rapidly than before the agreement.

KEY FIGURES AND TABLE

Figure 32.1   Opportunity Cost in Farmland, 757
Figure 32.2   Opportunity Cost in Mobilia, 758
Figure 32.3   International Trade in Cars, 759
Figure 32.4   Expanding Consumption Possibilities, 760
Figure 32.6   The Effects of a Tariff, 764
Figure 32.7   The Effects of a Quota, 766
Table 32.2   Net Exports, the Government Budget, Saving, and Investment, 774

KEY TERMS

Dumping, 768
Exports, 756
General Agreement on Tariffs and Trade, 763
Imports, 756
Infant-industry argument, 767
Net exports, 756
Nontariff barrier, 763
North American Free Trade Agreement, 764
Quota, 766
Tariff, 763
Terms of trade, 758
Voluntary export restraint, 766
World Trade Organization, 763

PROBLEMS

Go to ⊗myeconlab for solutions to odd-numbered problems and additional exercises.

1. The table provides information about Virtual Reality's production possibilities.

TV sets (per day)		Computers (per day)
0	and	36
10	and	35
20	and	33
30	and	30
40	and	26
50	and	21
60	and	15
70	and	8
80	and	0

a. Calculate Virtual Reality's opportunity cost of a TV set when it produces 10 sets a day.
b. Calculate Virtual Reality's opportunity cost of a TV set when it produces 40 sets a day.
c. Calculate Virtual Reality's opportunity cost of a TV set when it produces 70 sets a day.
d. Using the answers to parts (a), (b), and (c), sketch the relationship between the opportunity cost of a TV set and the quantity of TV sets produced in Virtual Reality.

2. The table provides information about Vital Sign's production possibilities.

TV sets (per day)		Computers (per day)
0	and	18.0
10	and	17.5
20	and	16.5
30	and	15.0
40	and	13.0
50	and	10.5
60	and	7.5
70	and	4.0
80	and	0

a. Calculate Vital Sign's opportunity cost of a TV set when it produces 10 sets a day.
b. Calculate Vital Sign's opportunity cost of a TV set when it produces 40 sets a day.
c. Calculate Vital Sign's opportunity cost of a TV set when it produces 70 sets a day.

d. Using the answers to parts (a), (b), and (c), sketch the relationship between the opportunity cost of a TV set and the quantity of TV sets produced in Vital Sign.

3. Suppose that with no international trade, Virtual Reality in problem 1 produces and consumes 10 TV sets a day and Vital Sign in problem 2 produces and consumes 60 TV sets a day. Now suppose that the two countries begin to trade with each other.
a. Which country exports TV sets?
b. What adjustments are made to the amount of each good produced by each country?
c. What adjustments are made to the amount of each good consumed by each country?
d. What can you say about the terms of trade (the price of a TV set expressed as computers per TV set) under free trade?

4. Suppose that with no international trade, Virtual Reality in problem 1 produces and consumes 50 TV sets a day and Vital Sign in problem 2 produces and consumes 20 TV sets a day. Now suppose that the two countries begin to trade with each other.
a. Which country exports TV sets?
b. What adjustments are made to the amount of each good produced by each country?
c. What adjustments are made to the amount of each good consumed by each country?
d. What can you say about the terms of trade (the price of a TV set expressed as computers per TV set) under free trade?

5. Compare the total quantities of each good produced in problems 1 and 2 with the total quantities of each good produced in problems 3 and 4.
a. Does free trade increase or decrease the total quantities of TV sets and computers produced in each case? Why?
b. What happens to the price of a TV set in Virtual Reality in each case? Why does it rise in one case and fall in the other?
c. What happens to the price of a computer in Vital Sign in each case? Why does it rise in one case and fall in the other?

6. Compare the international trade in problem 3 with that in problem 4.
a. Why does Virtual Reality export TV sets in one case and import them in the other case?
b. Do the TV producers or the computer producers gain in each case?
c. Do consumers gain in each case?

7. The figure depicts the world market for soybeans. With free trade, what is the world price of soybeans, the quantities exported and imported, and the balance of trade?

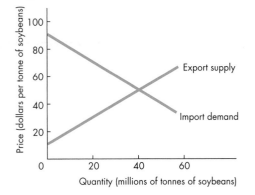

8. If in problem 7, a tariff of $20 per tonne is imposed on imported soybean, what is the world price of soybeans, the quantity of soybean imports, the price in the importing country, and the tariff revenue?

9. The Silecon, whose currency is the grain, conducted the following transactions in 2002:

Item	Billions of grains
Net exports of goods and services	250
Borrowing from the rest of the world	–60
Lending to the rest of the world	200
Change in official reserves	–10

What are the current account, capital account, and official settlements balances?

10. Spin, whose currency is the wheel, conducted the following transactions in 2002:

Item	Billions of wheels
Net exports of goods and services	20
Borrowing from the rest of the world	4
Lending to the rest of the world	24
Change in official reserves	0

What are the current account, capital account, and official settlements balances?

CRITICAL THINKING

1. Study *Reading Between the Lines* on pp. 778–779 and then answer the following questions:
   a. Why did the United States impose a tariff on lumber imports from Canada?
   b. What are the effects of the tariff on lumber?
   c. Who are the winners and who are the losers from the tariff on lumber?
   d. Modify the figures on page 779 to show the effects of a Canadian subsidy to lumber producers on the consumer surplus, producer surplus, and deadweight loss in the United States.

WEB EXERCISES

Use the links on [myeconlab] **to work the following exercises.**

1. Visit the Web site of the World Trade Organization and obtain information about the latest round of trade talks on freeing trade in agricultural products.
   a. What is the argument for ending agricultural subsidies in rich countries?
   b. Why is the European Union so opposed to dismantling farm subsidies?
   c. Why do you think Australia and New Zealand have ended farm subsidies?
   d. What is Canada's position of farm subsidies? What accounts for Canada's position?

2. Obtain information to write a NAFTA report card on agriculture. Then answer the following questions:
   a. What does NAFTA seek to achieve in agriculture trade?
   b. What has NAFTA achieved to date?
   c. What are the obstacles to greater gains for North American trade in agricultural products?
   d. Would you vote to maintain NAFTA? Why or why not?
   e. Would you vote to expand NAFTA to include other countries? Why or why not?

AGGREGATE SUPPLY, ECONOMIC GROWTH, AND INTERNATIONAL TRADE

PART 9

Expanding the Frontier

Economics is about how we cope with scarcity. We cope by making choices that balance marginal benefits and marginal costs so that we use our scarce resources efficiently.

These choices determine how much work we do; how hard we work at school to learn the mental skills that form our human capital and that determine the kinds of jobs we get and the incomes we earn; and how much we save for future big-ticket expenditures. These choices also determine how much businesses and governments spend on new capital—on auto assembly lines, computers and fibre cables for improved Internet services, shopping malls, highways, bridges, and tunnels; and how intensively existing capital and natural resources are used and therefore how quickly they wear out or are used up. Most significant of all, these choices determine the problems that scientists, engineers, and other inventors work on to develop new technologies.

All the choices we've just described determine two vital measures of economic performance:

- Real GDP
- Economic growth

Real GDP is determined by the quantity of labour, the quantity of capital, and the state of technological knowledge. And economic growth is determined by growth in the quantity of labour, capital accumulation, and technological advances.

Economic growth, maintained at a steady rate over a number of decades, is the single most powerful influence on any society. It brings a transformation that continues to amaze thoughtful people. Economic growth that is maintained at a rapid rate can transform a society in years, not decades. Such transformations are taking place right now in many Asian countries. These transformations are economic miracles.

The three chapters in this part studied the foundations of aggregate supply, the miracle of rapid economic growth and the forces that shape our capacity to produce goods and services, and the gains from international trade and the national balance of payments. Chapter 30 explained how labour market equilibrium determines potential GDP and derives the aggregate supply curves. Chapter 31 studied the process of economic growth in the fast-growing economies of Asia and Canada. It explained how growth is influenced by technological change and the incentives that stimulate it. Chapter 32 explained how all nations can benefit from free international trade, reviewed the free trade versus protection debate, and explained the source of a nation's international deficit.

The global economy is big news these days. And it has always attracted attention. On the next pages, you can meet the economist who first understood comparative advantage, David Ricardo. And you can meet one of Canada's leading international economists, Dan Trefler of the University of Toronto.

Gains from International Trade

THE ECONOMIST

David Ricardo *(1772–1832) was a
highly successful 27-year-old stockbroker
when he stumbled on a copy of Adam Smith's*
Wealth of Nations *(see p. 54) on a weekend
visit to the country. He was immediately
hooked and went on to become the most cele-
brated economist of his age and one of the
all-time great economists. One of his many
contributions was to develop the principle of
comparative advantage, the foundation on
which the modern theory of international
trade is built. The example he used to illustrate this principle was the trade between
England and Portugal in cloth and wine.*

*The World Trade Organization (WTO)
and its predecessor, General Agreement on
Tariffs and Trade, were established as a reaction
against the devastation wrought by beggar-thy-
neighbour tariffs imposed during the 1930s.
But the WTO and the goals that it pursues are
also triumphs for the logic first worked out by
Smith and Ricardo.*

THE ISSUES

Until the mid-eighteenth century, it was generally believed that the purpose of international trade was to keep exports greater than
imports and pile up gold. If gold was accumulated, it was believed, the nation would
prosper; if gold was lost through an international deficit, the nation would be drained of
money and impoverished. These beliefs are
called *mercantilism*, and the *mercantilists*
were pamphleteers who advocated with mis-
sionary fervor the pursuit of an international
surplus. If exports did not exceed imports,
the mercantilists wanted imports restricted.

In the 1740s, David Hume explained
that as the quantity of money (gold) changes,
so also does the price level, and the nation's
real wealth is unaffected. In the 1770s, Adam
Smith argued that import restrictions would
lower the gains from specialization and
make a nation poorer. Thirty years later,
David Ricardo proved the law of comparative advantage and demonstrated the superi-
ority of free trade. Mercantilism was
intellectually bankrupt but remained politically powerful.

Gradually, through the nineteenth century, the mercantilist influence waned and
North America and Western Europe prospered in an environment of increasingly free
international trade. But despite remarkable
advances in economic understanding, mercantilism never quite died. It had a brief and
devastating revival in the 1920s and 1930s
when tariff hikes brought about the collapse
of international trade and accentuated the
Great Depression. It subsided again after
World War II with the establishment of the
General Agreement on Tariffs and Trade
(GATT).

But mercantilism lingers on. The often-
expressed view that the United States should

restrict Chinese imports and reduce its deficit with China and the fear that NAFTA will bring economic ruin to Canada are modern manifestations of mercantilism. It would be interesting to have David Hume, Adam Smith, and David Ricardo commenting on these views. But we know what they would say—the same things that they said to the eighteenth-century mercantilists. And they would still be right today.

THEN

In the eighteenth century, when mercantilists and economists were debating the pros and cons of free international exchange, the transportation technology that was available limited the gains from international trade. Sailing ships with tiny cargo holds took close to a month to cross the Atlantic Ocean. But the potential gains were large, and so was the incentive to cut shipping costs. By the 1850s, the clipper ship had been developed, cutting the journey from Boston to Liverpool to only $12^{1}/_{4}$ days. Half a century later, 10,000-ton steamships were sailing between North America and England in just 4 days. As sailing times and costs declined, the gains from international trade increased and the volume of trade expanded.

NOW

The container ship has revolutionized international trade and contributed to its continued expansion. Today, most goods cross the oceans in containers—metal boxes—packed into and piled on top of ships like this one. Container technology has cut the cost of ocean shipping by economizing on handling and by making cargoes harder to steal, thereby lowering insurance costs. It is unlikely that there would be much international trade in goods such as television sets and DVD players without this technology. High-value and perishable cargoes such as flowers and fresh foods, as well as urgent courier packages, travel by air. Every day, dozens of cargo-laden 747s fly between every major North American city and to destinations across the Atlantic and Pacific oceans.

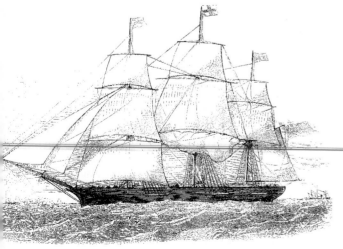

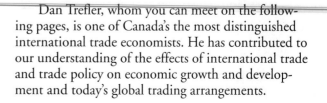

Dan Trefler, whom you can meet on the following pages, is one of Canada's the most distinguished international trade economists. He has contributed to our understanding of the effects of international trade and trade policy on economic growth and development and today's global trading arrangements.

785

Dan Trefler *is the J. Douglas and Ruth Grant Canada Research Chair in Competitiveness and Prosperity at the University of Toronto's Rotman School of Management. Born in Toronto, he was an undergraduate at the University of Toronto and a graduate student at Cambridge University and the University of California, Los Angeles.*

Professor Trefler is a Research Fellow at the Canadian Institute for Advanced Research and a Research Associate at the National Bureau of Economic Research. He also serves on the Ontario Task Force on Competitiveness, Productivity, and Economic Progress. He was the winner of the Canadian Economics Association's Rae Award for Excellence in Research and is a co-editor of the Journal of International Economics.

Professor Trefler's research is broad but focuses on policy levers for promoting Canadian competitiveness.

Michael Parkin and Robin Bade talked with Dan Trefler about his work and the light that it sheds on international trade issues such as offshoring and NAFTA.

Dan Trefler

Dan, what attracted you to economics?

Throughout my life, including when I was a teenager, I've been interested in how social systems work and what makes some societies so much more successful than others.

Economics offers one of several perspectives on that question. What is so nice about the economic perspective is that it tries to combine a whole bunch of nifty theories about what makes a society successful with evidence-based data-driven analysis that is often lacking in other approaches.

So why is it that Africa has done so poorly over the years? We often use very vague terms like colonial heritage or poor institutions, but if you gave me a large-scale database to analyze the problem, I'd be like a pig at the trough, delighted to really think about it.

Why did you decide to focus on international economics?

In part, because of a profound interest in development economics, which is so tightly linked to international trade. But more specifically, as a young man just starting out in economics, the hot topic of the day was the 1988 General Election which was fought on the issue of should Canada have a free trade agreement with the United States, after more than 100 years of protectionism.

Who has had the greatest influence on your development as an economist?

Again, as a teenager I was thinking about society in political science and sociological terms until I read a book by Che Guevara (now back in fashion), who said that if you really want to understand society you have to understand economics. The best place to think about that is to be doing things like reading the *Wall Street Journal*, and from there it was downhill. I was completely entranced by the economic approach.

Why should Canadians care about international trade?

Because it is where little things make a big difference. I think most of us would like to think that we have solutions to all of society's problems, which are magic bullets. In fact, the way to make Canada an even greater place is to make it even a little bit more productive, say 10 to15 percent more productive. Even a 10 percent increase in our productivity would generate for us upwards of $100 billion in revenue to play with. With $100 billion, think of what you could do. You could, if you're a new conservative, eliminate all corporate taxes, which would cost maybe about $25 billion. If you were very left leaning, you could pour huge amounts of money into single moms, natives, immigrants, and male high school dropouts—the four poorest groups in our country.

> " *Little things make a big difference. ... Even a 10 percent increase in our productivity would generate for us upwards of $100 billion in revenue to play with. ... Interntional trade is one of the biggest drivers of productivity.* "

You would have plenty of money left to drive an agenda for children if you were so inclined; lots of money left for redistributing to our have-not provinces like Newfoundland. You could run every single one of these things that I've mentioned at a cadillac level of service or delivery with $100 billion.

So worrying about productivity is really worrying about how we're going to feed our social agenda. And then that's where trade comes in. International trade is one of the biggest drivers of productivity, and it does so in two ways. First, it pressures our companies to become more innovative than they ever have been; and second, it supports our companies by providing them with the possibility of accessing larger markets, say like the U.S. market or the Chinese market.

So I think about international trade as a way of pressuring firms to be more competitive and in supporting them in entering the foreign markets.

Let's talk about the aspect of international economic activity that scares most people: offshoring. First, is it really new, or has it been around a long time? Or, what is new about it?

You know I read recently in the back of a news magazine an advertisement saying "offshore your personal life." They provided dating services for people!

We hear a lot of hype around offshoring. There are two aspects of it that are new. One is that the pace at which we are seeing manufacturing rise in low-wage countries like China is really breathtaking. That's both wonderful and scary. It's wonderful for these poor countries, which are suddenly finding themselves to be more affluent. It's a little scary for Canadian workers in the manufacturing sector.

The other aspect that is really fundamentally new and we've never seen it before is the tradability of services. The idea that somebody sitting in, say, Bangalore, India, is providing services to us is truly remarkable. And it speaks to the word "globalization" in a way that I think no other statement does. Nothing like that has ever been seen in history.

How big is the offshoring of services?

The Bangalore example turned out to be the exception to the rule. First of all, offshoring is not that large. There are different ways of doing the accounting, but if you think about offshoring of services, which is not all of offshoring, it accounts for only about 10 percent of our international trade. It's a small amount though it is growing fast and that's why people are so interested in it.

The second aspect of offshoring of services is that 85 percent of it goes to other rich countries, like the United States, so only a small portion of it is with countries like India. But that is changing rapidly. So right now, it's not important. Where we'll be in the future, that's another question.

What are the effects of offshoring on unemployment and wages?

The unemployment rate fluctuates for reasons that have very little to do with international trade. That is very obvious if you just plot the data.

Offshoring does have an impact on wages, but much less of an impact than people think. There is a small group of people out there, maybe less than 5 percent of the population, who has been hammered by international trade, seeing their jobs displaced and wages absolutely collapse under the weight to Chinese competition. That is the exception.

The interesting thing about offshoring of services is what impact it will have on wages because now we're seeing international trade affecting the wages of the very skilled. That is something new. That is not something we've ever seen before. It is too early to say for sure what the impacts are but the early research suggests that it will have a very large impact on wages and a moderate impact on employment.

Let's now turn to another big source of discussion and concern: NAFTA. What is the latest tally on its benefits and costs?

NAFTA was my teething grounds in economics—I spent years and years studying it. There are many aspects of it that interest people. Let's start with the narrowest and simplest and that is its affect on employment, wages, and productivity. NAFTA has had a large effect on displacing workers. That is, the shipping of workers from low value-added activities, activities that were once protected, into higher value-added activities. Some workers were definitely displaced. And it hurts if you're unemployed for six months, looking for a new job. That's a big hit.

There's been absolutely no affect of the free trade agreement on wages, which to me was a big surprise since I was expecting that we would be competing with labour from south of the Mason-Dixon Line in the United States.

The surprise has been the huge impact on productivity and that impact has been upward of 6 percent for manufacturing as a whole, which is a very, very large number. The idea that a single government policy like liberalizing trade could have such a big impact on productivity is to me remarkable and a testament to what government can do when it puts its mind to it.

Now there is also a larger issue about what is sometimes called the "Trade and ..." agenda, which deals with things like the environment and sovereignty issues where we retain our rights over water and so on. Those have turned out so far to be a non-issue.

What advice do you have for a student who is just starting to study economics? Is economics a good subject in which to major?

Economics works extremely well with the social sciences. It works with sociology, it works with political science, and it's starting to work with areas that are more surprising, which is psychology and the natural sciences; we're getting an increased insight in that area. What advice do I have? It would be to read a lot. Becoming knowledgeable is the best way to have fun.

What would you suggest students read?

Read books, read books. People all around you are writing books that are acceptable to very general audiences. Go out and read some books on neuroscience and economics, or sociology and economics, or political science. If you're interested in economic development, read books about the new institutionalism. If you're interested in international trade, read Helpman's *The Mystery of Economic Growth* or Jared Diamond's *Guns, Germs, and Steel*. Or if you're interested in something more historical, read David S. Landes, *The Wealth and Poverty of Nations*.

What can a student do to make a difference?

When it comes to international trade, it's very important to know that you have a huge impact through activism, that you can do it through going out there and demonstrating on the lines every time there is an international trade agreement. But it's important to become informed so that you know exactly why you're out there demonstrating.

You can also make a difference through consumer activism—that is things like eco-labelling, insisting on it or making the effort to try to find out where the goods that you use are produced, or even something simple like going to Second Cup or Starbucks and saying "what you're doing for fair trade in coffee is not nearly enough, you could do a lot more."

CANADIAN
ECONOMY
DATABASE

CANADIAN ECONOMY DATABASE

The following data tables provide a description of some of the main features of the Canadian economy from 1926 to 2001.

You can make graphs of these data by using *Economics in Action* on the Parkin–Bade Web site. To do so, open the table of contents page for *any* chapter, click on Data Graphing and then click on Canada Historical.

These data are updated annually on the Parkin–Bade Web site.

Sources

CANSIM series: Statistics Canada, Ottawa

HSC series: Statistics Canada, *Historical Statistics of Canada*, Second Edition, F. H. Leacy (ed.), Ottawa, 1983.

HSC(1) series: The MacMillan Company of Canada Limited, *Historical Statistics of Canada*, M.C. Urquhart (ed.), Toronto, 1965.

A break in a series is indicated by [b].

Variables

1. Real GDP
HSC series F55 and CANSIM series v1992292. The data for 1926–1960 are F55 multiplied by the 1961 ratio of v1992292 to F55.

2. Real consumption expenditure
HSC series F33 and CANSIM series v1992262. The data for 1926–1960 are F33 multiplied by the 1961 ratio of v1992262 to F33.

3. Real investment
HSC is F55 minus the sum of F33, F34, and F51 plus F52; CANSIM series is v1992292 minus the sum of v1992262, v1992268, 1992282 plus v1992286. The data for 1926–1960 are *HSC* multiplied by the 1961 ratio of CANSIM to *HSC*.

4. Real government expenditure
HSC series F34 and CANSIM series v1992268. The data for 1926–1960 are F34 multiplied by the 1961 ratio of v1992268 to F34.

5. Real exports
HSC series F51 and CANSIM series v1992282. The data for 1926–1960 are F51 multiplied by the 1961 ratio of v1992282 to F51.

6. Real imports
HSC series F52 and CANSIM series v1992286. The data for 1926–1960 are F51 multiplied by the 1961 ratio of v1992286 to F52.

7. Real net exports
Real exports *minus* real imports.

8. Potential GDP
Real GDP trends and authors' assumptions and calculations.

9. Fluctuations around potential GDP
Percentage deviation of real GDP from potential GDP.

10. Real GDP growth rate
Annual percentage change in real GDP.

11. GDP deflator
HSC series K172 and CANSIM series v647710 and v3860248. The data for 1961–1980 are v647710 multiplied by the 1981 ratio of v3860248 to v647710. The data for 1926–1960 are K172 multiplied by the 1961 ratio of the above calculation to K172.

12. CPI
Statistics Canada, CANSIM series v737344.

13. Inflation rate
Annual percentage change in the GDP deflator.

14. Inflation rate
Annual percentage change in the CPI.

15. Labour force
CANSIM series v21051 and v2461098.

16. Labour force participation rate
CANSIM series v21051, v21056, and v2461245.

17. Average weekly hours
HSC series E128, E129, E130, E131, E132, E133, E134, E135; Statistics Canada, CANSIM series v2461119 and v2641490, and authors' calculations.

18. Unemployment rate
HSC series D127, D132, and D491 and CANSIM series v2461224.

19. Long-term interest rate
HSC(1) series H605, *HSC* series J475, and Bank of Canada series B14013.

20. Short-term interest rate
HSC series J471 and Bank of Canada series B14060.

21. Federal government revenues
HSC series H18 and CANSIM series v499985.

22. Federal government outlays
HSC series H34 and CANSIM series v500016.

23. Federal government surplus(+)/deficit(-)
HSC series H18 and H34 and CANSIM series v499985 and v500016.

24. Gross federal debt
CANSIM series v151537.

25. M1
Bank of Canada series B2033.

26. M2+
Bank of Canada series B2037.

27. M1 velocity
Series 1 multiplied by series 11 divided by series 25.

28. M2+ velocity
Series 1 multiplied by series 11 divided by series 26.

29. Exchange rate
HSC series J562 and CANSIM series v37426.

30. Current account
HSC series G83 and CANSIM series v114421.

Year		1926	1927	1928	1929	1930	1931	1932	1933	1934	1935
Real GDP (billions of 1997 dollars)	1	61.2	67.0	73.1	73.4	70.3	61.4	55.0	51.3	57.6	62.1
Real consumption expenditure (billions of 1997 dollars)	2	35.6	39.8	43.6	46.3	44.3	42.2	38.9	37.9	39.9	41.6
Real investment (billions of 1997 dollars)	3	12.4	14.5	16.3	14.4	12.7	4.2	1.0	0.0	2.8	4.5
Real government expenditures (billions of 1997 dollars)	4	10.0	10.5	10.6	11.9	13.0	13.8	13.3	11.2	11.9	12.4
Real exports (billions of 1997 dollars)	5	12.1	12.2	13.8	13.0	11.3	10.1	9.4	9.5	10.7	11.8
Real imports (billions of 1997 dollars)	6	8.9	9.9	11.1	12.1	11.0	8.8	7.6	7.2	7.7	8.2
Real net exports (billions of 1997 dollars)	7	3.2	2.3	2.7	0.9	0.3	1.3	1.8	2.2	3.0	3.5
Potential GDP (billions of 1997 dollars)	8	62.0	63.8	65.7	67.7	69.7	71.8	73.9	76.1	78.4	80.8
Fluctuations around potential GDP (percentage)	9	−1.2	5.0	11.3	8.5	0.8	−14.5	−25.6	−32.6	−26.6	−23.2
Real GDP growth rate (percent per year)	10	—	9.5	9.1	0.4	−4.3	−12.7	−10.4	−6.7	12.1	7.8
GDP deflator (1997 = 100)	11	8.7	8.6	8.5	8.6	8.4	7.9	7.1	7.0	7.1	7.1
CPI (1992 = 100)	12	10.9	10.8	10.8	11.0	10.9	9.8	8.9	8.5	8.6	8.7
Inflation rate (GDP deflator percent per year)	13	—	−1.1	−0.6	1.1	−2.5	−6.2	−9.3	−1.7	1.4	0.3
Inflation rate (CPI percent per year)	14	0	−0.9	0	1.9	−0.9	−10.1	−9.2	−4.5	1.2	1.2
Labour force (millions)	15	3.7	3.8	3.9	4.0	4.1	4.2	4.2	4.3	4.3	4.4
Labour force participation rate (percentage)	16	57.8	57.9	58.0	58.1	58.2	58.3	58.2	58.0	57.9	57.8
Average weekly hours (hours per week)	17	—	—	—	—	—	—	—	—	—	—
Unemployment rate (percentage)	18	2.9	1.8	1.7	2.9	9.1	11.6	17.6	19.3	14.5	14.2
Long-term interest rate (percent per year)	19	4.9	4.6	4.5	4.9	4.7	4.6	5.1	4.6	4.0	3.6
Short-term interest rate (percent per year)	20	—	—	—	—	—	—	—	—	2.5	1.5
Federal government revenues (billions of dollars)	21	0.4	0.4	0.5	0.5	0.4	0.3	0.3	0.3	0.4	0.4
Federal government outlays (billions of dollars)	22	0.4	0.4	0.4	0.4	0.4	0.4	0.5	0.5	0.5	0.5
Federal government surplus (+)/deficit(−) (billions of dollars)	23	0	0.1	0.1	0	−0.1	−0.1	−0.2	−0.1	−0.1	−0.2
Gross federal debt (billions of dollars)	24	2.8	2.8	2.7	2.7	2.6	2.7	2.9	3.1	3.2	3.5
M1 (billions of dollars)	25	—	—	—	—	—	—	—	—	—	—
M2+ (billions of dollars)	26	—	—	—	—	—	—	—	—	—	—
M1 velocity (GDP/M1)	27	—	—	—	—	—	—	—	—	—	—
M2+ velocity (GDP/M2+)	28	—	—	—	—	—	—	—	—	—	—
Exchange rate (U.S. dollars per Canadian dollar)	29	1.00	1.00	1.00	1.00	1.00	0.96	0.88	0.92	1.01	0.99
Current account balance (billions of dollars)	30	0.1	0	0	−0.3	−0.3	−0.2	−0.1	0	0.1	0.1

	1936	1937	1938	1939	1940	1941	1942	1943	1944	1945	1946	1947	1948	1949	
	64.8	71.3	71.9	77.2	88.1	100.8	119.5	124.3	129.2	126.3	123.0	128.2	131.4	136.4	1
	43.5	46.2	45.6	46.9	50.3	53.7	55.1	56.7	60.8	66.9	74.4	79.6	77.7	82.1	2
	4.0	8.3	8.8	11.3	6.4	0.5	−20.7	−29.9	−38.0	−19.0	9.5	19.5	23.6	23.4	3
	12.5	12.6	14.1	15.0	26.5	38.3	80.2	87.7	100.7	69.3	32.8	24.7	23.4	25.9	4
	14.2	14.5	13.1	14.4	16.4	21.6	19.3	26.8	25.9	25.2	21.2	21.0	21.7	20.4	5
	9.3	10.3	9.6	10.3	11.5	13.3	14.3	17.0	20.2	16.0	14.8	16.7	15.0	15.4	6
	4.8	4.2	3.4	4.1	4.9	8.3	5.0	9.8	5.7	9.2	6.3	4.4	6.7	5.0	7
	83.2	85.7	88.2	90.9	93.6	97.3	101.1	105.1	109.3	113.7	118.3	123.2	128.2	133.6	8
	−22.1	−16.7	−18.5	−15.0	−5.8	3.6	18.2	18.2	18.2	11.1	3.9	4.1	2.4	2.1	9
	4.4	10.0	0.8	7.4	14.1	14.4	18.6	4.0	4.0	−2.2	−2.7	4.3	2.5	3.8	10
	7.4	7.6	7.6	7.5	7.9	8.5	8.9	9.2	9.4	9.7	10.0	10.8	12.2	12.7	11
	8.8	9.1	9.2	9.2	9.5	10.1	10.5	10.7	10.8	10.9	11.2	12.3	14.0	14.5	12
	3.3	2.6	0	−0.9	4.7	7.9	4.5	3.5	3.1	2.5	2.9	8.8	12.3	4.3	13
	1.1	3.4	1.1	0	3.3	6.3	4.0	1.9	0.9	0.9	2.8	9.8	13.8	3.6	14
	4.5	4.5	4.6	4.6	4.6	4.5	4.6	4.6	4.5	4.5	4.8	4.9	5.0	5.2	15
	57.6	57.5	57.4	57.2	56.6	55.4	56.5	58.0	57.4	56.2	55.0	54.9	54.6	54.4	16
	—	—	—	—	—	—	—	—	—	44.1	42.7	42.5	42.3	42.2	17
	12.8	9.1	11.4	11.4	9.0	4.1	2.7	1.4	1.2	1.4	[b]3.4	2.2	2.3	2.8	18
	[b]3.0	3.2	3.1	3.2	3.3	3.1	3.1	3.0	3.0	2.9	2.6	2.6	2.9	2.8	19
	0.9	0.7	0.6	0.7	0.7	0.6	0.5	0.5	0.4	0.4	0.4	0.4	0.4	0.5	20
	0.5	0.5	0.5	0.6	0.9	1.5	2.3	2.8	2.7	3.0	3.0	2.9	2.8	2.6	21
	0.5	0.5	0.6	0.7	1.3	1.9	4.4	5.3	5.2	5.1	2.6	2.2	2.2	2.4	22
	−0.1	0	−0.1	−0.1	−0.4	−0.4	−2.1	−2.6	−2.6	−2.1	0.4	0.7	0.6	0.1	23
	3.5	3.6	3.6	3.7	4.0	5.0	6.6	8.8	11.8	14.9	17.9	17.7	17.2	16.9	24
	—	—	—	—	—	—	—	—	—	—	—	—	—	—	25
	—	—	—	—	—	—	—	—	—	—	—	—	—	—	26
	—	—	—	—	—	—	—	—	—	—	—	—	—	—	27
	—	—	—	—	—	—	—	—	—	—	—	—	—	—	28
	1.00	1.00	0.99	0.96	0.90	0.90	0.90	0.90	0.90	0.91	1.00	1.00	1.00	0.97	29
	0.2	0.2	0.1	0.1	0.2	0.5	0.1	0.7	0.1	0.7	[b]0.3	0.0	0.4	0.2	30

Year		1950	1951	1952	1953	1954	1955	1956	1957	1958	1959
Real GDP (billions of 1997 dollars)	1	146.7	154.1	167.8	176.5	174.3	190.7	206.9	211.7	216.6	224.8
Real consumption expenditure (billions of 1997 dollars)	2	87.5	88.2	94.4	100.9	104.6	113.6	122.1	126.6	131.2	138.5
Real investment (billions of 1997 dollars)	3	27.8	26.2	23.4	26.0	21.8	29.3	37.5	38.0	35.2	38.0
Real government expenditures (billions of 1997 dollars)	4	27.9	36.4	44.8	46.2	44.4	45.4	46.6	45.8	47.2	46.8
Real exports (billions of 1997 dollars)	5	20.3	22.2	24.7	24.5	23.6	25.4	27.3	27.5	27.4	28.5
Real imports (billions of 1997 dollars)	6	16.8	18.9	19.5	21.2	20.2	22.9	26.5	26.2	24.4	26.9
Real net exports (billions of 1997 dollars)	7	3.5	3.3	5.2	3.3	3.4	2.5	0.7	1.3	3.0	1.6
Potential GDP (billions of 1997 dollars)	8	139.1	145.0	151.1	157.6	164.4	171.5	179.0	186.9	195.3	204.1
Fluctuations around potential GDP (percentage)	9	5.5	6.3	11.0	12.0	6.0	11.2	15.5	13.3	10.9	10.2
Real GDP growth rate (percent per year)	10	7.6	5.0	8.9	5.1	−1.2	9.4	8.4	2.4	2.3	3.8
GDP deflator (1997 = 100)	11	13.0	14.5	15.1	15.1	15.3	15.4	16.0	16.3	16.6	16.9
CPI (1992 = 100)	12	14.9	16.4	16.9	16.7	16.8	16.8	17.1	17.6	18.0	18.3
Inflation rate (GDP deflator percent per year)	13	2.4	11.3	4.4	−0.2	1.6	0.6	3.7	2.1	1.5	2.0
Inflation rate (CPI percent per year)	14	2.8	10.1	3.0	−1.2	0.6	0	1.8	2.9	2.3	1.7
Labour force (millions)	15	5.2	5.2	5.3	5.4	5.5	5.6	5.8	6.0	6.1	6.2
Labour force participation rate (percentage)	16	53.7	53.7	53.5	53.1	52.9	52.9	53.5	54.0	53.9	53.8
Average weekly hours (hours per week)	17	42.3	41.7	41.5	41.3	40.7	41.0	41.0	40.4	40.2	40.7
Unemployment rate (percentage)	18	3.6	2.4	2.9	3.0	4.6	4.4	3.4	4.6	7.0	6.0
Long-term interest rate (percent per year)	19	2.8	3.2	3.6	3.7	3.1	3.1	3.6	4.2	4.5	5.0
Short-term interest rate (percent per year)	20	0.6	0.8	1.1	1.7	1.4	1.6	2.9	3.8	2.3	4.8
Federal government revenues (billions of dollars)	21	3.1	4.0	4.6	4.7	4.4	4.7	5.5	5.4	5.1	5.8
Federal government outlays (billions of dollars)	22	2.9	3.8	4.6	4.7	4.7	4.8	5.2	5.5	6.0	6.3
Federal government surplus (+)/deficit(−) (billions of dollars)	23	0.2	0.2	−0.1	0	−0.2	−0.1	0.3	−0.1	−0.8	−0.4
Gross federal debt (billions of dollars)	24	16.7	16.7	16.8	17.4	17.6	17.6	18.7	18.0	18.0	19.7
M1 (billions of dollars)	25	—	—	—	4.2	4.4	4.8	4.8	4.8	5.4	5.2
M2+ (billions of dollars)	26	—	—	—	—	—	—	—	—	—	—
M1 velocity (GDP/M1)	27	—	—	—	6.3	6.1	6.1	6.9	7.2	6.6	7.3
M2+ velocity (GDP/M2+)	28	—	—	—	—	—	—	—	—	—	—
Exchange rate (U.S. dollars per Canadian dollar)	29	[b]0.95	0.95	1.02	1.02	1.03	1.01	1.02	1.04	1.03	1.04
Current account balance (billions of dollars)	30	−0.3	−0.5	0.2	−0.4	−0.4	−0.7	−1.3	−1.4	−1.1	−1.4

	1960	1961	1962	1963	1964	1965	1966	1967	1968	1969	1970	1971	1972	1973	
	231.3	245.2	262.4	276.3	294.2	312.9	333.7	343.5	360.2	378.3	389.8	405.9	428.0	457.8	1
	143.3	152.7	160.4	167.0	175.7	185.8	194.9	202.0	210.7	220.5	224.6	236.7	253.0	270.0	2
	37.3	34.1	36.7	39.0	44.4	51.0	56.2	52.2	53.6	59.4	56.8	61.2	65.6	75.9	3
	47.9	64.0	67.4	69.3	72.3	76.8	83.8	90.5	95.8	99.0	106.2	110.5	113.7	117.5	4
	29.7	39.0	40.8	44.4	50.5	52.8	60.0	66.3	74.3	80.3	87.8	91.9	99.8	109.8	5
	26.9	38.5	39.3	40.0	45.1	51.1	58.0	61.2	67.4	76.2	75.0	80.0	91.4	104.7	6
	2.8	0.5	1.5	4.4	5.4	1.7	2.0	5.2	6.9	4.1	12.7	11.9	8.3	5.1	7
	212.0	248.3	262.2	275.0	290.4	306.4	325.8	337.0	355.9	373.4	389.6	406.5	426.8	451.8	8
	9.1	−1.2	0.1	0.5	1.3	2.1	2.4	1.9	1.2	1.3	0.1	−0.2	0.3	1.3	9
	2.9	2.8	7.0	5.3	6.5	6.4	6.6	2.9	4.9	5.0	3.0	4.1	5.4	7.0	10
	17.1	16.8	17.0	17.4	17.9	18.5	19.4	20.3	21.1	22.2	23.1	24.3	25.7	28.2	11
	18.5	18.7	18.9	19.2	19.6	20.0	20.8	21.5	22.4	23.4	24.2	24.9	26.1	28.1	12
	1.3	0.4	1.4	2.0	2.9	3.6	4.9	4.5	4.1	4.8	4.4	4.8	5.9	9.7	13
	1.1	1.1	1.1	1.6	2.1	2.0	4.0	3.4	4.2	4.5	3.4	2.9	4.8	7.7	14
	6.4	6.5	6.6	6.7	6.9	7.1	7.4	7.7	7.9	8.2	8.4	8.6	8.9	9.3	15
	54.2	54.1	53.9	53.8	54.1	54.4	55.1	55.5	55.5	55.8	55.8	56.1	56.5	57.5	16
	40.7	40.5	40.3	40.1	40.1	40.0	39.7	38.9	38.5	37.9	37.3	37.1	37.2	36.6	17
	7.0	7.1	5.9	5.5	4.7	3.9	3.6	4.1	4.8	4.7	5.9	6.4	6.3	5.6	18
	5.1	5.0	5.1	5.1	5.1	5.3	5.7	6.0	6.7	7.6	7.9	7.0	7.2	7.6	19
	3.2	2.8	4.0	3.6	3.7	4.0	5.0	4.6	6.3	7.1	6.1	3.6	3.5	5.4	20
	6.2	6.6	6.7	7.0	8.0	8.8	9.6	10.5	11.7	13.9	14.9	16.5	18.8	21.9	21
	6.6	7.1	7.6	7.7	8.1	8.6	9.8	11.0	12.2	13.2	15.1	17.2	19.6	21.8	22
	−0.3	−0.5	−0.9	−0.7	−0.1	0.2	−0.2	−0.5	−0.5	0.7	−0.2	−0.7	−0.9	0.1	23
	20.4	20.9	22.8	24.5	26.2	26.8	27.7	29.8	32.0	34.4	35.8	39.9	43.8	46.2	24
	5.5	5.9	6.1	6.3	6.7	7.1	7.7	8.4	8.9	9.7	9.9	11.0	12.7	14.6	25
	—	—	—	—	—	—	—	—	32.2	35.6	38.9	43.8	49.8	58.0	26
	7.2	6.9	7.3	7.6	7.8	8.1	8.4	8.2	8.5	8.7	9.1	9.0	8.6	8.8	27
	—	—	—	—	—	—	—	—	2.4	2.4	2.3	2.2	2.2	2.2	28
	1.03	0.99	0.94	0.93	0.93	0.93	0.93	0.93	0.93	0.93	0.96	0.99	1.01	1.00	29
	−1.2	−1.1	−1.2	−0.9	−0.5	−1.8	−1.7	−1.4	−1.1	−2.1	0.5	−1.0	−2.4	−2.1	30

Year		1974	1975	1976	1977	1978	1979	1980	1981	1982	1983
Real GDP (billions of 1997 dollars)	1	474.7	483.3	508.4	526.0	546.8	567.6	579.9	600.3	583.1	598.9
Real consumption expenditure (billions of 1997 dollars)	2	283.5	294.3	309.4	318.0	327.5	335.0	340.7	344.8	336.1	344.9
Real investment (billions of 1997 dollars)	3	84.9	84.5	91.6	91.7	92.4	106.8	103.2	112.4	71.9	83.6
Real government expenditures (billions of 1997 dollars)	4	124.7	132.6	134.5	140.4	142.5	143.6	148.3	150.3	154.3	155.9
Real exports (billions of 1997 dollars)	5	104.8	96.1	103.6	110.1	121.0	125.4	126.6	128.9	126.9	134.4
Real imports (billions of 1997 dollars)	6	115.3	111.8	118.8	118.4	121.9	130.4	126.3	129.5	108.6	119.4
Real net exports (billions of 1997 dollars)	7	−10.5	−15.7	−15.3	−8.3	−0.9	−5.0	0.4	−0.6	18.2	14.9
Potential GDP (billions of 1997 dollars)	8	466.0	481.5	504.9	525.7	547.1	560.7	569.1	587.3	604.9	623.2
Fluctuations around potential GDP (percentage)	9	1.8	0.4	0.7	0.1	−0.1	1.2	1.9	2.2	−3.6	−3.9
Real GDP growth rate (percent per year)	10	3.7	1.8	5.2	3.5	4.0	3.8	2.2	3.5	−2.9	2.7
GDP deflator (1997 = 100)	11	32.5	35.9	39.3	42.0	44.8	49.3	54.2	60.1	65.1	68.7
CPI (1992 = 100)	12	31.1	34.5	37.1	40.0	43.6	47.6	52.4	58.9	65.3	69.1
Inflation rate (GDP deflator percent per year)	13	15.2	10.7	9.5	6.8	6.6	10.0	10.1	10.8	8.5	5.4
Inflation rate (CPI percent per year)	14	10.7	10.9	7.5	7.8	9.0	9.2	10.1	12.4	10.9	5.8
Labour force (millions)	15	9.6	10.0	10.5	10.8	11.2	11.5	11.9	12.2	12.3	12.5
Labour force participation rate (percentage)	16	58.3	58.8	61.5	61.8	62.6	63.6	64.2	65.0	64.4	64.7
Average weekly hours (hours per week)	17	35.7	35.2	35.3	35.3	35.7	35.7	35.1	34.6	34.4	34.5
Unemployment rate (percentage)	18	5.4	7.1	7.1	8.0	8.4	7.5	7.5	7.6	11.1	11.9
Long-term interest rate (percent per year)	19	8.9	9.0	9.2	9.8	10.1	10.9	13.3	16.3	15.9	12.7
Short-term interest rate (percent per year)	20	7.8	7.4	8.9	7.4	8.6	11.5	12.7	17.8	13.9	9.3
Federal government revenues (billions of dollars)	21	29.0	30.9	34.5	35.3	36.7	42.0	49.1	63.4	65.1	67.4
Federal government outlays (billions of dollars)	22	28.4	35.4	38.7	43.5	48.2	52.5	60.8	71.7	83.6	91.0
Federal government surplus (+)/deficit(−) (billions of dollars)	23	0.6	−4.5	−4.2	−8.2	−11.4	−10.4	−11.8	−8.3	−18.5	−23.6
Gross federal debt (billions of dollars)	24	49.1	55.1	61.9	69.7	82.4	100.5	110.6	127.7	144.5	173.1
M1 (billions of dollars)	25	16.2	18.3	19.7	21.2	23.5	25.0	26.9	27.8	27.0	29.5
M2+ (billions of dollars)	26	70.0	81.5	94.5	110.7	127.3	149.0	174.8	201.0	218.6	235.4
M1 velocity (GDP/M1)	27	9.5	9.5	10.2	10.4	10.4	11.2	11.7	13.0	14.0	14.0
M2+ velocity (GDP/M2+)	28	2.2	2.1	2.1	2.0	1.9	1.9	1.8	1.8	1.7	1.7
Exchange rate (U.S. dollars per Canadian dollar)	29	1.02	0.98	1.01	0.94	0.88	0.85	0.86	0.83	0.81	0.81
Current account balance (billions of dollars)	30	−4.5	−8.3	−7.5	−7.4	−9.4	−9.8	−7.1	−15.0	2.3	−3.1

1984	1985	1986	1987	1988	1989	1990	1991	1992	1993	1994	1995	1996	1997	
633.8	664.1	680.1	709.1	744.3	763.8	765.3	749.3	755.8	773.5	810.7	833.5	847.0	882.7	1
359.5	377.3	391.4	407.7	425.3	439.9	444.9	437.9	444.6	452.6	466.3	475.9	488.2	510.7	2
95.5	103.0	107.6	121.3	133.7	143.1	128.3	114.9	110.6	114.4	126.4	132.5	133.6	162.9	3
158.1	165.8	168.5	171.1	179.1	185.3	192.5	198.4	199.8	199.7	199.0	197.3	194.3	191.9	4
159.1	166.7	173.9	179.0	195.0	196.9	206.1	209.8	224.9	249.2	280.9	304.7	321.8	348.6	5
139.8	151.5	162.4	171.1	194.1	205.5	209.7	214.9	224.9	241.5	260.9	275.9	290.0	331.3	6
19.3	15.3	11.5	7.9	0.9	−8.6	−3.5	−5.1	−0.1	7.8	20.0	28.9	31.8	17.3	7
642.1	661.4	681.5	702.7	725.5	739.4	751.0	761.5	772.9	788.5	807.5	831.0	859.0	890.7	8
−1.3	0.4	−0.2	0.9	2.6	3.3	1.9	−1.6	−2.2	−1.9	0.4	0.3	−1.4	−0.9	9
5.8	4.8	2.4	4.3	5.0	2.6	0.2	−2.1	0.9	2.3	4.8	2.8	1.6	4.2	10
70.9	73.1	75.4	78.8	82.4	86.1	88.8	91.5	92.7	94.0	95.1	97.2	98.8	100.0	11
72.1	75.0	78.1	81.5	84.8	89.0	93.3	98.5	100.0	101.8	102.0	104.2	105.8	107.6	12
3.3	3.1	3.0	4.6	4.5	4.5	3.2	3.0	1.3	1.4	1.1	2.3	1.6	1.2	13
4.3	4.0	4.1	4.4	4.0	5.0	4.8	5.6	1.5	1.8	0.2	2.2	1.5	1.7	14
12.7	13.0	13.3	13.5	13.8	14.1	14.2	14.3	14.3	14.4	14.6	14.7	14.8	15.1	15
65.0	65.5	66.0	66.4	66.8	67.2	67.1	66.5	65.7	65.4	65.2	64.9	64.7	64.9	16
34.5	34.7	34.7	34.1	34.7	35.1	34.6	33.9	33.4	33.8	34.3	34.0	34.2	34.2	17
11.3	10.6	9.7	8.8	7.8	7.5	8.2	10.3	11.2	11.4	10.3	9.4	9.6	9.2	18
13.5	11.7	10.4	10.7	10.9	10.8	11.9	10.8	9.9	8.9	9.4	9.0	8.1	7.0	19
11.1	9.5	9.0	8.2	9.4	12.0	12.8	8.9	6.5	4.9	5.4	7.0	4.3	3.2	20
73.5	80.2	88.6	97.3	106.6	113.7	120.9	125.8	130.1	128.7	131.9	140.3	148.0	162.6	21
102.2	112.3	114.4	120.6	128.9	138.5	151.5	161.2	164.4	167.2	165.9	172.4	166.1	160.1	22
−28.7	−32.2	−25.8	−23.3	−22.4	−24.8	−30.6	−35.4	−34.4	−38.5	−34.0	−32.1	−18.1	2.5	23
209.3	250.5	284.0	318.3	349.9	380.0	406.6	444.6	476.1	514.4	557.6	595.9	634.9	651.1	24
30.1	31.2	33.5	37.5	39.3	40.4	40.9	42.0	45.0	49.3	55.8	59.4	66.7	78.0	25
252.0	277.7	306.2	341.6	374.2	426.7	477.0	518.0	548.3	571.3	582.1	604.4	631.1	636.6	26
14.9	15.6	15.3	14.9	15.6	16.3	16.6	16.3	15.6	14.8	13.8	13.6	12.5	11.3	27
1.8	1.7	1.7	1.6	1.6	1.5	1.4	1.3	1.3	1.3	1.3	1.3	1.3	1.4	28
0.77	0.73	0.72	0.75	0.81	0.84	0.86	0.87	0.83	0.78	0.73	0.73	0.73	0.72	29
−1.7	−7.8	−15.5	−17.8	−18.3	−25.8	−23.1	−25.6	−25.4	−28.1	−17.7	−6.1	4.6	−11.4	30

Year		1998	1999	2000	2001	2002	2003	2004
Real GDP (billions of 1997 dollars)	1	918.9	969.8	1,020.5	1,038.7	1,070.8	1,092.4	1,124.4
Real consumption expenditure (billions of 1997 dollars)	2	524.8	544.8	566.7	579.5	600.7	619.4	640.6
Real investment (billions of 1997 dollars)	3	165.1	175.6	190.6	180.1	185.5	206.1	220.0
Real government expenditures (billions of 1997 dollars)	4	197.2	204.1	210.6	220.6	227.7	234.8	241.8
Real exports (billions of 1997 dollars)	5	380.4	421.0	458.6	445.0	449.3	439.8	461.7
Real imports (billions of 1997 dollars)	6	348.1	375.2	405.7	384.9	390.7	406.7	439.6
Real net exports (billions of 1997 dollars)	7	32.3	45.8	52.9	60.1	58.6	33.1	22.1
Potential GDP (billions of 1997 dollars)	8	926.3	963.0	999.5	1,034.6	1,063.3	1,095.7	1,128.9
Fluctuations around potential GDP (percentage)	9	−0.8	0.7	2.1	0.4	0.7	−0.3	−0.4
Real GDP growth rate (percent per year)	10	4.1	5.5	5.2	1.8	3.1	2.0	2.9
GDP deflator (1997 = 100)	11	99.6	101.3	105.5	106.7	107.8	111.3	114.7
CPI (1992 = 100)	12	108.6	110.5	113.5	116.4	119.0	122.3	124.6
Inflation rate (GDP deflator percent per year)	13	−0.4	1.7	4.1	1.1	1.0	3.3	3.1
Inflation rate (CPI percent per year)	14	0.9	1.7	2.7	2.6	2.2	2.8	1.9
Labour force (millions)	15	15.3	15.6	15.8	16.1	16.6	17.0	17.2
Labour force participation rate (percentage)	16	65.1	65.6	65.9	65.9	66.9	67.5	67.6
Average weekly hours (hours per week)	17	34.0	34.2	34.5	33.8	33.5	32.9	33.3
Unemployment rate (percentage)	18	8.4	7.6	6.9	7.2	7.7	7.6	7.2
Long-term interest rate (percent per year)	19	6.2	6.6	7.1	7.1	7.0	6.5	6.1
Short-term interest rate (percent per year)	20	4.7	4.7	5.5	3.9	2.5	2.9	2.3
Federal government revenues (billions of dollars)	21	167.5	177.7	195.7	193.9	191.6	196.2	207.3
Federal government outlays (billions of dollars)	22	163.7	171.9	179.3	184.5	184.3	195.6	199.5
Federal government surplus (+)/deficit(−) (billions of dollars)	23	3.8	5.8	16.4	9.5	7.3	0.6	7.8
Gross federal debt (billions of dollars)	24	645.7	648.4	648.2	644.9	640.5	629.6	628.8
M1 (billions of dollars)	25	86.0	92.6	106.2	119.0	133.0	143.6	161.4
M2+ (billions of dollars)	26	629.6	652.4	691.0	736.5	791.4	828.3	867.1
M1 velocity (GDP/M1)	27	10.6	10.6	10.1	9.3	8.7	8.5	8.0
M2+ velocity (GDP/M2+)	28	1.5	1.5	1.6	1.5	1.5	1.5	1.5
Exchange rate (U.S. dollars per Canadian dollar)	29	0.67	0.67	0.67	0.65	0.64	0.71	0.77
Current account balance (billions of dollars)	30	−11.4	2.6	29.3	25.1	21.1	18.4	28.8

GLOSSARY

Above full-employment equilibrium A macroeconomic equilibrium in which real GDP exceeds potential GDP. (p. 519)

Absolute advantage A person has an absolute advantage if that person is more productive than another person. (p. 42)

After-tax income Total income minus tax payments by households to governments. (p. 420)

Aggregate demand The relationship between the quantity of real GDP demanded and the price level. (p. 513)

Aggregate hours The total number of hours worked by all the people employed, both full time and part time, during a year. (p. 491)

Aggregate planned expenditure The expenditure that households, firms, governments, and foreigners plan to undertake in given circumstances. It is the sum of planned consumption expenditure, planned investment, planned government expenditures on goods and services, and planned exports minus planned imports. (p. 541)

Aggregate production function The relationship between the quantity of real GDP supplied and the quantities of labour and capital and the state of technology. (pp. 508, 739)

Allocative efficiency A situation in which we cannot produce more of any good without giving up some of another good that we value more highly. (p. 39)

Anti-combine law A law that regulates and prohibits certain kinds of market behaviour, such as monopoly and monopolistic practices. (p. 326)

Automated Clearing Settlement System (ACSS) A system through which all payments not processed by the LVTS are handled. (p. 596)

Automatic fiscal policy A change in fiscal policy that is triggered by the state of the economy. (p. 570)

Automatic stabilizers Mechanisms that stabilize real GDP without explicit action by the government. (p. 574)

Autonomous expenditure The sum of those components of aggregate planned expenditure that are not influenced by real GDP. Autonomous expenditure equals the sum of investment, government expenditures, exports, and the autonomous parts of consumption expenditure and imports. (p. 543)

Autonomous taxes Taxes that do not vary with real GDP. (p. 570)

Autonomous tax multiplier The magnification effect of a change in autonomous taxes on equilibrium expenditure and real GDP. (p. 572)

Average cost pricing rule A rule that sets price to cover cost including normal profit, which means setting the price equal to average total cost. (pp. 279, 329)

Average fixed cost Total fixed cost per unit of output. (p. 226)

Average product The average product of a factor of production. It equals total product divided by the quantity of the factor employed. (p. 221)

Average tax rate The percentage of income that is paid in tax. (p. 431)

Average total cost Total cost per unit of output. (p. 226)

Average variable cost Total variable cost per unit of output. (p. 226)

Balanced budget A government budget in which revenues and outlays are equal. (p. 565)

Bank rate The interest rate that the Bank of Canada charges the chartered banks on the reserves it lends them. (p. 660)

Barriers to entry Legal or natural constraints that protect a firm from potential competitors. (p. 264)

Barter The direct exchange of one good or service for other goods and services. (p. 590)

Base period The period in which the CPI is defined to be 100. (p. 498)

Below full-employment equilibrium A macroeconomic equilibrium in which potential GDP exceeds real GDP. (p. 518)

Big tradeoff The conflict between equity and efficiency. (pp. 10, 115, 433)

Bilateral monopoly A situation in which a single seller (a monopoly) faces a single buyer (a monopsony). (p. 417)

Black market An illegal trading arrangement in which the price exceeds the legally imposed price ceiling. (p. 126)

Budget deficit A government's budget balance that is negative—outlays exceed revenues. (p. 565)

Budget line The limits to a household's consumption choices. (p. 172)

Budget surplus A government's budget balance that is positive—revenues exceed outlays. (p. 565)

Business cycle The periodic but irregular up-and-down movement in production and jobs. (p. 448)

Canadian interest rate differential A gap equal to the Canadian interest rate minus the foreign interest rate. (p. 619)

Capital The tools, equipment, buildings, and other constructions that businesses now use to produce goods and services. (p. 4)

Capital accumulation The growth of capital resources, which includes human capital. (p. 40)

Capital consumption The decrease in the capital stock that results from wear and tear and obsolescence. (p. 469)

Capture theory A theory of regulation that states that the regulations are supplied to satisfy the demand of producers to maximize producer surplus—to maximize economic profit. (p. 327)

Cartel A group of firms that has entered into a collusive agreement to restrict output and increase prices and profits. (p. 297)

Central bank A public authority that supervises financial institutions and markets and conducts monetary policy. (p. 595)

Ceteris paribus Other things being equal—all other relevant things remaining the same. (p. 13)

Chain-weighted output index An index that uses the prices of two adjacent years to calculate the real GDP growth rate. (p. 474)

Change in demand A change in buyers' plans that occurs when some influence on those plans other than the price of the good changes. It is illustrated by a shift of the demand curve. (p. 62)

Change in supply A change in sellers' plans that occurs when some influence on those plans other than the price of the good changes. It is illustrated by a shift of the supply curve. (p. 67)

Change in the quantity demanded A change in buyers' plans that occurs when the price of a good changes but all other influences on buyers' plans remain unchanged. It is illustrated by a movement along the demand curve. (p. 65)

Change in the quantity supplied A change in sellers' plans that occurs when the price of a good changes but all other influences on sellers' plans remain unchanged. It is illustrated by a movement along the supply curve. (p. 68)

Chartered bank A private firm, chartered under the Bank Act of 1992 to receive deposits and make loans. (p. 593)

Classical growth theory A theory of economic growth based on the view that real GDP growth is temporary and that when real GDP per person increases above subsistence level, a population explosion brings real GDP back to subsistence level. (p. 743)

Coase theorem The proposition that if property rights exist, if only a small number of parties are involved, and transactions costs are low, then private transactions are efficient. (p. 351)

Collusive agreement An agreement between two (or more) producers to restrict output, raise the price, and increase profits. (p. 302)

Command system A method of organizing production that uses a managerial hierarchy—resources are allocated by order (command) of someone in authority. (pp. 104, 203)

Common resource A resource that is rival and nonexcludable. (p. 364)

Comparative advantage A person or country has a comparative advantage in an activity if that person or country can perform the activity at a lower opportunity cost than anyone else or any other country. (p. 42)

Competitive market A market that has many buyers and many sellers, so no single buyer or seller can influence the price. (p. 60)

Complement A good that is used in conjunction with another good. (p. 63)

Constant returns to scale Features of a firm's technology that lead to constant long-run average cost as output increases. When constant returns to scale are present, the *LRAC* curve is horizontal. (p. 233)

Consumer equilibrium A situation in which a consumer has allocated all his or her available income in the way that, given the prices of goods and services, maximizes his or her total utility. (p. 158)

Consumer Price Index (CPI) An index that measures the average of the prices paid by urban consumers for a fixed "basket" of the consumer goods and services. (p. 498)

Consumer surplus The value of a good minus the price paid for it, summed over the quantity bought. (p. 107)

Consumption expenditure The total payment for consumer goods and services. (p. 467)

Consumption function The relationship between consumption expenditure and disposable income, other things remaining the same. (p. 536)

Contestable market A market in which firms can enter and leave so easily that firms in the market face competition from potential entrants. (p. 310)

Contractionary fiscal policy A decrease in government expenditures or an increase in taxes. (p. 577)

Cooperative equilibrium The outcome of a game in which the players make and share the monopoly profit. (p. 309)

Copyright A government-sanctioned exclusive right granted to the inventor of a good, service, or productive process to produce, use, and sell the invention for a given number of years. (p. 357)

Core inflation A measure of inflation based on the CPI excluding the eight most volatile prices–the prices of fruit, vegetables, gasoline, fuel oil, natural gas, mortgage interest, intercity transportation, and tobacco—and also excluding changes in indirect taxes—taxes such as GST, HST, and provincial sales taxes. (p. 656)

Cost-push inflation An inflation that results from an initial increase in costs. (p. 635)

Crawling peg A policy regime that selects a target path for the exchange rate with intervention in the foreign exchange market to achieve that path. (p. 624)

Credit union A cooperative organization that operates under the Co-operative Credit Association Act of 1992 and that receives deposits and makes loans to its members. (p. 593)

Cross elasticity of demand The responsiveness of the demand for a good to a change in the price of a substitute or complement, other things remaining the same. It is calculated as the percentage change in the quantity demanded of the good divided by the percentage change in the price of the substitute or complement. (p. 91)

Cross-section graph A graph that shows the values of an economic variable for different groups in a population at a point in time. (p. 18)

Crowding in The tendency for expansionary fiscal policy to increase investment. (p. 683)

Crowding out The tendency for an expansionary fiscal policy action to decrease investment. (p. 683)

Crown Corporation A publicly owned firm in Canada. (p. 326)

Currency The coins and Bank of Canada notes that we use today. (p. 591)

Currency appreciation The rise in the value of one currency in terms of another currency. (p. 613)

Currency depreciation The fall in the value of one currency in terms of another currency. (p. 613)

Currency drain ratio The ratio of currency to deposits. (p. 597)

Currency union A merger of the currencies of a number of countries to form a single money and avoid foreign exchange transactions. (p. 624)

Current account A record of exports minus imports and interest payments paid to and received from abroad. (p. 457)

Cyclical surplus or deficit The actual surplus or deficit minus the structural surplus or deficit. (p. 575)

Cyclical unemployment The fluctuations in unemployment over the business cycle. (p. 496)

Deadweight loss A measure of inefficiency. It is equal to the decrease in consumer surplus and producer surplus that results from an inefficient level of production. (p. 111)

Deflation A negative inflation rate—a process in which the price level is falling. (p. 455)

Demand The relationship between the quantity of a good that consumers plan to buy and the price of the good when all other influences on buyers' plans remain the same. It is described by a demand schedule and illustrated by a demand curve. (p. 61)

Demand curve A curve that shows the relationship between the quantity demanded of a good and its price when all other influences on consumers' planned purchases remain the same. (p. 62)

Demand for labour The relationship between the quantity of labour demanded and the real wage rate when all other influences on firms' hiring plans remain the same. (p. 709)

Demand for money curve The relationship between the quantity of money demanded and the interest rate when all other influences on the amount of money that people wish to hold remain the same. (p. 602)

Demand-pull inflation An inflation that results from an initial increase in aggregate demand. (p. 633)

Depository institution A firm that takes deposits from households and firms and makes loans to other households and firms. (p. 593)

Depreciation The decrease in the capital stock that results from wear and tear and obsolescence. (p. 469)

Derived demand Demand for a factor of production, which is derived from the demand for the goods and services produced by that factor. (p. 388)

Desired reserve ratio The ratio of reserves to deposits that banks wish to hold. (p. 597)

Diminishing marginal rate of substitution The general tendency for a person to be willing to give up less of good y to get one more unit of good x, and at the same time remain indifferent, as the quantity of good x increases. (p. 176)

Diminishing marginal returns The tendency for the marginal product of an additional unit of a factor of production to be less than the marginal product of the previous unit of the factor. (p. 223)

Diminishing marginal utility The decrease in marginal utility as the quantity consumed increases. (p. 156)

Direct relationship A relationship between two variables that move in the same direction. (p. 20)

Discounting The conversion of a future amount of money to its present value. (p. 398)

Discouraged worker A person who does not have a job, is available for work, and is willing to work but who has given up the effort to find work. (pp. 453, 490)

Discretionary fiscal policy A policy action that is initiated by an act of Parliament. (p. 570)

Diseconomies of scale Features of a firm's technology that lead to rising long-run average cost as output increases. (p. 232)

Disposable income Aggregate income minus taxes plus transfer payments. (pp. 515, 536)

Dominant strategy equilibrium A Nash equilibrium in which the best strategy for each player is to cheat (deny) regardless of the strategy of the other player. (p. 308)

Dumping The sale by a foreign firm of exports at a lower price than the cost of production. (p. 768)

Duopoly A market structure in which two producers of a good or service compete. (p. 296)

Dynamic comparative advantage A comparative advantage that a person or country possesses as a result of having specialized in a particular activity and then, as a result of learning-by-doing, having become the producer with the lowest opportunity cost. (p. 45)

Earnings sharing regulation A regulation that if a firm's profits rise above a target level, they must be shared with the firm's customers. (p. 332)

Economic depreciation The change in the market value of capital over a given period. (p. 198)

Economic efficiency A situation that occurs when the firm produces a given output at the least cost. (p. 201)

Economic growth The expansion of production possibilities that results from capital accumulation and technological change. (pp. 40, 447)

Economic growth rate The percentage change in the quantity of goods and services produced from one year to the next. (p. 476)

Economic model A description of some aspect of the economic world

that includes only those features of the world that are needed for the purpose at hand. (p. 12)

Economic profit A firm's total revenue minus its opportunity cost. (p. 199)

Economic rent The income received by the owner of a factor of production over and above the amount required to induce that owner to offer the factor for use. (p. 406)

Economics The social science that studies the choices that we make as we cope with *scarcity* and the *incentives* that influence and reconcile those choices. (p. 2)

Economic theory A generalization that summarizes what we think we understand about the economic choices that people make and the performance of industries and entire economies. (p. 12)

Economic welfare A comprehensive measure of the general state of economic well-being. (p. 476)

Economies of scale Features of a firm's technology that lead to a falling long-run average cost as output increases. (pp. 213, 232)

Economies of scope Decreases in average total cost that occur when a firm uses specialized resources to produce a range of goods and services. (p. 213)

Efficiency wage A real wage rate that is set above the full-employment equilibrium wage rate and that balances the costs and benefits of this higher wage rate to maximize the firm's profit. (p. 720)

Elastic demand Demand with a price elasticity greater than 1; other things remaining the same, the percentage change in the quantity demanded exceeds the percentage change in price. (p. 87)

Elasticity of supply The responsiveness of the quantity supplied of a good to a change in its price, other things remaining the same. (p. 94)

Employment-to-population ratio The percentage of people of working age who have jobs. (p. 490)

Entrepreneurship The human resource that organizes the other three factors of production: labour, land, and capital. (p. 4)

Equation of exchange An equation that states that the quantity of money multiplied by the velocity of circulation equals GDP. (p. 638)

Equilibrium expenditure The level of aggregate expenditure that occurs when aggregate planned expenditure equals real GDP. (p. 544)

Equilibrium price The price at which the quantity demanded equals the quantity supplied. (p. 70)

Equilibrium quantity The quantity bought and sold at the equilibrium price. (p. 70)

Excess reserves A bank's actual reserves minus its desired reserves. (p. 597)

Excludable A good or service or a resource is excludable if it is possible to prevent someone from enjoying the benefit of it. (p. 364)

Expansion A business cycle phase between a trough and a peak—a period in which real GDP increases. (p. 448)

Expansionary fiscal policy An increase in government expenditures or a decrease in taxes. (p. 577)

Exports The goods and services that we sell to people in other countries. (pp. 468, 756)

External diseconomies Factors outside the control of a firm that raise the firm's costs as the industry produces a larger output. (p. 253)

External economies Factors beyond the control of a firm that lower the firm's costs as the industry produces a larger output. (p. 253)

Externality A cost or a benefit that arises from production and falls on someone other than the producer, or a cost or a benefit that arises from consumption and falls on someone other than the consumer. (p. 346)

Factors of production The resources used to produce goods and services. (p. 3)

Farm marketing board A regulatory agency that intervenes in an agricultural market to stabilize the price of an agricultural product. (p. 138)

Federal budget The annual statement of the outlays and revenues of the government of Canada, together with the laws and regulations that approve and support those outlays and revenues. (p. 564)

Final good An item that is bought by its final user during the specified time period. (p. 466)

Financial innovation The development of new financial products—new ways of borrowing and lending. (p. 601)

Firm An economic unit that hires factors of production and organizes those factors to produce and sell goods and services. (pp. 45, 198)

Fiscal policy The use of the federal budget to achieve macroeconomic objectives such as full employment, sustained long-term economic growth, and price level stability by setting and changing taxes, making transfer payments, and purchasing goods and services. (pp. 459, 515, 564)

Fixed exchange rate A policy regime in which the value of the exchange rate is decided by the government or central bank and the unregulated forces of demand and supply are blocked by direct intervention in the foreign exchange market. (p. 623)

Flexible exchange rate A policy regime in which the value of the exchange rate is determined by demand and supply with no direct intervention in the foreign exchange market by the central bank. (p. 623)

Flow A quantity per unit of time. (p. 469)

Foreign currency The notes, coins and bank deposits in the currency of another country. (p. 612)

Foreign exchange market The market in which the currency of one country is exchanged for the currency of another. (p. 612)

Foreign exchange rate The price at which one currency exchanges for another. (p. 612)

Four-firm concentration ratio A measure of market power that is calculated as the percentage of the value of sales accounted for by the four largest firms in an industry. (p. 208)

Free-rider problem The absence of an incentive for people to pay for what they consume. (p. 364)

Frictional unemployment The unemployment that arises from normal labour turnover—from people entering and leaving the labour force and from the ongoing creation and destruction of jobs. (p. 495)

Full employment A situation in which the quantity of labour demanded equals the quantity supplied. At full employment, there is no cyclical unemployment—all unemployment is frictional, structural, and seasonal. (p. 496)

Game theory A tool that economists use to analyze strategic behaviour—behaviour that takes into account the expected behaviour of others and the recognition of mutual interdependence. (p. 300)

GDP deflator One measure of the price level, which is the average of current-year prices as a percentage of base-year prices. (p. 474)

General Agreement on Tariffs and Trade An international agreement signed in 1947 to reduce tariffs on international trade. (p. 763)

Goods and services All the objects that people value and produce to satisfy their wants. (p. 3)

Government budget deficit The deficit that arises when the government spends more than it collects in taxes. (p. 457)

Government budget surplus The surplus that arises when the government collects more in taxes than it spends. (p. 457)

Government debt The total amount of borrowing that the government has undertaken. It equals the sum of past budget deficits minus the sum of past budget surpluses. (p. 567)

Government expenditures Goods and services bought by the government. (p. 468)

Government expenditures multiplier The magnification effect of a change in government expenditures on goods and services on equilibrium expenditure and real GDP (p. 570)

Government failure A situation in which government actions result in inefficiency. (p. 325)

Great Depression A decade (1929–1939) of high unemployment and stagnant production throughout the world economy. (p. 446)

Gross domestic product (GDP) The market value of all final goods and services produced within a country during a given time period. (p. 466)

Gross investment The total amount spent on purchases of new capital and on replacing depreciated capital. (p. 469)

Growth accounting A method of calculating how much real GDP growth results from growth of labour and capital and how much is attributable to technological change. (p. 739)

Growth rate cycle downturn A pronounced, pervasive, and persistent decline in the growth rate of aggregate economic activity. (p. 486)

Growth recession A situation in which the growth rate of real GDP remains positive but slows so that real GDP falls below potential GDP. (p. 448)

Herfindahl–Hirschman Index A measure of market power that is calculated as the square of the market share of each firm (as a percentage) summed over the largest 50 firms (or over all firms if there are fewer than 50) in a market. (p. 208)

Human capital The knowledge and skill that people obtain from education, on-the-job training, and work experience. (pp. 3, 707)

Implicit rental rate The firm's opportunity cost of using its own capital. (p. 198)

Imports The goods and services that we buy from people in other countries. (pp. 468, 756)

Incentive A reward that encourages or a penalty that discourages an action. (p. 2)

Incentive system A method of organizing production that uses a market-like mechanism inside the firm. (p. 203)

Income effect The effect of a change in income on consumption, other things remaining the same. (p. 180)

Income elasticity of demand The responsiveness of demand to a change in income, other things remaining the same. It is calculated as the percentage change in the quantity demanded divided by the percentage change in income. (p. 92)

Indifference curve A line that shows combinations of goods among which a consumer is indifferent. (p. 175)

Individual transferable quota (ITQ) A production limit that is assigned to an individual who is free to transfer the quota to someone else. (p. 374)

Induced expenditure The sum of the components of aggregate planned expenditure that vary with real GDP. Induced expenditure equals consumption expenditure minus imports. (p. 543)

Induced taxes Taxes that vary with real GDP. (p. 573)

Inelastic demand A demand with a price elasticity between 0 and 1; the percentage change in the quantity demanded is less than the percentage change in price. (p. 87)

Infant-industry argument The argument that it is necessary to protect a new industry to enable it to grow into a mature industry that can compete in world markets. (p. 767)

Inferior good A good for which demand decreases as income increases. (p. 64)

Inflation A process in which the price level is rising and money is losing value. (p. 455)

Inflation rate The percentage change in the price level from one year to the next. (p. 500)

Inflationary gap The amount by which real GDP exceeds potential GDP. (p. 519)

Instrument rule A decision rule for monetary policy that sets the policy instrument at a level that is based on the current state of the economy. (p. 659)

Intellectual property rights Property rights for discoveries owned by the creators of knowledge. (p. 357)

Interest The income that capital earns. (p. 4)

Interest rate The amount received by a lender and paid by a borrower expressed as a percentage of the amount of the loan. (p. 604)

Interest rate parity A situation in which the interest rates on assets in different currencies are equal when exchange rate changes are taken into account. (p. 622)

Interest-sensitive expenditure curve The relationship between aggregate expenditure plans and the real interest rate when all other influences on expenditure plans remain the same. (p. 667)

Intermediate good An item that is produced by one firm, bought by another firm, and used as a compo-

nent of a final good or service. (p. 466)

International crowding out The tendency for an expansionary fiscal policy to decrease net exports. (p. 683)

Inverse relationship A relationship between variables that move in opposite directions. (p. 21)

Investment The purchase of new plant, equipment, and buildings and additions to inventories. (p. 468)

Job rationing The practice of paying a real wage rate above the equilibrium level and then rationing jobs by some method. (p. 720)

Job search The activity of looking for an acceptable vacant job. (p. 719)

Keynesian A macroeconomist who regards the economy as being inherently unstable and requiring active government intervention to achieve stability. (p. 688)

***k*-percent rule** A rule that makes the quantity of money grow at a rate of *k* percent a year, where *k* equals the growth rate of potential GDP. (p. 671)

Labour The work time and work effort that people devote to producing goods and services. (p. 3)

Labour force The sum of the people who are employed and who are unemployed. (pp. 452, 488)

Labour force participation rate The percentage of the working-age population who are members of the labour force. (p. 490)

Labour productivity Real GDP per hour of labour. (pp. 707, 739)

Labour union An organized group of workers whose purpose is to increase wages and to influence other job conditions. (p. 413)

Land All the gifts of nature that we use to produce goods and services. (p. 3)

Large Value Tranfer System (LVTS) An electronic payments system that enables financial institutions and their customers to make large payments instantly and with sure knowledge that the payment has been made. (p. 596)

Law of demand Other things remaining the same, the higher the price of a good, the smaller is the quantity demanded of it. (p. 61)

Law of diminishing returns As a firm uses more of a variable input, with a given quantity of other inputs (fixed inputs), the marginal product of the variable input eventually diminishes. (pp. 223, 709, 740)

Law of supply Other things remaining the same, the higher the price of a good, the greater is the quantity supplied of it. (p. 66)

Learning-by-doing People become more productive in an activity (learn) just by repeatedly producing a particular good or service (doing). (pp. 45, 707)

Legal monopoly A market structure in which there is one firm and entry is restricted by the granting of a public franchise, government licence, patent, or copyright. (p. 264)

Lender of last resort The Bank of Canada stands ready to make loans to banks when the banking system as a whole is short of reserves. (p. 595)

Limit pricing The practice of setting the price at the highest level that inflicts a loss on an entrant. (p. 311)

Linear relationship A relationship between two variables that is illustrated by a straight line. (p. 20)

Liquidity The property of being instantly convertible into a means of payment with little loss in value. (p. 592)

Living wage An hourly wage rate that enables a person who works a 40-hour work week to rent adequate housing for not more than 30 percent of the amount earned. (p. 131)

Long run A period of time in which the quantities of all resources can be varied. (p. 220)

Long-run aggregate supply curve The relationship between the quantity of real GDP supplied and the price level in the long run when real GDP equals potential GDP. (pp. 508, 713)

Long-run average cost curve The relationship between the lowest attainable average total cost and output when both plant size and labour are varied. (p. 231)

Long-run industry supply curve A curve that shows how the quantity supplied by an industry varies as the market price varies after all the possible adjustments have been made, including changes in plant size and the number of firms in the industry. (p. 253)

Long-run macroeconomic equilibrium A situation that occurs when real GDP equals potential GDP— the economy is on its long-run aggregate supply curve. (p. 517)

Long-run neutrality The proposition that in the long run, a change in the quantity of money changes the price level and leaves all real variables unchanged. (p. 691)

Long-run Phillips curve A curve that shows the relationship between inflation and unemployment when the actual inflation rate equals the expected inflation rate. (p. 646)

Lorenz curve A curve that graphs the cumulative percentage of income or wealth against the cumulative percentage of households. (p. 421)

Low-income cutoff The income level, determined separately for different types of families (for example, single persons, couples, one parent) that is selected such that families with incomes below that limit normally spend 55 percent or more of their income on food, shelter, and clothing. (p. 424)

Lucas wedge The accumulated loss of output that results from a slowdown in the growth rate of real GDP per person. (p. 451)

M1 A measure of money that consists of currency held outside the banks plus demand deposits at chartered banks that are owned by individuals and businesses. (p. 591)

M2+ A measure of money that consists of M1 plus personal savings deposits, and nonpersonal notice deposits at chartered banks plus all types of deposits at trust and mortgage loan companies, credit unions, caisses populaires, and other financial institutions. (p. 591)

Macroeconomic long run A time frame that is sufficiently long for real GDP to return to potential GDP so that full employment prevails. (p. 508)

Macroeconomics The study of the performance of the national economy and the global economy. (p. 2)

Macroeconomic short run A period during which real GDP has fallen below or risen above potential GDP. (p. 509)

Margin When a choice is changed by a small amount or by a little at a time, the choice is made at the margin. (p. 11)

Marginal benefit The benefit that a person receives from consuming one more unit of a good or service. It is measured as the maximum amount that a person is willing to pay for one more unit of the good or service. (pp. 11, 38)

Marginal benefit curve A curve that shows the relationship between the marginal benefit of a good and the quantity of that good consumed. (p. 38)

Marginal cost The opportunity cost of producing one more unit of a good or service. It is the best alternative forgone. It is calculated as the increase in total cost divided by the increase in output. (pp. 11, 37, 226)

Marginal cost pricing rule A rule that sets the price of a good or service equal to the marginal cost of producing it. (pp. 278, 329)

Marginal external benefit The benefit from an additional unit of a good or service that people other than the consumer enjoy. (p. 353)

Marginal external cost The cost of producing an additional unit of a good or service that falls on people other than the producer. (p. 349)

Marginal private benefit The benefit from an additional unit of a good or service that the consumer of that good or service receives. (p. 353)

Marginal private cost The cost of producing an additional unit of a good or service that is borne by the producer of that good or service. (p. 349)

Marginal product The increase in total product that results from a one-unit increase in the variable input, with all other inputs remaining the same. It is calculated as the increase in total product divided by the increase in the variable input employed, when the quantities of all other inputs are constant. (p. 221)

Marginal product of labour The additional real GDP produced by an additional hour of labour when all other influences on production remain the same. (p. 709)

Marginal propensity to consume The fraction of a change in disposable income that is consumed. It is calculated as the change in consumption expenditure divided by the change in disposable income. (p. 538)

Marginal propensity to import The fraction of an increase in real GDP that is spent on imports. (p. 541)

Marginal propensity to save The fraction of an increase in disposable income that is saved. It is calculated as the change in saving divided by

the change in disposable income. (p. 538)

Marginal rate of substitution The rate at which a person will give up good y (the good measured on the y-axis) to get an additional unit of good x (the good measured on the x-axis) and at the same time remain indifferent (remain on the same indifference curve). (p. 176)

Marginal revenue The change in total revenue that results from a one-unit increase in the quantity sold. It is calculated as the change in total revenue divided by the change in quantity sold. (p. 240)

Marginal revenue product The change in total revenue that results from employing one more unit of a factor of production (labour) while the quantity of all other factors remains the same. It is calculated as the increase in total revenue divided by the increase in the quantity of the factor (labour). (p. 390)

Marginal social benefit The marginal benefit enjoyed by society—by the consumer of a good or service (marginal private benefit) plus the marginal benefit enjoyed by others (marginal external benefit). (p. 353)

Marginal social cost The marginal cost incurred by the entire society— by the producer and by everyone else on whom the cost falls— and is the sum of marginal private cost and marginal external cost. (p. 349)

Marginal utility The change in total utility resulting from a one-unit increase in the quantity of a good consumed. (p. 156)

Marginal utility per dollar The marginal utility from a good divided by its price. (p. 158)

Market Any arrangement that enables buyers and sellers to get information and to do business with each other. (p. 46)

Market failure A state in which the market does not allocate resources efficiently. (p. 324)

Market income The wages, interest, rent, and profit earned in factor markets and before paying income taxes. (p. 420)

Market power The ability to influence the market, and in particular the market price, by influencing the total quantity offered for sale. (p. 264)

McCallum rule A rule that makes the growth rate of the monetary base respond to the long-term average growth rate of real GDP and medium-term changes in the velocity of circulation of the monetary base. (p. 670)

Means of payment A method of settling a debt. (p. 590)

Microeconomics The study of the choices that individuals and businesses make, the way these choices interact, and the influence governments exert on them. (p. 2)

Minimum efficient scale The smallest quantity of output at which the long-run average cost curve reaches its lowest level. (p. 233)

Minimum wage A regulation that makes the hiring of labour below a specified wage rate illegal. (pp. 130, 721)

Monetarist A macroeconomist who believes that fluctuations in the quantity of money are the main source of economic fluctuations. (p. 688)

Monetary base The sum of the Bank of Canada notes outside the Bank of Canada, chartered banks' deposits at the Bank of Canada, and coins held by households, firms, and banks. (p. 597)

Monetary policy The attempt to control inflation and moderate the business cycle by changing the quantity of money and adjusting interest rates and the exchange rate. (pp. 459, 515, 606)

Money Any commodity or token that is generally acceptable as the means of payment. (pp. 46, 590)

Money multiplier The ratio of the change in the quantity of money to the change in the monetary base. (p. 600)

Money price The number of dollars that must be given up in exchange for a good or service. (p. 60)

Money wage rate The number of dollars that an hour of labour earns. (p. 709)

Monopolistic competition A market structure in which a large number of firms compete by making similar but slightly different products. (pp. 207, 286)

Monopoly A market structure in which there is one firm, which produces a good or service that has no close substitutes and in which the firm is protected from competition by a barrier preventing the entry of new firms. (pp. 207, 264)

Monopsony A market in which there is a single buyer. (p. 416)

Multiplier The amount by which a change in autonomous expenditure is magnified or multiplied to determine the change in equilibrium expenditure and real GDP. (p. 546)

Nash equilibrium The outcome of a game that occurs when player A takes the best possible action given the action of player B and player B takes the best possible action given the action of player A. (p. 301)

National saving The sum of private saving (saving by households and businesses) and government saving. (p. 469)

Natural monopoly A monopoly that occurs when one firm can supply the entire market at a lower price than two or more firms can. (p. 264)

Natural rate of unemployment The unemployment rate when the economy is at full employment. There is no cyclical unemployment; all unemployment is frictional, structural, and seasonal. (pp. 496, 508)

Negative externality An externality that arises from either production or

consumption and that imposes an external cost. (p. 346)

Negative relationship A relationship between variables that move in opposite directions. (p. 21)

Neoclassical growth theory A theory of economic growth that proposes that real GDP per person grows because technological change induces a level of saving and investment that makes capital per hour of labour grow. (p. 745)

Net exports The value of exports minus the value of imports. (pp. 468, 756)

Net investment Net increase in the capital stock—gross investment minus depreciation. (p. 469)

Net present value The present value of the future flow of marginal revenue product generated by capital minus the cost of the capital. (p. 400)

Net taxes Taxes paid to governments minus transfer payments received from governments. (p. 468)

New growth theory A theory of economic growth based on the idea that real GDP per person grows because of the choices that people make in the pursuit of profit and that growth can persist indefinitely. (p. 747)

Nominal GDP The value of the final goods and services produced in a given year valued at the prices that prevailed in that same year. It is a more precise name for GDP. (p. 473)

Nominal interest rate The percentage return on an asset such as a bond expressed in terms of money. (p. 665)

Nonexcludable A good or service or a resource is nonexcludable if it is impossible (or extremely costly) to prevent someone from benefiting from it. (p. 364)

Nonrenewable natural resources Natural resources that can be used only once and that cannot be replaced once they have been used. (p. 403)

Nonrival A good or service or a resource is nonrival if its use by one person does not decrease the quantity available for someone else. (p. 364)

Nontariff barrier Any action other than a tariff that restricts international trade. (p. 763)

Normal good A good for which demand increases as income increases. (p. 64)

Normal profit The expected return for supplying entrepreneurial ability. (p. 199)

North American Free Trade Agreement An agreement, which became effective on January 1, 1994, to eliminate all barriers to international trade between the United States, Canada, and Mexico after a 15-year phasing-in period. (p. 764)

Oligopoly A market structure in which a small number of firms compete. (pp. 207, 296)

One-third rule The rule that, with no change in technology, a 1 percent increase in capital per hour of labour brings, on the average, a one-third of 1 percent increase in real GDP per hour of labour. (p. 740)

Open market operation The purchase or sale of government of Canada securities—Treasury bills and government bonds—by the Bank of Canada from or to a chartered bank or the public. (p. 660)

Operating band The target overnight loans rate plus or minus 0.25 percentage points. (p. 660)

Opportunity cost The highest-valued alternative that we give up to get something. (p. 10)

Output gap Real GDP minus potential GDP. (p. 451)

Overnight loans rate The interest rate on overnight loans that members of the LVTS (big banks) make to each other. (p. 658)

Patent A government-sanctioned exclusive right granted to the inventor of a good, service, or productive process to produce, use, and sell the invention for a given number of years. (p. 357)

Payments system The system through which banks make payments to each other to settle transactions by their customers. (p. 595)

Payoff matrix A table that shows the payoffs for every possible action by each player for every possible action by each other player. (p. 300)

Perfect competition A market in which there are many firms each selling an identical product; there are many buyers; there are no restrictions on entry into the industry; firms in the industry have no advantage over potential new entrants; and firms and buyers are well informed about the price of each firm's product. (pp. 207, 240)

Perfectly elastic demand Demand with an infinite price elasticity; the quantity demanded changes by an infinitely large percentage in response to a tiny price change. (p. 87)

Perfectly inelastic demand Demand with a price elasticity of zero; the quantity demanded remains constant when the price changes. (p. 86)

Perfect price discrimination Price discrimination that extracts the entire consumer surplus. (p. 275)

Phillips curve A curve that shows a relationship between inflation and unemployment. (p. 644)

Pigovian taxes Taxes that are used as an incentive for producers to cut back on an activity that creates an external cost. (p. 352)

Policy conflict A situation in which the government and the Bank of Canada pursue different goals and the actions of one make it harder for the other to achieve its goals. (p. 692)

Policy coordination A situation in which the government and the Bank

of Canada work together to achieve a common set of goals. (p. 692)

Political equilibrium The outcome that results from the choices of voters, firms, politicians, and bureaucrats. (p. 326)

Positive externality An externality that arises from either production or consumption and that provides an external benefit. (p. 346)

Positive relationship A relationship between two variables that move in the same direction. (p. 20)

Potential GDP The value of production when all the economy's labour, capital, land, and entrepreneurial ability are fully employed; the quantity of real GDP at full employment. (pp. 447, 497)

Poverty A state in which a household's income is too low to be able to buy the quantities of food, shelter, and clothing that are deemed necessary. (p. 424)

Preferences A description of a person's likes and dislikes. (p. 38)

Present value The amount of money that, if invested today, will grow to be as large as a given future amount when the interest that it will earn is taken into account. (p. 398)

Price cap regulation A regulation that specifies the highest price that the firm is permitted to set. (p. 330)

Price ceiling A regulation that makes it illegal to charge a price higher than a specified level. (p. 125)

Price discrimination The practice of selling different units of a good or service for different prices or of charging one customer different prices for different quantities bought. (p. 265)

Price effect The effect of a change in the price on the quantity of a good consumed, other things remaining the same. (p. 179)

Price elasticity of demand A units-free measure of the responsiveness of the quantity demanded of a good to

a change in its price, when all other influences on buyers' plans remain the same. (p. 84)

Price floor A regulation that makes it illegal to charge a price lower than a specified level. (p. 130)

Price level The average level of prices as measured by a price index. (pp. 455, 474)

Price taker A firm that cannot influence the price of the good or service it produces. (p. 240)

Principal–agent problem The problem of devising compensation rules that induce an agent to act in the best interest of a principal. (p. 204)

Principle of minimum differentiation The tendency for competitors to make themselves identical as they try to appeal to the maximum number of clients or voters. (p. 367)

Private good A good or service that is both rival and excludable. (p. 364)

Producer surplus The price of a good minus the opportunity cost of producing it, summed over the quantity sold. (p. 109)

Product differentiation Making a product slightly different from the product of a competing firm. (pp. 207, 286)

Production efficiency A situation in which the economy cannot produce more of one good without producing less of some other good. (p. 35)

Production function The relationship between real GDP and the quantity of labour employed when all other influences on production remain the same. (p. 706)

Production possibilities frontier The boundary between the combinations of goods and services that can be produced and the combinations that cannot. (p. 34)

Production quota An upper limit to the quantity of a good that may be produced in a specified period. (p. 139)

Productivity curve A relationship that shows how real GDP per hour of labour changes as the amount of capital per hour of labour changes with a given state of technology. (p. 739)

Productivity growth slowdown A situation in which the growth rate of output per person sags. (p. 447)

Profit The income earned by entrepreneurship. (p. 4)

Progressive income tax A tax on income at an average rate that increases with the level of income. (p. 431)

Property rights Social arrangements that govern the ownership, use, and disposal of resources or factors of production, goods, and services that are enforceable in the courts. (pp. 46, 350)

Proportional income tax A tax on income at a constant average rate, regardless of the level of income. (p. 431)

Provincial budget The annual statement of the outlays and revenues of a provincial government, together with the laws and regulations that approve and support those outlays and revenues. (p. 564)

Public good A good or service that is both nonrival and nonexcludable—it can be consumed simultaneously by everyone and from which no one can be excluded. (p. 364)

Public provision The production of a good or service by a public authority that receives its revenue from the government. (p. 355)

Purchasing power parity The equal value of different monies. (p. 622)

Quantity demanded The amount of a good or service that consumers plan to buy during a given time period at a particular price. (p. 61)

Quantity of labour demanded The number of labour hours hired by all the firms in the economy. (p. 709)

Quantity of labour supplied The number of labour hours that all households in the economy plan to work. (p. 711)

Quantity supplied The amount of a good or service that producers plan to sell during a given time period at a particular price. (p. 66)

Quantity theory of money The proposition that in the long run, an increase in the quantity of money brings an equal percentage increase in the price level. (p. 638)

Quota A quantitative restriction on the import of a particular good, which specifies the maximum amount that can be imported in a given time period. (p. 766)

Rand Formula A requirement that all workers represented by a union must pay union dues, whether they join the union or not. (p. 413)

Rate of return regulation A regulation that requires the firm to justify its price by showing that the price enables it to earn a specified target percent return on its capital. (p. 330)

Rational expectation The most accurate forecast possible, a forecast that uses all the available information, including knowledge of the relevant economic forces that influence the variable being forecasted. (p. 641)

Rational ignorance The decision not to acquire information because the cost of doing so exceeds the expected benefit. (p. 368)

Real exchange rate The relative price of the GDP baskets of goods and services in two countries. (p. 671)

Real GDP The value of final goods and services produced in a given year when valued at constant prices. (pp. 447, 473)

Real gross domestic product (real GDP) The value of final goods and services produced in a given year when valued at constant prices. (pp. 447, 473)

Real income A household's income expressed as a quantity of goods that the household can afford to buy. (pp. 155, 173)

Real interest rate The percentage return on an asset expressed in terms of what money will buy. It is the nominal interest rate adjusted for inflation and is approximately equal to the nominal interest rate minus the inflation rate. (p. 665)

Real wage rate The quantity of goods and services that an hour's work can buy. It is equal to the money wage rate divided by the price level and multiplied by 100. (pp. 492, 709)

Recession A period during which real GDP decreases—the growth rate of real GDP is negative—for at least two successive quarters. (pp. 448)

Recessionary gap The amount by which potential GDP exceeds real GDP. (p. 518)

Regressive income tax A tax on income at an average rate that decreases with the level of income. (p. 431)

Regulation Rules administered by a government agency to influence economic activity by determining price, product standards and types, and conditions under which a new firm may enter an industry. (p. 326)

Relative price The ratio of the price of one good or service to the price of another good or service. A relative price is an opportunity cost. (pp. 60, 154, 173)

Renewable natural resources Natural resources that can be used repeatedly without depleting what is available for future use. (p. 403)

Rent The income that land earns. (p. 4)

Rent ceiling A regulation that makes it illegal to charge a rent higher than a specified level. (p. 125)

Rent seeking Any attempt to capture a consumer surplus, a producer surplus, or an economic profit. (p. 272)

Reserve ratio The fraction of a bank's total deposits that are held in reserves. (p. 597)

Reserves Cash in a bank's vault plus the bank's deposits at the Bank of Canada. (p. 593)

Rival A good or service or a resource is rival if its use by one person decreases the quantity available for someone else. (p. 364)

Saving The amount of income that households have left after they have paid their taxes and bought their consumption goods and services. (p. 468)

Saving function The relationship between saving and disposable income, other things remaining the same. (p. 536)

Scarcity The state in which the resources available are insufficient to satisfy people's wants. (p. 2)

Scatter diagram A diagram that plots the value of one variable against the value of another. (p. 19)

Search activity The time spent looking for someone with whom to do business. (p. 126)

Seasonal unemployment Unemployment that arises because the number of jobs available has decreased because of the season. (p. 496)

Self-interest The choices that you think are best for you. (p. 5)

Settlements balances rate The interest rate that the Bank of Canada pays banks on their reserve deposits at the Bank of Canada. (p. 660)

Short run The short run in microeconomics has two meanings. For the firm, it is the period of time in which the quantity of at least one input is fixed and the quantities of the other inputs can be varied. The fixed input is usually capital—that is, the firm has a given plant size. For the industry, the short run is the period of time in which each firm has a given plant size and the num-

ber of firms in the industry is fixed. (p. 220)

Short-run aggregate supply curve A curve that shows the relationship between the quantity of real GDP supplied and the price level in the short run when the money wage rate, other resource prices, and potential GDP remain constant. (pp. 509, 713)

Short-run industry supply curve A curve that shows the quantity supplied by the industry at each price when the plant size of each firm and the number of firms in the industry remain the same. (p. 247)

Short-run macroeconomic equilibrium A situation that occurs when the quantity of real GDP demanded equals the quantity of real GDP supplied—at the point of intersection of the AD curve and the SAS curve. (p. 516)

Short-run Phillips curve A curve that shows the tradeoff between inflation and unemployment, when the expected inflation rate and the natural rate of unemployment remain the same. (p. 644)

Shutdown point The output and price at which the firm just covers its total variable cost. In the short run, the firm is indifferent between producing the profit-maximizing output and shutting down temporarily. (p. 246)

Signal An action taken by an informed person (or firm) to send a message to uninformed people. (p. 294)

Single-price monopoly A monopoly that must sell each unit of its output for the same price to all its customers. (p. 265)

Slope The change in the value of the variable measured on the y-axis divided by the change in the value of the variable measured on the x-axis. (p. 24)

Social interest Choices that are the best for society as a whole. (p. 5)

Social interest theory A theory that politicians supply the regulation that achieves an efficient allocation of resources. (p. 327)

Stock A quantity that exists at a point in time. (p. 469)

Strategies All the possible actions of each player in a game. (p. 300)

Structural surplus or deficit The budget balance that would occur if the economy were at full employment and real GDP were equal to potential GDP. (p. 575)

Structural unemployment The unemployment that arises when changes in technology or international competition change the skills needed to perform jobs or change the locations of jobs. (p. 496)

Subsidy A payment that the government makes to private producers. (pp. 138, 356)

Subsistence real wage rate The minimum real wage rate needed to maintain life. (p. 744)

Substitute A good that can be used in place of another good. (p. 63)

Substitution effect The effect of a change in price of a good or service on the quantity bought when the consumer (hypothetically) remains indifferent between the original and the new consumption situations—that is, the consumer remains on the same indifference curve. (p. 181)

Sunk cost The past cost of buying a plant that has no resale value. (p. 220)

Supply The relationship between the quantity of a good that producers plan to sell and the price of the good when all other influences on producers' plans remain the same. It is described by a supply schedule and illustrated by a supply curve. (p. 66)

Supply curve A curve that shows the relationship between the quantity supplied and the price of a good when all other influences on producers' planned sales remain the same. (p. 66)

Supply of labour The relationship between the quantity of labour supplied and the real wage rate when all other influences on work plans remain the same. (p. 711)

Symmetry principle A requirement that people in similar situations be treated similarly. (p. 116)

Targeting rule A decision rule for monetary policy that sets the policy instrument at a level that makes the forecast of the ultimate policy target equal to the target. (p. 659)

Tariff A tax that is imposed by the importing country when an imported good crosses its international boundary. (p. 763)

Tax incidence The division of the burden of the tax between the buyer and the seller. (p. 132)

Taylor rule A rule that sets the overnight rate in response to only the current inflation rate and the current estimate of the output gap. (p. 670)

Technological change The development of new goods and of better ways of producing goods and services. (p. 40)

Technological efficiency A situation that occurs when the firm produces a given output by using the least amount of inputs. (p. 201)

Technology Any method of producing a good or service. (p. 200)

Terms of trade The quantity of goods and services that a country exports to pay for its imports of goods and services. (p. 758)

Time-series graph A graph that measures time (for example, months or years) on the *x*-axis and the variable or variables in which we are interested on the *y*-axis. (p. 18)

Total cost The cost of all the productive resources that a firm uses. (p. 225)

Total fixed cost The cost of the firm's fixed inputs. (p. 225)

Total income Market income plus cash payments to households by governments. (p. 420)

Total product The total output produced by a firm in a given period of time. (p. 221)

Total revenue The value of a firm's sales. It is calculated as the price of the good multiplied by the quantity sold. (pp. 88, 240)

Total revenue test A method of estimating the price elasticity of demand by observing the change in total revenue that results from a change in the price, when all other influences on the quantity sold remain the same. (p. 88)

Total utility The total benefit that a person gets from the consumption of goods and services. (p. 156)

Total variable cost The cost of all the firm's variable inputs. (p. 225)

Tradeoff A constraint that involves giving up one thing to get something else. (p. 9)

Transactions costs The costs that arise from finding someone with whom to do business, of reaching an agreement about the price and other aspects of the exchange, and of ensuring that the terms of the agreement are fulfilled. The opportunity costs of conducting a transaction. (pp. 113, 212, 351)

Trend The general tendency for a variable to move in one direction. (p. 18)

Trust and mortgage loan company A privately owned depository institution that operates under the Trust and Loan Companies Act of 1992. (p. 593)

Unemployment A state in which a person does not have a job but is available for work, willing to work, and has made some effort to find work within the previous four weeks. (p. 452)

Unemployment rate The percentage of the people in the labour force who are unemployed. (pp. 452, 489)

Unit elastic demand Demand with a price elasticity of 1; the percentage change in the quantity demanded equals the percentage change in price. (p. 86)

Utilitarianism A principle that states that we should strive to achieve "the greatest happiness for the greatest number of people." (p. 114)

Utility The benefit or satisfaction that a person gets from the consumption of a good or service. (p. 156)

Velocity of circulation The average number of times a dollar of money is used annually to buy the goods and services that make up GDP. (p. 638)

Voluntary export restraint An agreement between two governments in which the government of the exporting country agrees to restrain the volume of its own exports. (p. 766)

Voucher A token that the government provides to households, which they can use to buy specified goods and services. (p. 356)

Wages The income that labour earns. (p. 4)

Wealth The market value of all the things that people own—the market value of their assets. (p. 469)

Working-age population The total number of people aged 15 years and over. (p. 488)

World Trade Organization An international organization that places greater obligations on its member countries to observe the GATT rules. (p. 763)

Note: Key terms and the pages on which they are defined are **bolded**. References to "*f*" denote a figure and "*t*" denote a table.

A

above full-employment equilibrium, 519, 692
absolute advantage, 42–45
absolute value, 86
acid rain, 347, 382
actual aggregate expenditure, 543–544
advertising
    brand names, 295
    described, 292
    efficiency, 295
    expenditures, 292–293, 293*f*
    and markup, 294*f*
    quality, as signal of, 294–295
    selling costs and demand, 294
    selling costs and total cost, 293, 293*f*
after-tax income, 420
age of householder, 425
aggregate demand, 513
    see also aggregate supply–aggregate demand model
    and aggregate cost-push inflation, 636, 636*f*
    changes in aggregate demand, 514–516, 515*f*, 553*f*
    and demand-pull inflation, 633
    and fiscal policy, 576–578, 577*f*
    fluctuations in, 520–521, 520*f*
    and government expenditures, 577*f*
    graphical illustration, 513*f*, 522*f*
    increase, in long run, 554–555
    increase, in short run, 554
    macroeconomic equilibrium, 679*f*
    and monetary policy transmission process, 668–669
    quantity of real GDP demanded, 513, 514
    substitution effects, 514
    wealth effect, 513–514
aggregate demand curve
    described, 513–514, 513*f*
    and price level, 554–555
    shifts of, 516, 552*f*
aggregate demand shock, 632
aggregate expenditure
    components of, 536
    described, 468
    formula, 558
    graphical illustration, 542*f*
    and the price level, 551–553
aggregate expenditure curve
    described, 542
    formula, 558
    graphical illustration, 558*f*
    slope of, 548, 550*f*, 571

    substitution effects, 551
    wealth effect, 551
aggregate expenditure model
    actual aggregate expenditure, 543–544
    aggregate planned expenditure and real GDP, 543
    convergence to equilibrium, 545
    described, 541, 542
    equilibrium expenditure, 544–545, 544*f*
    planned expenditure, 543–544
aggregate expenditure schedule, 542
aggregate hours, 491–492, 491*f*
aggregate income, 468
aggregate planned expenditure, 541, 543
aggregate production function, 508, 739
aggregate supply
    see also aggregate supply–aggregate demand model
    aggregate production function, 508
    capital, change in quantity of, 511
    changes in, 511–512
    and cost-push inflation, 635
    fluctuations in, 521, 521*f*
    full-employment quantity of labour, change in, 511
    fundamentals of, 508
    graphical illustration, 522*f*
    and labour market, 709–714
    long-run aggregate supply, 508–509, 509*f*, 510, 510*f*
    long-run aggregate supply curve, 713–714, 713*f*
    macroeconomic equilibrium, 679*f*
    money wage rate, changes in, 512, 512*f*
    potential GDP, changes in, 511, 511*f*
    resource prices, changes in, 512, 512*f*
    short-run aggregate supply, 509, 510, 510*f*
    short-run aggregate supply curve, 713–714, 713*f*
    technological change, 512
aggregate supply–aggregate demand model
    above full-employment equilibrium, 519
    aggregate demand, fluctuations in, 520–521, 520*f*
    aggregate supply, fluctuations in, 521, 521*f*
    business cycle, 518–519, 519*f*, 523
    economic growth, 522
    evolving Canadian economy, 1961–2004, 523
    inflation, 508, 523
    Kyoto Protocol, 524–525
    long-run equilibrium, 518
    short-run Phillips curve, 645, 645*f*
    supply-side effects of tax cuts, 579–581, 580*f*
aggregate supply–aggregate demand model (*AS–AD* model)
    concepts used by, 508

    economic growth, 518
    inflation, 518
aggregate supply curves. *See* long-run aggregate supply curve; short-run aggregate supply curve
aggregate supply shock, 632
agricultural markets
    farm marketing board, 138
    harvest fluctuations, 137–138, 137*f*
    production quota, 139, 139*f*
    subsidies, 138, 138*f*
Agricultural Revolution, 6, 53
AIDS, 8
air pollution, 347–348, 348*f*
Akerlof, George, 650
Alchian, Armen, 213
allocative efficiency, 39, 39*f*
Allowance, 431
Allowance for the Survivor, 431
Anarchy, State, and Utopia (Nozick), 116
Andreesen, Marc, 747
anti-combine law, 326, 338–339, 339*t*
anticipated inflation
    costs of, 642–643
    described, 641–642, 642*f*
    tax effects, 643
    transactions costs, 643
    uncertainty, increased, 643
Asia-Pacific Economic Cooperation, 764
assortative mating, 430
Aten, Bettina, 478
Automated Clearing Settlement System (ACSS), 596
automatic fiscal policy, 570
automatic stabilizers, 574–576
autonomous consumption, 536
autonomous consumption expenditure, 666
autonomous expenditure, 543, 546, 558
autonomous tax multiplier, 572–573, 573*f*, 585
autonomous taxes, 570
autonomous transfer payments, 573, 585
average cost, 226–227, 227*f*
average cost pricing rule, 279, 329–330, 330*f*
average fixed cost, 226
average price, 85–86
average product, 221
average product curve, 224, 224*f*
average quantity, 85–86
average tax rate, 431
average total cost, 226
average total cost curve, 226–227, 227*f*, 231
average variable cost, 226
axes, 17

B

balance of international payments
    balance of payments, 1984-2004, 773*f*

balance of payments account, 772–773, 772*t*
capital account, 772
creditor nation, 774
current account, 772
current account balance, 772, 774–775, 774*t*
debtor nation, 774
net borrower, 774
net lender, 774
official Canadian reserves, 772
official settlements account, 772
twin deficits, 775, 775*f*
balance of payments account, 772–773, 772*t*
balanced budget, 565, 576
bank mergers, 339
Bank of Canada
see also monetary policy
balance sheet, 595
bank notes, issuer of, 595
bank rate, 660
banker to banks and government, 595
core inflation, 656
decision-making process, 659–660
described, 595
economists, 658
Governing Council, 657–658
instrument rule, 659
interest rate target, 605
lender of last resort, 595
monetary base, 597
and monetary policy, 459
open market operations, 660–661, 661*f*
operating band, 660
quantity of money target, 605
settlement balances rate, 660
targeting rule, 659–660
Bank of Canada Act, 656
Bank of Montreal, 339, 593
Bank of Nova Scotia, 593
bank rate, 660
banking system
Bank of Canada, 595
depository institutions, 593–594
described, 593
payments system, 595–596
banks
bank rate, 660
central bank, 595
costs of monitoring borrowers, 594
creation of deposits, 596–597
desired currency drain ratio, 597
desired reserve ratio, 597
desired reserves, 597
economic functions, 594
excess reserves, 597
goal of, 593
liquidity, creation of, 594
loans, 593–594, 596–597
market for reserves, 662, 662*f*
minimization of borrowing costs, 594
monetary base, 597
money creation process, 597–599, 598*f,* 599*f*
pooling risk, 594
required reserve ratio, 597
reserve ratio, 597

reserves, 593–594
as term, 593
bar chart, 18
barriers to entry, 264
and concentration measures, 210
legal barriers to entry, 264
monopoly, 264–265
natural barriers to entry, 264–265
oligopoly, 296
Barro, Robert, 643
barter, 590
base period, 498
base year, 473–474
basis points, 659*n*
BCE Inc., 340
Beaudry, Paul, 150–152
Bell Canada, 234–235
Bell Canada Enterprises, 338
bell-shaped distribution, 420
below full-employment equilibrium, 518, 692
benefits
of economic growth, 452
of education, 48–49, 49*f*
external benefits, 112–113
marginal benefit. *See* marginal benefit
marginal external benefit, 353
marginal private benefit, 353
marginal social benefit, 353
private benefits, 353–355
product innovation, 292
social benefits, 353–355
Bentham, Jeremy, 192–193
Berners-Lee, Tim, 197
best affordable point, 178*f,* 190
big tradeoff, 10, 115, 433
bilateral monopoly, 417
Bina, Eric, 747
black market, 126
boat rides, 166–167
Boorstin, Daniel J., 147
Bouey, Gerald, 455
Bowlus, Audra J., 496*n*
brand names, 295
Brazil, 701
break-even point, 242
broadband providers, 340–341
budget
government budget. *See* government budgets
household's budget, 154–155
budget deficit, 565, 574–575, 574*f*
budget equation, 173–174
budget line, 154, 172, 172*f*
budget maximization
marginal cost pricing, 336
at zero price, 336
budget surplus, 565
bureaucracy model of public enterprise, 336–337
bureaucratic overprovision, 368*f*
bureaucrats, 325–326, 368
business cycle, 448
aggregate supply–aggregate demand model, 518–519, 519*f,* 523
budget deficit, 574–575, 574*f*
dates, 486

described, 448, 448*f,* 486
expansion, 550
forecasts, 479
growth rate cycles, 486
job creation and destruction, 452
recession, 550
turning points, 549–550
two views of Canadian business cycle, 487*f*
business investment, 471
business organization, 204–206, 205*t*

C
Canada
anti-combine law, 338, 339*t*
balance of payments account, 772*t*
business cycle, 448, 448*f*
capital market trends, 397*f*
concentration measures, 209, 209*f*
cost-push inflation, 637
current account, 457
demand for money, 603–604, 603*f,* 606–607
demand-pull inflation, 635
economic growth in, 41, 41*f,* 447, 447*f,* 522, 734*f*
fluctuations in, 447, 447*f*
income distribution, 420*f*
inflation, 455, 455*f*
labour market trends, 389*f*
labour productivity, 717–718
long-term economic growth, 449*f*
money, 591–592
Phillips curve, 647, 647*f*
population, 717–718
production function, 708*f*
productivity growth slowdown and speedup, 741–742, 741*f*
quintile shares, 421*f*
regulation in, 327
tariffs, history of, 763–764 763*f*
total government sector, 568
unemployment, 453, 453*f*
Canada Assistance Plan, 431
Canada Child Tax Benefit program, 431
Canada Packers Inc., 339
Canada Post, 264
Canada/Quebec Pension Plans, 431
Canada–United States Free Trade Agreement, 776
Canada–U.S. productivity gap, 722–723
Canadian Auto Workers, 415
Canadian Charter of Rights and Freedoms, 477
Canadian Congress of Labour, 413
Canadian consumption function, 540, 540*f*
Canadian dollar
see also foreign exchange market
appreciating (2002–2005), 621, 621*f*
and business outlook, 626–627
Canadian dollar–U.S. dollar exchange rate, 612, 613*f*
changes in demand, 619, 619*f*
changes in supply, 620, 620*f*
demand curve, 616, 616*f*
depreciating (1991–2002), 621, 621*f*
supply curve, 617, 617*f*
Canadian economy
business cycles, 523

economic growth, 522
evolving economy, 1961–2004, 523
growth in, 734
inflation, 523
multiplier and, 556–557
Canadian interest rate differential, 619
Canadian Labour Congress, 413
Canadian National (CN) Railroad, 337
Canadian Pacific Ltd., 204, 210–211, 337
Canadian Payments Association (CPA),
595–596
capital, 4
accumulation, and classical growth theory,
744–745
change in quantity of, 511
demand curve, 401
demand for capital, 397–398, 401*f*
financial capital, 397
illustration of, 470*f*
and income tax, 580
increase in, 717
investment in new capital, 737–738
meaning of, 469
physical capital, 397, 707, 716
substitutability of, for labour, 394
supply curve of capital, 402
supply of capital, 402
unequal ownership of capital, 430
capital account, 772
capital accumulation, 40
capital consumption, 469
capital markets
Canadian capital market trends, 397*f*
changes in demand and supply, 403
decision to buy, 400–401
demand curve for capital, 401
demand for capital, 397–398
discounting, 398–400
equilibrium, 402*f*
firm's demand for capital, 401*f*
interest rate and, 40
interest rate changes, 401
market demand for capital, 401*f*
net present value, 400
present value, 398–400
supply curve of capital, 402
supply of capital, 402
unanticipated inflation, and financial capital market, 640–641
capture theory, 327, 332, 333–334
Card, David, 131, 496*n*, 721
Carlyle, Thomas, 440
cartel, 297, 332–333
cartel regulation, 332–334
causation, 20
central bank, 595
central planning, 5–6, 45
ceteris paribus, **13,** 26–27
chain linking, 474
chain-weighted output index, 474
change in demand, 62
capital markets, 403
vs. change in quantity demanded, 64–65,
65*f*
and change in supply, opposite
direction, 75, 75*f*

and change in supply, same direction, 74,
74*f*
changes in aggregate demand, 514–516,
515*f*
changes in demand for labour, 393, 393*t*,
415
effects of, 72–73, 72*f*
expected future income, 64
expected future prices, 63–64
income, 64
increase in, 63*f*
labour unions and, 415
perfect competition, 248
permanent change in demand, 252–253,
253*f*
population, 64
price, effect on, 94
quantity, effect on, 72–73, 72*f*, 94
related goods, prices of, 63
shift in demand curve, 65
supply, effect on, 72–73, 72*f*
change in supply, 67
capital markets, 403
and change in demand, opposite
direction, 75, 75*f*
and change in demand, same
direction, 74, 74*f*
vs. change in the quantity supplied, 68–69,
69*f*
changes in aggregate supply, 511–512
effects of, 73, 73*f*
expected future prices, 68
graphical illustration, 68*f*
prices of productive resources, 67
prices of related goods produced, 67–68
suppliers, number of, 68
supply of labour, 395–396
technology and, 68
change in the quantity demanded, 64–65,
65*f*
change in the quantity supplied, 68–69, 69*f*
chartered bank, 593
see also banks
cheating, 304–305, 304*f*
cheques, 592
chicken game, 308, 308*f*
children, number of, 425
China
central planning in, 5
competition in, 312–313
Cultural Revolution, 5
real GDP, 478, 479*f*
choices
changes from, 10
at the margin, 11
and new growth theory, 747
perfect competition, 256
public choice, and political marketplace,
325–326, 325*f*
responding to incentives, 11
and self-interest, 5
and social interest, 5
and tradeoffs, 9
utility-maximizing choice, 158
work-leisure choices, 182–183
Chrysler, 338
CIBC, 593

cigarette tax, 133
circular flow of expenditure and income,
467–468, 467*f*
circular flows through markets, 46, 47*f*
classical growth theory, 743
basic concepts of, 743
and capital accumulation, 744–745
graphical illustration, 744*f*
population growth, 743–744
and productivity curve, 744
subsistence real wage rate, 744
Clean Air Act, 353
close substitutes, 177, 177*f*, 240, 264
Co-operative Credit Association Act, 593
Coase, Ronald, 382–383
Coase theorem, 351
collective bargaining, 413
collusion
cartel, 332–333
monopolistic competition, impossibility in,
286
monopoly profits, 303*f*
oligopoly, 297, 333*f*
price-fixing game, 302–304
profit maximization, 303, 303*f*
collusive agreement, 302
command system, 104, 203
commodity substitution bias, 501
common resources, 364
described, 324
efficient use of, 373–375
individual transferable quota (ITQ),
374–375, 375*f*
political equilibrium, 375
property rights, 373–374
public choice, 375
quotas, 374, 374*f*
sustainable production, 370–371, 370*t*,
371*f*
tragedy of the commons, 364, 370–375
comparative advantage, 42–45, 757, 758,
761
competition
in China, 312–313
currency union, effect of, 624
and efficiency, 256–257, 257*f*
monopolistic competition. *See* monopolistic competition
monopoly. *See* monopoly
oligopoly. *See* oligopoly
perfect competition. *See* perfect competition
Competition Act, 1986, 339*t*
competition policy
anti-combine law, 338–339
economic theory of government, 324–326
economic theory of regulation, 326–327
monopoly regulation, 326–327
oligopoly regulation, 326–327
public ownership, 335–337
regulation and deregulation, 327–334
Competition Tribunal cases, 338
competitive environment
concentration measures, 208–211
market structures, 207–208
competitive equilibrium, 110, 110*f*, 256
competitive market, 60, 110–113

complements, **63**
 and cross-elasticity of demand, 92
 perfect complements, 177–178, 177*f*
 in production, 68
concentration measures
 barriers to entry, 210
 Canadian economy, 209, 209*f*
 firm turnover, 210
 four-firm concentration ratio, 208, 208*t*
 geographic scope of market, 210
 Herfindahl–Hirschman Index (HHI),
  208–209
 limitations of, 209–211
 market and industry correspondence,
  210–211
 oligopoly, 297
constant-cost industry, 254*f*
constant returns to scale, 233
Constitution of Canada, 478
constraints, 200
consumer behaviour
 income effect, 180, 180*f*, 181
 predictions of, 178–182, 178*f*
 price effect, 179–180, 179*f*
 rational decision makers, 192–193
 substitution effect, 181, 181*f*
consumer efficiency, 164
consumer equilibrium, 158
Consumer Price Index (CPI), 498
 base period, 498
 biased CPI, 501
 calculation of, 499–500, 499*t*
 consequences of bias, 501
 construction of, 498–500
 CPI basket, selection of, 498–499, 498*f*
 described, 455
 formula, 499
 inflation, measurement of, 500, 500*f*
 magnitude of bias, 501
 monthly CPI report, 502–503
 monthly price survey, 499
 reading the numbers, 498
consumer surplus, 107, 107*f*, 164, 165,
  273–274
consumption
 autonomous consumption, 536
 changes in, and gains from international
  trade, 759–761
 as function of real GDP, 540
 induced consumption, 536
 marginal propensity to consume, 538, 538*f*
consumption expenditure, 467, 469,
  539–540, 666
consumption function, 536, 537*f*, 539*f*, 540,
  540*f*, 558
consumption plans, 536–538
consumption possibilities, 154, 154*f*,
  172–174, 172*f*, 760, 760*f*
contest, 104
contestable market, 310–311, 311*f*
contractionary fiscal policy, 577
convergent geometric series, 600*n*
cooperative equilibrium, 309
coordinates, 17*f*
coordinating decisions, 46
copyright, 264, **357**
core inflation, 656

corporate income taxes, 564
corporate profits, 472
corporate scandals, 7–8
corporation, 205
correlation, 20
cost curves
 average total cost curve, 226–227, 227*f*,
  231
 long-run average cost curve, 231, 232,
  232*f*
 and product curves, 228*f*
 shifts in, 228–229
cost-push inflation, 635
 aggregate demand response, 636, 636*f*
 in Canada, 637
 initial effect of decrease in aggregate supply,
  635
 and price level, 636*f*
 process, 636
 spiral, 637*f*
 stagflation, 635
costs
 advertising, 292–293, 293*f*
 average cost, 226–227, 227*f*
 average fixed cost, 226
 average total cost, 226
 average variable cost, 226
 of economic growth, 40, 452
 of education, 48–49, 49*f*
 explicit costs, 198
 external cost, 112, 349, 349*f*, 350*f*
 glossary of, 229*t*
 implicit costs, 198
 inflation, 456
 long-run cost, 230–233
 marginal cost. *See* marginal cost
 marginal external cost, 349
 marginal social cost, 349
 owner's resources, 199
 private costs, 349
 product innovation, 292
 selling costs, 293–294, 293*f*
 short-run costs, 225–229
 sunk cost, 220
 total cost, 225, 225*f*, 243*f*
 total fixed cost, 225
 total variable cost, 225
 transactions costs, 113, 212–213
 unemployment, 454
Courchene, Thomas J., 624
Cournot, Antoine-Augustine, 148, 318
CP Express and Transport, 204
CPI basket, 498–499, 498*f*
crawling peg, 624, 671
credit cards, 592
credit union, 593
creditor nation, 774
cross elasticity of demand, 91–92, 91*f*
cross exchange rates, 613–614, 613*f*, 614*f*
cross-section graph, 18, 19*f*
crowding in, 683
crowding out, 683, 690–691
Crown Corporation, 326
 bureaucratic, 336–337, 336*f*
 compromise outcome, 337
 described, 335
 efficiency, 335–336, 335*f*

 examples of, 335
 privatization, 337
 profit maximization, 337
 in reality, 337
currency, 591
currency appreciation, 613, 621, 621*f*
currency depreciation, 613, 621, 621*f*
currency drain ratio, 597
currency union, 624–625
current account, 457, 772
 current account balance, 772, 774–775, 774*t*
 Currie, Janet, 442–444
 curved line, slope of, 25–26, 25*f*
cyclical surplus or deficit, 575–576, 575*f*,
  576
cyclical unemployment, 496

D
Darwin, Charles, 440
De Beers, 265
deadweight loss, 111–112, 271
debit cards, 592
debt, 430
debt interest, 565
debtor nation, 774
decentralized coordination, 45
decision time frames, 220
decreasing-cost industry, 254*f*
deficits
 budget deficit, 565, 574–575, 574*f*
 cyclical deficit, 575–576, 575*f*, 576
 government budget deficit, 457, 458*f*
 government deficits around the world,
  569*f*
 structural deficit, 575–576, 575*f*
 temporary cyclical deficit, 575
 twin deficits, 775, 775*f*
deflation, 455
demand, 61
 aggregate demand. *See* aggregate demand
 for capital, 397–398, 401*f*
 change in demand. *See* change in demand
 change in the quantity demanded, 64–65,
  65*f*
 and consumer surplus, 107, 107*f*
 demand schedule, 62
 derived demand, 388
 described, 61
 elasticity. *See* elasticities of demand
 for factor of production, 388
 in foreign exchange market, 615
 for high-skilled and low-skilled labour,
  426
 individual demand, 106–107, 106*f*
 for labour. *See* demand for labour
 law of demand, 61, 148–149
 and marginal benefit, 106–107
 and marginal revenue, 266*f*
 market demand, 106–107, 106*f*, 394
 for money, 601–604, 606–607
 in perfect competition, 241*f*
 pollution-free environment, 347
 price elasticity. *See* price elasticity of
  demand
 quantity demanded, 61, 64–65
 for regulation, 326
 and selling costs, 294

and value, 106
and willingness to pay, 106
demand and supply theory
    predicting changes in price and quantity,
        72–75
    price of oil, 76–77
demand curve, 62
    for Canadian dollars, 616, 616*f*
    capital demand curve, 401
    demand for money curve. *See* demand for
        money curve
    graphical illustration, 62*f*
    and income effect, 180, 180*f*
    kinked demand curve model, 298, 298*f*
    labour demand curve, 391
    as marginal benefit curve, 106
    market demand curve, 107
    mathematics of, 78
    movement along, 65
    and price effect, 179–180, 179*f*
    shift of, 65
    straight-line demand curve, elasticity along,
        87, 87*f*
demand effects, 580–581
demand equation, 78
demand for labour, 709
    change in, and labour unions, 415
    changes in, 393, 393*t*, 415, 711
    diminishing marginal product, 710–711
    elasticity of, 394
    graphical illustration, 709*f*
    high-skilled labour, 426
    human capital, 426
    low-skilled labour, 426
    marginal product, 710, 710*f*
    quantity of labour demanded, 709
demand for money, 603–604, 603*f*, 606–607
demand for money curve, 602
    changes in, 602*f*
    graphical illustration, 602*f*
    shifts in, 602
demand-pull inflation, 633
    in Canada, 635
    initial effect of increase in aggregate
        demand, 633
    money wage rate response, 633–634
    process, 634
    rise in price level, 633*f*
    spiral, 634*f*
demand schedule, 62
Demsetz, 213
Deng Xiaoping, 5
depository institutions, 593–594
    see also banks
deposits, 591, 596–597
depreciation, 469
depression, 449
deregulation, 334
derived demand, 388, 389
desired currency drain ratio, 597
desired reserve ratio, 597
desired reserves, 597
developing economies, 450
diamonds and water, 164–165
diminishing marginal product, 710–711
diminishing marginal product of capital, 230

**diminishing marginal rate of substitution,
    176**
diminishing marginal returns, 223
diminishing marginal revenue product, 390
diminishing marginal utility, 156–157
diminishing returns, 230
direct relationship, 20–21, 21*f*
direct tax, 472
disappearing invisible hand, 307
discounting, 398–400
discouraged workers, 453, 490
The Discoverers (Boorstin), 147
discretionary fiscal policy, 570, 574
discrimination, 127, 429–430, 429*f*
diseconomies of scale, 232–233
disposable income, 515, 536
dispute-settling mechanisms, 776
divisible goods, 172
dollar. *See* Canadian dollar
domestic product at market prices, 472
dominant firm oligopoly, 298–299, 299*f*
dominant strategy equilibrium, 308
double coincidence of wants, 590
double counting, 466
drugs, 140–141, 140*f*
dumping, 768
duopolists' dilemma, 305–306
duopoly, 296, 296*f*
Dupuit, Jules, 149
duration of poverty, 425, 425*f*
dynamic comparative advantage, 45, 767

E
e-books, 184–185
earnings sharing regulation, 332
East Germany, 6
eBay, 263
economic accounting concepts, 198–199,
    199*t*
economic coordination, 45–47
Economic Cycle Research Institute (ECRI),
    486
economic depreciation, 198–199
economic efficiency, 201–202
economic growth, 40, 447
    aggregate supply-aggregate demand model,
        508, 522
    around the world, 449–450, 450*f*,
        735–736
    Asia, catchup in, 736, 736*f*
    benefits of, 452
    business cycle, 448, 448*f*
    in Canada, 41, 41*f*, 447, 447*f*, 522, 734*f*
    causes of, 737–738
    cost of, 40, 452
    forecasting, 750–751
    graphical illustration, 40*f*
    growth accounting, 739–742
    growth rates over time, 449–450
    growth theories, 743–749
    in Hong Kong, 41, 41*f*
    incentive system, 737
    investment in human capital, 738
    investment in new capital, 737–738
    long-term economic growth in Canada,
        449*f*
    long-term growth trends, 734–736

Lucas wedge, 451, 451*f*
    and markets, 737
    measurement of, 447
    monetary exchange facilities, 737
    new technologies, discovery of, 738
    Okun gap, 451, 451*f*
    persistent differences in growth rates, 450
    potential GDP, growth of, 447
    preconditions for, 737
    property rights, 737
    saving, 737–738
    and standard of living, 40
economic growth rate, 476
    business cycle forecasts, 479
    economic welfare comparisons, 476–478
    international comparisons, 478–479
economic inequality
    discrimination, 429–430, 429*f*
    human capital, 426–428
    income distribution, 420, 420*f*
    income Lorenz curve, 421–422, 421*f*
    income redistribution, 431–433
    low-income cutoff, 424
    measurement of, 420–426
    poverty, 424–425, 424*f*, 425*f*
    skill differentials, 427*f*
    sources of, 426–430
    trends in inequality, 423, 424*f*
    unequal ownership of capital, 430
    wealth, distribution of, 422
economic model, 12–13, 20–23
economic profit, 199
    break-even point, 242
    monopolistic competition, 288*f*
    monopoly, 303, 303*f*
    and perfect competition, 240–241
    residual income economic profit, 388
    in single-price monopoly, 268
    and total revenue and total cost, 243*f*
economic rent, 406–407, 407*f*
economic science
    agreement and disagreement, 14
    cause and effect, 13
    ceteris paribus, 13
    economic model, 12–13
    economic theory, 12
    fallacy of composition, 13
    normative statements, 12
    observation and measurement, 12
    obstacles and pitfalls, 13–14
    post hoc fallacy, 13–14
    testing models, 12–13
economic theory, 12
economic theory of government
    common resources, 324
    described, 324
    externalities, 324
    free-rider problem, 324
    government failure, 325
    income redistribution, 325
    market failure, 324
    monopoly regulation, 324
    oligopoly, regulations of, 324
    public choice, and political marketplace,
        325–326, 325*f*
    public goods, 324
economic theory of regulation, 326–327

economic way of thinking
  choices, and change, 10
  choices, and tradeoffs, 9
  human nature, incentives, and
    institutions, 11
  margin, choosing at, 11
  opportunity cost, 10
  responding to incentives, 11
  what, how and for whom tradeoffs, 9–10
economic wealth, sources of, 54–55
economic welfare, 476–478
economics, 2
  definition of, 2
  macroeconomics, 2
  microeconomics, 2
  scarcity and, 2
  self-interest, and the social interest, 5–8
  as social science, 12–14
  two big questions, 3–8
  what, how, and for whom, 3–5
economies of scale, 213, 232
  gains from international trade, 762
  long-run cost, 232–233
  monopoly, 277–278
economies of scope, 213, 277–278
economies of team production, 213
ecosystem, 347
education
  costs and benefits of, 48–49, 49f
  improvement in quality, 742
  and poverty, 425
  returns from, 427
efficiency
  advertising, 295
  brand names, 295
  competitive equilibrium, 110, 110f
  competitive market, 110–113
  consumer efficiency, 164
  Crown corporation, 335–336, 335f
  demand and marginal benefit, 106–107
  economic efficiency, 201–202
  and fairness, 116
  monopolistic competition, 291
  obstacles to, 112–113
  paradox of value, 164–165, 165f
  perfect competition, 256–257, 271, 271f
  and product innovation, 292
  public goods, efficient quantity of, 366,
    367f
  and regulation of natural monopoly,
    278–279
  resource allocation methods, 104–105
  single-price monopoly, 271, 271f
  supply and marginal cost, 108–109
  and taxes, 112, 136, 136f
  technological efficiency, 201
efficiency wage, 720–721
Ehrlich, Paul, 440
elastic demand, 86–87, 86f, 267
elastic supply, 95f
elasticities of demand
  for CDs, 98–99
  cross elasticity of demand, 91–92, 91f
  glossary, 97t
  income elasticity of demand, 92–93
  labour, 394
  minus sign and elasticity, 86

price elasticity of demand. *See* price elastic-
    ity of demand
  for the product, 394
elasticity of supply, 94
  calculation of, 94–95
  elastic supply, 95f
  formula, 94
  glossary, 97t
  inelastic supply, 95f
  influencing factors, 95–96
  perfectly elastic supply, 95f, 135
  perfectly inelastic supply, 95f, 135
  range of, 95
  and taxes, 135, 135f
  time frame for supply decisions, 96
  unit elastic supply, 95f
emission charges, 352
emission permits, 353
emission standards, 382
employment
  full employment. *See* full employment
  and the labour force, 1960–2004, 489f
  and product concepts, 221–224
  and real GDP, 706–708
  with sticky wages, 727
employment argument, 767
Employment Insurance, 133, 431
employment-to-population ratio, 490
energy price shocks, 742
energy products, 776
Enron, 7
entrants, 493
entrepreneurship, 4
entry
  barriers to entry. *See* barriers to entry
  monopolistic competition, 287
  perfect competition, 249–250, 249f
environmental externalities, 382–383
Environmental Protection Agency (EPA), 353
environmental quality, 477
environmental regulation, 742, 769
equality of opportunity, 116
equation of exchange, 638
equilibrium
  above full-employment equilibrium, 692
  below full-employment equilibrium, 518,
    692
  best deal for buyers and sellers, 71
  capital market equilibrium, 402f
  competitive equilibrium, 110, 110f, 256
  consumer equilibrium, 158
  cooperative equilibrium, 309
  described, 70
  dominant strategy equilibrium, 308
  equilibrium expenditure, 544–545, 544f
  equilibrium price, 70, 79
  equilibrium quantity, 70, 79
  equilibrium regulation, 327
  foreign exchange market, 618
  free trade equilibrium, 761
  full-employment equilibrium, 712
  GDP, and price level, 553–555
  graphical illustration, 70f
  labour market, 396, 712
  long-run equilibrium, 251, 251f
  macroeconomic equilibrium, 516–521,
    678–679

  in market for reserves, 662, 662f
  mathematics of, 79
  money market equilibrium, 605, 605f
  Nash equilibrium, 301
  political equilibrium, 326
  price adjustments, 71
  price as regulator, 70–71
  rent-seeking equilibrium, 272–273, 273f
  short-run equilibrium, 248, 248f
  short-run equilibrium in labour market,
    726–727
  simultaneous equilibrium, 678–679
equilibrium cross exchange rates, 618, 618f
equilibrium expenditure, 544–545, 544f,
    559, 559f, 584
equilibrium price, 70, 79
equilibrium quantity, 70, 79
equilibrium regulation, 327
equity
  big tradeoff, 115
  fair results, 114–115
  of markets, 114–117
  symmetry principle, 116
  utilitarianism, 114–115, 115f
Ethiopia, 118–119
excess capacity, 290–291, 290f
excess reserves, 597
exchange rate policy
  crawling peg, 624
  currency union, 624–625
  fixed exchange rate, 623–624
  flexible exchange rate, 623
exchange rate targeting rule, 671
exchange rates
  Canadian dollar–U.S. dollar exchange rate,
    612, 613f
  changes in, 620–621
  changes in demand and supply, 619–622,
    619f
  cross exchange rates, 613–614, 613f, 614f
  effects, 692
  equilibrium cross exchange rates, 618,
    618f
  expectations, 622
  expected future exchange rate, 619, 620
  fiscal policy effectiveness, 689
  fluctuations in, 619–622, 621f, 665
  interest rate parity, 622
  and international crowding out, 683
  monetary policy effectiveness, 689
  and monetary policy transmission, 665
  and money, 687
  purchasing power parity (PPP), 622
  real exchange rate, 671
excludable, 364
exit
  monopolistic competition, 287
  perfect competition, 249f, 250
expansion, 448, 486, 550
expansionary fiscal policy, 577, 680–682,
    680f, 681f, 690–691
  see also fiscal policy
expansionary monetary policy, 684–687, 684f,
    685f, 686f, 691
  see also monetary policy
expectations
  and change in aggregate demand, 514–515

exchange rates, 622
rational expectation, 641
expected future exchange rate, 619, 620
expected future income, 64, 402
expected future prices, 63–64, 68
expected profit effect, 616, 617
expenditure
    actual aggregate expenditure, 543–544
    aggregate expenditure, 468, 536
    aggregate planned expenditure, 541
    autonomous expenditure, 543, 546, 558
    consumption expenditure, 467, 469
    and elasticity, 89
    equilibrium expenditure at fixed price level,
        541–545
    on goods and services, 565
    government expenditures, 468, 471
    induced expenditure, 543, 546, 570–571
    and interest rate, 679f
    interest-sensitive expenditure curve, 667
    personal expenditures, 471
    planned expenditure, 543–544
expenditure approach, 471, 471t
expenditure multipliers
    equilibrium expenditure at fixed price level,
        541–545
    expenditure plans and GDP, 536–541
    the multiplier, 546–550
    the multiplier and price level, 551–555
expenditure plans
    consumption plans, 536–538
    and gross domestic product (GDP),
        536–541
    and interest rates, 665–667, 667f
    saving plans, 536–538
explicit costs, 198
exports, 468, 756
    net exports, 468, 471, 667, 756
    world demand for Canadian exports,
        619
exports effect, 616
external benefits, 112–113, 353–357, 354f
    see also externalities
external cost, 112, 349, 349f, 350f
    see also externalities
external diseconomies, 253–255
external economies, 253–255
externalities, 346
    copyright, 357
    economic theory of government, 324
    and efficiency, 112
    environmental externalities, 382–383
    external benefits, 112–113, 353–357,
        354f
    external cost, 112, 349, 349f, 350f
    government actions, 352–353, 355–357
    marketable permits, 352–353
    negative consumption externalities, 346
    negative externality, 346
    negative production externalities, 346
    patent, 357
    pollution, 347–352
    positive consumption externalities, 346
    positive externality, 346, 353–357
    positive production externalities, 346
    private subsidies, 356
    public provision, 355–356, 355f

taxes, 352, 353f
    voucher, 356–357, 356f
extreme Keynesian hypothesis, 688
extreme monetarist hypothesis, 689

F
factor markets
    capital markets, 397–403
    demand and supply, 388f
    derived demand, 388
    described, 46
    economic rent, 406–407, 407f
    interaction of demand and supply, 406–407
    labour markets, 389–396, 413–416
    large and small incomes, 406–407
    natural resource markets, 403–405
    opportunity cost, 406–407, 407f
factor prices, 388, 393
factors of production, 3
    capital, 4
    demand for, 388
    derived demand, 388
    entrepreneurship, 4
    income from, 4
    labour, 3
    land, 3
    markets for. See factor markets
    trading of, 388
fair results, 114–115, 127
fair rules, 116, 127
fairness, 114–117
fallacy of composition, 13, 138
Family Supplement program, 431
farm marketing board, 138
farmers' income, 472
father of economics. See Smith, Adam
federal budget, 564–565, 564f
    see also government budgets
federal regulatory agencies, 328t
final good, 466
financial flows, 468
financial innovation, 601
financial property, 46
firm, 45, 198
    business organization, types of, 204–206,
        205t, 206f
    competitive environment, 207–211
    constraints, 200
    economic problem, 198–200
    economic profit, 199
    economies of scale, 213
    economies of scope, 213
    goal of, 198
    in long run, 242
    and markets, 212–213
    and opportunity cost, 198–199
    organization of production, 203–204
    perfect competition decisions, 242–248
    political marketplace, 325
    principal–agent problem, 204
    profit, measurement of, 198
    in short run, 242
    short-run supply curve (perfect competi-
        tion), 246, 246f
    transaction costs, 212–213
firm turnover, 210
first-come, first-served, 104–105

fiscal policy, 459, 515, 564
    and aggregate demand, 576–578,
        577f
    automatic fiscal policy, 570
    automatic stabilizers, 574–576
    and change in aggregate demand, 515
    contractionary fiscal policy, 577
    credibility, 694–695
    crowding in, 683
    crowding out, 683
    demand effects, 580–581
    discretionary fiscal policy, 570, 574
    economic adjustment to, 682f
    effectiveness, 687
    exchange rate effectiveness, 689
    expansionary fiscal policy, 577, 680–682,
        680f, 681f, 690–691
    first round effects, 680, 680f
    fiscal expansion at potential GDP, 578–579
    at full employment, 690–691, 690f
    interest rate effectiveness, 689
    international crowding out, 683
    limitations of, 579
    other fiscal policies, 683
    and potential GDP, 579–580
    process, 564
    real GDP and price level, 578f
    second round effects, 680–681, 681f
    in short run, 680–683
    supply-side effects, 579–581, 580f
fiscal policy multipliers
    algebra of, 584–585
    autonomous tax multiplier, 572–573, 573f,
        585
    autonomous transfer payments, 585
    equilibrium expenditure, 584
    government expenditures multiplier,
        570–572, 571t, 572f, 584–585
    heating multiplier, 582–583
    and international trade, 574
    and price level, 576–579
fixed exchange rate, 623–624
fixed prices, 541
flat-rate income tax, 431
flexible exchange rate, 623
flow, 493f
flow, 469
flow supply, 404
fluctuations
    in Canada, 447, 447f
    of real GDP around potential GDP, 448
"for whom" tradeoffs, 9–10
force, 105
forecasting
    economic growth, 750–751
    inflation, 641
    rational expectation, 641
foreign currency, 612, 612f
foreign exchange market, 612
    see also Canadian dollar
    changes in demand, 619, 619f
    changes in supply, 620, 620f
    demand, 615
    demand and supply, 615
    demand curve for Canadian dollars, 616,
        616f
    equilibrium cross exchange rates, 618, 618f

expected profit effect, 616, 617
exports effect, 616
imports effect, 617
intervention, 623*f*
law of demand, 615–616
law of supply, 617
market equilibrium, 618
supply, 615, 617
supply curve for Canadian dollars, 617, 617*f*
foreign exchange rate, 612
see also exchange rates
foreign exchange risk, 625
45° line, 536
four-firm concentration ratio, 208, 208*t*, 297
four-fold classification, 364, 364*f*
free-rider problem, 364
benefits of public goods, 365–366, 365*f*
bureaucrats, 368
described, 113, 324, 365
efficient quantity of public goods, 366, 367*f*
political equilibrium, 369
principle of minimum differentiation, 367
rational ignorance, 368
free trade. *See* international trade
free trade equilibrium, 761
frictional unemployment, 495–496
Friedman, Milton, 356, 671, 688, 700–701
full employment, 496
aggregate supply curves, 713–714, 713*f*
in Canada, 1980 and 2004, 718*f*
crowding out, 690–691
departure from, 640
expansionary fiscal policy at, 690–691, 690*f*
expansionary monetary policy, 691
and potential GDP, 712, 713*f*
unemployment at full employment, 508, 719–721
full-employment equilibrium, 712
full-employment quantity of labour, 511

G
gains from international trade
balanced trade, 759
calculation of, 761
cheaper to buy than to produce, 758
comparative advantage, 757, 761
consumption, changes in, 759–761
diversity of taste, 762
economies of scale, 762
expanding consumption possibilities, 760, 760*f*
free trade equilibrium, 761
gains fro both countries, 761
in practice, 761–762
production, changes in, 759–761
terms of trade, 758–759
trade in similar goods, 762
gains from trade
achievement of, 43–45
competitive advantage, 42
dynamic comparative advantage, 45
graphical illustration, 44*f*

international trade. *See* gains from international trade
specialization, 42
game theory, 300
chicken game, 308, 308*f*
contestable market, 310–311, 311*f*
cooperative equilibrium, 309
disappearing invisible hand, 307
dominant strategy equilibrium, 308
duopolists' dilemma, 305–306
games, features of, 300
Nash equilibrium, 301, 305–306
payoff matrix, 300, 301*t*, 305, 306*t*
price-fixing game, 302–306
and price wars, 310
prisoners' dilemma, 300–301, 301*t*
punishment, 309
R&D game, 306–307, 307*t*
repeated duopoly game, 309–310
sequential game, 310–311
strategies, 300
tit-for-tat strategy, 309
trigger strategy, 309
GDP. *See* gross domestic product (GDP)
GDP deflator, 474
General Agreement on Tariffs and Trade (GATT), 763, 784
General Theory of Employment, Interest, and Money (Keynes), 446, 459, 688
geographic scope of market, 210
geographical patterns of international trade, 756
Germany, 643, 700, 701
global perspective
comparative advantage, 761
economic growth, 449–450, 450*f*, 735–736
government budgets, 569, 569*f*
government deficits, 569*f*
inflation, 456, 456*f*
money growth and inflation, 639*f*
real GDP growth, 735–736
unemployment, 454
global warming, 348
globalization
of production decisions, 6
self-interest, and the social interest, 6
goods
classification of, 364
complement, 63
divisible goods, 172
excludable, 364
final good, 466
four-fold classification, 364, 364*f*
inferior good, 64, 182
inferior goods, 92
intermediate good, 466
international trade in, 756
luxuries, 89
necessities, 89
nonexcludable, 364
nonrival, 364
normal good, 64
private goods, 364
public goods. *See* public goods
rival, 364
similar goods, 762
substitute, 63

goods and services, 3
consumers of, 4
factors of production, 3–4
trends in what we produce, 3, 3*f*
goods markets, 46
Google, 263, 280–281
Governing Council, 657–658
government
see also regulation
growth of, 369
income redistribution, 431–433
inefficient overprovision, 369
license, 264
voter preferences, 369
government budget deficit, 457, 458, 458*f*
government budget surplus, 457, 458, 458*f*
government budgets
balanced budget, 565, 576
budget deficit, 574–575, 574*f*
budget making, 564
current account balance, 774*t*
cyclical surplus or deficit, 575–576, 575*f*, 576
deficit, 565, 569*f*
federal budget, 564
global perspective, 569, 569*f*
government debt, 567–568, 567*f*
highlights of 2005 budget, 564–565, 564*t*
historical perspective, 565–569
outlays, 565, 566–567, 567*f*
provincial budget, 564, 568–569, 568*f*
public capital stock, 568
revenues, 564, 566, 566*f*
structural surplus or deficit, 575–576, 575*f*
surplus, 565
temporary cyclical surplus or deficit, 575
total government budgets, 569*f*
government debt, 567–568, 567*f*
government expenditures, 468, 471, 565, 577*f*
government expenditures multiplier, 584–585
government expenditures multiplier, 570–572, 571*t*, 572*f*
government failure, 325
government sector balance, 774
graphs
axes, 17
bar chart, 18
ceteris paribus, 26–27
coordinates, 17*f*
correlation and causation, 20
cross-section graph, 18, 19*f*
described, 17
direct relationship, 20–21, 21*f*
in economic models, 20–23
inverse relationship, 21–22, 22*f*
linear relationship, 20–21, 28, 28*f*
making a graph, 17*f*
maximum and minimum points, 22, 23*f*
misleading graphs, 20
negative relationship, 21–22, 22*f*
origin, 17
positive relationship, 20–21, 21*f*
scatter diagrams, 19–20, 19*f*
slope, 24–26
three or more variables, 26–27, 27*f*
time-series graph, 18, 18*f*

trend, 18
two-variable graph, 17
unrelated variables, 23, 23f
x-axis, 17
y-axis, 17
y-axis intercept, 29
Great Depression, 446, 449, 486, 530, 784
gross domestic product (GDP), 466
   Canadian GDP balloon, 475f
   and circular flow of expenditure and
      income, 467–468, 467f
   equilibrium GDP, and price level,
      553–555, 577–578
   expenditure approach, 471, 471t
   and expenditure plans, 536–541
   final goods and services, 466
   financial flows, 468
   in a given time period, 466
   gross, meaning of, 469–470
   growth of, 470
   income approach, 471–472, 472f
   investment, financing of, 468–469
   market value, 466
   measurement of, 471–472
   nominal GDP, 473
   potential GDP. See potential GDP
   produced within a country, 466
   quarterly GDP report, 480–481
   real gross domestic product, 447
   see also real GDP
gross investment, 469
growth. See economic growth
growth accounting, 739
   achievement of faster growth, 742
   aggregate production function, 739
   labour productivity, 739
   productivity curve, 739–741, 740f
   productivity growth slowdown and
      speedup, 741–742
   purpose of, 739
growth rate cycle downturn, 486
growth recession, 448
growth theories
   classical growth theory, 743–745, 744f
   described, 743
   neoclassical growth theory, 745–747, 746f
   new growth theory, 747–749
Guaranteed Income Supplement (GIS), 431
guns versus butter, 9

H
Hamermesh, Daniel, 131, 721
Hargreaves, James, 531
Harris, Richard, 624
health, 477
Herfindahl–Hirschman Index (HHI),
   208–209, 297
Heston, Alan, 478
high-skilled labour
   demand for, 426
   skill differentials, 427f
   supply of, 426
   wage rates, 426–427
high-technology industries, 742
HIV/AIDS, 8
Holmstrom, Bengt, 317, 320–322
Hong Kong, economic growth in, 41, 41f

Hotelling, Harold, 405, 440
Hotelling Principle, 404–405, 440
household production, 476
households
   differences in degree of specialization, 430
   saving, 468
   types of, 425
household's budget
   budget line, 154, 172, 172f
   consumption possibilities, 154, 154f
   price and income changes, 154–155, 155f
   real income, 173
   relative price, 154–155, 173
housing markets
   black market, 126
   equilibrium rent, 124
   long-run adjustments, 125
   price ceiling, 125
   regulation of, 125–126
   rent ceiling, 125, 127–128, 127f
   and rent ceilings, 124–128
   San Francisco earthquake, 124, 125f
   search activity, 126
"how" tradeoffs, 9
Howitt, Peter, 532–534, 643
Hoxby, Caroline M., 384–386
human capital, 3, 4f, **707**
   as capital resource, 40
   demand for labour, 426
   differences in, and inequality, 427–428
   and economic inequality, 426–428
   education, 427
   inequality trends, 428, 428f
   investment in, 738
   learning-by-doing, 707
   lost human capital, 454
   quantity of, and potential GDP, 511
   skill differentials, 427f
   supply of labour, 426
   training, 427
   wage rates, 426–427
human nature, 11
Hume, David, 784, 785
Hurricane Rita, 408–409
hyperinflation, 457, 643, 700

I
IBM, 250
illegal goods, 140–141, 140f
implicit costs, 198
implicit rental rate, 198
import function, 541, 558
import restrictions, 415
imports, 468, 756
   Canadian demand for, 620
   marginal propensity to import, 541, 574
   and multiplier, 548–549
imports effect, 617
incentive, 2
   and human nature, 11
   innovation, 277
   reconciliation of self-interest and social
      interest, 11
   response to, 11
incentive pay, 204
incentive system, 203

income
   see also economic inequality
   after-tax income, 420
   aggregate income, 468
   annual income, 423
   categories of, 471–472
   and demand, 64
   disposable income, 515, 536
   distribution of. See income distribution
   expected future income, 64, 402
   and factor prices, 388
   from factors of production, 4
   farmers' income, 472
   income change, 155, 155f, 174, 174f
   investment, 472
   large incomes, 406–407
   lifetime income, 423
   Lorenz curve, 421–422, 421f, 422f
   market income, 420
   mean income, 420
   median income, 420
   mode income, 420
   net domestic income at factor cost, 472
   from non-farm unincorporated
      businesses, 472
   proportion spent, and elasticity, 90
   real income, 155, 173
   redistribution of income. See income redis-
      tribution
   and saving decisions, 402
   small incomes, 406–407
   sources of, 425
   total income, 425
   vs. wealth, 422–423
income approach, 471–472, 472f
income distribution
   after-tax income, 420, 420f
   bell-shaped distribution, 420
   income distribution trends, 428, 428f
   positively skewed distribution, 420
income effect, 180
   calculation of, 181
   and change in demand, 180f
   and demand, 61
   described, 61
   high wage rate, 183
   isolation of, 181f
   supply of labour, 395
income elastic demand, 92
income elasticity of demand, 92
   income elastic demand, 92
   inferior goods, 92
   public goods, 369
   real-world examples, 93, 93f, 93t
   in ten countries, 93f
income inelastic demand, 92
income maintenance programs, 431
income redistribution
   big tradeoff, 433
   economic theory of government, 325
   income maintenance programs, 431
   income taxes, 431
   scale of, 432, 432f
   subsidized services, 431–432
   and unanticipated inflation, 640
income taxes, 431, 434–435, 549
   see also taxes

income-time budget line, 182, 183*f*
increasing-cost industry, 254*f*
increasing marginal returns, 222–223
indifference curve, 175
   graphical illustration, 175*f*
   marginal rate of substitution *(MRS)*, 176,
      176*f*
   and marginal utility, 189–190, 189*f*
   preference maps, 175–178, 175*f*
   and preferences, 189–190, 189*f*
indirect tax, 472, 564
individual demand, 106–107, 106*f*
individual supply, 108–109, 108*f*
individual transferable quota (ITQ),
   374–375, 375*f*
indivisible goods, 172
induced consumption, 536
induced expenditure, 543, 546, 570–571
induced taxes, 573
industrial economies, 454*f*
Industrial Revolution, 6, 53, 530, 531
inefficiency
   deadweight loss, 111–112
   external benefit, 354*f*
   external cost, 350*f*
   government failure, 325
   minimum wage, 130
   monopoly, 271*f*
   overproduction, 112, 112*f*
   rent ceiling, 127, 127*f*
   tariffs, 765
   underproduction, 111, 112*f*
inefficient overprovision, 369
inelastic demand, 86–87, 86*f*, 267
inelastic supply, 95*f*
inequality. *See* economic inequality
infant-industry argument, 767
inferior good, 64, 92, 182
inflation, 455
   aggregate demand shock, 632
   aggregate supply–aggregate demand model,
      508, 523
   aggregate supply shock, 632
   anticipated inflation, 641–644, 642*f*
   around the world, 456, 456*f*
   in Canada, 455, 455*f*
   core inflation, 656
   cost-push inflation, 635–637
   costs of, 456
   demand-pull inflation, 633–635
   effects of, 640–644
   forecasting inflation, 641
   hyperinflation, 457, 643, 700
   inflation–unemployment tradeoff,
      650–651
   influence of, 447
   and interest rates, 648–649, 648*f*
   measurement of, and CPI, 500, 500*f*
   and monetary policy, 656
   and money growth, 638–639, 639*f*
   natural rate of unemployment, changes in,
      646, 647*f*
   nominal interest rate, influence on, 649
   as ongoing process, 632
   overadjustment for, 476
   Phillips curve, 644–648
   price level, change i, 632, 632*f*

problem of, 456–457
   quantity theory of money, 638–639
   stagflation, 635
   unanticipated inflation, 640–641, 642
   understanding inflation, 700–701
   and unemployment, 644–648
inflation-control target
   avoiding inflation with, 701
   controversy, 657
   and outcome, 657*f*
   rationale for, 656–657
inflation rate, 500
inflation–unemployment tradeoff, 650–651
inflationary gap, 519, 692
information constraints, 200
Information Revolution, 6–7, 53, 531
inheritances, 430
innovation, 264, 277, 292
institutions, role of, 11
instrument rule, 659
Intel Corporation, 310
intellectual property, 46
intellectual property rights, 357
interdependence, 297
interest, 4, 472
interest rate, 604
   Bank of Canada target, 605
   bank rate, 660
   and capital markets, 40
   changes, 401
   consumption expenditure, 666
   currency union, effect of, 625
   determination, 604–605, 649
   effects, 692
   and exchange rate fluctuations, 619,
      620
   and expenditure, 679*f*
   and expenditure plans, 665–667, 667*f*
   fiscal policy effectiveness, 689
   fluctuations in, and monetary policy trans-
      missions, 663–664, 664*f*
   formula, 604
   and inflation, 648–649, 648*f*
   monetary policy effectiveness, 689
   and money, 679*f*
   as money holding influence, 601
   and money market equilibrium, 605,
      605*f*
   and net exports, 667
   nominal interest rate, 649, 665–666
   and opportunity cost, 666
   overnight rate, 596
   paradox, 672–673
   and real GDP growth, 669*f*
   real interest rate, 665–666
   and saving decisions, 402
   Treasury bill rate, 664
interest rate parity, 622
interest-sensitive expenditure curve, 667
intermediate good, 466
intermediate position, 689
international crowding out, 683
International Panel on Climate Change
   (IPCC), 348
international substitution, 551
international surplus and deficit, 457–458,
   458*f*

international trade
   balance of international payments,
      772–775
   encouragement of, and economic growth,
      742
   and fiscal policy multipliers, 574
   gains from, 757–762
   geographical patterns, 756
   in goods, 756
   net exports and international
      borrowing, 756
   nontariff barrier, 763, 766, 776
   North American Free Trade Agreement,
      776–777
   patterns, 756
   protectionism. *See* protectionism
   quotas, 766, 766*f*
   restrictions. *See* protectionism
   in services, 756, 776
   tariffs, 763–765, 778–779
   terms of trade, 758–759
   trends, 756
   volume of trade, 756
   voluntary export restraint (VER), 766
intertemporal substitution, 551
invention, 264, 277
inverse relationship, 21–22, 22*f*
investment, 468
   business investment, 471
   financing of, 468–469
   gross investment, 469
   illustration of, 470*f*
   income, 472, 564
   interest rate, effect of, 666
   meaning of, 469
   net investment, 469
   in new capital, 737–738
investment securities, 594
invisible hand, 111
involuntary part-time rate, 489

J
job leavers, 493
job losers, 493
job rationing, 720–721
job search, 719–720, 719*f*
jobs, 452
John Labatt Ltd., 339
joint unlimited liability, 205

K
k-percent rule, 671
Kennedy Round, 763
Keynes, John Maynard, 446, 459, 530–531,
   688
Keynesian, 688
Keynesian–monetarist controversy, 688–689
Kimberly-Clark, 306–307
kinked demand curve model, 298, 298*f*
knowledge
   copyright, 357
   and diminishing returns, 747–748
   external benefits, 353–357, 354*f*
   government actions in face of external ben-
      efits, 355–357
   marginal external benefit, 353

marginal private benefit, 353
marginal social benefit, 353
patent, 357
private benefits, 353–355
private subsidies, 356
public provision, 355–356, 355f
social benefits, 353–355
voucher, 356–357, 356f
Krueger, Alan, 131, 721
Kyoto Protocol, 524–525

L
labour, 3
demand for labour. *See* demand for labour
intensity, 394
marginal product of labour, 390, 709
marginal revenue product, 390, 390t
substitutability of capital for, 394
supply for high-skilled and low-skilled
labour, 426
supply of labour. *See* supply of labour
Labour Council of Canada, 413
labour demand. *See* demand for labour
labour demand curve, 391
labour force, 452, 488
employment and unemployment,
1960–2004, 489f
entrants, 493
re-entrants, 493
labour force participation, 712
labour force participation rate, 490
labour force status, 425
Labour Force Survey, 488
labour market
aggregate hours, 491–492, 491f
and aggregate supply, 709–714
Canadian labour market trends, 389f
changes in demand for labour, 393, 393t
changes in supply of labour, 395–396
changing face of, 490f
demand for high-skilled and low-skilled
labour, 426
demand for labour, 389, 391f, 396,
709–711, 709f
discrimination, 429–430, 429f
elasticity of demand for labour, 394
equilibrium, 396, 712
equilibrium trends, 396
flows, 493f
full-employment equilibrium, 712
human capital, 426–428
income effect, 395
indicators, 488–491
labour demand curve, 391
labour supply curve, 183, 183f, 395, 395f
living wage, 131
and long-run aggregate supply, 725f
long-run supply of labour, 128–129
low-skilled workers, 128, 129f
marginal revenue product, 390, 390t
market demand, 394
market power in, 413–416
market supply of labour curve, 395
minimum wage, 130–131, 130f
monopsony, 416–418, 416f
and potential GDP, 712, 713f
profit maximization, 392–393

quantity of labour hours employed,
709–714
in short run, 727f
and short-run aggregate supply, 727–729,
728f
short-run equilibrium, 726–727
short-run supply of labour, 128
stick wages, 727
substitution effect, 395
supply for high-skilled and low-skilled
labour, 426
supply of labour, 394–396, 396, 711–712
taxes, 579–580
unanticipated inflation, 640
labour productivity, 707, 739
in Canada, 717–718
Canada–U.S. productivity gap, 722–723
effects of increase in, 716, 717f
growth accounting, 739
and human capital, 707–708, 716
increase in, 708f, 715–716
and long-run aggregate supply, 726
one-third rule, 740–741
physical capital and, 707, 716
and potential GDP, 715–716
production function, shifts in, 708
productivity curve, 739–741, 740f
productivity growth slowdown, 741–742,
741f
real GDP per hour of labour, 739, 739f
and technology, 708, 716
labour supply. *See* supply of labour
labour supply curve, 183, 183f, 395, 395f
labour union, 413
bilateral monopoly, 417
binding arbitration, 413
change in demand for labour, 415
closed shop, 413
collective bargaining, 413
in competitive labour market, 414–415,
414f
constraints, 414
the local, 413
lockout, 413
minimum wage, support, 415
and monopsony, 417
objectives, 413–418
open shop, 413
Rand Formula, 413
union–nonunion wage differentials,
415–416
union shop, 413
land, 3, 404f
land pollution, 348–349
Lardner, Dionysius, 148
Large Value Transfer System (LVTS), 596
law of demand, 61, 148–149, 615–616
law of diminishing returns, 223, 226, **709,**
710, **740**
law of supply, 66, 148–149, 617
learning-by-doing, 45, 707, 767
legal barriers to entry, 264
legal monopoly, 264
legalization of drugs, 141
leisure time, 477, 706, 707f
lender of last resort, 595
Levitt, Steven D., 194–196

life expectancy, 477
limit pricing, 311
limited liability, 205
linear equation, 28
linear relationship, 20–21, 28, 28f
liquid assets, 592, 594
liquidity, 592, 594
liquidity trap, 688
living wage, 131
loans, 593–594, 596–597, 665
long run, 220, 242
long-run adjustments, 249
long-run aggregate supply
changes in, 726, 729
described, 508–509
and labour market, 725f
and labour productivity, 726
labour supply, changes in, 726
long-run aggregate supply curve, 508, 509f,
713
deriving, 724–726, 725f
described, 508–509
full employment and, 713–714, 713f
movements along, 510, 510f
and potential GDP, 580
long-run average cost curve, 231, 232,
232f
long-run cost
constant returns to scale, 233
diseconomies of scale, 232–233
economies of scale, 232–233
long-run average cost curve, 231, 232,
232f
minimum efficient scale, 233
production function, 230, 230t
and short-run cost, 230–231
long-run decisions in perfect competition,
242
long-run equilibrium, 251, 251f
long-run industry supply curve, 253, 254f
long-run macroeconomic equilibrium, 517,
517f
long-run neutrality, 691
long-run Phillips curve, 646, 646f
long-run supply curve, 96
long-run supply of labour, 128–129
long-term contracts, 204
long-term goals, 446
long-term growth trends, 734–736
Lorenz curve, 421–422, 421f, 422f
lottery, 105, 127
low-income cutoff, 424
low-skilled labour
decrease in demand for, 128
demand for, 426
market for, 129f
minimum wages and, 415
skill differentials, 427f
supply of, 426
wage rates, 426–427
Lucas, Robert E. Jr., 531
Lucas wedge, 451, 451f
luxuries, 89

M
M1, 591
M2+, 591

macroeconomic equilibrium
    aggregate supply and aggregate demand, 679*f*
    below full-employment equilibrium, 518
    long-run macroeconomic equilibrium, 517, 517*f*
    money and the interest rate, 679*f*
    short-run macroeconomic equilibrium, 516–517, 517*f*, 678
    simultaneous equilibrium, 678–679
macroeconomic long run, 508
macroeconomic policies
    exchange rate effects, 692
    extreme Keynesian hypothesis, 688
    extreme monetarist hypothesis, 689
    fiscal policy. *See* fiscal policy
    interest rate effects, 692
    intermediate position, 689
    Keynesian–monetarist controversy, 688–689
    monetary and fiscal tensions, 694–695
    monetary policy. *See* monetary policy
    policy conflicts, 692–693
    policy coordination, 692
    policy interaction risk, 693
macroeconomic short run, 509
macroeconomics, 2
    growth and fluctuations, 447–452
    inflation, 455–457
    issues of, 446
    jobs and unemployment, 452–454
    long-term goals, 446
    origins of, 446
    policy challenges and tools, 459
    revolution in, 530–531
    short-term goals, 446
    surpluses and deficits, 457–458
majority rule, 104
Malthus, Thomas Robert, 440–441, 743
maple syrup, 258–259
margin, 11
marginal analysis, 160, 244
marginal benefit, 11, 38
    and demand, 106–107
    demand curve and, 62
    described, 365
    marginal external benefit, 353
    marginal private benefit, 353
    marginal social benefit, 353
    and preferences, 38, 38*f*
    principle of decreasing marginal benefit, 38
marginal benefit curve, 38, 38*f*
marginal cost, 11, 226, 227*f*
    marginal external cost, 349
    marginal private cost, 349
    marginal social cost, 349
    and production possibilities frontier *(PPF)*, 37, 37*f*
    and supply, 108–109
marginal cost pricing rule, 278, 329
marginal external benefit, 353
marginal external cost, 349
marginal private benefit, 353
marginal private cost, 349
marginal product, 221, 710, 710*f*
marginal product curve, 222–223, 223*f*
marginal product of capital, 230

marginal product of labour, 390, **709**
marginal propensity to consume, 538, 538*f*
marginal propensity to import, 541, 574
marginal propensity to save, 538–539, 538*f*
marginal rate of substitution *(MRS)*, **176,** 176*f*, 184–185
marginal revenue, 240
    and demand, 266*f*
    described, 240–241
    and elasticity, 267, 267*f*
    and price, 266, 266*f*
    single-price monopoly, 266
marginal revenue product, 390, 390*t*
marginal revenue product curve, 391
marginal social benefit, 353, 372
marginal social benefit *(MSB)* curve, 107
marginal social cost, 349
marginal social cost *(MSC)* curve, 109
marginal tax rate, 573
marginal utility, 156, 157*f*
marginal utility model
    best affordable point, 190
    boat rides, 166–167
    efficiency, concept of, 164–165
    and indifference curves, 189–190, 189*f*
    predictions, 160–164
    summary of, 163*t*
marginal utility per dollar, 158–159, 159*f*, 159*t*
market and industry correspondence, 210–211
market constraints, 200
market demand, 106–107, 106*f*, 394
market economy
    vs. central planning, 6
    circular flows in, 47*f*
    economic coordination, 45–47
market equilibrium. *See* equilibrium
market failure, 324
market for reserves, 662, 662*f*
market income, 420
market intervention. *See* competition policy
market power, 264–265
    broadband providers, 340–341
    issues, 318–319
    in labour market, 413–416
market price, 104
market structure
    see also specific market structures
    concentration measures, 208–211
    monopolistic competition, 207
    monopoly, 207
    in North American economy, 211, 211*f*
    oligopoly, 207
    perfect competition, 207
    table of, 210*t*
market supply, 108–109, 108*f*
market supply of labour curve, 395
market value, 466
marketable permits, 352–353
marketing, 286–287, 292–295
markets, 46
    agricultural market, 137–139
    alternatives to, 113
    black market, 126
    buyers and seller, 60

    capital markets, 397–403
    circular flows through markets, 46, 47*f*
    and competitive environment, 207–211
    competitive market, 60
    contestable market, 310–311, 311*f*
    coordination, 212
    and economic growth, 737
    factor markets, 46
    fairness of, 114–117
    and firms, 212–213
    foreign exchange market. *See* foreign exchange market
    goods markets, 46
    housing markets, 124–128
    illegal goods, 140–141, 140*f*
    labour market, 128–131, 389–396
    labour markets, 413–416
    monopsony, 416–418
    natural resource markets, 403–405
    and prices, 60
markup, 290*f*, 291, 294*f*
Marshall, Alfred, 148–149
maximum point, 22, 23*f*
McCallum, Bennet T., 670
McCallum rule, 670
mean income, 420
means of payment, 590
measurement, 12
median income, 420
medium of exchange, 590
mercantilism, 784–785
mercantilists, 784
microeconomics, 2
Microsoft Corporation, 207, 264
minimum efficient scale, 233, 240
minimum point, 22, 23*f*
minimum supply-price, 108
minimum wage, 130–131, 130*f*, 142–143, 415, 417–418, 417*f*, **721**
minus sign, and elasticity, 86
mode income, 420
momentary supply curve, 96, 137
monetarist, 688
monetary base, 597
monetary base instrument rule, 670
monetary exchange facilities, 737
monetary policy, 459, 515
    see also Bank of Canada
    in action, 672–673
    actual inflation, 656
    alternative strategies, 670–671
    Bank of Canada Act, 656
    Bank of Canada economists, 658
    bank rate, 660
    and change in aggregate demand, 515
    conduct of, 658–662
    consultations with government, 658
    credibility, 694–695
    economic adjustment, 686*f*
    effectiveness, 688
    exchange rate effectiveness, 689
    exchange rate targeting rule, 671
    expansionary monetary policy, 684–687, 684*f*, 685*f*, 686*f*, 691
    expenditure and interest rate, 679*f*
    first round effects, 684*f*

at full employment, 691
Governing Council of Bank of Canada, 657–658
inflation-control target, 656–657, 657f
interest rate effectiveness, 689
k-percent rule, 671
McCallum rule, 670
monetary base instrument rule, 670
money and exchange rate, 687
money targeting rule, 671
objective, 656–657
open market operations, 660–661, 661f
operating band, 660
overnight rate, 658–659, 659f
overnight rate instrument rule, 670
overnight rate target, achievement of, 660–661
policy instrument, choice of, 658
real exchange rate, 671
responsibility for, 657–658
rules, vs. discretion, 671
second round effects, 685–687, 685f
settlement balances rate, 660
shocks needing, 625
in short run, 684–687
Taylor rule, 670
monetary policy transmission process
change in aggregate demand, 668–669
consumption expenditure, 666
exchange rate fluctuations, 665
final effect of interest rate cut, 668f
interest rate and expenditure plans, 665–667
interest rate and opportunity cost, 666
interest rate fluctuations, 663–664, 664f
interest-sensitive expenditure curve, 667
investment, 666
long-term interest rates, 664
money and loans, 665
overnight rate and spending, 667
overview, 663, 663f
and price level, 668–669
and real GDP, 668–669
time lags in adjustment process, 669
Treasury bill rate, 664
money, 46, 590
banks, and creation of money, 596–600
in Canada today, 591–592
currency, 591
demand for money, 601–604
deposits, 591, 592
and exchange rate, 687
growth of, and inflation, 638–639, 639f
influences on holding money, 601
and interest rate, 679f
liquidity, 592
long-run neutrality, 691
M1, 591
M2+, 591
as medium of exchange, 590
and monetary policy transmission process, 665
nominal money, 601
not money, 592
official measures of, 591–592, 591f

quantity of money target, 605
quantity theory of money, 638–639
real money, 601
store of value, 591
unit of account, 590–591, 590t
money creation process, 597–599, 598f, 599f
money holding influences
financial innovation, 601
interest rate, 601
price level, 601
real GDP, 601
money market equilibrium, 605, 605f
money multiplier, 599–600
money price, 60
money targeting rule, 671
money wage rate, 709
adjustment of, and full employment, 725
calculation of, 492
changes in, and short-run aggregate supply, 729
changes in, effect of, 512, 512f
demand-pull inflation, response to, 633–634
monopolistic competition, 207, 286
advertising, 292–295
brand names, 295
collusion, impossibility of, 286
efficiency, 291
entry, 287
examples of, 287, 287f
excess capacity, 290–291, 290f
exit, 287
ignoring other firms, 286
innovation, 292
large number of firms, 286
marketing, 286–287, 292–295
markup, 290f, 291
output and price decision, 288–291
output and price in long run, 289f
vs. perfect competition, 290–291
price, competition on, 286
product development, 292–295
product differentiation, 286
profit maximization, 288–289
quality, competition on, 286
short-run economic loss, 289f
short-run economic profit, 288f
short-run output and price decision, 288
small market share, 286
zero economic profit, 289–290, 289f
monopoly, 207, 264
average cost pricing rule, 279
barriers to entry, 264–265
bilateral monopoly, 417
concentration ratio, 208
creation of, 272
economic profit, 303, 303f
economies of scale, 277–278
economies of scope, 277–278
and efficiency, 113
elastic demand, 267
examples of, 264
features of, 264–265
gains from monopoly, 277–278
incentives to innovation, 277
inefficiency, 271f
legal monopoly, 264

and market power, 264–265
natural monopoly, 264–265, 265f, 278–279, 296, 328–332, 329f, 330f, 331f
no close substitutes, 264
policy issues, 277–279
price discrimination, 265, 273–276
price-setting strategies, 265
purchase of, 272
regulation, 278–279, 279f, 324, 326–327
single-price monopoly. See single-price monopoly
monopsony, 416
bilateral monopoly, 417
labour market, 416f
and minimum wage, 417–418, 417f
tendencies, 417
and unions, 417
Moore's law, 7
Morgenstern, Oskar, 300
movement along demand curve, 65
multiplier, 546
see also expenditure multipliers; fiscal policy multipliers
aggregate demand, long-run increase, 554–555
aggregate demand, short-run increase in, 554f
algebra of, 558–559, 559f
basic idea of, 546
business cycle turning points, 549–550
and Canadian economy, 556–557
equilibrium GDP, and price level, 553–555
graphical illustration, 547f
greater than one, 547
and imports, 548–549
income taxes and, 549
long run, 555f
monetary multiplier, 608
multiplier effect, 546
and the price level, 551–555
short run, 554f
size of, 547
and slope of aggregate expenditure curve, 548, 550f
multiplier effect, 546
multiplier process, 549f
Murphy, Kevin, 131, 721

N
Nash, John, 301, 307
Nash equilibrium, 301, 305–306
National Bank of Canada, 593
National Bureau of Economic Research (NBER), 486
national culture, protection of, 769
National Income and Expenditure Accounts, 471–472
national saving, 469
National Science and Engineering Research Council of Canada, 742
national security argument, 768
natural barriers to entry, 264–265
natural monopoly, 264
average cost pricing, 330f
creation of, 296
described, 264–265

graphical illustration, 265f
inflating cost, 331f
marginal cost pricing, 331f
price cap regulation, 331f
regulation of, 278–279, 279f, 328–332
natural oligopoly, 296, 296f
natural rate of unemployment, 496, 508,
646, 647f, 719
natural resources markets
categories of, 403
known stock, 404
nonrenewable natural resources, 404, 405f
price and Hotelling Principle, 404–405
renewable natural resources, 403–404
stock of a natural resource, 404
necessities, 89
negative externalities, 346
negative consumption externalities, 346
negative production externalities, 346
pollution, 347–352
negative relationship, 21–22, 22f, 29, 29f
neoclassical growth theory, 745
basic concepts, 745–746
graphical illustration, 746f
population growth, 745
problem with, 747
and productivity curve, 746
target rate of return and saving, 745
and technological change, 745
net benefit, 366
net borrower, 774
net domestic income at factor cost, 472
net domestic product, 469–470
net exports, 468, 471, 667, 756, 774
net investment, 469
net lender, 774
net present value, 400
net taxes, 468
New Economy, 6–7, 741
new goods bias, 501
new growth theory, 747
discoveries and choices, 747
discoveries and profits, 747
discoveries as public capital good, 747
graphical illustration, 748f
knowledge capital, and diminishing
returns, 747–748
perpetual motion economy, 748–749, 749f
and productivity curve, 748
nominal GDP, 473
nominal interest rate, 649, **665**–666
nominal money, 601
nonexcludable, 364
nonrenewable natural resources, 403, 404,
405f
nonrival, 364
nontariff barrier, 763, 766, 776
normal good, 64
normal profit, 199
normative statements, 12
Nortel Networks, 203, 210, 213, 214–215
**North American Free Trade Agreement
(NAFTA),** 541, 621, **764,** 776–777
Nozick, Robert, 116
NutraSweet, 338

O
observation, 12
official Canadian reserves, 772
official settlements account, 772
oil industry, 408–409
oil prices, 76–77
Okun gap, 451, 451f
Old Age Security (OAS), 431
oligopoly, 207, 296
barriers to entry, 296
chicken game, 308, 308f
collusion, 297, 333f
cooperative equilibrium, 309
disappearing invisible hand, 307
dominant firm oligopoly, 298–299, 299f
dominant strategy equilibrium, 308
duopolists' dilemma, 305–306
duopoly, 296, 296f
examples of, 297, 297f
features of, 296
game theory, 300–311
illegal cartels, 332
kinked demand curve model, 298, 298f
Nash equilibrium, 301, 305–306
natural oligopoly, 296, 296f
price-fixing game, 302–306
price wars, 310
prisoners' dilemma, 300–301, 301t
punishment, 309
R&D game, 306–307, 307t
regulation, 324, 326–327
repeated duopoly game, 309–310
sequential game, 310–311
small number of firms, 297
traditional oligopoly models, 298–299
one-third rule, 740–741
OPEC (Organization of Petroleum Exporting
Countries), 332, 455
open market operations, 660–661, 661f
operating band, 660
opportunity cost, 10
and comparative advantage, 757
cost of owner's resources, 199
described, 60
economic depreciation, 198–199
and economic rent, 406–407, 407f
explicit costs, 198
factor markets, 406–407, 407f
implicit costs, 198
implicit rental rate, 198
increasing, 36
and interest rate, 666
of leisure, 395
measurement of, 757, 757f
production possibilities frontier, 757, 757f
and production possibilities frontier (PPF),
35–36
as ratio, 35–36
relative price, 60
search time and, 126
organization of production, 203–204
origin, 17
outlet substitution bias, 501
output
see also output and price decision
and external cost, 349
in monopolistic competition, 288–291

in perfect competition, 248–251
price of, 393
product concepts and, 221
profit-maximizing output, 242–243
short-run cost, 225–229
short-run technology constraint, 221
in single-price monopoly, 270, 270f
output and price decision
monopolistic competition, 288–291
perfect competition, 270
single-price monopoly, 266–269, 268t,
269f
output gap, 451, 518, 519
outsourcing, 212
overnight loans, 593–594
overnight loans rate, 658–659, 659f
overnight rate, 596, 667
overnight rate instrument rule, 670
overproduction, 112, 112f
ownership, 204

P
paradox of value, 164–165, 165f
partnership, 204–205
patent, 264, **357**
payments system, 595–596
payoff matrix, 300, 301t, 305, 306t
peak, 448
People's Republic of China. *See* China
percentage change, 86
perfect competition, 207, 240
causes of, 240
change in demand, 248
choices, 256
competitive equilibrium, 256
concentration ratio, 208
demand in, 241f
economic profit, 240–241
efficiency, 256–257, 271, 271f
efficient allocation, 256–257, 257f
entry, effects of, 249–250, 249f
excess capacity, 290–291, 290f
exit, effects of, 249f, 250
external economies and diseconomies,
253–255
firm decisions in, 242–248
firm short-run supply curve, 246, 246f
long-run adjustments, 249
long-run changes in price and
quantity, 253, 254f
long-run decisions, 242
long-run equilibrium, 251, 251f
long-run industry supply curve, 253, 254f
maple syrup, 258–259
marginal analysis, 244
markup, 290f, 291
vs. monopolistic competition, 290–291
output and price, 270
output in, 248–251
permanent change in demand, 252–253,
253f
plant size, changes in, 250–251, 251f
preferences, changes in, 252–255
price in, 241f, 248–251
price takers, 240
profit in, 248–251

profit-maximizing output, 242–243, 244, 244*f*
resources, use of, 256
revenue in, 241*f*
short-run decisions, 242
short-run equilibrium, 248, 248*f*
short-run industry supply curve, 247, 247*f*
short run profit outcomes, 245, 245*f*
vs. single-price monopoly, 270–273
technological advances, 252–255
perfect price discrimination, 275–276, 276*f*
perfect substitutes, 177, 177*f*, 240
perfectly elastic demand, 86*f*, **87,** 134
perfectly elastic supply, 95*f*, 135
perfectly inelastic demand, 86, 86*f*, 134
perfectly inelastic supply, 95*f*, 135
perpetual motion economy, 748–749, 749*f*
perpetuity, 604
personal characteristics, 105
personal expenditures, 471
personal income taxes, 564
Peterson, Janet, 433
Phillips curve, 644
in Canada, 647, 647*f*
long-run Phillips curve, 646, 646*f*
natural rate of unemployment, changes in, 646, 647*f*
short-run Phillips curve, 644–645, 644*f*, 645*f*, 646*f*
phone industry, 234–235
physical capital, 707, 716
Pigou, Arthur Cecil, 352
Pigovian taxes, 352
planned expenditure, 543–544
plant size, 250–251, 251*f*
policy conflicts, 692–693
policy coordination, 692
policy interaction risk, 693
political equilibrium, 326, 369, 375
political freedom, 477–478
political marketplace, 325–326, 325*f*
politicians, 325
pollution
acid rain, 347
air pollution, 347–348, 348*f*
air pollution debate, 358–359
Coase theorem, 351
demand for pollution-free environment, 347
economics of, 349–353
emission charges, 352
external cost, 349, 349*f*, 350*f*
global warming, 348
government actions in face of external costs, 352–353
land pollution, 348–349
marginal external cost, 349
marginal private cost, 349
marginal social cost, 349
marketable permits, 352–353
private costs, 349
and production, 350
property rights, 350, 351*f*
sources of, 347–349
taxes, 352, 353*f*
water pollution, 348
pooling risk, 594

population
in Canada, 717–718
classical growth theory of population growth, 743–744
and demand, 64
increase in, 717
and increase in potential GDP, 714–715, 715*f*
neoclassical economics of population growth, 745
subsistence real wage rate, 744
population growth, 440–441
population survey, 488
positive externalities, 346
knowledge, 353–357
positive consumption externalities, 346
positive production externalities, 346
positive relationship, 20–21, 21*f*, 29
positively skewed distribution, 420
post hoc fallacy, 13–14
potential entry, 210
potential GDP, 447, 497
changes in, 511, 511*f*, 714–718
described, 508
and fiscal policy, 579–580
fluctuations of real GDP around, 448
and human capital, 511
increases in, 714–718
and labour market, 712, 713*f*
labour productivity, increase in, 715–716
and long-run aggregate supply curve, 580
population increase and, 714–715, 715*f*
poverty, 424–425, 424*f*, 425*f*
preference map, 175–178, 175*f*
preferences, 38
best affordable point, 190
changes in, and technological advances, 252–255
diversity of, and gains from international trade, 762
and indifference curves, 175–178, 189–190
marginal rate of substitution *(MRS)*, 176, 176*f*
marginal utility model, 189–190
preference map, 175–178, 175*f*
and utility, 156–157
voter preferences, 369
present value, 398–400
price
see also output and price decision
adjustments, 71
average cost pricing rule, 279, 329–330, 330*f*
average price, 85–86
change in demand, effect of, 72–73, 72*f*, 94
change in supply, effects of, 73, 73*f*, 84*f*
changes in demand and supply, opposite direction, 75, 75*f*
changes in demand and supply, same direction, 74, 74*f*
expected future prices, 63–64, 68
falling resource prices, 405*f*
of firm's output, 393
fixed prices, 541
and Hotelling Principle, 404–405

limit pricing, 311
long-run changes, 253, 254*f*
marginal cost pricing rule, 278–279, 329
and marginal revenue, 266, 266*f*
market price. *See* market price
and markets, 60
minimum supply price, 67
minimum supply-price, 108
money price, 60
monopolistic competition, 286
in monopolistic competition, 288–291
in monopoly, 265
oil prices, 76–77
in perfect competition, 241*f*, 248–251
prediction of changes in, 72–75
price change, 155, 155*f*, 173–174, 174*f*
productive resources, 229
of productive resources. and supply, 67
regulations, and efficiency, 112
as regulator, 70–71
related goods, 63
related goods produced, 67–68
relative price, 60, 173, 509
and shortage, 71
in single-price monopoly, 270, 270*f*
single-price monopoly decision, 266–269, 269*f*
and surplus, 71
two-part tariff, 279
vs. value, 106
price cap regulation, 330–332, 331*f*
price ceiling, 125, 330–332, 331*f*
price discrimination, 265
among groups of buyers, 274
among units of a good, 274
and consumer surplus, 273–274
graphical illustration, 275*f*
and marginal cost pricing rule, 278–279, 329
in monopoly, 273–276
perfect price discrimination, 275–276, 276*f*
profiting by, 274–275, 274*f*
price effect, 179–180, 179*f*
price elasticity of demand, 84
average price, 85–86
average quantity, 85–86
calculation of, 85, 85*f*
closeness of substitutes, 89
elastic demand, 86–87, 86*f*, 267
and expenditure, 89
formula, 85
inelastic demand, 86–87, 86*f*, 267
influencing factors, 89–90
and marginal revenue, 267, 267*f*
perfectly elastic demand, 86*f*, 87, 134
perfectly inelastic demand, 86, 86*f*, 134
proportion of income spent, 90
real-world price elasticities of demand, 89*t*
straight-line demand curve, elasticity along, 87, 87*f*
and taxes, 134, 134*f*
in ten countries, 90*f*
time elapsed since price change, 90
total revenue, 88, 88*f*
unit elastic demand, 86, 86*f*, 267
units-free measure, 86

price-fixing game, 302–306
price floor, 130
price level, 455, 474
 and aggregate expenditure, 551–553
 calculation of, 474–475
 and cost-push inflation, 636*f*
 and demand-pull inflation, 633*f*
 equilibrium expenditure at fixed price level, 541–545
 and equilibrium GDP, 553–555, 577–578
 and fiscal policy multipliers, 576–579
 GDP deflator, 474
 and inflation, 632, 632*f*
 and inflation rate, 632
 and monetary policy transmission process, 668–669
 as money holding influence, 601
 and the multiplier, 551–555
 and stagflation, 635
price takers, 240
price wars, 310
principal–agent problem, 204
principle of decreasing marginal benefit, 38
principle of minimum differentiation, 367
prisoners' dilemma, 300–301, 301*t*
private benefits, 353–355
private costs, 349
private goods, 364
private sector balance, 775
privatization, 337
Procter & Gamble, 306–307
producer surplus, 109, 109*f*, 406
product concepts
 average product, 221
 marginal product, 221
 product curves, 221–224
 total product, 221
product curves
 average product curve, 224, 224*f*
 described, 221
 graphical illustration, 228*f*
 marginal product curve, 222–223, 223*f*
 total product curve, 222, 222*f*
product development, 292–295
product differentiation, 207, 286
product innovation. *See* innovation
product schedules, 221
production
 changes in, and gains from international trade, 759–761
 economies of team production, 213
 household production, 476
 organization of production, 203–204
production efficiency, 35
production function, 230, 230*t*, **706,** 707*f*, 708, 708*f*
production possibilities
 allocative efficiency, 37–39
 economic coordination, 45–47
 economic growth, 40–41
 gains from trade, 42–45
 limits to, 34–36
 real GDP and leisure time, 706, 707*f*
production possibilities frontier *(PPF)*, **34**
 allocative efficiency, 37–39, 39*f*
 described, 34–35
 graphical illustration, 34*f*

 and marginal cost, 37, 37*f*
 and opportunity cost, 35–36
 opportunity cost, measurement of, 757, 757*f*
 preferences, and marginal benefit, 38, 38*f*
 production efficiency, 35
 tradeoff, 35
production quota, 139, 139*f*, 374, 374*f*, **766,** 766*f*
production technology, 393
productive resources, 229
productivity. *See* labour productivity
productivity changes, 707–708
productivity curve, 739–741, 740*f*, 744, 746, 748
productivity growth slowdown, 447, 492, 741–742, 741*f*
productivity growth speedup, 741
professional association, 413
profit, 4
 corporate profits, 472
 economic profit. *See* economic profit
 expected profit effect, 616, 617
 measurement of, 198
 and new growth theory, 747
 normal profit, 199
 in perfect competition, 248–251
 price discrimination, 274–275, 274*f*
 short run profit outcomes, 245, 245*f*
profit maximization
 collusion and, 303
 Crown corporation, 337
 labour market, 392–393
 monopolistic competition, 288–289
 perfect competition, 242–243, 244, 244*f*
 and regulation of natural monopoly, 278
 single-price monopoly, 268
profit-maximizing output, 242–243, 244, 244*f*
progressive income tax, 431
prohibition, 141
property rights, 46, 350, 351*f*, 373–374, 737
property tax, 570
proportional income tax, 431
proportionate change, 86
protectionism
 case against protectionism, 767–771
 compensation of losers, 770–771
 competition with cheap foreign labour, 768–769
 diversity and stability, 769
 dumping argument, 768
 employment argument, 767
 exploitation of developing countries, prevention of, 769
 infant-industry argument, 767
 lax environmental standards, 769
 national culture, protection of, 769
 national security argument, 768
 nontariff barrier, 763, 766, 776
 quotas, 766, 766*f*
 reasons for restrictions, 769–770
 rent seeking, 770
 tariff revenue, 769–770
 tariffs, 763–765, 778–779
 trade deficit, avoidance of, 771

provincial budget, 564, 568–569, 568*f*
public choice theory, 325–326, 325*f*, 368, 369, 375
public franchise, 264
public goods, 364
 benefits of, 365–366, 365*f*
 bureaucrats, 368
 described, 113, 324
 discoveries as, 747
 efficient quantity, 366, 367*f*
 free-rider problem, 113, 324, 364, 365–369
 income elasticity of demand, 369
 political equilibrium, 369
 principle of minimum differentiation, 367
 private provision by market, 366
 public provision by majority vote, 366–367
 rational ignorance, 368
public ownership
 see also Crown corporation
 bureaucracy model of public enterprise, 336–337
 described, 326
public provision, 355–356, 355*f*, 366–367
punishment, 309
purchasing power parity (PPP), 478, **622,** 671

Q
quality
 advertising as signal of, 294–295
 of education, improvements in, 742
 monopolistic competition, 286
quality change bias, 501
quantity
 average quantity, 85–86
 capital, change in quantity of, 511
 change in demand, effect of, 72–73, 72*f*, 94
 change in supply, effect of, 73, 73*f*, 84*f*
 changes in demand and supply, opposite direction, 75, 75*f*
 changes in demand and supply, same direction, 74, 74*f*
 efficient quantity of public goods, 366, 367*f*
 equilibrium quantity, 70, 79
 full-employment quantity of labour, change in, 511
 of human capital, and potential GDP, 511
 long-run changes, 253, 254*f*
 prediction of changes in, 72–75
 quantity of money target, 605
quantity demanded, 61, 64–65
quantity of labour demanded, 709
quantity of labour supplied, 711
quantity of real GDP demanded, 513, 514
quantity regulations, 112
quantity supplied, 66
quantity theory of money, 638
 equation of exchange, 638
 evidence on, 638–639
 and McCallum rule, 670
 velocity of circulation, 638
queue, 127
quintiles, 420, 421*f*
quotas, 139, 139*f*, 374, 374*f*, **766,** 766*f*

R
rainforests, 376–377
Ramsey, Frank, 745
Rand Formula, 413
rate of return regulation, 330
rational decision makers, 192–193
rational expectation, 641
rational ignorance, 368
Rawls, John, 115
Rawski, Thomas, 478–479
R&D game, 306–307, 307*t*
re-entrants, 493
real exchange rate, 671
real GDP, 447, 473
  aggregate expenditure model, 541–545
  aggregate planned expenditure, 543
  base-year prices value of, 473–474
  calculation of, 473
  chain-weighted output index, 474
  changes in potential GDP, 714–718
  and consumption, 540
  economic growth rate, calculation of,
      476–479
  economic welfare comparisons, 476–478
  and employment, 706–708
  and expenditure plans, 536–540
  fixed price level, 541–545
  fluctuations, 448
  growth in, and interest rates, 669*f*
  growth in world economy, 735–736
  international comparisons, 478–479
  and leisure time, 706, 707*f*
  and monetary policy transmission process,
      668–669
  as money holding influence, 601
  per hour of labour, 739, 739*f*
  PPP prices, 478
  and the price level, 473–475
  production function, 706
  production possibilities, 706, 707*f*
  productivity changes, 707–708
  and quantity of labour employed, 706–708
  quantity of real GDP demanded, 513, 514
  recession, working definition of, 486
  short-run changes in quantity of real GDP
      supplies, 729
  and unemployment, 497, 497*f*
real gross domestic product. *See* real GDP
real income, 155, 173
real interest rate, 665–666
real money, 601
real property, 46
real wage rate, 492, 492*f,* 509, **709**
recession, 448, 449, 486, 550
recessionary gap, 518
redistribution of surpluses, 272
regressive income tax, 431
regulation, 326
  average cost pricing rule, 329–330, 330*f*
  capture theory, 327, 332, 333–334
  cartel regulation, 332–334
  conservative perspective, 327
  demand for, 326
  earnings sharing regulation, 332
  economic theory of regulation, 326–327
  environmental regulation, 742, 769
  equilibrium regulation, 327

federal regulatory agencies, 328*t*
liberal perspective, 327
marginal cost pricing rule, 329
of monopoly, 324, 326–327
of natural monopoly, 278–279, 279*f,*
    328–332, 329*f,* 330*f,* 331*f*
of oligopoly, 324, 326–327
predictions, 334
price cap regulation, 330–332, 331*f*
rate of return regulation, 330
regulatory process, 327–328
scope of, 327
in social interest, 329–330
social interest theory, 327, 332, 333–334
supply of, 326
regulatory process, 327–328
relative price, 60, 154–155, **173,** 509
renewable natural resources, 403–404
rent, 4
rent ceiling, 125
  black market, 126
  fairness of, 127
  graphical illustration, 126*f*
  inefficiency of, 127, 127*f*
  in practice, 128
rent seeking, 272, 770
rent-seeking equilibrium, 272–273,
    273*f*
repeated duopoly game, 309–310
required reserve ratio, 597
research and development, 742
reservation wage, 394
reserve ratio, 597
reserves, 593–594, 597, 662, 662*f*
resource allocation methods
  command system, 104
  contest, 104
  first-come, first-served, 104–105
  force, 105
  lottery, 105
  majority rule, 104
  market price, 104
  personal characteristics, 105
resources
  allocative efficiency, 37–39, 39*f*
  classification of, 364
  common resources, 324, 364
  cost of, 199
  excludable, 364
  four-fold classification, 364, 364*f*
  misallocation of, 35
  natural resource markets, 403–405
  nonexcludable, 364
  nonrenewable natural resources, 403
  nonrival, 364
  perfect competition, 256
  productive resources, 67, 229
  renewable natural resources, 403–404
  rival, 364
  substitution possibilities, 95–96
revenue
  government budgets, 564, 566, 566*f*
  marginal revenue, 240–241, 266
  in perfect competition, 241*f*
  tariff revenue, 769–770
  total revenue, 88, 88*f,* 240, 243*f,* 266
Ricardo, David, 440, 743, 784–785

rice index, 60
Riddell, Craig W., 496*n*
rival, 364
Rogers Communications Inc., 340
Romer, Paul, 357*n,* 747
Roth, John, 203
Royal Bank of Canada, 339, 593

S
San Francisco earthquake, 124, 125*f*
saving, 468
  and economic growth, 737–738
  marginal propensity to save, 538–539,
      538*f*
  national saving, 469
  other influences on, 539–540
  stimulation of, 742
  target rate of, 745
saving function, 536–537, 537*f,* 539*f*
saving plans, 536–538
Say, Jean-Baptiste, 530
Say's Law, 530
scarcity, 2
scatter diagrams, 19–20, 19*f*
Schumpeter, Joseph, 747
search activity, 126
seasonal unemployment, 496
self-interest, 5, 11, 103, 113
selling costs
  and demand, 294
  and total cost, 293, 293*f*
September 11, 2001, 7
sequential game, 310–311
services
  increases in, 3
  international trade in, 756, 776
settlement balances rate, 660
shift of demand curve, 65
shocks
  aggregate demand shock, 632
  aggregate supply shock, 632
  energy price shocks, 742
  needing national monetary policy, 625
short run, 220
  firm and industry, 242
  losses in, 245
  profit in, 245
short-run aggregate supply
  changes in, 729
  described, 509, 510*f*
  and labour market, 727–729, 728*f*
  short-run equilibrium in labour
      market, 726–727
**short-run aggregate supply curve, 509,
    713**
  deriving, 727–729, 728*f*
  and full employment, 713–714, 713*f*
  movements along, 510, 510*f*
  shape of, 729
short-run cost
  average cost, 226–227, 227*f*
  average total cost curve, 226–227, 227*f,*
      231
  cost curves, 228–229, 228*f*
  for different quantities of capital, 231*f*
  and long-run cost, 230–231
  marginal cost, 226, 227*f*

product curves, 228–229, 228f
total cost, 225, 225f
short-run decisions in perfect competition, 242
short-run equilibrium, 248, 248f
short-run equilibrium in labour market, 726–727
short-run fiscal policy, 680–683
short-run industry supply curve, 247, 247f
short-run macroeconomic equilibrium, 516–517, 517f, 678
short-run monetary policy, 684–687
short-run Phillips curve, 644–645, 644f, 645f, 646f
short-run supply curve, 96, 246, 246f
short-run supply of labour, 128
short-run technology constraint, 221–224
short-term goals, 446
shortage, and price, 71
shutdown point, 246
signal, 294–295
similar goods, 762
Simon, Julian, 440–441
simultaneous equilibrium, 678–679
single-price monopoly, 265
  see also monopoly
  vs. competition, 270–273
  efficiency and, 271, 271f
  elastic demand, 267
  marginal revenue and elasticity, 267, 267f
  marginal revenue equals marginal cost, 268
  output and price, 270, 270f
  output and price decision, 266–269, 268t, 269f
  price and marginal revenue, 266, 266f
  profit maximization, 268
  redistribution of surpluses, 272
  rent seeking, 272
  rent-seeking equilibrium, 272–273, 273f
skill differentials, 427f
slope, 24
  across an arc, 25–26, 26f
  curved line, 25–26, 25f
  of a line, 28–29, 28f
  at a point, 25, 25f
  straight line, 24–25, 24f
Smith, Adam, 5, 13, 54–55, 111, 164, 318, 459, 743, 784, 785
smog, 382
social interest, 5, 11, 103, 339
social interest theory, 327, 332, 333–334, 369
social justice, 477–478
social loss, 112
social science. *See* economic science
social security programs, 431
sole proprietorship, 204
Solow, Robert, 740, 745
sovereignty, loss of, 625
Soviet Union, central planning in, 5–6
special interest, 339
specialization
  described, 42
  and gains from trade, 42–45
stagnation, 741
sticky wages, 727
stock, 469

store of value, 591
straight line
  from equations to, 28–29
  negative relationship, 29, 29f
  position of, 29
  positive relationship, 29
  slope, 24–25, 24f, 28–29, 28f
strategic behaviour, 300
strategies, 300
structural slump, 720
structural surplus or deficit, 575–576, 575f
structural unemployment, 496
subsidies, 138, 356
  agricultural markets, 138
  described, 472
  and efficiency, 112
  external benefit, response to, 356
  graphical illustration, 138f
  trade negotiations on, 776
subsidized services, 431–432
subsistence real wage rate, 744
substitutes, 63
  close substitutes, 177, 177f, 240, 264
  closeness of, and elasticity of demand, 89
  commodity substitution bias, 501
  and cross-elasticity of demand, 91
  degree of substitutability, 177–178, 177f
  international substitution, 551
  intertemporal substitution, 551
  perfect substitutes, 177, 177f
  resource substitution possibilities, 95–96
substitutes in production, 67–68
substitution effect, 181
  and aggregate demand curve, 514
  aggregate expenditure and price level, 551–552
  and demand, 61
  described, 61
  high wage rate, 183
  interest rates and, 664
  international substitution, 551
  intertemporal substitution, 551
  isolation of, 181f
  supply of labour, 395
Summers, Lawrence H., 56–58
Summers, Robert, 478
sunk cost, 220
suppliers, number of, 68
supply, 66
  aggregate supply. *See* aggregate supply
  of capital, 402
  change in supply. *See* change in supply
  change in the quantity supplied, 68–69, 69f
  elasticity of supply. *See* elasticity of supply
  flow supply, 404
  in foreign exchange market, 615, 617
  of high-skilled and low-skilled labour, 426
  individual supply, 108–109, 108f
  of labour, 394, 396
  labour supply, 182, 183f
  of land, 404f
  law of supply, 66, 148–149
  and marginal cost, 108–109
  market supply, 108–109, 108f
  minimum supply price, 67
  and minimum supply-price, 108

nonrenewable natural resources, 404, 405f
producer surplus, 109, 109f
quantity supplied, 66
of regulation, 326
renewable natural resources, 403–404
supply curve, 66–67, 67f
supply schedule, 66
supply and demand theory. *See* demand and supply theory
supply curve, 66
  for Canadian dollars, 617, 617f
  capital supply curve, 402
  described, 66–67, 67f
  labour supply curve, 183, 183f, 395, 395f
  long-run industry supply curve, 253, 254f
  long-run supply curve, 96
  as marginal cost curve, 108
  market supply curve, 108, 109
  mathematics of, 78
  momentary supply curve, 96, 137
  short-run industry supply curve, 247, 247f
  short-run supply curve, 96, 246, 246f
supply equation, 78
supply of labour, 711
  change in supply, 395–396
  graphical illustration of, 711
  hours per person, 712
  human capital, 426
  income effect, 395
  labour force participation, 712
  labour supply response, 712
  and long-run aggregate supply, 726
  long-run supply of labour, 128–129
  market supply of labour curve, 395
  quantity of labour supplied, 711
  short-run supply of labour, 128
  substitution effect, 395
  work–leisure choices, 182, 183f
supply schedule, 66
supply-side effects of fiscal policy, 579–581, 580f
surplus
  budget surplus, 565
  consumer surplus. *See* consumer surplus
  cyclical surplus, 575–576, 575f, 576
  government budget surplus, 457, 458f
  international surplus, 457–458
  and price, 71
  redistribution of, 272
  structural surplus, 575–576, 575f
  temporary cyclical surplus, 575
sustainable production, 370–371, 370t, 371f
symmetry principle, 116

T
target rate of return and saving, 745
targeting rule, 659–660
tariffs, 763
  application of, 764–765
  effects of, 764f
  history of, 763–764 763f
  inefficiency and, 765
  lumber industry, 778–779
  revenue from, 769–770
tax incidence, 132
tax rates, 573

taxes
    and anticipated inflation, 643
    autonomous taxes, 570
    average tax rate, 431
    on buyers, 133, 133*f*
    and Canada–U.S. productivity gap,
        722–723
    and capital, 580
    corporate income taxes, 564
    direct tax, 472
    division of, and elasticity of demand, 134
    division of, and elasticity of supply, 135,
        135*f*
    on drugs, 141
    and efficiency, 112, 136, 136*f*
    equivalence of tax on buyers and
        sellers, 133
    and externalities, 352
    flat-rate income tax, 431
    and income redistribution, 431
    income taxes, 431, 434–435, 549
    indirect tax, 472, 564
    induced taxes, 573
    and multiplier, 549
    net taxes, 468
    personal income taxes, 564
    Pigovian taxes, 352
    pollution, 352, 353*f*
    in practice, 136
    progressive income tax, 431
    property tax, 570
    proportional income tax, 431
    regressive income tax, 431
    on sellers, 132, 132*f*
    supply-side effects of tax cuts, 579–581,
        580*f*
    tax incidence, 132
Taylor, John B., 670
Taylor rule, 670
TD Canada Trust, 593
technological change, 40
    implementation process, 255
    and increased production, 512
    and neoclassical growth theory, 745
    and productivity, 717–718
    during productivity growth slowdown, 742
    structural slump, 720
technological efficiency, 201
technology, 200
    and changes in supply, 68
    convergence, 219
    cost curves, shifts in, 228–229
    economic growth, and discovery of new
        technologies, 738
    and labour productivity, 708, 716
    production technology, 393
    and structural slump, 720
technology constraints
    described, 200
    short-run technology constraint, 221–224
temporary cyclical surplus or deficit, 575
temporary plant shutdown, 246
terms of trade, 758–759
A Theory of Justice (Rawls), 115
Thomson, Ken, 419
time lags, 669
time-series graph, 18, 18*f*

tit-for-tat strategy, 309
Tokyo Round, 763
Toronto Stock Exchange, 147
total benefit, 365
total cost, 225, 225*f*, 243*f*, 293, 293*f*
total fixed cost, 225
total government sector, 568
total income, 420
total product, 221
total product curve, 222, 222*f*
total revenue, 88, 88*f*, **240,** 243*f*, 266
total revenue test, 88
total utility, 156, 157*f*, 189*f*
total variable cost, 225
tradeoff, 9
    along production possibilities frontier
        (PPF), 35
    big tradeoff, 10, 115, 433
    "for whom" tradeoffs, 9–10
    guns *versus* butter, 9
    "how" tradeoffs, 9
    inflation–unemployment tradeoff, 650–651
    "what" tradeoffs, 9
tragedy of the commons
    described, 113, 370
    efficient outcome, 373–375
    efficient use of the commons, 372, 373*f*
    individual transferable quota (ITQ),
        374–375, 375*f*
    marginal social benefit, 372
    original tragedy of the commons, 370
    overfishing equilibrium, 371–372
    political equilibrium, 375
    property rights, 373–374
    public choice, 375
    quotas, 374, 374*f*
    rainforests, 376–377
    sustainable production, 370–371, 370*t*,
        371*f*
training, 427
Traité d'économie politique (Say), 530
transactions costs, 113, 212–213, **351,** 624,
    643
transfer payments, 468, 565, 573
transition economies, 450
transparency, 624
Treasury bill rate, 664
A Treatise in Political Economy (Say), 530
Trefler, Dan, 786–787
trend, 18
trigger strategy, 309
tropical rainforests, 8
trough, 448
trust and mortgage loan company, 593
twin deficits, 775, 775*f*
two big economic questions
    self-interest, and the social interest, 5–8
    what, how, and for whom, 3–5
two-part tariff, 279, 329

U
unanticipated inflation
    in financial capital market, 640–641
    full employment, departure from, 640
    increases in aggregate demand, 642
    in labour market, 640
    and redistribution of income, 640

underground economy, 477
underproduction, 111, 112*f*
unemployment, 452
    around the world, 454
    in Canada, 453, 453*f*
    compensation, 720
    costs of, 454
    cyclical unemployment, 496
    demographic change, 720
    demographics of, 494–495, 495*f*
    described, 493
    by duration, 494*f*
    duration of, 494
    frictional unemployment, 495–496
    industrial economies, 454*f*
    and inflation, 644–648
    inflation–unemployment tradeoff,
        650–651
    job rationing, 720–721
    job search, 719–720, 719*f*
    and the labour force, 1960-2004, 489*f*
    lost human capital, 454
    lost production and incomes, 454
    and minimum wage, 130, 130*f*
    natural rate of unemployment, 646, 647*f*
    Phillips curve, 644–648
    problem of, 454
    and real GDP, 497, 497*f*
    by reason, 494*f*
    seasonal unemployment, 496
    sources of, 493–494
    structural change, 720
    structural unemployment, 496
    types of, 495–496
unemployment rate, 452, 489
    decline in, and worker shortage, 460–461
    discouraged workers, 453
    imperfect measure, 453
    natural rate of unemployment, 496, 508,
        719
union–nonunion wage differentials, 415–416
unions. *See* labour union
unit elastic demand, 86, 86*f*, 267
unit elastic supply, 95*f*
unit of account, 590–591, 590*t*
United States
    real GDP in, 478–479
    trade with. *See* North American Free Trade
        Agreement (NAFTA)
units-free measure, 86
unlimited liability, 204
Uruguay Round, 763
utilitarianism, 114–115, 115*f*
utility, 156
    diminishing marginal utility, 156–157
    existence of, 190
    marginal utility, 156, 157*f*
    marginal utility per dollar, 158–159, 159*f*,
        159*t*
    marginal utility theory, 160–164, 163*t*
    maximization of, 158–160, 190
    and preferences, 156–157
    temperature analogy, 164
    total utility, 156, 157*f*
    units of utility, 160
utility-maximizing choice, 158

V

value
  and demand, 106
  paradox of value, 164–165, 165*f*
  vs. price, 106
variables
  negative relationship, 21–22, 22*f*
  positive relationship, 20–21, 21*f*
  three or more variables, 26–27, 27*f*
  unrelated variables, 23, 23*f*
velocity of circulation, 638
VoIP, 234–235
Volcker, Paul, 455
voluntary export restraint (VER), 766
von Neumann, John, 300, 317, 318–319
voter preferences, 369
voucher, 356–357, 356*f*

W

wage differentials
  and discrimination, 429
  high-skilled *vs.* low-skilled labour,
    426–427
  and skill differentials, 427*f*

wages, 4
  bargaining over, and CPI changes, 501
  efficiency wage, 720–721
  living wage, 131
  minimum wage, 130–131, 130*f*, 415,
    417–418, 417*f*, 721
  money wage rate, 492, 512, 512*f*, 709,
    725, 729
  real wage rate, 492, 492*f*, 509, 709
  reservation wage, 394
  sticky wages, 727
  subsistence real wage rate, 744
  union-nonunion wage differentials, 415–416
wages, salaries and supplementary labour
    income, 471
wants, 61
water pollution, 348
water shortages, 8, 116–117
wealth, 469
  annual wealth, 423
  distribution of, 422
  vs. income, 422–423
  and income taxes, 434–435
  lifetime wealth, 423
  Lorenz curve, 422*f*

marriage and wealth concentration, 430
wealth effect, 513–514, 551
Wealth of Nations (Smith), 5, 13, 54, 111, 459
Welch, Finis, 131, 721
welfare challenges, 433
welfare programs, 431
West Germany, 6
"what" tradeoffs, 9
willingness to pay, 106
women, and wages, 429–430
Woodford, Michael, 702–704
work–leisure choices, 182–183
worker shortage, 460–461
Workers' Compensation programs, 431
working-age population, 488
World Trade Organization (WTO), 763
WorldCom, 7

X

x-axis, 17

Y

y-axis, 17
y-axis intercept, 29

CREDITS

Photo Credits

Part 1: p. 54, Corbis-Bettmann; p. 55 (left), Culver Pictures; p. 55 (right), Bruce Ando/Tony Stone Images.

Part 2: p. 148, Stock Montage; p. 149 (left), Courtesy Stoddart Publishing Co. Limited, from *Canada: The Missing Years*; p. 149 (right), PhotoDisc, Inc.

Part 3: p. 192, Corbis-Bettmann; p. 193 (left), Keystone-Mass Collection (V22542) UCR/California Museum of Photography, University of California, Riverside; p. 193 (right), China Tourism Press/Getty Images.

Part 4: p. 207 (left), PhotoDisc, Inc.; p. 207 (left, inset), Dick Morton; p. 207 (right), Dick Morton; p. 207 (right, inset), © Reuters New Media; p. 215 (top), Jonathan Hayward/CP Photo Archive; p. 215 (bottom), Bloomberg News/Landov; p. 318, Stock Montage; p. 319 (left), Culver Pictures; p. 319 (right), Don Wilson/West Stock.

Part 5: p. 382, David Joel/David Joel Photography, Inc.; p. 383 (left), Jim Baron/The Image Finders; p. 383 (right), Patrick Mullen; p. 384, E. S. Lee.

Part 6: p. 440, Corbis-Bettmann; p. 441 (left), National Archives of Canada/PA-030176; p. 441 (right), Mark E. Gibson.

Part 7: p. 530, Stock Montage; p. 531 (left), Corbis/Bettmann; p. 531 (right), Mug Shots, First Light.

Part 8: p. 582, CP PHOTO/Tom Hanson; p. 615, AP/Wide World Photos; p. 700, Marshall Henrichs/Addison-Wesley; p. 701 (left), UPI/Corbis-Bettmann; p. 701 (right), © Carlos Humberto TDC/Contact Press Images.

Part 9: p. 784, Corbis-Bettman; p. 785 (left), North Wind Pictures Archives; p. 785 (right), © M. Timothy O'Keefe/ Weststock.

Additional Figure and Table Credits

p. 150, Photo and interview: Reprinted by permission of Professor Paul Beaudry.

p. 409, Figures 1–3: *Historical Statistics on the United States from Colonial Times to 1970*, U.S. Department of Energy Information, U.S. Bureau of Labour Statistics, University of Michigan Document Center, and Oilnergy at www.oilnergy.com/1obrent.htm.

p. 532, Photo and interview: Reprinted by permission of Professor Peter Howitt.